1 MONTH OF FREE READING

at
www.ForgottenBooks.com

By purchasing this book you are eligible for one month membership to ForgottenBooks.com, giving you unlimited access to our entire collection of over 1,000,000 titles via our web site and mobile apps.

To claim your free month visit:
www.forgottenbooks.com/free917375

* Offer is valid for 45 days from date of purchase. Terms and conditions apply.

ISBN 978-0-266-97056-9
PIBN 10917375

This book is a reproduction of an important historical work. Forgotten Books uses state-of-the-art technology to digitally reconstruct the work, preserving the original format whilst repairing imperfections present in the aged copy. In rare cases, an imperfection in the original, such as a blemish or missing page, may be replicated in our edition. We do, however, repair the vast majority of imperfections successfully; any imperfections that remain are intentionally left to preserve the state of such historical works.

Forgotten Books is a registered trademark of FB &c Ltd.
Copyright © 2018 FB &c Ltd.
FB &c Ltd, Dalton House, 60 Windsor Avenue, London, SW19 2RR.
Company number 08720141. Registered in England and Wales.

For support please visit www.forgottenbooks.com

THE COMMONHEALTH

VOLUME 20-23
No. 1

JAN.-FEB.-MAR.
1933-1936

Cancer

MASSACHUSETTS
DEPARTMENT OF PUBLIC HEALTH

THE COMMONHEALTH

QUARTERLY BULLETIN OF THE MASSACHUSETTS DEPARTMENT OF
PUBLIC HEALTH
Sent Free to any Citizen of the State
Entered as second-class matter at Boston Postoffice.

M. LUISE DIEZ, M.D., DIRECTOR OF DIVISION OF CHILD HYGIENE, EDITOR.
Room 545 State House, Boston, Mass.

CONTENTS

	PAGE
Foreword, by George H. Bigelow, M.D.	3
Biopsy in Mammary Cancer, by James Ewing, M.D.	4
Cancer of the Stomach, by J. Shelton Horsley, M.D.	5

Medical Section:
Three Cured Cases of Carcinoma of Cervix, by C. F. Lynch, M.D.,
    E. W. Beauchamp, M.D. and W. J. Kisiel, M.D. . . . 7
Worcester Cancer Clinic Committee . . . 8
A State-Aided Cancer Clinic, by William T. Hopkins, M.D., F.A.C.S. 9
The Lowell Clinic, by John H. Lambert, M.D. . 10
Pondville Hospital Cured Cancer Clinic, by Ernest M. Daland, M.D. 11
Cancer of the Lip and Skin, by Ernest M. Daland, M.D. . . 16
Worcester North Cancer Clinic Committee . 25
Cancer Service in General Hospitals, by Curtis C. Tripp, M.D. . 25
Why a Cancer Clinic, by J. Forrest Burnham, M.D. . . . 26
The Pittsfield Clinics, by C. H. Richardson, M.D. . 28
The Teaching Service in a Cancer Clinic, by Harry F. Friedman, M.D. 29
Brockton Cancer Clinic Committee, by Michael F. Barrett, M.D. . 30

Educational Section:
Clinic Publicity, by Frederic Edwards . . . 31
Progress in Lynn, by Margaret Read Vincent . . 32
Neighborly Service at Pondville, by Mrs. Ralph Bullard . 32
Plans for 1933, by Mildred E. Kennedy—for the Gardner Committee 33
Educational Work, by Mrs. James F. Bailey 34
Plans of a New Committee, by Edith L. Minsky . . 35
Work of the Boston Committee, by Margaret H. Tracy . . 35
Cancer Publicity in Brockton, by William T. Card . . 36

Social Service Section:
Social Service in the State Cancer Program, by Eleanor E. Kelly . 36
What Social Work Means in the Worcester North Cancer Clinics, by
    Olive Twichell . 37
Social Service in the Worcester Cancer Clinics, by Gertrude J. Carney 37
Social Service in the New Bedford Cancer Clinic, by Ida G. Dudelson 38
Social Service in the Lowell Cancer Clinics, by Muriel Eales . 38
What Social Service Means to the Springfield Cancer Clinic, by Alice
    M. Drapeau . 39
Social Service in the Lawrence Cancer Clinic, by Angie M. Richardson 39
The Social Worker's Part in Securing Early Treatment for Cancer
    Patients, by Mrs. Dorothy A. Oates . 40
Social Service in the Tumor Clinic of the Boston Dispensary, by
    Bernice E. Cross . 41
"Eventually, Why Not Now?", by Rosamond Tatro . 42
Pondville Hospital Social Service Department, by Neil A. Fountain 43
Berkshire County Cancer Clinics, by Rosamond Tatro . . 44
National Institute of Health . . . 44
Maternal Deaths in Massachusetts . 45
Neighborhood House Health Activities, by Ruth R. Kent . . 46

Editorial Comment:
The "Cancer Cure" Always with Us . . . 47
What Another Campaign? Appendicitis? . . 48

Book Notes:
The Student's Handbook on Nursing Case Studies . 48
Growth and Development of the Child—Part I—General Considerations 48
Education for Healthful Living in the Public Schools of Bellevue-
    Yorkville, 1927-1931 . 49
Report of Division of Food and Drugs, October-November-December, 1932 50

FOREWORD
By George H. Bigelow, M.D.

For over a decade now there has been an intensifying of interest in this country and abroad in the problem connected with the shocking increase in the cancer death rate. State, national and international organizations have all devoted themselves to this matter, much research has been undertaken, much has been written for professional and lay consumption. From being a word that one was almost ostracized for using, "cancer" is now brought into the conversation frequently with no more emotion than "tuberculosis". This has all influenced the public attitude toward the disease.

Six years ago, due primarily to sincere, widespread, nonprofessional interest that demanded that the life-saving knowledge that we have should be put to work, the matter was agitated in the Legislature, investigated, and then formulated into statutes. As a result a Massachusetts cancer program was drawn up on the advice of a carefully selected representative group of lay and professional men and women. A hospital and clinics have been opened, field investigations have been made extensively on cancer and other chronic diseases, and through the widest possible cooperation an intensive educational campaign has been carried on. What has been the result of the expenditure of this considerable money and considerably more energy?

Last year over 1,000 patients were cared for in the State Hospital at Pondville and the year ended, as it had begun, with a heavy waiting list. In the out-patient department 3,500 more patients were seen. Another 3,400 were seen in the fifteen state-aided clinics. Could it be that these represent a group of patients who were previously not being served or was it that the general hospitals were turning over their cancer work to the State and going on to other fields? A study showed that during the period of the program the number of cancer patients cared for annually in the general hospitals of the State increased 36 per cent. This was 50 per cent more than the similar increase in general hospitals outside of Massachusetts studied by the American Society for the Control of Cancer. We can say, then, that there has been an unprecedented increase in hospital care due to the public demand for service to cancer and that 50 per cent of this increase was due to the intensive educational campaign carried on in the State.

But has this demand for service accomplished anything? To our astonishment we find that since 1926 there has been practically no increase in the death rate from cancer in Massachusetts when adjustments are made for age and sex. This is the first time that records of the State for this disease show anything like such a lag in increase over any such period of time. However, it might be said that this was a biological phenomenon indicating that cancer had reached the saturation point in the population and would have happened anyway whether the campaign had been put on or not. The cynic would say that at least the campaign had not prevented the improvement.

However, the figures go a little farther than that and show that the most marked improvement in the death rate has been found in the accessible rather than the inaccessible cancers. In other words, the improvement has been found in cancers in those locations where our present knowledge offers the most in the way of prevention and cure. Had the thing been merely biological one would have expected that the improvement would have occurred in all forms of cancer rather than most markedly in those where our knowledge is most effective.

It is, then, perhaps safe to say that as a result of the campaign people are coming forward for service as never before and we can begin to detect the results of this service through lessened deaths.

However, there is no cause for complacency. Too many of our hospital beds and waiting lists are clogged with incurables who waited because they thought the early signs and symptoms unimportant, because they were distracted during the critical period when cure was possible by charlatans and quacks, because they were distracted by the well-meaning and knavish neighbor's home remedy, because they were persuaded to fear the "bloodthirsty knife" of the surgeon when that knife could have been life-saving, because of economics when service is available without economic let or hindrance, because of a thousand and one irrelative matters. In spite of the cured cancer clinics, there is still too much delay produced by professional pessimism. There is still too much difficulty in persuading the older people who have fixed aversions to hospitals and the discussion of what they consider unpleasant and hopeless. Were our knowledge fully put to use we could double annually the cures. There is still far too little money available for research in this humanly important field and there is still far too great a gap between the knowledge that we have and its application. We should feel vastly encouraged by what has happened and should pledge renewed energies to the task, to the end that the promise of accomplishments of the last five years may be eclipsed by those of the five years to come.

BIOPSY IN MAMMARY CANCER
BY JAMES EWING, M.D.

The extent and severity of the radical operation for mammary cancer calls for a positive diagnosis in every case. Since women are now coming earlier for diagnosis of mammary disease, and often before the characteristic clinical symptoms of established cancer have developed, the diagnosis of these conditions has become more difficult and biopsies are more frequently required.

The practice of removing apparently benign nodules from the breast in a doctor's office and waiting two or three days for a report from a distant pathologist often leads to serious situations, and, in the opinion of some surgeons, may imperil the patient's chances for a cure even by a radical operation. The mechanical trauma from such a biopsy may well dislodge cancer cells and cut across and loosen cancerous lymphatics, while the delay of some days gives opportunity for the dislodged cells to reach the distant lymph nodes. The hyperemia of the inflammatory process may also stimulate tumor growth and facilitate the local growth and even the dislodgement of more active tumor cells. There have been some observations which indicate that these undesirable events actually occur and it is reasonable to assume that they do occur. Therefore the conservative surgeon will not remove a tumor nodule from the breast except in a surgical operating room where he is prepared to have an immediate diagnosis made and the proper operation performed at the same time.

There is a difference of opinion regarding the best method of performing the operation for a biopsy of the breast. Some surgeons prefer to cut directly into the tumor, make the diagnosis on the gross appearance which is usually specific, or cut out a piece of the tumor for frozen section. If the tumor proves to be cancer, the wound is closed over a sponge soaked in 10% formalin. They then discard the instruments and gloves used in the exploration, prepare the skin anew, and proceed with the operation indicated. This is a very direct and expeditious method. It avoids much trauma inevitable in a local excision which requires cutting on all sides of the tumor nodule. In the case of bulky tumors it may be the best method.

In the case of small tumors I think it is safer to remove the whole tumor, together with a wide area of normal breast tissue, using extreme care not to squeeze or roughly handle the cancerous mass. This procedure avoids cutting into cancerous tissue, and if it is done with extreme care not to squeeze the tumor, cancer cells should not be dislodged.

An experienced surgeon or pathologist should be able to recognize the great majority of malignant tumors of the breast by gross examination of the cut surface of the tumor. Unless he can do this it is obvious that the tissue chosen for microscopic section may not contain the malignant tumor. Therefore great importance attaches to the gross diagnosis, which should be relied upon wherever possible. The extent of the disease also can be told only by gross examination. The cicatricial character, resistance, opacity or translucency, and the chalky streaks of carcinoma are generally specific. Frozen section is therefore often unnecessary but should be made in all cases which are in any respect doubtful to the particular surgeon or pathologist concerned. This diagnosis should be made at the operation and the appropriate procedure carried out immediately.

There are some lesions in the breast in which it is difficult for any surgeon or pathologist to state positively whether the condition is malignant or benign. Hence the surgeon must not assume that by obtaining a microscopic diagnosis he has secured positive information. In such cases the clinical data, age of patient, extent and duration of the disease, condition of lymph nodes, and especially the gross characters of the lesion should be given much importance in the decision. Under these circumstances some surgeons would err on the side of caution and perform the radical operation. I believe it is unfair to the patient to perform a radical mastectomy unless the diagnosis of carcinoma is positive. There are many precancerous and suspicious lesions in the breast which are clinically benign, while a true carcinoma is nearly always obvious to a pathologist of adequate experience. When a substantial doubt exists about the nature of a microscopic section of a breast tumor, it is generally not cancer.

CANCER OF THE STOMACH
BY J. SHELTON HORSLEY, M.D.

Deaths from cancer are increasing. There are now in the United States about 120,000 deaths from cancer each year, one-fourth to one-third of them being from cancer of the stomach.

In the fight against cancer, the most powerful of the captains of the men of death is cancer of the stomach.

Gastric cancer occurs more frequently in men than in women. Clinically it may be divided into two classes: (1) the kind of cancer that gives a history of indigestion, frequently resembling the history of peptic ulcer, for several years before the cancer becomes obvious; (2) the cancer of the stomach in which gastric symptoms appear only a few months before the disease is detected. The first type represents about 25 to 30 per cent of all gastric cancers. The second type comprises about 70 to 75 per cent of the gastric cancers.

Elsewhere in the body it seems to be true that cancer does not originate directly from normal healthy tissue. In regions that we can inspect, as the mouth, tongue, skin, rectum and lower sigmoid, cancer arises on a pre-existing benign lesion such as a patch of leukoplakia, a wart, a mole, an ulcer or a polyp-like growth. It is probable that cancer in the stomach follows this same general law. In the interior of the stomach, which cannot be satisfactorily inspected, benign growths or even ulcers may exist for years, especially if in the "silent areas" of the stomach, without creating symptoms until cancerous change and rapid growth have set in. The lesser curvature of the stomach, where gastric peristalsis begins, is the important motor region and about 80 per cent of all stomach complaints are due to interference with its peristalsis. A growth or lesion of any kind in the narrow pyloric end of the stomach may also cause symptoms because of partial obstructions. Roentgenologists say that any ulcer along the greater curvature of the stomach capable of demonstration by

X-ray is practically always malignant, while many of the ulcers on the lesser curvature are benign.

It is generally recognized that some gastric cancers have their origin in benign peptic ulcers. The ratio of this incidence, however, is a subject of much dispute. It is true, too, that there is a low-grade cancer of the stomach which ulcerates early and cannot be distinguished grossly even at operation from a benign ulcer, microscopic examination being necessary to make a diagnosis. In the opinion of Holmes and Hampton, roentgenologists of the Massachusetts General Hospital, and of many gastro-enterologists, the difficulty in differentiating between early cancer and peptic ulcer is so great as to call for surgical excision, the only known means of curing gastric cancer, unless the suspected lesion responds to medical treatment within a few weeks.

Because of the proximity of the liver and pancreas to the stomach and because, also, gastric cancers are usually not very radio-sensitive, efficient radiation treatment cannot be given gastric cancer, so the only means of cure is excision by partial gastrectomy. In some rare instances a total gastrectomy is justifiable.

If a patient reaches the "tropic of cancer," say 35 years of age, and begins to complain of vague symptoms of indigestion, such as belching, nausea, water-brash, heart-burn, sometimes vomiting, pain and discomfort in the upper abdomen, whether coming on at a regular time after meals or not, he should receive a careful examination by a competent general practitioner. In the majority of cases this stomach trouble will be found to be due to something other than a gastric lesion, and can be cured by appropriate medical measures. If, however, the patient is not relieved of his complaints after faithfully following the advised treatment for two or three weeks, his stomach and intestine should be examined with X-rays by someone fully competent to do this.

If cancer is found, an operation should be done as soon as possible by a surgeon of experience in gastric surgery. If the lesion appears to be a peptic ulcer, medical treatment may be instituted for a few weeks; then, if improvement as noted by X-rays and clinically is not marked, the lesion should be removed by a partial gastrectomy.

If the patient has been having stomach symptoms for many years, and reaches the age of 35 years, the same routine should be enforced.

In the early stages of disease the diagnosis is difficult, but it is in the early stages that the diagnosis is important so that proper treatment can be given. It has been shown by Dr. Margaret Warwick that in about 23 per cent of cancers of the stomach coming to necropsy the cancer is still confined to the stomach, and that many of these deaths result from perforation of the cancer and peritonitis, and not from the constitutional effects of cancer. It seems probable that, if at necropsy 23 per cent of gastric cancers are still limited to the stomach, an earlier diagnosis and a proper operation would uncover a larger percentage of cases in which the cancer was confined to the stomach and could be cured by partial gastrectomy.

It is only by adopting some plan to follow through to a definite diagnosis and treatment the earliest signs of stomach trouble that the enormous mortality from gastric cancer can be reduced.

SPRINGFIELD CANCER COMMITTEE
March 4, 1927
CHAIRMAN, CHARLES F. LYNCH, M.D.

THREE CURED CASES OF CARCINOMA OF CERVIX

By C. F. LYNCH, M.D., E. C. BEAUCHAMP, M.D.
and W. J. KISIEL, M.D.

Cancer is probably the most discussed medical topic of the day. Practically every medical journal contains a discussion of some phase of this scourge. In all medical and surgical conventions, it occupies a prominent place. Research laboratories of all kinds seem to bend their energies toward this goal. Because it has to be considered in some form or other in differential diagnosis—every practitioner has it ever in mind. Such earnest endeavor should not be, and is not, without some fruit.

There may be discussions as to type of treatment, and to modality of procedure, but on one point all are agreed: the earlier the diagnosis, the better the prognosis. Probably the greatest field of attack lies in public education. Abnormal growths, and unusual discharges must not be permitted to go on unmentioned to a medical adviser. "Do not wait for pain," we believe constitutes a fitting slogan. Pain means pressure, and pressure already means considerable development of the disease.

The cases of cured cancer of the cervix (four and one half to five years) reported here bear out two salient points: (1) that we possess in radium an effective means of treatment, and frequently of cure; (2) that the lay mind (alas! sometimes the medical) is not keyed up to demand thorough investigation of early stage of disease.

First Case: Mrs. C. M.—Age 59—had a hysterectomy performed in 1915, from which she recovered uneventfully. No malignancy is reported at that time; her health continued good, until six months before admission, when she developed occasional vaginal bleeding. This irregular bleeding was scant and unassociated with pain. It was accompanied by a slight foul-odored discharge. The day preceding her admission she had a severe hemorrhage and on August 29, 1928, the cervix was patent, moderately indurated. Coming from it was a mass about the size of an egg yolk, which was irregular, granular and bleeding freely on manipulation. The growth was removed and the cervix curetted on August 31, 1928. The pathological diagnosis confirmed the clinical opinion: Carcinoma of the Cervix. September 7, 1928, a capsule containing 50 mgs. of radium was inserted into the cervix for twenty-four hours. On October 20, 1928, 15 mgs. of radium, in needles, was thrust in the cervix for twenty-four hours. In 1929 she received the usual course of deep X-ray treatments. On August 3, 1929, though the cervix seemed entirely healed, the patient had complained of seeing a little blood and another radium application of 50 mgs. in capsule form was advised and applied to the cervix. In March 1931, patient returned to the hospital with a fissure in ano. At this time considerable thickening of the recto-vaginal wall was found, and about three inches from the vulvar orifice there was a small fistula, a burn resulting from the last radium application. Since this time the patient has been in no way incapacitated. She carries on usual occupation and has no complaint. Physical examination fails to reveal any further cervical trouble and the small fistulous tract is healed.

Second Case: Mrs. A. S.—Age 42—came under observation September 23, 1928, complaining of vaginal bleeding. She had given birth to three children. Since the last child, several years ago, she noticed rather profuse leukorrhea and for the past five years she has had moderate irregular bleeding. Intercourse always provoked bleeding. She had no pain other than a vague pelvic discomfort. Physical examination was negative except the cervix. It presented evidence of an old stellate laceration. It was thickened and moderately indurated, particularly on the right side. Here the tissue was very friable, and digital examination provoked bleeding. There was no infiltration of the vaginal vault. The uterus was slightly enlarged, but freely moveable. A biopsy was taken September 24, 1932—Diagnosis—Microscopic: Squamous Cell Carcinoma of Cervix. On October 5, 1928, 50 mgs. of radium, in capsule, was inserted into the cervix for twenty-four hours. On November 2, 1928, 50 mgs. of radium in capsule was inserted in the cervical canal and 25 mgs. of radium, in needles, was thrust in the cervical tissue, both of these remaining for twenty-four hours. From this time, until January 19, 1929, she received a series of nine X-ray treatments, covering the right lower abdomen, left lower abdomen, and perineal area. Her bleeding gradually ceased, never to recur. She has been examined at regular intervals. There is no evidence of further involvement of cervix, the patient has no complaints and, without effort, she is carrying on her usual duties.

Third Case: Mrs. F. P.—Present age 31—first seen in June of 1927. Her third child was born August 21, 1926. In September she began to bleed irregularly. Her physician failed to examine her and recommended douches. This she did without improvement. In June she consulted one of us, complaining of loss of weight, feeling tired out, irregular vaginal bleeding. The patient was definitely anemic. After examination, a provisional diagnosis of Carcinoma of Cervix was made. Patient examined at the Mercy Hospital Cancer Clinic, from which she was admitted to the Surgical Service for biopsy, which revealed a Squamous Cell Carcinoma of Cervix. Patient was referred to Pondville, where she received a radium treatment (dosage unknown to us). During the rest of 1927, she was quite miserable, complaining of a continuance of irregular bleeding, of definite pain in the pelvis and lower back. In December of this year, after a severe hemorrhage, she was admitted to the Springfield Hospital for a second application of radium. Fifty mgs. in capsule form was applied to the cervix. During early 1928 she was bedridden. She looked very poorly. Pain was prominent in the lower abdomen, in the sacral region and in the vagina. She still had occasional slight vaginal bleeding. In June 1928, patient was doing quite well, general condition had improved to the point where she was going out for short walks. She put on considerable weight and gradually resumed her household duties. In 1929, she was so much improved, as to be quite unrecognizable to people who had seen her in 1927. In October of 1929, her condition appeared cured except for small spot on the posterior lip of the cervix, which still bled fairly easily on probing. This small area has disappeared and regular examinations have failed to reveal any reappearance of the cancer. In December 1932, her last examination was negative. This patient received no X-ray treatment. From a practically moribund and seemingly hopeless individual, she has become an active and healthy mother, fulfilling her duties to the family.

In terminating the report of these cases, we wish to express our thanks and appreciation to Mr. Frederic Edwards, and to Miss Alice Drapeau. Their enthusiasm in cancer work, and their willing co-operation, have been of the greatest value in the local cancer program.

WORCESTER CANCER CLINIC COMMITTEE
March 4, 1927
CHAIRMAN, ERNEST L. HUNT, M.D.

The situation in Worcester differs materially from that of other cancer clinic cities (except Boston), in that there has been a daily clinic in one or even two of the five local hospitals since March, 1927. In consequence, there has been difficulty in securing newspaper space for announcements of clinics. This is not owing in any sense to lack of cooperation on the part of the press, but is due to the lack of news value inherent in the announcement of a clinic which is held daily. On the other hand, the Worcester clinics have been rather generally used as consultation centers by the medical profession of the city and surrounding towns.

LYNN CANCER CLINIC COMMITTEE
April 14, 1927
CHAIRMAN, WILLIAM T. HOPKINS, M.D., F.A.C.S.

A STATE-AIDED CANCER CLINIC

All Massachusetts State-aided cancer clinics have a similar set-up. Varying conditions, however, make for some differences in details of operation.

The Lynn Cancer Clinic is conducted under the management of a committee of five members of the Lynn Medical Fraternity, acting in cooperation with the Department of Public Health of the Commonwealth. In endeavoring to secure the better control of cancer, the most outstanding need appeared to be for more correct information concerning cancer on the part of the public and of the medical profession. The prevailing impression seemed to be that a diagnosis of cancer was equivalent to a sentence of death.

An educational campaign was started consisting of the formation of a lay educational committee composed of interested welfare-minded men and women in the communities which it was hoped to serve. An effort was made to interest service clubs and other social and welfare organizations and talks were given wherever an audience would consent to listen. Newspaper publicity was very generously contributed by the two daily papers in Lynn, and one in Salem. An occasional public luncheon was held at which speakers of note addressed the gathering.

The cancer hysteria, reports of which sometimes reach us, we have not encountered, although about seventeen hundred patients have passed through our clinic.

In the operation of the clinic the first requisite seemed to be to provide competent diagnostic service, and the three chiefs of the surgical service of Lynn Hospital were selected to personally conduct the clinic, serving four months each in rotation, with the services of the entire hospital staff available as required. In addition, a member of the staff of the Huntington Hospital was engaged to visit the clinic once each month as consultant. The object was to assure a qualified opinion in the interest of the patient, to afford opportunity for improvement in the diagnostic skill of the clinician and to inspire greater confidence in the community in general and on the part of the medical profession in our vicinity. This feature has been continued to the present time.

No charge of any kind has been made thus far to patients, except that those able to pay the hospital for X-ray service are expected to do so. For those requiring X-ray service and unable to pay, the hospital furnishes such services without charge upon request of the clinic. The hospital also provides without charge quarters in which the clinic is held, equipment, dressings, etc., and services of nurses at the clinic.

The next important problem was to provide adequate social service. In this respect we feel that we have been fortunate in our personnel. Our follow-up ceases only with the life of the patient.

After the clinic had been in operation for a year, its value to the community was recognized by a financial contribution from the Welfare Federation of Greater Lynn, and this has been continued with the exception of one year of severe depression.

To guard against serious results from possible errors in diagnosis, we have adopted the policy of regarding all doubtful lesions as cancerous until proved otherwise. In questionable breast tumors, for instance, we operate with a pathologist present who makes a rapid frozen section diagnosis which determines the extent of the operation. Ours is a diagnostic clinic, and for treatment patients are referred to the family doctor, to the local hospital or to some other hospital. Whenever a patient receives a diagnosis of cancer a letter stating the facts is immediately sent to the family doctor, if the patient has one.

The clinic began to function on April 22, 1927, and has since been held weekly. As to the curability of cancer we have no opinion as to the percentage. We do not consider anything less than a five-year cure. Upon that basis we are restricted to the cases coming to our clinic during the first eight months of its activity. In this period we saw sixty-five cancers of many sorts and degrees of progress. Of these 65, adequately treated in 1927, twenty-nine were known to be living and free from evidence of recurrence on January 1, 1933. These figures, while trustworthy in themselves, should not be used as a basis of computation concerning the curability of cancer in general, for many of them were skin cancer, noted for its amenability to cure, and many adjustments would be necessary as to delay in treatment, variety of malignancy, grade, anatomical location, particular tissue invaded, metastases and other considerations. These figures are here introduced merely as evidence in support of the contention that a diagnosis of cancer does not of necessity carry with it a certainty of fatality to the patient from that cause. If that fact may be considered to be established, then an opportunity is afforded to introduce into our educational program a far more hopeful note, upon a sound basis. If this will be accepted by the public generally, it will modify the dread of the subject of cancer and thus should operate to lessen the delay in seeking a qualified opinion.

In an attempt at evaluation of our clinic, my estimate would be that we have saved some lives, relieved many persons, have been instrumental in providing terminal comfort and care, and perhaps have made some impression in disseminating more correct information concerning cancer.

LOWELL CANCER COMMITTEE
May 27, 1927
CHAIRMAN, JOHN H. LAMBERT, M.D.

THE LOWELL CLINIC

The cancer clinic established in May, 1927, at the Lowell General Hospital was one of the first in the chain of State-aided cancer clinics. Work has been carried on continuously in a weekly clinic since that time.

As evidence of the systematic activities of a strong associate committee, regular newspaper announcements of the clinic, and other educational efforts have been made and the attendance in consequence has been large and especially even, averaging between forty and fifty a month, but some months it goes well over sixty.

At least two members of the clinic staff are always in attendance at the clinic, if possible, every patient being examined by two or more physicians of the senior staff when possible. In case there is a disagreement in respect to diagnosis, further examination is made and the patient's condition more closely studied. If a diagnosis cannot be made the patient is referred for further study either by X-ray examination, exploratory incision or by some other method. No treatment is given in the clinic, hospital cases being admitted to the hospital of choice while every individual referred to the clinic by a private physician or who expresses a choice of family physician is referred for treatment back to him with the clinic diagnosis and recommendations for treatment. In addition to the regular staff a group of younger physicians are being trained in the methods of the clinic by being assigned to work with the various members of the regular staff at the clinics.

Lowell offers an excellent example among the Massachusetts State-aided cancer clinics of the theory set forth by the American College of Surgeons that the diagnosis of early cancer should be made only after examination by a number of individual physicians in consultation.

PONDVILLE HOSPITAL

SUPERINTENDENT, GEORGE M. SULLIVAN, M.D.

June 21, 1927

PONDVILLE HOSPITAL CURED CANCER CLINIC

Held on April 5, 1932

BY ERNEST M. DALAND, M.D.

The meeting was held in the Recreation Building of the Pondville Hospital. Fifty physicians and five nurses were present. Dr. Ernest M. Daland, who presided, stated that no five-year cures would be shown, because the hospital has been running less than five years. However, most of the patients shown have been free of their disease for three or four years since treatment was given. A small group of patients were shown to demonstrate that much palliation can be given even though cure cannot be expected.

A brief review of the history, policies and work of the hospital was given. The hospital was opened in June 1927 with ninety beds but last year twenty-five more beds were added. For four years, the hospital has been filled to capacity with a long list of patients awaiting admission.

The requirements for admission to the hospital are three: The person must have a malignancy or a question of malignancy; he must have been a resident of the State for two out of the previous three years; and he must be referred by a physician. Patients who come to the clinic may come without recommendation of a physician, and the clinic makes a free examination and diagnosis. If any treatment is to be given, there is a charge made for that on the basis of one day in the hospital. The patients pay at the rate of $10.50 a week, or $1.50 a day, if they can afford to pay that. If not, the cities and towns where they have their residence pay at the rate of $17.50 a week. If they have no legal settlement, then they are taken care of as State patients.

The hospital has a resident staff consisting of the superintendent, who is a trained medical man and who also has executive ability so that he appreciates the medical and administrative side of our problems, four resident surgeons and one resident pathologist. We are shortly to have a medical resident. These are all men who have had hospital training before coming here. The visiting staff is made up of a group of seventeen men, all men in practice in other cities, mostly in Boston. These men come here at stated times during the week, a group of about ten making two visits a week, averaging a full half day at each visit. Others visit once a week or whenever the occasion arises.

Clinics

This clinic is one of the chain of fifteen State-aided clinics that is conducted throughout the State. In all these clinics, it is possible for a person to get free diagnosis and recommendation for treatment. We take complete histories and do complete physical examinations, even though the lesion is a superficial one on the face. We see a great many non-malignant conditions. If possible, a diagnosis is made and the patient is sent back to his physician or to any physician he may select if not sent by one, with the recommendation for treatment. If the patient has malignancy or suspicious malignancy, he can then be sent into the hospital and treatment carried out if the doctor so wishes.

Hospital Patients

Patients admitted to the hospital come under several groups:

First, the patient with the early, operable, curable lesion. This type, of course, we like to see come in. It is quite essential that we have a certain percentage of this type of patient in the hospital for the benefit of other patients, the doctors and the nurses. We are getting an increasingly large number of patients who have early, curable lesions.

Second, there is the type of patient who has had treatment elsewhere, but who has not received complete cure. The time has arrived when more drastic radiation or operation is needed, and by giving such treatment, some hope of cure can still be offered.

The third type is sent in as an advanced case. We have learned that while we have respect for the diagnoses of other men, it is quite worth while to repeat all examinations that have been made. A patient with an inoperable, advanced malignancy of the stomach is put through the same routine examinations, if his condition permits, that the early, new patient is put through. We check up on the diagnosis, and in some cases we do not agree; and in other cases, we do not agree with the type of treatment that has been advised. Perhaps we advise operation where it has not been advised before. In the routine check-up on this class of patient, we have many pleasant surprises, for some have no cancer.

Emergencies

We have a number of people who require emergency surgery. We have patients with malignancies of the stomach or large intestines for which gastrostomies or cecostomies are required and laryngeal obstructions for which tracheotomies are required. I believe there are ten or fifteen patients with artificial openings in the hospital at all times. We had one patient in the hospital who had a tracheotomy and gastrostomy. We had a large prostate which gave us a great deal of concern. He was kept on constant drainage for some time. We thought a suprapubic cystotomy would be necessary along with the gastrostomy and tracheotomy, but it never did come to that.

Palliative Treatment

The last group of patients must be classed as palliative cases. On these we have done palliative operations to remove their symptoms. Some of these have pleased us very much by going on for a period of years without having any recurrence. We feel we should treat patients' lesions regardless of whether we think that they are going to become five-year cures. The five-year cures are dividends received by the doctor and the patient for taking a lesion early and treating it radically. We certainly would not refuse to treat any patient because we thought he would have only four years of life. We must not think too much of the standard of five years. Some people whom we think we may relieve for two years may get a complete cure.

We have, also, cases who can receive palliation with the hope of cure by X-radiation or radium treatment. X-ray treatment for metastatic malignancy is very efficacious in relieving pain. We have many patients with breast or prostatic metastases and other patients where surgery does not seem wise, where radiation is not only palliative, but gives a very definite chance of relief and cure. There are a certain number of patients who require surgery for the relief of pain. X-ray and other methods having failed, we call on the neurological surgeon, who does some type of nerve operation, as alcohol injections, cervical rhizotomies, and chordotomies. These are all operations which have a very definite place in this type of hospital.

Bedside Nursing

Then there is also a type of patient in the hospital who does not need so much the care of the surgeon as he does nursing care. During the first two months that the hospital was open, the patients came in faster than the equipment did. Our X-ray machine was not ready, the radium was not here, and the surgical equipment was not in. We had to carry on with only medical and nursing care. We were surprised to find out how much good we had done without the use of some of these other agents. A patient with an ulcerating, foul lesion of the breast, with a good deal of pain, can be made quite comfortable by frequent dressings, by removal of the slough, and by thorough irrigation of the wound. It requires good nursing to care for a bed patient for a year and still have the skin stay in good condition.

Drug Treatment

Patients using large amounts of morphine on admission can be relieved so that they use only aspirin or codeine. Aspirin is a very valuable drug for the type of pain these patients have. The average patient who has been in the hospital a month uses less narcotics than on admission, and the number of patients who get a considerable amount is always very small.

Length of Stay

The average length of stay of a patient is forty-one days. During the last year, in the main hospital, we treated six hundred twenty-six new patients and some four hundred old patients. Many of these old patients came in for a period of one or two months several times during the year, coming in for a series of X-ray treatments. In the out-patient department there were eight hundred fifty new patients and many old ones with a total of twenty-eight hundred visits.

Skin Cases

Dr. Richard Dresser showed five cases of rather extensive skin cancer, in each of which radiation had destroyed the lesion. None of these have passed the three year period, so that, while cure is expected, they were not shown as cured cases.

The first patient presented, on admission, a lesion 1.5x1x1 cm. at the inner canthus and bridge of the nose. Biopsy showed a basal cell carcinoma. It was treated by inserting radium needles of platinum into the growth parallel to the surface. A dosage of 150 mghrs. was given and there has been no recurrence in eighteen months.

The second patient had been treated for a lesion involving the outer half of the lower eyelid with involvement of the conjunctiva and moderate ectropion. The eyeball was protected by a lead shield and the lesion was treated by X-ray. One area showed persistent induration and this was treated twice by radium with no recurrence for one year.

The third patient had a similar lesion at the outer canthus with another on the face. She received one X-ray treatment and three by radium and she has been well for sixteen months.

The other two patients had skin cancers of the face and nose. Both of these cleared up under radium treatment and there has been no recurrence for one year.

Biopsy is desirable but is not always made. One dose of radium or X-ray is better than multiple doses, as the tissues become radio-resistant and subsequent doses are not as effective as the first. After a lesion has had two or three treatments and has not healed, surgery should be used. All these patients should be followed five years, up to that time there is danger of recurrence, particularly around the periphery. Treatment of the recurrence is usually satisfactorily accomplished.

Urological

Dr. Roger Graves demonstrated three urological cases. The first was a man of 54 on whom a nephrectomy had been done four years ago for hypernephroma. His first sympton was hematuria, for which he consulted his doctor immediately. A pyelogram showed a defect which was considered pathological and operation was done at once. Blood in the urine is never normal and should never be regarded as such. It must not be considered that it comes from some simple cause until a complete urological examination has been made. Early diagnosis is essential if a renal neoplasm is to be cured.

Two cases of cancer of the penis were shown. Cancer of the penis represents from one to three per cent of cancer in males. Fifteen cases have been seen at Pondville in five years. As is usually the case, none of these patients had been circumcised early in life. This suggests chronic irritation as the etiological factor. The first sign is a foul discharge from beneath the prepuce, usually without any pain or bleeding. Biopsy with a cautery knife may be necessary to clinch the diagnosis.

Treatment of the early lesion confined to the skin of the prepuce can be carried out by radium. Careful watch must be kept of the inguinal glands. The first case presented belonged to this group—a man of 58 years. On two occasions, radium was inserted into the growth on his penis, with X-ray treatments to the groins. The lesion has remained healed for nearly four years.

Where the lesion is more extensive, where it involves the glans penis or the deep fascia of the penis, surgery is preferable to radiation. Partial amputation or complete extirpation must be done, depending on the extent of the disease. The second patient illustrated this type—an extensive, sloughing carcinoma of the glans and corona with enlarged glands. Nine months ago radical amputation of the penis with implantation of the urethra in the perineum was done. The glands in both groins were dissected out. High voltage X-ray treatments were then given over the healed incisions. Pathologically the penis showed epidermoid carcinoma, Grade II, with no metastases to the glands. There has been no recurrence in nine months.

Surgical Cases

The general surgical cases were presented by Doctors Ernest Daland and Horatio Rogers. Twelve patients free from recurrence for three years or more were presented, twelve patients relieved for from one to three years, and five patients on whom palliative procedures had been carried out.

Six patients who had had a radical breast amputation with a dissection of the axilla were shown in the first group. One had received a preoperative series of X-ray treatments and another one postoperative series. The others received no radiation. X-radiation is not used as a routine measure postoperatively in breast cancers. In those cases where an inadequate operation before admission has been followed by radical operation here, and where cancer of the breast occurs in young women, we have used it. It has also been given in some of the very malignant types of cancer. Dr. Dresser feels that if one is going to give X-radiation, one wants to give it with a vengeance. Unless there is definite disease present, he does not feel that he wants to give three or four erythemas of X-radiation just on the chance that it may be good. He feels that it may do some harm. If immunity has been developed to radiation given as a postoperative measure, then it will have very little effect as a curative method if given for recurrent disease.

Radical operation on the breast consists of removal of the entire breast, the skin over it and the fascia beneath it, together with the entire pectoralis minor muscle and all the pectoralis major except that part arising from the clavicle, and the contents of the axilla with the exception of the long thoracic and subscapular nerves.

Two patients who had been operated on for cancer of the lip were shown. One was a man of 77 on whom a V-excision of the growth had been done. This was a Grade I lesion—a low grade growth. Our policy in small growths of this type is to deal only with the lip lesion unless glands can be palpated. In this patient a constant watch has been kept but none have appeared. The other patient underwent a bilateral dissection of the glands of the neck in addition to the lip operation for a midline lesion of moderately high malignancy. The pathologist reported no cancer in the glands and the patient has remained well.

Results

We have recently looked over some end results of carcinoma of the lip, particularly from the Massachusetts General Hospital. The figures run like this: Of the malignancies of the lip where an operation has been done on the lip and nothing has been done for the glands, the percentage of five-year cures is sixty. Where the lip is operated on and where the glands are dissected but where no cancer is found in the glands, the percentage is from 88 to 93 per cent. In cases where glands do show malignancy the results are around 30 per cent for five-year cures.

The other patients demonstrated in this group were: (1) a man with a large basal cell carcinoma of the back treated by excision and skin graft; (2) a man on whom an interscapulothoracic (shoulder girdle) amputation had been done for fibrosarcoma; (3) a man with cancer of the tongue, treated by electrocoagulation without neck dissection, (4) a carcinoma of the upper jaw and antrum treated by electrocoagulation and radium.

In the second group of patients, well less than three years, were shown cases of carcinoma of the face (3), nose, breast, upper lip, lower lip, mouth, sarcoma of the parotid, and carcinoma of the sigmoid—all treated by operation.

Our policy is to excise some of the superficial skin cancers if excision would not give too great deformity, but to treat the majority by radiation. We do not attempt to distinguish between the basal cell and the squamous cell lesions for they appear to react equally well to radiation. One patient was shown who had developed a recurrence following a radical breast operation. This recurrence has apparently been destroyed by X-ray. A recurrent carcinoma of the nose under treatment by radiation was also presented.

Gynecological

Doctors Joe V. Meigs and Langdon Parsons presented six gynecological patients. The first with carcinoma of the vagina is free of disease for three years following the use of radium seeds. This is the only patient alive any length of time after treatment for this disease that Dr. Meigs has found at Pondville or the Massachusetts General Hospital. The prognosis in cancer of the vagina is extremely poor.

Two women were shown who were well three and four years after radium treatment for cancer of the cervix.

In favorable cases of carcinoma of the cervix, we can do as well with radium as can be done by hysterectomy. There is very little choice between the two, except the mortality and morbidity is very much less with radium than it is with surgery. In cases which are more extensive, the results are very bad with surgery and almost as bad with radium. In cases involving the cervix, vagina, and broad ligaments, surgery is not even thought of. Most of the cases we see here, of course, are extensive. Many of them have been treated elsewhere. We do what we can to help them. Some of them are alive and well, going on for three years. In carcinoma of the cervix, if we find a patient with a history lasting over six months, we feel that patient is in an inoperable group and will probably not get well.

The efficacy of complete hysterectomy for cancer of the fundus was demonstrated by two patients well for three and two and a half years. Another patient had had a supravaginal hysterectomy for the same disease but came to us for persistent bleeding from the cervix. She was given radium treatment to the cervix, but she would have done better if she had received a complete hysterectomy in the first place.

Doctor Meigs' Comment

The prognosis in adenocarcinoma of the body of the uterus is very different from that of cancer of the cervix. In carcinoma of the body of the uterus we expect to get very much better results. We do not have enough cases here to give statistics but I can give you some from the Massachusetts General Hospital. These cases are practically all operated upon in our clinic here and our results seem to me to show that surgery is better than radium. We have at the General 78 per cent of five-year cures in this particular group of cases taking the three groups together—50 per cent of the rapidly growing ones; 65 per cent of the moderately growing ones; and 89 per cent of the slowly growing ones. In other words this tumor is particularly favorable to surgery. A lot of men are treating these cases with radium. A lot have been treated with radium at the Huntington Memorial Hospital. In cases of obese patients, patients with heart disease who could not stand ether, it is justifiable to use radium. Contrast our statistics of 75 per cent, total cures for five years, with Heyman's in Stockholm who has only been able to cure 60 per cent of the favorable cases which could not be operated upon. This is a picked group of the best cases he had in the clinic which could not be operated upon.

CANCER OF THE LIP AND SKIN
By Ernest M. Daland, M.D.

Cancer of the Lip

Many cancers of the lip arise from lesions which are apparently trivial in themselves. Such conditions as keratoses, chronic ulcers and fissures, leukoplakia and areas of chronic irritation are definitely precancerous lesions. As such they demand treatment. The danger lies in the erroneous diagnosis of precancer when the condition is a cancerous one.

A keratosis is a thickening or scaling of the outer layers of the dry portion of the mucous membrane of the lip. The scale is thick and tenacious and it may be sensitive. It may become ulcerated and heal with difficulty. It is more common in men, particularly smokers. Cigarettes often stick to it and tear it off when removed, leaving an ulceration. Many keratoses may be softened and destroyed by the use of ointments. Others require radium in mild doses.

Chronic ulcers and fissures of several weeks duration and not responding to washes and salves must be viewed with suspicion and treated by radiation or excision.

Leukoplakia, frequently present inside the mouth as well as on the lip, is frequently caused or increased by the use of tobacco and may be cured by stopping its use. It is probably best treated by desiccation or coagulation if it does not respond to simpler methods within a short time. Radium is sometimes used quite effectively, but it has been disappointing in many instances and we have practically discarded it for this purpose.

Cancer of the lip is about fifty times as common in men as in women. It occurs much more often on the lower lip than on the upper and is more serious when on the lower lip. It may appear at any age, but is more common after forty. It is more common in users of tobacco and in individuals with foul mouths and bad teeth.

As stated above, it may develop on a benign ulcer of long standing or on a keratosis or leukoplakia. Any nodule, ulcer, persistent cold sore, persistent chapping or deformity of the lip must be considered cancer until proven otherwise.

Ewing[1] describes two clinical types of epidermoid carcinoma of the lip, the papillary and the ulcerative infiltrating type. The papillary type is a wart-like elevated lesion situated on the epidermis and for a long period is unaccompanied by a deep or subepithelial induration. It extends slowly in all diameters, finally ulcerates, penetrates the underlying tissue, involves the nodes and then resembles the second type.

The second type begins as a broad thickening of the epidermal layer, with early dense infiltration of the deeper structures and with crater-like ulceration surrounded by a definite, indurated border. It advances more rapidly than the papillary type, involves the lymphatic structures earlier and is surrounded by an area of edema. It may become infected and often undergoes necrosis.

Basal cell carcinoma begins on the cutaneous border of the lip and acts like a skin cancer. It rarely metastisizes to glands and is treated like other skin cancers.

A differential diagnosis must be made between syphilis, tuberculosis and chronic infection, in addition to the precancerous conditions mentioned. A chancre may be diagnosed by a proper dark field examination and by the extensive early acute glandular involvement. Tertiary syphilis gives a positive Wassermann test, but it must be remembered that cancer and syphilis may both be present. In the presence of suspected cancer and a positive Wassermann, a biopsy must be done. A tuberculous ulcer is usually very painful and is always secondary to extensive tuberculosis of the lungs or larynx.

Biopsy on lip lesions is not a desirable procedure if it can be avoided, and, if done, one should be prepared to proceed with treatment within a very short time. Complete removal or "total biopsy" is far better in the small lesions. It can be done under novocaine and is probably the best treatment, whatever the lesion.

Cancer may appear on any part of the lip. It is most serious when it extends onto the mucous membrane toward the gum or when it invades the mucosa at the corner of the mouth. However, the seriousness of cancer of the lip lies chiefly in the fact that it spreads into the lymph nodes of the neck with great rapidity. Cancer in the center of the lip metastasizes into the submental glands, then to the submaxillary glands on either side and to the upper and lower cervical groups, both superficial and deep. If the lesion is located on one side only, it may skip the submental glands and spread to the chain of glands on one side only.

In examining the lip and neck for cancer the following methods may be of help: Careful, *gentle* palpation of the lip between the thumb and forefinger reveals an area of inelastic, pearly induration when cancer is present, even in the early stages. The edge of the lip is rolled gently back and forth and if no pearly edge appears, it is quite likely that cancer is not present.

External palpation for glands of the neck is not very satisfactory unless the glands are large. A better method is to insert the forefinger of one hand into the floor of the mouth lateral and anterior to the tongue and to palpate the tissues between this finger and the fingers of the other hand. One quickly learns to recognize the normal submaxillary salivary gland and to note the presence of other glands. The typical cancerous gland is hard, but the gland may be fairly soft during the early stages of invasion. Glands in the neck must be considered cancerous until proven otherwise.

Broders[2] and others have done some interesting work on the grading of lip cancer into four groups, according to the degree of malignancy. A study is made microscopically of the amount of differentiation shown by the cells of the new growth, the difference in the size and shape of the cells, the staining of their nuclei, the number of mitoses, etc. The more the tendency to assume normal structures, the less is the degree of malignancy. Cases grouped in Grade I are the warty, papillary type which rarely metastasizes to the glands. In some of these, it is not necessary to remove the glands unless they become enlarged. Much interest has been aroused by this new classification, but one must not carry his enthusiasm too far, for, as Greenough has remarked, one must not forget that they are all cancer in whatever group they are placed.

Treatment

There is much difference of opinion as to treatment. Many men favor radium treatment to the lip, others desiccation and others excision. We grant that radium will usually destroy and heal a cancer of the lip. We do not feel that the result is as lasting as surgical removal. We have little experience with desiccation but more with electrocoagulation, particularly in the extensive cases. If one is to be *radical enough* with these measures, one must create a considerable defect on the lip. Why not remove surgically and correct the defect at the same time? We value the opportunity to obtain a pathological specimen for study enough to favor surgical excision in preference to the other methods mentioned.

We must warn against the use of cancer pastes, cancer salves, herb remedies, and the like. Every year scores of patients in this State lose their right to existence because these remedies are used. We realize that some primary cancers are healed by the use of these agents, but no consideration is given to the deposits in the glands. A few months later a gland appears in the neck. The patient does not associate it with his primary lesion and postpones treatment until too late.

We advise surgical removal of all cancers of the lip, either by a V or a rectangular incision, the excision to extend through the full thickness of the lip and to include at least one half inch of normal tissue on all sides of the lesion. If a wide excision is done of a large lesion it may be necessary to resort to a plastic operation to close the defect.

In regard to the glands of the neck, some physicians feel that no treatment is of any use. Others use radiation, and still others use radiation at first and operation if glands increase during the radiation. With the exception of the small lesions which, on removal, prove to be Grade I cancers, we advise a neck dissection on all cases if the physical condition warrants it. We include the large Grade I lesions in this group. If we suspect a Grade I lesion, it is removed under novocaine, otherwise the lip lesion and the glands are removed at one sitting, either under general or local anaesthesia. If the lesion lies well to one side of the lip, dissection of the glands on that side is sufficient. The presence of the lesion near the center of the lip calls for dissection of both sides of the neck down to the level of the bifurcation of the carotid. For lesions of long standing, wherever their location on the lip, bilateral dissection is indicated.

The Neck Dissection

A curved incision is made under the jaw from beneath the chin, on the opposite side, parallel with the jaw, back to the sternomastoid muscle. The skin and fat flaps are dissected upward and downward. The sternomastoid muscle is exposed as is the tip of the parotid gland and the angle of the jaw. The triangular space between these landmarks contains some of the upper cervical glands and should be cleared out. The dissection is carried down the sternomastoid muscle for about two inches. Then all the fat and glandular tissue is swept forward to beyond the midline. The internal jugular vein is cleared and the facial vein ligated. The platysma should be removed and all tissues up to the edge of the jaw swept forward. The external and anterior jugular veins are ligated and cut, the facial artery at its entrance into the submaxillary gland is divided and the submaxillary gland removed. The lower dissection passes just below the digastric muscle and tendon, follows up the belly of one digastric for a short distance, but then includes the tissues in the submental space, which lie between the bellies of the two digastrics. When the submaxillary gland is removed care must be taken not to cut the lingual nerve which lies along the upper border of the inner half of the gland. This is well covered by fascia and may be easily retracted and missed if not looked for. Drainage is accomplished through a stab wound at the lowest portion of the dissected area. The skin is closed. Very little deformity follows this dissection.

Results of Operative Treatment at the Massachusetts General Hospital

Two series of cases have been studied and reported in recent years, the first by Simmons and Daland[3] and the second by Shedden[4]. In the first series there were 187 cases but only 131 are available for final results. Local excision of the growth was done in 33 cases with 20 three-year cures (66 per cent). Removal of the primary growth combined with neck dissection produced 87 per cent three-year cures when no cancer was found in the glands (63 of 72 cases). When cancer was present in the glands, 5 of 19 patients (26 per cent) survived three years.

It is not always possible to tell by clinical examination whether the glands are involved or not. In 24 cases in this group, no glands could be palpated before operation and yet in six (25 per cent) they were found at operation. Palpable glands did not necessarily mean that cancer was present; for many of these palpable glands were found to be inflammatory.

Shedden in an analysis of a later group of 107 cases found but 38 per cent three-year cures in the cases on whom the lip alone was operated on. Dissection of the glands was done in the remainder of the cases but in only 10 per cent was cancer found. There were 88 per cent alive and well where no cancer was found and 57 per cent where cancer was present in the glands.

Combining these two series, giving 200 known results, the results were 49 per cent on the simple lip operation, 42 per cent where the glands were cancerous and 87 per cent when no cancer was present in the glands. However, these are three-year, not five-year cures. Figuring on the longer time the results would not be quite as good, although recurrence after three years is uncommon.

Results of Operative Treatment at the Pondville Hospital

Taylor has studied the end results of all cancers of the lip operated on at the Pondville Hospital between July 1, 1927 and July 1, 1929 and is preparing the report for publication. Nineteen cases are available for end-result studies. The percentage of three-year cures in these nineteen cases, all with pathological studies, is 94.7. All patients (nine) in whom a simple V excision was done without a neck dissection survived three years. Three out of four patients who had V excisions and neck dissections with cancer in the glands were three-year cures. Six patients who had the same operation, but in whom no cancer was found in the glands, survived three years.

Results in Other Clinics

In 1865 Thiersch[6] stated that 10 per cent of the patients with cancer of the lip remained well for three years at least. In 1885 Woerner[7], from the Tuebinger Clinic, reported 350 operations on 277 individuals with 32 per cent three-year cures. Fricke[6] in 1898 found 55 per cent cured for the same time in his 128 cases.

Crile in 1906 described the block dissection of the lymph nodes and lymph-bearing areolar tissue. Twelve of his 46 cases (26 per cent) were well for three years, several of whom had extensive glandular involvement.

Bloodgood[7] reviewed the results of 44 cancers of the lip treated surgically. In 11 cases, the lip lesion was excised but the glands were untreated. Sixty-three per cent remained well five years, but 27 per cent died from metastases in the glands. Twenty-one patients, in addition to excision of the local lesion, had a glandular dissection with no cancer in the glands. All but one of these (95 per cent) were cured for at least five years. Twelve patients had cancer in their glands at operation. Six of these (50 per cent) remained well.

Broders[8] traced 58 per cent of 537 lip cancers treated by operation at the Mayo Clinic. Of the 306 traced patients, 169 (55 per cent) remained well (length of time not stated). Of those who died, many died of other causes, but at least half of them died of recurrence of their lip cancer. Seventeen per cent of those having glandular metastases at operation remained well. No patient in his series who had more than one group of lymph nodes involved was reported living.

Broders[2], in the article referred to, announced his classification according to the degree of differentiation of the cells, a classification widely in use at the present time. In his Grade I cases, the most differentiated type, there were no deaths; Grade II, 54.9 per cent deaths; Grade III, 84.2 per cent; and in Grade IV all patients died. In his series of 449 neck dissections (not all these patients were traced), the glands were involved in 23 per cent.

Sistrunk[4], also reporting from the Mayo Clinic, stated that where the neck was dissected and no cancer found in the glands, 90 per cent were cured for five to eight years.

Brewer[5], reviewing statistics of cases operated on at the Roosevelt and Presbyterian Hospitals in New York, the Mayo Clinic, Johns Hopkins Hospital and others found 66 per cent five-year cures in the group where the lip alone was operated on. If the glands were dissected and no cancer found, the cures rose to 92 per cent while, if cancerous glands were removed, cures were only 34 per cent in five years.

Figi[9], in a more recent report from the Mayo Clinic, states that approximately 90 per cent are cured if the glands are not involved and approximately 50 per cent if cancer is present. No definite series of results is given. The present policy is to excise lip cancer of all grades unless the size of the lesion or the patient's condition forbids it. In that case interstitial radiation and external radiation is used. If the lesion is extensive, a cautery excision is done down to the bone, followed six months later by a plastic closure. The submental glands and the submaxillary glands on both sides are dissected out. If they are involved, the next lower group is removed.

Stevens[10] does not give the number in his series treated by electrothermic surgery, but reports 80 per cent five-year cures in the superficial lesions, 40 per cent in the deeply invading lesions without glands and 11 per cent in the cases with metastatic glands. The three groups average 44 per cent five-year cures.

Schreiner[11] reports on the results of irradiation of cancer of the lip at the New York State Institute for the Study of Malignant Disease. Of 65 cases where the lip alone was involved, 68 per cent were well for at least five years. Of 23 cases in which the glands were enlarged but movable, 13 per cent were cured for five years. Where the disease was extensive with involvement of the deeper structures 3 per cent were cured of eight cases.

Berven, Heyman and Thoreus[12], report on the cancers of the lip treated by radium at the Radiumhemmet, Stockholm, from 1909 to 1923. Radium was applied to the surface of the tumor on dental plastic mass with a filter of gold and platinum having a filtration equivalent of 1 mm. lead. Certain of the more extensive lesions were also treated by radium at a distance, as were the gland-bearing areas. They divided their cases into the superficial cancers on which they report 80 per cent five-year cures and the infiltrating cancers, 41 per cent of whom are alive and well for five years. They state that more than one half of the second group were inoperable when treatment was first attempted. The present technique consists in embedding radium needles into the primary tumor.

Pendergrass[13] reports in great detail on the treatment of lip cancer by radiation. He advises against dissection of the glands because it is a mutilating operation. His results are inconclusive. He selects 58 of 172 cases treated as the most favorable in the series. All but three of these are well but for how long a time he does not state. There are also three untraced cases.

Quick[14] reports from the Memorial Hospital, New York, that cancer of the lip is treated by filtered radium to the lesion if it is superficial, filtered interstitial radium if it is more extensive. Very large lesions are radiated, then excised and closed by a plastic operation. All necks where glands are not palpable are radiated. If a gland with an intact capsule is palpable, a unilateral dissection is done. Glands with cancer invading the capsule are considered inoperable and are treated by the implantation of radium with external radiation as well. Quick believes that the radical neck dissection is unnecessary and gives no better results than a dissection of the submental and submaxillary groups plus the upper deep cervical group. He does not give his end results.

Pancoast[15] advises radium to the lip and radium packs followed by X-ray treatment to the neck. He later coagulates the local lesion. If radiation does not cause the glands to disappear, he dissects the neck. He does not state his results.

Forsell[16] states that he knows of no lip cancers with glandular metastases that have been cured by radium.

Montgomery and Culver[17] treated 60 cases with radium. They do not state whether or not the glands were involved but they report 80 per cent free from recurrence at the end of five years.

Conclusion

1. Persisting ulcers, leukoplakia, or tumors of the lip may be cancer and must be treated as such until proven otherwise.

2. If the lesion is treated before it has spread to the glands and if only the lip is treated, there is a 60 per cent chance of cure. If treated equally early but combined with a dissection of the glands, there is a 90 per cent chance of cure.

3. The percentage of cures obtained in all operable cases which are traced five years is approximately seventy.

4. Inasmuch as many patients have inoperable lesions when they are first admitted, it is probable that not more than 50 per cent of all the patients with cancer of the lip who appear for treatment survive the five year period.

Cancer of the Lip

TABLE I—*Excision only. No treatment of glands.*

	No. cases	Duration of cures	Per cent cured
Bloodgood	11	5 years	63
Brewer	—	5 years	66
Simmons and Daland	33	3 years	60
Shedden	12	3 years	38
Taylor	7	3 years	100

TABLE II—*Excision lip lesion with dissection of glands.*
No cancer in glands

	No. cases	Duration of cures	Per cent cured
Bloodgood	12	5 years	95
Sistrunk	—	5 years	90
Brewer	—	5 years	92
Simmons and Daland	72	3 years	87
Shedden	52	3 years	88
Taylor	6	3 years	100

Cancer in glands

	No. cases	Duration of cures	Per cent cured
Bloodgood	12	5 years	50
Brewer	—	5 years	34
Simmons and Daland	19	3 years	26
Shedden	7	3 years	57
Taylor	4	3 years	75

Bibliography

1. EWING, *Neoplastic Diseases*.
2. BRODERS, *Squamous Cell Epithelioma of the Lip*, J.A.M.A. 74:656, Mar. 6, '20.
3. SIMMONS AND DALAND, *The Results of Operations for Cancer of the Lip at the Massachusetts General Hospital from 1909 to 1919*, Surg. Gynec. & Obst. 35:766-771, Dec. '22.
4. SHEDDEN, *The Results of Surgical Treatment of Epithelioma of the Lip*. Boston M. & S.J. 196:262-270, Feb. 17 '27.
5. TAYLOR, *Unpublished report*.
6. QUOTED BY BREWER, *Carcinoma of the Lip and Cheek*. Surg. Gynec. & Obst. 36:169-184, Feb. '23.
7. BLOODGOOD, *Cancer of the lower lip*. Boston M. & S.J. 1914, CLXX, 49-51. *Carcinoma of the lower lip; its diagnosis and operative treatment*. Surg. Gynec. and Obst. 1914, XVIII, pp. 404-422.
8. SISTRUNK, *The Results of the Surgical Treatment of Epithelioma of the Lip*. Ann. Surg. 73:521, May 1921.
9. FIGI, *Collected Papers of the Mayo Clinic*, XXI, 1929, p. 724.
10. STEVENS, *Electrothermic Surgery in Management of Carcinomata of the Lip*. Am. J. Surg. 7:831-835, December 1929.
11. SCHREINER AND SIMPSON, *End Results of Irradiation of Cancer of Lip*. Radiol. Rev. & Chicago M. Rec. 51:235-245, June 1929.
12. BERVEN, HEYMAN & THORÆUS, *The Technique in the Treatment of Tumors at Radiumhemmet, Stockholm, 1929*. P. A. Norstedt and Söner.
13. PENDERGRASS, *Epidermoid Carcinoma (epithelioma) of Lip*. S. Clin. N. Amer. 7:117-163, February 1927.
14. QUICK, *Clinical Reports from Memorial Hospital, New York City*. Am. J. Cancer 15:229-270, January 1931.
15. PANCOAST, *Modern Treatment of Cancer of the Lip*. Surg. Gynec. & Obst. 34:589-593, May 1922.
16. FORSELL, Acta Radiologica, 1928, Sup. II.
17. MONTGOMERY AND CULVER, *Epithelioma of the Lip Treated with Radium*. California and West. Med. 22:628-631, December 1924.

CANCER OF THE SKIN

We should first consider briefly the precancerous conditions. It is commonly believed that certain keratoses, papillomas, moles and "warts" are forerunners of skin cancer.

We should distinguish between tyo types of keratoses, the seborrhoeic and the senile. The seborrhoeic keratosis is characterized by an overgrowth of the horny layer of the skin, irregularity of the prickle cell layer of epithelium without invasion of the corium, absence of pain and by an increased pigmentation. There is a mild inflammatory reaction. This type of keratosis is soft to palpate, feels greasy, is often multiple. It rarely becomes cancerous.

A senile keratosis shows a similar heaping up of the outer layer with microscopic changes in the dermis, but it is tender and rough to the touch, it causes an itching sensation and shows some inflammatory reaction. It does not show pigmentation, it is easily pulled off with resulting soreness around the base. It may be softened by ointments, but the lesion reappears repeatedly. This type of lesion may persist for years, but it usually changes into a squamous cell cancer. Both types occur most often on the exposed surfaces of the body.

Arsenical keratoses arise years after a patient has taken arsenic for medical purposes. They resemble the senile keratoses except that they occur all over the body, chiefly on the hands and soles. They do not respond well to treatment and almost invariably become cancerous if not destroyed.

A lesion often considered by the patient to be a mole may be a beginning seborrhoeic keratosis. Removal of this type of lesion is usually requested for cosmetic purposes. Radium is very efficacious in destroying either type of keratosis, the dosage required being very slight. Desiccation is a valuable aid in treating these benign skin conditions.

It has commonly been stated that skin cancer is found more commonly in men, particularly in out-of-door workers. The writer in an analysis of two hundred and sixty-five cases found a slight preponderance in men, but about half the men and all of the women were indoor workers. It does seem likely that certain of the outdoor workers are much more likely to have multiple and more serious lesions than the others. Skin cancers are most likely to occur on the exposed surfaces, and are commonest on the face above a line drawn through the angles of the mouth.

Cancer of the skin may occur at any age after maturity, but is usually found after forty and much more commonly after sixty.

There are two main types of skin cancer—the prickle cell or squamous cell cancer and the basal cell type. It is not always possible to distinguish between the two types clinically. The treatment of the local lesion is the same, whichever the type. Apparently it makes no difference as to the effectiveness of radiation. However, the basal cell type rarely ever spreads to the glands, but occasionally the squamous cell type does. The occurrence of metastases is hardly common enough to warrant a dissection of the glands as a preventive measure when the lesion is on the face, but careful watch must be kept on the glands of the neck.

The basal cell lesion or rodent ulcer is characterized by a tiny ulceration over which a scab forms. There is a heaping up of the cells around the periphery. After a while the scab comes off and the ulcer becomes larger. The raised edge advances a little further and the entire lesion becomes larger and more irregular. Later the ulceration and induration extend deeper and involve deeper layers. The exact extent of the lesion is difficult to determine clinically, so that wide removal is necessary to cure it. Basal cell carcinomas occur chiefly on the face.

The squamous cell lesion is much more indefinite in appearance and is apt to have an irregular outline. It may begin as an ulceration or as a papillary lesion or a combination of the two. The surface is covered with a dirty grayish slough, it tends to bleed easily and the edge is indurated. The clinical course is more rapid than the other type and the lesion may metastasize to the glands. Some lesions may show both types of growth when examined microscopically. Lesions in the area one inch in front of the ear, on the hands or feet, vulva, scrotum or penis are usually of the squamous cell type and are apt to spread to the adjacent glands.

Treatment

Without question, every case of skin cancer which has not extended beneath the skin should be cured if the patient is cooperative and completes his treatment. The agents used are surgical excision, radium, X-ray and electrothermic methods. Any of these, in experienced hands, is satisfactory.

For lesions on the forehead, ears, lower cheeks, neck and hands surgical excision is preferable unless the excision will deform other structures. Surgical excision can be done under local anaesthesia, the wound is quickly healed with the minimum amount of discomfort or disability, the result is usually satisfactory and we have the advantage of a pathological examination. If radiation fails, surgery must be resorted to, whatever deformity is created. Glandular dissection should be done for cancers of the skin of the hand, foot, vulva, penis and scrotum.

Desiccation of superficial lesions is advocated by some men. This may at times be satisfactory. The only reason for using it is to prevent a bad scar and the danger is that the surface destruction be not carried deep enough to cure the lesion. For more extensive lesions electrocoagulation is of great help and frequently accomplishes a cure when the usual excision or radiation fails.

For lesions on the nose, upper lip, eyelids and adjacent parts of the face radium is undoubtedly the treatment of choice. As a rule, heavily screened radium is used, although in some clinics bare radium tubes are still used. For the usual skin cancer, a radium dosage should be used sufficient to destroy the lesion in one treatment or two at the most. Mild doses of radium will temporarily heal a skin cancer but a much heavier dose is necessary to make the result permanent.

In the hands of experienced radiologists, X-radiation will accomplish practically the same results as radium. It is necessary to give doses of X-rays proportionate to the radium doses. This method does not lend itself to all cases because of technical difficulties. Tissues soon develop an immunity to X-ray or radium and unless vigorous treatment is given at first, failure follows.

Curetting a skin cancer is unscientific and frequently results in recurrence and metastasis.

Results

The only statistics of results available are from the Collis P. Huntington Memorial Hospital[1], from which are reported results on 265 cases treated by radium in 1917 and 1918. The average age was 60, with 144 over 60. Of the 265 cases, results were obtained at the end of three years on 203. Seventy eight were followed for a full five years, with but one recurrence between the three and five year period.

In Class A, where the lesion was limited to the skin and not encroaching on neighboring structures of 138 cases, 112 were cured by radium and 4 by excision after radiation. This gave 84 per cent cures for three years. In Class B, where there is some fixation or encroachment on a second structure, there were 39 cases. Fifteen were cured by radium and four by radium plus excision, a total of 48 per cent. Class C comprised the cases with deep fixation. None were cured by radium, but one with operation after radium—but 3 per cent of the whole group.

Summarizing the results, 84 per cent of the early, favorable cases were cured, 48 per cent of the moderately advanced and but 3 per cent of the advanced cases. Combining these figures gives 67 per cent of the total traced cases.

Results in Other Clinics

Berven and Heyman[2] and Forsell[3] report 86 per cent permanent cures (five years or more) in superficial skin cancers and 51 per cent in the infiltrating forms. Ninety-five per cent of the patients in the first group, who did not interrupt treatment before it was completed, were cured.

A report from the State Institute for the Study of Malignant Disease at Buffalo[4] states that, if skin cancer were treated early, 95 to 100 per cent should remain well for five years or more. As it is, of 307 cases appearing favorable for cure 86 per cent did remain well five years after radium treatment. There were also 33 far advanced cases and only 39 per cent were cured for five years.

Bibliography

1. DALAND, *End Results of Radium Treatment of Skin Cancer*, Journal A. M. A. Vol. 86, February 13, 1926, p. 471.
2. BERVEN AND HEYMAN, *Report on Cases Radiologically Treated at Radiumhemmet, Stockholm, 1929*.
3. FORSELL, Acta Radiologica, 1928 Sup: II.
4. Health News, N. Y. State Department of Health, February 1, 1932.

WORCESTER NORTH CANCER CLINIC COMMITTEE
February 7, 1928

CHAIRMAN, FREDERICK H. THOMPSON, M.D.

When the question arose of providing cancer diagnostic service in the Worcester North district, it was deemed advisable that each of the three larger communities—Fitchburg, Gardner and Leominster—should arrange for a clinic in its local hospital. This proposal met a cordial response from the hospitals, and a clinic has been held in weekly rotation in one of these three hospitals since February, 1928.

While the attendance in these clinics has been numerically smaller than in some of the more populous areas, the clinics in Fitchburg and Gardner are apparently adequately serving the needs of their immediate neighborhoods and the clinics have been regularly announced in the local papers. The growth of the Leominster clinic has been slower. With the organization of a new associate committee larger attendance is looked for in the near future.

NEW BEDFORD CANCER CLINIC COMMITTEE
March 14, 1928

CHAIRMAN, A. H. MANDELL, M.D.

CANCER SERVICE IN GENERAL HOSPITALS
BY CURTIS C. TRIPP, M.D.

In the running of the New Bedford Cancer Clinic it has occurred to me that there are two changes which might be advantageously introduced to improve the service that is being rendered to cancer patients. As our clinic is now organized, cases requiring biopsy are referred to their own physicians or to the surgical clinic of the local hospital's recommendation. The patients who are in the private patient class should, of course, be referred to their own physicians for any or all necessary treatment, as at present. But many of our cases are dependent on charity clinics for treatment and I believe that we can treat these patients more efficiently and save time, clinic visits, and unnecessary shuttling about, by having our cancer clinic prepared to do simple surgery, such as taking biopsies and removing small superficial tumors instead of referring such cases to other clinics. Such procedures are essentially diagnostic in character and should form a part of the function of a diagnostic clinic.

In our clinic now we follow all positive cases of cancer at intervals from the time they are first seen, and the greatest gap in our contact with these patients is the most important time when they are receiving their first active treatment. Thereafter they are followed to an end-result, and further treatment is advised as indicated. It would seem reasonable that a group of men, interested in cancer work, who see these patients for diagnosis and who will eventually follow many of them through until the disease is ended, would be best qualified to treat them, and where a clinic is held in a hospital which will eventually provide treatment in the ward services for many of its cases, as. is the situation here, it would seem reasonable that the clinic staff should have some contact with the actual treatment of the charity cases which enter the wards. I would consider the most efficient arrangement to be the establishment of a definite cancer service in the general hospitals where clinics are conducted, and feel that the importance and difficulties of cancer treatment warrant such a service. Its organization should be similar to, and preferably identical with, the present cancer clinic group, comprising surgeon, radiologist, and consultants in pathology, gynecology, urology, dermatology, and internal medicine. This would provide an interested and cooperating group which would discuss each case individually, direct the entire course of treatment, and especially help to coordinate the work of the surgeon and radiologist. It would also give a satisfactory opportunity for pre- and postoperative study, offer the best available treatment and after-care and would carry each case through from its first arrival at the clinic to the final check-up under the direction of the same group.

LAWRENCE CANCER CLINIC COMMITTEE
April 24, 1928

CHAIRMAN, J. FORREST BURNHAM, M.D.

WHY A CANCER CLINIC

When the Massachusetts State Legislature passed a bill which commissioned the Massachusetts State Department of Public Health to institute State-aided cancer clinics in Massachusetts, the whole matter was an untried affair.

The problem of cancer and its train of woeful consequences has been the subject of very much discussion by medical and social organizations everywhere, and the proponents of the measure brought forward sufficient evidence as to the probable value of the State's assistance to the medical and social agencies interested in this serious disease, outlined a program of possible partial control of the malady; and presented this information to the lawmakers in such a convincing manner, that the legislation was passed by both houses and the bill was approved by the Governor.

In searching for the most suitable agent to handle this big proposition, the State Department of Public Health was selected, under the terms of the bill, to execute the details thereof. Time has demonstrated that a wise choice of a vehicle for the carrying out of the provisions of the act, was made. Suitable funds are appropriated for certain necessary expenditures.

In the State's earlier attacks on tuberculosis and its problem of control and care, the commission plan was adopted, and it was a success; and yet the later method of presenting a medical (cancer) proposition to the State's medical (State Department of Public Health) organization has proved its value. It was apparent that the organization of the Department was already in existence, with its machinery and personnel and the taking over of one more subject meant the addition of such new medical and clerical assistance only as was required. With his usual energy the Commissioner of Health attacked the problem of organization, and as a result today, seven years later the entire system, as arranged, is proceeding smoothly in an orderly manner.

The two elements necessary to convince were the practicing physicians and the reputable hospitals. Like other new and untried plans which have been presented to them in the past, the physicians looked askance at the movement, often suspecting that it might be another attempt tending to a separation of their patients from them, to the eventual disaster of the latter. Most physicians of any years of experience have had socialistic problems of various natures presented to them, and having suffered because of them, are unwilling to further inconvenience their patients, even when the original intention was good.

In the Lawrence district a year was necessary to convince the majority of the good physicians that the scheme was workable and of value to patient and physician.

The underlying principle now being so widely accepted, of permitting physicians to be in charge of, and manage or define the methods of handling, and specify the limits of all organizations where medical treatment of individuals is concerned, was early made plain by the Commissioner as applicable to the proposed clinics.

In all medico-social clinics everywhere the physician, today, has determined that the best good to the patient occurs when the nurse, the social worker, the attachés of health departments, medical or lay, are, collectively, instruments in the hands of the skillful, honest physician to be used as a part of the cure. Like drugs, the knife, mental therapeutics, and food, all are prescribed in varying doses as particular patients need, after study of the cases by the careful physician.

A cause of certain cases of mental anguish, accompanied by obvious financial depression on the part of physicians, has followed the unpleasant results to the patient, of contact with certain forms of mass treatment and irregular lay official advice. This situation is often caused by lack of cooperation between the family physician and official medical departments. The physician is usually correct but uninformed of the scope of the work ordered by the department, and the subaltern is usually incorrect but working as best he can, while lacking a medical viewpoint. It is almost idle to hope to give any lay individual a complete medical viewpoint, short of the medical school training. It has been generally accepted that the true specialist in medicine should have a period of general training as a general practitioner, and it is not beyond reason to expect that the medical health officer should have a similar background.

Recent developments in this State have made it more hopeful that the patient and public generally will be in a position to obtain nearer 100% efficiency in treatment, since the Massachusetts Medical Society has provided a Committee on Public Relations, which committee has already secured good cooperation with the Department of Public Health.

The family physician has been accomplishing his humanitarian work since the period of the Great Physician, and regardless of a recent edict as to what will be done to him, he plans to carry on.

The Lawrence Cancer Clinic has operated successfully for five years, has gained and kept the confidence of the surrounding medical profession and has acquired a good reputation among patients and public.

From the beginning, the management of the Lawrence General Hospital has offered every possible encouragement to the clinic, its buildings, nurses, executives, social workers, Roentgen Ray Department, internes, beds, dressings when needed, and its every facility found in an approved hospital of 150 beds.

The medical staff gave earnest thought to the plan, and having accepted the responsibilities involved, entered into the matter with enthusiasm and has carried it on creditably, while the entire personnel of thirty-eight is ready to do its part when required.

The lines of the clinic have been defined as those of the Essex North District Medical Society. This includes three cities and eleven towns with a population of 208,246 and a medical population of 229 physicians.

An important function which the clinic has developed is its use as a place for postgraduate instruction, including theoretical, didactic and practical. Physicians whose lives are spent largely in diagnostic and operative cancer work have conducted Demonstration Clinics upon the occasion of the regular and special clinics at the Lawrence General Hospital. To the general practitioner in our community, as elsewhere, the opportunities of examining and treating manifold cases of cancer, near cancer, and benign growths are, in the nature of events, more or less limited, and yet a certain knowledge of diagnosis and treatment of such cases is essential to the welfare of his clientele. The information gained from our Demonstration Clinics has been found invaluable and has been eagerly taken when offered, and attending physicians have appreciated the opportunity. Such clinics have had as many as thirty physicians present and interested.

The Commonwealth of Massachusetts appears to occupy the happy position, as in many advances in medical lines in the interest of health, of a leader in solving the cancer control problem. Some of the other states have given the matter consideration later, and are following programs aimed at the same target. New York, Illinois, New Hampshire and California are working on this humane medical problem and it bids fair to be a country-wide effort whose value will eventually be reflected in increased health to our citizens. Our vital statistics should later show better morbidity and mortality figures, as has been noticed everywhere in tuberculosis and venereal diseases, both of which diseases have experienced medical broadside attacks of a similar nature.

In conclusion it is fair to remark that there appears to be no question now but that in the years during which cancer clinics have been established they have demonstrated their value to patient, public and physician. Also, the funds appropriated by certain states, as well as auxiliary money furnished by other organizations, and the uncounted financial resources represented by the contributions of the facilities of charity hospitals, and the time and services of many physicians, entirely uncompensated in coin of the realm, have caused marked progress in supporting the fight of humanity vs. cancer.

Lastly, we must never forget that the interest of the patient is the prime desideratum in all these medical problems, including cancer, and that the cardinal premise, argument and decision is one which has been very clearly enunciated in an extract from the Final Report of the Commission on Medical Education, under the chairmanship of President Lowell of Harvard University.

This valuable study has been in progress since 1925 and in its summary just released this self truth is promulgated:

"Sound medical service can be rendered only when a single physician assumes the direct responsibility for a given patient."

BERKSHIRE COUNTY CANCER CLINIC COMMITTEE
May 31, 1928
CHAIRMAN, C. H. RICHARDSON, M.D.

THE PITTSFIELD CLINICS

The clinics in Berkshire County have been held weekly in rotation at the three Pittsfield hospitals, and monthly at the North Adams Hospital during the past year. The clinics have been well attended, considering the population. The conditions in Berkshire are a little different from congested cities in that people have not been educated to attend clinics as they have in the larger cities.

The number of people, who think they might have cancer, going to their private physician or surgeon, has increased very materially so that the real good done by the clinics is the publicity of the subject of cancer, which drives the possible sufferer to early investigation of his condition.

Our committee feels that we can get more publicity in the newspapers by not having the clinics so frequently and they therefore have been changed to every two weeks, rotating at the three Pittsfield hospitals for the coming year.

Dr. Thomas P. Hennelly, the former chairman of the committee for Berkshire County, was very attentive and very much interested and his death was a great loss to the committee. The writer has been elected chairman of the committee in Dr. Hennelly's place.

BOSTON DISPENSARY TUMOR CLINIC
July 1, 1928
SURGEON-IN-CHIEF, WILLIAM M. SHEDDEN, M.D.

THE TEACHING SERVICE IN A CANCER CLINIC
BY HARRY F. FRIEDMAN, M.D.

The medical student receives very little instruction in the basic facts and accepted methods of diagnosis and treatment of cancer. He is grilled in the fundamental medical sciences in order that he may have an appreciation of the symptoms, pathology, and treatment of the various diseases.

He is weighed down by the enormous amount of literature he must consume and the conflicting ideas therein expressed. Yet, with it all, if he is clever, he will at once see that the practice of medicine is not an exact science, that there are very few diseases in which there is a known cause and specific cure, and that his object, unless he becomes a purely scientific investigator, must resolve itself into preventing disease or effecting symptomatic relief until those natural processes come into play and effect a cure. So it is today that preventive medicine stands foremost in the realm of medical practice.

The student receives thorough instruction, both didactic and clinical, in the more common diseases such as tuberculosis, heart disease, pneumonia, rheumatism, diseases of the kidneys, liver, blood, etc. He has opportunity to observe these diseases in their various stages and to note the effects of treatment.

He can give the origin and insertion of numerous muscles, their blood supply and function, as well as trace the various nerves. His chemistry and physiology are well grounded, and the student of a Class A medical school, if he is industrious, can pass the examination of any State Board of Registration without embarrassment.

The inspiration of great teachers and investigators is ever in his memory, and he applies their precepts in the practice of his profession.

It is manifestly impossible for the student of medicine to familiarize himself thoroughly with all of its branches. He learns to treat the more common diseases, those with which he is most apt to come in contact in his daily work.

The one disease that he knows absolutely nothing about, dreads the word, treats it indifferently or not at all, is cancer. The average medical student receives no direct instruction in cancer, and the average doctor of medicine has only a vague idea of the present accepted methods of diagnosis and treatment. Now, what should be the attitude of the medical school in this matter? Is the school to stand by and see the rising incidence and mortality from cancer unchallenged? Is she to allow her students to enter practice with such insufficient knowledge of its diagnosis and treatment? Is she to depend on outside aid from a few State clinics or privately endowed cancer hospitals for the enlightenment of her students? Massachusetts leads in the diagnosis and treatment of her cancer sick. The fine facilities that the State offers for the diagnosis and treatment of cancer are not generally appreciated by the profession or public, though to my knowledge there is no organized plan of teaching in any of these institutions. Many hospitals have cancer clinics for the benefit of their patients, splendidly equipped and staffed, but how many offer to the student and profession a teaching service? To those of us who are actively engaged in the cancer problem, the wisdom of an organized teaching program is vital. The medical student and practitioner must receive proper instruction in the diagnosis and treatment of cancer if we are to lessen its mortality.

There should be a separate department for the teaching of cancer, its diagnosis and treatment, in every medical school in connection with one or more of its associated hospitals. The guidance of this department should be under one head, with representatives of the various branches of medicine cooperating in teaching the type of cancer which comes under their jurisdiction. The radiologist should teach the radiology of cancer; the pathologist, the pathology of cancer; the surgeon, the surgery of cancer; and so on.

The recognition of the precancerous lesion, the early cancer and its treatment should be stressed. The proper method of cancer prevention is the physician's responsibility, and to him alone must we look for its solution. No amount of education of the public will suffice if we are to neglect or ill-advise them when they come to us for advice. The incidence of cancer of the uterine cervix in women who have borne children would become nil if these cases were examined at definite intervals after their confinement, and such simple remedial defects as tears and inflammations corrected immediately. Yet cancer of the cervix continues to take its toll, and usually at a time of life when the mother is most needed in the home. A good obstetrician never sees a cancer of the cervix in a patient whom he has delivered; only the neglected cases develop cancer. Cancer of the lip, mouth, and tongue can be prevented by the removal of all irritations, especially diseased teeth and poorly fitting dentures.

It is an easy matter to instill into the minds of the student definite axioms which will guide him in the prevention and help him towards the diagnosis and cure. I have heard a great many doctors say, "Why go to a lecture on cancer? They tell you to get it early, be radical in your treatment, and then, well—maybe you will effect a cure." This statement is true. In telling them to get it early, we should instruct them how to recognize it early, the art of prevention, early recognition, and adequate accepted treatment. There are some cases of cancer you cannot cure no matter how early you recognize them. Fortunately these cases are not common.

If the cases of cancer now existing in Massachusetts had had early diagnosis, quick and adequate treatment, and should early recognition and proper treatment be applied to all cases that will develop this year, the estimated deaths would be reduced at least thirty per cent. As I have said, you can educate the public to consult a physician early, but unless that physician can make the correct diagnosis and institute proper treatment, the result will be unsatisfactory.

Cancer is not a self-limited disease. It is progressive and, unless eradicated, will terminate fatally. If proper instruction is given, one can safely say that the incidence of cancer will drop decidedly, and the mortality rate correspondingly decrease.

BROCKTON CANCER CLINIC COMMITTEE
June 12, 1930

CHAIRMAN, MICHAEL F. BARRETT, M.D.

Of the State-aided cancer clinics throughout Massachusetts, the one in Brockton is the most recent, being established June 1930. The number of problems we have to present at this time, therefore, is not sufficient to draw satisfactory conclusions.

The policy is to center the clinic around the general practitioner by assisting him in a more detailed diagnosis. All patients having a family physician are referred to him by letter covering findings and opinion, and the field of treatment is left to his discretion. However, the clinic is able in many instances to help the family physician in arranging for early, adequate treatment.

Figures from the annual report of 1932 show that from June 1930 to December 1932, 123 of the 756 patients examined at the clinic were diagnosed cancer. Of these diagnosed cancer all but seven received treatment approved by the clinic. It is certain that the splendid cooperation of the local physicians, the persistent effort of the Educational Committee, and and the continued publicity contribute largely toward the success of the clinic.

SPRINGFIELD ASSOCIATE CANCER COMMITTEE
SECRETARY, FREDERIC EDWARDS

CLINIC PUBLICITY
BY FREDERIC EDWARDS

In any publicity campaign the main purpose, of course, is to get before the general public an idea of what it is all about. Obviously, therefore, in our campaign for the control of cancer, the chief objectives of an educational program should be to acquaint as many people as possible with the knowledge that cancer is curable, if discovered early and treated immediately, and that there are already available in Massachusetts facilities for early diagnosis and medical and hospital care.

From a long experience with the campaign against tuberculosis, we in Springfield are of the opinion that the same sort of extensive and intensive methods which have been so successfully applied in that crusade can be as successfully used in the campaign against cancer. Our experience, however, has demonstrated that better results are secured through the printed and the spoken word than through any other advertising methods. By the printed word we mean particularly use of the press, and by the spoken word continuous informal talks before such groups as service clubs, women's clubs, parent teacher associations and the like, whose members really form a large group of missionaries able and willing to spread the gospel of educational cancer publicity to a widespread, interested group of people. That the foregoing statement is true is evidenced continually by the fact that visitors to the office of the Springfield district cancer committee, and to the cancer clinics themselves, account for their visits by having either seen in a paper, or learned through someone who has heard the story, what the cancer committee is endeavoring to accomplish.

Throughout the entire Connecticut Valley we are extremely fortunate in having a splendidly cooperative press, which is both socially minded and public spirited. Invariably, every paper in our district will print nearly every line we give them pertaining to the Massachusetts Cancer Program. In addition, our papers print not only all syndicated articles pertaining to the studies, or the control, or the cure of cancer, but they also publish regularly almost every article sent them through the Associated Press relative to the work of scientists, research laboratories and medical schools which are endeavoring to find solutions to the problem. From the increasing attendance at clinics whenever special time and thought is given to newspaper publicity, it is evident that such a source of information is not only worth while but that it pays great dividends. Of course, all such educational publicity should be continuous because it has been proven over and over again that sporadic attempts to arouse enthusiasm, or even interest, are simply expedients, and that whenever interest or enthusiasm is merely temporarily aroused it quickly wanes and dissipates itself.

Certain key people who control or influence large groups are always worth contacting. We refer especially to directors of visiting nurse associations, officers of industrial nurses' clubs, general agents for large insurance companies and the chief executives of all health and welfare organizations who have administrative control over large groups of workers, particularly nurses. Again, it is the story of educating a comparatively small group of missionaries whose influence is so widespread that the gospel of cancer educational publicity can be pretty thoroughly disseminated. Moreover, the employees of such executives having daily direct contact with so many families and individuals are always in a position to detect apparent danger signals of cancers and refer such suspects either to their own family physicians, or to the State-aided clinics.

There are, of course, many ways to broadcast educational publicity. The opinion of the Springfield committee, however, and experience has proved it wise, clearly shows that it is much better to settle after careful trial on a few effective means rather than to scatter the efforts throughout many diversified, but ineffectual, methods.

LYNN CANCER CLINIC ASSOCIATION
CHAIRMAN, MARGARET READ VINCENT

PROGRESS IN LYNN

At a luncheon meeting in March, 1927, the Lynn Educational Committee was organized. For over five years now it has been growing in membership and strength of accomplishment in cooperating with the Massachusetts Department of Public Health and with the Cancer Committee of the Lynn Medical Fraternity who operate our Cancer Clinic.

Through its subcommittees, Educational, Social Service, and Publicity, it has carried on its educational and preventive work by contacting public groups in Lynn and the surrounding district, which includes the towns of Swampscott, Nahant, Saugus, Marblehead, Salem, Peabody, Beverly, Danvers, Rockport and Gloucester. Our clinic has received and aided patients from all of these places.

Biennial luncheon meetings, sponsored by the Allied Service Council, and weekly publicity, generously given by our newspapers, seem to have had the most successful results in our city in bringing the good work of our cancer clinic before the public. It was during Achievement Week in April, 1932, that our largest and most successful luncheon meeting was held.

The informal, quarterly committee meetings are well attended, full of discussion, interest and inspiration.

The Educational Committee has received some financial aid from the Lynn Community Fund Association since the first year, but last April the Lynn Cancer Clinic Association was incorporated to take over the work of the unincorporated Educational Committee, and it was granted an associate membership by the Lynn Community Fund Association. This assures us of a small yearly fund with which to aid the more unfortunate clinic patients who have no means for transportation to the Pondville Hospital or other places of treatment. Since the State funds are restricted to the diagnostic side of cancer, this separate fund prevents any delay between diagnosis and treatment.

The Lynn Cancer Clinic Association believes it is making progress. It believes that interest is increasing among the people in its district, and that the results of our educational campaign are, however slowly, beginning to be felt.

SOCIAL SERVICE COMMITTEE OF PONDVILLE HOSPITAL
CHAIRMAN, MRS. RALPH BULLARD

NEIGHBORLY SERVICE AT PONDVILLE

Because of the isolated position of Pondville Hospital, Dr. Bigelow recognized the need of personal contact for the staff and workers with the people in the immediate vicinity, and the Hospital's need of the interest of the community. A group of women from near-by towns, the parish priest and local minister were invited to form the Social Service Committee.

The purpose of the Committee is to keep the community informed about the hospital, the work it is doing, it needs, and to spread the gospel of friendliness. The members meet once a month to conduct any business and plan for future activities. On the first three Fridays of each month the Committee members and friends of the Hospital meet to make dressings, of which an enormous amount is used in the Hospital.

When the Committee was first organized, an appeal for money was made to clubs and church organizations. The members of the Committee assessed themselves ten dollars each in order to create a fund called the "Cheer Fund." The money is used to furnish certain little luxuries for the pleasure and comfort of the patients and employees. In order to continue the Fund, card parties have been given from time to time, and friends of the Hospital have generously contributed making it possible for the Committee to do certain things that the State cannot do.

At Christmas time each patient is remembered with a gift—this year bed jackets for the women and slippers for the men. On each holiday some small appropriate gift is provided to brighten up the trays—such as flowers at Easter, May baskets on May Day, heart-shaped boxes filled with candy for Valentine's Day. Transportation is provided when necessary, eyeglasses mended, cigars, cigarettes, and newspapers provided for patients unable to buy them themselves.

During the summer months, near-by Garden Clubs have kept the Hospital bright with flowers. Friends of the Hospital have given entertainments of all kinds, including Sunday Concerts. Puzzles, games, cards and reading material of all kinds have been given.

The Committee started the library, now consisting of several hundred volumes, by soliciting books from Women's Clubs throughout the State. Individuals, libraries and book shops send books and current magazines from time to time. The Cheer Fund contributes five dollars monthly for the purchase of new books. Members and friends have given magazine subscriptions. The superintendent, recognizing the need for bedside library service, provided the services of a part-time librarian and bought a book cart.

The Committee bought dishes and an electric plate for the nurses' home; several parties have been given for the nurses and employees; equipment for sports of several kinds was provided, and a victrola brought for the Recreation Hall.

These are a few of the ways by which the Social Service Committee has tried to brighten the lives of the patients and those caring for them.

GARDNER ASSOCIATE CANCER COMMITTEE
CHAIRMAN, MRS. GEORGE C. SWEENEY

PLANS FOR 1933
BY MILDRED E. KENNEDY
For the Gardner Committee

While it is an accepted fact that the newspaper is the best medium for cancer publicity, the Gardner Associate Cancer Committee is of the opinion that much can be done in addition to put over its cancer educational program.

The Committee, made up of representative citizens of Gardner and surrounding towns, has a definite program lined up for this year.

In addition to newspaper publicity, they plan to work through all the organized groups in the community, from the largest club down to the smallest social or church group. An outline of a five-minute talk has been given to each committee member. This outline covers the object of the clinic, who is eligible to attend, the time of the clinic, the danger signals of cancer, the need for early diagnosis and treatment of cancer, the accepted types of treatment, the danger of "Quacks", the value of social work, a few facts about the Pondville Hospital and ends by repeating the time and place of the clinic.

Each member will be assigned to give this short talk to certain groups. A chart has been prepared, listing every organization in Gardner, its leader, time and place of meeting, average attendance, member assigned to speak, and attendance. This same information, listed on a card, is given to the member addressing the group. After the meeting, the attendance is filled in on the card and it is returned to the chairman, who lists it on the chart. As the clinic is held every third week, it is hoped to give this talk to each organization meeting the week preceding the clinic.

After one year of organized effort, the Gardner Clinic attendance has increased from thirty-two new patients in 1932 to sixty-nine in 1933. With this plan, it is hoped that the people of the Gardner zone will become cancer minded and that they will be informed of the facilities which are available in Gardner and in the State.

LAWRENCE ASSOCIATE CANCER COMMITTEE
CHAIRMAN, MRS. JAMES F. BAILEY

EDUCATIONAL WORK

The educational work of the Lawrence Associate Cancer Committee has been carried on through several channels. At the beginning of our work we contacted all the mills, factories and department stores and through the cooperation of their agents and nurses, distributed in the pay envelopes of all workers the printed matter on cancer, giving the symptoms of cancer and the importance of early diagnosis and treatment. An article on cancer and an advertisement of our clinic has appeared twice a month in fifteen newspapers—some of the newspapers are printed in foreign languages. Recently we have added another newspaper from Reading, which is on the borderline of our district, and just now we are beginning to get results from this additional advertising. The newspapers have been of very great assistance in the development of the clinic.

The International Institute, through their work with the foreign born in classes and other outlets, have brought many patients to our clinic and their workers who are nearly all foreign born themselves have acted as interpreters, when necessary, at our clinics.

Public speakers from the State House have met with several clubs and committee groups to discuss cancer. Every social agency in our territory has been visited personally by some member of the committee and had the clinic work explained and also been given generous amounts of cancer literature for distribution.

The State's provision for a visiting consultant from Boston whenever requested has been the means of increasing the interest of our doctors in cancer. We usually have a list on file of doctors who make a request to be notified when a special clinic is to be held and about every three months or oftener when a clinic is held there is a good attendance of from twenty-four to thirty-six visiting doctors, several of them bringing along their own patients on whom they wish advice regarding diagnosis or treatment. Four out-of-state doctors have visited our clinics (three from New Hampshire where the cancer program is still quite limited and also one physician from Vermont). We have noticed a decided growing interest on the part of our doctors in this subject of cancer.

NORTH ADAMS ASSOCIATE CANCER COMMITTEE
CHAIRMAN, MRS. ARTHUR F. NOONE

PLANS OF A NEW COMMITTEE
BY EDITH L. MINSKY, SECRETARY

The North Adams Educational Committee was organized about a year ago. It is still in its infancy but is achieving very good results in its short period of activity. Its membership is composed of women representing all sections of the city, including the outlying towns and villages, thereby enabling the educational work of the committee to reach all the people. There are industrial nurses in the group who carry the educational work into the shops and factories and reach both the employers and employees, as well as their families through them. The insurance nurses and agents have aided the committee by distributing literature, while making their visits from home to home.

We owe a great deal to the immensely important part which the local newspaper has played in spreading cancer knowledge by its willingness to allot us plenty of newspaper space in very prominent pages of the paper.

Since the committee has been organized more interest has been created in the fight for stamping out cancer or at least getting it in its earliest stages. The people are alert to any possible symptoms of the disease and are more willing to visit the clinic held monthly at the local hospital, thus giving the doctors an opportunity to advise as to proper treatment and in many cases affecting a permanent cure.

Results such as the following prove to the committee that their splendid cooperation and efforts warrant continued work. In 1930, seven patients visited the local clinic, which meets but once a month; in 1931, twenty-six; and in nine months of 1932, thirty patients were examined, showing a steady gain resulting from the spreading of knowledge.

EDUCATIONAL COMMITTEE ON CANCER OF BOSTON HEALTH LEAGUE
CHAIRMAN, ANNA C. PALMER, M.D.

WORK OF THE BOSTON COMMITTEE
BY MARGARET H. TRACY, SECRETARY

The first meeting of this Committee was held in June 1931. During the season of 1931-1932 the Committee sponsored the public meeting in Symphony Hall during "Cancer Week."

In addition talks on cancer were given by this Committee in various parts of the city under the auspices of the Boston City Health Department. These meetings opened with a health film, then the talk, which was followed by a funny film that amused both the older persons and the children, the latter being admitted after the talk. Through the generosity of the American Society for the Control of Cancer, literature in English, Italian, Polish and Yiddish was distributed at these meetings and it was interesting to note how much more attention some of the older persons paid to the booklet printed in their native language than to the picture shown.

In the season 1932-1933 we are speaking at the numerous Settlement Houses in Boston. Five talks have already been given and we expect four or five more dates before the end of the season. In conjunction with the project of the State Health Department, to reach the biology students in college, this Committee has arranged for a talk on the biological aspect of cancer at the Massachusetts College of Pharmacy and Simmons College.

Two copies of the Cancer Bulletin have been published and have been well received.

BROCKTON ASSOCIATE CANCER COMMITTEE
CHAIRMAN, GEORGE H. LEACH

CANCER PUBLICITY IN BROCKTON
BY WILLIAM T. CARD

The imperative need of early diagnosis has been the theme of the publicity of the lay committee of the Brockton Cancer Clinic during the nearly three years of its existence.

The local press has cooperated generously in enabling the committee to get its story over to the citizens of Brockton and the outlying towns served by the clinic. Reading notices telling some of the simpler cancer symptoms have been published regularly, each concluding with a plea that every individual who suspects a cancerous growth give himself the benefit of the doubt and immediately visit the clinic for advice as to treatment or for reassurance as to a negative condition.

That this publicity is read is proven by the fact that attendance at the cancer clinic drops markedly if, as occasionally happens, these reading notices fail to appear in the papers.

Would that it were possible to know and to publish the total number of days by which the lives of human beings are shortened because of failure to learn the facts at once and neglect in acting promptly where action is necessary.

How tragic it is to attempt to estimate what those unnecessarily lost days of life and health might have held for these foolish victims of their own fear, carelessness, or indifference for their loved ones and for a world which needed them.

To educate people along the lines we have laid down is a task the importance of which it is impossible to overestimate.

SOCIAL SERVICE IN THE STATE CANCER PROGRAM
BY ELEANOR E. KELLY
Supervisor of Social Service

In cancer, as in every disease, early diagnosis and prompt treatment are dependent not only upon the doctor's examination and recommendation as to treatment, but upon the patient's carrying out this advice.

In doing this, however, the patient is influenced by social and environmental conditions—an important fact which must be taken into consideration.

The availability of community resources, the patient's attitude, and that of his family, as well as their resourcefulness in meeting his medical social problem, all condition the effectivness of the medical service in his case.

It is because of this relationship between the medical and social problems that medical social service has been recognized as essential to the State Cancer Program.

In accordance with the minimum requirements for the State-aided Cancer Clinics, social service forms a part of each clinic, and individualization is thus made possible in medical social study, diagnosis and treatment.

Last year these clinic social workers initiated social treatment for approximately 700* patients. In addition, about 5,000* interviews were held with the patient or others concerned with his problem for the purpose of interpreting the medical social plan, community resources, etc., and about 7,100* interviews in connection with the follow-up of patients needing treatment or patients under observation. Some form of service was rendered also to 618* patients who had not attended clinic. This figure indicates largely service requested by private physicians.

* These figures are exclusive of Pondville.

At Pondville, social service is carried on by three medical social workers in accordance with the recognized functions of the hospital social worker.

The clinics outside of Pondville, however, vary as to attendance, territory covered, and frequency of clinic meetings—with the result that in one community a full-time social worker is required; in another the social work is covered by a part-time worker; and in still another, one social worker covers three clinics.

The close cooperation between the Pondville and clinic social workers and this office makes for better service to the individual and the community.

The work is described by the social workers in the following articles.

WHAT SOCIAL WORK MEANS IN THE WORCESTER NORTH CANCER CLINICS

By Olive Twichell

The social worker is responsible for social case treatment whenever the need is indicated, for medical follow-up of patients, and for collecting statistical data used in the studies made by the State Department of Public Health.

Her first responsibility is to the patient diagnosed cancer—to make certain he understands the doctor's recommendations and the urgency of following them, to assist him in arranging for hospitalization when necessary, and to remove any obstacles in the way of his carrying out the doctor's recommendation promptly.

The social worker visits all cancer patients in the home, gives encouragement and helps to create constructive attitudes.

The majority of the patients attending the Worcester North clinics, if found to have cancer, are referred to Pondville Hospital for treatment. The social worker arranges transportation for these patients, and frequently takes the patient to the hospital herself. She also arranges for transportation of patients to the clinic at Pondville when they are requested to return there for observation or treatment.

Patients having diagnoses other than cancer are also followed up by the social worker. She arranges for hospitalization, if necessary, or follows up the patient to the extent of getting him to return to his family physician for the prescribed treatment.

All cancer patients are followed for the rest of their lives, and records are kept on every patient.

SOCIAL SERVICE IN THE WORCESTER CANCER CLINICS

By Gertrude J. Carney

In 1927, the Cancer Clinics were organized in six hospitals with a clinic held daily. The need of social service was felt to be of great importance and two months later a worker was secured to act as a medium between the clinic and patient, to understand his needs and help him to solve the many problems that arise to delay treatment. This community was very fortunate in having a group of young women interested in this phase of work who provided the worker's salary, taxi service for clinic patients, and transportation to Pondville Hospital when necessary. Co-operation from social agencies, welfare boards, local and out-of-town physicians has been commendable.

For the past two years, the majority of clinic patients have been receiving aid from the welfare department or a private charitable organization. To help the patient and his family to adjust themselves to the situation arising from his illness is a problem that is solved by using tactful methods, to bring about contentment in the home, to aid with the budget, and try to provide the family with clothing and other necessities whenever possible.

Cooperation in regard to the hospitalization of the patient on the part of the family has occasionally been a problem among the foreign speaking group; due to the fact that the patient has an incurable cancer, they do not wish to pay for care when funds are available. The importance of medical and nursing care printed in the various languages would enlighten these people and give them a better understanding of the treatment and care necessary to control the disease.

SOCIAL SERVICE IN THE NEW BEDFORD CANCER CLINIC
By Ida G. Dudelson

One of the most dreadful problems that we are facing right now—not only here in New Bedford, but in social service departments everywhere—is the unemployment situation in relation to the physical welfare of the people with whom we come in contact. They are so discouraged and so worried about their daily existence that they are giving no thought to their physical well-being. They are ill, but finances trouble them more. They are wretched, but keeping a roof over their heads is uppermost in their minds. How can we meet this problem? We have had to step in and get weekly aid from welfare departments for families that had no income at all. We have had to have aid supplemented by welfare agencies where there was barely enough to keep them going. We have had to clothe and roof families. All these things we have had to do before we could attempt to aid them physically for it was impossible to make them e the danger of their disease when they were worried about material things.

Our task, however, is not completed when they finally realize the danger there is in cancer and when they realize that early treatment may mean life. Fear of hospitals, doctors, and clinics, when they have never had the use of these, is not easily overcome. A hospital to many means the end of everything—surgery and radium, even worse than the end.

In treating patients who have cancer we go through a primary and high school education as it were, for in all problems of health it is only through education that we open people's minds to so treat their bodies that li for themselves, their children, and their families can be prolonged.fe

SOCIAL SERVICE IN THE LOWELL CANCER CLINIC
By Muriel Eales

The Lowell Cancer Clinic is a clinic for diagnosis only. Every patient coming to this clinic is examined by two or more physicians. After the examination each one is referred by the doctor in the clinic to the clinic social worker, who explains to him the recommendations of the staff physician and, if necessary, helps the patient to carry out these recommendations.

Any patient referred to the clinic by a private physician or known to a local physician is referred back and a report of the clinic findings sent to that physician. Others are referred directly to doctors or hospitals where recommended treatment may be obtained.

The worker always tries to interpret the patient's condition and the importance of early treatment to the patient and his family, will make appointments for his examination, treatment, and hospitalization, and, if necessary, arrange for transportation. If there is any question of the patient's inability to finance the advised treatment the worker makes a social investigation to determine his financial status or eligibility for free care and guides the patient in arranging for treatment.

In Lowell, if the patient is eligible for hospitalization this may be arranged through the Public Welfare Department. In some instances the general hospitals have free beds available for acute cases and local physicians are always quite willing to give reduced rates or free treatment where the need is apparent. If the social findings suggest it the worker enlists the cooperation of the local charitable agencies, so that the patient or his family may have necessary material aid during the time the patient is incapacitated because of treatment.

All clinic patients having positive diagnoses of cancer are visited by the social worker several times a year, some more often than others, as condition indicates. Contact is maintained with patients having precancerous conditions until treatment has been instituted and favorable results obtained. Those having deferred diagnoses are followed until a diagnosis has been made by the clinic or acceptable to the clinic staff.

WHAT SOCIAL SERVICE MEANS TO THE SPRINGFIELD CANCER CLINIC

By ALICE M. DRAPEAU

One of the most constructive projects we have in connection with our cancer clinics is the department of social service. Beyond question there is great need for such service, because it is the means of helping to solve such vital problems as:—securing home care for the family while the mother is away; financial aid, hospitalization for the patient without means, and transportation to Pondville. Many requests are also received for assistance in matters that have no connection with cancer. For example, one former patient asked aid in having a feeble-minded child placed in a State institution.

Social Service also means a more gratifying end result in the treatment of cancer by removing obstacles which might stand in the way of early and adequate care of the patient. Private physicians are recognizing the benefit of such service by referring to the clinic their own patients who need social service assistance. In some instances doctors have brought their problems to the worker and asked her advice.

The greatest problem of the Springfield clinic district is transportation to Pondville on account of the distance, cost and time consumed in making the two hundred mile round trip. Many patients, especially those with skin cancers, could easily be treated in the out-patient department if the hospital were not so far removed from our Western Massachusetts towns. The lack of free use of radium for patients who cannot pay the fee charged by private physicians is another big problem. Even our local hospitals have no radium available except through private sources.

Despite our problems, however, we in the Springfield district, through the splendid cooperation of the members of our medical profession, our hospitals, and our laymen are overcoming our obstacles one by one to a very gratifying degree.

SOCIAL SERVICE IN THE LAWRENCE CANCER CLINIC

By ANGIE M. RICHARDSON

Social work in the cancer clinic at Lawrence differs little from the other clinics throughout the State. It is recognized as an important adjunct to the medical service. The worker's responsibility involves social case treatment and medical follow-up of the patient. She also has charge of the records which are kept on a uniform State basis in order that they can be used for statistical purposes by the State Health Department.

When the doctor has made a diagnosis of cancer, the social worker assists him by making a plan to carry out his recommendation promptly. She must make certain that the patient has understood the recommendation the doctor has made and realizes the importance of early treatment.

If there are any obstacles that will prevent the patient from starting treatment, it is the social worker's duty to help him to overcome these. She assists him in arranging for hospitalization when necessary. This may be at a local hospital; if, however, treatment is required at another institution, she often arranges for transportation. There is close co-operation with Pondville.

There are many personal problems that a social worker is able to solve, because her interest extends to the home as well.

In no field of medicine is a careful follow-up of the patient as essential as in the treatment of malignant disease.

LYNN CANCER CLINIC

THE SOCIAL WORKER'S PART IN SECURING EARLY TREATMENT FOR CANCER PATIENTS

BY MRS. DOROTHY A. OATES

The importance of the element of time in cancer is stressed so often that a social worker in a cancer clinic should consider it her primary duty to arrange for treatment for patients as quickly as possible after the recommendation for treatment has been made by the doctor. The duration of symptoms prior to patient's visit to clinic can be lessened in time only by effective education of the public, but the shortening of the time between the clinic visit and treatment is the duty of the social worker.

All sorts of social problems are allied with the patient's reason for deferring treatment, and the social worker should be especially well fitted by her training and experience to deal with the problems. Often a patient feels that he or she cannot afford treatment or transportation for treatment or is too feeble to go to another city by train or trolley for specialized treatment. Again, there is no one to care for the family during hospitalization. All these things can be adjusted by a social worker through careful investigation, reporting facts to hospitals in order that they may adjust their rates, contacting the relief agencies for help in any financial problem affecting the home, etc. If the doctor has been able to impress on the patient at the time of examination the importance of immediate treatment, the patient's attitude toward treatment is more easily influenced and the obstacles in the way of treatment are more easily removed. The social worker's knowledge of the different specialized hospitals, the kinds of treatment, etc., helps in explaining the situation to the patient and his family.

A study of the annual reports of the past five years of the Lynn clinic, from April 22, 1927 to January 1, 1933 has been made. Three hundred and seventy-one patients are listed as having been diagnosed cancer at the clinic. Fifty-two of this number had no treatment recommended, either because of a postoperative condition with no evidence of recurrence or because treatment was no longer of any avail. One hundred eighty-seven, or 58.6 per cent of the remainder, were treated within a week; thirty-nine within two weeks, and twenty-six within one month. Therefore, two hundred fifty-two patients, or 68.8 per cent were treated within one month. Of the remaining sixty-seven, thirty-four received treatment later than one month after visit to clinic and the remaining thirty-three are recorded as having no treatment. Since the social workers follow all patients refusing treatment, hoping to persuade the patient to follow the advice of the clinic, these figures may be subject to change. Some have been treated since the publishing of the annual reports and some have died before treatment could be arranged.

In addition to the work with the cancer patients the social worker has an almost equally important duty to those patients whose diagnoses are deferred and those diagnosed as having precancerous conditions. These latter often need more careful persuasion than those diagnosed cancer for they are apt to minimize their condition and refuse treatment more persistently. If it is true that a day's delay reduces the chance for cure in different types of cancer, it behooves a social worker to strive to arrange treatment for every patient within as short a time as possible.

SOCIAL SERVICE IN THE TUMOR CLINIC OF THE BOSTON DISPENSARY

By Bernice E. Cross

The year 1932 has shown definite and encouraging advances in the care of patients with cancer—earlier diagnosis, more regular treatment and better understanding of the seriousness of the disease. Whether this is due to the radio and newspaper publicity which has been conducted by the State, or to the general increase over the country of the awakening to "cancer consciousness" cannot be definitely determined. This is shown in some degree by the following figures, illustrating an increase in patients coming to clinic for diagnosis, and a decrease in those refusing treatment and later returning:

	1931	1932
New cases treated	189	194
Old cases reinstated	20	11
Consultations	32	51

The social work of the clinic falls into three categories:

A. *Interpretative Service:*

This is a routine on all patients and is necessary to insure regular attendance to clinic, understanding of diagnosis and meaning of treatment. The case of Mrs. A. illustrates this point:

A woman of 69 came to the clinic with her married daughter, having been referred through the Medical Department. Examination showed inoperable carcinoma of the breast and X-radiation was advised. Patient came for one treatment and did not return—personal letter elicited no response. Home visit was made and patient stated her only relief came from her hot water bottle and X-ray treatment had done nothing for her. The disease was explained to the daughter and the value and action of treatment shown to patient. After interpretation patient was willing to continue with X-radiation, plus the hot water bottle.

B. *Medical Follow-up:*

Every patient diagnosed cancer is followed periodically for life through the clinic, when discharged to another State clinic. A record is kept on each patient and he is checked through private doctor, local hospital or personal contact. At present there are many such people on list. Every effort is made to have patient return for diagnosis if it is not made at the first visit. For example:

Mrs. X was seen in the clinic. Diagnosis was deferred and the patient advised to enter the hospital for dilatation and curetage and biopsy of cervix. As she worked by the day, and was the support of an invalid husband, she felt it impossible to take the time off for hospitalization. All efforts to interpret to patient and husband were unsuccessful. One of her employers was interested in the situation and through her, arrangements were made for patient to follow the medical recommendations.

C. *Individual Case Treatment:*

This again may be divided into two parts, constructive and palliative, being largely dependent upon the stage of disease and the medical prognosis.

The following case will illustrate palliative case treatment:

Mrs. Y., is a woman of 55, with inoperable carcinoma of the breast, living in a tenement in the South End. Her husband, aged 73, was the only person to care for her. Transportation to clinic was arranged and paid for through a special Cancer Fund, as the family was receiving $8.00 a week city aid. Old age assistance was secured for the husband and the patient was placed on straight city aid increasing the income to $11.00 a week. Insurance was carried by the Boston Dispensary until this arrangement was put through. The case was followed for several months when the carcinoma metastasized to the knee, causing a fracture and rendering patient an invalid. The Shut-In Society, a private organization for care of invalids, was interested in patient and provided a wheel chair to permit patient to get to the kitchen and supervise her husband's housekeeping, which was a great source of worry to her during her entire period of bed care. Her husband refused all offers to have the laundry done and a community health nurse assisted in the nursing care of the patient. The family is still a unit, each member devoted to the other, leaning upon each other for support. Diagnosis and poor prognosis was explained by a physician to her husband, but he refuses to believe it and is still eagerly awaiting patient's recovery.

Constructive case work may be illustrated by family adjustments, completion of medical care, patient's facing of responsibility, etc. Such work may be done either in cooperation with other community agencies or within the family group.

The cooperation of other hospitals in the care of clinic patients is worthy of mention. During the year, 51 patients were referred to other hospitals—16 in the months of October to December. Of these none were refused, although only one was able to pay for hospital care.

Some difficulty has been encountered in securing supplementation of city aid over a long period for cancer patients, as the general impression is that the case is incurable and the patient should be in a chronic hospital. The special fund in the clinic is available for the purpose, but it seems to be a problem that should be met by an outside agency.

Friends and relatives seem to be more of a resource in these cases than in any others, probably because of the nature of the disease and the sympathy which is aroused by such a diagnosis.

BROCKTON CANCER CLINIC

"EVENTUALLY, WHY NOT NOW?"

BY ROSAMOND TATRO

Social Worker, State Department of Public Health

"I'll let it go a while", reiterates the patient.

Time and a social worker are rivals. Delay is one factor in cancer that the social worker dreads. Why? Because to her it means the patient is daily losing his chance for cure. His reasons may be fear, apathy, stubbornness, or the constant cry of today—unemployment, no money. But these unfortunate attitudes must be overcome if the fight for health is to continue. Who is to do it? At the clinic, the doctor has told the patient his condition and has advised suitable treatment. The social worker has further explained the doctor's interpretation to the patient but rather than come to an immediate decision he preferred to return home and talk it over with his family.

It is regrettable that time enters and plays a dual trick. It nullifies the patient's fear of imminent danger and yet maliciously allows the cancer to progress. Then re-enters the rival, the social worker. In her visits to the home she sees the patient in his familiar surroundings. It is there that he can best tell her his fear of cancer, dread of an operation, and as for X-ray and radium, well, he just refuses to "chance his life with new fangled experiments." The social worker tries to find ways and means of combatting these reasons for delay so that she may secure available treatment for the patient.

In Brockton the group just exemplified above has delayed from six months to a year after attending the clinic. Of this group of seven patients requiring more intensive follow-up, four have now started treatment thus allying themselves with the social worker in her struggle against time and the avoidable loss of life resulting from delay.

Brockton has been fortunate, however, through the cooperation of the clinic and family physician, through private and public social agencies, Pondville Hospital and other institutions to have secured treatment promptly; sixty-eight per cent of the patients diagnosed cancer having been treated within a week after their first visit to the clinic.

It will only be through education and continued follow-up that we will change the patient's slogan from "eventually" to "why not now?"

PONDVILLE HOSPITAL SOCIAL SERVICE DEPARTMENT
By Neil A. Fountain

The Social Service Department at Pondville differs from most of the other clinics in that it serves both the out-patient and the house patient.

In the clinic the social worker sees each new patient before he is examined and helps him if need be, in carrying out the doctor's advice.

One day a young woman, mother of six children, came to the clinic. Diagnosis could not be established until after operation. She was anxious to get well but thought she could not leave her family. After talking the situation over with the patient and her husband, this plan was made: the three oldest boys would remain at home with the father, a neighbor said she would care for one small child and the other two were placed with the patient's aunt. The Department of Public Welfare agreed to pay the children's board. She was admitted to the hospital. Cancer was ruled out, but she needed surgical attention. Arrangements were made for her transfer to a general hospital and for care in a convalescent home after her discharge.

All house patients are known to the social workers and effort is made to know the nearest relative. Her service to the patient varies in importance from a slight service to helping make it possible for the patient to accept treatment; finding a home and money for patient able to live a fairly normal life but unable to earn his living. Sometimes a small errand is but the stepping stone to a very real problem.

An old gentleman asked for a copy of Shakespeare with large print—this was provided. Sometime afterward he came to the worker saying, "You got the book I wanted and had my glasses mended, perhaps you can tell me what to do now." The doctor had told him that he could be discharged in a short time. He wanted to go but had no money and no home. He was a fine type of man, well educated and had held good positions. His wife's long illness and his own had used up all his savings. He was too proud to borrow from friends, knowing he could never repay. It was arranged, through an agency interested in old men, to place him in a nursing home until time for further treatment. After his second admittance to this hospital, he felt so much better that he wished to return to a small hotel where he had formerly lived. The Old Age Pension was secured for him and this, supplemented by a sum from the former interested agency, made it possible.

Because of the long waiting list, each patient is visited in his home either by a Pondville social worker or one from some other clinic nearest his home, in order to determine which patient presents the greatest need.

A telephone call from the State House told of a pitiful case. The father of a family was very ill and the family in need. A home visit was made and the family found to be living in a nice, well furnished and cared for home. The patient was in a comfortable attractive bedroom overlooking the town and surrounding country. The patient was suffering, but he wished to remain at home as long as possible. His doctor came on call and the district nurse called daily. The wife, son and daughter were working, but the wife's work was in the evening so that he was never left alone. A friend, thinking he was doing a kindness had telephoned and in his eagerness had given a false impression of the situation.

One of the most important duties of the social worker is the "follow-up". Sometimes she learns that the patient does not return to the clinic because he does not understand the importance of keeping under observation, or he cannot get transportation, etc.

One woman wrote that she could not come because she had no way of getting here. She was visited and found to be living in a cottage in the woods. The worker arranged with the Department of Public Welfare to bring her. Obstacles such as this can almost always be overcome.

All house patients are discharged both medically and socially—no patient ever leaves Pondville unless it is made reasonably certain that he will have adequate care.

BERKSHIRE COUNTY CANCER CLINICS

BY ROSAMOND TATRO

Social Worker, State Department of Public Health

There is at present no social service in Berkshire County. However, because of the necessity of routine follow-up of all cancer patients, and the importance of early treatment, an attempt has been made to place the patients under supervision of a cooperating local agency.

In Pittsfield, the Visiting Nurse Association is assuming responsibility for arranging treatment for patients referred from the three clinics. They also are making the periodic follow-up visits.

The Southern Berkshire Health Unit, with headquarters at Great Barrington has accepted the work of follow-up in the towns included in the Unit. In the towns where there is a separate nursing association, the work will be done by the individual nurse in that community.

Turning to the northern section of Berkshire County, in North Adams the district nurse will do the necessary visiting and likewise the individual nurse in each surrounding town. In each instance the clinic patients are referred to the nursing associations, through the courtesy of the hospitals.

In addition there are the records and reports. A clinic secretary has been employed who will attend the clinics for routine clerical procedure and be responsible for all correspondence and reports.

NATIONAL INSTITUTE OF HEALTH

"The National Institute of Health was created by Congress in 1930. It is an outgrowth and enlargement of the old Hygienic Laboratory of the Public Health Service, and is the scientific research division of the Service. Its function is to ascertain the cause, prevention and cure of diseases affecting human beings. The act which brought it into existence provided for an appropriation of $750,000, now being spent in providing more adequate facilities for the Institute, and authorized the Secretary of the Treasury to accept gifts for research in problems relating to the health of man.

"The Conference Board of the National Institute of Health is an unofficial, voluntary organization of public spirited men whose aim is to assist the Public Health Service, through the National Institute of Health, to perform its noble work in the conservation of public health.

"It is the mission of this Board to inform the people of America of the accomplishments of the Public Health Service in the past, and to point the way to its increased activities and greater service in the future aided by larger resources.

"The Conference Board does not solicit or accept subscriptions. The expense of its operations has been provided by generous philanthropists.

Its sole purpose is to make known the aims and aspirations of the National Institute of Health, which is attempting to conquer disease and give longer life and more happiness to all men. Sums given to the Institute—little or big, from the widow's mite to the large gifts of the rich—must be sent direct to the Treasurer of the United States, Washington, D. C., and marked 'Gift to National Institute of Health.' Funds so contributed will then be expended by the Government as desired by the donors. *The legal restrictions thrown around such expenditures assure donors that their contributions will be devoted to the purpose intended without the deduction of one cent for commissions or overhead.*

"Government scientists have made extremely valuable discoveries concerning such diseases as malaria, hookworm, tularaemia (rabbit fever), undulant fever, psittacosis (parrot fever), typhus, Rocky Mountain spotted fever, and have done much to solve the sanitation problems of the country."

MATERNAL DEATHS IN MASSACHUSETTS

The following figures have been copied from the Annual Report on the Vital Statistics of Massachusetts for the years ending December 31, 1930 and December 31, 1931. The year 1931 is the first year in which the new classification of causes of death is used. This classification does not, of course, affect in any way the number of deaths under each cause.

Maternal Deaths in Massachusetts, 1930

Accidents of pregnancy		42
Abortion	17	
Ectopic gestation	20	
Others under this title	5	
Puerperal hemorrhage		61
Other accidents of labor		66
Caesarean section	25	
Other surgical operations and instrumental delivery	10	
Others under this title	31	
Puerperal septicemia		141
Puerperal phlegmasia alba dolens, embolus, sudden death		58
Puerperal albuminuria and convulsions		68
Puerperal diseases of the breast		1
Total		**437**

Maternal death rate — 5.9 per 1,000 live births.
Infant death rate — 60.3 per 1,000 live births.
(4,440 deaths)

Maternal Deaths in Massachusetts, 1931

Abortion with septic conditions		24
Abortion without mention of septic conditions (to include hemorrhage)		18
Ectopic gestation		7
With septic conditions specified	0	
Without mention of septic conditions	7	
Other accidents of pregnancy (not to include hemorrhage)		3
Puerperal hemorrhage		49
Placenta praevia	18	
Other puerperal hemorrhages	31	
Puerperal septicemia (not specified as due to abortion)		95
Puerperal septicemia and pyemia	94	
Puerperal tetanus	1	
Puerperal albuminuria and eclampsia		52

Other toxemias of pregnancy		41
Puerperal phlegmasia alba dolens, embolus, sudden death (not specified as septic)		62
Phlegmasia alba dolens	3	
Embolism and thrombosis	59	
Other accidents of childbirth		57
Caesarean operation	22	
Others	35	
Others and unspecified conditions of the puerperal state		0
Total		408

In any statement of the causes of maternal deaths it quickly becomes obvious that only by studying each individual case can convincing information be obtained in regard to possible prevention.

Four hundred and eight mothers died in Massachusetts in 1931, making the maternal death rate for that year 5.9 per 1,000 live births. The rate was the same for the year 1930. Infant deaths to the number of 3,803 occurred in 1931, making an *infant death rate of 54.8, the lowest rate ever reported for this State*. It will be of great interest to see if this rate holds during the subsequent years of economic trouble. More mothers are in the homes caring for their babies; more information on baby care is being distributed constantly in one way or another; and the feeling of many nurses is that more mothers are nursing their infants. These items may have some bearing on the present rate but there are still many puzzling problems in connection with prematurity and first month deaths.

NEIGHBORHOOD HOUSE HEALTH ACTIVITIES

BY RUTH R. KENT

West Springfield Neighborhood House Association

The Child Welfare Department of the Neighborhood House, West Springfield, is part of a threefold community program of public health nursing, family case work, and recreation.

The house and offices are at 647 Main Street. In addition, the first floor of the Meadow Street School is used for the Educational-Recreational Department activities, and one room at Mittineague School is used one afternoon a week for Well Child Conferences.

The Staff of the Neighborhood House consists of the executive secretary, two graduate nurses, one case worker, the director of the educational-recreational department, an office secretary, and sixteen volunteer workers.

The Family Welfare Department deals with families and individuals whose difficulties make them liable to become dependent, or prevent their achieving normal family life.

The Educational-Recreational program aims to supply normal recreational and extra curricular educational activities for young people in a section where few such opportunities exist.

The program of this department is flexible so that adjustments may be made during the year which will add to the interest of the club members.

The formation of a group, known as the Community Youth Council, composed of representatives from all organizations sponsoring leisure time activities for young people, has aided in the broadening of the program. The various organizations pooled their facilities. In this way the clubs at Neighborhood House were afforded the use of the gymnasiums at the Junior and Senior High Schools for basket ball practice, and the swimming pool at the Community Y. M. C. A.

Sewing classes for the purpose of teaching mothers how to make over clothes have been formed as a new project of this department.

The Child Welfare Department carries on a health program for children from birth to six years of age. This service includes nursing conferences and home visits for the purpose of teaching the local mothers the proper care of their babies and young children.

The well child conferences are held twice each week—one in the West end, and one in the more thickly settled center of the town. Attendance at the conferences is limited to well children. The age groups admitted include the children from three weeks to school age. No fee is charged for the service.

It is the aim of the department to see that every child attending the conferences is given a complete physicial examination at least once each year. A record is made of any physical defect found and arrangements for treatment are made.

If the family cannot afford to pay, or does not have a regular physician, the case is referred to the proper agency for treatment.

Since the Neighborhood House Association is one of twenty-eight agencies of the Community Chest, it is possible at all times to supplement the health service with assistance from not only the other departments of the Neighborhood House, but with any of the affiliating agencies.

This is particularly fortunate because of the increasingly large number of patients who cannot financially arrange for treatment.

The greater part of the nurses' time on duty is devoted to home visiting. Approximately 2,500 home visits were made during the past year. These visits included the supervision of treatment recommended by the physicians, advice on feeding, and observation and advice regarding the formation of proper health habits.

The effect of the health supervisory visits is apparent in the interest that the majority of parents are manifesting in providing essential foods and proper care for their children.

During the past year, because of lack of employment, many of the fathers have been present when the nurses have made visits in the homes. Thus the nurses were afforded a splendid contact with both parents, and the father has been made to realize that the health of his children is his particular problem.

Because of the pressure of work at the Neighborhood House during the past two years, it has been necessary to eliminate the number of Committee meetings. One large group, known as the Advisory Committee, was formed by uniting members of the nursing, the educational and recreational and case committees. This group meets monthly and each supervisor presents the problems of her own department.

These meetings are very stimulating and keep the community informed as to the work of the Neighborhood House Association.

Editorial Comment

The "Cancer Cure" Always with Us.—"Cure for a Cancer." "Take the narrow-leafed dock root, wash it clean; boil it soft in rain or spring water. Wash the ulcer with this decoction, as warm as the patient can bear, and fill the cavity with the liquor for ten minutes. Then scrape off the pulp of the root; bruise it fine; spread it on gauze and lay it on so as to bring the poultice in contact with every part of the ulcer. Then spread a fine cloth, dipped in the liquor, over it and repeat the process two or three times in twenty-four hours. At each dressing the patient should drink a wine glass full of tea of the same root, with one-third of a glass of port wine, sweetened with honey, to prevent laxness.

Its efficacy on the wife of Reverend Eli Forbes of Gloucester is sufficient to remove all doubts from the most distrustful."

The above was copied from the Farmer's Almanack of 1803. The insatiable yearning of the human race for one specific cure for cancer is still with us. It breaks out at frequent intervals as is revealed in two newspaper headlines picked at random from the grist of a week's clippings: "Cancer Machine Guarantees Cure, Doctor Reveals" and "Growth Retarded by New Compound".

As we read on, however, we learn in the first instance that this guarantee is offered only "if the machine proves successful," in the second, that "much remained to be done in experimenting with the compound," and that "whether or not it will be found useful in retarding abnormal growth (such as cancer) is in the laps of the gods."

Still the headlines, always a sensitive index to public appeal, tell the story of the universal craving for some assurance that the all-potent cure for cancer is at hand.

What, Another Campaign? Appendicitis? The increasing prominence of appendicitis as a cause of death, particularly in the lower age groups, is alarming. One of the important causes of this is our inveterate habit of self-medication. Any pain in the region vaguely and Anglo-Saxonly described as "the belly" means a laxative or a purge, for a "good clean out". The mortality following removal of the appendix is low when no purgative has been used and increases with the number taken. We must teach people that if they have such a pain hot and cold local applications are apparently innocuous, but medication without medical advice is folly. (If such a one cannot leave his intestinal tract alone, an enema is far safer than drugging from above which only adds to the confusion.)

Last year in Philadelphia a campaign of public education against self-medication for abdominal pain was put on by the Medical and Pharmaceutical Societies in cooperation with the Department of Health. Studies of appendicitis deaths before and after the campaign showed that it was distinctly worth while. Such studies are being made in Massachusetts and such a campaign is planned for Massachusetts in April. A fool and his money can be parted but can a fool, with a pain in his belly, be kept from his drug?

Book Notes

THE STUDENT'S HANDBOOK ON NURSING CASE STUDIES. Second edition, revised. by Deborah McLurg Jensen, R.N., B.S. $1.00. 129 pp. Macmillan Co.

This is a very valuable book for training school students. Recognizing the patient as an individual and studying his needs, physical, mental, social and economic, is certainly an asset and is a tremendous help to both patient and nurse. Of course, it requires time to make case studies but it is well worth the effort.

Having the nurse taught to recognize social problems and that there is a Social Service Exchange that serves as a clearing house is of tremendous importance.

The book is very interesting, readable, and of real value.

GROWTH AND DEVELOPMENT OF THE CHILD—Part I—GENERAL CONSIDERATIONS. White House Conference Publication. $3.00. 380 pp. The Century Co.

The amount of valuable information gathered into this one introductory volume on Growth and Development of the Child is almost appalling! It contains a wealth of material interesting and useful to all who are working for improvement along child hygiene lines.

There are a few important points, knowledge of which we may well bear in mind constantly, and first of all, is the lack of anywhere nearly complete knowledge of all the factors in growth and development in the prenatal and postnatal periods and also during adolescence. These life periods are felt to be the most neglected today.

The importance of a clear picture of the normal child taken as a whole and of each child as an individual, is many times emphasized. Each child is a different person, sex being the first differentiation, then age, then the individual inheritance and reaction to an environment. Inheritance varies always, hence the interaction of inheritance and environment which produces such wide differences even in children of the same race and family. We have, as yet, no standards ready which sufficiently take into account all these differences. Averages have pretty much served their day. They have not helped us as much as we expected, whether height-weight measurement, I.Q., or what not.

In estimating what range of variation in growth and development is normal, individual study of each child gives the final word. The practical question is how shall we get this adequately done for all children? At present it looks hopeless but we can at least advocate it is an ideal and also we can allay the worries of many anxious parents who unfortunately have been trained in the fear of their children "falling below average" in growth or accomplishment.

The following topics are taken up in this book which is the first in a series of four on this subject: Heredity and Its Interaction with Environment; Identical and Fraternal Twins; Prematurity; Human Types; The Development of Physiological Stability; Temperature Regulation of the Body; Sleep and Repose; Fatigue; Organized Athletics During School Age; Photodynamic Activity of Light and Its Use as a Therapeutic Agent; The Influence of Atmospheric Conditions; Difficulties in Relating the Behavior of Children to Home Environment; Socio-Economic Factors Influencing Growth and Development; Immunity and Age; Disease in Relation to Growth and Development.

Comprehensive references follow each section and there is an index.

EDUCATION FOR HEALTHFUL LIVING IN THE PUBLIC SCHOOLS OF BELLEVUE-YORKVILLE 1927-1931 by Nina B. Lamkin. $.55 postpaid. 58 pp. Bellevue-Yorkville Health Demonstration, 325 E. 38th Street, New York, N. Y.

The development of a program of health education in the public schools of the Bellevue-Yorkville District was a four-year cooperative project carried on by the Board of Education, the Department of Health, the Bellevue-Yorkville Health Demonstration and other agencies.

This monograph by Miss Lamkin, the consultant, contains a much condensed account of this arduous undertaking worked out under numerous handicaps. One wishes that the account might have been more detailed, nevertheless it makes profitable reading for those interested in programs of health education.

REPORT OF DIVISION OF FOOD AND DRUGS

During the months of October, November and December 1932, samples were collected in 162 cities and towns.

There were 741 samples of milk examined, of which 62 were below standard; from 4 samples the cream had been in part removed, and 1 sample contained added water. There were 23 samples of Grade A milk examined, all of which were above the legal standard of 4.00% fat. There were 1,082 bacteriological examinations made of milk. There were 65 samples examined for hemolytic bacteria, all of which were negative.

There were 874 samples of food examined, of which 188 were adulterated or misbranded. These consisted of 103 samples of eggs, 24 samples of which were sold as fresh eggs but were not fresh, 59 samples were cold storage not so marked and 20 samples were decomposed; 1 sample of horse radish which contained coloring and was incorrectly labeled; 28 samples of hamburg steak, all of which contained a compound of sulphur dioxide not properly labeled and 1 sample of which was also decomposed; 14 samples of sausage, 11 of which contained a compound of sulphur dioxide not properly labeled and 3 samples contained starch in excess of 2 per cent; 2 samples of liver which were decomposed; 7 samples of butter, 3 samples of which were below the legal standard in milk fat, and 4 samples were rancid, 1 sample of which was also below the legal standard in milk fat; 1 sample of maple syrup which contained cane sugar; 2 samples of dried fruits which contained sulphur dioxide; 2 samples of olive oil which contained cottonseed oil; and 28 samples of vinegar which were below the legal standard in acetic acid.

There were 9 samples of drugs examined, of which 5 were adulterated or misbranded. These consisted of 1 sample of lime water which did not conform to the U. S. P. requirements; 1 sample of "Crazy Crystals", the composition of which did not conform to that advertised; 1 sample of ether which contained aldehyde; 1 sample of spiritus frumenti which contained diethylphthalate; and 1 sample of camphorated oil which did not conform to the U. S. P. requirements.

The police departments submitted 1,072 samples of liquor for examination, 1,056 of which were above 0.5% in alcohol. The police departments also submitted 28 samples of narcotics, etc., for examination, 1 of which contained codein; 9 contained heroin; 2 contained papaverine; 1 sample of bread contained lead and arsenic; 3 samples of flour were examined for lead with negative results; 1 sample of oil, 1 sample of white powder, 1 sample of candy, 1 sample of a brown liquid, and 1 sample of salt cake, were all examined for poisons with negative results; 4 samples, 2 of which were cigarettes, were all examined for alkaloids with negative results; 1 sample of pills contained caffeine; 1 sample consisted of water and a trace of oil of lemon; and 1 sample of lard was examined for lead with negative results.

One sample of water which contained a deposit of crystalline calcium carbonate was submitted from the District Attorney's Office, Cambridge.

One sample of yellow-brown semi-solid material, identified as soap containing alcohol and a phenol compound, was submitted by the Department of Public Safety; a heating pad was submitted by the Department of Labor and Industries; and 1 sample of coffee drink examined for poisons with negative results was submitted by the Gardner State Colony.

There were 88 cities and towns visited for the inspection of pasteurizing plants, and 281 plants were inspected.

There were 104 hearings held pertaining to violations of the laws.

There were 90 convictions for violations of the law, $1,273 in fines being imposed.

Albert Mylott of Abington; John L. Toner of Nantucket; Nicholas

Rauh of Wilbraham, were all convicted for violations of the milk laws. John L. Toner of Nantucket appealed his case.

Roy Curley of Hudson; Oscar Laipson of Worcester; Harry Feldman of Everett; Forest Lake Dairy Company, Incorporated, of Palmer; Hugh A. Rodden of Salem; Albert J. Gage, 3 cases, of Pembroke; Antonio La Rose and Emile La Rose of Dracut; Joseph Fila of Thorndike; F. B. Mallory, Incorporated, of Springfield; J. F. McAdams and Brother, Incorporated, of Chelsea; William Rogers of Fairhaven; Sylvia Fortier, 3 cases, of Fall River; Miles Burnett of North Adams; Calixte Desmarais of Swansea; Elizabeth Charbonneau, 2 cases, and Adelard Beland of Lowell; John O. Soares and John Voloza of Somerset; and George Zervas, 2 cases, of Ipswich, were all convicted for violations of the pasteurization law and regulations. The two cases of John E. Lombard of Ipswich, and John W. Pratt, 1 case, of Peabody, were filed without finding. Roy Curley of Hudson appealed his case. Calixte Desmarais of Swansea, John O. Soares and John Voloza of Somerset, Elizabeth Charbonneau, 2 cases, and Adelard Beland of Lowell, all pleaded guilty and were placed on probation. Sylvia Fortier, 2 cases, of Fall River, was given suspended sentence to May 3rd, 1933; and George Zervas, 2 cases, of Ipswich, was given suspended sentence for one year.

Benjamin Cohen of Chelsea; John Dobosz of Holyoke; William Alter, Joseph Charnas and Guiseppe D'Angelo, all of Roxbury; Harry Selansky of Melrose; M. M. Mades Company, Incorporated, of Everett; George Eskow of Taunton; H. L. Dakin & Company, Anthony Gill and Anthony Rydziel, all of Worcester; First National Stores, Incorporated, of Peabody; The Great Atlantic & Pacific Tea Company of Lawrence; Harry Simon and Samuel Risman of Dorchester; M. Winer Company of Revere; John Marcinek of Thorndike; Abriham Less, Joseph Berger, Jacob Kronick, Harry Levitte, Joseph Tallarico and Henry Kronick, all of North Adams; John Leal of East Providence, Rhode Island; First National Stores, Incorporated, and Wasel Kopka of Salem; Cambridge Provision Company, Incorporated, 2 cases, and Louis Abramowitz of Cambridge; and Louis P. Labbe of Fall River, were all convicted for violations of the food laws. Benjamin Cohen of Chelsea; Cambridge Provision Company, Incorporated, 2 cases, of Cambridge; and Wasel Kopka of Salem, all appealed their cases. Samuel Risman of Dorchester was placed on probation.

Puritan Cake Company, Incorporated, and James S. Rousokis of Cambridge; Apollo Cake Specialties, Incorporated, of Charlestown; Paramount Baking Corporation of Roxbury; and Peterkofsky, Incorporated, of Brighton, were all convicted for using decomposed eggs in the manufacture of food products. James S. Rousokis of Cambridge appealed his case.

Hathaway Baking Company of Cambridge was convicted for violation of the bakery laws.

Morris Gallup of Taunton; John Klys of Indian Orchard; Paul Jacobs, Peter Kariofiles, James Van Dyk Company, and Isaac Widlansky, all of Springfield; Philip Jacobs, Nicholas Legadinos, and H. L. Dakin & Company, all of Worcester; Max Comman of Cambridge; Harry Katz of Roxbury; and Henry Kronick of North Adams, were all convicted for false advertising. Philip Jacobs of Worcester appealed his case.

Peter Boukalis, The Gloria Chain Stores, Incorporated, George Peters, Morris Di Pinto, all of Worcester; Samuel Fine and Isaac Silverman of Revere; Cudahy Packing Company of South Boston; John Glynn of Charlestown; and Leon Albert of Mattapan, were all convicted for violations of the cold storage laws. John Glynn of Charlestown was placed on probation until May 18th, 1933.

Jose Fenandes and George C. Phillips of Norton; and Ralph Sarro of

52

Mansfield, were all convicted for violations of the slaughtering laws. Jose Fenandes of Norton appealed his case.

Samuel Tublin of Fall River was convicted for violation of the mattress law.

In accordance with Section 25, Chapter 111 of the General Laws, the following is the list of articles of adulterated food collected in original packages from manufacturers, wholesalers, or producers:

Butter which was below the legal standard in milk fat was obtained as follows:

Three samples from The Great Atlantic & Pacific Tea Company of Lawrence; and 2 samples from The Great Atlantic & Pacific Tea Company of Springfield.

One sample of butter which was below the legal standard in milk fat and was also decomposed was obtained from The Great Atlantic & Pacific Tea Company of Lawrence.

Olive oil which contained cottonseed oil was obtained as follows:

One sample each, from Steven Sturgis and John Zedros, both of Lynn.

One sample of maple syrup which contained cane sugar was obtained from Nicholas Lagadinos of Worcester.

Hamburg steak which contained a compound of sulphur dioxide not properly labeled was obtained as follows:

One sample each, from Rood & Woodbury of Springfield; Abraham Sweet, Wellworth Market, Incorporated, and Devon's Meat Market, all of Roxbury; The Great Atlantic & Pacific Tea Company of Natick; Benjamin Cohen, Anthony Gill, Hyman Karp, and Consumers Provision Stores, Incorporated, all of Worcester; Moro's Meat Market of Framingham; Abe Cramer, Samuel Richton, and Simon Kronick, all of North Adams; Isaac Goldstein and Sirloin Stores of Everett; Louis Abramotiz of Cambridge; Harry Simon, Isador Shwartz, Isaac Bassimer, Alter Brothers, and Samuel Risman, all of Dorchester; Frank Hollis and Andrew Rudkosky of Chelsea; Harry Gillis of Boston; and Abriham Hodas of Greenfield; and 2 samples were obtained from Harry Levitte of North Adams.

One sample of hamburg steak which contained a compound of sulphur dioxide not properly labeled and was also decomposed was obtained from Cambridge Provision Company, Incorporated, of Cambridge.

Sausage which contained a compound of sulphur dioxide not properly labeled was obtained as follows:

Two samples from D. Petrini & Company of Boston; and 1 sample each, from A. Albertelli & Company of Boston; and Wellworth Market, Incorporated, of Roxbury.

Sausage which contained starch in excess of 2 per cent was obtained as follows:

One sample each, from Peter L. Berlo of South Boston; and Harry L. Bradbury of Lawrence.

Liver which was decomposed was obtained as follows:

One sample each, from Chicago Butchers of Roxbury; and Dakin's Bakery & Delicatessen of Worcester.

Vinegar which was low in acid was obtained as follows:

Six samples from R. I. Sales Company of Providence, R. I.; 4 samples from Carbon Products Company of Providence, R. I.; 3 samples from A. Dupuis of Fall River; 2 samples each, from Red Cross Products Company, and Louis P. Labbe, both of Fall River; and Progress Pickling & Vinegar Company of East Providence, R. I.; and 1 sample each, from Pure Products Company of West Springfield; Pure Food Service Company, and B. & L. Products Company, both of Fall River; and Lugi Pasquelli of Worcester.

There were twelve confiscations, consisting of 40 pounds of decomposed beef; 60 pounds of decomposed beef sweet breads; 10 pounds of decomposed pickled lambs' tongues; 400 pounds of decomposed chickens; 25 pounds of decomposed chickens; 908 pounds of decomposed fowl; 20 pounds of decomposed haddock; 30 pounds of decomposed haddock fillets; 90 pounds of decomposed haddock fillets; 625 pounds of decomposed halibut; 300 pounds of decomposed mackerel; and 100 pounds of decomposed mullet.

The licensed cold storage warehouses reported the following amounts of food placed in storage during September, 1932:—382,230 dozens of case eggs; 204,847 pounds of broken out eggs; 861,860 pounds of butter; 817,059 pounds of poultry; 1,467,730 pounds of fresh meat and fresh meat products; and 5,785,031 pounds of fresh food fish.

There was on hand October 1, 1932:—4,910,670 dozens of case eggs; 2,160,409 pounds of broken out eggs; 7,863,823 pounds of butter; 2,677,250¾ pounds of poultry; 3,080,070 pounds of fresh meat and fresh meat products; and 23,114,249 pounds of fresh food fish.

The licensed cold storage warehouses reported the following amounts of food placed in storage during October, 1932:—420,210 dozens of case eggs; 325,135 pounds of broken out eggs; 804,040 pounds of butter; 1,099,934 pounds of poultry; 1,752,915½ pounds of fresh meat and fresh meat products; and 2,389,832 pounds of fresh food fish.

There was on hand November 1, 1932:—2,924,280 dozens of case eggs; 1,834,715 pounds of broken out eggs; 5,788,934 pounds of butter; 2,917,274 pounds of poultry; 2,889,617 pounds of fresh meat and fresh meat products; and 21,355,916 pounds of fresh food fish.

The licensed cold storage warehouses reported the following amounts of food placed in storage during November, 1932:—282,030 dozens of case eggs; 283,647 pounds of broken out eggs; 415,103 pounds of butter; 3,536,558 pounds of poultry; 2,537,980 pounds of fresh meat and fresh meat products; and 1,496,273 pounds of fresh food fish.

There was on hand December 1, 1932:—1,060,860 dozens of case eggs; 1,517,133 pounds of broken out eggs; 3,280,482 pounds of butter; 5,479,165¼ pounds of poultry; 3,026,554½ pounds of fresh meat and fresh meat products; and 17,652,581 pounds of fresh food fish.

MASSACHUSETTS DEPARTMENT OF PUBLIC HEALTH

Commissioner of Public Health, GEORGE H. BIGELOW, M.D.

Public Health Council

GEORGE H. BIGELOW, M. D., *Chairman*

ROGER I. LEE, M.D.   RICHARD P. STRONG, M.D.
SYLVESTER E. RYAN, M.D.   JAMES L. TIGHE.
FRANCIS H. LALLY, M.D.   GORDON HUTCHINS.

Secretary, ALICE M. NELSON.

Division of Administration	Under direction of Commissioner.
Division of Sanitary Engineering	Director and Chief Engineer, ARTHUR D. WESTON, C.E.
Division of Communicable Diseases	Director, GAYLORD W. ANDERSON, M.D.
Division of Water and Sewage Laboratories	Director and Chemist, H. W. CLARK
Division of Biologic Laboratories	Director and Pathologist, BENJAMIN WHITE, Ph.D.
Division of Food and Drugs	Director and Analyst, HERMANN C. LYTHGOE, S.B.
Division of Child Hygiene	Director, M. LUISE DIEZ, M.D.
Division of Tuberculosis	Director, ALTON S. POPE, M.D.
Division of Adult Hygiene	Director, HERBERT L. LOMBARD, M.D.

State District Health Officers

The Southeastern District	RICHARD P. MACKNIGHT, M.D., New Bedford.
The Metropolitan District	CHARLES B. MACK, M.D., Boston.
The Northeastern District	ROBERT E. ARCHIBALD, M.D., Lynn.
The Worcester County District	OSCAR A. DUDLEY, M.D., Worcester.
The Connecticut Valley District	HAROLD E. MINER, M.D., Springfield.
The Berkshire District	WALTER W. LEE, M.D., No. Adams.

PUBLICATION OF THIS DOCUMENT APPROVED BY THE COMMISSION ON ADMINISTRATION AND FINANC
5500. 3-'33. Order 7969.

THE COMMONHEALTH

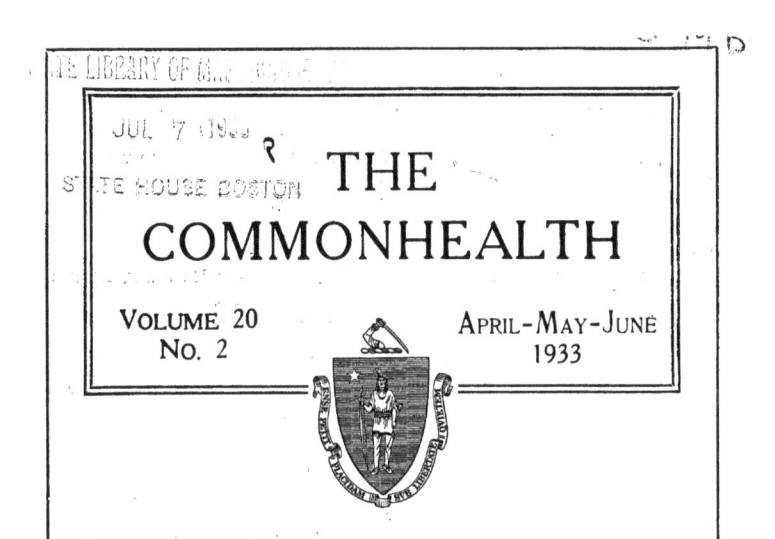

VOLUME 20
No. 2

APRIL-MAY-JUNE
1933

Control of Gonorrhea and Syphilis

MASSACHUSETTS
DEPARTMENT OF PUBLIC HEALTH

THE COMMONHEALTH

QUARTERLY BULLETIN OF THE MASSACHUSETTS DEPARTMENT OF
PUBLIC HEALTH
Sent Free to any Citizen of the State
Entered as second class matter at Boston Postoffice.

M. LUISE DIEZ, M.D., DIRECTOR OF DIVISION OF CHILD HYGIENE, EDITOR.
Room 545 State House, Boston, Mass.

CONTENTS
PAGE

Some Diseases We Don't Talk About—and Why Not. The Prevalence of
  Gonorrhea and Syphilis 57
Gonorrhea and Syphilis. A Description of the Two Diseases . . . 59
Congenital Syphilis 62
The Control of Gonorrhea and Syphilis 64
Public Health Nursing and the Medical Aspects of Social Hygiene . . 67
Syphilis. What the Public Health Nurse Should Know About the Patient
  and the Disease 71
Familial Syphilis. Significant Facts for the Public Health Nurse . . 74
Syphilis. Some Facts Regarding Diagnosis and Treatment . . . 77
Syphilis. A Review 82
Facts About Gonorrhea 84
The Public Health Nurse and the Community Social Hygiene Program . 87
The Public Health Nurse and the Educational Phases of a Social Hygiene
  Program 92
The Nurse in the Control of Gonorrhea and Syphilis. As the Health Officer Sees Her 95
Economic Aspects of the Management of Syphilis 101
Minimum Standards for Clinics for the Treatment of Gonorrhea and
  Syphilis 108
Editorial Comment:
  Radio Broadcasts. Public Information 116
  The Nurse in the Control of Gonorrhea and Syphilis . . . 116
  Economic Aspects of the Management of Syphilis 116
  Minimum Standards for Clinics for the Treatment of Gonorrhea and
    Syphilis 116
  Massachusetts Society for Social Hygiene 117
Report of the Division of Food and Drugs, January-February-March, 1933 118

SOME DISEASES WE DON'T TALK ABOUT—AND WHY NOT
THE PREVALENCE OF GONORRHEA AND SYPHILIS
Radio Broadcast, Station WBZ, December 24, 1930

N. A. NELSON, M.D.

There are few diseases which affect large numbers of people that we do not discuss publicly at one time or another. Some of them we talk less and less about, such as yellow fever which Dr. Gorgas practically wiped off the face of the earth not so many years ago. Others are talked about only as some emergency arises, such as an epidemic of smallpox in a community which has neglected the important business of vaccination. There are some diseases, like infantile paralysis, which we discuss only to express fear of them because we know so little about them.

There are two diseases, however, that affect more people than any other except, perhaps, the common cold and its complications, but about which we have talked very little until recently. During the war we did have something to say about gonorrhea and syphilis, but almost wholly in their relation to the welfare of the soldier and the sailor. Since then, students of public health have investigated the relation of these diseases to the civilian population, and it is because of what they have discovered that these diseases once more are receiving public attention and their control has come to be considered one of the major public health problems of today.

Gonorrhea is as old as history. Syphilis is probably as old, but its early history is not as clear. In 1493 a physician of Barcelona, Spain, treated the pilot and several sailors of Columbus' fleet, for a new disease, contracted in the West Indies. Not long after, an outbreak of this disease occurred in Italy, following the invasion of the army of King Charles. It soon became epidemic in all of Europe, and the foundation was laid for the present prevalence of this disease over the entire world.

All through their history both these diseases have been associated in the public mind only with immoral men and women. There is no doubt that much of their spread has been through those who have been morally delinquent. But to assume that they are to be found only among such men and women, is to assume what most decidedly is not so. They are to be found in all levels of society, from the rich to the poor; from the intelligent to the feebleminded; from the guilty to the innocent. There is good reason to believe that at least half a million people in the State of Massachusetts have been infected with gonorrhea or syphilis during the past ten years.

Our records show that more than one-third of those infected are women, and that while eight out of ten men are infected while they are single, more than half the women infected are married. Everybody knows that women are as faithful to their marriage obligations as men. The truth is that men, infected when single, after some but not enough treatment, think they are cured, marry and infect their brides. Surely these women, infected through marriage, cannot be considered as paying the penalty of wrong conduct! There is no sadder chapter in the history of medicine than that of gonorrhea in women, with its trail of major surgery, wrecked health and childless homes. Two authorities in this country insist that, statistically, half the men you meet have had, have, or will have gonorrhea at some time in their lives. If that is true, or even half true, it would seem that women might well ask of their prospective husbands, "What of health do you bring me?" as well as "What of wealth?"

There are other tragedies. The clinics and doctors' offices of this State can produce records of hundreds of little girls, from a few days to ten or twelve years of age, who have been infected. Morally innocent of any wrong, they have been infected by careless or uninformed adults.

They are doomed to months and sometimes to years of treatment, suffering, and exclusion from school.

There is no mother who does not dread the appearance of infantile paralysis in the community. Syphilis kills or cripples far more children in every level of society than infantile paralysis and destroys countless others even before they are born. Certainly these innocents cannot be held morally responsible for their misfortune!

But how guilty are the guilty? Both these diseases are found most frequently in boys 20 and 21 years of age and among girls 19 and 20 years of age. Two out of every three cases of gonorrhea reported in women are in women under 25 years of age! When we consider that most children are taught everything to fit them for life except how to meet life itself, is it any wonder that sex leads them astray? Our boys and girls step out of our homes at the age of five or six years into a world of sex with a stork or a doctor's bag as their only sex information. And with an incomprehensible obstinacy their parents close their eyes to what they know is going on, while the "wise" playmate, the sex novel and moving picture and the divorce news provide a rotten substitute for the decent sex education, built on character, which should have been given them.

What is it that makes us believe that, in spite of our own experiences, our children will grow up in wholesome innocence of the sordid interpretations of sex, when the sewers of indecent misinformation are always spouting forth their filth, and the sources of wholesome information are stopped by an exasperating, stupid prudishness! Why should we wonder that there is petting which knows no limit, promiscuity, gonorrhea, syphilis, blasted hopes and unhappy futures, with remorse to keep company with misery! What must our disillusioned boys and girls think of us who, knowing better, allow them to face alone an impulse as old and as big as life itself,—the urge of life to reproduce itself?

Sex properly finds its expression in the finest things in the world. We are proud that we are men and women; we are happy to announce to all who will read or listen that a son or a daughter has been born to us; we find pleasure in romance; we delight in the rebirth of nature in the spring; we long for love, for a home and for a family. Then how can we be ashamed of sex? Why do we not teach our children that sex is all these splendid things and not at all the purely physical and vulgar thing that twisted minds and vicious characters are making it appear to be?

There is a solution of the problem of gonorrhea and syphilis. Just as tuberculosis is being routed by intelligent public action, so can these two diseases be routed by intelligent public action. When you are willing to drag them into the open where you can study them and their causes, you will find ways of controlling them. When men learn that women will no longer accept disease as a wedding gift, they will avoid exposure to disease, or they will be sure of cure before they marry. When fathers and mothers become as concerned over who is teaching their children the things that make character, as they are over who is teaching them arithmetic, instead of leaving it to every Tom, Dick and Harry, then children will be taught to think of sex as decent and treat it with the wholesome respect which is its due.

Will you let your daughter destroy her hope for happiness by allowing her, in her ignorance, to stumble into some temptation from which she may find it impossible to retreat? Or will you sigh with relief that she is at last safely married, even though it may prove that she has at the same time become wedded to disease? That has been the experience of a multitude of daughters. Will your son offer to his family health and the joy of living, or disease with all that follows in its path? The sons of many good fathers and mothers are laying the foundation for futures of unhappiness.

Some things are being done, and there will be discovered other things that may be done to solve these problems of human relationships. There are twenty-six clinics in Massachusetts where those who cannot afford to pay a doctor may be treated. Support these clinics and see to it that the quality and adequacy of the service that they offer is all that it should be. It is important that those who are infected be taught the necessity of immediate and persistent treatment for their own sakes and for the protection of others. Is your community doing what it should be doing to make this information available to those who need it? Some druggists still treat or prescribe treatment for these diseases concerning which they know nothing. What are the druggists in your community doing? A few newspapers have the courage to print facts about gonorrhea and syphilis. What are your newspapers telling you? Is your hospital one of the few which will provide beds for human beings sick with these diseases, or does it close its door against them as so many hospitals do? A few cities are providing social and nursing service for the unfortunates who need it, as they are doing for the tuberculous. If yours is not, why not?

The Massachusetts Department of Public Health is doing all that it can to keep patients under treatment and to make treatment readily available to all who need it. The Massachusetts Society for Social Hygiene, with offices in the Little Building, Boston, is doing all that it can to tell parents and young people that sex-character is important not only in the control of gonorrhea and syphilis but also to the happiness of our homes. Support this society, for when people have learned that training of children in sex-character is as necessary as training in honesty or chivalry or industry, there will be little necessity for concern about gonorrhea and syphilis.

The ultimate control of these diseases, therefore, is just as far away, or just as near at hand as you, mothers and fathers, want it to be. But until the day arrives when character universally rules sex, those who become infected owe themselves immediate and careful medical attention if they would regain their health. They have, too, the serious responsibility of preventing the spread of their infections. They are urged to seek immediately, the advice, not of the druggist or of a friend, but of a competent physician. These diseases are curable, but much permanent damage may be done unless treatment is begun soon after infection takes place and kept up, not only until the symptoms have disappeared, but until the doctor pronounces a cure. Those who do not have the strength of character which will keep them from danger should remember that extra-marital sex relationship must be considered as an exposure to infection. Gonorrhea and syphilis are diseases. Those who are infected with them are sick persons in need of the best of care. Those who are well should avoid exposure just as carefully as they would avoid exposure to any other dangerous and crippling and killing disease.

GONORRHEA AND SYPHILIS
A DESCRIPTION OF THE TWO DISEASES
Radio Broadcast, Station WEEI, August 12, 1932

N. A. NELSON, M.D.

The Massachusetts Department of Public Health has long recognized the importance of gonorrhea and syphilis as public health problems. During the past fifteen years the Department has built up a program for their control which includes financial aid to fourteen of the twenty-six public clinics in the State, the distribution of drugs for treatment, the maintenance of diagnostic laboratories, lecture service and the distribution to patients, the medical profession and the public of informative literature.

In 1492 Columbus discovered America. In 1493 a physician of Barcelona, Spain, treated the pilot of Columbus' fleet and several of the sailors, for a new disease contracted in the West Indies. This disease, syphilis, soon became epidemic over all of Europe.

Gonorrhea is as old as history. Clear descriptions of it are to be found in the earlier books of the Old Testament. Yet today public health and medical authorities are finding the control of this disease one of the most difficult of problems. In fact gonorrhea and syphilis, together, constitute, without doubt, the largest and most baffling public health problem which civilization has yet faced.

Both diseases are reported by physicians to the Department just as diphtheria or any other communicable disease is reported, with this difference, that so long as the patient remains under medical care and does not expose others to his infection, his name and address are not included in the report. The information received is used only for studying the size and nature of the problem and for determining what progress is being made in control.

More than 200,000 cases of syphilis are now reported annually in the United States. During the ten years ending with 1931 there were reported 279,000 more cases of syphilis than of scarlet fever, 950,000 more than of diphtheria, and 1,640,000 more than of typhoid fever. Astounding figures! They are still more astonishing when it is noted that while scarlet fever and diphtheria are quite well reported, syphilis and gonorrhea are the most incompletely reported diseases. It is estimated, that there are always half a million persons in this country under medical care for syphilis, and that approximately one in every ten or twelve persons has this disease. Gonorrhea is at least two or three times as prevalent as syphilis. Certainly measles is the only reportable communicable disease which can approach either of these two in prevalence.

Last year in Massachusetts 4,500 cases of syphilis and 7,200 cases of gonorrhea were reported. The most optimistic estimates indicate that not more than a quarter of the cases actually under medical care in this State are reported and that approximately 50,000 cases of the two diseases should have been reported.

One of the chief difficulties in the control of gonorrhea and syphilis is the general misunderstanding of them. People associate them only with immorality, and feel that infection is a suitable reward to those who do not behave. That is often an unfair and dangerous point of view, as will be evident from the following:—

During the last ten years at least 15,000 of those reported in Massachusetts as having these diseases, acquired their infections innocently. Nearly 2,000 of them were children born with syphilis; at least 1,000 of them were young girls, the majority of them under ten years of age, infected with gonorrhea by careless parents or attendants. Some 12,000 or more were married women infected by husbands who thought their own infections were cured before they married, or who were not aware that they had the disease.

To these 15,000 innocently infected, whose cases were reported, must be added at least four times as many more, among those whose infections have not been reported. It seems high time that some public attention should be given to these dangerous diseases which, in ten years, apparently have been the cause of the innocent infection of 75,000 residents of Massachusetts, many thousands of them children.

Syphilis is a dangerous, communicable disease. It is caused by a germ which travels through the blood. It may destroy any part of the body if not treated promptly and properly. If it is untreated or inadequately treated, it develops in three stages:—

In the first stage, the germs go through the skin at the point of inoculation. There they multiply, many of them passing into the blood and to all parts of the body. Two to six weeks later a sore appears where the germs first went through the skin. This sore is the first sign of syphilis. It may be of any size from a small pimple or "cold sore" to a large ulcer. It is called a chancre. Many chancres, especially in women, are never noticed, and syphilis may be discovered only when the later stages appear, or a blood test is made. The germs of the disease are scattered throughout the body long before this first sign appears. The sore may heal without treatment and the patient unfortunately thinks that the disease is cured.

A few weeks later some or all of the symptoms of the second stage may appear. They are skin rashes, canker-like sores in the mouth, headache, fever, pain in the bones, and falling hair and eyebrows. The sores in the mouth or on other moist surfaces are very dangerous as they may contain thousands of the germs. Kissing a person in the second stage of this disease may result readily in infection.

If the disease is not promptly treated, these second stage symptoms may disappear and return several times, each recurrence causing more damage than the others. Sometimes the symptoms of this stage are so mild that they are not noticed, but the final outcome of the disease, if not treated properly, is just as serious in these cases as in those with marked symptoms.

The first and second stages of the disease are the most dangerous to others because of the open sores, but at the same time offer to the patient the greatest chance for cure. It is most unfortunate, that, in the present state of public knowledge, only one of every three patients under medical care is in the early stage of infection. The other two are approaching, or have passed into the third stage when their infections are discovered.

The signs of the second stage will disappear, eventually, even without treatment. Again the patient may think he is cured. Years later, however, there may develop locomotor ataxia, general paralysis of the insane or other forms of syphilis of the brain, nerves, heart, blood-vessels, bones, eyes, liver, or any other part of the body. Untreated or poorly treated syphilis is almost certain to develop into some form of the third stage.

Syphilis is curable when proper treatment is begun during the first stage or early in the second stage. The progress of the disease may be stopped by treatment in the third stage, but much of the damage already done never can be repaired. In any stage this disease requires treatment and then watching up to five years or more.

In 1910 a drug was discovered which is still the most useful in the treatment of syphilis. It is known as "606" because the discoverer made 606 experiments before he hit upon the successful combination of chemicals. Other drugs are used in association with "606" since this is so powerful that it cannot be given continuously over long periods.

The most favorable case requires at least a year and preferably from fifteen to eighteen months of constant treatment. Many experts insist that the patient with first or second stage syphilis should be treated continuously until the blood tests have been negative for at least one year. After treatment is stopped blood tests must be made at regular intervals for two or three years or more to be sure of cure.

Gonorrhea is also a dangerous, communicable disease, caused by a germ. It has no relationship to syphilis although both diseases frequently are caught at the same time.

The symptoms of this disease are discharge of pus, and pain or burning on emptying the bladder. These early signs appear from five to seven days after exposure and are frequently so mild in women that they are missed entirely.

The disease quickly becomes chronic, spreading to all parts of the genito-urinary system. In men it leads to chronic inflammation of the prostate gland, sometimes to stricture, not infrequently to a severe and obstinate form of rheumatism and occasionally to a fatal form of heart disease. Most men make light of gonorrhea because the early signs soon disappear. They do not realize that many chronic ailments are the result of the earlier acute infection.

In women gonorrhea leads to serious and often dangerous complications. Among them are troublesome disturbances of the female periodic functions and years or a lifetime of backache, abdominal pains and other so-called "female troubles", all too often leading to the operating table for the removal of tubes, ovaries and even the entire internal reproductive system. If women were aware of the enormous burden of poor health they are carrying because of gonorrhea, there might be greater hope for the eventual control of this disease through insistence on healthy husbands.

The treatment of gonorrhea is not as satisfactory, from the point of view of the public health, as that for syphilis. The drug "606" quickly heals the open sores of syphilis, but so long as a patient has gonorrhea the disease is easily spread, in fact, it is most dangerous when the symptoms have disappeared because the patient thinks it is cured. Only a competent doctor, aided by laboratory tests, can decide when the danger is past. Many weeks, usually months, and occasionally years are required for the cure of gonorrhea, depending to a great extent upon the conduct of the patient.

In gonorrhea and syphilis, then, we have the most prevalent of reportable communicable diseases, both of which attack the innocent as well as the morally delinquent. They are both very dangerous and require early discovery and prompt and constant treatment until cure is certain. They are both greatly misunderstood by most people and it will be only through better understanding that their control will finally be brought about. Will you not interest yourself in the control of these diseases at least to the extent of learning more about them? Informed public opinion and public support are of the greatest value to the medical profession and the health authorities in their efforts to control any disease. Call Capitol 4600 or write the Massachusetts Department of Public Health, State House, Boston, for literature or other forms of information.

CONGENITAL SYPHILIS

Radio Broadcast, Station WEEI, September 30, 1932

N. A. NELSON, M.D.

Not long ago a man went to a doctor for treatment for a difficulty which he had. In making a note of the man's medical and family history it was discovered that his wife had never given birth to a living child. All of her six pregnancies had ended either in miscarriages or in babies born dead. She was again expecting to become a mother. Both husband and wife were very anxious to have children.

Blood tests soon convinced the doctor that the man had syphilis, and he was placed under treatment. He was urged to have his wife come in for a blood test, but this she refused to do. The next baby was born dead. Then she agreed to an examination and it was found that she had syphilis. Treatment was begun and continued regularly throughout her next pregnancy. This family now has a living and healthy baby.

Just the other day a ten-year old girl was admitted to an institution for the blind. Her eyesight had been failing for some time, but treatment for her condition had been neglected. She was born with syphilis, but the disease had not become active until ten years later when it destroyed her sight.

Nine hundred and forty-four cases of congenital syphilis have been reported in Massachusetts during the past three years (1930, 1931, 1932). If this form of the disease is reported as incompletely as other forms, about four thousand should have been recorded. In spite of poor reporting, one hundred more deaths of children have been recorded as due to syphilis than to infantile paralysis during the last ten years. If infantile paralysis were as prevalent, year after year, as congenital syphilis is known to be, there would be public panic.

Congenital syphilis is a tragedy of motherhood and a destroyer of children. It is one of several reasons why the control of syphilis has been accepted as a public health problem. Syphilis is one of the most publicly misunderstood of diseases.

There are reliable figures to show that at least half a million people in the United States are under treatment for syphilis at the present moment. About one in every ten persons in this country has or has had the disease. Nearly half of them are women. At least half of these women have been infected through marriage with men who thought they were cured before they married, or who did not know they had the disease. Ninety-five out of every hundred syphilitic women are infected during the years when they may become mothers. It is little wonder that so many children are born with the disease.

The continued slaughter of babies by congenital syphilis is inexcusable because it is entirely preventable. The little country of Denmark with a population about that of the State of Massachusetts, has almost completely wiped out this form of the disease. Proper treatment of the expectant mother, if begun early enough, will almost invariably result in the prevention of syphilis in the baby. One of the most striking examples of this fact was described at the beginning of this talk. Let me give it further emphasis with the following account of the experiences of a group of two hundred women who had syphilis. These two hundred women had had six hundred pregnancies. Four hundred and fifty of them ended in the death of the baby before birth or soon thereafter. Most of the living one hundred and fifty babies had syphilis and only a few of them lived to be more than five years old. Some of those who lived are mentally defective, some are blind, some are deaf, some in various other degrees of ill health. These same women were given treatment for syphilis during their next one hundred and sixty pregnancies. One hundred and fifty of their babies were born alive. None of them had syphilis. What a difference! It is dramatic, isn't it, in its difference! Yet in this country and in this State syphilis is permitted to take its regular toll of child health, child eyesight, child minds and child lives, year after year, simply because of public misunderstanding and public disinterest.

Syphilis very strangely quiets down so much in women when they are to have babies that the physician can rarely discover the disease by physical examination. The only way in which it can be discovered is by blood tests. Since so many women have syphilis, most of them without knowing it, every expectant mother should have the test the moment she discovers that she is to become a mother. This taking of blood tests should become as much a part of the care of a prospective mother as the putting of drops in the eyes has become a part of the care of the new-born baby. No woman need fear the test. In those who do not have syphilis it will be negative. Those who do have the disease should welcome its discovery if they wish to have living and healthy babies.

Many physicians fear to suggest a blood test to their patients because patients so often become indignant at what they believe to be an implication that the doctor suspects the infection. There is no such implication. Doctors have discovered that this disease is to be found among all classes of people and that it is never safe to assume that it is not present in a given patient. Those who have the disease rarely know it. It is a serious thing to allow a woman to go through all the trials of expectant motherhood only to have it end in the preventable disaster of congenital syphilis. Those women who again and again have given birth to dead or diseased babies because of syphilis are the victims of a public misunderstanding which has effectively prevented physicians from discovering their infections in time. Most of them would have felt insulted if the doctor had suggested a blood test. Yet when their babies were born dead, or when, later in life the signs of disease appeared, there was no escaping the fact that they had syphilis.

If the doctor suggests a blood test, his suggestion should be accepted. He cannot decide without it who does and who does not have the disease. The test should be a regular part of the attention he gives to all expectant mothers. Sooner or later he will discover some who need treatment.

Congenital syphilis makes its appearance in the child at various ages. The baby becomes infected from the mother before it is born. The disease may kill the baby before birth. The child may be born alive but live only a short time, from a few minutes to a few weeks or months. Or it may appear perfectly healthy at birth only to have the disease appear weeks, months or years later. It is a too common experience in clinics and doctors' offices to see children who are mentally defective due to syphilis. It too often happens that a child of eight to ten or twelve years suddenly develops trouble with its eyes or hearing and unless proper treatment is begun at once, becomes permanently blind or deaf. Too many children suffer ill health in innumerable other ways because they were born with syphilis. There are enough other handicaps to childhood without permitting the preventable diseases to go on disabling and destroying life and health.

There is some evidence that progress is being made in Massachusetts toward the prevention of congenital syphilis. Not nearly so many women are found to have syphilis among those who attend the various maternity hospitals, as was the case ten years ago. The medical profession, the clinics and the State Department of Public Health together have brought about the treatment of thousands of cases of syphilis. This not only has brought cure to many of them but has prevented the spread of the disease in many instances. Then, too, many women are being treated during pregnancy so that congenital syphilis may be prevented. But in spite of all these signs of progress, and in spite of the fact that only a small number of all the cases come to our official attention, more than nine hundred cases of congenital syphilis were reported during the last three years. That is not a record to be proud of in this day when so much is being said and done for child health. A simple blood test made when each of these mothers first discovered that she was pregnant would have led to treatment. All of these cases represent needless unhappiness for three times as many people—their mothers, their fathers and themselves.

The Massachusetts Department of Public Health is seriously engaged in an effort to control syphilis and gonorrhea. Every physician who sees the damage caused by these diseases desires to see them controlled. But the doctor cannot treat syphilis unless he is given an opportunity to discover it. Until people become informed concerning syphilis, two out of every three infected persons will continue to come to medical attention in the late rather than the early and more readily curable stages, the mental disease hospitals will continue annually to receive hundreds of patients with syphilis of the nervous system; the destruction of the heart and blood vessels in middle age will go on; babies will die or they will live only to meet disaster or destruction at another time and the bill for the treatment of syphilis and its end results will continue to be counted in the millions of dollars.

Besides aiding financially fourteen of the twenty-six public clinics in the State, distributing drugs for treatment, maintaining diagnostic laboratories and assisting the physician in every way possible, your State Department of Public Health will do all that it can to inform you concerning syphilis and gonorrhea. Call Capitol 4600 or write to the Department at the State House, Boston, for literature or other forms of information.

THE CONTROL OF GONORRHEA AND SYPHILIS

Radio Broadcast, Station WEEI, October 16, 1931

N. A. NELSON, M.D.

Sixteen years ago, Dr. Eugene R. Kelley, late Commissioner of Public Health, predicted that if accurate data were available, we would be dismayed at the prevalence of these two diseases. The information which has accumulated since that time, warrants his prediction. Syphilis alone, poorly reported as it is, is on the face of reports more prevalent than scarlet fever or diphtheria and several times more prevalent than typhoid fever or smallpox, in the United States. Gonorrhea is two or three times as prevalent as syphilis. There is abundant evidence that there are always more than a million people under medical care in this country for one or the other of these diseases, not to mention at least an equal number not under treatment. It appears that no less than a million and a half new cases of gonorrhea come to medical attention every year in the United States.

In 1915 the State Wassermann Laboratory was opened. It was desired to make this all important, but exceedingly costly blood test freely available to any patient at the request of any physician licensed to practice medicine in Massachusetts. Some indication that it has filled a great need may be seen in the 100,000 tests for syphilis made at the Laboratory in the single year of 1930.

In 1916, the General Court, by special act, appropriated $10,000 to be expended under the direction of the State Department of Public Health in the purchase or the manufacture of arsphenamine, popularly known as "606". This drug is the most effective medication known for the treatment of syphilis, but up to the time of its free distribution by the State its cost was far too much for the average patient to pay. Since 1916 the Department has distributed nearly a million doses of this drug to hospitals, clinics and physicians.

The bacteriological laboratory, in addition to making tests for diphtheria, typhoid fever, tuberculosis, and so on, also examines material sent in by physicians all over the State, for the germs of gonorrhea. Thousands of these examinations are made in this laboratory each year, in addition to other thousands examined in local board of health laboratories, hospitals and physicians' offices.

In 1918, these diseases were declared by the Department of Public Health to be diseases dangerous to the public health, and therefore reportable. The time had come when some sort of bookkeeping had to be done if our problem was to be measured; for it is only in knowing the size and nature of a problem that a sound solution of it may be evolved. Public policy made it advisable that the names and addresses of persons with these diseases should not be required in the reports. Quarantine for the many months and sometimes years required to cure gonorrhea and syphilis is out of the question. It is more important for the moment to know how many cases there are under treatment, how they are distributed according to age, sex and marital state, and in what stages of the disease medical attention is first sought, than to know who the patients are. The diseases must be understood before radical procedures can be adopted for their control.

During the thirteen years that have passed there have been reported in Massachusetts 100,000 cases of gonorrhea and 40,000 cases of syphilis. At the present rate, more than 11,000 cases of the two diseases will be reported this year. There is abundant evidence that even now, not more than a quarter of the cases under medical care are actually reported each year in this State. If 11,000 cases of smallpox or of infantile paralysis or typhoid fever were reported in a single year in Massachusetts, the public outcry would be, like that famous shot in 1775, heard round the world.

From this total of 140,000 reports of gonorrhea and syphilis received, we have learned, among other things:—

That they are diseases of youth, the greatest number of cases occurring in boys at 20 years of age and in girls at 19 years of age;

That two out of every three women who have gonorrhea are less than 25 years of age;

That one out of every ten women who have this disease is a girl under 14 years of age; girls and even babies are innocently infected by careless parents or attendants who have the disease;

That two out of every three women who have gonorrhea or syphilis are infected through marriage by men who thought they were cured before they married;

That two out of every three patients with syphilis come to medical attention from one to 20 years too late, when the most communicable and most curable stage of the disease is long since passed;

That half the patients with gonorrhea come to medical attention six months or more too late, when the disease has spread so deeply that cure is exceedingly difficult;

That patients not only neglect to seek medical care in time, but stop treatment as soon as the visible signs of disease have disappeared, although months and even years of further treatment may be required for cure.

In 1918, as a result of the war-time enthusiasm for keeping the soldier and sailor fit to fight, a number of clinics were opened throughout the country for the treatment of those who could not afford private medical care. With two or three exceptions, the Massachusetts clinics are still in operation and new ones have been opened until there are, at present, 27 of them scattered throughout the State. Fourteen of these are aided financially through the State Department of Public Health in order that residents of the smaller communities, where clinics cannot be maintained, may receive treatment. These fourteen clinics admit about 5,000 new patients every year. Most of these clinics have nurses or social workers who are kept busy urging delinquent patients to resume treatment, discovering new cases in the families of patients, and advising treatment to those who can be identified as sources of infection.

We do not believe that Massachusetts druggists accept the serious and illegal responsibility for prescribing for and treating these diseases to the extent that they do in some other parts of the country. There is evidence, however, that too many druggists do practice in this field of medicine for the sake of an ill-earned dollar. The Massachusetts Pharmaceutical Association has taken a firm stand with the Department of Public Health in its attempt to discourage this practice. Through its cooperation more than 400 of the 2,000 druggists in the State are distributing the Department's literature to all who seek their advice concerning these two diseases.

Behind all this more or less concrete and material structure there is being carried on a great campaign of information, limited to a great extent, unfortunately, to those who already are infected. During the last two or three years more than 200,000 booklets, describing the nature and treatment of these diseases have been distributed to physicians and clinics for the instruction of their patients. At the same time, some 60,000 other booklets describing up-to-date methods of treating these diseases, have been mailed to the physicians of this State. Several hundred physicians and nurses have heard talks on this subject, and in cooperation with the Massachusetts Society for Social Hygiene, thousands of persons have been told of the importance of the problems which these diseases present.

Unfortunately, due to generations of prudery and false modesty, it is still very difficult to persuade many of those who control such channels of public health education as newspapers, magazines, and so on, to permit their use for public information concerning gonorrhea and syphilis. Here and there a courageous editor or radio station director has permitted the use of his facilities for this purpose. Surprisingly the public reaction has always been favorable, not a single protest having been registered at any time. It is our experience that people are willing to hear the truth about these diseases and it is easy to tell the truth without in any way being obscene or without at any time using objectionable language.

Thousands of innocent people are being infected with these diseases. They are both widely prevalent among all classes and levels of society. Your daughter may marry a man who honestly thought he was cured and there is evidence that even your son may marry a woman who is unaware that she ever had gonorrhea or syphilis. Congenital syphilis in children has come like a thunderbolt out of a blue sky to many an unsuspecting father and mother. These diseases are by no means confined to those women who lead dishonorable lives nor to the men who associate with them. The following story is true, and by no means an uncommon one so far as it involves the innocently infected person:—

A young nurse burned her thumb while on duty. The burn failed to heal and when, some weeks later a rash broke out, it was discovered that the nurse had syphilis. It developed that she had been caring for a baby with a highly dangerous form of congenital syphilis, from which she had acquired her infection. The baby's mother, a young, newly married woman, had syphilis, of course. It was learned that her husband had had a tiny sore, which to him was insignificant, and which had healed readily some time before he had married. He did not suspect syphilis. He did not knowingly infect his innocent wife. She did not knowingly infect her innocent baby. The baby did not knowingly infect the nurse who did nothing more reprehensible than her duty as a member of a noble profession. Of four persons who acquired syphilis, three were innocent of the least wrong. The young husband was not the conscious cause of their disaster. Think it over. Syphilis and gonorrhea are no respectors of persons nor of morality.

If you approve of public information concerning these two dangerous and prevalent diseases, or wish further information concerning them, write to the Massachusetts Department of Public Health, State House, Boston, or in care of this station, or to the Massachusetts Society for Social Hygiene, Little Building, Boston.

PUBLIC HEALTH NURSING AND THE MEDICAL ASPECTS OF SOCIAL HYGIENE*

BY GLADYS CRAIN, R.N.

Assistant Director, National Organization for Public Health Nursing

Editorial Note: Home study, group conferences, staff education—call it what you will the desire of public health nurses to prepare themselves for better service is everywhere apparent. There is no field in which public health nurses are showing a greater interest than in that of social hygiene. We therefore take pride in offering a series of articles for group discussion or individual study, with leading questions and suggested reference reading, by Miss Crain, who is a member of the N.O.P.H.N. staff working on a joint project with the American Social Hygiene Association.

It goes without saying that Miss Crain is ready to answer questions on this subject or send a wider reading list to those interested. The second article in this series will appear in August, its general subject—*Syphilis*.

The modern graduate nurse, whatever her particular field of interest, is being recognized as a potential influence in the control and prevention of those factors which undermine the health and stability of individuals and families. For this reason, problems in the realm of social hygiene are engaging her attention. Efforts are being made to include social hygiene material in undergraduate courses, and nurses actively engaged in public health are asking for staff education programs which can be used for individual or group study.

Because of the needs of the latter group, PUBLIC HEALTH NURSING is planning to publish suggestions for staff discussion on the various aspects of social hygiene as they apply to nursing. It is certain that the medical phases of this subject concern us for syphilis and gonorrhea are communicable diseases which must be dealt with as effectively as other scourges of mankind which are being controlled and in some instances almost entirely eradicated. The magnitude of the problems of syphilis and gonorrhea are appreciated and methods for a successful attack known and available especially for syphilis. The need is to use the resources and apply the knowledge which we have at hand. Inertia of professional and lay groups is everywhere evident and is largely due to certain misconceptions: It is thought that these diseases are limited to the vicious and outcast; the problem is linked with prostitution alone; the victims are branded as moral delinquents who deserve their fate.

The Facts

The facts are that in this country about 1 per cent of the population, or 1,227,000 individuals, are at a specified time under care for syphilis and gonorrhea, and that these figures do not take into account the vast number of unreported, unrecognized, and self-treated cases; that clinics and private physicians are daily testifying to the prevalence of innocent infections and that any untreated case is a source of infection endangering the community as surely as typhoid fever or tuberculosis.

Interesting studies have been made comparing the prevalence of syphilis with other common communicable diseases. The most striking figures are those published by Dr. Nels Nelson of Massachusetts in 1930. He reviewed the morbidity reports over a period of eight years in 42 states, and found that syphilis exceeded scarlet fever by 35,000 cases, diphtheria by 390,000 cases, and in 21 states exceeded tuberculosis by 78,000 cases. In a second study made at the same time he showed that for every 100 cases of typhoid fever, smallpox, diphtheria and scarlet fever together, there were 95 cases of syphilis and gonorrhea.

These figures alone indicate the importance of the venereal diseases as health problems, but when statistics are studied in terms of age groups the situation becomes even more impressive.

Syphilis and gonorrhea are primarily diseases of youth. Studies made in New York State, Massachusetts and other sections of the country show that the peak of prevalence of these diseases is between the ages of 17 and 24 years.

This is comment enough upon the shortcomings of the home, the school, environmental influences, and recreational facilities to safeguard these young people.

Syphilis not only attacks youth but is a destroyer of life. Osler stated that it is the "captain of the men of death." We have only recognized this fact in recent years, for syphilis imitates other diseases and deaths recorded under numerous other diagnoses may be due to the spirochæte.

For example, it has been estimated that 25 per cent of deaths diagnosed as angina pectoris, 10 per cent of the deaths from Bright's disease, and 50 per cent of the deaths from congenital debility may actually be due to syphilis. One does not think of comparing syphilis with infantile paralysis as a cause of death in children under 15 years of age, and yet research in one community showed that during a period of five years there were 480 deaths among this group of children from infantile paralysis and 575 deaths from syphilis.

Every effort is being made, and rightly, to control infantile paralysis, but because syphilis kills case by case with no epidemic flare-ups, the importance of concerted action toward its eradication has not been recognized. The economic and social cost of syphilis and gonorrhea is stupendous. Millions of dollars are spent each year to care for the insane, the crippled and otherwise incapacitated. However, the loss to the community and family, especially where syphilis is concerned, cannot be estimated. This disease cuts life expectancy in half, and the death of the breadwinner means broken homes and dependent children.

The Nurse's Approach

The nurse's approach to syphilis and gonorrhea should not be different from her attack on tuberculosis, typhoid or scarlet fever. She may assist in reporting by referring suspicious cases which are not under medical care to the health officer. The ability to assist requires a knowledge of the diseases themselves and a keen appreciation of ethical relationships and prerogatives. She may assist in giving medical and nursing care and treatment, by attendance at clinic, by giving intelligent bedside care, and by demonstrations and treatments in the home. She will make her work of lasting value by constructive teaching and thereby send the patient out into the community, or leave him in his home, with a clear understanding of the nature of his disease, a practical program for carrying out treatment and for protecting others, and last but not least, the courage to carry on.

Case-Finding

One phase of the medical program in which the nurse is preeminently useful is in case-finding and case-holding. Syphilis and gonorrhea are familial diseases, and one case develops from another. Therefore, in dealing with these diseases, we cannot confine our efforts to one individual. In planning for a case-finding program many organizations begin with the prenatal patient and the eradication of congenital syphilis. Syphilis is a disease which can be passed directly from mother to child *in utero*, and in its most virulent form may destroy the product of conception. It is known that usually the more recently the mother has acquired the disease prior to conception, the more damage will be done to the fœtus, and that after five or six years the power of transmission lessens. However, cases have been cited showing the birth of syphilitic infants as late as the twentieth year of the mother's infection.. Therefore, the only certain control of the disease is treatment of the pregnant syphilitic woman as this has a profound effect in lessening the power of transmission. Dr. Moore of Johns Hopkins found that where adequate treatment was given to a group of 440 pregnant syphilitic women, only 3.4 per cent of the off-spring had syphilis, and 96.6 per cent were normal living children. It should be iterated and reiterated that the time factor in treatment is all-important. The nurse's problem is not how to treat a syphilitic woman, but rather how to get all patients examined early in pregnancy, by the fifth month at least, for after this time the effectiveness of anti-syphilitic measures is less sure. To prevent congenital syphilis the disease must be diagnosed in the mother. Syphilis in pregnancy is difficult to recognize, and usually causes the patient little inconvenience. Therefore, the only way to discover cases is by employing a routine Wassermann or any of the more recent precipitation tests.

In clinics where these diagnostic procedures are used, 3 to 23 per cent of all pregnant women have been found to have syphilis, and in certain areas this figure rises as high as 32 to 50 per cent. Difficulties which develop in getting the ignorant or foreign-born mother under care early tax all the resourcefulness, skill and insight of the nurse, for only by constant teaching and a real understanding of the patient's point of view can the barriers of ancient taboos and superstitions be broken down.

A second problem concerns the husbands of syphilitic patients. They are usually neglected because they are so frequently away from home when the nurse calls, and yet they may be a source of infection to other members of their families. Every effort should be made to get this group examined. Then if our work is to be complete, the children born prior to the present pregnancy must receive attention, and after the birth of the new baby, it also should be examined, treated if a positive diagnosis of syphilis is made, and supervised over a period of years.

To summarize the part of the nurse in case-finding in familial syphilis:

1. Stress the importance of medical supervision early in pregnancy for all prenatal patients.

2. Teach the importance of all procedures in a complete prenatal examination including the Wassermann.

3. Interpret the diagnosis of syphilis in terms of the patient's understanding, stressing the importance of treatment from the standpoint of the health of the new baby and reiterating the hopeful aspects of the situation.

4. Keep the mother faithful to treatment throughout pregnancy by continued encouragement and friendly help. This may include making arrangements for someone to accompany her to clinic, planning for care of the children who must be left at home; and seeing that financial adjustments and social conplications are taken care of.

5. Remember that the mental health of the patient is as important as her physical well being, by foreseeing worries and fears that may arise in connection with the diagnosis and helping the patient to face the situation calmly and constructively.

6. Teach the importance of continuing treatment after the postpartum period.

7. See that the new-born baby is examined and has adequate supervision and treatment.

8. Arrange for the examination of contacts—the father and children.

The nurse is influential insofar as she has the capacity to "hear the worst or the best in human nature and accepts it neither as worst nor best but as life."

Dr. Stephen Rushmore in discussing the value of the nurse as a teacher says:

"The whole teaching of the nurse is given special point in the presence of pregnancy because to the normal woman anything that affects her unborn baby is of utmost importance. Of these great opportunites we have scarcely begun to take advantage. Here indeed the primitive method of one pupil and one teacher sitting down together and talking it over surpasses in effectiveness anything devised in later times."

In all case-finding efforts, we begin with the patient. Gonorrhea presents somewhat different problems from syphilis but again the disease concerns the entire family or household.

The first case known to the nurse might be a child with cervico-vaginitis and her efforts would not only be directed toward treatment of the patient but also teaching the parents the facts of the disease, the importance of precautionary measures, and the need for examination of other members of the family to rule out gonorrhea. In the majority of instances when a child has this form of vaginitis the source of infection is in the home.

The types of case-finding which I have mentioned are within the province of every nurse. The more technical form of epidemiological search for sources of infection is still looked upon as demanding unusual qualifications and preparation, and therefore will not be emphasized here.

In the field of communicable disease control, sanitary codes, and positive health teaching play an important part along with the strictly medical measures, and the intelligent worker will know state and local laws which have to do with the venereal diseases and conditions in her community which make police and court activities necessary.

The effectiveness of the nurse's efforts in the educational phases of the program depends upon ethical relationships, a background of scientific knowledge, a sane approach to all situations, an ability to interpret and skill in presenting facts from the angle of the individual's interest and understanding.

It goes without saying that the nurse does not work alone in the program for control. In fact the success of her work depends upon her resourcefulness in cooperating with, and supplementing the efforts of health officer, private physician, clinic, social worker and all others in the community.

Suggestions for Staff Discussion

1. What local ordinances have you in your community requiring the reporting of syphilis and gonorrhea?

2. How many cases of syphilis and gonorrhea were reported in your community in 1931? In 1930?

3. What are the local agencies which are taking part in controlling these diseases? What is your relationship to these groups?

4. What is your particular contribution as an individual or organization in this phase of health work?

5. Discuss one of your family case histories in which syphilis or gonorrhea is a problem. Show case-finding methods used. What contribution did other agencies make to a solution of this case? How essential was the contribution of the nurse in this instance?

References

American Journal of Public Health, February, 1932. Articles by Parran, Thomas; Nelson, N. A.; and Munson, William L.

Nelson, N. A. *What can be done about Gonorrhea and Syphilis?* Mass. Dept. of Health and U.S.P.H.S. May be purchased from the American Social Hygiene Association, 450 Seventh Avenue, New York City. 10 cents.

Hidden Costs in Industry. American Social Hygiene Association, 450 Seventh Avenue, New York City. 10 cents.

Usilton, L. J. *Prevalence of Venereal Disease in the U. S.* Reprint No. 27. 5 cents. United States Public Health Service, U. S. Government Printing Office, Washington, D. C.

Snow, W. F. *The Venereal Diseases, Their Medical, Nursing and Community Aspects.* Funk & Wagnalls, N. Y. 1914. (National Health Series).

SYPHILIS*

What the Public Health Nurse Should Know About the Patient and the Disease

By GLADYS CRAIN, R.N.

Assistant Director, National Organization for Public Health Nursing

There is a challenge to public health nurses in the scientific facts regarding the control and eradication of syphilis, a disease which has for centuries diverted attention from its power and prevalence by masquerading under many confusing diagnoses.

Dr. Edward Keyes very recently made the statement that approximately nine per cent of the population of New York State is infected with syphilis and 81,000 new cases are added each year. Other states show equally impressive figures in spite of inadequate methods of reporting.

It has been stated on many occasions that there is no other single disease which causes a greater degree of human unhappiness, total disability and loss of earning capacity. On the other hand, there is no single disease for which there is a more accurate means for confirming clinical diagnosis, for rendering the patient non-infectious by specific drugs, arresting the destructive spread of the causative organism, and, under favorable conditions, effecting remarkable cures.

Here is a disease which might become rare in one generation if all health workers prepared for an attack upon it. It is cheering to enumerate some of the effective weapons which are at hand:

1. For diagnosis: the dark field miscroscope, the Wassermann and precipitation tests.

2. For routine treatments: the arsenobenzenes, bismuth, mercury, and the iodides.

3. For neurosyphilis: Tryparsamide, malaria therapy, and diathermy.

4. For public protection: the arsenobenzenes which kill the spirochæte and render the infectious lesions of syphilitic patients sterile.

It has been said that the Roman Legion was superior to the Greek Phalanx because every man in it was an accomplished warrior who could if alone give admirable account of himself. Public health nurses are potentially powerful legionaries, but success demands individual knowledge of the habits of the enemy and a planned method of attack based upon that knowledge. Syphilis has been known to the civilized world since 1495, and yet until the latter part of the nineteenth century

---

* Reprinted through the courtesy of Public Health Nursing from the issue of August, 1932,

and the first decade of the twentieth, slow progress had been made in the scientific knowledge of its cause, modes of transmission, and means of control and care. However, with the animal experimentations of Metchnikoff and Roux in 1903 and the discovery of the causative organism by Schaudinn and Hoffman in 1905 there followed a number of dramatic and valuable contributions such as the perfection of the complement fixation test by Wassermann, and the discovery of "606" salvarsan or arsphenamine by Ehrlich.

Today the emphasis is upon the early rather than the late manifestations of syphilis, for early diagnosis and treatment gives the greatest chance for cure, and also insures public health protection.

It is obvious that the brief discussion of syphilis which follows is inadequate, but a few facts regarding its clinical course may be helpful in refreshing the memory and in leading to further study.

Dr. Louis Chargin in an interesting study of 444 syphilitic patients found that a total of 60 per cent were apparently cured and the greatest number of cures, amounting to 90 per cent, were in the primary seronegative group. It goes without saying that the public should be as thoroughly acquainted with the earliest manifestations of this disease as they are of cancer and tuberculosis, and impressed in a like manner with the hopefulness of early treatment. Syphilis is caused by the *treponema pallidum*, or as it is more frequently designated the *spirochœta pallida*, an anærobic corkscrew-shaped organism which has an extremely low viability outside the human body. It is killed by a temperature of 123° F., by weak soap solutions, weak antiseptics, and even tap water. It is killed quickly by drying or exposure to sunlight. This fortunate fragility has been a protection to mankind against such a complete universality of the disease as is found in tuberculosis. The spirochæte is spread by intimate contact of person with person, and only comparatively rarely by household utensils and other articles of personal use.

Dr. John Stokes in discussing the habits of the organism says:

"Anærobiosis and moisture make (syphilis) a disease of intimate contacts, for only in the mouth and vagina and under the foreskin are found year in and year out the biologic conditions which perpetuate the infection. It is well worth while in discussing syphilis with patients whose perspective is much distorted ... to direct their attention to this aspect of the matter. It is not a divine moral purpose or a satanic punitive ingenuity that connects syphilis with genital activities, but a mere biologic accident, no more significant in the last analysis than the fact that potatoes grow in sandy loam."

Because of the social stigma, and exaggerated notions regarding the results of a syphilitic infection, it is not uncommon for patients to develop anxiety neuroses and negativistic attitudes toward treatment. Psychiatrists say that a seemingly uncoöperative patient may be so because of mechanisms over which he has no control. The only way to obviate such reactions is to anticipate his fears and misconceptions, and lay the facts of the situation clearly before him.

The period of incubation in syphilis is about three weeks, during which the patient has no discomfort and the activities of the organisms are hidden. At the end of this time the primary sore appears, invariably at the site of the organism's entry into the body. The lesion looks harmless enough but is actually teeming with spirochætes. One drop of serum from the chancre, placed under the lens of a dark field microscope, will show myriads of dancing particles gleaming silver white, and coiled in perfect symmetry.

Approximately six to eight weeks after the appearance of the chancre the early secondary stage is heralded by a generalized rash. This may be macular, papular, pustular, or mixed—it may also resemble any one of a number of common skin diseases such as impetigo contagiosa, pityriasis rosa, and psoriasis. Such masquerading results in mistakes in diagnosis which are tragic for the patient and his contacts.

To refer to Dr. Chargin's study again, 61 per cent of patients seen in the early secondary state were apparently cured, while those who started treatment after the third month of the disease were only 45 per cent curable. Infectious lesions such as chancres, flat condylamata, mucous patches, and a rash that is crusted or oozing (a dry rash is non-infectious) make the early stages of syphilis very important from a public health angle, and the nurse who has a high index of suspicion plus a scientific background of knowledge may be instrumental in uncovering unsuspected sources of infection by getting such patients under medical care at the earliest possible moment.

In untreated cases of syphilis infectious lesions may appear at intervals over a period of five years. After this time there is usually a period of latency when the patient has no symptoms. However, the organisms continue their destructive work under cover. Certain strains of the spirochæte cause tertiary gummas, while others are responsible for the degenerative changes in parasyphilis (cardiovascular damage or involvement of the brain and spinal cord). It is well to remember that these late lesions of syphilis are non-infectious.

The results of syphilis at any stage when no steps are taken to control it are serious indeed. Miscarriages, stillbirths, malformed infants, blindness, deafness, apoplexy, aneurisms, cardiac disease, locomotor ataxia, general paralysis, and insanity are some of the charges which may be laid at its door. There is nothing more tragic, however, than the breaking down of a fine intellect, or the collapse of an individual in a responsible position. In the former the loss to society is inestimable, in the latter may rest the beginnings of a community catastrophe. One writer sums up the situation as follows: "Civilization has paid dearly when in the brains of our great ones syphilis has provoked wars or prevented sonatas."

Questions for Discussion

1. What concurrent disinfection would you teach in a home where there is a case of early secondary syphilis?
2. What would you do with valuable books which have been used constantly by an infectious syphilitic patient?
3. How would you convince a syphilitic patient of the importance of bringing his contacts to a physician or clinic for examination? Write out briefly what you would include in your teaching and use for group discussion.
4. A patient with late secondary syphilis, receiving arsphenamine treatment at a clinic, was discharged from his job in a shoe factory, when his employer accidentally learned of his diagnosis. Was this a necessary health measure? If the employer later asked for your advice about the case what facts would you present for or against reinstating the patient?
5. A patient, who came into a clinic on June 20, 1932, with a primary lesion of the lip which had developed within a day or so, named three friends as possible sources of his infection. The first he had not seen since November 27, 1931; the second since May 28, 1932; and the third he had taken out on a party on June the 9th. Which contact would you be especially interested in getting under treatment at once?

References

*Stokes, John. *Dermatology and Syphilology for Nurses*. W. B. Saunders Co., Philadelphia, Pa. $2.50.

Parks. W. H. *Public Health and Hygiene*. Lea & Febiger, Philadelphia, Pa., 1928. $9.00.

Rosenau, M. J. *Preventive Medicine and Hygiene*. D. Appleton & Co., New York, 1927. $10.00.

N. O. P. H. N. *Manual of Public Health Nursing*. The Macmillan Co., New York, N. Y., 1932. $1.50.

The Public Health Nurse, March, 1931, page 150.

We remind our readers that N. O. P. H. N. members may borrow books for a three weeks period from the National Health Library, 450 Seventh Avenue, New York City, for the cost of wrapping and mailing.

*If funds are limited and only one book can be purchased, this general text book will be found helpful.

The next article will deal with family syphilis and include congenital s hilis.

FAMILIAL SYPHILIS*
Significant Facts for the Public Health Nurse
BY GLADYS CRAIN, R.N.
Assistant Director, National Organization for Public Health Nursing

Every public health nurse accepts the seeming paradox that "the best way to cure a disease is to prevent it." The facts of syphilis create a gloomy picture until we remember that the prevention of one aspect of this disease—congenital syphilis—is comparatively simple and under favorable conditions almost certain of success. Dr. Walter Clarke in discussing the brilliant discoveries in this field, says that they constitute at once "a triumph of medical science, and a challenge to all medical and social agencies caring for women and children. The triumph consists in saving 95 out of 100 infants threatened by congenital syphilis. The challenge consists in the opportunity to apply modern diagnostic and therapeutic measures to every pregnant syphilitic woman. Thus the ...unborn child is given an opportunity for life and health."

The problem of preventing syphilis in the parents of these children is a more complicated one, which involves laws eradicating prostitution, and marriage laws controlling infected persons. It has been estimated that 90 per cent of syphilis in the married is the result of ante-marital infection and the lack of adequate treatment, and that more than 50 per cent of the pregnant syphilitic women who attend clinics are innocently infected. Some states have instituted marriage laws requiring the contracting parties to present certificates showing freedom from any venereal disease, but these laws will be of little value until the public is educated not only in regard to the facts of syphilis and the dangers of a vicious environment, but also to demand clinical and serological examinations of all those about to marry, and the assurance of adequate treatment and long time supervision of those infected.

The question as to when it is safe for a syphilitic patient to marry is difficult to answer, and must be decided by the physician in each individual case. Three to five years after infection has been the rule when treatment has been adequate, but a rigid adherence to this has proved impracticable in many instances. Some authorities have suggested that a better solution for the protection of parents and children would be a program of regulated marriage. In such instances the contracting parties would receive explicit instructions, which would include the importance of abstinence from intimate contacts, except when the patient is undergoing an active course of arsphenamine treatment, the desirability of close medical supervision for the family, and the necessity for long time regular treatment.

In discussing familial syphilis nurses often ask whether it is possible for a healthy woman to have a syphilitic child. At one time it was thought that the infection of the fetus might be of paternal origin alone, but today most syphilologists agree that a syphilitic infant presupposes a mother with a general syphilitic infection, with the strong probability that the father has the disease also.

The reason for confusion regarding the origin of the disease in congenital syphilitics is that the infection is so often extremely mild in the mother and may be entirely hidden. Occasionally the Wassermann test is negative or only weakly positive, and the physician must rely upon a previous history of possible miscarriages, stillbirths, or delicate infants for this diagnosis. Many such patients, wholly unaware of their infection, and discouraged that previous pregnancies have ended in disaster, may, under anti-syphilitic treatment (begun before the fifth month of pregnancy), have a normal, healthy infant.

---
* Reprinted through the courtesy of Public Health Nursing from the issue of October, 1932.

The Question of Breast Feeding

Another question which has been debated pro and con is whether the milk of a syphilitic woman may infect a non-syphilitic child. Rosenau in his "Preventive Medicine and Hygiene" makes the statement that "The milk of a syphilitic woman must be regarded as infectious since it is well known that a syphilitic wet nurse without lesions will almost surely infect a healthy child." Although this point is controversial, the fact that such infections may occur would suggest the importance of Wassermann tests for all women who supply milk stations with breast milk.

Colle's law that a healthy mother can nurse her syphilitic infant without danger to herself, means in the light of present-day knowledge, that this is possible because the presence of the disease in her blood stream gives her an immunity to further infection. Her apparent health illustrates the deceptive cunning of the spirochæte. Profeta's law that a healthy child of a syphilitic mother may be nursed by her and yet not become infected may be explained in a similar way—the infant already has congenital syphilis. The above observations do not take into consideration those infrequent cases where the infant of a syphilitic woman has escaped infection.

From the standpoint of prevention, questions regarding the breast feeding of these babies are frequently raised. In such cases the decision must be left to the physician in charge, and may depend upon the recency of the mother's infection, the amount of treatment which she has had, and the social situations involved. The procedure of the nurse will be to check carefully with the physician regarding his instructions in the matter and see to it that the mother follows such orders accurately, for each case must be considered individually.

An important consideration in those families where syphilis has been discovered, is the possibility of infection in more than one member. In teaching the need for examination and treatment of contacts, many delicate and difficult situations will be brought to light. However, by approaching the family on the basis of health alone, attacking the problem as one would tuberculosis or routine corrective and preventive work, the tactful nurse can, in most instances, gain the family's confidence and coöperation.

The Child Welfare Program

In her efforts toward the eradication of congenital syphilis the nurse must go farther afield than her work with the prenatal patient and families where there is a recognized case of syphilis. She must be ever on the watch for and alert to the danger signs of congenital syphilis in her infant welfare, preschool and school contacts as well.

Dr. John Stokes in reviewing the prevalence of syphilis estimates that three children in one hundred have the disease, and in city populations, 3 to 4 per cent. It is important to save these unfortunate individuals from further ravages of the spirochæte—such as blindness, deafness, deformity, and insanity—by early adequate treatment.

In child welfare work the reduction of infant mortality rates is considered a valuable indication of effective health measures. Researches of scientists have shown that syphilis is the most important single factor in the causation of fetal death. J. Whitridge Williams in an early study at Johns Hopkins found that 34.4 per cent of all deaths occurring between "the period of viability and the expiration of the first two weeks of the puerperium" were due to this disease, and McCord found 45 per cent of such deaths among negro infants chargeable to the same cause.

Review of Symptoms

A brief summary of some of the manifestations of congenital syphilis in those cases where the fetus did not receive the benefits of antisyphilitic treatment by way of the mother's blood stream may be helpful. Many of the aspects depend upon the recency of the mother's infection at the time of conception. The most virulent forms of the disease are those which result in early abortions, stillbirths, macerated fetuses, and in infants born with cutaneous or visceral lesions, or with such malformations as hare lip, spina bifida, and hydrocephalus.

The classic type of puny, weazened infant with its wrinkled simianesque face and skin the color of café-au-lait is not as common as was once thought—but does represent a severe infection. Such infants, when liveborn, live only a few hours or a day or two after birth. Treatment is usually unavailing, for syphilis causes death in at least 90 per cent of the cases. However, it is greater tragedy for the 10 per cent who survive —both from the standpoint of the child and also his family. Long ago Fournier said that "there is nothing more dangerous to its environment than a syphilitic infant."

When the power of an infection in the mother has been lessened by time, the pregnancy may result in the birth of a child presenting no clinical evidence of syphilis. In one-third of these cases the cord Wassermann is negative at birth, but a blood test after a period of six weeks may be strongly positive.

Within a few days or weeks, however, clinical signs of early congenital syphilis may also appear. The most characteristic of these are loss of weight, bullous eruptions on the palms and soles, a high pitched cry, feebleness, pseudo-paralysis of the extremities, snuffles which persist, eruptions about the mouth which on healing leave radiating scars or rhagades. All symptoms except such as are caused by actual destruction of tissue may disappear without treatment, and the parents may consider the child cured.

Unfortunately, months or possibly years later the tardive type of the disease will make itself evident. Often symptoms will not appear until the tenth or twelfth year, and in some instances manifestations of congenital syphilis are not observed until the twentieth or thirtieth year of life. Dr. Winston Rutledge in an article in the *Southern Medical Journal* for August, 1932, makes the following interesting statement in his conclusions: "Because of the high percentage of congenital syphilitics who remain symptom free, and sero-negative for months and years, we feel justified in treating all children of syphilitic parents."

Interstitial keratitis, eighth nerve deafness and Hutchinsonian teeth are three important symptoms of this late type of the disease, which taken together form a diagnostic triad. Other common stigmata are sabre shins, mulberry-like molars, saddle-nose, a high-arched palate and prominent frontal bones. As a general rule cardiovascular symptoms are rare in congenital syphilis, but involvement of the brain and spinal cord is seen in juvenile tabes and paresis.

Social Implications Present a Challenge

There are many social maladjustments which may be ascribed to congenital syphilis. An infant with contagious lesions such as mucous patches, condylomata, oozing eruptions and snuffles is a source of danger to others who must be protected from him. However, as years go on this danger of infection lessens, although the general public is overfearful of anyone with this disease, and the school child may suffer handicaps and humiliation when his diagnosis becomes known. As a matter of fact there is little danger of infection in late childhood and after, and these children should be allowed to mingle freely with others in school and in play. They may later marry and have children free from syphilis, for the danger of the disease being handed on to the third generation is extremely slight.

Syphilis in the family causes more unhappiness than any other single disease. Aside from the fears, the worries, and attacks of conscience in the parents which make for an unwholesome home environment, and the possible loss of earning capacity in the father because of the disease, there is also the chance that disfiguring stigmata in the child may cause social as well as physical disability. This may be responsible for years of sensitiveness and bitterness, with a resulting damage to personality when the child finally learns their true significance.

Surely there is a challenge to the nurse and social worker in this field; for in the words of Dr. Hugh S. Cumming, "No problem touching the question of social betterment is free from complications of the venereal diseases. Since these complications can not be ignored it becomes the duty of all intelligent men and women to assist in the fight to which the Federal government, the states, the counties, and municipalities are by law committed."

Questions for Discussion

1. Are routine Wassermann tests used as a part of all prenatal examinations in your community? Of general medical examinations?
2. What local provision is made for the treatment of the pregnant syphilitic woman? Are there plans for the follow-up of delinquents, for examination of contacts, for supervision of new-born babies of these women?
3. What would be your procedure if you discovered a baby two weeks old with snuffles and eruptions on palms and soles?
4. What would you do about a school child who has a persistent case of pink eye?
5. Review one of your own cases, considering the following points:
   a. Instructions regarding the facts of the disease, general hygiene, treatment and concurrent disinfection.
   b. Plans for examination of contacts.
   c. Plans for social adjustments.
   d. Consideration of mental hygiene of individual members.
   e. Plans for coöperation with physicians and other agencies interested.

References

Congenital Syphilis. J. F. Schamberg, M.D., and Carroll S. Wright, M.D. Reprint No. 17, Superintendent of Documents, United States Government Printing Office, Washington, D. C., 1929. 5 cents.

The Prevention of Congenital Syphilis. Walter Clarke, M.D. American Social Hygiene Association, 450 Seventh Avenue, New York City. 10 cents.

Can Congenital Syphilis Be Prevented? Eugene S. Coler, M.D., Reprint No. 21. Superintendent of Documents, United States Government Printing Office, Washington, D. C., 1930. 5 cents.

Stokes, John. *Dermatology and Syphilology for Nurses.* W. B. Saunders Co., 1930. Pages 193-205.

Social Hygiene and the Prevention of Blindness. William F. Snow, M.D. American Social Hygiene Association, 450 Seventh Avenue, New York City. 10 cents.

Emotional Disturbances Accompanying Syphilis. Austin M. Cheever, M.D. "American Journal of Nursing," May, 1930.

Stokes, John. *Modern Clinical Syphilology.* W. B. Saunders Co. May be borrowed from National Health Library by members of N.O.P.H.N., 450 Seventh Avenue, New York City.

SYPHILIS*

Some Facts Regarding Diagnosis and Treatment

BY GLADYS CRAIN, R.N.

Assistant Director, National Organization for Public Health Nursing

Some one has said that a cultured man or woman is one who knows "something about everything and everything about something." This definition might well be applied to the public health nurse, who needs an impressive background of knowledge to cope with the varied situations which come to her attention.

Although the diagnosis and treatment of syphilis are prerogatives of the physician, the public health nurse should be familiar with the common methods in use.

---

* Reprinted through the courtesy of Public Health Nursing from the issue of November, 1932.

Method of Diagnosis

It is interesting to remember that up to 1906 there was no serum test for the diagnosis of syphilis. During that year, however, Bordet and Genjou finished their studies on complement fixation and immunity. Later Wassermann, Neisser, and Bruch applied these findings to syphilis and developed the Wassermann test which with the later precipitation tests has been such a valuable aid in the diagnosis of the secondary and late stages of the disease.

The accurate diagnosis of the early seronegative stage of syphilis has been made possible through the perfection of the dark field microscope. By a special method of concentrating light upon the field to be observed and by use of the highest power oil immersion lens, one may see a host of spirochætes in the clear serum obtained from a primary syphilitic lesion. Since the success of the treatment of syphilis is invariably and directly in proportion to the promptness with which it is begun, the dark field examination for accuracy and speed of diagnosis is extremely important. While the dark field is possibly the most accurate method for recognizing the *treponema pallidum*, it is not always practicable. In such cases stained smears have had considerable success and are being adopted in a number of centers.

The Wassermann and other blood tests which rely upon the phenomenon of complement fixation or precipitation, are, of course, indirect methods of diagnosis in contradistinction to the dark field which is a direct and certain method. Blood tests are an effective but not an infallible means of determining the presence of syphilis, and positive reactions must be interpreted in the light of the patient's history, together with painstaking clinical observations.

The Wassermann Test

The test most frequently employed is the Wassermann, which has in recent years been modified and improved by Kolmer and others. It is a very complicated laboratory procedure and requires six different reagents to perform it. These are guinea pig serum, rabbit serum, an extract of beef heart or other muscle tissue, sheep's blood corpuscles, human serum, and physiological saline. So many animal reagents add to the cost of the test, making it prohibitive in some communities, and also rendering standardization difficult.

Another disadvantage of the Wassermann test is that it must be performed in two separate steps which take many hours to complete. In spite of these facts it has great value and when used routinely in medical and other diagnostic clinics brings to light many unsuspected cases of syphilis and clears up numerous mysteries where treatment for some ailment which syphilis has simulated, proves unavailing or baffling.

The complexity of the Wassermann test has served as an incentive to scientists to develop a more simple and if possible more dependable test for syphilis. Most of the attempts have been directed toward precipitation reactions. Those most frequently employed in this country are the Kahn, the Hinton, and the Kline. The Hinton test is highly sensitive in its reactions, and it has considerable prestige in the East— especially in New England.

The Kahn is much more widely employed and in some laboratories is the only test in use. It has certain advantages over the Wassermann, which have contributed to its ready adoption. It takes less than one hour to complete; there is but one step required in its performance; and only three reagents are used. These are extract from normal muscle tissue, which is standardized, human serum, and physiological saline.

The Kline test is much like the Kahn but is performed in half the time, and the reaction is observed under the microscope. An important advantage of the Kline is that a very small amount of blood is necessary for the test. Experiments with finger blood are being perfected, and hold interesting possibilities for the future. Several test tubes with controls are used to demonstrate the reaction of the Wassermann, Kahn, and Hinton.

Nurses frequently ask what a four-plus Wassermann and Kahn look like in the test tube. It would be interesting to go into the fascinating details of these tests, but space will not allow this. Suffice it to say that in a positive Wassermann the fluid in the tube is clear and colorless, with sheep's corpuscles settled in the bottom. In a negative Wassermann there is a laking of the blood corpuscles and the fluid is red in color. A four-plus Kahn shows a heavy precipitate in the mixture, while a negative Kahn is without precipitate.

The best practice according to outstanding syphilologists is to employ more than one type of test for each specimen of blood examined.

Interpretation of Tests

Some points for the public health nurse to remember in interpreting blood tests are that they are no guide to the infectiousness or non-infectiousness of a patient; that a single positive test should not be taken as diagnostic; that several positives mean syphilis, and call for treatment; that a negative test in a patient under treatment is not a proof of cure, nor is it an index of any patient's real condition or final diagnosis.

It was at one time thought that patients with such diseases as scarlet fever, tuberculosis, malaria, jaundice, and also women in the last months of pregnancy might show a positive Wassermann test, even though free from syphilis. This viewpoint is today discredited. It is highly probable that these patients also have a syphilitic infection.

It is the usual practice to test the spinal fluid of each syphilitic patient within the first year of his infection—to discover whether the disease has spread to the nervous system. Some clinics perform this test as frequently as every six months. Specimens of fluid are obtained by lumbar or cistern punctures.

Another interesting test tube procedure which has developed in connection with the spinal fluid is the colloidal gold reaction. This test by a curve of changing color indicates whether paresis or tabes is developing.

It is encouraging to realize that in these ways the physician may early become aware of the beginnings of spirochætal activity in the brain or cord, and start special treatment at once to prevent further damage.

Treatment

In dealing with the treatment of syphilis two points of view must be considered:

1. The Public Health and community interest in the control of a communicable disease.
2. The patient's interest in his own cure.

The arsenobenzenes which include Ehrlich's "606" (Salvarsan or arsphenamine), neoarsphenamine ("914"), and sulpharsphenamine are the most effective drugs in use both from the standpoint of the cure of the patient and the safety of the community. The first two are usually given intravenously, and the last intramuscularly. A few injections of these drugs render dangerous lesions non-infectious by paralyzing and killing spirochætes. These drugs also have a tonic effect on the patient, so that often after a short course of treatment he feels unusually well and as the lesions quickly disappear he has a tendency to think himself cured. It is very difficult at this point to get him to continue treatment. However, it is said that inadequate treatment is worse than no treatment, since it tends to hasten nerve involvement. Also when treatment is discontinued too soon, relapses may occur with infectious lesions which again make the patient a menace to the community.

In connection with the use of arsphenamine present practice includes bismuth—a heavy metal which is given intramuscularly. This drug not only kills the organisms of syphilis, but also builds up the body's resistance to the disease. As a spirochæticide it is not considered as powerful as arsphenamine, but in certain combinations such as "bismarsen" remarkable results have been demonstrated in those Wassermann-fast cases over which arsphenamine has had little apparent effect.

A third drug is mercury, which has practically no power over the germ itself but is a tonic for stimulating the natural protective forces of the body.

Iodides in various combinations are also useful in syphilis as they dissolve tertiary lesions, relieve pain in periostitis and are valuable in the treatment of cardiovascular and neurosyphilis.

Neurosyphilis used to be hopeless and fatal manifestation of the disease. However, since 1921 the use of tryparsamide, malaria therapy and diathermy have produced excellent results. In a study of 542 mental patients treated with tryparsamide 36 per cent were so improved that they were again able to adjust to a normal community life. Research regarding the efficiency of malaria therapy shows about the same percentage of improvement.

Reactions to Treatment

There are occasional reactions to treatment with which public health nurses should be familiar. The severe headache following the lumbar puncture can usually be avoided when small gauge needles are used, and the patient rests flat in bed for at least twenty-four hours after the operation.

Some of the reactions following the injection of arsphenamine are due to faulty preparation of equipment, and poor technique; others may result from indiscretions on the patient's part.

Early symptoms of intolerance to the arsenobenzenes are general malaise, headache, nausea, and nitritoid crisis. The latter reaction is recognized by flushing of the face, swelling of the lips, choking, coughing, difficulty in breathing, and cardiac distress. The theory usually put forward is that this is a protein or anaphylactic intolerance. Adrenalin gives almost instant relief. Later reactions may simulate nephritis, jaundice, and various dermatoses.

The commoner forms of reaction to mercury and bismuth are stomatitis, kidney complications and gastro-intestinal disturbances. In bismuth intolerance a blue line showing along the margin of the gums means the beginning of trouble.

A grave reaction in tryparsamide treatment is eye involvement, which may begin with a slight irritation and go on to a gradual narrowing of the field of vision and final blindness.

The important thing for the nurse to remember is that any abnormal symptoms which a patient, who is under treatment, may complain of, are worth noting, and reporting to the physician in charge.

Home Visiting

There is as a rule very little actual nursing care to be given to syphilitic patients in their homes, as they are, in the majority of cases, ambulatory and quite able to do for themselves. For those occasional patients who need bedside care, the skills which are acceptable in medical, surgical, and mental disease nursing apply. For example, the nursing care of a heart case does not change in principle because the patient's lesion is syphilitic in origin.

In 90 per cent of the cases brought to her attention in the field, the public health nurse's role will be that of teacher. In such instances the content of her home visits will include the following:

1. An investigation of the home situation to ascertain whether it is favorable from the standpoint of treatment; and whether instructions given by the clinic or private physician can be adapted to the limitations of the environment.

2. Teaching the facts of the disease; what it is; how it is spread; the possibility of cure; the value of adequate treatment and the results of inadequate treatment.
3. Demonstrating precautionary measures if the disease is in a communicable stage; and assisting the patient with plans for carrying them out under the possible difficulties of his home surroundings.
4. Demonstrating special treatments.
5. Teaching personal hygiene and general health measures.
6. Extending preventive teaching to all members of the family since disease is a family matter.

Dr. David Lees reiterates the importance of good hygiene and the maintenance of good health as an aid in the cure of syphilis and a preventive of intolerance to drugs. Congenital syphilitics especially need good food, fresh air, sunshine, cod liver oil, and plenty of rest, if satisfactory results are to be obtained.

Special teaching of mouth hygiene is necessary—and all carious and broken teeth should be attended to. A clean mouth, brushing the teeth three times a day, and using an astringent mouth wash are aids in preventing stomatitis.

The omitting of all food for several hours before treatment and the avoidance of alcohol are also preventives of untoward reactions to the drugs.

Tact and skill in teaching are prerequisites in working with these families. It is a common error to try to force an issue, when one is impatient for results. It is also easy to confuse teaching and telling. A patient is never motivated by a string of facts. New ideas—better modes of living—must be related to his interests, and framed within the restrictions of his environment, his intelligence, and knowledge. Only then will he see their value for himself, and *act*. Only then can the nurse consider that she has taught.

Questions

1. What is the average length of time that patients with syphilis continue treatment in your own organization?
2. What are the reasons that patients give for lapses? List these in the order of frequency.
3. What can you do in the light of these reasons to improve case holding among this group?
4. Outline what you would tell a patient who thought he was cured after a few injections of arsphenamine; one who had an unfortunate reaction to treatment and refused further injections; one who has had one negative Wassermann after a course of treatment; a pregnant syphilitic mother who feels perfectly well and can see no reason for hospital care or medicine.
5. How would you explain the value of a routine Wassermann to a pregnant woman?

References

Stokes, John: *Dermatology and Syphilology for Nurses.* Saunders, 1930. Pp. 182-192, 206-249.

Pugh, Stokes, Brown and Carnell: *The Patient's Reasons for Lapse in Treatment.* "American Journal of Syphilis," Vol. 14, Oct., 1930, p. 438.

Miller, Virginia Boyer, R.N.: *Tests for Syphilis, An Explanation of the Wassermann.* "American Journal of Nursing," Vol. 30, June, 1930, pp. 707-712.

Kennedy, Katherine E., R.N.: *Tests for Syphilis, The Kahn Test.* "American Journal of Nursing." Vol. 30, June, 1930, pp. 713-714.

A Positive Wassermann by a Victim. "Survey," September 15, 1931, Vol. 66, p. 545.

Stokes, John: *Instructions to Clinic Patients.* "The Public Health Nurse," Vol. 23, March, 1931 p. 150.

SYPHILIS*
A Review

Editorial Note: Like every good teacher, Miss Crain sees value in a "review quiz". Here are fifty posers on syphilis for the December study program in social hygiene. We suggest giving each correct answer the value of two points and seeing if you can score a hundred. Or perhaps, an old fashioned spelling bee, dividing your staff into two teams, would—to change the figure of speech—sugar the pill. Answers may be found in the July, August, October and November numbers of *Public Health Nursing* and in Stokes: "Dermatology and Syphilology for Nurses," or your questions may be referred to Miss Crain at the N.O.P.H.N.

1. How many centuries elapsed between the first known outbreak of syphilis in Europe and the discovery of the causative organism of the disease?
2. What six scientists made outstanding contributions to an understanding of syphilis in the first decade of the twentieth century?
3. How does the treponema pallidum compare with the tubercle bacillus in ability to survive under conditions outside the human body? What significance has this from the standpoint of chance infection?
4. Give three conditions especially favorable to the prolongation of the life of the spirochaeta pallida outside the human body?
5. What are four common and effective means of killing the spirochaeta pallida outside the human body?
6. How is syphilis transmitted?
7. Why is the term venereal as applied to syphilis a misnomer?
8. What does the first visible skin reaction to the spirochete indicate as to the probable length of time the patient has had the disease? What is the lesion called and what are accompanying symptoms?
9. How soon after exposure to syphilis do the organisms get into the blood stream?
10. Can syphilis in any stage of the disease be considered a local infection? Give reasons to support your answer.
11. What is the difference between chancre and chancroid?
12. What is the public health significance of chancroid?
13. Has a negative Wassermann report on the blood specimen of a patient with a genital lesion diagnostic value? Give reason for answer.
14. How can a diagnosis be accurately and directly confirmed in the seronegative stage of primary syphilis?
15. What is the importance of the early treatment of syphilitic patients from the standpoint of public health protection and the cure of the disease?
16. What is the usual period of time which elapses between exposure to syphilis and the appearance of so-called secondary symptoms?
17. Name three common infectious lesions of syphilis.
18. Give precautionary measures which the nurse should establish for her own protection, and that of others in caring for a patient with infectious lesions.
19. What is the length of time during which a patient may be a potential source of infection to others?
20. What common skin lesions may syphilitic eruptions resemble?
21. Are moist and dry lesions equally infectious? In this connection, how dangerous to others in the waiting room is a clinic patient with a macular syphilitic rash?
22. How infectious are discharges from a tertiary gumma? Are they a real source of danger to the nurse who does the dressing? Would the method of handling such soiled dressings differ from that of an osteomyelitis case?

---
* Reprinted through the courtesy of Public Health Nursing from the issue of December, 1932.

23. Are there any non-infectious lesions of syphilis?
24. Does a positive Wassermann reaction determine the infectiousness or non-infectiousness of a patient?
25. What lesions of congenital syphilis are considered infectious?
26. Should children discovered in school with tardive congenital syphilis be excluded? Give reason for answer.
27. What form of syphilis is considered a fatal manifestation of the disease and competes with neurosyphilis in its capacity to disable its victims?
28. What four diseases of heart and blood vessels may be of syphilitic origin and are important causes of death?
29. Give the name and three characteristic symptoms of syphilis of the spinal cord.
30. Give range of time between exposure to syphilis and spinal cord involvement. What procedure is used to determine such involvement?
31. What symptoms are common when syphilis attacks the cortex of the brain?
32. What is the significance of the phrase—Syphilis is a familial disease?
33. What are two important steps to take in the prevention of congenital syphilis?
34. How early in the pregnancy of a syphilitic patient should treatment be instituted in order to prevent the extension of the disease to placenta and fetus?
35. Can you justify the practice of beginning antisyphilitic treatment as late as the eighth month of pregnancy? What would be its value to the mother? To the baby?
36. What facts in the history of a prenatal patient would lead one to suspect the presence of a syphilitic infection?
37. How reliable is a cord Wassermann test?
38. What are three significant manifestations of fetal syphilis? Of infantile syphilis?
39. What is the Hutchinsonian triad?
40. What may cause defects of the upper central incisors besides syphilis?
41. Sabre shins may be confused as a symptom of what other disease? The incipient stage of interstitial keratitis as a symptom of what other disease?
42. What are rhagades? How caused?
43. What can you say about the significance of the paternal origin of congenital syphilis?
44. Could a mother with late syphilis have healthy children? Give reasons for answer.
45. Does a course of treatment given throughout pregnancy cure a syphilitic woman?
46. Is a patient considered infectious while receiving a routine course of arsphenamine?
47. How can you justify the practice of supervising and treating all children (whether they show evidence of syphilis or not) born of untreated syphilitic mothers?
48. Distinguish in general terms between the following: Wassermann, Kahn, Kline, Hinton and colloidal gold tests.
49. From the standpoint of cure or the arrest of syphilis, and the protection of community health, give one fact about each of the following; mercury bismuth, neoarsphenamine, typarsamide, malaria therapy.
50. What are early signs of intolerance to bismuth, arsphenamine, tryparsamide, mercury?

FACTS ABOUT GONORRHEA*

BY GLADYS CRAIN, R.N.

Assistant Director, National Organization for Public Health Nursing

Gonorrhea has been fitly called the "Fourth Great Plague," for according to reliable figures it is afflicting at any given time "more persons than ever have been, or will be, the victims of cancer, tuberculosis, and syphilis combined."

This is a disease which ranks second to measles in prevalence and is reported six times as frequently as typhoid fever.

Dr. Taliaferro Clark has given as the attack rate for gonorrhea 679,000 new cases a year, for the country as a whole. As this is based on surveys of known cases under treatment, the estimate is only a minimum one.

Although there are five times as many new cases among the male population as among the female, the real social significance of the disease lies in its prevalence among women. The tremendous toll in suffering and even death from various complications following a primary infection cannot be estimated. At least forty per cent of the cases of sterility in women can be laid at the door of this disease and fifty per cent of all gynecological operations are a result of gonococcal infections. The disease in male patients is not, generally speaking, as serious as in the female, but with unskillful treatment severe complications and sterility may occur.

The fact that gonorrhea is a menace to individual health and efficiency and endemic in all communities is not widely understood. Indeed the fallacy persists that this disease is no more serious than a common cold and that it is after all confined to the vicious and outcast alone.

Public health and other professional groups have in many instances failed to face the facts and accept the problem of controlling this communicable disease, both because of its unpleasant connotation, and the discouraging aspects of its treatment and cure. However, ignoring the situation will not help it, and until gonorrhea is put on the same basis as the other communicable diseases from the standpoint of education of the public in preventive measures, the establishment of easily available treatment centers in all communities, the setting up of standards for diagnosis and treatment and definite criteria for cure, no real progress in its eradication can be made.

Characteristics of the Gonococcus

One writer has said that like the poor we have the gonorrheic with us always. In fact, this disease is as old as the human race, and man is its only reservoir. Unlike the spirochæta pallida, the gonococcus will not thrive when inoculated into lower animals, and this fact has hindered research and prevented progress.

The organism, an intracellular gram-negative diplococcus, was discovered by Neisser in 1879. Dr. P. S. Pelouze protests against its name—gonococcus—which he says means a "berry-like organism that produces an involuntary flow of semen." He adds with finality, "It is not and it does not." This organism is differentiated from other cocci by its arrangement in pairs, its predilection for very special culture media, its presence within the protoplasm of cells and its reaction to the gram stain.

The gonococcus is a fragile anærobe. It abhors aridity, and is destroyed by mild disinfectants, soap and water. It is intolerant to any unsuitable media, and although it lives for some time on moist surfaces, it dies quickly when exposed to sun and air. The organism thrives best upon columnar epithelial cells. Since this type of mucous membrane is found in the lining of the genito-urinary system, gonorrhea is chiefly confined to these areas. There is no natural immunity to this disease, but its virulence depends somewhat upon the individual's physical condition.

---

* Reprinted through the courtesy of Public Health Nursing from the issue of January, 1933.

Modes of transmission include sexual and other intimate contacts. Chance infections in adults are comparatively rare, although occasionally the disease may be acquired by using contaminated articles. This statement does not apply to those cases acquired in childhood. Here accidental infections are the rule.

The progress of a gonococcal infection in the adult may be summarized as follows: a period of local inflammation, a period of extension through the genito-urinary tract, and possibly, later, a generalized infection involving the joints, tendons, muscles, and rarely the heart. An important point to remember is that the gonococcus may live for years in the tissues of the human body in a latent state, only to become virulent and active again when transferred to the healthy tissues of another individual. This makes the disease treacherous and formidable.

Early Symptoms of Infection

The period of incubation for gonorrhea ranges from twelve hours to a week, the average time being from five to seven days. The urethral orifice is usually the primary point of infection. The first symptoms are those attending any local inflammation. There are redness, itching, burning and pain of the parts affected. The pain becomes intense on urination. These symptoms last two or three days and possibly by the fifth there is a discharge of mucus and pus, and the external genitalia become swollen. From this point of primary infection the organisms may extend into the uterus, fallopian tubes, ovaries, and even involve the peritoneal cavity in the female. In the male, an extension from the anterior urethra through the posterior urethra, the prostate gland, the vas deferens, and finally the epididymis may occur.

Gonorrhea causes sterility by occluding the fallopian tubes in women and blocking the epididymis in men. The disease is more serious in women than men chiefly because of the anatomical structures involved, and also because pregnancy and the normal cycle of menstruation predispose the female to a vast extension of infection. When the disease becomes generalized, any portion of the body may be invaded. However, the usual manifestation is a gonorrheal arthritis which is crippling and often resists the most vigorous and prolonged treatment. Gonorrheal endocarditis and general septicemia are grave but rare complications which, when they occur, usually result in death.

In order to have any real understanding of the course of gonorrhea, it is necessary to be able to visualize the anatomy of the urogenital structures in both sexes. Such a review is beyond the limits of this paper. Suffice it to say that the gonococcus progresses easily along the genito-urinary tract because of the continuity of columnar or transitional epithelium which is its favorite habitat. Also, it thrives in the deep glands of Batholin, Skene, and Maboth in the female and in Cowper's glands and other mucous pockets in the male. The organism does not live as a rule upon the surface of mucous membrane but penetrates the intracellular spaces into the submucosa, where it lies buried. This fact is significant from the standpoint of treatment.

Treatment

In the past, it was thought that the organism was killed by the use of certain antiseptics which were instilled into the genito-urinary tract. This led to the fallacy that the stronger the drug the sooner the cure. Such practice resulted in irreparable injuries. There is no drug that is a specific for the gonococcus as arsphenamine is for the spirochæta pallida. No drug has been found which will actually reach the organism in the submucosa. The purpose of treatment is to cleanse and stimulate the tissues in order that they may be better able to fight the infection. Mucous membrane is extremely delicate and is easily inflamed and traumatized by harsh methods. It must be reiterated that mildness of solutions and extreme gentleness in administering them is one of the most important elements in the treatment of these cases and in the prevention of an upward extension of the infection.

It would be only confusing to go into the details of treatment, and the drugs employed. Their name is legion and each has its advocates. Besides silver preparations, potassium permanganate, etc., diathermy and vaccines are being employed with increasing success if we can judge by reports. Destruction of the infected glands which are chronic foci of infection is accomplished by means of cauterization or incision. Also in severe complications, major operations may be a last resort.

Essentials in the early treatment of female patients are rest in bed, scrupulous cleanliness, and a bland diet. Irrigations of the external genitalia three or four times a day with hot normal saline, boric acid, or sodium bicarbonate, or hot sitz baths are used to allay inflammation and cleanse the parts. Douches are not given until after the acute stage of the disease is past. The treatment of the male patient is the same in principle—emphasis being placed on scrupulous cleanliness and the use of mild solutions for irrigating. For both sexes, abstinence from alcohol and sex activity are important. In the last analysis, however, our best ally for cure is an untraumatized mucous membrane, for here originates largely, if not solely, the curative processes which will eliminate the disease.

Manifestations of the Disease

There are several other infections which cause symptoms similar to gonorrhea and therefore a diagnosis of this disease can never be made safely until the gonococcus has been identified in the discharges of the patient. This is accomplished by special staining processes and use of the microscope. In chronic cases of gonorrhea when it is difficult to find the organism, a complement fixation test is used which is comparable to the Wassermann in method but which has not yet reached its degree of accuracy.

Gonorrhea like syphilis is a family disease and is one of the greatest enemies of childhood. As has been stated, it not only prevents life, but the presence of the disease in the mother may result in an infection of the eyes of the newborn. Ophthalmia neonatorum* is, however, entirely preventable if a silver preparation is dropped into the eyes of the baby at birth. An unskillful irrigation of the eyes may give a false sense of security and result in a tragedy. Every portion of the conjunctival sac must be reached if the drug is to be effective. Observation of the baby's eyes during the first two weeks of life is important and any discharge or inflammation should receive careful attention and suitable treatment whether it is due to the gonococcus or not.

Another serious manifestation of gonorrhea in children is vaginitis or vulvovaginitis in little girls and rarely urethritis in little boys. It is well to remember that vaginitis may be caused by a number of organisms. In fact, one large clinic reports that at least fifty per cent of the vaginitis cases which it admits are caused by other organisms or etiological factors which in no way implicate the gonococcus. Lack of personal hygiene is one of the elements to consider in cases of non-specific origin. Dr. Brunet has estimated that five per cent of the children in poor communities have gonorrheal vulvovaginitis, but that this disease is comparatively negligible in the better sections. The reason for this difference lies in bad housing, crowded sleeping quarters and poor hygiene.

Little girls are very susceptible to chance infections because before the age of puberty the genitalia are poorly developed, and protected only by columnar epithelium. After puberty, the cells change to the squamous type, which is resistant to the gonococcus—hence the rarity of accidental infection in adults. The most frequent source of infection in children is found in some other members of the family. Children may acquire gonorrhea by sleeping with an infected individual, or through contaminated

---
* See article on this disease in Public Health Nursing for December, 1932.

articles such as sheets, towels, toilet seats, etc. Teaching the importance of examination of contacts is as much a part of the program for controlling this disease as is the actual cure of the patient.

The first symptoms in the child are similar to those in the adult and, therefore, need not be repeated. Fortunately, the disease rarely progresses beyond the cervix in children. It is, however, highly resistant and may take many months to cure. Numerous types of treatment are in vogue, from the conservative sitz bath and boric powder to the intensive use of douches and instillations. Whatever the method employed, it is necessary to demonstrate each step to the mother who may be giving care to the child between the nurse's visits. Especial emphasis should be placed upon the need of extreme gentleness and patience in giving treatment, also the importance of the daily bath, clean clothes, and increased fluid intake and a nourishing diet. Plans should be worked out for the protection of other members of the family and the mother or whoever is responsible for the patient should be warned about possible eye involvement if scrupulous care is not maintained.

The mental health of the child is a highly important consideration also. Much unhappiness could be avoided if this phase of the problem received the attention that it deserves. Feelings of inferiority, and a false sense of guilt may be developed which will be difficult to combat later and which may deeply affect the personality of the child. Often the mother has a highly emotional attitude toward the situation and only by a sane interpretation of facts can the nurse help her to a wholesome understanding of the problem. Everything should be done to keep the daily routine of the child as normal as possible. She should have outdoor recreation, indoor amusement, and an opportunity to continue her studies when she is excluded from school.

Public health nurses have an important part to play in the control of gonorrhea as it affects the family, particularly when problems touch upon maternal and child welfare. Prerequisites to success include a wholesome attitude, an understanding of the disease—its ethical, personal, and social complications—skill in teaching, a thoughtful, kindly, tactful approach to those afflicted, and last but not least the ability to "work honestly and earnestly with other agencies engaged in relieving humanity of this great menace."

Questions for Discussion

1. What are some of the complications which may arise in a pregnant patient with a gonococcal infection?
2. Report on an actual case history where vaginitis has been discovered in one of the children in the family. Discuss your contact with the family, plans for the care of the child in the home, and relationships with interested agencies. What other health and social situations did you find in this family? Had they any bearing upon the specific disease problem?

References

Stokes, John—*Dermatology and Syphilology for Nurses*. Saunders, 1930. pp. 156-166.

Brunet and Dickinson—*Gonorrhea in the Female*. U. S. Government Printing Office, Washington, D. C., 5 cents.

Pelouze, P. S.—*Gonococcal Infection in the Male*. U. S. Government Printing Office, Washington, D. C., 5 cents.

THE PUBLIC HEALTH NURSE AND THE COMMUNITY SOCIAL HYGIENE PROGRAM*

BY GLADYS L. CRAIN, R.N.

Assistant Director, National Organization for Public Health Nursing

Public health nursing, whatever else it may be, is a community service which has developed in response to real needs.

---
* Reprinted through the courtesy of Public Health Nursing from the issue of February, 1933,

Therefore, its continued growth depends upon the ability of its members to adapt themselves to changing conditions, to interpret trends, and to meet new conceptions of community health promotion with foresight and intelligence. Whatever contribution the public health nurse gives to her community must enrich, or add to, but not duplicate what is already being done for the welfare of individuals and families. This does not mean that her program is a restricted one, for through coöperative relationships, a keen awareness of lacks, and an ability to stimulate the development of better community health facilities she greatly extends her influence and usefulness.

During the past few years social hygiene activities, especially as they relate to the control of syphilis and gonococcal infections, have been gaining recognition as major public health concerns. Signs of the times point to an aroused interest among a variety of health and social workers, probation officers, and other professional and lay groups who are earnestly studying methods for controlling the diseases and the abolishment of environmental influences which encourage their spread.

Public health nurses are not lagging behind in this movement, for by means of study programs, staff education and extension courses, they are preparing to meet this new challenge. It is obvious that education in the medical and nursing facts of the diseases, syphilis and gonorrhea, is a necessary prerequisite for intelligent participation in a community social hygiene program, but this is not enough. Knowledge of what has been accepted as a workable community program for the control of these diseases is quite as important; also what is actually being done in the community to which the nurse belongs, what is left undone, and what part of this program is basically a public health nursing job. In order to build her service upon a solid rock of fundamental needs, a careful survey of resources should be made.

Present community programs in the field of social hygiene have their common origin in the "American Plan" which was evolved during the World War, to control the spread of syphilis and gonorrhea in the army. This threefold plan included:

Education of the soldiers regarding the venereal diseases, their prevention and cure; also education in a saner approach to sex.

Control of prostitution, the eradication of other vicious environmental influences, and the establishment of wholesome recreational facilities.

The setting up of clinics for diagnosis and treatment of infected individuals, and the teaching of prophylactic measures.

The phenomenal success of this program in reducing the number of cases of venereal disease in the army resulted in the adoption of a modification of these measures by civil communities. This movement was furthered by the Chamberlain-Kahn Act which made it possible for the Federal Government to subsidize states in order that bureaus for the control of the venereal diseases might be established and maintained. This subsidy was available from 1919 to 1921.

Today most communities have developed a program which embodies the three elements considered basic to a successful combating of syphilis and gonorrhea. These measures are:

Medical measures which are the first line of defense and include epidemiological practice (reporting of all cases, search for sources of infection and examination of contacts), diagnostic service in state and local laboratories; and hospital and clinic facilities for treatment of infected individuals.

Legal measures which include laws and ordinances for the suppression of prostitution and for quarantining infectious and recalcitrant patients.

Educational measures for teaching the public the nature of the diseases, syphilis and gonorrhea, the importance of preventive measures, early diagnosis and adequate treatment; the promotion of sex character education for children and the training of parents, teachers, etc., for the task.

No local agency is carrying the entire burden of this complicated program. It is a community enterprise in which both official and non-official groups have a share. The ultimate responsibility for the control of disease and the protection of the health of the community rests with the health department. The health officer should be looked to as a leader and his approval sought in all projects which private agencies, in this field, are contemplating. Also, they should adopt such standards as will conform to the requirements of the local sanitary code.

The following questions summarize some of the major activities in a community social hygiene program. It goes without saying that rural areas and small towns will not have as many of these resources as the larger cities, but the state or county often is prepared to give far more assistance in the solution of social hygiene problems than local groups are aware of.

I. *Medical measures in your community*
   A. The Health Department:
      1. Is there a bureau or division for venereal disease control?
      2. If not, how is this public health problem handled?
      3. Is there provision for epidemiological investigations? Are nurses employed in this field?
      4. Is there an official diagnostic laboratory?
      5. What are the provisions for the treatment of indigent patients in the city? In rural areas?
      6. Is the reporting of cases of syphilis and gonorrhea enforced?
      7. How many cases were reported last year?
      8. What is the content of the sanitary code?
      9. Does the health department maintain its own clinics or subsidize hospital and private clinics for the treatment of syphilis and gonorrhea?
      10. How are lapsed cases and recalcitrant patients handled? How does a knowledge of these facts assist the nurse in her own program and the solution of individual problems?

   B. Private clinics attached to hospitals or dispensaries:
      1. How many treat syphilis? Gonorrhea?
      2. On what days are clinics held? Are there evening clinics?
      3. Standards:
         a. Methods, diagnosis, and treatment.
         b. Case holding, investigation of sources of infection, attention to contacts, lapsed cases.
         c. What percentage of cases remains under treatment until cured?
         d. Constructive teaching in clinics.
         e. Program for the detection of syphilis in pregnancy and the prevention of congenital syphilis.
         f. Program for patients with gonorrhea, especially prenatals and children with gonorrheal vaginitis.
         g. Is there social service follow-up?
         h. Is there nursing follow-up?
         i. What coöperative arrangements have been worked out with public health nursing groups? If there are none, is there a field for service here?

   C. Private Physicians:
      1. Are they treating syphilis and gonorrhea? What plans have they for case holding? Examinations of contacts? Sources of infection and lapsed cases?
      2. Is there a field for public health nursing service in the follow-up of private physicians' cases?

   D. Public Health Nursing Groups (School nurses, industrial nurses, health department nurses, visiting nurses, etc.):
      1. What are these groups contributing in the way of follow-up, case finding, family health teaching, the prevention of congenital syphilis, work with gonorrheal vaginitis cases including individual and group teaching of adults, etc.? What coöperative relationships have been established to coördinate the work done in this field?

II. *Legal protective and recreational measures*
  A. What are the laws regarding the control of infectious individuals, food handlers, reporting of cases, etc? Regarding interstate travel of infectious patients?
  B. Laws for controlling prostitution and other vicious elements in the environment.
  C. Court and health department activities in this field.
  D. Work of policewomen and probation officers, etc.
    1. What is being done for young sex offenders in the way of rehabilitation?
  E. Are there citizens' committees active in this field?
  F. Are parks, playgrounds, dance halls, and other places of amusement supervised?
  G. What provisions for wholesome recreation are found in churches, clubs, settlements, Y.W.C.A. and Y.M.C.A.'s, Boy Scout organizations, etc.

III. *Educational measures*
  A. Health Department: Are there pamphlets, films, exhibits, lectures, etc., available here?
  B. Libraries: Is this a source for books and articles on social hygiene?
  C. Social hygiene societies: What can be obtained in the way of books and pamphlets, speakers for clubs, etc.? Is there a consultation service?
  D. Schools: Is sex education integrated in the school curricula?
  E. Churches and other character-building organizations:
    1. What is being done to guide boy and girl relationships?
    2. Are women's clubs, parents' organizations, etc., studying sex education problems?

Although the public health nurse must have an intelligent grasp of the broad aspects of a social hygiene program, and the types of agencies participating in these phases, her chief concern will be in the realm of communicable disease control, and she will coöperate most closely with institutions dealing with the problems which complicate this activity.

Most nursing organizations where a social hygiene program has been established have set up the following objectives:

1. To assist in finding all cases of syphilis and gonorrhea and all contacts.
2. To assist in arranging for medical supervision, early diagnosis, treatment and follow-up.
3. To assist in securing complete reporting of all cases.
4. To secure nursing care and supervision in the home.
5. To assist in giving constructive individual and family health teaching.

The emphasis, however, has been different depending upon community needs and resources.

The following are a few of the actual services which public health nursing organizations are giving in the field of social hygiene:

I. A complete follow-up service for all cases of syphilis and gonorrhea attending public venereal disease clinics.

II. A follow-up service in connection with private clinics for all cases of syphilis and gonorrhea presenting a family health or nursing problem. Such cases would include all congenital syphilitics, all cases where there are children in the family, all cases of gonorrheal vaginitis, all cases where there are dressings, treatments, or bedside care. This type of coöperative project usually supplements the work of the social service worker who handles complicated social situations, etc.

III. A service in connection with an existing prenatal program, emphasis being placed upon the prevention of congenital syphilis. Early examinations, routine Wassermann tests, close supervision, attention to all contacts when syphilis is present in the mother, and special planning for the new-born baby are a few of the activities here. This involves coöperative planning with prenatal clinics, reports on Wassermann findings, progress of treatment, complications, etc.

IV. A follow-up service for private physicians' cases.

V. A service recently under consideration in a private organization involved a small group of syphilitic families. These were selected for the purpose of studying content and method of health teaching most effective with this group, number of visits necessary, reasons for lapses in treatment, care of contacts, and the complicating health and social problems which present obstacles to treatment and cure and prevent a complete adjustment of the family.

In studying community programs for the control of syphilis and gonorrhea, it is evident that the least developed services are those which might be listed under family health and prevention. The major emphasis, in many places, is still upon mass treatment of individuals. Public health nurses are especially equipped to assist in filling this serious gap. In these times of economic insecurity, new services cannot be developed but the existing program can be enriched.

A generalized nursing service provides ample opportunity for case finding and family teaching through its prenatal and child welfare programs alone.

The industrial nurse has an opportunity to do preventive work if she has developed a sensitiveness to symptoms which deviate from the normal and may mean a syphilitic or gonococcal infection, through advice regarding the importance of physical examinations and other health teaching.

The school nurse may also contribute to the program through case finding and arranging for home supervision of congenital syphilitics.

The rural nurse has a challenging task, along with all the others mentioned, of stimulating the development of adequate treatment facilities by presenting striking situations which show the need.

Whatever coöperative services are developed in public health nursing organizations, it is necessary to consider them from the standpoint of benefit to the agencies concerned, and to the community, and their value in developing a more satisfactory service to patients and their families. In summing up her chapter on venereal disease work in her textbook, "Public Health Nursing," Miss Mary S. Gardner presents a challenge worth considering, which we quote:

"Nursing has a wonderful tradition which has come down to it through the ages, that wherever human suffering exists, there it is a nurse's privilege to be. Perhaps that privilege can be no better exercised than in ministering to a class of patients whose physical suffering is augmented by the fact that a stigma is attached to the disease which attacked them. By this ministry a nurse may gain a personal understanding that will perhaps help her to do her part in bringing the venereal diseases out of their present hiding places into the full light of day, where they may be fought and vanquished as have so many other scourges of mankind."

Questions for Discussion

1. What has been accomplished in your community in social hygiene? (Summary of resources)
2. What are the gaps in the community program as you see it?
3. What particular contributions can your organization make in the light of these facts? What might your personal contribution be?
4. What is your organization doing in this field at the present time? (Summarize activities)
5. What are the next steps to take?

References

Snow, William F. *Venereal Diseases—Medical, Nursing, and Community Aspects.* Funk & Wagnalls Company. 30 cents.

Stokes, John. *Dermatology and Syphilology for Nurses.* pp. 265-269.

Winslow, C.-E. A. *Social Hygiene.* American Social Hygiene Association, 450 Seventh Avenue, New York City. 10 cents.

Law Enforcement in Social Hygiene. American Social Hygiene Association, 450 Seventh Avenue, New York City. 10 cents.

Gardner, Mary S. *Public Health Nursing.* The Macmillan Company, 1924. pp. 378-393.

A Social Hygiene Program for New York State. Reprint from Report, New York State Health Commission, 1932.

Byington, Margaret. *What Social Workers Should Know About Their Community.* Russell Sage Foundation, New York City. 25 cents.

Objectives in Public Health Nursing. National Organization for Public Health Nursing, 450 Seventh Avenue, New York City. Free.

THE PUBLIC HEALTH NURSE AND THE EDUCATIONAL PHASES OF A SOCIAL HYGIENE PROGRAM*

BY GLADYS L. CRAIN, R.N.

Assistant Director, National Organization for Public Health Nursing

The relation of the public health nurse to the medical aspects of a social hygiene program is comparatively simple to define, for her role in the control of syphilis and gonorrhea is not very different from that of her work with tuberculosis or any other disease which endangers the health of the community. She has a legitimate part also in such educational activities as are concerned with the dispelling of fallacies, and the teaching of facts about these diseases, and with creating a more wholesome and hopeful attitude toward them.

However, there is considerable perplexity regarding that part of a social hygiene program which has to do with sex instruction and sex character training.

The nurse's help is not infrequently solicited here because it is assumed that her scientific training has prepared her for the task. In her intimate contact with homes she is constantly meeting and cannot ignore questions of a sex-social nature which not only have to do with child training but also adolescent misconceptions, and adult maladjustments.

Outside of the home she is being asked to lecture to adult and school groups on sex education problems, and is called upon to take the parents' place in instructing boys and girls at adolescence in the physiological and psychological changes which they have not been prepared to understand or taught to accept as a matter of course. Public health nurses are troubled not only about the wisdom of such wholesale teaching, but also about their ability to handle sex instruction adequately under any circumstances, and its logical place in their recognized services to the community. How much such activity is a legitimate part of a public health nurse's work can be answered only by an examination of its adaptation to her regular family health program, and of her personal preparation and fitness.

Definite Preparation for the Task

Those to whom sex education is entrusted need definite qualifications for the task such as a wholesome balanced attitude toward sex as a normal factor in life, a scientific spirit, an educational background in which the biological, psychological, sociological and ethical aspects of sex have been synthesized, and with all this a wise philosophy, and a sensitiveness to individuals and situations. There has been a good deal of experimentation in sex education, and a knowledge of present trends and established standards must be part of the equipment of those who would venture to give advice in this field, in order that such anachronisms as "sex talks," "sex courses," and a wholesale delivery of the facts of life at one sitting are not urged as a solution of individual or school problems.

Unfortunately, it is the rare person who has all of these qualifications and contrary to popular belief a nurse's training in most instances has been quite as inadequate in this field as that of the public whom she serves. She brings to the subject of sex as do most of us—according to Karl de Schweinitz, "Kinks, embarrassments and personal perplexities which have been acquired in the process of adjusting the most powerful and individualistic of emotions to the exigencies of our social environment."

It is very easy in meeting with an ignorance greater than one's own to be carried away by an over-balanced enthusiasm to "spread the glad tidings;" or when one has a smattering of knowledge and a missionary urge, to get beyond one's depth in a discussion of complicated, intimate

---

* Reprinted through the courtesy of Public Health Nursing from the issue of March, 1933.

personal relationships and maladjustments. All such teaching by an untrained person, although kindly in intention, may do infinite harm. Complicated problems whether they occur in the realm of the physical, the mental or sex-social, need expert help and the public health nurse is rendering her best service when she is able to recognize danger signs, know resources, and arrange for the kind of assistance that most adequately meets the situation.

Parental Responsibility

In the field of sex character training and sex instruction of children, it is an accepted fact that the chief responsibility belongs first to the home and second to the school in coöperation with the parent. Parents, because of the inadequacies of their own training need help—and such organizations as Parent-Teacher Associations and women's clubs, in a number of communities, are trying to meet this need through study programs, institutes and special speakers.

Although there are limits, let us say, to the public health nurse's usefulness as a sex educator, there are also opportunities which she cannot overlook in her relationships to parents and schools. The fact that her advice is sought offers a challenge to prepare herself for the task of creating right attitudes toward problems small and large in the realm of sex which are brought to her attention. The only person who can straighten out the kinks in another's thinking is the one who has solved his own problems. A sane wholesome attitude can do more to dispel perplexities than a volume of didactic teaching.

As a family health worker it is important for the nurse to think through her program and the daily drama which she witnesses, and attempt to see at what points her assistance in an interpretation of problems, which have a sex significance to parents and teachers, may be a logical part of her work.

Relationship to Daily Work

The following are a few very simple illustrations to show how the work of the nurse is bound up with that part of sex education which naturally falls within the realm of general hygiene, mental and physical.

The Maternity Program:
 A. The prenatal patient
   1. Teaching the young prenatal patient facts about the physiology of pregnancy.
   2. Creating a wholesome scientific attitude toward reproduction.
   3. Dispelling fears and misconceptions.
   4. Helping the patient with plans for telling her children about the coming of the new baby, and giving them a real share in preparing for this event.
 B. The new-born baby
   1. Seeing that the infant's sex organs are normal, and explaining the importance of a physician's care if there are adhesions or other abnormalities.
   2. Teaching the proper care of the genital organs as part of routine bath demonstrations.
   3. Teaching the mother correct names for the genital organs and other parts of the body so that she will not be embarrassed by the lack of a proper vocabulary.
   4. Emphasizing the fact that all character training begins with the establishing of regular habits of eating, sleeping and eliminating.

Child Welfare Program:
 A. The child in the home
   1. Creating wholesome attitudes toward the first questions of children which seem to parents to have a sex significance. Explaining that such questions are symptoms of an awakening curiosity about everything, and that they should be answered as briefly, simply, honestly, and objectively as any other type of question which the child may ask.

2. Suggesting to the mother well chosen literature which may help her with these early questions and problems, and give her a better understanding and perspective.
3. Teaching that one of the most important factors in giving the child the right start is in the attitude of parents and the atmosphere of the home.
4. Emphasizing the importance of habit training: that the breaking of undesirable habits is not accomplished by nagging, slapping, or frightening the child, that such methods fix habits. *For example:* Explaining to the mother who is upset when her little child is discovered handling his sex organs, that this is as innocent and natural as touching any other part of his body, that the way to prevent such a habit becoming fixed is by seeing that he is kept clean, that his clothes fit properly and that he has enough to keep him occupied and happy during his waking hours, and otherwise not to pay too much attention to it.

B. The child in school
1. Creating a sane attitude among the teachers toward problems of child behavior which are discovered, such as masturbation, sex play among groups of children, etc.
2. Urging that such problems be treated individually and constructively by looking for *causes* rather than at the thing itself, and by working closely with the parents.
3. When called upon to give "sex talks," tactfully suggesting the better method of dealing with immediate problems individually, and the importance of working out eventually a plan for integrating sex education material in "nature studies," civics, home economics, etc.
4. Pointing out that the problems of adolescence cannot be solved alone by teaching the facts of bodily development and hygiene, and the significance of all this to the individual and society.

Example: Ruth, aged 15, was in high school. She was doing poor work. She flirted outrageously with the boys and shocked her teachers. She ran away for long automobile rides with older men who were not fit companions for her. The principal of the school did not know what to do about her as many complaints were coming to his ears, so he referred her to the school nurse and asked her to warn the child about the end results of her rash actions. The nurse was wise, however, and looked to causes. The coöperation of the child, the parents, and a guidance clinic for older children were gained. Ruth's I.Q. was 130 and she had unusual artistic ability which her parents were scornful of. She had been conscientiously taught all the "facts of life" which she needed, but her Scottish parents, who were very matter of fact, were forcing her to train for secretarial work when she wanted to become an artist, hence the unconscious revolt. Her teachers were given a key to the situation and adjustments were made in her school studies. Today she is a successful student in an important art school and is happy and adjusted.

One might go on multiplying illustrations of this kind indefinitely. Other types of work with other age groups bring equal opportunities. In the last analysis the contribution of the nurse to the field of sex education is an *attitude;* a skill in helping people to help themselves, an ability to recognize untoward actions as symptoms of some maladjustment, or the outgrowth of a natural urge; and a conviction that sex education is not a matter of an hour, a day or a year, but a life process that begins with birth.

In order to give this kind of service, the nurse already in the field must plan for her own re-education. For the nurse of the future we can do no better than to say with Miss Winifred Rand:

"Let us turn back to our educational institutions, high schools, colleges, training schools, and with one voice cry we must be taught that we may teach... Otherwise, public health nurses will not be able to take the next step forward—and not to take it would be intolerable."

Bibliography

For the Adult

Social Hygiene in Schools—White House Conference on Child Health and Protection, Century Company, New York City, 1932.

Emery—*Revising Our Attitude Toward Sex*—National Committee for Mental Hygiene, 450 Seventh Avenue, New York City. 15 cents.

Stokes, John—*Dermatology and Syphilology for Nurses*—Chapter 27.

For Child Training

Child Questions and Their Answers—American Social Hygiene Association, 450 Seventh Avenue, New York City. 10 cents.

de Schweinitz, Karl—*Dangers and Advantages of Sex Instruction*—National Committee for Mental Hygiene, 450 Seventh Avenue, New York City. 15 cents.

A Vocabulary for Family Use in Early Sex Education—Women's Coöperative Alliance. 212 Citizens Building, Minneapolis, Minn.

Richards, E. L., M.D.—*Behavior Aspects of Child Conduct*—Macmillan. $2.50.

Taft—*Some Undesirable Habits and Suggestions as to Treatment*—National Committee for Mental Hygiene, 450 Seventh Avenue, New York City. 15 cents.

Tiebout—*Preparing the Child for Adolescenec*—National Committee for Mental Hygiene, 450 Seventh Avenue, New York City. 5 cents.

Gruenberg, B. C. —*Parents—Sex Education*—American Social Hygiene Association, 450 Seventh Avenue, New York City.

Cady, B. C.—*The Way Life Begins*—American Social Hygiene Association, 450 Seventh Avenue, New York City. $1.50.

de Schweinitz, Karl—*Growing Up*—Macmillan. $1.50.

Toward Helping the Adolescent

The Boy Problem, 10 cents; *Your Daughter's Mother*, 10 cents; *Training Youth for Parenthood*, 10 cents—American Social Hygiene Association, 450 Seventh Avenue, New York City.

Growing Up in the World Today, 20 cents—Massachusetts Social Hygiene Society, 1150 Little Building, Boston, Mass.

Thom, Douglas—*Normal Youth and Its Everyday Problems*—Appleton. $2.50.

Preparation for Marriage

Choosing a Home Partner, 10 cents; *The Question of Petting*, 15 cents. American Social Hygiene Association, 450 Seventh Avenue, New York City.

Exner, Max—*The Sexual Side of Marriage*—Norton. $2.50.

Royden, Maude—*Sex and Common Sense*.

THE NURSE IN THE CONTROL OF GONORRHEA AND SYPHILIS*

As the Health Officer Sees Her

N. A. NELSON, M.D.

Assistant Director, Division of Communicable Diseases
Massachusetts Department of Public Health

The problems surrounding the control of gonorrhea and syphilis have been discussed during the past year by Miss Gladys Crain in an excellent series of papers in PUBLIC HEALTH NURSING.** This paper will deal more specifically with some of the administrative problems which perplex the health officer and for the solution of which he must lean heavily upon the coöperation of the nurse.

---

* Reprinted through the courtesy of Public Health Nursing from the issue of April, 1933.
** Public Health Nursing and the Medical Aspects of Social Hygiene. July, 1932.
  Syphilis. What the Public Health Nurse Should Know about the Patient and the Disease, August, 1932.
  Familial Syphilis. October, 1932.
  Syphilis. Some Facts Regarding Diagnosis and Treatment. November, 1932.
  Facts about Gonorrhea. January, 1933.
  The Community and the Social Hygiene Program. February, 1933.
  Educational Phases of the Social Hygiene Program. March, 1933.

The nurse, like the physician, is no longer bound to the care only of those who, being obviously ill, seek her services. Whether she does private duty or institutional, industrial, community, or public health nursing, she thinks in terms of health; positive health more than mere return to health. The obviously sick, and especially those with communicable disease, are only the hub around which the opportunity revolves for building a broad, constructive program for community health.

It is a privilege to see a child return from the valley of the shadow of a diptheritic death under one's expert ministrations, but it is a greater privilege to know that as a result of one's teachings and toxin-antitoxin, ten thousand children will never enter that valley. It is of utmost importance to provide sanatoria for the tuberculous who come to medical attention. But it is more soundly satisfying to reach out into the families from whence these patients come, to discover the early, more hopeful cases and, through careful supervision of the exposed, to prevent further spread of the infection. The patient with typhoid fever must be the reason for searching for the carrier or for the environmental source of his infection for the sake of public health.

Unique Problems of Prevention

Gonorrhea and syphilis occupy unique positions as communicable diseases. Their communicability is quite limited, compared to that of most of the others, yet they are prevalent beyond all imagination. They are spread largely through the most universally desired and the most intimate of personal contacts, sexual intercourse, too frequently, but by no means always promiscuous. For this reason case-finding and steering to medical care is often difficult beyond description. The duration of these infections makes the cost of treatment a serious obstacle to adequate treatment. Their prevention reaches into the very foundation of human existence and has to overcome sex appetite, sex ignorance, and sex prudery. The fog of ignorance is so thick about these diseases that even those who battle against therapeutic contraception and therapeutic abortion do not seem to realize the fact that gonorrhea is the greatest of all sterilizers and syphilis the greatest of abortionists. It is apparent that the control of these diseases must depend in great measure upon public information.

For reasons obvious only to the editors, newspapers and magazines, the usual channels of much public health information, remain closed to any discussion of gonorrhea and syphilis. Authors of sound, sane educational material are few and the subject is difficult. Much of the story, therefore, must be passed on by word of mouth. The nurse, well thought of by her public, enjoying unusual confidence, reaching into even the smallest village and hamlet, and already engaged in teaching public health, becomes the most logical and valuable teacher in this field. A good teacher, however, must herself be informed.

Curative medicine is preventive medicine only in a very limited sense. The proper management of a case of communicable disease prevents any further spread of the infection from that particular source. The difficulty lies in the fact that the infection is spread before the disease is recognized by some competent medical authority. The control of typhoid fever, smallpox, and diphtheria depends upon the application of measures which reduce the possibility of infections to the lowest possible minimum. Gonorrhea and syphilis will not be controlled solely through the treatment of infections as they occur and can be discovered. Resort to medical control alone is like bailing out the kitchen when the water pipe has burst, instead of shutting off the water and fixing the pipe. Social hygiene, sex hygiene, sex character-building aim to shut off the source of gonorrhea and syphilis and to fix the attitude of society toward sex so that its use will be directed along its proper channels. Social hygiene thus is true preventive medicine so far as these diseases are concerned.

Control of Known and Discoverable Cases

The health officer, however, sees three major problems to be dealt with in the control of gonorrhea and syphilis. There is no specific immunization with which to protect, all at once, the whole population. The most urgent need, therefore, is to control known and discoverable cases. Both diseases are prevalent beyond calculation. They are constantly being spread. Hundreds of thousands of infections have been diagnosed and are receiving treatment or are in need of it. Other hundreds of thousands will appear tomorrow for treatment. Still other hundreds of thousands might be discovered through adequate case-finding. Women are being infected through marriage, young girls are suffering from innocently acquired gonorrheal infections, babies are being born with congenital syphilis. All these provide an immediate problem calling for all the available resources of the health department. Clinics must be established and maintained; patients must be taught the nature of their infections, what is required as to treatment, and what constitutes proper conduct; delinquent patients, contacts, and spreaders of infection must be followed up; syphilis in pregnant women must be treated for the prevention of congenital syphilis; the medical profession needs instruction in the proper management of both diseases; laboratory services must be provided; and diagnostic procedures improved; the therapeutic armamentarium is inadequate; hospitalization must be provided for, administrative technique developed, and epidemiological studies made. All these, and more, constitute a medical problem of immense proportions.

Public Education

The second major problem is that of public education in the nature of gonorrhea and syphilis. From a purely medical point of view this consists of awakening the public to the prevalence of these dangerous, communicable diseases, the frequency with which they attack the innocent, the importance of immediate and continued medical observation after exposure and the necessity for prolonged and regular treatment. This is education simply as to the nature of two communicable diseases. It is primarily the problem of the health officer and the medical profession, assisted and prompted by the social hygiene association just as the tuberculosis society assists and prompts in the program for the control of tuberculosis.

The third major problem, reaching through future generations, and much broader than the mere control of disease, is the development of the social hygiene program. Gonorrhea and syphilis are only two symptoms, so to speak, of sex ignorance, feeblemindedness, incorrigibility, and family maladjustment, just as premarital and promiscuous sexual intercourse, illegitimacy, marital incompatibility, separation, divorce, and many other social evils are symptoms of sex ignorance, feeblemindedness, incorrigibility, and family maladjustment. Eliminate gonorrhea and syphilis through some as yet undiscovered method of immunization and the others still remain. The social hygienist, therefore, has a much broader and deeper problem to solve than that of the more specific protection of the public health.

For many reasons, administrative, economic, and related to the limitation of the field, the health officer cannot assume the responsibility for the development of such a broad program. He should support and encourage it, however, since it may become the ultimate solution of his problem of the control of gonorrhea and syphilis.

The Nurse's Share of Responsibility

The nurse, as the lieutenant of the health officer, must work beside him for the medical control of these diseases and in the education of the public concerning them. She should be informed in social hygiene and be represented in social hygiene councils. But she cannot assume, any more than the health officer can, the responsibility for carrying out a broad social hygiene program. She should be able to distinguish between a public health and behavior problem. The feebleminded, the sexually precocious, the prostitute, are fundamentally problems in behavior albeit they may be spreaders of disease. Whenever it is feasible the nurse should call upon such agencies as are especially equipped to deal with these problems. The simple treatment of their infections is no solution of the problem which they present.

The teaching of sex-character to children is not the nurse's business. That is social hygiene and looks to results that reach far beyond the control of disease. It requires special aptitude and special training. It is dangerous in the hands of any but the most competent. If trained teachers are not available, it is much safer to direct the parent to sources of sound material and let the teaching be done around the family fireside. Encourage parents to teach sex character, but do not substitute for them unless the occasion be a most unusual one.

Too much direct concern over social problems often destroys the nurse's effectiveness as a protector of the public health. A nurse learned from a young man the identity of the alleged source of his infection. The girl was found to be pregnant. The nurse succeeded in securing a court order compelling the young man to support the baby, but she was no longer able to supervise his further treatment because she had lost his confidence in her as a nurse. The nurse does not assume the responsibility for correcting the social ills of the community when they are not related to problems in public health. They should be referred quietly to the proper agency without the participation of the nurse becoming obvious. It is safest to take only such steps as may be necessary to accomplish the adequate treatment of known cases, to discover and bring new cases to medical care and to prevent new infections so far as possible.

Follow-up of Cases

When the nurse must be both nurse and social worker in her community she must decide when to stop doing social work in order not to neglect nursing. The solution of difficult social problems for a few may mean less in terms of community health than the expenditure of the same amount of time toward the return to treatment of many who need only simple explanations and guidance and in the finding of cases to be discovered just around the corner.

Perhaps the most routine of the nurse's duties will be the follow-up of cases lapsing treatment. A great deal of sympathetic understanding is essential to success. The patient readily disappears if he begins to feel the heel of authority on his neck. The further control of a patient that cannot be found is obviously impossible. This tendency to keep out of official sight is demonstrated by the frequency of false identification. (In Massachusetts only 47 per cent of nearly 10,000 delinquent patients followed through the State and local health departments could be located.) Consequently the patient is disturbed by the mere fact that the nurse has found him at all, if he is found.

Correct and Complete Information

In the second place, the information which patients receive in the average doctor's office or in the average clinic consists chiefly of a statement of the diagnosis that the disease is communicable and that they must "return next week for treatment." Patients rarely understand that the disappearance of annoying signs and symptoms is not indicative of cure. The nurse or health officer who summarily orders the patient to return to treatment has not changed his opinion that he is in no further need of treatment. The instruction must be supplied that has been lacking from the beginning. Calvin Coolidge is said to have remarked that he would like to see a little more of law observance and a little less of law enforcement. To observe a law one must first understand and be in sympathy with its purpose. The enlightened patient is more likely to observe the "laws" of good conduct and regular treatment than the uninformed patient is likely to submit long to arbitrary law enforcement. The control of tuberculosis has followed the understanding acceptance by the public of services which it has been taught are essential to the cure and prevention of a prevalent and dangerous communicable disease.

Enforced treatment is no guarantee of good conduct; witness the patients who resume sexual intercourse the moment the acute symptoms have subsided. Innumerable husbands and wives labor under the false impression that sex excitement or actual intercourse, using a condom, is permissible even though treatment is still going on. It is the patient's understanding of the whole problem that counts, not merely the fact that he may appear regularly for treatment.

Change in Approach

The search for "sources of infection" also requires understanding. It is unfortunate that the term "source of infection" ever came into use in this connection. It is the most antagonistic approach that could possibly be made. A person who is accused of having infected another is quite naturally on the defensive. There is so much anxiety to disclaim responsibility for another's injury that there is both vocal and mental denial of the possibility that they themselves may be infected. It is a perfectly understandable reaction. It is often an unjust accusation. The patient, on being questioned as to his exposures, naturally thinks of the last one. The incubation period of either disease is long enough and variable enough so that his contacts during that period may have been many. The last partner may have been exposed to his infection rather than have been the cause of it. Or the patient may have an acute recurrence of an old, neglected infection which he mistakes for a new one. All his recent contacts may then be victims of the patient's infection.

It is always safest to approach a contact, whether or not the alleged source of an infection, as the possible victim of an infection. Certainly every "source of infection" must at some time previously have been the victim of another's infection. The person thus approached is concerned, in his or her own interest, as the offended party. As there is no need for defense against accusation, the advice to seek medical attention is more readily accepted. It is never necessary to identify the source of the information and it is wisest not to do so unless ordered by a court. It is better to think always in terms of case-finding than in the uncertain and often unjust term of search for the "source of infection."

Follow-up of a Private Physician's Cases

The follow-up of patients for the private physician is another nursing problem. Physicians do not have that service available which clinics find indispensable, yet their patients are in the same need of it. The community nurse and the private duty nurse already have a partnership with the physician which they might well extend to include the control of gonorrhea and syphilis. The health department nurse has a similar opportunity, but her relationship with the physician is less concrete. Regretably much of communicable disease nursing is done under direct supervision of the health department to the practical exclusion of the physician in charge of the case. It is important that the nurse represent the physician rather than her agency, in contacting the private physician's cases of gonorrhea and syphilis. The identity of the patient must never be divulged by the nurse even to her agency.* Nor should she attempt to refer cases to clinics or settle any of the problems surrounding the patient except as specifically authorized or directed to do so by the physician.

Protection of the Public

Much that is ridiculous is done by uninformed officials who suddenly become active in the control of gonorrhea and syphilis. There is not the least reason for the removal of a patient with gonorrhea from his occupation for the protection of the public health unless the occupation is that of nursing or personal attendance upon small girls. Among adults gonorrhea is spread only through sexual intercourse or related contacts of a sexual nature. It is never spread through food, nor through any of the usual occupational or social contacts.

Syphilis, however, is communicable in other close personal contacts, in its early stages. The most dangerous early lesions are those of secondary syphilis and of primary syphilis of the mouth or exposed parts of the body. Every patient with exposed or oral lesions of early syphilis should be hospitalized or isolated at home until treatment has healed the lesions and keeps them healed. Thereafter the patient should be permitted to return to work so long as treatment is regular.

The dismissal from any occupation as dangerous to his fellow-employees, of any patient in whom the only evidence of infection is positive blood tests is unfair and ridiculous. If the patient is under treatment he is safer than the person who becomes infected today and who during the next few months will have open lesions and fails to seek medical attention. Even the open lesions of late syphilis are rarely dangerous in ordinary social and occupational contacts.

Except as a case-finding procedure, the use of the routine blood test in food handlers and other occupations has no bearing upon the protection of the public health from an occupational point of view. Few early cases will be discovered by an annual examination of that kind and it leaves a false sense of security. The industrial nurse, however, will be interested in the discovery and treatment of infections for the sake of reducing inefficiency, time lost and the cost of compensable injury aggravated by the complication of gonorrhea or syphilis. She may do much toward correcting the attitude of employers toward the continued employment of infected persons. Case-finding in the families of infected employees or in their sexual contacts is essential, of course, to a completed job.

It is the opinion of many authorities that the exclusion of young girls from school because of gonorrheal infection is not warranted by any evidence that this disease is spread in the school. It exists there, certainly, but probably as the result of exposure outside of school. Exclusion deprives these children of months of education and often results in their social ostracism and the ruin of family reputations. Apparently many of the so-called gonorrheal infections are transplants of non-gonorrheal organisms normally found in the upper respiratory tract, which makes the label of gonorrhea all the more unjust. Children are being compelled by a tradition not supported by fact, to suffer all sorts of public indignity, especially in the smaller communities where the information rapidly becomes public property. This matter deserves serious study, for it seems apparent that a grave injustice is being done.

Importance of Prompt Prenatal Treatment

It is quite unnecessary to indulge in any detailed discussion of congenital syphilis since Miss Crain has done it so well. However, as a result of studies which are being made, it appears that it is not enough

---

* Editor's Note: "The identity of the patient must never be divulged by the nurse, even to her agency."
With Dr. Nelson's concurrence, we are throwing open this question to general discussion. Won't you let us know how you feel about the feasibility of carrying out this suggestion?

that the blood test be made routine in pregnancy for the control of congenital syphilis. Some of the best of prenatal clinics permit such delays between the taking of the specimen of blood and the eventual treatment of the patient that the value of the test is completely nullified. The prenatal nurse must not be satisfied simply that the test has been made. She must be forever on the alert to see to it that the patient is brought immediately to treatment. That may involve complete reorganization of everything from the system of laboratory reporting, through record keeping, to the location and hours of the coöperating syphilis clinic or of the prenatal clinic . Some of the failures of organization and administration to take advantage of evidence of infection in pregnant woman, are astounding.

Indifference of Family Physician

I cannot close without some mention of the nurse's most frequent question, "What can I do when the family physician fails to see or refuses to recognize the need for examination of certain of my patients or their families?" Frankly, I cannot answer that question. The health officer frequently is faced with the same problem. It is most discouraging to secure the identity of a contact, have the local health officer persuade the patient to go to a physician who, on the strength of an incomplete physical examination or of a single negative smear, declares the contact free of infection. One physician refused to examine a woman who was reasonably suspected of being infected because he "had known her all her life, had delivered all her babies and knew her to be a respectable woman who couldn't possibly have gonorrhea." Fortunately not all physicians have that point of view, but the management of both gonorrhea and syphilis has long been neglected in the medical schools. Many physicians still feel that case-finding in gonorrhea and syphilis is "snooping" into the private lives of their patients. It may be trite to quote that "Rome was not built in a day," but it is to the point. So simple a procedure as immunization against diphtheria is not universally promoted by the medical profession.

No doubt also, the nurse antagonizes the physician on occasion by presuming to diagnose and to advise when both are the physician's prerogatives. I sometimes wonder why physicians and nurses do not get together around the conference table more often. Do physicians ask the nurse to present her problems at the meetings of the medical society? Does the nurse invite the president of the medical society into her councils? Perhaps here is another opportunity for the nurse to take the initiative and to start something.

ECONOMIC ASPECTS OF THE MANAGEMENT OF SYPHILIS*

ALBERT KEIDEL, M.D.

Baltimore

Conjectural estimates of the prevalence of venereal disease in the United States bid fair shortly to be replaced by more accurate information on the basis of surveys conducted by the United States Public Health Service jointly with the American Social Hygiene Association. The results obtained from a survey of twenty-five communities with a population of almost 25,000,000 have just been summarized by Usilton.[1] She arrives at the appalling conclusion that there are each year in this country 423,000 fresh infections with syphilis, the annual rate of attack being 3.46 per thousand of the population. If this figure is applied to the census reports of the numbers of the population of different age groups, it is

---

* Read at the Fifty-Fourth Annual Meeting of the American Dermatological Association, Toronto, Canada, June, 1931.
* Reprinted through the courtesy of Archives of Dermatology and Syphilology, from Vol. 25, pp. 470-479, March, 1932.
[1]. Usilton, Lida J.: Ven. Dis. Inform. 11:543, 1930.

easy to estimate that well over 10 per cent of the adults of the country are, or have at one time been, infected with syphilis.

Of the various methods for the control of syphilis available to the physician, only one is of great practical importance, that is, adequate treatment of the infectious patient. Prophylaxis, education, repression of prostitution and other methods of social hygiene all play, or can be made to play, a valuable role in diminishing the incidence of fresh infections; but for the physician, the important thing is treatment. If it were possible promptly to arrive at a diagnosis in all patients with infectious syphilis, and immediately to institute treatment destroying the organisms in infectious lesions, with reasonable assurance against relapse, syphilis would become an almost negligible factor in public health. The knowledge of how to accomplish this feat and the weapons with which to do it are already at hand; obviously, however, they are not being successfully applied. I believe that one of the chief reasons for failure is the high cost of the medical care, and that the element of cost prevents not only the proper treatment of many patients, but even the recognition of the syphilitic condition.

The question at once arises, What constitutes infectiousness in syphilis? It is as yet unanswerable. Early syphilis (primary, secondary or relapsing), of course; but is the patient with latent or late syphilis a carrier who may transmit the infection to others? At times he certainly is, as is witnessed by numerous tragic family stories. What of the pregnant woman with no lesions but a positive Wassermann reaction of the blood? She may not be infectious for her sexual partner, but she is certainly so for her child in utero. From the practical standpoint, the syphilologist can I believe, take only one position; namely, that while early syphilis is surely infectious, latent and late syphilis are at least potentially so, and that control of the disease will not be accomplished until all such patients are recognized as syphilitic and brought under treatment.

Aside from the obviously impossible step of educating all practicing physicians to the point of diagnostic expertness equivalent to that of the syphilologist, how is syphilis to be recognized? It occurred to me that the average large dispensary service might serve as a cross-section of the general practice of medicine in illustrating the complaints that brought the patient to a physician, and the basis on which a diagnosis of syphilis was made. Accordingly, I have surveyed the last 1,000 consecutive admissions to the syphilis clinic of the Johns Hopkins Hospital, from the standpoint of the referring clinic, and the reason which that clinic had for transferring the patient to the syphilis clinic. Slightly more than one fifth of the patients entered the hospital with a complaint that indicated the desirability of a general medical examination. Among these 209 medical cases, the diagnosis of syphilis was made in 134, or 64 per cent, only by virtue of the fact that a routine Wassermann test of the blood was done. The obstetric department accounted for 59 of 1,000 cases; in 55 of these 59 women, or 95 per cent, a positive Wassermann reaction was the only evidence of syphilis. The other referring clinics do not use the Wassermann test as a routine; when syphilis is diagnosed, it is usually on the basis of a definite history, or unmistakable lesions. Even so, among the 664 patients sent to the syphilis clinic from all sources other than the medical or obstetric clinics, no less than 35 per cent would have gone unrecognized as syphilitic except for the Wassermann test of the blood. These sources, of course, include in their material 22 per cent of the cases of early syphilis in which the diagnosis can usually be made without the aid of the Wassermann test. If one limits the discussion to late syphilis, Turner's[2] figures from the syphilis clinic of Johns Hopkins Hospital show that among 6,420 patients with late syphilis, the diagnosis was

[2] Turner, T. B.: The Race and Sex Distribution of the Lesions of Syphilis in 10,000 Cases, Bull. Johns Hopkins Hosp. 46:159, 1930.

latent syphilis, made solely because of a positive Wassermann test of the blood in 53 per cent.

It is unnecessary to consider these figures further. They tell a story that the syphilologist has been stressing for years; namely, that thousands of cases of syphilis are unrecognized and untreated because of the failure of physicians to perform the Wassermann test more frequently as a routine. This is true even of large hospital services, such as that at Johns Hopkins, where the only outpatient clinics employing the test as a routine are the medical, obstetric and, recently, dermatologic. Some years ago, with a smaller dispensary clientele than at present, Moore and I[3] estimated that approximately 3,000 patients per year were passing through the outpatient department of Johns Hopkins with unrecognized syphilis. In private medical practice the Wassermann test is applied as a routine by only a few internists. Failure to employ it more widely is due partly to an entangling of medical and moral ideas, partly to the obvious fact that many contacts between patient and physician are for minor reasons which do not call for a general examination, and partly because of the expense entailed. The question of cost is, I believe, of paramount importance.

Cost of Laboratory Tests

The practicing physician may send specimens for the Wassermann test either to a city, county or state health department, or to a private laboratory. If the former, the cost to the patient is nothing, unless, as is too often the case, the physician makes a charge which he retains; if the latter, the cost is usually $5. There is much to be said, from the standpoint of public health, not only for free Wassermann service, but for absolutely free treatment for all patients with venereal disease—a procedure already adopted in Denmark and England. In this country, such an extension of the idea of state medicine would call forth violent protest from the medical profession and is, moreover, unlikely with our system of state and local government. Unless the public health authorities are prepared to take over the whole question of the control of venereal disease, however, there seems to be as much cause for protest against free Wassermann service for private patients, able to pay a fee, as against free urinalyses, chemical examinations of the blood or roentgen examinations. A patient who can afford to pay for a Wassermann test should pay for it.

How much should he pay? The charge of $5 persists, partly through long established custom, partly through the multiplication of small laboratories, each doing only a few tests, and thus keeping the cost artificially high because of proportionately high overhead expenses. The actual cost of doing a quantitatively titered Wassermann test of the blood, with an additional flocculation test, in a small but efficient laboratory doing 200 tests per month, is $1.63 apiece. If 500 tests per month were run the estimated cost would be 66 cents. The serologic laboratory at the Johns Hopkins Hospital, doing over 50,000 tests per year, does them at an average total cost of 29 cents each. Obviously, the prevailing fees for Wassermann tests are too high. The solution lies in a reduction of the small laboratories doing a few tests, and the centralization of this work in several larger laboratories in big cities, where the saving represented by the volume of work done can be passed on to the patient.

Cost of Treatment for Syphilis

Bringing down the cost of diagnostic laboratory procedures is the simplest element of the problem of control of syphilis. There remains the much more complex question of the cost of treatment. How largely this looms in the mind of the average syphilitic patient can only be appreciated by

---
[3] Keidel, A., and Moore, J. E.; The Wassermann Reaction in the Johns Hopkins Hospital, Bull. Johns Hopkins Hosp. 34:16, 1923.

one who is in constant contact with both private and so-called charity clinic patients.

What does it cost to be treated for syphilis? Generally speaking, the average patient in this country has two available alternatives. He may go to a large clinic, where he can be treated free if his circumstances warrant it, but where he is usually called on to pay something toward the cost of his care, or he can seek private medical attention. The actual cost of treating a patient at the Johns Hopkins Hospital amounts to $1.03 per visit, including the cost of special drugs and of all necessary laboratory procedures. A patient with early syphilis must make an average total of seventy-six visits, over a period of twenty-seven months. This brings the cost to $78, a not inconsiderable sum for the class of patients under discussion, and a staggering impossibility if two or more members of the family group must be treated, as is frequently the case.

In private practice, the cheapest available medical service in Baltimore could provide this same service for $305, if all Wassermann tests necessary for diagnosis and treatment were performed free of charge in the laboratory of the health department. Practically all of this expense would fall within the first fifteen months. This assumes that the original examination is charged at $10, each injection of an arsphenamine product at $5 and each injection of mercury or bismuth, at $2.50. Incidentally, experience leads me to believe that few physicians are willing to treat patients for fees as low as this. If Wassermann tests must be charged also, the total minimum cost rises from $305 to $380. Little experience in medical economics is necessary to realize that this sort of fee schedule is possible only for the physician who treats a great many syphilitic patients, thus reducing his overhead cost, or for the physician who, treating only a few patients, does it badly.

These are the minimum fees of private practice. The average fees for the same amount of treatment on the basis of Baltimore standards might fairly be put at $650, again almost all concentrated in a period of fifteen months. The prevailing fee schedule in this instance is $10 for an injection of an arsphenamine and $5 for one of bismuth or mercury, with other fees in proportion.

The amount of treatment considered here is that for an uncomplicated case of early syphilis. If there are any complications from treatment, if the spinal fluid is discovered to be positive, if more than one patient in the family is to be treated, the cost mounts with what seems to the frightened patient to be almost geometrical progression. Moreover, only one third of the new patients in general medical practice each year have early syphilis (Usilton[1]); two-thirds have late syphilis. Here the total average duration of treatment rises from fifteen to twenty-four months or more, and the total cost from a minimum of $305 or an average of $650, to $480 or $1,050.

These sums begin to mount up to figures that are difficult even for patients in the upper level of wage earners. If the problem is one of neurosyphilis, with perhaps hospitalization, fever or intraspinal therapy, ophthalmologic consultations, etc., it is little wonder that the average patient in moderate circumstances is consumed by a panicky fear of his inability to carry out what is demanded of him. Nothing need be said of average, high or maximum fees. Patients able to afford $2,000 or $3,000 a year for medical care present no economic problem.

To what extent do these two types of medical service, clinic and private, meet the public demand for medical attention for syphilis? To what extent does their failure to meet the demand, if present, influence the incidence of fresh syphilitic infections, or cause further economic loss to the individual, the family or the community, by virtue of the fact that the patient abandons treatment when his money runs out, and subsequently breaks down because of his disease? These are largely unanswerable questions, at least in any accurate fashion. Eighty-seven per cent of the persons of both sexes gainfully employed in the United States in 1918 received incomes under $2,000 per year.[4] Taking the country as a whole, 66 per cent of the patients with venereal disease are being treated (1925-1930) at the hands of private physicians and 33 per cent in clinics. Obviously, the 66 per cent under private care do not all belong to the 13 per cent of the population earning more than $2,000 per year. Equally obviously, many such patients are either incurring a financial obligation they cannot meet, or they are taking treatment as far as their means permit, and then abandoning it regardless of whether they are "cured" or even noninfectious. The latter course is the disastrous one from the standpoint of public health. That it frequently happens is only too clear to one with a large syphilologic experience. Many patients are dismissed by their physicians while still hopelessly inadequately treated, because they are no longer able to pay their bills. Many others stop treatment voluntarily for the same reason. Some of them with more intelligence than pride come to a free clinic to complete their treatment. More of them, especially those of the "white collar" class unfortunately do not, sometimes because of the shame of receiving charity, sometimes because unable to lose time from work to attend clinics at inconvenient hours, sometimes because of the publicity involved and sometimes because of reluctance to mingle with lower caste white patients or with Negroes.

It seems apparent from these considerations that to an even greater extent than in other forms of medical care, the main problem lies, not with the poor man who can be treated at cost or even free, nor with the well-to-do, to whom the expenditure of money for expert care is no object, but with the middle class, the great bulk of the population. Current medical literature attests the interest which the cost of medical care has for the general public and the medical profession; and the formation of a committee of distinguished physicians and laymen to consider this question speaks for the prevalent desire to do something constructive about it.

From the special standpoint of the management of the syphilitic patient, there are several steps that physicians can properly take. For many years dermatologists, notably Stokes, have been ceaselessly advocating the simplification of methods of treatment. This does not necessarily mean a search for new and more potent spirocheticidal drugs, which can properly be left in the hands of the experimental chemotherapist, but rather the elaboration of simpler methods of treatment with the drugs already at hand. For example, many dermatologists have repeatedly stressed the superiority of arsphenamine to neoarsphenamine, and have devoted much time to a consideration of results of treatment with arsphenamine to prove this point. They have perhaps lost sight of the fact that the relatively complex technic of administration of arsphenamine weighs more heavily with the average practitioner than its reputed therapeutic superiority, and that he insists on using the simpler neoarsphenamine, even though no such accurate data as to its efficiency are available. From the practical standpoint, the time spent in eulogizing arsphenamine, which the practitioner will not use, might be more profitably employed in studying the results obtainable from neoarshpenamine, which he will use, and in elaborating a method of treatment with the simpler drug which will produce results comparable to those obtainable with the more complex. As clinicians dealing with large numbers of syphilitic patients, this would seem distinctly the task of the dermatologist.

The physician who undertakes the treatment of patients with syphilis must discuss the financial problem with his patient from several angles. He must adapt methods of treatment to his patient's financial ability to carry them out. The administration of iodides by the intravenous route may, in some instances, be slightly more advantageous than to give them by mouth; but the one means an outlay of $3 or $4 to the pharmacist for the drug, and the other the payment of $50 or $100 to the intravenous

---
[4] Bigelow, G. H.: Why the Pay Clinic, Hosp. Soc. Serv. 8:1, 1923.

therapeutist for an equivalent amount of drug. Is the gain to the patient from the more complex method worth what it costs? The intramuscular or intravenous administration of soluble mercurial salts has a distinct place in therapy; but the physician must conscientiously decide whether thirty or forty such injections, which must be given at frequent intervals, will really be worth more to the patient's health than eight or ten intramuscular injections of an insoluble salt or a course of inunctions.

The physician who starts the treatment of a syphilitic patient has a moral and public health responsibility to see the case through to a finish. The first conversation with the patient, after the diagnosis has been established, should include a frank discussion of what treatment will probably be necessary, barring complications, and of its probable cost. In some cases, it has worked satisfactorily to do away with a set fee schedule for special procedures of treatment and, instead, to outline probable total minimum and maximum costs, and from this to work out a monthly average fee. In this case a patient may be told, not that injections of arsphenamine will be $5, $10 or $15 apiece, but that his treatment and subsequent follow up, over a period of two and one-half years, will cost an average of $15, $25 or $35 per month, for example. If the patient, on hearing what is necessary, finds himself unable to meet the fees demanded, the physician responsible for the diagnosis is under an absolute obligation to make other arrangements for him to be properly treated either by revising his own schedule of fees downward or by referring him to a less expensive practitioner or to a clinic. It is indefensible to treat the patient until his funds are exhausted and then drop him.

The expense of carrying on the private practice of medicine is, however, sufficiently great and there is a definite point past which the physician cannot be expected to go. With the best intentions in the world on his part to keep his fees as low as is consistent with his expenses, and to extend credit whenever necessary, he is often unable to provide the long term care and the relatively costly drugs which the syphilitic person in moderate circumstances must have. There are many cultured and educated people who are unable to finance adequate medical care, and who refuse to be the recipients of charity, either from private or from state agencies. Under existing circumstances, the majority of them go without treatment, are self-treated or resort to quackery.

The Pay Clinic

The obvious method of bringing together the physician who wants to provide adequate medical care and the patient in moderate circumstances who wants to receive it is the pay clinic. Such an institution can furnish expert medical service and, if its volume of work is sufficiently high, can even operate at a substantial profit on fees that are impossibly low for the individual practitioner. This point is amply proved by a famous example in one of our large cities, which undertakes the management of venereal disease in general. Here treatment for early syphilis, identical with that given at the Johns Hopkins Hospital, can be furnished at a total cost of $155. This is as compared with a cost of $78 in the charity clinic at Johns Hopkins or a minimum cost of $305 to a private patient. That the public seems to appreciate the service provided is amply illustrated by the fact that at this particular pay clinic about 20,000 new patients per year are received. It is estimated that 75 per cent of these patients have annual incomes of less than $2,000, and it is highly probable that few patients actually able to pay the prevailing fees of private practice attend the clinic.

To operate successfully, the pay clinic, in addition to furnishing competent medical care, must be available to patients at hours that conflict least with the necessity for earning a living; it must furnish privacy for the patient to a degree impossible in the charity clinic, and it must be able to attract its clientele. The classification of syphilis as a venereal disease and the fact that it is associated in lay and medical minds alike with the sexual act make it impossible for a pay clinic for syphilis or for venereal disease in general to attract patients as can similar institutions with more general medical aims. The satisfied syphilitic patient does not often tell his syphilitic friends that he is pleased with his treatment and advise them to go to the same place; indeed, he is unlikely to know which of his friends has syphilis. The only ways in which the average syphilitic patient in moderate circumstances can be made aware that a pay clinic for his treatment exists are through being informed by the physician who makes the diagnosis or through advertising sponsored by the clinic.

It is generally felt throughout the medical profession that advertising by posters or in the lay press, as heretofore conducted, has been objectionable. Perhaps some way that will have the cooperation of physicians can be found to resolve the difficulty. It has been suggested that simple announcements might be utilized, stating, for example, that persons suspecting that they may have syphilis (or venereal disease) should be examined and treated if necessary, and that the available agencies for treatment in a given community be listed, beginning with "your private physician, or if you cannot afford private medical care, the following institutions," these institutions, free, part-pay and pay, being named in alphabetical order, with their addresses and hours of availability.

Other elements of antagonism of practicing physicians toward the idea of the pay clinic might also be eliminated. The type of pay clinic suggested should be sponsored by the medical profession itself rather than by lay philanthropists. It should meticulously limit its activities to patients falling within the appropriate income class, rejecting those able to finance adequate private medical care. It should scrupulously avoid intrusion into other fields of medical practice. Its professional activities should be directed by experts, and positions on its staff should be open to competent and reputable physicians who might profitably regard a few years of association with it as postgraduate education. Finally, the members of the staff should be adequately compensated for their services.

The pay clinic seems so adequate a solution to the problem of the management of syphilis for patients in moderate circumstances that it is desirable for the medical profession, and especially for syphilologists, to consider it carefully. If the idea of the pay clinic does not meet with approval, it is the duty of the medical profession to offer a satisfactory alternative. If none is offered, pay clinics are likely to be the outcome, or perhaps even less agreeable solutions sponsored from outside the ranks of the medical profession.

Summary

The cost of the diagnosis and treatment of syphilis is a major factor in our inadequate control of the infection. The Wassermann test often is not employed in diagnosis because it costs $5, whereas it can be done accurately for as little as 29 cents. In most American cities, treatment facilities for syphilis are available only in free or part-pay clinics, at a representative one of which the cost of the treatment for early syphilis is $78; or in private practice, in which the estimated minimum cost of equivalent treatment is $305. The average cost of private treatment for the same type of patient is more than $600. Many patients of the moderate income class are inadequately treated because they cannot afford to complete the necessary treatment in private hands, and will not accept the alternative of free or part-pay clinics.

Suggested steps in the solution of this problem are: (1) simplification of existing methods of treatment; (2) the choice of the simpler and less expensive method of treatment, provided this does not entail a sacrifice of therapeutic efficiency; (3) the realization by the physician who undertakes the treatment of a syphilitic patient that he must see that treatment through to completion by one or another means; (4) the establishment of pay clinics in centers with a large population.

Certain of the prevailing objections to the pay clinic are briefly mentioned, and remedies are suggested.

MINIMUM STANDARDS FOR CLINICS FOR THE TREATMENT OF GONORRHEA AND SYPHILIS

The Massachusetts Department of Public Health

Foreword

There is no doubt as to the need for public clinics for the treatment of gonorrhea and syphilis. Several such clinics have been maintained in Massachusetts for many years. State aid has been given to a majority of them for nearly fifteen years on the principle that in those clinics, residents of communities too small for the maintenance of their own clinics may have treatment if they are unable to pay a physician.

The quality of the medical service offered by public clinics should be at least equal to that which is expected from the medical profession at large. Preferably it should approach that which is given by specialists in the particular field.

Further, since gonorrhea and syphilis are communicable diseases, dangerous to the public health, there falls upon the public clinic the responsibility for keeping the patient under treatment, and for the discovery, within reason, of as many contacts and sources of infection as can be identified. Public policy is opposed to the disclosure of the identity of the coöperative patient. Thus the control of the patient and the discovery of his contacts and the source of his infection is taken out of official hands.

The Department believes that it is time that some "yardstick" should be applied to the services of those clinics already in operation, as well as of those which may apply for State aid or recognition in the future. The following are considered to represent the minimum acceptable standards for the conduct of a clinic for the treatment of gonorrhea or syphilis.

Naturally, since clinics vary in size and in resources, it is impossible to prescribe uniform quantitative standards. These are essentially qualitative. It must be left to a study of each clinic separately to determine how well each meets the needs of its particular community. Subsidy will be continued or considered for only those clinics which meet these standards. Any clinic directories published by the Department will contain information concerning only those clinics which meet these standards.

Effective February 14, 1933

THE MASSACHUSETTS DEPARTMENT OF PUBLIC HEALTH

GEORGE H. BIGELOW,
Commissioner.

Note:—These Standards have been approved by:—
The Public Health Committee of the Massachusetts Medical Society.
The Neisserian Medical Society of Massachusetts.
The New England Dermatological Society.
The American Social Hygiene Association.
The Massachusetts Society for Social Hygiene.
The New England Section of the American Association of Hospital Social Workers.
The Boston Health League.
And a large group of social workers, nurses and individual physicians specializing in the treatment of gonorrhea or syphilis.

Location and Responsible Agency

1. Except in unusual circumstances, subsidy will be considered only for clinics located in communities of at least 30,000 population.
2. Subsidy will be considered only for clinics maintained and operated by:—
    (a) The local board of health itself, or jointly with some local hospital, preferably, in either case, as a part of the out-patient department of a hospital; or
    (b) By a city hospital or a general hospital or a general dispensary, as a part of its out-patient department.

Clinic Hours

1. Clinics should function at least as follows:—
    (a) So that each patient with syphilis may have at least one treatment per week. Arrangements should be made for treatment at least twice a week, at the clinic or elsewhere, of patients with open, early syphilis.
    (b) So that each patient with gonorrhea may have at least one treatment per week. Arrangements should be made for treatment at least three times a week, at the clinic or elsewhere, of male patients with acute gonorrhea.
    (c) At least one clinic in a given community should have adequate evening clinic service (after five o'clock p. m.) or subsidy will not be considered for any of them. Preference in subsidy will be given the clinic with evening sessions.
    (d) While it is preferable that the sexes be treated for gonorrhea at different sessions, their treatment at the same session is permissible, provided that by means of separate dressing rooms and the utmost care in routing patients through the treatment room, any embarrassment of a patient is avoided.

Clinic Equipment

1. The minimum equipment of a clinic should be:—
    (a) Rooms
        (1) Waiting room(s) for patients, preferably but not necessarily separate for the sexes.
        (2) Consultation room(s) for physician and social worker.
        (3) Dressing room(s) separate for the sexes if both sexes are treated at the same session. Sections of the examining or treatment rooms may be screened off for dressing rooms.
        (4) Examining room(s). The consultation room or treatment room may be used for examination if strict privacy for the patient is possible.
        (5) Treatment room(s).
        (6) Convenient toilet facilities.
    (b) Medical Equipment
        *(1) Microscope, dark field condenser, stains, etc.
        *(2) Equipment for urine examination.
        (3) Syringes, needles, gauze, gloves, catheters, sounds, irrigators, specula, etc., in sufficient quantity for uninterrupted procedure.
        (4) Sterilizer.
        (5) Running hot and cold water.
        (6) Tables for examination and treatment, properly lighted.
        (7) Couch or table for patients who have reactions to treatment.
    (c) Clerical Equipment
        (1) Desk(s) and filing cabinet(s) for records and correspondence, with lock and key.
        (2) Suitable forms for diagnostic and treatment records (see "Reports and Records").
    *Unless available in a convenient laboratory elsewhere.

Clinic Personnel

There is nothing so important as the quality and attitude of the clinic personnel. It has been noted repeatedly, that though a clinic is poorly located and its equipment the most elementary, it is a success if the personnel is interested and takes time to give individual attention to, and to gain the confidence of the patient in a spirit of kindly concern. That is what makes for success in the private practice of medicine. Nothing kills a clinic as quickly as lack of interest, perfunctory contact with the patient, boredom or, on the other hand, that "hard-boiled" roughness or abruptness which is so likely to develop through long association with these diseases.

The attitude of the physician reflects itself throughout the entire personnel. His point of view must be broader than simply that of physician in relation to the patient and include the public health. The patient naturally turns to him for full information concerning the disease. The instruction of the patient cannot be left entirely to the social worker or nurse. If the matter is not of sufficient weight to receive the attention of the physician as a part of the medical problem, the patient attaches less importance to it, coming from some other member of the staff. The nature of the disease, the treatment required, the importance of conduct and regularity of attendance, the importance to themselves and to the public health of treatment for the contacts and the source of infection, must be touched upon by the physician. Thus the way is opened for more detailed discussion by the social worker or nurse, of such problems as may be left to them to handle.

Gonorrhea and syphilis are communicable diseases. This the patient must understand and the clinic personnel keep constantly in mind. Delinquencies in attendance and the treatment of contacts and sources of infection are as much a part of the problem of control as the treatment of those patients who attend. Consequently the personnel of the clinic must include someone whose responsibility it is to attend to this phase of the management of the case. It is well established that certain of these problems can be handled adequately only by a medical social worker. Some patients are delinquent because of economic or social conditions which require adjustment. Difficult social problems often surround the elimination of the source of infection. On occasion the combined resources of several agencies may be needed to satisfy the needs of a given case. None but a properly trained medical social worker can do this work.

On the other hand, much of this work takes time. It is poor public health procedure to give so much attention to a few cases that many others are totally neglected. It is the opinion of the Department that when the resources of the clinic are so limited that adequate personnel to do complete social service cannot be afforded, first consideration should be given the majority of patients needing simpler forms of follow-up. Other community resources should be utilized in the solution of the more complex problems. A large part of the routine clinic follow-up can be done by a properly qualified public health nurse. For the present, for those clinics which cannot afford adequate social service, the Department will accept a properly qualified public health nurse as minimum follow-up personnel. Any clinic which can afford a medical social worker should have one. Consideration for subsidy will be determined by the extent to which the clinic has made provision for social service consistent with its resources.

The minimum personnel should be:—

1. A competent physician who should be the clinic chief and who should have adequate medical assistance according to the demands of the clinic.

2. A graduate nurse who should assist the physician, prepare pa-

tients, etc., and who may also keep the clinic records if the services of a clinic clerk are not available.

3. A medical social worker whose qualifications should be determined according to standards set by the American Association of Hospital Social Workers.

4. Until such a time as it is possible to secure the services of a qualified medical social worker, routine follow-up service may be provided through a public health nurse who should be qualified as follows:—

(a) She should have completed satisfactorily a one-year course in public health nursing and have had at least one year of satisfactory experience, under supervision, in a public health nursing agency; or

(b) She should be a graduate nurse with exceptional qualifications who has had at least two years of satisfactory experience, under supervision, in a public health nursing agency.

5. In either case, any candidate who has not had six months' experience in the management of gonorrhea and syphilis, should secure this experience, under supervision, immediately following appointment.

NOTE:—See appendix for functions of medical social worker and public health nurse.

Admission of Patients

1. Subsidy will be considered only if the services of the clinic are available to otherwise eligible residents of other communities who can more conveniently attend the said clinic than any other public clinic (See 6-c).

2. All persons who apply for diagnosis should be admitted and examined, regardless of residence, or of previous treatment elsewhere for other conditions, or of ability to pay a physician for treatment. Gonorrhea and syphilis are communicable diseases and must be diagnosed at the earliest opportunity for the sake of the patient and for the protection of the public health. If the applicant is refused examination at the clinic, several days may elapse before he appears or can be admitted for examination elsewhere. If he has early syphilis or some forms of gonorrhea, delay may be very serious, certainly to the patient, and very likely to those whom he has infected or may expose to infection. If the symptoms or signs of early syphilis or of acute gonorrhea are mild or subsiding, they may have so nearly disappeared in a few days as to delay or prevent diagnosis. And above all, the patient must understand, from the beginning, that communicable disease deserves immediate attention, or he will be little impressed, later on, by urgent requests to return to treatment. It is inconceivable that a patient likely to have smallpox or diphtheria would be referred for examination elsewhere at a later date. Gonorrhea and syphilis, especially in their acute stages, deserve the same consideration as any other acute, communicable disease.

3. If a diagnosis can be made at the first visit, the first treatment may be given at that time. The patient may then be referred (if he should be), together with a summary of his record, to the physician or clinic to be responsible for his care. His failure to report elsewhere for treatment should result in his being reported immediately to the State Department of Public Health as having prematurely discontinued treatment.

4. If a diagnosis cannot be made at the first visit, and the patient is not entitled to treatment at the diagnostic clinic, it should be left to the discretion of the clinic chief to complete the diagnosis or to refer the patient at once to the appropriate place for further observation.

5. No patient should be admitted for examination or treatment who has been under treatment elsewhere for the present infection, except for good reason, such as:—

(a) Inability to continue paying the average fee charged by physicians in the area;

(b) Permanent or temporary change of residence, or some occupational factor, which makes attendance at the former clinic illogical or unreasonable:

(c) Improper or emergency acceptance of the case originally, as out of its sphere of service, by the former clinic;

(d) At the request of the previously responsible physician or clinic for valid reason.

6. Any person admitted for examination should be retained as a patient of the diagnostic clinic if:—

(a) Found to be infected with gonorrhea or syphilis, or suffering from a condition suspected to be gonorrheal or syphilitic (this should not prohibit transfer to the urological, gynecological, skin or other out-patient services maintained by the agency, if gonorrhea and syphilis are ruled out); and

(b) After reasonable investigation it is found that the patient is unable to pay the average fee charged by physicians in the area, taking into account the long time required for treatment as well as the economic status of the patient; and

(c) The patient is a resident of the area logically served by the clinic, taking into account the location of other "free" clinics, and transportation facilities. Patients should be referred to the most readily accessible clinic. Exceptions to this may be made in case of employment or temporary residence in the area, which makes attendance at the otherwise logical clinic impracticable.

Fees

1. No patient should be denied treatment because of inability to pay a fee.

2. Boards of health of communities from which patients come who are unable to pay a fee should be willing to pay a fee covering the cost of the service rendered or else provide treatment for the patient elsewhere. (Chapter 111, Sections 32, 116, 117 and 118, General Laws.) The agreement for such payment should be made between the board of health concerned and the clinic. No patient should be denied treatment at a subsidized clinic because of failure of the board of health to pay a fee. However, if there is a clinic in the community of the patient's residence, supported by public funds (city hospital or board of health clinic) no other clinic should charge that local board of health for the treatment of indigent patients. Such patients as are unable to pay and the clinic unwilling to retain, should be referred to the publicly supported clinic.

3. Obviously no fee should be charged for medication supplied by the State Department of Public Health, nor for work done in the State or other public laboratories.

4. Exceptions. The standards as to fees apply only to State subsidized clinics, except that Section 3 shall apply to all clinics.

Note:—The law requires that fees collected in clinics maintained and operated by local boards of health shall revert to the city or town treasury. They may not be applied to the maintenance of the clinic except by special appropriation.

Reports and Records

1. All cases of gonorrhea and syphilis diagnosed or treated at the clinic must be reported to the State Department of Public Health as required by the Regulations of the Department, and on forms as prescribed.

2. A report of certain clinic statistics should be made to the State Department of Public Health once a month, on forms provided by the Department.

3. Detailed individual records should be kept for each case admitted to the clinic. The minimum record should contain the essential social

data, history of the present infection, physical and laboratory examinations, diagnosis, an exact account and date of each treatment, reactions to treatment, note of lapses from treatment, final disposition of the case, and a statement .that will indicate that an effort has been made to identify the contacts, and, in gonorrhea and early syphilis, the source of infection.

4. Patients who discontinue treatment prematurely, and identified sources of infection must be reported by name and address to the Department as required by regulations of the Department, if after reasonable effort on the part of the clinic the patient (or source of infection) is still not under medical care.

Instruction of the Patient

1. The physician should explain to the patient, as soon as a diagnosis of gonorrhea or syphilis is made:—
    (a) The nature of the disease;
  *(b) The conduct required of the patient;
    (c) The general nature of treatment; the importance of regular attendance; of calling the physician's attention to any reactions to treatment; and the importance of adequate treatment;
    (d) Any medication or treatment to be taken at home;
    (e) The importance of discovering contact infections;
    (f) The importance of treatment for the source of infection.

2. The social worker should review with the patient the information and instructions given by the physician to determine whether they have been interpreted correctly by the patient.

3. The nurse, if so directed by the physician, may explain the details of home treatment to women(douches, sitz-baths, etc.).

Consultation and Hospitalization

Satisfactory arrangements should be made for at least:—
1. Special examinations (cardiac, neurologic, ophthalmologic, urologic, etc.)
2. Spinal puncture and spinal fluid examinations.
3. Hospitalization of openly communicable early syphilis.

Syphilis

1. Equipment for dark field examination should be available in the clinic, or so near at hand that a patient suspected to have primary syphilis or open secondary syphilis may be conducted to the laboratory for examination the moment it is indicated.

2. No patient with clinical primary syphilis should be treated locally or systemically for syphilis until clinical diagnosis has been confirmed by dark field examination or by serological study, or by confrontation.

3. A diagnosis of late syphilis should not be made or ruled out on the result of a single serological examination of the blood.

4. If history or clinical evidence suggests syphilis, and laboratory confirmation of diagnosis is not possible, the patient should be advised that the examination is not complete without a spinal fluid examination.

5. One or the arsenicals (arsphenamine, sulpharsphenamine, neoarsphenamine, silverarsphenamine, bismarsen, etc.) and either bismuth or mercury or both should constitute the essential anti-syphilitic therapy in early (primary and secondary) syphilis, unless definitely contraindicated by the condition of the patient or the sensitivity of the patient to the drug. This is not intended to discourage controlled research in therapy but only to apply to the routine of the clinic until other forms of therapy may be approved by syphilologists in general.

6. Prior to each contemplated treatment, especially with arsenical,

---

* If gonorrhea or early syphilis is suspected, conduct should be discussed at the patient's first visit, even though the diagnosis has not been completed.

the patient should be questioned in regard to such symptoms as itching, rashes, nausea, vomiting, diarrhea, jaundice, persistent pain, or visual disturbance, and physical examination should be made if indicated.

7. Urine examination (albumin and cytology at least) should be made not less than once each two months during regular treatment, and especially during the exhibition of mercury or bismuth.

8. Treatment of early syphilis should be continued, preferably without "vacations", until the blood serology has been persistently negative for at least six months, and preferably for one year. The only exceptions to this rule should be:—contraindications to intensive treatment, or cases which, after at least two years of treatment appear to be "Wassermann-fast".

9. Patients should be advised that evidence of "cure" is incomplete without spinal fluid examination made at least a year following the date of infection.

10. No patient should be discharged as "cured" until the physical and serological examinations have remained persistently negative for at least three years.

11. Women of child-bearing age should be advised to have medical observation throughout every subsequent pregnancy regardless of "cure" of syphilis.

Gonorrhea

The difficulties attending the diagnosis of gonorrhea and the determination of its cure are well known. Since there are no exact clinical or laboratory procedures through the use of which the presence or absence of the disease or its cure may be exactly determined, it becomes necessary to depend frequently on clinical judgment for the answers to these questions. The following "Standards" for the diagnosis and cure of gonorrhea are not mathematically nor scientifically exact. They are rather a definition of what has been found to be sound as the result of the considerable experience of a number of physicians who treat gonorrhea.

1. The possibility of gonorrheal infection in a new female patient should not be dismissed unless the history and clinical findings (urethra, Skene's glands, Bartholin glands, cervix, pelvis) are definitely negative and at least three consecutive weekly smears from the urethra and cervix (one just before or just following the menstrual period) are free from the gonococcus and contain less than five leucocytes per oil immersion field (unless there is definite pathology of other origin to account for the presence of pus).

2. The possibility of gonorrheal infection in a new male patient should not be dismissed unless the history and clinical findings (urethra, epididymis and prostate gland) are definitely negative and at least three prostatic smears are free from the gonococcus and contain less than five leucocytes per oil immersion field (unless there is definite pathology of other origin to account for the presence of pus).

3. No female patient should be discharged as "cured" of a gonorrheal infection until clinical findings are negative and weekly urethral and cervical smears over at least three months, treatment being suspended, are persistently free from the gonococcus and contain less than five leucocytes per oil immersion field (unless there is definite pathology of other origin to account for the presence of pus).

4. No male patient who has had posterior urethritis should be discharged as "cured" of a gonorrheal infection until clinical findings are negative and prostatic smears, treatment being suspended, taken twice a month for at least three months, are negative for the gonococcus and contain less than five leucocytes per oil immersion field. The persistence of a marked prostatic infection six months after the disappearance of the gonococcus in a well-behaved patient who has had at least six months of regular treatment and provocative examination, may be reason for his transfer to a urological clinic.

Appendix
1. Functions of a medical social worker.

(a) Social admitting service (including financial eligibility).

(b) Social review of all patients in clinic—considering patient's ability to cooperate effectively in the physician's plan of treatment.

(c) Interpretation of medical social aspects of patient's problem to the patient, his family, the physician and, when indicated to community agencies.

(d) Full social examination and social treatment when indicated.

(e) Follow-up, including such social adjustments as can be made without full social examination.

(f) Responsibility for examination of as many contacts (especially familial) and of sources of infection of early syphilis and gonorrhea, as possible.

(g) Cooperating with appropriate agencies in community problems.

(h) Social aspects of clinic management.

2. Functions of the alternative public health nurse.

(a) Admitting service (including financial eligibility).

(b) Social review of all patients in clinic—considering patient's ability to cooperate effectively in the physician's plan of treatment.

(c) Interpreting of medical social aspects of patient's problem to the patient, his family, the physician, and when indicated, to community agencies.

(d) Referring to social agencies for social examination and social treatment.

(e) Follow-up, including social adjustments which can be made without full social examination.

(f) Responsibility for examination of as many contacts (especially familial) and of sources of infection of early syphilis and gonorrhea, as possible.

(g) Cooperating with appropriate agencies in community problems.

(h) Clinic management.

Editorial Comment

Radio Broadcasts. Public Information. It is probable that some day newspaper editors will become as broad-minded as radio station directors. In the meantime, however, since the newspapers are open to almost any sort of "sex news" but closed to the sort of sound public information concerning gonorrhea and syphilis that we have found to be much in demand, we are happy to be able now and then to talk directly to the people of the State about these two diseases. It has been interesting to note that in spite of their entire frankness, not a single complaint has been received from our radio audiences against these broadcasts of public information. In fact an appreciable number of favorable comments, requests for further information and at least one commendatory newspaper editorial have followed the broadcasts. The few newspapers in the country which have opened their columns to a frank discussion of the problem which these diseases present have suffered not the least unfavorable criticism. People must somehow be informed concerning gonorrhea and syphilis both of which are communicable diseases which affect large numbers of the morally innocent, as do other communicable diseases. A large number of reprints of these four radio broadcasts are available for distribution.

The Nurse in the Control of Gonorrhea and Syphilis. It is with a great deal of pleasure that we offer to the nurses of Massachusetts a series of papers written by Miss Gladys Crain, R.N., Assistant Director of the National Organization for Public Health Nursing, together with a discussion of the nurse's relationship to the control of these diseases as the health officer sees it. The literature is notoriously lacking in sound material and we congratulate Miss Crain on her ability to prepare material sufficiently non-technical to be readily understandable and yet sufficiently comprehensive to serve as a rather full guide to the nurse who has responsibilities in this field. The material should be equally valuable to the social worker or to any one interested in the maintenance of the public health. A large supply of reprints of this series of papers is available for distribution.

Economic Aspects of the Management of Syphilis. Through the courtesy of Archives of Dermatology and Syphilology and of Dr. Albert Keidel, the author, we are permitted to reprint this paper, which considers some of the economic difficulties confronting the patient with syphilis. There is much food for thought here for the medical profession and no little argument for the maintenance of public clinics. "Indigency" as it is related to syphilis is quite a different thing from indigency in relation to the more acute communicable diseases which require expenditure for medical service over a relatively short time. We hope that some day someone with Dr. Keidel's understanding and experience will perform a similar service for patients with gonorrhea. It may be pertinent to note that Dr. Keidel is not, nor, as far as we are aware, never has been a health officer.

Minimum Standards for Clinics for the Treatment of Gonorrhea and Syphilis. After fifteen years of public clinics for patients with gonorrhea or syphilis, a number of which have been aided financially over the years by the Massachusetts Department of Public Health, certain minimum standards for the operation of these clinics have been proposed. After wide review by many physicians, social workers, nurses and health officials, these standards have emerged as printed in this issue of The Commonhealth. The introductory statement defines their purpose. Minimum standards may be dangerous in that they may be taken by the smugly complacent as maximum standards. On the other hand, those clinics which seek to progress will do so with or without minimum standards, while the smugly complacent are probably now subminimal and may be raised to a higher level of service. It is better to have them smugly complacent at a higher level than that which they now occupy.

Massachusetts Society for Social Hygiene. Reorganized in 1928, this Society has, we are confident, worked itself into a position of leadership among social hygiene societies in this country. With a field staff of three lecturers, with its contribution of "Growing Up in the World Today" to social hygiene literature for adolescents, with its support of and financial assistance to medical follow-up service at the Lowell and Fall River clinics, with its joint study with the Community Health Association of the follow-up service in the Boston clinics, with its study of the treatment of pregnant women with syphilis, and with its proposed plan for the wide-spread distribution of literature for public information, it has become a most important factor in the program not only for the control of gonorrhea and syphilis but also in the laying of a ground work in sex hygiene and sex character building that is invaluable.

REPORT OF DIVISION OF FOOD AND DRUGS

During the months of January, February and March 1933, samples were collected in 225 cities and towns.

There were 1,135 samples of milk examined, of which 101 were below standard; from 13 samples the cream had been in part removed, and 1 sample contained added water. There were 53 samples of Grade A milk examined, 2 samples of which were below the legal standard of 4.00% fat. There were 965 bacteriological examinations made of milk, 1 of cream, 20 of hamburg steak, and 1 of canned apple sauce. There were 54 samples examined for hemolytic bacteria, 53 of which were negative, and 1 positive.

There were 904 samples of food examined, of which 106 were adulterated or misbranded. These consisted of 2 samples of butter which were below the legal standard in milk fat; 1 sample of chocolate milk which was made with skimmed milk and incorrectly labeled; 15 samples of eggs, 11 samples of which were cold storage not marked, 1 of which was also decomposed, 1 sample which was sold as fresh eggs but was not fresh, and 3 samples were decomposed; 26 samples of hamburg steak, 15 of which contained a compound of sulphur dioxide not properly labeled, 4 samples were decomposed, 1 of which also contained a compound of sulphur dioxide not properly labeled, and 7 samples were watered, 2 of which also contained a compound of sulphur dioxide. not properly labeled; 49 samples of sausage, 28 samples of which contained a compound of sulphur dioxide not properly labeled, 1 sample of which also contained starch in excess of 2 per cent, 3 samples were decomposed, 11 samples contained added color, and 7 samples contained starch in excess of 2 per cent; 1 sample of liver which was decomposed; 1 sample of maple syrup which contained cane sugar; 2 samples of extract of vanilla consisting in part of coumarin and containing no vanilla resins; and 9 samples of vinegar, 5 of which were below the legal standard in acetic acid, 3 contained added color, 2 of which also were below the legal standard in acetic acid, and 1 sample was not pure cider vinegar and was adulterated with added caramel color.

There were 6 samples of drugs examined, of which 1 was adulterated. This was a sample of camphorated oil which did not conform to the U. S. P. requirements.

The police departments submitted 783 samples of liquor for examination, 776 of which were above 0.5% in alcohol. The police departments also submitted 7 samples of narcotics, etc., for examination, 3 of which contained heroin, 1 contained gum opium, 1 contained sulphuric acid, 1 contained morphine, and 1 sample of tobacco was examined for narcotics with negative results.

There were 121 cities and towns visited for the inspection of pasteurizing plants, and 382 plants were inspected.

There were 107 hearings held pertaining to violations of the laws.

There were 84 convictions for violations of the law, $1,080 in fines being imposed.

Robert Catherwood of Lowell; Joseph A. Rogers of Haverhill; Sylvio Fortier of Fall River; Farmers' Dairy, Incorporated, of New Bedford; Holyoke Producers Dairy Company of Holyoke; Model Dairy, Incorporated, 2 cases of Pittsfield; and David M. Watt, 2 cases, of Barre, were all convicted for violations of the pasteurization law and regulations. The two cases of Lottie Mioduszewski of North Saugus were filed without finding.

Charles A. David of Springfield; Peter Geokos, Basil Panis, and Joseph P. Sousa, all of Cambridge; Charles O'Connor and Ernest F. Rioux of North Attleboro; Joseph Conto and Patrick W. O'Connell, 2 cases, of East Taunton; and Sylvio Fortier of Fall River; were all convicted for violations of the milk laws. Patrick W. O'Connell of East Taunton appealed one case.

Pure Products Company, Incorporated, 4 cases, of West Springfield; The Great Atlantic & Pacific Tea Company, 2 cases, Swift & Company, Armour & Company, Phillip Pesecetta, and Stefano Maggipant, all of Springfield; The Great Atlantic & Pacific Tea Company and Frank H. Rice of Greenfield; T. A. Dewire & Son Company of Somerville; Samuel White of Winthrop; Samuel Andrews and Antony Poretti of Waltham; Keve Kessler of Malden; John Obartuck of Gilbertville; William Czerwonka of Holyoke; John Freni, Nathan Alpert, New England Provision Company, and Charles De Rosa, all of Boston; Peter L. Berlo, 2 cases, of South Boston; Frank Zambello of East Boston; Economy Grocery Store of Medford; Henry Stavely of Fitchburg; Joseph Halpern and Benjamin Stolzberg of Haverhill; Victor Brogi, 2 cases, of Taunton; Aaron Medelbaum, Anthony Rolka, Philip Keimach, Andrew Rudkosky, William Mezikolsky, Morris Rubin, Herman Spivack, and Abraham Kaufman, all of Chelsea; Stravos Stergis and Abraham A. Marks of Lynn; and Irving Ross of Allston, were all convicted for violations of the food laws. New England Provision Company of Boston appealed their case. Herman Spivack and Abraham Kaufman of Chelsea; and Samuel White of Winthrop, were given suspended sentences.

Samuel Abbott of Roxbury; and Thomas F. Sheridan of Watertown, were convicted for false advertising.

Paul Avenzino Company, Incorporated, of Cambridge; Charles Bucci and Frank Bonerba of Beverly; Bernard Burnstin, Grand Union Company, Thomas Govoni, and Swift & Company, all of Springfield, Nicholas Calebrese and Gerard Longo of Medford; Barney Cohen of Brighton; Armour & Company of Boston; J. S. Contas Brothers, Incorporated, of Waltham; Hyman Hoffman of Roxbury; Stephen Ingemi of Salem; Mary Kagin and Stefan Kumko of Holyoke; Angelo Rizzo of Everett; and Michael L. Murray of Taunton, were all convicted for violations of the cold storage laws. Frank Bonerba of Beverly, Barney Cohen of Brighton; Hyman Hoffman of Roxbury; and Stephen Ingemi of Salem, all appealed their cases.

Post Taste-T Foods, Incorporated, and Ludwig Danten of Newton, were convicted for violations of the bakery laws. Ludwig Danten of Newton pleaded guilty and was placed on probation.

In accordance with Section 25, Chapter 111 of the General Laws, the following is the list of articles of adulterated food collected in original packages from manufacturers, wholesalers, or producers:

Butter which was below the legal standard in milk fat was obtained as follows:

One sample each, from Swift & Company, and Rood & Woodbury, both of Springfield.

One sample of chocolate milk which was made with skimmed milk and incorrectly labeled was obtained from Rix Milk Company of Westfield.

One sample of maple syrup which contained cane sugar was obtained from F. W. Woolworth of Boston.

One sample of liver which was decomposed was obtained from The Great Atlantic & Pacific Tea Company of Springfield.

Hamburg steak which contained a compound of sulphur dioxide not properly labeled was obtained as follows:

One sample each, from Joseph Elton and Benjamin Stolzberg of Haverhill; Victor Brogi of Taunton; John Kaplan of Woburn; Joseph Rosenburg and Joseph Bataglia of Boston; Joseph Mazzariello of East Boston; Blossom Meat Market and Abraham Shapiro of Lynn; and Samuel Schwalb, Philip Keimack, Aaron Mandelbaum, Abrahám Kaufman, Morris Mezikofsky, and Herman Spivack, all of Chelsea.

Hamburg steak which contained added water was obtained as follows: One sample each, from Central Beef Market and Abraham A. Marks of Lynn; The Great Atlantic & Pacific Tea Company of Worcester, and H. Alpert of Boston.

Hamburg steak which was decomposed was obtained as follows:
One sample each, from Public Market of Allston; Keve Kessler of Malden; and Wheeler Square Market of Waltham.

Hamurg steak which contained a compound of sulphur dioxide not properly labeled and also contained added water was obtained as follows:
One sample each, from Nathan Fishman of Allston; and Empire Beef Company of Worcester.

One sample of hamburg steak which contained a compound of sulphur dioxide not properly labeled and was also decomposed was obtained from James A. Steinberg of Worcester.

Sausage which contained a compound of sulphur dioxide not properly labeled was obtained as follows:
Three samples from H. Alpert & Company of Boston; 2 samples from N. Maggioli of Medford; and 1 sample each, from Nathan Alpert, Nathan N. Alpert, Charles De Rosa, John Freni, A. Albertelli & Company, D. Petrino & Company, Supreme Public Market, Cuillo Market, and Joseph Reinholtz, all of Boston; East Boston Public Meat Market and Frank Zambello of East Boston; Gloria Chain Store of Beverly; Rose De Luca of Somerville; Globe Market of Springfield, and Antonio Giovino of Cambridge.

Sausage which contained starch in excess of 2 per cent was obtained as follows:
Two samples each, from John Obartuck of Gilbertville; and Henry Stavely of Fitchburg; and 1 sample from Sunnyside Market of Taunton.

Sausage which contained added color was obtained as follows:
Four samples from New England Provision Company of Boston; 1 sample each, from First National Store of Stoughton, Salem, and Somerville; and Colonial Provision Company, Incorporated, of Boston.

Sausage which was decomposed was obtained from Malden Square Market of Malden.

One sample of sausage which contained starch in excess of 2 per cent and also contained a compound of sulphur dioxide not properly labeled was obtained from Sunnyside Market of Taunton.

Vinegar which was low in acid was obtained as follows:
Three samples from Pure Products Company, Incorporated, of West Springfield; and 1 sample from Carbon Products Company of Providence, Rhode Island.

One sample of vinegar which contained added color was obtained from Pure Products Company, Incorporated, of West Springfield.

One sample of vinegar which was low in acid and contained added color was obtained from Pure Products Company, Incorporated, of West Springfield.

One sample of vinegar which was not pure cider vinegar and was adulterated with added carmel color was obtained from Progress Pickling & Vinegar Company of Providence, Rhode Island.

There were ten confiscations, consisting of 3 pounds of decomposed beef liver; 18 pounds of decomposed chicken; 260 pounds of decomposed chickens and fowl; 39 pounds of decomposed chickens' legs; 364 pounds of decomposed cooked chicken paste; 176 pounds of decomposed cooked chicken paste; 495 pounds of decomposed cooked chicken paste; 350 pounds of decomposed pork kidneys; 230 pounds of decomposed pigs' feet; and 70 pounds of decomposed cooked spaghetti.

The licensed cold storage warehouses reported the following amounts of food placed in storage during December, 1932:— 389,940 dozens of case eggs; 341,100 pounds of broken out eggs; 267,497 pounds of butter; 3,274,570 pounds of poultry; 3,186,370½ pounds of fresh meat and fresh meat products; and 1,559,703 pounds of fresh food fish.

There was on hand January 1, 1933:—187,080 dozens of case eggs; 1,251,034 pounds of broken out eggs; 1,432,800 pounds of butter; 7,651,-134 pounds of poultry; 4,578,887 pounds of fresh meat and fresh meat products; and 14,253,381 pounds of fresh food fish.

The licensed cold storage warehouses reported the following amounts of food placed in storage during January 1933:—97,290 dozens of case eggs; 196,223 pounds of broken out eggs; 301,518 pounds of butter; 1,943,617 pounds of poultry; 2,917,163½ pounds of fresh meat and fresh meat products; and 2,381,658 pounds of fresh food fish.

There was on hand February 1, 1933:—39,600 dozens of case eggs; 899,866 pounds of broken out eggs; 669,818 pounds of butter; 7,816,088 pounds of poultry; 5,463,564 pounds of fresh meat and fresh meat products; and 10,682,289 pounds of fresh food fish.

The licensed cold storage warehouses reported the following amounts of food placed in storage during February, 1933:—212,280 dozens of case eggs; 413,480 pounds of broken out eggs; 310,818 pounds of butter; 903,358 pounds of poultry; 2,884,124½ pounds of fresh meat and fresh meat products; and 1,846,918 pounds of fresh food fish.

There was on hand March 1, 1933:—121,470 dozens of case eggs; 803,653 pounds of broken out eggs; 413,250 pounds of butter; 6,547,068 pounds of poultry; 5,688,652½ pounds of fresh meat and fresh meat products; and 6,720,207 pounds of fresh food fish.

MASSACHUSETTS DEPARTMENT OF PUBLIC HEALTH

Commissioner of Public Health, GEORGE H. BIGELOW, M.D.

Public Health Council

GEORGE H. BIGELOW, M. D., *Chairman*

ROGER I. LEE, M.D.
SYLVESTER E. RYAN, M.D.
FRANCIS H. LALLY, M.D.
RICHARD P. STRONG, M.D.
JAMES L. TIGHE.
GORDON HUTCHINS.

Secretary, ALICE M. NELSON.

Division of Administration	Under direction of Commissioner.
Division of Sanitary Engineering	Director and Chief Engineer, ARTHUR D. WESTON, C.E.
Division of Communicable Diseases	Director, GAYLORD W. ANDERSON, M.D.
Division of Water and Sewage Laboratories	Director and Chemist, H. W. CLARK
Division of Biologic Laboratories	Director and Pathologist, BENJAMIN WHITE, Ph.D.
Division of Food and Drugs	Director and Analyst, HERMANN C. LYTHGOE, S.B.
Division of Child Hygiene	Director, M. LUISE DIEZ, M.D.
Division of Tuberculosis	Director, ALTON S. POPE, M.D.
Division of Adult Hygiene	Director, HERBERT L. LOMBARD, M.D.

State District Health Officers

The Southeastern District	RICHARD P. MACKNIGHT, M.D., New Bedford.
The Metropolitan District	CHARLES B. MACK, M.D., Boston.
The Northeastern District	ROBERT E. ARCHIBALD, M.D., Lynn.
The Worcester County District	OSCAR A. DUDLEY, M.D., Worcester.
The Connecticut Valley District	HAROLD E. MINER, M.D., Springfield.
The Berkshire District	WALTER W. LEE, M.D., No. Adams.

PUBLICATION OF THIS DOCUMENT APPROVED BY THE COMMISSION ON ADMINISTRATION AND FINANCE
5000. 5-'33. Order 8483.

THE COMMONHEALTH

VOLUME 20   JULY - AUG. - SEPT.
No. 3   1933

Epidemiology

MASSACHUSETTS
DEPARTMENT OF PUBLIC HEALTH

THE COMMONHEALTH

QUARTERLY BULLETIN OF THE MASSACHUSETTS DEPARTMENT OF
PUBLIC HEALTH

Sent Free to any Citizen of the State

Entered as second class matter at Boston Postoffice.

M. LUISE DIEZ, M.D., DIRECTOR OF DIVISION OF CHILD HYGIENE, EDITOR.
Room 545 State House, Boston, Mass.

CONTENTS

	PAGE
Foreword	125
Epidemiology	125
Typhoid Fever	126
Gastro-Enteritis	141
Bacillary Dysentery	145
Streptococcic Infections	148
Smallpox	153
Epidemiology in the Control of Tuberculosis	155
Gonorrhea and Syphilis	157
Epidemiology in Chronic Disease	163
Epidemiological Approach to Dental Caries	165
News Notes	
National Organization for Public Health Nursing	167
American Red Cross	167
At Last Something Is to Be Done about Gonorrhea!	167
Book Note	
Prophylactic Odontotomy	168
Report of the Division of Food and Drugs, April, May, June, 1933	169

FOREWORD

In presenting this epidemiological number of The Commonhealth, the Massachusetts Department of Public Health is not attempting to bring out a complete case book of epidemiology. To do so would be presumptuous, as the field is too large to come within the scope of any one group. Nor has it been assumed that a complete epidemiological picture of any one disease has been presented. The desire which has motivated the preparation of this issue has been simply to make available for others some of the epidemiological data which has accumulated in the Departmental files.

Much of the material has never been previously published, as it hardly warranted the usual formal type of essay. Yet in the file of every department may be found many brief bits which may be helpful to others who are interested in disease prevention.

The material has been presented in case form for purposes of simplicity and ease of reference. In a few instances certain errors which temporarily obscured the picture have been emphasized merely to point out certain pitfalls to be avoided. Man learns only through careful review of his mistakes; to turn his back on them is to delay progress. If the material here presented for review is of any assistance to others faced with epidemiological problems, the work entailed in its preparation will have been well rewarded.

EPIDEMIOLOGY

Epidemiology is the science of the occurrence of disease. It attempts to determine the conditions under which disease may develop, the cause of it, the predisposing factors and those natural phenomena which tend to prevent it. The aim of epidemiological research is thus to answer the very important question "Why does a disease occur?"

Originally, epidemiological study was limited to the so-called epidemic diseases, those which were obviously communicable, spreading through a population. From the earliest time man had striven to learn the reason why the plagues and pestilences occurred so that he might guard himself against them. Although many of his theories as to the ultimate cause of these diseases may seem somewhat naive in the light of our present knowledge as to bacteria, we should not forget that many of the essential epidemiological facts were discovered and put to use. Long before the discovery of the plasmodium of malaria and the recognition of the mosquito vector, it had been recognized that malaria was associated with swampy lands. Many very primitive peoples had learned to avoid the low-lying countries during the summer months. The discovery, centuries later, that it was the mosquitoes breeding in these swamps rather than the supposedly bad air (mal aria) emanating from them that caused the disease was but a refinement of knowledge which permits us to direct our control measures with greater precision. Similarly with typhoid fever, the clear-cut epidemiological observations of William Budd which preceded the recognition of the importance of bacteria as a cause of disease, pointed the way to the prevention of this disease, which was, at the time, the most important single cause of death.

With the development of the sciences of bacteriology and immunology, epidemiological research has pushed ahead rapidly. No longer have our observations been limited to the study of the environmental factors. We have been enabled to learn some of the very vital factors which determine individual resistance to disease. We have been permitted to study the bacteria as they entered the body, observe their effect in the human system, trace them as they left the body and observe their extra-corporeal habitat. The factors which have acted on these bacteria both inside and outside the body have come under study, as well as the response of the system to the presence of these invaders. In this way our store of epidemiological knowledge has been tremendously enriched but with each addition there have been opened new avenues for investigation which may lead to an even clearer understanding of the disease. Rich as may be our knowledge of some diseases, we have probably but scratched the surface even of those which we think we understand the best. In the case of some diseases we are quite frankly wandering through a forest, and although the trail may at times seem somewhat more clear than formerly we still stumble against obstacles which as yet we have not surmounted. The importance of careful observation and controlled research of even the most minute points cannot be overstressed if we are to broaden our knowledge and learn those vital factors which are essential for disease prevention.

It would be unfortunate, however, were we to assume that epidemiological research must be limited to those diseases caused by microörganisms. To do so would be to lose sight of one of the most fruitful fields for discovery. Underlying every disease condition are certain epidemiological factors which are deserving of study. The recent developments in the science of nutrition have furnished striking examples of the possibilities of epidemiological research in non-infectious diseases, with results of far-reaching importance in prevention. Every disease process has a reason for its development and unless the factors which determine this departure from the normal are understood, little systematic progress in prevention can be made. Just as important as the discovery of the cause of cancer is the recognition of those elements which predispose toward its development. Together they constitute the epidemiology of the disease. Neither is complete without the other. According to the extent to which they are understood will prevention be possible.

There is no royal road of epidemiology. Although certain methods of study are applicable to all conditions, each disease, just as it has peculiarities which distinguish it from other diseases, has the special characteristics which modify the epidemiological approach. All facts which may shed light on the problem of why the disease occurs must be studied thoroughly and the truths learned interpreted in the light of other knowledge. It is only through such study of the facts underlying the occurrence of disease that progress will be made in man's fight for disease prevention.

TYPHOID FEVER

As has been frequently pointed out by Rosenau, a typhoid infection occurs as the result of a short circuit between the intestinal tract of one person and the alimentary canal of another. Every typhoid infection means that the organisms which are given off from a typhoid case or carrier are taken into the mouth of the new victim. The problem for the epidemiologist is to discover this short circuit, to solve the problem of whence came these bacteria.

Ultimately every case of typhoid fever is traceable to another case or carrier, as no reservoir of the disease is known outside of the human race. In former years in this State, and even today in other parts of the world, many of the cases are due to other cases whose excreta pollute water intended for drinking. Such an event is extremely rare in Massachusetts today, owing to the extensive development of public water supplies and sewage disposal systems. Consequently the few cases today that are traceable to other cases occur primarily among family contacts. With the more universal observance of anti-typhoid vaccination of these contacts, such cases are of less frequent occurrence.

The greater part of the residual typhoid in the State is due, without doubt, to direct or indirect contact with carriers of the disease. It is probably a safe estimate that approximately one thousand such carriers are living in this State today; less than one hundred of these are known. Every case of typhoid offers an opportunity to recognize one of these carriers. Such recognition means that the carrier, being appraised of the condition, will be far less likely to impart the infection to others. Yet discovery of these carriers presents many difficulties. The majority of the cases now occurring in this State have little, if any, apparent connection with one another. When a group of cases occurs the discovery of a common factor is relatively easy and will narrow the search. The sporadic cases which constitute the major part of our present typhoid problem offer few such clues. Our present day society is so organized that scores of persons may have handled the food consumed during a single week. The discovery of which one of these (assuming that they may all be found) may be a typhoid carrier, is a problem beset with such difficulties that failure is more frequently the reward than is success. Yet it is these difficulties and the vital importance of discovering a carrier, who, if unrecognized, might infect others, that should inspire the investigator to the most careful and thorough search.

Ultimately, of course, we may look forward with reasonable assurance to the time when typhoid fever will be even more rare than today. In a state in which 97% of the population live in communities with public water supplies and 85% in those with public sewage disposal facilities, and in which 85% of the milk is pasteurized, we may feel with some assurance that we will see no return of those major epidemics of typhoid. So long as the number of cases can be kept at the present low figure, or even lower, the number of carriers in the community will rapidly decrease, not through discovery and cure but through death from natural processes. Each year more unrecognized carriers die of natural processes than are created in virtue of recent infections. The community is thus rapidly and surely sterilizing itself of typhoid carriers and may confidently look forward to the time when even our present low rates will appear large in comparison. Until such time the discovery of the sources of typhoid infections will continue to offer a challenge to the ingenuity of the epidemiologist.

Polluted Water Supply

In L (85,000 population), seven cases of typhoid appeared as follows:

Report	Name	Age	Onset	Incubation period
Sept. 26	A. F.	15	Sept. 14	17 days
Sept. 26	C. G.	14	Sept. 25	28 days
Sept. 30	J. C.	12	Sept. 16	19 days
Oct. 1	V. Z.	11	Sept. 13	16 days
Oct. 1	R. B.	11	Sept. 17	20 days
Oct. 6	S. R.	8	Sept. 16	19 days
Oct. 11	A. B.	13	Sept. 26	29 days

After the first two or three cases appeared it became evident that aside from the fact that all lived in the same city the only common factor was their attendance at a picnic held on August 28. As other cases were recognized it was found that they too had been at the picnic, which had been attended by between two and three thousand children as guests of the playground department. Everybody at the picnic had brought his or her own lunch, precluding the possibility of the cases being due to a carrier who had infected the food served. Although it was possible to buy refreshments at the picnic grounds, at least four of the group insisted that they had purchased nothing as they had no money. On repeated questioning as to the water which they had drunk all acknowledged having drunk from a certain faucet apart from the regular drinking fountains. Although others who escaped typhoid had used this water, some of them, as well as some of the victims, had had an acute diarrhea a day of so after the picnic. The faucet described was readily located and found to be part of a separate water system derived from a river known to be polluted and intended only for purposes of flushing the toilets and sprinkling the grounds. It had, however, not been labelled to show that the water was not safe for drinking.

Discussion:—In the above instances two factors pointed strongly toward a water-borne infection, the incubation period and the preliminary diarrhea. Water-borne typhoid tends to have a longer incubation period than does that due to infection spread through milk or other foods. When it became apparent that the only factor in common had been attendance at the picnic, the incubation period could be readily estimated. Had this been a food-borne outbreak, although some of the cases might have had a long incubation period, some cases could have been expected in which the period was much shorter. That none such were found pointed toward a water-borne infection.

It is a common observation that in a community outbreak of water-borne typhoid a wave of gastro-intestinal conditions precedes the appearance of the cases of typhoid. (The experience of Olean, N. Y., described by Dean in the April, 1931, issue of the American Journal of Public Health, page 390, presents a striking example of this phenomenon.) In the case of these children, careful questioning brought out the fact that certain brothers and sisters who had escaped typhoid, though using water from this faucet, had experienced the diarrhea 24 to 48 hours later. Although little is known as to the factors which cause this diarrhea, it is so well recognized as a forerunner of water-borne typhoid that such an occurrence in a community merits careful study to rule out the possibility of pollution of the water supply. It should not be inferred, however, that every instance of a community outbreak of gastro-enteritis is a forewarning of typhoid, or proof of sewage pollution of the water supply. Such, in fact, is far from the case. Such an assumption would unjustly cast suspicion on many perfectly satisfactory supplies. Much remains to be learned of these outbreaks. The alert health officer and water supply official will, however, remember that such occurrences may, in some instances, be a forerunner of typhoid and investigate them carefully.

The above outbreak serves to call attention also to the menace of polluted water supplies which are accessible to the public. If such must exist they should be carefully labelled to minimize the possibility of their use. In this instance there was nothing about the faucet to suggest that this water differed in any regard from that elsewhere used in the picnic grounds. It is hardly to be wondered that persons brought up to look upon the water obtained from the faucet as safe for drinking should have used this polluted supply without question as to its safety.

Water Polluted Through Faulty Cross Connection

City L, population 85,000, had for a number of years an incidence of typhoid somewhat above the average for the State. Little notice was therefore taken of the first few cases of the following series:

Date of report	Name	Age	Occupation
Jan. 15	C. D.	18	Mill worker
Feb. 7	A. B.	43	" "
Feb. 11	J. F.	27	" "
Mar. 10	C. B.	20	.. ..
Mar. 11	F. A.	30	.. ..
Mar. 15	S. R.	21	
Mar. 28	A. P.	23	
Mar. 28	N. B.	30	
Apr. 10	E. L.	30	"
Apr. 10	G. C.	23	.. "

That they were mill workers excited little attention in a city of mills. Three weeks intervened between the first and second, then four days between the second and third. As these latter two knew each other they might have had a common source. When a month later cases reappeared it became apparent that these must be more than sporadic cases without connection one with the other. All of the cases were employed in the same mill (which employed hundreds of workers) and, even more important, all worked in the same section. Obviously then, certain factors were at work in this section of the mill which were leading to typhoid fever·among those here employed. As the conditions under which their meals were eaten at noon were the same as elsewhere in the factory the possibility of a carrier in the mill being responsible for the infections was very remote. This left as the most likely source of the infection the water supply, which, however, was the same in all sections of the mill. Samples of water taken from bubblers in this section where the cases of typhoid had occurred showed evidence of pollution; specimens from bubblers in other sections were safe for drinking. Careful tracing of the pipes in and leading to this section showed that there existed a cross connection between the city supply and an emergency supply which, because it was intended for fire purposes only, had been obtained from the cheapest possible source, namely, the river which was known to be grossly polluted. A single-hinged check valve, designed to prevent the polluted water from entering the pipes carrying the pure water, had become so crusted with tubercles of rust that it failed to make a tight seal. The grossly polluted water had thus entered the water supply of this section, contaminating the whole system. When the connection was broken the outbreak stopped promptly.

Discussion:—Viewed in retrospect, and after all the cases have been brought to light, any typhoid outbreak appears simple of solution. Most of the above cases, however, did not appear until after the cause of the outbreak had become apparent. The long incubation period of water-borne typhoid, averaging 14-17 days, makes it inevitable that many cases of the disease which would have aided in the investigation will not appear until too late to be of assistance.

In the above instance the first case apparently excited little suspicion, being considered as "just another case of typhoid". The second and third, occurring together in friends, were apparently considered related, but that they worked in the same mill was thought to be pure chance. That a month elapsed without additional cases being reported must have substantiated this belief. When, however, additional cases began to appear in rapid succession it was quickly apparent that certain factors were in operation which had been overlooked. The outbreak illustrates well the danger of a too ready conclusion that the case in question was infected from unrecognizable sources.

These cases also emphasize the danger that lies in the cross connections which exist between pure and polluted water \supplies. In order to obtain low fire insurance rates a dual source of water for fire purposes is installed. To pipe the two supplies to all corners of the mill with sprinkler connections on both is expensive. A far cheaper solution is found through connecting the two systems so that if the pressure falls too low in the city supply within the mills, the emergency fire pumps may come into action to furnish water for the other supply. As this is intended only for fire purposes it is obtained from the cheapest available source which is usually the river along which the mill is located. In almost every instance the water of this river is so polluted as to render it unsafe for drinking. In order that the emergency use of this extra supply shall not contaminate the mains of the pure supply, an automatic check valve is installed. This often consists of a hinged clapper which is supposed to seat upon a metal cuff whenever the pressure of the polluted supply exceeds that of the pure, thus preventing mixing in the mains. Thus the only mixing which can occur is within the mill itself, or if the valve is so located, within the sprinkler system of the mill.

Although the theory underlying these valves is sound, experience shows that they do not always function as intended. If, as is frequently the case, the valve on the cuff is made of iron, the constant contact with the water results in the formation of irregularly shaped tubercles of rust. These may become several millimeters in thickness and prevent the valve from closing properly. Thus whenever, either because of actual use in extinguishing a fire or at the time of testing the condition of the fire pumps the pressure on the polluted side exceeds that on the pure, water which is unsafe for human consumption leaks through and may at times cause typhoid in those who may consume it.

Such hazards may be averted by (1) entire separation of the systems, which is expensive, (2) the installation of automatic chlorinators which start to function whenever the fire pumps are started, or (3) the installation of double check valves of noncorrosible material, installed some distance apart so that a foreign object which might obstruct one valve would not affect the other, and most important of all so installed that they can be periodically tested to prove that the valves are operating properly. So long as such cross connections exist it is imperative that the valves to protect the pure supply be tested frequently.

Milk Infected by a Carrier

Three cases of typhoid fever occurring in school children in a town of 6,000 population focussed attention upon the source of milk furnished at the school, as this was apparently the only food that the cases had in common. This milk was obtained from the R farm, which left much to be desired from the point of view of cleanliness. Although Mrs. R gave a history of having had typhoid fever a number of years prior, her stool and urine specimens were consistently negative. As the investigation progressed, however, additional cases appeared in the town, 23 cases being ultimately reported. All but a few of the school children had been obtaining raw milk from the J route, either in their homes or place of employment. Further investigation showed that J had frequently sold milk to R, so that some of that used in the schools might have been produced on the J farm. A temporary helper on this farm, who had told a fellow employee of having had typhoid several years earlier, had left the farm before the investigation was made. He was finally located and found to be a typhoid carrier. As he knew no other mode of livelihood than dairy work he submitted to gall bladder removal to be cured of his carrier condition. The bile was found to be positive for typhoid organisms both before and at the time of operation. Gall stones were present. He was followed with monthly specimens for over a year. All of these as well as a bile specimen a year after operation were negative for typhoid, attesting to the cure of his carrier condition.

Discussion:—The above is a typical outbreak of a milk-borne typhoid, the milk being infected by an unrecognized carrier. The exact time and mode of infection of the milk is usually difficult or impossible to determine. In some instances as above, it may be in the course of the milking, the infection being transferred from the hands of a carrier employed as a milker. If so-called "wet milking" is resorted to, the chances of such infection are increased. In other instances infection may occur during the course of the bottling or even the capping if this is done by hand. Such accidental infections are virtually impossible to prevent in spite of the utmost precautions. Cleanliness, mechanical processing of the milk, and testing of milk handlers minimize the chances. Pasteurization through its destruction of typhoid and other pathogenic organisms supplements the other safeguards, throwing around the milk supply a factor of safety not obtainable in any other way.

This outbreak illustrates the necessity of detailed and careful investigation of the exact source of any milk under suspicion. It is common practice among milk dealers to purchase from one another as extra amounts may be required. In any investigation of a milk route it is therefore necessary to inquire carefully as to supplementary supplies.

Cure of the carrier condition, as above, is the ideal solution of such a problem. Non-surgical measures of cure are notoriously unsuccessful. As the infection usually is located in the gall bladder, removal of this organ usually results in cure of the carrier state. As almost invariably such carriers have gall stones (of fourteen known carriers who have come to operation in this state all have had stones), the operation is of benefit for the carrier as well as for the protection of the public health. Before operation is undertaken it is well to make certain by examination of bile obtained by duodenal tube that the infection is actually located in the biliary tract. In this way operation on the purely intestinal carrier who could obviously not be benefited by gall bladder removal may be avoided. After operation it is well to make certain through repeated stool examinations and through further bile examination that the carrier condition has been cured. The examination of the bile specimen is especially important as was found in another state, a carrier being released from supervision after operation on the basis of repeated negative stool specimens, only to find later, in connection with another outbreak, that she was still a carrier, as proven by a positive bile specimen. The cure of carriers is a worth-while undertaking if used selectively so as to limit it to those who have a reasonable prospect of cure, and if such carriers are followed with sufficient care afterwards to make certain that a cure has been accomplished.

Milk Infected by Unrecognized Case

On investigation of a case of typhoid fever in the person of M. T., age 5, it was found that whereas all the other members of the family had been using pasteurized milk, this one child had been fed raw milk because she was below "standard" physically and needed "building up". This milk had been obtained from a neighbor who had a single cow. The rest of the milk from this cow had been distributed in three directions. Part had been sold to a family of foreign extraction whose racial custom it was to boil all milk before use. A second part was used at the farmer's home entirely for cooking, neither he nor his wife using milk in any other way. The remainder had been fed to the chickens. Thus the only milk from this source used raw was consumed by the child that developed typhoid. Shortly before the case occurred the farmer had employed a man, among whose duties was that of milking. He had been feeling poorly for some time but had continued at work, being unwilling to "give in". He had finally left about a week before the child became sick with typhoid. He was located about two months later and acknowledged having felt poorly for several weeks, though he had not consulted a physician. He had now completely recovered. Although repeated stool and urine specimens were negative for typhoid, his Widal reaction was strongly positive.

Discussion:—Although it is impossible to prove that this milker actually had typhoid, the history of the illness which he "fought off" and the strongly positive Widal reaction would indicate that in all probability he continued at work while ill with an unrecognized typhoid fever. Before he was finally located he had had ample time to recover from a temporary carrier condition. The case illustrates well the menace attendant upon the continuance at work of a milk handler who is suffering from an undiagnosed illness. Much as persons may be proud of their ability to keep at work without "giving in," to do so may, as in this instance, constitute a distinct hazard to others.

Contact With a Case

G. G., age 7, developed typhoid fever about November 4, the source of the infection being undiscovered. On November 13 he was admitted to a hospital where the diagnosis was made and the case reported on November 16. No attempt was made to inoculate the thirteen other members of the family. Additional cases developed as follows:

Onset	Name	Age	Relation
Nov. 17	P. G.	42	father
Nov. 22	C. G.	15	sister
Nov. 25	R. G.	40	mother
Nov. 28	Y. G.	5	sister
Nov. 28	S. G.	4	brother
Nov. 28	H. G.	12	brother
Dec. 15	F. G.	10	brother
Dec. 24	D. G.	3	sister
Dec. 27	M. G.	8	brother
Dec. 28	B. G.	1	sister

Discussion: Of thirteen family members in contact with the original case, ten contracted the infection. The dates of onset strongly suggest that all were secondary infections due to contact with the original case. The father with an onset 13 days after the first might have been either a secondary case or infected at the same time with a longer incubation period. The same is true for those with onsets varying from November 22 to November 28, though here the difference of three weeks is much more suggestive of secondary cases. The last four are unquestionably secondary.

Many of these cases might have been prevented had all members of the family been immunized as soon as the first case was recognized. No one knows exactly the time when immunity is produced by typhoid vaccine. It is hard to say therefore that it would have prevented or altered any of those cases occurring within two weeks of the discovery of the first case. It would certainly have prevented the last four cases.

The exact value of immunization after infection has occurred is a matter which merits further study. One of the best reports on this subject is to be found in the work of Crouch in the Public Health Reports for October 10, 1930, who found that among those inoculated after infection had occurred there was a slight protective value and a definite tendency toward a lessening of the severity of the infection. It is certainly common experience that, if all family contacts of a case of typhoid are inoculated promptly, secondary cases rarely occur.

Repeated Cases From One Carrier

Mrs. X was found to be a typhoid carrier in 1926, suspicion being directed toward her in the course of the investigation of the source of infection of her two grandchildren. On inquiring carefully into her history it was learned that she had had typhoid fever in August, 1899. The following month her daughter contracted the infection. In October, her husband and two sons were taken sick. No further cases occurred among her contacts until 1907 when three cases of typhoid occurred in a family taking milk from the X farm. In 1911, another daughter had typhoid. August, 1913, a grandson who often ate at Mrs. X's house contracted the disease. Another case apparently due to the milk, occurred the same year, Mrs. X having washed the milk pails and other utensils. Likewise in 1913, a visitor at the X home developed typhoid. The next year a farm hand was infected. Finally, in 1926, the two grandchildren referred to above contracted typhoid fever.

Discussion:—The foregoing trail of typhoid due to one carrier is strongly suggestive of the tale of "Typhoid Mary". Only the fact that but rarely did she prepare food for others than members of her own family (who had already been infected) prevented a wider spread of the infection. Had it been earlier noticed that repeated cases of typhoid were occurring in this family, the carrier might have been discovered years before the infections which led to her recognition. Investigation of any case of typhoid is incomplete unless a detailed search is made for previous cases in relatives not necessarily members of the household. In this instance had the investigator of the 1926 cases, finding that the mother who had had typhoid was not a carrier, been satisfied as to his inability to find the source of the infection, the carrier would have escaped detection and might well have caused other cases in the future, as she had in the past. Inquiries as to other relatives who had had typhoid brought to light the chain of events leading to the recognition of the carrier.

Chance Infections From Carriers

A. Mrs. M., aged 48, was found to be a carrier in connection with the investigation of a typhoid outbreak in a girl's college. All of the eleven cases were among girls or employees who had been eating in the lunch room, in which Mrs. M. was employed as the cook. Her Widal showed partial agglutination (microscopic method) and two stool specimens were both positive for typhoid bacilli. She denied having had typhoid fever and when first questioned denied any protracted illness. On subsequent questioning, it was learned that her first husband had died twenty-two years prior of an illness considered to have been tuberculosis, though its total duration was less than one month. Immediately following his death she was ill in bed for about two months with malaise and weakness. No definite diagnosis of her condition had been made, though it had been variously pronounced as grippe, nervous breakdown and exhaustion. For the ten years following his death, she was employed by this same college, principally in a food-handling capacity. No outbreaks of typhoid occurred in the college at this time. She then remarried, but three years prior to the current outbreak she resumed her work, taking a place as cook in a small restaurant in a large city. It was impossible to determine possible typhoid infections caused in this way, though there was never any suspicion directed toward the restaurant. After working here for a little over a year, she obtained a position as cook in a lunch room of a large department store, staying there a year and a half. This lunch room was patronized by public and employees alike, several hundred meals being served each noon. The presence or absence of cases among the public eating here was impossible to determine, but during the year and a half no cases of typhoid occurred among the several hundred employees. Mrs M. then entered the employ of the college, working for about a month in connection with the summer session and then assuming charge of the lunch room when the regular term opened the latter part of September. She continued to work there until she was removed on November 14. Several hundred girls ate there daily. The circumstances surrounding the cases proved almost beyond doubt that all of them were caused by a single article of food (presumably chicken croquettes) prepared by Mrs. M. on October 23. In other words, there was no evidence that she may have caused infections on more than a single day, and she almost certainly did not cause infection on any of the subsequent 22 days before discovery of her carrier condition.

B. Mrs. C., aged 58, had had typhoid fever twenty-one years ago. The discovery of her carrier condition resulted from an investigation of a case of typhoid fever in the person of her niece, a girl of twelve. Two weeks before the onset of her illness she had spent a few days in a summer camp with her aunt and grandmother, both of whom had had typhoid. Stool specimens from Mrs. C. were positive for B. typhosus, from the grandmother repeatedly negative. No known cases of typhoid fever had occurred in Mrs. C.'s family following her illness 21 years ago. For several years she had been very active in women's work in her church, frequently helping in the preparation of church suppers and recently having had complete charge of the same. Her principal interest and pleasure lay in the preparation of these suppers. At no time had any cases of typhoid been connected with these suppers, nor had there been any outbreaks of typhoid in this community for many years. The few cases of typhoid that had occurred in this town (a suburban community of 16,000 population) had all been of a sporadic nature (only 16 cases during the preceding ten years) so that it is hard to believe that her participation in church suppers had ever caused unrecognized outbreaks.

C. Mrs. R., aged 65, had had typhoid 29 years prior to her discovery as a carrier. It was not possible to trace her contacts with any degree of certainty for more than the eight preceding years. During this interval she had been employed as cook successively in two related families. In neither had there been extensive entertaining though relatives, had frequently been present for meals. Until the incident that led to the discovery of her carrier condition, no cases of typhoid had ever occurred among the members of either family, their relatives or dinner guests. Her discovery came as the result of investigation of the source of infection of a young man who shortly before his onset had visited for several days in the home where she was employed as cook and housekeeper. Her stools were positive for B. typhosus.

All three of the above carriers were persons noted for the cleanliness of their households and the neatness of their persons. The attention to cleanliness which characterized them was such as in each instance to be specially noted by those investigating the cases.

Discussion:—Owing to the dramatic nature of the story of "Typhoid Mary" it has been too often assumed that typhoid carriers usually leave behind them a somewhat extensive trail of disease, especially if they have been employed in a food handling occupation. Fortunately such is not the case, as illustrated by the three carriers here described. Frequently it is impossible to determine the extent to which infections have been caused owing to the fact that the group exposed to infection cannot be reached for study. In these instances, however, there seems little doubt as to the fact that although the carriers had been handling food for public consumption for a number of years, few if any infections had been caused before the incident that led to the discovery of the carrier condition.

The ability of a carrier to handle food without causing infections is quite apparent when the factors underlying the transmission of the infection are considered. In order that infection of another person shall occur the organisms must be passed in living condition from the body of the carrier, must be transferred to the hands, incompletely removed by washing, transferred before they have had time to die to a food that is to be eaten raw or incompletely cooked, and finally taken into the mouth of a person susceptible to typhoid fever. All of these variable factors must occur at the same time in order to complete the chain of events leading to typhoid infection from a carrier. If the chain is broken at any one of the many links infection at that particular time will not take place.

This obviously is not to be construed as minimizing the danger from the employment of a carrier in a public food handling capacity. This is so well known as to require no further emphasis. These instances are cited merely as examples of the fact that handling of food for a number of years without causing infection is not proof that a person is not a carrier or excuse for failing to investigate a possible carrier condition.

Infection of Family Contact by Carrier

A. In August, J. H. had typhoid fever, the source of his infection being undetermined. Although hospitalized he was released from supervision by the board of health without adequate cultures to determine whether or not he was still a carrier. In December of the same year his daughter developed typhoid fever, at which time stool and urine specimens were obtained from her father. The stool specimens were found to be positive showing him to be a carrier. As he had but recently recovered and might therefore be merely a transient carrier, additional specimens were obtained a year later which were likewise found to contain typhoid organisms.

B. On investigating a case of typhoid in the person of a man of 22, it was found that his mother with whom he was living had had typhoid fever seven years prior. No release specimens had been obtained from her during convalescence. Stool specimens submitted at the time of her son's illness showed her to be a typhoid carrier.

Discussion:—In both of the above instances the second case of typhoid within the family might readily have been prevented. It is hardly exaggeration to say that they were due to negligence. Healthy carriers of typhoid fever as spreaders of disease have been recognized for over 25 years. It is well known that a certain number of those who recover from the infection continue as carriers, the number being estimated as varying from 2 to 10%. The former figure is more nearly consistent with experience in this State. It is common practice in many states to consider as convalescent carriers those who are shedding the organisms during the first year after recovery and as permanent or chronic carriers those still positive after a year. Although Garbat in his monograph on typhoid carriers (Rockefeller Institute Monograph No. 16, 1922), considers that any person still shedding the organisms three months after the infection is a permanent carrier, there is considerable evidence that spontaneous cures, though infrequent, may occur after that time.

After a year, however, cure of the carrier condition without removal of the gall bladder seldom, if ever, occurs. In view of these facts, repetition of which seems almost superfluous, it is surprising to find that many cases of typhoid even today are released from supervision without an attempt being made to detect a possible carrier state.

Infections From Convalescent Carriers

A. J. S., age 4, developed typhoid fever about December 1. Careful questioning as to other cases of sickness in the family brought out the fact that A. S., his father, had been sick for a few weeks about a month earlier, the case being considered one of grippe or influenza. His Widal reaction was positive; typhoid organisms were found in the stool specimens. Additional stool specimens were obtained at frequent intervals during the next year, all of them being positive for typhoid, showing him to be a chronic carrier.

B. Three members of a family of seven developed typhoid fever. About a month prior their mother had taken a position requiring her absence from home most of the day. A friend, H. M., had come to live with them at this time to do the housework. For about six weeks before coming to them she had been sick at home. No physician had been in attendance. On the development of typhoid in the home to which she went, stool specimens were obtained from her and found to be positive for typhoid organisms. These continued to be positive for several weeks, ultimately becoming negative, indicating that her carrier condition was merely transient during her convalescence.

Discussion:—One of the most important aspects of any epidemiological investigation is the search for unrecognized cases which might have been the source of the case in question. Most diseases may occur in such mild atypical forms as to escape detection or recognition unless attention is focused on them. To ignore these is often to overlook the true source of the infection. In the former instance this would have been particularly unfortunate in that the father was ultimately shown to be a chronic typhoid carrier. Of course it is possible that he might have been a carrier as result of an unrecognized infection at an earlier date, and that the illness which preceded his son's typhoid infection was actually grippe or influenza as considered by the attending physician. This is a question which cannot be solved. There remains, however, the fact that in both instances search for other cases in the family revealed persons who were carrying the infection, and might, if unrecognized, have infected other persons.

Permanent Carrier at Four Years of Age

In July 1928, J. B., aged four, contracted typhoid fever. The source of his infection was not found. Stool cultures taken since his recovery have been consistently positive for typhoid organisms. In September 1929, a woman who had visited the home and come into rather intimate contact with J. B. through holding him on her lap developed typhoid fever. A few months later two playmates of J. B. developed typhoid. Two years intervened without cases of typhoid appearing in his contacts. In August, 1932, a child with whom he had played contracted typhoid. About the same time a child in a neighboring town with whom he had played while visiting with his mother developed the disease. A month later still another playmate came down with typhoid.

Discussion:—The above case emphasizes the fact, too often overlooked, that young persons may become permanent typhoid carriers, although it is true that most carriers are adults and usually in middle life, no age is spared. In this instance a boy of four became a chronic carrier as evidenced by the laboratory findings and the trail of typhoid which he left among his associates. At such an age the sense of cleanliness is so poorly developed, and the intellectual level is so unable to grasp a concept as difficult as that of the typhoid carrier state, that little cooperation from the child can be expected. Unfortunately in this instance the parents who should have grasped the significance of the situation seemed as lacking in appreciation of its seriousness as did the child. Had it not been for the refusal of the school committee to accept this boy as a pupil, unquestionably many more cases of typhoid would have been caused by him.

Carrier Employed in Restaurant

The city of Y (population 35,000), had been relatively free of typhoid fever for a number of years, averaging barely one case per year. In the ten months period March to December of one year, ten cases occurred as follows:

Date of report	Onset	Initial	Age	Occupation
Apr. 6	Mar. 28	E. B.	19	Oiler
Apr. 17	Apr. 6	M. S.	23	Weaver
July 19	July 3	R. C.	9	Student
Aug. 26	Aug. 16	L. G.	9	Student
Sept. 18	Sept. 6	A. L.	18	Clerk
Sept. 28	Sept. 3	P. T.	18	Laborer
Nov. 7	Oct. 1	E. P.	22	Carpenter
Nov. 7	Oct. 20	A. W.	6	Student
Nov. 7	Oct. 25	H. S.	32	Accountant
Dec. 2	Nov. 11	B. D.	11	Student

These patients were not acquainted with each other. Although they lived in rather widely separated sections of the city, none were from homes in the upper economic level. In almost every instance it was found that the person sick had eaten somewhere out of town, had been swimming in obviously polluted water or had drunk water of questionable safety. On review of the whole situation it was brought out that A. L., listed originally as a "clerk", was employed as a counter-man in a small restaurant which specialized on light lunches, largely frankforts, hamburg and other inexpensive dishes, usually consumed at the counter. This boy had been employed here for barely a month before he contracted typhoid fever. He obtained all of his meals at the lunch counter as part payment of his wages. Further investigation of this restaurant showed that the others employed there were a Mrs. T. and her daughter. They shared the responsibility for the cooking. Mrs. T. had had typhoid fever approximately twenty years prior. Two years later her daughter had contracted the infection, other members of the family escaping. Repeated stool specimens from Mrs. T. were consistently positive for typhoid organisms showing her to be a carrier. Her daughter's specimens were negative. On further questioning of the patients, who had been sick in preceding months it was impossible to connect any further cases with this restaurant. All, however, acknowledged having attended the moving picture theatre which adjoined it, and admitted the possibility that they might have stopped in for a frankfort or other sandwich after the show. Mrs. T. had purchased this restaurant in February, 1929. The cases began to appear in March. She was discovered in December, ceasing to work immediately. One case of typhoid, previously infected, was recognized a few days later. From this time until 22 months later no cases of typhoid occurred in the city.

Discussion:—Although the matter is one which does not admit of proof, it is reasonable to believe that in this instance the one carrier was probably the source of the infection of the majority of the cases. The sudden increase in typhoid fever occurred coincidental with her assuming a place as a public food handler. The cases ceased to occur as soon as she stopped handling food for public consumption. This seems more than mere chance. That the other cases did not recall eating at this lunch counter, does not conclusively prove that they were not connected, owing to the well recognized limit in human ability to remember details of events which were at the moment of apparently little significance. One needs only to attempt to make a complete list of places where he has eaten during the previous month to recognize the difficulty in such matters. In many of these instances several months had elapsed before the patients were questioned as to this particular restaurant.

This outbreak illustrates well the difficulties in finding the source of infection of cases which are not closely connected. Under the present organization of society several hundred persons may have handled the food that is eaten during the course of a month. It is therefore only mere chance, as above, that may direct the investigation toward a carrier employed in such a position. In this instance the infection of a fellow employee furnished the clue, yet even this would have been missed except for somewhat detailed questioning as to the patient's occupation. Only by careful and thorough questioning will such carriers ever be discovered.

Typhoid Carrier without Known History of Infection

Within a period of four days four cases of typhoid fever appeared among 125 pupils attending a private school. The only factor that was apparently common to all four was that all had had their lunches in the school dining room (two were day pupils having no meals at the school other than at noon). In the dining room they had been scattered at different tables, suggesting that the infection must have come from some person in the kitchen rather than from a person handling food in the dining room. Stool and urine specimens from all those employed in the kitchen, and later from other employees of the school and farms furnishing the milk were consistently negative. Finally a kitchen helper who had been employed for about four weeks before the outbreak and who had been discharged before the cases began to appear, came forward, because as she said, she had heard of the cases and that all the others in the kitchen had been examined so thought she also should be tested. Her stool specimens yielded almost a pure culture of typhoid organisms. She denied having been ill recently nor could she recall any protracted illness that might have been typhoid fever that escaped recognition. As she had of her own volition submitted to examination it is reasonable to believe that she was truthful in her statement that even though she was a chronic typhoid carrier she had not had typhoid fever to the best of her knowledge. .

Discussion:—That a person is a chronic typhoid carrier means that at some time in the past there has been a typhoid infection. Infection, however, does not necessarily mean the development of a recognized illness. In a given group of cases, all of which have derived their infections from a common source the cases may vary from the severe and even fatal type to the extremely mild ambulatory type which would have completely escaped recognition had not a determined search been made for it. It is apparent, however, that such cases may develop the chronic carrier state just as readily as do those with typical and severe cases of the disease. Proven carriers who have no recollection of typhoid fever or any other protracted illness are encountered so frequently that in any search for a carrier the source of infection may be frequently missed if attention is paid solely to those who recall having had typhoid.

The outbreak described above might, of course, have been avoided had the school authorities required an examination of all prospective food handlers before employment. In this climate there is one disease, typhoid fever, which may be frequently spread by food handlers. Although other diseases may be occasionally so spread they are of far less importance and prevention is infinitely more difficult. Examination of food handlers is but an empty gesture unless special attention is paid to the detection of a possible typhoid carrier condition. If this matter is dismissed with the mere denial of previous typhoid, certain carriers will inevitably be missed. Proof that a stool or urine specimen submitted to the laboratory actually came from the person in question is often difficult. In the Widal reaction there is frequently a useful guide in pointing the way toward the discovery of a carrier. In this State, 90% of the proven carriers (exclusive of those discovered through examination of specimens taken during convalescence) show an abnormal Widal reaction. Thus in a community such as Massachusetts in which typhoid immunization is rarely carried out, a Widal reaction which is not frankly negative may well excite suspicion as to the existence of a possible carrier state. It has the advantage that it is readily performed and that there is no question as to the origin of the specimen. In the above instance a Widal examination on the carrier showed a partial agglutination. The carrier state was proven by the isolation of typhoid bacilli from the feces. Had this school at that time, as it does now, required that as a prerequisite to employment in the kitchen, the person shall have been tested for a possible typhoid carrier condition, the four cases of typhoid that occurred would have been avoided.

Carrier Infections

A. B. L. developed typhoid fever on Sept. 1. As she had been in Maine from July 10 to September 1 it was apparent that the infection had been contracted there. The case was listed on the local board of health records as infected in another community and the matter closed. When a further investigation was made to obtain such information as might assist the Maine authorities in locating a possible source of infection of other persons, it was found that about three years prior her sister had come to live with her and the two had spent the summer together. This sister had had typhoid fever. Repeated stool specimens, and ultimately two bile specimens were consistently positive for typhoid organisms, showing this sister to be a carrier.

B. E. S. was admitted to the Quincy hospital as a case of suspected typhoid fever. Prompt investigation of the case by a representative of the Quincy Board of Health brought out the fact that this man had been working on a dredge along the Cape. It was also learned that other members of the crew had been sick, one of them being in a metropolitan hospital with an undiagnosed illness. This information was immediately relayed to the State Department of Public Health. Investigation of the crew of the dredge showed the cook to be a typhoid carrier. He had accompanied the dredge from an out-of-state port, the bulk of the crew having been acquired after reaching the Cape. Three cases were ultimately found in this group of about one dozen men.

Discussion:—The only purpose of epidemiological investigation of typhoid cases is to find the source of infection so that others will not be similarly infected. These cases represent the extremes in such investigations. In the former instance the investigator was too anxious to have a clean typhoid record for his community. Finding that the person was infected outside of the state, the matter was immediately dropped without even inquiring as to possible sources of infection, recognition of which would prevent infection of other persons. Ironically the source lay not in another state but in that very community for which he was so anxious to have a clean record. Undiscovered this person might easily have caused further cases.

The thoroughness of the investigation on the part of the Quincy Board of Health furnishes a very refreshing contrast. Although the case was obviously not infected in Quincy, and had been brought there only for hospitalization purposes, detailed information was obtained as to possible sources of infection. The one type of investigation served a useful purpose in that through it a carrier was found who, if undiscovered, might easily have caused more cases. The other type of investigation was but an empty form, serving no useful purpose.

Carrier or Contact Infection?

On October 12, A. S., a mill worker in a city of 100,000 population, developed typhoid fever. As his meals had been obtained largely in restaurants the names of which he could not recall it seemed apparent that this was a case infected from an undeterminable source. On October 21, E. B. developed typhoid fever and on October 24, B. B., his wife, likewise became ill. Mr. and Mrs. B. had been living for about two months at the home of his grandmother, M. M.; as both were working in factories, all of the cooking was done by the grandmother. The fourth member of the household, G. M., a granddaughter, was a close friend of A. S., the first case of typhoid. She and her grandmother both escaped the infection. The only time when the three persons who were ultimately sick were together was on October 12 when they, accompanied by Mr. and Mrs. B, had been to a park to see some fireworks. On this occasion, A. S., who was already feeling somewhat miserable from the first symptoms of what was later found to be typhoid, had purchased candy and popcorn which he shared with the group. On subsequent questioning it became apparent that he had at various times while calling upon G. M., eaten food prepared by M. M. She denied having had typhoid but acknowledged a protracted illness twenty-six years prior. Examination of her stool specimens showed her to be a typhoid carrier.

Discussion:—The mere fact that two weeks have intervened between the onset of cases within a single group does not necessarily mean that the latter are secondary to the former. The incubation period of typhoid is conventionally stated as varying from seven to twenty-three days, yet periods as short as three days and as long as thirty days have been encountered. Especially important and frequently overlooked is the fact that various members of a group having a single common exposure may present both extremes of incubation periods. In one instance in Massachusetts following a banquet the incubation periods of those who had no other connection with each other than the banquet, varied from four to twenty-nine days. In the instance cited above, assumption that because of the two weeks interval between the cases, those occurring later must have been secondary to the first case, would have only turned attention away from a carrier, who, in all probability, was the source of infection of the entire group.

The factor which first turned suspicion upon the grandmother was the fact that the granddaughter, G. M., who had had far more frequent contact with the original case than had her cousins, should have escaped. It would have been reasonable to assume that had A. S. been the source of infection of the others through so casual a contact she would likewise have been infected. It was especially significant that whereas the granddaughter had been living with the grandmother for many years, in fact since early childhood, the cousins had been in the household only two months and A. S., her friend, had been introduced to her barely six weeks prior. Thus of the group of five in or connected with the household, only those developed typhoid fever who had recently come within the circle. Apparently the granddaughter had, through repeated small doses of infection, established a resistance to typhoid without at any time manifesting any symptoms of the disease. This phenomenon is frequently encountered, the families of carriers apparently escaping infection; yet when a new and susceptible person is introduced into the family group, this person frequently contracts the disease. The most plausible explanation must lie in a resistance established through ingestion of doses of organisms too small to produce recognizable clinical symptoms, yet repeated frequently enough to produce a high degree of resistance. It is unfortunate that the Widal reaction is not a sufficiently accurate measure of immunity to be of use in measuring such a resistance.

Infection of Unimmunized Nurses

A. On January 13, R. M., a student nurse in hospital X, contracted typhoid fever and died. As she had during her hours off duty eaten at many restaurants and roadside stands, it was at first assumed that she might have contracted the infection in this manner. Her fiancé who had accompanied her on these occasions escaped. On February 5, Mrs. Z. and her daughter were admitted to the same hospital, ill with typhoid fever of at least two weeks duration. On January 3, Mr. Z. had come to this hospital where he had died following an operation for what was supposed to be appendicitis. Miss M. the nurse who died of typhoid had been on night duty in the ward where Mr. Z. was ill; she had not been immunized against typhoid fever. Although the matter is one which cannot be conclusively proven it is probable in the above instances that Mr. Z's illness was typhoid fever, that his wife and daughter contracted their infections from him and that Miss M. likewise was infected while caring for him.

B. On October 6, R. S., a student nurse in hospital Y, contracted typhoid fever. About two weeks prior she had given the admission care to a patient whose illness was subsequently diagnosed as typhoid fever. Miss S. had not been immunized against typhoid fever.

C. On October 5, B. R., a student nurse in hospital Z, and like the two nurses above not immunized against typhoid, contracted the disease while working on a ward containing two recognized cases of typhoid.

Discussion:—Although it is impossible to prove that all of the above infections were contracted in line of duty, such an inference is well founded. Typhoid fever was at one time one of the hazards of the nursing profession. Today, failure to protect the attendants of a case or those who may be exposed to an unrecognized case reflects little credit upon the hospital in which they are employed. In all well conducted hospitals, immunization of the nurses against typhoid, as against smallpox, diphtheria and, to an increasing extent, scarlet fever, is carried on as a matter of routine.

GASTRO-ENTERITIS

The term "food poisoning" as it is popularly used, covers a wide variety of conditions, ranging from bacillary dysentery to chemical poisonings having no relation to food. If we leave out of consideration the two extremes we have a group of conditions, formerly referred to as ptomaine poisoning, characterized by sudden onset, vomiting and diarrhea. In most instances several members of a family or group may be affected almost simultaneously.

With the discard years ago of the theory of ptomaines (chemical products of the decomposition of meat) there grew up a mass of evidence to associate such conditions with bacteria of the colon-typhoid group, those most frequently incriminated being B. enteritidis, B. aertrycke, and B. suipestifer. That illness followed the ingestion of food that had been cooked led to the discovery of the existence of heat stable toxins, chemical products of the bacteria which might cause severe irritation of the gastro-intestinal tract. Such infections have been more frequently reported in the foreign literature where there has appeared a strong tendency to ascribe the ultimate source of the infection to animal reservoirs. So strong is this tendency that the possibility of human carriers has at times been categorically denied.

In recent years another type of infection has come into prominence with the discovery by Jordan and his coworkers that in some instances the so-called poisonings might be due to heat stable toxins formed by certain staphylococci. Unfortunately as no laboratory test is known other than the feeding of toxic filtrate to human volunteers, progress along this line has been slow.

There remains, however, a large group of gastro-intestinal conditions, often occurring in epidemic proportions in which the explanation is far less obvious. As these are often clinically indistinguishable from the more conventional case of "food poisoning", there is a temptation to feel that the latter term is after all but an epidemiological description. The whole group is one which needs much further study before the tangled skein can be unravelled. The following cases are but samples of a few of the diverse conditions within this group.

Gastro-Enteritis Apparently Water-Borne
Cause Unknown

In C, a town of 3,000 population, about 500 cases of vomiting and diarrhea occurred within a single week. In many instances several members of a family were involved. There was nothing distinctive about the age distribution of the cases, the youngest being a baby of a few months and many cases appearing among elderly persons. Both sexes were equally affected. The earliest case had begun on a Friday, with more on subsequent days. School absences were most numerous on Monday, Tuesday and Wednesday, falling off rapidly thereafter. After Thursday no new cases occurred.

The distribution in the town depended more upon density of population than on any other factor. Although the majority of the cases occurred within a half mile radius of the center of the village, no inhabited street was altogether free of cases. In one section of the town which, however, derived its water supply from an adjoining community, no cases occurred. Similarly those families in the distant parts of the town and dependent upon private wells were spared except for the children who attended school in the village and while there used the public supply.

Examination of a sample of water taken at the time of the outbreak showed no evidence of pollution by either bacteriological or chemical tests.

Discussion:—Had these cases followed a banquet in which all had participated the clinical diagnosis would unquestionably have been food poisoning and careful search made for the organisms commonly associated with these conditions. In this instance the epidemiological evidence ruled out the possibility of a food infection, pointing very strongly to a water-borne source. Although there seems little doubt of the fact that the condition, whether due to a chemical irritation or a bacterial infection was associated with the water, the tests showed no evidence of pollution or any departure from the normal analyses made over some thirty previous years. As no chemicals were added to the water there was no possibility of overdosage. Perhaps had samples been obtained earlier some pollution would have been found. This seems somewhat unlikely owing to the fact that the supply was from driven wells in good condition, never previously associated with similar disturbances during the thirty years of their use. Furthermore during the two and a half years that have since elapsed the same wells have been used without further trouble.

Although the conclusion seems unescapable that the water was involved, the real cause of the condition must at present remain unknown. This is not an isolated instance as similar outbreaks have been encountered elsewhere. In some instances they have followed the blowing-off of the mains, yet this so frequently occurs without trouble that it is difficult to ascribe any etiological significance thereto. Perhaps further research may cast some light upon the cause of such outbreaks.

Gastro-Enteritis Due to Polluted Water

A. In F., a village of some 500 inhabitants, repeated outbreaks of gastro-enteritis had occurred for a number of years. Following each outbreak the householders had for a while boiled all the water from the privately owned supply. The owners of this had been repeatedly warned that it was open to pollution, its filtration was inadequate and that chlorination was essential. Ultimately about 100 cases of vomiting and diarrhea occurred at which time it was found that much of the water had been pumped directly from the stream into the mains without a semblance of filtration or chlorination. The cases as before were confined entirely to those using this water supply.

B. In N., a village of 2000, numerous cases of gastro-enteritis occurred among those using the water supply. Another village in the same township, but with a separate supply, and those using private wells escaped the condition. A few days prior, a heavy storm had severely scoured the watershed upon which (contrary to advice) the water company had permitted lumbering operations. Evidences of possible pollution were still apparent.

Discussion:—These two outbreaks illustrate well the types of gastro-enteritis due to the drinking of a sewage polluted water supply. As was pointed out when discussing typhoid fever a water-borne outbreak may frequently be preceded by a wave of gastro-enteritis, the exact nature of which is not understood but apparently due to the sewage pollution. If the pollution carries with it typhoid organisms from cases or carriers, typhoid may follow. If not, the gastro-enteritis may be the only result. In these two instances there was no question of the pollution of the supply as shown by the presence of bacteria characteristic of sewage. Nothing less than good fortune dictated that none of this should be from typhoid cases or carriers. In these instances, though the source of infection was known to be the polluted water, the clinical picture of the cases was indistinguishable from that seen in many cases of so-called "food poisoning."

Milk Borne Gastro-Enteritis

During a four-day period, 16 members of five related households were afflicted with a gastro-enteritis characterized by malaise, headache, abdominal discomfort, nausea, vomiting, diarrhea and moderate residual prostration. The acute symptoms lasted from 24 to 48 hours. The first case appeared on April 15, M. A., a farmer and dairyman, being roused from his sleep by vomiting and diarrhea. He was ill for two days, during which time he continued at his work caring for the B estate. This included the milking of the two cows and the straining and bottling of the milk. One of his grandchildren, who lived with him, was taken sick on April 17, two others on April 19. Four other members of the household escaped.

In the B household, eight out of ten members (including week-end guests) were affected. One of those escaping was a small baby whose milk came from a different source. The milk and cream used by the others came from the estate farm and was handled by M. A. All of the household, except two servants, arrived on April 17 and were taken sick on April 18 or 19.

The C household (son of owner B) was situated about two miles distant. They had not been at the B household for a meal. The milk used had come from the family estate. It was used raw by the householder and his wife, who were taken sick on April 19 and 18th respectively. The baby, age 4 months, whose milk had been boiled, was not affected.

The D and E families were neighbors of farmer A. In each household one out of five members was affected, sickening on April 19. In each instance the person ill was a child who on April 16th had attended a children's party at household A. No other members of these families had had any contact with the A family. The milk in each instance was derived from an outside source.

The outbreak was not brought to light until April 20th by which time all of the cases had virtually recovered, the guests having returned to the city. Stool specimens were obtained from five persons who were still suffering from a diarrhea, but yielded no organisms of the paratyphoid dysentery group. Similarly specimens from M. A., the first case, were negative.

Discussion.:—In three of the above households there was no factor in common other than the consumption of raw milk from a common source. The person who had cared for the milk had been ill a few days before with a similar condition and while sick had continued handling the milk. In the other two households the only persons sick had attended a party in the home of the first case. This combination of circumstances renders inescapable the conclusion that the illness had been spread through the vehicle of the raw milk and that the farmer who continued at work while sick had in all probability infected the supply. This explanation derives especially strong support from the fact that cases of identical illness occurred simultaneously in a household two miles distant having nothing in common with the other group except the milk supply.

Unfortunately no more exact diagnosis of the condition can be made than to call it a gastro-enteritis. Clinically it was no different from those cases following the consumption of water which is apparently polluted, nor does it differ from the typical "food poisoning". In the absence of definite bacteriological findings exact diagnosis is impossible. It differs from the more frequently occurring outbreaks only in the fact that in this instance raw milk was the vehicle for the spread of the infection.

"Food-Poisoning"

In three large and entirely unconnected industrial plants 151 cases of severe gastro-enteritis occurred on the same afternoon. The onset was in all instances within an hour after the lunch period. Predominant symptoms were acute abdominal cramps with vomiting and diarrhea. The only factor in common to the three groups was the purchase of box lunches from a single company, which on the day in question had sold no lunches at any other plants. All of those sick had eaten these box lunches, employees bringing their own lunches or eating elsewhere being unaffected. Questioning of 120 of those sick yielded the following information as to foods eaten:

Food	Number eating	Per cent ill
Jelly sandwich	90	75%
Ham sandwich	92	77%
Beef sandwich	88	73%
Pear	89	74%
Fig-newton	89	74%
Chocolate cream pie	116	97%

Even more significant than the above findings was the fact that 24 of these persons had eaten nothing but the cream pie. The four that were sick but had not eaten the pie were but mildly affected, complaining of "sour stomach". Their illness was apparently more sympathetic than real. Examination of the filling of the cream pie yielded an organism of the colon group, a staphylococcus and a streptococcus. Cultures of the food handlers yielded negative results. Chemical analysis of the pie showed no recognizable chemical poison.

Discussion:—The above outbreak is an example of a severe form of food poisoning. The onset within an hour after eating the pie, which was unquestionably the responsible agent, strongly suggests the presence of some chemical substance which was extremely irritating to the gastric mucosa. That the chemical irritant may have been a toxin produced by bacterial growth is possible. The more recent discovery by Jordan (to whom samples of this pie were submitted) that staphylococci can produce a soluble toxin resistant to heat, adds importance to the fact that staphylococci were found in the cream pie. At the time of the outbreak no attention was paid to this organism.

Outbreaks similar to the above have been frequently described due to the consumption of bakery products containing cream fillings. This material which is not thoroughly cooked is apparently readily contaminated and may even serve as a culture medium. The frequent practice of keeping the filling overnight before filling it into the final product may well add to the hazard.

Mild Carbon Monoxide Poisoning Simulating Food Poisoning

A. Poisoning following the consumption of dandelion greens dug from under a tree that had been sprayed with an arsenic solution was at first blamed for severe intestinal symptoms in all members of a family of five. Two weeks prior the physician had been called to attend two children that were unconscious. Both revived after rather severe vomiting. No diagnosis was made. On the second occasion all five members of the family had been found unconscious around the dining room table. As they were revived all showed a severe vomiting. Examination of the premises showed that the rooms were tightly sealed and that the water heater had been operating for several hours. Neither the kitchen stove nor the gas water heater were provided with any form of vent.

B. Two ladies sharing an apartment purchased some grapes from a street vender. Shortly after eating these both were attacked with severe nausea and vomiting, accompanied by loss of consciousness. A nurse who came to care for them was similarly affected within 48 hours. Owing to the recent purchase of the grapes it was at once assumed that these were the cause, especially as the nurse had eaten a few that were left. Examination of the apartment showed an unvented gas heater of a type incapable of caring for the gas pressure of the system in which it was installed. It was recommended that the heater be replaced or that when in use, ventilation for the apartment be provided. These suggestions were ignored owing to an insistence that the grapes had been the cause of the illness. Two weeks later after use of the heater without simultaneous ventilation of the apartment both ladies had a repetition of their previous illnesses, with severe nausea and vomiting.

C. Of three men occupying a ship at anchor two were found dead in their bunks. The third had severe nausea, vomiting and dizziness. A beef stew which the three had shared the previous evening was at first blamed especially as there had been some question as to its taste. The two that died had occupied bunks in the galley, where a wood fire had been kept all night. The one who escaped had slept in an adjoining room. Spectroscopic examination of the blood of the victims showed it to contain appreciable quantities of carbon monoxide. A fire was rebuilt in the stove, the drafts and hatches set as on the night of the tragedy and after a few hours samples of air taken in various parts of the cabins. Those from the bunks where the two men had died showed carbon monoxide present in dangerous proportions; in the other bunk somewhat less amounts were found.

Discussion:—All of the above three cases were at first considered as "ptomaine poisoning". In each instance it was possible to find some article of food that appeared at first glance as a plausible source of the trouble. Yet in each instance too ready an assumption that food was involved would merely have led the investigation away from the true nature of the condition, a carbon monoxide poisoning. Because of the popular attention given to the fatal cases of carbon monoxide poisoning due to the exhaust fumes of an auto in a closed room, the symptoms of a somewhat milder form of the poisoning have received somewhat less attention than they deserve. Though in most of the above instances the loss of consciousness might have suggested the true cause, some of those affected showed only a severe vomiting, which might readily have been interpreted as the result of a rather extreme type of food poisoning. That no diarrhea later occurred would naturally weigh against a food infection.

These cases are presented merely as examples of chemical poisonings which closely simulate the conventional food infections. Similar instances due to the ingestion of very minute amounts of potassium cyanide have been described by Williams (Journal of The American Medical Association, March 1, 1930 p. 627) In these instances the cyanide was a part of a silver polish which had apparently been incompletely removed from certain eating utensils.

BACILLARY DYSENTERY

Because bacillary dysentery has never been as prevalent in this State as in warmer climates, where environmental conditions are more favorable to its spread, and since the incidence has been still farther reduced by protecting water supplies and pasteurizing milk, it is easy to lose sight of the importance of the occasional outbreaks which do occur. One reason why this disease is more likely to escape notice is that the Shiga strain, which is responsible for the more severe type, is seldom found here. The strains usually isolated are the Flexner and Hiss-Y varieties. Because the organisms in this group are so closely related, it has been impossible to separate them into distinct strains. There has been a tendency, therefore, to be content to know that the organism isolated is a member of the group and call it paradysentery strain or a Flexner strain, using the term Flexner in its broadest sense. While usually less virulent, these organisms often cause fatal infections in infants and in the aged. Individual cases due to the Sonne strains are occasionally seen.

Family Outbreaks — Source Undetermined

A. In a family consisting of the grandparents, parents and five children, the grandmother was the first to show symptoms. She had a severe diarrhea and was quite weakened by the infection. A week later the grandfather had a light attack. A week later the mother had intestinal cramps and diarrhea, while the father had only nausea and vomiting. About the time the parents were at the height of their illness two small children began to have symptoms. One had a mild attack. The other became violently ill and died two days later. The illness of the family was not brought to official notice until after the death of the child and it was then too late to find the source of the original case. The succeeding cases were no doubt contact infections. Three weeks later another child had a similar gastro-intestinal upset and a dysentery bacillus of the Flexner group was isolated from a stool sample obtained from the child. It is reasonable to believe that the preceding cases were likewise due to the same organism.

B. Two children in a family became suddenly ill, vomited, complained of cramps and began to evacuate watery stools streaked with blood. The younger child became progressively worse and died forty-eight hours later. By this time the mother and another child were ill and the three were removed to a hospital. Two days later an infant and the remaining older child were also showing symptoms. The infant died within three days but all the others recovered.

Investigation of the water, milk and foods of the family failed to disclose the source of the organisms causing the original cases. Again the succeeding cases were probably contact infections.

C. A child of two and a half years became suddenly ill of cramps, vomiting and diarrhea. The temperature rose rapidly and the child became more and more prostrated, dying forty-eight hours later. The next day after the first child became ill, his sister, aged four, complained of similar symptoms. She was ill for three or four days and passed through an uneventful convalescence. A third child, aged five, who became ill two days after the second, had an attack very similar to the first and likewise died within forty-eight hours of the onset. The mother became ill about the time the third child began to complain, had a diarrhea for three or four days, and then recovered. The father and two older children escaped the infection.

It would appear that the two smaller children contracted the disease about the same time and that the other two cases were secondary. Search for the source of the infection was unavailing. No other cases occurred among those who were using the same milk. The children had not been away from home for a meal and no unusual articles of diet had been introduced into the home. The water supply, while not entirely satisfactory, did not appear to be involved.

Cultures taken from the intestine of the second child to succumb contained a dysentery bacillus belonging to the paradysentery group. It was felt that all of the other cases were caused by the same organism.

Discussion:—In each of these outbreaks a dysentry bacillus gained entrance into a family in some undetermined way. After the first case others contracted the illness by contact or through contaminated articles in the household. The cases varied from a mild diarrhea in the adults to fulminating infection ending in death in young children. These outbreaks emphasize the necessity of taking proper precautions when diarrhea breaks out in a family, particularly if there are young children.

Family Outbreak — Probably Spread by Water

A child of two became ill and developed a purging diarrhea. Two days later the mother became ill and in the succeeding two days three other children developed similar symptoms. Only two members of the family escaped the infection. Three of the children were so acutely ill that they were removed to a hospital, but they all eventually recovered.

The family had not been away from home for a meal, nor had they had any unusual foods in their home. No visitors except near neighbors had been in their home and there were no similar illnesses in the neighborhood. No fresh milk had been used as the family was in poor circumstances and usually used canned milk. The only thing upon which suspicion fell was the water supply. Water was used from a well across the street which was located in a barnyard. Animals came to the pump to drink and when the pump had to be primed, water was dipped from the horse trough. A few days later three other cases of diarrhea occurred in a family using water from the pump, but whether they were infected by the water supply or were contact cases from association with the family already ill could not be determined. One of the three, a woman of fifty-three, died, and bacillary dysentery was given as one of the causes of death. The well was condemned and ordered closed up.

Discussion:—Water-borne dysentery occurs very infrequently in Massachusetts because only a small proportion of the total population have to depend upon wells and unprotected supplies. Those cases which do occur are usually among persons who use water from wells and springs improperly guarded against surface pollution.

Institutional Outbreak — Spread by Contact

From June to October, one hundred cases of dysentery, with eighteen deaths, occurred in a mental disease hospital caring for 1750 patients. At first the cases were limited largely to a single ward—an infirmary ward caring for debilitated and bedridden patients. The epidemic was completely checked for a time after the initial outbreak and no additional cases were reported for over a month. When new cases began to occur practically every building in the institution was involved. Attendants on the male side were the first to become ill so it would seem that they were responsible for introducing the infection into those buildings. No doubt the spread on the female side occurred in the same way. The highest incidence of cases was in the wards where the patients did not go to the general dining rooms. The patients on these wards were less cooperative and at the same time less careful of personal hygiene than those going to the general dining room. The facilities for cleaning and sterilizing dishes on the wards was entirely inadequate and the chance of spreading an intestinal organism was very great. There was no explosive increase of cases at any time during the outbreak, from one to six new cases being the usual number reported each day.

An interesting feature of the outbreak was that the employees and stronger patients showed only mild symptoms, whereas many of the debilitated patients were acutely ill, some of them dying as a result of the infection.

Discussion:—The manner of spread of the infection in the institution would seem to eliminate the central kitchen, the water supply, and the milk supply as vehicles of transfer. If any of these had been involved, the outbreak would have been a much more explosive one, whereas the infection smoldered along all summer with small peaks at certain times. Such a course suggests very strongly that the transfer was largely by contact, with some spread in individual wards through the dishes and food served on the ward.

Institutional Outbreak — Spread by Milk

In a period of six weeks, over 125 cases of dysentery occurred in a mental disease hospital caring for over 2,000 patients. There were 17 deaths more or less directly attributable to the infection. The cases were distributed throughout the hospital, no group being entirely spared. Employees and more robust patients had very mild symptoms. Weaker and older patients became acutely ill and the fatalities were among this group.

Milk was one of the first vehicles suggested as the probable means of spread. Investigation showed that there was no diarrhea among the dairy herds owned by the hospital, and the bacteriological examinations showed that the milk in the dairy before and after pasteurization was satisfactory. Samples taken from the icebox in the kitchen also showed low counts. However, samples taken from the tables where the patients were eating contained from 500,000 to 1,000,000 bacteria, and dysentery bacilli of the Flexner group were identified in cultures from the milk.

All food handlers and milk handlers were examined in hope of locating a carrier. None of the 172 individuals examined were harboring dysentery bacilli. One patient sick early in the epidemic had a positive agglutination test with the Flexner bacillus. Before his illness and death he had been an active worker in the kitchen, usually distributing milk from the icebox to the various eating places.

Discussion:—It seems very likely that the patient who handled the milk may have been responsible for the widespread distribution of the infection. Just how he became infected and whether or not some other case or carrier also came in contact with the milk can not be determined. Many of the later cases were, of course, due to contact with those who became ill earlier. When the milk was properly safeguarded, the epidemic was soon ended.

Institutional Outbreak — Apparently Spread by Food

During two months a large number of cases of mild diarrhea occurred in a college of over 1,000 students. The cases were limited to two dormitories served by a single kitchen. The infection was so mild that the students did not report to the college physician until a few cases of a more severe nature occurred. Investigation then disclosed the fact that the malady had been prevalent for over a month. A check up of the cooks and other food handlers brought to light the fact that one of the maids was harboring a dysentery bacillus of the paradysentery group. A similar organism was isolated from two students who were ill at the time.

Discussion:—This outbreak illustrates the fact that dysentery in institutions of young healthy adults is likely to be very mild, due probably to the resistance of the individuals attacked. It appears likely that the infection was spread by food contaminated by a carrier or a mild case. Whether the maid found harboring the dysentery bacillus was responsible for the outbreak or whether she acquired the organism during the outbreak can not be determined.

STREPTOCOCCIC INFECTIONS

Hemolytic streptococci are responsible for a variety of infections. A striking characteristic of milk and food-borne epidemics due to these organisms is that instead of their producing a single type of infection in each epidemic, there may frequently be cases more or less representative of all varieties. While there may be a certain amount of specificity in the various strains so that a scarlet fever strain will produce scarlet fever and an epidemicus strain will produce septic sore throat, it is almost necessary to conclude that there must be a considerable amount of overlapping of toxic and infective characteristics. Were this not true, the epidemics would be limited more closely to a single type of infection.

It is unfortunate that a simple and accurate method of identifying each of the various strains has not been developed. This difficulty makes it impossible to eliminate the coincidental streptococcic infections derived, perhaps, from other sources and having no relation to the epidemic. Even so the epidemiology of the cases often suggests that the atypical cases seen are actually a part of the epidemic.

To account for this wide variety of clinical manifestations, it is necessary to postulate that the variations are largely due to differences in the resistance of the host rather than to differences in the characteristics of the causative organism. Facts accumulated from various epidemics would seem to substantiate this view. For instance, in milk-borne scarlet fever outbreaks, infants and small children usually have scarlet fever while adults in the families have only sore throat. Moreover, those giving a history of previous scarlet fever usually escape the rash even though they may have sore throat. The incubation period tends to be shorter in the young than in the old.

I. Scarlet Fever

Milk-Borne Infections of Varied Types

A. Some 70 cases of scarlet fever occurred on the milk route of a dealer whose milk went into three communities. There were nine cases among ten families in the town (population 6,500) in which the dairy farm was located. Seven additional persons had severe sore throat and four developed enlarged glands in the neck without particular throat symptoms.

In a neighboring community (population 21,000), a dealer was in the habit of buying 16 quarts of milk from the above milk farm and mixing it with his morning milking. The night and morning milkings were bottled separately. No cases occurred among those who were known to receive only bottles from the night milking. Five persons who took milk from this dealer had scarlet fever. One had septic sore throat and died of septicemia. Another had erysipelas.

In the city (population 70,000), where most of the milk from the farm was delivered, more than 50 cases of scarlet fever were found on the milk route and there were, in addition, many patients with sore throat, swollen cervical glands and other evidences of hemolytic streptococcus infection. A survey among customers of other milk dealers revealed practically no cases of throat infections.

In attempting to discover the sources of the organisms, it was found that the two members of the family who milked the cows had raw, inflamed throats and throat cultures showed that they were carrying hemolytic streptococci. One cow in the dairy herd was found to have mastitis and cultures from the infected quarter yielded hemolytic streptococci. The farmer claimed that milk from the infected cow had not been used for two weeks. Whether the organisms came from the milkers or from the infected cow will never be proved. The farm produced 160 quarts of milk per day, all of which was sold raw. The infected milkers were excluded from the dairy barn, the cow was ordered slaughtered, and the milk pasteurized. The occurrence of new cases ceased in less than a week. Hemolytic streptococci were found in the udder of the cow after slaughter.

B. Fifty-seven cases of scarlet fever occurred on a milk route of only 75 quarts. Thirty-seven of the cases occurred in the town (population 3,600) in which the milk was produced and 20 cases in an adjoining town (population 3,200). The high attack rate among those who used the raw milk is shown in the following table:

Attack Rate among Users of Infected Milk

Ages	No. of Persons in Household	No. Who used Milk	Scarlet Fever	Sore Throat	Total infections	Scarlet Fever	Sore Throat	Total infections
0-4	24	20	15	4	19	75	20	95
5-9	14	14	9	2	11	64	14	79
10-14	19	19	10	5	15	53	26	79
15-19	15	15	5	5	10	33	33	67
20-24	16	16	6	3	9	38	19	56
25 & over	79	64	12	19	31	19	30	48
Total	167	148	57	38	95	39	26	64

That the supply was heavily infected is suggested by the short incubation period as well as the high attack rate. In most cases, the period was apparently less than 48 hours and children were often ill in 24 hours. One adult died of complicating broncho-pneumonia and septicemia.

Search was made for the source of the organisms. There had apparently been no illness in the milk dealer's home during the weeks preceding the outbreak and there were no throat infections at the time of the investigation. There had been two cases of scarlet fever on the milk route just before the outbreak. Two cows in the dairy herd were found to have mastitis; one was harboring hemolytic streptococci, the organisms being found on the first sample taken from her and again after she was slaughtered. Because the epidemic began two days after the other cow was put into the milking line, it is not unlikely that she may also have harbored the same organisms earlier, even though none were found at the time of the investigation. It is probable, therefore, that the outbreak was caused by the organisms from one or both of the cows. Just how they became infected could not be demonstrated. The two cows were slaughtered, and the milk was ordered to be pasteurized. The outbreak came to an abrupt end.

Discussion:—These two epidemics illustrate the protean character of streptococcic infections spread by milk. The type of infection varied all the way from unmistakable scarlet fever with the characteristic rash, throat, tongue, fever, prostration, desquamation, and complicating otitis or adenitis, through the various milder forms in which some of the usual features were missing, to the other extreme where there was only a mild sore throat. In addition, there were sore throats with such complications as pharyngeal abscess, erysipelas, broncho-pneumonia and septicemia. There was hardly a form of streptococcic infection of the upper respiratory tract which was not seen. The high attack rates and short incubation periods are characteristic of milk-borne epidemics.

Spread by Milk, Probably Infected after Pasteurization

Nine cases of scarlet fever occurred on a pasteurized milk route in a city of 65,000. A visit to the homes of about half of the customers disclosed the fact that there was hardly a family using the milk in which there had not been some kind of upper respiratory tract infection. Children particularly were affected.

It was discovered that the milk dealer produced all of his milk on his own farm and that he did not handle the milk after it was delivered at the pasteurizing plant. He employed a man to deliver the milk who had no connection with the farm but picked up the milk at the pasteurizing plant after it was bottled. Careful questioning disclosed that fact that during June and July there had been some kind of an eruptive disorder among the individuals who lived on the milk farm and their nearby neighbors. This condition was said to be German measles. The dealer himself was one of the last ones to have the eruption, his rash appearing shortly before the middle of July. During all this time no such rashes were occurring among his milk customers.

About August 1, the man who owned the pasteurizing plant also had what he thought was German measles. He was not ill enough to stop work or call a physician. He continued to supervise the pasteurization of the milk and did a portion of the work himself. The milk was cooled by running over the exposed pipes of the aerator and cooler and was then bottled and capped by a hand-operated machine, so that it is conceivable that infection of the milk could have occurred after pasteurization. About a week later, cases of scarlet fever began to occur among customers using the milk supply mentioned above. There were no cases on the two other milk routes which were also pasteurized at this plant. The milk of the other two routes was mixed and pasteurized together. A number of customers of one of the other dealers were visited and no cases of illness of any kind were found in the households. Some kind of accident must apparently have happened to one milk supply, therefore, and not to the others, but it was impossible to determine whether the milk was infected by a member of the family of the milk dealer or by the owner of the pasteurizing plant.

Discussion:—Even though disease spread by pasteurized milk is extremely rare, the possibility of its existence should never be overlooked. No process is fool-proof, especially if it depends to some extent upon a human factor. The effectiveness of pasteurization is well proven by the extreme rarity of conditions such as the above, especially when it is remembered that many of those operating pasteurization plants have very little special training to qualify them for the work.

Except for the fact that it was on a pasteurized milk route, this outbreak varies very little from the characteristics illustrated in the two preceding epidemics.

Infection Spread through Food

In June, 1926, three outbreaks of scarlet fever occurred simultaneously in three separate cities. All of the individuals ill had attended banquets served by the same caterer on the same night. At least 138 persons out of 592 possibly exposed were ill, 98 with scarlet fever, the remainder with streptococcic infections without a rash. The incubation was short, in many cases being less than 24 hours.

The only article of food served at all of the three banquets, and not at four others prepared by the same caterer the same night, was lobster salad. Six employees of the establishment were found to have hemolytic streptococci in their throats, but it was impossible to say that they had not been infected after the outbreak since the cultures were not made until a week had elapsed after the serving of the banquets. The most probable explanation is that some employee was carrying the organism when the food was being prepared and infected the lobster salad.

Discussion:—Here again other types of streptococcic infection are present, contracted apparently from the same sources and produced by the same organism as the frank cases of scarlet fever seen in the outbreak. The salad was not all equally contaminated apparently, since a quarter of those exposed were quite severely affected while the other three-quarters showed no evidence of infection. Foods of this kind which are not eaten for some time after cooking and which have sufficient moisture to protect the bacteria have been responsible for a number of outbreaks, especially typhoid fever.

II. Septic Sore Throat

Septic sore throat is often considered an epidemiological rather than a clinical entity. Under such circumstances the term refers to a severe throat infection, often with complications, and due to the consumption of milk infected with hemolytic streptococcus epidemicus. It is unlikely, however, that such a narrow definition can be defended in the light of recent investigations. Pilot and his associates have repeatedly isolated the epidemicus strain of streptococci from the throats of persons whose infections were in no way due to infected milk. In some instances the same organisms have been found in the throats of healthy carriers. These findings naturally suggest that sporadic types of the infection may occur, spread through the same type of human contacts as are diphtheria or scarlet fever, and that the more frequently recognized milk-borne outbreaks develop simply through an udder infection with this organism resulting in a massive infection of the milk. It should be remembered, however, that in contradistinction to scarlet fever, secondary contact cases occur but rarely. Similarly, interest in the infections due to the epidemicus strain should not divert attention away from outbreaks which are clinically and epidemiologically similar but due to other strains of hemolytic streptococci.

Mild Sore Throat Spread by Milk Apparently Infected by Milker

In March, 1930, 178 cases of sore throat occurred in a town of 3,000 population. Of these, 164 cases were among members of families who used one milk supply. The case rate for this dealer was 55 cases per 100 quarts, while the highest rate for any other dealer was 7 per 100 quarts. Of the 331 persons in the families visited, 170 became ill, which is an attack rate of 51 per cent. Several developed cervical adenitis or otitis media as complications. There were no deaths.

The throat of one of the milkers was found to show evidence of a subsiding infection, and hemolytic streptococci were found in cultures from both milkers. The throat of the man who bottled and capped the milk was negative. No cows showed any evidence of mastitis nor were hemolytic streptococci present in their milk. While there was abundant evidence that the milk was infected, it was impossible at the time of the investigation to demonstrate the method by which the organisms got into the milk. It is quite possible, however, that one of the milk handlers was responsible.

Severe Sore Throat Due to Milk from Infected Cow

Of 23 persons using milk from a single cow owned by a neighbor, 20 contracted septic sore throat. The cow was cared for and milked by a hired man, and the milk in turn was handled by the housekeeper. The hired man claimed that the cow was in good condition, and when his attention was called to the mastitis in one quarter of the udder, he insisted that it was of no consequence. However, it was demonstrated that there were hemolytic streptococci both in the cow's udder and in the throat of the milker and the supposition was that the udder had been infected by the milker. At any rate, he apparently did not get the organisms, which he carried, from the cow because he used another milk supply in his own home, and moreover, he claimed not to have had a sore throat.

The attack rate was exceedingly high, 82 per cent of those known to have used the milk becoming ill. The owner of the cow and one of his daughters were victims of the disease, one dying of broncho-pneumonia and the other of septicemia. A third person died of erysipelas and septicemia. One other person was on the danger list because of pneumonia, but finally recovered. One unusual feature of the outbreak is the fact that it was largely adults in the older age groups who were exposed and became ill. The youngest person ill was a girl of eighteen.

Probable Effect of Dilution in Modifying Infection

In a town of 2,500 population, within a period of twenty-one days, seventeen cases of sore throat occurred. All but one case were on the milk route of one dealer. He delivered 1,080 quarts per day, 680 quarts being pasteurized and 400 quarts being raw. Thirteen of those ill were using raw milk and three claimed to have used the pasteurized milk. The only complication noted was cervical adenitis which occurred in seven cases.

Examination of the dairy herd failed to throw suspicion on any particular cow. Pooled samples from the cows were collected and one of the samples was found to contain hemolytic streptococci. Additional samples were taken from each cow whose milk was represented in the positive pooled sample. One cow was found to be harboring hemolytic streptococci. She was slaughtered, and on autopsy an abscess was found in one quarter of the udder from which the organisms were again isolated. A farm hand who occasionally helped with the milking gave a history of "a bad sore throat" three weeks before the outbreak. Again it is very probable that an udder infection was responsible for the outbreak.

Discussion:—In this group of outbreaks, we are apparently dealing with organisms which do not have the power of producing the skin rash seen in scarlet fever, but in most other respects the effects of infection are practically identical. The epidemiology is essentially the same. A person carrying the organism can usually be located on the milk farm or in the dairy and, in a large number of instances, a cow harboring the organisms is found in the dairy herd. When the milk supply is small, the attack rate is high, and the infection tends to be more severe. On the other hand, dilution in a large supply gives, a somewhat milder infection, and the attack rate is lower.

SMALLPOX

Outstanding among the epidemiological characteristics of smallpox is the striking protection afforded by vaccination. So successful has this been in preventing the disease that most latter day studies have been associated with this phase of the subject. We thus see a picture much altered from that of smallpox as encountered in a non-protected community. We are inclined to forget that normally smallpox has many epidemiological features simulating measles, notably age distribution and universal susceptibility. Like measles and in sharp contradistinction to diphtheria and scarlet fever, resistance does not develop without a frank attack of the disease, except such as may be artificially induced by vaccination. In the few instances here presented no effort has been made to do more than to bring forth additional evidence of the long duration of protection conferred by a single vaccination. It should be emphasized that in these few instances it was a mild type of smallpox against which the resistance was manifested. The question whether a similar resistance would occur for a more malignant type is not answered, though the bulk of evidence from other sources would suggest that it might not be of so high a level over so long a period of years.

Individual Protection Due to Vaccination

During the early part of December, Mrs. V. and her baby left Staatsburg, N. Y. to visit at Mrs. V's home in Williamstown. Shortly afterwards Mr. V. developed what was considered to be grippe. After spending two days in bed he began to feel better so decided to rejoin his

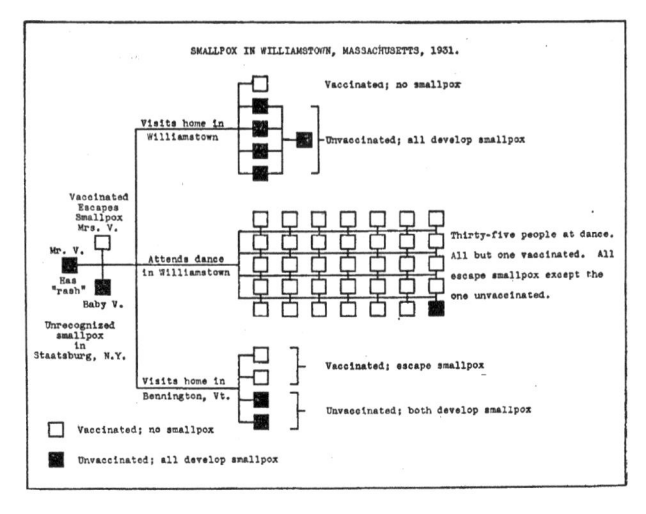

SMALLPOX IN WILLIAMSTOWN, MASSACHUSETTS, 1931.

family in Williamstown. Although he noticed the development of a rash on his body he paid no attention to it. He travelled by train to Bennington, Vermont where he stayed from 2 A.M. to 7 A.M. at the home of his sister. He then proceeded by bus to Williamstown, where he stayed for a few days. As he was feeling much better the night of his arrival he accompanied his wife to a dance. He and his family then returned to Staatsburg where he consulted his physician about the rash. A diagnosis of mild smallpox was made, which prompted an investigation of his Vermont and Massachusetts contacts. In Bennington, at the home of his sister, she, and her husband, both vaccinated, escaped. Their two children, unvaccinated, developed smallpox about two weeks later. At his wife's home, four children developed smallpox some two weeks after his visit; a baby contracted it some two weeks later, presumably infected by its brothers and sisters rather than by Mr. V. None of these had ever been vaccinated. Only the mother-in-law escaped; she had been vaccinated as a child. Of the thirty-five guests at the dance all but one had been vaccinated; this one contracted smallpox. Finally, in his own family, the baby came down with smallpox after their return to New York; his wife, who had been vaccinated some two years prior, escaped.

Discussion:—Few epidemiological investigations yield results which are one hundred per cent perfect. There are usually exceptional cases of susceptible persons who, though intimately exposed, escape infection, thus furnishing fuel to the flames of those who would doubt. Likewise there are instances of supposedly immune persons who contract the disease. To the person who attacks the problem with an open mind, these instances, rather than vitiating the remaining evidence, merely emphasize the fact that resistance is but a relative matter. What we call immunity is simply that level of resistance necessary to protect the individual from such a dose of infection as might be encountered under the usual circumstances of spread. It never implies an absolute protection against unlimited quantities of infection.

The above instance is particularly striking as an illustration of the high level of resistance against smallpox due to a single vaccination many years prior. Although the evidence is not presented as to the number of years that had elapsed since vaccination all of those attending the dance were young adults who had been vaccinated at the time of their admission to school, as required by law. The certainty with which the infection singled out the unvaccinated, while sparing the vaccinated, even though the exposure was presumably equal for all, is a striking example of the protection afforded by vaccination.

Community Protection Due to Vaccination

In the early part of 1932, some sixty cases of smallpox appeared in one section of Fitchburg. To prevent its further spread, vaccination of all residents was carried out, during the course of which data as to previous vaccination was obtained. Correlation of this with the reported cases yielded the following results:

	Number of Persons	Number of Cases Smallpox	Case Rate per 100,000 Population
Unvaccinated	5,457	57	1,048
Vaccinated over 40 years prior	4,926	3	61
Vaccinated during past 40 years	29,558	0	0

Discussion:—These figures furnish a very striking proof of the community protection which comes from a single vaccination in childhood. The majority of these had been vaccinated upon admission to the public schools. They had not been vaccinated since that time. As the city had been free of smallpox they had not had an opportunity to reenforce their resistance through exposure to the disease, the protection which they enjoyed being due solely to the previous vaccination. The form of smallpox which was present in Fitchburg was mild. As the evidence available (see especially Chapin and Smith, J. Prev. Med. 6:273, 1932) strongly suggests that this may be entirely different from severe and malignant smallpox, it would be hazardous to draw a conclusion that so high a level of resistance would persist against this latter type, as was evidenced in Fitchburg against the mild form.

Immunity of Long Duration following Vaccination

Of seven persons travelling from Florida to Massachusetts by automobile, three were found ill with smallpox on their arrival, and a fourth convalescent. None of these had ever been vaccinated. The other three had been vaccinated four, thirteen and sixty-four years previously. In spite of the fact that the entire group had been exposed to a known case of smallpox in Florida before their departure, and that the three had shared the confining quarters of a small five-passenger car with the four that had smallpox, they did not contract the infection. On subsequent vaccination all three showed a reaction of immunity.

Discussion:—The question of the duration of immunity following vaccination is one which occurs frequently, yet cannot be answered dogmatically. The figure most frequently quoted is seven years. In one of the above cases it was at least sixty-four years. Though this may be an extreme case, showing merely that under certain conditions the resistance may be of such long duration, the evidence here presented as well as that shown by the experience in Fitchburg and Williamstown show that so far as concerns community protection in a state such as Massachusetts, the effective immunity may be of much greater duration than the conventional seven years.

EPIDEMIOLOGY IN THE CONTROL OF TUBERCULOSIS

The greatest progress made in the control of tuberculosis during the past decade has been due to a more general recognition of the fact that the disease is as truly communicable as scarlet fever or diphtheria. For more than fifty years we have known that the tubercle bacillus is the only cause of tuberculosis, yet we have gone on treating the disease as though it were not contagious. When a case of tuberculosis has been diagnosed and sent to the sanatorium, and the doctor has given instructions for the disinfection of the patient's clothing and room, nothing more has been considered necessary until another case occurred in the family. The tendency of tuberculosis to "run in families" has been ascribed to "heredity" or "predisposition" and the obvious fact of infection generally overlooked.

If every case of tuberculosis had a rash or developed a cough within a week of infection, the problem of control would be relatively simple. Unfortunately, the incubation period is a matter of months or years, and by the time symptoms or physical signs warrant a diagnosis the patient has often infected other members of his family and helped to assure the immortality of tuberculosis. It would be as rational to hospitalize the recognized case of typhoid fever and forget the other members of his family who might be incubating the disease as it is to limit our control measures in tuberculosis to the clinical case.

During the past few years several organizations have adopted examination of family contacts as a method of case-finding in tuberculosis. In Tennessee, Bishop and Gass found that 23 per cent of the contacts of reported cases were suffering from tuberculosis. At the Middlesex County Sanatorium, Remick has been able to secure the examination of the family contacts of practically all of his patients on admission. There he has found approximately 20 per cent of such contacts had either the pulmonary or childhood type of tuberculosis. Furthermore, he has found a much larger proportion of these cases in an early stage of the disease than his patients admitted through the usual channels. To be of value contact examinations must include X-rays of the chest. A diagnosis that waits for symptoms and physical signs is often too late to be of benefit to the patient.

The spread of tuberculosis in families is well illustrated by a few cases which have recently occurred in the diagnostic work of the Department of Public Health:

1. **Unsuspected Spread from the Open Case:**

In the spring of 1932 a physician in a Connecticut Valley city referred a man, 39, to the Out-Patient Department of Westfield State Sanatorium for diagnosis. The patient was found to be suffering from moderately advanced tuberculosis, and it was suggested to the doctor that he send in the other members of the family for examination. The patient's wife was found to have a chronic, fibroid type of tuberculosis, apparently the source of her husband's infection. Two daughters, aged 12 and 14, had early pulmonary tuberculosis, and two younger children, the childhood type of tuberculosis. Only two members of the family were free from disease. Without the routine examination of contacts in this family none of the secondary cases would have been discovered until they had developed clinical signs of tuberculosis and their best chance for recovery was gone.

2. **The Chronic Carrier of Tuberculosis:**

In the course of routine school examinations by the Chadwick Clinics in a small coast town in 1927, two girls in a family were found to have pulmonary tuberculosis and a sister was classified as suspicious. The family history revealed that three older sisters had died of tuberculosis in the past five years. Three younger children were well at the time of examination. The father, though working, gave a history of chronic cough, but refused examination. The older of the two girls found to have tuberculosis in 1927 died in 1930 and the younger in 1932. The father, after a long illness, died of "heart disease" in 1932, but one physician who saw him occasionally said he unquestionably had tuberculosis. From the history it appeared that the father's cough preceded the illness of his children, and that he was the previously unsuspected source of the infection which resulted in the death of five of his daughters.

Because a large part of the infection with tuberculosis takes place in the home the plan of the Chadwick Clinics has been modified to include examination of family contacts whenever tuberculosis is found in a school child. Such a procedure is time consuming, but often makes it possible to find the source of infection and really stop the spread of the disease in a given family. A few examples will illustrate the method:

3. **The Infected Child as a Guide to the Source of Infection:**

A boy of 8 was found in the school examinations to have hilum tuberculosis. History showed that his mother had died of tuberculosis in 1930, and his grandmother in 1931. On examination the grandfather proved to have fibroid tuberculosis, and two aunts and an uncle active pulmonary tuberculosis. Another aunt is now in a sanatorium with the disease. Out of the eight members of two families in this house only two had escaped tuberculosis.

4. **The Value of a Well-Taken History:**

In a certain high school, a girl of 16 reacted to the tuberculin test and a history was obtained that her father had died of tuberculosis the previous year. Examination of other members of the family showed that a sister of 18 had unsuspected pulmonary tuberculosis.

Through the employment of epidemiological methods we thus have two approaches for the discovery of tuberculosis: First, the examination of contacts of known cases who may be suffering from undetected tuberculosis; second, the examination of members of the families of school children found to have tuberculosis who often have been infected by their parents. The importance of studying the family as a unit is well brought out in a series of 110 cases of children with pulmonary tuberculosis seen in the State Follow-Up Clinic. Seventy per cent of these examinations disclosed the source of infection in some other member of the family. To control tuberculosis it is not enough to diagnose and hospitalize the frank case; every possible effort must be made to determine the source of infection and to locate other contacts who may already be harboring unsuspected disease. Because infection requires relatively intimate or prolonged contact wth a sputum-positive case, and the incubation period of the disease is a matter of months instead of days, the epidemiology of tuberculosis is seldom as obvious as that of smallpox or typhoid fever. A clear grasp of the principles involved is, however, just as essential to an understanding of the disease and the formulation of sound control measures.

GONORRHEA AND SYPHILIS

In principle, the epidemiology of gonorrhea and syphilis is the same as that of any communicable disease. It seeks to answer two questions:—(1) From whom did the patient get the infection? (2) To whom has the patient given the disease? From a purely epidemiological point of view, the fact that the majority of infections with gonorrhea and syphilis are acquired through sexual intercourse should greatly simplify the problem of case-finding. The search is limited to the relatively few persons with whom the patient has been in sexual or other very intimate relationship. Actually, however, various medical and social factors intervene to complicate or to obstruct case-finding in a large proportion of cases.

The first and most effective obstacle is the public notion that infection with gonorrhea or syphilis is irrefutable evidence of misconduct. This notion, unfortunately, is also too prevalent among physicians, nurses, social workers and health officials. Consequently although most infections in women are acquired through marriage and many infections with syphilis in both sexes are congenital, no patient wants the fact of his infection to become known to any other than the physician to whom he has gone for treatment. To require the identification of all patients to the health officer would either drive them away from proper medical attention or would encourage the already too common practice of giving false names and addresses. (More than half of the 10,000 patients reported by name in Massachusetts in the last three years, for having lapsed treatment, could not be found because of false identification.)

The health officer, therefore, must delegate to the treating physician or to the clinic social worker, this important business of case-finding. Except as he may have access to clinic records or is successful in persuading physicians to report, he may have little knowledge of how effectively this work is being done. Certainly he lacks any such detailed grasp of, or control over, the situation as he has, for instance, in typhoid fever, diphtheria, smallpox or even tuberculosis.

Even the physician who sincerely tries to do as complete a job of case-finding as possible, and the clinic social worker whose business it is to do it, find themselves confronted by many obstacles to satisfactory epidemiology. These have their origins in several sources among which may be mentioned the disease itself, the patient, the alleged source of infection, the alleged intimate contacts of the patient, the health official and the physician. It is encouraging, nevertheless, to know that almost unbelievable success in case-finding has been the reward of those physicians and social workers who are sufficiently interested to follow through instead of giving up at the first evidence that the search is going to be difficult.

The following cases are offered to illustrate the successes and the failures of epidemiology in gonorrhea and syphilis. They are taken from the records of several clinics and from the experiences of the State Department of Public Health.

Value of Routine Blood Test

Case 1—A young married woman was being examined in a clinic for a gynecological condition. Routine blood tests showed that she had syphilis, and the syphilis clinic made a diagnosis of syphilis in the secondary stage. Her husband was examined and found to be free from the disease. This woman at first refused to identify her extramarital sexual partner, but after many visits to the clinic and repeated interviews with the social worker, she gave his name and that of the physician with whom he was supposed to be under treatment. The physician informed the social worker that the man had lapsed treatment. Shortly thereafter, however, he was returned to the physician.

Comment:

This case demonstrates:—
(1) That women are not always infected by their husbands.
(2) That it may require great patience and persistence to secure the confidence of the patient and thus proceed with case-finding.
(3) That although the sexual partner may be thought to be under treatment it is essential to make certain of it.
(4) That prompt discovery of this infection through the routine use of blood tests prevented the almost certain eventual infection of the husband. Thus blood tests are important in case-finding.

Detection of Early Syphilis through Routine Examination of Contacts

Case 2—A married man appeared at a clinic with a genital sore, which was diagnosed through darkfield examination as primary syphilis. For nine months he had been separated from his wife who, however, had returned to him two weeks prior to his appearance at the clinic. He named as a sexual partner a married woman, separated from her husband, who had been his housekeeper during his wife's absence. This woman was found to have secondary syphilis. Her young son was found to be free from infection. The wife of the original patient was examined three days after the patient first appeared but at that time presented no evidence of infection. One month later, however, during one of several follow-up examinations, she presented the sore of primary syphilis. Her three children, aged 4, 6 and 8, were free from infection. The three patients have been under regular treatment and are responding favorably.

Comment:

This case illustrates three very important points:—
(1) That the diagnosis of primary syphilis by darkfield (when the blood is still probably negative) makes it possible not only to start treatment at the most favorable moment and to prevent the further spread of infection, but also to find related cases quickly.
(2) That it is always necessary, because of the long incubation period of syphilis (2 to 6 weeks), to examine repeatedly any recently exposed persons. Since the primary sore may be missed, especially in women, physical examinations and blood tests should be made regularly for at least three months after the last exposure.
(3) That the social worker in charge of this case saw to it that every person was examined who had been in intimate contact with any of the three infected persons. Children, especially, may be exposed to the infections of others in the household through kissing, etc.

Case-Finding through Examination of Contacts

Case 3—A young married woman with an eruption on her body was found by a clinic physician to have secondary syphilis. She claimed to have been infected by a girl friend living with her who had used the family douche bag. As the patient's sister used this douche bag also, she was examined and found to have secondary syphilis. The husbands of both sisters were examined and both had syphilis. The girl friend who was thought to be the source of infection did not have the disease.

Comment:
This case teaches:—
(1) That an alleged "source of infection" may, after all, not be the source of infection and thus every possible lead should be followed. It may never be determined who had the original infection in this family, but, at any rate, four cases were found where only the original patient might have been if the social worker had been content with the examination of the girl friend who proved to be free from infection. It is worth thinking of the congenital syphilis which might have resulted should the infections in these two young married couples have gone undiscovered and untreated.

Infection Innocently Contracted

Case 4—A middle-aged married woman had acute gonorrhea. She was persuaded to have her husband examined and he was found to have the disease. Since it was impossible to secure an admission of extramarital intercourse from him, the wife was questioned further. She admitted that she had had intercourse with a neighbor. Examination was suggested to the neighbor, but his 21 year old feebleminded daughter appeared instead. She had gonorrhea and admitted frequent sexual contacts with her father. The father was then examined by a private physician and found to have gonorrhea. The girl was removed from her home and is under the care of a social agency. No legal action could be taken against the father since the testimony of the feebleminded girl was said to be inacceptable.

Comment:
This case teaches:—
(1) That husbands may be innocently infected by their wives.
(2) That to have assumed that the husband was the source of the wife's infection would have left the infections in the neighbor and his daughter, as well as an intolerable situation, undiscovered.

Gonorrhea in Childhood Secondary to Infected Family Contact

Case 5—A three-year old girl was found, at a clinic, to have gonorrhea. Her mother had gonorrhea. Blood tests for syphilis were negative for both. The father was examined and found to have gonorrhea which he admitted having contracted out West some months before. (The State Department of Health communicated this information to the western State Department of Health with the result that the source of infection was located and placed under treatment.) The father's blood was tested and he was found to have syphilis also. He had been neglecting treatment for congenital syphilis in spite of the fact that his eyes were involved. A one-year old baby in the family had neither disease.

Comment:
This case illustrates four important epidemiological points:—
(1) That children (especially girls) are innocently infected with gonorrhea by infected adults. (In Massachusetts 10% of all reported gonorrhea in the female is in girls under 14 years of age.) Also, the father of the child had congenital syphilis which he acquired before birth from his mother. (In Massachusetts about 8% of all reported syphilis is congenital syphilis.)

(2) That if a child has gonorrhea search should be made at once for the infection in other members of the family. This is usually best begun with the mother.
(3) That sources of infection in distant places may be brought to treatment through the aid of departments of health.
(4) That routine blood tests for syphilis are of utmost importance in discovering neglected or unsuspected syphilis.

Gonorrhea Found through Examination of Family Contacts

Case 6—A married man, aged 27, was found to have gonorrhea. His wife was examined and found to be infected and pregnant. The children were examined and the oldest girl found to have the disease. The six-year old sister of the patient's wife also had gonorrhea as did also the nineteen-year old brother.

Comment:
This case is the reverse of Case No. 5 since the innocently infected wife and children were brought to medical care as the result of casefinding following the discovery of the infection in an adult male.

Neglected Gonorrheal Infection Spread to Family Contacts

Case 7—A sixteen year old boy was operated upon in a hospital for acute gonorrheal epididymitis. His parents were informed that the operation was for appendicitis. He was allowed to return to his home of four rooms, occupied by ten persons, three of them young girls. In a few weeks the three year old girl was brought to the hospital with gonorrheal vaginitis and a gonorrheal eye infection. Even this did not appear to excite anyone and two weeks later the nine year old sister was brought in with gonorrheal vaginitis. Then the family was examined and proper instructions given.

Comment:
A suggestion of what neglect of the epidemiological aspects of a case may mean to the community is to be found in the fact that this case cost the Community Health Association $160 for 174 visits to this family and cost the city $145 for the hospitalization of the two children—a total of $305. One child has permanently impaired vision.

Congenital Syphilis Due to Neglected Infection of Mother

Case 8—A middle-aged man was treated for late syphilis for two years. His statement that his wife and seven children were well was accepted and no follow-up was done. Later, one of his children developed interstitial keratitis. Then examination of the family disclosed syphilis in the mother, definite congenital syphilis in two other children and a cardiac condition due to syphilis in the baby.

Comment:
Discovery and treatment of the infections in the children would have prevented the development of interstitial keratitis. Treatment of the mother during pregnancy, at least, probably would have given her a healthy baby.

Gonorrhea is a Disease of the "Teens"

Case 9—A seventeen year old junior high school student was named as a possible source of infection by a male clinic patient who had gonorrhea. She was examined and found to have the disease. She named four other contacts, two of whom were examined in the clinic and put under treatment. Another was examined and placed under medical care by a private physician. The fourth could not be located. The girl eventually was sent to an institution as a behavior problem.

Comment:
This case, in addition to illustrating what can be done by follow-up,

also indicates something of the age of those who are infected. This was a seventeen year old girl. Three out of every four women reported as having gonorrhea are under twenty-five years of age and two out of every three are under twenty years of age.

"Respectability" is no Guarantee of Freedom from Gonorrhea or Syphilis

Case 10—A physician, treating a male patient for gonorrhea, learned the identity of the alleged source of infection. The State Department of Public Health was notified and the local board of health asked to advise medical attention. The woman was found and persuaded to see a physician, which she did. This physician wrote the State Department of Health that he would not even examine the woman as he knew her to be a respectable married woman whom he had known for many years and all of whose children he had delivered. Eventually another physician found that the woman had gonorrhea.

Comment:
Case-finding must never be neglected because of appearances or the presumption that infection cannot exist because of the social standing of the person allegedly involved. Many a difficult piece of epidemiology, requiring patience and persistence on the part of physicians, social workers and health officials has come to naught because some other physician has refused to take the matter seriously. Dependence upon the negative smear, especially in the female, failure to examine the male prostate or to make blood tests, has effectively stopped case-finding in altogether too many instances.

Innocent Extra-Genital Infection

Case 11—A nurse in a large hospital burned her thumb on an alcohol lamp while preparing medication for a baby. The burn failed to heal, and five weeks later, when a rash came out on her body, it was discovered that she had syphilis and that the primary sore was in the burn on the thumb. It was then found that the baby had "snuffles", the running nose of congenital syphilis in a highly communicable stage. The baby's mother was examined and, of course, found to have syphilis. The husband also had syphilis which he had acquired before marriage.

A most discouraging feature of this case was the prudish point of view of the superintendent of one of the hospitals at which this nurse was receiving training as an affiliate. It was the intention of this superintendent to refuse her further training at that hospital because she had syphilis, in spite of the fact that treatment soon made the disease non-communicable so far as any nursing contacts were concerned. It required some rather pointed correspondence and conferences to change this attitude so that the nurse might go on with her training. Unfortunately this superintendent's objection arose more from a feeling that the nurse's reputation was damaged than from any fear that the disease made her dangerous to her patients!

Comment:
This case illustrates several most important points:—
(1) That syphilis is, in many cases, not a venereal disease. The nurse, the baby and the mother were innocent victims of a communicable, not venereal, disease.
(2) That through search for the cause of infection in the nurse, the disease was discovered in the baby and mother and father in time to save them from eventual disaster as a result of untreated syphilis.
(3) That the mother of a congenitally syphilitic baby always has syphilis, though she may have been infected innocently by her husband.
(4) That if this mother had had a blood test done during the early part of her pregnancy, the baby might have been born healthy

through treatment of the mother and at least two innocent persons, the baby and the nurse, saved from infection. If the mother's pregnancy had come to medical attention too late to prevent the baby's infection, at least it would have been possible to take precautions which would have prevented the infection of the nurse. Case-finding should be begun at the first possible moment.
(5) Every pregnant woman should have blood tests made the moment she comes to medical attention, and the earlier that is in pregnancy, the better, especially if she is found to have syphilis.
(6) That no person should be denied employment simply because they have syphilis, provided they are under treatment and have no open lesions of early (primary or secondary) syphilis.
(7) That prudishness has no place in the attitude, of those who should know better, toward persons with syphilis. The disease is neither a crime nor is it by any means necessarily evidence of any misconduct whatever.

The above cases are only a few of hundreds that may be found in the records of clinics and physicians. They do not by any means present a complete picture of the difficulties which confront the epidemiologist, or of the immense amount of patient work that this type of epidemiology requires. They will help to demonstrate what can be accomplished if the physician or nurse or social worker or health officer has the will to go ahead, the sympathetic attitude which wins the patient's confidence and the tact which is so necessary in the approach to the alleged contacts of the patient.

Summary

Eleven cases are reported to illustrate what can be accomplished in the epidemiology of gonorrhea and syphilis by those who are interested, patient, persistent and tactful. The following points, in particular, are emphasized:—
(1) That the disease itself, either because of a long incubation period or because of moderate symptoms which encourage delay in seeking medical attention, may obstruct case-finding.
 (Case 1 and 5. The value of the routine blood test.)
 (Case 2. The long incubation period of syphilis.)
 (Case 8. Asymptomatic congenital and maternal syphilis.)
(2) That the patient may attempt to avoid identifying the person from whom the infection may have been acquired or the persons to whom the infection may have been given. (Of course, in the case of intercourse while greatly intoxicated or with unknown "pick-ups" identification of these persons may be impossible.) (Cases 1 & 4).
(3) That the patient may have an honest but erroneous idea of where the infection was acquired. (Case 3).
(4) That it is not safe to assume that the husband is necessarily the source of his wife's infection (Case 1) even though he himself may have the disease. (Case 4).
(5) That health departments may help in case-finding. (Case 5).
(6) That the infection of innocent persons may be prevented by prompt diagnosis and case-finding. Cases 1, 2, 6, 7, 8 and 11).
(7) That lack of interest on the part of any person responsible for any part of case-finding, whether it be the physician, social worker or health officer, will bring to naught all the effort of the others and result in the further spread of infection as well as in disaster for the untreated cases. (Cases 7, 8, 10 and 11).
(8) That congenital syphilis can be or could have been prevented by finding and treating syphilis in the mother. (Cases 5, 8, and 11).
(9) That children are frequently infected innocently by parents, relatives or attendants who have gonorrhea. (Cases 5, 6 and 7).
(10) That responsibility for case-finding has not ceased until every possible lead has been exhausted. (all cases).

Acknowledgment

The courtesy of the clinics which sent in many case records is acknowledged. Limited space precluded the use of all the material which they made available for this study.

EPIDEMIOLOGY IN CHRONIC DISEASE

The patient died of cancer of the uterus. Her history shows that she was born in Northern Europe; had an exceedingly nervous temperament; had gonorrhea when she was sixteen years of age; married when she was twenty; received a tear at the birth of her first child which was never repaired; had two other children; and then used contraceptives for the remainder of her childbearing period. Her diet contained no vegetables except potato, and she drank one quart of tea daily. Her teeth had been removed a few months before the cancer was discovered and all of them had pus roots. Her mother died of cancer of the uterus. Her paternal aunt had cancer of the breast. What caused the patient's cancer?

The examination of her record, or that of any other individual, fails to give the answer, save in the mind of some enthusiast with a pet hobby. The physician who believes that uterine tears are the cause of all cancers of the uterus immediately points to the tear and forgets the rest of the history. Another physician who believes diet to be an etiological factor points to the lack of vegetables and thinks his point is proven. The vast majority, however, admit that they do not know the cause. They realize uterine tears, contraceptives, and gonorrhea may at times cause irritation and chronic irritation is believed to be a precancerous condition. Heredity may be of importance. Foci of infection and dietary habits may so alter the body metabolism that cancer develops. Other variables as yet unthought of may be the cause. They do not know.

It is only by collecting the histories of a large number of individuals—some with cancer, some without—and comparing the records, item by item, that we are able to arrive at results approaching soundness. Even so, we are not sure that a given person had cancer as the diagnosis in many cases was only clinical. In other cases we wonder if some individuals without cancer would have developed the disease had they lived a few months longer. If all the individuals with cancer had uterine tears and all the individuals without cancer did not, and if all the other variables were equally distributed between the two groups, conclusions would be easy. This is never the case, and an elaborate analysis is required before even tentative conclusions can be postulated, and such conclusions must be made subject to reservation, with a keen realization of the inadequacy of much of the data. This is epidemiology as applied to chronic disease.

The science of epidemiology for many years was limited to the study of epidemics, and only comparatively recently has included other diseases. This broader interpretation of the word is justified from its Greek derivation, as well as from the fact that the methods of approach are nearly identical whether studying acute or chronic disease. The study of the epidemic diseases is easier as the search for the source can be limited to short periods of time, while in chronic disease they may cover a lifetime and the element of human fallibility increases with time.

Epidemiology studies the incidence of disease in relation to local environment, personal habits, history, and individual traits. It attempts to get a better understanding of the nature, source, and means of spread of the disease, and to learn under what conditions it can be best checked. In clinical medicine the unit is the individual. In epidemiology the unit is a population and mass phenomena must be studied.

During the past six years the Massachusetts Department of Public Health has been making intensive epidemiological studies in chronic disease. Some of these studies were of short duration, while others required years. The most extensive study was a survey of chronic disease conducted in fifty-one cities and towns in Massachusetts. This study covered a four-year period and information was obtained by a house-to-house canvass of 75,000 individuals.

Factors dealing with the life history of individuals were obtained in the survey and morbidity figures were computed for those who had these factors and those who did not. It is shown that among individuals with former attacks of rheumatic fever, frequent sore throats, growing pains, frequent colds, malaria, typhoid, diphtheria, and scarlet fever the chronic disease attack rate is higher than among those not having had these diseases. Individuals who, over a period of years, have eaten the protective foods (leafy vegetables, milk, citrous fruits) have lower rates than those who have not. Individuals who have had bad teeth and tonsils throughout life have higher rates than those who have not. Individuals with nervous temperaments have much higher chronic disease rates than those with phlegmatic temperaments. The disease rate among those who have exercised a great deal is much lower than among those who have had very little exercise. The overweights and the underweights have more chronic disease than the normal weights. Individuals who had chronic indigestion have higher chronic disease rates than those who had not, and the regular users of laxatives higher rates than the non-users. Among individuals with an hereditary history of chronic disease there is more chronic disease than among those with no such history.

This rough grouping of all chronic diseases does not portray the etiology of individual diseases and it would be well for similar information to be obtained for these diseases.

At the present time the Department is collecting epidemiological data from cancer patients, rheumatism patients, and controls. This material will be studied to determine whether or not there are sufficient differences to warrant etiological consideration.

Irritation has long been considered an exciting cause of cancer and chronic irritation from ill-fitting plates, ragged teeth, spectacles, corsets, and uterine tears will be studied as well as the relation of pre-existing diseases and foci of infection to rheumatism and cancer. It is hoped to show whether or not there are marked differences between the groups in exercise, recreation, bowel and eating habits. Heredity history of the individual will be studied in both sexes, and among the females dysmenorrhea, leukorrhea, childbearing, abscessed breasts, and lacerated cervices. Many cross sections can be made from this material as the presence of other diseases is given in the records.

The practicability of such studies is easily seen. In several previous studies the data indicate that women with uterine tears are more apt to have cancer of the uterus than others. Such a finding warrants the repairing of such tears as a preventive measure. Cancer of the buccal cavity is believed to be more prevalent among tobacco users with unclean mouths. While it may be impossible to greatly limit the use of tobacco, it should be easy to instruct tobacco users to have the dentist clean their teeth at frequent intervals. Certain parts of our population have more cancer than others. Racial factors are of importance, and among the groups having high cancer rates educational activities should be stressed.

Joslin[*] finds more diabetes among the children of diabetic parents than among the general population. This would point toward greater responsibility on the part of the parents in seeing that their children were examined at frequent intervals.

Heart disease may follow diseased tonsils. The removal of these may prevent a damaged heart. In the chronic disease survey, unhygienic living was closely associated with the degenerative diseases. This argues a more intensive campaign for proper living.

These are but examples of how epidemiological methods can be used to lower disease incidence. Epidemiology is endeavoring to shed additional light on chronic disease. The epidemiologist is continually searching for the cause of the disease in order that he may decrease its prevalence.

---

[*] Joslin, Elliott P. Treatment of Diabetes Mellitus. Lea and Febiger, Phila. 1928.

From time immemorial it has been the custom of people to reason that because some event followed some other event, the preceding one was the cause.

Sumner, in his "Folkways," related that in Molamba, Africa, pestilence broke out shortly after the death of a Portuguese there. So certain were the natives that this death caused the pestilence, they took every precaution to prevent any other white man from dying in their country. Again he tells of another instance on the Nicobar Islands when some natives who had just begun to make pottery died. From that time on the art of pottery making was given up and never again attempted.

But one does not need to revert to ancient times and primitive people for examples of the "post hoc ergo propter hoc" form of reasoning. We are constantly finding specimens of it in all walks of life, and particularly in cancer theorizing. For instance, a little child had cancer. Her grandmother cared for her and later developed cancer. This caused the statement that the grandmother contracted the disease from the child. On another occasion, a mother had a cancer and later her daughter developed one, which resulted in the claim that heredity was the cause. Three brothers, also, had cancer, and the fourth, who did not, attributed his freedom from the disease to the fact that he drank alcohol while his brothers did not. These and similar theories must be either established or disproved by epidemiological methods.

This is the task of the epidemiologist—to separate the true from the false, to clarify the unknown, and to assist medicine in the conquest of disease.

EPIDEMIOLOGICAL APPROACH TO DENTAL CARIES

The epidemiological approach to the problems of disease prevention offers a means of intelligent program planning. For few phases of public health is this seen to better advantage than in the field of dental hygiene. Here the apparently unrelated problems of correction of existing dental defects and provisions for adequate nutrition are so closely interwoven that any program which fails to correlate the two factors falls far short of the goal which it should attain. Although our knowledge of the nutritional factors in the growth of teeth and their resistance to caries is still in the developmental stage, certain information is already in our possession which should be used in every dental hygiene program.

The following data gathered in a survey in a community of 3,000 present in very simple form the use of epidemiological methods in the development of such a program.

Grade	Children Examined	Defects Corrected	Non-carious Cases	Carious Cases
1 and 2	116	2	5	109
3	54	3	0	51
4	48	3	3	42
5 and 6	110	9	3	98
Totals	328	17	11	300

*Cases Requiring Immediate Attention**

Grade	Enamel Defects in Permanent Teeth	Visible abscesses (emergency cases)
1 and 2	53	5
3	17	4
4	0	6
5 and 6	0	8
Totals	70	23

* See Dental Policy approved by the Dental Advisory Committee of the Department of Public Health.

A survey such as the above gives a picture of the need for operative work. In order to prevent, so far as possible, further development of caries, attention must, however, be given to the nutritional needs of the group.

The carious cases were classified as follows:

Grade	Active Caries	Rampant Caries	Partly Arrested
1 and 2	91	8	10
3	37	5	8
4	45	2	5
5 and 6	46	0	34
Totals	219	15	57

All cases of rampant caries and others showing decalcification areas, gingival caries or generally inflamed gums were selected for careful study. The following table shows the distribution of these so-called "nutrition cases" (Miner).

Grade	Children Examined	Nutrition Cases	Per Cent
1 and 2	116	40	34%
3	54	14	26%
4	48	9	17%
5 and 6	110	31	28%
Totals	328	94	28%

These cases were further studied by a nutritionist to determine the dietary deficiencies which were contributing to the development of caries. Information was obtained as follows on 72 of the 94 cases.

	Number of Children	Per Cent
Milk:		
1 qt. or more daily	16	20%
1 pt. to 1 qt. daily	24	30%
Less than 1 pint	32	44%
Fresh fruit:		
Daily	15	19%
Almost daily	21	27%
Only occasionally	36	49%
Dark bread and cereals	54	71%
Eggs:		
Daily	9	12%
3-4 a week	24	30%
Only occasionally	39	53%
Raw vegetables daily	3	4%
Tomatoes weekly or oftener	32	41%

The underlying causes for lack of foods were then studied to determine whether this was due to poor discipline, to anorexia, or to economic conditions with the following result:

Too many sweets	22	28%
Poor food habits	20	26%
Family needed budget advice as to food	54	71%

The above tables contain the data essential to the establishment of a well balanced and comprehensive dental health program. They show both the operative and nutritional needs. Just as an epidemiological investigation of a case of typhoid may reveal the sources of the disease and prevent further infections, so in this case an exceedingly simple epidemiological study of the dental caries in a group paved the way for the development of adequate preventive measures.

News Notes

NATIONAL ORGANIZATION FOR PUBLIC HEALTH NURSING

A complete bibliography of reference material published by the National Organization for Public Health Nursing in PUBLIC HEALTH NURSING and LISTENING IN, relating to the adjustments in the practice of public health nursing made necessary by the economic situation has been prepared by the National Organization for Public Health Nursing.

Nurses having access to the magazine and wishing to inform themselves on the changes wrought in their profession throughout the United States during the last two years should write for this bibliography.

Among the pertinent and engrossing subjects it lists are: Salaries, hours on duty, vacation, relief giving, changes in program, sources of support and budgets. Copies may be secured from the N. O. P. H. N., 450 Seventh Avenue, New York, N. Y.

New Mexico leads the states in enrollment in the N. O. P. H. N. with every public health nurse within its borders a member for 1933. Rhode Island is second with 96 per cent; District of Columbia 87 per cent, third; and Oklahoma and Iowa fourth and fifth with 72 per cent and 69 per cent respectively. Michigan for all its banking difficulties is a close sixth with 68 per cent.

Fourteen states are more than half enrolled and in half the states 40 per cent or more of the public health nurses are members. Total enrollment now exceeds 6,300.

AMERICAN RED CROSS

The annual Roll Call of the American National Red Cross, to enroll members for 1934, will be conducted by the Chapters throughout the Nation from November 11 through November 30th, 1933.

AT LAST SOMETHING IS TO BE DONE ABOUT GONORRHEA!

A Committee for Survey of Research on the Gonococcus and Gonococcal Infections has been formed by the Division of Medical Sciences of the National Research Council, in cooperation with the American Social Hygiene Association. Its purpose is to collect, analyze, and collate the facts already established and the efforts now in progress to add to knowledge of the gonococcus and gonococcal infections, especially as regards bacteriology, pathology, immunity, mechanism of infection, and some of the forms of therapy. Attention will be concentrated chiefly on work done in the United States. At the close of the preliminary survey the Committee, with the assistance of a conference of experts, will compile a report with the object of stimulating interest in the study of the gonococcus, or providing a point of departure and of suggesting promising leads for further investigation. The survey will cover the literature, but it is hoped that unpublished work, and studies which were incomplete or whose results were inconclusive, may also be included.

Dr. Stanhope Bayne-Jones, Chairman, earnestly invites the co-operation of workers interested in this field. Other members of the Committee are Dr. Edward L. Keyes, Dr. Walter Clarke, Secretary, and Dr. Francis Blake, Chairman of the Division, ex-officio. Headquarters have been established at Room 1101, 450 Seventh Avenue, New York, where communications and reprints will be welcomed.

Book Note

PROPHYLACTIC ODONTOTOMY, produced by the Hyatt Study Club of New York. $1.50. 104 pp. The Macmillan Company.

Under the above title, the Hyatt Study Club of New York has published an "operative manual" with the avowed intention of explaining "a practical and simple procedure for the prevention of caries in pit and fissure cavities".

As we all know, decay of teeth or dental caries, is one of the most baffling problems with which all members of the Healing Art—not just dentists—are confronted.

To a consideration of this vexed question, the Hyatt Study Club of New York has devoted several years of work. It may be that the practice of the procedures outlined in this book will be the beginning of a new era in dentistry and in any case, the Club should remember with comfort the Browning maxim, " 'Tis not what a man does that exalts him; but what a man *would* do."

The Study Club's idea is to initiate a movement having as its object the helping of our children, the future men and women, to have better teeth and mouth health. Any practical method of carrying such a noble idea to fruition may well be described as bringing about a new birth in health measures.

While space is too limited to give an exhaustive analysis of this work, it is hoped that there will be sufficient room to frame a review of some of the outstanding features.

(1) The conclusions and suggestions are based on statistics laboriously compiled and guaranteed: and yet there are many people who denounce statistics on principle. It would perhaps be better to discard the word statistics altogether and speak of *Facts*—and facts are stubborn things to contend with!

(2) An outstanding feature of the work is the emphasis laid on the management of children. Herein, in our opinion, is the crux of the situation. Dentistry for children has not been taken seriously enough by a large majority of the dental profession, who, instead of fostering the development and early supervision of the dental organ, have confined themselves to repair of the said organ when broken down and diseased. For pity's sake, let us have more practitioners interested in Mouth Health for Children.

(3) Another point of major importance is the Economics of Odontotomy; and this is discussed ably from the viewpoint of the patient and the dentists.

The authors discuss the persistency of Tradition as a force, and suggest that in many instances Tradition has no justifiable excuse for existence. Let us remember that because a thing has always been done in a certain way is no proof that it cannot be done in another and a better way.

(4) The chapters on Examination Technique, Preparation of Cavities, Filling Materials, all merit the closest study.

(5) Chapter 11 on Terminology is important, as any discussion of the language of the part must be.

It is safe to say that a large proportion of the indifference to certain phases of our problems is due to a want of clear definitions and a standardized phraseology.

(6) In summing up, one reviewer at least is of the opinion that, if a moiety of the dental profession would take this Manual to their hearts and carry out all the details therein expounded, it would enhance to a tremendous extent the health and well-being of our long-suffering population.

There is no reasonable doubt as to an unhygienic condition being at least one potent factor in dental disease; and all means possible should be used to counteract that handicap in health. At the present time the other factor of nutrition, with all its ramifications into Biology, Endocrinology, Sympathetic and Para-Sympathetic Nervous Systems, in short Metabolism, is in such an embryonic stage that we are not in a position to give definite and all-conclusive opinions.

But all *can* give serious consideration to *Prophylactic Odontotomy*.

E. Melville Quinby, M.R.C.S., L.R.C.P., D.M.D.
President, Massachusetts Dental Hygiene Council.

REPORT OF DIVISION OF FOOD AND DRUGS

During the months of April, May and June 1933, samples were collected in 218 cities and towns.

There were 1,781 samples of milk examined, of which 193 were below standard; from 18 samples the cream had been in part removed, and 11 samples contained added water. There were 108 samples of Grade A milk examined, 3 samples of which were below the legal standard of 4.00% fat. There were 1,047 bacteriological examinations made of milk, and 12 of hamburg steak. There were 2 samples examined for hemolytic bacteria, both of which were negative.

There were 533 samples of food examined, of which 65 were adulterated or misbranded. These consisted of 7 samples of extract of vanilla, 6 samples of which contained coumarin, and 1 sample was low in vanillin; 30 samples of sausage, 2 samples of which contained a compound of sulphur dioxide not properly labeled, 4 samples contained starch in excess of 2 per cent, 1 sample was decomposed, and 23 samples contained added color; 14 samples of hamburg steak, 2 samples of which contained a compound of sulphur dioxide not properly labeled, 7 samples contained water, 2 of which also contained a compound of sulphur dioxide not properly labeled, and 5 samples were decomposed, 1 of which also contained water; 2 samples of liver which were decomposed; 1 sample of bread which contained part of a cigarette; 3 samples of salad oil which were misbranded; 1 sample of dried apricots which contained sulphur dioxide not properly labeled; 4 samples of eggs which were sold as fresh eggs but were not fresh; 1 sample of maple syrup which contained cane sugar; 1 sample of canned sweet corn which was in a state of advanced fermentation; and 1 sample of vinegar which contained added color.

There were 11 samples of drugs examined, of which 3 samples were adulterated. These consisted of 2 samples of cottonseed oil which did not conform to the requirements of the U. S. Pharmacopoeia, and 1 miscellaneous sample identified as Atropin.

The police departments submitted 666 samples of liquor for examination, 662 of which were above 0.5% in alcohol. The police departments also submitted 20 samples of narcotics, etc., for examination, 8 samples of which contained heroin, 1 sample of which also contained powdered sugar; 1 sample contained morphine sulphate; 1 sample contained bichloride of mercury; 1 sample contained ergot; 1 sample contained ergot and quinine; 1 sample contained ergot, oil of savin, iron and aloe; 1 sample contained 4.85% water and 35.6 hydrocyanic acid; 1 sample contained fine sand, free carbon, resins, sand clay, and iron (ferric) chloride; 1 sample contained sugar; 1 sample of liquor was found to contain no methyl alcohol; 1 sample was found to contain no alkaloidal drugs; 1 sample of cigarette was found to contain no narcotics; and another sample was found to contain no narcotics.

There were 122 cities and towns visited for the inspection of pasteurizing plants, and 345 plants were inspected.

There were 64 hearings held pertaining to violations of the laws.

There were 70 convictions for violations of the law, $1,260 in fines being imposed.

Hermit Mahar and James Secaras of Pittsfield; Henry C. Carreau of

East Douglas; Frank G. Clark of Huntington; Adam Dobrosielski of Salem; Charles Nimmo of Lawrence; Badger Farms Creameries of Newburyport; James Yeanecopolos of Berkley; and Stanley Peret of Chicopee, were all convicted for violations of the milk laws. Henry C. Carreau of East Douglas appealed his case.

F. B. Mallory, Incorporated, of Springfield; J. F. McAdams Brothers, Incorporated, of Chelsea; Richard A. Stinson of Uxbridge; and Herlihy Brothers, Incorporated of Somerville, were all convicted for violations of the Grade A Milk regulations.

Albert T. Magee, 2 cases, and James B. Crane of Leominster; Hazen K. Richardson of Middleton; F. B. Mallory, Incorporated, of Springfield; Max Bookless of Pittsfield; Owen Clifford of Ludlow; John M. Texeira of Fairhaven; John Sheehan of Holyoke; Hancock Milk Company, 2 cases, and Edgar W. Hancock of Wakefield; Antonio Karafiles of Chelmsford; Allen W. Houghton of North Amherst; Nook Farm Corporation, 2 cases, of Plymouth; and John Sudol, 2 cases, of Groveland, were all convicted for violations of the pasteurization laws and regulations. John Sudol of Groveland appealed one of his cases.

F. W. Woolworth Company, Colonial Provision Company, Incorporated, New England Provision Company, Gloria Chain Stores, Incorporated; Nathan Alpert and David Gallis, all of Boston; Peter L. Berlo of South Boston; Joseph Di Pietro of East Boston; Samuel Cohen and Barney Kupperstein of Roxbury; Leo Berlin of Chelsea; John Kaplan of Woburn; James A. Steinberg, Consumers Provision Stores, Incorporated, and The Great Atlantic & Pacific Tea Company of Worcester; First National Stores, Incorporated, of Salem; Samuel Berger, M. M. Mades Company, Incorporated, Balkus Sausage & Provision Company, and Warren Hixon & Company, Incorporated, all of Lynn; Benjamin Gold, 2 cases, and Keve Kessler, 2 cases, of Malden; Joseph Frodema of Springfield; The Fred F. Field Holsteins Dutchland Farms Trustees of Newtonville; Nathan Fishman, 2 cases, of Allston; Frank Hummer, U. & S. Beef & Provision Company, Incorporated, and John Wohrle, all of Pittsfield; Julius Neuhart of Lawrence; Springfield Provision Company of Chicopee; and James V. Veloza of Fall River, were all convicted for violations of the food laws. First National Stores, Incorporated, of Salem appealed their case. John Kaplan of Woburn; and Leo Berlin of Chelsea, were given suspended sentences.

Charles Rabinowitz of Pittsfield was convicted for violation of the bakery laws.

Peter Boukalis of Worcester was convicted for false advertising.

Ivy Pharmacy, Incorporated, 2 cases, of Roxbury, was convicted for violation of the drug laws.

Leo Kollman of Pittsfield was convicted for violation of the soft drink laws.

In accordance with Section 25, Chapter 111 of the General Laws, the following is the list of articles of adulterated food collected in original packages, from manufacturers, wholesalers, or producers:

Hamburg steak which contained a compound of sulphur dioxide not properly labeled was obtained as follows:
One sample each, from David Gallis of Boston, and Morris Mindick of Roxbury.

Hamburg steak which contained added water was obtained as follows:
One sample each, from M. I. Bassinov of Roxbury; Transfer Market and Smith's Food Shop of Cambridge; Harry Gillis of Boston; and Moro's Market of Milford.

Hamburg steak which was decomposed was obtained as follows:
One sample each, from The Great Atlantic & Pacific Tea Company, Consumers Provision Store, Incorporated, and Mindick's Market, all of Worcester; and Sirloin Stores of Lynn.

Hamburg steak which contained a compound of sulphur dioxide not

properly labeled and also contained added water was obtained as follows:
One sample each, from Abraham Rozen of Boston; and Samuel Berkman of Roxbury.
One sample of hamburg steak which was decomposed and also contained added water was obtained from Samuel Berger of Lynn.
Sausage which contained added color was obtained as follows:
Four samples from Springfield Provision Company of Chicopee; 3 samples each, from U. & S. Beef & Provision Company, Incorporated, and John Wohrle of Pittsfield; 2 samples, from James V. Veloza of Fall River; and 1 sample each, from H. L. Handy of Springfield; U. S. Sausage Company and Frank Hummer of Pittsfield; Balkus Sausage & Provision Company of Lynn; and Julius Neuhart of Lawrence.
Sausage which contained starch in excess of 2 per cent was obtained as follows:
One sample each, from James V. Veloza and Globe Provision Company of Fall River; and Peter L. Berlo of South Boston.
One sample of sausage which was decomposed was obtained from Warren Hixon Company of Lynn.
One sample of sausage which contained a compound of sulphur dioxide not properly labeled was obtained from Louis Sawlsky of South Boston.
Liver which was decomposed was obtained as follows:
One sample each, from Consumer's Provision Store, Incorporated, of Worcester; and Warren F. Hixon, Incorporated, of Lynn.
One sample of maple syrup which contained cane sugar was obtained from The Fred F. Field Holsteins Dutchland Farms Trustees at Newtonville.
One sample of dried apricots which contained sulphur dioxide not properly labeled was obtained from Grand Union Company at Lee.
One sample of bread which contained part of a cigarette was obtained from Paramount Baking Company of Roxbury.
One sample of vinegar which contained added color was obtained from Pure Products Company, Incorporated, of West Springfield.
Vanilla extract which contained coumarin was obtained as follows:
One sample each, from Garb Drug Company of Cambridge; and Roma Extract Company of Boston.
There were five confiscations, consisting of six pounds of decomposed bologna; sixteen pounds of decomposed frankforts; six pounds of decomposed ham ends; eight pounds of decomposed lamb; and four pounds of decomposed liver.
The licensed cold storage warehouses reported the following amounts of food placed in storage during March, 1933:—1,241,610 dozens of case eggs; 695,736 pounds of broken out eggs; 266,164 pounds of butter; 852,838 pounds of poultry; 2,060,430 pounds of fresh meat and fresh meat products; and 2,845,787 pounds of fresh food fish.
There was on hand April 1, 1933:—1,245,930 dozens of case eggs; 958,391 pounds of broken out eggs; 294,935 pounds of butter; 5,085,874 pounds of poultry; 4,955,470½ pounds of fresh meat and fresh meat products; and 5,501,629 pounds of fresh food fish.
The licensed cold storage warehouses reported the following amounts of food placed in storage during April, 1933:—3,194,040 dozens of case eggs; 1,137,400 pounds of broken out eggs; 303,113 pounds of butter; 892,515 pounds of poultry; 2,802,680 pounds of fresh meat and fresh meat products; and 3,489,681 pounds of fresh food fish.
There was on hand May 1, 1933:—4,300,440 dozens of case eggs; 1,427,786 pounds of broken out eggs; 371,722 pounds of butter; 3,717,829 pounds of poultry; 5,267,901½ pounds of fresh meat and fresh meat products; and 5,752,113 pounds of fresh food fish.
The licensed cold storage warehouses reported the following amounts

of food placed in storage during May, 1933:— 2,998,531 dozens of case eggs; 1,469,442 pounds of broken out eggs; 1,597,435 pounds of butter; 2,012,583 pounds of poultry; 4,620,330 pounds of fresh meat and fresh meat products; and 6,750,515 pounds of fresh food fish.

There was on hand June 1, 1933:—7,148,760 dozens of case eggs; 2,083,140 pounds of broken out eggs; 1,709,959 pounds of butter; 3,658,696 pounds of poultry; 6,830,526 pounds of fresh meat and fresh meat products; and 10,040,403 pounds of fresh food fish.

MASSACHUSETTS DEPARTMENT OF PUBLIC HEALTH

Commissioner of Public Health, GEORGE H. BIGELOW, M.D.

Public Health Council

GEORGE H. BIGELOW, M. D., *Chairman*

ROGER I. LEE, M.D.
SYLVESTER E. RYAN, M.D.
FRANCIS H. LALLY, M.D.

RICHARD P. STRONG, M.D.
JAMES L. TIGHE.
GORDON HUTCHINS.

Secretary, ALICE M. NELSON

Division of Administration	Under direction of Commissioner.
Division of Sanitary Engineering	Director and Chief Engineer, ARTHUR D. WESTON, C.E.
Division of Communicable Diseases	Director, GAYLORD W. ANDERSON, M.D.
Division of Water and Sewage Laboratories	Director and Chemist, H. W. CLARK
Division of Biologic Laboratories	Director and Pathologist, BENJAMIN WHITE, Ph.D.
Division of Food and Drugs	Director and Analyst, HERMANN C. LYTHGOE, S.B.
Division of Child Hygiene	Director, M. LUISE DIEZ, M.D.
Division of Tuberculosis	Director, ALTON S. POPE, M.D.
Division of Adult Hygiene	Director, HERBERT L. LOMBARD, M.D.

State District Health Officers

The Southeastern District	RICHARD P. MACKNIGHT, M.D., New Bedford.
The Metropolitan District	CHARLES B. MACK, M.D., Boston
The Northeastern District	ROBERT E. ARCHIBALD, M.D., Lynn.
The Worcester County District	OSCAR A. DUDLEY, M.D., Worcester.
The Connecticut Valley District	HAROLD E. MINER, M.D., Springfield.
The Berkshire District	WALTER W. LEE, M.D., No. Adams.

THE COMMONHEALTH

VOLUME 20   OCT. - NOV. - DEC.
No. 4   1933

The Handicapped

MASSACHUSETTS
DEPARTMENT OF PUBLIC HEALTH

THE COMMONHEALTH
QUARTERLY BULLETIN OF THE MASSACHUSETTS DEPARTMENT OF
PUBLIC HEALTH
Sent Free to any Citizen of the State
Entered as second class matter at Boston Postoffice.

M. LUISE DIEZ, M.D., DIRECTOR OF DIVISION OF CHILD HYGIENE, EDITOR.
Room 545 State House, Boston, Mass.

CONTENTS

	PAGE
Community Care of the Handicapped, by Herbert C. Parsons	177
What the Social Worker Can Do for the Handicapped, by Eleanor E. Kelly	179
A Nutrition Program, by Agnes Early	181
Cardiac Child, by T. Duckett Jones, M.D.	184
Occupational Therapy, by Caroline N. Shaw	186
Vocational Guidance for the Tuberculous Child, by Leon A. Alley, M.D.	187
The Sheltered Workshop of the Boston Tuberculosis Association, by Bernice W. Billings, R.N. and Esther L. Frutkoff	189
The Cooperative Workrooms, Inc., by Hazel Newton	191
Traveling School Clinics for the Examination of Retarded Children in the Public Schools, by Neil A. Dayton, M.D.	193
The Prevention of Crime — The Gangster in the Making, by L. Vernon Briggs, M.D.	198
The Maladjusted School Child and His Needs, by Anna King	201
The Rest and Nutrition Program in the Boston Public Schools, by Clara Loitman, M.D.	206
Physical Education for the Handicapped, by Carl L. Schrader	210
Vocational Rehabilitation for Persons Disabled in Industry or Otherwise, by Robert O. Small	212
Atypical Children and Their Education, by Arthur B. Lord	215
The Massachusetts Hospital School, Its Program and Results, by Ruth Park	217
The Annual Census of Physically Handicapped Children, by Margaret MacDonald	219
Relief of Unemployment in Massachusetts by Water Supply, Sewerage and Hospitalization Construction	221
Community and Nursing Standards for Maternity Care	223
The Difference Between Tweedledum and Tweedledee, by N. A. Nelson, M.D.	225
Report of the Division of Food and Drugs, July, August and September 1933	228
Index	234

COMMUNITY CARE OF THE HANDICAPPED
BY HERBERT C. PARSONS
Executive Secretary Massachusetts Child Labor Committee

Unmistakably the movement towards community provision for the care of those whose condition or conduct constitutes a social claim continues as a major objective in both policy and practice. The speed of its advance may not be measured but these are evidence that it is being accelerated. Compulsion comes from both economic and humanitarian sources. Remote indeed is the time when the institution was the receptacle for about all the community problem cases, so far as they were discovered to need any form of treatment or restraint. Relief of the poor moved out of the almshouse to the foster-home. The dependent child was freed from the orphanage to the community. The less threatening violator of law was given correction under normal conditions against the abnormal one of the jail. But along with these assumptions of care there has come a sense of new problems, of new responsibilities, to be undertaken either institutionally or within community bounds. Towards these, still coming more clearly within the range of social vision, the first impulse is that they shall be kept from institutional care to the fullest extent consistent with their greatest good and, as well, the community's gain. The institutional burden, as to certain subjects of care, has become so heavy as to compel other provisions but this pressure is not a greater force than the humanitarian consideration. They move together towards the end that the institution shall in all regards take its place as a last, as against the first, resort.

As matters now stand, there are certain forms of physical handicap, the subjects of which are primarily recognized as having community claim. As to these, the resort to the institution is remote and exceptional. Such are the blind. The Massachusetts statute as to the victims of defective eyesight is a distinct social chapter. It long ago passed out of question that sight-impairment at birth shall be systematically prevented. Beyond this the provisions for the blind in education are highly specialized, as are also those for their industrial employment. The outcome is that institutional care, developed as it is to a high level of individual culture, bears a numerical relation to the whole problem that is extremely fractional. Somewhat less distinctly are the victims of aural defect given consideration, but as to these institutional provision is justifiably small.

The recent and thorough census of the crippled, in itself a fine social enterprise, has revealed an appealing situation and distinctly a community one. The fractional proportion in the school at Canton, which is justifiably the object of state pride, leaves the margin for community meeting of a cultural need as one of challenging interest. Awareness of the claim of the tubercular upon community interest has been an achievement of the years, which obviously demands a sustained attention.

The mentally handicapped are an unsolved problem, chiefly because the institutional provision is far short of clear needs. The outcome of the situation is that either there must be additional provision or livelier action towards community care, or both. It may be ignorant to express an opinion that a more extended parole from the schools for the feeble-minded should be brought about. When the average stay in the state's industrial training schools is to be reckoned in months, fewer than twelve in the two more juvenile ones, and it is a settled policy to release on parole thus soon, it is fair to question if the requirement of training at the feeble-minded schools could not wisely be relaxed, in terms of years.

In modern classification the delinquent are included among the handicapped. Such was the White House Conference grouping. So taken, the problems of the juvenile sessions of the district courts gain social importance. There is now in process a movement to bring the treatment of delinquency up from the dead level where it has stayed static for a quarter century. In any plan for progress here, the development of community resources for constructive care after determination of delinquency is a prime factor. The broad issue of prevention through community equipment can, at the moment, be given only a passing salute. It involves many possibilities, including the development of the nerve connection between the schools and the courts, quite too casual as it now is. The clinical station stands somewhere between the two — in theory, but not in Massachusetts. Elsewhere the relationship between the clinic, the court and the school is now recognized and operated.

It would relieve anxious minds among those who care about the welfare of children and their protection against injuries which put their future in peril, if there could be any assurance that we are not now developing new handicaps. To an extent that is just becoming evident, and not yet in its full measure, the depression has resulted in damaging undernourishment of children and its near relative, malnutrition. Reports that are by no means inclusive are definite to a startling extent. They reveal that, not in one, but in several of our cities, there are hundreds of children who show the damage of being underfed. In some cases the reports are statistical, as in one of our large cities, where the percentage of clearly undernourished children has grown seriously in recent years and has broken over sectional bounds. It is found no longer alone in the districts where the "poorer" people are located but in sections of the city which are rated "well-to-do". In another city, totally lacking in provision for either the discovery or the correction of this semi-starving, the unofficial observer reports an extremity, which relief officials refuse to so much as note.

Possibly the handicap of being underfed or wrongly fed falls outside the list this brief discussion is supposed to cover. But it does not stand apart from the causes of handicap which are within the traditional definition. It cannot be separated from the health injuries that are its end effects. The community has an inescapable obligation, in the first place, to know what is happening to childhood and, in the second place, to deal with it. One experimental enterprise in the employment of a community nutritional director, proved that parents gratefully respond to such service and take home, in the full sense of that phrase, the practical instruction given them.

The progress of community care for the handicapped, which was gaining ground of permanent value in terms of future health, happiness and usefulness, has been stalled by the reduction in facilities. The outcome cannot be other than a future strain and financial burden because of the increase of institutional loads, not to mention accumulation of ills and disadvantages not to be so directly reckoned.

Even under the restrictions which somehow cut most deeply at the points of greatest service to childhood, and in the face of the greater need present conditions produce, the urgency of community as against institutional care cannot be relaxed. Indeed in its fuller development is involved the largest economies possible to be brought about. Beyond the immediate and obvious prudence of relieving institutional care is protection against eventual burdens. And beyond that is the possible gain that runs beyond dollar calculation — the gain in human fitness for life.

Community social interests should be pooled. The present conditions are causing widespread nervous activity on the part of organizations with special interests, each of them a commendable interest. There is imminent peril that instead of the service to the disadvantaged being more effective it will be uneven and unbalanced, leaving gaps of neglect, and by no means making sure that the many interests will have a well proportioned attention. The Massachusetts Child Council, made up of some twenty-five leaders in the fields of child interest, is undertaking to secure this balance on problems in general. Its main purpose is to bring a like balance in the communities by securing the full and frank consideration of problems and resources in a united group made up of those who, in public and private positions of responsibility, can view them in their due relation. Somehow and everywhere that equilibrium should be brought about in order that the interest in the handicapped and service to them shall be just as effective as it is possible to accomplish.

WHAT THE SOCIAL WORKER CAN DO FOR THE HANDICAPPED

BY ELEANOR E. KELLY
Supervisor of Social Service
Massachusetts Department of Public Health

A little girl crying on her first day at school because she sees that the other children run and play as she cannot do . . . A blind youth struggling through college with the added expense of hiring "seeing" eyes to read the lessons and "seeing" guides to accompany him home . . . A young girl bitterly drawing into the little world within herself because, in the business world and in the social life of her contemporaries, a serious disfigurement causes her to be politely shunned . . . A youth with low mentality led unwittingly into crime . . . A family man, discouraged by repeated failures to secure work where he knows men are wanted — (he knows the politely veiled refusals mean, "We can't afford the accident risk of employing a cripple.") . . . Handicapped, all of them!

These are typical of the situations with which social workers are constantly dealing.

We are using the word "handicapped" in a very limited sense, for after all, there are other handicaps, such as unfortunate personality traits, less apparent mental defects and physical characteristics, which are sometimes even more crippling to the individual possessor of them than are some of the more obvious handicaps! These too, social workers are dealing with in the everyday problems of case work.

Of first importance in work with the handicapped is the consideration of John Jones not as "one of the handicapped," but as "John Jones who has a paralyzed right arm." This individualization is the basis of all social case work. It is only, too, through a knowledge of the problems of handicapped individuals that one is able properly to interpret the needs of the handicapped as a group.

The social worker, as I see it, has a threefold opportunity in this field: service to the individual; interpretation of the needs of the group; and contribution towards efforts to prevent certain handicaps.

Handicapped persons have, of course, the same social problems to meet as those who are not handicapped, and the social worker deals with these personal and environmental conditions in the same way by the use of the case work method, considering the individual as part of a family unit and as a member of his particular community. There are, however, certain special points to be considered in this field.

First, in working with the individual, she must understand his particular handicap, with the physiological and psychological factors involved.

Is the handicap temporary or permanent? To what extent is mechanical compensation possible? To what extent will the handicap interfere with his normal activities?

In the case of a patient with a cardiac condition, for example, what type of work, if any, will the doctor approve for the patient? Under what working conditions is it safe for him to accept employment?

If the client is partially blind, is his vision limited in range or in degree? Is he one of those who see better at twilight than in the daytime? Is his vision consistently strong every day or is it seriously affected by fatigue?

Will another man need continued treatment, or avoidance of undue strain; or is the handicap such that, once he has accepted the fact, he may well learn to forget it? A leg amputation is certainly a serious matter, but with mechanical compensation a man may accept the loss and carry on as before; whereas, a tuberculous hip may need constant sparing and repeated periods of treatment.

Upon the answers to questions such as these will depend somewhat the ability of the handicapped person to make his own adjustment socially and economically.

The social worker sometimes needs to help the client to understand his own handicap. She first assures herself that he has had competent medical advice if indicated; that he understands any plan of treatment which has been made, and knows his physical limitations.

The social worker sometimes finds that through ignorance, or for financial reasons, a handicap has been accepted when medical care would have completely removed the person from the group of the handicapped. Especially has this been true in the case of children. Many of these cases, however, are now being discovered early through the increasingly effective school health programs and public health nursing services and the growing custom of medical supervision of the well child.

The social worker must be familiar with the resources which exist for medical diagnosis and treatment, especially for the individual who is unable to secure the services of the private doctor.

Here, there is very close interplay between the hospital social worker and the non-medical social worker who may be planning with the handicapped person, the hospital social worker assuming responsibility for interpreting any medical plan both to the patient and to the other social worker, and presenting to the doctor the social factors in the case which may be of significance.

Sometimes the patient is unwilling to accept the doctor's statement that nothing can be done for him and the social worker can render the patient a very real service if she is able to help him to accept the truth. Otherwise, he may start on a "shopping tour," spending time and money going from one doctor or hospital to another, or he may follow the ever-ready advice of friends to try patent cures of one sort or another, thus postponing the period of adjustment and growing more and more discouraged as each new attempt fails.

If the social worker is to be of help to the handicapped person, she must gain his confidence and usually that of his family. This is the first step towards helping him to gain confidence in himself and to set about planning for what may be to him a new form of life. To secure this confidence she must herself be convinced that what she is trying to accomplish is worthwhile.

To find oneself, for instance, without accustomed sight or hearing must be an almost overwhelming experience; and what a shock to the young man just beginning his life work to learn that a crippling disease has left him without the power to walk! As soon as possible these persons should be helped to realize the power of their remaining faculties. The now deaf musician must know that he can earn his living by some other means even though the joy of music may never again be his; and he must be encouraged to learn lip reading in order that he may not lose contact with his friends and may be able to talk with his future employers.

The social worker will put the newly handicapped man in touch with the resources for rehabilitation and training in order that his particular aptitudes may be studied and possibilities for training or for immediate employment may be opened up to him. Similarly, new opportunities may be found for the individual who, though not recently handicapped may have failed to receive adequate education or training.

Sometimes financial assistance must be 'sought for braces or other appliances. In many cases the social worker assists the client in learning his rights in the matter of compensation for injury.

The newly handicapped person and the one who has long since grown accustomed to his handicap have some very different problems to face. Fear and embarrassment are more potent to the former, loneliness and the sense of defeat more deadening; whereas, the latter may have acquired a fine mastery of himself. The former may start out with fine high courage; whereas repeated discouragements may have embittered the other.

They have also, however, many problems in common. Such persons often have a feeling of inferiority just because they think they are different from other people. Perhaps the social worker can help in pointing out that the difference is apparent only—not real. Fundamentally, the man with one arm is just like the man with both arms—if he *is* a man!

Of great importance is the attitude of the person's family and friends, for often those who care most for him do him the greatest harm by over-sentimental solicitude which increases his feeling of inferiority and dependence.

The man in a wheel chair may still be able to dress himself. The blind man can still walk and does not want to sit and be waited upon. Thus the social worker must often interpret to his family the needs of the handicapped person—especially his need to be recognized as a normal human being. He may learn to ignore the handicap. If only others, too, would forget it!

Effective social service for the handicapped person, whether the handicap be physical or mental, means long-time planning, and mobilization of the numerous resources which exist for the purpose of helping him towards the highest measure of achievement.

The social worker's knowledge of many individual situations among the handicapped enables her to present the needs of the group upon a factual basis. For instance, in time of general unemployment, the handicapped have little hope of jobs although their need of work and their ability may be as great. In such times they must be far more skilled than the nonhandicapped if they are to secure work. Again, one unsatisfactory handicapped employee may cause discrimination against the whole group; or a beggar, if he happens to be handicapped, may create a most unfortunate public attitude toward the group. People are usually very willing to give money or pity but are not always so ready to give understanding and opportunity.

Although resources for certain types of handicapped are well organized, there are still serious lacks. For the blind, the deaf, and the physically crippled child, much is being done, but for the epileptic and diabetic child, for instance, social resources are still very inadequate. Education for these children and for cardiac children may be seriously interfered with unless special attention is given to the problem of those who can ill afford the added handicap of poor education. These and other needs of the group, the social worker is in a position to point out to a public which is becoming increasingly aware of its responsibility toward all social problems.

In prevention also the social worker can make a very definite contribution. Because of her contact with families in their homes, she is in a position to discover conditions which if neglected might mean later one more handicapped person. She facilitates early diagnosis and treatment in individual cases, and she presents social data which may be of significance in the educational or legislative programs directed toward prevention of physical or mental handicaps.

The trained social worker, then, because of her understanding of human relationships and knowledge of social and economic forces at work, has both an opportunity and a responsibility for constructive service to the handicapped.

A NUTRITION PROGRAM

BY AGNES EARLY

Formerly Community Nutritionist
Lawrence, Massachusetts

Last spring, a meeting of local social, educational and welfare leaders in the city of Lawrence met with representatives from the Massachusetts State Departments of Public Welfare, Public Health and Education to discuss their nutrition needs and to plan a program of relief. Previous to this meeting, various local groups had been endeavoring to help meet the nutrition needs of the school children. A group of city nurses were furnishing breakfasts to needy children in one section of the city and in another, a group of teachers were supporting a similar project. Families who had been receiving milk through various social agencies had to be cut off from this supply because of lack of funds. The number of families receiving aid from the Welfare Department was large; the city was in financial difficulty and the food budgets were of necessity quite restricted. Local grocers, market and milk men were not receiving money on accounts which had run for over a period of many months. Yet withal, everyone was sympathetic and trying in his individual way to help the situation as much as possible. This, then, was the situation when a worker was sent to Lawrence in May for the Massachusetts Child Council, to formulate a nutrition program.

A local nutrition committee was formed with a representative from each of the local social service agencies, as well as from the city Welfare Department, the School Department, the manager of the City Gardens and the Chamber of Commerce. The first step taken in the program was the organization of nutrition classes for homemakers in dependent families. These classes were started on May 15 in three of the city's public schools. Class members were personally visited by agents of the local social agencies, that is, the Tuberculosis League, City Mission, Catholic Charities and International Institute. The women were enrolled in the school centre nearest their homes. In all, ninety-four women were registered for the classes. There was an average weekly attendance of forty-five members. Six of the local practical art teachers volunteered their services as instructors.

About fifteen children were brought to the various classes by the mothers who had no one at home to take care of them. In the high school, a continuation school girl took charge of these children and served them a meal from the menu prepared by the mothers. An interesting feature of this service was that some of the children who wouldn't eat when with the mother, perhaps because of her food prejudice, ate heartily when with the other children; so incidentally, some food habit training was given. The mothers were greatly interested in this phase of the lessons. All of the women expressed a desire for further food training in the fall and spoke of other friends and neighbors whom they thought would like to share in the training.

The classes met from 1:45 to 4.30 P.M. once each week from May through June. Instruction was given in buying, preparing and serving foods which would give the best health protection for the minimum expenditure. Three meals, namely, breakfast, dinner and supper were prepared and served for each day in the week. The food budget was planned so that women learned to plan ahead so as to get variety and at the same time save money, time and effort. The menus were planned by the Vocational Division of the State Department of Education based on a grocery order approved by the Massachusetts Department of Public Health to show the proper food combinations for well balanced and adequate meals at a minimum cost. At every session, discussions were held regarding variations of that particular day's menu and the women were told what to add to the menus to make them more satisfying when they had more food money. Emphasis was given in the instruction to the selection of foods which would best meet the food requirements of all the family, especially the children. The importance of milk, bread and cereals, vegetables and fruit in the low cost diets was emphasized.

On June 7, a group of nineteen Italian mothers met in another school. These mothers were not familiar with American foods nor food habits. Some did not speak English, but an interpreter was present who helped in the instruction. An effort was made to impress upon these mothers the food value of fresh milk and the necessity of proper health habits such as cleanliness, rest, fresh air, etc. in relation to food. A simple food demonstration was given at each of these meetings at which a milk dish and cereal dish were prepared and served. During the summer, follow-up visits were made to the homes of the women who attended the nutrition classes. Almost without exception the women asked for more work this fall and reported using the food practices learned in the classes as well as an effort to improve the food habits of the family, such as the inclusion of more vegetables, some of them raw, and the use of more milk. Since most of these families have wage earners back at work they can maintain their standards, but the need of continued follow-up is imperative. The city is planning to meet this need by offering this fall units in low cost meals in their evening school program.

On June 14, Professor Cole of Massachusetts State College gave a canning demonstration to a group of fifty women who had been invited by the nutrition leaders to attend. Of this group, twelve volunteered to serve as leaders for the Community Canning project.

The city of Lawrence had more than 900 subsistence gardens allotted to applicants from the city's welfare agencies. Seeds were purchased by the city Welfare Department and plowing, fertilizing and watering facilities were given by the city. In order to care for the surplus crops of the community gardens, a survey was made to determine a proper location for canning kitchens. It was at first thought advisable to have two kitchens located in different parts of the city. Permission was given by the school authorities to use a building for this purpose. However, as the opening of the school came before the end of the canning season, another location was sought.

As it was desirable to have the work of canning carried on in proximity to the gardens, available buildings were sought in their neighborhood. Very fortunately, such a building was found at the Essex County Training School, housing the original institutional kitchen. Permission was obtained from the County Commissioners to use the building and Superintendent Tetler generously cooperated in every way to make the building available.

The building was cleaned and the equipment set up and connected by men from the Welfare Department who worked industriously so that it might be opened on the appointed date. Since this building was connected by steam with the main plant of the institution, the major fuel problem was solved. The site of the original sink proved an ideal location for a hot water tank which was built locally. This tank was constructed with a capacity for processing over 200 cans at a time. The tank was conveniently located near windows so that the cans could be slid, immediately after processing, down a trough to a hogshead of cold water to cool them. Plans were submitted to the local tinsmith to construct lifters of sheet iron to lift the cans from their steam heated bath. A disused copper caldron was scoured and made ready for use and as it was heated by steam it proved an ideal place to blanche vegetables. A local furniture store loaned a three-burner gasoline stove for additional cooking facilities. Two sinks were in the room and a number of work tables were borrowed, besides a clock, scales, dishpans and other utensils.

In July, the Mayor called a meeting at which the question of the city's approval of purchasing cans was considered. It was agreed that a sum of from $400 to $500 might be allotted for the project. It was decided to purchase 10,000 cans and three sealers, as well as some cooking kettles and other necessary small equipment.

On August 16, the canning kitchen was first opened. Men from the Welfare Department, working in shifts, operated the sealers. The average number of women and men using the kitchen were from twenty to thirty per day and the average daily number of cans turned out, from 300 to 400.

Each worker received a certain number of cans for his day's work when he was working for the kitchen. If working for himself, the kitchen exacted a toll of one can for every ten put up. A limit of one hundred cans was set for each family using the kitchen. Many families thus helped to provide for the coming winter by taking their garden surplus to the kitchen and giving their time to prepare and can their produce or by bartering their time for a certain number of cans of the donated produce. Much produce was donated to the kitchen by neighboring market gardeners, as well as by private garden owners.

On September 1, a local leader, Mrs. Walter Dean, became supervisor of the kitchen and under her able leadership the work continued throughout the month. At the end of September over 9,900 cans of tomatoes, beans, carrots and beets had been prepared. Several hundred cans of produce were given by the kitchen to each of the following local agencies: the City Home, the Catholic Charities and the City Mission for distribution in relief work this winter.

CARDIAC CHILD
BY T. DUCKETT JONES, M.D.
House of the Good Samaritan
Boston, Mass.

It may be well to state at the outset that the large volume or problem of heart disease in children is the result of heart disease of the acquired type rather than congenital defects of the heart. The scope of this short article will therefore be limited to acquired heart disease in children, which indicates rheumatic heart disease.

Rheumatic heart disease is the result of rheumatic fever, and consists of changes in all three layers of the heart: endocardium, myocardium, and pericardium. In addition, there are extensive changes during rheumatic fever in other organs, especially the liver, and throughout the blood vessels. The symptomatology hence is not limited to the heart, and usually is very protean in character. Children from five to fifteen years of age are very prone to rheumatic fever, and the disease shows a very strong tendency to repeated recurrences during this age period. The disease may remain active for varying periods from several months to several years. Between 85% and 90% of those individuals exhibiting manifestations of rheumatic fever, show on examination heart disease of the rheumatic type. This heart disease is usually permanent. The recurrences of rheumatic fever are associated, at least in 75% of the instances, with infection of the upper respiratory tract (sore throat, colds, etc.). The cause is as yet not definitely known.

The above introduction is given merely to give an indication of what one is really dealing with when we discuss the problem of the cardiac child. While the disease is very prevalent and the mortality high (21% in 1,000 cases over a ten-year period, House of Good Samaritan series), the majority of children do not develop sufficient heart disease to prevent their leading moderately active lives, and in fact, well over 50% are able ultimately to lead a normally active physical life.

The care of the acutely ill child with rheumatic fever and active heart disease is well known to medical men, and hospitalization as a rule is necessary, largely because it is impossible to give adequate care to a very ill individual in the homes where rheumatic fever is prevalent (the disease is predominant on the whole among the industrial classes).

The actual medical assistance, therefore, resolves itself into the care of the child during the chronic low-grade forms of active rheumatic fever and heart disease, measures of importance in promoting general health when there is no active disease, and attempts at preventing recurrences of rheumatic fever. In addition, there are other factors of importance which may be discussed under appropriate headings, such as the education of parents and patient, actual schooling, vocational guidance, and the psychology of the individual with rheumatic heart disease.

The protean manifestations of rheumatic fever have been mentioned. In no stage of the disease is this seen more definitely than in the chronic low-grade or continuous form, which usually in children follows the acute illness. Continuation of active rheumatic fever is presumptive evidence of active heart disease. Some of the major symptoms may be listed: joint pains of varying degrees and severity, low-grade fever, nosebleeds, subcutaneous nodules, rashes (various forms of erythema multiforme), moderate anemia, anorexia, vomiting, precordial pain, abdominal pain, failure to gain weight, etc. In addition, there is usually laboratory evidence of active infection long after the clinical symptoms have subsided.

While there is no general medical agreement upon the form of therapy necessary during this stage of the disease, the large number of physicians devoting any appreciable time and attention to this disease, feel that rest in bed so long as there is evidence of active infection is the most important feature. Common sense would seem to indicate this and it is merely following, perhaps, the most important of all therapeutic measures. Consistently good results may be obtained if this procedure is carried out. It is, however, difficult to obtain, as it means months of restriction of activity. This may be impossible and difficult in the home, and require hospitalization. This feature of the disease is fairly comparable to the type of care given in tuberculosis. In addition to the benefit from prolonged rest, the education of the patient is an important factor. It is especially important to protect children with continuous rheumatic fever from contact with individuals having acute respiratory infection.

When there is no longer any active rheumatic fever, the child is gradually returned to whatever degree of physical activity his permanent heart damage will permit (as a rule limitation of competitive sports is eventually the only restriction), and a resumption of school work. At this period it is wise to better the home conditions as much as is possible. The child should sleep alone and better still in a room alone. A well balanced diet is beneficial to general health. A quart of milk daily, some fresh fruit, and fresh vegetables are insisted upon whenever possible. At this stage it is wise also to instruct the parent and child concerning the recurring nature of the disease, the importance of avoiding respiratory infection, and that medical aid should be sought should respiratory infection or any symptoms of rheumatic fever occur. The picture should be presented as helpful and in no sense as a hopeless proposition. The outcome of the individual case may depend in a large degree upon this education, and it should be done thoroughly and by some one thoroughly familiar with the disease. Upon it rests the most important feature of helping the individual patient—intelligent cooperation.

At the present time our knowledge as to how best prevent recurrences of rheumatic fever is scanty. The association of tonsillitis, sore throats, colds, etc., with these recurrences, justifies instilling into the minds of both parents and child, that all people with acute respiratory infections should be zealously avoided. Inquiry into the respiratory history of a family, will at times bring out information that some one member has frequent colds and sore throats. It is even wise, in some instances, to have tonsillectomy performed in another member of the family in an attempt to protect the cardiac child. It is notoriously difficult to prevent the spread of respiratory infection through a family, especially in crowded quarters with many small children. Despite this the family should be made to realize the importance of striving hard to do so.

The problem of school is a difficult, but essential one. Children who, because of active rheumatic fever, lose much time from school, should have as much instruction as possible in an effort to keep them up in their studies. During the past several years much has been accomplished through visiting teachers going into the home. This program might well be further increased. Except during acute severe illness, school at home or hospital is possible. This has long been recognized by the House of the Good Samaritan and the Robert Bent Brigham Hospital, where instruction is given. It is indeed pathetic to see an older child, who will be able to lead an active life, unwilling to continue at school because of the age of classmates being several years younger. Nor can such a child be blamed, for it is a definite invitation to a feeling of inferiority. The urgent attempt should always be made to keep the child as nearly as possible up in his or her studies.

With the proper education of child and parent, and the introduction to the child of suitable interests and handicrafts during the long periods of bed rest, it should be possible to prevent any great psychological alteration because of this recurring and chronic disease. This requires much education and substitution, but is a necessary and worthy aim.

In a small number of children it is necessary to provide vocational guidance and instruction. This group has not only a poor prognosis as regards length of life, but is unable to carry on any appreciable physical activity. Efforts here are directed toward making these children ultimately self-supporting by means of a sedentary occupation.

The problem of the cardiac child is a large and difficult one. It is, however, hopeful and much assistance can be given. We have in addition, a right to expect an increase in our knowledge of heart disease within a few years, and it is the hope and purpose of many students of the disease that we may be able to more materially assist these patients.

OCCUPATIONAL THERAPY

BY CAROLINE N. SHAW
Director of Occupational Therapy
Robert Bent Brigham Hospital, Boston, Mass.

Occupational Therapy seems a long name for a very normal bit of work. It may be defined as "any activity, mental or physical, definitely prescribed and guided for the distinct purpose of contributing to and hastening recovery from disease." In the strictest sense the occupational therapy aide's medicine kit is a kit of crafts, offering incentives to patients to undertake some normal activity. It has played a very real part in recent years and is playing an increasing part in the recovery of the handicapped patient.

There is not space here to enlarge on the occupational therapy field — greatest in the mental hospitals, constantly increasing in tuberculosis, general and children's hospitals. Here I wish to emphasize the need and use of occupational therapy for those with functional handicaps, due either to accident, industry or disease, such as the widespread foe, arthritis. People inquire as to the line of demarcation between occupational therapy and physiotherapy. In orthopedic work the departments dovetail but need neither overlap nor conflict. The physiotherapist gives her patients both active and passive exercises. The occupational therapist provides means for her patient to get active exercise (in the strictest sense by means of crafts) but she does not do passive work with her patient. There are varying distinct steps in occupational therapy work which it is well to remember.

First comes hospital treatment:
    (a) for the patient in bed,
    (b) for the wheelchair patient,
    (c) for the ambulatory patient who can do work in the hospital shop.

If special gifts or interests of the patient can be discovered which at the same time can be developed medically for his functional benefit, so much the better.

Hospital work for orthopedic patients is done on the doctor's prescription. The *method* of doing the crafts is of the first importance so that the patient may obtain the greatest possible functional benefit. This phase of the work should not be commercialized, but be regarded as treatment only.

An orthopedic specialist in Boston has said, "Probably the greatest use for occupational therapy is to secure normal movements in joints when they are limited through disease, after fractures, splints, casts, operations and arthritis. Because
    1. The work can be made to produce every known movement of any joint in the body.
    2. It can be graded to any desired effort.
    3. It can be controlled."

When the patient is discharged from the hospital he may still need definite functional treatment, best gained by a normal use (or use tending toward normality) of muscles or joints. Perhaps a patient has never had to be hospitalized, but has some functional handicap. At this point the curative work shop is a most important asset to the patient . . . our second distinct step in treatment. Here his activity is guided by trained workers under doctor's prescription. Such shops can materially aid in the recovery of industrial accident cases. In Milwaukee, Wisconsin, there is such a shop, excellently organized. In it physiotherapy and occupational therapy cooperate in the treatment of the patient. Industrial concerns send their accident cases to it. Other such shops are being started—and one could well be used in this community.

The Sheltered Workshop might be called another step in the patient's recovery, but not really the occupational therapy worker's problem. Here the patient tests himself out before being subjected to the strain of competition. The Sheltered Workshop of the Boston Tuberculosis Association is a good illustration.

Also prevocational and rehabilitation and reeducation in the industrial field are continuations rather than parts of the occupational therapist's program. The occupational therapist should cooperate with the social service departments to use all available agencies in the community in planning for the patient's re-entry as a useful unit in community life.

VOCATIONAL GUIDANCE FOR THE TUBERCULOUS CHILD

BY LEON A. ALLEY, M.D.

Superintendent, Lakeville State Sanatorium

The various forms of extra-pulmonary tuberculosis produce many and varied handicaps of all degrees. In the bony structures of the body, the most common is the loss of motion either in whole or in part of one or more joints. These joints may be in the weight-bearing structures; for example, the hip, knee, sacro-iliac, ankle, or small bones of the feet. Or they may be in the upper extremities; for example, the shoulder, elbow, wrist, or small bones of the hands. Or again the handicap may be due to immobilization of the spine. Lesions high in the spine are followed by a stiff neck and lesions in the middle or low spine result in a stiff back.

As tuberculosis attacks the soft tissues in various parts of the body as well as the bony structures, handicaps are noted particularly in those cases where involvement has taken place in the eyes and ears as well as those cases of tuberculosis of the skin resulting in marked disfigurement especially of the exposed surfaces of the body. Contractures are often the result of these conditions necessitating excision of the diseased tissue. These contractures may also follow skin grafting especially when the part removed is extensive or when secondary contractures result from operation.

Children of all ages who have a partial or total loss of vision are taught to read by the Braille method. Typewriting has also been found practical. The deaf child is taught lip reading and has an educational program directing his activities into those channels in which his handicap will be one of the least hindrance.

Our problem is to carry out so far as it is practical, without interfering with the treatment for which the patient is primarily admitted to the sanatorium, methods and measures of theoretical as well as practical instruction in those subjects that may be properly classified as assisting in the formation of the ground work for vocations of one sort or another. This may be called Vocational Guidance as it has as often as possible a "job objective." Much of the work must of necessity be of a fundamental nature but at all times leads and points to a definite goal.

In the sanatorium, we particularly direct our energies with children and young adults toward building up the proper educational foundations in order that following their discharge they may be properly equipped to carry on courses as furnished by the State Department of Education in Vocational Guidance with definite job objectives. Bearing in mind that the patient is primarily tuberculous, the education and training must be along such lines that his or her handicap may be overcome but at the same time the type of occupation must be so selected as to avoid, so far as possible, the chances of future breakdowns not only at the previous site of the disease but also in any other part of the body due to the fatigue and strain of a poorly selected occupation. We must remember that he has already shown, at least temporarily, the lack of sufficient resistance to prevent the development of an active tuberculous lesion. More than the handicap must therefore be considered.

Because of the popularity of the treatment for diseased joints by surgical ankylosis which results in the elimination of all motion from a joint, the child who has lost the function of an ankle, knee, or hip must, of course, be trained for an occupation that does not require the active use of these joints.

Watch repairing, mechanical drawing, blue printing, mimeographing, poultry raising, sign painting, leather work and handicraft are some of the courses that have been especially selected and chosen for patients recovering from tuberculosis of the bones and joints. The use of power machines for wood working is very popular with the older boys regardless of the handicap. Ship and aeroplane modeling opens a very wide field for the individual to display skill and talent.

Both theoretical and practical instructions for older boys are carried on in brace making which has proven to be a field of occupation that is not overcrowded and in which there is always a demand for a well-trained brace maker. The art of brace making and the development of appliances for various types of cripples is an occupation with but few, if any, contraindications for a person with handicaps resulting from any form of extra-pulmonary tuberculosis. Practical instructions in electrical engineering are available in the institution with its own power plant generating its own electrical supply and maintaining the equipment for its distribution.

The making and assembling of jewelry is an art readily acquired and is practical for the patient with but little academic foundation. Hand painting and decorating of china and parchment are practical and appeal to the aesthetic type of person. There are many outlets for artistic work of this type. Bookbinding is instructive and popular with both boys and girls of a wide range of ages.

Older children receive instructions by means of especially arranged Red Cross Courses in Home Hygiene which prove to be of inestimable value in every home that is fortunate enough to have at least one member of the family so trained. They also have the opportunity of learning and practicing the duties of the attendant nurse in caring for the sick.

Telephone switchboard instructions have been found most practical and popular especially among girls. This is a vocation that may be successfully followed for many years, as is also various types of office work, especially card filing, cataloguing, library cataloguing, and so forth.

Children with abdominal or renal tuberculosis because of the nature of their disease must follow a sedentary life and must therefore be educated and trained for those occupations best fitted for their condition.

For all children up to sixteen years of age, graded school work is available. Particular attention is paid to the most important academic subjects because of the limited time available each day for instruction rather than to use the time for many of the subjects now taught in the public schools.

The value of any safe occupation that will instill and reestablish confidence in the handicapped cannot be estimated as many of the physical handicaps can be markedly exaggerated by the mental point of view of the individual. On the other hand the handicapped child or young adult must be taught his or her limitation in order that he or she may so live and work as to guard and maintain that degree of good health that has required months and in many cases years to acquire. The maintainance of good health is much more to be desired than that type of work that is more remunerative for a few years time but may eventually be the cause of many months or years of suffering or disability. The most important phase of education and training of the handicapped individual is that which teaches him how to live a long and useful life.

THE SHELTERED WORKSHOP OF THE BOSTON TUBERCULOSIS ASSOCIATION

BY BERNICE W. BILLINGS, R.N. AND ESTHER L. FRUTKOFF

Boston Tuberculosis Association

The Sheltered Workshop conducted by the Boston Tuberculosis Association was started in September 1930. The loan of a school building and yard at 35 Tyler Street, Boston, was secured from the city, and the shop itself was financed through private funds.

Object

The object of this shop was to provide training and suitable employment for patients who had been treated for tuberculosis in sanatoria or at home and had become well enough to work but were not yet strong enough to return to full-time jobs.

Admission

A ruling was made that each patient should be admitted upon request of a physician and accompanied by a medical statement with a recommendation as to the number of hours of work which he was thought able to do. In the beginning several patients who were too sick to work were admitted to the shop but as soon as arrangements could be made for these sick patients to have sanatorium or home care, they were discharged. Greater care has been observed since then on the admission of patients, and at present all of those who are working at the shop are arrested and quiescent cases of tuberculosis.

Mental Condition

Mental tests were made on all patients admitted in the first three months. These tests seemed to have little or no value. Many of them were of foreign extraction and did not understand the questions. Several of the most intelligent patients at the shop had a mental age of ten years. These tests are not now given, but if there is any question regarding the mentality of a particular patient, a special mental examination is made.

Care

Since many of these patients have but a scanty breakfast they are served a mid-morning lunch of a glass of milk and crackers. A hearty dinner at 12 o'clock is also provided, and the patients are obliged to take one hour's rest each day.

Clinics and Follow-Up

The Association furnishes a physician to examine these patients on their entrance to the shop and from time to time thereafter. The service of a trained public health worker is provided to supervise these patients in the shop, to find work for them on their discharge from the shop and to visit them in their homes.

Teaching

A teacher with a background of eight years of experience in carpentry and one year's training in the School of Manual Arts, is engaged to teach the men carpentry. A graduate of a School of Domestic Science and Dressmaking is employed to teach sewing to the women.

Pay of Patients

All of the patients are paid on entrance 18c. an hour and 60 per cent of them are now being paid from 22c. to 50c. an hour. Lunch and dinner are free.

Admission and Discharge

Since the opening of the Sheltered Shop, eighty-five patients have been employed, and of these, thirty-two are there at present. Thirty-one of the fifty-three who were discharged are well and able to work. The remainder were those who were discharged as unsuited for the shop, either from active tuberculosis or because of handicaps other than tuberculosis.

One of our former working patients is now employed in a linen room of a Boston institution. The training which she received at the shop enabled her to hold her job. Many of the patients returned to their old occupations after they had worked up to full time at the shop and were discharged by the clinic physician as able to work outside.

Sales

A saleswoman with seven years' experience in retail stores is employed to buy the raw materials for the shop and to sell the finished products. She also supervises the women's department and has charge of the parking space. It has been found impossible to fill large orders on time since the patients can not be hurried. The work has, therefore, been confined to taking orders and selling finished products at bazaars and at sales.

Parking Space

The Association was given permission to use the school yard as a parking space and this has given employment to men patients who have recovered from tuberculosis.

Receipts

In the first year the sale of goods and receipts from the parking space brought in $4,051.96. In the second year the receipts from the same sources were $5,586.09, and in the year 1933 it is estimated that $6,000 will be received.

Cost

It cost, exclusive of the amount received from sales and parking space, $19,122.42 to maintain the shop for the first full year. Twenty-seven patients were cared for. In 1932 the daily average of patients was increased to thirty-two. With the increase in the receipts from the sales and parking space, the cost for maintaining the shop was $20,042.08.

Boarders

The budget for 1933 was reduced and consequently but twenty-five patients could be cared for. Since there were fourteen applicants who could not be admitted for at least six months, a plan was devised to secure from interested agencies and persons, subsidies to cover the cost of food and carfares for the patients on the waiting list, thus admitting them at once. The shop has employed an average of five extra patients provided for in this way. As soon as vacancies have occurred, these patients were placed on the shop payroll. We believe this plan has been an excellent one as it has enabled these patients to live and work under wholesome conditions for from three to six months earlier than if they had awaited regular admission.

Value of Shop

We believe the shop has done much to restore the confidence and courage of those patients who have been in sanatoria for years and become timid and fearful of breaking down. It gives excellent training to young men and women in trades which will help them to earn a living after their discharge from the shop. It has raised the living standard of both the patients and their families. Many of the patients who were entirely dependent on their families or the charitable agencies have learned to assume responsibility and are not only self-supporting but aid in the support of their families. The follow-up worker reports that the general health of the shop patients has been greatly improved, and that among other things, dental work has been completed and glasses have been secured when needed.

We look forward eventually to increasing the number of patients to at least fifty and to including boarding patients from cities and towns in Greater Boston. Although the shop may never be self-supporting, we believe that in time it will meet the greater part of its cost through the admission of more patients, better and quicker work and consequently an increase in sales.

THE COOPERATIVE WORKROOMS, INC.

BY HAZEL NEWTON

The Cooperative Workrooms, Inc.

Jobs have always been pretty important things to all of us — "The right job for the right person" has been for years a matter of interest to employers, teachers and vocational guidance workers, as well as to employees themselves.

How infinitely much more important has employment become in the last three years, when depression has made it a question of any job at all, whether one is fitted for it or not! To a certain extent, the abnormal conditions during a depression period are present all the time in the lives of people who are in any way handicapped in the struggle to earn a living. The Cooperative Workrooms, Inc., knows this well, for this is the field in which all its efforts are expended. This social agency was organized more than fifty years ago by a group of Boston ladies "to ameliorate the condition of the poor." To that end friendly visiting was carried on by a corps of volunteer visitors, soon destined to ally themselves with what is now the Family Welfare Society, organized a few years after the Cooperative Workrooms was chartered.

More and more, then, the efforts of the Cooperative Workrooms, Inc., were turned toward employment problems of the handicapped until now, at 36 Washington Street, Boston, busy workrooms give evidence of how the need is being met. Here are electric sewing machines so easy to run that even though a leg, crippled by infantile paralysis, is in irons, it becomes no obstacle to turning out a well-made garment. Totally deaf girls can read the lips of the instructors or have directions written out. The tremors of a cerebral palsy have been steadied remarkably by mechanical repetition in the operation of the button-hole machine. Inspection is accomplished by two girls working together. One was born with no left arm, the other has almost total loss of use of her right because of Parkinsonian syndrome.

So it goes through the processes of learning and practicing a trade that can be useful in the industrial or commercial world — for in recent years the Workrooms has been called upon to help other people than those whose ability and interest indicated factory work. For example, a telephone operator, both arms and both legs affected by poliomyelitis, does not need to walk much, writes messages with her left hand, and by wearing a head-set manages to accomplish very efficient work. The policy has always been to serve as widely as possible, so there are no limits of race, creed, residence or age. Neither are there restrictions as to the form of handicap. Often an invisible handicap may be a more serious obstacle to good adjustment at work than an obvious one such as the withered hand of spastic paralysis.

So the Workrooms includes the mental and social difficulties also in its attempts to help. Psychoneurosis in any of its manifestations, slight or grave, may make an employer feel only that his worker is a nuisance, a whiner, or a trouble maker. To have the symptoms understood may give the sufferer more insight into his own condition so that he can adjust to his work and his fellow workers so satisfactorily that his real ability is released in wider channels.

The hospital clinics begin this process of course, but the Workrooms is frequently called upon to continue under conditions approximating those in industry.

Human beings are so complex that one cannot say "This is a case of tuberculosis of the spine and should have light work", and consider the problem solved when such work has been obtained. People cannot be neatly docketed in this way. Many times it has been the experience of the Workrooms to have a problem of physical trouble presented, to have tried to solve it on the basis of physical adjustment, only to find that until the more delicate, subtle personality adjustments were made the problem still remained. On the other hand, a client has sometimes come solely because he recognized a personality difficulty in himself which he had never suspected was caused by a physical condition until the careful social case work carried on at the Workrooms revealed it. This case work includes the using of all possible resources to achieve so complete a rehabilitation that it includes that feeling of happiness and proper self-satisfaction in the individual which comes only with as complete a mental, physical, and social adjustment as can be achieved.

Sometimes these resources mean that the aid of relief agencies is asked, or that a hospital clinic gives a complete physical examination. It may be that the long-continued friendly contact of an agency specializing in family situations is needed, or that the help of an agency caring for children is called in. Perhaps the recreations offered by a settlement house are necessary, or the evening study classes of the public school system. In any event the Workrooms tries to supplement its endeavors with others so that all needs are met. The Workrooms pays wages to every one employed, based, at first, not on production, but on earnest effort. In time this wage is increased so that it does bear some relation to the amount produced.

The Workrooms does not think of itself as a sheltered workshop where its trainees remain indefinitely in an atmosphere adjusted to them. On the contrary it so tries to adjust its clients to normal conditions in industry that they may successfully carry on after they leave the Workrooms.

Not all clients are susceptible of training. Some are too old ever to hope to find a place in the competitive world again. These are given simple work for only a few days each week, solely for the therapeutic value of occupation, of feeling that they are still of some use even in a limited way, and for the change of scene from their meagre home surroundings that the Workrooms affords. The small wage they are given is often a considerable proportion of their entire budget.

Home sewing is given, too, to a number of women. Most of these are in great financial need owing to illness, unemployment of the normal wage earner, or of other conditions beyond their control. In compliance with the law on home work in the Commonwealth of Massachusetts each of them is licensed by the Board of Labor and Industries, and in addition the social worker of the Workrooms takes special pains to make sure that home conditions are suitable, that no contagious diseases are present, that children are not being neglected and that the worker's own strength is not being overtaxed.

Sincere as the desire of the Workrooms is to be of as great usefulness as possible, it is inevitably limited by financial conditions. Fortunately, a fund has been established for the payment of staff salaries, and the contributions of interested people, formerly personally, but now through the joint fund-raising carried on in Boston, are a substantial help. Sales of the products of clients more nearly determine the amount available for training purposes than any other form of income. These products include such items as hospital patients' shirts, operating room gowns, nurses' uniforms, waitresses' uniforms, smocks, housedresses, and children's dresses. They are sold wherever customers can be found for them, priced at a rate to compete fairly with the goods of profit-making organizations. The Workrooms is a charity, and therefore will never be on a paying basis because of the constant turnover of unskilled handicapped people who cannot produce the equivalent of what they are paid.

In many instances the greater the need for social service, the greater the expense during the period of training. Materials to make the garments are an unavoidable expense but every effort is made, both in their purchase and in all other expenses incidental to the carrying on of the affairs of the Workrooms, that every cent possible is turned into wages for clients.

TRAVELING SCHOOL CLINICS FOR THE EXAMINATION OF RETARDED CHILDREN IN THE PUBLIC SCHOOLS

BY NEIL A. DAYTON, M.D.

Director, Division of Mental Deficiency
Massachusetts Department of Mental Diseases

The Division of Mental Deficiency supervises the activities of fifteen traveling psychiatric school clinics coming under the Department of Mental Diseases. These clinics have been in operation for eighteen years, and have been state wide in their function since 1921, or a period of eleven years.

The Massachusetts School Clinic System was devised and placed in operation by the late Doctor Walter E. Fernald, who sent out the first traveling clinic from the Waverley School on December 15, 1914. In 1917, the late Doctor George L. Wallace sent out the second traveling clinic from the Wrentham State School. As time went on, however, it soon became evident that these two clinics could not examine all the backward children in the public schools of the entire State, and the formation of additional units became imperative. Doctor Fernald placed the matter before the Commissioner of Mental Diseases, Doctor George M. Kline, and in 1921, as a result of their collaboration, traveling clinics were created to operate from each of the fourteen institutions under the Department of Mental Diseases. Thus, for the first time, an adequate state wide system for the examination of all retarded children was made possible. The fifteenth clinic was added in January, 1928.

Doctor Kline saw that the withdrawal of a psychiatrist from the medical staffs of the various hospitals was impracticable and, therefore, increased the quota of each institution by one physician and one psychologist to carry on this important work. Doctor Payson Smith, Commissioner of Education, took an active part in framing the law relating to retarded children and in outlining and enforcing the school clinic regulations which have contributed so materially to the school clinic system.

The General Court of 1919 enacted a law to legalize the operation of the clinics in the public school system. This law was later amended by the Legislature in 1922, and again in 1931. It now reads as follows:

Chapter 71, section 46, General Laws (as amended by chapter 231, acts of 1922, and chapter 358, acts of 1931) "The school committee of every town shall annually ascertain, *under regulations prescribed by the Department of Education and the Department of Mental Diseases,* the number of children three years or more retarded in mental development in attendance upon its public schools, or of school age and resident therein. At the beginning of each school year, the committee of every town where there are ten or more such children shall establish special classes for their instruction according to their mental attainments, under regulations prescribed by the department. A child appearing to be mentally retarded in any less degree may, upon request of the superintendent of schools of the town where he attends school, be examined under such regulations as may be prescribed by the department of education and the department of mental diseases. No child under the control of the department of public welfare or of the child welfare division of the institutions department of the city of Boston who is three years or more retarded in mental development within the meaning of this section shall, after complaint made by the school committee to the department of public welfare or said division, be placed in a town which is not required to maintain a special class as provided for in this section. (Approved May 26, 1931)."

With the amendment of 1931, radical changes in the school clinic law which had been under consideration for a good many years were affected. Reference is made particularly to that section permitting examinations of children less than three years retarded. Quite often problem cases have come to the attention of the school authorities needing examination and care, but who could not be examined under the restrictions of the previous law. We feel that this change is one of the most constructive moves ever made in this particular field. While it doubtlessly increases the work of the clinic, still the increased scope of the service will more than justify any slight added expense.

The Department of Education has outlined certain regulations dealing with examinations and special class provision. The first paragraph of these regulations applies in particular to the school clinics under the supervision of this Division. It reads as follows: "1· The school committee shall require the examination of all children of school age residing in the town who appear to be three or more years retarded in mental development. *The examination shall be given by the State Department of Mental Diseases or an examiner approved by that Department."*

The growth in the number of examinations completed by the traveling clinics each year is outlined in Table I. The striking increase in 1921 is due, of course, to the fact that fourteen clinics became operative at that time, where only two had been operative previous to 1921. We note that in 1932 over 6,000 retarded children were examined by the various clinics.

Graph I outlines the accumulation of examinations. It shows that a total of 63,723 examinations of retarded children have been conducted by the clinics during the eighteen years of operation.

There has been a steady increase of interest throughout the State in the work which is being done by our traveling clinics. Superintendents now welcome any assistance which the clinics can give, and have become enthusiastic supporters of this system of examining retarded children. They were not long in recognizing the fact that the service provided is detached from the local school organization and, as such, can provide an examination which is wholly impersonal. In the past parents of retarded children have been sometimes critical of the decisions made by the local school superintendent in reference to the class placement of retarded

TABLE I. — Number of School Clinic Examinations, 1915-1932

Year	Number of Examinations	Year	Number of Examinations
1915	126	1924	4567
1916	307	1925	4395
1917	259	1926	4652
1918	210	1927	5638
1919	247	1928	6286
1920	269	1929	6259
1921	2284	1930	6527
1922	4836	1931	6439
1923	4343	1932	6079

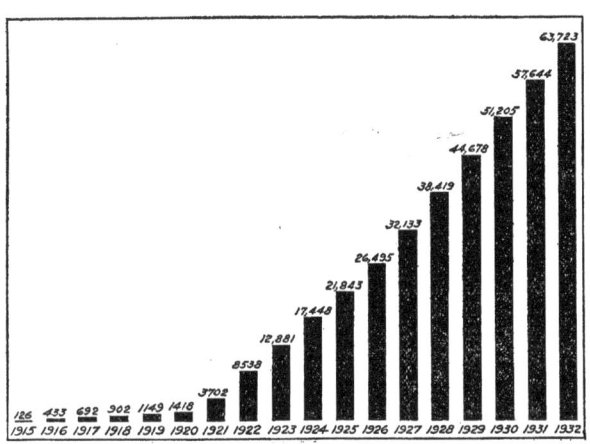

GRAPH I. — CUMULATIVE GRAPH OF SCHOOL CLINIC EXAMINATIONS, 1915-1932.

children. They are proving to be less critical of the decisions of our clinic psychiatrists. They recognize that the decisions are based on very complete medical and psychiatric examinations by a clinic which is not a part of the local school organization.

It is a standard practice for the psychiatrists of the traveling clinics to invite the parents of children examined to come to the schools and to confer with them following the examinations. Many parents cooperate in this matter, and have come to a better understanding of their children when behavior problems and other difficulties are interpreted to them by the psychiatrist.

Total Examinations During 1932

Table II reveals that a total of 6,079 examinations were conducted by all clinics during the year 1932. Of these examinations, 4,461 were first examinations and 1,618 were reexaminations. The sex difference is noticeable in that 4,126 or 67 per cent of all examinations were males and 1,953 or 32 per cent were females.

We observe that 2,885 or 47 per cent of all examinations were recommended for special classes: 47 per cent of the males and 48 per cent of the females. Two hundred seventy-six or 4.5 per cent of all examinations were recommended for placement within a State school: 3.6 per cent of the males and 6.4 per cent of the females. Other recommendations fell into such small groupings that they are not given in detail. However, the twenty or more other recommendations used made up 48 per cent of the total number. Considering these figures as a whole, we note that *2,885 children were recommended for special classes in Massachusetts during a single school year*. As the total number of children already in special classes in the towns having examinations during 1932 is now 5,111, we can see the great need for additional special class provision. That is, in a single year we recommend 2,885 children for special class, and this number is over 56 per cent of the number of children already in special classes.

TABLE II — School Clinic Examinations Conducted during Year Ended November 30, 1932, by Institution, Status of Recommendation, and Sex.

INSTITUTIONS	Total Examinations			Recommended for Special Classes			Recommended for Institutional Care			Other Recommendations		
	Total	Male	Female	T.	M.	F.	T.	M.	F.	T.	M.	F.
Belchertown	401	269	132	201	145	56	58	25	33	142	99	43
Boston Psychopathic	113	83	30	12	10	2	–	–	–	101	73	28
Boston State	410	274	136	137	86	51	20	11	9	253	177	76
Danvers	324	224	100	148	102	46	15	11	4	161	111	50
Foxborough	515	361	154	171	111	60	8	2	6	336	248	88
Gardner	261	181	80	62	43	19	11	5	6	188	133	55
Grafton	295	177	118	153	100	53	16	9	7	126	68	58
Medfield	360	238	122	247	166	81	6	4	2	107	68	39
Monson	304	215	89	197	132	65	7	6	1	100	77	23
Northampton	443	306	137	189	124	65	15	8	7	239	174	65
Taunton	309	231	78	122	87	35	2	2	–	185	142	43
Walter E. Fernald	1355	896	459	829	550	279	61	35	26	465	311	154
Westborough	117	79	38	27	18	9	3	2	1	87	59	28
Worcester	265	178	87	147	95	52	19	13	6	99	70	29
Wrentham	607	414	193	243	169	74	35	18	17	329	227	102
Total	6079	4126	1953	2885	1938	947	276	151	125	2918	2037	881
Per cent	100.0	100.0	100.0	47.5	47.0	48.5	4.5	3.6	6.4	48.0	49.4	45.1

Personnel of Clinics, 1932, by Institutions

In Table III we present the personnel of the various clinics for the year 1932. This is being done as it may serve as a directory to any individuals or schools who are interested in having their retarded children examined. Applications for the services of these clinics may be sent to the Department of Education or to the writer of this communication. Over the past few years the workers of these clinics have done remarkable work in dealing with the many difficult situations met with, and have richly deserved the expressed gratitude of the many communities in which they have done their work. The infinite variety of child problems coming to them has required a versatility of judgment rarely demanded of psychiatrists. However, they have met these problems in a manner which has reflected credit on themselves and their respective institutions.

We must recall that the matter of diagnosis of mental deficiency is always an extremely delicate matter. Parents rarely recognize that mental retardation is in the same category as any other physical disturbance, such as congenital hip disease, for example. Their extreme sensitiveness on this question makes it necessary that the psychiatrist emphasize the possibilities of a carefully outlined training program, and keep to the fore the more hopeful aspects and possible accomplishment to be attained through specialized instruction. The recognition of the child's retardation and his placement in the proper school classes may easily mark the upturn in the child's life. The workers who have studied these cases and who have made the required decisions have rendered an inestimable service to these children. We have not observed the results to be attained long enough to say that we know what intensive training under a specialized program can do for a retarded child.

TABLE III — Personnel of Traveling School Clinics, by Institution, for Year Ended November 30, 1932.

Institution	Psychiatrist in Charge	Psychologist	Social Worker
Belchertown	Herbert L. Flynn, M.D.	May Buckler	Dorothy Peese
Boston Psychopathic	Mary Palmer, M.D.	Viola M. Jones	Mrs. Grover Curtis
Boston State	Alberta S. Guibord, M.D.	Edith B. James	Florence Armstrong and staff
Danvers	Edgar C. Yerbury, M.D. Doris M. Sidwell, M.D.	Dorothy MacLeod Marion Krauzer Mrs. Mildred Carpenter Lucy Sanborn Alice Schoenfuss	
Foxborough	Cornelia B. J. Schorer, M.D.	Eleanor Culbert Minnie Radner	Rebecca Russakoff Ruth Holmes Sadye Salutzky
Gardner	William A. Hunter, M.D.	Aurelia Boles	
Grafton	Anna C. Wellington, M.D.	Emaline L. Kelly	
Medfield	George A. Troxell, M.D.	Frances Allen Reed	Mary A. Morris Sibyl H. Wardwell
Monson	Lucie G. Forrer, M.D.	Marion Zerbe Dorothy H. Roche	Lula P. Hayes Teresa Cotter
Northampton	Harriet W. Whitney, M.D.	Maryalys S. Parker	Adelaide Putnam
Taunton	Olga E. Steinecke, M.D.	Margaret Chapin Charlotte Foye	Emma Lowe
Walter E. Fernald	Esther S. B. Woodward, M.D.	Elizabeth A. Bicknell	
Westborough	Betsy Coffin, M.D.	Adelaide Proctor	Pauline F. Barry
Worcester	Lonnie O. Farrar, M.D.	David Shakow Mary S. Millard Helen Laskey Frances Merrick	Elizabeth Marvel
Wrentham	Alice M. Patterson, M.D.	Beatrice N. Wolfson	

The clinic personnel can have the satisfaction of knowing that they have done the pioneer work in this field in a most highly satisfactory manner. They have rendered invaluable service, not only to children, but to parents, to school officials, and to the community in general, as well.

Summary

In summarizing, we may say that the traveling school clinics for the examination of retarded children have rendered a great service to the communities in Massachusetts over the past eighteen years of their operation. Over the past few years they have examined over 6,000 retarded children each year, and altogether have examined a grand total of over 63,000 children. It is almost impossible to estimate the value of a community service of this type. Now that the law regarding the examination of retarded children has been changed so that problem and behavior difficulties may be referred, the public schools have at their call a highly specialized clinic to help them in settling their many troublesome questions in reference to child problems. In providing special classes for retarded children, the Department of Education and the various school systems have done a remarkable piece of work. It is becoming increasingly evident that the backward child when placed in a proper environment and taught in an understanding manner, as is only possible in special class work, the percentage of behavior difficulties among the mentally defective decreases quite markedly. All retarded and backward children should have the benefit of a complete and thorough psychiatric examination at an early date. In this way we can feel quite sure that future difficulties are going to be largely obviated.

THE PREVENTION OF CRIME
THE GANGSTER IN THE MAKING*

By L. Vernon Briggs, M.D.

Boston, Massachusetts

Much has been written on the prevention of crime, and numerous commissions have been appointed and investigations and surveys made to make some plan for reducing the enormous incidence of crime, especially among youths and juveniles. So far as I know, all the work for the prevention of crime up to the present time has made not even a dent in the crime record nor reduced the continual increase in the numbers of gangsters responsible for holdups, assaults and murders.

The commissions for the prevention of crime appointed by the different branches of our government have consisted for the most part of people who, having no real experience with the criminal, have had to depend upon evidence presented to them by criminologists, volunteer enthusiasts, one-sided specialists or people with a hobby. They have had to sift this hearsay evidence and from it formulate plans or reports which have usually been pigeonholed and in any case have had little practical value. We must look at this great question in a practical way. Let us discard assumptions, theories and plans for reforming the already hardened criminal and strike at the source from which gangsters and other young criminals develop.

In the prevention of crime we have never struck at the source in a practical way. In the examination of hundreds of criminals I have found that a great majority of them, old as well as young, and especially the young gangsters of today, began their criminal careers between the ages of ten and twenty; and recently some are beginning at an even earlier age. Many of these young gangsters are well brought up until the time of their school life. They often do well at school; many graduate from the grammar school and some few have spent one or two years in the high school. There is no question of mental deficiency in the majority of these cases. Hundreds of boys who graduate from grammar school or who leave the high school before graduation on account of economic or other troubles in their families, walk out into the world with no prospect of employment, and not a soul reaches out a hand to help them. Of those who graduate, some immediately find employment through the influence of parents or friends or fill vacant positions waiting for such material. But there is a large group of those who have no friends to give them jobs and whose families are not able to help them. Right here is where many of these young gangsters start their careers. Discouraged after making every effort to obtain legitimate employment and usually being in unfavorable environment, they either join the corner gang or get suggestions from moving pictures, radio stories or details of sensational front-page newspaper accounts of the adventure of crime. Many of the boys they meet on the corner are graduates of our so-called "reform schools" who talk over with them the crimes they see depicted in the movies, hear over the radio or read in the papers; or they tell of their own experiences as to the easy way of making money and of the thrill they get from wild rides in stolen automobiles or from holdups.

Ordinarily the young gangsters do not care for safe-blowing or housebreaking, though sometimes they do even these. What most of them want is the thrill, even though there is no financial gain from their adventures. If caught early in their career they are usually sent to one of the so called "reform schools" which have proved to be schools for education in crime. I can not tell you the large number of the boys whom I have examined who, at twelve, fourteen or sixteen years of age, were sent to one of these "reform schools" for appropriating an automobile for a joy ride or some other

* Abbreviated from a paper read at the Fall Meeting of the New England Society of Psychiatry, at Providence, Rhode Island, October 6, 1933.

minor delinquency and who have told me that there they met other boys more experienced in crime than themselves, who had told them exciting stories about the more serious crimes of holdup or burglary and who then and there planned with them a life of crime together after their discharge. Some boys even make their escape from these schools so that they may immediately begin their holdups and depredations, and as little effort is made to return them to the schools they are free to pursue their avocations until they are finally convicted of some serious crime. Miss Grace Abbott, head of the Children's Bureau at Washington rightly said that reformatories often made bad youngsters worse and good ones weak.

Another link in the development of the young gangster is the want of classification of these boys after their first arrest. Thrown together with hardened criminals in jails or prisons, they listen to the tales of their companions with admiration and the desire of emulation. I remember not long ago seeing a thirteen-year-old boy walking round and round the yard of one of our jails hand-in-hand with an extremely unpleasant tough-looking character. I called the boy to me and asked, "What are you here for?" He replied, "For stealing candy and cigarettes from a store in the West End. I expect to go to court tomorrow." I asked, "Who is your companion? What is he saying to you?" He answered, "Gee! He's a great guy; he's been in prison a great many times. He has been telling me of robbing men, and he has killed two in his getaways. Gee! He's a great man!"

More than a hundred boys between fourteen and sixteen years of age are held unnecessarily in the Charles Street Jail every year, and nearly as many in the Middlesex County Jail at East Cambridge. The exploitation of crime news today reaches every home in the land. The prominence given this sort of news and the sensational manner of presenting it makes the gangster the hero of many susceptible young minds. I am not going into the question of the after-care or the reform of these young gangsters for I am writing on prevention; we must take this group at the source and protect its members from the temptation of an environment which educates them in crime or gives them the desire for such thrill and inspiration.

We know how ready and eager the community and even the legislators are to punish these young offenders after they are caught and to provide the money for their arrests, many trials and temporary segregations where they are fed and clothed and often educated for further deeds of violence at great expense to the taxpayers. We know the large number of organizations whose object is the reform of criminals and the different welfare organizations which contribute to the support of their families, but pay little attention to the prevention of delinquencies.

My plan would be for all these organizations, or the communities which they represent, to get together and organize a personnel who would be on hand when these boys are graduated or leave school prematurely to take them by the hand and guide them into normal pursuits. When boys are about to leave school, for whatever cause, blank questionnaires should be furnished them to fill out which would inform the teacher what plans or desires each boy has for the immediate future. The boy for whom arrangements have not already been made, as shown by his reply, should have his questionnaire card turned over to the members of the follow-up committee, in whose hands the boy should be placed until they are assured that he is protected from evil influence and has a proper place in the community. Any amount of money which is needed to organize and maintain intelligently a system which would take care of these boys and make them an asset rather than a liability to the community should be considered trivial.

I agree with Professor Sayre that "the orthodox and acceptable methods of our day are not materially reducing crime," and that "we must attack the problem during childhood." But I believe that the next step must be some plan to help the group who, when they graduate or leave school, are now lost because of neglect.

A campaign should be started at once to educate our censors of moving pictures, radio stories, etc., to the serious dangers of crime pictures and stories, which are probably now the cause of much crime in this State. Some of these young gangsters have told me that when gangster business was dull and they were not meeting with much success they went to see "crime pictures" to be pepped up and get inspiration and encouragement and to learn new methods for their work. They don't mind whether or not the story has a moral and the burglar is caught and punished; that does not interest them. What they want are the details and mechanism of the crimes. Attorney General Bushnell some years ago urged the enactment of a law which he said "absolutely would prohibit children in the formative period of their lives from attending moving pictures which painted violations of law in attractive colors." Some time ago a new code of movie conduct was ratified by the Directors of the Motion Picture Producers and Distributors of America, Inc. The code, an announcement said, will determine the character of motion pictures exhibited in 22,000 theaters in this country. Among other provisions, scenes of passion shall not be introduced when not essential to the plot. The sanctity of the institution of marriage and the home shall be upheld. Crimes against law shall never be presented in such a way as to show sympathy with the crime as against law or justice. Acts of murder or brutality shall be presented only in such a way as will not inspire imitation; methods of crime shall not be presented in explicit detail on the screen, revenge in modern times shall not be justified as a motive." Anybody who attends the movies will be surprised at the interpretation put on the films by this body of Directors.

If the radio and more especially the moving pictures are not responsible for the education in crime of children under ten years of age, I would like to have someone tell me how these youngsters get the information which they use so effectively to carry out crimes requiring a knowledge and skill which it would be impossible for them to have without some information or suggestion.

The court rooms of our cities are also schools for criminals. Youths bent on a criminal life can learn the methods of old and experienced wrongdoers in the court room. In notorious cases, especially holdups with a lot of thrill in them, you will find the court rooms crowded with gangsters in the making who are there learning the technique of criminal adventure; and even the corridors adjacent to these court rooms are filled with hardened and embryo criminals, waiting their turn for seats in the courtrooms.

A survey of crime items in the daily press in New York city made four years ago, showed that 4,412 items, covering 89,622 inches of space were published in the twelve leading newspapers in a single month; the percentages of crime news in relation to the whole varied from 11.87% in the Evening Telegram to 33.11% in the Daily News. Undoubtedly these percentages would be much higher today.

I feel sure, after these many years of experience, that if organization could be so perfected by the State or the communities therein, that these boys should be given a friendly hand at the time they need it, which they virtually never receive today, instead of the unlimited attention paid to them later, it would be only a few years before we should see a lowering of the incidence of crime in Massachusetts. Only by such means of attacking crime at its source can real prevention be brought about. As the State now looks after the defective eyes, teeth, etc. of our school children, let it also look after the morals and the future of the comparatively few graduates of our schools who are without friends or moral guidance at the most critical period of their lives.

THE MALADJUSTED SCHOOL CHILD AND HIS NEEDS*

BY ANNA KING
Director of Social Service, Austen Riggs Foundation, Inc.

What do you, school superintendents, physicians, physical directors, want from me, a child guidance worker, in this paper? Much mental hygiene literature is available to you free, or at nominal cost, through the National and State Mental Hygiene Societies, the Commonwealth Fund and other groups who are working with you for the child. What more can the experience of a child guidance worker contribute which will be of use to you in recognizing and helping those school children who show some maladjustment?

To answer this question certain general considerations stand out: First, it is important to review the fundamental purpose of education. I think we would agree that the objective might be defined as the development of strong, individual citizens, well equipped to carry on and achieve —to live fully—in this new world. The objective is not academic grades nor standardization; we no not fall into the error of those students of whom the wise professor said, "They work to pass and not to know. They do pass; they don't know."

We would, doubtless, all agree that the school system with its intricate developments, ramifications and problems of organization, exists for no purpose other than to serve the development of the child. Though this is the objective, by the nature of human organizations, every teacher and other school officer has to work within the scope of the system. The system, moreover, is often handicapped by lack of funds, the inertia of large bodies, too large classes, and certain administrative requirements which are necessary for order but which are a constant tax upon the strength of the faculty, tending to obscure the real objectives toward which they strive.

There is a further consideration in regard to the public school system as a means toward the end of the education of the child: School attendance is required by law. The school has authority. Parents must send their child to school; the child must come; the teacher must take him and teach him or give reason for failure to do so. Neither teacher nor parent may take the attitude about school attendance that this can be "taken or left." This very authority and necessity is often a complication. We Americans have the tradition of independence and individualism. We do not accept authority easily except as we ourselves have delegated it and in a republic this authority requiring school attendance seems too remote to be always satisfying either to individual teacher or parent when all is not harmonious in the child's school education. Discipline of a compulsory sort the school can use, and by means of it can get a negative compliance, but not the type of free cooperation and initiative in working out problems which is the greatest ally to education in weathering difficulties. The child may be led to the fountain of knowledge but cannot be forced to drink.

On the score of authority, the child guidance clinic is happily free. No parent need use the clinic. No school need accept the recommendations; hence the child who does come, the parents and school who do wish this help, have an ally free from the antagonisms that authority may create. For this very reason sometimes the clinic can contribute what the school has recommended but cannot win.

In addition to these general considerations of the fundamental purpose of education—the complications that a large organization such as the school system must face, and the handicap of authority—there is yet one more consideration which it is important to bear in mind: the school faculty is human. It is composed of high-minded, devoted, well-trained individuals who have not thereby lost their human inheritance of aspira-

---
* Talk given at the School Hygiene Conferences, November 15th and 16th, 1932 in Pittsfield and Westfield.

tions, loyalties, cares, fears, doubts and hopes. By nature of their position of leadership and authority it is sometimes assumed that they must always be right and perfect! They are asked to achieve a stupendous and sometimes almost impossible task. Any discussion which presupposes perfection and complete adjustment on the part of the teacher is dealing with unreality. Teachers, like the rest of the world, are people and deserve the sympathy, understanding, tolerance and comradeship that all human beings must have if they are to work together to the best of their capacity in this adventure of life.

So much for certain general considerations.

Now, if, bearing these in mind we try to discuss the maladjusted school child we must again define terms. It is not necessary to point out that the title doubtless means the maladjusted child in school. But what do we mean by maladjustment? A recent study made of the teachers' reports on what misbehavior among their pupils bothered them most, emphasized such infractions of discipline and lack of respect for authority as whispering, speaking out of turn, acting "smart". I am sure that all of us would agree that while these may be more inconvenient than shyness, suspicion, or cowardice, they are less serious signs of maladjustment.

In considering what is maladjustment, we must think, maladjusted to what? To their teacher? To their comrades? To airplanes? To themselves? To cities? To farm life? In that delightful book by Kenneth Graham, The Golden Age, the world is looked at with the eyes of children, and grown-ups are the maladjusted individuals because they do not fit into the children's world except as "the Olympians," strange, gigantic figures usually living aloof in a cloudy world of their own, but occasionally descending to interfere with the delightful and legitimate activities of the young by arbitrary and capricious acts, such as secreting the dead mouse in the parlor grand piano.

Would we not agree that the term "maladjusted" should be "maladjusted to life," and that to know what constitutes maladjustment we must be able to define what we mean by life?

Professor W. T. Councilman of Harvard, in his book for laymen, Disease and Its Causes, points out that to define disease one must define that which it attacks—life—and he quotes Herbert Spencer's definition of life;- "Life is a continuous adjustment of internal relations to external conditions." And the essential properties of life he defines as the properties of being adaptable and individual. He shows how all living things are dependent on external conditions, but have within themselves the tools with which to adjust to these conditions; the higher in the animal scale, the finer the development of the tool to adjust, the tool being the central nervous system.

The highest unit developed in life, the baby, is born completely dependent, the center of his universe. He is equipped to adjust but has to learn to use this equipment. Of course, at birth, the most important of the external conditions which enable him to survive are his parents. His education for life means learning gradually to become self-dependent, to take his own place in the world as a social being and to modify, maintain and develop his own identity in the face of external conditions which are themselves changing and becoming more complex as his individual life evolves.

With the baby, what is the "internal relations" part of his life and how do the "external conditions"—the parents and the situations they control—need to act to help these to get properly under way in a progressive habit of adjusting? The internal relations—the whole child—is a body-mind machine articulated by its central nervous system which functions as a telephone system. Through this nervous system the child responds to stimuli of various kinds and receives the education which his environment gives.

The education of the body, habits of hygiene—teeth, diet, and so forth—I am not discussing. The education of the mind has two phases. Too often it is not recognized that the mind has two parts. The intelligence is not the oldest part of the mind though it has longest been the subject of conscious education. This is the part of the mind that makes man supreme, that gives him his power to talk, his memory, his reason, his capacity for abstract thinking. Individuals are born with different degrees of intelligence, but in spite of this variation in native capacity each individual has the opportunity to develop, to go far, by the proper culture of whatever native capacity he has. The other part of the human mind is far older than the intelligence and has for long been taken so for granted that it is only within recent times that there has been emphasis on the scientific study of its laws of growth, and of methods for its education. I refer to the instinctive life.

There are many definitions of instinct. You probably are familiar with some such definition as the following: "An inherited tendency to act in a predetermined, specific way in response to certain stimuli." Every instinct has three parts, the reception of the stimulus, the reaction in consciousness or "emotion", and the tendency to expression of this emotion in action. For example, we all know both by subjective and objective observation such feelings as anger, fear, love, curiosity, self-assertion. We know that these are aroused by some external stimuli or some thought as a stimulus. We know the intensity of the emotion that accompanies each one of these instincts and the tendency to expression in action, both within our body and externally, that goes with these. We know the blush, the quickened heart beat, the actual physiological expression as well as the sharp word, the sudden motion, the act which seems necessary at the moment but on which we spend much afterthought to explain to ourselves and others.

Now what is the attitude today toward instincts? Even some educated people have a benighted idea that instincts are something to be rid of. They fail to recognize that in human beings it is the instincts which are the dynamo that enables the human being to go where his intelligence wills. Without instincts a human being, no matter how high his intelligence, is as static as a genius at the wheel of an automobile with no engine. There is an extraordinary amount of misinformation common on this subject of instincts. One hears parents say that children "should not feel" in a given way. Individuals are ashamed of the feelings they have within them and think they must be queer to feel like that! Today there is an increasing understanding that in this art of human adjustment we cannot always control the stimuli or the situation in which we are; we cannot control our emotion—that part of our instinct which is our feeling about the stimulus; but we, as human beings, can control and choose how we shall act, how we shall express that emotion.

It is in the third part of the instinct, its expression in action, that education has its opportunity. The wise parent helps the child from earliest infancy to accept his feelings and to choose a way of expressing these feelings that will make for enduring satisfaction; the parent helps him to learn to stand certain discomforts of the moment for the sake of certain more important and enduring satisfactions. He helps the child to build up an increasing sense of security and power through skillful direction in the matter of expressing his feelings. All children like to achieve. They like to be considered grown-up. They like to think that in not crying when they are hurt or in giving up a toy to a little sister to make her happy they are acting as their parents would act. They can get a progressive satisfaction in achievement in the fun of this game and very early they learn to have a practical understanding that instincts are often in conflict either with each other, with their intelligence, or with their environment. The little boy who is jealous of his new brother because he has to divide his parents' attention with him can forget his jealous vindictiveness in the satisfaction of the new honor of taking his mother's place watching the baby while she is called away for a few minutes.

Now, returning to our term *the maladjusted child* and thinking of it in relation to our definition of life, "the continuous adjustment of internal relations to external conditions", we recognize that the maladjustment may occur either in the "internal relations" or in the "external conditions." When a given child does not make the usual degree of adjustment we call him maladjusted, but it is often the parent or the environment and not the child that really should be described as maladjusted. Most children, in body, intelligence, and instincts are so-called "normal" at birth; but it is what the environment, through the parents and others, does to this "normal" being that causes the maladjustment.

You, who greet the children who have already travelled five or six years on their life voyage, know a few of the common maladjustments that have been developed before school age. You know the child who has been babied at home, who wants to continue to be the center of the stage, who wants his mother, that is, who still seeks an infantile type of security. You know the child who won't mind, who is not adjusted to being one of the group, who wants to be the boss of everbody, who can't get on either with the teachers or with the other children. You know the child who is hungry for attention, who isn't loved at home, the child whose only form of importance is that of being "smarty". You all know also the more serious sorts of maladjustment, the child who won't play, who is solitary, who is withdrawing from the voyage instead of sailing forth on his adventure, however bumptiously or faultily.

But when we think of what has happened to a child in those first six years, how far he has had to go in changing his own place in the world from the center of his own circle and from complete security of infancy where every need is met to being one of a large group of young strangers entering a new world in the schoolroom, our wonder is not at the number who are maladjusted but at the resilience of the human organism which makes most somehow to fit in. If any adult were asked in six years to make a correspondingly large shift in his relation to life, could he possibly survive?

The child of six when he enters school is making his first great change of environment. He goes into a new physical set-up, strange walls and tables and books and, more important, a new leader in authority and new comrades, many of them. He has to take a new place in his universe; he may experience new feelings that he has never known before, the fear of failure, the strain of competition, jealousy of those who have more in possessions, in brains or in looks, perhaps a sense of neglect. In this new environment the two major factors are not the familiar parents and brothers and sisters but a strange teacher and strange children.

Now what can this environment do to help him to continue in his lessons of adjustment? What does he need from his teacher? All children need help from their teachers but the maladjusted child needs this in greater measure. A few needs stand out above all others:

First: He needs understanding.

This understanding is of two kinds. First, intellectual curiosity; why is he what he is? A physician once said to a psychiatrist speaking of a nervous patient who had interrupted him repeatedly on the telephone; "Don't you get irritated at her for acting this way?" "Oh, no," said the psychiatrist, "When I entered psychiatry I forgot the meaning of the word irritation." "What did you put in its place?", asked the physician. "Intellectual curiosity," replied the psychiatrist.

This type of intellectual curiosity will lead to knowing why the child is as he is. What is his bodily capacity? What is his intellectual capacity? And here I repeat that I cannot digress to discuss the use and abuse of intelligence tests. In addition to studying the child's intellectual equipment, it is fascinating to discover to what extent one can create out of one's imagination the world in which the child lives, what his body of knowledge is.

One little boy in the first grade was asked a simple problem in arithmetic by the young teacher who had come recently from the city to a rural school.

"Johnny, there are forty sheep in a pasture and one jumps over the fence; how many are left?"

The answer, prompt and unquestioning, "None."

"Think, Johnny. You know that. Forty sheep, and one jumped over the fence. How many are there still in the pasture?"

Again, sturdy and secure, "None."

Sadly the teacher shook her head. "Johnny, I'm afraid you don't know your arithmetic. There are thirty-nine left."

Firmly and vehemently Johnny shook his head. "Teacher, that isn't so. You don't know sheep. There are none left."

In the child's world the facts in the question are much more important than an abstract mathematical question! He did know sheep and he was more interested in sheep than in substraction.

To supplement intellectual curiosity and go hand in hand with it another type of understanding is needed—emotional understanding—the feeling of comradeship with the child in his adventure. You remember the boy's definition of a friend: "A friend is a fellow what knows you but likes you." The capacity of the teacher to feel *with* him and not simply *at* him, the sympathy and understanding born of a strong humanity within, the capacity for play, for suffering, for interest in continued learning to live, a generous faith in life and in his contribution to life and in his ability to go on learning—all these are implicit in an emotional understanding which meets the needs of a child. Children know, by standards surer than any standards that education has devised, whether the teacher has this emotional understanding, whether the teacher is, as they say somewhat disrespectfully, "a regular guy."

Second: Along with understanding, the child needs leadership.

He needs the teacher to help him develop the use of intelligence, to introduce him to the new world of fact and thought in which he is learning to live, and to give him a new type of security based on his power of independence and not on the weakness of dependence. How the teacher recognizes and uses the leadership that superior maturity and prestige of position give, is one of the measures of his success. If he can avoid building on competition, fear of failure, jealousy and tale-bearing and can build up on the positive side of the child's emotions—if he can supplement what the parents do at home, making his new position of authority an alliance with them to help the child to self-reliance—if he can give the child, by his own love of it, a sense of satisfaction in good workmanship, and in the delight of comradeship—if, in short, the teacher can develop in the child a sense of good sportsmanship and has the ingenuity which enables him to bring out the peculiar aptitudes of that given child, the sense of humor which sees things in perspective, and finally the capacity to add an admixture of wise neglect, he is a leader whom his pupils will never forget.

What the teacher is as a performing human being is more to the child than what he teaches; in the measure that he practices what he teaches, will he be one of the enduring allies in the life of that child.

But some needs of the school child, the teacher cannot meet. The child seeks the comradeship of his own group and their approval. The child is a social animal and only as his instinct to belong to the group and his ability to take the discipline of his peers are developed, has he learned to accept his place in the world.

One cannot conclude a discussion of the needs of the maladjusted child without mentioning another factor. We cannot see the child's needs without thinking also of his contribution.

In the world of health, mental as well as physical, it is through the study of those who deviate conspicuously that science learns how to stabilize and develop to a fuller degree the health of the rest. It is in this "pathological laboratory" that the way is first shown to prevent similar deviation in others; and it is only by what they contribute to scientific knowledge that these "different" children contribute; the school system and the individual teacher have a heavy load.

There is an inevitable tendency in large bodies to become static and unwieldy. These young noncomformists jolt us out of any possibility of becoming routine-minded. How we are able to stretch ourselves sufficiently to meet their needs is one measure of success of the school system and its capacity for growth. Beyond the contributions these make to the school system, these young people, these so-called maladjusted young people, contribute to all of us. Life for all of us is still the continuous adjustment of internal relations to external conditions; and not only America but all organized society in these post-war days is learning to live in a new and unknown world. These maladjusted children may be one of the danger signals to point out where civilization itself is not adjusted. As we learn how to help these children to find their adjustment in a new and intricate world, they may lead us to see how civilization should be modified if the human race is to continue to live and grow in the new external conditions of the world today.

Bibliography

1. Books and pamphlets on Mental Hygiene suggested by the Massachusetts Society for Mental Hygiene, 4 Joy Street, Boston.
   (Both of these are on mimeographed lists.)
2. Commonwealth Fund publications, 41 East 57th Street, New York City.
3. National Committee for Mental Hygiene publications, 450 Seventh Ave., New York City.
4. Children's Bureau, Department of Labor, Washington, D. C.
5. Child Study Association of America, 54 West 70th Street, New York City.
6. The Parents' Magazine, 114 East 32nd Street, New York City.
7. The Survey, 112 East 19th Street, New York City.

THE REST AND NUTRITION PROGRAM IN THE BOSTON PUBLIC SCHOOLS

By Clara Loitman, M.D.

Medical Supervisor of Nutrition, Boston Public Schools

"He who helps a child helps humanity with an immediateness which no other help given to human creature in any other stage of human life can possibly give again." (Phillips Brooks)

The Rest and Nutrition Program of the Boston Public Schools has as its main purpose the prevention and control of tuberculosis and malnutrition among the school children.

The program was first organized in 1926 by the writer, who was the first Medical Supervisor of Nutrition of the Boston Public Schools. This program affords a practical and efficient method of providing rest and nutrition and the practice of health habits during the school day for selected children.

The children who are chosen for the Rest and Nutrition Groups fall into one or more of the following classes:
1. Tuberculosis
   (a) Children diagnosed as having latent or suspicious tuberculosis, but who are considered well enough to attend public school.
   (b) Children who have been in contact with a tuberculosis patient.
   (c) Children who have a family history of tuberculosis.
2. Malnutrition of Underpar
   The selection of children in this group depends on several factors.
   (a) Physical examination of the child with consideration of general appearance and attitude, muscle tone, amount of subcutaneous fat, posture, color of mucous membrane and skin, etc.

(b) History as to whether child is easily fatigued, hyper-irritable, has frequent illnesses, etc.
(c) Consideration, whenever possible, of social and familial body traits. We know that we do not all conform to one body type; some are the bull dog type, others are the wolf hound type, and each child must be considered individually.
(d) Weight.
There is still too much attention given to actual body weight and the erroneously called normal weight which is merely an average weight. Children who are 7% or more underweight according to the standard tables are referred for examination for the Rest and Nutrition Group. Many of these children manifest no signs or symptoms of being underpar or malnourished. On the other hand many children who are up to, or even above their average weight showed definite signs and symptoms of being malnourished. The past and present rate of gain is considered more important than actual weight.

Unfortunately, there are no reliable standards for the diagnosis of the malnourished child. Therefore the diagnosis must depend largely on the experience and personal equation of the physician making the diagnosis. The optimum in physical health, rather than the average, should be the goal we should set for our children.

3. Organic Cardiac
These children with organic cardiac lesions are selected because it is felt that increased physical rest will be beneficial to them.

4. Convalescent Children
This includes children returning to school after surgical operations or medical illnesses, such as chorea and rheumatic fever.

5. Miscellaneous Group
This group includes children referred for various reasons by teachers, clinics, private physicians and social agencies. Children manifesting nervous instability, children with orthopedic defects, or poor health habits are in this group. Teachers are encouraged to refer children who manifest behavior changes such as increased irritability or apathy or who appear to fatigue easily. In this way many children who may be showing the first signs of malnutrition may be helped.

It is far wiser to build a protective fence around the top of the precipice than to have an ambulance awaiting at the bottom.

The Rest and Nutrition Program affords a practical and satisfactory method of helping children for whom increased rest and nutrition during the school day are desirable. One or more rooms are set apart for the use of the children in the Rest and Nutrition Groups and in these rooms the food is prepared and served and the children rest. The children attend their regular school classes. This means a great deal to the child whose physical condition permits him to attend public schools. There is no segregation from his fellow school mates, which is greatly appreciated by both the children and their parents.

In the morning the children attend their regular school classes. In the mid-morning, about twenty minutes before the mid-morning school recess, the children come to the Rest and Nutrition room. This room is equipped with an army cot and blanket for each child. The room has been thoroughly aired, the windows opened, and usually the sun is streaming in when the children arrive. Shoes are removed and the children take their places on the cots for a half hour rest. Little eyes close and a soft sigh may be heard here and there, there is the rustle of turning bodies and soon all are relaxed, many actually asleep. After the rest the children put on their shoes, wash and wipe their hands and take their places for mid-morning lunch, properly seated at a table. This mid-morning lunch consists of a simple sandwich, unsweetened crackers, milk or weak cocoa or fruit, depending on the weather. After the lunch the children join the other school children at morning recess, returning to their classes with the rest of the school population.

At noonday, while the other children go home, the children who attend the Rest and Nutrition Group remain in school. They return to the rest room again and rest from one half to one hour. They again wash their hands and are ready for a nutritious noonday meal. One noon, they may have a savory beef stew with vegetables, a tempting pudding, milk and bread and butter, or again they may have an attractively arranged and colorful vegetable plate, cheese and luscious gingerbread with whipped cream, and of course, a drink and bread and butter. After dinner the children go out into the school yard and return for the regular afternoon session.

The noonday period takes no time from school lessons. The mid-morning period includes about twenty minutes of the regular recess and therefore interferes but little with the school program. In the intermediate schools, the children have the mid-morning lunch but may be excused from the mid-morning rest. The actual time and duration of the rest periods varies in different schools, depending on the individual school program. Children from all grades in the school may attend the Rest and Nutrition Group and children may be entered or discharged from the Rest and Nutrition Group as their physical condition requires, with minimum alteration in the regular school program.

The children in the Rest and Nutrition Groups are in immediate charge of nutrition attendants who are civil service appointees. These women buy, prepare and serve the food and care for the children during the rest periods. The attendants are under the supervision of the Medical Supervisor of Nutrition, who directly supervises their work and meets with them individually and in general meetings to discuss topics pertinent to the Rest and Nutrition Program.

The Rest and Nutrition Program offers a practical method for the practice of health habits. The children learn about proper meal planning and proper table manners. The children are not only told about washing their hands before eating, about sitting properly at the table and about chewing their food properly but actually practice these health habits. Also at these rest and eating periods the importance of cooperation is learned.

Very infrequently is there any difficulty with the children concerning the food served. When a child refuses a food because he is unaccustomed to it the problem is approached with patience and training. In one school there are children of twenty-seven nationalities and many of these are represented in the Rest and Nutrition Class. A dark-eyed Mexican lad, a Chinese girl, a Syrian, a Lithuanian, an Armenian, a fair-haired Nordic, and an American, sitting at one table for noonday lunch! Surely, it is too much to expect that all these children from different homes and backgrounds will eat the same food with the same eagerness.

Occasionally we meet the overindulged child of oversolicitous parents who is accustomed to have each mouthful of food spooned in with a story or a promise or a threat. The problems of these children are treated individually. It is not at all uncommon to have some child ask, "Gee, how do you make this cabbage salad? It's swell!" or to have a mother call to express her gratitude because Johnny ate vegetables in school or because Helen was so much less irritable and slept better at night.

Not only is it important to carry out this program in school but it is also important to secure home cooperation and to stimulate the child's own interest in his welfare so that he may practice health habits outside of school. When a child is referred for the Rest and Nutrition Group he is given a physical examination by the Medical Supervisor of Nutrition to determine his nutritional status. His nutrition, physical defects and known exposure or contact with tuberculosis is recorded. Additional physical examinations are made whenever necessary, as when a child fails to make expected progress and before discharge from the Group. Also these children are weighed monthly, heights recorded tri-yearly, by the school nurse.

Home cooperation is secured through the school nurses. The nurse secures parental permission to have the child in Rest and Nutrition Group, explains the purpose of the program, cooperates in the correction of defects and helps in innumerable other ways. The nurses are a very important factor in the success of the Rest and Nutrition Program and too much praise cannot be given them and their supervisor, Miss Helen McCaffrey, for their support and cooperation.

At the organization of a new class a mothers' meeting, (usually attended by mothers, fathers, neighbors and little sisters and brothers) is held in the school by the Medical Supervisor of Nutrition. At these meetings the school program is explained and a general discussion of nutrition and health follows. Additional mothers' meetings are held from time to time, and individual interviews with mothers are held whenever necessary for welfare of the child. Also, there are simple talks with children on healthe

In all the work with the children, health is the important factor. Illnesses, physical defects and bad habits are never stressed. In fact, many of the children call the Rest and Nutrition Group the Health Club. Great care is always taken to maintain the child's respect for his parents and his home in discussing home food and health habits.

In 1926 the writer organized two Rest and Nutrition Groups. The physical and mental improvement manifested by the children in these groups was so definite that teachers and parents were most enthusiastic in their approval of the program. The success of these two groups merited the increase in the number of Rest and Nutrition Groups so that now there are twenty-five Rest and Nutrition Groups. During the school season of 1932-33, 1,001 children attended the Rest and Nutrition Group, for one month or longer. The average stay in the class was 23.18 weeks and on this time the average gain in weight per child was 4.20 pounds.

These children were classified as follows:

Malnutrition	769
Tuberculosis group	121
Organic cardiacs	56
Convalescents	28
Miscellaneous	73*

*Of these, 10 children had an organic cardiac lesion and were malnourished, and 36 were malnourished and belonged to the tuberculosis group.

In addition 2,269 extra dinners and 82,963 extra mid-morning lunches were served to needy children.

To many persons gain in weight means a great deal, but this is only one factor in estimating a child's physical progress and improvement, other factors are important, as improvement in appearance, color, posture and muscular tone, and general attitude. Teachers and mothers report less irritability in the children, a greater alertness, and greater activity with less fatigue than before. As one mother said, "She is a happier child since she has been in the Rest and Nutrition Group!"

After all, that is what we want to see, a happy, well child for health is so necessary to all the duties as well as pleasures of life.

PHYSICAL EDUCATION FOR THE HANDICAPPED

By Carl L. Schrader

Supervisor of Physical Education
Massachusetts Department of Education

The part that physical education plays in the service of those handicapped for the natural participation of living, may best be stated in a twofold way. First, what it may achieve in restoring handicapped individuals to normal; second, what it may achieve in making possible a participation in recreational and health-maintaining activities for those who are permanently handicapped.

Accepting physical education, that is, exercise, as a phase of hygienic living, it becomes necessary to accept as fact the statement that exercise is capable of influencing the living habits of an individual in many ways. Wholesome exercise, carried on intelligently and under good conditions, tends to increase the demand for food and drink. If in the health education, which now supposedly accompanies physical education, there has been instruction about the proper kind of food and drink, this stimulation through exercise might well be accepted as an aid to healthy growth. Wholesome and vigorous activity likewise makes its demand for ample sleep. It is necessary for us to recognize the difference between being physically tired and being nervously or mentally fatigued. Vigorous exercise leads to the desire for a refreshing bath, not so much for the sake of cleanliness as for the stimulating reaction which is bound to follow.

It is often held that the habit of clothing oneself is affected by active participation in wholesome physical activities. When the circulation is kept keen there is less need for heavy clothing, which at best interferes with proper ventilation of the body.

We have to accept well-being as being based on experience, and when this experience has resulted from something we have done, rather than from what nature herself has done, our habits of living are likely to be influenced for the better.

The more complete a physical examination is in the schools, the more opportunity there is for detecting handicaps, particularly those that fall within the range of being overcome by prescribed means. Some of the most common handicaps that occur in the life of the child and where physical education might be an aid, are in the field of postural deviation from the normal. Ample opportunity for the use of all extremities, those calling into play the larger muscle groups, will do much to maintain the normal appearance in carriage. Where there have been handicaps to prevent the erect growth, it is necessary to ascertain the cause if possible, in order to find the necessary aid. We know that frequently the cause is that of malnutrition, in which case the most effective aid is the proper kind and quantity of food. The proper dosage of exercise in this instance will likewise stimulate a healthy appetite, a procedure with which the nutrition worker should become thoroughly familiar. These exercises are not aimed at postural correction by force, but rather are intended to stimulate the desire for food.

The main purpose of physical education in counteracting posturally abnormal tendencies is to maintain or increase muscle tone. Hence, the effects should be, and usually are toward a general body building, with such special efforts for selected individuals as tend toward correction. We are not at all certain of the extent to which we can influence structure. We do feel quite convinced that when muscular tone is keen and well balanced, and no striking faulty habits have been acquired, we meet an acceptable good carriage.

In the process of physical education the effort is made to have pupils recognize good form in whatever they are engaged. There is good and poor form in every activity the body is capable of performing. Dancing, skating, swimming, vaulting, horseback riding, walking, throwing, sitting, etc., all may be performed so that they are beautiful in their execution, or they may appear slovenly and ugly. Since poor posture, insofar as it is not due to disease, is mainly an aesthetic offence, we may well assume that persistent effort to have youth and adults recognize and be conscious of good and bad form will be a big factor in an effort for correction. The pathological claim is not so well founded as recent studies seem to indicate. There is no one posture that is correct; hence, to aid everyone to assume for himself the best possible posture rather than the best conceivable posture is our effort.

Much has been achieved in foot correction in the schools. Feet play a great part in the effort for erect carriage. In addition to the general exercises that tend to strengthen the muscles of the feet, there are special exercises prescribed and designed to overcome harmful deviations.

The more intimate the relation is between the teacher of physical education and the pupils, the more can be achieved in assisting the individual to overcome handicaps. Not so very long ago teachers of physical education who insisted on the participation of boys and girls suffering from some permanent physical handicap were charged with being cruel and heartless. Today the handicapped share in all the activities, and are found to react as joyfully as do the normal children. They are encouraged to develop their normal portions of the body as much as possible. One needs but to visit a school for crippled children, and see them play the same games that normal children play, to be convinced of the wisdom of the present attitude toward these children. One may see whole baseball teams on which no player has two legs, and be amazed at the technique which has been developed. Even the blind play games, jump for height and distance, run races, swim, etc. To be sure, this all requires planning, but it is worth while to make it possible for this group to share in living which hitherto has been denied them.

Physical education teachers are trained to discern the special needs of children, and to teach accordingly. They need the support of the principal, other teachers, school physician, and school nurse, and surely that of the home. The school physician particularly should aid in convincing mothers of the advantage that lies in their child's participating in the activity program. Play is a birthright of every child, irrespective of handicaps, and it is the school's business to capitalize whatever equipment nature may have granted the child.

There are social handicaps which are not so easily discernible as some of the physical. Many of these fall within the range of mental hygiene and can be curbed or even eradicated. Large numbers of children live in an environment where neither home nor community furnish opportunity for a guided social atmosphere, and it is to the public schools that we must look for fulfillment of this need. Physical education provides an experience laboratory for many of the good citizenship traits. The physical education program is based in the main upon activity, and the community judges a citizen by his actions, not by what he thinks. Action is in the open, is visible, hence it can be directed and corrected if necessary. Character and citizenship are largely based upon experience, and the playground and gymnasium can create many situations which resemble civic reality. In these places the children are not merely seated as in a classroom, with a necessary plan for order, but they are in action under a marked degree of freedom. Whatever their traits or quirks are, whether timidity, selfishness, boastfulness, cheating, or other minus qualities, they will manifest themselves here, and the trained leader will know how to curb them by the various set-ups of activities which can be devised.

Obedience of law is a prime necessity for success in a play program, and in the repetition of this playing in strict accordance with rules lies the hope of creating habits of right doing. In a fast game there is no time to deliberate whether to foul or not to foul; consequently, all actions are habit or experience. All the good qualities we think of in connection with good citizenship, loyalty, chivalry, fair play, determination, courage, etc., do not just happen to exist with most people, but are acquirable through experience, and can become permanent property. In play there is opportunity to place the timid child in situations where he discovers that he can do some things as well as others can, and then have confidence in himself. On the other hand, the bully needs to be placed in situations where he will be the under-dog, and thus gain respect for the rights and abilities of others. It is a problem of diagnosis. The special need has to be determined, and a possible remedy may follow.

It is no idle twaddle to point out these possibilities, for there is ample evidence. It depends first of all on the leadership for such a program, and on the community's willingness to furnish the facilities for it. Physical education has been well defined as being a way of living. To educate merely to earn a living would leave a drab world to live in. If it were possible to accumulate the signatures of all the men and women who have experienced the result of a wholesome physically active life themselves, we would have a volume of evidence that would shut out all doubt. That there are excesses goes without saying; any good thing becomes an evil when carried to excess. This, too, physical education aims to prevent by placing competition within safe bounds and keeping it under the control of the school, rather than trusting it to the fans of Main Street. A better understanding on the part of the public in general, and the parents in particular, will enable those engaged in teaching health and physical education to come nearer achieving these desirable objectives.

VOCATIONAL REHABILITATION FOR PERSONS DISABLED IN INDUSTRY OR OTHERWISE

By Robert O. Small

Director, Division of Vocational Education
Massachusetts Department of Education

The Law and Its Administration

By an Act of the Legislature approved by the Governor, May 25, 1921, and effective August 25, 1921, the Commonwealth of Massachusetts accepted the provisions of an Act of Congress to promote vocational rehabilitation of persons disabled in industry and otherwise, and their return to civil employment. For this purpose the Commissioner and Advisory Board of Education are constituted and designated as the State Board for Vocational Education, and directed to cooperate with the Federal Board for Vocational Education and to establish and maintain or to assist in establishing and maintaining such courses as it may deem advisable and necessary. The work is carried on directly by the Rehabilitation Section of the Division of Vocational Education.

What Vocational Rehabilitation Means

Vocational rehabilitation means the readjustment and return of the handicapped individual to his proper place in the productive forces of the day; this being accomplished through the training and development of his remaining abilities. This training is offered free of charge to those who may take advantage of it and affords the handicapped person the opportunity to reestablish himself and to become an independent, self-supporting and worthy citizen. Vocational rehabilitation involves no charity, as it is in a sense an extension of the public school system to give the handicapped civilians of the State an opportunity to reestablish themselves.

Who Is Eligible for Rehabilitation

The services of the Rehabilitation Section are available for any resident of Massachusetts, of legal employable age, either male or female, who has a physical disability which is a vocational handicap and who reasonably may be expected to be fitted for remunerative employment.

The physical disability may be the result of an industrial accident, a public accident such as an automobile or railroad accident, or it may be the result of a disease or a defect existing from birth.

The disabled persons must be of an age at which they may be legally employed, sixteen years in most cases, and it must be reasonable to expect that after rehabilitation they will be able to engage in suitable occupations.

At this time it is held that the following persons are not eligible for this service:

(a) Aged or helpless persons requiring permanent or custodial care.
(b) Any inmate of a state institution or any person confined in a correctional or penal institution.
(c) Any person deemed not susceptible of rehabilitation.
(d) Persons under the age of fourteen, and in some instances, sixteen years.

How Rehabilitation Is Accomplished

Each handicapped person is studied as an individual and an attempt is made to draw up a rehabilitation program that will meet the needs of that individual.

One of the important steps in rehabilitation is the selection of a suitable occupation for the future. The selection depends upon many factors among them the handicapped person's disability, education, natural aptitudes, previous industrial experience and the opportunities for employment in the particular line of work. The Rehabilitation Section helps the handicapped person to give the proper consideration to those factors and to choose an occupation in which he may expect to be successful.

The Rehabilitation Section then provides whatever training is necessary to prepare the particular person for the particular occupation. The training is designed and planned to fit the person not only for useful employment but to meet the requirements of a specific vocation.

Where and What Type of Training Is Given

The necessary training is arranged as near as possible to the place of residence of the handicapped individual. It may embody any one or a combination of two or more of the following forms:

Institutional Training. This type of training offers an opportunity to enter upon a suitable course of training in trade, technical, agricultural or commercial schools, either day or evening.

Employment Training. Frequently, training under actual working conditions is found to be the most feasible type. It is known as employment training and is given on the job, in a factory, shop or commercial establishment under the direct supervision of a cooperative employer with whom the Rehabilitation Section has arranged an approved training program.

Correspondence Training. Instruction may be given through correspondence courses. They are used occasionally during convalescence and in preparation for more intensive vocational training.

Tutorial Training. Occasionally it may be found necessary to provide a tutor, for example, as a supplement to a correspondence course, or where the handicap of the person in training is of such a nature that for the time being he cannot readily reach other training agencies.

Survey of Service

The services of the Rehabilitation Section available for the handicapped consist of the following:

(a) Counsel upon training or placement in the former occupation or a new one.
(b) An opportunity to enter upon a suitable course of training in trade, technical, agricultural, or commercial schools; in industrial or commercial establishments; by correspondence courses; or by tutors.

(c) Supervision and guidance during training so that the greatest benefit may be derived therefrom.
(d) Help in securing placement when the course of training has been successfully completed.
(e) Advice and assistance in securing artificial limbs and other orthopedic and prosthetic appliances at minimum cost and inconvenience.
(f) Financial aid for maintenance during rehabilitation of such persons as are deemed able to profit by training.

In addition to the personal service which is rendered, the Rehabilitation Section may bear whatever expenses are necessarily incurred for tuition and for instructional supplies, such as books, etc. Under certain conditions it may pay part of the cost of artificial limbs and appliances and may contribute to the support of persons able to profit by training.

Persons injured in industry and to whom the provisions of the Workmen's Compensation Act apply are not deprived in any way of the rights under that act by accepting training or other services offered by the Rehabilitation Section.

Policy Regarding General and Professional Courses

The Rehabilitation Section does not plan to give education which is mainly academic or cultural. It limits the courses given to such as will directly assist the handicapped person to acquire the skill and related technical knowledge which will enable him to enter upon a selected occupation efficiently. Since the aim is to prepare the trainees vocationally, it is only as general education has a direct and immediate bearing rather than a preliminary and preparatory relationship that it may be considered.

It is also a general principle in rehabilitation cases that the final objective should not be too remote in point of time. On a request for professional training, full consideration must be given to the following factors viewed from the standpoint of the profession and of the candidate:
(a) Pertinent economic conditions.
(b) Physical and mental capacity required.
(c) Educational background.
(d) Length and type of training necessary.

The Rehabilitation Section stands ready at all times to advise on the desirability and feasibility of professional training for any particular individual.

The value of such special opportunities and specialized training for the physically handicapped is well evidenced as shown by the results of those applicants who have applied themselves and who have completed rehabilitation programs under the supervision of the Department. Training has been given in 149 different occupations. Nine of the more common are:

Show Card Writing	Painting	Carpentry
Automobile Repairing	Agriculture	Electrical Work
Watch Repairing	Drafting	Shoe Repairing

Following is a summary of the work of the Rehabilitation Section from August 1921 to September 30, 1933:

Contacts 54,492
Prospects listed 7,181
Cases registered 2,953
Registrants put in training 1,552
Registrants placed after training 761
Registrants placed without training 526
Registrants rehabilitated 1,257
Registrants closed for all other causes 1,267

Applications for Rehabilitation

Applications for persons over sixteen years of age, eligible for vocational rehabilitation, should be made to the Rehabilitation Section. Application may be made in person or by mail, by the handicapped person himself, or in behalf of such person by a physician, hospital, social worker, employer, insurance company, fraternal organization, friend or relative, or by an interested citizen or agency. It is not necessary to use any special form or blank in making application. All that is required is that the name, address, age and nature of disability of the handicapped person be forwarded to the Department of Education, Rehabilitation Section, 20 Somerset Street, Boston, Mass. Direct communication with the handicapped person will then be established and arrangements will be made for a personal interview with a representative of the Department.

ATYPICAL CHILDREN AND THEIR EDUCATION
By Arthur B. Lord
Supervisor of Special Schools and Classes
Massachusetts Department of Education

Schools for the Deaf

On October 1, 1933, there were 585 children being educated in the schools for the deaf at the expense of the Commonwealth. The registration was as follows:

American School	11	Clarke School	114
Beverly School	77	Horace Mann School	183
Boston School	200		

Children who are deaf are placed in these institutions by the Department of Education and their instruction is under its supervision. During the past few years progress has been made in several fields. We find that in three of the Massachusetts schools classes for retarded children are maintained; that there has been a marked expansion of manual and domestic arts and handwork in many classes and a considerable amount of modern equipment for work with the deaf has been purchased by the several schools. It is now possible for the child with normal mentality who is deaf to be taught speech and lip reading. After such instruction, these children are able to attend their local high schools or trade schools with normal children and take their place in the community. The personnel of the teaching force is year by year coming nearer to the qualifications which the Department believes is necessary for teachers in special education, which is graduation from normal school or college with at least one year of specialized training in the field in which the teacher is to work.

Day Classes for the Deaf

The second step in the education of the deaf is by means of day classes established in certain cities. These classes are located in school buildings with regular classes. This gives the deaf children an opportunity not only to take some of the academic and handwork with the normal children but also to mingle with them in the various activities of the school. The day class offers deaf children an opportunity to receive instruction which is similar to that offered in schools for the deaf but with the opportunity of remaining at home and having the advantages of home training and supervision. Such classes are located at:

Lynn	21	Springfield	15
New Bedford	9	Worcester	23

No attempt has been made to carry the instruction of children in Day Classes for the Deaf beyond the fourth grade and in some cases not beyond the second. When they have completed the work offered by the Day Class, they are transferred to the Horace Mann School or one of the boarding schools.

Lip Reading Classes

A field in which much has been done in the past few years is that of teaching lip reading to hard-of-hearing children in the public schools. In this work a teacher visits the various buildings in a school system and children who are hard-of-hearing meet with her for from thirty to forty-five minutes for instruction in reading the lips. To many boys and girls it is quite essential that they have this instruction; otherwise, they would be unable to continue in the public schools. Many of these cases of deafness are progressive and while the children may be able to hear fairly well at the present time, such will not be the case a few years from now. Lip reading therefore is of vital importance to them. Teachers of lip reading are employed in the following towns and cities: Boston, Cambridge, Chelsea, Fall River, Lynn, New Bedford, Newton, Somerville, Springfield, Waltham, West Springfield, Everett and Watertown. There is a decided need for an extension of this service and it is hoped that many other towns and cities will find it possible to employ a teacher either part or full time. The use of the audiometer has proved very effective in discovering children who need this instruction.

School for the Blind

Education for the blind is provided by the State. Children who are so handicapped are sent to the Perkins Institution for the Blind at Watertown where they receive the equivalent of a public school education. Many of these students take up college work. At the present time, there are 177 pupils at Perkins Institution who have been placed there by the State.

Sight Saving Classes

Massachusetts has thirty-eight Sight Saving Classes in nineteen cities and the town of Brookline. There are twelve neighboring cities and towns providing for one or more children with visual handicap in these classes.

The enrollment at present is 485 pupils. Classes are in the following cities: Boston, Brockton, Brookline, Cambridge, Chelsea, Everett, Framingham, Fall River, Holyoke, Lowell, Lynn, Medford, New Bedford, Newton, Revere, Salem, Somerville, Springfield, Watertown, Worcester.

These classes are for children whose vision cannot be improved beyond 20/50 and where visual defect is not greater than 20/200.

Application should be made to the State Division of the Blind *after examination*.

Home Instruction for Physically Handicapped Children

In 1930 the Legislature enacted a law which provides for the education of physically handicapped children in their homes. The law requires that the School Committees take a census of such children each year. If it is found that there are five or more such children who are unable to attend school, teachers shall be sent to their homes to give them instruction. If there are less than five such children, the town may provide home instruction. The last report which has been compiled showed that forty-one towns and cities had offered such instruction to physically handicapped children.

The Department requires that teachers for this work shall have been graduated from normal school or had equivalent training and in addition thereto have had three years of teaching experience in the public schools. Children to the number of five hundred and six are receiving instruction.

The periods of time given to each child vary as follows:

Number of towns	Hours per week	Number of towns	Hours per week
4	1 to 1-3/4	1	4
13	2	9	5
10	3	5	No report

These children in the majority of cases are making remarkable progress. With but an hour or two a week of instruction, children are keeping up to grade. Such children apparently look upon this opportunity for instruction as a privilege. As a result they make every effort to take advantage of it. Too often the so-called normal child in school looks upon his educational opportunity as a "right" rather than a privilege. This, perhaps, explains the fact that crippled children, notwithstanding their handicaps, outstrip their more fortunate brothers. Numerous cases have come to the attention of the Department which demonstrates the great happiness which this extension of educational opportunities is bringing into the lives of these shut-in children.

THE MASSACHUSETTS HOSPITAL SCHOOL, ITS PROGRAM AND RESULTS

BY RUTH PARK

Social Worker, Massachusetts Hospital School

The program of the Hospital School is the outgrowth of more than twenty-five years of experience in the care and training of crippled children. It is always flexible enough so that changing circumstances may be met by changes in its method of application. It is kept as any educational plan should be, in a living and developing rather than in a fixed state. It also has its roots in some very definite and permanent principles governing life and growth, as these were observed by scientific workers at the time of its formulation.

When the institution was opened on December 1, 1907 by proclamation of the Governor, it was fortunate in being established as the result of legislation which had been guided by far-sighted surgeons and others who were interested in the end results of any program for the relief of crippled children. From the beginning, the men, who worked on the shaping of a plan for a Hospital School for all the children of the Commonwealth who were able to use the advantages there offered, had in mind the nature of their problem. As the result of observations in their own practice the Boston surgeons who guided the formulation of the program for the training of the crippled children of the State realized that long periods of time were needed even in completing recovery in improvable cases. Permanent crippling deformity when it occurs in a child of school age calls even more urgently for a long-continued plan of treatment. Provision was accordingly made for a scheme of training in school and out, which should touch the lives of the children admitted to the school on more than the ground of mere treatment of disability. As an early report of the trustees says, "For the education of these children to a position of usefulness in an American community, it is necessary not only that they should be trained to labor and handicrafts, but that they should be given the broadest aims."

Training for children admitted to the Hospital School is arranged for in many other places than in classrooms. Having provided an environment where food, shelter, and clothing should make for health, and where all necessary medical, surgical and nursing care should be constantly at hand, the founders used this as a basis for the upbuilding of habits of mental health. Most of the patients received would be of an age for common-school study, so provision was made for complete academic instruction in elementary studies from the first through the eighth grades. This provision has been adequate in a large majority of cases through twenty-five years, and is still the basis of the instruction given. Some extension of educational opportunity has been made at either end, and there is now kindergarten work with a preschool group, and vocational clerical work of high school grade with a few selected cases after they have received the eighth grade diploma of graduation, but for the great number of pupils, the present provision is adequate. It is considered a mistaken idea to keep even handicapped pupils too long in a specially sheltered environment.

Education through play has a large place in the scheme of things at the Hospital School. Country surroundings like a farming village give all the children a chance to have, under safeguards and not too ostentatious supervision, an opportunity to swing, to climb, to dig in the dirt and to lie down under pine trees. Baseball was found to be possible, swimming, campfire groups and Boy Scout activities have from time to time played a part not only in amusing the children, but in improving morale, and developing initiative and a sense of responsibility. Music and drama have been agencies of worth in the pupils lives, and instruction in arts and handicrafts has played a leading part.

In planning industrial and vocational work for the pupils, the founders felt that the most valuable and elastic program would be one which should develop out of the daily work of the school, and which should be close enough to the life of each girl and boy to be recognized as necessary and comprehensible. For children under the age of adolescence, trade instruction of a stereotyped form is not desirable. For handicapped children, no work can be considered without leaving much freedom of adaptation in accordance with type of disability, strength available for productive work and native tastes and inclinations. The outgrowth of these principles has been a system of voluntary apprenticeship, giving prevocational tastes of various occupations. The older boys are glad to try their hand at milking, painting a roof, nailing on shingles, or driving an automobile. The girls in their cottages have practical domestic training, in all the household arts. They learn skilled use of their hands in weaving, sewing and embroidery. They help in the office and learn to handle a telephone switchboard. The older pupils in need of such training are carefully and individually studied for assignment by the physicians in charge. Everyone in contact with a pupil is instructed to regard himself as a teacher. By the time a pupil is ready to leave the school there is a well-rounded picture of his traits of character, tastes, and capacities in the possession of those responsible for his guidance.

A school that sends out its graduates from the grammar grades must expect to wait a long time before perceiving results. The members of the first class, 1912, are now in their thirties, those of the later classes are still completing their education elsewhere, or just beginning trials at self-support. But time enough has passed to allow a fair evaluation. Of the several hundred graduates of the school, there are a few exceptions from the list of class after class which numbers young men and women who have learned, sometimes in the face of almost insuperable difficulties, to overlook their disabilities, to develop the value of what they can do, and to show that after all, the sum of a man's accomplishment depends mainly upon his intellectual adaptability, his morale, and his attitude toward work and life. Some very severely handicapped graduates have been among the most successful. Many have married, and judging from observation have maintained on the whole a stable and admirable type of home life. Most professions and many industries are represented among them. There are teachers, lawyers, one doctor. There are independent business men, office managers, and a Federal auditor. There are chauffeurs, telegraphers, printers, cooks, telephone operators, seamstresses, stenographers, and farmers. One man with extreme handicap is the industrial secretary for a large metropolitan philanthropic organization, and a woman, also with great disability, is assistant to the head of a college English department. Such success as can be found in the ranks of the Hospital School graduates has been won against odds, with the handicap of suffering and blight falling in the normally happy and carefree time of childhood and early youth. That these men and women have shown the courage and patience to find their way through life with good cheer and breadth of mind, inspires those who know them, and furnishes fresh evidence as to the worth and possibilities of human nature.

THE ANNUAL CENSUS OF PHYSICALLY HANDICAPPED CHILDREN

BY MARGARET MAC DONALD

Supervisor of Social Service for Crippled Children
Massachusetts Department of Public Welfare

Early in 1930 there was a demand for legislation calling for the instruction of certain severely crippled children in their homes. Previous to 1930 such instruction had been provided by the school boards in a number of Massachusetts cities, the school authorities in Holyoke being the pioneers in that work in this State. It was, therefore, quite natural that parents and friends of crippled children elsewhere should demand legislation requiring their cities to do likewise.

At the time of this demand, a State-wide Survey of Crippled Children in Massachusetts was being made under the Department of Public Welfare* and although it was very far from completion information already gathered seemed to warrant legislation which would call for an annual census of crippled children and would provide for the teaching of certain crippled children in their homes. It was found, for instance, that while the majority of the children already listed in the survey were having adequate medical attention, an appreciable number of them were not receiving any treatment; that the majority of the children not under treatment had had an initial medical examination and treatment had been started, but for various reasons been dropped or, at best, had been carried on only spasmodically. Among the reasons for lack of treatment were parental prejudice or indifference, lack of funds and, in some instances, lack of follow-up work in busy clinics. It was felt, therefore, that an annual census of crippled children would bring these as well as new victims of crippling to light and would assist in maintaining the continuity of treatment which is so important in crippling conditions.

It was also found that while many of the crippled children already reported were attending the regular public schools, and a large proportion of the more severely handicapped were being cared for either at the Massachusetts Hospital School at Canton, or in one of the privately conducted schools in the State such as The Industrial School for Crippled Children, The Berkshire School for Crippled Children and The New England Peabody Home, there were, nevertheless, a considerable number of children who were not receiving education. In this number were included children who, in spite of all that medical science could do for them, were doomed to a life of complete dependency upon others. Usually the parents of these children preferred to make them comfortable and happy at home instead of sending them to an institution, and it was not unusual to find that these children were growing up illiterate. In addition to these, there were those boys and girls who were obliged to lose much time in school because of operative treatment or treatment which entailed long periods of inactivity. In some instances they had experienced so many such enforced absences that they fell far behind their classmates and, in discouragement, dropped out of school at an early age, when under normal conditions they would have continued their education through high school at least. In such cases the demand for home instruction was felt to be justified.

The following law, therefore, was enacted by the State Legislature and became effective August 1st, 1930:

General Laws, Chapter 71,
Section 46A.

"The school committee of every town shall annually ascertain under regulations prescribed by the department and the commissioner of public

---
* House Document No. 401—Final report of the Department of Public Welfare relative to the Number and Care of Crippled Children.

welfare, the number of children of school age and resident therein who are crippled. In any town where, at the beginning of any school year, there are five or more children so crippled as to make attendance at a public school not feasible, and who are not otherwise provided for, the school committee shall, and in any town where there are less than five such children may, employ a teacher or teachers, on full or part time, who shall with the approval in each case of the department and the said commissioner, offer instruction to said children in their homes or at such places and under such conditions as the committee may arrange."

In April 1932, the law was amended to read "physically handicapped" instead of "crippled". This was done to insure the benefits of the law to children suffering from cardiac disabilities, chorea, and other medical conditions of not a strictly crippling nature.

As the law calls for the approval in each case of the departments of education and public welfare it is necessary for an investigation to be made in all cases. A Supervisor of Social Service for Crippled Children has been appointed in the Department of Public Welfare for this purpose and the investigations are made with these questions in mind: -

What are the needs of this child from the standpoints of treatment and education?

Is the child having adequate medical attention: Is everything possible being done to reduce the amount of handicap he has so he may live a more nearly normal life?

What are his educational needs? Does he need the opportunity of going on with his studies at home during an enforced and extended absence from the public school to which he may be expected to return upon the completion of his convalescence? It it possible to arrange for him to attend the regular public school with some adjustment, such as allowing him to bring his lunch, thus necessitating the trip between his home and the school being made but twice instead of four times?

Is he a child who, in spite of all that medical science can do for him, is bound to be a permanent cripple and therefore one who should have special training as a crippled child, in order to be able to take his place in society as a self-respecting, self-supporting citizen?

It is the intention of the departments of education and public welfare that approval for home instruction shall be given only in cases where some better solution of the child's educational problem can not be found.

Whenever home instruction is approved an effort is made to contact with the teacher and to help her to understand the child's condition so that she may teach him more intelligently. Very often the teacher has never seen children handicapped in the way these children are, whom she is called upon to teach in their homes, and she is very much at a loss to know how much to attempt with them. The teacher, therefore, nearly always welcomes these contacts and once the contact is made, frequently calls for further conferences about the children. The aim is, of course, to have the doctor, the parents, and the teacher, all working together in the interest of the child so, whenever possible, those responsible for the medical supervision of the child are consulted and their recommendations sought.

While there is no doubt that this law is proving to be a decided aid to the solution of the problems of many handicapped children, those who assist in the administration of it are increasingly aware of the fact that there are still certain handicapped children whose problems are not being satisfactorily solved, but they feel that the opportunity which the law provides for the accumulation of information regarding these problems, gives it an added value. The accumulation of such information will serve as a basis for the formulation of further legislation for handicapped children as the need is demonstrated.

RELIEF OF UNEMPLOYMENT IN MASSACHUSETTS BY WATER SUPPLY, SEWERAGE AND HOSPITALIZATION CONSTRUCTION

Through the medium of the "National Industrial Recovery Act", the President was authorized to expend $3,300,000,000 for the construction of public works. To effectuate the title of the act, some $2,000,000,000 were to be distributed to states, counties and municipalities to finance comprehensive programs of public works construction. Section 202 of this act provided as follows:

(a) "construction, repair and improvement of public highways, parkways, public buildings, and any publicly owned instrumentalities and facilities."

(b) ". . . purification of waters, construction of sewage-disposal plants."

(c) "any projects of the character heretofore constructed or carried on either directly by public authority or with public aid to serve the interests of the general public."

(d) "construction under public regulation or control of low-cost housing and slum-clearance projects."

(e) "any projects . . . of any character heretofore eligible for loans under subsection (a) of section 201 of the Emergency Relief and Construction Act of 1932 . . ., and paragraph (3) of subsection (a) shall . . . be held to include loans for construction or completion of reservoirs and pumping plants."

To carry out this work in Massachusetts, the State Legislature passed an act, known as Chapter 366 of the Acts of 1933, and in accordance with this act there was set up a State Emergency Finance Board to pass upon all municipal projects to be financed under the National Industrial Recovery Act. It is interesting to note that of some $39,405,502 worth of projects submitted by cities and towns to the Emergency Finance Board, $15,158,345 related to matters of water supply, sewerage, refuse disposal and hospitalization. These projects and the action taken by the Emergency Finance Board in relation thereto are shown on the appended table.

APPLICATIONS FOR PUBLIC WORKS PROJECTS OF PUBLIC HEALTH NATURE PRESENTED TO EMERGENCY FINANCE BOARD TO DATE, NOVEMBER 6, 1933

(App. — Approved. FAB — Sent to Federal Advisory Board.)

Place	Project	Amount	Decision
Abington	Water System Improvements	$ 33,500	Vote to come
Adams	Water Supply Reservoirs	300,000	Vote to come
Baldwinsville	Water Supply System	160,000	Pending legislation
Boston	Sewer Construction	3,000,000	Revised for $1,000,000
Boston	City Hospital Improvements	2,000,000	
Boston	High Pressure Mains	800,000	
Brookline	Surface Water Drains (Grant)	4,260	App. 9/26 FAB 10/4
Brookline	Sewer Construction	14,000	App. 9/26 FAB 10/4
Brookline	Relaying Water Mains	31,000	App. 9/26 FAB 10/4
Chelmsford	Water Supply District	75,000	App. 9/26 FAB 10/4
Georgetown	Public Water Works	130,000	App. 9/26 FAB 10/4
Gloucester	Relaying Water Mains	100,000	App. 10/31 FAB 11/2
Gloucester	Sewer Construction	100,000	App. 10/31 FAB 11/2
Gt. Barrington	Water Supply Facilities	60,000	App. 10/23 FAB 11/6
Haverhill	Sewers and Storm Drains	30,000	Awaiting Vote
Lexington	Erection of Standpipe	40,000	App. 9/27 FAB 10/4
Lexington	Sewer Construction	46,000	App. 9/27 FAB 10/4
Lowell	Water Works Improvements	811,140	Disapproved
Lowell	Sewer Construction	740,000	App. 11/3 for $140,000
Marlborough	Sewage Improvements	25,000	App. 9/1 FAB 9/5
Marlborough	Surface Water Drains	7,500	Disapproved 10/18
Marlborough	Relaying Water Mains	25,000	App. 10/18 FAB 10/24
Medford	New Drain Construction	75,000	Vote to come

Place	Project	Amount	Decision
Milford	Sewage Disposal Unit	78,250	Refused 10/10
Natick	Sewage Plant	174,000	On the Table
New Bedford	Water Works Improvements	500,000	App. 10/10 FAB 10/23
New Bedford	Sewer Construction	21,000	App. 11/3
Newburyport	Water Filtration Plant	60,000	App. 9/20 FAB 9/21
Newton	Refuse Incinerator	200,000	App. 10/20 FAB 10/24
Newton	Sewer Construction	115,000	App. 11/3 FAB 11/4
North Adams	Sewers and Sewage Plant	373,000	App. 9/13 FAB 9/18
North Andover	Water Main Extensions	15,000	App. 10/6 FAB 10/16
Norwood	Sewer Construction	25,000	App. 11/3
Paxton	Water Supply System	85,000	App. 9/13 FAB 9/18
Pittsfield	Sewage Disposal Plant	250,000	New Application Coming
Quincy	Sewer Construction	339,200	App. 10/3 FAB 10/6
Quincy	Storm Water Sewers	159,000	App. 10/3 FAB 10/6
Somerville	Incinerator	216,000	
Somerville	Sewer Drains Garfield Ave.	6,020	
Somerville	Sewer Drains Stone Avenue	13,070	
Somerville	Sewer Drains Fremont St.	10,880	
Somerville	Sewer Drains Glenwood Rd.	7,850	
Somerville	Sewer Drains Partridge Ave.	8,000	
Somerville	Sewer Drains Kidder and Willow Ave.	4,960	
Somerville	Sewer Drains Josephine Ave.	4,980	
Somerville	Sewer Drains Jay Street	3,600	
Somerville	Sewer Drains Rogers & Morrison Aves.	13,250	
Somerville	Sewer Drains Waverly Street	20,000	
Somerville	Sewer Drains Boston & Lowell Railroad	30,000	
Somerville	Sewer Drains Gorham Street	6,500	
Somerville	Sewer Drains Paulina Street	7,000	
Somerville	Sewer Drains Raymond Avenue	9,650	
Somerville	Water Mains Curtis Street	2,300	
Somerville	Water Mains Kimball Street	4,900	
Somerville	Water Mains Porter Street	7,400	
Somerville	Water Mains Crown Street	5,000	
Somerville	Water Mains Brastow Avenue	5,000	
Somerville	Water Mains Lowell Street	10,200	
Somerville	Water Mains Spring Street	6,100	
Somerville	Water Mains Atherton Street	2,300	
Somerville	Water Mains Benton Road	6,300	
Somerville	Water Mains Joy Street	7,000	
Somerville	Water Mains Maple Street	4,900	
Somerville	Water Mains Wyatt Street	4,700	
Somerville	Water Mains Perry Street	4,700	
Somerville	Water Mains Oak Street	6,300	
Somerville	Water Mains Hanson Street	5,400	
Somerville	Water Mains Skehan Street	2,300	
Somerville	Water Mains Calvin Street	4,900	
Somerville	Water Mains Dimick Street	6,400	
Somerville	Water Mains Buckingham Street	2,300	
Somerville	Water Mains Grant Street	9,700	
Somerville	Water Mains Garfield Avenue	7,000	
Somerville	Water Mains Glen Street	16,200	
Somerville	Water Mains Mystic Avenue	6,300	
Somerville	Water Mains Broadway	7,000	
Somerville	Water Mains Raymond Avenue	9,250	
Somerville	Water Mains North Street	1,800	
Somerville	Separate Sewer System Perry Street	7,360	
Somerville	Separate Sewer System Endicott Ave.	2,350	
Somerville	Separate Sewer System Wheatland St.	11,200	
Somerville	Separate Sewer System Grant Street	13,200	
Somerville	Water Mains Jacques Street	16,200	
Springfield	Construction of Sewers	423,700	App. 9/20 FAB 9/21
Taunton	Mill River Improvement	103,000	App. 9/26 FAB 10/4
Taunton	Sewage Disposal Plant	420,000	Disapproved
Taunton	Weir Village Sewers	100,000	Tabled
Townsend	Water Works System	154,000	App. 10/5 FAB 10/16
Sturbridge	Water Supply System (Grant)	18,840	App. 10/19 FAB 10/24
Wakefield	Replacing Water Pipes	100,000	App. 9/26 FAB 10/4

Walpole	Lateral Sewers	125,000	Vote coming	
Williamstown	Sewer Construction	35,000	App. 10/31 FAB 11/2	
Winthrop	Sewer and Street Construction	90,520	App. 10/31 FAB 11/2	
Worcester	Bath House and Sewer Construction	80,000	Temp. Held	
Worcester	Contagious Diseases Ward	300,000		
Worcester	Surgical and Maternity Ward	600,000		
Worcester	Water Main Construction	140,000	App. 10/2 $138,573 FAB 10/5	
Worcester	Sewer Construction	662,388	App. 10/3 for $251,343	
Worcester	Sewage Treatment Plant	53,107		
Waltham	Water System Improvements	108,000	App. 10/31 $98,000	
Waltham	New Drains	79,520	App. 11/1 $33,520	
Woburn	Extension Trunk Sewer	100,000	App. 10/30 FAB 11/2	

FOREWORD

We are bringing to your attention the Community and Nursing Standards for Maternity Care as recommended by the Committee of the Massachusetts Medical Society and published in the New England Journal of Medicine, August 3, 1933.

This is a very valuable contribution to public health literature and these standards should be adopted by every community which has the health of its mothers and children at heart.

Talk it over with your physicians, your nursing organizations, your hospitals and community leaders and organize for their adoption.

COMMUNITY AND NURSING STANDARDS FOR MATERNITY CARE*

At the request of the State Department of Public Health the Obstetrical Section of the Massachusetts Medical Society authorized the appointment of an Advisory Committee to the Department, at the Annual Meeting in 1932. This Committee was asked by the Department to recommend community and nursing standards for maternity care and, after careful consideration, submits the following:

FRANK A. PEMBERTON, M.D., *Chairman* CHARLES E. MONGAN, M.D.
RICHARD S. BENNER, M.D. JOSEPH W. O'CONNOR, M.D.
THOMAS H. GOETHALS, M.D. ALONZO K. PAINE, M.D.
FREDERICK J. LYNCH, M.D. LOUIS E. PHANEUF, M.D.
The Committee.

COMMUNITY AND NURSING STANDARDS FOR MATERNITY CARE

I. General Principles

1. The aim of adequate maternity care is the minimum of mental and physical discomfort for every woman during pregnancy; the maximum of mental and physical fitness at its termination, with the reward of a well baby and the knowledge whereby she may keep herself and her baby well.

2. Every organization and individual giving maternity care should make a conscientious and coordinated effort directly or indirectly to teach the community the value of and the need for medical and nursing care from the time pregnancy is suspected.

3. While independent centers giving prenatal care are at times necessary, it is important that such centers have a definite working agreement with hospital services for the reception of patients and their subsequent treatment.

4. Community planning for maternity care is necessary.

5. To clear up the considerable confusion, public health nursing is here defined.

"Public health nursing is an organized community service rendered by graduate nurses to the individual, family and community. This service includes the interpretation and application of medical, sanitary

* Reprinted from the New England Journal of Medicine, Vol. 209, No. 5, pp. 257-258, Aug. 3, 1933

and social procedures for the correction of defects, prevention of disease and the promotion of health, and may include skilled care of the sick in their homes."

(Definition by the National Organization for Public Health Nursing)

II. Organization of Community Resources

1. Each city and town or group of towns should have a local committee on maternity care which may be a sub-committee of a community health council, if such exists. This committee should be composed of representatives of the medical society, the hospital, the boards of public welfare and public health, the visiting nursing association and other appropriate professional and lay groups or individuals. This committee should serve as a clearing house for information, should endeavor to develop improved facilities for obstetrical care where these are deficient or lacking, and should stimulate the adoption of uniform standards by those engaged in maternity work.

2. In addition to private practitioners, beds for obstetrical care should be available in an adequate hospital or hospitals. The departments of public welfare should pay for adequate service to the indigent.

3. For those unable to pay for service individually there should be clinic service, preferably in a hospital giving obstetrical care, available for prenatal and postnatal service, to which physicians may send private patients if they so desire.

4. Through hospitals, visiting nursing associations and other appropriate community agencies, or through an association of two or more of these agencies, a continuous prenatal, delivery and postnatal service should be available.

III. Prenatal Nursing Care

If the patient is not under medical supervision, the nurse must make every effort to get the patient under the care of a physician as soon as possible. If the patient is unable to employ a physician, she should then be sent to an appropriate prenatal clinic.

Each organization offering prenatal nursing service should have a definite policy which has been passed upon by the local professional group as a whole or by the special committee. The visits by the nurse to the patient before she has placed herself under medical care should consist of efforts to get the patient under care, and such instruction as may be necessary to accomplish this.

Home visits by a supervised public health nurse in accordance with the physician's instructions are desirable. If the doctor requests, such visits may include:

1. Checking up on the condition of the patient by noting the following:
   Temperature, pulse, respiration
   Inspection of mouth
   Blood pressure
   Condition of breasts and care of nipples
   Movement of fetus
   Presence of edema and varicosities
   Danger Signs:
     Headache
     Change in mental attitude
     Dyspnoea
     Epigastric pain
     Nausea—vomiting (time occurrence)
     Vaginal discharge—character and amount
     Bleeding
     Constipation
   Food
   General hygiene
   Urinalysis—for the presence of albumin or sugar.

The nurse's visit is of increased value if she sends a report of her findings and advice to the doctor or hospital caring for the patient.

2. Determining the needs of the patient in relation to her home, in order to help solve any problem that may effect the health or happiness of the expectant mother.

3. Advising about the preparation for delivery if home delivery is planned; helping to make any plans which may be necessary if the patient is to go to the hospital, such as placing children.

4. Arranging for supplementary care at time of delivery and during the postpartum period.

5. Instructing the patient regarding the symptoms which indicate the onset of labor and informing her of the importance of reporting to the doctor or the hospital if these come on. (Rupture of membranes, even without pains being present, calls for attendance of the doctor or visit to the hospital.)

IV. Nursing Delivery Care

At the time of delivery the duties of the public health nurse and attendants are to assist the physician and carry out his instructions. It must be recognized that the demands of obstetrical nursing care in the home are very exacting, and may materially interfere with the general public health nursing program. It is, therefore, well for the community to consider having available special arrangements for this type of nursing service, properly supervised.

V. After-Care Nursing

Care of patients after delivery should include careful inspection and supervision and every effort should be made to guard against complications. To this end, public health nursing care should include:

For the Mother:
a. A daily bed bath with warm water and soap.
b. Perineal cleansing and dressing according to approved method, after using bedpan and as often as necessary.
c. Daily inspection of breasts and nipples.
d. Temperature, pulse, respiration.
e. Other detailed observation of the patient with immediate report to the physician of any abnormalities or change in the patient's condition.
f. Instruction and demonstration of postpartum care for the patient delivered at home, to the person assuming responsibility for the care of the patient.

For Baby:
a. Daily bath.
b. Temperature taken daily if desired.
c. Inspection of eyes, mouth, cord.
d. Inspection of stools.
e. Training the mother to nurse her baby.
f. Regular weighing every other day to determine whether sufficient milk has been obtained.

THE DIFFERENCE BETWEEN TWEEDLEDUM AND TWEEDLEDEE

Radio Broadcast, Station W. E. E. I., October 27, 1933

N. A. NELSON, M.D.

Assistant Director, Division of Communicable Diseases

A genealogist—you know—one of those persons who will find out for you whether or not your great-great-grandfather came over in the Mayflower, was asked, once upon a time, to look up the family tree of a socially very prominent lady. He did—and was very much upset by what he found. He told a friend that he had discovered that one of this fine lady's relatives—not very distant, either—had died in prison in the electric chair. Said the genealogist to his friend, "I can't tell her that. She'll never forgive me for finding it out, and it will mean the end of any business from her or her friends. What in the world am I going to do?" The friend thought a minute. Then he said, "That's easy. Tell her that he occupied the chair of applied electricity at one of our leading public institutions."

Perhaps in this case it didn't make any real difference that the lady went away happy in the belief that her dear relative had been the professor of electricity in a leading university. There are occasions when, for practical purposes, there is little difference, as the expression goes, between Tweedledum and Tweedledee.

There are times, however, when these twins may not be in any way identical. Tweedledum may be tall and thin, as it were, and Tweedledee may be short and fat. For instance, twenty-five or thirty years ago, people talked (or rather, they whispered) about "Consumption" and "The White Plague". Those who had the disease were looked upon as social outcasts. No wonder! They had consumption! They were being consumed; eaten up! They were victims of the White Plague, rushing rapidly onward to meet Death! No healthy person wanted anything to do with plagues or with Death!

Fortunately, there were a few thoughtful people who refused to think of those unfortunate sick in such a negative, inconsiderate, hopeless way. One of those thoughtful people was Dr. Trudeau. He had the disease himself. He wasn't ready to be consumed by anything except a burning desire to help others like himself. With that hopeful attitude to give him faith, he discovered that people didn't have to be consumed by this disease. They could be cured! And out of that discovery came the even greater one, that it could be prevented!

But if consumptives were no longer being consumed since they were being cured, how could we go on using the name, consumption? Ridiculous! Well, if they didn't have consumption, what did they have? They had tuberculosis! What a difference! Nothing in that word to bring up, a mental picture of fatalistic hopelessness. Nothing obnoxious or unpleasant or horrifying in that name. It is just the name of a disease, just as appendicitis is the name of a disease. And you all know now that when people began to say "tuberculosis", instead of "consumption", they began to build sanatoria; to improve housing and living conditions; they began to open clinics and to see to the protection of children who were being exposed to infection. The result? Tuberculosis kills only a quarter as many people in Massachusetts per one hundred thousand of population, as it did thirty years ago, and every year sees a lower death rate.

In this case, then, Tweedledum Consumption and Tweedledee Tuberculosis are quite different characters. They refer to the same disease, it is true, but what a difference they make in point of view and in human progress!

Now for another, but equally serious example. The Registrar of Vital Statistics at the State House has the death certificates of hundreds of children who have died of a very common disease. They were all born with it. The State hospitals for the feebleminded, the homes for the blind, clinics and physicians everywhere have records of thousands of children who were born with it. In my own office in the State Department of Public Health I have the records of nearly one thousand children who are now under treatment for this same disease.

Another disease attacks the eyes of at least forty babies under one year of age every year in this State, some of whom are made permanently blind. In addition, the State Department of Public Health receives reports that nearly three hundred little girls, most of them under ten years of age, are infected with this disease every year.

These two diseases with which thousands of children in this country are born, year after year, or are otherwise innocently infected, are known to people as venereal diseases! Think of it! Venereal diseases! Let us see what Webster's unabridged dictionary says about that word "venereal". "Of and pertaining to venery, or sexual love". How in the world can these thousands of children be said to have venereal disease, when their infections have been acquired through birth or in some other manner equally far removed from any sex behavior on their parts! Not only is it utterly ridiculous, but it most unfairly applies a word to them which, through the years has come to mean something quite obnoxious and indecent. The so-called venereal diseases have long been associated in the public mind with men and women of loose morals. The minute the words are spoken the mind almost automatically thinks of sexual misconduct on the part of the one who is infected. Nothing makes me boil so much as to have some thoughtless person call me on the telephone to ask what to do for a baby with venereal disease. In this day and age it is the aim of the Society to protect children from the unpleasant,   t we fasten   a label upon them.

Doctors, dentists and nurses not at all infrequently catch syphilis from the patients they treat. I could tell you of a physician who caught it from a woman he was attending at childbirth; of a surgeon who cut his finger while operating on a young man who had it; of a dentist who caught it through working in the mouth of a patient in the early stages of the disease; of a nurse who got the germs into a burn on her thumb from a new-born baby that had syphilis; of the young lady who caught it through kissing her sweetheart; of the child who became infected through the kiss of its aunt! At least fifteen per cent of all infections with this disease are the result of contacts, between people, that have nothing to do with sex whatever. How can they be said to have venereal disease?

Let us look into this matter a little further. We know that at this moment there are more than one million people in the United States under treatment for gonorrhea and syphilis. Nearly half of those who are infected are women. At least two-thirds of these women were infected, after marriage, by husbands who either did not know they were infected or thought they were cured. Now these married women have venereal disease if we accept Webster's definition of the word venereal as pertaining to sexual love. But they most certainly do not have venereal disease if we accept the popular meaning of the word which means loose morals. These women had every moral and legal right to the relationships with their husbands through which they became infected. They, also, are being labeled, thoughtlessly and inhumanely, by implication, as having been guilty of serious misconduct.

I might go on to discuss the responsibility of Society for the hundreds of thousands of infections with gonorrhea and syphilis among boys and girls whose only sex education at home has been the fairy story of the stork and the doctor's bag. It is true that they may be said, in one sense, to have venereal disease. But too many of them have it because the very thoughtlessness and prudishness which has produced the term "venereal disease" has also denied them the information which might have saved them from gonorrhea and syphilis.

Let us, for a moment, look at those words, gonorrhea and syphilis, that people and newspapers and magazines seem to fear so much. What is gonorrhea? It is a disease of the eye in many new-born babies. It is a disease of certain delicate membranes in young, innocently infected girls and in babies. I have two friends, both doctors, who have lost the sight of an eye by getting the germs of gonorrhea into them from flying drops of pus, during the examination or treatment of patients. It is a disease of married women who have been infected by their husbands. The word, gonorrhea, says nothing about the manner in which the disease is acquired. It has no unfair, no obnoxious, no harmful implications. It is the name of a disease which may be caught by perfectly moral people, just as tuberculosis may be caught by perfectly decent people. The word consumption suggested hopelessness to people. The words venereal disease suggest immorality. The name, tuberculosis, changed the public point of view to one of hopefulness. The name, gonorrhea, because it carries no slur on character, will let people hear the pleas of the multitude of innocently infected, that something be done to stop this blinding, sterilizing, home-wrecking, health-destroying disease from going any further.

What is syphilis? It is a disease of the blood which kills babies before they are born or when they are a few weeks or months old. It is a disease which makes children blind, deaf, feebleminded, insane, or leaves them with weak, unhealthy and crippled bodies. It is a disease which, in its early stages, may be spread by a kiss. Doctors, dentists and nurses catch it from patients. Brides catch it from their uncured husbands. The word, syphilis, is the name of a very common disease, and makes no slanderous insinuations as to how it may have been acquired. If people will use it because they understand that, the innocently infected will no longer be compelled to hang their heads in the shame which is now so wrongfully and thoughtlessly hung upon them. Osler, the great physician, has said that "even the sinner is entitled to Christian treatment". How much more is he or she entitled to Christian treatment who has been innocently infected with gonorrhea or syphilis.

There may not be much difference between Tweedledum and Tweedledee, so far as many of the foolish arguments of this world are concerned. But in the use of the words, venereal disease, and the names, gonorrhea and syphilis, there is a difference in point of view which means everything to what our attitude is going to be toward those unfortunates who have them.

REPORT OF THE DIVISION OF FOOD AND DRUGS

During the months of July, August and September 1933, samples were collected in 169 cities and towns.

There were 1,214 samples of milk examined, of which 268 were below standard, from 25 samples the cream had been in part removed, 7 samples contained added water, and 12 samples were skimmed milk below the legal standard. There were 74 samples of Grade A milk examined, 6 samples of which were below the legal standard of 4.00% fat. There were 930 bacteriological examinations made of milk, 706 of which complied with the requirements.

There were 434 samples of food examined, of which 136 were adulterated or misbranded. These consisted of 1 sample of alimentary pastes, which was low in egg solids; 8 samples of marshmallow which contained benzoic acid; 11 samples of eggs, 8 of which were sold as fresh eggs but were not fresh, and 3 samples were cold storage not so marked; 2 samples of butter which were low in fat; 1 sample of blueberry pie which contained a greenish-blue mold; 3 samples of olives which were decomposed; 1 sample of vanilla which contained coumarin, vanillin and no resin; 1 sample of ice cream which was low in fat; 37 samples of hamburg steak, 1 sample of sausage, 8 samples of liver, 1 sample of pork chops, 1 sample of soup meat, 3 samples of beef suet, and 2 samples of pork kidney, all of which were decomposed; 29 samples of hamburg steak, 6 samples of which contained sodium sulphite in excess of one tenth of one per cent and also contained added water and were decomposed, 3 samples which contained sodium sulphite in excess of one tenth of one per cent and were also decomposed, 2 samples which contained sodium sulphite in excess of one tenth of one per cent and also contained added water, 4 samples which contained added water two of which were also decomposed, and 14 samples contained sodium sulphite in excess of one tenth of one per cent, 17 samples of hamburg steak which were not properly labeled, 1 sample of which contained a compound of sulphur dioxide, added water and was also decomposed, 10 samples which contained a compound of sulphur dioxide, 3 of which were also decomposed, and 6 samples contained a compound of sulphur dioxide; 2 samples of sausage which contained sodium sulphite in excess of one tenth of one per cent, 6 samples of sausage which contained a compound of sulphur dioxide not properly labeled, and 1 sample of sausage which contained starch in excess of 2 per cent.

There were 2 samples of miscellaneous drugs examined, of which 1 sample was adulterated. This was a sample of eye wash which did not correspond to the prescription.

The police departments submitted 816 samples of liquor for examination, 812 of which were above 0.5% in alcohol. The police departments also submitted 13 samples to be analyzed for poisons or drugs, 1 sample of which contained opium, 11 samples contained heroin, and 1 sample of white powder was talc.

There were 66 cities and towns visited for the inspection of pasteurizing plants and 218 plants were inspected.

There were 106 hearings held pertaining to violations of the laws.

There were 66 convictions for violations of the law, $1,325 in fines being imposed.

Fred J. Castine and Oliver Superchi of Orange; Alice G. Collins and Mark E. McCarron of Woburn; Drauffis Dilyannis of Hull; George Phillips of Salisbury; Charles Quong of Athol; Andrew C. Reed of Danvers; D. William J. Shea of Oak Bluffs; and Joseph L. Walker of Hyannis, were all convicted for violations of the milk laws.

James W. Kirschner of Pittsfield was convicted for violation of the Grade A Milk regulations.

Maynard W. Lane, 2 cases, of Ipswich; Forest Lake Dairy Company, Incorporated, 2 cases, of Palmer; G. Fred Sumner, 2 cases, of South Attleboro; B. M. Frye, Incorporated, of Leominster; Julio Olivera of Fall River; and James B. Crane of Leominster, were all convicted for violations of the pasteurization laws and regulations.

John Pakalika of Arlington; Barney Burstine and John Zolta of Springfield; Albert Siegel and Lewis Abrams of Cambridge; Morris Shawachman and Frank Hollis of Chelsea; Samuel Berkman of Roxbury; Consumers Provision Company, Brockelman Brothers, 3 cases, and Mitchell Mindick, all of Worcester; The Great Atlantic & Pacific Tea Company, Isadore Solomon, and Atter Brothers, all of Gardner; The Great Atlantic & Pacific Tea Company, 2 cases, and Grand Union Company, of Pittsfield; Louis Sawelsky of South Boston; Abraham Rozen, Touraine Lunch, Incorporated, Hyman Alpert, Chamberlain & Company, Incorporated, 2 cases, Roma Extract Company, Incorporated, Three Millers Company, Max White, Joseph Reinholtz, and Morris Marienberg, all of Boston; Morris Libowitz, 3 cases, of Lawrence; The Great Atlantic & Pacific Tea Company of Leominster; Brockelman Brothers, Incorporated, and The Great Atlantic & Pacific Tea Company, 2 cases, of Fitchburg; Growers Outlet, Incorporated, and Orphir Tessier of Holyoke; Nathan Greenbaum of Amesbury; Julius Cohen of Everett; and Samuel Berger of Lynn, were all convicted for violations of the food laws. Touraine Lunch, Incorporated, Hyman Alpert, Morris Marienberg, Joseph Reinholtz, and Max White, all of Boston; Frank Hollis of Chelsea; Samuel Berkman of Roxbury; and Julius Cohen of Everett, all appealed their cases. The case of Economy Grocery Stores Company of Billerica was continued without finding for one year.

Grand Union Company of Pittsfield, and Samuel Berkman of Roxbury, were convicted for false advertising. Samuel Berkman of Roxbury appealed his case.

James W. Kirschner of Pittsfield was convicted for misbranding.

Three Millers Company of Boston was convicted for violation of the sanitary food law.

In accordance with Section 25, Chapter 111 of the General Laws, the following is the list of articles of adulterated food collected in original packages from manufacturers, wholesalers, or producers:

Two samples of milk from which a portion of the cream had been removed were produced by Mark E. McCarron of Woburn.

One sample of butter which was below the legal standard in milk fat was obtained from National Creamery Company of Somerville.

One sample of vanilla extract which contained coumarin, vanillin and no resin was obtained from A. R. Perdigao of Stoughton.

One sample of olives, and 2 samples of brine from olives, were obtained from G. Zuffante Company of Boston.

Marshmallow which contained a compound of benzoic acid was obtained as follows:

Four samples from Three Millers Lowell Company of Boston, and 1 sample from Angelus-Campfire Company of Chicago.

One sample of beef flank which was decomposed was obtained from Brockelman Brothers of Gardner.

One sample each of beef suet which was decomposed was obtained from Wellworth Market of Roxbury, and Joseph P. Eaton of Boston.

One sample of pork chops which was decomposed was obtained from from Atter Brothers of Gardner.

One sample of soup meat which was decomposed was obtained from City Public Market of Gardner.

Liver which was decomposed was obtained as follows:

One sample each, from Brockelman Brothers (Lincoln Square Market), Consumers Provision Company, Incorporated, Worcester Public Market, and Atlantic & Pacific Market, all of Worcester; Northampton Public Market of Northampton; The Great Atlantic & Pacific Tea Company of Pittsfield; United Butchers of Attleboro; Edwin Gralnick of Allston.

Pork kidney which was decomposed was obtained as follows:

One sample each, from Armour & Company and Max Belkin, both of Boston.

Hamburg steak which was decomposed was obtained as follows:

Two samples each, from The Great Atlantic & Pacific Tea Company of Fitchburg, and Wellworth Market of Roxbury; and 1 sample each, from The Great Atlantic & Pacific Tea Company of Gardner, Pittsfield, Leominster and North Attleboro; Brockelman Brothers, Incorporated, of Gardner, Leominster, Fitchburg, and Brockelman Brothers, Incorporated, (Lincoln Square Market) of Worcester; Premier Market of Lawrence; City Public Market of Gardner; Front Street Market, Worcester Public Market, and Louis' Market, all of Worcester; J. E. Ram's Incorporated, of Lee; Berkman's Market,, Incorporated, and Barney Gross, of Roxbury; Growers Outlet, Incorporated, and Orphir Tessier of Holyoke; Grand Union Company of Pittsfield; Blackstone Supply Company of Chelsea; Max White, Hyman Alpert, Joseph Reinholtz, and Morris Marienberg, all of Boston; Robert Kravitz, Bristol Market, and Manhattan Market, all of New Bedford; Hyman Goldkrand of Medford; and Nathan Greenman of Amesbury.

Hamburg steak which contained sodium sulphite in excess of one tenth of one per cent was obtained as follows:

One sample each, from Sigda Brothers and George Pasko of Holyoke; Mohican Beef Company, Lewis Goldman, Samuel Baker, Mrs. Lena Costello, and Jack Levy, all of Lynn; Pleasant Street Market, Incorporated, of Northampton; Abraham Kaufman of Chelsea; Benney Sack of Salem; Malden Square Market of Malden, Alter Brothers of Roxbury; Abram Cohen of New Bedford; and Phillip Schwachman of Boston.

Hamburg steak which contained sodium sulphite in excess of one tenth of one per cent, and also contained added water and was decomposed, was obtained as follows:

One sample each, from Nathan Sirkins, Ideal Provision Company, Incorporated, Estate of E. Cohen, and Israel Dores, all of Roxbury; Celia Kaizer (Fulton Market) of Chelsea; and Benjamin Stoltzberg of Haverhill.

Hamburg steak which contained sodium sulphite in excess of one tenth of one per cent and also contained added water was obtained as follows:

One sample each, from Harry Simon and Isaac Bassinov of Roxbury.

Hamburg steak which contained sodium sulphite in excess of one tenth of one per cent and was also decomposed was obtained as follows:

One sample each, from Clinton Market of Chelsea, Handy Dandy Stores, Incorporated, of Haverhill; M. Jacobson & Sons of Worcester; and David Gallis of Boston.

Hamburg steak which contained added water and was also decomposed was obtained as follows:

One sample each, from Woburn Provision Company of Everett; and Edwin Gralnick of Allston.

Hamburg steak which contained added water was obtained as follows:

One sample each, from Grade A Market of Lowell; and Aaron Mendelbaum of Chelsea.

Hamburg steak which contained a compound of sulphur dioxide not properly labeled was obtained as follows:

Two samples, from Empire Beef Company of Worcester; 1 sample each, from Julius Cohen of Everett; Shafran & Sons and Louis Segal of Roxbury; Fairburn's Market and Clinton Market of Lawrence; Alex Goldstein of Worcester; Bessie Keimach, Morris Shawackman, and Frank S. Hollis, all of Chelsea; Harry Lampert of Somerville; and Sirloin Stores of Malden.

Hamburg steak which contained a compound of sulphur dioxide not properly labeled and was also decomposed was obtained as follows:

One sample each, from Sirloin Stores of Everett; and Nathan Herman of New Bedford.

One sample of hamburg steak which contained a compound of sulphur dioxide not properly labeled, also contained added water and was decomposed, was obtained from Morris Libowitz (Clinton Market) of Lawrence.

Sausage which contained a compound of sulphur dioxide not properly labeled was obtained as follows:

One sample each, from Mary Berger of Lynn; Big Bear Meat Department, Incorporated, of Medford; Harry Selansky of Melrose; Morris Marienberg of Boston; and S. R. Berkman of Roxbury.

One sample of sausage which contained sodium sulphite in excess of one tenth of one per cent was obtained from United Provision of Holyoke.

One sample of sausage which was decomposed was obtained from Israel Dores of Roxbury.

There were thirteen confiscations, as follows:—35½ pounds of decomposed fowl; 138 pounds of tainted roasters; 500 pounds of beef affected with peritonitis; 200 pounds of decomposed beef; 45 pounds of decomposed beef livers; 9 pounds of decomposed liver; ¾ pound of decomposed Polish balogna; ½ pound of decomposed pork sausage; 2 pounds of decomposed hamburg steak; and 9,031 pounds of decomposed mackerel.

The licensed cold storage warehouses reported the following amounts of food placed in storage during June, 1933:—1,211,190 dozens of case eggs; 1,967,151 pounds of broken out eggs; 5,366,571 pounds of butter; 1,942,186 pounds of poultry; 3,762,749 pounds of fresh meat and fresh meat products; and 7,108,729 pounds of fresh food fish.

There was on hand July 1, 1933:—7,961,970 dozens of case eggs; 3,286,539 pounds of broken out eggs; 6,601,772 pounds of butter; 4,330,837 pounds of poultry; 8,654,576½ pounds of fresh meat and fresh meat products; and 15,090,380 pounds of fresh food fish.

The licensed cold storage warehouses reported the following amounts of food placed in storage during July, 1933:—908,160 dozens of case eggs; 1,093,368 pounds of broken out eggs; 4,695,928 pounds of butter; 1,639,784 pounds of poultry; 3,589,291½ pounds of fresh meat and fresh meat products; and 8,119,745 pounds of fresh food fish.

There was on hand August 1, 1933:—8,049,120 dozens of case eggs;

3,688,334 pounds of broken out eggs; 10,560,377 pounds of butter; 4,667,913 pounds of poultry; 9,289,641½ pounds of fresh meat and fresh meat products; and 20,393,978 pounds of fresh food fish.

The licensed cold storage warehouses reported the following amounts of food placed in storage during August, 1933:—595,140 dozens of case eggs; 462,832 pounds of broken out eggs; 2,681,973 pounds of butter; 1,211,186 pounds of poultry; 2,353,692½ pounds of fresh meat and fresh meat products; and 6,936,694 pounds of fresh food fish.

There was on hand September 1, 1933:—7,152,330 dozens of case eggs; 3,316,993 pounds of broken out eggs; 12,025,573 pounds of butter; 4,544,665 pounds of poultry; 8,353,295 pounds of fresh meat and fresh meat products; and 23,069,411 pounds of fresh food fish.

MASSACHUSETTS DEPARTMENT OF PUBLIC HEALTH

Commissioner of Public Health, HENRY D. CHADWICK, M.D.

Public Health Council

HENRY D. CHADWICK, M.D., *Chairman*

ROGER I. LEE, M.D.
SYLVESTER E. RYAN, M.D.
FRANCIS H. LALLY, M.D.

RICHARD P. STRONG, M.D.
JAMES L. TIGHE.
GORDON HUTCHINS.

Secretary, ALICE M. NELSON

Division of Administration	Under direction of Commissioner.
Division of Sanitary Engineering	Director and Chief Engineer, ARTHUR D. WESTON, C.E.
Division of Communicable Diseases	Director, GAYLORD W. ANDERSON, M.D.
Division of Biologic Laboratories	Director and Pathologist, BENJAMIN WHITE, Ph.D.
Division of Food and Drugs	Director and Analyst, HERMANN C. LYTHGOE, S.B.
Division of Child Hygiene	Director, M. LUISE DIEZ, M.D.
Division of Tuberculosis	Director, ALTON S. POPE, M.D.
Division of Adult Hygiene	Director, HERBERT L. LOMBARD, M.D.

State District Health Officers

The Southeastern District	RICHARD P. MACKNIGHT, M.D., New Bedford.
The Metropolitan District	CHARLES B. MACK, M.D., Boston
The Northeastern District	ROBERT E. ARCHIBALD, M.D., Lynn.
The Worcester County District	OSCAR A. DUDLEY, M.D., Worcester.
The Connecticut Valley District	HAROLD E. MINER, M.D., Springfield.
The Berkshire District	WALTER W. LEE, M.D., No. Adams.

INDEX

	PAGE
Alley, Leon A., Vocational Guidance for the Tuberculous Child	187
American Red Cross.	167
Annual Census of Physically Handicapped Children, by Margaret MacDonald	219
Appendicitis? What, Another Campaign	48
At Last Something Is To Be Done About Gonorrhea	167
Atypical Children and Their Education, by Arthur B. Lord	215
Beauchamp, E. W., M.D., Lynch, C. F., M.D., and Kisiel, W. J., M.D., Three Cured Cases of Carcinoma of Cervix	7
Berkshire County Cancer Clinic Committee	28
Berkshire County Cancer Clinics, by Rosamond Tatro	44
Bigelow, George H., M.D., Foreword to Cancer Number	3
Billings, Bernice W. and Esther L. Frutkoff, The Sheltered Workshop of the Boston Tuberculosis Association	189
Biopsy in Mammary Cancer, by James Ewing, M.D.	4
Book Notes:	
Education for Healthful Living in the Public Schools of Bellevue-Yorkville 1927-1931, by Nina B. Lamkin	49
Growth and Development of the Child — Part I — General Considerations, White House Conference Publication	48
Prophylactic Odontotomy, produced by the Hyatt Study Club	168
Student's Handbook on Nursing Case Studies, by Deborah McLurg Jensen, R.N., B.S.	48
Boston Committee (Cancer), Work of the, By Margaret H. Tracy	35
Boston Dispensary, Social Service in the Tumor Clinic of the, by Bernice E. Cross	41
Boston Dispensary Tumor Clinic	29
Boston Health League, Educational Committee on Cancer of	35
Boston Public Schools, The Rest and Nutrition Program in, by Clara Loitman, M.D.	206
Boston Tuberculosis Association, The Sheltered Workshop of the, by Bernice W. Billings and Esther L. Frutkoff	189
Briggs, L. Vernon, M.D., The Prevention of Crime – The Gangster in the Making	198
Brockton Associate Cancer Committee	36
Brockton Cancer Clinic	42
Brockton Cancer Clinic Committee	30
Brockton, Cancer Publicity in, by William T. Card	36
Cancer — See Cancer Number	1
Of the Lip and Skin, by Ernest M. Daland, M.D.	16
Mammary, Biopsy in, by James Ewing, M.D.	4
Of the Stomach, by J. Shelton Horsley, M.D.	5
Cancer Clinic — See Clinics	
Cancer Clinic Committees — See Clinic Committees	
Cancer Committees, Associate — See Committees, Associate Cancer	
"Cancer Cure" Always With Us	47
Cancer Patients, The Social Worker's Part in Securing Early Treatment for, by Mrs. Dorothy A. Oates	40
Cancer Program, Social Service in the State, by Eleanor E. Kelly	36
Cancer Publicity in Brockton, by William T. Card	36
Cancer Service in General Hospitals, by Curtis C. Tripp, M.D.	25
Carcinoma of Cervix, Three Cured Cases of, by C. F. Lynch, M.D., E. W. Beauchamp, M.D. and W. J. Kisiel, M.D.	7
Card, William T., Cancer Publicity in Brockton	36
Cardiac Child, by T. Duckett Jones, M.D.	184
Carney, Gertrude J., Social Service in the Worcester Cancer Clinics	37
Census, Annual, of Physically Handicapped Children, by Margaret MacDonald	219
Cervix, Carcinoma of, Three Cured Cases, by C. F. Lynch, M.D., E. W. Beauchamp, M.D. and W. J. Kisiel, M.D.	7
Chronic Disease, Epidemiology of	163
Clinic, Teaching Service in a Cancer, by Harry F. Friedman, M.D.	29
Clinic, Why a Cancer	26
Clinic Association, Lynn Cancer	32

	PAGE
Clinic Committees:	
Berkshire County Cancer	28
Brockton Cancer	30
Lawrence Cancer	26
Lynn Cancer	9
New Bedford Cancer	25
Worcester Cancer	8
Worcester North Cancer	25
Clinic Publicity, by Frederic Edwards	31
Clinics:	
Berkshire County Cancer, by Rosamond Tatro	44
Boston Dispensary Tumor	29
Social Service in the, by Bernice E. Cross	41
Brockton Cancer	42
Lawrence Cancer, Social Service in the, by Angie M. Richardson	39
Lowell Cancer	10
Social Service in the, by Muriel Eales	38
Lynn Cancer	40
New Bedford Cancer, Social Service in the, by Ida G. Dudelson	38
Pittsfield Cancer	28
Pondville Hospital Cured Cancer, by Ernest M. Daland, M.D.	11
Springfield Cancer, What Social Service Means to the, by Alice M. Drapeau	39
Worcester Cancer, Social Service in the, by Gertrude J. Carney	37
Worcester North Cancer, What Social Work Means in the, by Olive Twichell	37
Clinics for the Treatment of Gonorrhea and Syphilis, Minimum Standards for	108, 116
Clinics, Travelling School, for the Examination of Retarded Children in the Public Schools, by Neil A. Dayton, M.D.	193
Committees, Associate Cancer:	
Brockton	36
Gardner	33
Lawrence	34
North Adams	35
Springfield	31
Community and Nursing Standards for Maternity Care	223
Community Care of the Handicapped, by Herbert C. Parsons	177
Congenital Syphilis, by N. A. Nelson, M.D.	62
Control of Gonorrhea and Syphilis, by N. A. Nelson, M.D.	64
Cooperative Workrooms, Inc., by Hazel Newton	191
Crain, Gladys L., R.N.	
Facts about Gonorrhea	84
Familial Syphilis. Significant Facts for the Public Health Nurse	74
Nurse in the Control of Gonorrhea and Syphilis. As the Health Officer Sees Her	95
Public Health Nurse and the Community Social Hygiene Program	87
Public Health Nurse and the Educational Phases of a Social Hygiene Program	92
Public Health Nurse and the Medical Aspects of Social Hygiene	67
Syphilis. A Review	82
Syphilis. Some Facts Regarding Diagnosis and Treatment	77
Syphilis. What the Public Health Nurse Should Know about the Patient and the Disease	71
Crime, The Prevention of — The Gangster in the Making, by L. Vernon Briggs, M.D.	198
Cross, Bernice E., Social Service in the Tumor Clinic of the Boston Dispensary	41
Daland Ernest M., M.D., Cancer of the Lip and Skin	16
Daland, Ernest M., M. D., Pondville Hospital Cured Cancer Clinic	11
Dayton, Neil A., M.D., Travelling School Clinics for the Examination of Retarded Children in the Public Schools	193
Dental Caries, Epidemiological Approach to	165
Difference Between Tweedledum and Tweedledee, by N. A. Nelson, M.D.	225
Drapeau, Alice M., What Social Service Means to the Springfield Cancer Clinic	39
Dudelson, Ida G., Social Service in the New Bedford Cancer Clinic	38

	PAGE
Dysentery, Bacillary, Epidemiology of	145
Eales, Muriel, Social Service in the Lowell Cancer Clinic	38
Early, Agnes, A Nutrition Program	181
Economic Aspects of the Management of Syphilis, By Albert Keidel, M.D.	101, 116

Editorial Comment.
  "Cancer Cure" Always with Us . . . 47
  Economic Aspects of the Management of Syphilis . . . 116
  Massachusetts Society for Social Hygiene . . . 117
  Minimum Standards for Clinics for the Treatment of Gonorrhea and Syphilis . . . 116
  Nurse in the Control of Gonorrhea and Syphilis . . . 116
  Radio Broadcasts. Public Information . . . 116
  What, Another Campaign? Appendicitis? . . . 48
Education for Healthful Living in the Public Schools of Bellevue-Yorkville 1927-1931, by Nina B. Lamkin (book note) . . . 49
Educational Committee on Cancer of the Boston Health League . . . 35
Educational Work of the Lawrence Associate Cancer Committee . . . 34
Edwards, Frederic, Clinic Publicity . . . 31
Epidemiology: . . . 125
  Chronic Disease . . . 163
  Dental Caries, Epidemiological approach to . . . 165
  Dysentery, Bacillary . . . 145
  Gastro-Enteritis . . . 141
  Gonorrhea and Syphilis . . . 157
  Smallpox . . . 153
  Streptococcic Infections . . . 148
  Tuberculosis . . . 155
  Typhoid Fever . . . 126
"Eventually, Why Not Now?", by Rosamond Tatro . . . 42
Ewing, James, M.D., Biopsy in Mammary Cancer . . . 4
Facts about Gonorrhea, by Gladys L. Crain, R.N. . . . 84
Familial Syphilis. Significant Facts for the Public Health Nurse, by Gladys L. Crain, R.N. . . . 74
Food and Drugs, Report of Division of:
  October-November-December, 1932 . . . 50
  January-February-March, 1933 . . . 118
  April-May-June, 1933 . . . 169
  July-August-September, 1933 . . . 228
Foreword to Cancer Number, by George H. Bigelow, M.D. . . . 3
Fountain, Neil A., Pondville Hospital Social Service Department . . . 43
Friedman, Harry F., M.D., The Teaching Service in a Cancer Clinic . . . 29
Frutkoff, Esther L., and Bernice W. Billings, R.N., The Sheltered Workshop of the Boston Tuberculosis Association . . . 189
Gardner Associate Cancer Committee, Plans for 1933, by Mildred E. Kennedy . . . 33
Gastro-Enteritis, Epidemiology of . . . 141
Gonorrhea
  At Last Something Is to be Done about . . . 167
  Difference Between Tweedledum and Tweedledee, by N. A. Nelson, M.D. . . . 225
  Epidemiology of . . . 157
  Facts about, by Gladys L. Crain, R.N. . . . 84
Gonorrhea and Syphilis
  Control of, by N. A. Nelson, M.D. . . . 64
  Description of the Two Diseases, by N. A. Nelson, M.D. . . . 59
  Minimum Standards for Clinics for the Treatment of . . . 108, 116
  Nurse in the Control of. As the Health Officer Sees Her, by Gladys L. Crain, R.N. . . . 95, 116
  Prevalence of. Some Diseases We Don't Talk About — And Why Not, by N. A. Nelson, M.D. . . . 57
Growth and Development of the Child — Part I — General Considerations, White House Conference Publication (book note) . . . 48
Handicapped Child — See Handicapped Number . . . 176
Health Activities, Neighborhood House, by Ruth R. Kent . . . 46
Horsley, J. Shelton, M.D., Cancer of of the Stomach . . . 5
Hospitals, Cancer Service in General, by Curtis C. Tripp, M.D. . . . 25

	PAGE
Jones, T. Duckett, M.D., The Cardiac Child	184
Keidel, Albert, M.D., Economic Aspects of the Management of Syphilis	101
Kelly, Eleanor E., Social Service in the State Cancer Program	36
Kelly, Eleanor E., What the Social Worker Can Do for the Handicapped	179
Kennedy, Mildred E., Plans for 1933 — Gardner Associate Cancer Committee	33
Kent, Ruth R., Neighborhood House Health Activities	44
King, Anna, The Maladjusted School Child and His Needs	201
Kisiel, W. J., M.D., Lynch, C.F., M.D., and Beauchamp, E. W., M.D. Three Cured Cases of Carcinoma of Cervix	7
Lawrence Associate Cancer Committee	34
Lawrence Cancer Clinic, Social Service in the, by Angie M. Richardson	39
Lawrence Cancer Clinic Committee	26
Lip and Skin, Cancer of, by Ernest M. Daland, M.D.	16
Loitman, Clara, M.D., The Rest and Nutrition Program in the Boston Public Schools	206
Lord, Arthur B., Atypical Children and Their Education	215
Lowell Cancer Clinic	10
Social Service in, by Muriel Eales	38
Lowell Cancer Committee	10
Lynch, C. F., M.D., Beauchamp, E. W., M.D. and Kisiel, W. J., M.D., Three Cured Cases of Carcinoma of Cervix	7
Lynn Cancer Clinic	40
Lynn Cancer Clinic Association, Progress in	32
Lynn Cancer Clinic Committee	9
MacDonald, Margaret, The Annual Census of Physically Handicapped Children	219
Maladjusted School Child and His Needs, by Anna King	201
Mammary Cancer, Biopsy in, by James Ewing, M.D.	4
Massachusetts Hospital School, Its Program and Results, by Ruth Park	217
Massachusetts Society for Social Hygiene	117
Maternal Deaths in Massachusetts — 1930, 1931	45
Maternity Care, Community and Nursing Standards for	223
Minimum Standards for Clinics for the Treatment of Gonorrhea and Syphilis	108
Minsky, Edith L., Plans of a New Committee (North Adams Associate Cancer Committee)	35
National Institute of Health	44
National Organization for Public Health Nursing	167
Neighbor House Health Activities, by Ruth R. Kent	46
Neighborly Service at Pondville	32
Nelson, N. A., M.D.	
Congenital Syphilis	62
Control of Gonorrhea and Syphilis	64
Difference Between Tweedledum and Tweedledee	225
Gonorrhea and Syphilis. A Description of the Two Diseases	59
Some Diseases We Don't Talk About — And Why Not. The Prevalence of Gonorrhea and Syphilis	57
New Bedford Cancer Clinic, Social Service in, by Ida G. Dudelson	38
New Bedford Cancer Clinic Committee	25
News Notes	
American Red Cross	167
Gonorrhea, At Last Something Is to be Done about	167
National Organization for Public Health Nursing	167
Newton, Hazel, The Cooperative Workrooms, Inc.	191
North Adams Associate Cancer Committee, Plans of a New Committee, by Edith L. Minsky	35
Nurse in the Control of Gonorrhea and Syphilis (editorial)	116
As the Health Officer Sees Her, by Gladys L. Crain, R.N.	95
Nursing Standards for Maternity Care, Community and	223
Nutrition and Rest Program in the Boston Public Schools, by Clara Loitman, M.D.	206
Nutrition Program, by Agnes Early	181
Oates, Mrs. Dorothy A. The Social Worker's Part in Securing Early Treatment for Cancer Patients	40
Occupational Therapy, by Caroline N. Shaw	186
Park, Ruth, The Massachusetts Hospital School, Its Program and Results	217

	PAGE
Parsons, Herbert C., Community Care of the Handicapped	177
Physical Education for the Handicapped, by Carl L. Schrader	210
Physically Handicapped Children, The Annual Census of, by Margaret MacDonald	219
Pittsfield Clinics (Cancer)	28
Pondville, Neighborly Service at	32
Pondville Hospital Cured Cancer Clinic, by Ernest M. Daland, M.D.	11
Pondville Hospital, Social Service Committee of	32
Pondville Hospital Social Service Department, by Neil A. Fountain	43
Prevention of Crime — The Gangster in the Making, by L. Vernon Briggs, M.D.	198
Prophylactic Odontotomy (book note)	168
Public Health Nurse	
And the Community Social Hygiene Program, by Gladys L. Crain, R.N.	87
And the Educational Phases of a Social Hygiene Program, by Gladys L. Crain, R.N.	92
And the Medical Aspects of Social Hygiene, by Gladys L. Crain, R.N.	67
Significant Facts on Familial Syphilis for the, by Gladys L. Crain, R.N.	74
What She Should Know about the Patient and the Disease (Syphilis) by Gladys L. Crain, R.N.	71
Publicity, Cancer, in Brockton, by William T. Card	86
Publicity, Clinic, by Frederic Edwards	31
Public Information (editorial)	116
Radio Broadcasts	57, 59, 62, 64, 225
Rehabilitation, Vocational, for Persons Disabled in Industry or Otherwise, by Robert O. Small	212
Relief of Unemployment in Massachusetts by Water Supply, Sewerage and Hospitalization Construction	221
Rest and Nutrition Program in the Boston Public Schools, by Clara Loitman, M.D.	206
Richardson, Angie M., Social Service in the Lawrence Cancer Clinic	39
Schrader, Carl L., Physical Education for the Handicapped	210
Shaw, Caroline N., Occupational Therapy	186
Sheltered Workshop of the Boston Tuberculosis Association, by Bernice W. Billings, R.N., and Esther L. Frutkoff	189
Skin, Cancer of the Lip and, by Ernest M. Daland, M.D.	16
Small, Robert O., Vocational Rehabilitation for Persons Disabled in Industry or Otherwise	212
Smallpox, Epidemiology of	153
Social Hygiene, Public Health Nursing and the Medical Aspects of, by Gladys L. Crain, R.N.	67
Social Hygiene Program	
The Public Health Nurse and the Community, by Gladys L. Crain, R.N.	87
The Public Health Nurse and the Educational Phases of a, by Gladys L. Crain, R.N.	92
Social Service	
In the Lawrence Cancer Clinic, by Angie M. Richardson	39
In the Lowell Cancer Clinic, by Muriel Eales	38
In the New Bedford Cancer Clinic, by Ida G. Dudelson	38
In the State Cancer Program, by Eleanor E. Kelly	36
In the Tumor Clinic of the Boston Dispensary, by Bernice E. Cross	41
In the Worcester Cancer Clinics, by Gertrude J. Carney	37
What It Means to the Springfield Cancer Clinic, by Alice M. Drapeau	39
Social Service Committee of the Pondville Hospital	32
Social Service Department, Pondville Hospital, by Neil A. Fountain	43
Social Work, What It Means in the Worcester North Cancer Clinics, by Olive Twichell	37
Social Worker, What the, Can Do for the Handicapped, by Eleanor E. Kelly	179
Social Worker's Part in Securing Early Treatment for Cancer Patients, by Mrs. Dorothy A. Oates	40
Some Diseases We Don't Talk About — And Why Not. The Prevalence of Gonorrhea and Syphilis, by N. A. Nelson, M.D.	57
Springfield Associate Cancer Committee	31
Springfield Cancer Clinic, What Social Service Means to the, by Alice M. Drapeau	39
Springfield Cancer Committee	7
Standards, Community and Nursing, for Maternity Care	223
Standards (Minimum) for Clinics for the Treatment of Gonorrhea and Syphilis	108, 116

	PAGE
State Cancer Program, Social Service in, by Eleanor E. Kelly	36
State-Aided Cancer Clinic	9
Stomach, Cancer of the, by J. Shelton Horsley, M.D.	5
Streptococcic Infections, Epidemiology of	148
Student's Handbook on Nursing Case Studies, by Deborah McLurg Jensen, R.N., B.S. (book note)	48

Syphilis
A Review	82
Congenital, by N. A. Nelson, M.D.	62
Control of Gonorrhea and, by N. A. Nelson, M.D.	64
Difference between Tweedledum and Tweedledee, by N. A. Nelson, M.D.	225
Economic Aspects of the Management of, by Albert Keidel, M.D.	101, 116
Epidemiology of	157
Familial. Significant Facts Regarding Diagnosis and Treatment of, by Gladys L. Crain, R.N.	74
Gonorrhea and. A Description of the Two Diseases, by N. A. Nelson, M.D.	59
Minimum Standards for Clinics for the Treatment of	108, 116
Nurse in the Control of Gonorrhea and. As the Health Officer Sees Her, by Gladys L. Crain, R.N.	95, 116
Some Facts Regarding Diagnosis and Treatment, by Gladys L. Crain, R.N.	77
Prevalence of Gonorrhea and. Some Diseases We Don't Talk About— And Why Not, by N. A. Nelson, M.D.	57
What the Public Health Nurse Should Know about the Patient and the Disease, by Gladys L. Crain, R.N.	71
Tatro, Rosamond, Berkshire County Cancer Clinics	44
Tatro Rosamond, "Eventually, Why Not Now?"	42
Teaching Service in a Cancer Clinic, by Harry F. Friedman, M.D.	29
Three Cured Cases of Carcinoma of Cervix, by C. F. Lynch, M.D., E.W. Beauchamp, M.D. and W. J. Kisiel, M.D.	7
Tracy, Margaret H., Work of the Boston (Cancer) Committee	35
Traveling School Clinics for the Examination of Retarded Children in the Public Schools, by Neil A. Dayton, M.D.	193
Tripp, Curtis C., M.D., Cancer Service in General Hospitals	25
Tuberculosis, Epidemiology of	155
Tuberculous Child, Vocational Guidance for the, by Leon A. Alley, M.D.	187
Twichell, Olive, What Social Work Means in the Worcester North Cancer Clinics	37
Typhoid Fever, Epidemiology of	126
Unemployment, Relief of, in Massachusetts, by Water Supply, Sewerage and Hospitalization Construction	221
Vocational Guidance for the Tuberculous Child, by Leon A. Alley, M.D.	187
Vocational Rehabilitation for Persons Disabled in Industry or Otherwise, by Robert O. Small	212
What, Another Campaign? Appendicitis?	48
What Social Service Means to the Springfield Cancer Clinics, by Alice M. Drapeau	39
What Social Work Means in the Worcester North Cancer Clinics, by Olive Twichell	37
What the Social Worker Can Do for the Handicapped, by Eleanor E. Kelly	179
White House Conference Publication. Growth and Development of the Child — Part I — General Considerations (book note)	48
Why a Cancer Clinic	26
Work of the Boston (Cancer) Committee, by Margaret H. Tracy	35
Workrooms, The Cooperative, by Hazel Newton	191
Worcester Cancer Clinic Committee	8
Worcester Cancer Clinics, Social Service in, by Gertrude J. Carney	37
Worcester North Cancer Clinic Committee	25
Worcester North Cancer Clinics, What Social Work Means in, by Olive Twichell	37

PUBLICATION OF THIS DOCUMENT APPROVED BY THE COMMISSION ON ADMINISTRATION AND FINANCE
6M. 12-'33. Order 9906.

THE COMMONHEALTH

VOLUME 21   JAN. - FEB. - MAR. -
No. 1 - 4   1934

ADULT HYGIENE

MASSACHUSETTS
DEPARTMENT OF PUBLIC HEALTH

THE COMMONHEALTH

QUARTERLY BULLETIN OF THE MASSACHUSETTS DEPARTMENT OF PUBLIC HEALTH

Sent Free to any Citizen of the State

Entered as second class matter at Boston Postoffice.

M. LUISE DIEZ, M.D., DIRECTOR OF DIVISION OF CHILD HYGIENE, EDITOR.

Room 545 State House, Boston, Mass.

CONTENTS

	PAGE
Resignation of Dr. Bigelow — Appointment of Dr. Chadwick	3
Appointment of Ada Boone Coffey, R.N.	4
The Care of the Skin, by William J. MacDonald, M.D.	4
Nerves, by Abraham Myerson, M.D.	6
Heart Disease, by Samuel H. Proger, M.D.	9
Can High Blood Pressure Be Avoided? by Laurence B. Ellis, M.D.	11
Arteriosclerosis, by Paul D. White, M.D.	13
The Truth About Bright's Disease, by James P. O'Hare, M.D.	15
The Cancer Problem, by Ernest M. Daland, M.D.	17
What the Public Should Know of Diabetes, by Elliott P. Joslin, M.D.	20
Arthritis, by Robert B. Osgood, M.D.	23
Chronic Rheumatism, by Eleanor J. Macdonald, A.B.	25
The Effects of Fatigue, by John H. Talbott, M.D.	28
Pyorrhoea, by E. Melville Quinby, M.R.C.S., L.R.C.P., D.M.D.	30
Why Gums Bleed, prepared by the Massachusetts Dental Hygiene Council	32
Hemorrhoids, by L. S. McKittrick, M.D.	33
What Price Health?, by Mary R. Lakeman, M.D.	36
What Shall We Eat?	43
The Radio, by Herbert L. Lombard, M.D.	44
News Note: American Public Health Association Annual Meeting	46
Report of Division of Food and Drugs, October, November, December 1933	47

It is with sincere regret that the Department records the resignation of Dr. George H. Bigelow as Commissioner of Public Health, regret tempered only by the pleasure of welcoming Dr. Henry D. Chadwick as his successor. For eight years Dr. Bigelow has directed the destinies of the Department. He succeeded to a rich heritage passed down by such distinguished predecessors as Drs. Bowdich, Walcott, McLaughlin and Kelley. During these eight years he enriched the heritage as never before in so short a time.

Striking as might be a resumé of the changes and advances that have characterized these years, no statistics can ever measure the contributions that Dr. Bigelow has made. Only those whose privilege it has been to be associated with him can know the devotion and the sacrifice that he has given to the cause of better health in the Commonwealth and the nation. The cause that he knew to be right he has championed with a contagious zeal and enthusiasm. Where he found misunderstanding and sincere difference of opinion he labored untiringly and patiently to arrive at that solution which was best for the public interest. The machinations of the insincere and fraudulent he has fought with a courage and a relentlessness that have commanded for him a respect even among those whom he opposed. For his associates he has been an inspiring leader whose devotion to the duties of his office has been matched only by the generosity of his friendship. It is thus with great regret that the Department accepts his departure, realizing that it must now share with others the rare privilege of his association. In his new and larger field of work Dr. Bigelow carries with him the affection and best wishes of his former associates, and to the Massachusetts General Hospital, its staff and its patients the Department extends its heartiest congratulations at the privilege that is to be theirs.

To Dr. Chadwick the Department extends its most cordial welcome. After an absence of four years he returns to the Commonwealth to which he has already given over twenty years of devoted service. No one could be better equipped to carry on the rich heritage of public health in Massachusetts.

ADA BOONE COFFEY, R. N.

Ada Boone Coffey, R.N., our Chief Consultant in Public Health Nursing comes to us from the New York State Department of Health.

During her twelve years' service in New York she organized and supervised maternal and child health activities and devoted much time to group teaching of public health nurses, student nurses and lay groups. Since 1929, as extension secretary in public health nursing, Miss Coffey organized and directed a comprehensive statewide plan of staff education.

Her academic education was received at the University of Oregon and her professional training at Presbyterian Hospital, New York City. Since that time she has held many supervisory and executive positions including twenty months' service in the A. E. F. She has had broad experience in hospital work, medical social service, and in the organization and direction of public health nursing services.

THE CARE OF THE SKIN
By WILLIAM J. MACDONALD, M.D.
Boston, Massachusetts

I wish to bring to your notice some of the unfortunate results of taking medicines without skilled advice. By medicine I mean pills, tonics, creams, lotions and allied preparations.

Recently a gentleman walked into my office with a strange and very disfiguring skin disease of the face. It had been diagnosed as tuberculosis, and indeed it did resemble that disease. To his amazement I called it a drug rash. Mind you, he was not by any means a devotee to morphine or cocaine. But, he was inveterately attached to a well known nerve tonic sold at all soda fountains and drug stores. This particular medicine is fraught with dire danger. It contains potassium bromide and acetanilid which can be harmful always in large and continuous doses, and often injurious even in small doses. Despite this fact, anyone can approach a soda fountain and obtain this drug without question. This man died shortly afterwards. Undoubtedly, he had slowly and unwittingly killed himself. Alcoholics, sufferers from headaches and nervous individuals would be well warned to steer clear of effervescing (so called) nerve tonics.

Indulgence in any medicine whatsoever is to be deplored, unless it is authorized by a physician. Literally, hundreds of thousands of people are the victims of unnecessary self-medication. Why intelligent individuals will really believe the specious advertisements contained, not only in printed matter, but also in charlatanistic radio talks, is a matter of amazement. Would you ask a plumber to fit you out with an Easter frock? Well, it is just as silly to let a layman prescribe for your ailments. We, in this fair country, are very inclined to become faddists. If a nerve tonic, a purgative pill, a skin lotion or some other medicine comes wrapped in an attractive manner, we accept it with open arms. If, to gull us still further, the names of foreign doctors are quoted as extra inducements, we are inclined to forget that the ethics of medicine forbid such charlatanism. Have you ever heard the names of British or American physicians in this connection? No—you certainly have not, unless under strictly correct circumstances. And, let me tell you this, the Vienna Medical Faculty has officially reproved those members whose names have been quoted by a certain yeast company, and forbidden them to give testimonials in future. Therefore, remember that it is folly to drug yourself without a proper medical diagnosis.

A short time ago a patient consulted me for a large cancer of the breast. You will be amazed when I tell you that she had been treating it with an ointment of her own choice. She died in agony one month later. The case was too far gone even for surgery. Quite recently another lady with an ulcerating breast cancer allowed herself to be guided by a neighbour's advice, and she too used an ointment. She was sent to a competent surgeon, and, I hope, will recover. Remember this, please, ointments will not cure cancer. It is dastardly and criminal for anyone to sell them for this purpose.

Visit a drug store some day and take note of the countless so called tonics, dyspeptic mixtures, bladder pills and so on. It is astounding that people will blithely go in, state their ailments across the counter to a druggist, and calmly take what to them may be virtual poison.

Most nerve tonics contain bromide or similar sedatives. A certain percentage of people will invariably acquire a skin disease if they take such medicine. I do not believe any disease whatsoever is caused by "so called" nerves. If you are ill, if you are nervous, if you have any ailment at all, secure an accurate medical diagnosis. But, do not indulge in the irrational habit of perpetually swallowing nerve tonics without proper advice.

How often do we hear of sore throats which quickly become diphtheritic? And occasionally, mark you well, the sore throat is syphilitic. Ignoring these facts, the public will fatuously indulge in gargles and sprays which are harmless, as a rule; but how do you know your throat affection is not a source of menace to yourself and others? In our hospitals children die of diphtheria only when the parents are neglectful and use gargles when antitoxin is called for. One would really believe we lived in ancient times and that black magic and incantations were still in use. Every sore throat should be inspected expertly, and if necessary, a culture for diphtheria germs should be done. This will not hurt the child. Rather may it save his life. During the war, in our hospitals, every soldier with a sore throat was carefully examined for diphtheria.

The Australian bush is vast and tropical, and there it was I once came upon an aged man, isolated from neighbours, dying, or apparently dying, in the agonies of acute obstruction of the bowel. His wife, paralyzed with terror, and quite helpless, did, however, unearth an enema syringe. By its use the obstruction was overcome and the man recovered. Why mention this incident? Because it dramatizes the folly of self-medication. This man, to relieve pain, took a violent purgative. He thereby precipitated an acute bowel obstruction. In the presence of abdominal pain, refrain from drastic purgatives. Acute appendicitis and other acute abdominal emergencies are positively made worse by such measures. Headache is a very common complaint. Likewise is it common to take aspirin and allied sedatives for its relief. It is not common sense to pamper a headache with possibly harmful drugs. There is always a cause for headache. Find out what it is and take the correct remedy.

At this point may I warn you of the indiscriminate use of ointments and lotions for the relief of skin diseases, facial blemishes, superfluous hair, sweating and ulceration of any sort. In all conscience it is sometimes hard even for an expert skin specialist to remedy certain ailments. But self-medication for the above conditions is bound to lead you into trouble. For instance, many remedies widely advertised for the cure of "Athlete's Foot" are very irritating and aggravate the disease. This affection merits individual attention, and, naturally, must be accurately diagnosed. The physician alone can recognize the disease. He alone can correctly treat it. It is a menace to the community. It is everywhere spreading with the rapidity of a forest fire. More precautions should be taken for its arrest. Most certainly it should receive expert attention.

I would most emphatically warn my lady listeners of the danger of certain depilators. All are not harmful. Some are. One in particular, used by many women is vicious, dangerous and leads to great suffering. It contains thallium acetate—a very deadly drug. Reports in medical journals emphasize the danger of depilatories containing thallium acetate. In Germany this drug is used as rat poison. I know no safe way to remove hair permanently except by the electric needle.

Freckle removers and bleaching creams are harmful if used persistently.

Most of them contain mercury. Some face powders contain mercury, lead and orris root. These are most atrociously harmful to certain people and cause distressing eruptions, and at times, brown staining of the skin. Some hair tonics will cause a violent inflammation of the scalp and neck and face. Perfumes, too, especially the cheaper variety, as well as certain toilet waters, will irritate the skin and cause unnecessary suffering. Mind you, the majority of the creams on the market are safe. The beauty parlors are not to be condemned by any means. But, beware of harmful toilet preparations. Your physician is aware of their danger and will advise you correctly.

Time and time again elderly people persist in applying creams and ointments given them by friends, to cure small growths that appear on the face. They fail to realize the cancerous nature of such maladies. I warn you most emphatically to leave them alone. They should be treated by a physician and by no one else. The layman who dares to interfere with such malignant growth is deserving of great censure. Surgery or radium are eminently splendid remedies for their eradication.

I am persistently asked if I believe cold cream is necessary for a healthy skin. Well, I do not. Certain dry skins, I know well, will not tolerate soap or water. But, I emphatically state that soap and hot water are not only valuable for the skin, but downright necessary. How can a cold cream help your skin? It cannot. If you rubbed very hard you might force some of it in. Even if you did, its chemical composition differs entirely from human fat and oil. The average man has a much cleaner skin than a woman, and this is due to vigorous soap and water cleansing and shaving. It is a very common thing to hear people blame skin diseases upon "too much acid in the blood", "the liver", or "poor blood". Such utterly inane ideas emanate from pure unadulterated ignorance. Half the time the reason for a poor skin is entirely internal, and cannot be stupidly guessed at. Laziness, late rising and retiring, overeating, overindulgence in alcohol, and overheated rooms are the causes of poor skins and facial blemishes. Our greatest difficulty is to make people realize this. It would appear as if the art of walking is becoming lost. Well, so too will complexions, unless the automobile is garaged and walking taken up as a national pastime. You simply cannot obtain a good healthy skin by cream alone. If your skin is bad, then there is something wrong with you or your food or your habits.

It would be just as well at this time and upon this occasion to advise people against overindulgence in tobacco. We do not in the least condemn this habit, but it might be well for everybody, and especially those of the fair sex, to curtail their smoking. Indulgence in tobacco, in moderation, I, personally, believe is harmless.

The guardians of public health in this and other countries are properly educated physicians. Do you good folks realize what would happen if this fight did not go on? You would die by the thousands of plague. You may be riddled with tuberculosis. Typhoid fever might decimate your homes. Mothers at childbirth might perish with septicemia. Our markets would be flooded with death-dealing drugs and obnoxious skin preparations. As it is, they creep in even now. But the American Medical Association and its branches are guarding your interest. Without your knowledge these dangers are being met and resisted tooth and nail. This fight against charlatanism goes on all the time. Please, I ask you, assist in the fight, by your hearty cooperation.

NERVES

By Abraham Myerson, M.D.

Boston, Massachusetts

There are certain diseases which are dreaded by every one, largely because they threaten life—such diseases as tuberculosis, cancer, heart disease, pneumonia, etc. Contrasted with these are diseases whose main and outstanding threat is to happiness and efficiency, since life itself is not shortened nor threatened by them. These diseases are lumped together in the lay mind under the term "nervousness", which, like many another widespread term, itself implies that here are nervous and mental disorders in which no alteration can be found in any part of the nervous system. In this particular, these conditions differ from such diseases as locomotor ataxia, cerebral hemorrhage and tumor of the brain, because there are marked changes in the structure of the nervous system in the latter troubles. One might compare the psychoneuroses to a watch which needed oiling or cleaning, or merely a winding up, as against one in which a vital part was broken.

These psychoneuroses are divided by physicians into three kinds: neurasthenia, psychasthenia, and hysteria. I am going to discuss only the first of these, neurasthenia, because it is the most common and the least difficult to understand of the three. It may be stated that fundamentally neurasthenia is marked by an increased liability to fatigue. The tired feeling that comes on with a minimum of exertion, worse on arising than on going to bed, is its distinguishing mark. Sleep, which should remove the fatigue of the day, does not; the victim takes half of his day to get going; and at night, when he should have the delicious drowsiness of bedtime, he is wide-awake and disinclined to go to bed or sleep. This fatigue enters into all functions of the mind and body. Fatigue of mind brings about lack of concentration, an inattention, and this brings about an inefficiency that worries the patient beyond words as portending a mental breakdown. Fatigue of purpose brings a listlessness of effort, a shirking of the strenuous, the more distressing because the victim is often enough an idealist with over-lofty purposes. Fatigue of mood is marked by depression of a mild kind, a liability to worry, a lack of enthusiasm for those one lives with or for the things formerly held dearest. And, finally, the fatigue is often marked by a lack of control over the emotional expression so that anger blazes forth more easily over trifles, and the tears come upon even a slight vexation. To be neurasthenic is to magnify the pins and pricks of life into calamities, and to be the victim of an abnormal state that is neither health nor disease.

In addition to this central group of symptoms are first, pains and aches of all kinds, which are really more often disagreeable feelings rather than true pains; second, changes in the appetite and in the condition of the bowels; third, insomnia or disturbed, restless slumber. We look to the bed as a refuge from our troubles, as a sanctuary wherein is rebuilt our strength. We may link work and sleep as the two complementary functions necessary for happiness. If sleep is disturbed, so is work, and with that our purposes are threatened. So disturbed sleep has not only its bodily effects, but has marked results in the effect on happiness.

Fundamental in the symptoms of neurasthenia is fear. This fear takes two main forms: first, the worry over the life situation in general, fear which extends to all the comings, goings, and doings of life, a form of fear-thought which is both a cause of neurasthenia and a symptom; second, a special form of worry called hypochondriacism, which essentially is fear about one's own health. The hypochondriac magnifies every flutter of his heart into heart disease, every stitch in his side into pleurisy, every cough into tuberculosis, every pain in the abdomen into cancer of the stomach, and every headache into the possibility of brain tumor or insanity.

Such are a few of the main symptoms of neurasthenia. It may range from mere fatigue, pain, and insomnia to a profound loss of energy, with fear, anxiety, and almost complete prostration.

We may discuss as causative of this condition certain fundamental situations. We must start with the statement that mind and body are one, that what happens to one physically may change the whole trend of thinking, feeling, and acting, and what happens to one mentally, either as an idea or emotion may change the workings of the body, disturbing sleep, digestion, and the coordinated action of the great organs of the body.

All mankind knows this in the sense that all language crystallizes these beliefs, but it is rarely taken into account either by medical men or the laity.

Thus, we may establish as causative of this state certain physical situations. It may follow exhausting illness, surgical operation, difficult childbirth, and in any situation which drains the energy and resources of the organism. Such conditions are common after influenza, pneumonia, and after those surgical operations where the patient is allowed too quickly to get back to his duties. One of the crying needs of every community is an institution where people may rest after an exhausting illness.

Just as surely as physical situations may cause neurasthenia, psychasthenia, or hysteria, so mental situations may cause them, and, in fact, are undoubtedly more important in the majority of cases in their genesis. There are situations in which fear arises as a sudden and overpowering emotion, such as the battlefield, or in the perilous places in industry, or on the streets of the cities, and occasionally even in the safest and coziest nook in the home. The traumatic neurosis, so-called, has its origin, at least in part, in the de-energizing result of fear, and in the persistence of the emotion for many and many a day to come. For fear may act as a most potent drug, and its physical effects range from the cold chill, the rapid heart, the sharp, painful respiration, and the all-gone feeling in the abdomen, to the most complete unconsciousness. Indeed, all emotions are as much physical as mental, and he is a shallow thinker and a poor physician who dismisses the emotional state of the patient as unworthy of his most careful and detailed attention.

But in addition to these sudden overpowering emotional states, there are more constant mental situations of a disagreeable kind. Whether there is a subconsciousness or not, this can be affirmed—that every human being is a pot boiling with desires, passions, lusts, wishes, purposes, ideas, and emotions, some of which he clearly recognizes and clearly admits, and some of which he does not clearly recognize and which he would deny. These desires, passions, purposes, etc., are not in harmony one with another; they are often irreconcilable, and one has to be smothered for the sake of the other. Thus, a sex feeling that is not legitimate, an illicit forbidden love has to be conquered for the sake of the purpose to be religious or good, or the desire to be respected. So one may struggle against a hatred for a person whom one should love—a husband, a wife, an invalid parent, or child whose care is a burden—and one refuses to recognize that there is such a struggle. So one may seek to suppress jealousy, envy of the nearest and dearest; soul-stirring, forbidden passions; secret revolt against morality and law which may (and often does) rage in the most puritanical breast.

In the theory of the subconscious these undesired thoughts, feelings, passions, wishes, are repressed and pushed into the innermost recesses of the being, out of the light of the conscious personality, but nevertheless, acting on the personality, distorting it, wearying it.

However this may be, there is struggle, conflict in every human breast, and especially difficult and undecided struggles in the case of the psychoneurotic. Literally, secretly, or otherwise he is a house divided against itself, de-energized by fear, disgust, revolt, and conflict. It is in these conflicts and their results that the major part of neurasthenia, psychasthenia, and hysteria arises, in disgust, dissatisfaction, impotent revolt, and the splitting of the personality that comes when one part of us cannot live harmoniously with other parts.

The task of the physician in these cases is first of all to diagnose the situation, to make sure that he is not dealing with organic disease masked by a psychoneurosis. Thus, it must be emphasized as fundamental that in no case should the diagnosis be made until organic situations are excluded.

Second, the physician must then discover the physical factors out of which the condition has, in part, its origin, in bad habits of eating or sleeping, in bad habits of work and play, in poorly conducted organic habits, such as the care of the bowels. He must take whatever steps seem necessary to cure loss of appetite, disturbed sleep, and must prescribe medicines, fresh air, massage, and exercise according to the physical situation.

Third, he must do far more than these things. He must probe into the life of the patient and discover the mental causes, the dissatisfactions, the revolts, the disgusts, the forbidden desires, and the dissociations and conflicts that are back of the symptoms. He must harmonize the personality of the patient, must reconcile the one phase to another, and bring about a philosophy of life, either of renunciation or achievement, that will meet the situation. He must teach control of emotions and inculcate new purposes and ambitions, or restore the old ones if these have disappeared. His is a task formerly relegated to priest and pastor, to teacher and philosopher, but he must be all of these things when he deals with the psychoneurotic, and from his capacity for understanding human nature, and from his ability to probe successfully into the dark, fiercely guarded corners of the human mind, will come the ability to deal with these conditions.

HEART DISEASE
By SAMUEL H. PROGER, M.D.
Boston, Massachusetts

The heart serves only one function, poets to the contrary notwithstanding. It is the pumping mechanism by which the substances which maintain life are sent out in the blood to the tissues in all parts of the body, and the gaseous waste products are sent to the lungs to be exhaled. The proper functioning of this pump for a normal span of life depends upon the satisfactory state of three things: (1) the valves within the heart, (2) the blood vessels through which the blood is pumped, and (3) the small blood vessels which supply the heart itself with nourishment. Thus it is that heart trouble may be the result of leaking or stiff valves, of increased pressure in the blood vessels with hardening of these vessels, or of narrowing and hardening of the small vessels which supply the gasoline, as it were, to the pumping heart.

The chief diseases which cause disturbance in the valves are rheumatic fever, St. Vitus' dance, known scientifically as chorea, and syphilis. As regards the arteries, increased or high blood pressure naturally produces a strain on the heart which has to pump blood into these arteries, thus causing what is called hypertensive or high blood pressure heart disease. The vessels which supply the heart itself with nourishment are called the coronary arteries, and disease or hardening of these arteries produces what is called angina pectoris and also cardiac or heart asthma. Complete blockage of a coronary artery causes a severe prolonged attack of heart pain known as coronary thrombosis.

According to the ages at which they develop, all heart diseases may be divided into four groups as follows: First, congenital heart disease, or heart disease which is present at birth and is due to various abnormalities in the development of the heart before birth. So-called blue babies usually have this type of heart disease. Second, rheumatic heart disease, which generally develops in childhood, usually as a result of rheumatic fever or St. Vitus' dance. Third, syphilitic heart disease, which is seen in young and middle-aged adults as a result of the venereal infection. Fourth, the heart disease which occurs in older people and is usually due either to high blood pressure, or hardening of the arteries, or both.

Now let us consider more closely each of these four groups. It is amazing how often people who are born with abnormal hearts live satisfactorily to a ripe age. The avoidance of infection and excesses of all sorts, and moderate limitation of activity frequently allow people with congenital heart disease to live a long and useful life. Gilbert, the famed musical composer of Cambridge, is an excellent example. Born with one of the more serious types of abnormality of the heart, he lived to be sixty years old, and all who know his music will attèst to the usefulness and happiness of his life.

In this section of the country rheumatic heart disease is very common. To those who have rheumatic heart disease, it is particularly important to avoid infections in general such as common colds, and thus perhaps avoid relapses of the infection which originally caused the heart disease, such as rheumatic fever and St. Vitus' dance, or chorea. While it is perhaps impossible absolutely to prevent these relapses, it is known that those who live a normal, well-balanced life with an abundance of fresh air, sunshine, good food, with regular hours, and under conditions of cleanliness, are less likely to have re-infections than those who do not. Also it seems that it is desirable for children with rheumatic heart disease to be somewhat overweight. They get along better with the extra weight. In the South, rheumatic heart disease is rare, because the infections which cause this heart disease are rare. Those in this section of the country who have rheumatic heart disease can generally avoid further rheumatic infections if they move to the warm southern climate. The person with rheumatic heart disease should keep in mind the following symptoms which may indicate active rheumatic infection: joint or muscle pains, sore throat, nervous twitching, fever, nose bleeds, vomiting, and loss of weight. When any of these symptoms appear, a physician should be called.

Rheumatic heart disease, even more than congenital heart disease, is compatible with a long and useful life. Many people with rheumatic heart disease live twenty, forty, and even fifty years after its onset, comfortably and without symptoms. This is especially true of those whose occupation does not require a great amount of physical exertion.

Syphilitic heart disease obviously can be prevented by simply avoiding the initial infection; that is, by avoiding syphilis. Once the heart disease has developed, treatment of the infection with specific drugs and limitation of activity are advised to delay heart failure. If syphilis is treated early and effectively, syphilitic heart disease may be prevented.

The heart disease of older people, that due to high blood pressure or hardening of the arteries, offers cause for considerable optimism. This type of heart disease is usually benign and of long standing. In fact, many people have this condition for many years without knowing that anything is wrong. They may first become aware of it through a physician to whom they have gone for some entirely unrelated symptom. In such a case, undue alarm may actually prove harmful. Even the more serious conditions associated with this type of heart disease, such as angina pectoris, need not doom the sufferer to permanent invalidism. While it is true that a person with angina pectoris may at any moment have a sudden fatal accident, it is also true that many live ten or even twenty years after the onset of the condition. For a person with angina pectoris to crawl within himself and anxiously await the fateful end is as unnecessary as for a normal person to live in dreadful anticipation of being run down and killed by an automobile. It is not only unnecessary, it is unfortunate, because the patient with angina pectoris not only makes his life miserable thereby, but the mere attitude of fearful anxiety or fateful resignation may actually shorten his years. On the other hand, cheerfulness, hope, and courage are always conducive to longer life.

Many people with high blood pressure and enlarged hearts are overweight. It is advisable for such people to reduce. This, of course, should be done under proper medical supervision. I might cite here the following wise words from Shakespeare: "Leave gourmandizing, know the grave doth gape for thee thrice wider than for other men." I say "wise words" because recent statistics based on analysis of many cases actually show that, as compared with people of normal size, three times as many fat people beyond middle age die before they reach eighty years of age, and most of these die of heart disease. Also, physicians of long ago realized that obesity is harmful. Witness this, written more than a hundred years ago by a famous English doctor (Cheyne): "Every man after fifty ought to begin and lessen at least the quantity of his aliment, and if he would continue free from great and dangerous distempers and preserve his senses and faculties clear to the last, he ought every seven years to go abating gradually and sensibly and at least descend out of life as he ascended it, even into a child diet." I might add that the principal "great and dangerous distemper" to avoid or to ameliorate under these circumstances is heart disease.

Now what are the early symptoms of heart disease, and how is one to recognize whether or not his heart is beginning to weaken? Dr. Joseph H. Pratt, of Boston, in a careful study of the earliest symptoms of heart disease, found that in the majority of cases shortness of breath is the first indication of heart trouble. Of course, most of us with normal hearts who are not in the best of physical trim become short of breath after even moderate exertion to which we are not accustomed. The shortness of breath which is significant of heart disease, however, is an increasing shortness of breath for which there is no other obvious cause such as gain in weight or disease elsewhere. Increasing shortness of breath should always act as a warning signal which calls for medical attention. There are other less common early symptoms of heart trouble which would take too much time to discuss adequately, and merely to mention them might cause unnecessary alarm; for many people with normal hearts may have some of these symptoms simply as a result of nervousness and frequently because of a fear of heart disease. Young and middle-aged people who suspect that they have heart disease because of heart pounding, irregular heart beats, breathlessness, pain over the heart, etc. are almost invariably wrong in their diagnosis. The determination of the significance of the symptoms in such cases must rest entirely with the physician.

Patients with heart disease frequently wonder, in regard to adjusting their activities, just how much they can do without harming themselves. In this connection, it is well to remember the advice of the great English heart specialist, Sir James MacKenzie, "A person with heart disease can do in safety what he can do in comfort."

CAN HIGH BLOOD PRESSURE BE AVOIDED?
By LAURENCE B. ELLIS, M.D.
Boston, Massachusetts

High blood pressure, or hypertension, has become one of the bugbears of present day life. It is feared with a great fear, made the more mysterious because of the lack of knowledge as to the cause of the condition and because of the multiplicity and generally unsatisfactory nature of the treatments advocated. That in general the fear which this disease arouses is justified can be demonstrated from a perusal of the statistics of the causes of death in this country. Heart disease leads all other causes of death and in persons of middle age and over, hypertension is the chief agent producing this heart disease. Apoplexy and Bright's disease of the kidneys occupy prominent places in mortality tables, and again high blood pressure is the factor responsible for the major part of these conditions. Insurance statistics, moreover, foretell with a high degree of accuracy, the increased hazard to life that is occasioned by every ten millimeter rise in blood pressure above the normal.

Unfortunately, in spite of diligent search and extensive experiment, the difficulties presented by this problem are such that the exact cause of high blood pressure is still unknown. Although much has been learned regarding the factors which influence its occurrence and the nature of the damage its produces in the human body, the final explanation as to why some people develop it and others don't is as yet unsolved. And until the cause is known it is unlikely that an absolute cure will be found. At present there is no cure for high blood pressure. Once it has developed to any marked degree it usually persists throughout life. But there are certain measures that can be taken and treatments that can be given which will frequently stay or slow down the progression of the condition and relieve the symptoms so that an individual who suffers from high blood pressure may frequently lead a relatively normal life in complete comfort for very many years. For that reason there is no cause for undue alarm to anyone who may suffer from it. If certain relatively minor readjustments are made in one's life and a few simple measures for treatment are taken, there is no reason why such a patient should not look forward to many years of useful life.

I have said that much is known regarding the nature of the changes caused by this condition in the body and the factors which influence its occurrence. High blood pressure is essentially a disease of the smallest arteries of the body and these arteries are usually affected in every organ and tissue throughout the body. It used to be considered that damage to the kidneys was chiefly responsible for the high pressure, and as a result most of the older forms of treatment were directed toward the kidneys alone. It is now appreciated that the disease is much more generalized instead of being limited to the kidneys so that today we treat the patient as a whole.

Among the factors which appear to be concerned in the production of high blood pressure, the nature of our present day life looms important. There is more hustle and bustle and hurry and worry about our twentieth century existence in this country than every before. It is significant that high blood pressure is more prevalent today than it was in past years and of more frequent occurrence in the United States than in Europe. Among the Chinese and in primitive races it is extremely rare. It is impossible to escape the conclusion that the rapid pace and the high degree of tension which permeate the routine of living in this country predispose to the development of vascular disease and high blood pressure. The average American is a very strenuous person when compared to the European and Asiatic. He rarely relaxes or devotes much time to the more contemplative modes of life. Even in his games he is keyed up to the highest degree. He is always doing something; when he is not, he is worrying about it. From childhood to old age his nervous system is in a constant state of activity and this activity affects all of the bodily organs and in particular the blood vessels. The much needed rest that the nervous system requires is lacking. It resembles only too closely the driving of an automobile at a constant excessive speed and without proper lubrication. And the result is the same in the two instances. The vital parts give out sooner than they should.

Anyone could easily call to mind many individuals who have driven themselves all their lives at a high speed and yet have never developed high blood pressure. It is quite true that by no means everyone will develop this condition. There must be some individual and constitutional peculiarity which predisposes certain persons to the disease. Just what this is cannot be said with certainty. Unquestionably there is an inherited tendency to develop the disease possessed by many people. For this reason, one way to avoid high blood pressure would be to pick one's ancestors with care. In addition, it is frequently found in people who are of the high-strung, neurotic, worrying type. In such people mental states such as worry and fear are especially prone to be reflected by a rise in blood pressure, which at first may be temporary but ultimately becomes permanent.

In most persons the development of high blood pressure probably is a combination of an individual with a susceptible constitution being exposed to external conditions of stress and tension. It is clear then, what measures should be taken to prevent the occurrence of this condition, so far as is possible in the light of our present knowledge. We can do little to change the personality of people, we cannot eliminate an inherited tendency toward vascular disease, but we can encourage a more calm and less strenuous mode of life. It is easy to preach this and difficult to carry it into effect in a society which is used to such a high pressure way of life as is ours. But it can be done as has been demonstrated repeatedly by individuals under the spur of the necessity of treating one or another disease. Like the supplanting of all bad habits by good ones only constant application and a regular regime will accomplish anything. People must learn to relax and rest. It is not so important that they actually increase their hours of sleep as that they develop the habit of relaxing at stated periods during the day when they are not actually at work, and particularly after meals. A philosophical outlook on life should be developed so that worrying about the inconsequential details will be eliminated. Excesses of all types should be avoided—too much eating, drinking, smoking, exercising, all are bad, not only in themselves but because they frequently betoken a nature which is always going to extremes. The ancient Greeks had a dictum that moderation in all things led to a happy life. This tenet has been brought into more modern times as one of the principles of humanistic philosophy. It would be well for the health of the nation if it were adopted widely.

Proper attention to the upkeep and repair of the human machine is important. Known bodily defects and diseases should be treated and unknown ones should be searched for. Periodic health examinations are the best way of discovering incipient troubles at a time when they can be easily cared for.

These remarks apply equally to persons who already are suffering from high blood pressure, as well as to the populace at large, any one of whom may develop this condition in the near or distant future. Since we do not know at what age the factors which produce high blood pressure begin to operate, these preventive measures should be instituted at as early an age as possible. It is much easier to replace bad habits by good ones in youth than in old age.

ARTERIOSCLEROSIS
By Paul D. White, M.D.
Boston, Massachusetts

Arteriosclerosis literally means hardening of the arteries, but this is only the end stage of a process of softening or weakening of the inner and middle arterial coats which may go on for many years before the hard lime salts are deposited. The condition is universal and the process of deterioration begins in youth.

Arteriosclerosis is not strictly abnormal if we think of it as a wearing-out process in very old persons, although in future centuries even this occurrence may be regarded as pathological if it begins within the first hundred years of life. According to our present ideas arteriosclerosis takes on serious significance if it causes important symptoms or signs, or disability or death before the age of seventy years, and the earlier the age the greater the significance. Much is said about it now-a-days and there is a general impression that it occurs more often at earlier ages than it used to do. This impression may be justified by facts, but we must consider two possible explanations other than that fewer persons escape the process; these explanations are first, that more persons now survive infancy with its illnesses which were once formidable but now are largely under control, some of these survivors having inherited poor arterial tissue; and second, that the diagnosis of "hardening of the arteries" is more easily, accurately, and often made now-a-days than formerly. Be that as it may, it does appear true that our fathers did not live so long as did our grandfathers, and that we are not living so long as did our fathers. The much vaunted increase in the duration of human life in our time is due wholly to the survival of many individuals through childhood and early adult life who would once have died of dysentery in infancy or of typhoid fever or some other such infectious disease afterwards. None of this increase in the duration of life is due to an increase of the life span itself. It is this problem that now demands our urgent attention. We must do something to prevent the appalling waste of life at its zenith; this waste of life is largely the direct result of arteriosclerosis.

Hardening of the arteries is not a modern disease; it existed in ancient days as evidenced by finding it in Egyptian mummies, but it was clearly recognized as a disease only in relatively modern times, that is, within the past two hundred years. However, that excessive nervous strain and faulty diet were causes of disability and death was known to the medical faculty of the University of Salerno in Southern Italy in the Middle Ages, even though the mechanism by which such disability was actually produced was not known. In an early English translation in 1541 of the "Regiment of Helthe" of Salerno one finds the following observations: "He that desireth helth of body must eschew and avoyde great charges, thought, and care. ...The second doctrine is to eschew anger. ...The thyrde doctryne is to eate and drynke sobrely. ...The fourth doctrine is to make a lyght souper. ...The fifth doctrine is to walke after meate. ...The sixth doctrine is to eschew slepe incontinent after meate. ...Finally the auctor sayth, that who so syl observe the forsayde doctrines, shall lyve longe in good helthe and prosperite."

Arteriosclerosis is widespread throughout the body and throughout the world, affecting all arteries and all races, although to different degrees. It attacks all kinds of animals, too, especially birds of many species. It occurs in man at all ages but naturally increasingly with advancing years. Both sexes are affected, but the male sex preponderantly at earlier ages, apparently because of the greater strain to which males are as a rule subjected.

The cause of arteriosclerosis is not clearly understood in most instances. Through "wear and tear" at points of unusual pressure, stretching, or bending, the wall weakens. Fat is deposited as "atheroma", which literally means pudding, in spots in the intima or inner wall, or the muscle of the media or middle coat undergoes change. In the course of time lime salts are deposited in these regions and the artery becomes stiff and narrowed. The chemistry of all this change is still obscure but certain factors are known which favor the onset of the transformation; these are excessive work, excessive blood pressure, diabetes, lead poisoning, syphilis in the case of certain arteries, and inherited tendency. Other factors have also been blamed but they are still open to question—they are excessive food, certain foods like protein taken to excess, tobacco, nervous strain in the case of the coronary arteries of the heart, and infectious diseases other than syphilis. Some day we shall have answers to these questions—at present they remain largely unsolved.

What are the symptoms and signs of arteriosclerosis? How does it show itself? Mostly through disturbance of function of whatever tissue or organ is affected by the decrease of blood supply resulting from the narrowing of the arteries. Of course, in some parts of the body as at the wrist or on the foot or on the forehead it is possible to feel the arteries and to judge how hard they are directly, but most of the important arteries of the body are internal and so not to be reached except sometimes by X-ray study or by special tests or by observations as to the function of the organs supplied by them.

Thus, it is obvious that the symptoms and signs of arteriosclerosis are legion and extend from the crown of the head to the soles of the feet. I shall now name instances of the more important or more obvious results of localized arteriosclerosis. Beginning with the head these are whitening of the hair due to local changes in the arteries supplying the hair follicles, loss of elasticity of the skin, apoplexy and various other disturbances of the brain due to hardening of the arteries there together with high blood pressure, cataracts in the eye from opacities of the lenses, and deafness from decrease in the blood supply to the inner and middle ears. In the thorax we find elongation and stiffening of the great artery called the aorta, angina pectoris and coronary thrombosis due to arteriosclerosis of the important little coronary arteries that supply the heart muscle with blood, and changes in the arteries of the lungs following extensive lung diseases and increased blood pressure in the lungs. Next, there is Bright's disease from affection of the small arteries of the kidneys. Finally in the extremities reference should be made to cramps in the muscles on exercise (called intermittent claudication) caused by sclerosis of the arteries going to the muscles, and finally to atrophy and even gangrene of the toes and fingers from marked changes in the arteries supplying the extremities. Frequently several organs may be affected at the same time but often only one is damaged to any notable degree. The most serious effects are on the heart and brain; of next importance is limitation of the blood supply to the kidneys.

The treatment of arteriosclerosis affords little that is curative. Alleviation is, however, often possible through various measures, particularly that of reducing the amount of work thrown upon the affected organs, as in the case of heart or kidneys. There are no magical drugs or remedies although from time immemorial such drugs or remedies have been advised. The fountain of youth has not yet been discovered. We must neither foster unwarranted hopes nor yet should we consider that nothing can be done when arteriosclerosis causes trouble. Frequently symptoms can be relieved and life prolonged for years by common sense measures known to all physicians.

Of far greater importance than the treatment of arteriosclerosis is, of course, its prevention. Since we know some of the factors behind it we can accomplish definite results in this very vital phase of preventive medicine. The two important points in this direction are first, the establishment of good habits of health in early life—exercise, rest, relaxation, diet, all in moderation; and second, the avoidance of infections and poisons (which may or may not include tobacco—no one knows for certain.) These are very difficult measures and at present are impossible to apply in full, but the more complete their fulfillment the more delayed the appearance of arteriosclerosis, always bearing in mind, however, that a large share of responsibility appears to be that of inheritance.

Finally, many individuals, perhaps justifiably at times, will not wish to carry out all the measures that may prevent their being early crippled or killed by arteriosclerosis. A carefully planned existence with a view only to health may be too humdrum. Last year in a radio message Dr. Harold Stevens quoted a verse of Edna St. Vincent Millay which well expresses this idea:

> "My candle burns at both ends;
> It will not last the night;
> But ah, my foes, and oh, my friends,
> It gives a lovely light!"

In the final analysis, however, the maximum of happiness and usefulness can be secured by heeding the simple sensible tenets of healthy living, thereby avoiding early disability and death with all the burden and misery that such trouble brings upon family, friends, and community.

THE TRUTH ABOUT BRIGHT'S DISEASE
By JAMES P. O'HARE, M.D.
Boston, Massachusetts

I do not know who selected this curious talk but I am sure I know why. *Undoubtedly* he had in mind that the purpose of this brief and necessarily sketchy talk is to try is dispel the misunderstandings and fears of the laity concerning Bright's disease. This disease, named after Richard Bright, is essentially a disturbance of kidney function which is to excrete waste products and to help maintain the chemical balance of the body. The mechanism by which this is accomplished comprises five *million* microscopic filtration units. In health, these work with far greater efficiency than any of the units in our finest electric light and power plants. Like the latter, the kidneys have a tremendous reserve indicated by the fact that many units may be expectantly idling, *some* working at only *part* capacity, others at *full* speed. But *all* are ready at a moment's notice for the "peak load."

I do not believe that any of you realize the *enormous* quantities of blood that pass daily through the kidneys to be freed from waste products. Actually ten to fifteen times your body weight must be exposed to these filters each twenty-four hours of the day.

Bright's disease or nephritis destroys the efficiency of this beautiful mechanism by destroying these filtration units.

For the sake of simplicity I am going to divide all the various types of nephritis into acute and chronic.

Acute Bright's Disease

Acute nephritis is an inflammatory disease occurring *chiefly* in children and young adults. Its cause is usually an infection—often a mild one—in the throat or upper respiratory passages. Tonsillitis and scarlet fever are among the commonest causes.

The nephritis begins when the infection is at an end, ten to fourteen days from the onset of the infection. If you are watching, at this time you may notice an unusual pallor and perhaps slight puffiness of the face or feet. Examination of the urine by the doctor discloses albumin and other evidences of kidney damage. Such damage is accompanied by retention of water and waste products in the tissues. These explain the *swellings* and the symptoms of *poisoning*.

Most patients, especially children, recover completely in a few weeks. A rare patient has such a severe process that the kidneys *shut down completely* and death occurs quickly. A few only pass on into chronic nephritis. This unfortunate result may arise from any of the three following causes:

(1) The acute stage may be *so mild* that it is never recognized.
(2) Treatment may be poor or poorly followed.
(3) The disease may become chronic in spite of the best of treatment.

The most important part of the care of these patients is *bed rest*. This must be maintained—if necessary *for months*—until the physician is thoroughly satisfied that *all signs of inflammation have ceased*. This is *not* easy because the patient is very soon without symptoms, feels well, and *cannot understand* the need of staying in bed. It is, however, *vitally* important because getting up too soon may cause him to lose his *only* chance to be cured.

Dietetic treatment is next in importance. This should be arranged not merely to *spare* the kidneys but with *due regard* to the needs of the rest of the body. Our diets, after the first few days, are *much* more liberal than they used to be ten years ago when the patient got nothing but milk for weeks.

Drug treatment is of least importance and only of value in the relief of particular symptoms and signs.

During convalescence all infectious foci should be removed and all new infections avoided. These tend to keep up the disease and often activate it.

Chronic Nephritis

In patients under thirty-five this disease is usually the result of an *acute* nephritis. *Beyond thirty-five* its origin is *entirely* different, the result of high blood pressure and generalized arteriosclerosis. Both types are very similar and eventually reach the same end point.

In the first type the acute inflammation in the kidneys continues unabated and slowly progressive destruction of these organs follows. These organs are no *longer* able to function properly and waste products pile up in the tissues producing symptoms of poisoning. At the same time the blood pressure rises and changes take place in the *arteries, heart, brain, eyes*, etc. Death is the final result.

In some patients chronic nephritis is of short duration lasting not more than two or three years. Many, however, with good care and treatment, live comfortably and well for *many, many* years. I am still following some of my patients whose original disease began fifteen or more years ago. I have heard of one man, still alive, who was diagnosed "chronic nephritis" twenty-seven years ago. So, although the disease may well be a serious one there is no need for pessimism. *Many* a patient has lived to *bury* the doctor who predicted *too pessimistic* an outlook for him.

In the second type of chronic nephritis occurring in older individuals the disease is *not* primarily in the *kidneys at all* but in the small arteries all over the body. As a result of this sclerosis of arteries there is a gradual diminution of the blood supply and hence nutrition to various organs including the kidneys. Degeneration of these organs necessarily follows. High blood pressure is associated with this parent disease which is called Vascular Hypertension.

In the past, many patients have been diagnosed chronic nephritis who really had little or no disease of the kidneys. Many of the symptoms commonly attributed to chronic Bright's disease should more accurately be attributed to the parallel disorders in the brain or heart.

Vascular hypertension is most often an inheritance, an inherited weakness of blood vessels aggravated by abuse of the circulation by too intense mental and perhaps physical strain. Without doubt, overeating also plays a part. High blood pressure and hardening of small arteries may be noted at thirty-five or even earlier years. If the arterial disease advances more rapidly in the brain, apoplexy is probable. If the circulation through the heart is more affected, heart disease is the result. If the disease becomes marked in the kidneys, chronic nephritis follows. Frequently one patient shows signs of several of these secondary disorders. Many more patients die from heart disease or shock than from inadequate kidney function. All of these disorders should be grouped together as part of one generalized circulatory disease—Vascular Hypertension.

How important this disease is is indicated by the fact that practically one person in every four over fifty years dies from some of its forms. Furthermore, our strenuous life with its mental strain and worries seems to be advancing the age incidence into the early thirties; yes, even into the twenties. Unless we learn to live more calmly, our span of life—recently increased by the control of the infectious diseases—will again decrease through quick wearing out of our circulatory machinery.

The duration of these various circulatory disorders is extremely variable. In a few patients the disease advances with great rapidity and "finis" is written in three to four years. In most, however, progress is quite slow—fifteen to twenty years is not rare. When chronic Bright's disease occurs, it is late and frequently not as serious as the other disturbances of the heart, brain, etc.

No discussion of the treatment of heart disease, hypertension, etc. is possible here. In a general way it can be said that anything that will make us live more sanely and worry less will decrease the incidence and slow down the progress of all these diseases.

Again, I am sure that if every adult thirty-five years or over would voluntarily or by compulsion have a physical examination each year we doctors would pick up these diseases in the early stages when cure is possible and treatment much more effective. It is truly pitiful at times to have a patient present himself late in the disease looking for help, when your examination discloses the architecture of his circulation largely destroyed. A routine examination a few years before might have disclosed the structural weaknesses which at that time might have been strengthened and protected.

The first step in the treatment of chronic nephritis should be a careful examination to estimate the degree of damage not in the kidneys alone but in the heart, brain, blood vessels, etc. If the disease is not too far advanced, much can be done in the way of supporting the circulation, decreasing strains, etc. by rest, exercise, diet and drugs.

The treatment of the kidneys is largely dietetic, striving to balance the intake of certain foods with the body needs and the decreased ability of the kidneys to handle the waste products. Chemical blood and urine tests are now available to help us estimate the degree of kidney dysfunction and the success of our dietetic efforts.

Drugs, while necessary in the treatment of other parts of the circulation, are, for the most part, harmful to the sick kidney.

Infections should, of course, be cleared up and new infections avoided.

Conclusion

Acute nephritis is usually serious only in that it may become chronic. Chronic nephritis, though a serious complex disease, can be, with good care, compatible with comfort for many years.

THE CANCER PROBLEM
By Ernest M. Daland, M.D.
Boston, Massachusetts

We do not know the exact cause of cancer, whether it is chemical, biological or bacterial. We do know that certain types of cancer may be caused by chronic irritation, as cancer of the mouth from carious teeth, that others are due to chemical irritation as cancer of the skin in tar workers. We have no evidence that cancer is caused by bacteria, but there is reason to believe that disordered biological processes in the tissues may be the causative factor.

There is much work to be done on this problem of the cause of cancer. First, much more must be known of the chemistry and biology of normal tissues. It is evident that one group of workers have got to tackle this problem with all the resources at hand and thousands are today at work on it.

But what of the thousands of patients who have cancer and who are developing it every day? Must they await the learning of the exact cause? Certainly not. We must use the knowledge that we already have of the ordinary habits of cancer cells and try to prevent their ravages.

Even better, suppose that we try to prevent cancer by removing conditions that are likely to become cancerous. At the Pondville Hospital in 1927, 1928 and 1929 we treated sixty-five patients with keratoses of the skin, known to be precancerous lesions. Three years later we find that none of these remain as precancerous lesions, and none of these patients have developed cancer. Cancer of the lip, tongue and mouth occur chiefly in that stratum of society that does not use proper mouth hygiene. Clean mouths with teeth properly attended to, or with properly fitting dental plates, and with no taint of syphilis rarely develop cancer. It is said that twenty per cent of all cancers of the breast develop in patients with previous cystic conditions in the breast. Operative treatment of the latter condition is a mild procedure compared with the radical operation required in cancer.

The badly lacerated uterine cervix with secondary erosion is a dangerous organ. Careful prolonged treatment, sometimes with and sometimes without operation will clear up this condition so that cancer will not develop. Other illustrations could be given, but suffice it to say that if an individual receives treatment for conditions that are definitely abnormal, there will be a great saving of individuals from death by cancer.

Cancer is a curable disease in most organs, if it is treated early. That is a fact that must be passed on to the layman, who hears of the cancer deaths but not of the cancer cures. At two recent congresses of the American College of Surgeons, sixty surgeons have reported 24,000 cases of cancer, which have been cured for five years or more. That number is a mere drop in the bucket of cured cancers. If a patient survives a five-year period after treatment, it is probable that he is cured, although in rare instances a cancer may recur at a later period in life.

Cancer has recently been compared with a fire. During the early minutes of a fire it is easily extinguished. The longer it goes on, the more difficult it is to stop it. A fierce fire may be extinguished if sufficient resources are available, but there remains a vast amount of destroyed property. So it is with cancer. The neglected cancer will have destroyed tissues which can never be replaced and in order to develop back-fires a barricade must be laid down in the surrounding normal tissues either by surgery or radiation.

First of all must come early diagnosis and if a diagnosis is to be made it is necessary that the physician see the patient. Why this delay of five months before seeing the doctor that we found in 370 cases at the Massachusetts General Hospital? There are three main reasons: (1) The belief that the condition amounted to nothing; (2) the fear that the physician might find a cancer and the inability of the patient to face the situation, based on his lack of appreciation that early cancer is curable; (3) the economic problem of securing treatment. The answers to the first two are obvious. The economic problem is difficult. Here in Massachusetts the Department of Public Health has offered free diagnosis for suspected cancer in more than a dozen centers in the State. Numerous other clinics offer free or nearly free diagnosis as well as treatment service at far below cost. At the central cancer hospital, treatment is refused nobody that is without funds. For people of moderate means the medical profession is always ready to give its service for what the patient can afford to pay. As far as the cost of treatment goes, there is no excuse for delay. As far as the loss of time and wages goes, the loss is but a tiny part of the economic loss if the patient is untreated, undergoes a long period of disability, subjects his family to endless trouble, ending with an undertaker's bill. We occasionally have to point out that coffins are expensive when a patient wishes to put off treatment, because of the expense involved.

Having decided to consult a physician, the next question is, which one. One must select a physician who has an adequate medical training, one who is progressive, who knows of the advances in medicine, one who reads the medical literature, and one who will be willing to consult with others if he cannot make a diagnosis. If the first doctor does not impress one with these qualifications, one should not hesitate to seek out another. Members of the various medical cults should be selected only if they have had a basic medical course of the prescribed four years. Under no circumstances should laymen with some pet herb, remedy, or paste be allowed to undertake the treatment. The results will be unsatisfactory and the time lost will assure a fatal outcome. It is doubtful if any layman has a remedy for cancer that has not been investigated by the medical profession, and found wanting. Lastly, there is no known medicine, external or internal, that has any effect on the course of a cancer.

The only methods of treating cancer successfully are by surgery, X-ray or radium or a combination of the three.

Now there is a group of patients who have neglected to come to their physician early or to have the treatment advised. Another group has come as early as they noticed symptoms, but unfortunately the disease had already progressed to a point where cure is not sure. Still another group comprises those that were inadequately treated in the first place, or who did not respond to good treatment and still have cancer. It must be admitted here that there are exceptions to the rule that cancer can be cured if treated early, for occasionally a cancerous growth goes on unhampered in spite of the best treatment that can be given.

This type of patient calls for careful thought and consultation. Something must be done for these people. Very radical operation, extensive treatment, by the high voltage X-ray, or by radium, may occasionally accomplish a seemingly miraculous result. One cannot tell which cases will be the ones to respond favorably and, therefore, all should be treated. Such symptoms as bleeding, discharge and pain are unendurable, and such measures as may clear up the symptoms must be instituted. The relief of pain may result in a marked prolongation of life. In the attempt to relieve the symptoms frequently it is found that a cure is secured.

I repeat that something must be done for this type of patient. We must not think in terms of permanent cure and hesitate to treat because of a fear of spoiling our percentage of cures. We must do the day's work and apply the treatment that today's situation calls for. It is well to take the patient into our confidence and point out that things do not look as favorable as we wish, but that we believe we can relieve the symptoms and possibly accomplish a cure. When explained in this way, the patient will be sure to cooperate. If the medical profession does not do something for this type of patient, some untrained person will try measures which may actually be harmful.

Finally, there is the advanced cancer patient, who, through his own delay, through inadequate treatment, or through no fault of anybody, arrives at the stage where he needs nursing and medical care. Possibly this can be carried out at home, and, if so, it is well. If such care means withdrawing another member of the family from gainful occupation in order to secure adequate home care, it is more economical to place the patient in an institution.

We do not believe in the segregation of the hopeless cases into separate hospitals or wards. The very sick patient or the very unsightly patient must be isolated in a separate room. The cancer patient rarely gives up hope; he desires to live. It is a tremendous help for him to see patients entering the hospital and leaving after X-ray treatment or operation. He may not realize that such treatment is only alleviatory. To him this patient has gone home and he awaits the time when he may do likewise. He does not realize that his case is hopeless until a short time before the end and there is little time to think of it. Careful nursing and sufficient treatment by medicines is a very important part of the care of this group of patients.

Summary

The handling of the cancer problem may be summarized as follows: (1) Research to learn more about the disease, (2) early diagnosis, (3) early, adequate treatment by competent physicians, (4) an attempt to do something for nearly every cancer patient in whom the disease is moderately advanced, and, (5) the care of the hopeless case.

WHAT THE PUBLIC SHOULD KNOW OF DIABETES
By ELLIOTT P. JOSLIN, M.D.
Boston, Massachusetts

The people of Massachusetts should know something about diabetes, because there are so many individuals in the State who have it. Our Board of Health estimates that the number is 14,000, and of the present population it is probable that three or four times as many more will develop it before or during their old age. There is a second and a better reason for becoming acquainted with this disease—if the patient thoroughly understands it, treatment is simplified and he can live a long, happy and useful life, whereas otherwise life may end suddenly, or disagreeable complications appear. Finally, the best reason of all for learning about diabetes is the strong possibility that, with knowledge concerning it, you may avoid it.

Diabetes is rare in childhood and two thirds of all the cases are above the age of forty years. We do not know how to prevent it in the young, but we do know that from forty onwards it is increasingly common if the individual is or has been fat. Therefore, the chances are overwhelming that you will not get diabetes, if your weight is kept within normal limits. Heredity also may be a factor, and two diabetics should not marry one another and have children; because theoretically, at least, all the children will become diabetic; if a diabetic marries a nondiabetic but of a diabetic family, half the children would be expected to acquire the disease; if two nondiabetics but of diabetic families marry, one quarter should develop diabetes. But if a diabetic marries a nondiabetic of a nondiabetic family, none of the children should ever have diabetes. There is this encouraging thought, namely, that if one hundred persons are predisposed or predestinated to have diabetes, the last three of the number will not develop it until they are over seventy years old. The element of heredity in diabetes is strong enough to make it doubly important for relatives of diabetics to control their weight and not get fat.

Diabetes comes on because the body ceases to get the benefit of the sugar which is formed out of the food. During health this sugar is used to keep us warm and to supply fuel for the muscles, including those of our heart, and for this purpose it is stored as animal starch (glycogen) in the liver and muscles, but if there is an extra supply it is changed to body fat just as hogs change to fat the sugar and starch which they get out of corn. This is a complicated process, which is marvelously regulated by the secretion of a gland, the pancreas, commonly known as the sweet bread. From this gland ten years ago a substance named insulin was extracted, and it is the lack of insulin produced by the pancreas which causes diabetes. In consequence, the sugar formed from the food collects in the blood of the diabetic and escapes unused in the urine. This can be prevented in part by eating less, particularly of sugar and starch, and by eating more fat, but if this does not correct the trouble, one can take insulin and in this way secure the full benefit of the diet.

Insulin is wonderful. Until it was discovered diabetic children lived only one or two years, but now they can live indefinitely and I know of more than a hundred who have had diabetes ten years. In one group of several hundred children whose diabetes began after insulin was available, in 1922, the mortality has been only one per hundred per year and in nearly every instance death was unrelated to diabetes or due to ignorance and carelessness. The lowest death rate for diabetes in Massachusetts for individuals under twenty years of age was in 1932, and amounted to 0.9 per 100,000 or 9 per million inhabitants. Insulin has also made over the lives of adults. These individuals are surely living twice as long as heretofore, and their lives are productive and independent. In fact, largely because the study of their diabetes has taught them so much about good hygiene, many of them have lived longer with their disease than would have been expected had they not had it.

Insulin is the only drug to be recommended for use in controlling diabetes. It is a drawback that it must be injected under the skin, but the results obtained are so striking that we should not grumble, but study its action and learn better how to use it while awaiting new discoveries which are sure to come. Where there was one doctor investigating diabetes a generation ago, there are one hundred today. If you are not satisfied with the rapidity of the progress in treatment already made, invest some of your money in your hospital or medical school to hurry it up.

The dietetic treatment of diabetes has made great strides since the introduction of insulin largely because of the new light it has thrown upon the disease. At one time to control diabetes the patients almost starved, but now the diet has grown to be so liberal that any diabetic can get plenty of food. The diet has improved in quality too, and today the diabetic is prescribed a satisfying amount of those previously forbidden foods which contain carbohydrate—starch and sugar. Generally the patient does better with insulin, but a goodly number either can do without insulin from the start, or later can give it up.

The diet in diabetes rests on one principle and no treatment succeeds if this is broken. The principle is this—overfeeding is harmful to a diabetic and must be avoided at all costs. Just as overeating helps to bring on diabetes, overeating makes it worse. Therefore, if more is taken of one kind of food, less must be taken of another; if the fat in the diet is increased the carbohydrate must be diminished and vice versa, or else the patient will receive too much food. These two classes of foodstuffs—fat and carbohydrate—are like children on the opposite ends of a seesaw. If one child goes up, the other child must come down. Some doctors give much fat and little carbohydrate and others give much carbohydrate and very little fat, but no doctor will prescribe much of both at the same time.

The dangers in the pathway of the diabetic are largely avoidable. If he neglects diet and insulin, he loses so much sugar in his urine that he runs down in strength and weight and becomes an easy prey for any disease. There is no necessity whatsoever for this. Should he deliberately or thoughtlessly break diet and overeat he may develop acid poisoning (diabetic coma) and before we had insulin practically always this meant death in a few hours or days. Fortunately today a large percentage of coma cases can be saved with the help of insulin. Intelligent diabetics know they can prevent going into coma. Whenever they feel ill from any cause they (1) call their doctor; (2) go to bed; (3) drink a cupful of hot liquid every hour; (4) move the bowels with an enema; (5) keep warm; and (6) secure the help of a nurse or someone else to care for them during these critical hours.

Just as diabetic coma comes on from overeating food, so it also arises from overeating one's own body as in the course of a fever. In any fever the patient is overeating, not of food, but of his own tissues. Furthermore during any infection the diabetes becomes temporarily more severe and insulin acts less well. Knowing this doctors teach their patients to take their insulin in larger doses or more frequently during infections and thus not only the harmfulness of the fever, but diabetic coma as well, is prevented. Coma also may come on if a patient accustomed to insulin, suddenly leaves it off and keeps on eating. Such a patient is then really overeating because it was due to his insulin that he was allowed to take his full diet.

Another danger, which fortunately seldom occurs in young diabetics, is diabetic gangrene. This is caused by poor circulation in the feet and the liability to slight injuries which an old person may not notice. Few elderly people realize that their sense of feeling for touch and pain, for heat and cold, is as dull as their hearing and their eyesight. Therefore, slight wounds in old people often go unseen or uncared for until the tiny sore has become so extensive that healing is out of the question and the amputation of a toe or a foot is necessary to save life. Gangrene takes a dreadful toll from diabetics, but to a large extent this is unnecessary. If the feet are washed every night, skin kept in good condition, anything unusual is discovered and can be treated in time. Instead of a beauty parlor for his face, the diabetic should visit a beauty parlor for his feet, and generally this means a visit to a chiropodist. The diabetic should keep his feet so clean that he would not be ashamed to ask the aid of the bright eyes and nimble fingers of his children or grand children to care for each individual toe.

The diabetic should be the cleanest citizen in the community. It pays him more than anyone else to be clean, because his skin is more vulnerable and thus more liable to infection. Injuries to the skin which would be harmless to an ordinary person may prove serious, heal slowly or not at all in a diabetic, and especially in that diabetic who has neglected treatment of his disease. Therefore, again I say it behooves the diabetic to be the cleanest citizen in the community.

First aid treatment of all injuries to a diabetic's skin is important. Avoid strong irritating antiseptics such as iodine. Some surgeons recommend the application of sterile gauze saturated with medicated alcohol or even one of the new antiseptics. Always consult a doctor for any redness, pain, swelling or other evidence of inflammation.

Why do we hear so much about diabetics today? It is very simple. There are many more of them about than ever before, because they all live so much longer. Only a few years ago one in five died the first year his diabetes began, but now only one in twenty-five. Then, too, we are finding more, because we are looking for them. In January 1922 I saw no cases whose diabetes began after seventy years of age, but in January 1931 there were thirteen. The insurance companies were the first to hunt for diabetics on a large scale, but today you can't get into college or into a prison, into a camp or gymnasium, without a test for the disease; and in fact, about the only places you can enter, unchallenged, are church and the movies, and at the latter you are likely to get a health talk, and at the former, if the church is alert, your body as well as your soul will be cared for because cleanliness comes next Godliness!

ARTHRITIS

By ROBERT B. OSGOOD, M.D.
Boston, Massachusetts

Arthritis means trouble with the joints. "Arthron" is the Greek word for a joint and arthritis means trouble with the joint, just as appendicitis means trouble with the appendix. Diseases that interfere with the free motion of our joints not only make us very uncomfortable, but they make us unable to be useful to other people and to earn our living. If they go on unchecked, they make cripples of us. Then other people have to wait on us and that interferes in turn with their *normal* activity. The kind of arthritis we shall talk about is often called chronic rheumatism. It is a very common trouble, more common than tuberculosis and cancer. It is probably the most important economic and social disease of the present time.

I once heard a policeman laying down the law of life to a coachman behind one of the houses on Beacon Street. The part of the conversation which I heard ran as follows:

The policeman said, "Everything you'll get in life is all planned out beforehand, just how long you are going to live, how many children you are going to have, how much money you are going to make, and how happy you are going to be."

"Yes, Mr. Officer," said the coachman, "that may be so, providing, of course, you don't die in the meantime."

A person who has chronic rheumatism or arthritis doesn't "die in the meantime" but must go on living crippled and in discomfort, if not in pain.

In England, during one year, the relief societies alone spent over ten million dollars in helping people suffering from rheumatic diseases, and these same diseases in one year caused a million weeks of idleness.

We must separate in our minds the kind of arthritis, or chronic rheumatism, which we are discussing this afternoon from the kind of arthritis which is called acute rheumatism or rheumatic fever. Rheumatic fever comes on quite suddenly with sharp pain and inflammation and swelling in the joints. It lasts a few weeks and then subsides, usually leaving the joints as free as ever and the patients often as well as ever, though it frequently affects their hearts.

Chronic arthritis, or chronic rheumatism, comes on often very slowly. Only one joint may be stiff for a day or two and not swollen or inflamed; then other joints feel stiff and the stiffness does not wear off and swelling comes on gradually.

There are two main types of this chronic rheumatism. One comes on earlier in life than the other. Children may have it and its first symptoms are usually felt before one is forty. It is usually a little more acute in its onset and progresses a little more rapidly than the other kind, and if it is unchecked, it is more crippling. Because the bones and muscles tend to waste away, it is called atrophic arthritis because atrophy means wasting.

The second kind is usually not noticed till people are over forty and at first they often pay very little attention to it unless it affects one of their weight-bearing joints like the knee. They may notice little bunches about the end joints of the fingers. Because lime is deposited about the edges of the joints and little overgrowths occur on the ends of the bones, it is called hypertrophic arthritis because hypertrophy means overgrowth.

It is important to pay attention to both these types of chronic rheumatism, for both may interfere with life, liberty and the pursuit of happiness.

Before we can make any common sense attempt to prevent these diseases or to treat them intelligently after they come on, we must know something about their causes. The reasons why we very briefly described the two types of chronic rheumatism or arthritis is because their causes and their treatment may be different. The commonest cause of the first type which comes on early in life and is called atrophic arthritis is something which makes the body less able to resist, or as we say, neutralizes any poisons which develop in the body. The healthy human body can take care of certain amounts of these poisons. It takes care of most bad oysters we may eat by causing a diarrhea that carries off the poison. We usually get over a common cold if we rest a day or two and drink plenty of water. If, however, these normal defense mechanisms of the body are weakened because we are overtired physically, or worried mentally, if we do not give our wonderful machines a chance to act normally because we sit or stand in a bad posture, if we have been weakened by exposure to cold and dampness or by some disease caused by germs, like grippe, or any other infection, then we may not be able to resist or neutralize these fatigue or germ poisons and the joints feel their effects. Some of the commonest causes of lowered resistance in the body, besides those we have mentioned, are improper food both in quantity and kind, imperfect action of the bowels, or constipation, too little exercise, too little fresh air, bad tonsils and bad teeth.

The commonest causes of the second type which usually comes on later in life and is called hypertrophic arthritis may be the poisons we described in the first type, but they do not so often arise from germs in the body. As we grow older, our organs do not take care of all kinds of poisons as well and we do not get rid of them as completely. Our organs act more sluggishly. Later in life the tissues of our joints do not stand injury or overuse as well. They tend to pile up lime because the heart does not pump as well, and the joints are not thoroughly flushed out by the blood. We are more likely to grow fat and flabby and our machines lag and sag.

What can we do to prevent both these types of arthritis or chronic rheumatism from coming on? I should say that the most important preventive measures were first, to avoid constantly driving our machinery too hard, and this applies to both our mental and our bodily machines. Second, to keep our machines "trued up" and in proper alignment, so that their complicated parts can work with the least amount of friction and the least amount of wear and tear. Third, to give our machines the most perfect kind of fuel. This means the type of food which gives us the greatest amount of energy when it is burned and leaves the least amount of wasteful, clogging residue after its useful energy has been extracted. The proper kind of food is rich in what we call vitamins. Fourth, to get rid of any colonies of harmful germs that may have settled in the tonsils, or sinuses or about the roots of the teeth, in the bowels, or anywhere else and are pouring into the blood more poison than we can take care of or neutralize.

These are the things which are the basic causes of most of the many chronic diseases, but one or more of them almost always exist before the joints begin to show signs of chronic rheumatism.

In the first type of chronic arthritis, called the atrophic type, the most common early causes are constant fatigue, poor body mechanics, improper food, improper action of the bowels and colonies of germs. In the second type of chronic arthritis, called the hypertrophic type, the most common early causes are imperfect elimination of the waste products of the body, improper and often excessive amounts of food, injury to the joints from accident or from an amount of use which is too much for the age and condition of the individual. Sometimes colonies of germs may play a part, but not as important a part as in the first type.

What should you do when your joints begin to feel stiff or painful or begin to swell. Consult your physician and do not be satisfied if he does nothing but give you medicine. Certain drugs may play an important part in the treatment of chronic rheumatism, but almost never will drugs or serums or vaccines alone overcome the basic causes of chronic rheumatism, nor will their use bring about a permanent cure in most cases. The disease must be attacked along various lines. A campaign must be planned to get rid of the underlying causes which we have mentioned.

When the disease is well advanced we shall probably not be able to hold it in check even by removing surgically the colonies of germs which may exist in the tonsils or teeth or elsewhere in the body. We must often do this, but treatment should begin, not end, with the removal of these colonies. If the joints tend to draw up and deformities are coming on, we can prevent many of them by proper treatment and braces. If they remain after the disease itself has been overcome we can restore some of their use and lessen the amount of crippling by special surgery, but we would emphasize the importance of catching the horse before he has escaped from the stable and torn up the delicate structures growing in the fields of the joints. Many of these can never be made to grow again after they have been seriously injured.

Are we doing anything to try make the public and their physicians realize this?

Yes, there is an international committee trying to get the fact of the economic importance of the disease before the public and to popularize among physicians the known and proved methods of treating the disease. An American branch called the American Committee for the Control of Rheumatism is hard at work at present. It is encouraging to know that this committee, made up of well known medical men and surgeons and research workers, feels optimistic concerning the future control of these diseases if physicians can be brought to look upon the disease as a generalized disease of which the joint symptoms are only one indication. If physicians can be stimulated to search out the basic causes and persistently to attack them by a combination of methods rather than by any *one* method, if the public can be induced to consult their physicians when the first fleeting symptoms of joint troubles begin, I think we may confidently expect that there will be less pitiful and wasteful crippling from the widespread disease called chronic rheumatism or arthritis.

CHRONIC RHEUMATISM
ELEANOR J. MACDONALD, A.B.
Statistician, Division of Adult Hygiene
Massachusetts Department of Public Health

Chronic rheumatism, the perennial cause of world-wide suffering and disability, has not received the attention it merits because rheumatism seems commonplace and lacks the dramatic appeal of such diseases as encephalitis, infantile paralysis, amoebic dysentery, or cancer. This disease is one that cripples but rarely kills; that is usually gradual in its onset and belies its own seriousness by its insidious approach; that seems to be as old as life itself and yet whose care and treatment is lamentably inadequate. Rheumatism is prevalent throughout the world and a Massachusetts sample showed that one out of every thirty-three individuals in Massachusetts was affected. The incidence, amount of hospitalization, and treatment for this disease in Massachusetts has been obtained from the chronic disease study in Massachusetts, in 1929, 1930 and 1931 by house-to-house surveys and reported by Bigelow and Lombard, and from a detailed study of cases of rheumatism from eighty-six hospitals in Massachusetts for the years 1928, 1929, and 1930.

Paleontology shows the neolithic man with his cave gout, the primeval Teuton and the early North American Indian with arthritis deformans.

Egyptian mummies show only too clearly the deformities of arthritis. A medical papyrus from Thebes of about 1550 B. C. actually describes arthritis deformans as "hardening of the joints and limbs" and continuing, recommends treatment to "make the joints limber."

In the field of rheumatism, the Humoral Theory of Physiology which has held the longest sway chronologically in the history of medicine has had special significance. The theory was familiar in Aristotle's day and was introduced into medicine by Hippocrates. It was the logical outgrowth of the doctrine of the four elements: earth, air, fire, and water. These elements applied to the body became dry, cold, hot, and moist. These four conditions were in combination known as the four humors or blood, yellow bile, phlegm, and black bile. Health meant a perfect balance of these component elements and illness was a lack of balance. Phlegm was synonymously called pituita, lymph, and rheum. "Rheum," derived from the Greek meant a defluxion. Pain was produced by the injurious qualities of impure blood seeking to pass off to the skin through the muscles and nerves. Venesection was the only fit method of treatment and required the evacuation of the offending humor by the appropriate channel. Gout was a local form of rheumatism and if insufficiently sound habits of living were common to an individual, gout would undoubtedly fall to his share. The term "rheumatism" itself was not introduced until 1578 when Guillame de Baillon in a treatise "De Rheumatismo et Pleuritide Dorsali" explained that rheumatism should be a separate classification in itself and must not continue to be confounded with catarrhus and arthritis as it had been until his time. He still persevered in the Humoral Theory of Physiology.

Regardless of whether it was called arthritis, gout, or catarrhus the problem of that disease which we know as rheumatism has persisted through the ages and is in the hands of this generation to recognize as an intensely serious problem.

Rheumatism has the highest morbidity of any of the chronic diseases and yet its mortality rate is extremely low with only one death in 500 from this cause. Females in Massachusetts have nearly twice as much rheumatism as males. There is much more rheumatism among the people living in the country. The highest rate is among the very poor. The rate improves noticeably with an ascending economic status. Sadly enough, those least able to cope with disability and suffering which needs care and treatment are those largely upon whom it is visited.

In view of the fact that the poor are the most numerous victims of rheumatism, it is not surprising that two-thirds of all those with the disease interviewed in the house-to-house survey were not receiving medical attention at the time they were interviewed, and well over one-third had received no medical attention for over a year. Of those who did not employ a physician, over one-half gave lack of confidence in medical ability to help them as the reason. This gives a clear picture of rheumatism in this State as furnished by the people themselves through house-to-house interviews.

The hospital records give another picture. On September 1, 1929, questionnaires were sent to hospitals representing 79 per cent of all hospital beds in the State, asking the number of rheumatism patients hospitalized on that date. There were 460 cases of rheumatism reported. A more detailed study of hospital records was made, covering all the cases of rheumatism admitted in eighty-six hospitals for the years 1928, 1929, and 1930. The beds in these hospitals comprise three-fourths of the general hospital beds in the State. In this period there were 4,144 cases of rheumatism hospitalized, 3,252 of which entered the hospital for this condition. Of this number, 25.7 per cent were classified as hypertrophic arthritis, 21.6 per cent as infectious; 10.4 per cent as atrophic; and 42.3 per cent "not stated." The median age of these individuals was highest in the hypertrophic group—males 60.7 years and females 60.1 years. The median age for the individuals in the atrophic group was younger—males

51.5 and females 53.0. The group with infectious arthritis was still younger—males 42.5 and females 42.8. Since the age distribution of the large "not stated" group was for males and females respectively 45.6 and 49.5, it is not unreasonable to assume that most of them would be distributed between the infectious and the atrophic types. The atrophic group remained longer in hospitals, averaging 23.7 days. The infectious group remained in the hospital for 18.8 days and the hypertrophic group for 16.0 days.

At discharge from the hospital, 74.7 per cent were considered improved or cured, 15.4 per cent were the same, 0.6 per cent were worse, 3.2 per cent were dead, and the condition of 6.1 per cent was unknown. The treatment furnished in the hospital is given in Table I and a comparison between hospital treatment and treatment recorded on the house-to-house survey is made. If two types of treatment were used, the more important was tabulated. "No treatment" was nearly as great in the hospital group as in the survey group. Surgery and apparatus were much greater in the hospital group. External applications were much greater in the survey group. Other types of treatment were substantially the same in both groups. Self-prescribing was limited to the survey group. In the hospitals, the hypertrophic group had the largest percentage receiving no treatment and a smaller percentage receiving surgery or apparatus than the other groups. The atrophic group had less surgery than the infectious group and more apparatus. With these exceptions, there is little difference between the groups.

The volume of the disease, the possibility of cure or alleviation under proper treatment, and the lack of medical attention for so large a part of this group point towards the need for the concerted action of every lay individual and every doctor in Massachusetts.

TABLE I.—*Therapy of Rheumatism Patients*

Therapy	Total Rheumatism Survey	Total	Hospital Survey Hypertrophic	Atrophic	Infectious	Not Stated
None	22.9	19.8	30.5	20.2	19.0	18.6
Surgery	0.1	14.3	7.0	10.0	17.8	18.1
Apparatus	4.3	19.9	17.6	25.8	18.6	20.6
Physiotherapy	15.1	18.5	19.9	18.4	19.7	16.8
Massage	6.5	3.7	2.0	2.1	2.3	5.8
Internal medicine (doctor)	17.3	15.5	14.7	13.7	14.9	16.7
External applications	16.0	2.8	2.4	2.1	4.1	2.5
Diet	1.2	0.5	0.5	0.7	1.0	0.2
Internal medicine (self-administered)	14.8					
Unknown	1.8	5.1	5.4	7.0	2.6	5.7

Bibliography

BIGELOW, GEORGE H., and LOMBARD, HERBERT L.: *Cancer and Other Chronic Diseases in Massachusetts*. Houghton Mifflin Co., Boston and New York, 1933.

BIGELOW, GEORGE H., and LOMBARD, HERBERT L.: *Chronic Rheumatism in Massachusetts*. New England Journal of Medicine, Vol. 203, No. 25, Dec. 18, 1930.

GARRISON, FIELDING H.: *An Introduction to the History of Medicine*. W. B. Saunders Co., Philadelphia and London, 1929.

NEWMAN, SIR GEORGE: *Rise of Preventive Medicine*. Oxford University Press, London, 1932.

RIDDELL, THE HON. WILLIAM RENWICK: *The Original Rheumatism*. Medical Journal and Record, Vol. CXXXVI, pages 518-519, Toronto, 1932.

SCUDAMORE, CHARLES. *A Treatise on the Nature and Cure of Gout and Rheumatism*. Edward Earle, Philadelphia, 1819.

THE EFFECTS OF FATIGUE
By JOHN H. TALBOTT, M.D.
Boston, Massachusetts

There are two significant types of fatigue that may be subjectively experienced by the human individual. These are, in the order of discussion, physical and functional fatigue. The first type is usually associated with physical exertion and the sensation is referred to the voluntary muscles. If the work has been strenuous the physiological changes that occur in the body may be quantitatively analyzed. The respiratory rate and heart rate will be increased with an added uptake of oxygen. The concentration of red and white cells in the blood likewise will be increased. There is another constituent of the blood that is altered in exercise which has recently been the subject of considerable study: this is an organic acid called lactic acid. It has been found that the concentration of this substance increases many fold in the muscles in the active state, and with the accumulation of lactic acid in the muscles there may be a spilling over into the blood stream. When lactic acid enters the blood stream it competes with a weaker acid, carbonic acid, and lowers the carbon dioxide content of the blood. Thus it can be said that important changes in the blood following muscular work are an increase of the red and white cells and lactic acid, and a lowering of the carbon dioxide combining power. But it is not possible at present to go further and say that one or all of these changes are responsible for the subjective sensation of physical fatigue.

The other type of fatigue that I wish to discuss is mental or functional. The division between physical and functional fatigue is not always exact, nor is it necessary in this instance that it should be. After a day's work of either physical or mental labor we may experience similar subjective sensations. And while the blood changes may be found after the physical labor, no significant changes are observed after mental labor. This evidence points against the known chemical changes as being primarily responsible for the subjective sensation of fatigue. It should be noted that while there may be important chemical changes in the cells of the nervous system in either type of fatigue, proof for this is not at present conclusive.

The assignment of seven or eight hours of work daily for most people in the social order today presupposes the ability of the average person to carry on for this period of time before the onset of fatigue. Some people, however, are not able to follow such a schedule, either the whole or in part. To these individuals who are chronically tired the name neurasthenia has been given. But it should be said at this time that while fatigue in these persons is generally an emotional reaction, fatigue may be a symptom of a disease requiring medical advice and care. Among the diseases in which fatigue is an early and significant symptom are Addison's Disease, Myasthenia Gravis and Effort Syndrome. Of more widespread experience is the feeling of fatigue that may be the onset of or accompany many acute and chronic diseases. The awareness of increased fatigability in an individual with a stable nervous system is a danger signal that should be promptly heeded.

After recognizing the sick person with organic disease and the neurasthenic who is chronically exhausted, let us consider the individual with a capacity for work greater than the average. Napoleon, Poincare, Edison and Theodore Roosevelt were men with such a reputation. Physiological data on such individuals are not at hand and casual observations are difficult to evaluate. In the absence of quantitative data on these persons let us examine the facts already recorded on certain athletes and their capacity for work. As an example, members of the world championship Yale crew for 1924 were able to row for a six-minute period using oxygen at a rate about twenty times the resting value. A Marathon race is another severe test of physical effort. In the twenty-six mile Boston Marathon a runner may consume more fuel in three hours than many laborers consume in a full day's work.

What accounts for the great difference in performance in the neurasthenic person who is chronically exhausted and the Marathon runner who may run eight to ten miles four times a week for months in preparation for a race? Constitutional endowment at birth may favor the man engaged in muscular work. Yet many athletes are physically normal and not physically perfect. The concentration of hormones in the body at any given time may be important. It has been known since the investigations of Dr. Cannon that in acute emergencies the hormone adrenalin may be increased and aid the person in adequately meeting a given situation. This increase of adrenalin may be significant early in a long contest but its effect probably is unimportant after this time.

There is another hormone from the adrenal gland only recently isolated that may be equally important in the prevention of fatigue in various individuals. The name of this hormone is cortin. Professor Hartman at Buffalo has found that cortin is decidedly beneficial when given to neurasthenic patients. This observation suggests a possible deficit of the hormone in this group of patients.

A third and equally important factor responsible for the differences in individual achievement is the speed of chemical processes in the body. At present indirect proof only is available confirming this assumption. Continued study of the physiology of muscular exercise and of the pathological physiology in thyroid disease may further substantiate this hypothesis.

But studies of the constitution, hormones and chemical processes do not fully explain the great variation in onset of fatigue in the neurasthenics and the athletes. Further investigation may associate it more clearly with one of the mentioned factors. In the absence of conclusive data let us examine certain accepted findings. In a period of prolonged patriotic stress as in 1917-1918, production of raw material reached a magnitude that was merely dreamed of ten years before. And the increased production of the nation was a direct function of the increased production of the individual. In the language of the runner, the nation had found its "second wind."

Professor William James in his interesting paper in the Philosophical Reviews of 1906 entitled "The Energies of Men," says, "If an unusual necessity forces us to press onward, a surprising thing occurs. The fatigue gets worse up to a certain point, when gradually or suddenly it passes away, and we are fresher than before. We have evidently tapped a level of new energy, masked until then by the fatigue-obstacle usually obeyed. There may be layer after layer of this experience. Mental activity shows the phenomenon as well as physical and in exceptional cases we may find, beyond the very extremity of fatigue-distress, amounts of ease and power that we never dreamed ourselves to own, sources of strength habitually not taxed at all because habitually we never push through the obstruction, never pass those early critical points." This is not the energy of youth but the energy of mature age. And the disturbing sociological phenomena during the years since the war should not be responsible for the onset of fatigue in this generation and period of world history. The fact is, however, that the wear and tear of modern life, made up of tension in business, worry, domestic difficulties and similar factors, are important causative agents in excessive fatigue. An intelligent understanding of these sociological phenomena would go far toward fortifying the individual against them.

In summary then it may be said that fatigue may be a useful physiological and psychological state but we need not become sensitized to it.

PYORRHOEA

By E. MELVILLE QUINBY, M.R.C.S., L.R.C.P., D.M.D.

Boston, Massachusetts

There are certain terms used by the "man in the street" to describe diseased conditions in connection with the teeth, and the supporting structures of the teeth, viz., the gums, the tooth-sockets, and the membrane covering the root surface of the teeth. The said names are caries or decay of teeth, and pyorrhoea, a disease or disintegration of gums, tooth-sockets and root membrane. Much more attention has been given to the prevention and treatment of caries than to the prevention and treatment of pyorrhoea, although probably as many teeth are lost, and systems poisoned by disease of the supporting tissues as in the case of caries or decay of teeth. From time immemorial disease of the gums has found mention in the writings of the ancients, in such terms as "loose teeth", "shaking teeth", and "hemorrhage of the gums." The first time that the term "pyorrhoea" was mentioned in this country was in a paper read by Dr. F. H. Rehwinkel in Chicago in 1877, entitled "Pyorrhea Alveolaris."[1]

Since that time oceans of literature have appeared on the subject, many causes for the disease suggested; and numberless treatments prescribed; but the problem is still unsolved, the causes still shrouded in mystery, and yet, as remarked previously, as many teeth are lost from pyorrhoea as from decay; and the dangers of systemic infection through absorption of poisons from pus pockets demands as much attention from members of the Healing Art as does caries of teeth with death of the nerve or pulp and ensuing abscess. Probably the need for such attention is greater, for the diseased tissue is so extensive in area—at least eight times the area of the tonsils, for example!

At what age does this disease present itself? Most people think of pyorrhoea as a disease of middle or late life! As a matter of cold fact, many children from eight to ten years exhibit symptoms such as redness and swelling of the gums; and this may affect the gums of a few teeth or many. Many children also present definite mobility of certain teeth, especially the front teeth, at an early age. Thus gingivitis, or gum inflammation, and alveolar (tooth-socket) disintegration which later in life results in loss of the teeth, should be looked for and carefully charted in examination of all mouths from the age of eight onward. Many patients between the ages of twenty-five and forty-five have complained to the dentist that the gums feel sore, and that a tooth or teeth have become loose, and yet the early symptoms of pyorrhoea manifest themselves to a careful observer frequently as soon as those of decay. There is no doubt, in other words, that many, many cases of pyorrhoea first diagnosed at twenty-five to forty-five years could have been avoided if there had been from the earliest visits to the dental office, a fifty-fifty examination of the *teeth* and the *supporting tissues*—the gums, the tooth-sockets and the pericemental membrane. In the latter examination, of course, X-ray films are required. (Everyone should have a radiographic survey once annually.)

What can be done to prevent, to alleviate or to cure this dread disease? Let it be understood at once, that no absolute cure is *possible* in cases where the loss of supporting tissue of the teeth is more than fifty per cent. The most that can be accomplished with the most careful treatment both by the dentist and the patient's faithful cooperation at home, is a restoration to function and health of the remaining structure. On the other hand, if taken in time and suitable measures adopted, there is no doubt of a successful issue. To make a long story short, there are three factors in treatment which *must* be considered in every case, viz.,

    (a) The building of the dental machine or nutrition
    (b) The arrangement of teeth or occlusion
    (c) The cleaning of teeth and massage of gums.

---

[1] Merritt.

I. *Nutrition.* Under this heading is included every condition of right living; the right elements in food, and the right assimilation thereof. Any systemic factor which interferes with nutrition must be treated before successful dealing with disease of supporting tissues of teeth can obtain. Powers of resistance must be established on a firm basis. The alignment of teeth must be cultivated from the earliest period of development of the dental machine, by supplying the elements of growth, and by giving exercise to the muscles of the jaws. N. B. Ninety per cent of dental machines are "out of gear."

A definite technique for removal of insoluble fragments of foodstuff mixed with mucin from the saliva, dead epithelium, lime salts and myriads of bacteria, must be established.

Furthermore this duty must be carried out by the patient daily, at least twice, after breakfast and before going to bed; and there must be no letting up for *one* day. Every person ought to see the dentist at least four times annually, and is strongly advised to ask the dentist to demonstrate the *right use* of the *right kind* of mouth cleanser in the mouth of the patient. The patient should demonstrate the technique used by himself or herself to the satisfaction of the dentist. The tongue must also be cleansed.

The moral to be deduced from all this is indicated in the slogan:
(a) Balanced diet
(b) Clean mouths
(c) Better dental machines for all.

Summary

1. Pyorrhoea must not be looked upon as a plague—a mark of Providential displeasure, and beyond redress!
2. On the contrary—this disease has a definite commencement with symptoms quite obvious to those who are *looking in that direction.*
3. Early recognition of symptoms is a *sine qua non* in prevention or cure of pyorrhoea.
4. Attention to *three factors* in every case: viz., (a) Nutrition, (b) Alignment of teeth, (c) Cleaning of teeth, gums and tongue, are absolutely necessary for success.
5. Dependence on use of medicaments, pastes, powders, lotions, etc., except as helps in the systemic and local treatments indicated, is to be deprecated most strongly!
6. There is no attempt made to *sterilize* or kill off the bacterial content of the average mouth; but every means possible should be utilized to neutralize the poisons or toxins which emanate from the decomposition and fermentation of foodstuff from three "squares" a day!
7. Pyorrhoea is *not an incurable* or a nonpreventable disease; and the sooner that one hundred millions of the U. S. A. who are unacquainted with mouth health, are educated in these points, the better for the health of future generations.
8. No mouth can be one hundred per cent efficient or healthy unless the *function* of the dental machine is unimpaired. For instance, when teeth are removed the resulting spaces *must be* filled.
9. In the last analysis—treatment should emphasize *health* measures, even though infection may be the most *obvious* cause of symptoms. These measures reduced to the lowest common denominator are:
   1. Universal attention to diet.
   2. Universal attention to cleanliness.

but the attention *must be universal* and thorough and encouraged *by all* members of the Healing Art.

WHY GUMS BLEED

If your gums bleed do not take the matter lightly. See your dentist at once. As you will see from the following list, there are many causes of bleeding gums. Sometimes it is merely a matter of local irritation. Other times tender gums are a symptom of pyorrhoea or malnutrition in its early stages. Early care will hasten a cure.

A. The apparent causes are found in the mouth itself or may be traced to some irritating local factor for which the individual himself is responsible.

The apparent causes are as follows:
1. Accumulations of tartar which cause bleeding by pressing and cutting the delicate gum tissues.
2. Cavities which go down to or under the gum line cause irritation and bleeding because of the sharp edges which they possess.
3. Overhanging fillings and crowns which press down on the gum tissue.
4. Broken down roots with sharp edges which irritate the tissues.
5. Irregular teeth which cause bleeding pockets to be formed between the teeth.
6. Lack of toothbrushing.
7. Improper toothbrushing.
8. Use of toothpicks and other such implements for "picking the teeth".
9. Improper use of dental floss.
10. Introduction of foreign materials into the mouth and the continuation of such a habit over a period of time; e. g., nails, pins, pencils, etc.
11. Mouth-breathing.
12. Overuse of the wind type of musical instruments.

B. Nonapparent causes are found in the body in some organ or tissue remote from the mouth. Many diseases will display symptoms in the mouth and bleeding gums may be a sign of trouble elsewhere in the body.

The more common nonapparent causes are as follows:
1. Blood diseases such as anemia.
2. Diseases of the ductless glands such as goitre.
3. Diabetes.
4. Kidney diseases.
5. Tuberculosis in the later stages.
6. Improper diet:
    (a) Lack of vitamins.
    (b) Lack of fresh vegetables.
    (c) Overabundance of carbohydrates.
7. Allergies—foods or drugs which cause skin and gum reactions in some individuals; e. g., strawberries, lobster, etc.
8. Lack of good general hygiene:
    (a) Lack of sleep.
    (b) Pernicious habits—excessive smoking, drinking, etc.

Prepared for the
Massachusetts Department of Public Health
By the
Massachusetts Dental Hygiene Council

HEMORRHOIDS

By L. S. MCKITTRICK, M.D.

Boston, Massachusetts

Definition

Hemorrhoids may be defined as groups of tortuous, dilated veins, or varicose tumors in the anal canal. They are arranged in clumps usually three in number, run lengthwise of the bowel; if internal they are covered entirely by the mucous membrane lining the intestines, if external, by skin, or if of the mixed variety they are covered partly by mucous membrane and partly by skin. They are found in both sexes, are rare in children, infrequent in adolescents, most common in young adults and people of middle age. They are frequently found in old age.

Causes

Any number of causes have been given for the development of hemorrhoids. Most of these are only of theoretical importance, many of them without foundation. They may all well be summed up, however, by saying that any condition such as a pregnancy, which obstructs the normal flow of blood from the vessels around the rectum and anus, or any activity such as lifting or straining which increases the pressure in these veins may result in the formation of hemorrhoids.

Symptoms

The most important single symptom of hemorrhoids and also the most common, is bleeding. It is the most important because it is also the most common symptom of a much more serious condition, cancer of the rectum. One can live uncomfortably for an indefinite period with occasional bleeding from hemorrhoids. The span of life and comfort is definitely limited, however, by cancer not properly treated. The bleeding from hemorrhoids is usually bright red, most frequently accompanies or immediately follows a movement of the bowels, may be small in amount and only noted on the toilet paper, or may be enough to drip into the water and to color it a deep red. Occasionally, the hemorrhoids may bleed into the lumen of the rectum so that a large clot will form, give the patient the desire to have a movement, and then be passed. The bleeding may or may not be accompanied by a protrusion from the rectum. Rarely is the hemorrhage severe enough to be serious, though occasionally there is sufficient bleeding to be very disturbing, at least to the patient who has it. On the other hand, should bleeding, even though relatively small in amount, continue over a long period of time, a very disturbing anemia may develop which will require active treatment.

Probably the next most characteristic symptom of internal hemorrhoids is the tendency to prolapse. By this we mean the protrusion of a soft, spongy, reddish-purple bunch externally. This is usually not painful, can as a rule be pushed back by gentle pressure, and most frequently accompanies the straining of a bowel movement. In the more severe cases these protrusions may form a rosette outside of the anus and if not immediately replaced, swelling may occur which will make reduction of the mass impossible, except by operation. This condition is known as strangulation. Occasionally these large protruding masses may ulcerate and at times become infected.

Pain is a symptom which most people seem to associate with hemorrhoids. Such is not the case. There may be a sensation of fullness or of slight discomfort, but uncomplicated hemorrhoids are not painful. If there is pain it means that either some other condition, such as a small, very sensitive ulcer or fissure is present, or that a blood vessel has ruptured producing a small, tender external tumor which cannot be reduced. This is known as a thrombosed hemorrhoid.

Itching may or may not be a symptom. This most annoying condition may be due to a number of conditions, hemorrhoids being only one. It is a symptom very commonly associated with hemorrhoids by the laity but actually one of the less characteristic symptoms of the condition we are discussing.

Diagnosis

Most people like to make their own diagnosis. Not long ago a middle-aged woman came to my office saying that she had had hemorrhoids for the past year which had not responded to treatment, but saying also that she had never seen a doctor. In explanation for this it was found that she had refused to see her doctor, had told her husband that she had hemorrhoids, and that he must go to the doctor and get something for them. The suppositories which the husband brought home gave only slight; temporary relief. This patient instead of having hemorrhoids had a cancer of the rectum. Through failure to have a careful examination and an accurate diagnosis one year was lost before proper treatment was obtained. It is, therefore, important that a careful examination be done before accepting a diagnosis of hemorrhoids. It is also important to realize that a patient may have both hemorrhoids and cancer, each of which is contributing to the bleeding. Age is no protection against the more serious condition. It is just as important for the young man or woman of twenty-five to have rectal bleeding accurately explained as it is for their parents or grandparents.

Usually it is very easy to make either diagnosis. It is only fair to say, however, that there are times when a patient may have bleeding due to hemorrhoids which can be accurately diagnosed only after several examinations, preferably done as near the time of the actual bleeding as possible. Examination in these cases must be done not only with the finger but also with a proctoscope, a small instrument with an electric light in the end which makes it possible to see the inside of the bowel and to examine its condition accurately. It is a very simple but important procedure.

Treatment

The treatment recommended depends upon a number of factors. Hemorrhoids that bleed frequently or profusely are in urgent need of treatment; whereas hemorrhoids which occur in the latter months of pregnancy often entirely disappear after childbirth. Small hemorrhoids with only occasional local discomfort or little bleeding respond well to a correction of diet, regulation of the bowels, and the use of local medication, usually in the form of suppositories. The method of treatment, therefore, must be selected according to the individual case. Some of the large prolapsing hemorrhoids can only be cured by operation, properly performed. On the other hand, the majority of internal hemorrhoids, if taken in the early stages, can be very satisfactorily treated by more conservative measures. Of the procedures available at the present time, there is little question but what a carefully done injection of a proper solution into each hemorrhoid by one trained in this work gives the most efficient results. On the other hand, the psychology of the average individual is such that the much more dramatic display occurring in the use of electricity gives to the latter an appeal entirely lacking in such a quietly efficient procedure as injection treatment.

In the injection method a solution which is anesthetic and at the same time produces considerable reaction in the nature of scar tissue is carefully injected into each individual hemorrhoid near its base. This is without discomfort to the patient, is readily done in the physician's office, is followed by little more than a feeling of fullness, and should give excellent results in carefully selected cases. It is desirable not to inject more than one or two hemorrhoids at one sitting. Two to four treatments usually suffice. This method has been used in hundreds of thousands of cases and in proper hands is a safe procedure. The immediate results are good. The patient, however, having this treatment should understand that the results are not always permanent. There is still no method of treatment which gives so high a percentage of permanent cures as operation. However, the injection method is so simple, can be done with so little discomfort to the patient, with no loss of time and at such small expense, that the average person will prefer chancing the possibility of subsequent injections to taking the time necessary for operation unless, of course, the hemorrhoids are of the type where operation is definitely indicated.

The electrical treatment of hemorrhoids, like injection, should be restricted to uncomplicated internal hemorrhoids. There are several different methods of applying electricity to hemorrhoids. Of these, the use of the high frequency current—either electrodessication or electrocoagulation—is most widely used. Inasmuch as these procedures hold no distinct advantage over other operative methods and require special apparatus and training, they will probably not replace the former in cases where operation is definitely indicated. Galvanism, another form of electricity used in these cases gives excellent results at times, but is less certain, takes much longer, and is so much more complicated than injection that it is not to be recommended.

The treatment of external hemorrhoids is quite different from that of internal hemorrhoids, and to use the conservative treatments just described might be dangerous. The external hemorrhoid should not be treated by electricity nor by injection. If the external hemorrhoid is the result of the rupture of a blood vessel in a small hemorrhoid on the outside with the easily felt, tender, painful swelling, it is best treated by injecting a small amount of novocain and removing the clot. Immediate relief from pain is obtained and within a few days the area is healed up. This does not require either going to the hospital or staying in bed and gives very satisfactory results. The other type of external hemorrhoid, consisting of tabs of flesh on the outside of the skin immediately around the anus, must be removed surgically. Injection of external hemorrhoids would result in painful ulcerations very slow to heal.

Summary

To summarize, hemorrhoids may be described as varicose tumors involving the veins in the anal canal. The most common symptoms are hemorrhage and prolapse. Hemorrhage is the most important because it is also a common symptom of the much more serious condition, cancer. Hemorrhoids may be divided into two groups, internal and external. The former are covered by the lining of the intestinal tract, the latter by skin. The former bleed and prolapse. Whenever bleeding occurs a careful examination must be done to exclude other causes of bleeding from the rectum. In treating internal hemorrhoids, the large extensive ones—particularly those protruding from the rectum—must be treated by some form of operation. Those less advanced, entirely internal, which tend to come out but are readily replaced, are satisfactorily treated in the office by the injection of a proper solution by one trained in its use. This method is definitely advocated in preference to any form of electrical treatment because it is safer, more certain, and less expensive. External hemorrhoids requiring treatment can be taken care of by operation only. Operation, however, for external hemorrhoids is a minor procedure.

WHAT PRICE HEALTH?

MARY R. LAKEMAN, M.D.
*Supervisor of Education
Division of Adult Hygiene*

How much would you be rated at,
In terms of honest wealth,
If for one dollar you could buy
One point of perfect health?
M. M. L.

Of late, an increasing number of people in Massachusetts have been seeking an answer to this question, keeping a personal health score month by month through a full year. It is an interesting game to discover where you stand in the matter of health according to an accepted standard, and then to try to bring your score, month by month, up toward the goal of 1000 points.

Though it would be sheer folly to assume that such an evaluation of personal health can serve as more than a rough index of one's general condition, it does, nevertheless, call attention to certain undeniable habits of which one is often unaware, and which may well be checked or guided, if one is to gain from life the greatest possible happiness and well-being, and give the greatest possible return in efficiency.

It is, of course, impossible to lay down in detail, rules of health which will apply to any large number of individuals. There are, however, certain fundamental principles which, without doubt, have a bearing on the satisfactions to be derived from everyday living, perhaps even on the length of time we shall spend in this old world. Beyond these fundamental principles, each person must be guided by his own distinctive needs, his abilities and limitations.

The object in this health game is this: taking off from where you are today—to improve your score, month by month, until the limit of your capacity is reached. The game is adapted to any person who has attained his full growth, not to children. If you can find competitors in your family or group of friends, so much the better.

Here are a few signs of health and some health habits by which you may, if you try, find an answer to the question, What Price Health?

I. Let us run through some of the points that go to make up the perfect score of 1000 points.

1. *Do you feel completely rested when you arise in the morning?*

We are accustomed to hear the opinion expressed that every grown person should have eight hours of sleep. This may, or may not apply to an individual. There was Thomas Edison for instance, who declared he did not need more than four or five hours. Perhaps others born under the same star can keep in prime condition with as little sleep as Mr. Edison! For the ordinary person, however, eight hours spent quietly in bed, even if not entirely in sleep, meet the everyday requirements and leave a safe margin for reserve force. When a group of young men were tested as to the quickness of their reaction to the spoken word after varying sleep periods, it was found that after four hours of sleep they had recovered all that they originally had of speed in response. When tests were made for accuracy and mental concentration, there was a different story to tell. Improvement in their faculties went on beyond four hours to six, and even to eight hours of sound sleep. We may infer from these studies that the manual worker doing routine tasks can carry on without seeming lessening of efficiency with less sleep than the executive, the student, or the teacher who must use his higher mental faculties.

There are different degrees and kinds of sleep too. Experiments at Colgate College[1] and elsewhere indicate that sleep is a complicated process, that we sleep in one part while awakening in another, as the sleep walker does, and that we profit less by sleep in a noisy place or in the presence of a bright light than in a quiet, dark room.

The real test of the adequacy of our habits of sleep comes in our ability to do the work of the following day. If we arise feeling rested, we have had enough sleep. The early morning hours without the proverbial setting-up of the morning coffee, are the ones which tell the story of recovery from the fatigue of the previous day. Physical fatigue is a matter of definite chemical change and sleep enables the blood to wash away the wastes created by the fatigue of the day.

2. *Can you do as much as your associates without undue fatigue?*

Are you one of those persons who are always tired, who declare they were "born tired"? If you are, and if you are as well a chronic worrier or if you are unhappy in your work or at home, the chances are that the state of tiredness is an emotional one. It would be a good idea to do some clear thinking to find out if you cannot adapt yourself to the inevitable, or better still, overcome existing difficulties. In order to overcome the difficulties, you must first bring them into the light. Then look them over from all points of view, decide what to do, and do it forthwith.

If there are no mental causes for that tired feeling, there may be some physical ones. Do you feel flushed in the afternoon? Have you a cough which continues after a fresh cold disappears? Do you become more short of breath than your friends in going up stairs or in climbing a hill? If the answer to any one of these questions is yes, go to your doctor and let him find out if anything is wrong. If there is no physical sign, look into your daily habits. Are you getting enough sleep, or do you have to be awakened by an alarm clock? If you are not ready to get up in the morning, try taking two or three unusually long nights in bed each week. This may serve as an antidote if you *must* abbreviate some of the other nights.

3. *Have you appetite for wholesome food?*

4. *Are you free from signs of indigestion?*

Normal hunger is a sensation caused by contractions of the muscles of the stomach when it becomes empty, hence if you expect to enjoy that pleasant experience, the stomach must be given a chance to empty itself, a process which requires several hours after eating. If we eat between meals, or while digestion is under way, we give the stomach a new task before it has completed the one on which it is at work. The digestive organs like some of us become confused and are likely to rebel when repeatedly asked to begin a new job before they have finished the old one.

Or if the mind is disturbed by worry or haste, the digestive fluids are not normally secreted. Experiments by Dr. Walter B. Cannon[2] show convincingly that when an animal is disturbed emotionally the flow of digestive fluids which would normally be poured into the stomach at the sight of food, is delayed or even suppressed. Attractive surroundings, tempting food, and a serene mind all help to send the correct message through the nervous system to the stomach, which will start the secretion of the gastric fluids necessary for digestion. It is well to look to the mental state when the usual appetite fails.

The process of digestion goes on without any awareness on our part and is far better done when we pay no attention to it. If we abuse our digestive organs by irregularity in eating or by eating when we are in a disturbed state of mind, we must be ready to take the consequences of our unwisdom. Everyone must learn for himself what are his own limitations, indigestion not accounted for by irregular habits or personal idiosyncrasies should be called to the attention of a physician. This is especially important if digestive upsets should become increasingly frequent or severe after the age of forty.

5. *Do you get on well with most people?*

What has that to do with health you ask? It has a lot to do with health.

people with whom he associates will inevitably be led away from health, physical and mental, not toward it. Perhaps he is very sensitive to slights, and feels he is being picked upon, finds it hard to get his neighbor's point of view. Failure to modify such "mindsets" as these, brings unhappiness, loneliness, and in their trail, nervous indigestion, vague aches and pains, and a host of other unwelcome accompaniments of a mind disturbed or not at peace with itself. So if you are one of these people who do not get on well with other folk, try a bit of self-criticism, looking for the faults in yourself, not in the other fellow. You are not responsible for his difficulties, you are for your own.

6. *Do you have confidence in yourself?*

For the person who lacks a reasonable appreciation of his own abilities, we know of no better way to fill that lack than to cultivate some particular skill or talent until he can excel in that field. Cultivate a hobby and learn to ride it with skill. Absorption in a hobby which has been mastered tends to carry a person on to the realization that every individual has a unique part to play in the game of life, which no other person can play quite so well as he himself.

7. *Are you free from persistent worry?*

Are you a worrier? If you are, learn to think not in circles, but in straight lines. Analyze your worry. Separate it into all its difficulties and obstacles. Sort these out as those which may be surmounted and those which are for the present insurmountable. Decide what you are going to do about them. Make a plan and start immediately to carry it out. Action is the great outlet which will break the "vicious circle" of worry or circular thinking.

8. *Can you relax at will?*

If you think you cannot relax, if you find your muscles are habitually tense when not in use, lie down on your back. Relax one finger, the next finger, the next, the right hand, the left hand, the arm, and continue this process until the whole body is relaxed. Practice this daily for a few minutes. In the midst of a busy day as well as at night it will rest you almost as much as a nap and will do much to encourage the habit of relaxing the muscles at will, and to bring the muscles under the control of the will.

9. *Is your skin clear? Natural color good?*

The skin is a great telltale. Apart from well defined skin diseases, the texture of the skin itself and the blood circulating beneath its outer layers speak eloquently of abounding health, and equally clearly betray poor elimination and food follies which we have committed wittingly or unwittingly. Not too much confidence is to be placed in the actual color of the skin or lips even if not concealed by make-up. There is great variation in the opacity of different skins. There is, however, a softness of texture and a quality of elasticity unmistakably identified with a healthy skin. Is yours like this?

10. *Is your vision good or corrected by glasses?*

What has eyesight to do with health? True, we may have good general health in spite of poor vision, but the handicap of imperfect vision is too great to be carried through life without making a vigorous effort to overcome it. Headaches and nervous symptoms are frequent accompaniments of uncorrected defects of vision and these are astonishingly common. The report of a study of a large number of college students[a] showed 40 per cent to have defective vision. Similarly among industrial workers 44.3 showed defects of vision. The causes of such a regrettable state of the eyes are many and far to seek, but none is probably more important than overfatigue in combination with poor lighting.

Furthermore, examination of the eyes at frequent intervals often brings to light minor troubles which may be easily corrected in their beginnings, hence, the desirability of a regular check-up of the eye sight.

11. *Can you hear ordinary conversation at a distance of 16 feet, with both ears?*

What is true of sight is equally true of hearing. Many hearing defects can be prevented by proper attention to trouble in the throat or nose, by prompt medical care for all forms of earache, and by the avoidance of high diving and prolonged swimming under water without protection of the ears. The slightest decrease of hearing should be brought to medical attention as soon as noticed, for such success as may be attained in preserving the hearing after changes in the inner ear have actually occurred can be won only by early and persistent treatment.

12. *Have you been free from infections, including colds?*

The common cold, that bane of civilized life, is still with us and likely to be for some years to come. Colds are about us on all sides from October to May. Everyone, at least occasionally, contracts one. Those who have been studying the nature of colds tell us that in this region, people in general average about two colds a year. Colds become increasingly abundant in October, subside somewhat during the early winter months only to increase both in severity and prevalence in February and March. Although we naturally assume that this increased prevalence at certain seasons is due to our climate, curiously enough, it is found that a similar seasonal variation occurs in other parts of the world, and in warm climates as well as cold. While defects of the nose or throat undoubtedly predispose one to frequent colds, the removal of such defects does not always prevent the repeated occurrence of colds. In short, the common cold is one of the unsolved problems of preventive medicine. Perhaps the best one can do to avoid colds is to follow the advice offered by Dr. George H. Bigelow while Commissioner of Public Health in Massachusetts:

"First of all, keep away from the person who has a cold. Avoid the cougher and sneezer. Never kiss on the mouth.

"Secondly, do not use a common towel or drinking cup. Do not borrow anyone's handkerchief. Especially baby should have his own handkerchief.

"Thirdly, keep your fingers away from your nose or mouth. As to treatment, take plenty of water, eat lightly, keep your bowels open, stay in bed if your temperature is above 99°, and call your doctor. Vaccines seem to help a small fraction, and if intelligently given apparently do no harm. Alkalis early in the disease may help with plenty of water, but again the treatment may be worse than the disease and needs medical supervision."

13. *Have you been free from constant or recurring pain?*

How many of us can say, as undoubtedly a few can, "I do not know what a headache is," and how many young women are on their jobs without discomfort every day in every month? We are inclined to be meekly submissive to handicaps of this everyday variety, without stopping to think that most of them can be avoided if we are willing to take pains to find out the cause and correct it. Why not track down the pain and remove the cause? Therein lies the way of escape from aches and pains.

14. *Has your posture been erect in sitting, and with weight on the balls of the feet in standing?*

It is not an easy matter to judge of one's own posture. If you have a friend who knows what good posture is, his criticism will be helpful. However, if you will take a sidewise glance in a long mirror as you stand beside it with head high, weight on the balls of the feet, with abdomen firm and chest up as if it were pulled from the ceiling, you will discover whether you are accomplishing what you are trying for. Try to "stand tall".

In a sitting position, the body should bend only at the kness and hips.

15. *Have you been free from foot troubles?*

If you have to answer no to this question, look first to your shoes. Shoes should fit easily, the sole should have a straight inner line in order to allow the long arch to attain its full height and to allow the great toe to keep its proper position. The heel should be broad enough to steady the foot, and low enough to provide a base for erect posture without bending at the knees. Next consider the angle at which the feet are placed in walking. Toes should point straight forward, not outward. In that way the best mechanical use is made of the foot. The joint at which the toes join the foot is like a hinge. When a gate sags its hinges are soon bent or pulled out of line and its fails to perform its function. It is the same with the foot when its hinge-joint is forced to work at an angle instead of straight forward.

16. *Have you been free from chronic infections, such as disease of gall bladder, tonsils, sinus infection, etc.?*
Any chronic infection should be carefully watched by a physician. Germs of the sort which cause chronic low-grade infections are bad company, and always subject to suspicion. Run them down to their headquarters.

17. *Have you been vaccinated against smallpox twice or more during your life time?*
In order that we may continue to enjoy our present freedom from the ravages of smallpox which once decimated our population, every child should be protected from this disease in early life. If vaccination is done during the first year and again at the age of seven or eight, reasonable protection is afforded for life except as direct exposure is threatened, as in times of epidemic.

18. *Have you been protected from typhoid fever either by having the disease or by three series of inoculations during your life time?*
Protection from typhoid fever by inoculation although often considered unnecessary in a locality in which the disease is rare, as in Massachusetts, is, nevertheless, a wise procedure, especially when a visit is to be made to some region where the disease is less well controlled. Only as the safety of each individual is assured, is the whole community protected.

These are some of the signs of health which taken together may be considered to indicate a sound body, ready to face the world with courage and the joy of living.

II. Now let us turn to some of our daily habits. Are we making the most of our physical assets as measured by the Signs of Health we have been considering?
Every day:
1. *Have you had a liberal amount of tomatoes, raw cabbage, lettuce or greens?*
2. *Have you eaten orange, grapefruit, pineapple or tomato at least once?*
3. *Have you eaten at least one vegetable besides potato?*
4. *Have you eaten at regular hours?*
5. *Have you taken at least a pint of milk, either as such or in combination?*
6. *Have you taken at least 3 pints of fluid?*
7. *Have you chewed your food thoroughly?*
8. *Have you had a natural bowel movement?*
9. *Have you felt comfortable after eating?*

If you have included all these things in your every day diet, and if you can answer in the affirmative all of these questions, you may be satisfied that you have stoked your engine to capacity and in return you may expect it to give good measure of service without annoying squeaks and groans.

10. *Have you averaged an hour out of doors?*
11. *Have you taken adequate active exercise?*

12. *Have you taken at least 10 hours each week for recreation?*
13. *Have you avoided excesses of all kinds?*

Every person must be his own judge of the amount and kind of exercise that is adequate for his own needs. We all agree, however, that we feel better and probably work more efficiently when we have spent some time in the open, and especially when we have indulged in some favorite form of recreation different from our daily work. This may be anything from a lively game of baseball for the young man shut up in the office most of the time and chafing for activity, to his father's mild contentment in raking up the lawn, or his mother's joy in gardening. Without some such outlet, it is difficult for the average individual to adjust himself to the complexities of present-day living.

Again each individual must define "excesses" for himself in relation to his own needs. In the matter of active exercise for instance, what is child's play for the young ball-player might be excess for his father, unthinkable for his mother. The key to a sound policy with regard to physical exercise is a stocktaking of one's whole physical make-up under the guidance of one's personal physician.

Of excesses in food—or drink—perhaps enough has already been said.

14. *Have you had a vacation with complete change of activity within the past year?*

There has been much discussion and wide disagreement as to the most desirable kind of vacation for a particular person. Perhaps after all, there is no more satisfying vacation than that which is found by the fortunate few in the daily enjoyment of absorbing and congenial work giving plenty of variety and satisfying human needs for constructive occupation. However, not many of us are able to make this perfect adjustment to everyday life, hence the need of a break in the daily routine. Change in the kind of activity appears to be the vital factor in a successful vacation rather than a change of scene. Some experience which offers an opportunity to indulge one's favorite tastes and desires, so often suppressed and frustrated in the work-a-day world, seems to bring the greatest reward in freshening one's outlook on life.

15. *Have you worn your clothing sufficiently loose so as not to impair circulation?*

We may be inclined to feel that there is no longer any temptation to a violation of this rule under the dictates of present-day fashion, but we still see men wearing stiff, tight collars which cannot fail to impair the circulation in parts above the collar, and we see stout ladies walking the street, trying to carry their weight, with how much misery to themselves we can only guess, on feet encased in shoes several sizes too small and designed for the ballroom rather than the sidewalk.

16. *Have you had a complete medical examination within the past year?*

17. *Has your dentist examined your teeth within six months?*

18. *If you have physical limitations, do you know them and have you lived within them?*

The periodic medical examination is really the crux of the whole problem of the preservation of such individual health as we have. Especially is this true with young children and with adults after the age of forty and on through life.

19. *If you had a cold or sore throat, with fever, did you remain in bed?*

If this precaution were generally followed, it might in large measure be the means of preventing the spread of colds and their complications, at the same time offering the victim of the cold his best chance of prompt recovery with exemption from the payment of a toll in the coin of chronic disease in later life.

The attitude toward his fellow-beings of a person suffering from a fresh cold serves as a good index of the intelligent application of health etiquette.

* * * * *

One writer on personal health has recently said,[4] "Though some afflictions cannot be prevented, probably 75 per cent can be warded off or controlled through hygiene and medical knowledge now at hand."

This ideal can be achieved only when each person acts as guardian of his own personal health. He must know where he stands, and this he must find out by means of a careful stocktaking by and with his own physician, one who is able to distinguish slight deviations from the normal and who is interested to help his patients preserve such health as they have, and to gain as much more as is possible. Together, patient and physician may outline a plan by which the individual learns to make the most of his assets and either to overcome, or to submit to his liabilities. It is in this way, through signs which only a physician can recognize that the chronic diseases to which persons of middle age are prone may often be detected in their beginnings, at a time when proper treatment may forestall possible disaster later on. To become acquainted with our physical machine and its complicated parts enable us the more skillfully to handle it. We hope the Health Score may serve as a first step toward such acquaintance and that it may aid each participant in his search for the best health of which he is capable. Is the game not worth playing? If you would like to join in, drop us a line asking for a copy of the Health Score Card.

THE HEALTH SCORE

Signs of Health

		Points
1.	Do you feel completely rested when you arise in the morning?	50
2.	Can you do as much as your associates without undue fatigue?	50
3.	Have you appetite for wholesome food?	30
4.	Are you free from signs of indigestion?	30
5.	Do you get on well with most people?	20
6.	Do you have confidence in yourself?	30
7.	Are you free from persistent worry?	30
8.	Can you relax at will?	30
9.	Is your skin clear? Natural color good?	20
10.	Is your vision good or corrected by glasses?	20
11.	Can you hear ordinary conversation at distance of 16 feet, with both ears?	20
12.	Have you been free from infections, including colds?	40
13.	Have you been free from constant or recurring pain?	30
14.	Has your posture been erect in sitting, and with weight on the balls of the feet in standing?	20
15.	Have you been free from foot troubles?	20
16.	Have you been free from chronic infections, such as gall bladder, tonsils, sinuses, etc.?	30
17.	Have you been vaccinated against smallpox twice or more during your life time?	20
18.	Have you been protected from typhoid fever either by having the disease or by three series of inoculations during your life time?	10
	"Signs of Health" Score	500

HEALTH HABITS

Every day:
Points

1. Have you had a liberal amount of tomatoes, raw cabbage, lettuce or greens? 40
2. Have you eaten orange, grapefruit, pineapple or tomato at least once? 40
3. Have you eaten at least one vegetable besides potato? . . 20
4. Have you eaten at regular hours? 20
5. Have you taken at least a pint of milk, either as such or in combination? 20
6. Have you taken at least 3 pints of fluid? 20
7. Have you chewed your food thoroughly? 10
8. Have you had a natural bowel movement? 30
9. Have you felt comfortable after eating? 20
10. Have you averaged an hour out of doors? 25
11. Have you taken adequate active exercise? 30

* * * * *

12. Have you taken at least 10 hours each week for recreation? . 20
13. Have you avoided excesses of all kinds? 30
14. Have you had a vacation with complete change of activity within the past year? 30
15. Have you worn your clothing sufficiently loose so as not to impair circulation? 20
16. Have you had a complete medical examination within the past year? 30
17. Has your dentist examined your teeth within 6 months? . . 25
18. If you have physical limitations, do you know them and have you lived within them? 30
19. If you had a cold or sore throat, with fever, did you remain in bed? 40

Health Habits Score 500
Signs of Health Score 500

Total Score 1000

References

[1] LAIRD, DONALD A., Ph.D., SC. D. and MULLER, CHARLES G., *Sleep*, New York: The John Day Company, 1930.
[2] CANNON, WALTER B., M.D., *Bodily Changes in Pain, Hunger, Fear and Rage*, New York: Appleton, 1915.
[3] SMILEY, DEAN FRANKLIN, GOULD, ADRIAN GORDON, and MELBY, ELIZABETH, *The Principles and Practice of Hygiene*, New York: Macmillan, 1930.
[4] HAYHURST, EMERY R., *Personal Health*, New York: McGraw Hill Book Company, 1927.

WHAT SHALL WE EAT?

Though most of us have come to recognize that the diet of growing children should contain certain food elements in generally accepted proportions, we are likely to overlook the fact that it also makes a difference what kind of food we grown-ups eat.

Dr. Henry C. Sherman has shown in feeding experiments with animals that by increasing certain elements in the diet, even beyond the amounts which have been found necessary to keep the creatures in good health, he has been able to increase physical vigor, quicken development and postpone the effects of old age. While there are material differences in the physiologic processes as between animals and human beings, nutritional principles apply in general to one as to the other.

The mature man or woman will do well to note now and again whether the daily diet includes:

Milk: At least one pint of milk, either as a drink, with cereals, in cocoa, in soups, sauces and puddings, or in any other form. Milk is the one common food which more than any other helps to supply the body needs for lime.
It contributes especially:
    Lime for bones and teeth,
    Protein for growth and repair of muscles and other parts of the body,
    Fat and sugar for energy,
    Vitamin A for health and vigor.

Cereals: Some whole grain, either as a cereal or in whole grain bread.
Whole grain, or "dark" bread or cereal gives:
    Iron for the blood,
    Starch for energy,
    Vitamin B for health and vigor.

Vegetables: Always one raw, and a leafy or yellow or green-colored vegetable, such as cabbage or lettuce, besides potato.
Vegetables, if one is a leafy or a raw vegetable, furnish:
    Lime for bones and teeth,
    Iron for healthy blood,
    Sugar for energy,
    Various vitamins for health and vigor.

Fruits: Fresh, canned or dried. An orange, grapefruit, pineapple or tomato (either fresh or canned) should be included for Vitamin C.
Fruits, if one is a tomato or an orange, give:
    Calcium for bones and teeth,
    Iron for healthy blood,
    Sugar for energy,
    Various vitamins for health and vigor.

Protein: Meat, fish, eggs, cheese, milk, nuts, and dried beans or peas. The proportionate amount of protein food in the diet should vary according to age and the actual bulk of the body. With advancing years and in hot weather the demand for protein food is lessened and it is wise to limit the amount taken.
Meat, fish, eggs, cheese, milk, nuts, and dried beans or peas give:
    Proteins for repair of body tissue,
    Iron for blood,
    Vitamin G for health and vigor.

Fats: About two tablespoonfuls of butter or cream, or a teaspoonful of cod liver oil every day, and occasionally servings of bacon and other fats, give:
    Fats for energy,
    Vitamins A and D for health and vigor.

Sweets: Natural sugars in molasses, honey, dried fruits and maple syrup give:
    Iron and minerals for healthy blood,
    Sugar for energy.
Refined sugar gives energy only.

After all, the sum and substance of a good, all-round diet for every day means a variety of foods which will include an abundance of vegetables and fruits and at least one pint of milk, and three or four eggs a week.

The person who is convinced that he owes his energy and sense of well-being in large measure to the food he eats, and who systematically chooses those foods best fitted to keep the body functioning at full capacity, is simply applying to his human mechanism the same intelligence which is expected of the stoker who supplies his furnace with that kind of fuel which gives best results in terms of heat and economy.

THE RADIO
HERBERT L. LOMBARD, M.D.
Director, Division of Adult Hygiene,
Massachusetts Department of Public Health

The evaluation of educational material of all types in public health is greatly to be desired. Various attempts to do this have been made at different times. The most significant one dealt with the relation of publicity to attendance at the State-aided cancer clinics. This brought out the fact that ten persons go to the State-aided cancer clinics as a result of newspaper publicity to every one who goes because of all other types of publicity combined.

There is the possibility that the exciting force which would send a person to a cancer clinic may differ from one which would change his daily habits of living. There is also the possibility that those who stated that they came to the State-aided cancer clinics because of articles they had read in the newspapers may have been sufficiently stimulated by other types of publicity in the past, and the final article they read in the newspapers was the culminating, rather than the sole, cause. The failure to remember frequent repetitions of an idea which may be presented in many different ways makes evaluation of educational work most difficult. An individual may hear on the radio that a lump is to be regarded as a possible cancer and years later, developing a lump, may not remember where the idea was first implanted. To actually measure the end results of publicity is practically impossible. The best that can be attained is far short of this. A measurement of the number of individuals listening to a radio program can be done. How many follow the advice given cannot be obtained.

For the past year the Massachusetts Department of Public Health has been attempting to obtain some measure of the value of the radio programs which have been given. Three broadcasts are given each week: one prepared by the Massachusetts Medical Society on some phase of medicine; another by the personnel of the Department on some phase of public health; and a third, the Health Forum, which answers questions that have been sent by the radio audience.

The answers given in the Health Forum are also printed in sixty-six newspapers in the State. During the year 1933, 389 individuals sent questions to the Department. Of this number 143 mentioned the Radio Health Forum, 70 the Newspaper Health Forum, while 176 did not state which prompted the correspondence. It is not known how this latter group should be allocated, to the radio or the newspaper, but if we assume the unknowns fall similarly to the knowns the radio appears to be of greater value than the newspaper. Requests to the Department for literature is an even stronger indication of the relative value of the radio. Sixty per cent came from radio listeners, 9 per cent from newspaper readers, and 31 per cent failed to mention whether radio or newspaper.

Questionnaires were sent to 2,810 individuals asking them if they listened to the various radio programs. Every family in one town of Metropolitan Boston was questioned and a random sample from the Boston Telephone Directory comprised the remainder. A response of 10 per cent was obtained from these questionnaires. It is impossible to determine whether those who did not answer were listeners in the same degree as those who did, or whether they all belong to the non-listener group.

The accompanying table shows the replies received. Two sets of percentages have been computed: the first based on the number who returned the questionnaire, and the second on the population to whom questionnaires were sent. If the sample returned is representative of the total group, the first set of percentages apply; if all those who did not answer belonged to the non-listener group, the second set applies. It is probable that the true figure lies somewhere between these two estimates.

A sample of Metropolitan Boston may not be indicative of Massachusetts as a whole, but the distribution of individuals who have replied to our Radio Health Forum suggests a State-wide character to our activities.

By adopting the smaller percentages, which we definitely feel to be too low, and assuming that these percentages would apply to Massachusetts as a whole, we estimate that at least twelve thousand individuals are regularly listening to one or more of the Department broadcasts. Similar computations give ten thousand regular listeners to the Massachusetts Medical Society broadcasts, slightly less to the Department broadcasts, and about seven thousand to the Health Forum. Inasmuch as all those who did not reply have been considered as non-listeners, these figures seem extremely conservative and, in all probability, the true figures are considerably greater.

The individuals were questioned as to listening to other health broadcasts. The only two which were mentioned by more than a few individuals were Dr. Bundesen with twenty listeners and Dr. Copeland with twenty-six. As these figures included both regular and occasional listeners, it is evident that the Massachusetts programs are more popular in this locality than the others.

The number of replies received were too small to make any but tentative conclusions, but they do indicate that health subjects on the radio are being listened to by a considerable part of the population.

Results of Radio Questionnaire

	Number Returned	Questionnaires Per Cent Returned	Per Cent Received
Regularly listened to all three of the broadcasts	15	5.0	0.5
Regularly listened to one or two of the broadcasts	18	6.0	0.6
Occasionally listened to one or more of the broadcasts	74	24.5	2.6
Never listened to any of the broadcasts	143	47.3	5.1
Did not answer questions	8	2.6	0.3
No radio	44	14.6	1.6
Total	302	100.0	10.7
Regularly listened to the Massachusetts Medical Society Broadcasts	28	9.3	1.0
Regularly listened to the Department broadcasts	27	8.9	1.0
Regularly listened to the Health Forum	20	6.6	0.7

News Note

American Public Health Association Annual Meeting

The American Public Health Association announces that its Sixty-third Annual Meeting will be held in Pasadena, California, September 3-6, 1934. The Western Branch of the American Public Health Association, with a membership of more than 1,200 from eleven western states, will hold its Fifth Annual Meeting at the same time.

Dr. J. D. Dunshee, Health Officer of Pasadena, has been appointed Chairman of the Local Committee on Arrangements. He will be assisted by Dr. John L. Pomeroy, President, and Dr. W. P. Shepard, Secretary of the Western Branch, and other prominent public health authorities on the west coast.

REPORT OF DIVISION OF FOOD AND DRUGS

During the months of October, November and December 1933, samples were collected in 180 cities and towns.

There were 1,159 samples of milk examined, of which 66 were below standard, from 10 samples the cream had been in part removed, and 1 sample contained added water. There were 61 samples of Grade A milk examined, 1 sample of which was below the legal standard of 4.00% fat. There were 974 bacteriological examinations made of milk, 868 of which complied with the requirements. There were 14 samples examined for hemolytic streptococci, all of which were negative.

There were 776 samples of food examined, of which 211 were adulterated or misbranded. These consisted of 3 samples of cream which were not labeled in accordance with the law; 59 samples of eggs, 13 of which were sold as fresh eggs but were not fresh, 4 were decomposed, and 42 samples were cold storage not so marked; 10 samples of vanilla extract, all of which contained coumarin; 2 samples of lemon extract which were adulterated and misbranded; 3 samples of maple syrup which contained cane sugar; 43 samples of hamburg steak, 12 samples of sausage, 1 sample of pork kidneys, and 14 samples of liver, all of which were decomposed; 45 samples of hamburg steak:—16 samples of which contained sodium sulphite in excess of one tenth of one per cent and 5 were also decomposed; 24 samples contained a compound of sulphur dioxide not properly labeled, 10 of which were also decomposed, and 3 samples also contained added water; and 5 samples contained added water, 1 sample of which also contained sodium sulphite in excess of one tenth of one per cent, and 2 samples were also decomposed; 16 samples of sausage, 13 of which contained a compound of sulphur dioxide not properly labeled, and 3 samples contained sodium sulphite in excess of one tenth of one per cent; 2 samples of dried fruit which contained sulphur dioxide not properly labeled; and 1 sample of beef which was decomposed.

There were 127 samples of drugs examined, of which 6 were adulterated. These consisted of 3 samples of camphorated oil, 2 samples of spirit of nitrous ether, and 1 sample of tincture of iodine, all of which did not conform to the U. S. P. requirements.

The police departments submitted 678 samples of liquor for examination. The police departments also submitted 26 samples to be analyzed for poisons or drugs, 1 sample of which contained opium, 1 sample contained morphine, 9 samples contained heroin, 1 sample contained heroin hydrochloride, 1 sample contained ethyl alcohol, 1 sample showed quinine sulphate, 2 samples contained a small amount of sugar, 1 sample of pork chops was examined for poison with negative results, 1 sample had the appearance of Cannabis Indica, and 8 samples were examined for narcotics or other poisons with negative results.

There were 84 cities and town visited for the inspection of pasteurizing plants, and 239 plants were inspected.

There were 60 hearings held pertaining to violations of the laws.

There were 126 convictions for violations of the law, $2,940 in fines being imposed.

Dutchland Farms, Incorporated, of Brockton; John Soares of Taunton; Arthur W. Cyr of Salem; Joseph Dobrowski of Adams; John C. Taylor of Bedford; and Adam Maslowski of New Junction, New Hampshire, were all convicted for violations of the milk laws.

Herlihy Brothers, Incorporated, of Somerville, was convicted for violation of the Grade A Milk regulations.

Harry Feldman, 3 cases, of Everett, was convicted for violations of the pasteurization laws and regulations. He appealed the three cases.

Fred L. Irons, 2 cases, and Harold Oxman of Malden; Julius E. Rams of Lee; H. L. Green Chain Stores, Incorporated, and The Great Atlantic & Pacific Tea Company of Pittsfield; Armour & Company, Max Belkins and Israel Swerdlick, all of Boston; William H. Cowddaire of Attleboro; Abraham Andelman, Frank Santos, The Great Atlantic & Pacific Tea Company, New England Markets, Incorporated, and Victor Alpert, all of Cambridge; Arthur Corey of Lawrence; Economy Grocery Company, 2 cases, and Benjamin Solomon of Greenfield; Julius Kronick, Samuel Richton and Harry Leavitte, all of North Adams; Henry E. L'Heureux of Salem; Morris Sawyer, George Eskow, and Saul Sawyer, all of Taunton; North Main Market, Incorporated, Samuel Abelson, Louis Market, Incorporated, The Great Atlantic & Pacific Tea Company, Empire Beef Company, 2 cases, Brockelman Brothers, Incorporated, 2 cases, and Israel Gillette, all of Worcester; The Great Atlantic & Pacific Tea Company of North Attleboro; The Great Atlantic & Pacific Tea Company, Massachusetts Mohican Company, and Harry Weinstein, all of Waltham; Brockelman Brothers, Incorporated, of Leominster; Hyman Goldkrand and Enrico Moro of Medford; Abraham Holland, Phillip Kaller, John Seaman, Barney Israel, Abraham Miller, Nathan Herman, 2 cases, Robert Kravitz, 2 cases, Samuel Schuster, 2 cases, and Leo Rocheleau, all of New Bedford; Max Hirsch, 3 cases, of Allston; Harry Brock, William Dee, Benjamin Gross, Hyman Racoff, Samuel R. Berkman, 3 cases, and Louis Siegal, 3 cases, all of Roxbury; Grand Union Stores, Incorporated, of Williamstown; Lewis Zass and Everybody's Market, Incorporated, 4 cases, of Fall River; Sarah Ferman (Lincoln Square Market) 2 cases, of Milford; John Gerogosian and John F. Ruggieri of Somerville; Woburn Provision Company, 2 cases, of Everett; Lewis Goldman and Jack Levy of Lynn; Alice Handler and Harry Ring of Brookline; August Kisiel of Ware; Needle & Davis, Incorporated, of Dorchester; and Edward Rossman, 2 cases, and Millie Shavitsky of Revere, were all convicted for violations of the food laws. Arthur Corey of Lawrence; Hyman Goldkrand of Medford; Samuel Schuster, 2 cases, of New Bedford; and Benjamin Gross, Hyman Racoff, and Samuel R. Berkman, 3 cases, all of Roxbury, all appealed their cases.

Harry Cohen of Greenfield; and Philip Vigoda of Brookline, were convicted for misbranding.

Harry Miller and M. Winer Company of Worcester; Samuel Richton of North Adams; Mary Britto of New Bedford; Samuel R. Berkman, Incorporated, and Samuel Feldman of Roxbury; and Massachusetts Mohican Company of Salem, were all convicted for false advertising.

Leo Raftery of Lee; Morris Corfine and Charles Risman of Revere; Armour & Company and Barney Greenberg of Fall River; Israel Cookis and James Samia of North Adams; Raymond Donoghue and Morris Finkle of Somerville; George Kelsey Company, Incorporated, of Pittsfield; John Kinder of Norwood; Frank Santos of Cambridge; and Philip Vigoda of Brookline, were all convicted for violations of the cold storage laws. Barney Greenberg of Fall River appealed his case.

Benjamin Libow and Philip Orenstein of Springfield; Morris and Samuel Milston of Lawrence; Lewis Pellett of Holyoke; and Joseph Weisman of Haverhill, were all convicted for violations of the mattress laws.

In accordance with Section 25, Chapter 111 of the General Laws, the following is the list of articles of adulterated food collected in original packages from manufacturers, wholesalers, or producers:

Two samples of cream which were incorrectly graded were obtained from C. L. Woodland of Watertown.

One sample of dried pears which contained sulphur dioxide not properly labeled was obtained from Growers Outlet of Greenfield.

One sample of lemon extract which was adulterated and misbranded was obtained from Famous Products Company of Malden.

Vanilla Extract which contained coumarin was obtained as follows:

Two samples from Clover Farms Stores of Waltham; and 1 sample each, from Clover Farms Stores of Sterling, Worcester, and West Brookfield, and Famous Products Company of Malden.

Maple Syrup which contained cane sugar was obtained as follows:

One sample each, from Grand Union Company of Pittsfield; Crown

Luncheonette of Worcester; and Harry Schneider of Roxbury.

Hamburg steak which was decomposed was obtained as follows:

One sample each, from Fred Uhlit, and The Great Atlantic & Pacific Tea Company of Pittsfield; United Meat Market (Maurice Foster), New England Markets, Incorporated, The Great Atlantic & Pacific Tea Company, Abraham Andelman, and Victor Alpert, all of Cambridge; Nathan Fishman of Allston; Lewis Goldman and Jack Levy (Clinton Market) of Lynn; Solin's Market, Incorporated (New York Cash Market) of Chicopee; Lincoln Square Market, Hyman Karp (Empire Beef Company), Brockelman Brothers, Samuel Abelson, and Jack Jacobson, all of Worcester; Alexander Beaudry and Arthur Gaudreault of Lowell; John Klys of Indian Orchard; Felix Pasay of Ware; The Great Atlantic & Pacific Tea Company, and Benjamin Solomon of Greenfield; Sarah Ferman (Lincoln Square Market) of Milford; Lewis Zass and Everybody's Super-Market of Fall River; Peoples Market, B. & M. Market, and Samuel Schuster, all of New Bedford; Harry Kronick of North Adams; Saul Sawyer of Taunton; Louis Public Market, The Great Atlantic & Pacific Tea Company, and Mohican Market, all of Waltham; Samuel Halpern of Westboro; Henry E. L'heurex of Salem; Malden Square Market of Malden; Brock's Market and Hyman Racoff of Roxbury; Woburn Provision Company, Incorporated, and Julius Cohen of Everett; and J. Shafran & Sons of Brookline; and 2 samples, from Economy Grocery Company of Greenfield.

Hamburg steak which contained a compound of sulphur dioxide not properly labeled and was also decomposed was obtained as follows:

One sample each, from Samuel Cohen of Boston; Nathan Needlman of Chelsea; The Great Atlantic & Pacific Tea Company of Malden; Enrico Moro (Moro Market) of Milford; Hyman Karp (Empire Beef Company) of Worcester; John F. Ruggieri of Somerville; Edward Rossman of Beachmont; Clover Farm Stores, and Robert Kravitz of New Bedford; and William Dee of Roxbury.

Hamburg steak which contained sodium sulphite in excess of one tenth of one per cent and was also decomposed was obtained as follows:

One sample each, from Israel Goldenberg of Boston; Abraham Miller of New Bedford; Needle & Davis, Incorporated, of Mattapan; Barron's Market of Cambridge; and Quality Market of Somerville.

Hamburg steak which contained added water and was also decomposed was obtained as follows:

One sample each, from Rood & Woodbury of Springfield; and Morris Sawyer of Taunton.

Hamburg steak which contained added water was obtained as follows:

One sample each, from Ganem's Market of Lawrence; and Benjamin Barron (Big Chief Store) of Chelsea.

Hamburg steak which contained a compound of sulphur dioxide not properly labeled and also contained added water was obtained as follows:

One sample each, from Max Baker of Roxbury, Abraham Shavitsky of Revere, and Harry Ring of Brookline.

Hamburg steak which contained sodium sulphite in excess of one tenth of one per cent and also contained added water was obtained as follows:

One sample, from Israel Swerdlick of Boston.

Hamburg steak which contained sodium sulphite in excess of one tenth of one per cent was obtained as follows:

Two samples, from Harry Leavitte of North Adams; and one sample each, from Sirloin Store of Malden; Clover Farm Stores of Ware; Max Comman of Cambridge; Mrs. Rebecca Wernick and Joseph Waldman of Roxbury; Peoples Cash Market and Simon Kronick of North Adams; Phillip Shwachman of Lynn; and Peoples Market of New Bedford.

Hamburg steak which contained a compound of sulphur dioxide not properly labeled was obtained as follows:

Two samples each, from The Great Atlantic & Pacific Tea Company of Springfield; and S. S. Kresge Company of Roxbury; and one sample each, from Stanley P. Chosek of Chicopee; George Eskow of Taunton; Sam Lipsky, Reuben Porter, and Mrs. Handler, all of Brookline; Smith's Food Shop of Cambridge; and Jacob Green of Roxbury.

Sausage which was decomposed was obtained as follows:

Three samples from John Klys of Indian Orchard; and one sample each, from H. L. Green Company of Pittsfield; Samuel Richton of North Adams; Economy Grocery Company of Greenfield; Sarah Ferman (Lincoln Square Market) of Milford; Store at 110 West Street, Chicopee; Shelburne Falls Public Market of Shelburne Falls; and Joseph Pasay of Ware.

Sausage which contained a compound of sulphur dioxide not properly labeled was obtained as follows:

Two samples, from Progresso Cash Market of Quincy; and one sample each, from Northampton Public Market and The Great Atlantic & Pacific Tea Company of Northampton; John F. Ruggieri, Quality Market, Jerry Di Sola, and Cosimo Nardella, all of Somerville; Big Chief Store of Chelsea; D. Petrini Company of Boston; Solin's Market (New York Cash Market), and Stanley P. Chosek of Chicopee.

Sausage which contained sodium sulphite in excess of one tenth of one per cent was obtained as follows:

One sample each, from Compton Market of Boston; William J. Lacroix of Chicopee Falls; and Max Comman of Cambridge.

Liver which was decomposed was obtained as follows:

Two samples, from Everybody's Super Market of Fall River; and one sample each, from Samuel Schuster of New Bedford; Brockelman Brothers of Worcester; Melvin's Market, Incorporated, and Francis J. Mello of Fall River; Samuel Dovner of Taunton; Solin's Market, Incorporated (New York Cash Market) of Chicopee; William J. Lacroix of Chicopee Falls; Rood & Woodbury of Springfield; Joseph Pasay of Ware; Blotner's Market of Beverly; Store at 238 Columbus Avenue, Pittsfield; and Wellworth Market of Roxbury.

One sample of pork kidneys which was decomposed was obtained from Tremont Market of Worcester.

One sample of dried fruits which contained sulphur dioxide not properly labeled was obtained from Grand Union Stores, Incorporated, of Williamstown.

There were seven confiscations, consisting of 250 pounds of decomposed carp; 3,500 pounds of dried out mackerel; 135 pounds of dried out sand eels; 500 pounds of dried out sardine herring; 950 pounds of decomposed shilli (canned fish); 200 pounds of dried out smelts; and 250 pounds of dried out red snappers.

The licensed cold storage warehouses reported the following amounts of food placed in storage during September, 1933:—284,730 dozens of case eggs; 445,800 pounds of broken out eggs; 901,973 pounds of butter; 1,033,190 pounds of poultry; 1,988,929½ pounds of fresh meat and fresh meat products; and 5,132,248 pounds of fresh food fish.

There was on hand October 1, 1933:—5,489,820 dozens of case eggs; 3,069,900 pounds of broken out eggs; 11,242,715 pounds of butter; 4,574,212 pounds of poultry; 6,248,331 pounds of fresh meat and fresh meat products; and 23,892,542 pounds of fresh food fish.

The licensed cold storage warehouses reported the following amounts of food placed in storage during October, 1933:—338,730 dozens of case eggs; 324,090 pounds of broken out eggs; 507,892 pounds of butter; 831,486 pounds of poultry, 1,623,791 pounds of fresh meat and fresh meat products; and 3,702,777 pounds of fresh food fish.

There was on hand November 1, 1933:—3,378,900 dozens of case eggs; 2,627,816 pounds of broken out eggs; 8,873,990 pounds of butter; 4,673,316 pounds of poultry; 4,437,241½ pounds of fresh meat and fresh meat products; and 22,100,008 pounds of fresh food fish.

The licensed cold storage warehouses reported the following amounts of food placed in storage during November, 1933:—340,200 dozens of case eggs; 417,878 pounds of broken out eggs; 618,379 pounds of butter; 2,378,872½ pounds of poultry; 2,985,753 pounds of fresh meat and fresh meat products; and 3,605,271 pounds of fresh food fish.

There was on hand December 1, 1933:—1,450,710 dozens of case eggs; 2,382,929 pounds of broken out eggs; 5,708,703 pounds of butter; 6,262,838½ pounds of poultry; 4,652,303¼ pounds of fresh meat and fresh meat products; and 20,155,005 pounds of fresh food fish.

MASSACHUSETTS DEPARTMENT OF PUBLIC HEALTH

Commissioner of Public Health, HENRY D. CHADWICK, M.D.

Public Health Council
HENRY D. CHADWICK, M.D., *Chairman*

ROGER I. LEE, M.D.
SYLVESTER E. RYAN, M.D.
FRANCIS H. LALLY, M.D.
RICHARD P. STRONG, M.D.
JAMES L. TIGHE.
GORDON HUTCHINS.

Secretary, ALICE M. NELSON

Division of Administration	Under direction of Commissioner.
Division of Sanitary Engineering	Director and Chief Engineer, ARTHUR D. WESTON, C.E.
Division of Communicable Diseases	Director, GAYLORD W. ANDERSON, M.D.
Division of Biologic Laboratories	Director and Pathologist, ELLIOTT S. ROBINSON, M.D.
Division of Food and Drugs	Director and Analyst, HERMANN C. LYTHGOE, S.B.
Division of Child Hygiene	Director, M. LUISE DIEZ, M.D.
Division of Tuberculosis	Director, ALTON S. POPE, M.D.
Division of Adult Hygiene	Director, HERBERT L. LOMBARD, M.D.

State District Health Officers

The Southeastern District	RICHARD P. MACKNIGHT, M.D., New Bedford.
The Metropolitan District	CHARLES B. MACK, M.D., Boston
The Northeastern District	ROBERT E. ARCHIBALD, M.D., Lynn.
The Worcester County District	OSCAR A. DUDLEY, M.D., Worcester.
The Connecticut Valley District	HAROLD E. MINER, M.D., Springfield.
The Berkshire District	WALTER W. LEE, M.D., No. Adams.

PUBLICATION OF THIS DOCUMENT APPROVED BY THE COMMISSION ON ADMINISTRATION AND FINANCE.
6M. 2-'34. Order 614.

THE COMMONHEALTH

VOLUME 21   APRIL-MAY-JUNE
No. 2   1934

DIABETES

MASSACHUSETTS DEPARTMENT OF PUBLIC HEALTH

THE COMMONHEALTH
QUARTERLY BULLETIN OF THE MASSACHUSETTS DEPARTMENT OF PUBLIC HEALTH

Sent Free to any Citizen of the State

Entered as second class matter at Boston Postoffice.

M. LUISE DIEZ, M.D., DIRECTOR OF DIVISION OF CHILD HYGIENE, EDITOR.

Room 545, State House, Boston, Mass.

CONTENTS

	PAGE
Diabetes, by Elliott P. Joslin, M.D.	56
The Historical Trend of Diabetes, by Eleanor J. Macdonald, A.B.	57
Diabetes in Massachusetts, by H. L. Lombard, M.D., Anne A. Boris, and Sadie Minsky	65
Treatment of Diabetes, by Elliot P. Joslin, M.D.	74
Diabetic Diets	76
Treatment of Diabetes Pays, by Elliott P. Joslin, M.D.	77
Insulin and Diabetes, by Elliott P. Joslin, M.D.	78
Cost of Diabetic Treatment, by Elliott P. Joslin, M.D.	81
Discharge Directions	82
Outline of Course of Talks for Diabetics	86
The Laboratory, by Hazel Hunt	88
Diabetic Coma, by Alexander Marble, M.D.	88
Coma, by George H. Bigelow, M.D.	93
Gangrene and Surgery in Diabetes, by Howard F. Root, M.D.	93
Tuberculosis in Diabetics, by Alton S. Pope, M.D.	96
Pregnancy in Diabetes, by Priscilla White, M.D.	98
Fractures in Elderly Diabetics, by H. F. Root, M.D., Priscilla White, M.D., and A. Marble, M.D.	101
Diabetic Child of Today, by Priscilla White, M.D.	103
Heredity of Diabetes, by Priscilla White, M.D.	109
Diabetic Camps, by Priscilla White, M.D.	111
Social Problems Facing Diabetic Patients, by Helen M. Bauer	114
What Do People Need to Know About Diabetes?, by Mary R. Lakeman, M.D.	117
Health Services of Tomorrow, by Thomas Parran, Jr., M.D.	120
Report of Division of Food and Drugs, January, February and March, 1934	127

At the request of the Massachusetts Department of Public Health I am submitting a group of papers upon diabetes for The Commonhealth from the George F. Baker Clinic. I am glad to comply but as a matter of fact my own part in the undertaking is represented simply by a letter to the Health Commissioner, Dr. Henry D. Chadwick, to which Dr. Lombard has given a title, a radio talk upon insulin, a short summary on the treatment of diabetes, a few words to show that treatment pays and a word upon the cost of diabetic treatment.

ELLIOTT P. JOSLIN.

DIABETES

ELLIOTT P. JOSLIN, M.D.

The accompanying chart shows what has been taking place with diabetes in Massachusetts during this century. For diabetics under twenty years of age the death rate in 1932 was the lowest yet attained and for those above the age of fifty it was the highest, due largely to the aging of our population. But progress must not cease. If the disease is even more vigorously treated with diet and insulin and the patient better informed regarding his own perils the mortality rates between the ages of twenty and forty-nine also can be lowered and the average age of those succumbing to the disease can be advanced. No case should be allowed to drift. Minor complications as well as serious infections and major operations will be tolerated if the diabetes is aggressively attacked and controlled by the adjustment of diet and insulin to the needs of the moment.

Cancer in a diabetic should be detected early and more than the usual percentage of cures obtained, because the doctor has the diabetic under constant supervision.

To tuberculosis the diabetic is subject today just as he was in the last century. He no longer leads a sheltered life. Always in obtaining the history one should inquire for contact with tuberculous cases, and never wait for physical signs in suspicious cases. An immediate X-ray alone will make possible an early diagnosis. General realization of this fact is still lacking. The former late diagnoses explain the supposed sudden advances of the tuberculous process in a diabetic. As a matter of fact, even cavities in a diabetic will heal and the disease become arrested. Surely secure an X-ray.

Gangrene is more hopeful in a diabetic than in a non-diabetic, because (1) it comes on more slowly, thus giving time for the formation of a collateral blood supply; (2) it frequently develops as a sequel to an inflammatory process which can be removed or healed; and (3) it is favored by the diabetes and this is susceptible to treatment. Little can be done for the purely senile type of gangrene. Diabetic gangrene can be prevented by avoidance of injuries to the feet, whereas this is far less a factor in senile gangrene which is so frequently embolic or thrombotic. The diabetic must be drilled to keep his feet clean and not to injure them with ill-fitting or worn out shoes and hot water bags or other appliances. The feet of a diabetic over forty years of age should be inspected at each visit to the doctor.

Diabetic coma today shows neglect on the part of someone. A death is as blamable as a death from diphtheria. Patients can avoid coma if they will report illness to their physician and he in turn will aggressively combat it. Insulin should never be wholly omitted just because one feels "sick" or does not eat a meal, particularly if sugar is present in the urine. Time is required quite as much as skill in treating coma. Recovery can be achieved only by painstakingly watching (1) the effect of insulin (20 to 50 units) from hour to hour upon the symptoms of the patient and upon the sugar in the urine or blood or better in both; (2) the effect upon the blood pressure of salt solution, solutions of glucose or even transfusion; (3) the tolerance of the stomach for liquids, often alone made possible by gastric lavage. If the doctor has not the time or the facilities for treating coma, then he should take advantage of a hospital. All hospitals should regard comas as emergencies and just as the visiting surgeons decide about all operations, so the visiting physicians should supervise the treatment of coma. The responsibility of treating diabetic coma should not be left in the hands of a house officer who may have never seen a case.

Diabetic fatalities from cancer, tuberculosis, gangrene and coma can be reduced and, in the case of coma, practically abolished, provided the patient is taught about his disease, follows his diet, takes insulin when necessary, and provided the doctor is always alert and when his own time is not available will ask a fellow practitioner to help him or will send the patient to a hospital.

DIABETES MELLITUS
By Age Groups
Massachusetts—1900-1932

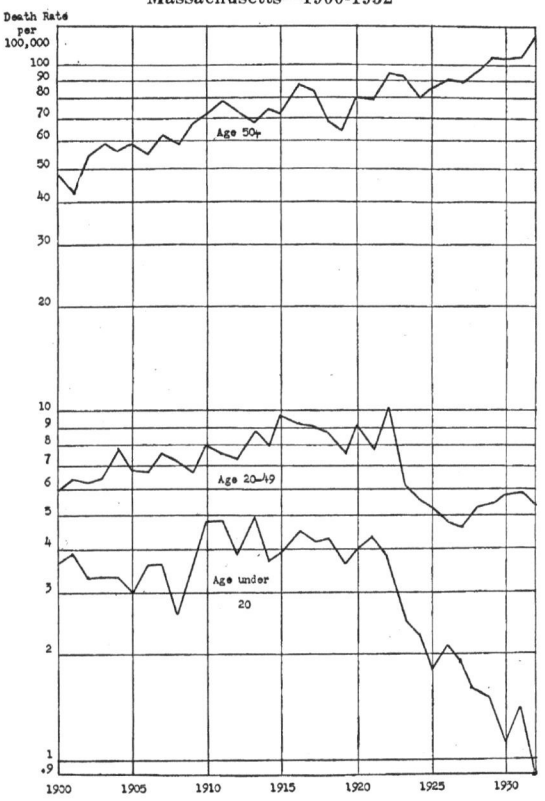

THE HISTORICAL TREND OF DIABETES
ELEANOR J. MACDONALD, A.B.
Statistician, Division of Adult Hygiene,
Massachusetts Department of Public Health

The dependence of advance on exact information derived from scientific and sound investigation is no more evident in any disease than in diabetes mellitus. Most unsupported statements, even if true, are disregarded by scientists today and this attitude toward unproved things is a common heritage with the past. It will be necessary to omit many investigators in the history of diabetes because their discoveries had no direct effect on the future of the disease.

In studying the records of the ancient writers, it is remarkable to find clinical descriptions of disease similar to those of today, but when one reads on, it becomes apparent that the description was the limit of information, for science was in a groping state and when it came upon problems that needed our present knowledge of anatomy, physiology, chemistry, and pathology to solve, these writers usually left the field of certain knowledge for that of conjecture, and the errors made in this natural way by respected and conscientious men left their mark on diabetes by retarding its eventual solution. The remarkable feature in the history of diabetes is the enormous number of serious men* who have worked on it and the two thousand years of patient study it represents.

"Diabetes mellitus is a disease of metabolism based on defect in the body's power to store and oxidize carbohydrates due to a decrease in the internal secretion of the pancreas, and marked by an abnormal amount of sugar in the blood and by the passage of an excessive amount of urine containing an excessive amount of sugar." The evolution of this definition is the story of diabetes.

Celsus defined the disease about 50 A. D. and advised treatment and a diet. He introduced one idea which has persisted—that the urine excreted exceeded the amount of liquid intake in the diet. Aretaeus of Cappadocia, writing in the first century, described diabetes among other diseases in the first part of his work, and suggested treatment for it in the second section. Aretaeus is the one who gave diabetes its name which, translated roughly from the Greek, means "to run through a siphon," and suggests clearly the picture of the disease in his mind. Osler quotes the translation of the description of diabetes given by Aretaeus as "melting down the flesh and bones into urine." Galen (131-201) had two patients with diabetes and from his experience described the disease as a weakness of the kidneys and introduced the idea that urine was unchanged drink. He called the disease "urinous diarrhea." In 200 A. D. a description of the disease was given in China by one of her greatest physicians, Tchang Tchong-king, who called it the "disease of thirst." Aëtius, about 550 A. D., introduced into therapy three measures that were in use for a long period thereafter—bleeding, emetics, and narcotics. Sweetness of diabetic urine was first mentioned in the Ayur Veda of Susruta in India in the sixth century B. C. It was called "Madhumeha" or "honey urine." This discovery of the outstanding symptom of diabetes was not generally known for another two thousand years, however, so, except for academic interest, it had no effect on the development of the disease.

The whole story of medical history was changed by the disruptive influence of the fall of Rome. This event has been explained frequently in its effect on religion, art, and literature. It had its special effect also on medical development. Up until the sixth century, each rising civilization assimilated the salient features of the declining one, until Rome came to be a blend of all the former civilizations. With her destruction by a new and barbarous people, all this accumulated culture was submerged and did not again appear until the Italian Renaissance.

The Benedictine monks at Monte Cassino, Italy, as early as the sixth century, had many medical manuscripts in their possession and studied them. It was the successors of this group of Benedictines who recognized the advantages of Salerno and established not only a monastery there but also a medical school. This school of Salerno, which was well established by the eleventh century, has handed down the records of its organization and of some of its great teachers. The founder of modern surgery, Roger of Parma, was one of their teachers. From Salerno, this awakened medical consciousness advanced first in Italy to the Universities of Bologna and Padua and then in France to Paris and Montpellier. The influence exerted by these schools was felt in all parts of Europe and many of the sciences later to be allied under the term medicine began to appear. Leonardo da Vinci with his paintings of the human body, Vesalius with his anatomy, Francis Bacon with his inductive reasoning, Harvey with his physiology, Malphighi with his anatomy, and Morgagni with his pathology—are all the results of this renaissance in medicine.

Thomas Willis (1621-1675), an Englishman, is the one who has been credited with the discovery that the urine of diabetics had the taste of honey or sugar. He did not think that it was sugar, but held to the idea that diabetes was a disease of the blood. He believed that the acid reaction of fermented wine was probably a cause of diabetes. Poor hygiene, worry, and nervous diseases were advanced by him also as causes of the disease. His suggestion for limitation of diet to "thicken the blood and supply salts" introduced the first undernutrition diet. Lime water was the alkali that he used for diabetics and marked the introduction of drugs in treatment of this disease. Though many times in earlier history the sweetish quality of diabetic urine was noted, it was not until Willis's introduction of the idea that it began to be used to its fullest extent in diagnosis. Until then polyuria, or any of a number of symptoms, were thought to have been diabetes, and only after the establishment of Willis's idea was the subsequent dietary regime possible.

It was just a century after Willis that Matthew Dobson, in 1776, finished the experiment by showing that sugar was present in the urine of diabetic patients and in addition, that the blood serum of diabetics had a sweet taste. Twelve years later (1788), Thomas Cawley, in the "London Medical Journal", wrote of his discovery of an atrophied pancreas, with calculi in its secretory ducts, in an autopsy on a diabetic. He however, thought that the disease was one of the kidneys. After Cawley, Bright, Lloyd, and Elliotson noted pancreatic lesions in autopsies, but none of these men established the relationship between lesions and diabetes.

In 1796, John Rollo, a surgeon in the English army, treated his first case of diabetes in a radically original way. He began by bleeding the patient and by careful confinement and rest at home. Then followed a strict diet, composed principally of rancid meat, intended to prevent the formation of sugar in the stomach.

One of the interesting features in the history of diabetes is that the first step toward the discovery of insulin was taken by one of the contemporaries of Willis. Conrad von Brunner, in 1683, removed the pancreas of a dog and observed the symptoms that followed. His detailed description of the condition of the depancreatized dog was a typical description of diabetes mellitus. From this period, toward the end of the seventeenth century, progress in diabetes developed along two distinct lines—experimentation with various types of diet and an inevitable trend toward the discovery of insulin through experimentation on animals and growing accuracy in laboratory research. There was not a distinct cleavage between the two lines of research, however, and many of the men experimenting on dogs applied their knowledge clinically and made contributions to the several theories of diet.

The theories on diagnosis and treatment, up to the era referred to by Elliott P. Joslin of Boston as the "Naunyn era," are worthy of mention for each of them had a temporary influence and doubtless, by trial and error, each had an integral part in the development of our present knowledge. Thomas Willis had suggested the first undernutrition diet; Richard Morton observed the hereditary character of the disease and suggested a milk diet; Richard Mead felt that diabetes was a disease of the liver and supported his contention by a supposed necropsy; Matthew

Dobson completed the study of Willis, discovered that not only the urine but the blood serum had a sweetish taste, and introduced the error that the diabetic must eat in excess to make up for the loss of nutritive material; Thomas Cawley made the first diagnosis of diabetes by the demonstration of sugar alone, and also demonstrated a pancreatic lesion in a diabetic necropsy; William Cullen added mellitus to the name of the disease, and felt that diabetes was a disease of the nervous system; John Brown added the idea of exercise as a form of treatment; Johann Peter Frank made a definite distinction between diabetes insipidus and diabetes mellitus; and Francis Home thought diabetes might be cured by a strictly meat diet, although he abandoned this idea before he had experimented with it enough to prove or disprove it.

The additions to diabetic knowledge through chemistry were necessary for later development, but need only be mentioned in this account. In 1857, Petters discovered acetone in diabetic urine. This was followed in a few years by the work of Kussmaul on acetonemia, of Stadelman, Külz, Minkowski, and Magnus-Levy on B-Oxybutyric acid in relation to diabetic coma.

Bernhard Naunyn, who was born in 1839, has given his name to an era in the development of diabetes, not because of any outstanding discovery, but because of his sound judgment, his application of existing knowledge, his outstanding pupils, and because of the discovery at his famous Strassburg school of the pancreatic gland as the seat of diabetic disease. The carbohydrate-free diet was rapidly becoming the accepted method of treatment in practically every country except Germany. Germany, as a whole, was opposed to the carbohydrate-free diet, but Naunyn supported this idea at first scientifically without taking into consideration the fact that any treatment which is too great a sacrifice to follow will be avoided by the average sick person, and later with modifications based on the individual sugar tolerance, and dietary needs. Notable among his pupils was Weintraud who disproved the theory advanced by Dobson that the caloric intake of a diabetic must be abnormal.

Naunyn's school held that diabetes was an inherited tendency, and that it was a functional disorder. The word acidosis was introduced by Naunyn. He judged the severity of cases by the degree of acidosis present. His diet consisted in the gradual withdrawal of carbohydrates. When the glycosuria cleared up, the patient was put on a diet with a gradual replacement of the carbohydrate until the minimum amount tolerated was restored. Naunyn's views on exercise agreed with those of some of his predecessors and consisted of walking, or mild exercise, if the patient were able, or complete rest if he were not. If the sugar did not clear up under this procedure, an undernutrition diet might be temporarily employed. When coma threatened, Naunyn advised giving up trying to get rid of the glycosuria and increased the carbohydrates. Naunyn agreed with some of his contemporaries and predecessors that fat was a main article of diet for diabetics, and as much as could be assimilated without causing indigestion should be used.

In 1902, von Noorden introduced the idea that a diet of oatmeal gruel caused the disappearance of glycosuria. This "oat cure" aroused comment and interest among the medical profession in which it had many followers. The real explanation seemed to be overlooked by most of the physicians—that it was probably the low caloric and protein value in the gruel that bettered the patient's condition.

Naunyn was sceptical of this cure, as he was of all the carbohydrate cures. From Rollo in 1796 down to his time, absence or presence of carbohydrates had been the basis of nearly every cure for diabetes. He held the theory that it was more likely undernutrition than any specific article of diet that caused the improved condition among diabetics. Von Noorden disagreed with the Naunyn school on the cause of acidosis and considered it something more than carbohydrate deficiency, but he agreed with Naunyn on the belief in the potency of fat in the diet. Both also agreed on the good results of an occasional fast day. Of the various men who advanced definite treatments for diabetes Naunyn, until 1914, probably had a larger following than any other.

The "Allen era," which extended from 1914 until 1922, was named for Frederick M. Allen. He and Joslin were discussing a case of Joslin's in which the diabetic patient had contracted tuberculosis. Joslin remarked that as the patient failed in strength from the tuberculosis, the diabetes improved. This case stimulated the experiment from which evolved the Allen fasting treatment. Allen produced a condition in animals which simulated human diabetes by partial pancreanectomy. He varied the disease from mild to severe, according to diet. His dogs died when fed liberally. When they were starved until glycosuria disappeared and then placed on a low diet, they felt better and there was no reappearance of the glycosuria. When this finding was applied to human beings, Allen drew the logical conclusion that no particular type of food was good or bad for a diabetic, but rather that a diabetic must always be limited in amount of diet.

In the light of recent events, this rationalization of Allen's experiment may not seem to be extraordinary, but when it is considered in view of the experience of Joslin who has had so large a clinical experience in the treatment of diabetes, it is a service the importance of which cannot be overestimated. To quote Joslin in speaking of the period following the onset of the Allen era, "During the next eight years the duration of life of my average diabetic increased one-fourth or the equivalent of slightly over one year. As the number of diabetics or pre-diabetics in the country was approximately 500,000, the establishment of this simple but far-reaching principle probably added half a million years to the lives of American diabetics."

The general adoption of the Allen treatment was largely due to Joslin. One outstanding difference in this diet from that of Naunyn is that fat was at first the only food withdrawn. The theory underlying the Allen fasting treatment was that diabetes is not only a disorder of carbohydrate assimilation, but of the whole metabolism generally. An increase in diet or in weight would, accordingly, constitute too great a strain on the disordered pancreas and, therefore, if the whole diet is lightened, more general improvement would be noted.

In the history of insulin following the observation by von Brunner, in 1683, that the removal of the pancreas in a dog caused typical diabetes, it was over a century before this connection was actually seen. In 1788, Cawley, an English physician, suggested a relationship between diabetes and the pancreas as a result of an observation he made that the pancreas of a person who had died of diabetes had atrophied and had calculi in its secretory ducts.

In 1845 Bouchardat formulated the theory that there exists a diabetes due to a disturbance of the pancreas. With attention thus being focused on the relationship of the pancreas to disease, numerous experiments were tried to see if the removal or ligation of the pancreas would cause diabetes.

Claude Bernard, in a series of papers published between 1849 and 1877, explained the metabolic changes of carbohydrates and announced his discovery of the glycogenic function of the liver. This knowledge had a definite bearing on the discovery of the cause of diabetes.

Although innumerable scientists were working on the subject, it was not until 1889 when Minkowski and von Mering carefully and completely extirpated the whole pancreas of the famous Strassburg dog that mankind was certain of the cause of diabetes. From this experiment it was learned that carbohydrate is formed out of protein in a fairly definite ratio; that levulose is the one type of carbohydrate which, when administered to a depancreatized dog, increases the glycogen in the liver; and that with only a fragment of the pancreas remaining, diabetes does not develop.

Histology was keeping pace with other advance and Paul Langerhans, in 1869, had discovered the division of the pancreas, since called the islands of Langerhans. The other type of cell contained in the acinous section of the pancreas was also known. Between 1889 and 1891, Giulio Vassale showed that there was a functional independence of the islands of Langerhans and the acinous cells of the pancreas. In 1893, Laguesse suspected that the islands of Langerhans produced an internal secretion. In 1899, Diamare and Laguesse, from studies of comparative anatomy, felt that the internal secretion from the islands of Langerhans effected metabolic changes of the carbohydrates, and showed that the islands were ductless glands like the thyroid or adrenals. Opie, in 1901, and Ssobolew, in 1902, from a study of several autopsies, stated that where diabetes was the result of a lesion of the pancreas, this lesion affected the islands of Langerhans, and where diabetes was not present, even though there were pancreatic lesions, these lesions were limited to the acinous portion of the pancreas. Ssobolew suggested that the pancreas of a new-born calf might be a fruitful source of the solution of the gland. All of these demonstrations proving that the islands of Langerhans are ductless glands and secrete something into the blood without which diabetes mellitus would develop, led to the suggestion by Sir Sharpey Schafer, in 1916, that this anti-diabetic hormone, as yet only an hypothetical secretion, should be named "insulin."

The development of insulin from this point was an attempt through chemical methods to find a substance, the presence of which was hypothetical, and the function of which had been negatively proved through experiments on the islands of Langerhans. One of the first experiments was that of Rennie and Fraser who used as a working basis the glands of certain fish which had been shown anatomically to be the same as the islands of Langerhans, and which were free from the secretions of the cells of the acinous section of the pancreas. They administered by mouth the extracts obtained and lost the benefit of them by the destructive reaction of the digestive juices, for it has since been proved that insulin is abundantly present in the glands with which they worked. One boy received some of the solution which they extracted subcutaneously and he derived benefit from it. Their other findings did not substantiate their original thesis, however, and their experiment was abandoned.

In 1908 there was a near discovery of insulin when Zeulzer extracted the pancreas with alcohol, thus saving it from destruction by digestive juices. Through experimentation, Zeulzer finally obtained an insulin extract which he injected in diabetic patients intravenously. Apparently, in view of our later knowledge, the peculiar symptoms which his diabetics developed were due to overdoses of the extract. However, his experiments were discontinued because of the reaction of patients to them.

Frederick G. Banting, assisted by C. H. Best, a young medical student, began a series of experiments in the laboratory of J. J. R. MacLeod of the Medical School of the University of Toronto. Banting was familiar with the experiments in which the ligation of the pancreatic ducts was followed by atrophy of the secretory digestive ducts, leaving the cells of the islands of Langerhans intact, and conceived the idea of using extracts of the atrophied glands. This investigator had an advantage the other earlier scientists did not have—"accurate micro-chemical methods of estimation of the percentage of sugar in the blood, an increase of which, ... is the cardinal symptom of diabetes."

The ducts connecting the pancreas and intestines of a dog were ligated, and a period of time long enough for the atrophy of the gland elapsed before Banting attempted to make solutions from the gland. When extracts from these glandular solutions were injected into diabetic dogs intravenously, there was an immediate approach to normal of the blood sugar of these dogs. This experiment was repeated several times with the same result before the conclusions were considered sound. Naturally, the number of atrophied glands would be limited and, therefore, unless some other method of obtaining insulin could be devised, the thing would be impractical.

Ssobolew had suggested that the pancreas of a new-born calf should be productive of large quantities of this substance, for the digestive processes do not begin until birth. Working on this knowledge, Banting and Best decided to try the pancreas of an unborn calf. This was done and various methods were used to purify the extract to remove all the irritants. The work of this chemical purification was accomplished by J. B. Collip. The product that relieves all the symptoms of diabetes was then ready.

It would seem that the greatest part of the work was accomplished at this stage, but there still remained the perfection of a system whereby insulin could be obtained from the pancreas of full grown cattle, and the perfection of a system whereby insulin could be produced on a large and commercial scale. For some time, although the original preparation of the extract was carried out seemingly to perfection, the quantity product was not the efficacious product of the early experiments. The laboratory of the Eli Lilly Company worked with the other experimenters for several months before it was discovered that the cause of the trouble was insufficient control of the degree of acidity at various stages of the extraction process. This acidity was eventually controlled by using isoelectric precipitation to purify—a process which is still in use.

At the present time, according to MacLeod, insulin is prepared in the following manner: "The pancreas is put through a meat chopper and collected in an equal volume of ordinary alcohol containing 25 cc. concentrated sulphuric acid for each kilogram of pancreas used. After being stirred for some time, the mixture is filtered, or centrifuged, and the alcohol is removed from the extract in a vacuum still. The watery residue is then mixed with ammonium sulphate (40 grams for each 100 c.c. of solution) whereby a precipitate containing most of the insulin separates out. The precipitate is collected and dissolved in water and reprecipitated with ammonium sulphate. This second precipitate is shaken with water containing sufficient ammonia to bring the pH value to between 6 and 8. By contrifuging, a clear watery solution is obtained from which insulin is precipitated, by adding acetic acid to bring pH to about 5. After standing some time at a low temperature the precipitated insulin is collected on a filter, redissolved in water containing sufficient hydrochloric acid to bring it into solution and reprecipitated by adjusting pH to between 5 and 6.... The end product ... is a practically colorless precipitate which can be dried in a vacuum desiccator and is of fairly uniform strength. A solution of this precipitate in dilute hydrochloric acid of an acidity greater than pH4.6 is the insulin of commerce. It is sold in solutions put up in sterile bottles and the solution is of such a strength that 1 cc. contains either 10, 20 or 40 units."

The intricacy of this process gives some idea of the cost of preparation and, subsequently, the cost to the individual of insulin. At present, many experiments are being carried on to discover a synthetic substitute. Abel and Geiling, at the present time working with crystalline insulin, are trying to find out the exact chemical elements in insulin. With this knowledge, it may be possible to manufacture a product direct from chemicals without the expense attached to the extraction process now in use.

The importance of international medical advance, sponsored by the League of Nations, is perfectly apparent in communicable diseases. It has its place in the treatment of diabetes, too. The Committee on the Standardization of Toxins, Drugs, etc., of the League of Nations, has defined a unit of insulin as one third of that amount of insulin which will lower the blood sugar to an average of 0.045 per cent within five hours of its injection. Thus, a person with diabetes mellitus can obtain accurate and uniform doses of insulin all over the world. Too great lowering of the blood sugar such as would follow the administration of too much insulin would cause excessive discomfort and, in some cases, convulsions. This is one of the reasons why diabetic patients educated in the care of their disease carry one or two lumps of sugar about with them to have on hand in case they feel weakness from too little sugar in their blood.

As to the status of diabetes in this latest era, called the "Banting era" after the name of its principal benefactor, it is not yet possible to say whether the islands of Langerhans can be replaced sufficiently to function as normal glands. It is known that even in the most severe conditions the treatment with insulin has brought patients back to normal, and Joslin has some cases where the use of insulin has been lessened and even stopped after a period of time, if the percentage of blood sugar is controlled by the diet.

The history of insulin in relation to diabetes has one of its most humane chapters in the benefit it has been to children. In most cases, diabetes has been a disease largely occurring in the degenerative period after forty years. In many cases, however, it has appeared in children. With them it has been, as a rule, a simple uncomplicated disease with a rapidly fatal termination. Insulin has restored these children not only to life, but to an active normal life. From the point of view of research, its value cannot be estimated. Before the Banting era, it was nearly impossible to study a case of pure, uncomplicated diabetes for any length of time, because these cases occurred only in young children, and most young children with the disease died in a year or two. Now they live and though they may always have to take insulin, a study of their health will clear up many of the points of the disease now in doubt, and make possible an improvement in the methods of treatment for both children and adults.

Bibliography

ALLEN, FREDERICK M.; STILLMAN, EDGAR; and FITZ, REGINALD: *Total Dietary Regulation in the Treatment of Diabetes*. The Rockefeller Institute for Medical Research, New York, 1919

DORLAND, W. A. NEWMAN: *The American Illustrated Medical Dictionary*. W. B. Saunders Company, Philadelphia and London, 1932

GARRISON, FIELDING H.: *History of Medicine*. W. B. Saunders Company, Philadelphia and London, 1929

JOSLIN, ELLIOTT P.: *Diabetes. Its Control by the Individual and by the State*. Harvard University Press, Cambridge, 1931.

JOSLIN, ELLIOTT P.: *The Treatment of Diabetes Mellitus*. Lea & Febiger, Philadelphia, 1928

LÉPINE, R.: *Le Diabète Sucré*. Félix Alcan, Ancienne Librarie Germer Baillière Et Cie, Paris, 1909.

MACLEOD, J. J. R.: *Insulin to the Rescue of the Diabetic*. Chemistry in Medicine, The Chemical Foundation, Inc., New York, 1928.

MCCRADIE, ANDREW ROSS: *The Discoveries in the Field of Diabetes Mellitus and Their Investigators*. Medical Life, Issue 45, June, 1924, American Society of Medical History, New York.

OSLER, SIR WILLIAM: *Principles and Practice of Medicine*. 1913 edition

WOODYATT, ROLLIN T.: *Diabetes Mellitus*. Cecil's Text-Book of Medicine, W. B. Saunders Company, Philadelphia and London, 1933

DIABETES IN MASSACHUSETTS

HERBERT L. LOMBARD, M.D., ANNE A. BORIS, and SADIE MINSKY,
*Division of Adult Hygiene,
Massachusetts Department of Public Health*

Knowledge of the epidemiology of diabetes is essential in any concerted attempt at control. Pertinent facts regarding the disease were obtained in the Massachusetts Chronic Disease Survey which included death records, hospital records and house-to-house visits in fifty-one cities and towns of the Commonwealth. Information was secured from approximately 75,000 individuals in 1929, 1930, and 1931. In 1929, the data covered every member of each family visited. In 1930 and 1931, the survey was limited to those over the age of forty. The presence of chronic disease was ascertained and information regarding care and treatment was obtained. Both sick and well were questioned regarding their habits of living in order to acquire some information on etiology. One-tenth of the total population and one-fourth of the population over forty had some form of chronic disease. Among the individuals interviewed, 9 out of every 1000 of those over forty and about 3 out of every 1000 of those of all ages had diabetes. In all cases the opinion of the individual questioned was accepted as a diagnosis, but over 97 per cent of those with diabetes admitted they had been told by a physician that they had the disease.

At any one time there are approximately 15,000 individuals in Massachusetts suffering with diabetes. While diabetes may occur at practically all ages, the highest rates are found in late adult life.

The death rates adjusted to age and sex to compensate for the changing age of the population indicate that diabetes has been increasing for many years. (Table I) The female rate has increased faster than the male. In both sexes, the adjusted rates showed the increase to be less than the crude rates. The rates by individual years since 1900 showed a remission in the rise in 1918 and 1919, and another one beginning in 1923. Among males, the subsequent increase following the drop in 1923 has not yet reached the 1922 level in the adjusted rates, while among females the 1922 rate was surpassed in 1932. An initial drop later followed by an increase in rate would be expected in a disease in which treatment prolongs life, but does not cure.

As the Manual of Joint Causes of Death gives diabetes precedence over most other diseases, the recorded deaths for diabetes include nearly all of the deaths of individuals who have had the disease, regardless of the immediate cause of death. In 1928, 1930, and 1932, 3,552 individuals died in Massachusetts who had had diabetes. Of this number, 88.6 per cent were certified as dying of diabetes, and the remaining 11.4 per cent of other conditions. Two fifths of this latter group were certified as dying of cancer, one-fourth of tuberculosis, and the rest of a few miscellaneous conditions—the most frequent being accidents and appendicitis. Realizing that once a person is diagnosed as a diabetic and in about nine times out of ten he will be certified as dying of this disease, the death rate cannot be expected to drop as long as the disease itself increases.

The efforts which have been expended to control the disease lie largely in treatment rather than prevention, and the results of treatment which may prolong life for many years will not be well portrayed in death charts. If treatment is sufficiently good as to cause individuals who would formerly have died in a lower age group to die in a higher, there will be improvement shown in these lower groups, but the higher cannot be lessened with the disease itself on the increase. Charts I and II show that just this situation has occurred in diabetes during the Banting era. Under the age of fifty there have been marked declines in

Table I

MORTALITY RATES, BY SEX, FOR DIABETES IN MASSACHUSETTS 1860-1933

Rate per 100,000

Year	Males Age, Sex Adjusted Rate*	Males Crude Rate	Females Age, Sex Adjusted Rate*	Females Crude Rate
1860	4.0	3.7	2.6	2.5
1870	5.1	5.0	2.7	2.7
1880	4.3	4.4	4.9	4.9
1890	7.4	7.6	8.9	9.0
1900	12.9	12.9	10.8	10.8
1901	9.6	9.6	12.7	12.7
1902	11.0	11.1	14.8	14.9
1903	12.3	12.4	15.1	15.2
1904	12.4	12.5	15.1	15.2
1905	11.7	11.7	15.7	15.9
1906	11.7	11.8	14.9	15.1
1907	12.4	12.5	17.2	17.4
1908	11.7	11.9	15.6	15.8
1909	12.4	12.4	18.1	18.4
1910	14.4	14.5	19.2	19.6
1911	16.7	16.9	19.6	20.0
1912	14.0	14.3	18.8	19.4
1913	15.4	15.8	19.7	19.5
1914	14.9	15.4	19.2	19.9
1915	15.6	16.3	20.0	20.9
1916	16.9	17.8	23.6	24.9
1917	17.6	18.4	22.1	23.4
1918	15.6	16.5	18.5	19.7
1919	13.6	14.4	17.6	18.8
1920	16.4	17.5	22.1	23.8
1921	14.0	15.2	22.7	24.6
1922	16.9	18.5	26.8	29.5
1923	14.3	16.1	23.7	26.7
1924	12.3	14.2	21.3	24.1
1925	13.7	15.9	20.5	23.8
1926	14.2	16.7	20.6	24.0
1927	12.1	14.3	22.2	26.3
1928	13.6	16.4	23.4	28.0
1929	13.2	16.1	25.4	30.9
1930	13.4	16.3	25.5	31.4
1931	14.5	18.1	24.9	31.0
1932	16.4	20.8	27.0	34.2
1933	15.2	19.4	28.8	36.7

* Adjusted to Massachusetts 1900 population.

the rates in both sexes, between fifty and sixty the rates have not altered greatly, but above sixty an upward trend is observed.

A much better estimate of the value of insulin can be obtained through studies on the duration of the disease and the average age at time of death. Joslin, in his private cases, found between the years 1922 and 1926 that the average duration was 7.6 years, while from 1926 to 1930 it was 8.4—an increase on the average of 0.2 years per year. From the Massachusetts death records a similar increase has been obtained, although both at the beginning and end of the periods studied the duration figures were lower than those furnished by Joslin. It is believed that Joslin's figures more nearly approach the correct duration than the Massachusetts death figures, as the duration obtained from the survey was greater by nearly a year than that furnished by the Massachusetts death records and, in addition, all these individuals were alive at the time of questioning.

The average age at time of death tells a similar story. (Table II) This figure gradually increased in the Naunyn era, continued to in-

Table II

AVERAGE AGE AT TIME OF DEATH OF INDIVIDUALS WITH DIABETES
Massachusetts 1850-1933

Year	Males	Females
1850	35.2	24.1
1860	45.9	29.0
1870	53.9	33.8
1880	48.9	40.3
1890	47.2	50.0
1900	52.8	51.4
1905	52.4	55.2
1910	49.8	56.4
1911	51.9	56.4
1912	52.6	57.1
1913	50.8	54.4
1914	54.8	55.9
1915	52.1	55.6
1916	54.4	57.2
1917	53.8	57.3
1918	53.4	55.6
1919	52.6	58.0
1920	54.3	57.5
1921	53.8	57.3
1922	54.5	58.6
1923	59.1	60.6
1924	59.0	59.8
1925	59.2	61.5
1926	61.5	61.8
1927	61.3	62.1
1928	61.3	62.2
1929	61.7	63.1
1930	62.7	63.6
1931	61.6	63.7
1932	64.0	65.2
1933	63.7	64.9

crease in the Allen era, and has again increased in the Banting era. The average age for males jumped over four years between 1922 and 1923. Between 1920 and 1930, the average age increased 15.5 per cent among males and 10.6 per cent among females. In the same period, the average age at time of death of individuals with cancer increased 0.3 per cent for males and 2.7 per cent for females; apoplexy 0.1 per cent for males and 0.4 per cent for females; heart disease 2.7 per cent for males and 4.6 per cent for females; nephritis 3.0 per cent for males and 3.3 per cent for females; and pulmonary tuberculosis 8.8 per cent for males and 5.1 per cent for females. This far greater increase in the average age of diabetics, combined with information on duration, seems adequate proof of what insulin is doing.

The diabetic rate in the survey showed no appreciable change in the various economic groups. This contrasted greatly with total chronic disease which had a far greater prevalence among the poor.

The diabetic death rate was greater in the city than in the country, but morbidity appeared about the same in both types of communities.

Of the individuals with diabetes, 5.5 per cent were found completely disabled and 29 per cent partially disabled. If these percentages were applied to the estimated cases of diabetes in Massachusetts, complete disability would be found in 850 individuals and partial disability in 4,300.

Diabetes was positively associated with heart disease and arteriosclerosis in both morbidity and mortality data. The mortality data also showed association with nephritis, apoplexy, tuberculosis, and cancer.

At the time of the survey, 77.8 per cent of the diabetics were under the care of physicians, as compared with 44.4 per cent of the total sick individuals found in the survey. Five per cent of those with diabetes were following the diet prescribed, in most cases, by physicians several years ago; only 1.0 per cent were receiving care in hospitals; 0.7 per cent employed Christian Science practitioners; 8.6 per cent were treating themselves; and 6.9 per cent were receiving no treatment. Females employed physicians slightly more than did males. Individuals with diabetes were receiving medical attention to a greater extent in the country than in the city.

Individuals who did not have a physician were questioned as to the reason. About one-tenth of the group said they were too poor to employ a physician; over one-third felt that the physician could not help them; and almost half of the group felt that their condition was not serious. The failure to recognize the need for medical attention by so large a part of this group indicates a need for further medical education.

During the year preceding the survey 4.8 per cent of those with diabetes employed nurses, and an additional 1.7 per cent needed nurses but could not obtain them because of economic reasons. Less than one-half of the nurses employed remained for more than three months.

About 7 per cent of the diabetics were hospitalized during the year preceding the survey. At the time of the survey, 98.5 per cent of the diabetics were being cared for at home. Of these, 12.8 per cent were living in homes unsuitable for their care.

On September 1, 1929, a census of the hospital population with this disease was taken by questionnaire. Replies were obtained from hospitals representing 79 per cent of all hospital beds in the State. In the hospitals that reported, there were 253 cases of diabetes—166 of these being in general hospitals. By assuming that the hospitals of various types not heard from had a number proportionate to those heard from, a theoretical number of cases for each type of hospital has been obtained. This gave 317 cases of diabetes in total hospitals, of which 206 were in general hospitals. The average stay in hospitals was 2.8 weeks for those admitted with diabetes and a similar duration for those admitted in which diabetes was found as additional pathology. Of all beds in these hospitals, 0.72 per cent were occupied by individuals admitted for diabetes, and 0.34 per cent by those in whom diabetes was a contributory factor. The disease was the primary cause for admission in 68.5 per cent of those with diabetes.

Questionnaires were sent to 435 nursing homes in Massachusetts, and replies were received from 35.4 per cent of these homes. The number of diabetic cases reported was 55, with a median stay of 3.8 months. Individuals with diabetes occupied 1.2 per cent of beds in these homes.

Among the wage-earners over forty in the survey sick with diabetes, 10.8 per cent were completely disabled economically and 7.5 per cent were partially disabled. Another measure of economic disability is the time lost from work during the year preceding the survey by wage-earners. Over one-fourth of the diabetic wage-earners lost an average of 6.2 months from their work during this period. Applying this figure to the total wage-earners in the survey gives 0.09 per cent of total working time lost by individuals with diabetes during the year, which for Massachusetts as a whole is approximately 677 years of work lost per year. The yearly money loss is over $800,000. These figures do not include time lost by wage-earners under forty or time lost by non-wage-earners. Neither does this estimate include expenditures for care and treatment.

The Massachusetts death records showed that 14 per cent of the diabetics who were Massachusetts residents died in cities or towns other than their usual residence. Of the individuals from other states who died in Massachusetts, 2.4 per cent were diabetics.

Adjusted mortality rates for diabetes for the thirty-four Registration States showed that the highest rates were in the northern part of the country.

In the Chronic Disease Survey, questions on heredity and environment were asked individuals over the age of forty in order to determine which of these factors, if any, were associated with chronic disease. The mere association does not necessarily signify causation, as two variables may be associated with one another simply because they are both associated with a third. However, such information as has been obtained is of some value in pointing toward possible etiological factors.

In 1930, histories were collected on 134 diabetics; in 1931, on 158. There have been matched five series of controls to each of these series of diabetics. The controls were identical with diabetics in respect to age and sex. The rates for the various factors studied have been computed in the diabetic series and in the controls. Information for some of the variables was obtained only in one year—in these series we have only one diabetic group and five controls. The differences between the rates of the diabetic cases and the controls have been computed with the standard deviations, and significance measured by the table of "t" of R. A. Fisher. (Table III)

Overweight showed the highest degree of significance of any of the variables studied. Many writers have mentioned this relationship, but some have questioned whether the overweight was the cause of the diabetes or whether the same syndromes which cause the diabetes also produce the obesity. Joslin feels overweight is of importance only in those with an hereditary history of diabetes.

Nervous temperament was highly associated with the disease. It is stated in Cecil's "Text-Book of Medicine" that "Depressive emotions, anxieties, fears, unhappiness arising from various causes—such as domestic infelicities, financial losses, etc., are notoriously capable of provoking the onset." Joslin considers exceptionally brilliant children to be good subjects for observations as they often come into the diabetic class. It is probable that the temperament of such children would, in most cases, be classified as nervous, and while our figures deal with adults they point to more diabetes among the nervous than the phlegmatic.

Table III FACTORS ON HEREDITY AND ENVIRONMENT IN DIABETES
Massachusetts Chronic Disease Survey   Rate per 100

Variables with Ten Controls	Diabetes	Controls	t	If t is:	Probability is:
Twenty per cent and more overweight	48.40 ± 4.26	17.40 ± 1.42	6.90		
Nervous temperament	55.90 ± 3.76	32.13 ± 1.25	6.00		
Heredity	9.71 ± 1.57	2.10 ± 0.52	4.61		
Indigestion	30.45 ± 4.04	16.97 ± 1.35	3.16	3.169	.01
Malaria	8.92 ± 1.60	3.67 ± 0.53	3.11		
Previous illness	44.95 ± 4.86	30.78 ± 1.62	2.77	2.764	.02
Frequent sore throats	8.61 ± 2.23	2.34 ± 0.74	2.67		
Little exercise	17.55 ± 3.74	7.11 ± 1.25	2.65		
Diphtheria	9.25 ± 1.23	5.96 ± 0.41	2.55		
Regular use of laxatives	42.90 ± 7.27	26.84 ± 2.42	2.10	2.228	.05
Scarlet fever	20.95 ± 4.22	13.94 ± 1.41	1.58		
Frequent colds	9.48 ± 2.43	5.65 ± 0.81	1.50		
Native born	67.40 ± 8.24	54.80 ± 2.75	1.45		
Poor	13.45 ± 4.00	10.20 ± 1.33	0.77	Not significant	
Typhoid fever	9.08 ± 2.94	6.76 ± 0.98	0.75		
Damp housing	7.59 ± 3.42	5.31 ± 1.14	0.63		
Bad teeth	37.60 ± 9.62	31.48 ± 3.21	0.60		
Rheumatic fever	3.64 ± 2.23	2.38 ± 0.74	0.54		
No regular dentistry	77.50 ± 6.59	73.90 ± 2.20	0.52		
Variables with Five Controls					
Bad tonsils	17.20 ± 1.83	3.69 ± 0.92	5.90	4.604	.01
Three and four native grandparents	40.20 ± 2.91	26.36 ± 1.46	3.80	3.747	.02
Native parents	46.60 ± 4.06	31.80 ± 2.03	2.92	2.776	.05
Non-protective foods	44.60 ± 6.11	43.26 ± 3.06	0.18	Not significant	
Dusty trade	3.73 ± 3.05	4.63 ± 1.53	-0.24		

Infections have frequently been mentioned as predisposing to the disease. Individuals who have had bad tonsils, malaria, frequent sore throats, and diphtheria all showed significantly more diabetes than their controls. The group that has had varying combinations of malaria, frequent sore throats, diphtheria, scarlet fever, frequent colds, typhoid fever, and rheumatic fever also showed significance. It is rather surprising to find bad tonsils strongly significant and bad teeth not significant, as infections from pus roots might be expected to have as great a connection with diabetes as tonsils.

Heredity showed a strong relationship. The heredity history was limited to parents, but it is sufficiently strong to warrant the belief that heredity is a real causal factor of diabetes. This view has been substantiated by many investigators. Joslin says, "Diabetes is hereditary. ... I suspect if we knew all the facts it would be shown that every diabetic had a diabetic relative." Apparently diabetes is more prevalent among the native born of native parents and native grandparents than the foreign born. The literature mentions higher rates among the Jews, but not among the native born of native ancestry. Nativity studies have largely been based on mortality rates. When such rates are studied in Massachusetts, the native born of native parents have significantly lower rates than the foreign born or the native born of foreign and mixed parents and the native born of foreign and mixed parents have higher rates than the foreign born. The discrepancy between morbidity and mortality rates by nativity is explainable by higher case fatality and earlier incidence among the foreign race stock groups. In the 1930 survey, the median duration for diabetes was 7 years 4.8 months for the native born of native parents; 5 years 3.6 months for the native born of foreign and mixed parents; and 7 years 9.6 months for the foreign born. The duration, as furnished by the death records for Massachusetts 1930, for diabetes was 4 years 2.0 months for the native born of native parents; 3 years 4.0 months for the native born of foreign and mixed parents; and 3 years 3.6 months for the foreign born. The median present age of the survey group with this disease was 62.7 years for the native born of native parents; 57.1 years for the native born of foreign and mixed parents; and 61.8 years for the foreign born. The median age at time of death for the 1930 mortality records was 68.9 years for the native born of native parents; 63.3 years for the native born of foreign and mixed parents; and 65.8 years for the foreign born. The nativity study indicates lower morbidity rates, higher case fatality, and earlier incidence among the foreign race stocks.

Lack of exercise was slightly associated with diabetes. Significance is not strong and the results obtained might indicate a definite connection with diabetes or an association with some of the other variables. The overweight person would probably exercise less than one of normal weight.

Indigestion showed a fairly strong association with diabetes. On the other hand, over 80 per cent of the diabetic individuals having this condition had, in addition, either nervous temperaments, obesity, or an hereditary history of diabetes. It is possible that long-continued indigestion may be a factor in this disease, but the results are by no means conclusive.

Either overweight, nervous temperament, or heredity were present in 78 per cent of the diabetic group. Inasmuch as heredity was measured by the history of father and mother only, it is probable that this figure would have been greater if other ancestors had been included. The control group had only 42 per cent in this category, making the significance very strong.

From the standpoint of prevention of diabetes, excessive overweight should be avoided, a more placid attitude toward living should be adopted, and all infections should receive prompt treatment. These measures are of added importance if an heredity history of the disease is present.

Chart I
MALE AGE SPECIFIC MORTALITY RATES FOR DIABETES
MASSACHUSETTS DEATHS, 1903-1933
Rate per 100,000

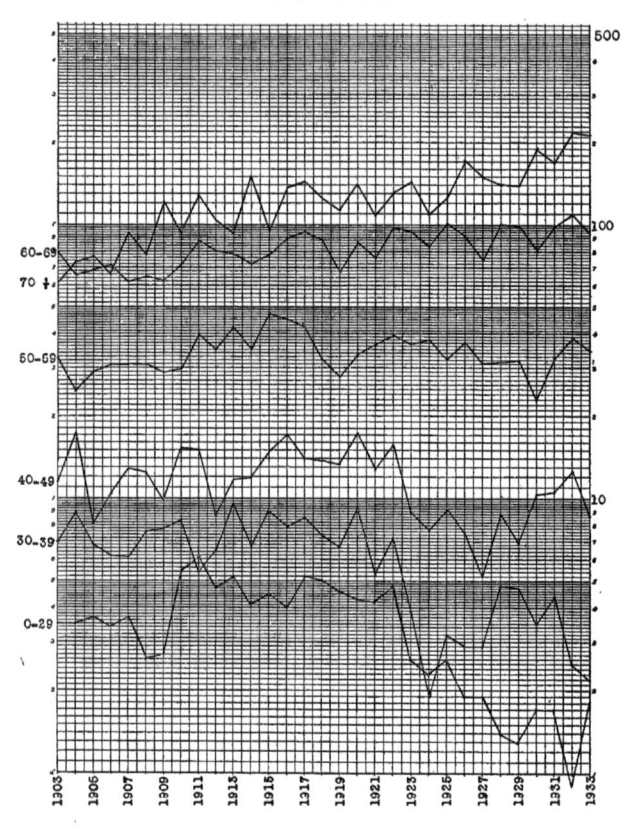

Bibliography

BIGELOW, GEORGE H., and LOMBARD, HERBERT L.: *Cancer and Other Chronic Diseases in Massachusetts*. Houghton Mifflin Company, Boston and New York, 1933

FISHER, R. A.: *Statistical Methods for Research Workers*. Oliver and Boyd, Edinburgh and London, 1925

JOSLIN, ELLIOTT P.: *A Diabetic Manual*. Lea & Febiger, Philadelphia, 1934

JOSLIN, ELLIOTT P.: *Fat and the Diabetic*. New England Journal of Medicine, Vol. 209, No. 11, September 14, 1933.

JOSLIN, ELLIOTT P.: *The Treatment of Diabetes Mellitus.* Lea & Febiger, Philadelphia, 1928
JOSLIN, ELLIOTT P., DUBLIN, LOUIS I., and MARKS, HERBERT H.: *Studies in Diabetes Mellitus.* II. Its Incidence and the Factors Underlying Its Variations. American Journal of The Medical Sciences, No. 4, Vol. 187, April, 1934
WOODYATT, ROLLIN T.: *Diabetes Mellitus.* Cecil's Text-Book of Medicine, W. B. Saunders Company, Philadelphia and London, 1933

Chart II
FEMALE AGE SPECIFIC MORTALITY RATES FOR DIABETES
MASSACHUSETTS DEATHS, 1903-1933
Rate per 100,000

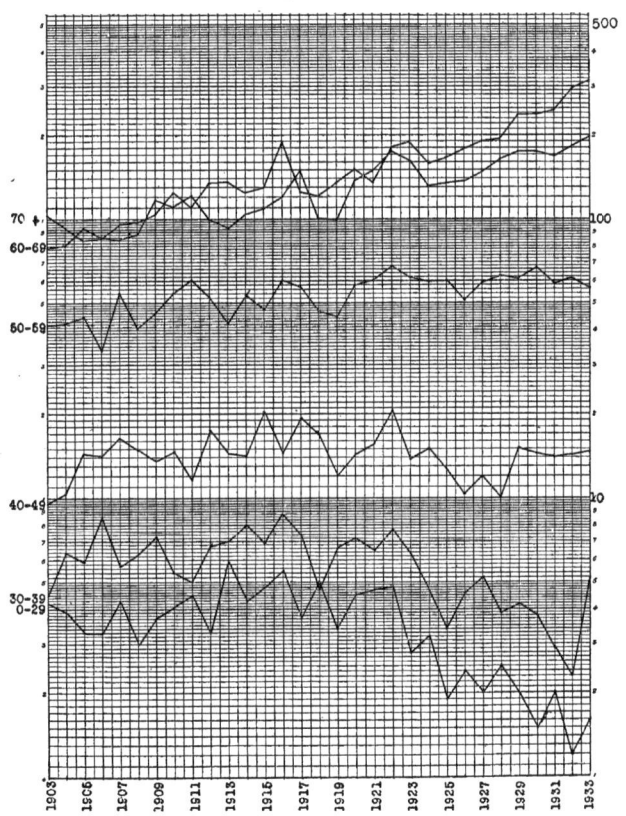

THE TREATMENT OF DIABETES
Elliott P. Joslin, M.D.
Boston, Mass.

Diet, insulin and exercise are the three agents at our disposal in the treatment of diabetes and success in their use depends upon the ability of the doctor and patient to adjust the three to each other.

The older the patient the more slowly should treatment begin. By this means sudden changes in the body fluids are prevented. One is always happy when the weight of the patient is constant for the first week unless one is overcoming the dehydration of coma and in that event a gain in weight is welcomed.

Diet

The diabetic diet is far simpler than often thought or taught. It should be a positive and not a negative diet. One tells the patient what to eat instead of what to avoid. In the doctor's mind there must be a clear conception of the proportion of carbohydrate, protein and fat which is to be prescribed, but there are any number of ways in which this can be conveyed to the patient. The fundamental dietetic principle is to avoid overfeeding. It matters little what measures for food are adopted. Scales and metric systems are the best in the end, but if the patient is averse to the same, lacks funds or is ignorant one can use a slice of bread, a standard biscuit or for liquids a tablespoon as a measure.

If a patient with a recently discovered diabetes should come to my office I should urge him (1) to go at once to the hospital; (2) place him upon a diet containing about 20 calories per kilogram body weight with carbohydrate at 100 to 130 grams, protein 50 to 60 grams and fat between 60 and 80 grams; (3) give him insulin 5 units before each meal; (4) collect the urine four times a day, morning, afternoon, evening, night, to determine the effect of the diet and insulin; (5) limit exercise to an amount consistent with his diet; and (6) start him upon his diabetic education. The diets usually employed are those outlined in Table 3 and the computations of the diets can be made from the food values in Tables 1 and 2. If the glycosuria did not decrease materially and daily, I should raise the insulin daily until this was accomplished even if the dose of insulin reached 20—15—20—5 units or more. Most patients become sugar free with as little as 10—10—10 units, few require 15—10—15—3 units.

So soon as it is evident by the falling glycosuria that the diabetes is coming under control one can increase the total calories by the addition of protein and fat, but it is seldom desirable to give more fat than is recorded opposite the carbohydrate allowed in Table 3. It seems paradoxical to increase the carbohydrate, protein and fat while glycosuria is present and one is endeavoring to get the patient sugar free, but the facts are this plan works. However, one advances above 120 grams carbohydrate cautiously. I suppose if the calories are deficient the body fat is drawn upon and that brings it about that the patient is upon a relatively high fat diet as compared with the carbohydrate and that in itself is deleterious.

When the adult patient is sugar free or shows only a few tenths per cent of sugar in the urine and is receiving a nearly maintenance diet, which ordinarily is about 30 calories per kilogram body weight, he can be sent home. It is always well to discharge a patient on somewhat too low a ration than too high a ration, but usually it is safer to increase the diet upon discharge by 5 or 10 grams of carbohydrate, protein and fat to guard against insulin reactions and such increases can generally be made without giving the patient too much food.

The dosage of insulin may change from day to day in the hospital but in order to avoid reactions it is well to lower it upon discharge. Most desirable is it to lessen the number of injections per day. Almost always one can get along with two injections, but if a third is required that is most conveniently administered upon retiring. The retiring dose is small 2, 3, 4 and almost never as much as 10 units. It is usually given without food and is prescribed so that the patient in the eight hours or more at night will be protected so that he can wake up sugar free. If a patient is sugar free on rising it implies he has glycogen stored in his liver and under such conditions the day is sure to progress more favorably than if he began it with hyperglycemia and glycosuria.

If a patient does not become sugar free with 30 units of insulin during twenty-four hours, seek (1) for errors in diet, (2) infections of any sort, whether general or local, (3) acidosis, (4) hyperthyroidism, (5) hemochromatosis. The last named condition is not nearly as rare as has been thought and the skin may show little of the typical brown pigmentation.

Exercise is of great help to the diabetic and especially of value when combined with insulin and a proper diet. Patients in bed are aided with exercise and the lack of it always raises difficulties in the management of diabetes. The patient crippled with rheumatism requires large doses of insulin and if his joints can be limbered and he can move about, the insulin can be lowered. A game of golf, Case 632 often told me, was the equal of 5 units.

Exercise is such a distinct aid in the treatment of diabetes that it should be recognized in the cost of the care of the patient. In hospitals patients are taught to exercise for their own good and outside of the hospital there is no reason why patients should not work and thus lessen the cost of their care. The whole scheme of caring for chronic patients and older invalids sooner or later must involve work on their part or else the expense will be overwhelming; and particularly should diabetic patients work if it is possible for them to do so because it is therapeutically advisable.

The advantages of exercise for diabetics are shown most plainly in the diabetic camps. We have found that our treatment of children goes far more smoothly in diabetic camps than it does in the hospital and to a considerable extent this is due to the introduction of exercise according to the need of the individual.

The average patient, based upon a group of thirty selected cases treated at the George F. Baker Clinic recently was found to be on a diet of carbohydrate 153 grams, protein 73 grams and fat 91 grams with insulin 26 units. At the present moment I should favor lowering rather than raising the carbohydrate in this diet adjusting the fat to compensate for the change.

If a diabetic does not do well, there is a reason, and one must not blame the treatment but seek for the explanation.

Week-end treatment for diabetics is quite satisfactory. In these times, when it is difficult to secure or hold a job, repeatedly patients have entered the hospital for a week-end treatment, coming in on a Friday afternoon and being discharged Sunday afternoon or early Monday morning. Most of the patients who have jobs are clever enough to gain a great deal of information in this short period. One day in a hospital spent in contact with other diabetics, seeing patients with gangrene, a patient with a carbuncle, perhaps another with diabetic coma or in hypoglycemia, will do more to instill a knowledge of diabetes than any amount of textbook teaching. Patients may not be able to read and write but they can see and hear and what they learn from observation and from interviews with other patients in the course of two days is astonishing.

The costs of medical care are likewise reduced during a hospital stay, because while being treated for and learning about diabetes all sorts of conditions which affect the diabetes adversely can be rectified. The teeth can be cleaned and if necessary extracted, bad tonsils can be removed, hyperthyroidism can be corrected. In children the appendix should be removed, if there is a distinct history of an attack, because of the confusion which always ensues when a child has diabetic coma and at the same time has discomfort in the abdomen. A few patients are discovered with gall stones. The eyes should be examined. Finally, every diabetic entering a hospital should have an X-ray of the chest because of the possibility of latent tuberculosis.

Table 1.[1]— **Foods Arranged Approximately According to Content of Carbohydrates**

Water, clear broths, coffee, tea, cocoa shells and cracked cocoa can be taken without allowance for food content.

Vegetables (fresh or canned)

1%–3%	5% / 3%–5%	10% *	15%	20%
Lettuce	Tomatoes	Str. Beans	Green Peas	Potatoes
Cucumbers	Water Cress	Brussels	Jerusalem	Shell Beans
Spinach	Sea Kale	Sprouts	Artichokes	Baked Beans
Asparagus	Cauliflower	Pumpkin	Parsnips	Green Corn
Rhubarb	Egg Plant	Turnip	Lima Beans	Boiled Rice
Endive	Cabbage	Kohl-Rabi	very young	Boiled
Marrow	Radishes	Squash		Macaroni
Sorrel	Leeks	Okra		
Sauerkraut	String Beans	Beets		
Beet Greens	very young	Carrots		
Dandelions	Broccoli	Onions		
Swiss Chard	French	Green Peas		
Celery	Artichokes	very young		
Mushrooms				

Fruits

Grapefruit		Strawberries	Raspberries	Bananas
		Lemons	Plums	Prunes
		Currants	Apricots	Ice Cream
		Cranberries	Pears	
		Peaches	Pineapple	
		Blackberries	Apples	
		Oranges	Blueberries	
			Cherries	

1 gram protein, 4 calories.
1 " carbohydrate, 4 "
1 " fat, 9 "
6.25 " protein contain 1g. nitrogen.

1 kilogram = 2.2 pounds.
30 grams g. or cubic centimeters c. c. = 1 ounce.
A patient "at rest" requires 25 calories per kilogram.

[1] Used with permission of Lea & Febiger.

* Reckon average carbohydrate in 5% veg. as 3%–of 10% veg. as 6%

Table 2.* — The Quantity of Carbohydrate, Protein and Fat and the Caloric Value of 30 Grams (1 ounce) of Foods in Common Use

30 grams 1 oz. Contain Approximately	Carbohydrates G.	Protein G.	Fat G.	Calories
Vegetables 5%	1	0.5	0	6
Vegetables 10%	2	0.5	0	10
Potato	6	1	0	28
Bread	18	3	0	84
Oatmeal, dry wgt.	20	5	2	118
Milk	1.5	1	1	19
Meat (cooked, lean)	0	8	5	77
Fish	0	6	0	24
Chicken (cooked lean)	0	8	3	59
Egg (one)	0	6	6	78
Cheese	0	8	11	131
Bacon	0	5	15	155
Cream, 20%	1	1	6	62
Cream, 40%	1	1	12	116
Butter	0	0	25	225
Oil	0	0	30	270

* Used with permission of Lea & Febiger

Table 3*
DIABETIC DIETS

DIETS	TOTAL DIET				CARBOHYDRATE (C)							PROTEIN and FAT (PF)				
	CARBO-HY-DRATE	PRO-TEIN	FAT	CALO-RIES	5% Vege-tables	10% Vege-tables	OR-ANGE	OAT-MEAL	PO-TATO	BREAD	MILK	EGG	MEAT	BACON	20% CREAM	BUT-TER
C1 PF1	110	50	61	1189	300	150	400	15	60	30	120	1	75		120	15
C2 PF2	122	55	73	1365	300	150	400	15	90	30	240	1	75		120	25
C3 PF3	131	60	81	1493	300	150	400	15	90	45	240	1	75	15	120	25
C4 PF4	140	73	92	1680	300	150	400	15	90	60	240	1	120	15	120	30
C5 PF5	151	82	99	1823	300		400	15	150	75	240	1	150	20	120	30
C6 PF6	160	85	104	1916	300		400	15	150	90	240	1	150	30	120	30
C7 PF7	172	95	121	2157	300		400	15	210	90	240	1	180	30	120	45

Approximate equivalents. 1 small orange (100 gms) = ½ banana (50 gms) = ½ saucer oatmeal (15 gms dry or 120 gms cooked) = 2 large saucers (300 gms) 5% vegetables = 1 large saucer (150 gms) 10% vegetables = potato size of egg = ½ slice (15 gms) bread.

* Used with permission of Lea & Febiger.

THE TREATMENT OF DIABETES PAYS
ELLIOTT P. JOSLIN, M.D.
Boston, Mass.

The treatment of diabetes is worth while. Years ago severe cases of diabetes were considered common, but today they are known to be rare. Indeed there are now apparently no severe cases of diabetes, because they are so well concealed by diet and insulin. The few cases, which actually are severe, we recognize are not such intrinsically, but because of complications such as infections and coma or because of associated diseases like hyperthyroidism, and haemochromatosis. Children present a second criterion of the usefulness of today's diabetic treatment. At present the yearly mortality of diabetic children is not far from one per cent, but before the introduction of insulin the yearly mortality was nearer 50 per cent in the best hands and 100 per cent as a rule. Chil-

teeth can be cleaned and if necessary extracted, bad tonsils can be removed, hyperthyroidism can be corrected. In children the appendix should be removed, if there is a distinct history of an attack, because of the confusion which always ensues when a child has diabetic coma and at the same time has discomfort in the abdomen. A few patients are discovered with gall stones. The eyes should be examined. Finally, every diabetic entering a hospital should have an X-ray of the chest because of the possibility of latent tuberculosis.

Table 1.[1]— **Foods Arranged Approximately According to Content of Carbohydrates**

Water, clear broths, coffee, tea, cocoa shells and cracked cocoa can be taken without allowance for food content.

Vegetables (fresh or canned)

1%–3%	5% 3%–5%	10%*	15%	20%
Lettuce	Tomatoes	Str. Beans	Green Peas	Potatoes
Cucumbers	Water Cress	Brussels	Jerusalem	Shell Beans
Spinach	Sea Kale	Sprouts	Artichokes	Baked Beans
Asparagus	Cauliflower	Pumpkin	Parsnips	Green Corn
Rhubarb	Egg Plant	Turnip	Lima Beans	Boiled Rice
Endive	Cabbage	Kohl-Rabi	very young	Boiled
Marrow	Radishes	Squash		Macaroni
Sorrel	Leeks	Okra		
Sauerkraut	String Beans	Beets		
Beet Greens	very young	Carrots		
Dandelions	Broccoli	Onions		
Swiss Chard	French	Green Peas		
Celery	Artichokes	very young		
Mushrooms				

		Fruits		
		Strawberries	Raspberries	Bananas
		Lemons	Plums	Prunes
Grapefruit		Currants	Apricots	Ice Cream
		Cranberries	Pears	
		Peaches	Pineapple	
		Blackberries	Apples	
		Oranges	Blueberries	
			Cherries	

1 gram protein, 4 calories.
1 "   carbohydrate, 4 "
1 "   fat, 9 "
6.25 " protein contain 1g. nitrogen.

1 kilogram = 2.2 pounds.
30 grams g. or cubic centimeters c. c. = 1 ounce.
A patient "at rest" requires 25 calories per kilogram.

[1] Used with permission of Lea & Febiger.
* Reckon average carbohydrate in 5% veg. as 3%–of 10% veg. as 6%

Table 2.* — The Quantity of Carbohydrate, Protein and Fat and the Caloric Value of 30 Grams (1 ounce) of Foods in Common Use

30 grams 1 oz. Contain Approximately	Carbohydrates G.	Protein G.	Fat G.	Calories
Vegetables 5%	1	0.5	0	6
Vegetables 10%	2	0.5	0	10
Potato	6	1	0	28
Bread	18	3	0	84
Oatmeal, dry wgt.	20	5	2	118
Milk	1.5	1	1	19
Meat (cooked, lean)	0	8	5	77
Fish	0	6	0	24
Chicken (cooked lean)	0	8	3	59
Egg (one)	0	6	6	78
Cheese	0	8	11	131
Bacon	0	5	15	155
Cream, 20%	1	1	6	62
Cream, 40%	1	1	12	116
Butter	0	0	25	225
Oil	0	0	30	270

* Used with permission of Lea & Febiger

Table 3*
DIABETIC DIETS

DIETS	TOTAL DIET				CARBOHYDRATE (C)							PROTEIN and FAT (PF)				
	CARBO-HY-DRATE	PRO-TEIN	FAT	CALO-RIES	5% Vege-tables	10% Vege-tables	OR-ANGE	OAT-MEAL	PO-TATO	BREAD	MILK	EGG	MEAT	BACON	20% CREAM	BUT-TER
C1 PF1	110	50	61	1189	300	150	400	15	60	30	120	1	75		120	15
C2 PF2	122	55	73	1365	300	150	400	15	90	30	240	1	75		120	25
C3 PF3	131	60	81	1493	300	150	400	15	90	45	240	1	75	15	120	25
C4 PF4	140	73	92	1680	300	150	400	15	90	60	240	1	120	15	120	30
C5 PF5	151	82	99	1823	300		400	15	150	75	240	1	150	20	120	30
C6 PF6	160	85	104	1916	300		400	15	150	90	240	1	150	30	120	30
C7 PF7	172	95	121	2157	300		400	15	210	90	240	1	180	30	120	45

Approximate equivalents. 1 small orange (100 gms) = ½ banana (50 gms) = ½ saucer oatmeal (15 gms dry or 120 gms cooked) = 2 large saucers (300 gms) 5% vegetables = 1 large saucer (150 gms) 10% vegetables = potato size of egg = ½ slice (15 gms) bread.

* Used with permission of Lea & Febiger.

THE TREATMENT OF DIABETES PAYS
ELLIOTT P. JOSLIN, M.D.
Boston, Mass.

The treatment of diabetes is worth while. Years ago severe cases of diabetes were considered common, but today they are known to be rare. Indeed there are now apparently no severe cases of diabetes, because they are so well concealed by diet and insulin. The few cases, which actually are severe, we recognize are not such intrinsically, but because of complications such as infections and coma or because of associated diseases like hyperthyroidism, and haemochromatosis. Children present a second criterion of the usefulness of today's diabetic treatment. At present the yearly mortality of diabetic children is not far from one per cent, but before the introduction of insulin the yearly mortality was nearer 50 per cent in the best hands and 100 per cent as a rule. Children likewise teach us very definitely that it is the uncontrolled diabetic who develops complications and dies. The third proof of the success of treatment is shown by the reduction of mortality from coma, gangrene and surgical operations, as well as by the reduction of deaths among those who acquire pneumonia, tuberculosis, or become pregnant.

Treatment pays the patient by increase in health and prolongation of life and the doctor by living evidence of his faithful effort and by added opportunities for earning a living.

INSULIN AND DIABETES*
ELLIOTT P. JOSLIN, M.D.
Boston, Mass.

This is in honor of Insulin's birthday—the birthday of insulin—a cheerful day for diabetics because insulin has made them healthy and useful instead of being sick and dependent. On February 1, or was it not really January 11, 1922, insulin was first injected into a human being by Banting and Best and with their discovery this winderful remedy became avaialble to mankind.

Insulin has doubled the duration of life of diabetics. Before insulin all diabetic children died and usually lived less than a year. Today with insulin diabetic children can live indefinitely.

What is insulin? Insulin is one of the secretions of the pancreas and when this is lacking diabetes results. It is formed in a group of cells of the pancreas called the Islands of Langerhans but these only constitute one-twentieth of the whole gland—not more than the weight of a Buffalo nickel. Up to the time of Banting and Best no one was able to extract insulin from the pancreas, because while attempting to do so it was destroyed by the remaining powerful, digestive ferments produced by that gland.

Pasteur said, "Chance helps the mind that is prepared," and the discovery of insulin again shows him to have been right. The discovery was the culmination of hard work of many men. Banting's mind was prepared, because he devised a method by which he could get rid of all the other digestive juices in the pancreas and thus extract insulin in pure form. He began his experiments in the Laboratory of Professor McLeod in the University of Toronto, Canada. Banting was not familiar with physiological methods. He was a surgeon, and so a medical student—a second year medical student—Charles H. Best helped him in his experiments. Most medical discoveries have been made by young men, but practically all discoveries in diabetes are due to youthful doctors.

Insulin was first obtained from a dog. Banting and Best tied the duct of the pancreas in a dog. The pancreas, you know, is the sweet bread and lies in the back part of the upper abdomen. In the following six weeks the whole of the gland, save the insulin producing cells, atrophied, became inactive, and at the end of that time Banting and Best extracted insulin from the remaining portion. This insulin extract they then injected into a diabetic dog and found their extract worked. There was a reduction of the sugar in the blood and of the sugar in the urine. They labored with feverish activity. Day after day through the hot summer of 1921 they carried on their experiments. I hold in my hands a copy of one of their experiments in which they noted the reduction of sugar in the blood and urine of a diabetic dog following the injection of their extract. Note the hours on the practical experiment. They are 1 a.m., 2 a.m., 3 a.m., and 4 a.m., and the blood sugar which had been 0.37 per cent had fallen to 0.21 per cent. I fear they did not keep to an eight-hour day or a thirty-hour week.

Every diabetic should love a dog because it was by experiments on

* Radio talk given over Station WBZ in February, 1934.

dogs that they live today. All through the summer and fall of 1921 Banting and Best struggled in the laboratory, perfected their technique, and finally, about six months after the beginning of their studies, twelve years ago today they injected their insulin into a human diabetic. The same effect was produced in him which they had found in diabetic animals. Later they were assisted by Professor Collip in the refinement of insulin so that when the Nobel prize was awarded for the discovery of insulin to Banting and McLeod, Banting divided his portion with the medical student, Charles H. Best, now Professor of Physiology in the University of Toronto, and Professor McLeod in whose laboratory the work was performed divided his portion with Dr. Collip.

The discovery of insulin spelled the death knell of quack diabetic remedies. Insulin will keep a diabetic dog alive, but quack diabetic remedies will not. No one can get me to test a quack remedy on a child when I know it will not work with a diabetic dog, and yet there are still quack remedies on the market which their producers urge doctors to give to their diabetic patients.

The action of insulin is strongest at an hour, but it lasts for eight hours. Many diabetics need it only once a day, because their own pancreas forms enough insulin to protect them for the balance of the day. Some diabetics need none. In the course of infections diabetics may need insulin every three hours, and in diabetic coma sometimes as often as every half-hour. Insulin brings down to normal the sugar in the blood and thus avoids the loss of sugar in the urine and makes the urine sugar free. Without insulin a severe diabetic loses the greater part of sugar and starch in his diet in the urine, and since sugar and starch (carbohydrate) constitute the chief part of our food, it is natural that he grows thin. To get rid of the sugar in the urine he must void large quantities of urine and this in turn makes him drink quarts and quarts of water. Increased sugar in the blood of a diabetic renders him liable to infections, not only lowers his resistance to general diseases like pneumonia, but makes him subject to boils and carbuncles. I know of a doctor who has been treating a diabetic patient seventy-one years old with pneumonia. A generation ago practically all diabetics with pneumonia died. This patient usually required 15 units of insulin daily, but last week during her pneumonia the requirement rose to 82 units, and despite eight days of high fever, seven and a half years of diabetes, and her age, she has recovered.

Think of what insulin has accomplished. Insulin has enabled a diabetic to get the value out of his food and this means that it has put a weak, thin, sick individual back to work—a precious privilege. Insulin has given a diabetic life itself. It has made him a productive factor in the community. It is less than thirty years ago that twenty-nine out of every one hundred diabetic patients entering one of the largest hospitals in Boston were carried out dead. Today the deaths from diabetes in such hospitals are a minimum. Formerly sixty out of every one hundred diabetics died of acid poisoning, diabetic coma, and all children who developed coma died. Today a death from diabetic coma is as needless as a death from diphtheria and the diabetic who lives on his diet and takes his insulin and keeps sugar free can avoid it. Even after it occurs insulin will save four out of five diabetics and in one group of ninety-seven children with diabetic coma, only one died.

What else has insulin done? Before the discovery of insulin it was seldom that a child lived one year with diabetes. Today children can live indefinitely and the modern diabetic child can go through school and college and lead a useful life. Before insulin diabetic children were the first to die. Now diabetic children live the longest because insulin protects them and the diabetics who die today are the old diabetics.

Insulin has reduced deaths from infections in diabetes. Before the discovery of insulin almost every diabetic who developed pneumonia died and every other diabetic died who had had a carbuncle, and when a diabetic needed a surgical operation or a diabetic woman was to be confined the doctors and the obstetrician threw up their hands in despair. Today it is almost as safe to operate upon a diabetic as upon a non-diabetic and this is due to insulin.

Insulin has doubled the length of life of diabetics. Before the discovery of insulin there were about 200,000 diabetics living in the United States. Today because of insulin there are approximately 400,000. But this does not tell the story. We know that in addition to the 400,000 living diabetics there are 2,000,000 other people in the United States who will develop the disease before they die. This shows the significance and importance of the discovery of insulin. At least one in fifty of the inhabitants of the United States are interested in insulin, and since each has five relatives, one in ten.

Why is it that there are more diabetics today than before insulin was discovered? Already I have partly answered that question. There are twice as many living because insulin has enabled them to live twice as long. Twelve years from now there may be twice as many more. But there is another reason and that is that diabetes is a disease of adult life. When I was born the average age at death in the community was about twenty-five years, today the average age at death is about 45 years. Diabetes is most common at fifty years. In other words, as the population in the United States grows older there are more and more people who live into the diabetic age zone and thus develop diabetes.

The prevention of diabetes in the future lies along two lines. First, diabetes is hereditary and two diabetics should not marry each other, but if a diabetic marries a non-diabetic in a non-diabetic family, their children are not expected to have diabetes. In the second place, diabetes in adults is a disease of the fat. If there is diabetes in your family when you are fair and forty keep thin. It is twice as common in old women as in old men. Since insulin the death rate in Massachusetts from diabetes has steadily fallen for all diabetics under the age of forty-five years; above forty-five years it has risen chiefly because of fat women. Therefore, if anyone in your family has diabetes, don't get fat and especially don't get fat if you are a woman with a diabetic heredity.

There are some dangers in the use of insulin just as there are some dangers in the use of ether. If one uses too much insulin it lowers the blood sugar too much and then a diabetic can get a reaction, become hungry, faint, tremble, sweat and get unconscious. A lump of sugar will bring him out of this state in an early stage. This condition is not peculiar to the effect of insulin, because it occurs with anyone who is on a deficient diet or after extreme exertion like the runners after a Marathon run. Little by little doctors and diabetic patients are getting better acquainted with the use of insulin and these reactions, and more and more they are avoided. The deaths from insulin reactions in the whole world are very few and I suspect it is understating their frequency to say that for one death from an insulin reaction there occur 10,000 deaths from diabetic coma.

Insulin does not work by mouth. It must be injected under the skin. Perhaps some day a method will be discovered by which a preparation of insulin or of some other gland will be found which will act as a substitute.

The discovery of insulin placed a great responsibility upon diabetics. Before it they were almost helpless. Now they are able to work, but this is not the whole story. Diabetics know that their lives depend upon insulin. In order to use it well they have been taken into hospitals or taught in doctors' offices a great deal of medicine. They know not only the complications of their diabetes, but incidentally they have had opportunities to learn other medical facts. Diabetics understand about their own diets and also they know what the proper diets are for other members of their households. But this is not all. Diabetics have learned that the disease is hereditary and that the chances are there is someone else living in their family who either has the disease or will develop it and it is up to them to help the family doctor detect the one in their family who has it, and by teaching all the others about the dangers of being fat in middle life to help prevent the acquirement. Moreover the duty of a diabetic does not end with his life. When he dies he should have an examination made of his body so that the doctors can learn what can be done to protect the rest of his family in generations to come. Never forget that an operation during life is attended with pain and is for the benefit of the individual, but an operation after death, an autopsy, is without pain, and is for the benefit of humanity and in the case of a diabetic is for the benefit of his descendants. Every diabetic should put in his will that he wishes an autopsy performed when he dies.

Years ago a young officer who had achieved signal success in his military training developed diabetes. Despite all his life's preparation, at the beginning of the War it seemed as if his studies had been fruitless. Let me tell you what this man did. Between 1914 and 1922 he kept himself alive as only was possible for a diabetic in those days—by almost starving. It seemed as if he was waging an absolutely hopeless fight, but he fought and fought on to keep his spark of life, although his weight dropped from 175 pounds to 110 pounds. Then insulin was discovered! That young officer failed to lead his company or his regiment in War, but by his example he has lived to lead a whole army of diabetics in Peace! An army is made up of soldiers. There are now 400,000 diabetic soldiers in this country. The army has many good leaders; it will win only if each soldier does his duty by himself and his neighbor.

THE COST OF DIABETIC TREATMENT
ELLIOTT P. JOSLIN, M.D.
Boston, Mass.

Much is said about the cost of diabetic treatment but this is warranted only to a moderate degree. The real cost comes in caring for the complications of the disease rather than for the disease itself. Diabetic coma implies neglect of treatment and an attack costs on the average $100; a neglected sore toe with its protracted healing costs a diabetic, the hospital or some one else, at least $300; the development of tuberculosis in a diabetic represents a yearly expenditure of $1,500, therefore:

Focus on the patient for the prevention of complications and save money. He alone knows whether he follows his diet and takes his insulin and exercise. He is the one who alone can protect himself from coma and injuries and can warn his doctor early of any sort of indisposition. Poor treatment is expensive. One child who was carelessly treated took 240 units of insulin a day and showed 5 per cent sugar in the urine and appeared sad and ill, but ten days later when sugar free with 44 units of insulin appeared happy and well.

Education and insulin have shortened hospital treatment from a four weeks' period to one week. For years there have been two or three classes for the diabetic patients each week, but now the talks are given daily beginning at 10.30 and ending at 11.15. An effort is made to assemble as many patients as possible for each class and seek to get their relatives as well. One talk is equal to a day of hospital care. Insulin, of course, has been the greater factor in shortening the period which is necessary to get control of the diabetes. One can truthfully say to a patient that ten cents invested in insulin is equal to the expense of a day in a hospital. If a patient objects to insulin, repeat this statement daily and prove it by showing him a case similar to his own who is receiving insulin and making greater and more rapid improvement and he will soon be convinced that he wishes to save money too. Class instruction helps much in such cases, because of the zeal of new converts to insulin in the audience. Often to save expense the patient can go home a day or two earlier than is the rule provided arrangement is made for the Wandering Diabetic Nurse to make a few visits in the home and thus teach the family.

Both the control of diabetes and the cost of treatment are favored by

DISCHARGE DIRECTIONS

NAME _____ ADDRESS _____ DATE _____

BREAKFAST			DINNER			SUPPER			NIGHT			TOTAL DAILY DIET	
INSULIN ___ UNITS			INSULIN ___ UNITS			INSULIN ___ UNITS			INSULIN ___ UNITS			C ___ P ___ F ___ CAL ___	
	GRAMS	PORTIONS		GRAMS	PORTIONS		GRAMS	PORTIONS		GRAMS	PORTIONS		GRAMS	PORTIONS
EGGS			EGGS			EGGS						EGGS		
MEAT, COOKED			MEAT, COOKED			MEAT, COOKED						MEAT, COOKED		
BACON			BACON			BACON						BACON		
5% VEG.			5% VEG.			5% VEG.						5% VEG.		
10% VEG.			10% VEG.			10% VEG.						10% VEG.		
OAT., DRY			OAT., DRY			OAT., DRY						OAT., DRY		
OAT., COOKED			OAT., COOKED			OAT., COOKED						OAT., COOKED		
UNEEDAS			UNEEDAS			UNEEDAS						UNEEDAS		
BUTTER			BUTTER			BUTTER						BUTTER		
CREAM, 20%			CREAM, 20%			CREAM, 20%						CREAM, 20%		
ORANGE			ORANGE			ORANGE						ORANGE		
GRAPEFRUIT			GRAPEFRUIT			GRAPEFRUIT						GRAPEFRUIT		
CHEESE			CHEESE			CHEESE						CHEESE		
POTATO			POTATO			POTATO						POTATO		
BREAD			BREAD			BREAD						BREAD		
MILK			MILK			MILK						MILK		

Special Medication _____

exercise and work. Theoretically it is often best to keep the patient at work and adjust diet and insulin to his occupation. If exercise is not taken in the hospital, allowance must be made for this when he goes home and diet enlarged or insulin reduced to prevent insulin reactions.

The cost of a diabetic diet need be little more than that of a non-diabetic diet. Fresh fruit it is true is desirable at each meal and this means usually grapefruit, orange, berries, a peach and in whole or in part an apple or banana. An egg can be taken at one meal and usually meat or cheese at the other two. Fresh vegetables are desirable, but cabbage, cucumbers, tomatoes, spinach and lettuce are not expensive. If the diabetic diet is said to be too expensive, because of these plain and desirable articles of food, it can also be said with equal pertinence that the ordinary diet without them is too cheap. Ten to fifteen cents extra allowance for daily food above the proper diet of a normal individual should be ample.

The cost of insulin for the average diabetic is not high. Thirty units is an average dose and this can be purchased for less than fifteen cents or half a cent a unit. As a rule the patients who take larger doses, namely, two or three times as much, are breaking their diet.

Special Instructions

The special instructions listed below are designed to help in preventing and distinguishing between diabetic coma and an insulin reaction. Remember that coma comes on gradually in days or hours, but an insulin reaction usually in less than an hour or in a few minutes. Coma comes from too much food and too little insulin: a reaction from too little food and too much insulin. In coma the urine contains sugar, but in a reaction although the first specimen may show sugar, a second specimen invariably will be sugar free or almost sugar free. The respiration in coma is heavy and deep but in insulin reaction is normal or in severe cases may be feeble.

I. To Prevent Diabetic Coma.
   A. Never omit insulin unless urine is sugar free. Keep to your diet and in case of an infection take more insulin if necessary to keep sugar free. It is imperative to test the urine frequently during an acute illness.
   B. If you feel sick and especially if you have FEVER, NAUSEA and VOMITING or severe pains in the abdomen: 1. Go to bed. 2. Call a doctor. 3. Take a cup of coffee, cocoa shells or broth every hour. Omit at least one-half your diet and instead take orange juice or oatmeal gruel. If the urine contains sugar, take insulin every hour under your doctor's direction. 4. Get someone, a relative, a friend or nurse to devote his entire time to you until you are well. 5. Move the bowels with an enema.

Carbohydrate Substitution Values

FOOD	CARBOHYDRATE 10 GM.	15 GM.
	GRAMS	GRAMS
GRAPEFRUIT PULP	200	300
STRAWBERRIES	150	225
WATERMELON	150	225
BLACKBERRIES	100	150
CANTALOUPE	100	150
ORANGE PULP	100	150
PEARS	100	150
PINEAPPLE	80	120
APRICOTS	75	115
CHERRIES	75	115
HONEYDEW MELON	75	115
PEACHES	75	115
RASPBERRIES	75	115
APPLE	65	100
BLUEBERRIES	65	100
BANANA	50	75
ICE CREAM	50	75
PLUMS	50	75
PRUNES	50	75

II. To Recognize and Treat an Insulin Reaction.
  A. CAUSES OF AN INSULIN REACTION.
    1. Too much insulin.
    2. Too little food or too long a period between insulin and food.
    3. Food given has been unabsorbed because of indigestion, vomiting or diarrhea.
    4. Unusual exercise.
  B. SYMPTOMS (may occur 1 to 8 hours after taking insulin).
    1. Trembling, nervousness, faintness, weakness, pallor, sweating, hunger, double vision, headache.
    2. Unconsciousness may occur if the reaction is severe.
  C. TREATMENT
    1. When the patient is conscious: Take the juice of an orange, one or more lumps of sugar, or one or more teaspoonfuls of corn syrup.
    2. In unconsciousness: If necessary give 0.5 c.c. adrenalin chloride 1:1000 solution hypodermically and repeat in 15 minutes. With return to consciousness as soon as possible give the juice of an orange by mouth. Ten per cent glucose solution may be given by rectum, under the skin or intravenously if the doctor so directs.
III. The best insurance a diabetic patient can have is to see his physician once a month. Take him this paper and a specimen of urine. Always carry this sheet with you or wear an identification tag with your Name, Address and the words—Diabetic Coma or Insulin Shock. Which?

Patients Taking Insulin Should Always Carry Two Lumps of Sugar

Treatment of Feet.

Hygiene of the Feet:—
  1. Wash feet daily with soap and water. Dry thoroughly, especially between toes, using pressure rather than vigorous rubbing.
  2. When thoroughly dry, rub with lanolin as often as necessary to keep skin soft and free from scales and dryness, but never render the feet tender. If the feet become too soft, rub once a day with alcohol.
  3. If the nails are brittle and dry, soften by soaking in warm water one-half hour each night and apply lanolin generously under and about the nails and bandage loosely. Clean nails with orange-wood sticks. Cut the nails only in a good light and after a bath, when the feet are very clean. Cut the nails straight across to avoid injury to the toes. If you go to a chiropodist tell him you have diabetes.
  4. All patients with overlapping toes or toes that are close together should separate them by lamb's wool. Patients with large joints or cramped-up toes should wear shoes without toe boxes and only vici kid leather.
  5. All patients over sixty should have daily rest periods at which time they should remove their shoes.
  6. Do not wear bed-room slippers when you ought to wear shoes. Slippers do not give proper support.
  7. Wear shoes of soft leather which fit and are not tight (neither narrow nor short). Wear new shoes one-half hour only on the first day and increase one hour daily. Do not step on floor with bare feet.
  8. Use bed socks instead of hot water bottles, bags or electric heaters.
  9. Every Sunday morning ask someone to examine your feet.
  10. After fifty years one hears less well, sees less well, and the sense of feeling is diminished. Remember this and be cautious about the feet.

Treatment of Corns and Callosities:—
1. Wear shoes which fit and cause no pressure.
2. Soak foot in warm, not hot, soapy water. Rub off with gauze or file off dead skin on or about callus or corn. Do not tear it off. Do not cut corns or callosities. Do not try to remove corns or calluses with patent or other medicines.
3. Prevent calluses under ball of foot.
    (a) by exercising such as curling and stretching toes twenty times a day,
    (b) by finishing each step on the toes and not on the ball of the foot.

Aids in Treatment of Imperfect Circulation:—Cold Feet:—
1. Exercises. Bend the foot down and up as far as it will go 6 times. Describe a circle to the left with the foot 6 times and then to the right. Repeat morning, noon, and night.
2. Massage with lanolin or cocoa butter.
3. Do not wear circular garters. Do not sit with knees crossed.
4. If you have had gangrene or been threatened with it, only allow yourself to be on your feet 2 hours in the morning, 2 hours in the afternoon, and 2 hours in the evening.

Treatment of Abrasions of the Skin:—
1. Proper first-aid treatment is of the utmost importance even in apparently minor injuries. Consult your physician immediately.
2. Avoid strong irritating antiseptics, such as sulpho-napthol and iodine.
3. As soon as possible after injury certain surgeons recommend the application of sterile gauze saturated with medicated alcohol or hexylresorcinol (S. T. 37). Keep wet for not more than thirty minutes by adding more of the antiseptic solution. Sterile gauze in sealed packets may be purchased at drug stores.
4. Elevate, and as much as possible until recovery, avoid using the foot.
5. Consult your doctor for any redness, pain, swelling, or other evidence of inflammation.

OUTLINE OF COURSE OF TALKS FOR DIABETICS

Topics considered each week in the diabetic classes held daily at the George F. Baker Clinic, New England Deaconess Hospital for patients and their relatives, for nurses and visiting doctors.

I. A. Definition. What is Diabetes?
    B. Etiology. Heredity. Inciting causes:
       obesity,
       infections,
       hyperthyroidism,
       hyperpituitarism.
    C. Diagnosis. Prove diabetes present or absent. Respect a reported analysis.
II. D. Sugar in Urine. Varieties. Total sugar lost in 24°. What this means. Demonstrate.
    E. Benedict Test. (a) method, interpretation (c) use of second specimen test.
                      (b) four-period test (morning, (d) best times to test and how often.
                          evening, afternoon, night)
    F. Blood Sugar. Advantages blood sugar over urine sugar. B.S. necessary for diagnosis.
       Comparison of sugar in the blood and glycogen in the liver.
III. G. Diet. Fundamental requirements of any permanent diet. Emphasize calorie needs, balance between C., P., and F., mineral requirements esp. Ca, Fe., I, H₂O. See Discharge Direction and Diet Card.
       A calorie measures the energy which may be derived from food. With one calorie a man can rise from a chair, turn a key in the door and sit down.
       Why weigh food? Who should weigh it?
       Weighing and estimating food compared. Equivalents in household portions.
       C. P. F. Cals.
       Weight: gain and loss. Long intervals between meals desirable.
    H. Treatment. Undernutrition—the foundation.

IV. I. Insulin   What it is   Source.   (e) Method of injection.
    (a) Who should take it?   (f) Site. Lumps. Atrophies.
    (b) Time, frequency, dose, omission   (g) Removal of broken needles.
    (c) One unit. U-10, U-20, U-40, Stress U-40.
    (d) An insulin syringe.

    Insulin should be continued even after the urine is sugar free in order to maintain weight, strength and provide growth. Some mild cases, particularly in later life, can get on without insulin, and some only require it during infections.
    Insulin is insurance.

  J. Insulin reactions. Causes. Symptoms. Treatment. See Discharge Directions.
     Coma and an insulin reaction compared.

V. K. Diabetic Coma. Cause. Prevention. Treatment. See Discharge Directions.

  L. Exercise. Regularity and Moderation. Remember a diabetic is driving three horses—Diet, Exercise and Insulin.

VI. M. Gangrene. See Discharge Directions for   (3) Imperfect circulation
                  (1) Hygiene of feet   (4) Abrasions of skin.
                  (2) Treatment of corns and
                      calluses

  N. Teeth.

  O. Skin. Boils. Carbuncles. Glycogen vs. sugar in the skin.

  P. Infections. Insulin during infections.
     Tuberculosis   (a) test children   (c) early diagnosis by X-ray.
                    (b) avoid contact

  Q. Neuritis. Avoid alcohol. Keep sugar free.

THE LABORATORY
HAZEL HUNT
Director Chemical Laboratory
New England Deaconess Hospital, Boston

The chemical laboratory plays a vital part in the successful treatment of diabetes. Proper diagnosis and therapy are almost impossible without it. Unfortunately it can be and often is a factor of considerable expense. That is because chemical laboratories are not used to the greatest advantage. It is only by doing chemical tests in large numbers that the cost per test can be kept down. The chief factor of expense is the time required of a trained technician. She, however, can do ten tests almost as quickly as one test and if ten are done the cost per test can be reduced almost 90 per cent. If a single blood sugar is determined once a week the actual cost of that single test may be almost prohibitive. If, however, blood sugar tests are done by the dozens, the cost of each becomes nominal.

If chemical laboratories equipped to do diabetic work are functioning at strategic points or at "diabetic islands of safety" and are actually kept busy by the doctors in the community, there is no reason why diabetic laboratory work should be costly. The average price charged for a blood sugar test in the average laboratory is five to ten dollars. Because of the few tests done that price is necessary. On the other hand, in a laboratory which serves a diabetic clinic the cost is one dollar or less per test.

It is by the adequate and free use of your laboratories that you will reduce the cost of laboratory work. Only when that happens can sufficient laboratory work be done on diabetic patients to follow successfully and efficiently the course of their disease and your treatment.

Practical Tests

The Usefulness of the Four Period Urine Test

Collect all the urine voided for twenty-four hours in four bottles as follows:

I   Urine between breakfast and dinner —M orning
II Urine from dinner to supper —A fternoon
III Urine from supper till bedtime —E vening
IV Urine voided during night and including specimen passed upon rising in the morning —N ight

Test urine in each bottle separately to decide from the presence of sugar when the dose of insulin should be changed or the diet altered.

The Two Specimen Test and What It Discloses

The diagnosis of an insulin reaction may be obscured because of sugar in the urine due to the retention by the bladder of urine secreted by the kidneys some hours earlier. Therefore, before deciding whether the patient at the moment is secreting urine with or without sugar or deciding between coma and an insulin reaction, secure a second specimen of urine. If this is sugar free, or nearly so, it will indicate a low blood sugar.

DIABETIC COMA
ALEXANDER MARBLE, M. D.
Boston, Mass.

That *diabetic coma is preventable* and that *deaths from diabetic coma are needless* have been stated repeatedly during the last decade. The truth of these statements is borne out by the decreasing mortality from diabetic coma as shown in the accompanying chart.

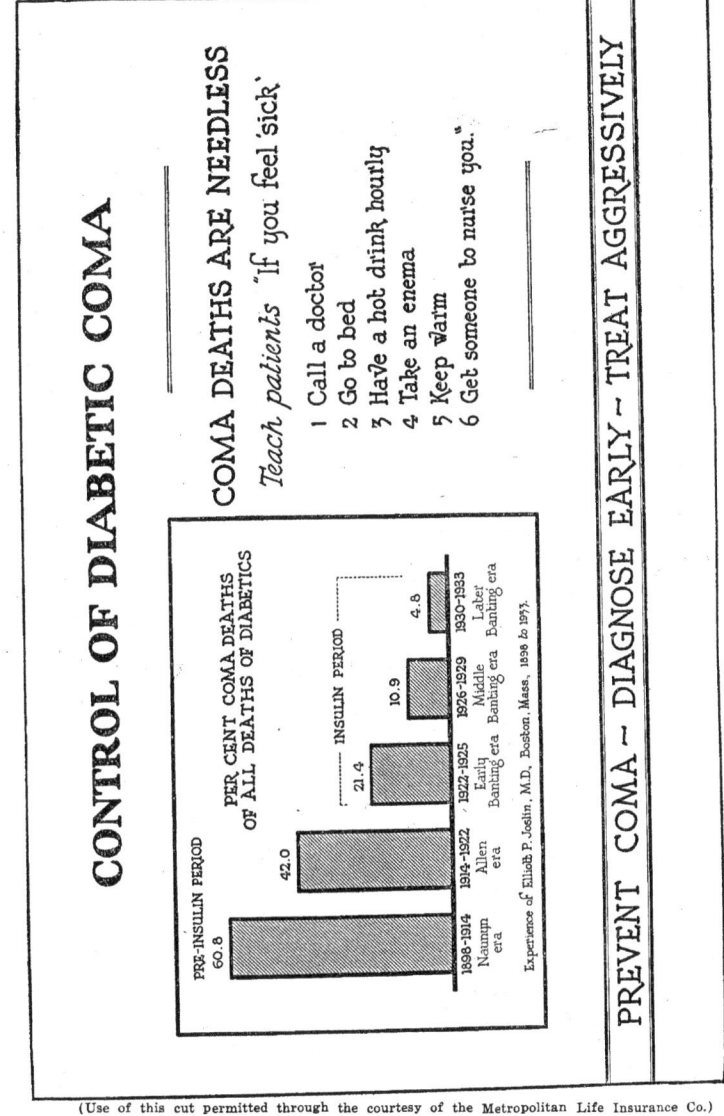

CONTROL OF DIABETIC COMA

COMA DEATHS ARE NEEDLESS

Teach patients "If you feel 'sick'

1. Call a doctor
2. Go to bed
3. Have a hot drink hourly
4. Take an enema
5. Keep warm
6. Get someone to nurse you."

PER CENT COMA DEATHS OF ALL DEATHS OF DIABETICS

PRE-INSULIN PERIOD
- 1898-1914 Naunyn era: 60.8
- 1914-1922 Allen era: 42.0

INSULIN PERIOD
- 1922-1925 Early Banting era: 21.4
- 1926-1929 Middle Banting era: 10.9
- 1930-1933 Later Banting era: 4.8

Experience of Elliott P. Joslin, M.D., Boston, Mass., 1898 to 1933.

PREVENT COMA ~ DIAGNOSE EARLY ~ TREAT AGGRESSIVELY

(Use of this cut permitted through the courtesy of the Metropolitan Life Insurance Co.)

It is evident from the above that before the introduction of the treatment of diabetes by undernutrition as suggested by Dr. F. M. Allen in 1914, over 60 per cent of all diabetics died in diabetic coma. In the period of the Allen method of treatment (1914-1922), 42 per cent of diabetics died in coma. Insulin revolutionized treatment and mortality statistics alike and in the latest group of patients studied (1930-1933), less than 5 per cent of diabetic deaths were in coma. Despite this lowered mortality, both doctor and patient must realize that diabetic coma is an antagonist worthy of great respect and that success in its control depends on prompt recognition and aggressive treatment. With insulin the treatment of diabetes is much easier but disastrous results follow when careful regulation is neglected.

Diabetic coma represents the end-result of uncontrolled diabetes. It is a condition of "acid-poisoning" in which the body is flooded with the incompletely oxidized products of the breakdown of fats. This in turn is due to the inability of the body of the diabetic to utilize carbohydrate in a normal fashion. Large quantities of sugar and "acetone bodies" accumulate in the blood and body tissues and are excreted in the urine.

Precipitating Factors

We teach patients that coma occurs because of (1) too much food, (2) too little insulin, or (3) infections. "Too much food" may mean deliberate breaking of diet or simply the innocent overeating of the person with undiagnosed diabetes. "Too little insulin" often means no insulin and here again the omission may not be a willful one. The influence of infections is real. Patients may be progressing serenely with diet, insulin and exercise well balanced when with the development of a carbuncle, pneumonia, upper respiratory infection or other acute febrile illness, acidosis may be precipitated.

Symptoms

There are no symptoms which are invariably found but usually the onset of definite acidosis is attended by malaise, nausea, vomiting and abdominal pain. If proper treatment is not instituted, the vomiting and abdominal pain continue and the breathing becomes labored. Respirations are of the long, deep, rapid Kussmaul ("air hunger") type. The saturation of the body with the "acetone bodies" is reflected in the fruity odor of the breath which sometimes is so marked that the peculiar smell in the sick room is apparent to those entering. Drowsiness comes, proceeds to stupor and passes finally into coma.

Signs

When first seen, the patient in full-blown diabetic coma presents a distressing picture. He lies in bed, unconscious, or semiconscious, often moaning as with pain, with a dry, cold skin, flushed drawn face, and obviously dehydrated tissues. The eyeballs are soft, the mouth and tongue are dry and present a dirty coating. At intervals the patient vomits dark brown material, obviously changed blood. On being turned or examined, cries as of pain may be occasioned. The abdominal findings may closely simulate those of acute appendicitis. The extremities are cold and the body temperature, in the absence of accompanying infection, is often below normal. The pulse is rapid and weak and the blood pressure low.

Laboratory Findings

The urine usually contains large but not extremely large amounts of sugar. A deep wine color is obtained with the addition of ferric chloride indicating the presence of large amounts of diabetic acid and acetone. The urinary sediment contains "showers" of granular casts. The blood sugar is high, although not always extraordinarily so. Values from 300 to 600 milligrams per cent are common: in one case the initial determination showed 1600 milligrams per cent. The carbon dioxide combining power of the blood plasma shows a marked reduction although there is no absolute parallelism between clinical and laboratory findings in this respect. Severe cases may have values of 10 volumes per cent or lower and values so low as not to permit accurate reading on the Van Slyke instrument are occasionally obtained. In the pre-insulin days it was noted that cases had almost always a bad prognosis if the carbon dioxide combining power of the plasma was 20 volumes per cent or below. The blood chloride is often appreciably lowered, due presumably to the persistent vomiting. The non-protein nitrogen of the blood may be increased. The white blood count is usually elevated.

Treatment

The patient in diabetic coma is a patient in shock. The body temperature is subnormal, the extremities cold, the pulse weak and rapid and the blood pressure low. Whatever else the treatment may be, due regard must be given to this phase of the condition. Immediately on admission to the hospital, the patient must be placed in a bed previously warmed. Warm blankets and bed-clothing must be used and the patient surrounded by hot water bottles so placed that there is no danger of burning the skin. Fluid in large amount must be provided but not more than 100 c.c. an hour should be allowed by mouth; hot liquids are preferable to cold. Often at first, however, because of vomiting no fluids can be given by mouth. Almost invariably physiological salt solution with or without added glucose, 5 or 10 per cent, must be given subcutaneously or intravenously in quantities which may amount to 3000 c.c. in twenty-four hours. If the blood pressure is extremely low, ephedrine sulphate may be given subcutaneously or intravenously, hourly if necessary, in doses of 25 to 50 mgm. As an emergency measure one or more doses of adrenalin hydrochloride (1-1000 solution) given subcutaneously in amounts of 0.5 to 1.0 c.c. or in smaller amounts intravenously may be necessary. Caffeine sodium benzoate may be administered subcutaneously in repeated doses of 0.45 gm. (7½ grains). In appropriate cases transfusion of whole blood should be considered to combat shock as in a non-diabetic emergency.

Specific treatment is provided with insulin. This must not be given in a half-hearted fashion. On admission a specimen of urine is obtained, by catheter if necessary, to test for sugar and diacetic acid. A large dose of insulin varying usually from 20 to 80 units should be given depending on the degree of acidosis. Occasionally a child with recent onset of diabetes and of coma requires less. Examination of the urine is repeated at half-hourly or hourly intervals during the first several hours and doses of insulin given according to the amount of sugar found. The unconscious patient may require 200 units within the first two hours and the total amount during the first twenty-four hours may be rarely as large as 1,000 units. On admission a determination of the blood sugar and of the carbon dioxide combining power of the blood plasma are made and these tests are repeated one or more times during the first hours of treatment in order at first to make the diagnosis and later to gauge progress of treatment. Access to a chemical laboratory in which analysis of urine and blood can be made promptly day or night is essential for best results and lowest mortality.

Gastric lavage should be carried out routinely. It accomplishes two results: first, nausea and vomiting are stopped and the way prepared for subsequent oral feeding and medication; and second, the frequent marked distention of the stomach with resulting pressure on the heart and other viscera is relieved. An enema should be given to clear out the lower bowel.

A most serious symptom is that of oliguria or anuria. To combat this the slow intravenous injection of warm 50 per cent glucose solution in amounts of 20 to 30 c.c. may be helpful. In cases in which there has been persistent vomiting with a resulting low blood plasma chloride, the intravenous injection one or twice of 50 c.c. of a 10 per cent solution of sodium chloride may stimulate the secretion of urine in a remarkable fashion.

Differential Diagnosis

An unconscious patient always presents a problem in diagnosis. When the patient is a known diabetic the possibility of diabetic coma comes quickly to the mind. One should not, however, forget that diabetic coma may be the first striking evidence of diabetes and the patient may be brought to the physician without any knowledge on the part of the family that diabetes is present. The past history and events leading up to the present illness are, nevertheless, of great value in calling attention to the correct diagnosis. In differential diagnosis one must consider the following: severe hypoglycemia, cerebral hemorrhage, uremia, meningitis, poisoning as by barbital, and toxicity from overwhelming infections. History, physical findings, examination of the urine, and determination of the blood sugar will allow ready diagnosis in almost every instance. In patients receiving insulin the differentiation between diabetic coma and an insulin reaction (hypoglycemia) may at times be confusing to the family of the patient and even to the doctor. It should be remembered that an insulin reaction occurs because of an excess of insulin and is accompanied by a low blood sugar and a sugar free urine. Whereas diabetic coma comes on gradually over a period of hours or days an insulin reaction is manifested in a matter of minutes. The symptoms of a usual insulin reaction are characteristic: nervousness, sweating, faintness, headache, hunger, and double vision. Only rarely does the condition progress to unconsciousness with or without convulsions. Although at the time of an insulin reaction the first specimen of urine may contain sugar, a second specimen obtained 15 or 20 minutes later will invariably be sugar free. Treatment, which consists in supplying readily available carbohydrate by mouth, under the skin, or by vein, gives prompt relief.

Prognosis

Among two hundred and twenty-one cases of diabetic coma treated with insulin between May 1923 and November 1932, there were twenty-nine deaths, a mortality of 13.1 per cent. As stated above, in the latest series of forty-two cases of coma seen between August, 1931 and November, 1932, death occurred in only two cases or in 4.8 per cent. The danger of coma increases steadily with age. Only three of the total of twenty-nine deaths in the whole series were in patients under twenty years of age and there were no deaths under ten years of age. The tremendous insult to the body produced by the acidosis is often too much for the individual with arteriosclerosis and a heart that is none too good. Nevertheless, the situation with the older patients is far from hopeless. A woman of seventy-three has been known to weather successfully an attack of diabetic coma. The longer a patient has been unconscious before treatment is begun, the worse is the outlook. After eight to twelve hours of unconsciousness without treatment, the prognosis must be regarded as grave. A low blood pressure, particularly one which does not rise or even falls despite treatment, is a bad prognostic sign. Accompanying heart or kidney disease, and particularly oliguria or anuria, indicate a poorer outlook. Other complications as severe infections, particularly in individuals past middle life, make for a worse prognosis. Marked acidosis as indicated by values for the carbon dioxide combining power of the blood plasma below 10 volumes per cent indicate, of course, a serious condition. A consideration of these various guides to prognosis leads to one conclusion, that to obtain the lowest mortality one must prevent diabetic coma by careful, day-by-day treatment of the diabetic condition, but that if coma does develop, it must be recognized early and treated promptly and energetically.

COMA
GEORGE H. BIGELOW, M. D.
Director, Massachusetts General Hospital

The unrecognized diabetic coma which still comes to the hospital is medically about as reprehensible as the case of diphtheria similarly unrecognized and untreated. The symptomatology which should arouse suspicion and the methods for precise diagnosis are to a certain extent analagous in the two diseases. The doctor unequivocably recognizes his responsibility in the diphtheria case and yet there is still too much complacency in regard to the neglected diabetic.

It has been shown again and again that diphtheria mortality increases with the day of the disease in which antitoxin is first administered. Similarly in diabetes delay is the essence of failure. Prompt recognition and specific treatment must be recognized as vitally in diabetes as in diphtheria.

GANGRENE AND SURGERY IN DIABETES
HOWARD F. ROOT, M. D.
Boston, Mass.

The development of complications frequently brings the diabetic to the physician. The diabetes may have been mild, producing few or no uncomfortable symptoms until a slight injury to a toe or a finger fails to heal or a painful boil develops. Then the careful physician who applies the rule—that the urine must always be tested—discovers the sugar.

Gangrene

Gangrene develops chiefly on an arteriosclerosic background, but it may occur in the young with little arteriosclerosis if the infection be severe enough. It seldom occurs without trauma such as pricking a blister, cutting a corn, a frost bite or burn. Even then it is usually accelerated by infection which could have been prevented had the hand or foot been carefully cleaned before it was touched.

It is a safe rule to teach a diabetic to keep his feet as clean as his face.

Diagnosis of Impending Gangrene

Mere calcification of the wall of the arteries of the legs as shown by X-ray is of little significance. The important question is whether occlusion of the arterial lumen or partial reduction of the lumina of many arterial branches has lowered the blood supply to the extremity involved.

The following table summarizes the more important points in diagnosis.

Diagnosis

Symptoms and Signs	Deficient Blood Supply	Normal Blood Supply
Intermittent claudication or cramps in calves on walking	+	0
Foot appears blanched or cadaveric on elevation and red or cyanotic when dependent	+	0
Pulsation in dorsalis pedis artery	0 or feeble	+
One foot is cooler than the other below a certain level	+	0

Osteomyelitis and Indolent Ulcers versus Gangrene

Any infection with purulent discharge on a toe or especially in close relationship to a joint or bone will almost certainly extend into and involve the joint or bone if it remains unhealed over two weeks. Therefore it is of major importance to treat energetically any such lesion as soon as it begins. Lesions of diabetic feet cannot be treated expectantly or by ambulatory methods unless they are very superficial or entirely free from infection. In such cases they will heal within ten days.

When infection in a callus, corn, or following some trauma has extended into a joint or bone causing osteomyelitis, whether or not the X-ray shows the lesion, it seldom will heal. Amputation of the toe as soon as the diagnosis is clearly established is then indicated. When the blood supply is good such cases of ostemyelitis may remain stationary for many weeks and the patient is loath to accept advice. The result is a long period of procrastination with suffering and expense ultimately leading sometimes to an extension of infection and loss of the entire foot. The decision as to the necessity of amputation must be arrived at early. Procrastination is the great enemy in treating diabetic feet.

Gangrene means the death of tissue usually with resulting black color. Superficial areas of gangrene may sometimes heal without an amputation. When gangrene of a toe or foot is associated with redness and swelling of the nearby tissues, and red streaks of lymphangitis extending up the leg, then delay in amputating the foot may cost a life. It is usually not difficult to convince the patient of the need for amputation because he or she suffers the pain.

Amputations through the thigh are done so quickly and with so little shock that almost any patient can withstand the operation. Postoperative deaths are almost always due to the fact that the long delay before operation has allowed the infection to extend by way of the lymphatics, blood stream or tendon sheaths above the level of amputation. It is the infection which kills and diabetes itself should never be the cause of death.

Surgery

There is almost no group of patients to whom the surgeon is so good a friend. Diabetics acquire infections of the skin or extremities easily and these require drainage; their bones are easily fractured; appendicitis and gallstones occur frequently. Retained pus is a grave menace to the diabetic because he develops septicemia so easily. Hence the treatment of every abscess and carbuncle should be considered surgical. Poultices, X-ray treatment and other measures are possibilities or makeshifts which sometimes serve a useful purpose, but the lesion should always be under surgical observation. When good surgical judgment indicates the need for operation, no delay should be permitted. It is delay and procrastination which are responsible for the many deaths from carbuncle.

Appendicitis is even more treacherous in the diabetic than the nondiabetic. The differential diagnosis between appendicitis and beginning diabetic coma is difficult. The urine will contain sugar and biacetic acid in coma, but both may also be present in appendicitis. The boardlike spasm of the abdomen in coma may simulate peritonitis due to rupture. Remember the danger of giving a cathartic to any patient with pain in the abdomen until the possibility of acute appendicitis is ruled out.

Differential Diagnosis of Diabetic Coma and Appendicitis

	Coma	Appendicitis
Abdominal pain	General	Localized first in epigastrium, later in lower right side
Tenderness and spasm	General; may be slight or extreme in degree	Localized over the appendix
Leucocytosis	Is often excessive	Present usually
Respiration	Air hunger	Normal
Skin and tongue	Dry	Not dry, although tongue may be coated
Rectal examination	Normal	Tenderness below pelvic brim sometimes present
Bowel movements	Obstipation	Constipation, sometimes diarrhea

Preparation of the diabetic for surgery requires (1) careful examination of the patient with special regard for the evidences of cardiovascular disease; (2) complete examination of urine, including sugar, diacetic acid, albumin and the sediment and an analysis of the blood for blood sugar and, if possible, for non-protein nitrogen; (3) diet including at least 100 grams carbohydrate during the twenty-four hours before operation; (4) care of the water metabolism so that sufficient liquids are given by hypodermoclysis or intravenous route to prevent dehydration; (5) the use of insulin if the urine contains sugar and the blood sugar is above normal.

For the patient who has been taking insulin, the dose may be increased by 25 per cent or more if glycosuria is marked. On the morning of operation, nothing is given by mouth if 100-150 grams carbohydrate have been retained during the preceding twenty-four hours. Insulin may be given in small amounts before operation, unless the urine is sugar free. After operation, orders for insulin should be contingent upon urinalysis. Thus a typical order is "Test the urine every four hours; if the Benedict test is red give 15 units insulin; if it is yellow give 10 units; if it is green give 5 units; if no sugar is present give no insulin." Thus the changing condition of the patient automatically is treated by insulin in doses suited to the glycosuria. Food after operation must be simple, such as oatmeal gruel (C.5%), orange juice (C.10%), ginger ale (C.10%), and skim milk (C.5%) with a total of 75 - 100 grams carbohydrate. Within forty-eight hours additions of egg, cream or toast may be made so that within a few days the usual diet may be resumed.

If glucose solution is administered intravenously insulin must not be given without a urine test or blood sugar analysis at the time. Hypoglycemia develops easily following glucose administration, as if the patients' pancreas were thereby stimulated to produce extra insulin. When such hypoglycemia develops postoperatively the symptoms may be atypical. Sudden mania, delirium, or mere stupor may occur without the usual premonitory hunger, sweating, trembling and weakness. The use of glucose solution intravenously is an absolute necessity in many cases and of great value in others. Rules adopted at one Boston hospital follow:

"During the twenty-four hours following an intravenous injection of glucose-containing solution, no insulin is to be given without a urine test showing the presence of sugar or a blood analysis. If it is not considered wise to catheterize for a urine specimen, the blood sugar should be determined by micro method if it is desired to save the veins. If the presence of glycosuria or acidosis indicates the need of administering insulin at the same time that the glucos solution is given, the dose given should be moderate, usually from 10 to 20 units. Later doses should be at four-hour intervals, the amount to be given depending upon the degree of glycosuria or hyperglycemia."

Spinal anesthesia gives great satisfaction for operations upon the extremities and lower abdomen. The absence of vomiting is valuable. Although the blood pressure may fall, recovery is usually prompt when the head is lowered. For upper abdominal surgery novocaine infiltration, followed by nitrous oxide and ether, is satisfactory.

TUBERCULOSIS IN DIABETICS
ALTON S. POPE, M.D.
Director, Division of Tuberculosis
Massachusetts Department of Public Health

It is small comfort to the diabetic patient to tell him that he is two or three times as likely to develop tuberculosis as the normal individual of his age, but it is essential to his safety that his physician recognize that simple fact. Forty years ago a diagnosis of tuberculosis carried with it practically no hope for the individual, but today it is recognized that early discovery is the first step in the successful treatment and prevention of that disease. Since the advent of insulin, even greater strides have been made in the control of diabetes and the successful treatment of tuberculosis in diabetics, as in non-diabetics, depends chiefly upon its early recognition.

In their extensive studies Dr. Elliott Joslin and his group have found active pulmonary tuberculosis in 2.8 per cent of their patients X-rayed. By means of questionnaires Dr. Joslin recently found that in the state and county tuberculosis sanatoria of Massachusetts one patient in every hundred has diabetes, as compared with one in three hundred of the general population. Females are more likely to develop tuberculosis in the teens, but after the age of twenty years males outnumber the females two to one. Even in late life tuberculosis is frequent if the diabetes is not controlled. Forty-seven of Dr. Joslin's cases developed tuberculosis after the age of sixty years. In diabetic children under fifteen tuberculosis proved to be thirteen times as common as in children of the same age examined in the Chadwick Clinics. Studies by Dr. Howard Root also indicate that as a rule tuberculosis is a complication of diabetes, rather than the reverse, for in 85 per cent of his cases the diabetes had preceded the tuberculosis.

The importance of diabetes as a predisposing cause of tuberculosis is obvious. For the past seventy-five years the death rate from tuberculosis in Massachusetts has been falling steadily. Since 1900 it has fallen over 70 per cent, while the mortality rate for diabetes in the Registration Area of the United States is now approximately three times as high as at the beginning of the century. In part, these changes can be explained by an increase in the average age of the population, but during the same period there has been a steady increase of deaths from diabetes among the tuberculous. In 1933 the diabetes mortality in one state and in thirty cities equalled or exceeded that from tuberculosis and in Brookline there have been as many or more deaths from diabetes for the past two years. Four years ago Dr. Dublin ventured the prophecy that in ten years the death rate from diabetes would exceed that from tuberculosis. The following diagram of the trends of these two diseases in Massachusetts would seem to justify such a statement:

TRENDS OF DEATH RATES FROM PULMONARY TUBERCULOSIS AND
FROM DIABETES, MASSACHUSETTS—1908–1932

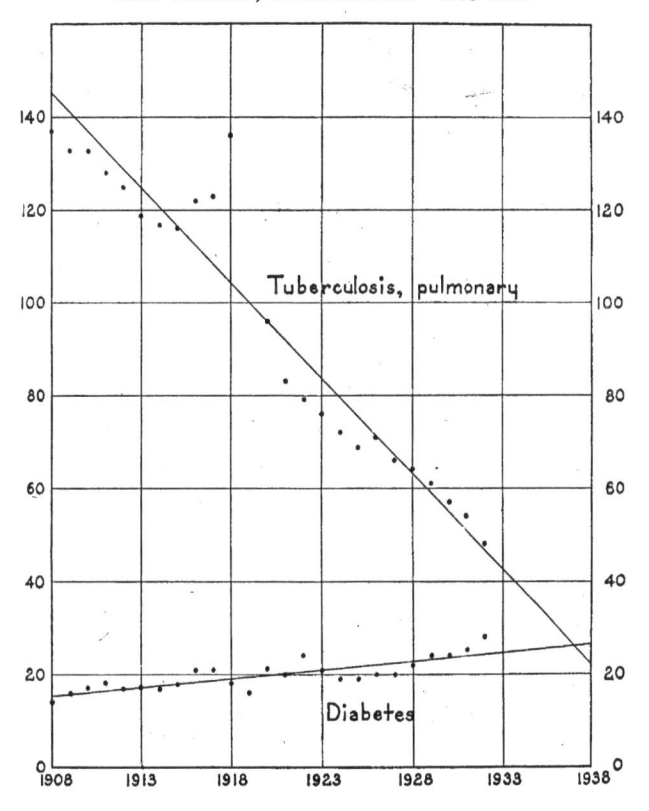

The outlook for the diabetic patient who has tuberculosis has changed completely in the past ten years. With insulin it is now possible to apply modern methods of tuberculosis treatment, including collapse therapy, with results approximating those obtained in the nondiabetic. Control of the diabetes is essential to successful treatment of the tuberculosis, and this is somewhat more difficult than in the average diabetic patient Nutrition must be maintained while exercise, one of the cardinal factors in the control of diabetes, must be suspended during the active stage of the pulmonary disease. Sanatorium experience has shown that diabetics often respond well to treatment and, if the tuberculosis is found at a reasonably early stage, a substantial number of patients secure an arrest of the disease. Dr. Root says that sanatorium treatment is a necessity and that their cases who have healed tuberculosis cavities have done so in sanatoria. Pneumothorax or thoracoplasty have been performed in many diabetics with increasingly favorable results.

The outlook for the diabetic individual who has tuberculosis depends chiefly upon the stage of his tuberculosis at the time it is discovered. Among patients with tuberculosis alone, the survival rate is about five times as high in those treated when their tuberculosis is in a minimal instead of an advanced stage. Unfortunately, among diabetics, tuberculosis is rarely found in an early stage. The symptoms are as insidious in diabetics as in nondiabetics, and early cases have rarely been discovered in diabetic patients because the X-ray was used too late. Incipient cases do well. Among ten such cases discovered at the Deaconess Hospital all but three have improved or remained stationary. Insulin has doubled the average length of life after the recognition of diabetes, but by prolonging the life of diabetics has made it possible for more of them to contract tuberculosis. On the other hand, the patient whose diabetes is well controlled is much less likely to develop tuberculosis than the diabetic with occasional acidosis and coma.

The prevention of tuberculosis in diabetics is essentially the same as the prevention of the disease in the general population. Of first importance is avoidance of infection through contact with open cases. X-ray examinations of all family contacts as well as the patient should be a routine procedure when the diagnosis of diabetes is established. In diabetic children tuberculosis must be sought for first by the skin test and second by X-ray. The Mantoux test was positive in 47 per cent of diabetic children both in Boston and Vienna. All such children should have an X-ray of the lungs, which should be repeated at the ages of 14 and 18 years. If they are in contact with an open case of tuberculosis in the family, at work, or at school, such contact must be broken by removal of the child. Such contact must always be sought diligently, because each source case discovered and isolated may save many other infections.

Good hygiene, including adequate diet, sufficient rest and regulated exercise are of special importance in maintaining the patient's resistance. Control of the diabetes by means of diet and insulin is essential. The risk of advanced tuberculosis can be greatly reduced by routine X-ray examination of the chest. Especially should we look for tuberculosis among the cases who have had coma or severe acidosis. One out of twelve may develop tuberculosis within three years. The coma cases must be followed for life with X-ray examinations once a year. In both diabetes and tuberculosis the patient must learn from his physician how to live successfully with his disease, for it is only by such individual effort that these two diseases can be further brought under control.

PREGNANCY IN DIABETES
PRISCILLA WHITE, M.D.
Boston, Mass.

Introduction

Nearly all physiological processes progress normally in controlled diabetes, notably the growth and development of the juvenile patient. If failure occurs one should find the cause and remedy the defect. One physiological process still baffles us with failure—that is the viability of the fetus of the diabetic mother. Although progress has been made and the failures reduced 50 per cent among patients who are under close observation, they still occur far more frequently in the diabetic than in the normal woman.

The four questions which are of greatest interest in the study of diabetes and pregnancy are: (1) is the patient truly diabetic, (2) is pregnancy ever a cause of the disease (3) does pregnancy alter the course of diabetes, and (4) why does the fetus die?

Glycosuria in Pregnancy

Glycosuria apparently benign in nature occurs so commonly in pregnancy that some writers go as far as to say that if enough specimens of urine of the pregnant patient are examined one or more will be found to contain sugar in amounts varying from traces to several per cent, and yet the blood sugar remains normal. The incidences reported vary from 35 per cent (Williams) to 65 per cent (R. Richardson) and 100 per cent (L. Chase). Generally this sugar is glucose. The theoretical factors which may produce this are first, lowered renal threshold which would not predispose to diabetes mellitus; second, hyperactivity of the posterior lobe of the pituitary gland which possesses the "diabetogenic factor." Third is hyperactivity of the thyroid. The latter two conditions are associated not only with glycosuria but also with hyperglycemia, and the hyperglycemia may disappear when hyperactivity of the gland ceases. Richardson goes so far as to report benign hyperglycemia in pregnancy. This is consistent with the endocrine background. Being conservatively trained, we would not dismiss the hyperglycemia or even the glycosuria lightly but would keep such patients under supervision. The fourth possible cause of glycosuria is damage to the liver incident to pregnancy. Glucose and lactose may be differentiated by fermentation; the former ferments and the latter does not.

Opposed to the view that pregnancy activates diabetes is the course found in some former juvenile diabetics, atypical cases, not requiring insulin. These patients have gone through pregnancies without development of the clinical signs of the disease. Furthermore, if pregnancy were found a factor one would suppose there would be a rise in the incidence of diabetes in women from twenty to forty years of age. Actually, more men than women develop diabetes prior to forty years of age in contrast to the predominance of women in later decades of onset. The evidence of fact outweighs the probabilities of theory.

The Onset of Diabetes by Decades

Decades	Males	Females
1	5.0	4.4
2	7.5	6.1
3	9.3	6.5
4	14.7	11.2
5	23.1	24.1

This brings us to the next problem of the course and treatment of diabetes during pregnancy. The question whether or not pregnancy alters the course of diabetes is still debatable. We must consider this in two phases—first, tolerance for carbohydrate, and second, predisposition to premature degenerative changes.

In the literature one finds reports of gains in tolerance for carbohydrate and an equal number of reports indicating losses in tolerance for carbohydrate. The fairly general consensus of opinion is that a loss occurs in the first trimester, a status which is stationary in the second, and either a gain or loss in the third. In the pregnant diabetic dog Carlson and Drennan were able to demonstrate a great gain in tolerance during pregnancy. That insulin circulates through the placenta of the mother is shown by the experiments of Pack and Barker. Insulin injected into the fetuses of a goat was followed by hypoglycemia in the mother. Some few patients in our series, notably one after coma, were able to give up insulin entirely in the last trimester. A crude analysis of our cases shows that half of the number with suitable records had milder diabetes during pregnancy than at any time before or since the pregnancy, but others have been more severe. Furthermore, we observed one patient for some weeks after the death of the fetus and her insulin requirement did not alter.

Pregnancy may injure the blood vessels of the eye, damage the heart, the liver or the kidneys. If the disease diabetes has just started this need not be expected, but we shall soon have to deal with a new problem—young diabetic women who at thirty may have had the disease for fifteen or even twenty years. Dr. Joslin has often remarked that for the true age of a diabetic one should add the duration of the disease, so at thirty such a pregnant woman might be forty-five or fifty years old so far as her heart and blood vessels are concerned. Of course, this paints the picture rather blackly. We know this is not the case if the patient has controlled diabetes. Unfortunately controlled diabetes in the young patient occurs too infrequently. In pregnancy the cholesterol is high. This is something we strive to avoid in diabetes. Illustrative of the danger of damage to the kidney is the fact that of our pregnant diabetics three have died of eclampsia and five others have had it.

The direct complications of diabetes, coma and hypoglycemia, are to be feared during pregnancy. The plasma combining power of the blood drops in pregnancy and in the diabetic with her faulty carbohydrate metabolism it is easy indeed for it to fall even to the low level of coma, 20 volumes per cent.

Hypoglycemia can result easily from the failure of the physician to take the lowered renal threshold into consideration, and in consequence lower the blood sugar excessively during the attempted desugarization.

The management of the disease diabetes during pregnancy is simplified by means of small divided meals, divided dosages of insulin, and a diet high in carbohydrate. Not only must one allow for the storage of glycogen in the mother, but also for that in the fetus. The glucose stored in the liver and muscles of the newborn infant is 35 gms. Beside this, glucose or glycogen is stored in the brain, the skin, and is present in the blood so that a crude estimate of the total amount of carbohydrate stored would be 50 gms. We must provide for this in the daily diet of the mother as an extra for the nutrition of her child. The patient must be kept under close observation by weekly visits to the clinic, and early hospitalization. Every effort should be made to control the weight of the mother thereby controlling the size of the baby. Patients with glycosuria which is apparently benign must be followed for three months after delivery.

Most important of all is a study of the outcome of these pregnancies. The diabetic mother does not die, but in only half of the cases does her child live. Among one hundred and forty-five diabetic women there have been two hundred and ten pregnancies with one hundred and nine living children. Forty-nine of these occurred before the use of insulin (1922) and sixty have occurred since. These cases have been scattered throughout the country and thus not under the supervision of any one group. There have been forty stillbirths and twenty-nine miscarriages, eighteen stillbirths prior to 1922, and twenty-four since that date. Sixteen of the miscarriage antedated 1922, and thirteen occurred later. There have been seventeen therapeutic abortions. Three patients died undelivered prior to insulin, and the outcome was unknown in thirteen. The living births prior to insulin were 59 per cent, and since insulin 63 per cent. The factors which may be responsible for fetal deaths are (1) mechanical, (2) chemical, and (3) structural.

Both living and dead babies were large, the average weights being 8.7 pounds for living babies and 10 pounds for stillbirths and infancy deaths. This increased size of the babies of diabetic mothers is so striking that some obstetricians call attention to the fact that it may indicate diabetes in the mother, and any mother who produces these large babies must be investigated for diabetes. One author has reported the condition as gigantism and observed changes in the fetal hypophysis.

Hydramnious occurs in diabetes, thus endangering the life of the child. Acidosis has been considered the cause of fetal death, but against this theory is the fact that half the patients who had acidosis or coma had living children. It is presumable to suppose that diabetic acidosis occurred more frequently in the pre-insulin era. Yet the outcome of the two eras was essentially the same. Supervised treatment helps, however, for in our own cases the child mortality has been 25 per cent.

The precipitating cause of diabetes is not the factor, for if it were, the patients with onset in pregnancy would have a worse outcome. The reverse is the case, for the longer the duration of the diabetes, the worse the prognosis for successful termination of pregnancy.

Age of the mother appears to be a factor, because the young and the old do worse than the intermediate group.

Age	Successful Outcome
Under 20	35 per cent
20 - 30	85 per cent
30 - 40	60 per cent
40+	50 per cent

Disease of the uterus may be a cause, namely endometritis or arterial disease.

Autopsies on these fetuses have revealed congenital defects of the heart, atresia of the gastro-intestinal tract, and defective development of the bones.

The greatest advance in treatment has been (1) the use of Cesarean section two weeks before term in all primiparae (in twelve cases there were no fatalities), and (2) the adequate control of diabetes, now rendered possible with the use of insulin.

FRACTURES IN ELDERLY DIABETICS

H. F. ROOT, M.D., P. WHITE, M.D., and A. MARBLE, M.D.

Boston, Mass.

Since reporting* two cases of crushing of the vertebrae with little or no antecedent trauma in elderly diabetics with generalized osteoporosis, a third case has appeared at the George F. Baker Clinic. More recently three patients with fractures not of the vertebrae were under treatment in the hospital at one time. These cases illustrate the ease with which fractures may occur in elderly diabetics and point the way toward their possible avoidance.

Mrs. A. L., Case No. 1916, aged 65 years, with diabetes of almost twenty years' duration, developed necrosis of one toe on the right foot in June, 1932. In the absence of sufficient blood supply to the foot, amputation of the leg was advised and refused. She then spent three months in another hospital, following which she returned home. From that time until February, 1934 she was confined to bed, the necrosis gradually advancing. On February 27, 1934 she re-entered the Deaconess Hospital with gangrene, fever, ascending infection, and underwent amputation of the right leg. The left leg showed atrophy and some edema. Convalescence was uneventful and she was driven home in her son's auto on April 8, 1934. When almost at the end of the drive, a truck struck the auto and she suffered a fracture of the shaft of the left femur. No one else in the car was injured and apparently the trauma to the thigh as she lay in the back seat was only slight. The atrophy and decalcification of the bone as shown by roentgenogram was extreme.

Mrs. K. P. B., Case No. 4577, aged 67 years, with diabetes of fourteen and a half years' duration fell down nine steps of a staircase at her home and fractured the right patella in addition to incurring minor bruises.

Mrs. B. P., Case No. 12575, aged 58 years, with diabetes of nine years' duration, while convalescing at home from "grippe," got out of bed, and fell in the bathroom striking her right leg. Roentgenograms showed a fracture of the right hip (comminuted intertrochanteric fracture with impaction).

Mrs. R. P., Case No. 6360, aged 62 years, with diabetes of fourteen years' duration, in April, 1931 had a large colloid adenomatous goitre removed. When first seen in September, 1927 she had partial paralysis of the bladder. The residual urine measured 900 c. c. Under treatment with constant drainage, followed later by frequent repeated catheterizations, the bladder condition improved. However, at times the residual urine measured as much as 2000 c.c. Roentgenogram of the spine in October, 1927 was normal except for arthritis and atrophy of bone. In January, 1934 she complained of a pain in the back and X-ray examination showed two areas of crushing at the first and second lumbar vertebrae. Other bones showed only rarefaction. No primary focus of carcinoma could be found. With rest in bed all pain became less and she has continued to be fairly comfortable except for cystitis since.

As mentioned elsewhere* factors which may influence calcium and phosphorus metabolism in diabetic patients are: (1) age of the patient, (2) activity of the patient, (3) amount of lime salts in the diet, (4) great excess in the diet of calcium over phosphorus, and vice versa, (5) achlorhydria or hypochlorhydria and diminished or lacking pancreatic lipolytic ferment, (6) prolonged diarrhea, (7) prolonged acidosis, (8) excessive fat in the diet, particularly if unabsorbed, (9) deficient or excessive supply of vitamin D substances.

None of the four patients described had had recent acidosis or diarrhea. None had, in so far as known, excessive fat in the diet. The significant facts as regards these patients would seem to be: all are women past middle life with ages ranging from fifty-eight to sixty-seven years; all have been obese in the past; all have in late years had little physical exercise and their lack of muscle tone is noticeable. In Case No. 1916 a confinement to bed of twenty months with consequent atrophy of bone and muscle may be held directly responsible for the osteoporosis and fragility of the bones. It is difficult to estimate with any degree of accuracy the amount of calcium, phosphorus, and Vitamin D substances received by these patients in the past several years but our impression is that the supply has been inadequate.

In *treatment*, in addition to appropriate measures as regards the fractures, the diets have been so arranged as to include sufficient calcium (at least 0.7 gm. daily) and Vitamin D substances. Each patient has received daily from 360 to 600 c.c. of milk and 90 to 300 c.c. of 20 per cent cream. Two patients have received respectively 30 and 60 grams of cheese daily. The amount of calcium from these foods thus averages from 0.53 to 0.82 gm. daily which is in addition to the calcium contained in the rest of the diet (approximately 0.4 gm. daily). Furthermore, we have given by mouth daily suitable doses of calcium gluconate and haliver oil or viosterol.

The diets of all patients should be checked at intervals to insure that they contain an adequate amount of lime salts and vitamin-containing foods. Physical activity within the ability of the patient should be encouraged and prolonged periods in bed avoided if at all possible. If long-continued bed rest is necessary, appropriate exercises or massage should be provided for. The diabetic condition should be kept under good control.

* Root, H F., White, P., and Marble A.: Abnormalities of Calcium Deposition in Diabetes Mellitus—Archives of Internal Medicine, 53s 46, 1934.

THE DIABETIC CHILD OF TODAY
PRISCILLA WHITE, M.D.
Boston, Mass.

Of all the phases of diabetes, the study of the juvenile patient is the most interesting, because the living diabetic child is in reality a new individual. Before the use of insulin in 1922, diabetic children when carefully treated lived on the average two years. Now they live indefinitely. The importance of the study of juvenile diabetes rests not in its frequency, since only one child in 8,000 develops the disease, but in its complexity and the fact that here alone we have pure diabetes. Consequently the child will reflect more clearly the true physiology, pathology and etiology of the disease than will the adult.

In order to show you how complicated is the problem of the young diabetic of today, to demonstrate how seldom even in childhood one treats the disease diabetes alone and to illustrate the vital diabetic problems of the moment, we have listed the diabetic patients who came to our clinic in a recent month. This happened to be in January, 1934, and we propose to confine the discussion to this small group rather than to the entire series of juvenile patients who have consulted Doctor Joslin from the year 1898 to 1934.

Our January juvenile practice was comprised of eighty-eight patients who presented the following problems either at the time of their examination or at some other time in their past diabetic careers:

1. The care of the uncomplicated diabetic.
2. The treatment of the direct complication of diabetes.
   Coma.
   Insulin shock.
3. The management of the indirect complications.
   Dwarfism.
   Arteriosclerosis.
   Cataracts.
   Xanthoma.
4. The control of emergencies.
   Acute infections.
   Chronic infections.
   Surgical complications.
5. The differentiation of diabetic from non-diabetic glycosurias.

The differential diagnosis of diabetes is obviously the first problem. This is important, because not every patient with sugar in the urine proves to be diabetic. Ordinarily our juvenile patients present no difficulties in diagnosis, since diabetes in childhood is a virulent disease with an acute or gradual onset instead of a slow onset as in the adult and the classical symptoms of polyuria, polyphagia, polydipsia, pruritus, loss of strength, weight and diminished vision are the same whether the patient is two or ninety. In infancy the disease is so virulent and the handicap from the lack of history so great that nearly every case is recognized only in coma. Rarely the parent observes stiffness or stickiness of the linen and if there is diabetes in the family suspects diabetes as a cause.

Illustrative of the patient who comes for diagnosis is Robert D., Case No. 12410 in whose urine a trace of sugar was found when the careful family physician did a complete routine urinary analysis because of petit mal. If this patient were diabetic it would be important to start treatment early and keep the case mild, if non-diabetic it would be unfortunate or even harmful to place him on a diabetic regimen.

The routine blood sugar taken three quarters of an hour p.c. was normal so a tolerance test was indicated. A sucrose or glucose tolerance test is preferably given fasting or at least four hours after a meal.

Under fifteen years of age the amount of glucose given is 1.8 grams per kilogram of body weight and of sucrose 1.3 grams per kilogram. The blood sugars are taken fasting one-half hour, one hour and two hours after the administration of the sugar. The interpretation of the curve is unfortunately not standard all over the world. Some clinics base the diagnosis on the rise, some on the fall, others on the entire curve. We rely upon the diagnosis at the peak of the curve. If the venous blood is 170 mgs. or the capillary blood 200 mgs. the diagnosis of diabetes is made. In this particular instance the blood sugars were normal and he was called an unclassified glycosuric, but was advised to keep under observation for a year. Had the blood sugar been normal and the urine never sugar free the diagnosis would have been that of a renal glycosuria, a benign condition requiring no treatment. Besides true glycosuria when the blood sugars are normal levulosuria and pentosuria must be excluded. These conditions are likewise benign and require no treatment.

While we are proceeding with the laboratory examination our physical examination may reveal suggestive evidence of the disease. The typical appearance of the untreated diabetic child at the first visit is this: He is tall for his age, underweight for height and age, generally mentally precocious. The skin is dry and wrinkled so that he appears older than his chronological age. The cheeks and lips may be cherry colored due to the acidosis. There is the general adenopathy commonly found in conditions associated with undernutrition: A functional, probably nutritional, systolic heart murmur is heard. The liver is readily felt three fingers' breadth below the costal margin. This enlargement of the liver is due to fatty infiltration. Often there is diastasis of the recti abdominal muscles. The patellar reflex may be hypoactive or absent due to degeneration of the nerves. The eyes are hypermetropic. The diagnosis established, our next problem is the treatment.

The treatment of the uncomplicated juvenile case is more involved than that of adult diabetes, because it consists of two phases, initial adjustment and periodic readjustment to allow for growth and development. Furthermore, one must contend with the greater physiological and emotional instability of the child. The actual principles of treatment employed in juvenile and adult diabetes are the same—diet, insulin and exercise. In the process of desugarization we still employ undernutrition prescribing for the child's initial diet 100 grams of carbohydrate, 1 gram of protein per kilogram of body weight and enough fat to yield 30 calories per kilogram. The diet is increased daily until the desired diet for age and size of the child is attained. Prolonged observation of cases under immediate control and with normal activity has demonstrated to our own satisfaction that the following diets permitted an average gain of from one-half to three-quarters pounds a month and fulfilled our own standards for controlled diabetes; namely, that the level of the sugar of the blood should be below 200 mgs., glycosuria less than 10 grams in twenty-four hours and the cholesterol content of the blood normal, 230 mgs. or below.

Age, yrs.	Cals./kg.	P./kg.	C.	P.	F.	Cals.
5	75	3.0	140	60	70	1400
10	65	2.5	160	70	80	1600
15	45	1.5	180	85	90	1800

Average Diet in Grams

You will notice this is a two to one carbohydrate fat ratio whereas the average non-diabetic's diet in this country is nearer 3:1. We still limit the carbohydrate to 200 grams, the protein to 100 and the fat to 110, and divide the total carbohydrate into one-fifth for breakfast, two-fifths at noon and at night.

A caloric increase of 5 to 10 per cent is made every six months or year according to the needs of the individual child so that he may grow two inches in height and six pounds in weight annually during childhood and double this amount during adolescence.

Insulin, to juvenile patients, is given continuously from the day of diagnosis and is considered the variable in treatment whereas the diet is the relative constant. We give the maximum dose one hour before breakfast, a slightly smaller dose one-half hour before the evening meal and, after the third year of diabetes, a few units at 10 o'clock or midnight. Sometimes an even distribution every eight hours is more efficient or the administration of insulin before each meal with or without the late night dose.

Rearrangements of carbohydrate during the three major meals or in accessory lunches, readjustments of insulin and exercise are made according to qualitative four-period tests (See section Laboratory P. 88) the level of the fasting blood sugar or one taken at eleven o'clock in the morning or four o'clock in the afternoon or an hour after a meal. There can be no pattern of treatment applicable for all cases. There can be no constant pattern for the same patient day in and day out for the regimen of the individual day governs the diabetic schedule.

The self discipline necessary for the successful treatment of diabetes is difficult in youth. This is well illustrated in this particular group of unselected cases, five having coma during the month, and one-quarter having had one or more attacks of coma. The case of George C., Case No. 10721, is typical. Following weeks of uncontrolled diabetes he developed a bad cold with fever. As soon as nausea and vomiting commenced he wrongly omitted insulin, and the mild acidosis progressed into coma.

Diabetic coma has primarily but a single cause, overeating. This, however, can be brought about in a variety of ways: (1) diet breaking, (2) omission of insulin, (3) infection, (4) starvation (the body overeating itself), (5) disease of the glycogen storage organs (liver, skin, muscles).

The cardinal signs and symptoms of coma are invariably present but differential diagnosis may be difficult for the nausea, vomiting, abdominal pain and leukocytosis simulate an acute surgical abdomen; the hyperpnoea, pneumonia, the traces of albumin and showers of coarse granular casts, nephritis. The diagnosis depends upon the level of the plasma combining power of the blood. In our clinic the diagnosis of coma is made when the combining power is 20 volumes per cent or below. This is an arbitrary figure selected because few patients whose plasma combining power fell to this level recovered prior to the use of insulin.

The treatment of coma in a child differs little from the treatment of coma in the adult: insulin early and in repeated doses, the amount depending upon the size and age of the patient and the duration of the diabetes as well as the clinical severity of the coma. From 5 to 40 units are given every fifteen minutes for two hours, then hourly until clinical improvement is evident. Actually from 30 to over 600 units have been given. Fluid is used to combat dehydration, from 500 to 6000 c.c. of normal salt solution by hypodermoclysis in the first twenty-four hours. Gastric lavage and enemata are employed to combat lack of gastro-intestinal tone. Adrenalin may be used to combat circulatory failure which, however, seldom occurs in childhood. Glucose may be resorted to to avert renal block, and carbohydrate given up to 100 grams by mouth in the first twenty-four hours.

In contrast to the case of George C. who omitted insulin during an infection is the case of George B., Case No. 2007, who better versed in diabetic treatment under the same circumstances increased his insulin (a little too much) to 50 units in a single dose. This happened to be a drill morning and during his exercise he collapsed, arrived in the hospital in an ambulance, was given glucose 20 c.c (50%) intravenously and recovered consciousness during the process of the administration of glucose.

The unconsciousness of diabetic coma must be differentiated from the unconsciousness of insulin shock, since the treatment of the two conditions is exactly opposite and delay in treatment of either may result in a fatality.

Although the diagnosis of these two conditions can be made absolutely by the laboratory data, the history and physical examination will give presumptive evidence while we are waiting for our laboratory reports or even, more important, if we are unable to obtain them.

The Differential Diagnosis of Diabetic Coma and Insulin Shock

	Diabetic Coma	Insulin Shock
Cause	Increase of diet	Reduction of diet
	Omission of insulin	Increase of insulin
	Infection	Increase of exercise
		Failure of absorption of food
History	Gradual loss of consciousness preceded by	Rapid loss of consciousness sometimes followed by vomiting
	Vomiting	Convulsions
	No convulsions	
Physical examination	Skin dry and flushed	Moist and pale
	Breathing hyperpnoeic	Shallow
	Pulse feeble	Full and bounding
	Blood pressure low	High
Laboratory	Blood sugar high	Low
	CO_2 under 20 volumes per cent	Normal or elevated.
	Urine sugar +++	+ or − (2nd specimen 0)
	Diacetic acid +++	0

Elaborate laboratory methods, however, may not be available, then one simple method differentiates the two conditions. The second of two urinary specimens in shock should be sugar free, and in coma not. The first specimen tested may be residual urine secreted by the kidneys before the drop in blood sugar occurred. The second specimen represents the true state of carbohydrate metabolism.

Mild shock is common. Beside the usual symptoms, nervousness, tremor, paraesthesias, diplopia, headache and sweating, the quiet child or the child in a tantrum must be considered hypoglycemic until proved otherwise. The treatment is self evident: Replacement of carbohydrate by mouth if the patient is conscious, by vein or under the skin if the patient is unconscious. To the unconscious patient we prefer to give a 50 per cent solution of glucose intravenously for this not only tends to replace the needed carbohydrate quickly, but also to combat the cerebral edema which occurs in severe cases of insulin shock.

Prevention of these complications is the up to date attitude and for this reason almost any degree of abnormal health in the juvenile patient must be considered an emergency. It is slight deviations from normal which precipitate acidosis and coma even in a fairly well controlled case in as short an interval as twelve or twenty-four hours. Therefore parents and patients besides being taught to notify the family physician immediately in case of illness must be taught simple rules for the management of such days. These are the same as our own rules for pre- and postoperative treatment—insulin every two, four or six hours depending upon the degree of reduction with the

Benedict test: For the child of fifteen years of age, 15 units if red or orange, 10 if yellow, 5 if yellow-green; to the child of ten years of age, 10 units if red or orange, 5 if yellow or yellow-green; to the child of five years of age, 5 units if red or orange, 3 if yellow. The diet should be reduced to carbohydrate 100 to 150 grams and a negligible amount of protein and fat. Such a diet could be one and one-half or two and a half quarts of milk in tweny-four hours.

So much for the direct complications, their treatment and prevention. The indirect complications, the premature degenerative changes command attention even more imperatively, because they are more tragic when they occur in youth and must be checked all the more vigorously, because of today's favorable evidence bearing upon the prognosis; namely, that decreasing severity of diabetes occurs when youthful cases have attained full growth and development.

Of these indirect complications dwarfism occurs most frequently and is the easiest to check, control and prevent. Fred G. Case No. 1616 is a striking example of the degree to which stunting in diabetes can occur. His disease commenced in 1919. In 1930 he was thirteen inches below height for age. The first six inches lacking can be accounted for by the fact that he was starved for the three years, 1919 to 1922 prior to the use of insulin, and the next seven inches by the transition period when undernutrition was still employed. At twenty years of age he is physically mature although still short, being five feet three inches.

Dwarfism is largely the result of the pre-insulin era but it occurs in the insulin era among those treated for periods without insulin and when the diet is persistently reduced to bring about sugar freedom. The most difficult lesson to teach parents is the following: When the child grows he requires more food and more insulin. In our own patients the dosage of insulin has doubled from infancy to fifteen years of age practically regardless of the duration of the disease. Any increase in insulin dosage indicates to the parents that the disease has become progressively worse and they will resort to all sorts of measures to reduce the dosage of insulin or at least to maintain it at the same level, actually placing a child of twelve upon a diet calorically inadequate for an infant of one.

It occurs, furthermore, in some children whose disease is uncontrolled because of diet breaking. This is mostly among the younger children, because they commit dietary indiscretions secretly and the dosage of insulin is not changed. The older children have become very adept at balancing diet and insulin under the same circumstances.

The onset of dwarfism is insidious, because at the commencement of diabetes the child is on the average two inches above the standard height for age. It would take three years of complete cessation of growth before the condition became apparent. These children grow a little, at the rate of 0.5 inches a year, therefore it is not until the fifth year of diabetes that the retardation is evident. This merely emphasizes the importance of checking annual rates of growth in diabetes as well as deviations from standards.

The treatment of the condition consists of a high caloric diet to counter-balance the high energy requirement. The basal metabolic rate of these pseudo dwarfs is 18 compared with 11 for all children and 2 for tall diabetic children.

Uncontrolled diabetes in childhood exacts its penalty immediately in the form of coma and carbuncles and abscesses. These disagreeable crises pass. So long as the child realizes he can recover he is relatively unconcerned for his future and often as not the experience fails to teach him the need of adherence to the diabetic schedule. Then uncontrolled diabetes exacts other remote penalties which may produce crippling or even death. Notable among such complications are cataracts, arteriosclerosis, involving retinal vessels, the coronaries and the vessels of the feet. There is also susceptibility to general infections such as tuberculosis.

The whole tragic course which occurs in diabetes is illustrated in the Case of Mary M., Case No. 4232, who had onset of diabetes at fourteen years in 1922, and was first seen by us in 1924. Her first hospital admission was in profound coma. From 1924 to 1928 she had coma three times and severe acidosis twice. Each attack was caused by diet breaking. An X-ray examination of the legs in 1925 showed no sclerosis after two years of badly controlled diabetes. In 1928 after six years of badly controlled disease there was a questionable trace by X-ray; in 1930 a definite trace and in 1932 a pipe stem artery. In 1928, cataracts were recognized. She also came in contact with a newly acquired sister-in-law who had unrecognized tuberculosis. With her uncontrolled disease her tissues were fertile soil for the tubercle bacillus. On X-ray an abscess was found in the lungs. She then spent twenty months at Rutland and her lesion became arrested. For two years she did well adhering to diet and insulin. Since then she has become discouraged, follows no form of treatment and the scar in the lungs is breaking down. In 1930 she had five carbuncles and in all has been operated upon eight times, for chronic tonsillitis, carbuncles and cataracts. Although she demonstrates that the diabetic can survive frequent attacks of acidosis and innumerable surgical operations, her tissues show the ravages of her uncontrolled diseases.

The diabetic child has really settled the controversy over diabetes as an etiological factor in the production of sclerosis and cataracts.

Arteriosclerosis is a rarity in young persons as shown by our own control group where none were found and by a review of the literature in which Pearl Zeek could find the records of only ninety-eight cases in non-diabetics covering a period of one hundred years. In ten years we have found thirty-six cases in juvenile diabetics. The common causes of sclerosis, nephritis, lues and sepsis have not occurred in our own cases. The two abnormal conditions which occur in diabetes are alterations of fat and of carbohydrate metabolism. In a comparison of our case we could find little clinical correlation between arteriosclerosis and high blood sugars, but arteriosclerosis occurred fifteen times more frequently in the group with high blood cholesterols. In the acidosis of uncontrolled diabetes the conditions are right for the redistribution of calcium from bone, union with cholesterol esters which are unsaturated fats, and final deposition in the blood vessels and in the lens of the eye. Therefore, our standards for the control of diabetes have come to be blood sugars below 200 milligrams and a cholesterol below 230 milligrams.

Cataracts have been recognized in twenty-four of the group of our children. Here again we have found a positive correlation between abnormality of cholesterol metabolism and frequency of cataracts, but our series is too small to be conclusive.

Hypercholesterolemia was a feature of the case No. 4232 just described, but another patient, Case No. 12383 had an even higher value, 1600 milligrams per 100 c.c, in fact, the highest in our records. He was first seen by us in January, 1934. For a year he had been living on a high fat diet without insulin. When his blood was withdrawn from the vein it looked like cream. Examination of eyes showed that rare lesion lipemia retinalis and his skin was covered with the diffuse yellow nodules characteristic of xanthoma diabeticorum, which on pathological examination consisted of cholesterin crystals. The lipemia retinalis disappeared in forty-eight hours. The xanthomata have just disappeared. At present the cholesterol is normal.

One child died in the hospital, Case No. 3078. Our entire juvenile mortality is 1 per cent a year. This patient illustrates the end results of uncontrolled diabetes, the others have illustrated its course. After twelve years of absolutely uncontrolled diabetes in which she had chronic acidosis, she developed perirectal abscesses, pyelonephritis, double otitis media, and mastoiditis and finally succumbed to pneumococcus meningitis. Autopsy confirmed clinical diagnosis revealing multiple abscesses of both kidneys, and beginning atheroma of the coronaries and the abdominal aorta. The pathological examination of the tissues in juvenile diabetes shows at first few irreversible changes in the pancreas. If the disease is uncontrolled, morphologically it is characterized by the faulty distribution of glycogen in the skin, liver and muscles and heart and the abnormal deposition of fat in the liver and reticulo-endothelial system and blood vessels. Histo chemical evidence of abnormal fat metabolism is greater in the child than in the adult.

Failures in the treatment of the young diabetic of today are not due to the type of treatment employed, but to the lack of treatment or uncontrolled disease. This we consider hopeful, because it can be remedied, yet control of diabetes depends upon the patient—an unfortunate situation in childhood since the child lacks wisdom. Therefore infinite tact, patience and understanding must be applied to the individual child and his problems.

THE HEREDITY OF DIABETES
PRISCILLA WHITE, M.D.
Boston, Mass.

In any discussion of the care of the diabetic child the inheritance of the disease must appear for it is this particular generation which must be taught to safeguard the next. It was the child in fact, who first convinced us of the importance of inheritance, revealed its latency, and suggested the mode of transmission.

The evidence of inheritance of diabetes is apparent in this group of eighty-eight children seen in January, 1934 for there were two pairs of homologous twins with diabetes, five children had a diabetic parent and five a diabetic sibling and there were five instances in which the disease had appeared in three generations.

The conclusions that diabetes is transmitted as a simple Mendelian recessive are based upon four facts:

1. The finding of a greater incidence of diabetes in families of a diabetic than in a control population.
2. The greater frequency of diabetes in both pairs of similar twins than in dissimilar twins.
3. The demonstration that the Mendelian law holds when applied to a large series of cases selected at random,
4. and that it holds when also applied to a small series of cases, not selected at random, but as a representative of the three types of Mendelian cross and whose families have been tested by routine analysis for accuracy of diagnosis and tolerance tests to reveal latent diabetes.

The statistically significant difference between the occurrence of diabetes in a diabetic and control population is that two per cent of the parents of our control population had diabetes whereas eight per cent of the parents of our diabetics had the disease. Diabetes occurred ten times more frequently in the brothers and sisters of diabetics than in the control group. Criticism of such data is often given—that we selected unfairly against diabetes. This is not actually the case and is substantiated by control series of German and English investigators.

The incidences of diabetes in the siblings of a control population, in the siblings of diabetic patients, in dissimilar and similar twins are compared in the following table:

The Incidence of Heredity in Diabetes in Various Groups

Population	Per Cent of Siblings with Diabetes
Control	0.6
Diabetic	6.0
Dissimilar twin	1.6
Similar twin	72

It is evident that a significant excess occurred in the group of similar twins.

The expected Mendelian ratios were found in our three types of crosses. Among the eight hundred families studied 4 per cent of diabetics were found in the siblings and in the children of diabetic X diabetic cross 24 per cent. If our data were complete we would have expected more—6 per cent in the first, 40 per cent in the second, and 100 per cent in the third, but this only if all members of the family had died after attaining old age. Actually our percentages are below this, but the significant factor is that the expected ratios were 1 to 2.5 to 6.1 and the actual were 1 to 2.4 to 5.7.

It is upon this one point and the concurrence of diabetes in both members of similar twins that the validity of the initial hypothesis rests, for if the basic etiology were due to an infection, trauma, nutrition, etc., it is highly improbable that these three ratios would be fulfilled in this manner and that the outcome would be such in similar twins.

Actually we have only identified one quarter of the diabetics expected and the next step is the attempt to find the missing patients. These two sources—some might have occurred in those individuals who died of other causes, and some will be found among people who have not reached the diabetic danger zone of middle life, and the remainder of the problem depends upon the time of age behavior of the disease and non-diabetic lethal factors.

The validity of the incidence curve is undoubted for in our curve occur about nine thousand of our own cases and our cases compare closely with those of other clinics, both here and abroad.

If we were dealing with a potentially diabetic population all the members of which had reached old age and who had died of no other cause we would expect the same curve. Actually this will not be the case so that a prediction curve has been constructed in the following manner: Each decade for one hundred persons represents one thousand yearly chances for the development of diabetes. Actually only four did develop diabetes, so that our expectation is not four in one hundred but four in one thousand yearly chances which must again be corrected for mortality of the decade. If we are correct, the potentially diabetic population of our group should fulfill the prediction. This is the diabetic X diabetic cross. Actually twenty-seven families were studied from this point of view and a curve constructed in the same manner with actual mortality included. The two curves were the same. From this we can predict the expected members in the two other crosses which would be essentially one half to one quarter our incidence curve.

What does this mean? It means that the eugenic control of diabetes is possible.

If a diabetic marries a diabetic, all of the children will eventually develop the disease. If a diabetic marries a carrier one half of the children will become diabetic. If two carriers marry one quarter may be diabetic, but if a diabetic marries a true non-diabetic none of the children should develop the disease.

This lesson must be carried to the children of diabetics for they represent true carriers of the disease.

Conclusions

Five points we wish to re-emphasize about diabetic children: (1) Deaths from coma and hypoglycemia and even their occurrences are needless; (2) diabetic dwarfism, an entity of the pre-insulin era, can occur in the insulin era, but is preventable; (3) premature degenerative changes occur even in childhood, but only when the disease is uncontrolled; (4) there appears to be a correlation between abnormalities of fat metabolism and premature degenerative changes; (5) diabetes is inherited as a single Mendelian recessive trait.

DIABETIC CAMPS
PRISCILLA WHITE, M.D.
Boston, Mass.

The Clara Barton Camp for Diabetic Children had its origin in 1932 when the searching minds of the Universalist Womens Missionary Society and the Young Peoples Religious Union read an article in the Boston Transcript. This article described the work being carried on at summer camps for diabetic children—so called "islands of safety" and carried with it a plea for the creation of similar units. Rightly these minds comprehended this as something very new and worth while—new because the living diabetic child is an entity of the past decade. Before the discovery of insulin ten years ago, in this country alone, 1,000 children died yearly of the disease. Today a thousand children contract the disease yearly but instead of dying in days, weeks, or months they are living indefinitely. Students of the disease know that in childhood there are many pitfalls for the patient and therefore the plea which appeared in the Transcript.

The Clara Barton Camp had been carrying on worth while work as a nutrition center for the underprivileged child but here was an even more vital problem—service for the handicapped child and perhaps a more appropriate memorial for the woman who was so medically minded that she had founded the American Red Cross. Interesting enough the writer of the plea for diabetic children was Doctor Joslin. Like Clara Barton he was a native of the town of Oxford. What could be more appropriate than that the work of these two people should be united at this center giving service to these handicapped children. An innovation at the homestead was started and the Spring of 1932 saw a corps of workers turning the homestead into a recreational-hospital unit.

That you may understand the full meaning and value of this work I wish to describe to you a little of the nature of diabetes and to tell you what it means to a child.

Diabetes is an inherited disease in which the food taken into the body is not utilized but converted into sugar and excreted. In the child starvation ensues with failure of growth and development and fairly rapid termination in death. All of this is due to the lack of insulin of the normal secretion of the islands of Langerhans in the pancreas. When the proper balance is established between diet and insulin the life and tissues of the child are those of normal individuals. But the self discipline necessary to the successful treatment of the disease is difficult in youth. Failures occur resulting in coma, susceptibility to infections, stunting of growth and development and premature aging—manifested by the formation of cataracts and aeriosclerosis. Let me repeat—these complications occur only when the disease is uncontrolled or untreated. Treated, the youthful body retains its normal functions and course of development. Therefore the child who will have this disease forever must be taught the rules of treatment, repeatedly checked, constantly encouraged and intelligently supervised.

Looking backward to the seven years prior to the foundation of the Clara Barton Camp we find our summer program was entirely recreational. The new venture was medical, recreational and educational.

*The original diabetic camp in New England was started by a New England Deaconess Hospital nurse and was entirely a private enterprise. The work had its origin in 1925 when this nurse, Mrs. E. B. Devine, took one child to her home for the summer. The result in this case was so successful and the child had such a good time that Doctor

---
* The first diabetic camp in the world was founded by Dr. Wendt in Michigan in 1924.

Joslin sent five children to her the next summer. With this beginning a thoroughly adequate but not elaborate organization was created. The camp building consists of a single unit having two dormitories with laboratories and showers, a dining room, kitchen and small laboratory. This camp is entirely recreational. There is no organized program. The activities of the day are planned on the spur of the moment and this works out very well for the younger children. The camp is located ideally on one of the lovely Ogunquit sand dunes. Thirty children may be cared for at a time.

In several regulation camps diabetic units have been established—notably two—Camp Teela Wooket for girls in Roxbury, Vermont and Camp Idlewild for boys in Lakeport, New Hampshire. Here ten or more children are cared for by New England Deaconess Hospital nurses. The diabetic children have participated in all activities, Teela Wooket featuring horseback riding, and Idlewild aqua-planing. They have done so well that they have won prizes for ability and also sportsmanship. These camps are especially suitable for the adolescent period and tend to weaken the child's belief that his life differs materially from the non-diabetic for, save that laboratory tests are done daily, diet charts kept and the diet weighed, their life had no departures from regular camp routine.

Differing-from these, the Clara Barton Camp supplements hospital treatment and is more appropriate for our most difficult cases. This is a free camp so far as the Universalist Church is concerned, but in a few instances children have paid a small fee. The camp accommodates about twenty-seven children at a time or fifty-four for a month each during the summer. The unit consists of the three dormitories, the large remodelled barn which provides a play room and dining room and a small but very modern laboratory where all emergency tests required in a general hospital can be performed for the children of the camp and nearby community. These tests are also demonstrated to any visitor who is medically trained and who wishes to acquire technique. The personnel consists of a head nurse with her two assistants, a dietitian, laboratory technician, counsellor and cook—all under the efficient supervision of a Camp Director. This year we hope to use diabetic nurses as the head nurse's assistants.

For this camp a definite health program must be planned before the season starts and the following questions asked:

1. Is this child's disease controlled as much as it should be? If the blood sugar and blood fat are high, the answer is no and the diet and insulin must be corrected to give the desired balance.

2. Are the growth and development normal? Unless the height is ideal for age, the weight for height and age, the answer is no. The diet must be corrected to increase the rate of growth.

3. Are there other defects—anemias, faulty posture, poor muscular development? Is the mental attitude right or is the child depressed or tending toward introspection?

of these problems must be considered and the appropriate program planned.

Thus the chief functions of the Clara Barton Camp are (1) the provision of a happy and safe vacation for the juvenile diabetic, (2) a release for the parents, (3) better diabetic training and education for the children, (4) the test of the adequacy of our own treatment, and (5) the teaching of the important phases of the treatment and course of juvenile diabetes.

One hundred per cent successes in happiness is inconsistent with human nature but the majority of the children had a very pleasant experience. It is a compliment to the personnel that two or three months before the opening of camp the former children campers write to ask if they may be included this year. This is a compliment, because the majority of children have been brought up with the excitement of movies, auto rides, beaches, all of which are missing in North Oxford. Provisions for vacations for the mothers and fathers of diabetic children are as important as those for the children. Vacations therefore are provided not only for the fifty-four children but for the one hundred and eight parents or theoretically for one hundred and sixty-two people. A diabetic child can never be out of the minds of parents unless he or she is protected against emergencies. Only in the hospital, the camp or home is he safe.

The third function has been improvement in the instruction of the young patient as well as the building of morale. Economic reasons have necessitated a reduction in the period of hospitalization to its present minimum of five or at most ten days and consequently the child has received instruction when his mental processes have been comparatively sluggish due to undernutrition or even acidosis. His diabetic education has thus often been incomplete. The camp can be utilized as a supplementary course in instruction. The nurses have very happily created a game attitude toward this and now every camp child can measure and administer his own insulin hypodermically and enjoys doing so, calculate and trade his diet, perform and interpret the Benedict test for sugar, recognize insulin reactions and treat them and knows the signs and symptoms of coma. At the same time every effort is made to keep diabetes in the background and normal living conditions are stressed for the children have crafts, fresh water swimming, picnics, hikes, etc.

The success of this venture cannot be measured at the close of the camp season but is known in the next twelve months for if successful not one of the children except in the presence of a severe infection should have coma. In two years only one Clara Barton camper has been treated at the New England Deaconess Hospital for coma!

Morale is strengthened by camp life. It is a relatively easy matter for the diabetic child to be obedient for a year. After this, the routine palls. He begins to visualize years of weighed diets, hypodermic injections, disagreeable reactions, limitation of activites. The recognition of a handicap grows on the child and discouragement ensues. When a group of these young children are brought together each one helps the other to rebuild courage.

In its fourth function, the investigation and critical analysis of our own methods of treatment the camp has been an invaluable scientific experiment giving us more knowledge of the food requirements necessary for the growth of the diabetic child than we had ever known before. In our first three week period in 1932 our children lost on the average of two pounds. We were not surprised at this for as a group they were well nourished. In the second group an even greater loss occurred in a week and it was evident that our diets were inadequate for activity. By the method of trial and error we found that a 15 per cent increase in food was necessary. Last year this was done immediately and the average gain was normal, one half pound a month, and now these diets are prescribed for our patients when they leave the hospital.

Last year beside planning a unit such as the one of the previous year we attempted something new and selected an additional group of diabetic children whose growth was stunted. Although nine out of every ten diabetic children grow and develop normally 10 per cent fall by the wayside and they perhaps more than any others should receive the benefit of prolonged supervised vacations. Stunting in growth amounting to from four to thirteen inches below the standard height for age occurred in sixty of our seven hundred children.

This condition has but one cause—undernutrition. This, however, can be brought about in a variety of ways but mainly one of four: first it may result from the undernutrition treatment of the pre-insulin era. For this the physician, parents and child are blameless because these children were starved in order that they might be kept alive. It occurs even in the insulin era when because of prejudice against insulin the child is treated for one or more years without it. But most frequently it results from the fact that parents persistently reduce diet rather than increase insulin to bring about sugar freedom. Perhaps the most difficult lesson to teach parents of diabetic children is the following— with increasing growth the requirement for food increases and consequently the need for insulin is greater. To the parents the increasing dosage of insulin indicates one thing only, increasing severity of diabetes and they resort to all sorts of measures to reduce insulin or at least to maintain it at the same level placing a child of twelve upon a diet of nine hundred calories which would be inadequate for an infant of one.

Then, too, it occurs among the children who have uncontrolled diabetes because of diet breaking.

In physical appearance these children are not abnormal. It is only when you ascertain the age of the patient that you realize that stunting has occurred. Those almost twenty years of age look like ten year old children.

Boys are more frequently affected. This is due to the fact that the total potentiality for growth in boys is greater than in girls (at sixteen years 62 inches for girls and 66 inches for boys).

The disease is often mild but the degree to which lack of control has occurred is evidenced by the fact that one out of four had had coma compared with one out of ten in our entire juvenile series and the fact that they were the victims of degenerative complications far more frequently and in fact these were ten times more frequent than in the average diabetic child.

Although no miracles were performed, —the children not growing inches at camp—the normal rate of growth in these dwarf children has been resumed. From past experience we know that acceleration in growth occurs late at from sixteen to twenty years rather than as it does in ordinary children at from twelve to sixteen years.

This year we will try something new. The children who develop complications have uncontrolled fat metabolism which we estimate by examination of the blood cholesterol and those children with high cholesterols will be given first choice.

The camp project for children stimulated other possibilities such as vacations for the adolescent or even for the adult diabetic. As conditions exist today such patients often plan to spend their vacations in the hospital as they actually do derive benefit not only from medical supervision, but also from the opportunity to relax their vigilance over their disease, which requires perpetual remembrance. Furthermore, it stimulates us to consider the foundation of a diabetic school where our young patients may be cared for and receive suitable vocational or professional training. In spite of the general optimism in the diabetic state today none of us can deny or fail to appreciate what this handicap means in the formative years.

SOCIAL PROBLEMS FACING DIABETIC PATIENTS
Helen Meredith Bauer
Social Service Department
Massachusetts General Hospital

When a patient learns from the doctor that he has diabetes, he is faced by an acute emergency demanding immediate adjustment to a new regime. This soon changes, however, into a chronic need, a new way of life. Naturally, if the patient is on an intellectual level where learning is easily assimilated and where he has resources—emotional, financial and environmental—so that treatment can be consummated effectively, there is no block to adjustment and to the carrying out of the diabetic regime. Unfortunately, however, many patients lack some one or more of the necessary adjuncts.

In chronic disease, such as diabetes, the social undercurrents of the medical situation play a particularly significant part. Medicine no longer treats a disease only, but the patient as a whole, so it is in the acquired knowledge of the patient and the power of utilizing that knowledge for the benefit of the patient that the medical social worker can give her unique contribution. The medical social worker is equipped to study both the patient and his environment, the way he is living, his racial and familial background which govern his reactions and feelings, his family and social relationships, his educational attainments and mental equipment as the basis for judgment as to the ability and probability of his carrying out medical recommendations intelligently. Disease is a failure of adaption both to conditions without the patient and those within. Since this is so, medical therapeutics often need to be augmented for those patients who have not complete resources within themselves by social guidance and by the coordinated and mutual participation of the patient and medical social worker in a plan which is balanced to meet the needs of the particular patient in his own particular environment.

To further medical treatment it may be necessary to remove strains in the patient's environment or help him overcome them, by more complete understanding, by encouragement or mental help and by financial assistance when it is necessary. It is especially urgent in the case of the diabetic patient to create or help to create an atmosphere free from worry, emotional conflicts and upsets, in order that the diabetic conditions will not be aggravated by emotional unhappiness or instability, since every sort of social problem may occur in the family of a diabetic. The ideal of his well-being is complete restoration to normal life and activities brought about by the intelligent following of the medical regime prescribed by the doctor, *in an environment from which all possible strain has been removed.*

The medical social worker's place in this program, as elsewhere, should be to help the patient as far as possible to overcome everything real or imaginary, which would interfere with his treatment. She should act as interpreter between the patient or patient group and the medical agents supervising his care, should provide means whereby financially and by social readjustment the physician's recommendations may be carried out, and through social study should be able to assist the patient to utilize all his assets and available strengths and to minimize or overcome his liabilities or weakness for his best adjustment to all phases of this chronic disease.

The financial strain under which some patients struggle is immeasurable. Many cannot make ends meet, regardless of the diabetic regime. Diet and insulin are financially out of the question. For this group, by the raising of money for diet and insulin and for buying urgently needed apparatus, the medical needs may be met and, as far as is possible the financial burden lifted from the shoulders of the careworn anxious patients. Many patients have to have complete change of environment. Grace was a young girl with diabetes whose family lived in a ramshackle house in what was almost a swamp. They lacked most of the necessities of life. Three younger brothers were sleeping on the floor with nothing but coats for bedding. The father would not allow any aid to be given to the family because of some political affiliations. When Grace had a severe bronchial infection sheets and blankets had to be hung on the walls to deaden the sound of the howling wind and to keep out the cold. It has been necessary to bring order out of chaos. Better living conditions have been found, work for the father provided and an order given, unknown to the father, to the grocery store for Grace's diabetic diet. Insulin has been provided. Grace has been watched over and carried through high school. She is now in a position to carry on for herself.

When a patient is faced with this chronic disease, fear plays a large part. Fear is a dread thing with which to live, and it is more or less commonly present in illness. Ignorance creates apprehension, and there is a fear reaction in the presence of the unknown. The patient needs all the help possible; he needs to be reassured, cheered, encouraged. He is often afraid of the very word diabetes, and either thinks he will have to diet, knowing little or nothing of the life-saving properties of insulin, or that the only thing necessary is to give himself plenty of insulin. There is fear in the method of treatment also. No one would take medicine by hypodermic syringe if he had the choice.

Racial food habits cause complications. An extreme case of this was shown by a Chinaman who found it very difficult to limit the amounts of rice which had hitherto formed the basis for his diet. Months of explanation and of actual food preparation in his home were needed. Later, on his return to China, plans were made whereby his insulin might be provided in his native country and his medical needs supervised. He was given an illustrated book made up of appropriate diets and of other matters pertaining to the diabetic regime, written in both English and Chinese.

Because of illness, the patient's variations from the normal standards of health, physical and often mental as well, have thrown him into a condition where he cannot always make his own plans or govern his own movements. His behavior may be incomprehensible to those who know little of illness and its effects on the mind.

A high school girl of sixteen, the middle child in a large family, where the father and two sisters had diabetes, seemed to undergo a complete personality change when she also was found to have the disease. She was irritable at home, had frequent crying spells and upset the entire family. She has needed constant psychological help to adjust to her new regime.

One woman, fifty years of age, has had a most difficult time because she had diabetes. At the time of onset her husband was dying and she had mortgaged their house to care for him. She did not wish to take the money to provide diet and insulin for herself, but found she could not let her medical needs go as she had to care for her husband. After his death she could not work, she had mental disturbances, the result, the doctors believed, of her age when the disease began. She has needed constant and continual encouragement in her daily adjustment, help so that she would not lose her house, provision of her diet and insulin, the smoothing out of the constant friction between her and her married daughter, due to her mental condition, and work that she could do at home to keep her happy and contented. The patient herself has gradually come to understand her own reactions and has learned to keep herself steady and control her emotions.

The outstanding factor in the treatment of diabetes is the self-control and willingness of the patient to follow the doctor's orders. Self-control is not always present at the beginning of the treatment and must be built up by a slow process which is dependent on the patient's understanding of his needs. It brings into play courage and a sense of responsibility. It may mean the overcoming of fear and the dread of being different from one's fellow men. Hard as all this is, it may lay the foundation, especially in the child, for future self-mastery that will make the entire life successful. The stage must be cleared for the diabetic patient to play a major role in the treatment of his disease. This done, the patient must understand that the fight is his, the victory possible, but that all his intelligence and self-control are needed to win. He must carry on his treatment himself, carefully following specific directions, daily growing in self-control. He must strive to attain the normal, sacrificing neither himself nor those around him to his medical needs.

The shame of having the disease, the hatred of being different from others, as well as lack of self-control, made William, age 14, hard to manage; and the life of his family unhappy. He broke his diabetic regime continually, started two consecutive school years by a period of hospitalization, due to carelessness in not sterilizing his needle properly. He would not allow anyone to mention his disease to him, was willful and self-assertive. It took two years of patient work to change his attitude toward the disease so that his own life would not be ruined eventually and so that his relations in the home could become more normal. A tutor was provided and other stimuli for his excellent mind. The success in his treatment was due in large measure to being able to have him keep up with his high school class the two years he was out of school.

School and work adjustment often have to be arranged for patients with diabetes. One man with a somewhat peculiar wife who cooked when and what she pleased for a meal, utterly regardless of any dietetic law or convention, was no help for her diabetic husband. It was necessary to have the hours of work changed for the patient so that he was away from home for both lunch and dinner. He so versed himself in the allotted amounts of food for the diabetic diet that he has been able to carry out the regime even when eating in restaurants.

Patients who can carry on the diabetic regime themselves seem to meet their Waterloo when amputation of a leg, because of diabetic gangrene, is necessary. Not only do they need help in adjusting to their terrific loss, but need to have artificial limbs provided and a new type of vocational rehabilitation so that they can continue to be self-supporting.

In these days of world depression and financial strain, the adjustments to new living conditions have become exceedingly difficult for many people the world over. This is especially true for some of those suffering from diabetes, where at all times the burden of the expense of treatment must be recognized and given serious consideration. It is not a matter of added expense for a day or a week, but probably for life, and it is always a question of how long some patients can meet the increased demands upon their financial resources for treatment of diabetes. Until science finds a less expensive method of treatment, the burden will be too great for many. In the meantime there is an opportunity indicated for preventive social work by checking the downward course of the individual, if the means for the necessary diet and insulin are given at the psychological moment.

In conclusion, the diabetic patient presents a stimulating challenge to himself, his physician and all those concerned in his cure and treatment. No one dealing with the patient can overlook the fact that this derangement of the metabolism is influenced by many factors: by the patient's environment, his manner of living, his hereditary food customs, his education and occupation, and perhaps by personality make-up and disturbances. The treatment must be individualized and synthesized by being built up on a consideration of the particular patient in his own unique setting, and the medical social worker can help by study of the situation, by guiding a change in the environmental factors which stand in the way of following medical treatment.

WHAT DO PEOPLE NEED TO KNOW ABOUT DIABETES?
MARY R. LAKEMAN, M.D.
Supervisor of Education in Adult Hygiene
Massachusetts Department of Public Health

The diabetic in Massachusetts is likely to be a fat woman between forty and sixty years of age, and rather above the average in mentality. The chances are that she is Jewish, and that she has a diabetic relative, parent or grandparent, aunt or uncle, brother or sister. She has never walked if she could ride and she does not care for any form of active exercise. Very likely she may have had an attack of gallstones.

Granted that diabetes occurs more often in the fat than in the lean, that the disease is hereditary, that more women have diabetes than men, that it is most common between the ages of forty and sixty and that the diabetic is often an overweight, highly intelligent individual— What of it? Does the knowing of all these things help to control diabetes?

Boldly we answer—Yes, it may. Obviously, however, we cannot in this generation overcome our inheritance. Every one of us, whether we like it or not, has inherited from his numerous ancestors all down through the ages a "pattern" of life. If, into that pattern there is woven the thread of predisposition to diabetes, one cannot remove that thread, but he can find out with what other threads it is interwoven and how it contributes to the whole life pattern.

That person who learns that diabetes has occurred in an ancestor or in the family of his or her life partner has made a discovery of great value to himself and to all who come after him. By keeping watch upon his bodily conditions and adapting his habits of living to this inherited tendency he may quite probably live a long, happy and successful life, whereas, blind to the meaning of such an hereditary predisposition, he is prone to stumble into serious physical difficulties from which he can be only partially rescued.

These facts must be appreciated by the people if the strong influence of heredity is ever to be weeded out from among the various factors underlying the development of the disease diabetes.

The person carrying this thread of diabetes in his life pattern will, if he is wise, select his personal physician in early years and keep closely in touch with him throughout his life. The first signs of diabetes are usually evident in the urine and blood long before symptoms occur. Hence people must learn that regular observation, preferably in the hands of the same physician at least once a year is a great safeguard against serious consequences, not alone for those who carry the tendency to hereditary disease, but for all of us.

People need to know the pros and cons of fat accumulation. At present there seems to be an over-swing of the pendulum toward a desire for slenderness, especially among young women already underweight. Between this extreme and the obese man or woman of forty and over, there is an ideal of sound nutrition free from a load of excess baggage in fat, which should be brought before the people.

Again, people need to know that infections are especially undesirable for those individuals who have a diabetic tendency and positively dangerous for the person who actually has diabetes. Infections aggravate diabetes and multiply many times the need for insulin in his treatment, as is frequently shown when a patient has a carbuncle.

In a recent study of the past history of diabetics in comparison with other people, it was found that severe sore throats, diphtheria, diseased tonsils and malaria were all more frequently mentioned by the diabetics than among a similar group of non-diabetics.

The lesson to be derived from this is that, as a safeguard, not alone from diabetes but from other chronic conditions as well, one should seek prompt treatment for all infections and should assure himself that he is free from after effects before dismissing his physician.

The "nervous temperament" so-called, is another thread which occurs very frequently in the life pattern of certain individuals. Whether or not the tense, high-strung individual owes this trait to his ancestors, to an over-active thyroid, or to continued worry or friction in every-day life, keeping the upper hand of one's nerves is a matter of self-control and character. The cultivation of poise, of a calm adaptability to the ups and downs of experience, is within the power of all of us and the earlier we begin that cultivation, the better for us whether we have a diabetic ancestral strain or not. One wise doctor in trying to help a neurotic patient gain self-control said, "Learn to turn your faucet way on, and then to shut it way off. Don't have dripping faucets. They are wasteful."

Among the people of this State, as of any other, are always those who already have diabetes. It is the duty of a Public Health Department to try to reach them and to tell them the importance of playing safe by keeping under the constant observation of a physician carefully chosen; that it is of vital importance that they learn with what diet, what amount and kind of exercise and rest, and what regime of daily life they are able to keep "sugar-free" and free from all symptoms of the disease. In diabetes the patient himself next to his physician is responible for his own life and physical condition. He cannot play the part of physician, but he is his doctor's indispensable assistant. No one but himself can recognize the first signs of oncoming coma. He must recognize the grave importance of keeping his feet absolutely clean and free from minor infections in order that he may ward off the danger of gangrene.

Even at the risk of creating undue alarm among those who may fear the disease diabetes with an unreasoning terror, we must tell people the early signs by which they may recognize the oncoming of diabetes.

The outstanding signs with which everyone should be familiar are— extreme thirst satisfied only by drinking great quantities of fluid, gnawing hunger, and the passage of an increased quantity of urine. These signs are accompanied by a loss in weight and strength. No one of them is always present, but any one, or especially two or more in combination, warrants immediate investigation.

If the people need to know these things, upon whom rests the responsibility for the teaching of them? Who indeed, when a physician has not been consulted unless upon their own representatives in matters of health, the health departments, or boards of health supported by the people, for the people.

The Massachusetts Department of Public Health, with the active co-operation of the Massachusetts Medical Society, is making an effort through the press, the radio, this magazine, The Commonhealth, and by the distribution of printed matter, to bring these facts to the knowledge of the people.

Much more might be done. Every community, large and small alike, might consider whether or not it has adequate medical and hospital facilities for the discovery of early cases of diabetes, and for the instruction of those who have the disease.

No longer is the prevention of disease the sole responsibility of a Board of Health. In all of the recent achievements in the control of disease problems, entire communities have been involved.

The great progress which has already been made in controlling such problems as those of tuberculosis, malaria, yellow fever, diphtheria has been brought about largely through general education and by coordinated community action. Similar advance awaits us as we face the problems of cancer, diabetes, heart disease, and other disease problems. The hypothetical fat lady, whose troubles we started out to discuss is somewhere in our midst. How is she to learn these things about her health she so much needs to know?

HEALTH SERVICES OF TOMORROW[1]
THOMAS PARRAN, JR., M.D.
New York State Commissioner of Health

It is not my purpose in this discussion either to attack or to defend current public health practice; nor have I any criticism whatever for the attitude of physicians concerning it. I feel that we have had enough of controversy; that in order to obtain a perspective of our several problems, we need to detach them, at least momentarily, from the exigencies of personal opinions and desires. It would seem to me that through a greater objectivity we may arrive at a clearer understanding of the past developments and present status of public health service. On the basis of that understanding, we should be able to analyze the trends of such service and to project the line of probable action. In the last analysis, each man must think this through for himself. He may find, as I have found in my effort to arrive at an objective interpretation, that his judgment of what is probable conflicts from time to time with his personal philosophy. Under such circumstances his acceptance of or opposition to the course of events must be predicated upon his intellectual honesty.

In the nation at large there is more than the usual need for openmindedness, for respect for the point of view unlike our own, as well as a courageous tenacity in adhering to what is truly valuable in established methods. That widely divergent views are held by many, physicians and laymen alike, concerning various public aspects of medicine, no one can deny. Today's forum serves to crystallize these views and should give all of us a broader concept.

On both sides of the controversy we can assume for the most part a sincere desire for medical progress; for better and more complete health services to all the people. Where disagreement exists, it concerns the methods and procedures which will contribute to this progress so ardently desired by all of us. Incomplete information and misinformation fan the flame. Extremists, whether reactionary or radical, do not contribute to progress. The usual result of their labors is to impede it.

It is well to bear in mind that our individual or collective views as doctors have had little weight in the past. Unless we improve the technique of making our views felt, they will have little weight in the future determination of the structure, scope, or content of public health. The people of each day and generation place an increasingly higher value on medical service. It would seem, however, that they consider themselves, as patients, as important a factor of medical service as we are. In consequence the medical profession conforms to the social system of which it is a part. Sigerist, expressing this point of view, recently said:

"There is one lesson that can be derived from history. It is this: that the physician's position in society is never determined by the physician himself, but by the society he is serving. We can oppose the development; we can retard it; but we will be unable to stop it."

From this there is apparent not only the futility of obstructing change but also of championing reforms which go beyond the current concepts of social responsibility. It is time that men should look to physicians themselves for guidance upon medical matters of public concern as well as those of private urgency. Nevertheless, the direction and distance we can lead toward a specific type of health service for tomorrow is limited sharply by the framework of tomorrow's social concepts.

Today's official health services reflect rather accurately our character as a nation.

Their diversity of form is in keeping with a similar diversity of

---
[1] Read before the Joint Conference of the American Academy of Political and Social Science and the College of Physicians of Philadelphia, Philadelphia, Pa., Feb. 7, 1934
Reprinted from "Public Health Reports," Vol. 49, No. 15, April 13, 1934 through courtesy of the U. S. Public Health Service.

political and social organization among the States, and even within a State.

Their incompleteness parallels the lack of concern for human rights and lack of confidence in government as an instrument for protecting human rights, which until recently characterized the popular mind.

Their individualistic idiosyncracies show, both in their weakness and in their strength, precisely the lack of regimentation which is to be expected from a nation of individualists.

Their sectional differences represent a difference in problems. Industrialization has brought the need for compensation and safety laws, unavoidable incursions into the health field. The transition from an agrarian to an industrial civilization brings a greater need for health service. Exotic diseases have given an impetus to public health work in the South. Many of the Western States, free from the yellow fever and the hookworm of the South, have been until recently too preoccupied with frontier problems to organize more than a perfunctory health service.

Tradition, too, has left its mark. The town meeting of early New England is reflected in the multiplicity of local health officers now found in these and adjacent States. Custom, also, helps to determine the quality and kind of service rendered. In many States and cities a change of administration entails a clean sweep in health department officials and major employees. Services periodically are disrupted and no long-range programs undertaken. In other States (New York is an example) it has become the custom to consider the health problem nonpartisan. The State health department has passed through many successive administrations without political changes in personnel or policy. Where partisan politics control the health department, there is the same control of other community services.

The lack of real professional leadership among those rendering health service probably is analogous to that in the medical profession as a whole; which, in turn, may be due to the low standards of professional education which prevailed until recent years among the rank and file.

If we add to these factors the difficulties of scientific appraisal inherent in many aspects of health service, as in many phases of medical practice, the gap between the present and the ideal in this country is easily understood.

Public health, too, is founded upon scientific discoveries which are comparatively recent. There is an inevitable cultural lag between the acquisition of knowledge and its application to the community; and, although the desire for life and health is a basic human emotion, the absence of disease, the prevention of an epidemic, the saving of life generally are rated as negative accomplishments. They are not dramatized in the public consciousness.

For a long time statesmen have expressed the thought that the care of the public health is a primary responsibility of government. Blackstone interpreted the legalistic aspect when he said: "The right to the enjoyment of health is a subdivision of the right of personal liberty, one of the absolute rights of persons."

These concepts mean that the community collectively should perform for its citizens (1) those services which are so important to the social organism that they cannot safely be left to the initiative of the individual uneducated or indifferent as to their importance and (2) those services which, because of their nature, the individual cannot provide for himself. So far, however, the performance of such services is more theory than fact. Public health has not been a major issue of our Government in the past. At the present time, when all human issues are coming to the fore, economic pressure—the necessity of providing a world fit to live in—has continued to shunt aside from public consciousness the present needless sacrifice of human life and efficiency by our inadequate use of scientific medicine. Current measures to restore minimum standards of living, however, are doing more to preserve the mental and physical health of the Nation than a frontal attack on disease alone.

Unfortunately, we have inaction and retrogression even in functions, such as control of communicable disease, which are generally accepted as appropriate spheres for governmental action; and in the line of private health protection, citizens have become increasingly unable to provide necessary medical service for themselves.

The distribution of present health and medical expenditures is distinctly inequitable, only 3 per cent of the total being made for preventive services, public and private. Out of a total per capita expenditure each year of $30 for all medical care, only $1 is spent for prevention. Quacks, nostrums, and patent medicines collect too large a part of the remainder.

Public health has not generally attracted the best of medical graduates. It has not in the past offered a satisfactory career because the financial rewards were modest and the openings not influenced by partisan politics were few. Before we can realize a completely sound health plan for tomorrow, we must raise up a new generation, not only of leaders but of well-trained men in the ranks.

Funds for the work have been scanty. Three fourths of our rural population have not even the elements of a public health service. Between 1931 and 1932 health budgets in cities and States, already inadequate for the proper conduct of minimum activities, declined, on the average, 17 per cent. In Alabama the cut was 50 per cent; in Mississippi and North Dakota, 75 per cent.

It is true that remarkable accomplishments have been made in the prevention of disease during the past 2 decades; but it is likewise true that these accomplishments are less than half of what is easily possible if all communities would provide for their citizens the health protective facilities now provided by a few communities.

A further increase in the life span by another 10 years is entirely possible. Of even greater economic importance are the disease and disability which can be prevented. Typhoid fever and diphtheria can be reduced to lower minima, the infant mortality rate can still be cut in half, two thirds of the present 13,000 maternal deaths can be prevented, the increasing incidence of the venereal diseases can be changed to a decreasing progression, the tuberculosis battle is only half won, and cancer can be better controlled.

The medical profession, as at present constituted, is increasingly unable to provide for all the people the minimum essentials of medical care without adding unbearably to the load of poorly paid and unpaid work it now carries. Three factors have contributed to this situation: First, although many human ailments can be treated satisfactorily with limited equipment, scientific advances have increased constantly the complexity and the cost of medical service. Second, the lowered income of a large part of the population has put medical care beyond the reach of an increasing number. As a result, many physicians, and dentists and nurses as well, find themselves today almost destitute. Third, people who are not ill and not confronted by a threat of illness are unwilling or uneducated to pay out of pocket for a preventive service.

Few will deny that our health system falls woefully short of results; yet there are those who would limit public health service to sanitation, quarantine, and the care of the insane and of other indigent sick. To accept this view is to ignore not only the inherent responsibility of government but the scientific factors and our considerable experience in public medical care. The quality of such service compares favorably with private treatment for the same class of patients in tuberculosis, sanatoria, mental disease hospitals, venereal disease clinics, public general hospitals, and immunization clinics.

It is no longer easy to secure applause by damning the Government because of its interference, without presenting valid evidence that alone and unaided by Government we can do a better job.

We may consider the potential scope of public health service as the application of biologic knowledge for the prevention and cure of disease and the promotion of health. In forecasting the health services of tomorrow, we need to determine what functions the Government can exercise better than other agencies to serve the health needs of the people. Society as a whole is indifferent to the squabble between public health officialdom and the medical hierarchy concerning the prerogatives of each. What happens to our present public health system or to the private practice of medicine, as we know them both today, will not be determined by the resolutions of medical societies nor by the recommendations of health officers.

It seems generally agreed that the current social and economic revolution cannot stop where it is. Are we to go forward during the coming years, veer left or right? We will not go back. We must assume that in any event we have faith in our capacity to adjust governmental forms to serve the people better than in the immediate past.

First, it is possible that the speedy return of economic prosperity may be accompanied by a revolt of trade and industry against onerous governmental control. As a result we may emerge with many of the forms and much of the formlessness of yesterday, the chief social residue of the recent tragic era being a somewhat better conception of individual rights and some means of preventing the more flagrant abuses and exploitations of those rights.

There is a second contingency—that we may continue our present trend toward a regulated capitalism with trade associations and cartels operating the economic system of the country under Government regulation and control. In such a system cooperative effort will be the dominant factor.

It must also be considered that we may show an incapacity for cooperative capitalistic effort. We may revolt against rigid regulation which fails to bring high profits in its wake. Recently, in an informal discussion of the subject, I heard a business man of major rank intimate that business as a whole may prove itself too dishonest to function under the regulations of an industrially controlled system. What then? Perhaps chaos as an interlude, but ultimately and possibly soon, a socialistic state.

Whatever the path we take, regardless of how earnestly as doctors we may fight for it or against it, the health service of tomorrow inevitably will conform to the governmental framework, whatever it may be.

If the political philosophy of yesterday again prevails, we shall, of course, continue the traditional forms of medicine and public health. The State will perform more completely, and better, I hope, the services which it now undertakes. New tasks will be added as the developing body of scientific knowledge and the needs of the people determine.

An essential part of this system, in my opinion, is the tools for better work which can be placed in the hands of the practicing physician. Among the aids which the most individualistic of doctors, in large numbers, have approved and used are the following: County general hospitals, managed by local medical boards and open to all citizens at a cost within their means; diagnostic laboratories, for clinical as well as communicable disease diagnosis; free biologic products and arsphenamines; community nursing; plus case finding and consultation service.

Such accessories to care as X-ray, laboratory, nursing, and hospital costs often outweigh the actual medical charges. If these accessories are furnished by the community, the medical bill frequently can be paid, the personal relationship of physician and patient retained, and the quality of medical service promoted. For it must be remembered that a patient may be able and willing to pay for an office call or for attendance at childbirth, yet be unable to negotiate for a cancer operation or the rehabilitation of a crippled child. For this reason it may prove very serviceable to the general practitioner for tax levies to supplement inadequate private subscriptions for the support of hospital and dispensary service; and for facilities now provided for the care of the insane, the aged, the tuberculous, and the venereally infected to be extended to other chronic and, therefore, expensive diseases.

But even under an economic system restored to familiar patterns there is an uncertain medical factor. During past months there have been some 5,000,000 families—about 18 per cent of the population—receiving from public funds all the necessities of life, including medical care. Under the happiest of conditions their restoration to self-support will be gradual. Having accepted free and, in about one third of the States, moderately adequate medical care—in many instances more freely available than in their whole previous experience, and of better quality than provided by the quacks and other questionable practitioners so often patronized by those in the low income classes—will they, having experienced such care, continue to insist upon it? The history of benefits to veterans gives us food for serious thought on this subject.

Under the traditional system the problem will grow more acute as to how both preventive and treatment needs will be met for the lower income classes. Medical societies will continue to advocate payment of fees from taxes to physicians for these purposes. The bogey of "State medicine" has been removed by acceptance of this principle. All of us now agree that public—that is, tax-supported—action is necessary. Witness the enthusiasm with which the Detroit plan has received medical approbation.

With acceptance of this principle there remain only three relatively minor issues as to method: First, should a particular service be rendered in the home and the doctor's office by any qualified physician on a fee basis paid by the public, or should it be rendered by part-time or full-time physicians? This issue will be resolved very simply. The taxpayer will choose the method which gives a satisfactory service at the lowest cost. This will vary; but, in general, experience has shown that preventive services now rendered by health departments can be done reasonably well and least expensively by organized clinics. In rural areas, on the other hand, the fee for service basis may prove best for certain disease conditions. We have not arrived at our present situation fortuitously.

It is agreed that individual attention, whether preventive or curative, by a skilled and interested physician is the best type of medical care. We should each of us prefer it, just as we should prefer a special nurse and a private hospital room, if we can afford it, when we ourselves are ill. Yet if we cannot pay for anything better, there is nothing inherently vicious about the general nursing service, the ward room, or preventive care and treatment in the clinic when otherwise the community and the individual would suffer from no service at all. In fact, provable progress against disease prevalence has been made thereby. Further, we can find skilled and interested physicians in the public service who treat patients as well as problems; we can find unskillful, uninterested physicians in private service to whom the patient is but a means for filling the pocketbook. The quality of any service depends upon the integrity and ability of its personnel. Neither public nor private medical service is all good or all bad.

The second issue in public medical care is at what income level shall we draw the line of eligibility? In measures to control a communicable disease the primary purpose is to protect the community. Hence, ability to pay for the treatment of smallpox or bubonic plague is purely a secondary consideration. Also, "ability to pay" for general medical care varies with the nature of the condition and therefore the cost of treatment.

A third issue is whether needed public medical service should be administered by a department of social welfare or by a department of health. I hold very strongly to the view that all public medical and health work should be done by the health department. Here we have the medical foundation which is lacking among social workers. Counterbalancing this, however, the social workers make out a good case for unifying medical relief with other relief and social reconstruction measures. This argument, plus the continued barrage of some medical groups to make prevention and not cure the objective of health service, may reduce health departments to the status of sanitary police, while the major health-promoting functions of the community are carried on by non-medical welfare agencies.

It is an interesting anomaly that if we move ahead and to the right, politically, the current of traditional medicine seems to carry the private practitioner farther and farther away from responsibility for preventive medicine in general and for treatment of disease which, if neglected, would be harmful to the community either because of its infectious nature or because the untreated individual or his family might become a public charge. The reason is simple. The doctor, of his own volition, has rendered long and valiant service for the poor and needy. Yet bound down as he is by the competitive system, we cannot expect him to assume the load of preventive services—nor do we find him volunteering to do it—when he finds it difficult to obtain reasonable compensation for what he does. Neither can the doctor's benevolence absorb the vast strata of those victims of technological maladministration whose sole asset is an uncertain wage at or below the bleakest living requirement.

If tax funds are available for the treatment of these cases, it is probable that the taxpayers' insistence on economy will result in the expenditure of these funds largely through the organized clinic rather than in the doctor's office, and for salaried physicians rather than fees for service.

If, on the other hand, the current economic revolution leads ahead, and left to a regulated capitalism, with industrial cooperation under Government control, then we almost certainly shall see various schemes of social insurance—old age, unemployment, and sickness.

The contest in this case will be over the nature and extent of supervision of the service, the extent of tax support, the freedom of choice and compensation of the physician, the restrictions on specialization, the voluntary or compulsory nature of the system, and the inclusion of cash as well as medical benefits.

Where most successful, sickness insurance requires the general practitioner as the keystone in providing a preventive and general medical service to the family as a unit, with reasonable and assured compensation. The work of health departments would be proportionately minimized in the treatment field as these services, paid for in advance, are available from the family physician.

In fact, is it not possible that the medical profession itself will be the prime advocate of sickness insurance as the least objectionable way of preserving the general practitioner and of attaining economic security? Here, then, is the paradox: As we move ahead along traditional lines, private medical practice is forced away from its preventive and many of its treatment functions by an expanding public health service. As we move to the left by abandoning traditional forms, private medical practice regains its traditional inclusive responsibility for both prevention and treatment, with a corresponding reduction in the scope of health-department functions.

The program of the British Medical Association entitled "A Medical Service for the Nation" deserves consideration if we anticipate this state of society.

If, through evolution or revolution we find ourselves to the extreme left and part of a socialist state tomorrow, then we doctors, too, will be socialists. Or, if we are not, our successors will be. State medicine will exist in the sense that the State will operate medical and health services in a manner comparable to our present system of public education. The medical recommendations contained in the platform of the British Labor Party give at least a rough idea of what this would be like. Or, if we recognize obvious differences in the level of medicine here and in Russia at the beginning of the World War, we may find some suggestions in the medical organization of that country.

What, then, is a doctor to do in a changing world? Is he to fight all suggested innovations as encroachments upon his livelihood? Will he have a voice in his own salvation, or is he but dust upon the wheel of circumstance?

You will notice that I said "doctor," not "private doctor," or "public health doctor." Good or bad, we are cut from the same cloth. We face transition of status and opportunity that will be far-reaching for each of us; but, as I said in the beginning, every man must think out for himself what lies ahead and what his personal attitude toward it will be. To my mind, these are the attitudes of an honest, earnest, well-trained doctor of today:

He is unafraid. The doctor's job, whether his present concern is private practice or public health, is of paramount importance in the Nation's welfare. Whatever the political framework of tomorrow, there will be a place for him and a place in the sun.

He continues to learn. He feels a maladjustment in the society he serves, and he seeks to understand it in the whole as well as in part. He considers with an open mind at least two sides of a suggestion—his own and the patient's. He is eager for new information; he faces facts.

He participates. If he is a practicing physician he is active in obtaining and maintaining a first-class health department for his community. If it is partisan-ridden, he helps to turn the rascals out and to change the rules so that a good job is possible. If he is a health officer, he keeps close to clinical medicine and medical research. He takes counsel with private physicians; he is familiar with their problems.

He plays fair. He is not petty himself nor will he tolerate the factional bitterness which has made so many a medical organization the synonym for strife.

And last, he looks ahead, in terms of the community and the Nation, as well as of himself and his profession. He is a good citizen.

You may think I have discussed a tomorrow that is too far away. Time alone can determine.

What I have attempted to do is to consider alternate political systems of which we will be a part, and to suggest different types of medical and health services within the framework which society places around us.

I have said that as doctors—as guild members—we have not in the past influenced the social structure in which we find ourselves; nor are our resolutions or recommendations likely to mold it tomorrow. When we speak as doctors alone, we have been suspected of self-interest. Yet as citizens we have full voice in the new order of things, and as doctors it is possible for us to implant in every citizen a respect for scientific medicine, for its potentialities, and for its practitioners, which will make easy the adjustments of tomorrow.

What we need is more evangelism in medicine, more concern for the citizen unserved, or poorly served. What we have had is a virulent sectarianism, a concern lest he be served by others who receive the reward.

Let us, then, study the needs of the people for health, consider the service which science has made possible and interpret to the people the best ways of applying science to health promotion. In doing this let us keep in mind two principles:

1. Progress made through evolution rests on a sounder basis than when the change is revolutionary.

2. The form of a program is not so important as the spirit. Drawn today, it may need to be modified tomorrow; but the ideals of that program, the spirit which conceived it, must be as unchanging as the tides.

REPORT OF DIVISION OF FOOD AND DRUGS

During the months of January, February and March 1934, samples were collected in 190 cities and towns.

There were 633 samples of milk examined, of which 85 were below standard, from 4 samples the cream had been in part removed, and 8 samples contained added water. There were 36 samples of Grade A milk examined, 1 sample of which was below the legal standard of 4.00% fat. There were 895 bacteriological examinations made of milk, 836 of which complied with the requirements. There were 5 samples examined for hemolytic streptococci, all of which were negative.

There were 752 samples of food examined, of which 195 were adulterated or misbranded. These consisted of 1 sample of butter which was below the legal standard in fat; 2 samples sold as butter which proved to be oleomargarine; 23 samples of eggs, 4 of which were sold as fresh eggs but were not fresh, and 19 samples were cold storage not so marked; 71 samples of confectionery, 60 of which enclosed a liquid containing more than one per cent of alcohol, and 2 samples also contained coal tar colors which were not certified by the U. S. Department of Agriculture; 6 samples of lemon extract, 5 of which were misbranded and 1 sample was low in oil; 10 samples of vanilla extract, 6 of which contained coumarin, and 4 samples were misbranded; 1 sample of orange extract which was misbranded; 1 sample of cream which was not labeled in accordance with the law; 4 samples of dried fruits which contained sulphur dioxide not properly labeled; 3 samples of pie filling which contained benzoic acid not so marked; 2 samples of fish which contained a compound of boron; 1 sample of olive oil which contained cottonseed oil; 35 samples of hamburg steak, 15 samples of which contained a compound of sulphur dioxide not properly labeled and 2 samples were also decomposed, 10 samples contained sodium sulphite in excess of one tenth of one per cent and 3 samples were also decomposed one of which was also watered, and 10 samples were decomposed and 1 sample was also watered; 40 samples of sausage, 10 samples of which contained a compound of sulphur dioxide not properly labeled and 1 sample was also decomposed, 5 samples contained sodium sulphite in excess of one tenth of one per cent, 7 samples were decomposed and 1 sample was also watered, 12 samples contained lungs, 1 sample contained color, and 5 samples contained starch in excess of 2 per cent; and 4 samples of liver and 2 samples of pork kidneys, all of which were decomposed.

There were 131 samples of drugs examined, of which 6 were adulterated. These consisted of 2 samples of spirit of nitrous ether, 1 sample of magnesium citrate solution, 1 sample of spirit of anise, 1 sample of syrup of hydriodic acid, and 1 sample of tincture of iodine, all of which did not conform to the U. S. P. requirements.

The police departments submitted 417 samples of liquor for examination. The police departments also submitted 30 samples to be analyzed for poisons or drugs, 21 samples of which contained heroin, 2 samples contained arsenic, 1 sample contained pieces of broken glass, 1 sample contained opium, 2 samples contained morphine, 1 sample contained ergot, oil of savin, ferrous sulphate and aloes, 1 sample contained water with a trace of gasoline, and 1 sample contained gasoline.

There were 91 cities and towns visited for the inspection of pasteurizing plants, and 305 plants were inspected.

There were 54 hearings held pertaining to violations of the laws.

There were 149 convictions for violations of the law, $3,172 in fines being imposed.

James Doyle of Dalton; Ernest Bascombe and John Joaquin of Fall River; Georgian Cafeteria, Incorporated, of Cambridge; and Ralph Tanner of Clarksburg, were all convicted for violations of the milk laws.

Monson Milk Company, Incorporated, of Monson; and Robert Steele of North Adams, were convicted for violations of the pasteurization laws and regulations.

Charles L. Woodland of Newton; Israel Ginsberg, Azer Drug Company, Henry Gretsky, Nathan Needleman, 2 cases, and Samuel Kaufman, all of Chelsea; Joseph Doll, Maurice Greenberg, and M. M. Mades Company, of Malden; Morris Fins, Ida Milne, and Mary Yakubowska of Salem; George Poulos of Lynn; Growers Outlet, Incorporated, of Greenfield; Max Baker and S. S. Kresge Company of Roxbury; Harry Selansky of Melrose; Benjamin L. Barron, Maurice Foster, Packers Outlet, Incorporated, 2 cases, and Michael La Magna, all of Cambridge; Peter Serena, Joseph Reinholtz, Morris Bernstein, Joseph Fried, Morris Goodfader, Italo Imperali, Anthony Albertelli, Harry Krivitsky, Abraham Gibson, Charles De Rosa, and Samuel Cohen, 2 cases, all of Boston; Rose De Luca, Jerry Di Sola and Harold Lampert, of Somerville; Nathan Fishman of Allston; Felix Pasay, 3 cases, of Ware; Economy Grocery Stores Company, and John Klys, 2 cases, of Springfield; William J. La Croix of Chicopee Falls; Francis J. Mello of Fall River; Myer Kronick of Orange; Albert Superski, Michael Kudla, Growers Outlet, Incorporated, John Moskal, and Dexter Food Corporation, all of Holyoke; Frank Andreottola and Economy Grocery Stores of Revere; Solin's Market, Incorporated, of Chicopee; Alexander Beaudry and Arthur Gaudreault of Lowell; Mrs. Sarah Ferman of Milford; Fred Uhlig of Pittsfield; The Great Atlantic & Pacific Tea Company, and David Gould of Worcester; Dominick Peluso, Antonio Buonanno and Cresenzo Savastano, all of Lawrence; Pleasant Street Market, Incorporated, Benjamin Silverman and The Great Atlantic and Pacific Tea Company, all of Northampton; and Benjamin Stolzberg of Haverhill, were all convicted for violations of the food laws. Nathan Needleman, 1 case, of Chelsea; Morris Fins, Ida Milne and Mary Yakubowska, all of Salem; George Poulos of Lynn; Harold Lampert of Somerville; and Antonio Buonanno of Lawrence, all appealed their cases.

Gilman & Moffett Company, William C. Anderson, Arthur Ballos, Martin W. Madden, David Berger, John Hamilton, Abraham Jones, George Pallas, and Walter E. Wilson, all of Worcester; George Becrelis of Leominster; Murray Roth, 2 cases, and Harry Sherman of Dorchester; Willam Bernstein (N. E. Cigar Company), Forbes & Wallace, Incorporated, Samuel Greenburg, Nemrow Brothers, Incorporated, Louis M. Shiff, Nicholas Stathis and Edward Viteralli, all of Springfield; Nicholas Bezreh and Morris Kramer of Cambridge; Stephen A. Bozicas, Harold Enright, and Eugene J. Murphy Company, all of Fitchburg; Edward J. Connolly of Lynn; Vincent J. Dimodica, David Starr, and Seymour Woodward, all of Boston; Leo Gaudette, Edmourd J. Giard, Louis Piageneni, and Gerolamo Soldani, all of Spencer; Benjamin Livingston, 2 cases, of Roxbury; Bay State Drug Company, Incorporated, of Palmer; and Phillip Winthrop of Brookline, were all convicted for violations of the confectionery law. Gilman & Moffett Company, William C. Anderson, Arthur Ballos, and David Berger, all of Worcester; Harry Sherman of Dorchester; Seymour Woodward of Boston; Leo Gaudette, Edmourd J. Giard, Louis Piageneni, and Gerolamo Soldani, all of Spencer; all appealed their cases.

Ludwig Dauten and Alphonse Freshette of Newton were convicted for violations of the bakery laws.

Charles Lazaros of Worcester; H. P. Hood & Sons, Incorporated, and Joseph Battaglia of Boston; and Achile Pirosseno of North Wilbraham, were all convicted for false advertising.

Nathan Davis of Salem was convicted for misbranding.

Max Baker of Roxbury; Lilly Beanstock and George Gervlis of Peabody; Douglingos S. Bettencourt, Frank S. Pontes, and Manuel Torres, all of Fall River; James Bruno of Springfield; Morris Stillman, Incorporated of Lynn; Hyman Cohen of Boston; Phillip Fresia, Manuel

Caidozo and Felix Cimici, all of Pittsfield; Jerry Di Sola, Peter Iacopocci, and Cosimo Nardella, all of Somerville; Chester Giberti and Saverio Santosuosso of Revere; Matthew J. Koszik of Greenfield; and Charles Bloom of Cambridge, were all convicted for violations of the cold storage laws. Saverio Santosuosso of Revere, appealed his case.

Diamond Mattress Company of Woonsocket, R. I.; Harry Miller, Morris Miller, Benjamin Malick and Samuel Weiner, all of Lynn; Springfield Mattress Company, Incorporated, of Springfield; Samuel Feinberg of Chelsea; Benjamin Florence of Boston; and Harry Rudnick of Roxbury, were all convicted for violations of the mattress laws. Benjamin Malick of Lynn appealed his case.

Isaac Broverman of Millis was convicted for violation of the slaughtering laws.

In accordance with Section 25, Chapter 111 of the General Laws, the following is the list of articles of adulterated food collected in original packages from manufacturers, wholesalers, or producers:

One sample of cream which was incorrectly graded was obtained from John A. Sellars of Lexington.

One sample of butter which was low in fat was obtained from Kussell's Creamery of Roxbury.

One sample of olive oil which contained cottonseed oil was obtained from Metropolitan Sales Company of Boston.

Pie filling which contained benzoic acid not properly marked was obtained as follows:

Two samples from Big Bear Meat Department, Incorporated, of Somerville; and 1 sample from Growers Outlet Company, Incorporated, of Holyoke.

Dried apricots which contained sulphur dioxide not properly labeled was obtained as follows:

One sample each, from Dexter Food Corporation (Popular Food Market) of Holyoke; Big Bear Grocery Department of Somerville; Commonwealth Grocery Company of Boston; and Consumers Wholesale Food Company, Incorporated, of Southbridge.

Vanilla Extract which contained coumarin was obtained as follows:

Five samples from Roma Extract Company of Boston; and one sample from Milton Sales Company of Springfield.

Lemon Extract which was misbranded was obtained as follows:

Two samples from Roma Extract Company of Boston; and one sample each, from Flav-O-Rite Company of Somerville, and Milton Sales Company of Springfield.

One sample of orange extract which was misbranded was obtained from Milton Sales Company of Springfield.

Pork Kidneys which were decomposed was obtained as follows:

One sample each, from Holyoke Provision Company and Albert Superski, both of Holyoke.

Liver which was decomposed was obtained as follows;

Two samples from Owl Trading Post (Packers Outlet Incorporated) of Cambridge; and one sample each, from Irving Ferman (Lincoln Square Market) of Milford, and Growers Outlet, Incorporated, of Holyoke.

Hamburg steak which contained a compound of sulphur dioxide not properly labeled was obtained as follows:

One sample each, from Isidore Dropkin of Roxbury; Samuel Kaufman and Ray Kaufman of Chelsea; Frank Cruz of Taunton; Gold Star Cash Market of East Boston; Harry Selansky of Melrose; Rose D'Luca of Somerville; Horne's Market of Cambridge; Sirloin Stores of Malden; Samuel Makowitz, M. Bornstein, and Harry Krivitsky, all of Boston; and Myer Kronick of Orange.

Hamburg Steak which contained a compound of sulphur dioxide not properly labeled and was also decomposed was obtained as follows:

One sample each, from Neck Market, Incorporated, of Charlestown; and William Wigod of Boston.

Hamburg steak which contained sodium sulphite in excess of one tenth of one per cent was obtained as follows:

One sample each, from Max White, Frank Kastan, and Irvin Kummel, all of Boston; Gold Star Cash Market of East Boston; Abraham Horne of North Cambridge; Hudson Market of Hudson; and Louis Goldman of Lynn.

Hamburg steak which contained sodium sulphite in excess of one tenth of one per cent and was also decomposed was obtained as follows:

One sample each, from Israel Ginsberg of Chelsea; and Max Most of Boston.

Hamburg steak which was decomposed was obtained as follows:

One sample each, from Economy Store of Revere; John A. Levy of Chelsea; The Great Atlantic & Pacific Tea Company, and Harold Lampert of Somerville; M. M. Mades Company, and John Levy of Lynn; Northampton Public Market and Pleasant Street Market, Incorporated, of Northampton; and Morris Goodfader of Boston.

One sample of hamburg steak which was decomposed and also watered was obtained from Moro Market of Milford.

One sample of hamburg steak which was decomposed, watered, and also contained sodium sulphite in excess of one tenth of one per cent was obtained from Morris Bloom of Lynn.

Sausage which contained a compound of sulphur dioxide not properly labeled was obtained as follows:

Two samples from Joseph Monsignore of Cambridge; and one sample each, from Rose D'Luca and Sirloin Store of Somerville; Renzo Moli and Gold Star Cash Market of East Boston; Holyoke Provision Company of Holyoke; and C. Cavigioti of Milford.

Sausage which contained sodium sulphite in excess of one tenth of one per cent was obtained as follows:

One sample each, from Frank Zambello of East Boston; and Rose De Luca of Somerville.

Sausage which was decomposed was obtained as follows:

One sample each, from G. Zuffante & Company and Big Bear Meat Department of Somerville; Andrew Rutkowsky of Chelsea; The Great Atlantic & Pacific Tea Company of Northampton; Benjamin Stolzberg of Haverhill; and New England Market, Incorporated, of Cambridge.

One sample of sausage which contained a compound of sulphur dioxide not properly labeled and was also decomposed was obtained from Herman Modest of Cambridge.

One sample of sausage which contained sodium sulphite in excess of one tenth of one per cent and was also decomposed and watered was obtained from Waltham Provision Company of Waltham.

Sausage which contained starch in excess of 2 per cent was obtained as follows:

One sample each, from Eli Warshaw and Public Market of East Boston; New England Market, Incorporated, of Cambridge; Atlantic Provision Company of Somerville; and John Levy of Lynn.

Sausage which contained lungs was obtained as follows:

One sample each, from Dominick Peluso, Antonio Buonanno, Chris Savastano and Crescenzo Savastano, all of Lawrence; and Abraham Gibson, Joseph Reinholtz, Joseph Fried, Serena Brothers, Italo Imperali, Charles De Rosa, and A. Albertelli, all of Boston.

The licensed cold storage warehouses reported the following amounts of food placed in storage during December 1933:—217,260 dozens of case eggs; 322,940 pounds of broken out eggs; 760,549 pounds of butter; 4,734,355 pounds of poultry; 3,957,563 pounds of fresh meat and fresh meat products; and 1,953,684 pounds of fresh food fish.

There was on hand January 1, 1934:—497,580 dozens of case eggs; 2,052,567 pounds of broken out eggs; 2,888,562 pounds of butter; 9,827,057½ pounds of poultry; 6,641,109 pounds of fresh meat and fresh meat products; and 15,773,427 pounds of fresh food fish.

The licensed cold storage warehouses reported the following amounts of food placed in storage during January, 1934:—284,430 dozens of case eggs; 341,968 pounds of broken out eggs; 807,818 pounds of butter, 2,313,392¼ pounds of poultry; 4,409,683¼ pounds of fresh meat and fresh meat products; and 2,084,955 pounds of fresh food fish.

There was on hand February 1, 1934:—15,120 dozens of case eggs; 1,635,382 pounds of broken out eggs; 1,885,372 pounds of butter; 10,212,144¼ pounds of poultry; 7,880,935¾ pounds of fresh meat and fresh meat products; and 10,919,171 pounds of fresh food fish.

The licensed cold storage warehouses reported the following amounts of food placed in storage during February, 1934:—165,930 dozens of case eggs; 419,970 pounds of broken out eggs; 434,732 pounds of butter; 1,238,729 pounds of poultry; 3,692,481½ pounds of fresh meat and fresh meat products; and 1,710,971 pounds of fresh food fish.

There was on hand March 1, 1934:—46,380 dozens of case eggs; 1,200,571 pounds of broken out eggs; 1,018,238 pounds of butter; 9,019,625¼ pounds of poultry; 8,049,568¼ pounds of fresh meat and fresh meat products; and 5,427,152 pounds of fresh food fish.

MASSACHUSETTS DEPARTMENT OF PUBLIC HEALTH

Commissioner of Public Health, HENRY D. CHADWICK, M.D.

Public Health Council

HENRY D. CHADWICK, M.D., *Chairman*

ROGER I. LEE, M.D. RICHARD P. STRONG, M.D.
SYLVESTER E. RYAN, M.D. JAMES L. TIGHE.
FRANCIS H. LALLY, M.D. GORDON HUTCHINS.

Secretary, ALICE M. NELSON

Division of Administration	Under direction of Commissioner.
Division of Sanitary Engineering	Director and Chief Engineer, ARTHUR D. WESTON, C.E.
Division of Communicable Diseases	Director, GAYLORD W. ANDERSON, M.D.
Division of Biologic Laboratories	Director and Pathologist, ELLIOTT S. ROBINSON, M.D.
Division of Food and Drugs	Director and Analyst, HERMANN C. LYTHGOE, S.B.
Division of Child Hygiene	Director, M. LUISE DIEZ, M.D.
Division of Tuberculosis	Director, ALTON S. POPE, M.D.
Division of Adult Hygiene	Director, HERBERT L. LOMBARD, M.D.

State District Health Officers

The Southeastern District	RICHARD P. MACKNIGHT, M.D., New Bedford.
The South Metropolitan District	GEORGE M. SULLIVAN, M.D., Stoughton.
The North Metropolitan District	CHARLES B. MACK, M.D., Boston
The Northeastern District	ROBERT E. ARCHIBALD, M.D., Lynn.
The Worcester County District	OSCAR A. DUDLEY, M.D., Worcester.
The Connecticut Valley District	HAROLD E. MINER, M.D., Springfield.
The Berkshire District	WALTER W. LEE, M.D., No. Adams.

PUBLICATION OF THIS DOCUMENT APPROVED BY THE COMMISSION ON ADMINISTRATION AND FINANCE.
14,000. 7-'34. Order 1745.

THE COMMONHEALTH

Volume 21
No. 3

July-Aug.-Sept.
1934

HEALTH EDUCATION

MASSACHUSETTS
DEPARTMENT OF PUBLIC HEALTH

THE COMMONHEALTH
QUARTERLY BULLETIN OF THE MASSACHUSETTS DEPARTMENT OF
PUBLIC HEALTH

Sent Free to any Citizen of the State

Entered as second class matter at Boston Postoffice.

M. LUISE DIEZ, M.D., DIRECTOR OF DIVISION OF CHILD HYGIENE, EDITOR.

Room 545, State House, Boston, Mass.

CONTENTS

	PAGE
Progressive Health Education, by Ada Boone Coffey, R. N.	135
Health Education Through a Community Health Department Publication, by Francis P. Denny, M.D.	137
Health Education by the Community Health Association, by Evangeline Morris	139
Health Education in a City Health Department, by Susan Murdock	142
Health Teaching in the Y W C A, by Rae E. Kaufer	146
Health Education by a Hospital Dispensary, by Mary Pfaffman	148
Health Education in the Field of Mental Hygiene, by Henry B. Elkind, M.D.	153
Health Education through Prenatal and Postnatal Letters and other Printed Material, by Susan M. Coffin, M.D.	155
School Lunch Survey — Children Fed by Wholesale with an Eye to Each's Particular Need, by Clara Sharpe Hough	156
Health Education through Demonstration, by Susan M. Coffin, M.D.	160
Art and Health Education, by John H. McCarthy	161
It Pays to Advertise, by Dorothea Nicoll	165
Protect Your Smile, by Eleanor G. McCarthy, D.H.	168
Health Education in the Schools, by John P. Sullivan, Ph.D.	169
The Conservation of the School Health Program, by Mabel C. Bragg	171
The Supervisor of Health Education — Responsibilities and Training, by C. E. Turner, M.A., Dr. P.H.	175
Health Education through the Classroom Teacher, by Mabel E. Turner	177
Health Education from the Aspect of the Physical Education Director, by Carl L. Schrader	179
The Preparation of Health Education Material for the Schools, by Jean V. Latimer, A.M.	182
Basic Considerations of the Junior High School Course of Study, by John P. Sullivan, Ph.D.	185
Health Education and Our High School Girl, by Albertine P. McKellar	189
Parent Education in Its Relation to Nursery Schools, by Mrs. T. Grafton Abbott	192
Health Education in Massachusetts as Pictured by 1933 Statistics, by Fredrika Moore, M.D.	194
Franklin County Demonstration—1927-1933, by Susan M. Coffin, M.D.	197
The Health Forum, by Henry D. Chadwick, M. D. and Herbert L. Lombard, M.D.	202
Editorial Comment:	
Visual Methods in Health Education	207
Report of the Division of Food and Drugs, April, May and June 1934	208

PROGRESSIVE HEALTH EDUCATION
ADA BOONE COFFEY, R. N.
Chief Consultant in Public Health Nursing
Massachusetts Department of Public Health

In this article I am confining my thoughts to some of the more practical aspects of health education which are within the range of my experience. The June, 1933, issue of the periodical *Education Method* reports the discussion of a jury-panel led by Dr. Courtis of the University of Michigan, having as the topic for discussion, "What is Progressive Education?" In the course of discussion the jury-panel reached a conclusion as to what a progressive educator is and I am using the conclusion as a sort of text. "A progressive educator is one who is dissatisfied with the aims, content and methods of education as they were and are, and is *creatively active* in devising a better education and in putting it into effect. Progressives are those who want to get somewhere and are on their way."

Let us carry this thought a step further and see what are some of the pre-requisites of progressive *health* educators, without which no *so-called* health educator is likely to get anywhere in particular, can scarcely be said to be on his way to any definite destination, and should he arrive somewhere by accident, probably would not know it.

Please bear in mind that I am considering the physical, mental, social and spiritual health of children and that the health educators under discussion are workers who are concerned with the development of the child in all of these aspects of health. As I see it, there are five essential pre-requisites which progressive health educators must possess.

First, they must have *much* more than a superficial knowledge of the basic scientific facts upon which health education is founded. A smattering of generalities is not a sufficient store to draw from when teaching the principles of health.

Second, they must have more than a speaking acquaintance with a set of psychological terms — rather a working knowledge of how behavior is formed and may be re-formed since indoctrination with facts alone will seldom, if ever, influence practice. If you don't believe this, analyze some of your own personal habits and, unless you are a paragon, you will find then many of your practices are contrary to your knowledge and to your teaching of others. Then, if you really want to improve your health behavior, figure out the reason for the inconsistency between your knowledge and practice. A group of us working on study outlines tried this out last spring in a series of conferences and were amazed at our own faulty health *mis*-behavior and we were all holding executive positions in the field of health education. It shocked some of us into searching for motives which actually would initiate, direct, and sustain health practices which we knew to be sound. What is true for such a professional group is even more true of the families we *think* we are influencing.

Third, they must make use of the recognized specific skills, technics, tools, and standards developed and set up by the particular professional group to which they belong so that they may be efficient and may bear the hall mark of professional workers rather than that of unskilled laborers. In such times as these, are agencies justified in asking public or private support for welfare and educational services unless progressive workers skilled in their professions are employed?

Fourth, they must have knowledge and vision enough to see that their own particular jobs are only a part of the whole contribution to health education. As St. Paul said, there are diversities of gifts, and those who possess maturity of mind will not foster what Dr. George H. Bigelow calls "professional trade-unionism". If we are sincerely concerned about the health and welfare of families, it makes no difference who turns the trick — if credit is sought it goes to the worker who can *forget* professional pigeon holes and think in terms of family needs. The professional worker whose learning is on such an obscure and rarefied plane that other professional workers cannot grasp enough of this specialized learning to pass on something of value to families when the occasion arises, had better reorganize his store of knowledge on a lower plane.

Fifth, they must make regular, periodic, fearless appraisal of their personal efforts and those of the organization and profession which they represent. Such appraisal presupposes that they began with clearly defined objectives since it is practically impossible to measure any effort which is not planned to accomplish some tangible and attainable goal—in other words, they must want to *get somewhere* and must be able from time to time to see how *far toward* that somewhere they have come.

Dr. Iago Galdston of New York University says that the purpose of any health education program is to influence behavior and he insists that behavior is essentially emotional rather than intellectual and that if we would teach health effectively we must take into consideration this emotional quality. Dr. Galdston cites several steps in the process of health education which need emphasis.

He says we must arouse curiosity or enlist awareness — in other words, what the psychologists call *readiness* is essential to learning process. If we are hungry, to eat is satisfying, and not to eat is annoying but at the end of a Thanksgiving dinner we are in a state of *unreadiness* to eat and another dinner would not only be annoying but distressing.

The child absorbed in play or in a book is not interested in coming instantly when called and needs some preparation to induce a state of readiness for coming. The prenatal patient who is overworked caring for other children and who feels secure because of her past successes in bearing children must have her interest enlisted before she is receptive to health instruction. Just how to enlist her interest is not always apparent and may be quite different with individual mothers but it is quite certain that it is first necessary to find out what drives are most influential in her emotional life and then present the hygiene of pregnancy in such a way that this emotion is involved. To be specific, what do parents want for themselves and their children which might give us some lead in motivating good prenatal and child hygiene? When preparing the outlines of the New York State staff education program on the psychological approach to child health my assistant and I decided we would ask as many married men and women as we could reach what they wanted out of their married life and by this means see if we could find some practical ways of popularizing prenatal and child hygiene. The results of this rather superficial study were quite enlightening and practically everyone questioned included the following points:

All wanted economic security. The Cost of Medical Care study made by the American Medical Association showed how devastating sickness is to economic security. Tuberculosis takes its highest toll from the age group who are heads of growing families and puerperal deaths come second to tuberculosis in women of this same age group — both of these risks threaten the security of the home — and both are preventable.

All (and especially emphasized by the men) wanted clean, orderly and pleasant homes. Mental or physical disability of any member of the family group spoils this picture.

Normal sexual life was emphasized. Women who have been subjected to unskilled or unplanned delivery with severe lacerations and other complications resulting are frequently indifferent or averse to normal marital relations for months following, and in some instances are never responsive again. All of us who have had experience in maternity work know this, but it is doubtful if the point is ever used to motivate good prenatal and obstetric care — although the sex instinct is recognized by all as one of the primary instincts. Gonorrhea, the greatest sterilizer, and syphilis, a great abortionist, are despoilers of the reproductive function, but we are more apt to use a puritanical moralistic approach in the prevention of these diseases rather than approaching them through the preservation of the sexual function. The relatively short period of time between sexual maturity and the average age of marriage should be pointed out to our youth in sex education, trying to get them to think in terms of the much longer period of happiness in marriage if venereal disease has not been acquired to make a happy marriage practically impossible.

Parents want their children to compare favorably with other children in physical fitness and scholastic attainments; in other words, they want the approval of their families, friends and neighbors (and this is another primary instinct, called by psychologists the herd instinct). They want their children to grow up feeling that they are well equipped for life without physical or emotional handicaps. Children are sure to blame their parents if through negligence they have poor teeth, faulty posture, other preventable orthopedic defects, disfiguring pox marks, squints, or preventable heart disease. The breach between the two generations can be bridged somewhat if parents can be made to see that their children will have greater respect for their opinion if there is evidence that they have utilized the most scientific health and educational facilities which were available.

Obviously, economic security, smoothly running homes, normal sexual life, and healthy happy children are *not* the products of homes broken or disorganized by death or disabling illnesses.

Perhaps these specific examples will illustrate the application of psychological principles to health education, and serve as a rather hastily constructed bridge between factual background and the motivation of healthful behavior.

What then shall we say, in summary, is meant by progressive health education?

Briefly, it is a service to individuals and groups given by trained personnel who recognize that the basic principles of the medical and social sciences must be translated into such form that the basic instincts of the individuals and groups will be aroused to form behavior patterns that will afford the greatest ultimate satisfactions in life.

In closing, may I say a word about the personal responsibility that each of us assumes by being in that privileged class of people who are employed. At no time in history has it been so clear who are the privileged class. We are — we who hold jobs and who draw regular salaries — and with privilege has always gone responsibility for the *under*privileged, and these are now the *un*employed. The most effective way that I know of to use this responsibility is by seeing to it that we *are* progressives and are utilizing every opportunity to improve our abilities to do expert jobs — that means we must support our professional organizations which can and do assemble the collective experience of our respective professions and make this available for our use. One is indeed provincial and limited in vision if he is not looking to others for help in solving the perplexing problems with which we are all faced at this time.

HEALTH EDUCATION THROUGH A COMMUNITY HEALTH DEPARTMENT PUBLICATION

FRANCIS P. DENNY, M. D.

Health Officer, Brookline, Massachusetts

There are two principal reasons for a Health Department Publication.

In the first place the Department needs some means of informing the public of the reasons and purposes of its regulations and activities in order to secure necessary support and cooperation.

In the second place the Department has at its disposal a great mass of information, ignorance of which on the part of the public results in much unnecessary sickness, and death. Many health officers feel that they must make some effort to get this information to their fellow citizens.

If there are one or more local newspapers with a large general circulation the Department may have a special column and so reach its public. There are many communities, however, where the people read chiefly the large metropolitan papers, so this method is not available, and if the printed word is to be used for health education, a health department publication must be resorted to.

Subject Matter

Almost always at the time of publication of the "Bulletin" — let us call it that for the sake of brevity — there are conditions existing which will suggest one or more of the subjects for discussion. For example, the unusual prevalence of some communicable diseases, poliomyelitis, measles, influenza, etc., a community drive for diphtheria or smallpox immunization or some new activity of the department, will readily suggest the subject for one or more leading articles.

There are certain important health lessons that need to be driven home repeatedly in any such publication: the early symptoms of cancer and tuberculosis, the dangers of overweight, the need of calling a physician for abdominal pain and the avoidance of laxatives, guarding against infection, taking care of "colds" to prevent pneumonia, first aid in emergencies, annual health examinations, and the like. Frequent write-ups on the various activities of the health department are desirable in order to keep the public informed and so secure their cooperation and support.

Statistical reports on morbidity and mortality may be included but they should be very brief and compact, otherwise they discourage the lay reader.

Articles for the Health Bulletin may be written by the editor or by various members of the Department. Public spirited physicians of well recognized standing in the community can often be induced to contribute and a few such signed articles by persons who are leaders in some special line help greatly to give weight and dignity to the publication.

In addition to articles written especially for the Bulletin an editor can find an enormous amount of health educational material upon which to draw. There are the publications of numerous state and municipal health departments which can be had for the asking and in exchange, and also many nonofficial publications. Many of these contain excellent articles which can be reprinted. Every writer of health educational material is only too glad to have his articles reprinted. In my experience consent can always be obtained to reprint even copyrighted material of this sort. Of course, due credit should always be given to this borrowed material.

Some illustrations are very desirable although they add to the expense. Certain individuals will only pick up printed matter to look at a picture, but once having done that they often begin to read.

Health publications vary greatly in their general style. Some follow the pattern of the daily press and the advertising sections of the periodicals, attracting attention by sensational methods; others are very conservative. Personally, I believe that a quiet dignified style is preferable and the advice so given is more likely to be followed than where the more sensational methods are employed.

Distribution

The publication of a good Health Bulletin is of no value unless it gets into the hands of those who will read it. The problem of its distribution is a difficult and serious one. Sending through the mail to a large and carefully prepared list is good but is very expensive, costing more than the printing. The bulletins may be given to the school children to take home. Many of them never get to the homes, and many of those adults one wishes to reach have no school children. Bulletins may be placed on store counters for free distribution, at the public library, and at the board of health office. All these various methods may be used in combination and will serve to get many copies distributed. Possibly in some communities Boy and Girl Scouts might be utilized.

In Brookline we have been fortunate in having an effective method of distribution which has not caused any additional expense. Having a town form of government — although the population is about 50,000 — the police department has been in the habit of distributing at every door the warrants for the town meetings and elections. They have also distributed four times a year the quarterly bulletins issued by the Health Department. This can readily be done by day patrolmen in a thickly settled community like ours where most of the doors are near the street without seriously interfering with the patrol of their districts.

Educational Value

It is always difficult to determine the true value of any educational measure. There are occasional straws, however, which indicate to the Health Department that they are getting results from their Health Bulletin, providing it is being widely distributed. For example, the results of the examination of the milk sold in the town are published in the Brookline Health Bulletin. Any dealer whose bacterial counts are high or whose butter fat has fallen is very certain to hear from his customers — a definite indication that the Bulletin is read. With this publication of the milk reports, cleanliness and efficient pasteurization have real money value to the dealers. The improvement in the milk supply of Brookline since the reports were first published in 1920 has been extraordinary. Then counts in the millions were frequent and counts in the hundreds unknown. During the last quarter the highest count was 42,000 and 41 per cent were in the hundreds.

The eating places in Brookline are scored as "excellent," "good," or "fair" and the results published. Here also we get evidence that the Bulletin is read.

In addition to such evidence as the above that the Bulletin is being read, we occasionally get indications that the advice given results in action. For instance, physicians have reported that patients have come to them for a health examination because they had read in the Bulletin that it was a good thing to do. At one such examination malignant disease was discovered. Patients coming to the Tuberculosis Dispensary have reported that they came because of what they read in the Bulletin. A grateful woman reported that she had a lump in the breast, read about the danger in the Bulletin, consulted a physician immediately, and had the lump removed.

Of course, it is only by the merest chance that such information reaches the Health Department but the mere fact that we do occasionally get such reports encourages us to believe that there are many other individuals who have been helped in the same way. The early diagnosis of a single case of cancer or tuberculosis is worth many thousands of Bulletins.

HEALTH EDUCATION BY THE COMMUNITY HEALTH ASSOCIATION

Evangeline Morris
Educational Director
Community Health Association

Mrs. Rose has recently come to the attention of our organization. She is twenty years old, has been married for one year and is now experiencing her first pregnancy. Her record states that she is a normal prenatal. This girl knows nothing of the physiological process of pregnancy, and her personal hygiene will bear improvement. Her diet is extremely poor, and her knowledge of infant care is negligible. But she has certain assets. She is young and ambitious and anxious to learn. This same anxiety for information will send her to wrong sources unless scientific guidance is readily available.

In recognition of the needs of this patient and the large group she typifies, the educational work of the Community Health Association begins with the pregnant woman. This program is carried out either in the home visit, which makes possible a highly individualized type of teaching, or through the organization of prenatal classes, offering the additional stimulation and incentive of class instruction. And no group is more receptive, more anxious to know of a better way, than these women, who attend in large and ever-increasing numbers the Mothers' Clubs of the various districts.

The material taught in these classes, which, incidentally, is the same for conferences in the home, covers a wide field. The plan of instruction makes it possible for patients who register as late as the seventh month of pregnancy to receive detailed information concerning every phase of prenatal care. The object of medical supervision, the value of an adequate diet in providing for the growth and development of the foetus, the prevention of constipation and control of weight, suitable clothing for the mother, the selection of a layette, preparation for home delivery, care of the infant including feeding, a budget and a daily schedule for the family are all included.

Important as this formal instruction may be, the clubs afford a broader service. Classes are supplemented by actual demonstration, illustrated by posters and amplified by the use of literature. Sewing groups are organized as a pre-class activity to teach actual methods of layette making. Nurse and nutrition worker are available to listen and whenever possible to help with the solution of individual problems. Refreshments are served, partly for their social value but more particularly to give the nutrition worker an additional opportunity to demonstrate the suitable selection and preparation of food.

This type of expansive teaching belongs particularly to pregnancy but the immediate postpartum period with the nurse in daily attendance offers an excellent opportunity for an intensified service. The presence of the new baby may and frequently does prove an overwhelming responsibility to the family. The nurse is able to interpret his needs and differentiate needs from desires, to plan his day and make his routine a part of the schedule for the family group. As the mother's strength returns, she is shown the value of good physical care, the importance of regularity and promptness in the feeding schedule, and the need of medical supervision both for herself and her infant.

One other opportunity for service to the newborn is provided in the two visits made to mothers delivered in the hospital. Since this service is given when the baby is approximately three weeks old and possibly for want of a better term, it is known as the "Third Week Visit." Since so much teaching must be accomplished in a limited time, a thoughtful plan has been evolved, which is followed in detail.

Preparation
1. An explanation of this service is given to the patient in Mothers' Club or during one of the home visits.
2. The nurse considers, with the aid of the prenatal record, the status of the individual mother:
    The needs of the untaught factory girl.
    The problems of the well-educated woman.

Demonstration
1. First Visit: The nurse undresses, bathes and dresses the baby, explaining each step in the process, and illustrating the proper method of handling.
2. Second Visit: The mother gives a return demonstration and receives encouragement in the form of constructive criticism.

Teaching Content
1. For the baby — routine of physical care and child training, supervision by family physician or clinic.
2. For the mother — emphasizing the importance of positive health, of postpartum care, of medical follow-up. Routine for breast feeding.
3. For the family — fitting the baby into his environment. An individual and highly important factor in the well-being of the entire family group.

The criterion of success in any undertaking is the actual accomplishment. The following case is cited as the zenith which we sometimes reach:

In some households with a new baby, 10:30 in the morning is a rather hectic time. But not with Mrs. Smith! She comes to her door through a tidy home, and she looks charming and rested. The only signs of a baby in this house are his sterile bottles of formula cooling at the sink and his small clothes flopping on the line. He himself is asleep on the porch. And Mrs. Smith is happy to explain the miracle of her good management. She learned so much at Mothers' Club and the nurse who came in to bathe the baby showed her all the rest. How satisfactory to look at this baby asleep in his bed, his hands and face already tanned by the sun, and his whole being radiating an air of peaceful security. And our work with this baby is completed unless he becomes ill. For the City Health Department follows every birth registration and assumes responsibility for infant welfare and preventive work with the preschool child.

While the emphasis in all public health teaching is on prevention, there remains for consideration the curative and corrective phases of our work. Five year old Jane and her family required this curative type of service. When Jane developed a gonorrheal cervico vaginitis, her mother was taught a suitable isolation technique, the exact procedures in nursing care, the importance of a good general health program for the patient, the fact that this condition in children has no social significance, and the certainty of a favorable prognosis under medical and nursing care.

Frequently the family needs for health supervision are multiple. The Certos were such a family. The trite comment — "a most completely disorganized home" — made by an experienced nurse accustomed to a congested district, is revealing. The young mother beginning her third pregnancy, overwhelmed with responsibilities and physical discomfort — the discouraged and irritable husband — the older child of three utterly untrained — and the year old baby, who cried incessantly were all living in cluttered rooms, existing on a badly balanced and expensive diet, and sinking from day to day into a deeper chaos. That was the situation four months ago. Today Mrs. Certos comes to the district office, bringing two unusually well adjusted children. She tells the supervisor that things are different in her home now, that since the nurse helped her train the baby, her husband has become interested and has helped with Tony, that both children have regular naps and go to bed at an early hour. She herself has time to rest and to finish her housework. And she adds with a shy smile, "I think we do better with this next baby."

It is the aim of this organization to provide a completely generalized service with each nurse equipped to carry every phase of this service to the families of her district. However, budget cases, a distinct specialty, are still carried by the nutrition workers. Such a case is represented by the Russos. This family of eight — with the father in poor physical condition requiring a high vitamin diet involving additional expense, and three of the children distinctly malnourished — are receiving $13.00 a week from the Overseers of Public Welfare, and supplementary assistance in the form of five quarts of milk daily and a certain amount of much needed clothing from the Family Welfare Society. Scientific knowledge of food values, skill in management and tact in teaching are all brought to play on this Herculean problem. Fourteen visits are made to the home, the mother adopts the suggestions made for food selection and the expenditure of her limited funds, and the family becomes accustomed to the essential protective foods to supplement those peculiar to their racial diet. The worker's final comment — "I believe these habits are now fixed and will last" — is significant.

Other cases might be cited illustrating the educational program with the convalescent child, with the cardiac and the infantile, or showing the approach to parental education and the problem of family relationships. It may, however, be sufficient to state that the nurses of this organization are alert to these and many other problems and that their daily visits have a definite content of practical teaching for their solution.

It is pertinent to consider in this connection the professional preparation of these nurses who compose the staff of the Community Health Association. They are graduates of high schools, of schools of nursing education and in addition have completed the Public Health Nursing course of an accredited college. This amount of preparation may seem formidable, but in reality it is only a beginning. To supplement and complete this training and to keep the nurses constantly informed of new developments in public health and allied fields, the organization provides for a continuous process of staff education.

This program of staff education is carried out under the leadership of the Director and her Assistant by four supervisors who have specialized in the fields of nutrition, orthopedics, mental health and social hygiene. The direct teaching of this group, who also act as consultants, is supplemented by the thirteen district supervisors, who are at all times available to the staff and whose practical experience in the handling of patients makes their advice of inestimable value.

If there is any direct formula for health education in family groups, we do not claim to have found it. Continuous growth to meet community needs, careful planning to prevent overlapping with the work of other agencies, change in keeping with modern economic and social trends are the factors which have shaped the educational work of the Community Health Association.

HEALTH EDUCATION IN A CITY HEALTH DEPARTMENT

SUSAN MURDOCK

Director, Health Education
Boston Health Department

In a city health department "health education" designates the procedures that teach to the community ways of gaining and preserving good health. Health education is daily becoming a more important factor in the work of the modern health department. It is recognized that if the health standards of the city are to be raised, if maternal and infant deaths are to be lessened, if we are to reduce the case and death rates of communicable diseases, if the degenerative diseases are to be kept under control, health education must be carried on. The health educator is now an important member of the staff of the progressive health department. The people in our cities should be taught how to make the best of the conditions under which necessity demands that they live — they should be instructed in personal and community hygiene so that by the absence of preventable disease and the worry and expense attached to it, their lives shall be fuller and happier ones.

A good health education program will eventually greatly reduce the cost of keeping a city healthy. It should embrace the whole community. Young and old, rich and poor, educated and uneducated should be considered. As many as possible of the many avenues of education open to the health educator should be used.

School health education is the branch of health education that is most widely known. Unless the school department undertakes a health program in its regular curriculum the teaching of health in the classroom, medical and nursing service must be arranged for, supervised and carried on by the health department. The school health program should include both public and parochial schools. In many instances the school department has no supervision over the parochial schools. In that case the health department is responsible for health education in parochial schools. Adequate medical and nursing service must be the first consideration of the health department in its school work. Next comes the classroom teaching of health. If the third step is neglected or omitted it greatly lessens the efficiency and efficaciousness of the work of both physicians and nurses. With teachers, nurses and doctors working together in the formation of good health habits among the children, the impartation of sound health knowledge, and the developing of healthy attitudes toward the children's personal health and their duty toward preserving good community health, a city has taken long strides toward raising its health standards. If the school department is responsible for the public schools, supervision of classroom teaching of health in parochial schools can be accomplished by the health department at minimum cost. One experienced, well-trained person can instruct teachers in ways of teaching health, distribute information and helpful material, and supervise the regular classroom work. If the city is not a large one this may be only a part-time job.

Because direct health education is by far the most successful of the various kinds of public health education it should be resorted to whenever possible. In the Boston Health Department we have organized a series of health talks for the people of the several Health Unit districts; namely, Charlestown, East Boston, North End, Roxbury, South Boston, South End and West End. These talks are given monthly in the Health Units to people who are reached through nurses, social workers, schools, newspapers and general health department activities. The health talks are given by an expert in the field being discussed or the health educator. The subject matter for such lectures is almost inexhaustible. The topic of "foods" alone will furnish material for several meetings. Then there is the prevention of communicable diseases; the value of early diagnosis and treatment in appendicitis, tuberculosis, cancer, etc.; the care of babies and children; and the necessity of having good, clean homes. The health talks are supplemented by a moving picture that emphasizes the lecture. This part of the program is generally followed by entertainment in the form of amusing moving pictures, readings or music.

We have found it a good plan to send speakers to talk with mothers' groups at settlement houses and clubs. The lecturers are physicians from the City Health Department who speak on subjects selected by the group leaders. In this way we are sure to give to the mothers something that they are anxious to have, and we are almost sure to be asked to arrange another talk. If we are approaching a foreign speaking group we try to talk to them in their own language for the feeling that the speaker knows and understands them seems to give them a confidence in us that we can obtain in no other way.

A splendid opportunity for "health educating" presents itself in city clinics — the health educator has a fertile field in those waiting their turn to see the doctor or dentist. Instructions arranged for particular age groups (if the patients are children) or to meet the needs of those attending a particular clinic should be constantly in readiness. If the information given is timely, and adapted to the needs of those attending the clinic, it is almost certain to bring the desired results. To carry on such instruction requires careful planning by the health educator. The work must be made interesting and appealing. Pictures, posters, stories and something to take home, either handwork or pertinent literature, all help to make the lesson more impressive.

If playground activity is part of the health department work or if a cooperative spirit exists between playground and health department officials, groups of children attending playgrounds may be reached in much the same way as those waiting for clinics. Here it is wiser to do health teaching from the story telling angle, or to do it through some handwork that emphasizes health habits, or by some method other than formal teaching.

The health educator must be ready to use all the facilities existing in her city to further her program, in fact it is possible to develop a splendid educational program using only the agencies that exist in a city the size of Boston. She must cooperate with the various professional, official, nonofficial and semicommercial groups that are working toward the gaining and maintaining of good health. In Boston we have worked with the State Department of Public Health, the American Red Cross, the Massachusetts Tuberculosis League, the Massachusetts Society for Social Hygiene, the Boston Health League, the New England Dairy Council, the East Boston Medical Society and various settlement house and church groups. The city health department should be willing to comply with the requests of those working within the city in furthering their health projects, but be careful to avoid any commercial relations.

Campaigns for diphtheria immunization, dental work, communicable disease control and the like, may be successfully carried out at a minimum cost to the health department if the cooperation of the agencies existing in a community is enlisted. In a campaign for education in regard to health examinations the members of the medical societies may be found willing to conduct the health examinations either in their own offices, charging a nominal fee, or to give free examinations in the health department quarters. They may be enlisted to give health talks to groups of people gathered through the efforts of social workers and health department. The social agencies will give the services of their workers for carrying on both lectures and health examinations. They may be willing to help in the publicity work which is necessary to health campaigns. A health campaign if carefully planned and executed with special attention to publicity will undoubtedly bring results that are gratifying to all those interested, the people themselves, the medical societies, the social agencies and the health department.

One of the most important tools in the hands of the city health department health educator is the newspaper. Practically every section of the newspaper can be used for health education. Feature stories, news items, stories, photographs, editorials and advertisements can all be used to advantage. Through the newspaper the public can be informed of health department activities, warned of impending epidemics, informed as to where they can obtain certain health services, told about preventable diseases and the value of early diagnosis and proper treatment in health protection, and advised regarding personal and community hygiene.

Careful, discriminating use of posters and health literature can be made a valuable part of the educational program. Clinic rooms or buildings given over to health purposes should be used for the displaying of health posters. Public buildings, settlement houses and school rooms are good places in which to hang them. The posters should be scientifically correct, attractive and colorful. They should be displayed with a thought as to whether the lesson in the poster is meant for those who will see it. Posters should not be allowed to remain too long in one place. A schedule 'may be worked out whereby all posters can be changed monthly.

Literature distributed by a health department must be carefully selected. If the department budget will allow it, the department can publish its own literature — otherwise material published by health agencies, insurance companies and state departments of health may be used successfully. The literature should be distributed according to some definite plan. If lectures or health lessons are to be given a repetition of the ideas stressed may be distributed for home reading. In such cases, if the talk is to be given in a foreign-speaking neighborhood, literature in the language of the people is best. I recall one instance where after a lecture on cancer we distributed pamphlets on the subject in Yiddish. After the literature had been distributed a comedy was shown on the screen and we were surprised to notice that the women were so interested in the little books that we had given them that they were paying little or no attention to the moving picture. Appropriate literature may be distributed at clinics and during health campaigns, such as a drive for toxin antitoxin or a tuberculosis campaign. It may be given out through schools, churches, clubs, factories, stores; or by nurses, social workers, inspectors and others working directly with the people. Health literature should be available wherever people are likely to ask for health information. Hundreds of thousands of pieces of literature can be distributed in the city during the course of a few months.

A health education reference library should be maintained for the use of the health educators employed by the city. This library should be made available to teachers, nurses, social workers and others who are likely to need it. It should be kept up to date with accounts of new educational projects and samples of useful material that is easily attainable.

Exhibits at clinics, in the front or rear of a lecture hall, at teachers' meetings, at mothers' clubs, settlement houses, clubs, etc., can be arranged by the city health department health educator. The exhibits may be arranged by the health department itself or they may be borrowed from the State Department of Public Health, or some private agency. The exhibit should be self explanatory but to reach a maximum of usefulness it should be accompanied by a person who can answer the questions of those looking at it.

With the continuance of health education or the adoption of a carefully planned health program in our cities there is no doubt but that health standards will be raised.

HEALTH TEACHING IN THE Y W C A
RAE E. KAUFER
Health Educational Secretary
Essex County Health Association, Inc.

When your time is your own in which to do as you please would you choose to solve a problem of health? This is the situation which confronts those who are interested in establishing a practical program in health education in the Y W C A. Most of the girls and young women who come to the Y W come with the desire to have a good time and to make new friends. Unless it is tactfully impressed upon them they are unaware of a need to learn more about their health or the health of the community. And yet, because they do come voluntarily they are particularly open to suggestion. The young adult becomes interested in health only after she begins to appreciate the way in which it will help her attain that which she desires.

It is the problem of the Y W C A, then, to interest girls in health, to arouse their enthusiasm, and to create a desire to solve with understanding the health problems of adult life. In this atmosphere of persuasion it is rather difficult to visualize any formal health program. However, the organization of the Y offers excellent opportunities for an organized health educational program as well as innumerable possibilities for incidental health teaching. This program under the direction of the Health Education Department should be formed in cooperation with representatives of the girls themselves. In some health teaching which we did recently in several industrial cities it was interesting to notice that when the term "health" was mentioned unaccompanied by an appropriate introduction these young women reacted just as unfavorably as children who had been exposed to "formal" health teaching. Yet these same young women responded enthusiastically to health teaching when they found they could discuss, informally, problems which were vital to them.

Health is so closely related to personal appearance that this subject proved to be a forceful reminder of the truth that every girl must be positively healthy to be really good looking — that all-inclusive health which incorporates their emotions, their minds, their social activity as well as their physical selves. The appeal of attractiveness is strong enough to interest all girls — be they in business, industry, high school or the home.

The Health Education Department should assume the responsibility of coordinating the entire health education program and of explaining the possibilities of this program to the various departments — the business and professional girls and women, the industrial girls and household employees, the younger girls, the international group and the adults.

The requirement that a medical examination must be received before participation in any active work furnishes an opportunity to stress the value of this protective measure. It is well worth the time expended for one of the examining physicians to meet informally with all groups of girls and to explain to them the purpose and value of an annual medical examination. At this time a health questionnaire such as the following may be discussed:

We need your ideas for Fall Program!*

1. Would you enjoy participating in a small discussion group on some phase of health that has proved a problem to girls today?
2. What subject would interest you most?
3. Are you needing light on some specific health program yourself?

* Boston Y W C A

If so, what is it? Should such information come through a class, or by conference with our examining physician?

4. Do you have an annual health examination? If so, do you follow up the recommendations made by the physician at that time?

Signed..................................

The response to this questionnaire from a group of business girls indicated that they were principally interested in the subjects of the type of diet which would keep them up to par, methods of relaxation, the attainment of poise, how to correct posture and foot defects and the care of the skin. That they would prefer to receive this information through small discussion groups was typical of their desire for sociability. These questionnaires are an excellent source on which to base the content matter of a series of informal group discussions.

The medical examination frequently shows remediable physical defects which would often be corrected if the girls were encouraged to secure the aid of their family physician or the various community health organizations. Interest may also be stimulated in the correction of posture and foot defects with the assistance of the health education department staff who also have the opportunity to emphasize the value of the reexamination.

The success of a well-rounded program depends upon the cooperation of all of the departments and committees within the Y as well as the health organizations in the community. It must be introduced in such a way that the girls feel it is their desire to develop such a program. We have found that with the assistance of health specialists a series of informal discussions under attractive titles are of interest to young women.

Under the topic of "Personal Appearance" a group of business girls in a Y W recently spent one hour a week for eight weeks discussing various phases of health in its relation to personal appearance. We endeavored to find the way in which the various aspects of health contribute to that secret force which makes a girl vital and interesting as well as good-looking. How appearance and attitude affect the personality of the young adult were first discussed and this led us to group the evidences of attractiveness. Here almost everything was mentioned from health to a sense of humor and from this list we knew we would want to include mental and social as well as physical hygiene in our discussions. A consideration of individual limitations and possibilities indicated that each girl must work with what she has and not with what she might have.

The second meeting began with a discussion of the skin, especially concerned with the way in which it is affected by food, exercise, cleanliness and rest. The interest regarding this subject was shown and many questions were discussed indicating the willingness of the girls to participate. Such popular newspaper articles as "You have to be well to be beautiful" were brought in and they received critical analysis based upon scientific facts, thus paving the way for a criticism of the modern advertisements as well as popular superstitions.

During each meeting one or two books from our health library regarding some phase of health were reviewed or recommended, resulting in the fact that many girls borrowed these. The films were well liked and aided in picturing the more technical aspects of many phases of personal and community health. In order to determine their knowledge the girls decided to answer the questions in a health knowledge test which had been prepared for use in the high school. After doing this they discovered that they had forgotten most of what they had learned about nutrition, bacteria, physiology and tuberculosis. Many were surprised to learn that tuberculosis is not inherited and that it is still the leading cause of death for young people between the ages of fifteen to twenty-five — the rate being twice as great for young women as for young men. They were interested to learn this and to realize that tuberculosis may be prevented through avoiding contact with the disease, maintaining good physical condition and by having an annual medical examination.

As the weeks went by the regular group members remained and new girls came into our discussions, apparently demonstrating that the subject of health may become popular when it is considered as a basis for something which is vital to young women. The health emphasis was discovered in such pamphlets as the "Good Looks Chart", the "Thirty Day Loveliness Test" and "Are You as Attractive as Nature Intended You to Be?" Correct nutrition, over, under and normal weight, social hygiene and mental health were each considered in its relation to health and personal appearance. As these meetings came to an end suggestions were made by the girls for their continuance, such subjects as social hygiene, mental relationship to health, and health of the family being suggested, indicating that the girls themselves realize the need for a study of the broader aspects of health.

This method of health teaching as well as this subject may be adapted for use with groups of high school or industrial girls. Planned with the aid of the girls the program should be organized for the entire year although it should be flexible enough to allow for alterations.

Of course, a program in health education includes many other phases which can only be mentioned here. Under the right circumstances films may be used, or a speaker will be of interest. A health library will appeal to a certain group while a bulletin board will attract others. A personal interview is the only way of reaching some girls while others may need only such general information as is spread through the use of the radio or in pamphlet or poster form.

The health week has its value in stimulating interest, especially if it is developed by the girls themselves. An exhibit should illustrate the effect of health upon the entire personality. This has been tried by actually setting the ordinary situations in which a girl finds herself — a living room stressing relaxation, the dining room and cafeteria emphasizing well balanced meals, a garden and camping scene showing the value of beauty and outdoor exercise, a dressing room stressing the value of cleanliness and an exhibit showing the community health resources. Many speakers and demonstrations took place during this week and it was most appropriately closed by a talk entitled "And charm lives on".

The incidental possibilities for health teaching are many — in the cooking classes, in the courses regarding poise as well as in the many groups which meet for sports and recreation. The opportunities which are offered to staff members for personal guidance are numerous in each department as well with the personal and vocational guidance counselors.

Education for health must continue throughout life — helping to make satisfactory adjustment among ever-shifting situations. Now that we are learning how young women may become interested in health we should endeavor to help them for they will not only help themselves but they will be an influence upon others.

HEALTH EDUCATION BY A HOSPITAL DISPENSARY
MARY PFAFFMANN
Health Educator
Boston Dispensary

The mass of human kind — men, women and children — that fills the clinic waiting room, demonstrates the need of giving out health knowledge. Watching the scene, the vision comes of the opportunity, amounting to an obligation, for hospital, dispensary, out-patient clinic and health centre to fortify treatment with another service, by means of health education. With the doctor, nurse and social worker there should be a teacher, to teach and interpret to the throngs, as they pass in and out, and as they wait for medical, dental or food treatment, the principles that help to protect and confirm the condition of health they are seeking. The number of such gathering places for people who are not well, the world over, indicates the extent of the educational service that needs to be rendered.

So many reasons favor the use of health education in the medical institution! There is the element of time — think of the sum total of the hours spent in clinic waiting rooms, six days of every week, by millions of people who would welcome employment for eye, ear, hand and mind, while waiting! There is the theory of the effectiveness of teaching concerning a need, when the need is uppermost in the consciousness of the person to be taught. The adult patient concerned for his health and all that depends upon it, the mother who has brought her child into the clinic, will be attentive, eager listeners to information given concerning the body's hygienic and food needs — and, further, will place the greater reliance upon it in that it has the endorsement of the medical institution or health centre.

The new knowledge which science is accumulating on health and nutrition should be interpreted to people, to the widest extent possible, in the interests of enlightenment in the matter of body needs and for greater satisfaction in every department of living — in work, recreation and leisure.

How often the medical record refers to "poor health habits" or "faulty food habits," and what a low status of health is thus designated! Here is work for the health educator; for the subject matter of health education concerns the proper food and health habits which the physician wishes his patients to apply in daily behavior, as an aid to the reconstruction and maintenance of health, as well as for prevention of disease, so akin is health education to preventive medicine.

How can health education be carried on in the clinic waiting room? As with all successful teaching, human interests must be utilized — the desire to be happy, to be busy at something, the pleasure in beautiful and interesting things and in things of special meaning, the love of color, the love of play, the interest in story and in motion. Utilizing these the health educator will devise means and methods of appeal to the patients, to the end of encouraging them to adopt proper food and health habits. She will create a cheerful and attractive environment, stimulating in ways favorable to her purpose. Painted tables and chairs, bookshelves and window hangings, for color; plants, flowers, books, maps, games, goldfish, a canary, to divert eye and mind; for the foreign-born something that relates to life in the native country — these will contribute to an environment in which it will be pleasant to sit for a while.

There will be pictures and posters to look at, designed to interpret a health principle and at the same time possessing high artistic merit. It is regrettable that the fine work of the Empire Marketing Board of London, which provided beautiful posters of the industries and products of the British Empire, including many related to food, has had to be discontinued. But from far and near, often from most unlikely sources, the health educator will gather a wealth of pictorial material, much of it of permanent value, and obtained at little cost or through the contribution of an interested friend glad to be able to serve. There is also satisfaction in creating material to meet a particular need, if only to the extent of formulating the idea, putting its execution into capably artistic hands.

The patient's appreciative comments will show that he recognizes not only the beauty and interest of such material but also its implications with respect to the performance of a health habit or the importance of certain foods — milk, fruit, vegetables, the whole grain products. Interested in such an environment, he becomes unreserved, reachable, suggestible, responsive to definite teaching.

And what of the methods for teaching patients of various age levels, various degrees of mental capacity and command of English — just as they come, for there can be no grading, except broadly between adult and child — and in the midst of clinic procedures?

It is clear that the form of presentation must have the characteristics of a common denominator in its power to reach the interest and understanding of all. In particular, methods must be most carefully studied to attain the utmost simplification in every form of presentation — in word, phrase and sentence, in speech and print, in explanation and demonstration. Visualization is important at every step, to hold and impress the mind through the eye, and repetition of important points through interesting means — never to the point of irksomeness. Essential knowledge concerning a subject of health must be given in one period, for the clientele is never the same from day to day, and this requires a study of how, in a short time, to give a great deal without overcrowding the mind. Always scientific accuracy must be guarded, and the spirit of every teaching process will be such as to surround good health practices with pleasant associations.

Let us demonstrate what may be done in the way of teaching children patients, while they wait for the doctor. Readily they will gather about the table with the health educator, who with subject matter for discussion prearranged will set them to thinking, say of our common need of sleep. The children will be encouraged to take part in the discussion, the teacher guiding them, somewhat as follows:

There will be delightful pictures to appreciate and talk about, pictures of sleeping children, of children on their way to bed, of the sleep habits of animals and birds — the bat asleep with head hanging downward, the young monkey soothed to sleep by its anxious mother. Yes, all creatures — birds, animals and people — sleep. They need to sleep — why? Well, think of the tired ship just returned from many months on the ocean (the teacher has a picture of a gallant ship to show). What does it probably need? Rest! Repair! (These words are recorded prominently.) Yes — and when it is emptied of passengers and cargo, sometimes it is put into a dry dock. (Here a picture of a dry dock is important, to visualize the unfamiliar.) What is done to the ship in dry dock? Yes — new parts are made to take the place of worn out parts, weak places are made strong until the ship is like new, and ready for another voyage to far countries.

The teacher asks: When does your body feel the way a tired ship feels? Yes — at evening time, after a day's work and play! And what does your body need then, and where do you put it? Yes, you put it to bed and to sleep for *rest* and *repair*. That is why you need sleep!

The children are amused with the analogy, which the teacher carries further.

The men who repair the ship — what do they use? Wood — nails — bolts — screws — paint — polish, yes. Now, what is used to repair your body? (No answer, and the teacher must reply to her question.) Food! Food! In food, especially in milk, fruit, vegetables and whole grain breads and cereals, your body finds the materials it will use to repair itself! And the repair work can be done best while you sleep. You wake up in the morning feeling — how? Yes, rested, repaired, new, like the ship, and ready for another day of play and work. That's how sleep helps you!

And remember this: while you sleep, you grow! The food materials that repair your body also help you to grow. (The word "growth" is listed under "rest" and "repair".) Plenty of sleep for rest, repair and growth — that's why you need sleep, every one.

Here can be interposed a little questionnaire:

Who needs most sleep, you or your grown-up brother or sister? Why? What will help to make each tomorrow happy for you? Why?

Some sort of picture or chart is needed to show and impress the proper bedtime for each one in the group of various ages — and it must have interest. The teacher has one that pictures all the children of all the world going to bed — here the 5, 6 and 7 year-olders, here the 8, 9 and 10 and here the 11, 12 and 13 year-old children, and under each group is stated the approved bedtime hour. As on a map each child locates himself on the chart and sees written underneath his proper bedtime. When his habit, as he reports it in reply to the teacher's query, does not correspond at all well to what it should be, there is opportunity for the teacher to confer with the mother, sitting near, in the spirit of a mutual desire to help the child. Often there are revealed home conditions unfavorable to good sleep habits, and often the mother cooperates for improvement in respect to sleeping conditions and the early bedtime.

Literature is drawn upon to help to make sleep and bedtime pleasantly anticipated by the child. Poetry ranges from the tired king who said that sleep is like a nurse (and is it not so, and like a doctor, too, urges the teacher, and finds the children in sympathy) to "The birds are silent in their nest and I must seek for mine." In the piece of handwork for each child, which may be taken home and which will be a reminder to him, and to others in the family, of his proper bedtime, the child will be happily absorbed until he is called to talk with the doctor.

In this fashion the teacher can work with children in the midst of clinic procedure — which they, absorbed in picture, talk, story, or handwork, will not heed — and under direct observation by the interested mothers and adult patients. And in plain sight of the mother, and especially for her to study, will be a picture chart, having beauty and interest, which will state distinctly the bedtime and the number of hours of sleep advisable for her children.

It is most important to interpret the new knowledge concerning the food constituents and their relations to the body's needs for growth and maintenance and energy. That children can understand and be greatly interested in the body's need of carbohydrate and fat, protein, calcium, iron, the vitamins and other essentials for health, and that this knowledge can be given them in a form in which they will be stimulated to apply it, with the cooperation of the mother, has been shown in the book, "Food and Your Body".* And in this book the common denominator form of presentation seems to have been attained, for its methods appeal to the adult as well as to the child.

Again — to demonstrate a piece of silent teaching by means of the exhibit — on the clinic walls are four sheets of mounting paper, of pleasing color, on which is mounted material that makes up a complete story of the need and manner of guarding against hand-to-mouth infection and the communicable diseases. In various pictures, carefully chosen, the exhibit shows hands — beautiful hands, hands that look clean, hands that are clever as they work, hands at rest. Under each is a brief comment, stated simply, easy to read. This fine-looking working woman — it's certain that her hands are clean, because her white cap and kerchief are so clean. Here is a picture of hands making bread, the fingers in the dough — I hope they are clean! — and another

---
* Pfaffman and Stern: Food and Your Body; Talks with Children. M. Barrows & Co. See also Teaching Nutrition to Boys and Girls by Mary Swartz Rose. Macmillan.

of children holding up their hands to one who is serving ice cream and cake, and saying, evidently, "Of course we washed our hands; we always wash our hands before we eat."

Here a brief talk in print carries on the story:

> Why should we wash our hands before eating — or before we touch food? Well, our fingers touch many, many things on which little living plants are growing, too small to see with our eyes, wonderful little plants that are called — yes, germs, or bacteria.
>
> What of that? Most kinds of bacteria are harmless, some help us, but there are a few that might make us sick if they should get inside the body. But how can they get inside the body?

Then comes a device to show how bacteria may enter the body by way of the fingers: a cut-out outline of a hand, with a line drawn from each finger tip to a printed comment (as in a cartoon) which refers to a possible source for gathering bacteria: the object picked up from the street, money received in change with a purchase, the ball that is tossed from hand to hand, spray from the cough or sneeze of a careless person, the door handles — walls — railings — store counters and other things that we touch.

Here the printed story is resumed with the suggestion of a familiar scene:

> And now at home, mother says to you, "Dinner is ready. Sit down."
>
> But your hands may be like this one that has been gathering bacteria! What will you do about it? Yes! Wash your hands! Always wash your hands before you eat — before you touch food — after you come from the toilet. On the last sheet of the exhibit is mounted a clean petri dish, underneath which is the inscription: A garden, ready to be planted. With what? With bacteria. How?

Beside it the picture of an open petri dish, with fingers pressing against the jelly, bears the inscription: This way.

Beside this is mounted a petri dish planted and incubated. It shows colonies of bacteria, and bears the inscription: The growing plants!

Then the story is resumed in print:

> They grew! They multiplied! How did they get there? Where did they come from? From the fingers that pressed against the soft, moist jelly. There are always bacteria clinging to our moist fingers — and some of them may be of the harmful kind. What shall we do about that?

Now comes a picture of Pasteur. His life and work have often been interpreted to patients as they wait for treatment, with the help of the excellent film strip loaned, with a delineascope, by our State Department of Health.[*]

The final paragraph of the exhibit's story follows:

> If we could ask Louis Pasteur, "How can we help to keep ourselves well?" — what might be his answer? He would probably say: "Keep your hands away from your face. Always wash them before you eat. Put only clean things in your mouth. These habits will help to keep you — and other people — safe from the kinds of sickness that spread from person to person."

This exhibit is studied well and understandingly by patients, adult and child. Such a statement has been made, and placed where all may read and study it, as a guide to the selection of foods that will fulfill the day's requirements for helping to maintain healthy development and

---
[*] This film strip concerning Pasteur, and others about Reed, Trudeau, Koch, are given to health workers by the Metropolitan Life Insurance Company, New York City.

energy, in both adult and child. It teaches food values very clearly, and for those who have little acquaintance with English the foods are visualized. The leaflet, "Feed Your Body to Protect Your Health," that is issued and distributed by the New England Dairy and Food Council, will furnish ideas for many excellent ways of spreading knowledge of the relations of food to the body.

Exhibits of this kind will be of permanent value, day and month in and out, to a changing clientele.

In Mothers' Meetings the health educator supplements her work with children, using the same teaching methods, for "we are all children".

What is good should be extended — and so the health educator will feel concerning the teaching of the principles of health. In the Boston Dispensary, opportunity is given the health educator to talk to student dietitians, students-in-training and graduate students in medicine, dentistry, home economics and public health, who will go away conscious of the possibilities of help to be gained from health education, wherever people come to seek advice about health and to people in all institutions.

HEALTH EDUCATION IN THE FIELD OF MENTAL HYGIENE
HENRY B. ELKIND, M. D.
Medical Director
Massachusetts Society for Mental Hygiene

The usual meaning of health education is the teaching of health facts, health habits, and healthy attitudes to school children. What is taught is largely in the realm of physical hygiene, although some attention is given to character education. Mental hygiene as such is rarely taught to school children.

Therefore health education in the field of mental hygiene will have in this article a somewhat different connotation than the teaching of mental hygiene to the school child, although some attention to this aspect will be given before the close of the article.

Health education in the field of mental hygiene has largely been the education of adults. The earliest organized attempts in this field were under the auspices of the National Committee for Mental Hygiene and date as far back as 1909. In 1908, however, we find what is perhaps the most effective piece of health education in this field — Clifford W. Beers' autobiography of a convalescing patient, called *A Mind that Found Itself*. It was this book, together with Mr. Beers' energetic efforts to focus public attention on the widespread problem of mental illness in the population, that brought about the organization of the National Committee.

From this time on, mental hygiene as an educational force in the community became more and more prominent. Under the leadership of Dr. Thomas W. Salmon, the first Medical Director of the National Committee, the first work of education was largely that of making surveys of the various states as to their care of the mentally ill. These surveys acquainted the public with the conditions found and offered recommendations for their improvement. This work was later taken up by State Societies for Mental Hygiene. Although the World War interrupted this work, its close initiated a new interest and a new educational effort — the education of the public as to the importance of the mental hygiene of childhood and the need of preventing mental illness and that human misery which is largely the result of mental factors.

This educational effort took various directions. Parents, educators, social workers, judges, probation officers, prison officials, and personnel executives in industry, were all included in this educational program. Clinics, lectures, lecture courses, often in cooperation with University

Extension, conferences, radio, posters, the publication of periodicals and the widespread dissemination of pamphlets and leaflets were the means employed.

Mental Hygiene, a quarterly, was the first periodical to be published in the sole interests of mental hygiene. Later came Bulletins of State Societies, much smaller in size, which reached an ever-increasing number of readers. Perhaps the most popular and most widely read piece of mental hygiene literature is Dr. Douglas A. Thom's "Habit Training Leaflets," first published in 1923. These have been of great value to parents and teachers. Much pamphlet material of similar nature has been made available, which runs a wide gamut of interests, from the preschool child to the mental hygiene of old age, and caters to the needs of all who are personally or professionally concerned with the human factor.

Two unique health education projects are *Understanding the Child* and *The Human Factor,* two quarterly periodicals published by the Massachusetts Society for Mental Hygiene. Publication of the latter was discontinued in 1931 because of the depression. Its purpose was to bring mental hygiene principles and practices to the personnel executive so that he might better understand the worker and more efficiently adjust him to his industrial environment. *Understanding the Child* was for three years sent free of charge to over 30,000 public school teachers of Massachusetts, in addition to a sizable number of paid subscribers outside of the State. It is now, however, on a self-supporting basis, the subscription fee charged being at cost. The purpose of the magazine is to disseminate mental hygiene information to school teachers with the hope that this new knowledge will become part of their pedagogy, and so raise the level of mental health in the State. Each number is devoted to a particular topic of practical importance to the classroom teacher, such as "Adolescence," "Discipline and the Child," "The Child and His Emotions," "Should Marks Be Abolished?" and "The First Years of School Life".

Mental hygiene is very difficult to teach children directly. Some work along this line was done by Miss Helen P. Taussig, formerly Visiting Teacher in the Department of Child Guidance, Newark, N. J. One difficulty, however, with the wide use of her technique is that few teachers have sufficient training and experience to apply it successfully. Perhaps a more practical and safer technique is that developed in 1928 by a group of Boston school teachers, called a "Council on the Educability of the Emotions," of which Dr. William F. Linehan, of Boston Teachers College, was chairman. Their first effort dealt with "Controlling Fear".

At the present time efforts to teach mental hygiene directly to school children should be looked upon as experimental. It is generally conceded that formal instruction in ways to behave and think is of little value. What is more vital is the life in and spirit of the school and the home; what is more fundamental is a deep feeling for moral values. Example is more effective than precept. The teacher's personality and her attitude towards her daily work and the pupils in her classroom affect the mental health of her children. The same may be said of parents.

This is not an exhaustive picture of health education in the field of mental hygiene, but it is typical of what may be found in a large part of this country and Canada. Its spread as an educative influence in modern life has been remarkably rapid as well as extensive. This is largely due to the great progress made in modern psychiatry, psychology, education, and social work. This progress is part of the great advance made in recent years in medicine and public health, and also reflects the humanitarianism of present times.

HEALTH EDUCATION THROUGH PRENATAL AND POSTNATAL LETTERS AND OTHER PRINTED MATERIAL

SUSAN M. COFFIN, M. D.
Consultant in Child Hygiene
Massachusetts Department of Public Health

Approximately 23,000 parents received prenatal and postnatal letters from the Massachusetts Department of Public Health during 1933. Each family thus served also received a copy of "Baby and You" and "One to Six", together with additional leaflets on habit training, dental care and protection from communicable diseases. This group included 6,100 expectant fathers who each had a special letter sent to them. One proud parent carried his in his vest pocket until the great event transpired, or so he told us! About 1,414 more families were given "by hand" appropriate printed material in connection with the examination of 1,716 children who attended the State Well Child Conferences.

The demand from local organizations and individuals for nutrition material including food lists, budgets, and low cost diets mounted into the thousands owing to economic conditions which made such advice seriously needed. Even churches and similar organizations made large use of health material, particularly that relating to preschool children, in their home visiting work; and the usual quantity of printed material was requested for school use, while private dentists asked for 62,000 copies of the leaflets that they use for distribution to their patients. And this is only one year's story!

Some interested citizen may well ask: "What do all these words on a er accomplish? Do we need so much printed information? Does it pay?"

It is true that direct teaching is and should be far more highly prized, but as by that method only a comparatively small per cent of our population can be reached, this printed matter does have its rightful place in health education. It is of value, too, in nailing the facts even when direct teaching can be done. Appropriate leaflets and pamphlets help to emphasize the points to be remembered in lesson, talk or demonstration and are eagerly accepted.

Every day many letters reach the Department from all parts of Massachusetts asking for material relating to health matters. They come from fathers and mothers, teachers, nurses, social workers and others, all of whom are seeking needed information. Many of the letters from parents are pathetic in their effort to make clear a need of knowledge and an honest desire to learn what is best to do for their children. These letters bear eloquent testimony to the growing feeling of a need for preparation in the job of being a parent. All receive prompt attention and publications suited to each are mailed with the replies.

"Yes," our inquiring citizen persists, "This is all very interesting, but is there any actual measure of the value of the mass of material furnished? How can any one be sure of its being used with benefit?"

We can, fortunately, show that there are at least two things which give us a reasonable measure of its use and value. The first is the steady and increasing demand. As stated above, requests are received in large numbers from both organizations and individuals. Former requests would not be repeated and new ones would not pile up if such material was not found to meet an actual need. This fact alone is a good indicator of "value received." And we surely cannot say that there are no other sources of such service today. Consider how many insurance companies and popular magazines offer attractive booklets on adult health, child care, nutrition, teeth, etc. Think what a large number of health talks, good ones many of them, too, emanate from the radio and later "burst into print"! But there seems to be a strong preference for the material coming from the State Department of Public Health as being better suited to local needs, which indeed it is because of the knowledge of special requirements that influences its careful preparation.

Our second measuring rod is the personal correspondence received. It is constant, endless, and every week brings its quota of letters of appreciation. Mrs. Green in Pittsfield asks that the prenatal letters be sent to her sister in Amesbury: "Because," she says, "they helped me so much; they have been my Bible!" One set of postnatal letters journeyed from family to family until they reached the Pacific coast and then hopped off to Australia.

Parents tell us how glad they are to learn that "our State Health Department" has material on child hygiene — they never say "Department of Public Health," by the way. The general feeling still seems to be that of the lady who remarked, "Public Health always makes one think of sewers and things," which, after all, may show a realization of its essential foundation in sanitation!

Occasionally along comes a brisk letter of criticism, like that of the keen young mother who took us to task for discrepant statements in two of our publications. More such letters of honest criticism and suggestion would be gladly welcomed.

Frequent revision of all printed matter is absolutely necessary to keep it from becoming stale and unprofitable stuff. One mother gaily produced a copy of "Baby and You," two or three editions back, and was much surprised to find how many changes had been made. "Babies do not change," she protested. "But knowledge does, and both grow," we explained.

Health education material has done its bit, too, in Americanization. Rarely nowadays do we get requests for "health books" in Italian, Polish or French, as we did frequently, some years ago. Recently a Polish mother asked for a baby book. She wanted to "learn health," she said. She was told that it would be in English and was asked: "Can you read English?" "Oh, no, not understand," she replied, "but" proudly, "my boy, he read all, everything, to me. He understand everything," and the boy, a lad of twelve or so, grinned cheerfully and said, with a regular Yankee twang, "Sure, I can read it to her good."

In health teaching as in medical teaching, standard "works" are very necessary, but here it is particularly necessary to have briefer material, frequently revised, for more popular use. Nurses, teachers and students, all have testified voluntarily to the value of this printed material and have remarked on the advantage of having it available in convenient form and under constant scrutiny and revision.

The primary aim of all publications of a Department of Public Health is, of course, prevention. Treatment and cure of diseases are not a part of its office, a fact that quite often has to be explained in considerable detail, though occasionally prevention and cure go happily hand in hand, as in rickets or malnutrition.

In fact, in every form of health education, whether by direct teaching, by demonstration or in individual study, well-chosen printed material fills no mean place. Without it we would be sadly at a loss to meet the modern cry for more and more information on keeping as fit as nature intends us to be.

SCHOOL LUNCH SURVEY
MARY SPALDING
Consultant in Nutrition
Massachusetts Department of Public Health

The following newspaper clipping, showing appreciation of the work of the lunchroom manager who is also the home economics teacher is a joy. This clipping was sent to the Department with Falmouth's School Lunch Survey Card. Such cards filled out in 306 cities and towns give us an idea of what more than 47,000 children are eating in our schools in Massachusetts.

As this survey showed that
>Only 1 child out of 4 had milk
>Only 1 child out of 5 had fruits and vegetables
>Only 1 child out of 5 had as long as twenty minutes for eating lunch
>Only 1 child out of 7 had dark bread
>Only 1 child out of 9 was getting a hot dish

there is plenty of work ahead for us this winter in bettering the lunches for school children.

Children Fed by Wholesale With an Eye to Each's Particular Need

CLARA SHARPE HOUGH

Falmouth Enterprise

A few years ago the lunchroom at the Junior High School provided only sandwiches and chocolate bars that could be purchased by school children to augment the lunches they brought from home. When hot dishes were added to this menu it still was available only to pupils of the High and Junior High schools. The elementary pupils, at the old Village school several blocks down the street, went home to their lunch or brought it with them. Then one day Mrs. Herbert McLane asked if her two small boys, just starting to school, might have a hot lunch over at the Junior high. These two little boys (Junior high and High school students now) were the first elementary school children to have lunch in the cafeteria. In another year Mrs. Florence I. Gay, village school principal, had arranged for all the elementary school children to lunch there. A year or so back the noon hour on Main Street was enlivened by the spectacle of long lines of school children, marshaled by their teachers across the street and through the library grounds to the Junior high for their lunch. Last year when the new elementary school was opened, one of its features was the big cafeteria and modern kitchen in the basement. Under direction of Mrs. Ruth H. Underwood several hundred elementary school children lunch there at 12:15 every school day, after the older pupils have had their meal between 11:15 and 12.

To the uninitiated that lunch hour is something like a juvenile bedlam. Long tables are lined with children. Long lines of children are marching along the counter with trays. Other children seem to be running back and forth from table to counter. The clamor of shrill little voices and the scamper of little feet fills the room. It is apparently confusion. But it is as a matter of fact orderly confusion. Mrs. Underwood, trim in her starched white uniform, unruffled by the constant stream of questions fired at her from both sides at once, presides at the wicket past which every child carries a tray. She has little stacks of cards before her, different colors. She has already seen that hot food is ready on the steam-table, that bottles of milk and chocolate, and cups of gelatine or custard for dessert are in the proper place. Pupil helpers serve the children as they march along. But the children who are learning to select their own lunches from the school menu, are closely superintended by the presiding genius in starchy white.

A seven-year-old balancing a tray containing a sandwich and a cup of gelatine stops to have her ticket punched, and asks for an ice-cream ticket. The ice-cream tickets are punched off on the lunch-ticket and redeemed at the counter after the rest of the lunch is eaten. But Mrs. Underwood looks at the tray. "No ice-cream, Betty, unless you have a hot dish or milk." Betty goes back and changes her sandwich for an appetizing plate of creamed tuna topped with a hot biscuit. She gets her ice-cream ticket. Another little girl asks for a ticket entitling her to ice-cream with chocolate sauce. A quick glance at her lunch-card. "No chocolate sauce today, you had it yesterday, you know your mother only wants you to have it once a week." A little boy runs up with a package of cheese crackers; he has finished his lunch and wants the crackers to take out-of-doors. "All right, Jimmy, you had your milk at lunch." Jimmy gets the cheese crackers.

Mrs. Underwood denies any special feat of memory in knowing what each child has eaten every day. It is true she has understandings with many parents. They can depend on her to see that little Sally doesn't have chocolate sauce more than once a week or that Junior does not fail to have a half-pint bottle of milk on his tray every noon. Parents who have not made any arrangement with her can also depend on her. She considers part of her job the supervision of the trays so that each child gets the lunch he should have. If children want to lunch on a sandwich and a dish of gelatine, all right. But if they do they don't get ice-cream. They don't have to take milk. But if they don't they are not allowed to buy a popcorn ball to take outside to eat. These rules seem to her quite simple, and she finds the children quite amenable to their enforcement. They learn very quickly that the price of the popcorn ball is the emptied bottle of milk as well as the nickel. There are also five-cent bags of potato chips that children who have eaten a proper lunch are allowed to buy. Mrs. Underwood does not allow younger children to have potato chips every day. But one mother called her and asked that she do just that for her little daughter. "Joan is so crazy for potato chips," she said, "that I wish you'd let her have them every day until she is tired of them, and then she'll get over it." So Joan is allowed to buy potato chips every day.

A number of children bring lunches from home and eat them at the cafeteria tables. Many more bring sandwiches and augment them with milk or hot soup. A large proportion line up with trays for their whole lunch. A nourishing lunch can be bought for 15 cents. Parents who send 75 cents to school with the child on Monday buy a week's card of lunches. For milk alone there is a card of another color, costing 5 cents a day. The room teachers keep the cards, marked with the child's name and pass them out at the noon hour. Mrs. Underwood collects them as they pass her with their laden trays. The day's lunch is punched off in her office after the lunch-period, and the cards are returned to the teachers. Thus the loss of cards from children's pockets or school books is obviated.

Every Friday a mimeograph copy of next week's menu is sent home by the children. Parents who are interested thus have the opportunity to check on what their children are eating. Some are interested enough to mark just what they want their children to eat each day. One little girl who is told to eat hot soup every day brings a thermos bottle with soup from home on the day school serves the kind of soup she doesn't like. Some children are provided with a 20-cent lunch each day. But the 15-cent lunch is the average, and will give a child hot soup, a sandwich, a bottle of milk; a hot dish, a bottle of milk, ice-cream or custard. One little boy marches by with a bottle of milk and two servings of creamed tuna. "Are you sure you can eat all that?" asks Mrs. Underwood before she takes his ticket. He nods eagerly. He knows he can eat two helpings of his favorite dish.

Once a month the hot dish is hot dogs, beloved of all children. Once a month there is hot chicken or turkey sandwich, with gravy. Some days the hot dish is roast lamb, sometimes it is creamed dried beef served with a baked potato. On Fridays there is fish or quahaug chowder. Another day the soup is corn chowder. One day there is macaroni and cheese, another American chop suey (which is spaghetti cooked with meat and tomatoes). There are always sandwiches, of enough variety that each child can find one nourishing item that he likes.

Off the big cafeteria is the little room with four good sized tables where the teachers in the two upper schools may buy the same lunches that the children have. Teachers from the village school eat with the children, one at the end of each table, and keep their charges in order. The older children, who have less supervision in their ordering, are expected to keep themselves in order while they eat.

The teachers finish their lunch and leave for the assembly period at 12. And then into the private dining-room Mrs. Underwood brings a little girl from the first grade who has found the big room so confusing that she could not eat her lunch. The lunch-room supervisor has found time, in spite of the close eye she keeps on all those children, to notice the troubled little girl who was in school for the first time and hadn't quite adjusted herself yet. Every day Mrs. Underwood brings her into the quiet room where she can eat her lunch peacefully until she has grown more accustomed to school life and the noisy presence of several hundred other children. A little boy, still very young and very shy, is brought in and seated at another table. He, too, will be adjusted to school routine in another few months, and will hold his own with the rest. But in the meantime Mrs. Underwood prescribes. She sees to it that the children who lunch in her cafeteria have their lunch.

There are also a half-dozen children for whom Mrs. Underwood made an appeal that has been answered by civic organizations. They are undernourished children whose parents could not afford to buy milk for them. These children now have daily milk-cards, identical with the cards held by more fortunate youngsters, so that no one guesses who they are as they march in line. Through donations from the Rotary Club, the Outlook Club, and the Salvation Army, they now have a bottle of milk daily with the lunch they bring from home. Mrs. Underwood, the watcher of the line, knew just which children needed it. She says that one sight of these children, the first day they held their cards and got that bottle of milk, would have amply repaid the donors.

That noon-hour, which most mothers of noisy families would consider a whole day's work, is just part of the job. There is plenty of other work to be done in the neat little office back of the kitchen. Here Mrs. Underwood and her secretary, Miss Anna Lumbert, keep books. They punch the lunch-cards of all the children; they keep the list of children who have lunch-cards; they have charge of the money paid, and they pay out the money for food; they order the supplies for the day's lunches. Mrs. Underwood plans her week's menu a week ahead and knows just what has to be ordered. Then, too, there are the helpers. There are the pupil assistants who help to serve food and clean up tables afterward, getting their own lunches in payment. There are kitchen helpers who are paid each week. No food is used a second day, except such things as roast meat which can be served in sandwiches or another form next day. Sandwiches and custards left over go to the pupil helpers. Milk, left over, is used next day in cooking. Each day's milk and milk chocolate drunk by the children is fresh that morning. But there is little left over. Long experience in just this sort of planning has made the supervisor an expert in knowing how much will be eaten each day.

The cafeteria not only is self-supporting, it pays its own way and pays the salaries of the two cooks, Mrs. Harold Leonard and Mrs. Thomas Sheehan, who make up those tasty soups and those hot rolls and that caramel custard that mothers of children hear about at home; and of the two paid kitchen helpers.

Mrs. Underwood who came here nine years ago after serving for two years as manager of the cafeteria in the Arlington junior high school, had her training at Simmons College. In addition to supervising the lunchroom, she gives classes in domestic science. After the lunchers have marched back to their classrooms, and the day's checking-up has been done, she might sit down and draw a long breath, you housewives would say.. No. She doesn't even sit down and begin to plan for next day. She briskly disposes of these noontime duties, and is all ready for a cooking class. A group of little girls is waiting for her in the spic and span demonstration kitchen where she will show them how to roll pie crust, or how to make molasses cookies, or how to set a luncheon table for six, or how to make cheese biscuit or chicken a la king or one of the other things that junior high girls are taught in their home economics course.

A year or so ago a salesman for a bakery which distributes cakes pretty widely got access to Mrs. Underwood and persuaded her to let him put a tray of his cup cakes on the lunch counter. She wouldn't contract for them, because she told him she knew they wouldn't be used in her cafeteria. He insisted that he be given a chance. He wanted to just put them out to see, then if they were the big success they should be he might have a customer in Mrs. Underwood. She finally consented. The frosted cup cakes were put on the counter with the other things, on a Thursday. The salesman came back the next Monday, sure of his success, ready to put through a contract. Just two cakes had been eaten. He charged Mrs. Underwood with not having them in sight on the counter. But they had been. They were where the Falmouth children could choose them instead of hot creamed beef or hot fish chowder or fresh chocolate custard if they wanted to. They hadn't wanted to. The salesman said he sold hundreds of dozens of them every week in this school and that. He could not understand it at all. It is, however, quite understandable to any thinking person who has watched the wheels working at noontime in the Village school cafeteria. The children in those other schools probably eat anything that comes along. They haven't any Mrs. Underwood there.

HEALTH EDUCATION THROUGH DEMONSTRATION
SUSAN M. COFFIN, M. D.
Consultant in Child Hygiene
Massachusetts Department of Public Health

There are three ways of learning: by seeing, hearing and doing. The ideal method combines all three. One morning, at home or in the hospital, a young mother, for the first time, sees her baby have his bath. A skillful nurse demonstrates the process quietly and slowly, explaining each step as she goes along. The value of this demonstration is increased immeasurably if the mother can have an opportunity to do the task herself once or twice under the nurse's supervision. This would also be the ideal method in any form of health teaching, but dealing as we do with groups or communities, we often have to be content with showing how the thing is done and explaining each procedure.

We find there is always with us the temptation to show too much at once, which, as experience has proved, creates only hurry and confusion. It is far better to demonstrate clearly a few essential points in feeding and guiding children, for example, than to attempt to cover many items at once, no matter how great the need appears to be.

Teaching by demonstration is aided very definitely by exhibit material sensibly chosen and attractively arranged. A mother brings her baby to a Well Child Conference for examination by the doctor, clad in many unnecessary garments — seven layers have sometimes been removed — and it helps to show her, right at the time, a baby doll properly dressed. A display of small children's clothing for summer and winter, toys, inexpensive and easy to keep clean, books and magazines for parents' use, (not just lists), an exhibit of the right food for a school child's lunch box, etc., these are all good examples of well-chosen material that can play an important part in a demonstration relating to child care and protection.

Any plan for a demonstration to the community as a whole should be preceded by vigorous preliminary publicity. Curiosity has to be stimulated in these days of a multiplicity of interests — the "law of diminishing returns" works here as elsewhere.

Suppose we wish to demonstrate the value of preparing children for school entrance by means of the "Summer Round-Up". Unless practically all the members of the community hear about it, nobody will come to see it and no one's interest will be sufficiently aroused to help in its development later as a permanent local responsibility. To make such a demonstration to the small group of local professional workers alone is to fail of the original aim which is to arouse general interest in a genuine community need.

Any demonstration should be kept as clear cut as possible in order to leave a definite impression in the minds of those who see it. Always, when possible, it should display actual proof of what may be accomplished by the procedures shown. The use of graphic posters and statistics in teaching nutrition, care of the teeth, protection from diphtheria, etc., is a valuable agent and makes prompt appeal to thoughtful observers. It is well to bear in mind in this connection the dictionary definition of a demonstration — "a public display by way of proof, example or instruction," only we would like to change "or" to "and" as we feel that all three are essential.

The greatest thing accomplished by a really successful demonstration is what, in actual fact, is its basic aim — to make other people feel they can go and do likewise. We are all children in that we often get discouraged if we cannot succeed fairly easily in doing the thing we have seen done. Again, simplicity and clearness are essential to success. A rather elaborate set-up is quite all right in an up-to-date city clinic, school, or mothers' club, but it may make the demonstration seem absolutely beyond reach in a small town or community. Hence, any sort of demonstration should be reasonably adapted to local resources as well as to local needs.

Keeping these few points in mind, health education through demonstration, intelligently carried out, can be of genuine value.

ART AND HEALTH EDUCATION
John H. McCarthy
Health Education Worker
Massachusetts Department of Public Health

We are living today in the greatest labor-saving, time-saving, and life-saving period in history. Invention after invention has developed rough ideas — dreams, if you will — into concrete realities. The early generations labored to make devices that would improve working conditions, and because of their efforts and the efforts of the succeeding generations, those same devices are now laboring for us. Practically all of our modern conveniences are the result of necessity. And the same is true of Art.

It is to be found in embryo in the strange tattooed symbols that cover the body of the savage, a necessity as a means of clan identification, individual identification, and a marking of rank. Next came the savage's efforts to give agreeable shape to the handle of his hatchet or knife — necessary because of his warlike existence; then his tracing of ornaments as a means of property identification. Later on he developed symmetry, a taste for color, reproduction of animals, first in the round, afterwards in relief and by means of drawing. Finally he essayed, though timidly, the imitation of the human figure and of vegetation. He now had developed his language, a language of pictures and symbols, a picture or poster alphabet before words — and today we are reading the histories of early nations by means of these same picture languages. Later generations developed art to a very high degree but as it improved it became less a necessity and more a luxury. During recent years people have gradually discovered possibilities in art in teaching, advertising, and selling. One of those possibilities now commonly used is Poster Work.

Poster Work

In health education the value of poster work cannot be overestimated. Posters are a universal language, adaptable to any nationality, any age, any intellect, and a group of any size. Almost 90 per cent of what we learn, we learn through the eye. Describe an animal to a group of twenty people who have never seen that particular animal or a picture of it, and your description will develop twenty animals, varying in shape and size according to the imaginative powers of the individual person, but show them a picture of that animal and they will grasp your description immediately and fit it to the picture. It is for that same reason that most people remember faces better than they do names.

Consequently, the poster is an able ally of every worker in health education and certain simple fundamentals of the good poster, once understood, can be easily carried out in the construction and use of both poster and chart.

Order

The first fundamental principle of good poster work, and one that is most sinned against, is order. A poster that has illustrative material and lettering scattered over it, perhaps for no other reason than to fill the available space, is disorderly. The mind cannot concentrate on any particular detail and this disorder reacts on the mind. For the same reason that a sick room is kept orderly and neat because of the mental effect on the patient, so should a poster be made orderly.

Lettering

The lettering should be simple and plain. Fancy type lettering is difficult to read, does not carry any distance, and requires more time to execute than a plain, solid type. The lettering should read horizontally, not diagonally or vertically and never Chinese style — one letter above the next. Careful thought will, in most cases, eliminate many unnecessary words. Some very clever posters tell their story without words.

Margins

The next factor is margins. Why have margins? What good are they? If there were no margins on posters, books, magazines, photographs, etc. the illustrations and printed matter would have to be handled. The margins keep the subject matter clean, frame the subject and keep it from scattering. They concentrate it and focus the attention on the subject. There is even a more important reason for the use of margins as Ruskin explained, in a masterly way — "This picture has something to say to you. In order that you may hear it, it is surrounded by a little silence." Picture a traffic policeman at night standing in a circle of light. The light is not on his feet, but surrounds his whole figure. He stands out clearly and distinctly because he is surrounded by a margin of silence. The silence is restful. It has the same effect as a pause in the spoken word. The pause between sentences is a silence, a margin, and makes the sentences stand out. Publishers realize this and the higher priced the edition, the better the margin.

Balance

Another factor is balance, a very important fundamental in good poster making. A horizontal line gives balance, and it is restful to the eye. A vertical line gives balance, and it is likewise restful. But a diagonal line does not have balance and it creates uneasiness, and is not restful. Just as a rolling ship causes physical unrest because of the lack of balance, an unbalanced poster causes mental unrest. A poster should have equal or balanced margins at the top and sides, and a deeper or wider margin at the bottom. The lettering should balance on a vertical line drawn through the center of the poster and the center of the illustration should be a little above the center of the poster. The human mind needs rest. Balance is the law of design that results in rest.

Simplicity

The next fundamental is simplicity. Make the poster simple and direct. Leave out all unnecessary details and strive to make the poster in outline or silhouette. Put a silence of soft tone around the picture so that the picture can talk. Make the treatment a decorative one rather than a photographic one, as a photographic poster is generally too soft. A simple study executed in simple relief is the most attractive poster.

Color

Color is a most important factor in good poster making because a poor choice and use of colors can ruin the finest executed illustration. Therefore a knowledge of color, its theory and application as applied to posters is most essential. Some people, sensitive to color, and with little or no knowledge of its theory and application, are able to combine colors into harmonious schemes, but for the majority who are not so fortunate the following should help in determining harmonious combinations. The primary colors are red, yellow and blue; the secondary colors, orange, green and purple; the tertiary colors, plum, russet and olive. Certain colors, such as red, yellow and orange, are more forceful than others and are called advancing colors. Blue, green and purple, less forceful, are called receding colors. The pure colors — primaries — advance more than the mixed colors — the secondaries and tertiaries. Besides color contrast there is a contrast of values. The term value, when used in reference to color, means its approach to light or dark. When a color approaches white it is called a tint; as it approaches black, a shade. The value of any color depends on its adjoining color. Dark colors used against light or light colors against dark are more forceful and striking. When any two primary colors are used to make a secondary, as yellow and blue to make green, the remaining primary becomes the complementary of the result of the combination; thus, red is the complementary of green, yellow the complementary of purple, and blue the complementary of orange. When two or more colors are used together it is called a color scheme. There are three types of color schemes: monochromatic, complementary and analogous. Monochromatic color schemes use different values of the same color, are restful but not very interesting. Complementary schemes use one primary and its complement, are striking and forceful, though less harmonious, because the colors are not related. Analogous schemes use any two primaries with the color obtained by mixing those primaries; thus red, yellow and orange, or red, blue and purple, or blue, yellow and green. This type of combination is more harmonious and pleasing because the colors are all related.

Appeal

There are three psychological principles of appeal which a poster must have to accomplish its work. First, it must have carrying power to attract attention; second, it must hold the attention long enough to leave an impression; third, it must have a definite favorable impression. The poster must accomplish all three to be successful.

Chart Making

At the present time there is a very apparent interest in chart making. As never before, various organizations have been forced to show more graphically the way that money is spent and the types of service given for that money. Not only organizations but physicians, dentists, nurses, instructors, teachers, coaches evidently have all found some use for this type of visual education as a finishing touch to any speech or lecture, illustrating comparisons necessary to drive home figures, percentages and ratios, illustrating local health conditions, the strong points and weak points of each community's health record, depicting graphically the prevalence of various diseases, the increase or lessening of cases and deaths, the importance of prevention, and so forth. Posters and charts can be used in innumerable places and be most successful, but some of the best fields for the richest returns are little used. People who are obliged to wait in places such as hospitals, dispensaries, physicians' and dentists' offices often lack occupation and their attention is easily obtainable for posters and charts which they might fail to notice under ordinary conditions. Good charts are self-explanatory and much clearer to the average person than a mass of figures and statistics. Thoughtful planning and careful execution in chart form of any phase of health education will certainly return rich dividends.

Of the many kinds of charts the following types have proved the most successful in health education. The simplest and most familiar form of illustrative material used by speakers is the statistical chart in which curves or bars bring out contrasts or similarities of various kinds. This type of chart, when so used, must be large enough so that the details are easily seen from the rear of the room. Chart maps are interesting to many people because of their long use in elementary education. Spot maps are satisfactory in illustrating the distribution of population, or in making comparisons of the extent of disease in the various sections of any particular area. Ranking of the different sections may be depicted by the method of shading and cross hatching — the black areas indicating the most backward sections, and the cross hatched those sections farther advanced, and the white those that have advanced most. The circle or pie chart is a familiar one, its sectors easily understood, and is commonly used for budgets. This type of chart, however, has one disadvantage: as the number of sectors increases, it becomes difficult to include figures and lettering so that they are easily read. There are also a number of other types of charts such as those planned on semilogarithmic cross section paper, but the types already mentioned generally prove best for poster chart purposes. Books have been written on the proper construction of charts but for the making of simple poster charts for the average person these few fundamentals should help.

The general arrangement should proceed from left to right and from bottom to top. Probably the vertical or horizontal bars requiring only a comparison of length and height are the most easily understood. When percentages are shown both the zero line and the hundred per cent line should be emphasized. The figures for the scales should be placed at the left and at the bottom. The title should be as clear and complete as possible. The fundamentals of poster making previously described apply also to the construction of good charts. Diagrams for non-technical groups should be exceedingly simple. Color not only adds greatly to the attractiveness of charts but may be used to make important factors stand out sharply. When black and white are used with colors, white intensifies and black lowers the intensity. When used with its complementary, a color is at its highest intensity; for instance, red with green, yellow with purple, and blue with orange.

Today the good poster or chart is one of the major forces in health education. A health message well thought out and well presented either in a chart or a poster is worth a hundred lectures, articles or pages of statistics to Mr. John Q. Public and his family.

IT PAYS TO ADVERTISE
DOROTHEA NICOLL
Nutritionist
Massachusetts Department of Public Health

Good advertising pays good dividends in public health as in any other business. An exhibit is one of the most vital kinds of advertising for the health worker. It is graphic! It "tells the world" in an interesting way. It is an interpreter worth using. It should be as much a routine part of any health worker's job as the annual report. It is, in fact, but one other way of keeping the public informed as to what you are doing, why you are doing it, or what the world is coming to — as far as health is concerned.

Exhibits range from very simple ones on a foot or two of bookshelf to the immense booths at fairs or expositions. But, simple or elaborate, they involve three things:

1. An idea or facts to be "put over".
2. An audience.
3. A bit of keen salesmanship.

Let's look at these three points separately.

The Idea

The basis of every exhibit is a single fact or idea that needs an audience. It may be the new Health Bookshelf at the Junior Library; or the ease with which the Jones' new twins can be bathed and dressed according to the way of the visiting nurse; or even the number of families over in Slab Valley that have had a case of measles since January.

To be worthy of exhibit the facts must be pertinent and they must be simply told. Suppose there are dozens of facts your audience should know. Select a few — weed out the merely interesting from the really vital. Prune them carefully. Make sure they are based on solid scientific truth — not fad or fancy. Then choose the most outstanding. If more than one is necessary to tell the complete story, be sure your exhibit has a central theme, and keep the others subordinate. Build around this central idea, tying every bit to it carefully. Or if you decide to run a series, have a "theme song". Interesting repetition is an aid in teaching. But make it interesting.

Facts concerning health may seem dry—water them with a bit of ingenuity and inspiration. What is commonplace to the health worker is often news to his audience, particularly if presented from a new angle. Building a camp site by the Scouts at camp may be hard work, but it's also a good lesson in public health, and one that is much more appreciated than any number of diagrams in a hygiene book. A model of the whole camp layout with red arrows for "Points of a Healthy Camp" made by the Scouts on their return may add to their dad's public health education too. Exhibits offer a grand chance for using volunteers and incidentally spreading health education in a wider circle.

Using maps with colored pins or flags is a common practice. But remember it is not to represent Joseph's coat of many colors — one or two facts at a time. It is better to tell only part of the story and tell it clearly than to crowd so much into your space that confusion results. If you have plenty of extra space, good! Simplicity is still the keynote. Select your material carefully and be sure it is related to the rest of the exhibit.

A hodge-podge of facts repels rather than attracts, no matter how vital they may be of themselves. You are selling these select ideas and facts to a wary audience whether children or adults. They must be carefully chosen, simply expressed and arranged to attract the most casual glance. Choose facts that mean something to your intended audience. Miss —— , over on High Hat Row may not care about the relative merits of Haliver Oil and sunshine in preventing rickets but she reads eagerly anything to do with "pink toothbrush". It concerns her. Make each exhibit fit its audience. If facts concerning pasteurized milk are just screaming to be told — exhibit them at the fair, the grange, or the Mothers' Club, not at the settlement workers' annual meeting. They may drink pasteurized milk — probably can't buy anything else in the city store —— but their greater interest is apt to be in sunny play places for little folks.

Speaking of Audiences

Be critical of your audience. Are they young or old, or a mixture of both? Are they clamoring for facts, or must you tempt them with your goods? Have they time to stop and read detailed signs, or must you plan so that "he who runs may read"?

Do they understand your language, or must you interpret it for them? Your everyday public health terms may be "Greek" to your next door neighbor even though English to you.

Will you expect them to digest all your facts on the spot, or do you intend to supply printed material to follow up your first contact?

Is your exhibit space in plain view, or must the public be enticed into it?

Considering these questions before exhibiting will make all the difference in the amount of attention you get and in your success as an exhibitor.

Then, too, who are you? Are you Johnny's teacher rounding out ten years of teaching everything, including health, at School District No. 2? If so, you are known to your audience, your word is law and more or less likely to be accepted. Use exhibits to add interest to your routine health work. Let the youngsters make the plans and carry them out. Loan them from room to room. A good school lunch packed by the sixth grade girls may be exchanged for the model of the bed, screen and movable window that the fourth grade boys made to show how to keep one's windows open even in cold weather and still be comfortable. Don't wait for Parents' Day. Everyday is a good day to exhibit health at school.

Or perhaps you are the milk inspector. The grange, the fair, the service clubs all offer you chances for exhibiting. Nothing to exhibit? Why not a couple of enlarged snapshots of the best milk plants displayed on the bulletin board near your office at the Town Hall. Or a few "Before and After" pictures. The more you can use well-made charts, maps or even actual equipment in talks the better your audience will understand your message.

Visiting nurses with a mothers' class have a splendid opportunity for exhibits. The articles can be handled, patterns made, short cuts and bright ideas exchanged. Your audience is anxious for the latest facts and often helpfully critical of them from a very experienced viewpoint.

Not one of the dozens of different health workers can afford to carry on without exhibits of one form or another. Whether your audience is likely to be responsive or balky, overcritical or too sweetly agreeable, casual passersby or earnest students, learned or laymen, exhibits are invaluable.

A Bit of Salesmanship

We can consider here only a few of the many kinds of exhibits. If these do not fit your needs, take a piece of an idea from here, a slice of experience from a fellow worker and mix well with plenty of inspiration. There are but few set rules for health exhibits:

1. Use outstanding facts based on scientific truth.
2. Show them as simply as possible.
3. Consider your audience carefully.

You may encounter certain rules when exhibiting at large conventions or expositions where signs must be of a certain size or coverings must be fire proofed, but these do not concern the usual exhibit. Those we are most interested in are:

1. The regular education feature.
2. The occasional publicity stunt.
3. The classroom equipment.

1. By "regular educational feature" we mean a place where an educational exhibit is displayed, and changed at regular intervals. This type of exhibit takes time and hard work to keep up, but is worth the pains because of the interest it creates, to say nothing of the questions it arouses. It is probably the most profitable for the money spent. It becomes a focal point in any teaching program. It sells your ideas for you. From the comments and questions, future exhibit ideas are gleaned. Here seasonal suggestions can be made — sun suits for the youngest — first-aid for the vacationist — Christmas sweets for the family. Every health organization can find a prominent spot in which to place such a feature. One week it may be a poster; the next, a more elaborate exhibit borrowed from some official agency. Have pertinent material and change it frequently. This should be truly educational and of great value in making the community more public health minded.

2. The publicity stunt is a temporary and usually spectacular affair. It may accompany the annual drive or some special occasion. Its great purpose is to win attention, but it is not necessarily educational. It is more apt to appeal entirely to the emotions instead of supplying factual material. It aims to arouse people to action but seldom follows up this first attack. This type has its place. It is the introduction — a way of saying "Hello". In order to get truly well acquainted, however, one of the other types of exhibit should follow this sort.

3. The last kind is that used as actual teaching material in a classroom. We will also include in this designation any exhibit used at a talk or series of lectures. It has a spokesman and does not need to speak for itself. Descriptive signs, so necessary to the first kind, are not needed here unless the articles are to be left out on display without the exhibitor present. Charts, models, actual articles of food, clothing, serums, bottles, in fact any such material make a lecture or talk much more graphic. It may be dolls and a sand table in the nursery school, white rats in the fifth grade, utensils for packing a lunch in the continuation school or factory, slides and microscopes at the community health day or a layette at the Visiting Nursing Association. There is no need to get in a rut in exhibiting for one exhibit seems to suggest still more.

The cost may range from little or nothing (thanks to generous souls who will loan a set of baby clothes, or a loaf of dark bread) to thousands of dollars, if one's budget allows. An exhibit showing the Red Cross nurse's seemingly unlimited use of newspapers is not only useful and inexpensive but actually fascinating. Wrapping paper, pressed, makes quite acceptable posters with a colored magazine picture and a bit of ink. They are fully as educational and often as attractive as if made with expensive Bristol board.

For the permanent exhibit a neutral colored background of plain paint, paper or cloth is best. Then, no matter what exhibit is put up, the color scheme will be attractive. Cream or buff color is to be preferred to plain white or a decided color. It gives a roomy appearance and shows less dirt than white. All exhibits, temporary or permanent should be artistically arranged as to color and placement if you wish to attract favorable attention. Remember they are your "ad" and your introduction. First impressions are often very lasting. Make a good one.

In summarizing it is well to note that as exhibitor you are not only a salesman but also a teacher. Be positive. Stress the right rather than the wrong — the pleasant rather than the gruesome, the do's, not the don'ts.

A successful health exhibit will always

1. Attract attention.
2. Have one outstanding theme.
3. Arouse a desire to know more about the subject and to do something about it as well.

Exhibits are lots of work, yes! But they bring astounding results if well planned. More success to them!

For help in planning exhibits, or loan of materials, posters, or films, write to the Massachusetts Department of Public Health, 546 State House, Boston, Mass.

PROTECT YOUR SMILE
ELEANOR G. MCCARTHY, D. H.
Consultant in Dental Hygiene
Massachusetts Department of Public Health

"Protect Your Smile" is the keynote of the Department's dental hygiene program of 1934 - 1935. This slogan, coined or borrowed in our effort to find a suitable name for a program in dental health for 4-H Clubs, is equally fitting for all age groups except perhaps the very young.

"Protect Your Smile" is more than a new program and it is more than an obvious attempt to hitch the wagon of dental care to the star of personal appearance. It is indicative of a change in our approach in dental health education and of our continuing insistence upon a program broad enough to embrace the many factors now believed indispensable to universal mouth health. Most of these factors can be grouped under the three headings of good nutrition, good home care and good dentistry. In these three ways do we protect our smiles.

Good physical health is but a means to our goal of clear minds and well integrated personalities. Good teeth are but a part of your smile. Your smile, the conveyor of cheer and happiness to those about you, is but an expression of your whole personality.

The "Protect Your Smile" program for 4-H Clubs is being planned as this issue of The Commonhealth goes to press. The Extension Service at the Massachusetts State College, the Massachusetts Dental Society and the Massachusetts Department of Public Health are working together on a plan which, as Mr. Farley, State 4-H Club leader has said, "is not just for this year or next year but possibly for five years or even more."

The 4-H Club leaders have chosen dental health as the focal point for their health program because of its importance and because a program for healthy teeth and gums is dependent upon, and results in, better general health. The program is threefold. The members will strive to protect their smiles through

Good nutrition
Careful daily home care of teeth and gums
Regular dental examinations and care.

The Department of Public Health has prepared an exhibit illustrating the types of food necessary for good nutrition, the tools needed for good home care and the protective services rendered by the family dentist. This will travel from Club to Club throughout the State.

The factual material on dental health that leaders and club members alike will need in carrying out the various activities in the program is being prepared. Activities for the Protect Your Smile Program will be correlated with other projects of the Club, some of which are Clothing, Food, Home Furnishing, Handicraft, Dairying, Poultry Raising, Gardening and Canning.

The Massachusetts Dental Society is working on plans for participation by dentists in every community where there are 4-H Clubs so that it will be possible for each club member to have his teeth and gums examined, at the beginning and again at the end of the program, so that he may know just what care his teeth need, just what measures are necessary for protecting his individual smile and how successful he has been in his attempt to improve the nutrition, health and appearance of his teeth and gums.

As mentioned in Mrs. McKellar's article, "Health Education and Our High School Girl", the 4-H Club national slogan is, "to make the best better." Their goals for the "Protect Your Smile" program are

>Cleaner teeth and healthier gums
>No new cavities
>All cavities filled.

The program, as planned, presents unlimited possibilities. The development of these possibilities will be through joint efforts of all concerned and especially through the initiative and resourcefulness of the individual club members.

HEALTH EDUCATION IN THE SCHOOLS
JOHN P. SULLIVAN, Ph.D.
Supervisor of Health Education
Boston School Department

We are all familiar with the rapid growth of the health education movement. But the reasons leading up to the acceptance of health education by the educators are worthy of attention. This place in the schools is herewith considered, first from a study of the nature of the child, and second, from a study of the nature of education.

Let us consider the attitude toward health objectives in education. Modern philosophers of education teach that the nature of the child is concerned with actual life situations and the nature of education should be concerned with preparing the child for the future by utilizing these real life situations. Too often has former school health work stressed knowledge, skills and techniques, with a failure to stress attitudes, ideals and conduct. Too often has it considered the present stage of development and neglected the future. Education should attempt to mould the individual from what he is to what he should be. Educators agree that all education should be centered around the mental, moral and physical development of the child. Past school health work has confined itself in too narrow a concept of physical development. It is necessary that we enlarge this concept. Steps are now under way to do this through health education.

Educators whose duty it was to draw up the curricula invariably listed health as the first objective of general education. Granted, however, that health is recognized as the first objective, the problem of organizing a working program which will result in improved health habits of our school children still remains. A new view must be considered to supplement the previous health work, and even to replace the ineffective former "blood and bone physiology" teachings. It must be new in spirit, in fundamental aims, in subject matter, in grade placement and in habit training. The child must be exposed to a health environment daily, that he may absorb unconsciously attitudes and ideals which shape his future life.

This new view with its needed program would require a careful consideration of the three previous agencies in education which led up to the health education movement; namely, (1) formal physical activity, (2) rise of informal activity, (3) introduction of health services, that is, doctor, dentist and nurse. Although these agencies satisfied in part the health objective, they did not satisfy fully either child nature or the nature of education.

The period of formal physical activity was introduced into the United States from Germany and Sweden during the nineteenth century. These formal systems were founded with a view of building up in our boys and girls, sound, vigorous and harmoniously developed bodies. Up to this time it was generally believed that regular daily exercise was all that was essential to attain and maintain health. These early systems of formal physical activities were accepted as complete health programs in themselves. But they did not prove natural to the child. Furthermore these formal systems did not recognize the growing nature of the child. An unfavorable reaction set in against this routinized and mechanized form of activity. Such systems of formal procedures, which were outgrowths of military formalism and of autocratic systems of European education, were destined to failure in the more democratic system in the United States.

Then occurred the rise of informal activities centering on play and the athletic movement. This change soon met with universal favor and has become "The American Spirit". This new influence has tended to promote the activities of play and athletics for their own sake and not for the purpose of correlating with the objectives of education and with the school's health program. As Dr. Thomas D. Wood so ably expresses it, "When physical education presents a program which is phychologically and physiologically sound and therefore pedagogically acceptable, it will find itself in organic relationship with education as a whole and with the other subjects or departments represented". This last of educational correlation was one of the weakest links. Although this system was a great improvement, and the fact that it is still in schools points to its worth, yet it failed to satisfy completely the nature of the child. Activity even though informal was not the "be all and end all" of a health program.

Next, medical inspection, the forerunner of present health services appeared on the horizon. It started in Boston in 1894 with the rise of epidemics among school children. The personnel of modern school health service is madeup for the most part of physicians, nurses and dentists. Its chief interest is in the machinery of modern medicine, dispensaries, clinics, physical examinations and control of communicable disease. The pupils usually come in contact with this health agency but once a year at the annual physical examination, and this only in a few systems. On other occasions the physicians, nurses and dentists meet the children only in emergencies. In other words, in the most ideal situation, this agency spends on an average of but twenty minutes a year with each individual. It is evident therefore that although the health service is filling an important place, as now organized it does not satisfy the full nature of the child nor fulfill the general objectives of education.

With the introduction and growth of such sciences as hygiene, bichemistry and bacteriology it was gradually realized that there were many elements concerned with healthful living, and that daily physical exercise, for example, is only one of these. The growth of medical sciences took from physical education, in a large measure, its initial function of being the only school agency to be concerned with the health of the child.

The health education movement which followed these three is founded on the theory that the fundamental basis of school health work, as of all school work, is teaching or guidance. This teaching of health in its broadest sense implies the following: teaching the child, through graded instruction, the fundamental of health knowledge, training the child to practice this health knowledge, and inculcating a correct attitude toward the meaning of positive health. The place of physical activities and health service as the sole school health agencies has thus been challenged. In other words, the child needs more than informal and formal activities and health service. The past has developed some fine activity programs, but at the same time there was little or no decreasing of physical defects.

These activity programs have their place but are not all sufficient. The child should be taught to think and act for himself in matters of health. Schools should not always emphasize doing for the child, but through guidance to lead the child to self guidance in health matters. Thus we see that the nature of the child and the nature of education demands a new agency which will better equip him in broad matters of health—personal, mental, social and moral, as well as physical. Health education is the new movement destined to fulfill this need of the child. It will not displace physical activities nor health services, but will complement them by unifying and coordinating them with its own field of endeavor, for the ultimate benefit of the child.

THE CONSERVATION ON THE SCHOOL HEALTH PROGRAM
MABEL C. BRAGG
Associate Professor of Education
School of Education, Boston University

Probably there was never a time when the conservation and improvement of the health of our school children were so important as they are at the beginning of this school year. We would have them fortified against the consequences of the evils of the times in which their childhood is being spent and from the discouragements of many of the homes from which they come. We would find for them all that persists of standards and opportunities for growth and success and happiness.

All homes are, of course, not included; yet the confusion of thinking, and the distress in regard to the future must influence all more or less as parents and community leaders confront each day as it comes and try valiantly to establish the children in the beliefs we know to be good and the practices that bring strength and power in the personal life. To the teachers comes the problem of maintaining their own poise and grace, perplexed as they are in many cases by the confusion of their personal affairs. But to the teachers, for these "children looking up, holding wonder like a cup" the responsibility and opportunity give them an escape and a refuge, and work for which they are absolutely necessary. The children are still ours, and our work is still in our hands.

In those communities where the care of the children and the best possible physical and emotional preparation for school is still continued, the teachers are set forward along their way and can readily begin with courage the social adjustment and the new knowledges and skills for which our schools are maintained.

In some communities the problem is more difficult. There are so many obstacles to learning that school life for many children is much harder than it needs to be. To make our school expenditures yield the greatest possible advantages, the condition of the children, the environment in which they are to learn and work, and the physical and mental cheer and courage of our teachers must be on the highest possible level that the community can afford to maintain. These are not the days to take away from the children anything that makes school life the greatest opportunity that it can be. These years will never come to them again, hence they must be the best that the community knows. There are parents, there are physicians and dentists, there are public health men and women and social service workers who will give as never before when the children's needs are revealed and the schools ask their help.

This means a study of the needs of the children. Each teacher will make a careful observation and record of the apparent condition of each child. She can know the background, the personal appearance, the apparent physical defects and the evident emotional response. Only so is she ready to teach each child the body of knowledge, the certain skills, the ways of living together that belong to that year of each child's life. Then, in close cooperation with the home, she does her best to help each child to reach the highest level of which he is capable. Both living and learning are her objectives and so school today means experiences and adventures in knowledge, opportunities for growth in skills and a greater chance for the increase of kindliness and generosity of spirit toward each other than we have ever known before. What we cannot have to work with is not our problem, what we do with what we have will reveal the success of our year's work.

The health problems in the schools present peculiar difficulties. In some communities where health programs have been carried on with courage and enthusiasm by teachers, school physicians, nurses and children to the very great satisfaction of the parents, reductions in appropriations have resulted in some of the health activities being cut from the school program. This has been true possibly because health teaching seems to the authorities a new subject and on this account, it must go. Another obstacle to a steady continuance of activities which arises is sometimes caused by the school administrators themselves. They allow some changed emphasis in subject matter material to displace health teaching and activities. Ambitious, forward-looking school officials who disregard the importance of the removal of physical obstacles to learning, and the establishment and maintenance of favorable environment in their enthusiasms over new experiments, may unconsciously cause their teachers to lessen their emphasis on the cooperation of the school with the home to help to secure healthy childhood. There are so many things to be done that this can be easily understood even of the most conscientious teachers. Yet it is fundamental that the boys and girls must have excellent physical condition, emotional stability, and good social adjustment in order that the schools may be successful.

In spite of the reduced health appropriations or changes in emphasis in the courses of study, the principals and teachers who know the value of health training and wish to carry it on can find a way. It can be motivated by their own plans as new ways of teaching what they must teach, and in the children's plans by helping them to find the best ways of doing their work under the best possible circumstances. Such schools cooperate with the homes or compensate for them by expecting of their pupils observance of the manners and customs that we know in regard to setting up right conditions for carrying on their work. The pupils themselves readily assume responsibility both for personal cleanliness and for cleanliness of environment. They learn the facts and develop an awareness of the best room temperature for work. In learning the good ways of living and working and playing together they learn the value and the satisfactions of sleep and rest, of proper food and exercise and sunshine, of fair play and generous spirit. These are good ways of living and surely all schools with high objectives consider such teaching a definite, vital part of their work.

The appropriate knowledge that answers the questions of the children as they grow on into the middle grades will be found as outcomes of many of their accepted subject studies. Social studies are rich in health situations and knowledge. Trips to dairy farms, fruit stores and grocery stores, together with many more such experiences, furnish valuable material for arousing and satisfying curiosity, supplying necessary knowledge and establishing desirable habits and practices. An understanding and appreciation of the ways in which the community furnishes play space and equipment, cares for waste disposal and makes and enforces regulations to protect the health of its people come from real contacts with personal situations and are found not alone in books, valuable as the books are for a fortification for the teacher and the standardization of knowledge.

Out of their experiences in their own families with the preparation for school each fall of new children entering school, and the correction of their own difficulties in order that school life may be most profitable, they learn greater appreciation of their family physicians and dentists, their school physicians and nurses, and the opportunities of clinics furnished by the Health Department. This appreciation is increased by really educational health examinations. Enthusiasm can be aroused by nurses, principals and teachers, cooperating with the pupils and encouraging them so that many physical defects will be corrected before the doctor comes rather than afterward. Thus it is that the annual health examination may come to mean that the doctors are coming to find as many perfect children in our building as possible and to help us all. Such work can be accomplished only when teachers and nurses instructed by the examiners know and study together the results of the examinations and cooperate with and supplement the work of the homes to secure correction. When these children and their parents learn the proper attitude and conduct and observations of regulations concerning communicable diseases, greater cooperation and observance of regulations can also be secured.

Through pupil responsibility and cooperation, teachers concerned that each child shall have his best possible chance for learning, family understanding and appreciation of the school health program, and emphasis of health work and requirements of results by the principal, it may be hoped that the health programs in the elementary schools will secure by the end of the sixth grade, certain established habits of living and satisfactory attitudes toward well-being. These will result in the best choices of conduct, and the appropriate knowledge that will fortify the pupils and teachers in the procedures, and will increase their interest and participation as their horizon widens and their opportunities and experiences increase.

Interest and cooperation in community health activities in addition to satisfactory health habits will contribute to the influences that will send to the secondary schools, students well equipped physically, mentally and socially for the learning situations that await them. Such conditions will come as a result of the wise health work carried on in the elementary schools, not only as a requirement by the high school but as a consequence of understanding and appreciation of the importance of helping to lay such foundations by both direct and indirect health teachings.

In the secondary schools, boys and girls and not subject matter are still the prime objects of importance. Again, understanding and emphasis by the principal, appreciation by him of the value of the contributions of all the health workers and contributing agencies are of the utmost value. Knowledge of the available help for individual pupils, emphasis of the subject and provision for health supervision and teaching in his school will go far toward establishing and conserving the health achievements of the elementary grades. They will also aid the pupils to meet the new physical and mental health problems at each new age level. While it is true that individual teachers or small groups working alone with zeal and personal concern, with interest in the needs of the individual pupil as well as in his reception of subject-matter knowledge can accomplish much, it is emphatically true that the real success for the high level of achievement in improved health environment and accomplishment rests upon the principal. His expectations, his requirements, his personal interest and his provision for the contribution of each subject-matter teacher, nurse, school physician, physical director and home room teacher really determine the power of the program. Health counsellors coordinate this work, raise the standard and increase the importance of the achievement in the eyes of the students, the uninterested teachers, if there be any, and arouse the pride of the community. While it is true that no school system can go farther or faster than its public wishes it to go, it still remains the privilege of the school administrators to accustom their people gradually to new emphasis in school life, insuring success to their new enterprises by close relation with familiar subject-matter experiences. Home economics taught from the right angle furnishes a fertile field for health work that will flourish in the homes of the community. Biology and general science give opportunities for knowledge backgrounds for practices considered necessary in the best regulated families and communities. Social studies with their health implications make immediate connections with closely related personal and community experiences and help to lay the foundation for more valuable health department work based on the increasing desires and understanding of the community. Physical education with its plays and games, its love of sunshine, its fostering of pride in growth and personal appearance, makes its very intimate, individual, valuable contribution. The doctors and the nurses with their preventive and remedial work establish themselves in the lives of the children as friends who are to be sought early rather than late. The psychologist helps to adjust individuals to their environment and so saves many a young person to happiness and usefulness. The home cooperates, understands and appreciates the influences at work to help them to establish their young people as valuable members of the community. The pupils themselves with habits, attitudes, appropriate knowledge that will enable them to meet life each day with strength, learn better how to make the right character choices and spend themselves for the best things in life. All these with the public and private agencies that help to the extent of their resources — all these are the vital forces of a functioning school health program brought to pass by an understanding of the needs of the children, and by the consecrated people who care about the health and the happiness of the children of their community to the extent that their first considerations in education are the removal of all possible obstacles to learning, and growth in knowledge and skill and kindliness.

To the objection that appropriations must be cut, we still have the homes and the schools and the health agencies who must not lower their standards of work during these troublous times. Our children's power must not be undermined; the adults must pay, if pay they must. New avenues are opening through which homes and schools are learning to make desirable choices and use of essential foods, the restoration of sleep and rest that will compensate for stress and strain is newly emphasized, standards of living are changed that will help many people to enjoy more the resources of their own homes, simpler recreations replace too great a stimulation of the emotional life with its accompanying sense of disappointment and frustration.

Little has been presented here of the ways of parents and teachers and nurses in accomplishing these results. These depend upon their preparation, their love for children and the understanding of their needs, upon their courage, and their power to lay the best possible foundation that no teaching may be lost. They depend on home interest and cooperation where fathers and mothers concern themselves in the school activities to the extent of helping to build necessary equipment for checking results or of preparing foods that some children may know how good some previously scorned vegetable may be. There are many ways in which needs can be discovered and plans made and carried out by pupils and teachers. Only a whole course of study would show how the teaching of health can be so motivated that it becomes the most important, the most fundamental group of activities in our school program. The mental, emotional and spiritual life of the students of our schools must be so strengthened that they will meet each day more valiantly, and solve more wisely the problems that lie before them.

Whatever cuts in appropriations are necessary, let them not be along health lines; whatever sacrifices must be made, let us not deprive the children of their fortifications for the best possible living. Let us conserve the health program!

THE SUPERVISOR OF HEALTH EDUCATION—RESPONSIBILITIES AND TRAINING

C. E. TURNER, M.A., Dr.P.H.
Professor of Biology and Public Health
Massachusetts Institute of Technology

"Health education should be in charge of the teacher under the sympathetic guidance of an efficient advisor or supervisor of health education, equipped with special and adequate professional training for this complex task."

This statement from the conclusions of the White House Conference on Child Health and Protection presents the combined opinion of national leaders in child health and in education. Why is such supervisory service needed, or, in other words, what are the responsibilities of such a supervisor?

The school department as well as the home must play its part in the health education of the child. When the child enters school we help to improve his health practices by direct training. As he goes through the grades we must continue the training and supply health information from grade to grade in accordance with his interests, responsibilities and mental capacity. The health education program must be a properly coordinated unit at all school levels and it must be so organized that each year presents a new approach with fresh interests to the child. The first responsibility, therefore, which can be adequately met only by a trained supervisor of health education is to establish a unified program of health training and instruction throughout the school system and to make this an integral part of general education.

There is need of health education supervision after the program has been set up if it is to function efficiently. A teacher can teach subtraction without knowing higher mathematics but he cannot answer correctly the questions of children in the field of health without a sound basic knowledge of physiology, hygiene and sanitation. The child asks "Does milk give me red blood?" The answer is "No." But behind that answer is a knowledge of nutrition on the part of the teacher that includes the information that iron is an essential element in which milk is deficient. Health education requires such a range of technical knowledge that special supervision is needed to see that health facts and not health fallacies are taught.

The importance of method in health education should not be undervalued. We are training as well as instructing. Inducing a child to get enough sleep is not at all like hearing a spelling lesson. Definite periods for hygiene are set aside beginning with grade four and must be wisely used, but health facts alone do not motivate health behavior. Much of the health training program must be scattered through the school day or developed in connection with opening exercises, school lunches, activity and rest. Without supervision and inspiring leadership these activities become haphazard, ineffective or nonexistent. The second responsibility of the health education supervisor, then, is to aid the classroom teacher in developing devices, subject matter, and methods for measuring the results of the health education program.

We have said that health education needs to be made a part of general education. It should also be made an integral part of the school health program. Some of the child's most valuable educational experiences come from a contact with the physician and the nurse. The teachers should know the nature of these experiences, help to prepare children for them, assist children to interpret them clearly and encourage children to act upon them wisely. The third responsibility of the health education supervisor, therefore, is to integrate the work of the classroom teacher with the other elements of the school health program. Such a person is a "Health Educator and Coordinator." Because he facilitates the work of the other health experts and because his constructive and creative leadership is reflected in the work of the whole body of classroom teachers, it is probable that the activities of no other health worker are productive of greater health benefits per dollar expended.

Training

There seems to be general agreement with the statement of the White House Conference that "supervisors of health education should have the usual training and experience of classroom teachers with a master's degree, or the full equivalent, in health education." Such a person "should be well trained in the sciences fundamental to health and in modern trends in supervision and curriculum building; and should have at least three years' experience in classroom teaching." In several schools it is now possible to secure a master's degree or its equivalent, the certificate in public health (C. P. H.) in the field of health education.

Training requirements for health-education supervisor are naturally divided into three phases: (1) training in health, (2) training in education, and (3) training in school health administration. If we are to develop a school health program for which the public health profession, the educators and the community have respect, supervisors must be trained soundly in educational method, subject matter and administrative principles.

Training in health should include a knowledge of the structure and function of the human body. This means a basic knowledge of modern physiology, built upon a background of biochemistry, gross and microscopic anatomy. The individual should also possess adequate training in nutrition, which rests primarily upon chemistry as a basic subject. A sound knowledge of mental hygiene, social hygiene and safety education is especially important.

In the public health field, knowledge ought to include general and sanitary bacteriology, the principles of municipal sanitation and public health administration, the biology of communicable diseases, and a sufficient knowledge of vital statistics to allow the supervisor to interpret the health status of the community and the state. We should add here some knowledge of public health social work, bordering on the field of social case work.

A thorough knowledge of child psychology, educational psychology and educational method is required if the supervisor is to command the respect of the teacher and contribute effectively to class activities when he visits the classroom. Furthermore, the supervisor needs a sound knowledge of the curriculum, its nature, its development, and its operation. The understanding of the individual differences in children, physical and mental, should be a part of his equipment, as well as a sound knowledge of the principles of modern supervision in the public school.

It is wise to insist upon teaching experience preparatory to work in health education supervision. The teaching profession like any other prefers to accept leadership and directions from a person with distinctive training and successful experience in its own professional field.

Instruction in school health administration will naturally be a part of the special graduate training of the supervisor. Specific training in the development and supervision of health education is a most important aspect. It is not possible for the supervisor of health education to be a physician, a nurse, a nutritionist, a dental hygienist, and a physical educator. It is not necessary that he should know the technique of the specialists who are working in the school. It is necessary that he understand what these various groups are doing and, more especially, how the classroom program in health education can be related to the medical, nursing, dental, physical education and nutrition services.

Obviously, some professional maturity is necessary for this field of work. A year of special work will supplement quite successfully the previous training for (1) the graduate of a teachers' college who has majored in science (chemistry, biology, and nutrition), or (2) the graduate of the liberal arts college who has a major in education with a minor in these sciences, or (3) the graduate in physical education from a school giving the bachelor's degree, or (4) a nurse with a bachelor's degree. It will be seen that nutritionists are included under the second classification. Some nurses who are also graduates of teachers' colleges have made outstanding contributions in this field of work. A one-year program of study is adequate for persons with these different kinds of previous training only if it is arranged individually for each student to supplement previous training with courses in the special subjects needed.

A thorough training in school health administration will provide opportunities for study in a school or department of public health which has relatively broad offerings in that field and in a school or department of education. From two such departments it is possible to build up a program of study which, when supplemented by special work in health education with practice teaching and when further supplemented by specific instruction in school health administration, provides a background upon which the individual can build a satisfactory professional experience.

We shall do well to remember in any consideration of this sort, that there is no substitute for native intelligence and that no program of study can make a person of limited ability into a professional worker of superior capacity. We should expect to find occasional individuals possessing high native intelligence, the ability to work well with other people, and the ability to profit by experience, who will have developed superior pieces of work in public school systems without ever having completed all of the desirable training requirements suggested above.

HEALTH EDUCATION THROUGH THE CLASSROOM TEACHER
MABEL E. TURNER
State Teachers College
Lowell, Massachusetts

"The classroom teacher is the keystone in the arch of health training." This is self evident because of the very nature of her position. Children will form habits of right living not by learning facts about life, but by doing things repeatedly with satisfactory results. The classroom teacher is the only one at school who is with the children long enough, and with groups small enough to carry through a program of habit training and to give support day by day to the health practices carried out at home. If we are ever to send forth from our elementary schools children who are proficient in the art of healthful living it must be very largely by and through the efforts of the individual classroom teachers.

In the past most teachers have fallen short of the realization of this achievement. This has largely been because school authorities have shown little concern about health and health practices. The teacher must emphasize in her teaching what her superior officers wish. In the past superintendents of school have been more concerned in the development of subject matter curricula and the various techniques and devices for gaining results in special fields rather than in thoroughgoing efforts to relate the work of the school to human needs. Much of the emphasis seems to have been based upon whims of superintendents rather than upon the real needs of the child for healthful living. Perhaps the conditions in the average school of the past are not as bad as J. P. Munroe states in his interesting book, *The Human Factor in Education*:

"Because the average school works against the health of our sons and daughters, we must strive all the harder to upbuild that health. Because the school tends to stunt the body and mind and even the soul of the child, we must work all the more to expand those. Because the school still depends on the old, bad stimulus of competition, we must emphasize all the more the beauty of cooperation, of each working for all and all for each. Because the school puts most of its emphasis upon using the head, we must do everything we can to provide opportunity for the body and the hands..."*

While we may not be guilty of all of these charges, yet it is nevertheless true that the schools of the past have been so highly artificial as to hinder the formation of the habits necessary for the promotion of health. We have often imparted the knowledge of hygiene and at the same time forced the formation of unhygienic habits. Health education in its true sense must be accepted by the administrative authorities of the school as a part of the educational program if it is to succeed. It is impossible for the teacher to develop a health education program without the support of her principal, general supervisors and superintendent.

If the school of the future is to make any genuine and adequate contribution to the furtherance of health it must provide for the formation of health habits, the imparting of health information, and the development of a health conscience. From the moment the child enters school effort must be centered on his forming desirable habits in the fields of both personal and social hygiene. He must form correct habits of posture, diet, elimination, exercise, rest, play, cleanliness, and the like. Along with these habits in which the physical aspect is prominent must go habits of mind which tend to conserve rather than to dissipate energy. The development of such a positive attitude toward health is possible only under the guidance of teachers who themselves possess it to the fullest measure, and who appreciate the significance of their work.

Since health education in the elementary school is the task primarily of the classroom teacher it is absolutely essential that she should have a clear understanding of all of the factors that enter into a well-rounded program in health. According to C. E. Turner in his *Principles of Health Education*, the duties of the classroom teacher with respect to pupil health are as follows:

"1. To assist in interpreting the school health program to the home.
2. To participate in the health examination of pupils.

---
* J. P. Munroe, *The Human Factor in Education* — p. 30.

3. To assist in the control of communicable diseases.
4. To support and further the work of the school health services through the program of health education in the classroom.
5. To assist in maintaining hygienic and sanitary conditions in the classroom.
6. To weigh and measure children or to supervise the children in doing it.
7. To conduct the daily health review.
8. To supervise the school lunch.
9. To conduct relaxation periods where necessary.
10. To supervise organized play as suggested by the physical education department.
11. To teach subject matter in health and hygiene.
12. To develop special health-training activities.
13. To correlate health with other subjects of the curriculum.
14. To furnish an example of health in herself."*

In order to carry out all of these duties in an efficient manner it will be necessary for teachers to have a knowledge of the fundamental subject matter in the related fields of health, as nutrition, community hygiene, social hygiene, mental hygiene, health of childhood and adolescence, school hygiene and sanitation, physical education, and personal hygiene. In addition to the subject-matter background a thorough course in health education methods is essential. Because of its broad scope health is one of the most difficult subjects to teach. The teacher who is to answer the questions of elementary school children correctly and within their understanding must be both informed and resourceful. It is a fallacious assumption that no specific knowledge is needed to teach health. Just to know the rules of the health game and to develop activities in connection with them is a long way from carrying out an adequate health education program.

While a basic knowledge in the field of health is absolutely necessary the classroom teacher must, in addition to this, feel a genuine spirit of devotion and enthusiasm for the health of her pupils if she is to achieve the highest success in her work. She should be interested, too, in supporting community health, and above all, her most important duty is to maintain her own good health. What she *is* speaks far louder to her pupils than what she says. In the last analysis, the success of her health teaching will depend to a large degree upon the spirit with which she carries it on. This would be true of her work in any field, but it is especially so in health.

Supervisors of health, school nurses, and other health specialists are necessary in the carrying out of a well-rounded health education program, but it is the classroom teacher alone who has the task of dealing intimately with the health of her children day-by-day throughout the school year. She needs the support of the health specialists — doctors, nurses, dentists, physical educators, nutritionists, and the rest in carrying out her work, but the strength of her program depends upon herself. If the arch of health training in her classroom is to be strong she must make it so.

HEALTH EDUCATION FROM THE ASPECT OF THE PHYSICAL EDUCATION DIRECTOR

CARL L. SCHRADER
State Supervisor of Physical Education
Massachusetts Department of Education

The trained teacher in the field of physical education recognizes the important place he may occupy in the endeavor to promote and main-

---
* C. E. Turner, *Principles of Health Education* — p. 273.

tain health. He has been taught to look upon the problem in a positive sense.

Physical education is usually thought of in terms of exercise, when in reality it should be conceived as a "way of living". However, exercise or more broadly, activity, is undoubtedly an essential factor in the scope of hygiene. Wholesome bodily activity results in healthy hygienic body cravings. Physical activity in its stimulating change of matter, or metabolism, creates an appetite for food, creates a desire for sleep, and a craving for the frequent and full bath — all surely vital health functions. It is in the intelligent use of activity, and the intelligent response to nature's demands, that the advantage lies. Abuse in either over or under doing will soon throw any bodily functions out of balance. The thoughtful physical education teacher will utilize these common experiences on the part of those whom he directs, toward an understanding of the simple logic, upon which well-being is based.

Health is a condition that has to be earned in order to be possessed. That is what makes it positive. To grossly violate nature's laws and then bolster up on artificial stimulants and pain-killers, is not keeping healthy, but is nothing short of illiteracy. Pain in its various degrees of severity, from the slight feeling of discomfort to the acute pain, is a blessing in disguise. It is nature's warning that something is wrong. To merely kill pain is but to defeat nature's purpose. It is in this sense that the interpretation of physical education, namely, a "way of living" is used. This over or under doing may be in any one of the mentioned aspects of hygiene: eating, sleeping, bathing, or exercise. Physical education, then, is interested in causing man to pursue his activities intelligently, so as to stimulate rather than undermine health.

To take short cuts has always been an American trait. In business as well as in play we accept a good thing and then immediately seek a way for achieving in a short time and in an extravagant way what was intended for a sane and safe procedure. Instead of going to the gymnasium or the golf links to leisurely enjoy the playing, man will rush from the running track in the gymnasium to the chest weights, then to the striking bag, lift heavy dumb-bells and what not, all in a brief space of time, coming out fatigued rather than refreshed. So the golfer rushes through thirty-six or even twice that many holes and boasts of it. The recreative element is lost, and instead of storing energy, it is squandered and physical bankruptcy may well result. The craving to create a record stifles many originally profitable types of recreation. The hiker who has for his goal the speed in which he may reach the mountain top or other distant goal, loses all that is recreation in hiking. When and where the element of play is lost we border the zone of danger. This does not mean that desirable goals can be reached without exertion, but it does mean that exhaustion is too big a price to pay for a vainglorious achievement.

It must be borne in mind that good health includes a healthy frame of mind. "Health Personality" it has been called. The old interpretation of health as that condition when one is not sick in bed is no longer acceptable. Instead, we think of health in abundance, so that at times we may be extravagant with it, employing this bank credit for tasks that require more than just the necessary energy to exist. All our personal "outs", such as irritability, impatience, nagging and overbearing fault-finding, which make us socially unpopular, may be traceable to some functional unbalance. Postural deficiencies are many times manifestations of slovenly and lazy habits. It is not only the face that mirrors personality. Erect bodily carriage portrays in a conspicuous manner an aliveness which is as attractive as is the facial expression. Both are decided business assets. While we are more or less helpless in changing our facial gifts, though face lifters promise otherwise, we can change our bodily bearing by balancing our muscle power, designed to carry us erect. Our bodily carriage is very easily affected. The state of emotion manifests itself outwardly by the bodily carriage. Whereas in sorrow, grief or pain our body assumes a collapsed or crushed position, with head low and eyes cast to the ground, walking in slow and deliberate step, joy forces the head high in the air, chest up, and a strong vigorous stride. The reverse is also true. A faulty posture provokes a downcast frame of mind. There is no vanity in striving for natural beauty such as intended here.

Physical education is concerned mainly with youth, for here it may mean a matter of a proper start in life, there being no, or at least few, faulty established habits. It is important that growth and development be aided by proper selection and dosage of activity. The well prepared and professionally minded teacher will endeavor to discern the individual needs and so occupy the pupil physically as to help him or her to reach his or her respective possible goal of man and womanhood. Any over or under doing, if anything, is more fatal here than with the adult. In the lower grades we permit the children to set their own pace, so to speak, or perhaps one should say "nature's pace." Children will run just so long and then deliberately allow themselves to be tagged, because they feel their limits. There is little danger, therefore, of being extravagant with the children's energy if we heed their own manifestations. It is in the later years, particularly in junior and senior high school, when in many instances physical education is sinning by urging youth to overdo. We have to take cognizance of the fact that growing and developing are energy-consuming processes, and whatever gross physical extravagance we urge or allow during these years, is very likely to interfere with nature's demand for growth. The difference between exertion and exhaustion need again be stressed here. Exertion in proper dosage stimulates growth, whereas exhaustion retards it. Schools and parents should be alert in not permitting children of junior or senior high school age to be exploited for school or local championships.

Competition is a desirable function in a physical education program. It must be kept within bounds, however. The game or sport must be fitted to the child rather than the other way around.

With the establishment of junior high schools many of the competitive evils that prevailed in the high school were adopted by the junior high school. Much headway has been made in correcting these mistakes, but the abuse is still too frequent to be ignored. Some of these errors are to play adult games too early, to play too long competitive schedules, to match teams out of class, and last but not least, to keep too little watch over physical condition. Football, unless modified, is no game for junior high school boys. Hockey is no game for junior high school girls. More than one competitive game a week is undesirable. To pit a weak team against a giant team is not only poor sport, but is unsafe and void of any satisfaction to the players on the losing side. To allow any individual to participate in strenuous interscholastic competition without expert medical advice is most unwise. On the girls' side particularly the tendency of urging participation beyond health safety is on the increase. In view of the fact that the tendency toward tuberculosis is on the increase among young girls, it would seem doubly important to protect the girls, and use every precaution to correct their living habits. Thorough physical examination of girls who are to be permitted to play on competing teams, and close watch on reactions while engaged in practice and playing, will prove to be valuable safety devices. Smaller communities, which usually do not have expert supervision, often err the most in maintaining competing teams with extreme schedules and late hours because of great distances to be travelled. The interest in such communities, which enthusiastically follow all the games, is centered mainly on the entertainment the sport affords, with little thought of the consequence to the young people.

Parents need to be aroused to understand the significance and purpose of physical education, of which play is a part, so as to recognize abuses when they exist. With a normal body and intelligent living, we can with safety undergo occasional strain, but with these two basic elements failing, the possibility of jeopardizing health is by no means remote. Evidence of overdoing on the part of young people does not usually follow immediately after excess, but is more often postponed, and manifests itself later in some deficiency, which prevents us later from doing the things we would like to do. The fact that youth is eager to do more and more should not deter us from using our more mature judgment. While management and supervision of the active play-life of children remains in the hands of school authorities, there is little danger of overemphasis, but when the management passes into the hands of town enthusiasts outside of school, both the objectives of play and its safety, are many times lost.

The Departments of Physical Education in our public schools which now command usually adequate equipment and expertly trained teachers are eager to have their efforts recognized as a health-building process in addition to the general educational objectives. Together with the school physician and nurse the life of young people is well protected, but only in so far as the community will do its part in aiding to have the healthy living practices promoted in school also carried on when the home is in control.

"Riches we wish to get,
Yet remain spendthrifts still,
We would have health and yet,
Still use our bodies ill."

THE PREPARATION OF HEALTH EDUCATION MATERIAL FOR THE SCHOOLS

JEAN V. LATIMER, A.M.
Educational Secretary
Massachusetts Tuberculosis League

Bertrand Brown in referring to "the four basic tasks in health education," says, "In any intelligently planned health educational effort, the following fundamental considerations must be present:

1. What ideas, images and emotional appeals must be conceived, accumulated, arranged, set forth and produced, and
2. Transmitted through what medium or by what means
3. To what audiences, in what locality or localities, in order
4. To accomplish what objectives?

Health education can be intelligently planned, and, as a consequence, effectively and economically pursued, only when each of these four fundamental component tasks is considered, not only as a separate factor in the educational process, but in its relation to each and all of the other basic tasks present."[1]

This is especially true in the preparation of health education materials for the schools. First of all it is pertinent to review the general objectives of school health education. Just what about health are we seeking to teach pupils through the medium of the schools? Why is it stated that health education is the first objective of modern education? What is the implication of the recognition? Where does it lead us? Such considerations are likely to result in more careful attention both as to content and methods of presentation of all health education materials.

If health education is to be thought of as "the sum of experience in school and elsewhere which favorably influences habits, attitudes and

---

[1] A New Deal in Health Education.— American Journal of Public Health, July, 1934.

knowledge related to individual, community and racial health," then the essential element in subject matter is to enrich these experiences so that they will have more significance and will, therefore, more likely result in deeper insights, appreciations and understandings. They should also provide for the future growth of each pupil. To reach these goals, therefore, should be the first point of reference in the preparation of health education material for the schools.

Again, it is necessary to further consider what are the specific objectives of each grade. Health education like all education must be thought of as a spiral process — in which repetition at a more advanced level is always necessary. Due care must be given to whether the material is suited to the age level of the children for whom it is intended. Does it enrich their present experience? Does it provide for the future growth of each pupil. This means not only an experimental knowledge of what ideas, knowledge and conceptions of health are best presented at various age levels, but it also means a checking up of the technical word lists of the general vocabularies of children at various periods of mental development. We have in the past been some times at fault in not employing more often technical or scientific terms, and in being too babyish in our treatment of health. Educators made this criticism of some of the health material which has been given them.

A supervisor of one of our largest and best known cities was recently heard to say that she doubted very much if the children received an adequate idea of roughage foods from the health stories in which foods were dramatically described as "inside scrubbing brushes". Analogies make health education material interesting and should continue to be used, but they are not enough. Should we not have as a more conscious goal, that of increasing the child's scientific health vocabulary? A checking up of current newspaper health articles surprises one at the use of scientific terms. If the masses of people read such, we might successfully hope to use such terms in the middle grades and secondary schools. Just now there is real need of enriching and strengthening material for presentation to upper grades and high school pupils.

In preparing health education material another difficult problem is to decide whether the material is to be addressed to the teacher or to the children. This must be decided or else the presentation is likely to be unsound. Would it not be a good plan if material prepared for children carry also supplementary adult teacher material? One of our tasks is to enrich and enlarge the teacher's own health scientific knowledge.

Not only a consideration of the audience to be addressed, but determining the accuracy of the health facts presented is fundamental. Here there are difficulties encountered. Recent articles by leaders in the field of medicine and public health have had a good deal to say about debunking much that is now being taught, because it is invalid, doubtful and actually false.[1] Dr. Donald B. Armstrong says, "In appraising so-called health facts, we want to be certain that they are true and that they are important."[2] He classifies a variety of so-called health facts into the following groups:

"1. Items in health practice that, certainly for our times and as far as we can see for the future, are scientifically certified facts.
2. Items whose probability is large, but where we are not quite certain of our facts. This group may include items that a previous generation accepted without question, but which we may now be unlearning, so to speak. It may also include

---

[1] Things to Forget in Health Teaching. — Warren E. Forsythe, M. D. Journal of Health and Physical Education, March, 1934. Also, The Journal of Outdoor Life, July, 1934.
[2] Health Facts — What to Tell. — American Journal of Public Health, March, 1932.

a group of near facts that increasing experience seems to make more and more probable, but about which we as yet have no final proof.
3. Items extensively used as facts, especially for commercial exploitation, but which we know either to be erroneous, or at least employed with misleading and perverting aims."

Today children in school, as a result of family, social tradition, or inaccurate classroom teaching certainly are full of many things about health which are not so. We might aim through our health education material of the future to try to get rid of this mass of misinformation. However, there are items of health about which we have a working knowledge, classified by Dr. Armstrong as a "B" fact, which may be used in teaching. All of us recognize with the immature mind, it is some times necessary to be assertive and even dogmatic. We never should with children, and even possibly with the general public, arouse too much scientific doubt which is so characteristic of the meticulous scientific or research style of writing. Health education material for school pupils must carry some degree of certainty, or else it is not convincing.

But, in preparing health education material we do not want to confine ourselves to the mere retelling of facts. The task of the health educator is even greater. Henry Adams declared, "Nothing in education is so astonishing as the amount of ignorance it accumulates in the form of inert facts." Especially is this true of health facts. Health materials which give insights and appreciations of the scientific method as applied to health education might well be an objective of the health education material, especially prepared for the secondary schools. Health facts and their application tend to change, some times very quickly, but the scientific method which enables the individual to understand and appreciate their applications remains relatively fixed.

Methods for the presentation of the material are also important. It has been said that people rarely act simply on the presentation of cold facts. They must be motivated. Children must be motivated by making the health information vital and related to the present interests. There must also be practical possibilities for application. A tub bath each day or oranges for breakfast stated as essentials for health are not always possible for each child. It would be tragically disappointing and certainly unscientific if we should seek to arouse a high school girl's interest by telling her if she developed maximum health she would become beautiful. But we can make an appeal by pointing out how certain elements of beauty — sparkling eyes, glossy hair, rosy cheeks and correct posture are manifestations of correct health habits and are to be improved upon by hygienic living.

Finally, in the presentation of health materials, we must understand and apply the techniques of all good writing. Unity of presentation is important. Particularly children cannot stand having too many loosely connected ideas presented to them at the same time. For this reason, in the monthly health bulletin which the League formerly published, we confine each issue to the making of one health idea or fact interesting. Similarly in the making of posters, it is far better to develop one basic idea. Wording on pictorial presentations is far more effective if it carries dramatic appeal, rather than several spread out ideas. Dramatic use of words to get a health conception across is useful. "Early Discovery, Early Recovery," as the title of an educational pamphlet for the high school, published by the National Tuberculosis Association, might well be cited as an example of such use.

There will always be need for revising health materials for school children, since, as has been said, we are dealing with a body of scientific facts which of themselves do not "stay put" but are constantly changing in light of new research. One can readily see the need of new materials presenting the current theories regarding ventilation, deep breathing, rough, bulky foods and many other items related to the teaching of hygiene.

Variety in repetition is also an important element, since people will always need to be reminded as well as told. The health educator will therefore constantly be preparing new materials. Our task is interesting in that it will never be completed. The possibilities for the use of health education materials in the school are now much greater than ever before.

BASIC CONSIDERATIONS OF THE JUNIOR HIGH SCHOOL COURSE OF STUDY

JOHN P. SULLIVAN, PH.D.

Supervisor of Health Education
Boston School Department

The need of organized courses of study in junior high schools is evident in the light of recent findings. The Research Department of the National Education Association finds in a curriculum study that health instruction is offered at least once a week as a required subject in nearly all junior high school grades. Even in the ninth grade it is offered as a constant in more programs than is any other subject except English.[1]

In the light of this authoritative information it is hard to understand the wholesale lack of courses of study in the junior high schools. In a survey completed in Massachusetts[2] it was found that only thirty-two per cent of the junior high schools had health courses of study.

The course of study is an important educational vehicle for unifying, coordinating and grading health content. It is equally necessary in the secondary grades as in the elementary. "A course of study consists of specifications and directions relating to educating children. Without a course of study a teacher works more or less in the dark. Although individually the teachers of a school system may be capable, industrious, and conscientious in their work, they will not, except by accident, coordinate their efforts in the best way unless they are provided with a good course of study."[3]

It can be truly said, that the course of study, supplemented by appropriate textbooks and teaching aids, is the best guarantee of what any particular school system aims to do in health teaching and training.

In the actual construction of a course of study for junior high schools, the supervisor finds himself in a veritable thicket of advocated theories.[4] Charters[5] and Bobbitt[6] would stress present needs of society as the starting point in making a course of study. Miriam[7] would emphasize the construction from the viewpoint of paidocentric (child centered) development. Bonser[8] would suggest a course based on fundamental life needs. They are not completely adequate. They fail in so far as they do not go beyond the orbit of present-day conditions and experience.

The job-analysis is urged by some educators as the most desirable method of determining the elements for the course of study. This method of determining such elements is open to criticism. While it is doubtless true that careful analysis of what children do is a valuable

[1] Creating a Curriculum for Adolescent Youth. Research Bull. of N E A , Vol. VI, No. 1, p. 52.
[2] Report, "Health Education Survey" — Mass. Tuberculosis League.
[3] Monroe, W. S., Making a Course of Study, p. 4.
[4] Cocking, W. D. — Administrative Procedure in Curriculum Making.
[5] Curriculum Construction, Chapt. I.
[6] How to Make a Curriculum, Chapters II-III.
[7] Child Life and Curriculum, Chapt. I.
[8] Elementary School Curriculum, Chapt. I.

contribution, nevertheless as a basis for procedure in course of study construction it fails in that it investigates the activity as it is now rather than as it should be. This is a fundamental error in procedure and would tend to strengthen and continue present practices, whether desirable or undesirable.

The following suggested procedure in constructing the junior high school course is based on the practices presented by the committee of the National Society for the Study of Education,[9] and supplemented by the biological and psychological principles and the laws of learning.[10]

Based on these the following procedure was undertaken in constructing the Boston course of study in health education for the junior high school grades:

1. Statement of objectives.
2. Examination of present courses of study.
3. Judgment of teachers and masters on selected topics.
4. Experimental teaching.
5. Health information test and teacher questionnaire for minimum of essentials and grade placement.
6. Course of study committee to bring course to completion.

The objectives as outlined by the Joint Committee[11] were the results of the best scientific investigation, and served as the objectives of this course of study:

1. To instruct children and youth so that they will conserve and improve their own health.
2. To establish in them the habits and principles of living which throughout their school life, and in later years, will assure that abundant vigor and vitality required for the greatest possible happiness and service in personal, family, and community life.
3. To influence parents and other adults, through the health education program for children, to adopt better habits and attitudes, so that the school may become an effective agency for the promotion of the social aspects of health education in the family and community as well as in the school itself.
4. To improve the individual and community life of the future; to insure a better second generation and a still better third generation — a healthier and fitter nation and race.

Dividing the field of health instruction into some of the major topics generally taught points to the range of placement. Table I shows the specific placement of the topics in some ten courses of study issued during the period 1927 to 1932. Four of the courses were for grades seven, eight and nine; six courses pertained to grades seven and eight.

While the grade placement of some topics varies, the placement of certain topics is found to be constant in median practice: home and school hygiene, for example, are taught almost entirely in the seventh grade, the nervous system in the eighth, and disease prevention and bacteria in the eighth and ninth. Is it not a reasonable assumption that the grade placements shown to be fairly constant in median practice, might suggest the most feasible placement?

These topics were sent to a representative group of junior high school masters and teachers. They were asked to group them under appropriate teaching units and assign the grade they thought best in the light of their experience. From the results of this source and with a realization that the foundation upon which to lay a health education course of

---
[9] 26th Yearbook, National Society for the Study of Education, Foundation of Curriculum Making. Part II — pp. 11-28.
[10] Basic Considerations of the Course of Study in Health Education. Education, Dec. 1933.
[11] Health Education.

study is a knowledge of the objectives for which you are going to train, the individual you are going to train, and the condition under which training is to be given, a mimeographed copy of a "Working Outline in Health Education for Grades VII, VIII and IX"[12] was prepared for experimental teaching. The following topic headings are suggestive of the experimental work considered suitable for the junior high schools.

Grade VII — Topic Headings
School Hygiene
Home Hygiene
Community Hygiene
Budgeting Time
Safety
Alcohol, Tobacco, and Patent Medicines
Vacation Time

Grade VIII — Topic Headings
Foods
Digestive System
Circulatory System
Respiratory System
Nervous System
Bony and Muscular System
Special Senses

Grade IX — Topic Headings
Public Health Agencies
Disease
Food Control
Health Heroes
Vocational Hygiene
Mental Health
Safety

This "Working Outline in Health Education" was distributed to some forty-nine schools having junior high classes for experimental teaching. At the end of the year two check-ups on the outline were offered. One was a health information test and the other a questionnaire to the teachers. This gave an approximate reaction from the teachers and pupils. These two sources afforded definite information and in the light of these two reactions, certain modifications were considered on the outline. These modifications necessitated the following changes. Physiology was divided among grades VII, VIII, and IX, and not concentrated in grade VIII. Furthermore, physiology topics were made to fit more appropriately the respective units. Thus bones and muscles were the physiological basis of the unit on posture. The following phases were made constant in all three grades, food, alcohol and tobacco, safety and first aid, mental health, and vacations. Personal hygiene was recommended for grade nine. Omission of vocational hygiene was considered as it was thought that personal hygiene would cover this phase sufficiently. The special senses were found too difficult for grade eight and more appropriate for the unit on personal hygiene in grade nine.

Out of the experience of this experimental teaching grew the necessity for realigning certain topics and for a more exhaustive study of the content. A course of study committee was then appointed by the superintendent to work under the direction of the supervisor of health education to further the "Working Outline" into a tentative course of study. The organization of this committee consisted of two groups.

---
[12]"A Working Outline in Health Education for Grades VII, VIII, IX," Boston School Dept. Boston.

The construction committee, composed of representatives from intermediate and senior high schools, was responsible for the actual construction. This committee worked in subcommittees according to grades developing objectives, content, activities, problems, references and the philosophy underlying the program. The supplementary committee composed of representatives from fields allied to health education acted in an advisory capacity to the construction committee. This cooperative undertaking made for a better understanding of the objectives of each field and prevented unnecessary overlapping of content.

In setting up the most desirable type of organization the committee agreed on the unit plan, with each unit allotted to an appropriate time for completion. This time element was one of the results of the experimental teaching. Furthermore it was suggested by a majority of the teachers in answering the questionnaire. Each unit began with the title and unit aim, followed by the specific objectives and basic activities. The course had table of contents, a list of the committees, and the Massachusetts Education Laws referring to health instruction and training. The teaching units followed, organized by grades. At the rear of the course a bibliography of pupil and teacher texts was added.

The following units represent the contents of the completed Tentative Course of Study as it is in use now:

Course of Study by Grades

GRADE VII
- Unit I — Health Education in School and other Public Buildings
- Unit II — Planning Time
- Unit III — A Model Home
- Unit IV — Health Education in the Neighborhood
- Unit V — Elementary First Aid
- Unit VI — Effects of Alcohol, Tobacco and Patent Medicines
- Unit VII — Vacation Time

GRADE VIII
- Unit I — Introduction to Year's Work
- Unit II — Posture and Its Needs
- Unit III — Nutrition
- Unit IV — The Digestive System
- Unit V — The Circulatory System
- Unit VI — The Nervous System and Mental Health
- Unit VII — Vacation Time

GRADE IX
- Unit I — Importance of Health
- Unit II — Mental Health
- Unit III — Personal Health
- Unit IV — Diet
- Unit V — Drugs, Tobacco, Alcohol and Narcotics
- Unit VI — Bacteria and Preventable Diseases
- Unit VII — Health Heroes
- Unit VIII — Safety
- Unit IX — First Aid
- Unit X — Public and Private Health Agencies

The supervisor supplemented this course with teaching aids. The list consisted of films, prepared simple experiments, models, graphs, and a library of approved source material. The films, with projectors and screens, prepared experiments, and charts are furnished the teachers on request. The library of approved source material is in the hands of each health education teacher. In addition the master of each school purchases the textbooks and other aids from his per capita allowance.

Thus the course of study, suitable texts and desirable teaching aids serve as a criterion of how one large school system is solving the health education program in the junior high school grades.

TABLE I

Grade Placement in Health Topics in Junior High Schools

Topics Of Health Teaching	A	B	C	D	E	F	G	H	I	J
Bones	7	8	–	–	8	7	8	8	7	7
Budgeting Time	–	7	7	–	–	–	–	–	–	–
Cells	7	8	–	–	–	–	7	9	–	–
Circulatory System	7	8	8	8	8	8	8	7	7	7
Cleanliness	–	7	7	–	7	–	–	7	–	–
Clothes	–	–	9	–	9	–	7-8	9	–	7
Community Hygiene	9	7	9	7	7	7	7	7	7	8
Digestive System	7	8	8	8	8	8	8	7	8	8
Disease—Bacteria	9	–	9	8	9	–	–	9	8	8
Fresh Air—Sun	–	7	–	–	7	7	7	7	–	–
Food	8	8	8	7	9	7	8	8	8	8
Health Heroes	9	7	8	8	9	–	–	9	8	8
Home Hygiene	7	–	7	7	7	8	–	7	–	7
Home Nursing	8	–	9	–	–	–	–	9	–	–
Industrial Hygiene	9	–	9	–	9	–	–	9	–	8
Joints	7	8	–	–	8	–	8	–	–	–
Mental Health	9	–	–	–	7	–	–	9	–	7
Muscles	7	8	8	8	7	7	8	8	7	7
Narcotics-Tobacco-Alcohol	9	–	7-8-9	7	7-8-9	–	7-8	7-8-9	7-8	8
Nervous System	8	8	9	–	8	8	8	8	8	8
Personal Hygiene	9	7	7	–	9	–	7	7	–	–
Rest-Sleep-Exercise	8	7	8	7	7	7	7	8	8	8
Posture	8	8	8	8	7	8	8	8	7	7
Respiratory System	7	8	7	8	9	7	8	7	7	7
Safety	8	7	7-8-9	7	8	7	7-8	8	7-8	7
First Aid	9	7	7-8-9	7	8	8	7-8	8	7-8	–
School Hygiene	7	7	7	–	8	–	–	–	7	7
Skin	8	8	9	7-8	7	7	7	9	–	–
Special Senses	8	8	9	8	9	8	–	9	8	8
Vacation Time	–	7	7-8	–	–	–	–	–	–	–

HEALTH EDUCATION AND OUR HIGH SCHOOL GIRL

ALBERTINE P. MCKELLAR

Public Health Education Worker
Massachusetts Department of Public Health

The high school girl, contrary to the rather prevalent opinion of many, is genuinely and sincerely interested in health — certainly not health merely for the sake of health, but as one girl said — "I want to be physically fit for my play and for my work so that I can get enjoyment and happiness out of life." Yes, the high school girl everywhere, whether in the large city or in the smallest of our rural towns, wants more than anything else, to be well, to have her beloved pep and a zest for living. She is, when once her interest has been aroused, not only eager to learn but enthusiastic in the application of the new knowledge. Especially is this so if some particularly desired result has become manifest — just the slightest amount of encouragement serves as an impetus that oftentimes involves almost unbelievable changes in habits.

The problem then in dealing with our high school girl is one of proper approach. The just exactly right entre must be made in order to penetrate that impregnable wall of sophistication and reach through the barrier of the know-it-all attitude. She will not tolerate methods used previously upon her in the grades, she refuses to be impressed in the slightest way by warnings or finger pointings of fear — she doesn't care to be bothered about studying the bodily functions or structure. We have failed, somehow, in our teaching, to make the health rules real vital life rules. She knows them, can glibly recite them, but almost invariably she utterly does not grasp the fact that after all by actually doing these simple things that she knows — has known for years — she could doubtless realize many of the desires nearest her heart. This chatter about milk and vegetables, plenty of sleep, not only seems childish but bores her. And she is most decidedly "fed-up" with any mention of health as most vividly illustrated by the groan — fairly stifled to be sure — but nevertheless always present, whenever a speaker is introduced to talk on health. But oh! the wide-eyed interest, the scribbling of notes, the literal swallowing of hook, line and sinker that accompanies any discussion relating to charm, to personal attractiveness, to protecting the smile, to the complexions, even to the curves of the high school girl! Tied up to any of those subjects the dull, despised health rules become new and alluring.

Food in relation to white gleaming teeth, and firm pink gums, to clear, glowing complexions, to bright, alive eyes, to glistening, silky hair, to well-built bodies free from sickness means something in the language that the high school girl speaks and understands. "Milk isn't half bad especially since I really had fewer cavities this last trip to the dentist and I've actually learned to eat spinach — remember all the iron in it!" Another one says, "There must be something to this line about more water — I tried it and several of the other things — a couple of fruits and raw vegetables and dark bread, and say! my constipation has really cleared up — no pills now for nearly three weeks. I've gone to bed earlier too, just sort of an experiment to see if it would make any difference and even though I loathe to admit it — when I get up in the morning I feel much more peppy as though going through the day would be fun. And parting with my daily after-school sundae and my candy lunch must have helped to dry up all my pimples. Am I thrilled with my new face. That alone is worth the trouble of doing some of the things I've known I should do for a long time."

Posture, discussed in the same breath with attractiveness, with poise and personality comes from the depths of boredom to the heights of enticement. Every girl is keen to look her very best and she knows that round shoulders or a drooped head or a protruding "middle" can ruin the best looking outfit she could possibly possess. Realizing that good posture is the net result of health, striving for better muscles and better muscular control is easier, after having got the "feel" of good posture and seen the difference in a full length mirror, especially when the looks of the new knitted suit is improved.

The vastly important question of sleep and rest involves tremendous problems that are not easily solved. Not only the gigantic demands upon the girls' mere twenty-four hours a day, but the customs and practices of the whole family complicate the situation. She knows that fatigue is an overwhelming obstacle to charm and when once she realizes that her vitality, her resistance to disease, her precious pep itself and the joy of living depend upon adequate sleep and rest she tries, to the best of her ability, to plan her activities, her homework, her dates, so that precious moments can be snatched for occasional rest and enough time left over for sleeping.

The precarious subject of personal cleanliness can be discussed in greatest detail when it is considered as the foundation of good grooming. Questions to do with charm, personal attractiveness, as well as with popularity, cannot help but include mention of scrupulous cleanliness—cleanliness of body, hands, hair and teeth.

These ideas were incorporated into a plan called the "Charm School" which has worked most successfully with the high school age girl in the 4H clubs. This organization, permeated with an indescribable eagerness to do, aroused by the common devotion to 4H ideals and standards, is a fine fertile field for experimentation. The fact that the girls are in 4H Club work asserts confidently the presence of sincerity, of ambition, and of eagerness — according to their slogan — "To make the best better." The plan consisted of two meetings some eight or ten weeks apart. At the first, the real meaning of the word charm is discussed in general, and in particular in relation to food, posture and grooming. Each girl in three individual conferences gives consideration to the quality and quantity of her diet. She writes the food that she has eaten for the past three meals and the nutritionist makes definite recommendations for improvement. Next, she meets the physical education instructor and her posture is examined. She is put into correct standing posture and special exercises are often suggested. And then her attention is called to good grooming, when the health education worker helps her with suggestions for care of the skin, hair, hands and teeth and with the selection and appropriateness of her costume. A score card is used, simply to indicate to the girl the amount of improvement made. Almost unbelievable changes have been made by the second meeting when the girls go through the same procedure of individual conferences. Cleared complexions, cleaner teeth, nicely manicured nails in place of bitten stubs, good looking low-heeled school shoes, improved posture are a few of the improvements that helped to create a noticeable general impression of good grooming and happiness.

This same plan was used with the girls coming to a social center from one of the most crowded sections of Boston. These girls, much older and very much more experienced, seem to grasp for individual help as eagerly as did their younger sisters — "Perhaps some of this will help me to get and to keep a job."

A group of unemployed girls were invited to attend a series of meetings by one of our private organizations. The Charm School material was presented in four meetings, the secretary was dubious about the attendance, but each time after the first, the room was filled and at the request of the girls the series were stretched to include two extra sessions.

In surroundings, very different from those described, the magic of charm again helped to improve health, and this time to give new interest and enjoyment to living that, at its best, takes spunk. In one of our sanatoria the girls, about high school age, from their beds and wheel chairs discussed the very same attributes, asked the very same kind of questions, showed the very same interest as their more active, but certainly no less enthusiastic, contemporaries.

In the more formal surroundings of the classroom a course in health education centering around the complexion can be planned to include essentials in physiology and hygiene. Beginning with the art of make-up, going through the construction and function of the skin, into circulation, digestion, assimilation and the nervous system. Again, health education material can be presented in relation to dieting—the study of the normal safe diet as compared to those of various faddists, and here is all the fascinating study of foods, their composition, their use in the body. "Protect your smile" is another possibility, bringing opportunity for almost endless discussion of nutrition, of home care, of care by the dentist in relation to dental health. At the end of courses similar to those outlined, in unsigned statements, over 95 per cent of the girls have always said that they have actually put into practice some of the theory discussed in class. Usually they say that they have improved in caring for their teeth, in their food habits and in their posture. Frankly they often say that an earlier bed time is just impossible, or that they just can't manage to get more sleep or rest.

In answer to the question, "What would you like a course in health education to include?" we hear: "I want to learn all about the skin." "Why do I have a toothache?" "Do high heels really hurt?" "Are there really bad diseases?" "Is it worse for girls to smoke than for boys?" "What about drinking?" "I hope to learn how to live better so that sometime I can be a healthy, intelligent mother."

They want to know and we want, to the best of our abilities, to tell them. Can we reach them, secure their confidence and help to prepare them for a world that is less safe, more difficult, more unstable than any woman has heretofore had to face — a world that not only demands that a woman be accomplished in domestic arts and social graces but be capable of earning a living as well.

PARENT EDUCATION IN ITS RELATION TO NURSERY SCHOOLS
Mrs. T. Grafton Abbott
Consultant in Child Management
Massachusetts Department of Education

For many years mothers have labored under the delusion that they were regarded as omniscient and should automatically know the solution of all children's problems simply because of the fact that they had borne offspring.

Times have changed rapidly in most respects but in regard to the training of parents for their jobs there has been, until recent years, little headway made. If you were to qualify for this profession (provided you considered it as such), I am sure you would not receive either a certificate or a diploma based on any training you might have received prior to marriage.

With the advent of Mental Hygiene, great progress has been made and parents are now not only willing to admit their fallibility in dealing with a problem in child management, but far more to their credit, they are coming seeking aid and guidance. Mothers may try to excuse Willie's bad temper on the score that "he is just like his father" but they are beginning to realize that this is not the correct answer and that people are at last seeing through their easy "alibi."

This new interest in Parent Education is spreading like wildfire. We see in that, too, some danger spots, as many parents not only feel their lack of knowledge but have developed as well feelings of guilt for their inadequacy. They should not, of course, take this attitude, but as we all know "a little learning is a dangerous thing."

Another group of young intelligent mothers is beginning to worry lest every symptom and manifestation "has a meaning all its own." They are very apt, in their zealousness, to magnify the unimportant and to notice too much. This is to be deplored.

One very hopeful sign, we observe, is the genuine eagerness on the part of *all* parents to gain further knowledge about their children.

Parent Education, as undertaken by the State Department of Education in Massachusetts in connection with the Emergency Education Program, centered about the Nursery Schools which were established in the State through Federal funds.

The objectives of the program were twofold: to help the parents of preschool children gain a better understanding of their children's problems, and to give to teachers on the job further knowledge of some of the mental hygiene principles underlying child management, thereby helping them to develop a technique in the handling of difficult situations as they might arise.

One very interesting fact in connection with the work in the State was that there could be found in any one given group of parents all ranges of educational opportunities, from the college graduate to the foreign born, having in common the keen desire to know more about the training and management of their children.

Another fact of interest was the difference in economic status in any given group, those with means mingling with people on the welfare and no class distinction of any sort being made when it came to a consideration of their children's needs. The eagerness for information cannot be overstated.

Many mothers attended these group meetings who had never previously come out for any meeting in connection with the schools. In a great many places permanent groups of mothers of preschool children have been organized. We are glad to reach the parents of little children so that we may start them early in a knowledge of habit training, discipline, and family attitudes, the points which our State program so strongly stressed. The needs of these parents are being met, the group discussions are along the lines of their interest, and various problems are taken up which most of the parents encounter in the training of their children.

We hope to develop, throughout the State, leaders in Parent Education who will be able to organize and lead study groups of mothers and fathers in their own communities.

Posters (thirty of them) were made under the direction of the Consultant, showing various problems in habit training, discipline and family attitudes, with rather specific suggestions given in the captions under the picture illustrating the point. We are greatly indebted to the Department of Public Health for their help in this connection and to Dr. Diez in particular for her never-failing interest and enthusiasm.

The posters have had a very wide showing already and have been on exhibition in many states. As a means of visual education we find them most effective, especially in working with the foreign born.

A handbook entitled "Guiding Principles of Child Management for Teachers" with suggested questions in working with parents, has been worked out and used extensively in the seminars held for teachers in different localities.

Only those places were visited which so requested this service through their superintendent of schools.

The work has been fascinating and of great interest. It is the type of work for which there is perpetual need. It offers both an opportunity and a challenge for service to those who are most eager to receive it.

One mother after a discussion group meeting said, "That lady saved my Willie from a beating." So if we did nothing else, at least we are justified as far as Willie is concerned.

The preschool children are also educating their parents through their Nursery School programs. One child said to his mother, "If you will say 'please' to me, I will say 'thank you'."

So who shall say that this effort is not in the right direction? We look for the answer, not in a few neurotic parents we may have gathered on the way, but in those eager conscientious, intelligent mothers who are clamoring at our doors for the help which should not be denied them.

HEALTH EDUCATION IN MASSACHUSETTS AS PICTURED BY 1933 STATISTICS

FREDRIKA MOORE, A.B., M.D.
Consultant in School Hygiene
Massachusetts Department of Public Health

Every other year superintendents, high school principals, nurses and dental workers fill out cheerfully or otherwise one of those destroyers of happiness, a questionnaire.

How much good cheer goes into the response is problematical, but plenty, if number and promptness of returns is an indication. In return there is sent out a summarized report of the figures which show, as far as figures can, certain facts about the school health programs in the State, so any place knowing its own figures can compare them with the figures for the State as a whole.

The reports are full of the meat which furnishes food for reflection for those who like to reflect. So much of this earnest reflection has been given to health education during the past year that a study has been made of the figures to see what information they would yield on State-wide practices in health education, "health education" here being used to mean not health instruction alone, but all educational procedures connected with the school health program.

The communities have been divided into groups:

	Population
Group I (a)	Cities 25,000 and above
Group I (b)	Cities 10,000 — 25,000
Group II	Towns 5,000 — 10,000
Group III	Towns under 5,000

Out of 355 questionnaires sent to superintendents, 317 were returned.

Like all other programs, that of health must depend, no matter how devoted the workers, to some extent upon money spent. Here the depression has apparently not seriously curtailed the budget. For health, exclusive of salaries of physical education teachers and money spent for sanitary buildings, the following amounts were spent per school child:

Group I (a) $2.50	Group II $1.22
Group I (b) 2.28	Group III 1.90

For $2.50 per child a large city can provide a very satisfactory health program with a full staff of physicians and nurses adequately paid for time enough to make their work educational, with several supervisors of health education, with clerical assistance for the professional workers, and yet have enough left for travel and supplies. This amount does not cover psychologists, dental hygienists, nutritionists, visiting teachers, etc.

It is a reasonable assumption then from the above table that the cities are able to finance a program where the doctors can take time to examine the children individually without hurry, talking to them during the examination in such a way that the procedure will create a desire for sound bodies and a willingness to do everything necessary to attain them.

The lesser amount spent by the towns permits a fairly adequate medical and nursing service with clerical help, but not much service from health education supervisors or other specialists. There is, therefore, an even stronger obligation upon doctor and nurse to make their work educational.

With, then, sufficient money being spent to provide a good minimum program, let us see if other figures show how far the program is educational. One of the chief functions of the nurse is to act as friend and teacher in the home. About half of her time should be devoted to this part of her work. This raises the question as to how many children a nurse can be expected to care for. The answer is about 2,000 for a full-time nurse. Of course, distance to be traveled, nature of the population, etc., have a bearing upon the question.

Actually, according to the replies, the numbers are as follows:

Average Number of Pupils Per Nurse

| Group I (a) | .... 2,100 | Group II | .... 1,600 |
| Group I (b) | .... 2,250 | Group III | .... 325 |

In Group III, the nurses are, naturally, on part time. According to the time of employment, even 325 children might be too many but as a matter of fact this does not happen. From these figures, it seems that the city nurses must be sufficiently hard pressed for time to make it necessary to choose between one activity or another and the question naturally arises as to which activity is curtailed. The better the educational background of the nurse the less likely is this to be the educational aspect of her work. Appreciation by the communities of the importance of training in relation to good service is shown as follows:

Number of Places Requiring the Following Qualifications of Their School Nurses

	Group I(a)	Group I(b)	Group II	Group III
Graduate Nurse	17(68%)	7(58%)	57(74%)	130(64%)
Registered	17(68%)	7(58%)	51(66%)	130(64%)
High School Diploma	4(16%)	2(16%)	18(24%)	39(18%)
Public Health Training	3(12%)	1(8%)	24(31%)	49(24%)
Training in School Nursing	3(12%)	2(16%)	14(18%)	34(16%)

These educational standards are not such as to be a matter of pride. Fortunately the percentage (83%) of graduate nurses working in the schools is higher than the standards indicate, but the educational background, apart from professional training required is surprisingly low for professional people who are required to meet teachers on their own ground.

It is true that classroom instruction in healthful living is primarily the teacher's job, but the teacher must depend upon the nurse for reference material and for assistance with content. A few people are "born teachers", but by and large the nurse who has not finished high school is suffering under a handicap and the town that employs her will suffer in its health education program. The nurse may compensate by a high degree of technical skill but prevention and education are the raison d'etre for a school health program.

For this reason school physicians also must add something to professional skill in detecting departures from the normal, that something being an understanding of child psychology with the ability to make their contacts with the school educational.

In Massachusetts the average number of children per physician is 1634, not too many to permit careful work. The time given to each child averages:

| Group I (a) | ...4 minutes | Group II | .....5 minutes |
| Group I (b) | ...6 minutes | Group III | .....5 minutes |

time enough for the encouraging or stimulating word.

In addition to this incidental teaching which means so much there should be more formal instruction in healthful living. It appears from the questionnaires that in Massachusetts 45 minutes per week is the average time given below Junior High School, in Junior High, 58 minutes. When it comes to Senior High, the situation is not so favorable. Healthfully speaking this is the forgotten group.

Two hundred and fifty questionnaires were sent to high school principals and 227 were returned and, alas, "the noes have it". No health course, 74%, and this is in spite of the fact that it is required by law. Where the course is given, the time allotted is as follows:

1 period ......20 places	4 periods ...... 3 places
2 periods ...... 3 places	5 periods ......20 places
3 periods ...... 2 places	

As to the year in which it is given, sophomore is the favorite with 19 aces; freshman with 12; junior with 8; senior with 11; and all years with 7.

The course is required in only 31 places. Instruction is by the physical education teacher in 12 places, by the nurse in 10. In the rest the responsibility is scattered.

When it comes to correlated health teaching, there is a more enthusiastic response. Practically all schools have it in connection with one or all of the following subjects in the order of frequency: Biology, General Science, Physical Education, Home Economics, Civics. Twenty-eight places have faculty health councils and twelve, students health councils.

Comment

1. Probably everyone will concede that the educational is the most important aspect of the school health program.

2. The average expenditure for health is sufficient for a good minimum program.

3. We know from continued observation of the nursing service that the majority of the nurses are doing earnest, conscientious work, but some are handicapped as members of a school system by lack of educational background. It is most decidedly the responsibility of the organized nursing profession to raise its standards but this does not absolve school committees from their responsibility in requiring high standards of education for the personnel in their schools.

4. More nursing service is needed in the city schools.

5. Since a greater amount of money is spent in the cities, the natural inference is that their school health programs are superior to the smaller places. This does not seem to be so.

6. The part-time doctor has on an average a small enough group in his charge to permit careful individual examinations. If he is hurrying or making wholesale examinations, the school committee should see that certain standards are made clear and that compensation is adequate for carrying them out.

7. The time allotment for health instruction is adequate up to senior high school.

8. Healthfully speaking, the senior high student is the forgotten child.

9. Hygiene is by law a required subject but is not taught in approximately three-fourths of the communities. It is the right of the high school graduate to have been prepared to earn a living, to perform the duties of citizenship, to found a family and to get satisfaction from life. Health as the result of healthful living personally and as a member of a family and of a community is fundamental. Health habit training in the grades is not sufficient. An elementary school child is not mature enough to grasp the implications of adult living.

10. Some correlated health teaching is carried on in practically all high schools.

11. The health education of the high school group requires serious consideration by school officials.

FRANKLIN COUNTY DEMONSTRATION
1927 - 1933

SUSAN M. COFFIN, M.D.
Consultant in Child Hygiene
Massachusetts Department of Public Health

In 1927 the Massachusetts Department of Public Health decided to conduct a Well Child Conference Demonstration in one county. Franklin County was chosen for this purpose, as it seemed to offer excellent opportunity for intensive teaching of child hygiene in an area containing both rural and small town communities. A preliminary study showed that many child health problems common to such communities all over the State existed. Need of more intensive teaching in the care of infants and preschool children, and need of guidance in using all available sources for child health and protection were the items specially noted.

Local nursing service, was, and still is, by no means adequate in all the towns served, but there was enough to make it reasonable to expect that a fair amount of nursing follow-up could be done, and such has proved the case in most instances. In fact, one aim of the conference service was to arouse interest in the need and value of generalized nursing service in all the communities.

It was planned to hold a yearly Well Child Conference in each of the twenty-six towns, except Greenfield, for a five-year period. This plan had to be modified to the extent of allowing six years for the five visits as they could not be completed in exactly five years. Greenfield was omitted because it already had an established health program. The ages of the children to be admitted to the demonstration conference were six months to six years. Of course, younger infants did often come, as mothers could not leave home without them.

One mother sent her two weeks' old baby with an obliging neighbor who was bringing her own four or five children with the message that she was "so sorry", she was not equal to coming herself, but she did not want the baby to "miss it!"

Population in the towns to be thus served ranged from little Monroe with a population of 173 to two towns with a population over 5,000. Total population of the twenty-five towns to be served was about 34,000. The occupations of most of the families seen were either farming, factory work, or small business interests, with the usual group of professional and larger business people found in New England towns.

As the Well Child Conferences were opened to every family in every town, attendance proved to be a good cross section of the population. Children from the families of the ministers, teachers, farmers, factory workers, store keepers, day laborers, all came, and the parents found they had many problems in common.

Nationalities were American, Polish, French, with a sprinkling of Italians and others.

One township might have several villages which sometimes necessitated holding the conference in more than one locality in order to overcome transportation difficulties. Help on transportation was frequently needed and was provided in part by local committees and obliging neighbors and sometimes by the State nurse's car. Frequently the fathers were away at work and the family Ford or horsedrawn vehicle was not available to bring mother and children to the clinic. The time for the conference was restricted as the roads had to be considered in many localities, except in the summer months. Even then, as late as July one year, chains were necessary to get the State car over the hill roads! Also the seasonal work of the people had to be taken into consideration, as many families felt they could not take "time off" for the conference during onion or berry picking, for example, especially as times grew hard and work was greatly needed.

In each town constant effort was made to form a permanent local committee representing the local official and nonofficial organizations, board of health, school committee, church, Grange, men and women's clubs, Parent-Teacher Association, etc. This was done through the combined efforts of the State Consultant Nurse and the State Department Health Education Worker with the local nurses and other interested persons. These committees have proved invaluable and are still "carrying on" in many instances. They often did most excellent work arranging for the place of the conference, assisting at the conference and in many cases making a house-to-house canvass to register the preschool children and interest the parents in the project.

Conferences were held in a great variety of places which oftentimes called for considerable ingenuity in arrangements for the workers and mothers. Church and town hall kitchens were especially coveted because of available running water and heat. Private homes were quite frequently offered for the use of the conferences and are associated in the minds of the workers with some very pleasant memories of New England hospitality. In one town the tiny village "lock-up" seemed to be the only convenient place and being centrally located, and on a level with the sidewalk, it proved quite satisfactory.

At first the idea of having a "well" child examined seemed almost ridiculous to many parents. The mother who spoke with most pride when she came to one of the conferences, was the one who was able to say, "My child has never seen a doctor since the day he was born."

An interesting change of thought often took place as subsequent visits were made to the conferences. Many parents grew to realize keenly the value of yearly examination and correction of defects. Frequently reports showed also how much earlier the family physician was being consulted when a child was ill or had suffered an accident. Perhaps most appreciated was the nutrition teaching, which helped mothers in buying and using food to the best advantage for the whole family. The remarks "I wish the conference came oftener", and "If only I'd known these things with my first baby", were heard at every session.

As in all Well Child Conferences, every child with defects was referred to the family physician and dentist for treatment. No medical treatment was suggested, but vaccination, diphtheria immunization and X-ray of tuberculosis contacts were urged in all cases where necessary. The individual record of each child examined was sent to the family physician year by year and every local physician received a notice and an invitation to visit the conferences. The physicians were also visited personally, by members of the staff from time to time, to get their opinion of the work being done.

Later, when a full-time dental hygienist was added to the Well Child Conference Unit, the same procedure was followed out in regard to the local dentists, also arrangements were made with the organization sponsoring the traveling dental service for schools in Franklin County to include as many of the preschool children as possible, and the service so obtained was largely responsible for the dental corrections made. The percentage of dental defects was frequently appalling there, as elsewhere.

The linking up of causative factors in dental and nutritional faults progressed steadily throughout the Demonstration and is felt to be one invaluable result of this piece of work. The point of emphasis shifted rapidly in dealing with all types of physical defects from simply finding defects and urging their correction, to actual prevention. We tried to make clear the value of a balanced diet and careful training from the baby's first week of life to help prevent the occurrence of defects, particularly those of nutrition and teeth, and with the older child we emphasized again the value of the same procedures to both prevent and arrest such conditions.

As these mothers so often brought the "new baby" along with the two and three year olds, there was a vivid opportunity to drive these lessons home and, too, each worker in turn brought up the importance of the mother's own health, particularly during the prenatal, postnatal and nursing periods. It is a mystery why so many women appear to accept with resignation such ills as loss of teeth, poor nutrition, pelvic injuries, etc. following child bearing. "But you have to expect these things," was the remark all too commonly heard among these mothers.

All of the towns had at least some school nursing service as required by law and eleven had a generalized nursing program under Red Cross supervision. Upon nursing follow-up by the local nurses, after the conference was over, depended the greater part of the results obtained, and this proved to be a problem of large proportions, especially in those towns having only school nursing. Nursing service gained steadily in quality during this five-year period in the majority of the towns.

Before each conference was held, the State Consultant Nurse met with the local nurse and the local committee, explained the aims of the Demonstration and helped with the preliminary planning for publicity, registration, and preparation for the clinic and the nursing follow-up. Publicity was soon found to be of very great importance and was carried on each year by means of house-to-house visits by local nurses or committee members, by talks, moving picture slides provided by the Department, local paper paragraphs, church announcements, and posters well distributed.

A preliminary publicity plan was also carried out. The State Health Education Worker spent at least two days in each town and when possible lived in one of the homes in order to get more closely in touch with the communities. In this way it was possible to visit all the leading people in each town, including members of the board of health, school committee, physicians, librarians and the presidents of all local organizations. Editors and newspaper correspondents were also interviewed and their help gained. Opportunities to speak to various groups were especially emphasized as important and included talks given to the Rotary Clubs, Kiwanis, Parent-Teacher Associations, Legion Auxiliary, Women's Clubs, "church supper" groups, one "quilting party", the Ladies' Aid Society and occasionally at a church service.

It was rather astonishing to discover how many organizations existed and how many social activities were going on in even the smallest communities, and it was early proved wise to guard against having conference dates conflict with other events.

The existing nursing service developed encouragingly along child hygiene lines during this period. Each year it stressed especially, more and more, the value of good nutrition in children as a protective measure.

As the work progressed a few more towns had generalized nursing service which, of course, helped enormously, but even today some quite large towns do not have such service. In those communities the school nurse frequently gave extra time to see the families after the conferences had been held. Sometimes an interested organization, such as the Women's Club, paid the local nurse for extra time in which to make follow-up calls on the families. At no time was it possible to obtain the amount of nursing service which would be needed for an ideal follow-up program, but all the same a large amount of such work was done and a great deal accomplished.

The number of physical defects shown by the children that were corrected in any one year did not look large on paper. But defects found one year and uncorrected that year were often attended to within the following two or three years, especially such defects as diseased or obstructive tonsils and adenoids and strabismus. "Depression" was on the way early in the game and was keenly felt before the Demonstration ended, which, of course, was a big handicap here, as elsewhere.

The principal aims of the Demonstration were as follows:
- To help arouse in each community a keener realization of the tremendous importance of good care of mother and child during the prenatal and nursing periods and the importance of infant and preschool hygiene.
- To find by physical examination what handicapping defects existed among infants and preschool children and to make clear the danger of neglecting such defects.
- To teach by demonstration and instruction the importance of right feeding and good habit training from birth on, and to show ways of accomplishing this with what resources were at hand.
- To start similar Well Child Conferences as local undertakings in those towns where it was a practical proposition.
- Finally, to learn by actual experience the best way to conduct such a demonstration in a town or county.

The procedure at the conferences was kept as simple as possible. Each child was weighed and measured, if cooperative, and had his history blank filled out by the consultant nurse. Physical examination by the doctor and dental hygienist followed. Discussion with the mother was an important part of the program. A large number of mothers were interested in requesting the prenatal and postnatal letters. So far as possible all their many questions were answered. Following the physical examinations, the nutritionist talked over the child's diet and eating habits with the mother or other relative present, and gave each suitable printed material to take home.

Special effort was made to have the children who were old enough to enter school the current year come to the conference in order that as many as possible might have their defects corrected before going to school. It was hoped in the beginning that a considerable number of children would be able to attend all five conferences, but the moving about of the families, many cases of illness, and a lack of interest in returning on the part of some parents, resulted in a small group who actually returned for each conference.

Changes in local nursing service also had a good deal to do with it as the "new" nurse often had not had time to visit the families before the conference and become acquainted with them. Some American mothers and many more Polish mothers needed such visits to make clear to them the need for yearly physical examination as this was very difficult for them to understand, especially if their children had shown no defects at the first examination. Many parents felt, too, that if the child was going to enter school within a year, it was not necessary to have examination as "everything would be fixed up" in school.

Of the 3,615 children seen during the Demonstration, 54 percent were examined once; 25 percent twice; 13 percent three times; 6 percent four times; and 2 percent had five examinations.

Defects

The defects found were checked on the State Well Child Conference Record and carefully tabulated later. Dental defects headed the list, and diseased or obstructive tonsils and adenoids came next; nutrition defects came third. Today we would doubtless emphasize more strongly dental defects as a part of nutrition failure and probably nutritional defects would be placed second, as has so often been the case in later work. (Economic distress had not, however, hit at nutrition as hard as in the last two years.)

Then followed skin, posture and other defects. No vision or hearing tests were made; habit difficulties such as abnormal bed wetting, prolonged sucking habits, temper tantrums, masturbation, were also noted and found to be of fairly common occurrence, but not limited to any special group, which was also true of the "fussy eaters".

Results

Correction of remediable defects depended on nursing follow-up and family interest and income. The greatest immediate obstacles encountered were lack of sufficient local nursing service-and a certain per cent of parents who could not grasp the need of correction of what often seemed to them unimportant defects. Financial difficulties were, of course, met frequently, but with a resourceful community nurse and parents who are cooperative, this obstacle can almost invariably be overcome.

The undernourished child who is "thin like his daddy", the child with nose and throat defects who "always has colds anyway", the child with strabismus who is "too young to bother with glasses", all are common examples of ignorance or neglect seen everywhere. The parents of these children needed much more teaching than they could receive at an annual Well Child Conference, and when adequate nursing follow-up was lacking, little was accomplished with them. There was, however, a very large group of interested parents eager to learn and to do.

The per cent of defects reported corrected year by year was 28 per cent the second year; 35 per cent the third year; 25 per cent the fourth year; and 34 per cent the final year. Many children who moved away and could not be followed directly were also found to have had their defects corrected when seen or heard from in other localities, but statistics were not compiled for this group.

Of the children who attended all five of the conferences, fifty-four were available for the special study made by a former member of the conference staff. Both the mothers and teachers of this little group were visited to learn what results could actually be ascertained.

The most encouraging thing obtained from this study was the fact that forty-two of the fifty-four mothers said the information obtained at the Well Child Conferences had been applied to the whole family. This is, of course, exactly what such a Demonstration hopes to accomplish — furnish instruction and material that will be of use to the family as a whole.

Two mothers of this small group said they saw no benefit in the conference service. Twenty-eight of the fifty-four children had had all defects corrected and sixteen had had partial correction. Eight others were under treatment or planned to have the needed medical or dental work done in the near future. All but five of the children had been to the dentist and all but one had had physical examination since being seen at the conference. Every child had been vaccinated and forty-one had had toxin antitoxin.

The twenty-eight children in this group who had had all defects corrected stood highest in behavior, attendance and scholarship, according to the teachers' reports, which, even in so small a group, seemed a fact of value. A teacher in speaking of one child whom we had examined five times and who had never shown any defects at the conferences said, "He is an outstanding child in every way."

Following the close of the Demonstration study (1933-1934), nine towns were financing their own Well Child Conferences and two towns were paying for a part of such service. In two towns a Summer Round-Up has been held for the entering school children and in one town a weighing and measuring clinic is being carried on by the nurse. Preschool administration of toxin antitoxin increased 50 per cent during the Demonstration period, not, of course, wholly due to this teaching but definitely aided by it.

Just a word in regard to records, reports and statistics. They are probably the least interesting part of an undertaking like this and they are certainly a great deal of work for all concerned, but they are extremely important. We learned that an adequate record sheet for each child to be examined, covering the whole number of years, is very essential and should be carefully worked out before starting. Brief narrative reports of each conference and a summary covering the nutritional, dental and statistical items, were made. These reports and summaries were necessary both for file reference and for use at later conferences and also at local committee and community meetings connected with the conference work.

What did we, the members of the Well Child Conference Unit, learn from our Franklin County experiences that would be of value to ourselves or others doing another similar piece of work? Condensed as much as possible, the following three things proved entirely essential to accomplishment:

Thorough preparation for every conference held, an interested local committee and nurse plus "good" publicity can accomplish miracles — almost!

Cooperation of all local official and private agencies and of the physicians and dentists. If cooperation is lacking from these necessary helpers, a plan of this sort had better be postponed until their interest and aid can be obtained (but never give up!).

Adequate nursing follow-up work, family visiting by competent and tactful nurses, as it is the only way we know of keeping in touch with the parents to encourage them and help them to find all available resources for the correction of defects.

Ignorance, indifference, poverty, these obstacles are always with us but they are not unsurmountable. We feel that there is no community in Massachusetts that is not capable of overcoming them for the sake of its children.

We could never tell the story of the Franklin County Demonstration without mention of Miss Mary Ayer, State Consultant Nurse for the Western District at the time of its inception and who, under the greatest of physical handicaps, worked so faithfully in its furtherance until she left us in 1930. Her pride and enthusiasm in this work sustained us all, State and community workers alike — and her gentle sense of humor brought us through smiling many a time! Her memory will remain when "demonstrations" are forgotten.

THE HEALTH FORUM*

HENRY D. CHADWICK, M. D., COMMISSIONER,
Massachusetts Department of Public Health
and
HERBERT L. LOMBARD, M. D., DIRECTOR,
Division of Adult Hygiene,
Massachusetts Department of Public Health

Whipple, in his "State Sanitation" published in 1917, said, "The Massachusetts State Board of Health has ever maintained a dignified and conservative attitude toward its publications, never having indulged in the use of cartoons, stories, or bright and catchy phrases, such as are found in many health bulletins; it has not 'written down' to what may be called the popular level, but has endeavored to instruct the physicians, believing that it was their province, in turn, to instruct the families to whom they minister, while it was for newspaper and magazine writers to present the facts of science in a form suitable for

---
*Printed with permission of the New England Journal of Medicine.

their readers. This has given to the publications of the Board a high scientific standing, which is better recognized in Europe, perhaps, than in this country."

Since that time, health departments, in general, have felt the need of going directly to the people with many problems, and the Massachusetts Legislature of 1929 amended the statutory duties of the State Department of Public Health to include dissemination of such information as it considers proper for diffusion among the people.

The Health Forum, started in 1930 as one other method for the dissemination of public health knowledge, was begun primarily as a radio project at W. E. E. I. After it was found that the newspapers would carry the questions and answers, it was adapted to both media of publicity. At the present time, it is printed in seventy newspapers.

A newspaper column, called the "Ways to Health," was started by the Department on February 24, 1919, and was published regularly until February 3, 1920. This column was limited to seven newspapers, and aroused much unfavorable feeling among physicians in the State. A successful and somewhat similar type of project regarding care of children, carried on by the Westchester County Children's Association, New York, was the incentive for the reestablishment of this form of publicity.

In the first year, 266 questions were received by the Health Forum; in the following year, 230; in the third year, 250; and in the year ending July 1, 1934, 617. The probable explanation for the great increase during the past year is the addition of the Boston Globe to the list of newspapers receiving the Forum, and a five minute Question Box on W. B. Z.

At the close of the first year, a review of the questions asked showed that the public was more interested in matters pertaining to disease than to public health. A large number of questions were of too personal a nature to be answered either through the newspaper or the radio, and personal letters were requested. The Department repeatedly attempted to curb such types of questions by reiterating that they could not be answered. As this did not suffice, the policy of the Department was changed.

Beginning in July, 1931, a foreword on some subject was prepared and the number of questions printed was decreased. This practice has continued to the present time. The Department also prepared questions on public health which were answered in place of many of the questions sent in.

In the four years of its existence, the Health Forum has received 1363 questions from the public. Diagnosis was requested by 253 individuals. Requests for the Department to outline treatment for a given disease was the substance of 361 letters. The Department was requested to furnish the name of a physician by 89 individuals and to outline a diet for a given disease by 114. Of the total 1363 questions, 817 or 60 per cent were outside the scope of the work of this Department.

From an educational standpoint, it is interesting to note which method of publicity stimulated the question. Our figures indicate 31 per cent radio, 22 per cent newspaper, and 47 per cent unknown. The unknown figure is so large that the information we have is not of great value. From such material as is available, considering that the unknown may have been reached by either newspaper or radio or possibly by both, it is felt that the radio and newspaper are probably of about equal weight. This, however, is by no means certain.

The average person asked 1.28 questions. Table I shows the method by which the questions were answered. As questions were answered by personal letter, by radio, or by the newspaper, or frequently by more than one of these media, the total number of answers given is much greater than the number of questions, and is 2232. Personal letters were sent to 972 individuals; the newspapers published 407 questions and answers; and the radio broadcast 853.

Wherever possible, questions have been answered by members of the Department, but about one-third of them (448) have been answered by specialists in various fields of medicine from whom the Department requested a reply.

Table II shows the type of questions asked in the Health Forum, the Ways to Health, the subjects of the Health Forum forewords, the subjects of literature requests, and the subjects of the Massachusetts Medical Society broadcasts. Although the latter broadcast is entirely separate from Health Forum activities, it is another way to instruct the public on medical matters, and there is a probability that some at least of the Health Forum questions were prompted by these talks.

In the May, 1934, issue of Hygeia appeared a list, in numerical order, of the twenty-five questions which were asked most frequently. A comparison of the questions received by the magazine with those received by the Department is shown in Table III.

Health Forum questions and requests for literature came from nearly half of the towns and cities in the State. The largest number came from Boston, Worcester, Springfield, Somerville, Lynn, Cambridge, and Brookline respectively. Sixty Health Forum questions originated outside of Massachusetts, but in New England; five in the United States, but outside of New England; and one came from outside of the United States. While questions came from widely separated geographical locations, the greater bulk of them were from eastern Massachusetts.

The Department has decided to change its policy again in regard to the Health Forum, as it has been found impossible to limit questions from the public to impersonal health matters. Beginning October 1st, no questions will be answered, and only discussions on timely topics will be used. In order to continue this as a Forum, the public will be invited to send in topics for discussion, and as many as seem practical will be used.

Table I.

Type of Answer Given to Health Forum Questions

August 1, 1930 — July 31, 1934

Personal letter	439
Newspaper	47
Radio	135
Letter and newspaper	12
Letter and radio	370
Newspaper and radio	197
Letter, newspaper, and radio	151
Unanswered as no address was given	12
Total	1,363

Table II.
Type of Information Sought

	Health Forum 1930-1934	Ways to Health 1919	Health Forum Forewords 1931-1934	Literature Requests 1933-1934	Mass. Medical Soc. Broadcasts 1931-1934
Accidents	1	2	3	0	4
Allergy	28	6	4	2	1
Anemia	14	2	0	1	1
Arthritis	131	6	5	223	2
Cancer	25	1	5	125	6
Cardiovascular renal disease	67	15	5	115	14
Communicable disease	0	1	3	3	2
Croup	0	2	0	0	0
Diabetes	20	1	5	28	2
Digestive diseases	99	20	4	47	5
Diphtheria	0	2	1	1	1
Endocrines	12	4	4	2	2
Erysipelas	1	0	1	0	0
Eye and ear diseases	21	14	1	2	5
Female genitals, diseases of	25	0	0	0	0
Genito-urinary diseases	20	2	0	0	0
Gonorrhea and syphilis	11	0	0	7	0
Hemorrhagic diseases	0	0	1	0	1
Hemorrhoids	9	2	1	5	1
Leprosy	0	0	0	1	0
Measles	0	1	3	3	2
Meningitis	0	0	2	0	1
Nervous and mental diseases	56	11	2	1	7
Nose, throat and mouth diseases	67	10	6	14	1
Nutritional diseases	0	1	2	0	0
Osteomyelitis, acute	0	0	1	0	0
Poliomyelitis, anterior	0	0	3	0	3
Rabies	0	1	3	2	1
Respiratory diseases, acute	10	12	7	8	5
Rheumatic fever	1	0	1	0	1
Scarlet fever	1	1	0	1	0
Skin, diseases of	146	37	4	8	0
Smallpox and vaccination	0	0	3	1	0
Trench fever	1	0	0	0	0
Tuberculosis	26	8	6	9	5
Typhoid fever	0	0	1	0	0
Varicose veins and phlebitis	16	2	0	1	0
Whooping cough	0	1	1	2	1
All other diseases	45	38	0	63	0
Total diseases	853	203	88	675	74
Symptoms given, asked diagnosis or treatment	253	99	0	0	0
Asked for doctor, no disease mentioned	25	7	0	0	0
Questions on normal diet and foods	73	51	12	283	6

Table II—Continued

	Health Forum 1930-1934	Ways to Health 1919	Health Forum Forewords 1931-1934	Literature Requests 1933-1934	Mass. Medical Soc. Broadcasts 1931-1934
Questions on drugs, cosmetics, and methods of therapy	43	21	0	1	4
Questions on public health, personal hygiene, and periodic health examination	60	89	52	379	41
Questions on body weight	34	22	0	0	2
Pregnancy	6	2	0	0	2
Headaches	0	0	1	0	1
Fatigue	0	0	2	0	2
Carbon monoxide gas	0	0	1	0	0
Hospitals	0	0	1	0	1
Quack doctors	0	0	2	0	3
Other questions	16	6	0	0	0
Total	510	297	71	663	62
Grand Total	1,363	500	159	1,338	136

Table III.
Comparison Between Hygeia and Health Forum Subjects

	Hygeia Order	Health Forum Order
Books and pamphlets	1	1
Diet and foods	2	5
Hair and scalp	3	39
Arthritis	4	6
"Beauty" questions	5	31
Sex	6	47
Drugs	7	20
Allergy	8	13
Physical therapy	9	44
Diseases peculiar to women	10	16
Constipation	11	31
Eyes and vision	12	26
Choosing a doctor	13	7
Diseases of heart and blood vessels	14	8
Mouth hygiene	15	11
Cancer	16	16
Ears and hearing	17	51
Infant and maternal hygiene	18	28
Tuberculosis	19	15
Cod liver oil preparations	20	0
Nose and sinuses	21	9
Diabetes	22	22
Thyroid gland and metabolism	23	31
Obesity and reducing	24	9
Acne and pimples	25	24

Editorial Comment

Visual Methods in Health Education. — If we differentiate between Health Propaganda and Health Education—and I think we ought to—the so-called Visual Aids appear in an altered light. When Public Health was concerned with crusades against insanitary conditions and unhygienic practices all the educational media—the poster, the exhibit, the demonstration, the stereopticon slide and the motion picture—had a prominent place in the educational program. When the objectives of Health Administration were to discourage spitting, sleeping in ill-ventilated rooms, the drinking of filthy milk and the like, the proposals could be dramatized in all the Visual Educational Mediums. The same was true when the aims had risen to a slightly higher level. We encouraged mothers to have their children vaccinated against smallpox and immunized against diphtheria through the same general publicity channels.

It is my conviction that the objectives of public hygiene are rapidly passing the broad propaganda stages not only in the matter of anti-spitting and the like, but in the immunization field as well. If this is true and we are approaching, or have reached, the stage when health education will be concerned largely with promoting good health habits on the part of the individual, the so-called Visual Aids become of less importance. If diet, rest and exercise are to be the objectives of health education, the individual must be given an understanding of the reasons for the health habits advocated and an opportunity to form the habits. Discussions of the physiological bases of good health habits do not lend themselves readily to the Visual Aid methods except in very limited applications.

A marked change is in evidence in modern educational mediums. For instance, instead of attempting to be a compendium of information, as the health poster of a decade ago did, the modern health poster is largely inspirational in nature attempting to make health attractive. (In a large collection of old and new posters I have some startling examples of this difference.) The same is true of the so-called health exhibit.

In the matter of motion pictures a similar trend is apparent. In the health propaganda days we had many agencies producing films designed to inspire parents to have their children immunized, etc. Most of these pictures are now antiquated in content and form, and are not being replaced by modern films. The conspicuous exception in the motion picture field is the Eastman Teaching Films. These, as you know, are designed to supplement the classroom teaching. They entail the study of a syllabus and require an explanation by the teacher. The examples which I have seen have satisfied me of the value of the Eastman Teaching Films, but I presume that their distribution is limited. Other than the Eastman Teaching Films I know of no new projects to extend the use of films as a method of health education.

A notable exception to all this is the use of posters, etc., in the waiting rooms of clinics, health centers, and the like. This is a special field, however, and I assume would not be of immediate interest to the majority of readers of The Commonhealth.—RAYMOND S. PATTERSON. Ph.D.

REPORT OF DIVISION OF FOOD AND DRUGS

During the months of April, May and June 1934, samples were collected in 225 cities and towns.

There were 1,643 samples of milk examined, of which 282 were below standard, from 27 samples the cream had been in part removed, and 16 samples contained added water. There were 103 samples of Grade A milk examined, 13 samples of which were below the legal standard of 4.00% fat. There were 1,298 bacteriological examinations made of milk, 1,031 of which complied with the requirements. There were 7 samples examined for hemolytic streptococci, 6 of which were negative and 1 positive.

There were 490 samples of food examined, 104 of which were adulterated. These consisted of 13 samples sold as butter which proved to be oleomargarine, colored; 1 sample of confectionery which was adulterated by the addition of paraffin; 6 samples of eggs which were sold as fresh eggs but were not fresh; 1 sample of vanilla extract which contained coumarin; 2 samples of lemon extract which were misbranded; 1 sample of maple syrup consisting in part of cane sugar syrup other than maple; 1 sample of cream puff which was sour; 1 sample of olive oil which contained cottonseed oil; 54 samples of hamburg steak, 13 samples of which contained sodium sulphite in excess of one tenth of one per cent and 6 samples were also decomposed, 36 samples were decomposed and 3 samples were also watered, 4 samples contained a compound of sulphur dioxide not properly labeled, and 1 sample was watered; 12 samples of sausage, 6 samples of which were decomposed, 4 samples contained color, 1 sample contained starch in excess of 2 per cent, and 1 sample contained a compound of sulphur dioxide not properly labeled; 11 samples of liver which were decomposed; and 1 sample of spice which was colored.

There were 5 samples of drugs examined, of which 3 were adulterated. These consisted of 2 samples of magnesium citrate, and 1 sample of spirit of nitrous ether, all of which did not conform to the U. S. P. requirements.

The police departments submitted 261 samples of liquor for examination. The police departments also submitted 25 samples to be analyzed for poisons or drugs, 9 samples of which contained heroin, 2 samples contained morphine sulphate, 3 samples contained opium, 1 sample contained caffein, 3 samples contained Cannabis indica, 3 samples were hop infusion, 1 sample contained ergot and oil of savin, 1 sample of yellow liquor was tested for arsenic with negative results, 1 sample was tested for alkaloids with negative results, and 1 sample of cigarettes was tested for added alkaloids with negative results.

There were 90 cities and towns visited for the inspection of pasteurizing plants, and 290 plants were inspected.

There were 62 hearings held pertaining to violations of the laws.

There were 90 convictions for violations of the law, $2,660 in fines being imposed.

Edgar S. Dimock of Oxford; Eugene Trahan of Westhampton; Frank Diani of Holliston; Eva Grechel of Ashfield; Hillside Dairy, Incorporated, of Marlborough; Stanley Malmosky of Bellingham; Winslow Chaffin of Brookfield; and Charles J. Duffy of Leicester, were all convicted for violations of the milk laws.

Herman Holder of Berlin; T. Dennehy & Sons of Quincy; Ernest Harnisch, 2 cases, and Fred Miller of Methuen; William C. Farrell and Napoleon Lavoie of Lowell; J. F. McAdams & Brothers of Chelsea; and Max Bookless of Pittsfield, were convicted for violations of the pasteurization laws and regulations.

Joseph W. Kirchner of Pittsfield was convicted for violation of the Grade A Milk Regulations. He appealed his case.

Big Bear Meat Department, Incorporated, and Atlantic Provision Company, Incorporated, of Somerville; Louis Market, Incorporated, of Webster; Growers Outlet, Incorporated, of Holyoke; Samuel Wernick of Roxbury; John A. Levy, 2 cases, Samuel Kline, 2 cases, Balkus Sausage & Provision Company, Louis Goldman, Israel Clebnik, M. M. Mades Corporation, and David Steinberg, all of Lynn; Abraham Horne, Herman Modest, Archie Alpert, Victor Alpert, and Cambridge Provision Company, all of Cambridge; Samuel Cohen, Harry Gillis, Chapin and Adams Corporation, John Freni, Frank S. Borgia, Irvin Kummel, G. Zuffante & Company, and James W. Ryan, 8 cases, all of Boston; E. Moro and C. Cavigicoti of Milford; Neck Market, Incorporated, 3 cases, and Alick Eidelman of Charlestown; Andrew Rutkowsky and Samuel Kaufman of Chelsea; City Provision Company, Incorporated, Aurila Filialt, Isaac Tillman, Main Street Market, Incorporated, 2 cases, Samuel Zimberg, and Abraham Askinas, all of Springfield; Renzo Moli of East Boston; Albert A. Leger, 3 cases, of Fall River; Chicopee Falls Public Market, Incorporated, 2 cases, and Harry Bellanger of Indian Orchard; Harry Weiner and Samuel Zellin of Allston; and Phillip Rosenberg of Dorchester, were all convicted for violations of the food laws. Louis Market, Incorporated, of Webster; Balkus Sausage and Provision Company, M. M. Mades Corporation, and David Steinberg, all of Lynn; Samuel Cohen, and James W. Ryan, 8 cases, of Boston; Allick Eidelman of Charlestown; Andrew Rutkowsky of Chelsea; City Provision Company, Incorporated, of Springfield; and Harry Weiner and Samuel Zellin of Allston, all appealed their cases.

City Provision Company, Incorporated, of Springfield was convicted for violation of the sanitary food law. This company appealed their case.

George Jamgochian of Somerville, and Spero Voudouris of Brookline, were convicted for false advertising.

Milton Brod of Springfield was convicted for misbranding.

Samuel Kidder & Company, Incorporated, of Charlestown; and Kimball Pharmacy, Incorporated, of Springfield, were convicted for violations of the drug laws.

B. Chesman & Son, Incorporated, of Boston was convicted for violation of the cold storage laws.

Salim Davis and Angelo Grasso of Agawam were convicted for violation of the slaughtering laws.

American Mattress Manufacturing Company of Boston; Eastern Mattress & Bed Spring Company of Lowell; Abraham Yaffa of Beverly; and Benjamin Cohen of Salem, were all convicted for violations of the mattress laws. Benjamin Cohen of Salem appealed his case.

In accordance with Section 25, Chapter 111 of the General Laws, the following is the list of articles of adulterated food collected in original packages from manufacturers, wholesalers, or producers.

Oleomargarine sold as butter was obtained as follows:

Two samples from Chapin & Adams, and one sample from Cudahy Packing Company, of Boston.

One sample of oleomargarine which was artificially colored was obtained from Albert Leger of Fall River.

One sample of lemon flavor which was misbranded was obtained from Broadway Sales Company of Boston.

One sample of maple syrup consisting in part of cane sugar syrup other than maple was obtained from Spero Voudouris of Brookline.

One sample of olive oil which contained cottonseed oil was obtained from Arthur Corey of Lawrence.

Liver which was decomposed was obtained as follows:

Two samples from Dakin's Market of Worcester; and one sample each, from Main Street Market, Incorporated, of Springfield; Louis Market, Incorporated, of Webster; Consumers Wholesale Food Company of

Southbridge; Christopher Perkins of Boston; Louis Zass of Fall River; City Public Market (Isador Solomon), and Brockelman Brothers of Gardner; Brockelman Brothers Market of Lawrence; and Kennedy's Market of Framingham.

Sausage which was decomposed was obtained as follows:
One sample each, from A. Gupposo & Company of Natick; Max Commans and New England Market, Incorporated, of Cambridge; Chicopee Falls Public Market, Incorporated, of Indian Orchard; and Abraham Askinas of Springfield.

Four samples of sausage which contained color were obtained from Balkus Sausage & Provision Company, Incorporated, of Lynn.

One sample of sausage which contained starch in excess of 2 per cent was obtained from Atlantic Provision Company of Somerville.

Hamburg steak which was decomposed was obtained as follows:
Two samples from Consumers Provision Company of Worcester; and one sample each, from Brockelman Brothers, North Main Market, Incorporated, Louis & Samuel Hodes, and Bernard Lerner, all of Worcester; Waltham Public Market of Waltham; Louis Rosenberg, Harry Gillis; Samuel H. Cohen, Star Market, Polly Wolf, and Max Most, all of Boston; People's Public Market of Fall River; City Public Market (Isador Solomon), and Brockelman Brothers, of Gardner; Myer Kronick of Orange; Main Street Market, Incorporated, Rood & Woodbury, Store at 1060 Main Street, and Auvila Filchrltz, all of Springfield; Harry Bellanger of Indian Orchard; Arthur Corey (Premium Market), and George Fairburn of Lawrence; Benjamin Stolzberg, Handy Dandy Store, Incorporated, and Parent Maloney, all of Haverhill; Harry Lampert of West Somerville; First National Stores of Somerville; Israel Clebnik and Samuel Kline of Lynn; Harry Weiner of Allston; Joseph Charness of Cambridge; and Abraham Sweet of Roxbury.

Hamburg steak which was decomposed and also watered was obtained as follows:
One sample each, from Benjamin Gross of Brookline; Waltham Provision Company of Waltham; and Neck Market, Incorporated, of Charlestown.

Hamburg steak which was decomposed and also contained sodium sulphite in excess of one tenth of one per cent was obtained as follows:
One sample each, from Allen's Market, Peter Gordon, Julius Smokler, and Ideal Market, all of Boston; and Rebecca Wernick of Roxbury.

Hamburg steak which contained sodium sulphite in excess of one tenth of one per cent was obtained as follows:
One sample each, from Polly Wolf and John Freni of Boston; Isaac Tillman of Springfield; Phillip Rosenberg of Dorchester; Joseph Charnas and Joseph Waldman of Roxbury; and Victor Alpert of Cambridge.

Hamburg steak which contained a compound of sulphur dioxide not properly labeled was obtained as follows:
One sample each, from Samuel Tallent of Springfield; Ettore Angelini of Fall River; Allick Eidelman of Charlestown; and Walter Needle of Dorchester.

One sample of hamburg steak which contained water was obtained from Alex Eidelman of Charlestown.

There were eight confiscations, consisting of 151 pounds of decomposed beef; 218 pounds of decomposed fowl; 13 pounds of decomposed cooked fowl; 44 pounds of decomposed pork; 1607 pounds of decomposed cooked pork in cans; 43 pounds of decomposed cut up turkey; 55 pounds of decomposed geese; and 215 pounds of decomposed moose meat.

The licensed cold storage warehouses reported the following amounts of food placed in storage during March, 1934:—688,260 dozens of case eggs; 521,243 pounds of broken out eggs; 328,564 pounds of butter; 980,121 pounds of poultry; 2,452,285 pounds of fresh meat and fresh meat products; and 4,011,371 pounds of fresh food fish.

There was on hand April 1, 1934:— 628,380 dozens of case eggs; 937,956 pounds of broken out eggs; 438,664 pounds of butter; 6,750,151¼ pounds of poultry; 7,606,616¾ pounds of fresh meat and fresh meat products; and 4,365,166 pounds of fresh food fish.

The licensed cold storage warehouses reported the following amounts of food placed in storage during April, 1934:—3,698,280 dozens of case eggs; 1,385,021 pounds of broken out eggs, 394,582 pounds of butter; 1,045,281 pounds of poultry; 2,104,702½ pounds of fresh meat and fresh meat products; and 4,199,979 pounds of fresh food fish.

There was on hand May 1, 1934:—4,213,830 dozens of case eggs; 1,514,398 pounds of broken out eggs; 346,259 pounds of butter; 4,622,785¼ pounds of poultry; 6,836,393½ pounds of fresh meat and fresh meat products; and 5,221,637 pounds of fresh food fish.

The licensed cold storage warehouses reported the following amounts of food placed in storage during May, 1934:—2,952,030 dozens of case eggs; 1,782,308 pounds of broken out eggs; 1,111,546 pounds of butter; 1,543,611 pounds of poultry; 4,168,414¼ pounds of fresh meat and fresh meat products; and 10,366,128 pounds of fresh food fish.

There was on hand June 1, 1934:—6,995,610 dozens of case eggs; 2,307,160 pounds of broken out eggs; 1,081,119 pounds of butter; 4,037,772¼ pounds of poultry; 7,771,061¼ pounds of fresh meat and fresh meat products; and 12,562,023 pounds of fresh food fish.

MASSACHUSETTS DEPARTMENT OF PUBLIC HEALTH

Commissioner of Public Health, HENRY D. CHADWICK, M.D.

Public Health Council

HENRY D. CHADWICK, M.D., *Chairman*

ROGER I. LEE, M.D. RICHARD P. STRONG, M.D.
SYLVESTER E. RYAN, M.D. JAMES L. TIGHE.
FRANCIS H. LALLY, M.D. GORDON HUTCHINS.

Secretary, ALICE M. NELSON

Division of Administration . . Under direction of Commissioner.
Division of Sanitary Engineering . Director and Chief Engineer,
   ARTHUR D. WESTON, C.E.
Division of Communicable Diseases Director,
   GAYLORD W. ANDERSON, M.D.
Division of Biologic Laboratories . Director and Pathologist,
   ELLIOTT S. ROBINSON, M.D.
Division of Food and Drugs . . Director and Analyst,
   HERMANN C. LYTHGOE, S.B.
Division of Child Hygiene . . Director, M. LUISE DIEZ, M.D.
Division of Tuberculosis . . Director, ALTON S. POPE, M.D.
Division of Adult Hygiene . . Director,
   HERBERT L. LOMBARD, M.D.

State District Health Officers

The Southeastern District .. RICHARD P. MACKNIGHT, M.D., New Bedford.
The South Metropolitan District . GEORGE M. SULLIVAN, M.D., Stoughton.
The North Metropolitan District . CHARLES B. MACK, M.D., Boston
The Northeastern District . . ROBERT E. ARCHIBALD, M.D., Lynn.
The Worcester County District . OSCAR A. DUDLEY, M.D., Worcester.
The Connecticut Valley District . HAROLD E. MINER, M.D., Springfield.
The Berkshire District ... WALTER W. LEE, M.D., No. Adams.

PUBLICATION OF THIS DOCUMENT APPROVED BY THE COMMISSION ON ADMINISTRATION AND FINANCE.
5000. 10-'34. Order 2595

THE COMMONHEALTH

Volume 21　　Oct.-Nov.-Dec.
No. 4　　　　1934

CANCER

MASSACHUSETTS
DEPARTMENT OF PUBLIC HEALTH

THE COMMONHEALTH

QUARTERLY BULLETIN OF THE MASSACHUSETTS DEPARTMENT OF
PUBLIC HEALTH

Sent Free to any Citizen of the State

Entered as second class matter at Boston Postoffice.

M. LUISE DIEZ, M.D., DIRECTOR OF DIVISION OF CHILD HYGIENE, EDITOR.

Room 545, State House, Boston, Mass.

CONTENTS

	PAGE
Foreword, Henry D. Chadwick, M. D.	215
Biopsy, Relation to Tumor Diagnosis, Shields Warren, M. D.	216
Bladder, Cancer of, Roger C. Graves, M. D.	217
Bone, Cancer of (Bone Sarcoma), Channing C. Simmons, M. D.	220
Brain, Cancer of, Gilbert Horrax, M. D.	225
Breast, Cancer of, Robert B. Greenough, M. D.	227
Cervix, Cancer of (Carcinoma of the Uterine Cervix), George A. Leland, Jr., M. D.	229
Clinic, Lowell Cancer, Lowell Clinic Staff	231
Educational Program on Cancer of the General Federation of Women's Clubs, Mary R. Lakeman, M. D.	232
Esophagus, Cancer of, Harris P. Mosher, M. D. and A. S. MacMillan, M. D.	234
Excerpts and Statistics on Cancer, Miss Frances A. Macdonald, A. B.	235
Eye, Cancer of (New Growths of the Eye), J. Herbert Waite, M.D.	244
Fundus, Cancer of (What the Physician Should Know about Cancer of the Fundus of the Uterus), Stephen Rushmore, M. D.	245
Historical Trends in Cancer, Miss Eleanor J. Macdonald, A. B.	247
Jaws, Cancer of, Varaztael H. Kazanjian, M. D.	265
Kidney, Cancer of, William C. Quinby, M. D. and Fletcher H. Colby, M. D.	269
Leukemias, Francis T. Hunter, M. D.	271
Lip, Cancer of, Ernest M. Daland, M. D.	274
Liver and Gall Bladder, Cancer of, Irving J. Walker, M. D.	278
Lung, Cancer of (Primary Carcinoma of the Lung), Edward D. Churchill, M. D.	279
Lymph Nodes, Cancer of (Primary Tumors of Lymph Nodes), Henry Jackson, Jr., M. D.	282
Mouth, Cancer of, Charles C. Lund, M. D.	284
Nasopharynx, Cancer of, Carl H. Ernlund, M. D.	286
Ovary, Cancer of, (Malignant Tumors of the Ovary, Joe V. Meigs, M. D.	289
Pancreas, Cancer of, Leland S. McKittrick, M. D.	291
Progress in Massachusetts Cancer Program, Henry D. Chadwick, M. D. and Herbert L. Lombard, M. D.	294
Prostate, Cancer of, George G. Smith, M. D.	299
Rectum and Colon, Cancer of, Daniel F. Jones, M. D.	301
Skin, Cancer of (Carcinoma of the Skin), Grantley W. Taylor, M .D.	304
Social Service in Cancer (Medical Social Service in the Cancer Clinic), Miss Eleanor E. Kelly	307
Stomach, Cancer of, Frank H. Lahey, M. D.	308
Thyroid, Cancer of (What the Physician Should Know about Cancer of the Thyroid), Howard M. Clute, M. D.	311
Report of Division of Food and Drugs, July, August and September, 1934	315

TO THE MEDICAL PROFESSION OF MASSACHUSETTS

The new policy of cancer control of the Massachusetts Department of Public Health has been perfected through the joint cooperation of the Department, the Cancer Committee of the Massachusetts Medical Society, the Massachusetts Branch of the American Society for the Control of Cancer, and many individual physicians and surgeons in the State.

This policy, which is outlined in this issue of "The Commonhealth" is based on the thesis that the practicing physician is the keyman in the cancer control movement. It is he who will first see the cancer case; it is he who must educate his patients to detect the early signs of the disease; it is he who must guide the patient to adequate therapy.

Group study is indicated in the diagnosis of cancer and the outlining of methods of treatment of the disease, for cancer is so complex a subject that the opinions of the surgeon, radiologist, and pathologist as well as that of the cancer specialist, are needed. The State-Aided Cancer Clinics in Massachusetts are prepared to furnish group diagnosis and advice on types of therapy as a consultation service for the physician.

The lay cancer committees of each town are to be known as the Cooperative Cancer Control Committees. They will arrange meetings, preferably in small groups, and invite the local physicians to discuss with them the subject of cancer.

This special issue of "The Commonhealth" has been prepared for physicians in the State to enable them to find easily accessible material on cancer, both for use in their general practice and for the preparation of short talks to the public.

HENRY D. CHADWICK, M. D.
Commissioner of Public Health

THE RELATION OF BIOPSY TO TUMOR DIAGNOSIS
By SHIELDS WARREN, M.D.
Boston, Massachusetts

When surgery was the only recognized treatment for malignant disease and when cases coming for treatment were practically all of advanced and obvious character, there was but little need for pathologic diagnosis based on examination of biopsy material. However, with the addition of X-ray and radium to the armamentarium of the practitioners treating cancer, and with the earlier appearance of the patients for treatment, often with lesions that cannot be definitely diagnosed in gross, the importance of pathological diagnosis has become much greater.

By biopsy we mean the removal of tumor tissue for the purpose of pathological diagnosis. Included in this definition should be the removal of entire nodules, such as a nodule from the breast or a polypoid mass from the rectum. The purpose of the biopsy is to guide treatment and give some idea as to prognosis.

In general, it may be said that wherever possible one should not cut through tumor tissue but remove the nodule under suspicion by cutting through the surrounding healthy tissues. In this way, spread into lymphatics, tissue spaces, or blood vessels will be, of course, minimized.

The use of aspiration biopsy, either simple aspiration with needle and syringe or by means of the so-called Hoffman punch, is to be discouraged except in those instances where a more satisfactory biopsy cannot be obtained. The advantages of aspiration biopsy are the simplicity of performance and lack of traumatization. The disadvantages are that it is difficult to tell whether the material obtained came from the tumor itself or from adjacent tissue, and it is also an added load on the pathologist, who has only small clusters of separate cells on which to make a diagnosis. Inasmuch as the relationship of cells to the surrounding tissue is of great importance in the diagnosis of malignancy, this obviously places the pathologist at a great disadvantage. For example, one sees in a certain type of intraductal hyperplasia of the breast, cells that are identical with those seen in carcinoma, but because of their relationship to the adjacent tissue, their lack of invasion, they cannot be considered malignant. Here, interpretation on the basis of aspiration biopsy, might well lead to an unnecessary radical operation. The chief value of aspiration biopsy, if it is to be done at all, is in cases where the diagnosis is already known and where radiation rather than surgical treatment is indicated. Thus, if after a cancer of the mouth has been treated, one later finds enlarged deep cervical nodes, an aspiration biopsy may be of service in establishing the diagnosis and in rendering unnecessary a fairly extensive operative procedure.

When one considers the precautions taken in biopsy in general, on theoretical grounds the crude method of pulling with a curet masses of tissue from the uterus for purposes of diagnosis should give rise to widespread dissemination of the tumor. However, uterine tumors that have undergone curettage do not seem to do worse than tumors elsewhere that have not been subjected to a similar degree of traumatization.

Obviously, the sooner the diagnosis can be given, the better for the patient. The ideal method would be widespread use of immediate frozen section diagnosis. However, this would be prohibitively expensive, as a pathologist must gain a considerable degree of proficiency in frozen section diagnosis, and well-trained men are too few to meet the needs. Moreover, there are certain instances in which the nature of the tumor makes it practically impossible to get results by the frozen section method capable of satisfactory interpretation and it is necessary to resort to the usual paraffin or celloidin techniques.

It is probable that no harm is done by the complete removal of a nodule of tumor tissue and a wait of a few days while the specimen is being sent to the laboratory and the report returned. Cauterization of the wound after biopsy may be advantageous. This will serve to kill any tumor cells which may be present and will serve to coagulate the tissue juices and blood in the exposed vessels and spaces that have been cut across.

Certain general precautions should be observed in the obtaining of a biopsy. First, it should be taken from the substance of the tumor itself. Wherever possible the entire nodule should be taken. Necrotic portions of the tumor should be avoided. If the removal is being done under local anesthesia, infiltration of the tumor with novocain or other anesthetic should be avoided, as this leads to a distortion of the structures. The biopsy specimen should preferably not be removed with a cautery or diathermy knife, but preferably be removed with sharp section, and, if cauterization is deemed advisable, this followed by immediate cauterization of the incision or a still wider excision with cautery and diathermy. The passage of the current or heat of the cauterization produces a marked distortion of the cells and leads to great difficulty in their diagnosis.

The Massachusetts State Tumor Diagnosis Service endeavors to send out its reports within 36 or 48 hours from the time the specimen is received. Containers with suitable fixing fluid and cards to identify the specimen may be obtained from either the district health officer or from the Department of Public Health at the State House. It is essential that the card accompanying the container should be completely filled out, as it is frequently necessary, in order to make a helpful and adequate diagnosis, to have the information available that is requested on the cards. We also stress the necessity of having the name of the patient filled out fully and accurately, as with many thousands of specimens, it is easy for confusion to take place unless this is done.

Certain terms in use by the Tumor Diagnosis Service may be perhaps properly explained here. Whenever possible, the grades of histologic malignancy of the epidermoid carcinomas are given. These cancers are classified on the basis of three grades. Grade I is the best differentiated, probably fairly resistant to radiation, slow to metastasize and of probably fairly slow clinical course, without tendency to the establishment of metastases. Grade II are moderately sensitive to radiation, apt to metastasize to the regional lymph nodes and sometimes beyond. Grade III are the least differentiated histologically, are apt to be sensitive to radiation, although highly malignant, and are apt to recur in a radioresistant form. They not infrequently metastasize widely. The prognosis is relatively poor.

In connection with carcinomas of glandular organs, such as the stomach, breast and prostate, two other terms are used: the adenocarcinoma, which implies a malignant epithelial tumor tending to form glands or alveoli; and carcinoma simplex, an epithelial tumor without differentiation towards glands or alveoli.

CANCER OF THE BLADDER
By ROGER C. GRAVES, M.D.
Boston, Massachusetts

The epithelial lining of the urinary bladder frequently gives rise to new growth. As yet, however, we have no knowledge concerning the underlying problems of etiology. Infection, vesical neck obstruction, calculi, diverticula, may serve on occasion as predisposing factors through the medium of chronic irritation, but they by no means tell the whole story as evidenced by the great number of individuals afflicted with these lesions, who do not develop tumors. There must be in addition some inherent condition which constitutes a predisposition towards growth. The possibilities of chronic irritation are best emphasized probably by the known high incidence of bladder tumors among those who work with aniline dyes. At the Pondville Hospital in the seven and one-half years of its existence, there have been ninety-two cases of bladder neoplasm, an average incidence for that institution of about one case for every month. Only eighteen of these patients were women.

The common new growths of the bladder vary histologically from the simplest benign papilloma to the most rapidly growing epidermoid carcinoma. The benign papilloma is always potentially malignant and therefore must be included in this discussion. It is convenient clinically to group them as papillary or infiltrating types. The papillary tumor arises from a relatively narrow stalk or pedicle and grows outwards into the bladder cavity, sometimes in bush-like formation which in advanced cases may fill the whole organ with villous growth. Malignant extension takes place around the base of the pedicle. It is a fact of supreme importance that the papillary carcinoma may be preceded for months or years by a benign papillary structure. Buerger, according to Ewing, has stated that thirty to thirty-six per cent of these carcinomas are so preceded. When one considers further that the patient with a benign papilloma may be readily cured, often by simple cystoscopic procedures, and that during its benign stage the tumor may signal its presence once or many times by urinary bleeding, it is obvious that the neglect of hematuria is inexcusable.

The infiltrating form of cancer, is as a rule, more resistant to treatment. It presents often as a sessile broad-based tumor, or as a fixed area of contracture, or as an ulcer, and it advances within the wall of the bladder rather than into its cavity. Tumors of the bladder may be single or multiple; multiplicity is more characteristic of the papillary variety, and multiplicity usually implies a lesser degree of malignancy, as compared with those cases in which but one tumor is found.

Metastases from carcinoma of the bladder occur more slowly and are less widespread in most instances than in the case of cancer of the prostate or testicle. This accounts for the clinical fact that one may find advanced disease in the bladder in an individual who still presents the outward appearance of good health. In fact, when degenerative changes take place in these patients, they are more often the result of lower ureteral occlusion by the growth and subsequent pyelonephritis, than of the direct effect of the cancer itself. As the primary tumor grows by direct extension beyond the limits of the bladder wall, it invades especially the adjacent pelvic structures and the regions of the distal ureters. It is probable that metastases occur first in most cases in the lymphatic system beginning in the pelvic nodes, though in advanced cases the process may spread to such distant organs as lungs and liver. Even bones are involved in occasional instances.

When the bladder tumor begins to signal its presence by local signs and symptoms, these may be variously expressed as disturbances of function—some change in the bladder habits of the individual; disturbances of control and abnormality of the urine. If there is increased frequency of urination, which is the most common derangement of function, it is because the neoplasm or blood clot or associated infection has heightened the irritability of the vesical musculature. Retention or incontinence in varying degree occur when the growth has invaded the sphincter region, or when it has obstructed mechanically the outlet of the bladder. I recall one case in which there was retention of urine caused by a small pedunculated tumor which lay across the urethral opening and closed it like a ball-valve, during the act of micturition.

Blood in the urine is the most important physical sign of new growth in the bladder. The hematuria may be gross or microscopic. Gross bleeding may be total, coloring the whole stream at a given voiding, or terminal. Terminal hematuria is observed sometimes when the tumor is situated at the vesical outlet where it is made to bleed chiefly at the close of the contraction which empties the bladder. The important fact to remember with reference to blood in the urine is that it is *never normal*, and that it is always dangerous to treat it merely with reassurance and medication. To be sure it may arise from some relatively simple source but it is unsafe to assume that such is the case until complete investigation has excluded the possibility of serious disease, and no consideration urges this more strongly than the early detection of malignancy. A direct cystoscopic inspection of the bladder requires but a few minutes and nowadays involves so little discomfort for the patient that there is seldom reason to withhold it when the signs and symptoms of possible tumor present themselves. Far better a negative examination than an undiscovered cancer.

Painful urination is not a common accompaniment of new growth in the bladder, especially in the early stages of the disease. It sometimes occurs with the advent of infection or following the deposition of urinary salts on the ulcerated sloughing surface of the tumor. Painless hematuria is still, as we have long been taught, a warning signal of the greatest importance.

The diagnosis in these cases is usually not difficult. It is made by inspection of the bladder through a small examining cystoscope. Cystograms made after bladder filling with an opaque solution are also an important aid in determining the size and extent of the lesion, and are particularly useful in those instances where, for one reason or another, the passage of a cystoscope is impossible or unwise. The complete investigation of a case before undertaking treatment includes, in addition, careful physical examination of the patient and laboratory studies which have to do especially with estimations of renal function. Finally, intravenous pyelo-ureterograms are made whenever safe, for the further invaluable information that may be obtained in this way concerning the upper levels of the urinary tract.

In the limited space allotted to this subject there is no place for detailed considerations of treatment, but the methods now generally employed may be discussed briefly.

Such transurethral procedures as fulguration with high-frequency current and cystoscopic implantation of radium seeds should be reserved, unqualifiedly, for small tumors so situated in the bladder as to be easily accessible to cystoscopic approach. My personal belief, however, is that, in general, treatment through the cystoscope should be confined to the treatment of the benign papilloma. While an occasional exception may be found in a very early malignant lesion or in a small postoperative area of recurrence, it is my feeling that the patient with cancer deserves the opportunity afforded only by open operation, of the most careful direct inspection of the growth and the most accurate application of the therapeutic agent to be employed, whether it be surgical excision, electrocoagulation, or radium.

Tumors confined to the superior, anterior, and antero-lateral surfaces of the bladder, and not involving the fixed trigonal and sphincter regions, may be dealt with satisfactorily by surgical resection, removing with the growth a wide margin of normal tissue. It is desirable to use cutting current for these dissections as an aid in the control of hemorrhage, and every effort must be made as in all these procedures within the bladder, to guard against injury of normal mucosa and to avoid the dissemination of tumor cells in the wound during the operation.

In the case of tumors in the region of the trigone and bladder neck, and the greater number of them are so situated, good results may be obtained with the combined use of electrocoagulation and radium. When the lesion has been carefully exposed to view through the suprapubic approach, the raised or papillary portions are best destroyed by coagulation or removed with cutting current, after which the entire area of the base of the growth is cauterized and thoroughly undermined with radium, usually in the form of gold or platinum seeds. Electrocoagulation and cauterization alone are not sufficient, as we frequently see cases of recurrence where the radium has been omitted from this program.

There is still another group of cases, small but definite, in which the carcinoma is still confined to the bladder but is so extensive or so unfavorably located in the bladder that there is no reasonable chance of cure by the ordinary methods of treatment. For such patients the only hope of completely eradicating the disease lies in total cystectomy, and the results with this procedure are increasingly encouraging. Removal of the bladder demands, of course, that new outlets must be provided for the urinary stream. There are three possibilities for each of which there are specific indications; nephrostomy; ureterostomy, which brings the ureters through the abdominal wall to open upon the skin; and ureteral transplantation to the rectosigmoid portion of the large bowel.

High voltage X-ray therapy in the treatment of cancer of the bladder is used often as a postoperative measure but its chief value lies in wholly inoperable cases where it is hoped by this means to lessen hemorrhage and to retard at least the progress of the growth.

Whatever the plan of treatment, it should be remembered that the patient who has had a bladder tumor must remain under observation and undergo cystoscopic inspection at gradually widening intervals over an indefinite period. This is essential to safety not only for the prompt discovery of recurrence at the original site, but also because of the chance that new tumors may form in the vesical mucosa that has once manifested a tendency in this direction. Finally, and in conclusion, it may be said that with present-day methods the results in this whole field are most promising. A very hopeful prognosis can now be given in those cases in which a diagnosis has been made promptly enough to permit treatment before the disease has progressed to its later stages. There can be reasonable expectancy of cure in the early lesions and even, in some instances, in the moderately advanced ones, while in the advanced cases more effective palliation may be accomplished than was formerly possible.

BONE SARCOMA
By CHANNING C. SIMMONS, M.D.
Boston, Massachusetts

To understand the formation of bone tumors it is necessary to bear in mind certain essential facts. Primary bone neoplasms are mesoblastic and the cell of origin is the embryonic fibroblast. Depending on the anatomic demand, the fibroblast, by differentiation, may form fibrous tissue, cartilage, bone or muscle. Owing to this fact varied forms of tissue may be seen in bone tumors and it is confusing when the qualifying adjectives such as myxo, chondro, osteo, osteoid, etc., are applied. It is much better to use the term "osteogenic tumor", as suggested by Ewing, meaning a tumor derived from tissue primarily intended to form bone for all true bone tumors.

The osteogenic tumors may be divided into the malignant (sarcoma) and nonmalignant forms. The following classification is a slight rearrangement of that adopted by the Registry of Bone Sarcoma of the American College of Surgeons:

Classification of Tumors of Bone

A. Tumors Originating in Bone
  1. Osteogenic Tumors
      Benign — osteoma, chondroma, etc.
      Malignant (osteogenic sarcoma) — periosteal, sclerosing, chondral, etc.
  2. Ewing's sarcoma
  3. Myeloma
  4. Unclassified malignant tumors
  5. Benign giant cell tumor

B. Other Tumors of Bone
  7. Metastatic Tumors — cancer, hypernephroma, lymphoma, etc.
  8. Parosteal Fibrosarcoma
  9. Odontoma, etc.
  10. Other conditions — subperiosteal hematoma, bone cyst (osteitis fibrosa cystica) Pagets, sarcoid, etc.

Benign Bone Tumors

The benign bone tumors are the osteomas and chondromas. They are of slow growth and cause no pain. The diagnosis is made by the X-ray. These tumors being composed of adult tissue, are not radio-sensitive and the proper treatment is complete excision if the tumor is a chondroma. An exostosis should be excised if in an accessible position.

Osteogenic Sarcoma

Osteogenic sarcoma is one of the most malignant forms of tumor. It is seen commonly near the epiphyseal ends of the long bones, particularly about the knee joint, but may arise in the shaft especially in the humerus. Osteogenic sarcoma is relatively rare in the jaw and in the flat bones, and when arising in these situations is somewhat less malignant than a similar tumor of the long bones. It is never seen in the phalanges. It is a disease of children and young adults, and is unusual in individuals over fifty, except in connection with Paget's Disease. A history of trauma immediately preceding the first symptom is often obtained, and while a single trauma is not an etiological factor in carcinoma it may have some relation to the formation of sarcoma and other bone tumors. The disease may originate in the medulla or beneath the periosteum but when the patient is first seen by a physician both the periosteum and medulla are always involved. It is best, therefore, not to use the terms "periosteal" and "central", but to consider all these growths in the larger group of osteogenic sarcoma. Microscopically, the tumors are composed of tissue in any or all degrees of transition between the embryonic fibroblast and adult bone cells. The degree of malignancy depends on the cellular portion of the tumor. Ewing distinguishes three subdivisions and applies the adjectives, fibrocellular, telangiectatic and sclerosing. Phemister mentions a chondral type. In the sclerosing and chondral forms bone and cartilage predominate and these tissues being of a more adult type the tumors are of slower growth and less malignant. Metastases take place through the blood stream and are almost invariably found in the lungs.

Symptoms:

The early symptoms of sarcoma of a long bone are pain or tumor or both, occurring in an otherwise healthy person. A common history is that of a slight injury followed in a few weeks by pain referred to the neighboring joint and not relieved by rest. Late symptoms are tumor with dilated superficial veins, cachexia and evidence of lung metastases.

X-ray:

The characteristic X-ray shows a tumor of the end of the diaphysis with both bone formation and bone destruction, one process usually predominating. The adjectives osteolytic and osteoblastic are often applied. The periosteum is dissected up and there may be ray formation beneath it. A characteristic appearance is seen at the upper limits of the tumor, the so-called reactive angle. The shadow of the shaft can usually be seen extending through the growth. The osteolytic form may resemble a giant cell tumor, especially when it is centrally situated in the external condyle of the femur, a common seat for both growths. The outlines, however, are not well defined and there is no expansion as is the case in giant cell tumor. Metastases in the chest are seen as round, dense areas in the lung.

Diagnosis:

Unexplained pain in a bone in a healthy young adult referred to the neighboring joint, following injury, not relieved by rest is very suggestive of osteogenic sarcoma and demands radiographic examination in every instance. The radiograph is the most important diagnostic procedure, but it is not always characteristic and should be interpreted by one with experience in the diagnosis of bone tumors and diseases. In elderly individuals with a demonstrable bone tumor, metastatic cancer and hypernephroma must be considered for they are the most common forms of bone tumor after forty-five. The possibility of syphilis should always be borne in mind. Osteomyelitis should also be considered as well as certain of the rare forms of bone diseases such a sarcoid, osteopoikylosis, Paget's disease, marble bones, etc. Subperiosteal hematoma is often difficult to differentiate from sarcoma even with the radiograph and many atypical cases will be seen. Preliminary biopsy in a suspected case of osteogenic sarcoma is a dangerous procedure. If biopsy is contemplated it should be done with a tourniquet in place and permission obtained for immediate amputation if the tumor proves to be malignant.

Prognosis:

The prognosis of true osteogenic sarcoma is poor following any method of treatment, death from lung metastases in from one to three years being the rule. Cures usually take place in the cases seen and treated radically at an early stage of the disease, and in the more differentiated forms, such as the chondral type of sarcoma, and the unclassified forms. The average case is rarely seen by a surgeon in less than two months from the onset of the disease and if our statistics of cures are to be improved the tumors must be recognized in the earliest stages. The patients are, also, slow to accept radical surgery, that is amputation, and valuable time is lost while other expedients are tried.

Treatment:

The accepted treatment at the present time is amputation, after biopsy, through the bone next proximal to the one diseased, or disarticulation. Amputation should not be done except for the relief of pain if there is any evidence of metastases. Osteogenic sarcoma is a radioresistant tumor, and although the growth may be somewhat retarded and pain relieved by radiation treatment cure is not to be expected. The osteolytic forms are somewhat more radiosensitive than the chondral and sclerosing types and radiation treatment may be employed in the incurable case. The value of pre- and postoperative prophylactic radiation has not been established at the present time. Of 65 cases of cured osteogenic sarcoma in the Registry all have been treated by radical surgery. The value of the treatment by the mixed toxins of streptococcus and the bacillus prodigiosus

(Coley serum) still remains to be proved. Many cured cases have been treated by these toxins but they have also been operated upon. At present, treatment by this method is not generally advocated.

Ewing Sarcoma

Ewing first distinguished this type of malignant bone tumor in 1922 and applied the name endothelial myeloma. It is probably the round cell sarcoma of the earlier writers. It is usually seen in males under twenty and is often mistaken for osteomyelitis. It occurs in any bone although it is more common in the shaft of the long bones or in the flat bones. The tumor causes bone destruction with no new bone formation, although there may be some reactive bone formation particularly in the fibula. Microscopically, it is composed of small, round cells with little cytoplasm, closely packed together, and contains no cartilage, osteoid or other bone tissues.

Symptoms:

The symptoms are intermittent pain and swelling often following injury. The part is hot, the temperature slightly elevated and the white blood count varies from 10,000 to 15,000. The picture closely resembles that of a low grade, acute osteomyelitis, and at operation the soft, cellular tissue is very suggestive of pus. The tumor progresses with remissions and in the later stages of the disease temperatures of 103 - 104 are not uncommon. Metastases occur in the lungs and other bones, the skull being a common seat. The disease may run a rapid course, but the average duration of life from onset is from two to three years.

X-ray:

The X-ray shows bone destruction. The shaft has a moth eaten appearance while the periosteum is raised and striated, giving the so-called onion skin appearance. When there is much reactive bone, ray formation may be seen beneath the periosteum but the usual picture strongly suggests osteomyelitis.

Diagnosis:

The diagnosis is made on the history, physical examination and X-ray findings.

Prognosis:

The prognosis is bad but depends somewhat on the type of disease and whether acute or chronic. Eleven per cent of the cases in the Registry of Bone Sarcoma are classed as five-year cures. All have been treated by radical surgery.

Treatment:

This tumor is very radiosensitive. Following radiation treatment the growth disappears, the bone assumes a relatively normal appearance by X-ray and the general condition of the patient improves. Recurrence and death from metastases, however, is the rule. Amputation, if no metastases can be demonstrated, is the treatment of choice as in other forms of sarcoma. Pre- and postoperative radiation treatment may be of more value in this type of tumor than in true osteogenic sarcoma, but the efficacy in preventing recurrence has not been proved. The metastases are at first as radiosensitive as the original tumor.

Unclassified Malignant Tumors

There is a certain group of tumors closely resembling true osteogenic sarcoma, which, clinically, cannot be distinguished from it, but which on microscopic examination present a somewhat different picture. The treatment of these tumors is the same as that of osteogenic sarcoma.

Multiple Myeloma

As the name implies this is a multiple tumor of a bone marrow probably originating from one type of cell. Occasionally, one bone only is involved. The tumors are composed of plasma cells, and sometimes similar tumors are found in the soft parts. The disease is most common in adult males.

Symptoms:

The symptoms are pain in the affected bone, tumor, anemia and those caused by deformity due to fracture or collapse of bone, such as the body of a vertebra. One of the above symptoms usually predominates in the individual case. The blood chemistry is normal except for an increase in the serum globulin and plasma cells are occasionally seen in the blood smear. Bence Jones bodies may be demonstrated in the urine in about 40 per cent of the cases. The course of the disease varies greatly according to whether it is the acute or chronic form. Death may occur in a few months or the disease progress slowly for many years.

X-ray:

The classical X-ray appearance is that of multiple, central bone destructive tumors, involving many of the flat and the long bones. Atypical forms are common and a definite diagnosis based on the radiographic findings may be impossible.

Prognosis:

The disease is uniformly fatal, but it is difficult to prophesy the length of life in a given case. The average duration of life is from two to six years. One case in the Registry of Bone Sarcoma is living in fair health sixteen years after the diagnosis was established by pathological examination.

Treatment:

The disease runs its course practically unaffected by treatment. Surgery may be employed as indicated to correct deformity. Radiation by either high voltage X-ray or radium pack is to be advised, and in certain cases the growths respond in a satisfactory manner. Many of the tumors, however, prove to be radioresistant. Treatment by Coley serum has been advocated.

Giant Cell Tumors

Giant cell tumor, formerly called sarcoma, is a nonmalignant tumor arising usually in the ends of the long bones. It occurs at any age but is most common in young adults. It is a medullary tumor of the epiphyseal end of the bone, causing bone destruction with distention of the cortex which may be entirely destroyed. It is limited by the epiphyseal or joint cartilage. The tumor is soft and often described as appearing like currant jelly, but may be yellowish, fibrous or cystic, the appearance being altered by pathological fracture. It is of slow growth and does not metastasize. A malignant variant is described. Microscopically, it is composed of granulation tissue containing foreign body giant cells which should not be confused with tumor giant cells. The cause is unknown, but a history of trauma is often obtained and it has been suggested that the tumor is due to an injury of the nutrient artery.

Symptoms:

The symptoms are those common to other bone tumors; namely, pain, tumor and pathological fracture.

X-ray:

The radiograph shows a centrally placed, bone destructive tumor, the cavity being divided by coarse trabeculae. The growth is limited by the joint cartilage above and the lower edge is sharply defined. The cortex is distended and absorbed, the transverse diameter of the tumor being equal to the longitudinal.

Diagnosis:

The diagnosis is made on the physical examination and the radiograph. Metastatic tumors, bone cysts, parathyroid disease and the central osteolytic osteogenic sarcoma are the principal conditions with which it may be confused. In an osteogenic sarcoma involving chiefly the medulla there is no distention of the cortex and the growth rarely extends to the joint cartilage.

Treatment:

The treatment lies between radiation or surgery. Good and bad results have been obtained by both methods. If the tumor is of the fibula or bones of the forearm, resection with or without bone graft is the treatment of choice, for a sufficient number of cases have undergone malignant changes to make total removal of the tumor advisable when possible. Curetting of the cavity which is then swabbed out with carbolic acid is the operation usually advised, but complete regeneration of bone does not occur even if the cavity is filled with bone chips. If radiation is employed it should be given by a radiologist conversant with the treatment of this type of tumor. In certain instances amputation is necessary.

Parosteal Sarcoma

This tumor is a fibrosarcoma arising in the outer layers of the periosteum and involving the bone secondarily. It is rare and somewhat less malignant than true bone sarcoma.

Metastatic Tumors

The possibility of a bone tumor being a metastasis from a malignant tumor of the soft parts should always be considered in adults. Any malignant tumor may give rise to bone metastases but certain forms of cancer seem to have the predilection to attack bone. Metastatic deposits in the pelvic bones and spine are common in cancer of the prostate. Cancer of the breast metastasizes to any bone in the body, and cancer of the thyroid commonly forms bone metastases often in the skull. Metastatic hypernephroma should be suspected in a bone destructive tumor in the shaft of a long bone. The possibility that an apparent bone tumor may represent some form of bone or generalized disease such as Paget's disease, malignant lymphoma or hyperparathyroidism should always be borne in mind.

CANCER OF THE BRAIN
By GILBERT HORRAX, M.D.
Boston, Massachusetts

In discussing "cancer of the brain," a few words of explanation are necessary in order that there may be no misunderstanding about the tumors with which we are dealing. This is particularly important, not only because of the great variety of brain tumors, but also since there is still prevalent the belief that all new growths within the intracranial cavity are more or less hopeless, and that only under the most fortunate circumstances can a permanent cure be obtained by their successful removal. It must be granted at once that all brain tumors regardless of type are serious lesions, and that success in operating upon them requires long and careful experience in the technique of this now highly developed branch of surgery. When, however, this experience has been gained, it is probably not too much to say that somewhat more than a third of all patients having brain tumors should be capable of being completely cured, another third brought back to useful life for many months or even years, while the remainder are incapable of being benefited. Furthermore, the general operative mortality to obtain these results should not be much over 10 per cent, although obviously in certain types of growth it is higher than in others.

The commonest forms of primary brain tumors are the gliomas which represent about 40 per cent of all intracranial new growths. About half of them are properly called malignant because they infiltrate the brain widely and therefore are almost never capable of complete removal. Until comparatively few years ago it was believed that all tumors comprehended under the general term "gliomas of the brain" came within this category. We now know that many gliomatous growths, some of them solid and others largely cystic but containing a solid portion of growth in the cyst wall are among the most benign of intracranial lesions, capable of complete and permanent excision. Likewise it is now possible with modern neurosurgical methods, especially since the advent of electrosurgery, to be much more radical in the treatment of these tumors, so that even those which in former years were perhaps entirely inoperable may be so dealt with as to give the patient a considerable period of wage-earning life.

In addition to the benign types of glioma there are large numbers of encapsulated intracranial growths such as meningiomas (dural endotheliomas), pituitary adenomas and acoustic neuromas,—to mention the more common varieties, the removal of which as a rule is quite feasible, and should result ordinarily in the patient's restoration to good health.

We now may consider true cancer (carcinoma) of the brain. It is almost never primary there, but about five per cent of all intracranial tumors are metastatic cancer which has its origin in some other organ of the body. Cancer of the lung and of the breast are the most frequent sources of secondary brain involvement.

In contradistinction to what has been said about other brain tumors, the chance of any great benefit to be derived from operations upon metastatic carcinoma is not good, the survival period of the patient as a rule being only a few months. Furthermore, there are likely to be multiple, small carcinomatous nodules in the brain, many of which could not be located and removed even if this seemed wise to do. Nevertheless there are at times single, large metastatic growths in the brain, and occasionally these may be removed intact. Such growths are likely to come from a slowly growing primary cancer of the lung, and patients have been known to remain in good health for as long as seven years after the brain tumor had been removed.

Because of the fact that so little can be accomplished in the vast majority of patients with true brain cancer, it is important, if possible, to know that one is dealing with this type of growth rather than with one of the more common forms of brain tumor. If the general physical examination or clinical history of the patient indicates cancer elsewhere in the body, the brain symptoms, such as headache, vomiting, sensory or motor paralyses, aphasia and the like are almost certainly due to metastatic cerebral involvement. Likewise if brain symptoms are present in a patient from whom a breast cancer has been removed with apparent success even five, ten or possibly more years previously, nevertheless the chances are still vastly greater that the brain condition has come from the original breast cancer rather than from a growth originating in the intracranial cavity.

From the foregoing it will be seen that the obvious way of eliminating cancer of the brain is to eliminate cancer elsewhere in the body at the earliest possible moment. This, however, is far from simple, because a metastatic brain tumor is not infrequently exposed and perhaps removed at operation although there have been no signs, symptoms or suggestions in the patient's history that would lead one to suspect a primary growth in some other organ.

Aside from the occasional removal of a single secondary cancerous growth in the brain, which may in rare instances give a fairly long survival period of useful life, the only other possible useful operative procedure is a decompression. This operation is sometimes undertaken to alleviate the extreme headaches and to preserve vision in patients who are known to have a brain metastasis. The period of survival is as a rule so short, however, that ordinarily the simplest and best thing for the patient is to be kept as comfortable as possible by the free use of any sedatives and hypnotics that will accomplish this end.

Nevertheless, after all that has been said, it must not be forgotten that rarely a patient may have had a successful operation for cancer elsewhere and subsequently develop brain symptoms which are due either to a primary brain growth or to a clot or some other type of vascular lesion. For this reason one must call upon his judgment in each individual case, taking all factors into consideration, together with careful physical and X-ray examinations in order to decide as to whether the patient should be given the benefit of an exploratory brain operation, since these explorations are now much less hazardous than they were even ten to fifteen years ago.

CANCER OF THE BREAST
By ROBERT B. GREENOUGH, M.D.
Boston, Massachusetts

Cancer of the breast is one of the most common and important forms of cancer which occur in women. Too often, however, its presence is not discovered even by the patient herself until it has reached such a degree of development that it has spread widely from its point of origin, and complete removal by operation has become impossible. This occurs in spite of the fact that the breast is an external organ and readily accessible to frequent examination. The fact that pain is *not* a characteristic symptom of early cancer of the breast is perhaps responsible for the delay on the part of the patient in seeking medical advice, but the chief reason is probably that early cancer presents itself only as a tumor in the breast, whereas a number of other conditions which are *not* cancer present this same symptom of a tumor in the breast also, and to the patient and even to the physician the diagnosis of cancer may be difficult or indeed impossible by external examination at this stage of the disease.

The earliest sign by which a lump in the breast can be recognized as being actually cancer is usually that it becomes adherent to the skin. This sign may present itself as a dimple or depression over the tumor, or as a mere loss of the normal mobility of the skin, such that on movement of the whole breast on the chest wall a drag on the skin over the tumor can be observed in a good light.

The next important symptom suggestive of cancer is the enlargement of one or more of the lymph nodes in the axilla on the affected side. This symptom is not always to be depended upon with certainty. Cancer of the breast may be present without palpable axillary nodes, and vice versa, axillary nodes may rarely be enlarged and palpable as a result of conditions other than cancer. In the majority of cases, however, the presence of enlarged nodes is a reliable indication of cancer.

Other early symptoms of cancer of the breast occur less frequently, such as bloody discharge from the nipple, which has been estimated to indicate cancer in about fifty per cent of all cases in which it is observed. Retraction of the nipple may take place as a result of the growth of cancer in the breast beneath, in the same way that adherence to the skin is brought about; this is a very suggestive symptom, but only rarely appears as an early sign of the disease. A breast in which cancer is developing may show gross change of contour in comparison with the other side, as by the presence of abnormal swelling or lump; or, on the contrary, the affected breast may be actually shrunken and smaller than the normal side, and the nipple of the cancerous breast may be appreciably higher than that of the other side. Finally, the development of eczema about the nipple (Paget's disease) may be an indication of the presence of cancer in the breast beneath.

The consistency of the tumor in cancer of the breast varies within wide limits, but is always harder and firmer than the surrounding breast tissue and lacks the elastic quality which is frequently associated with cysts and benign tumors; cancer is more fixed and less mobile in the breast tissue and does not give the same sensation of encapsulation, as does a benign tumor or a cyst.

With the progress of time, and the further development of the disease, cancer of the breast extends beyond its point of origin by continuous growth and infiltration of the surrounding structures, such as the skin, the fascia and the muscles of the chest wall. Extension or permeation through the lymph-channels carries it to the axillary lymph nodes of the affected side, across the sternum to the opposite breast, or through the perforating lymphatics which accompany the internal mammary vessels into the anterior mediastinum, and, more rarely, from the upper hemisphere of the breast, directly to the lymph nodes above the clavicle. Once established in the lymph nodes cancer extends as a rule in the direction of the lymph stream, to involve the nodes which are next in line. Occasionally, owing to blocking of lymphatic channels, a bizarre or retrograde course of extension may be observed. Progression of the disease downward and inward to the epigastrium and eventually to the liver has been observed.

Through the blood vessels extension and remote metastases may occur, not only in the bones of the skeleton (cranium, spine, clavicle, ribs, pelvis, femur and humerus) but also to the lung, the brain and occasionally to other internal organs. The most common sites for internal metastasis are the lungs pleura and mediastinum and the liver, although bone involvement is by no means unusual.

Consideration of the many possible lines of extension of cancer from its origin in the breast makes it necessary to give careful study to every patient suspected of having breast cancer in order to discover evidence of metastases which will contraindicate attempts by surgery to obtain a radical cure. This study should include not only a complete physical examination, but a careful clinical history with questions directed to the discovery of any abnormality of function which could possibly indicate remote metastasis. X-ray studies of the chest, spine, pelvis and hips, cranium and shoulder girdle should be a routine procedure in every case before radical operation is attempted.

With this brief statement of the significant signs and symptoms of cancer of the breast, we must acknowledge that the more certain the diagnosis of cancer, based upon these findings, the more unfavorable the outlook for the permanent cure of the disease. In round numbers, based upon the experience of well-known clinics, it may be said that approximately three out of four, or seventy-five per cent of cases of cancer of the breast in which the disease is still confined to the breast at the time of radical operation, will be alive and well at the end of the five-year period; whereas only about one in four, or twenty-five per cent of cases with involvement of the axillary nodes, will be in this fortunate situation. The legitimate conclusion to be drawn from these figures is that we must not wait for characteristic symptoms to develop by which we can make the positive diagnosis of cancer of the breast.

We must depend upon exploratory operation. It is true that transillumination of the breast and soft part X-rays are an aid in the study of suspected cases, but as yet these methods are to be relied upon only in the hands of the most experienced observers, and even then, as a rule only when they are in agreement with the clinical evidence derived from other data.

There are many methods of performing a biopsy on a suspected breast tumor; varying from the aspiration-punch technique advocated at the Memorial Hospital in New York, to the open exploratory incision or excision employed more widely over the country. In any case, delay between the biopsy and the radical operation is to be avoided; immediate pathological examination by frozen sections should be available and the surgeon who attempts to operate on suspected cancer of the breast without these resources, except under conditions which demand emergency procedure, fails to provide for his patient the opportunity to which every woman should be entitled; namely, that of being cured of cancer of the breast by the employment of such measures as are known to medical science to be effective in promoting successful results in the treatment of this common form of cancer.

CARCINOMA OF THE UTERINE CERVIX
BY GEORGE A. LELAND, JR., M.D.
Boston, Massachusetts

Incidence

Statistical studies show the incidence of carcinoma of the cervix to be greater in women who have borne children than in those who have had no pregnancies. This fact is so well known and has been taken for granted so automatically that the tendency is to forget that carcinoma of the cervix often occurs in women who have never been pregnant. It has been emphasized that the age incidence is greater between the years of forty to fifty-five than in earlier or later decades. The more the cancer problem is studied the more it becomes apparent that the term "cancer age" is fallacious. The incidence of carcinoma of the cervix in women below thirty years of age is by no means uncommon. Nor should one believe that a case at such an early age is, because of that fact, unsusceptible to cure. Any case that is neglected by the patient in not calling attention to her symptoms, or is neglected by the physician in not appreciating the significance of the symptoms, usually results disastrously. In young persons the early recognition on the part of the patient as well as the physician can and does result in cured cases. A definite proportion of all cases seems to begin in the immediate postpartum period of multiparous women. Appreciation of this fact on the part of the attending physician may well result in the earlier detection of many such cases.

Prevention

Although, as indicated above, one must not be lulled into a feeling of safety in a case of a nulliparous patient, nevertheless, it is, of course, true that the greatest danger exists with the women who have been pregnant. This danger apparently increases not so much with the number of pregnancies, as with the degree of damage which the cervix has suffered at the time of any one delivery. A badly torn, everted cervix is necessarily subject to more irritation with each succeeding menstrual period than is the more nearly normal cervix. Such cervices should always be regarded as a menace and should receive adequate attention before the degenerative changes consequent upon the menopause take place. Just what adequate attention may mean must be determined individually for each and every case. Such procedures include cauterization, simple repair, amputation of the cervix, repair combined with supravaginal hysterectomy and complete hysterectomy by either the abdominal or vaginal approach.

Absolute avoidance of carcinoma of the cervix necessarily can be accomplished only by complete removal of the cervix. Such a radical procedure is obviously unwise in every instance. The judgment of the attending surgeon will necessarily determine the type of procedure indicated in a given case. The frequency of recurrence of pelvic tumors very strongly suggests that the surgeon should have a specific reason for leaving in any part of the uterus.

Early Diagnosis

Symptomatically it is practically always found that the patient has suffered abnormal discharge of blood. This commonly occurs as a slightly excessive menstrual period or is noted at the time of intercourse. Too often these early warnings are disregarded and the patient waits until considerable bleeding, foul discharge, or even pelvic pain become only too obvious.

The physical signs which should arouse the suspicion of the physician are free bleeding upon palpation, hardness to palpation, and proliferation of tissue anywhere on the exocervix either on the vaginal mucous membrane or upon the mucous membrane of the everted canal. The evidence to be obtained by the use of Lugol solution is too indefinite to be fully relied upon. The stain is, of course, not taken by everted canal mucous membrane. When the stain is not taken by the normal vaginal mucous membrane of the exocervix the test should be regarded as positive, and an adequate investigation made. Such an investigation may include not merely the removal of a small segment of the cervix, but may necessitate the complete examination of the entire exocervix. It is only by such a complete examination that a malignant or premalignant condition can be satisfactorily ruled out.

The rectal examination is a procedure by which many an early carcinoma may be distinguished from chronic cervicitis occurring in the badly lacerated cervix. In the case of malignant disease there is usually to be noted by rectum a definite infiltration of edema about the cervix especially at the base of the broad ligaments. This edema is absent in the case of chronic cervicitis. Physicians examining the cervix for question of malignant disease should thoroughly train themselves in the rectal examination of this type of case. Not only may this form of examination detect an early and otherwise unsuspected case of carcinoma, but it will also indicate in the more advanced case the exact degree of extension of the disease.

Treatment

As in all instances of malignant disease in accessible structures of the body the extent of disease at the time treatment is instituted will determine the nature of that treatment. For carcinoma of the cervix both surgery and radium offer excellent chances for cure in the favorable cases. Occasionally a case deemed to be unfavorable for operation will be cured by the application of radium. It is well recognized that radium with or without deep therapy X-ray as an accessory offers the greatest possible palliative relief to the cases of carcinoma of the cervix that are unquestionably advanced beyond the curable group. The use of radium has now been on trial over a long enough period of time to have demonstrated that the post-radium cures are as effective as those obtained by operation. The dangers incident to the application of radium are so much less than those following a major surgical operation that radium has now come to be almost universally recognized as the procedure of choice. In this connection it is to be noted, however, that radium, like the aseptic scalpel, is of importance not alone in its inherent properties but quite as much in the skill with which it is used. Accuracy in the application of radium both in form and dosage is essential in the treatment of all types of cancer. This rule is especially true in the multiplicity of the problems connected with the treatment of carcinoma of the cervix.

Prognosis

In the early cases of carcinoma of the cervix it may be confidently expected that five-year cures will be obtained in at least 50 per cent of the cases. Such cases include for the most part those in which the disease has involved the cervix only. A large proportion of those cases in which the disease has but barely invaded the vaginal wall beyond the cervix, or has but slightly passed from the endocervix up into the uterine cavity, will likewise fall into this favorable group where cures may be expected. As soon as the disease has invaded the lymphatic tissues of the pericervical and broad ligament regions, the outlook for favorable permanent results at once drops to very nearly nil. This is true whether the case is treated by surgery or by radium, although on the whole in this group those treated by radium are definitely better off. The richness of the lymphatic circulation leading away from the cervix along the path of the ureters very quickly enables the cancer cells to spread from the cervix to the outlying tissues. This rapid spread accounts for the relatively small proportion of favorable cases of carcinoma of the cervix seen in any clinic. The realization of this point emphasizes the necessity for the early recognition of the precancerous cervix and the immediate subjection of suspicious tissue to the microscope.

THE LOWELL CANCER CLINIC
Prepared by Members of the Clinic Staff

The Lowell Cancer Clinic was organized under the auspices of the State Department of Public Health in 1927, with a cancer committee made up of physicians appointed by the Middlesex North District Medical Society as its representatives. Since there are three Class A hospitals of nearly the same size in Lowell, these hospitals all were represented in this original committee. In the formation of the original staff for the Clinic, two surgeons and a medical man were named to represent each hospital and the services were so arranged that each group took four months apiece. Since the inception of the Clinic there have been some changes in the staff by reason of resignation and death, but the same system has always been retained of keeping a group of three doctors wherever possible for filling each service. When the Clinic was started, there were also appointed as consultants, specialists in eye, ear, nose and throat work, genito-urinary work, roentgenology, radiology, pathology and dentistry, and arrangements were made for referring cases when necessary to the skin specialist who is consultant to the Lowell General Hospital.

By arrangement with the hospital authorities, the Clinic has been held in the Out-Patient Department of the Lowell General Hospital once each week on Friday at 10 A. M. In the department of the hospital where the Clinic is held, there are a considerable number of well-lighted and heated examining rooms with facilities for doing table examinations and bed and couch examinations at the same time.

First, the patient's history is taken, usually by an experienced volunteer worker and the patient is made ready in one of the rooms by a nurse. The history is then read by one of the group of physicians and further details obtained if necessary. The patient is then examined by the entire group with a nurse in attendance. The case is then discussed in a separate room and each member gives his opinion independently; the discussion is carried on until an agreement is reached as to the diagnosis and the form of treatment advised. This is then dictated to the regular clerk of the Clinic, in the presence of the Clinic's social worker, so that if there are any obscure points she may get them cleared up immediately. The patient is then turned over to the social worker who carries out, as far as possible, the directions of the examining group. Any case requiring further investigation by a specialist is referred at once to one of the consulting specialists; the pathologist, radiologist and roentgenologist are usually in the hospital and easily called in if it is considered advisable.

The so-called chief of the Clinic has endeavored to work with each group in turn for a part of the time in order to coordinate the methods throughout the various services. This year a series of staff conferences has been started to consider and discuss various problems arising in the Clinic. The Clinic staff has been reorganized, its numbers increased, and the services divided to make each service two months instead of four. Under this reorganization, there is in each group one of the older men who has had the most experience in the Cancer Clinic and two younger men who have had less experience in the Clinic, still following out the group idea of examining all patients and striving to interest a larger and younger group of men to carry on in the years to come.

Physicians who have referred patients, and those who are interested in the Clinic, have always been welcome to attend, although no special clinics are arranged for their particular benefit.

EDUCATIONAL PROGRAM ON CANCER OF THE GENERAL FEDERATION OF WOMEN'S CLUBS
By Mary R. Lakeman, M.D.
Epidemiologist, Division of Adult Hygiene,
Massachusetts Department of Public Health

The General Federation of Women's Clubs has this year launched a vigorous campaign for cancer education through its Division of Public Health of which Mrs. Carl W. Illig, Jr., of Massachusetts, is chairman.

The program as outlined by this Division has been given wide circulation among Women's Clubs all over the United States. It carries with it the recommendation that every Club devote at least one meeting each season for the consideration of the cancer problem.

Its program has three distinct phases:—The duty of every clubwoman in the campaign against cancer is:

First: Inform herself of how best to protect herself against cancer. This is done:
  (A) By learning how to avoid situations which contribute to its incidence:
    (1) By careful skin hygiene.
    (2) By careful hygiene of the mouth cavity.
    (3) By periodic examination of tissues and organs of the body most likely to be the site of cancerous growth.
  (B) By increasing many fold the chances for its successful treatment:
    (1) By learning how to recognize danger signals which may mean early symptoms of its presence:
      (a) Any sore which will not heal.
      (b) Any lump on the breast.
      (c) Any wart, wen, or mole which shows any sudden or unusual degree of growth.
      (d) Any unusual or irregular discharge from any of the body openings.
    (2) By reporting to a skilled physician or clinic for immediate diagnosis and treatment.

Second: Spread to her friends and family information as to the nature, incidence, and treatment of cancer. This is done:
- (A) By individual effort through:
  - (1) Spreading pamphlets (to be distributed by the General Federation).
  - (2) Conversation and personal influence.
- (B) By fostering the Federation's program as follows:
  - (1) An annual cancer meeting before every Women's Club. This would include talks on various subjects such as:
    - (a) What women can do about cancer.
    - (b) Recent progress in cancer research.
    - (c) The nature and incidence of cancer.
    - (d) The prevention of cancer.
    - (e) The value of periodic health examinations.
  - (2) Radio talks on various cancer topics.
  - (3) Use of movie films showing:
    - (a) The difference between normal and cancerous growth.
    - (b) The growth of living tissue outside of the body.
  - (4) Cancer talks before service clubs, church groups, high schools, colleges, Parent-Teacher Associations, etc.
  - (5) Educational cancer exhibits at various gatherings.

Third: Help encourage the establishment and maintenance of additional facilities for public education in cancer and for its diagnosis and treatment:
- (A) By voluntary contribution of ten cents per annum by every Club member. These contributions will form "The General Federation of Women's Clubs Cancer Control Fund."

The Cancer Education Program, according to the custom of the General Federation, has received the approval of an Advisory Board on Public Health and Child Welfare which is composed of leaders in eighteen national health and child welfare organizations under the chairmanship of Surgeon-General Hugh S. Cumming of the United States Public Health Service.

The Cancer Program was started in 1934, and through the co-operation of the forty-nine State Federation Chairmen of Public Health, it has progressed rapidly. The slogan which the Federation has adopted for its Cancer Program is: "Cancer Thrives on Ignorance. Fight It With Knowledge."

The program has been adopted in Arkansas, California, Florida, Illinois, Indiana, Kansas, Kentucky, Louisiana, Maine, Massachusetts, Mississippi, Missouri, Nebraska, New Hampshire, New York, North Carolina, Ohio, Pennsylvania, Tennessee, and Wisconsin.

As the membership of the Federation is mostly made up of women in the prime of life, the fight against cancer would make a strong appeal. Realizing that since 1900, tuberculosis, through educational activities, has decreased rapidly throughout the United States, it was felt that through the interest and promotion of educational facilities, the General Federation could make a similar fight against cancer.

The money collected by the Clubs is to be turned in to the Division of Public Health of the General Federation for the purpose of forming "The General Federation of Women's Clubs Cancer Control Fund." This fund will not be used until a sufficient amount has been received. The Advisory Board will then recommend to the Executive Board of the General Federation how the fund should be used—whether for scholarships, educational facilities, or other purposes.

CANCER OF THE ESOPHAGUS
BY H. P. MOSHER, M. D.
and
A. S. MACMILLAN M. D.
Boston, Massachusetts

Cancer of the esophagus leads to one of the most hideous deaths to which the human race is exposed, namely death from starvation. Its only symptom is gradual increase in difficulty in swallowing, accompanied by increasing emaciation until the patient dies of starvation. A few cases die from hemorrhage caused by the cancer eroding one of the great vessels coming from the heart. In the terminal stage there may be some pain, but pain is not a prominent symptom.

The statistics of the Massachusetts General Hospital and the Massachusetts Eye and Ear Infirmary show that in every 115 patients applying for treatment, one patient comes for difficulty in swallowing. There are, of course, other causes of difficulty in swallowing than cancer. These generally are some form of non-cancerous stricture. However, in a thousand cases of patients examined for difficulty in swallowing, 350 or 40 per cent were cases of cancer. The peak of the cancer age comes between fifty and seventy years. The extremes are thirty years, and ninety.

The duration of the difficulty in swallowing before patients report for examination averages five months. This is due to the fact that patients adapt their food to their changing ability to swallow, and so report for examination late. It is imperative, in this type of cancer, as in all others, that the diagnosis should be made early.

Men, in the proportion of six to one, are subject to cancer of the esophagus. The new growth has no point of election in the esophagus, that is, it occurs in all parts with equal frequency.

There are two forms of carcinoma in the esophagus. The first arises from the epithelium, or the epidermoid, and the second arises from the glands. Epidermoid carcinoma is eight times more frequent than the glandular type.

The diagnosis is readily made by the X-ray examination. In fact, carcinoma of the esophagus is the easiest of all X-ray diagnoses to make. Its characteristic is obstruction of the esophagus above which the esophageal walls are extremely ragged and irregular. The reduced esophageal opening is centrally placed.

In the diseases of the esophagus as they are tabulated at the Massachusetts General Hospital

40% are cancer	5% are burns
15% are fibrosis lower end	4% are pulsion pouches
13% are webs	3% are extrinsic causes
11% are fibrosis upper third	2% are ulcers
6% are paralysis	1% are traction pouches

The rate of cancer deaths per 100,000 in the government statistics published in 1929 were as follows:

21.4 stomach	3.0 buccal cavity
14.6 intestine and peritoneum	2.5 skin
13.7 female genital organs	2.1 lungs and pleura
8.8 breast	1.5 esophagus
8.8 liver and gall bladder	.9 pharynx
3.7 prostate	.8 larynx

The treatment of cancer has been extremely disappointing for many years. At first it consisted in the removal of the cancerous growth through the esophagoscope to restore the patient's ability to swallow. Then came the implantation of radium seeds, and finally, the use of the X-ray.

Preliminary to these procedures, if the patient is practically starving, it is necessary to open the stomach and to place a feeding tube in it. Then the procedures just mentioned are instituted according to the preference of the surgeon. The writer, personally, has never seen a cure of cancer of the esophagus. Within the last six months, however, massive doses of X-ray have caused the apparent disappearance of epidermoid cancer in two cases treated at the Massachusetts General Hospital. No results have been obtained in the glandular type. Only time will tell whether this is anything more than a temporary improvement.

Thoracic surgery is making very rapid strides, and it is the hope of all physicians that the surgeons working in this field will soon be able to deal surgically with this disease owing to their improved technique and better methods of approach.

EXCERPTS AND STATISTICS ON CANCER
Compiled by
FRANCES A. MACDONALD, A. B.,
Field Epidemiologist, Division of Adult Hygiene
Massachusetts Department of Public Health

"Cancer is not evenly distributed throughout the country. In 1924-1927 the age adjusted rates placed New York first, Massachusetts second, and South Carolina last. Of the thirty-four Registration States the half having the highest rates are in the northern part of the country, while the remaining half includes the Southern States and a few of the Central States. It is probable that a part of the differences in rates in cancer may be due to diagnosis, but doubtless other factors are of more importance."[1]

MASSACHUSETTS CANCER DEATHS, 1933
By Age and Sex

AGE GROUPS	MALE Deaths	Percentage Distribution	FEMALE Deaths	Percentage Distribution	TOTAL Deaths	Percentage Distribution
-10	18	0.3	6	0.1	24	0.4
10-19	7	0.1	12	0.2	19	0.3
20-29	29	0.5	28	0.4	57	0.9
30-39	68	1.1	180	2.8	248	3.9
40-49	250	3.9	434	6.8	684	10.7
50-59	543	8.5	769	12.1	1,312	20.6
60-69	927	14.5	1,030	16.2	1,957	30.7
70-79	729	11.4	807	12.6	1,536	24.0
80+	208	3.3	337	5.3	545	8.6
Total	2,779	43.6	3,603	56.5	6,382	100.1

Increase of Cancer

"There have probably been greater differences of opinion and more statistical papers written on increase of cancer than any other phase of the cancer problem. Investigators working on the etiology of cancer are extremely interested in whether or not the disease is increasing beyond such increase as is bound to occur in aging populations."

"It is admitted by all statisticians that erroneous diagnosis does play an important part in cancer statistics, but to many of them the conviction is strong that the error is not sufficiently great to account for all of the remaining increase."[1]

MASSACHUSETTS AGE, SEX ADJUSTED CANCER DEATH RATES
Adjusted to Massachusetts 1900 Population
Rate per 100,000

Year	Male	Female	Total
1900	50.2	91.6	71.5
1901	50.6	93.7	72.7
1902	47.9	97.0	73.0
1903	50.9	97.8	75.0
1904	54.2	102.9	79.2
1905	55.5	103.7	80.3
1906	63.1	99.5	81.8
1907	58.9	108.7	84.4
1908	59.9	108.7	84.9
1909	60.3	108.5	85.0
1910	63.7	111.3	88.1
1911	68.8	112.1	91.0
1912	63.5	117.6	91.3
1913	71.5	119.7	96.2
1914	70.9	119.6	95.9
1915	73.7	119.5	97.2
1916	77.1	126.5	102.5
1917	76.2	127.0	102.3
1918	78.6	123.2	101.5
1919	77.9	120.5	99.7
1920	84.5	128.6	107.1
1921	85.9	129.4	108.2
1922	83.5	126.9	105.8
1923	85.4	125.8	106.1
1924	92.2	127.5	110.3
1925	89.6	130.0	110.4
1926	94.3	127.5	111.4
1927	92.5	128.9	111.1
1928	94.3	128.8	112.0
1929	93.3	127.4	110.8
1930	96.8	125.4	111.5
1931	93.6	126.2	110.3
1932	97.1	129.1	113.5
1933	102.0	128.6	115.6

During the last thirteen years the female rate shows no increase.

Nativity

"The adjusted rates for foreign born as a whole and the children of foreign born are much higher than those of native born of native parents, although there is apparently a difference between different nationalities of the foreign born."[1]

AGE, SEX ADJUSTED CANCER MORTALITY RATES IN BOSTON, BY NATIVITY
Ten-Year Average
Rate per 100,000

Nativity	Male	Female
Irish	146.1	149.8
English	118.5	166.8

Italian	71.2	99.8
Russian	125.7	118.5
Teuton	132.0	136.0
Scandinavian	127.2	110.5
Canadian	129.2	169.5
Total Foreign Born	124.0	143.5
Native Born of Native Parents	64.6	107.5
Native Born of Foreign Parents	145.3	177.8 [1]

Conjugal State

"In each country the rate of mortality upon unmarried women is higher than upon married when proper allowance is made for the numbers of women of each civil state living in each age-group. By the method of partial correlation applied to administrative units of population, it also appeared that the rate of mortality (age standardised) was negatively correlated with an index of fertility. By the use of the clinical material, it was possible to prove that the fertility of the married women who developed cancer of the breast was significantly less than that of the married women of the control group, when full allowance has been made for age, length of exposure to risk of pregnancy and the possible direct influence of the disease itself. All these results are mutually confirmatory and establish beyond doubt that a fertility below the normal for the particular nation is associated with increased liability to cancer of the breast. Whether the relation signifies a general greater liability to cancer in the case of breasts which have never developed for purposes of lactation or characterises a particular innate physiological type cannot, of course, be determined by statistical analysis alone."

"As a whole, the death rates show that unmarried women are relatively little affected by cancer of the cervix, and the disease is almost confined to women who have been pregnant. It is known that cancer of the body of the uterus is relatively more common among single women, and it is probable that the data for single women relate very largely to disease of this part of the organ alone."[3]

Causation of Cancer

"The search for the distribution of cancer in all forms of life has revealed much to suggest that it is a biologic phenomenon not dependent on any single specific factor and that it is a cellular defensive reaction to a local abnormal environment which is not efficiently eliminated by multicellular organization. The wide range of the disease suggests further that the many very different specific causes vary perhaps with species, habits, geography, organs, tissues and portals of entry. Although possibly quite different, they produce tissue destruction with consequent attempts at regeneration, during the partial failure of which the cells take on a migratory and individualistic phase which eventually destroys the whole organism of which they have been a part. This is, of course, not an unheard of phenomenon of life and is not characteristic alone of cells but of much larger units such as human beings.

"The pure experimentalists have confirmed the old empirical ideas that chronic irritation and heredity play parts although the mechanism of heredity may still be under discussion. Despite this progress, a specific cause of human cancer has not been discovered; no means of producing immunity has been established; there is no means of making the diagnosis early other than with a microscope; there is no specific method of treatment and no immediate practical means of preventing the disease through knowledge of genetics. In my opinion one of their greatest functions is censorship of the many 'cancer cures' that too readily gain publicity; I have seen excellent physicians and surgeons become prematurely enthusiastic and sincerely advocate immature spectacular ideas relative to the cause, diagnosis and treatment of cancer."[4]

Heredity

"Another obstacle is the general assumption that cancer is the result of hereditary tendencies which express themselves in the so-called spontaneous outbreak of the disease. One need not depreciate the importance of the experimental evidence regarding hereditary factors in cancer in order to remove this hindrance to the prevention of the disease. The importance of heredity must be accepted in a considerable list of less frequent forms of cancer, as recently enumerated by Wells. One may cheerfully accept all the data secured by Slye and others regarding the influence of heredity in mouse tumors, intensified by selective breeding, and still see that the hereditary tendency is not the disease itself, that the usual exciting factors must be brought into play, and that in hereditarily predisposed subjects the preventable factors may be successfully excluded.

"It appears that the human race enjoys a general susceptibility to the disease, which, however, rarely expresses itself unless extraneous exciting factors are brought into action, while the hereditary tendency may be present to an extreme degree without result unless some of these factors are at work. Nevertheless I do not believe that heredity can be dismissed from practical consideration in the origin of cancer. It is probably sound advice to offer the public, that when there is a strong tendency to cancer in the family the members of that family may well take unusual precautions against the disease. Nothing in the genetic study of cancer seems to justify the general interdiction of intermarriages among such families. It is important to remember that individuals inherit the family habits and environment of their forebears, and that these factors may explain some of the observations suggesting an influence of heredity."[5]

Contagion

"Another far more serious obstacle is the widespread assumption of the parasitic theory of the origin of cancer. If cancer is due to the action of an unknown, microscopic, perhaps ultramicroscopic, universal parasite, then effectual prevention must wait upon its discovery. At the present day, I have no hesitation in committing myself without reservation against this theory. With most general pathologists, I regard it as incompatible with the known facts about cancer. The assumption of a universal cancer parasite can be held only by those who assume in addition that cancer is a single disease, comparable to syphilis or tuberculosis. This assumption appears to be untenable. Cancer is not a single pathological entity, but a great group of diseases, of very varied origin and course. Virchow divided biological processes into three grand classes: normal growth and functional changes, inflammation, and neoplasia. Neoplastic reaction of tissue cells is comparable to inflammatory reaction. There are about as many neoplastic diseases as infectious diseases, and no more reason for assuming a single origin for the one than for the other group. If there were less anticipation of the imminent discovery of the universal cancer parasite, fewer announcements of its demonstration, and more recognition of the specific exciting factors in cancer, the cause of cancer control would be benefited."[6]

Trauma

"The traumatic origin of malignant tumours forms a voluminous and highly controversial chapter. Avoiding the controversies, it must be admitted that sarcomas of bone and brain, and more rarely still, carcinomas, arise after single traumas, but how the injury produces this result escapes adequate explanation. Some form of tissue predisposition is probably an essential factor.

"The subject of traumatic cancer greatly needs critical study from the statistical, clinical and pathological sides."[6]

Public Attitude in Cancer

"The layman knows of the many cases that are not cured, whether an attempt at cure by operation has been made or not, but he rarely knows of the cured cases, for the reason that the individual who has been relieved of the disease by operation goes about his or her business as well as ever, and disguises so far as possible, the loss of the organ or the scar of the operation by which his or her life was saved. It is difficult to controvert this personal experience of the individual by assertions of the possibilities or probabilities of cure, but it must be done if the public is to understand the actual facts of the cancer problem. Every physician should feel it his duty to make these facts clear to the laymen within his reach."[7]

ATTENDANCE AT STATE-AIDED CANCER CLINICS, 1933

Total patients	3,921
Cancer	973
Precancerous lesions	453
Deferred diagnosis	112
Undiagnosed	28
No pathology	172
Post-operative, no evidence of recurrence	102
All other conditions	2,081
Percentage with cancer	24.8
Percentage with precancerous lesions	11.6
Median age of total clinic patients	49.4
Median age of cancer patients	61.0

MEDIAN DURATION IN MONTHS BETWEEN FIRST SYMPTOM AND FIRST VISIT TO PHYSICIAN AND FIRST VISIT TO CLINIC, BY LOCATION OF CANCER, 1933

Location of Cancer	Median Duration Before First Visit to Physician	Median Duration Before First Visit to Clinic
Buccal cavity	6.0	7.1
Digestive tract	4.1	6.9
Respiratory system	4.0*	8.5*
Uterus	4.3	6.9
Other female genital organs	5.5*	6.8*
Breast	3.4	6.0
Male genito-urinary organs	6.1*	8.8
Skin	12.5	18.5
Other and unspecified organs	4.8	9.0
Total Patients**	6.2	9.4 [8]

* Based on less than 25 cases.
** Some individuals had more than one cancer.

Cancer Patients
Reason for Coming to Clinic, 1933

Reason	Percentage*
Physician	68.3
Friends or relatives	8.6
Newspapers	10.4
All others	22.3

* Does not total to 100 per cent as some individuals gave more than one reason.[8]

Cancer Patients
Symptoms that First Brought Patient to Clinic, 1933

Symptoms	Percentage*
Swelling	35.6
Ulceration	34.0
Discharge and bleeding	17.2
Pain	28.3
Deformity	7.5
Loss of weight	11.3
Malaise	4.3
Observation	4.2
Itching	1.6
Scaly skin	2.4
Others	10.0
Unknown	0.3

* Does not total to 100 per cent as multiple symptoms were given by some patients.[8]

Contact of Cancer Patients with Physician, 1933

	Percentage
Referred by physician to clinic:	
One physician consulted	39.2
More than one physician consulted	29.2
Not referred by physician to clinic:	
One or more physicians consulted	16.4
No physicians consulted	15.2 [8]

Cancer Patients
Reason for Delay Between First Symptom and First Visit to Physician, 1929

Reason	Percentage
Thought it other conditions	48.2
Felt delay short	11.6
Negligence	10.4
Symptoms not severe	8.6
Ignorance	5.4
Fear	4.5
Economics	2.7
Used home remedies	2.7
Miscellaneous	2.4
Bad advice	1.8
Opposed to physicians	1.8

Percentage of Cancer Patients Alive Five Years After Coming to Massachusetts State-Aided Cancer Clinics*

Location of Cancer	Percentage
Buccal cavity	33
Digestive tract	4
Respiratory system	0
Uterus	24

Other female genital organs	30
Breast	23
Male genito-urinary organs	12
Skin	66
Other and unspecified organs	29

* This does not represent cures as some have active cancer.

Treatment of Cancer

"As a result of the intensive study of cancer which has been going on all over the world in special cancer hospitals and research institutes during the past ten years, the treatment of cancer has been refined and developed to an extent that is perhaps not generally appreciated by members of the medical profession who have not kept closely in touch with this special line of work.

"These improvements in the treatment of cancer, moreover, have resulted not from any one epoch-making discovery in regard to the cause of cancer (unfortunately, no such discovery has yet been made); but rather by the better utilization and co-ordination of methods of treatment already known to us, combined with a more intelligent application of those methods in the light of the advances in the knowledge of the disease which have been made during this period, and by a close and co-ordinated application of the group consultation method of dealing with the disease. The treatment of cancer is admittedly no longer a 'one man job,' and the marked improvements in treatment have resulted chiefly from the organization of groups of physicians and scientists ... each competent in his own field; but working in consultation with free and frank discussion, to determine the methods best adapted to achieve the desired result in the individual case. This is the chief factor in the development of cancer therapy in recent years, and as this principle is further accepted, and more and more such groups of cancer workers are organized still further developments and refinements of treatment may confidently be expected with a corresponding increased efficiency, and a resulting diminution in the mortality of this disease.'"

"Cancer Cures"

"Drugs of all kinds have been employed both for local administration by injection or as caustic pastes and for more general constitutional effects. In some the active agent is known as creosote; in others the remedy is secret. The compounds are sold at high prices to physicians or to laymen who are sufficiently credulous to purchase them. No series of authentic cures of cancer has yet been demonstrated by any of these methods.

"Attempts to cure cancer, or to influence its growth, by diet have been widely advocated but with no success. When we realize the widespread occurrence of cancer in the animal kingdom, affecting herbivorous as well as carnivorous animals, of the most varied diet, we see how futile is the attempt to prevent or to cure cancer by any modification of diet in man.

"Perhaps the most ridiculous of all of the fake cancer cures is that which depends on a theory of electrical vibration supposed to exist in human tissues. No scientific evidence of the existence of such vibration can be shown, but a whole system of diagnosis and treatment of disease has been constructed which reaps a rich harvest for certain practitioners, while giving imaginary relief only to the imaginary diseases which are diagnosed by its own peculiar methods.

"Finally, the fake 'cancer cures,' herb and Indian doctors, increase the mortality from cancer. It is charitable to suppose that those who exploit these methods do so rather from ignorance than by intention;

but the result is the same in any case. The patient is encouraged to expect relief, until his money is exhausted and his disease is too far advanced for cure by any known method of treatment.'"

Hospitalization

"Two studies of eighty-six general hospitals in Massachusetts conducted five years apart show an improvement in the hospitalization of cancer." In 1923-1925, 4093 individuals were admitted to these hospitals for cancer, and in 1928-1930, 5479 individuals, an increase of 33.9 per cent.[1]

Prevention

"A rational basis for the prevention of cancer lies in the fact that the major forms of the disease are due to some form of chronic irritation. It is a sane and profitable and yet tedious occupation, that has long been pursued, to investigate these chronic irritations that lead to cancer. While in many instances, we have rather accurate information regarding them, in many other conditions our knowledge is very unprecise and even impressionistic. Generally the knowledge is based on clinical observation, but in some cases it is supported by experimental data, while in others there is hardly any real information available.

"In the intelligent treatment of precancerous diseases and precancerous lesions the medical profession is daily performing a service of great importance in the prevention of cancer. The list of these conditions is very long and their significance generally well organized. Yet in all the medical specialties this service is often very defective, and there is little doubt but that much more could be accomplished if the education of physicians was made more specific regarding the dangers of these conditions when untreated."

"Among preventable cancers the most obvious is the intra-oral group. It has long been known that cancers of the lip, mouth, tongue, and tonsil are due to bad teeth, tobacco, and syphilis, and the importance is, I think, in the order named. Experience in a large clinic for these diseases reveals, on the average, an astonishing degree of irritation due to these factors. Broken, decayed, and projecting teeth continually tear the adjacent mucosa. Sound teeth slightly out of alignment, but with sharp edges, are often responsible. Pyorrhea often adds an effective irritant, especially in cancer of the floor of the mouth. Elaborate plates containing various metallic alloys are particularly irritating to some mouths."

"Cancer of the lip is nearly always caused by the irritation of tobacco but a prominent predisposing factor is seborrhoeic dermatitis and inflammation of the vermilion border."

"Cancer of the external genitals in both sexes is nearly always traceable to various forms of uncleanliness of these organs. Circumcision would reduce the incidence of cancer in the male about 2 per cent."

"In the origin of cancers of the skin predisposition plays a large part. The predisposing factors are found in an abundance of suppressed hair follicles which give rise to many rodent ulcers; in the special sensitiveness of certain skins to the effects of wind and sunlight (seaman's skin, xeroderma); in the overdevelopment of sweat and sebaceous glands in persons with oily skins (seborrhoeic dermatitis), and in the occurrence of congenital pigmented moles. None of these predisposing conditions are very obscure or beyond the comprehension of a layman. With all of them the factor of chronic irritation in some form is generally necessary for the outbreak of cancer."

"The main factor in the causation of cervical cancer is the presence of cervical lacerations, especially neglected ones."

"There are two resources available, the insistent repair of cervical lesions after childbirth, and periodic examinations, during and after the child-bearing period. Since cervical cancer develops abruptly, and advances to a serious condition in many cases within a few weeks or months, these examinations must be made at least every six months, in suspicious cases, and once a year in others."

"A particularly pernicious belief widely held among women of all classes is that bleeding often marks the onset of the menopause. More often it is the signal of well established and ulcerating cancer."

"The same conditions in the mouth that lead to buccal cancer are often found in oesophageal and gastric cancer. Alcohol, tobacco, and the bolting of hot, irritating, imperfectly masticated food must be regarded as highly important in the causation of oesophageal cancer. To preach to the public the correction of such habits and conditions seems to be the sole method of attack on this very frequent malady."

"Experienced clinicians point out that gastric cancer arises in two types of subjects, one with an athletic stomach, the other with an irritable stomach that has long given trouble. Heredity may play a part in gastric cancer, probably as much through the inheritance of dietary habits as from any intrinsic tendency toward cancer."

"While present data do not seem to warrant us in attributing the majority of rectal cancers to chronic constipation alone, it is safe to urge that this condition should be avoided for the direct purpose of preventing cancer. The rectal and intestinal cancers of young adults seem referable to other and uncontrollable factors."

"From the dissection of many cancerous breasts I have long been impressed by the evidence of stagnation in the ducts leading from the cancerous area, but it must be admitted that in many breasts, especially atrophic organs, the gross evidence of stagnation has not been clear."

"We have thus clinical, anatomical, and experimental data indicating that stagnation of secretions is a prime factor in the causation of chronic mastitis and mammary cancer, and a basis is thus laid for the hygiene of the breast and the prevention of mammary cancer."[5]

Bibliography

[1] BIGELOW, GEORGE H., and LOMBARD, HERBERT L.: *Cancer and Other Chronic Diseases in Massachusetts*. Houghton Mifflin Company, Boston and New York, 1933.

[2] BIGELOW, GEORGE H., and LOMBARD, HERBERT L.: *Change in the Massachusetts Cancer Trend*. New England Journal of Medicine, Vol. 210, No. 10, March 8, 1934.

[3] *Report on the Work of the Cancer Commission for the Years 1923 to 1927*. League of Nations Health Organization, Health III. 17., Geneva, 1927.

[4] MACCARTY, WILLIAM C.: *The Cancer Problem*. Journal of the American Medical Association, Vol. 103, No. 13, September 29, 1934.

[5] EWING, JAMES: *The Prevention of Cancer*. Cancer Control, Lake Mohonk Conference, 1926. Surgical Publishing Company, Chicago, 1927.

[6] EWING, JAMES: *The Causal and Formal Genesis of Cancer*. Cancer Conference, London, 1928. William Wood and Company, New York, 1928.

[7] *Essential Facts About Cancer*. American Society for the Control of Cancer, Bulletin 14, Revised January, 1924.

[8] *Annual Report of the Massachusetts Department of Public Health*, 1933.

[9] GREENOUGH, ROBERT B.: *Modern Cancer Therapy*: A Resume. New England Journal of Medicine, December 26, 1929.

NEW GROWTHS OF THE EYE

BY J. HERBERT WAITE, M. D.

Boston, Massachusetts

New growths, primary and metastatic, spare the crystalline lens and nearly always the cornea, but involve in great variety the other tissues of the eye and adnexa. While not common, new growths in this region appear during early childhood and after midlife.

The most disastrous new growth of the first years of life is the retinoblastoma, sometimes incorrectly called "glioma retinae," a tumor involving the neuro-epithelium of the retina and extending early along the sclera-perforating vessels into the orbit or along the optic nerve into the cranium. It is disastrous because its appearance within the eye is seldom recognized early, because it is bilaterial in one-quarter of the cases, and because of its tendency to invade the cranial cavity. The presence of the growing tumor within the eye may make itself known to the parents by replacing the normally black pupil with a whitish cast, or through secondary glaucoma intervening to bring about a semi-dilated pupil, shallow anterior chamber, and in some cases injection of the vessels of the anterior segment of the eyeball. Examination of a small child must be made with the aid of general anaesthesia, if sufficient care is to be taken to differentiate between retinoblastoma and pseudoglioma, the extensive connective tissue, proliferation following suppuration. Before administering the anaesthetic, the pupil of each eye should be dilated with one per cent solution of homatropine. Then with anaesthesia, each fundus should be carefully studied, and tonometric measurements of ocular pressures should be made. If the findings support the diagnosis of tumor, the affected eye should be enucleated with a long nerve stump. To make sure that extension has not already taken place along the optic nerve, the stump should be sectioned and reported at once by a pathologist.

Of less urgency are the dermoid tumors which may appear during childhood, usually in the conjunctiva at the corneal margin, or subcutaneously at the upper outer rim of the orbit. These new growths cause trouble only through displacement of adjacent parts, and through disfigurement. They represent skin elements in abnormal sites, and may contain hair and sebaceous material. Complete removal is usually possible by careful dissection.

Abnormal pigmentations may appear in the ocular tissues of children. Diffuse and extensive pigmentation of the iris-ciliary body-choroid may slowly make one eye darker than its mate, and show typical "goose-flesh" topography on the anterior surface of the iris under sufficient magnification. Of all published cases of melanosis uvea, 30 per cent have been observed to develop epibulbar or intraocular melanosarcoma. Therefore, eyes of this type require careful follow-up. Local collections of chromatophores, called naevi, may be found on lids, conjunctiva, or iris. Little attention is paid to them if they do not increase in size or density. However, it is recognized that a benign naevus may become a malignant sarcoma, particularly if located in the conjunctiva near the corneal margin. Before excising a naevus at this site, one should carefully define its extent by careful slit-lamp examination with a microscope, so that the entire naevus may be totally removed.

After midlife, the important new growths in this region are the carcinomata of the eyelids and conjunctiva, and the sarcomata of the uveal tract.

The most common malignant tumor of eyelid or conjunctiva in older patients is the epithelioma, which takes its origin usually where one epithelium metamorphoses into another type. Sites for predilection are therefore the lid margin where skin undergoes transition into mu-

cous membrane, and the limbus where conjunctival epithelium undergoes transition into corneal epithelium. The tumor shows little tendency to metastasize except to regional lymph nodes, but does tend to erode the deeper tissues. A barrier to such erosion is interposed in Bowman's membrane of the cornea, and the cornea may become completely surrounded if tumor cells gain access to Tenon's capsule.
Epithelioma may be treated successfully by radium, X-ray, or excision. If the growth is upon the eyeball, the treatment of choice would seem to be excision, followed by careful cauterization of the entire tumor area.

In older patients, malignant epithelial growth may arise primarily in the accessory epithelial structures, the hair follicles and the sebaceous glands. On account of the tendency to ulcerate and invade, this growth is commonly called rodent ulcer. It usually appears as a small papule near the inner canthus, ulcerates, and is soon covered by a bloody crust. If the crust is removed, it is found that the edges of the ulcer are firm and elevated. The growth rapidly invades and destroys the underlying tissues, muscles, tear passages, and bony orbit, and eventually the eyeball itself.

Sarcoma may arise in any portion of the uveal tract, and is more commonly found in the choroid than in the iris or ciliary body. Sarcoma has been observed in patients as young as two years and as old as eighty-four years, but it is most frequently found between the ages of forty and sixty years. In the iris or ciliary body, sarcoma brings about an early secondary glaucoma, due to obstruction of the free escape of aqueous from the filtration angle. In the choroid, sarcoma produces at first a local defect in the corresponding visual field, and later, on account of its vascularity and serum-rich transudate into the ocular fluids it may cause a rise in ocular pressure. Extensive detachment of the retina, and cataract formation are also sequels. In every patient past forty, with one sound eye, and one affected eye, whether the affliction appears to be cataract, glaucoma, or detached retina, one must always suspect sarcoma as the underlying and original cause, and attempt to rule out its suspected presence by transillumination. Since metastasis may occur by the blood stream at any time, the only rational treatment for sarcoma of the uveal tract is to remove the eye at once.

Carcinomata which have involved the chest may metastasize to the choroid, and usually the metastasis is bilateral, and consists of a flat thickening of the posterior pole of the choroid with detachment of the retina. The patient is usually in the stage of general carcinomatosis, and treatment is therefore symptomatic.

WHAT THE PHYSICIAN SHOULD KNOW ABOUT CANCER OF THE FUNDUS OF THE UTERUS
BY STEPHEN RUSHMORE, M. D.
Boston, Massachusetts

Cancer of the fundus of the uterus can be cured—*if* certain conditions are fulfilled. It is the conditions which have to be fulfilled that are of immediate interest to the physician. The growth must be detected when it is eradicable; and the patient's general condition must be such that removal is reasonably safe.

The physician should remember in the first place, that although cancer of the fundus occasionally undergoes spontaneous cure, this is a rare occurrence, and there is no practical justification for expecting this result in any given case.

In the second place, cancer not cured grows progressively and causes death, often with great suffering. It is not a disease which is merely a slight inconvenience, remaining stationary for years.

In the third place, it occurs in a part of the body not directly accessible to touch or sight, and therefore indirect methods of diagnosis are required. Inspection of the inside of the uterus is not practicable.

It occurs more frequently after forty-five than before that age and about half the cases have been reported between fifty and sixty. Cancer of the cervix is about fifteen times as frequent as cancer of the fundus. Usually cancer of the fundus originates in the fundus; rarely does it extend up from the cervix without showing marked involvement in the cervix, and very rarely is it due to extension from outside the uterus. It is for a relatively long period of its growth localized, slow growing, not tending to metastasize and therefore amenable to treatment.

It occurs more frequently in married than in unmarried women; and in married women pregnancy seems to be a predisposing condition, although not with the overwhelming force that it is in cancer of the cervix.

It occurs in about 2 per cent of all myoma cases; and myoma occurs in 20 to 25 per cent of all carcinoma of the fundus cases. This concurrence is, therefore, worthy of clinical attention.

It has no characteristic symptoms. It is sometimes accompanied by pain, but often the pain is due to other causes. Pain due to cancer of the body of the uterus occurs when the growth has extended beyond the uterus to other organs or structures, and when the uterus, attempting to expel polypoid masses, undergoes painful contractions.

The symptoms often are increase in discharge, or beginning of discharge, many times watery in character, and bleeding between menstrual periods. If bleeding and discharge occur after the menopause, and examination of the cervix shows no sign of a growth there, the patient should be regarded as having potential cancer of the fundus until adequate examination for exclusion has been made.

The probability is that such a patient does not have cancer of the fundus, but cancer is so serious that no chance of overlooking it should be taken. The probability is that some benign (non-cancerous) condition is the cause of the bleeding.

If a patient has bleeding from the uterus after the menopause, and a myoma is found on examination, the bleeding is probably not due to the myoma but may be due to cancer of the fundus. The patient should be given a general anaesthetic and subjected to a thorough curettage of the uterus. The cervix should be well dilated and the size and shape of the uterine cavity, and firmness and consistency of the uterine wall noted carefully. Every portion of the lining of the uterus should be gone over carefully with a curet small enough to enter the corners and sharp enough to remove the endometrium without undue force.

Every bit of tissue should be sent to the laboratory at once for examination; or, if the laboratory is not immediately accessible, the tissue should be placed at once in suitable hardening fluid. The curettage should be performed carefully, not casually; it is a "minor operation" only in the immediate risk to the patient's life.

Numerous failures to detect cancer when present have been reported. They are generally regarded as due to defect of the operator rather than defect of the method or of the pathologist.

The tissue should be submitted to a competent pathologist for microscopical examination. The diagnosis should not be made on the gross appearance of the tissue.

If cancer is found to be present, the patient should, in general, be subjected to hysterectomy, preferably by the abdominal route, after closure of the cervical canal from below by suture. If on abdominal exploration, the growth seems eradicable, removal of the uterus without wide dissection of tissue is indicated.

Radium may be tried if operation is contraindicated. Ordinarily it is not satisfactory. There is first the difficulty of determining the exact position of the malignant area. Then the growth may be unexpectedly massive and not suitable for radiation. On the other side, is the generally highly satisfactory result of operation, relatively low immediate mortality, and considerable percentage of ultimate cures.

It is probable that more ultimate cures have followed neglect or delayed treatment in this than in almost any other form of cancer, but this is no justification for putting off for even a week the finding out of what is actually the matter in any patient suspected of having cancer of the fundus.

HISTORICAL TRENDS IN CANCER
BY ELEANOR J. MACDONALD, A. B.,
*Statistician, Division of Adult Hygiene,
Massachusetts Department of Public Health*

The development of knowledge concerning a disease is generally based on the exact state of knowledge of a period for a foundation, with the additions of the forward-looking pioneers of that period furnishing the setting for the next period. In cancer, as in other diseases, and even as in industrial, governmental, and literary fields the comprehensive state of the whole civilized world has had a direct bearing. It was as recently as the seventeenth century that Francis Bacon, the English philosopher, said with complete conviction, "I have taken all knowledge to be 'my province'." It was nearly two hundred years later before students felt that specialization was necessary for the greatest advance in a given subject; that, except in rare cases, general knowledge must be the object of the student for a background upon which his own more or less limited specialty must be developed.

The history of cancer might be said to have one underlying trend from the beginning to the present time—the general trend of theories relating to the causation of cancer. The separation of the specialties of gross and microscopic pathology and cancer surgery is a development occurring about the beginning of the nineteenth century, and was followed a century later by radiology. The cleavage between surgery and the general trend of causation is not as clearly defined as in pathology and radiology. In considering this trend some of the early practitioners who performed outstanding operations for cancer will be mentioned as an introduction to the definite development of the trend of surgery in cancer. The historical trends in cancer will be developed with this thought in mind, as follows:

1. General trend of theories relating to cancer.
2. Trend of gross and microscopic pathology.
3. Trend of surgery in cancer.
4. Trend of radiology in cancer.
5. Trend of present control measures in cancer.

The popular definition, according to "Webster's International Dictionary," describes cancer as a "malignant growth of tissue, usually ulcerating, tending to spread by local invasion and also through the lymph and blood stream, associated with general ill health and progressive emaciation;—so called originally because of the veins and hardened tissue extending from it, compared by the ancients to the claws of a crab; ..."

In a paper on "The Life History of Cancer" by David Arthur Welsh, a physician of Edinburgh, a few salient thoughts are set forth. In part he said, "What is it that starts the cancer cell on its malignant career? ... We do not know. Under the microscope we can see the birth of a cancer, we can see it grow, we can see it spread, we can see it invade and destroy the healthy tissues, we can tell cancer cells from tissue cells, we can classify and grade the different types of cancer and tumor growth. Whole chapters in the life history of cancer are open to our view. But the chapters that we are most anxious to read are closed.

"These are the chapters on the ultimate cause and on the essential nature of cancer. Perhaps the analogy that is easiest to follow is to look upon cancer as a local rebellion of a group of discontented cells within that commonwealth of working cells which form the human body. The rebellious cells throw off all restraint; and, if the local riot be not promptly checked by heroic measures, it may develop into a generalized invasion which destroys the whole commonwealth."

This picture of cancer is the cumulation of the knowledge of the ages. The fossil bones of extinct animals prove beyond doubt that cancer has been in existence from prehistoric times. Pathological lesions including tumors have been recognized among the prehistoric mammals. Burton J. Lee said, "These remains were the first to attract the attention of early paleontologists and the relics found in them were for a long time supposed to be evidences of the universal flood, which, according to Hebrew tradition, had destroyed all animal life. In the Mesozoic era, or age of reptiles (6,000,000 to 12,000,000 years ago), the bones of the monosaurs, dinosaurs, pleisosaurs, phytosaurs and other reptiles show lesions resembling the modern forms of osteoma, osteosarcoma and hemangioma of bone. The evidences of bone cancer increase with each succeeding geological period through the Cenozoic and Holozoic eras until, in the Egyptian, benign and malignant tumors of the soft parts are discovered."

In the Ancient Indian Epic, the Ramayana of about 2000 B.C., a disease was described which resembled cancer. The Ancient Indians were the first group to leave us a systematic presentation of diseases. Although their knowledge of anatomy was slight, they were doing outstanding work in surgery. Neoplasmic extirpation was mentioned, as was an ointment of arsenic compounds, and cautery for treatment of growths.

Egyptian medical theories have been preserved in the Ebers Papyrus of 1500 B.C. Anatomy was so little understood by them that any swelling was considered a cancer. The ointment, composed of arsenic and vinegar, which they used as treatment for external cancer, was named "Egyptian Ointment," and used until the sixteenth century. The first specific description of a particular type of cancer was an inscription from the library of Nineveh of about 800 B.C. in which carcinoma of the breast was recognized.

The terms "cancer" meaning benign tumor, and "carcinoma" meaning malignant tumor were first used by Hippocrates.

General Trend

After Hippocrates, the early centuries produced many original theorists on cancer. The interesting thing about cancer, as about diabetes, is the enormous number of earnest students who have pondered the problem. No matter how irrelevant some of the hypotheses may seem in the light of subsequent development, there are few among them which do not merit serious contemplation, and admiration for the physicians who thought of them.

Cato, a prominent Roman in the first century, described the healing properties of cabbage. Celsus, a Roman contemporary of Christ, described his belief in the clinical appearance of external cancer and advised operation for the less severe forms such as cancer of the lip. It was he who introduced the idea that cancer could be diagnosed by the inefficacy of therapy—if you cut it out and it grew again, it was cancer. Galen, also a Roman, dogmatized the old humoral physiology wherein the body was thought to have been composed of four fluids— blood, mucus, yellow and black bile— and specified black bile as the offending agent causing cancer. This theory of the atra bilis, or black bile, was the dominating influence on cancer etiology and therapy for a thousand years. Some of Galen's ideas are still important as, for example, his warning that cancer must be diagnosed at the beginning. He believed that cancer was a constitutional disease and vaguely recognized secondary growths. For therapy he advised a restricted diet, blood letting, cautery, and opium salves for severe pain. He devised a classification for tumors which was in use for over a thousand years.

Leonides, a native of Alexandria, 180 A.D., was responsible for popularizing surgery in cancer and approached modern methods in his excision of breast cancer. Oribasius, in the fourth century, expressed the opinion that cancer was generally incurable except in its earliest stages. Aëtius, in the sixth century, gave a nearly-authentic description of cancer of the rectum. Paul of Ægina, in the seventh century, stated that cancer could occur in every internal and external place.

The three best known men of the Arabian school to whom much historical credit is ascribed in popularizing medical information were Rhazes, Avicenna, and Avenzoar. Rhazes, of the ninth and tenth centuries, systematized the works of Hippocrates and Galen. Avicenna, of the tenth and eleventh centuries, left one of the best works on medicine until the fifteenth century. In cancer, he believed that the early stages were curable through internal therapy, diet, and blood letting. He advocated the use of arsenic internally. For open, external cancers he used plasters. Avenzoar, of the eleventh and twelfth centuries, introduced probe therapy and rectal feeding in cancer of the esophagus and stomach.

Petrocellus, of the School of Salerno, in the twelfth century, was the first to make digital examination in the case of cancer of the rectum. Roger of Parma, of the same school, in the twelfth century, sometimes called the "Father of Surgery," advised against the operation on all hidden cancers.

The thirteenth, fourteenth, fifteenth, and sixteenth centuries produced Lanfranchi, Florentinus, di Vigo, Fallopius, and other famous physicians. Sennert, practicing in the sixteenth and seventeenth centuries, introduced the much-mooted question of the contagiousness of cancer.

Fabricius Hildanus, in the sixteenth and seventeenth centuries, who was a remarkable anatomist, has recorded in his works some detailed and authentic operations for cancer. Lee said of him that he "was the first to practice a complete axillary dissection in the treatment of mammary cancer." A Dutch contemporary, Nicholas Tulpius, spent much of his life working on cancer. He gave exact clinical descriptions of the disease. In the case of cancer of the bladder, he was the first to recognize and diagnose it in life. He also subscribed to the theory of cancer contagion. Another contemporary was Severinus, who was the first to distinguish between cancer and benign tumors of the breast.

England, at the period of the Renaissance, introduced a new departure in cancer therapy. In the works of William Clowes, personal physician to Queen Elizabeth, was mentioned the remarkable cure of a cancer through the consecration of the Queen. This was, undoubtedly, an outgrowth of the idea that the French Queen, in the same manner, had cured tuberculosis.

Caustics were commonly used in all cauteries during this Renaissance Period.

The main addition to existing cancer knowledge by Paracelsus, the controversial Swiss alchemist and physician, was that cancer developed as a result of a superfluity of mineral salt in the blood seeking an outlet. Van Helmont, his follower, first distinguished cancer from leprosy.

Descartes, the philosopher, introduced the sour lymph theory, the study of which occupied all investigators for 150 years. The theory was as follows: "It was assumed that extravascular lymph coagulated through some process and became hard, and that then scirrhus arose, which was mild; if the lymph, however, fermented, or became sour, or otherwise contained some acid substance, severe cancer developed. The severity, therefore, was dependent on the quality of the lymph, on its thickness, its fermentation, its alkalescence and its acidity. Pathological anatomy played no role in this theory."

The lymph theory was subjected to a variety of experiments. Among the earliest was that in which the lymph was coagulated through heat. A froth was produced. Froth was produced when tumors were boiled. Therefore, it was concluded that tumors were lymphatic in origin without any more direct proof. Many practitioners who noted the difference between benign and malignant tumors could not content themselves with this theory, so the hypothesis naturally followed that it was not the lymph but the degeneration of the lymph that caused cancer. Antoine Louis, the second director of the Academy of Surgery in Paris, subscribed to this theory as did Le Dran, who proved the local character of the disease, with special reference to skin cancer, and who sought to prove that many of the reported cures in medical literature had not really been cancer at all. Astruc, another contemporary, cited as indirect causes of cancer, trauma, scabies, and constipation. This man also distinguished cysts from cancer.

With Morgagni, the Italian pathological anatomist, came not only the basis of pathological anatomy, but also a concentration of attention on cancer of the internal organs. He led the way in the study of the gross pathology of tumors, and his example was followed by Le Dran, Bayle, and Laennec in France, and by John Hunter, Wardrop, Hodgkin, and Cooper in England. Morgagni was the first to begin opposition to the Cartesian lymph theory. He offered no substitute, but rested his case with the recognition that an impasse had been reached.

In 1773, the Academy of Lyon raised as a problem for theses discussion, "What is Cancer?" Wolff considered that the prize-winning thesis of Bernard Peyrilhe was handled with genius. Peyrilhe, a chemist, was working for his Ph.D. degree, and afterward became professor of chemistry in the School of Health in Paris. Peyrilhe showed that it was not feasible to continue research along the paths already trod; that a new path would have to be sought. The four potential directions which research should follow were:

1. The sources of cancer poison.
2. The ascertainment of its nature.
3. The way in which it works.
4. The best method of cure.

Peyrilhe clearly described the clinical appearances of the early and late stages. He still adhered to the lymph theory in part, though he believed that it could not be a case of spontaneous degeneration of the lymph, but must be instead the result of a specific cancer virus. He tried to establish this idea experimentally, but finally decided that the lymph, through a lack of motion, coagulated and when dampness reached it, it decayed.

Peyrilhe was the first author to attempt a solution to the problem of cancer through experimentation on animals. He produced a wound on the back of a dog, and injected it with matter from a breast cancer. His landlady, who could not stand the howling of the dog, drowned the animal before the experiment could be concluded.

Boerhaave, working in Holland contemporaneously with Morgagni, introduced the idea that inflammation played a large part in pathology of cancer. It arose, he felt, in the rubbing of the blood in the smallest vessels as a result of mechanical injury, or blood which had been amassed through obstruction, and that the seat of the inflammation was in the lymph vessels.

The theory of Sylvius was based on the chemical constituents of the body. Fermentation was the chief cause of all functions. Even the motion of the blood was caused through the fermentation of alkali from the liver, and acid from the saliva. This was a natural outgrowth of humoral pathology.

Friedrich Hoffmann, another of the famous German physicians, developed an interesting system and introduced it in 1718. It was a combination of the three most popular medical theories after the black bile era,—i.e., the Cartesian theory of sour lymph, the mechanical theory, and the chemical theory. He believed strongly in the heredity of cancer. The first reference to the theory of heredity found in the literature was in the refutation of it by Daniel Sennert (1572-1637). Sennert disagreed with a case cited by Zacutus Lisitanus in which Lisitanus stated that a daughter had contracted cancer from her mother not through contagion but through an hereditary infection.

Great Britain's contributions in the eighteenth century were chiefly from Alexander Monro of the famous family of surgeons in Edinburgh, commonly known as Monro Primus, Secundus, and Tertius who clearly defined lymph stasis and said it caused cancer; and John Hunter, who advanced a well-thought-out thesis on coagulated lymph. "According to Hunter, when blood coagulated it became divided into two substances,—into blood water and into coagulated lymph. Hunter attributed no further biological significance to the red blood corpuscles. This lymph also played a large part in inflammation. . . . The source of the blood of cancer was 'coagulated lymph'." Since coagulated lymph came from the enlarged vessels, Hunter attempted compression of the vessels to shut off the nourishment of the tumor.

The impetus that Hunter gave to the study of cancer among the English surgeons prompted the formation, in the early nineteenth century, of a society of its most outstanding physicians. This society was called the "Society for Investigating the Nature and Cure of Cancer" (1802) and was composed of such outstanding men as Baillie, Sims, Willan, Home, Sharpe, Pearson, Abernethy, Denman, and others. Every well-known physician in England received a questionnaire of thirteen questions of which the ten most important follow:

"1. The diagnostic symptoms of cancer.
2. The nature of cancer, especially pathologically-anatomically.
3. Is cancer a primary disease or can other diseases develop into cancer?
4. Is cancer hereditary?
5. Is cancer contagious?
6. Is cancer related to other diseases?
7. Is there a stage in which cancer is only local, and does cancer have the tendency to produce the same tumors in other parts of the body?
8. Influence of the climate and the environs on the spread of cancer.
9. Is there a predispositioning temperament?
10. Do animals have cancer?"

The Society was working about one hundred years ahead of its time, and dissolved in 1806 because of lack of cooperation. Home, of the original Society, was one of the first to use the microscope in order to become familiar with the finer anatomical structure of cancer.

The late eighteenth and early nineteenth centuries witnessed an unprecedented progress in the description and classification of cancer. Pott's description of chimney-sweep's cancer has become a classic. This was but one of many accurate clinical diagnoses of the time. Another innovation of this period was the establishment of the first hospital exclusively for patients with cancer. Jean Godinot, a canon of the Cathedral of Rheims, had devoted his life to caring for the poor, and at his death left money for erecting and maintaining a cancer hospital. It was opened in 1740 with twelve beds. Cancer was popularly thought to be contagious at this period, and in 1779 this hospital was moved outside the city. It was called the Hôpital Saint Louis. Until 1846 it was used for cancer patients only.

In England, the first cancer service in a general hospital was established in 1792. John Howard, a surgeon and pupil of the famous Pott, suggested that some of the airy, unused wards of the Middlesex Hospital be appropriated for patients with cancer, where they might remain "until either relieved by art or released by death." In addition, he secured 3500 pounds for maintenance. Interest grew in this cancer work and Middlesex Hospital has, through the Cancer Research Laboratories and the Bland-Sutton Institute of Pathology, become one of the most famous clinics of the world.

John A. Paris, in 1822, described arsenic cancer in man and animals in Cornwall, England. He noticed that horses and cows in the neighborhood of the copper smelting factories lost their hoofs, and even suffered from a cancerous condition of the rump. The smelters were frequently afflicted with cancer of the scrotum. It was 1888 before Hutchinson recognized arsenic as the irritating agent in this form of cancer.

Between 1872 and 1875, the theory of Julius Friedrich Cohnheim that there was a congenital foundation for cancer began to gain in prestige. In 1877, Cohnheim published a text book on pathology in which he presented this embryonal theory of the origin of cancer. Cohnheim, the favorite pupil of Virchow, did not agree with his teacher that cancer could be caused by inflammation alone. He felt that in an early stage in the development of the embryo, certain cells were not properly allocated. These cells being embryonic in character, had a remarkable ability to proliferate, and this proliferation was cancer. This theory has been modified by various observers.

The transitional period of the nineteenth to the twentieth century was accompanied by changes in methods of research, and changes in methods of treatment. The period that was popularizing the telephone and rapid transit was also forging ahead in medicine. One of the last theories preceding this era was that cancer might be induced by parasites. Reginald H. Harrison, in 1889, described pathologically five infected gall bladders, four of which had carcinoma. He had noted the frequency of carcinoma of the bladder among patients with Bilharziasis. These five patients had died of Bilharziasis, a disease common among the Egyptians, caused by the severe and long-continued irritation of the deposition on the walls of the bladder and rectum of the eggs of the parasite Bilharzia haematobia. On the basis of these observations, Harrison suggested that the parasite might be the predisposing irritant. In 1905 a paper was published in which Carl Goebel verified these findings, basing his opinion on a larger number of cases. More recently, cancer of the liver, also caused by flukes, was discovered among the Chinese.

Animal experimentation, which had been tried without success by

Peyrilhe in 1773 and by Dupuytren in 1807, was successfully launched by Arthur Hanau in 1889. He was a lecturer at the University of Zurich and published a paper in which he described the transplantation of spontaneous carcinoma of the vulva of a rat to the testes of two male rats. His work was not recognized and he committed suicide. There were several other experimenters in this field, but the ability to inoculate rats with sarcoma was not established beyond a doubt until 1901 by Leo Loeb, in America, and by Jensen, in Denmark, in 1903. These experimenters carried mice with cancer through nineteen or more generations without changing the microscopic structure of the sarcoma. Jensen pointed out that he had effected his reproduction of the sarcoma by actual transplantation of the parenchymal cells of the original tumor, some of which lived and started the new tumor.

Peyton Rous, working on forty spontaneous tumors of chickens, five of which were transplantable, at the Rockefeller Institute between 1910 and 1914, showed that these tumors could be transplanted by extracts of the tumor tissue from which all cells had been removed. One of these tumors, a pure spindle-cell sarcoma called Chicken Tumor I or, more commonly, Rous sarcoma, has been a source of intense investigation ever since.

In 1913, Johannes Fibiger, professor of pathology in the University of Copenhagen, found at autopsy large papillomas of the stomach in three wild rats. Careful study showed that the stomach contained a parasitic worm of the nematode group. The effect of these nematode worms in the development of malignant tumors was first noticed by Borrel in 1910. Five years of intensive work on Fibiger's part proved that this nematode, during its evolution, used a particular type of cockroach as the intermediate host. Fibiger thus produced gastric papillomas and carcinoma by feeding these cockroaches to rats. Other sarcomas have been produced in rats by feeding them with cysticercus fasciolaris. Cancer of the gall bladder has been produced in guinea pigs by the insertion of human gallstones.

Katsusaburo Yamagiwa and Koichi Ichikawa were the first to produce true carcinoma from coal tar irritation. The effect of scarlet red dyes on tissue proliferation had been demonstrated and workers for nearly twenty years had been attempting this, but it was first accomplished in 1916 by painting the ears of rabbits with coal tar. Leitch has since produced malignant growths in laboratory animals by potassium arsenite, paraffin, and other "carcinogens." All of these experiments emphasize, aside from the point in question, how valid Virchow's irritation theory still is.

Darwin's "Origin of Species" and Galton's "Law of Ancestral Heredity" were heralded by scientists when they were produced. Contemporaneously with Darwin, Gregor Mendel, Abbot of Brünn in Moravia, was working on the law of inheritance. He communicated his great law to the Society of Naturalists at Brünn in 1865. This law did not become generally known until 1900 when De Vries arrived at it independently. Two years later, Mendel's original papers were translated, and his work received its just acclaim.

Five years later, in 1907, the first significant study on the heredity of mouse cancer appeared in the "Journal of Medical Research." Ernest Edward Tyzzer showed in this article that by crossing cancerous mice families could be produced with an abnormally high incidence of spontaneous tumors. This was the beginning of the experimental study of heredity in mouse cancer.

Clarence C. Little and Maud Slye are prominent present-day investigators of genetics in cancer through experiments with mice. Dr. Little started his strain of mice in 1909. Miss Slye has a long strain of mice, and published her earliest material about 1913. These are but two of many serious workers on this subject, but the true genetic picture of cancer still remains a question.

Trend of Gross and Microscopic Pathology

The first attempt at a systematic monograph on pathology was written by Matthew Baillie in 1793. A nephew of the Hunters, he carried on the tradition of the famous family, and based his work on 'the preparations in the Hunters' museum. There had been earlier attempts to set forth pathology, but they had been largely limited to unallied case reports. Baillie stated that he was going to limit himself to "an account of the morbid changes of structure which take place. . . . This will be done according to a local arrangement, very much in the same manner as if we were describing natural structure." Baillie included descriptions and engravings of the gross morphology of cancer of the esophagus, stomach, and bladder.

Marie-François-Xavier Bichat, the famous French anatomist, who died in 1802 at thirty-one years of age, introduced in his short span of life the consideration of body structure in terms of the tissues of which it was composed. This was a new departure from the former methods in which disease pathology was described in terms of organs and systems of organs. In the case of cancer, Bichat taught that the tissue was the seat of the disease and differentiated between the stroma, or frame work of an organ, and the chyma, or essential elements of an organ. Bichat, without the use of a microscope, recognized that tumors must be composed of the common unit of structure,—the cell.

In the evolution of pathology of cancer, many excellent monographs on individual types of cancer have appeared. The distinction between pulmonary tuberculosis and cancer of the lung was established by Laennec, a general pathologist, in 1815. He was the first to recognize that melanoma was a distinct type of cancer. His autopsy experience was extensive.

Sir Astley Paston Cooper, surgeon to Guy's Hospital, London, published two deservedly famous books on diseases and anatomy of the breast in 1829 and 1840, respectively. The first volume dealt with benign tumors and inflammatory conditions, and is notable especially for the first clear diagnostic account of fibro-adenoma, and a classic description of chronic cystic mastitis. The second book is famous for its authoritative description of the structure of the breast. In 1830 appeared Cooper's work, "Observations on the Structure and Diseases of the Testis." He described accurately the means of early diagnosis, the natural history, and course of metastasis of cancer of the testicle.

In 1829, Joseph Claude Anthelm Récamier used the term "metastasis" to describe secondary growths. It was he who first described invasion of the veins by cancer, and who noted that chronic irritation of supernumerary organs resulted in cancer. The introduction of the achromatic microscope by Selligues and Chevalier, in 1824, opened the way that has led to the present time in steady progress in histology and to a better knowledge of cell structure. In 1665, Hooke had discovered the cell as a unit of vegetable structure. Raspail, in 1827, examined adipose tissue and discovered the analogy to cell growth in vegetable life.

In 1832, Thomas Hodgkin presented a paper "On Some Morbid Appearances of the Absorbent Glands and Spleen." Samuel Wilks, biographer of Guy's Hospital, later applied Hodgkin's name to malignant lymphogranuloma, a case of which Hodgkin had included in the above study, although he made no claim to having conclusively isolated and described the disease. In fact, this distinction was not accomplished beyond question until 1898, when Carl Sternberg, in an excellent monograph, distinguished Hodgkin's disease from aleukemic leukemia, or pseudoleukemia, with which it had been confused. Sternberg gave perfectly accurate descriptions with one exception,—he thought he had found tubercle bacilli in most of his cases.

Johannes Müller, a contemporary of Hodgkin, was working in the Royal Museum of Berlin on a rearrangement of tumors. He was dissatisfied with their classification and reclassified them, basing his opinions on their histological appearance. He published, in 1838, the first extensive microscopical study of diseased tissue, and established the part of the cell in tumors. The same year, two of his pupils, Schwann and Schleiden, published their work on the physiology of the cell in plant and animal life. Müller was almost prophetic in his knowledge of cancer.

In 1849, after seven years' work, John Hughes Bennett, published one of the earliest English monographs on the pathology of cancer. He described fifty-six tumors, their clinical history, operation, and follow-up. He failed to recognize carcinoma of the skin. Some of his recommendations as to cancer therapy are still sound.

One of the earliest students of cancer of the skin and mucous surfaces was the Copenhagen pathologist, Adolph Hannover, a pupil of Müller. Hannover felt that these tumors were different from cancer, because he could not find "the specific cancer cell." He called this group "epithelioma," and included both basal and squamous cell carcinoma. Although he made the initial error of calling this group non-cancers, he gave valuable gross and microscopical descriptions and did much toward bringing diagnosis by biopsy into prominence.

In 1855, Manuel Garcia, a singing teacher, devised a mirror on a long handle, by the use of which he studied the movements of the larynx. Two years later, Ludwig Türck, a neurologist in the University of Vienna, demonstrated laryngeal lesions with a similar mirror. The next year, Johann Czermak, professor of physiology in the University at Pest, improved on this method by inventing the perforated concave head-mirror. Both Czermak and Turck described laryngeal tumors viewed by this method.

Charles-Philippe Robin described the histogenesis of carcinoma of the kidney in 1855, and Ernst Leberecht Wagner laid the foundations of knowledge of the pathology of uterine cancer in 1858.

John Adams, a surgeon to the London Hospital, and one of the prominent contributors to the gross pathology of the prostate, was the first to distinguish between hypertrophied prostate and cancer of the prostate.

Velpeau, in 1854, professor of medicine at Paris and a leading French surgeon of the early nineteenth century, emphasized for the first time in France the difference between fibro-adenoma and carcinoma.

In 1855, Billroth, who had come under Müller's influence in pathologic histology, published his first report. He was assistant to the surgeon, Langenbeck, and had Langenbeck's operative specimens to work with. His first paper classified and described polyps, and made it clear that they did not degenerate, as a rule, into carcinoma. His interest in tumors continued through his long career as a surgeon. Living as he did in the developmental period of microscopic pathology and antiseptic surgery, he assimilated the advances as they came, and contributed more to the subject of tumors than any other surgeon.

Samuel W. Gross, of Philadelphia, a lecturer on surgical pathology, wrote the first comprehensive account of bone sarcoma in 1879. In 1880 he published the first book in English on tumors of the breast which demonstrated the relationship between microscopic diagnosis and clinical knowledge. At a time when cancer of the breast was generally considered incurable, Gross proved by his records that about

10 per cent of his patients were alive and well three years after operation. He insisted on the removal of the whole breast and all the axillary glands in every case of breast cancer.

In 1883, Anton Wolfler gave the first sound classification of thyroid tumors. Wolfler was later professor of surgery at Graz and at Prague and became justly famous for his work in thyroid and gastro-intestinal surgery.

Müller's most famous pupil was Rudolph Ludwig Karl Virchow. He sensed the importance of the microscopical approach to pathology, and his book, "Cellular Pathology," published in 1858, is probably the most important single work in the history of medicine. When Virchow began the study of medicine, cellular structure was vaguely recognized, but was confused in origin with the essential primary fluid of the humoral theory. Virchow disregarded this idea and with the famous "Omnis cellula e cellula" established the cell on its own—as the unit in which disease processes operate.

Virchow described tumors as a proliferation of cells of connective tissue, as a result of some irritating element or secretion. Virchow divided tumors into two classes: the homologous, resulting from a proliferation of a type of cell already present; and the heterologous, resulting from a change in character to cells of a different type. The first group he classed benign generally; and the second group, malignant. Virchow's belief that all malignant tumors arose heterologously from connective tissue aroused such controversy that it was a moot question among German pathologists for a quarter of a century. Virchow did not comprehend the mechanism of metastasis, although he recognized cancer cell emboli in the blood stream and the spread of a primary cancer to a second site. What Garrison describes as "the dynamic phase of Virchow's doctrine, or chronic irritation," is considered as sound today as it was a century ago.

In 1865, Thiersch, German professor of surgery at Erlangen and Leipzig, modified Virchow's theory somewhat by showing that the cells of a carcinoma were derived from epithelium and not from connective tissue. Thiersch is notable for other reasons. He demonstrated that the occurrence of secondary foci of carcinoma in lymph nodes was the result of metastasis of carcinoma cells, and he was one of the first to apply Lister's antiseptic method. Professor Wilhelm Waldeyer, of Breslau, completed Thiersch's work in 1872. He showed that metastasis might occur through the lymph, as well as the blood. Thiersch had shown that the cells of an epithelial carcinoma were derived from epithelium rather than connective tissue. Waldeyer confirmed this epithelium as the source of epithelial tumors in internal organs. Waldeyer also demonstrated that metastasis occurred by direct extension and embolism with the lymph and blood vessels acting as channels.

Embryonal adenomyo-sarcoma of the kidney was first described by Carl Joseph Eberth in 1872. Eberth was one of the most famous of the German pathologists, and the demonstrator of the typhoid bacillus.

In 1874, Sir James Paget described that breast condition which bears his name. Paget is one of the best known among English physicians, for his book on surgical pathology was widely used as a text book. His fame rested on his diagnostic ability.

In 1874, Sappey, professor of anatomy at Paris, added signally to the knowledge of the lymphatics. William Hunter, around 1746, had demonstrated the independence of lymphatics from arteries and veins by means of injections of mercury. This led to an increased enthusiasm in the study of the lymphatics. In 1787, Mascagni published his great book on the lymphatics. This was the authority on the subject for almost a century, when Sappey made public his work on the subject. Sappey, by improved technique, was able to ascertain and chart further details of the lymphatics in many parts of the body so accurately, that, with the newly aroused consciousness on the part of the surgeons of the importance of lymphatic drainage in cancer therapy, and the use of these charts, many early radical operations were planned.

In 1896, a further advance was made in the knowledge of the anatomy of the lymphatics by Gerota of Berlin. Until his experiments, many of the finer lymphatics had been ruptured by the force necessary to inject mercury and other materials. He used capillary pipets of glass and injected through them such materials as Prussian blue, suspended in turpentine and ether. By this means, experiments were performed which gave regional lymphatic information of extreme importance in cancer surgery. Within five years, papers appeared clearing up the confusion about exact lymphatic structure in the nose, cheek, lip, tongue, breast, stomach, cecum, colon, rectum, uterus, and other organs. This knowledge was a necessary precursor of the radical block dissections in which not only the tumor mass itself, but all its ramifications subject to metastases were to be removed in order to effect permanent recovery.

In 1888, Sir Byrom Bramwell published a monograph entitled, "Intracranial Tumors." Bramwell was a lecturer in the School of Medicine in Edinburgh, had had nineteen years of intensive clinical experience, and had been a pathologist for three years to the Edinburgh Royal Infirmary. Harvey Cushing has called this the outstanding clinical treatise on intracranial tumors of that early period in the development of brain surgery, and advised that neurologists refer to it when some unusual clinical condition arose.

Hans Kundrat gave the description of lymphosarcoma, which is still in use, in a paper published in 1893.

In 1902, in a book on "The Microscopic Diagnosis of Malignant Tumors," David von Hansemann, a German professor, founded the modern trend of grading tumors according to their degree of malignancy. He correlated the degree of anaplasia, or change from a specific histologic type of cell, with the degree of malignancy.

The same year, another German pathologist, Maximilian Borst, wrote in two volumes an outstanding work on the pathology of tumors, giving a comprehensive picture of the natural history and pathology of cancer as it stood at the date of writing.

In 1903, Edmund Krompecher, professor at the University of Budapest, wrote a monograph in which he separated from other epidermal cancers, the group which retained the structure of the basal cells. These he called "basal-cell carcinomas." This marked a definite improvement in the classification of tumors.

The development of gross and microscopic pathology in the last few years has been omitted because of the inadvisability of selecting outstanding works when proximity to them makes fair evaluation impossible.

Trend in Surgery

Surgery has been the preëminent method of treatment in cancer from the time of the ancient Ebers Papyrus, and the historical trend of the disease shows surgeons to have been active in investigations, the results of which would improve their therapeutic resources and surgical technique. It is significant that the first group to organize in large numbers to investigate the cause and nature of cancer should have been England's most outstanding surgeons.

Celsus, in the first century, has left excellent descriptions of operations for lip and other cancers. Leonides, of Alexandria, in the second century, and Guy de Chauliac, in the fourteenth century, both outstanding surgeons, left descriptions of operations on cancers. Paré, in the sixteenth century, operated only on accessible cancers. Hildanus, of the late sixteenth and early seventeenth centuries, did the first axillary dissection for breast cancer. Severinus, a contemporary of Hildanus, a great surgeon, first differentiated between benign and malignant tumors of the breast. He operated for benign tumors because he thought they might become malignant.

Le Dran, one of the most enlightened surgeons of the eighteenth century, wrote an excellent treatise on the nature and treatment of cancer. He felt cancer was only local in its early stages, that it spread by way of the lymphatics to regional nodes, and from there to the general circulation. He described the general route of metastasis in breast carcinoma. He cut out the involved nodes, but felt that when they were involved, the case was generally incurable. Le Dran was an earnest educator in opposing therapy, other than surgery, which he considered impractical. Le Dran showed a great advance over previous knowledge in cancer. Récamier, who was the first to recognize with clarity the extension of cancer and to use the term "metastasis," was an outstanding surgeon.

John C. Warren, of Boston, Massachusetts, a pupil of Cooper and professor of anatomy and surgery at Harvard University, devoted much of his life to the surgical treatment of tumors. In 1837, he published the first American work on cancer, "Surgical Observations on Tumours, with Cases and Operations." It was Warren who performed the operation introducing the use of ether in surgery, and the operation itself was on a vascular tumor of the neck.

In 1830, Jacques L. Lisfranc read a paper in which he described perineal resection of the rectum for cancer. Having first carried out elaborate studies to ascertain the height of the peritoneal reflection from the rectum in men and women, and to make sure of the chief vessels encountered, he had operated on nine cases, six of which operations were successful.

In 1841, Auguste B. Bérard presented the first comprehensive treatise on parotid tumors. Bérard had perfected his technique for operative removal which he believed was necessary, and based the paper on fifty-two reports which he had collected. He had learned to control hemorrhage by careful ligation of vessels, supplemented by pressure. He felt that injury to the facial nerve was the only thing to be feared in parotid tumors.

The first intestinal resection for cancer was performed on the sigmoid in 1833 by Jean François Reybard. The patient lived for six months in comfort, then died of recurrence. The Royal Academy of Medicine verified this operation.

George McClellan, one of America's most distinguished surgeons and founder of Jefferson Medical College, between 1826 and 1846 removed the parotid entirely in eleven cases, and partially in thirty cases, with only one operative death. The operative mortality had been very high before this time and the average surgeon had seen only three or four cases.

One of the most important pioneers in the modern field of surgery in cancer was Charles Hewitt Moore of Middlesex Hospital, London. His paper, "On the Influence of Inadequate Operations on the Theory of Cancer," which appeared in 1867, laid the groundwork for the present methods. In case of breast tumor, he directed the operator to remove the breast itself, the adjoining skin, pectoral muscle, lymphatics, and axillary glands. This was to be done all in one piece without cutting into the main tumor. His own country did not accept his teachings until thirty years later, after America and Continental Europe had generally adopted it.

Billroth, a pioneer in visceral surgery, was one of the first to use

Listerism. He made the first resection of the esophagus in 1872, and the first resection of the pylorus for cancer which was successful, in 1881. Among his many achievements were the first total laryngectomy, and the first abdominal resection of a bladder tumor. Billroth published the results of his works yearly, and had an inestimable influence on cancer surgery.

Billroth's assistant, Alexander von Winiwarter, was appointed by him to make a study of the 548 cases of carcinoma which he had treated at his clinic between 1867 and 1876. This account, presented in 1878, is famous for its presentation of the end results of cancer surgery. He showed 4.7 per cent of the 170 breast cancer patients alive and well at the end of three years. This was the first time anything as comprehensive as this study had been done.

Richard von Volkmann, in 1875, published a description in his general surgical text book of three cases of scrotal cancer among distillers of tar and paraffin, in the district of Halle. The dermatitis preceding the initial lesion was also discussed. This surgeon was one of the first to publish his follow-up records for operations for breast cancer.

The first successful abdominal hysterectomy for cancer was performed by Wilhelm Alexander Freund in 1878. There had been several operations of this sort previously, but none with the rational plan and Listerian antisepsis of Freund. The patient was alive and well twenty-six years later.

The development of diagnosis and treatment of cancer of the bladder depended on the perfecting of one of the means of diagnosis—the cystoscope. In 1884, Sir Henry Thompson, an English surgeon, devised an operation which cured some of his patients. His report of twenty cases is a meritorious pre-cystoscopic work.

In 1886, after years of experimenting, Max Nitze, in Berlin, perfected a cystoscope and in 1889 published a classic paper on the subject. Thereafter, this instrument enabled the diagnosis of bladder cancers.

In 1891, Albarran, professor of urology at Paris, made a fundamental contribution to the knowledge of bladder tumors. He described their pathology, the use of the cystoscope in diagnosis, the well-considered operative procedure by suprapubic cystotomy, and gave a follow-up study of nearly one hundred cases.

Until ten years after the introduction of Lister's antisepsis, brain surgery was limited to the relief of brain pressure by trephining. The decade between 1870 and 1880 marked the beginnings of study of the physiology of the brain. Only with this knowledge could brain lesions be clinically recognized. Fritsch and Hitzig, in Germany, and Ferrier, in England, were outstanding experimenters in this field. Hughlings Jackson used this knowledge clinically with great success.

In 1884, with the advantages of following these pioneers, it was possible for Alexander H. Bennett, the son of a Scotch physician, and a brilliant student in clinical neurology, to diagnose a tumor of the brain, and for Sir Rickman John Godlee, a nephew of Lister, to remove it surgically. This same year, Sir Victor Horsley began some experiments on monkeys for the purpose of studying cerebral localization. For two years, Horsley continued this experimenting, incidentally perfecting a technique which made him an expert operator on human brains. In 1886, following his first operation on May 25, Horsley had performed ten operations with the loss of only one patient. The next year, he removed a tumor of the spinal cord successfully. This was the first operation of its kind that was ever done.

William Stewart Halsted's description of the operation for cancer of the breast, in the Johns Hopkins Hospital Reports in 1891, has been called the greatest contribution to the treatment of breast cancer. Halsted was a surgeon in Baltimore, Maryland. For breast cancer he advised wide skin excision, removal of the pectoralis major and division of the pectoralis minor, and the complete dissection of the axilla.

Themistokles Gluck, a German surgeon, devised an operation for laryngectomy and published his paper on the subject in 1899, eleven years after the death of Kaiser Friedrich from cancer of the larynx.

Mikulicz, one of Billroth's most brilliant assistants, contributed much to cancer surgery. He was the first to carry out plastic reconstruction of the esophagus following the removal of the carcinoma. His operation was described in a paper published in 1903.

In 1899, Quénu, of Paris, published the second of two volumes on "Surgery of the Rectum," in which he described resection of the rectum by the abdominal perineal route. He mentioned removal of nodes along the iliac vessels, but made no specific attempt to remove the regional lymph nodes. The mortality was high in the hands of most operators, until the desirability of removing adequately the regional lymph nodes was emphasized by C. H. Mayo.

This account of surgery in cancer sketches the general trend up to the twentieth century. The intense and comprehensive work of many outstanding surgeons who have contributed to this field has necessarily been omitted.

Trend in Radiology

A new and radical addition to cancer therapy and diagnosis was discovered in the last decade of the nineteenth century, and introduced to practical use in the first decade of the twentieth century. In 1899, Tage Sjögren treated an elderly man with advanced epithelioma of the cheek with Roentgen rays. This had been definitely diagnosed by microscopic examination. The lesion healed rapidly. This was the first successful use of X-rays in actual cancer.

The first reported case of the use of radium in cancer was made known in 1903 by S. W. Goldberg and E. S. London. Goldberg had applied radium to his forearm and developed an ulcer which was very slow to heal. These two investigators felt that radium would have a definite effect on cancerous epithelium. They treated two basal cell carcinomas of the face, both of which healed. Thus the potentialities of this new and valuable method of treatment of cancer were demonstrated.

In 1906, Max Otten reported on thirteen proved cases of primary carcinoma of the lung which had been diagnosed by Roentgen rays and verified by autopsy. This was the first time that this lesion had been so accurately demonstrated. It marked a definite forward step in knowledge of cancer of the lung, since roentgenography is so essential to its early diagnosis.

While the evolution of the ideas culminating in Roentgen rays may well be said to have begun 600 years before Christ in the earliest concept of electricity, it remained for Herschel, Crookes, and Roentgen to bring them to a point of usefulness.

Sir John Herschel noticed that a peculiar blue light was diffused from a colorless solution of quinine sulphate. Professor George Stokes explained that this blue light was composed of vibrations originally too rapid to be visible which were slowed down within the limits of perceptibility as they passed through the liquid.

In 1874 and 1875, Professor William Crookes, who had discovered thallium in 1861, was working on electric rays He devised a vacuum tube in which he placed rubies, phenakite, and some other suitable objects upon which electrical discharges were directed. These enclosed objects then glowed with a brilliant light. He then found that a ray from the negative pole of an electric machine would cause a Crookes bulb itself to shine with a vivid golden-green ray.

Crookes performed his experiments in a London laboratory before a group of colleagues. Immediately, hundreds of experiments with the Crookes tube followed. In 1894, Professor Philipp Lenard discovered that from the Crookes tube, with which he was experimenting, a cathode ray emerged which passed easily through a thin aluminum plate. Hertz had found that thin sheets of metal were virtually transparent to his electric waves. Lenard found this was a property of the cathode ray and in a much higher degree. It was also learned that the ultra-violet ray of ordinary light has the peculiar power of causing the gases through which it travels to become conductors of electricity, with the effect of discharging an electrified metallic plate. Cathode rays showed this property. The still more remarkable ray of Roentgen is also associated with these rays.

Late on the night of November 8, 1895, Professor Wilhelm Conrad Roentgen was working alone in his laboratory at the University of Würzburg on the problem of cathode rays from a vacuum tube. His own words, as recounted in "McClure's Magazine," April, 1896, follow: "I was working with a Crookes tube covered by a shield of black cardboard. A piece of barium platino-cyanide paper lay on the bench there. I had been passing a current through the tube, and I noticed a peculiar black line across the paper.... The effect was one which could only be produced, in ordinary parlance, by the passage of light.... I assumed that the effect must have come from the tube, since its character indicated that it could come from nowhere else. I tested it. In a few minutes there was no doubt about it. Rays were coming from the tube which had a luminescent effect upon the paper." He called them "X-ray." After discovering their existence, Roentgen studied the potentialities of X-rays. He found out that they penetrated paper, wood, and cloth easily, the thickness of the substance making no perceptible difference within reasonable limits. Since X-rays penetrated all other substances, they were tried on the human body and penetrated it readily.

Roentgen had called attention to the fact that X-rays proceeded from those parts of the tube where the glass showed the most fluorescence. It was thought that the existence of the rays might be dependent on previously acquired fluorescence, and many experimenters tried to ascertain with Balmain dyes, which were known to become luminous after exposure to the light, whether or not results similar to those of Roentgen could be obtained.

In 1896, Antoine Henri Becquerel exposed a number of phosphorescent substances covered with black paper under a photographic plate with negative results. He repeated this type of experiment, using uranium salts and two layers of black paper with a small silver plate between the uranium and the photographic plate. He obtained a distinct photographic effect.

This successful experiment did not establish the relation of the rays to previous fluorescence, for Becquerel obtained the same results regardless of whether he used uranium which had been exposed to the light, or uranium which had been kept some time in darkness and could not possibly have stored up luminescence. He had discovered uranium, or Becquerel rays.

Madame Marie Curie was a senior student at the Municipal School of Physics and Technical Chemistry in Paris at the time Becquerel was doing these experiments. For her doctoral thesis she chose "Radio-Activity," a term of her own creation. Her husband was professor of physics. They had devised a delicate instrument for the detection of electric rays.

Professor and Madame Curie, at Becquerel's request, investigated all the chemical elements and showed that except with uranium and thorium, no appreciable effect indicating rays could be obtained. Many of the minerals showed noticeable action in this direction. They observed that uranium pitchblende was much more radioactive than other uranium and thorium compounds. Assuming that this excessive radioactivity was due to the presence in the pitchblende of a small amount of some unknown element, they worked on this thesis, and in 1898 separated first a substance which they called "polonium" and then that substance exhibiting an astonishing degree of radioactivity, which they called "radium."

Radium is a solid white metal. It is extracted from pitchblende as a salt,—radium chloride. It maintains a temperature several degrees above the surrounding atmosphere, and is a spontaneous source of three distinct kinds of rays,—alpha, beta, and gamma, and also of a radioactive gas called "radium emanation." The gamma rays are comparable to Roentgen rays, passing through many substances opaque to light. The beta rays are less penetrating than the gamma rays, and are similar to cathode rays. The penetrating power of the alpha rays is very slight.

In 1903, George Perthes, one of the early workers in X-ray for cancer therapy, presented an excellent paper on radiosensitivity. He had experimented on his own fingers, and on animals. He introduced the idea that since the main difference between normal epithelial cells and carcinoma cells was in the increased ability of the cancer cell to grow, it was possible that this function of the cell might be the one injured by radiation.

By 1906, when superficial forms of cancer were being treated in greater numbers by radiation, it became apparent that there were outstanding differences in radiosensitivity. Jean Bergonié and Louis Tribondeau worked out the following law explaining this phenomenon: "The greater the reproductive activity of cells, the more prolonged the process of karyokinesis, and the less definitely fixed their morphology and functions, the more intense is the action of X-rays upon them." Bergonié was famous in the field of radiology from the beginning. He was a physician and physicist, and held the chair of medical physics in the University of Bordeaux. In 1904, he published a paper on the therapeutic use of X-rays in breast and face cancer.

X-ray has a chapter of special significance in the diagnosis of cancer of the stomach. Many investigators had been engaged in developing fluoroscopy. In 1904, H. Rieder reported that he had, by feeding his patients bismuth mixed with milk or mashed potato, made accurate studies through fluoroscopy in the shape and movements of the stomach and intestines.

Guido Holzknecht adopted Rieder's method. He had developed fluoroscopy to a point of practical usefulness in studies of the stomach. The series of papers immediately following embodied the basic principles of the diagnosis by X-ray of gastric lesions. He published them in his own journal. In 1908 he collaborated with S. Jonas on the first book on roentgenological descriptions of carcinoma of the stomach to be published. His efforts to make roentgenology a medical specialty, so recognized by universities, did more for the cause than any other single thing. His death in 1931 from X-ray burns marked him as another martyr to science.

The first specimen of radium brought to the United States was purchased by a patient of Dr. Manges and Dr. Willy Meyer in New York. This was presented, in 1903, to Manges, who in turn gave it to the New York Academy of Medicine. The same year, Robert Abbe, of Columbia University, purchased 150 milligrams of radium barium chloride from the Curie Laboratory. He experimented on germinating seeds, ants, trout, pollywogs, and mice, and on normal human skin. He treated inoperable cancer of the breast with radium and noted the changes. He also noted the destruction of cancer cells around the site of the radium tubes, and the fibrous hyperplasia. Abbe, in 1904, also wrote that from his clinical observation, "superficial epithelioma, rodent ulcer and small recurrent cancer nodules can be caused to disappear." He also proved that beta rays from radium are the effective force in cell destruction.

Henri Dominici added signally to radiation therapy by the discovery of the principle of filtration in 1908. He devised a means of excluding both the alpha and beta rays, allowing only the deeply-penetrating gamma rays to pass. Applying these gamma rays to tumors, he found little change in the overlying structures, while the tissues in the deep-seated tumor regressed. He made extensive histologic studies of the effect of radium and its emanations on various body tissues.

The next twenty years were years of research in the application of radiation. The original X-ray equipment was superseded by the Coolidge Tube in 1912, devised by the American physicist, W. D. Coolidge. In 1927, the first volume of "Archives de l'institut du radium de l'universite de Paris et de la fondation Curie," of which Claude Regaud is director, was published. It contained comprehensive histologic studies of the effect of radiation on the different adult tissues in man, and in laboratory animals by Claude Regaud and Antoine Lacassagne, which may be said to form the basis of the modern concept of radiosensitivity of neoplastic disease. In 1930, Gösta Forssell published an authoritative and comprehensive statement on the use of radiotherapy in the treatment of cancer, based on the results of five years' work at the famous Radiumhemmet in Stockholm.

Trend of Present Control Measures in Cancer

The present era marks the convergence of all the trends in cancer to a concentration on the subject, unprecedented in its history. Research, special cancer hospitals, and clinics are already established in many countries of the world. Symposiums and international conferences to which the leaders in research, diagnosis, treatment, and organization have come, have added to the general feeling that although cancer is the problem of every small community, it is also international in its aspects. A Cancer Commission was appointed early in the Health Organization of the League of Nations, and various sub-committees are reporting the results of their investigations. The United States Public Health Service is at work on the problem. Individual states are developing cancer programs. The American Society for the Control of Cancer since 1913 has conducted educational campaigns, and, recently, has added epidemiological investigations.

In the face of the actual problem, more must be done. Research requires funds; hospital facilities are inadequate; diagnosis is too often delayed; and public apathy must be overcome. The present trend in cancer is toward group specialization. There is a difference of opinion as to the best method for accomplishing this. Some feel there should be only a few centers, as, for example, four in the United States, while others feel there should be innumerable centers. The common ground remains the constantly growing recognition that cancer therapy demands group opinion.

Time and research have witnessed the separation of disease after disease from that group originally included under the nomenclature of "cancer." Malignant disease itself, more clearly defined, remains. The association of cancer with life—of the cell as the root of involvement, of the resemblance of cancer growth to cell growth, of the difference of cells themselves, and of the difference of the several types of cancer—is recognized. Among some physicians the belief is held that therapy will never extend beyond the utilization of present knowledge. Others look to an epoch-making discovery which will overturn present concepts.

It was in about 1875 that Sir John Erichsen declared in a public address that operative surgery had nearly reached its furthest possible limits of development. The failure of this prophesy may find a parallel in cancer. Schereschewsky voices the thoughts of many serious investigators in the field in the following statement:

"That the cancer death rate will continue to increase in the future as it has in the past is not to be supposed. Physical, chemical, and biologic processes all tend to a state of equilibrium. So in the case of cancer when the forces which are tending to raise the human race to a new and higher level of susceptibility have spent themselves, we may expect no further increase in the rate, at least from the operations of these causes. And, lying concealed in these evils, as in Pandora's Box, there is still the hope in the hearts of the medical profession and of the students of the public health that to-morrow, next month, or next year the true defense against this relentless foe will be vouchsafed us."

Bibliography

ADAIR, FRANK E.: *Progress of Research in Cancer and Its Significance for the Layman.* Hospital Social Service, September, 1933.

ADAIR, FRANK E. (Edited by): *Cancer.* J. B. Lippincott Company, Philadelphia, Montreal and London, 1931.

BETT, W. R. (Edited by): *A Short History of Some Common Diseases.* Oxford University Press, London: Humphrey Milford, 1934.

BLOODGOOD, JOSEPH COLT: *Cancer as a Public Health Problem.* Campaign Notes of the American Society for the Control of Cancer, Vol. XI, No. 5, May, 1929.

BREWSTER, E. T.: *Some Recent Aspects of Darwinism.* Atlantic Monthly, April, 1904.

BRODERS, ALBERT C.: *Practical Points on the Microscopic Grading of Carcinoma.* New York State Journal of Medicine, June 1, 1932.

CANCER CONTROL. *Lake Mohonk Conference, 1926.* The Surgical Publishing Company, Chicago, 1927.

CRAMER, W.: *The Comparative Study of Cancer.* The Cancer Review (England), June, 1932.

CRAMER W.: *The Prevention of Cancer.* The Lancet (England), January 6, 1934.

CURIE, MADAME: *Modern Theories of Electricity and Matter.* Annual Report, Smithsonian Institution, 1905-1906.

EWING, JAMES. *Some Results of Cancer Research.* Bulletin of the American Society for the Control of Cancer, Vol. XV, No. 7, July, 1933.

EWING, JAMES. *The Prevention of Cancer.* The Forum, New York, March, 1927.

EWING, JAMES: *Neoplastic Diseases.* W. B. Saunders Company, Philadelphia, 1928.

GARRISON, FIELDING H.: *An Introduction to the History of Medicine.* W. B. Saunders Company, Philadelphia and London, 1929.

GARRISON, FIELDING H.: *The History of Cancer.* Bulletin of the New York Academy of Medicine, Vol. II, No. 4, April, 1926.

GESCHICKTER, CHARLES F.: *Recent Work on Cancer.* Journal of the American Medical Association, Vol. 94, No. 5, February 1, 1930.

GIBSON, ANNA L.: *Radium, Radon, Radiumtherapy.* American Journal of Nursing, August, 1930.

HAAGENSEN, CUSHMAN D.: *An Exhibit of Important Books, Papers, and Memorabilia Illustrating the Evolution of the Knowledge of Cancer.* The American Journal of Cancer, Vol. XVIII, No. 1, May, 1933.

HIMSTEDT, FRANZ: *Radioactivity.* Annual Report, Smithsonian Institution, 1905-1906.
HIRSCH, ISAAC SETH: *Wilhelm Konrad Roentgen.* Bulletin of the American Society for the Control of Cancer, Vol. XII, No. 4, April, 1930.
HOFFMAN, FREDERICK L.: *The Mortality from Cancer Throughout the World.* The Prudential Press, Newark, N. J., 1915.
ILES, G.: *Flame, Electricity and the Camera, Chapter 24.* Doubleday, Page and Company, New York.
JACKSON, HENRY, JR.: *Cancer and the General Practitioner.* New England Journal of Medicine, Vol. 211, No. 5, August 2, 1934.
KRUMBHAAR, E. B.: *Real and False Progress in Cancer Research.* American Journal of Cancer, September, 1933.
LEAGUE OF NATIONS: *Health Organization: Cancer Commission*—Reports submitted by the Radiological Sub-Commission, Geneva, 1929.
LEAGUE OF NATIONS: *Health Organization:* International Health Year Book, Geneva, 1930.
LEAGUE OF NATIONS: *Health Organization: Protective Measures Against Dangers Resulting from the Use of Radium, Roentgen and Ultraviolet Rays,* Geneva, 1931.
LEE, BURTON J.: *Cancer—A Community Health Problem.* Bulletin of the American Society for the Control of Cancer, Vol. XV, No. 8, August, 1933.
LEE, BURTON, J.: *The Indications for Surgery and the Indications for Irradiation in the Treatment of Cancer.* Bulletin of the American Society for the Control of Cancer, Vol. XIII, No. 7, July, 1931.
LITERATURE OF CANCER, THE: Reprinted from Campaign Notes, American Society for the Control of Cancer, August, 1928.
LONG, ESMOND R.: *A History of Pathology.* The Williams and Wilkins Company, Baltimore, 1928.
MOYNIHAN, LORD BERKELEY: *The Future of Surgery.* Bulletin of the American Society for the Control of Cancer, Vol. XIII, No. 7, July, 1931.
Report of the Activities of the American Society for the Control of Cancer: 1929-1933. Bulletin of the American Society for the Control of Cancer, Vol. XV, No. 10, October, 1933.
Report of the International Conference on Cancer, London, 1928. William Wood and Company, New York.
SCHERESCHEWSKY, J. W.: *The Course of Cancer Mortality in the Ten Original Registration States for the 21-Year Period, 1900-1920.* United States Public Health Service Bulletin, No. 155, Washington, D. C., 1925.
SEELIG, MAJOR G.: *Medicine, An Historical Outline.* The Williams and Wilkins Company, Baltimore, 1931.
SKINNER, EDWARD H.: *The Fetich of a Cancer Cure.* Bulletin of the American Society for the Control of Cancer, Vol. XV, No. 9, September, 1933.
WELSH, DAVID ARTHUR: *The Life History of Cancer.* Medical Journal of Australia, April 26, 1930.
WOLFF, JACOB: *Die Lehre von der Krebskrankheit* in four volumes, published in 1907-1911-1913-1928 respectively—Gustav Fischer, Jena.

CANCER OF THE JAWS

By V. H. KAZANJIAN, M. D.

Boston, Massachusetts

Malignant tumors of the jaws originate either as a proliferation of epithelial cells (carcinoma) or of connective tissue cells (sarcoma). For the purpose of this discussion only the carcinomata will be considered, since these form the large majority of jaw malignancies encountered in clinical practice. While a wide variety of benign tumors of the jaws has been described in the literature, only those which are relatively frequent of occurrence and which have some bearing on differential diagnosis with carcinoma will be mentioned.

Etiology

Although the exact causes of cancer have never been determined, chronic irritation of some form or other is generally accepted by experts as the most consistent factor. Four sources of chronic irritation appear to be most frequently associated with cancers of the jaws and buccal cavity: syphilis; mechanical irritations, such as poorly constructed dental plates, overhanging fillings, or ill-fitting crowns; tobacco; and miserable mouth hygiene as evidenced by widespread periodontal disease. These are mentioned in the reverse order of their importance.

The role of syphilis in cancer of the jaws is relatively unimportant of itself.

Mechanical irritations have, in the past, been unduly blamed as a predisposing cause of mouth cancer, but the evidence is by no means conclusive. Clinical observation will show cases where cancer has developed from the apparent irritation of the sharp edges of a brokendown tooth; yet in other cases patients have worn badly fitting dental restorations for many years without untoward results; and in still other cases, cancer has developed in edentulous patients who have been wearing well-constructed dentures.

The theory that tobacco smoking may have a definite relationship to the incidence of mouth cancers is based upon extensive clinical and experimental observations. For example, men are far more susceptible to cancer of the jaws than women, and the smoking habit is more common among men. The increased prevalence of smoking among women will undoubtedly affect the number of buccal cancers occurring among them. Leukoplakia, which results from the continued irritation of the mucous membrane of the mouth by tobacco smoking, is definitely regarded as a precancerous lesion. In the early stages of this disease, the tissues are slightly pale, wrinkled and scaly. Later the epithelium becomes more thickened and raised above the level of the surrounding normal tissue and is covered with grayish white patches. If this process is unchecked, the affected part undergoes degenerative changes either in the form of mouth papillomas or an erosive type of cancer.

Widespread dental disease and poor mouth hygiene appear, however, to be consistently associated with the incidence of cancer of the mouth. It is a common observation that the great majority of patients suffering from carcinoma of the jaws have been very neglectful of the health of their mouths. Consequently adequate care of the teeth and gums, particularly for those patients approaching middle or old age, becomes of paramount importance as a factor in preventing cancer of the mouth and jaws.

Certain it is that if any one of the four above-mentioned sources of chronic irritation may produce carcinoma of the oral cavity, a combination of several of them is even more serious. Unquestionably, therefore, badly diseased mouths and poor mouth hygiene, especially when mechanical irritation and the continued use of tobacco are superimposed, should be regarded with suspicion.

Diagnosis

In the advanced stages, cancer is relatively easy to diagnose, but at that time it may be too late to provide effective assistance to the patient. The greatest effort, therefore, should be concentrated in detecting early lesions, and these are often difficult to differentiate from nonmalignant lesions. Fortunately, owing to the exposed position of the mouth, the opportunity for discovering precancerous or early cancerous lesions is greater than in any other part of the body, except the skin.

Three types of jaw carcinomata are differentiated. The first type usually originates from the mucous membrane covering of the alveolar processes or palate, and does not essentially differ in its clinical picture from carcinoma of other parts of the buccal cavity. Its clinical course, however, is slower, and the percentage of cures is greater than from carcinoma of the tongue or other mobile parts of the mouth. This statement applies more to maxillary lesions than to those of the mandible where the condition is often more serious. Its first appearance is usually a small wart-like mass on the gum margins which soon exhibits small papillary projections. As it grows larger, it tends to project into the oral cavity with comparatively little infiltration into the deeper tissues. Eventually, however, erosion and ulceration take place. This type normally originates from the center of a well-developed leukoplakia. It grows rather slowly and is less malignant unless it is constantly irritated by sharp edges of broken-down teeth.

In the second or erosion type of carcinoma, the lesion may start as a simple granuloma and may protrude from the side of a tooth or a socket of a recently extracted tooth. It bleeds easily, and as it grows larger, the central area becomes ulcerated. These ulcers are commonly deeper than ordinary ones, and the margins are more or less uneven, elevated and indurated. The entire mass soon becomes adherent to the periosteum. Ordinary ulcers of the mouth are more superficial in clinical appearance, do not have zones of induration at the periphery, and are susceptible to ordinary medication. Pain is a variable symptom in early cancer as it may be totally absent. This type is moderately malignant.

The third type is characterized by deep infiltration of the tissues and often appears in edentulous mouths. The patient becomes conscious of it when he experiences pain and discomfort and when he has difficulty in wearing artificial dentures. Examination shows slightly inflamed mucous membranes, projecting below the normal outline of the alveolar ridge. Digital pressure reveals a definite soft mass which has already caused diffused absorption of the bone. This type shows practically no tendency to ulcerate, rather extending into the bony tissue. In the upper jaw, it may involve the maxillary sinuses, in which case early diagnosis may be delayed until the lesion has advanced far enough to extend into the nasal cavity or the canine fossa. In the lower jaw, definite enlargement of the mandible is noticeable. Not infrequently patients complain of neuralgic pain. The main diagnostic point in this type of carcinoma is a soft mass accompanied by rapid absorption of the bone and by pain. The X-ray picture is characteristic and shows uneven decalcification of the bone. Biopsy examination is, of course, conclusive for all types of carcinoma.

Differential Diagnosis

Of the large number of benign mouth tumors, some of which may be regarded as percancerous lesions, four types may be confused with cancer. They are: chronic hypertrophy of the gingivae; hypertrophic fibrous tissues; epulis of fibromas; and cysts, dentigerous, radicular and multilocular.

Chronic hypertrophy of the gingivae is invariably caused by mechanical irritation from ill-fitting dental restorations or from pressure of salivary calculi complicated with bacterial invasion. These lesions are usually quite congested, bleed easily and, at times, assume considerable size. They rarely become ulcerated, however, and do not have the hard indurated irregular margins so typical of early cancer. Moreover, when the irritation is removed, healing is rapid. Hypertrophic fibrous tissue of varying size, even resembling hard papillomata, is often seen at the anterior aspect of the alveolar ridges in edentulous patients. Such lesions have a broad base covered with normal looking mucous membrane resembling more or less keloid scars. They are not painful and are caused by ill-fitting dentures worn for a long period of time. In spite of their prevalence, they are not known to undergo degenerative changes.

Under the general term epulis are grouped many benign connective tissue tumors, or fibromata. They are projecting masses between or in the proximity of the teeth, and originate in the periosteum or the peridental membrane. Uusually they have a fairly narrow base, and the surface mucosa is hard, shiny, normal in color, or may be vascular and congested. They sometimes assume considerable size. These tumors resemble the papillomatous type of carcinoma, yet their rate of growth is slow. They seldom cause distortion of the bone, and microscopically show either fibrous tissue or benign giant cells.

Benign cystic tumors are quite common in the jaws. They may grow to considerable size causing extensive absorption of the bone, and superficially, they resemble the penetrating type of carcinoma. Radicular cysts develop at the root end of an infected tooth. Dentigerous cysts usually result from an unerupted tooth which is generally found attached to the wall of the cystic sac. Both these types grow slowly but may assume large size, occasionally in the upper jaw displacing the maxillary sinus. Aside from causing local damage, they are not known to produce malignancy. Usually the X-ray picture is sufficient for diagnosis, as these cysts show a well-defined cavity surrounded by sharply outlined bony tissue.

Multilocular cysts, or adamantinomas, are true epithelial tumors, originating from the epithelial cells of the enamel organs. Their growth is uneven and lobulated. They are locally malignant and are known to undergo malignant degeneration, even invading neighboring glands. They occur usually in young adults and are found more frequently in the mandible. They grow slowly but are capable of assuming great size. The X-ray picture is characteristic.

Treatment

In general, the treatment of carcinoma of the jaws is a surgical problem. As soon as discovered, the entire lesion should be removed by electrocoagulation. Not infrequently it is necessary to resect a part of the mandible even in moderately advanced cases, and under such conditions, the glands of the neck should be resected as well. The majority of operations for cancer of the upper jaw can be performed through the mouth without an external incision. If a considerable portion of the maxilla is involved, surgical diathermy is advisable.

As an adjunct to surgery, radiation, either by radium or X-ray treatment, is an accepted therapeutic measure.

In inoperable cases of carcinoma, the reduction of pain, caused usually by involvements of the nerve terminations, comes under the charge of the attending physician. For this purpose, it is important to keep the ulcerations free from sloughing. Pastes, consisting, for example, of powdered aspirin mixed with glycerine and saturated on gauze, may be inserted in the cavity. In extreme cases, hypnotics may be used, including alcohol injections into the nerve trunks where feasible.

Attempts at Prevention

By far the most important factors in the constant effort to prevent or at least control cancer are early diagnosis and early treatment. Here the general practitioner of medicine or dentistry can perform a valuable service to his patients. The early recognition of precancerous or cancerous lesions is a serious responsibility which only the man who comes in frequent association with his patients can assume. Important points to remember, therefore, are: first, the establishment of good mouth hygiene, the moderation of the use of tobacco. and the elimination of mechanical irritations resulting from poor dental restoration; second, the viewing with suspicion of any persistent chronic ulceration or sore which fails to respond to local treatment; third, knowledge of the precancerous lesions; and fourth, the vital necessity of referring questionable cases to proper authorities for more thorough examination and diagnosis.

Only by persistent care and watchfulness will the ravages of cancer be lessened and perhaps brought under control.

CANCER OF THE KIDNEY
BY WILLIAM C. QUINBY, M. D.
and
FLETCHER H. COLBY, M. D.
Boston, Massachusetts

Classified broadly, neoplasms of the kidney are in two groups and most of them are to be regarded as cancer. These growths involve (1) the pelvis of the kidney and (2) the parenchyma, or solid portion. Other types of malignant growths of the kidneys are encountered, such as the Wilms tumor, most frequently seen in children either at birth or during the first year of life. These are teratoid in character with a histological appearance either sarcomatous or carcinomatous, and their growth is very rapid and malignant. Benign tumors of the kidney parenchyma are rare, the only one of clinical significance being the adenoma which occasionally reaches a large size simulating the more common malignant growths.

Neoplasms which arise in the kidney pelvis are relatively rare. They are of two types, papilloma and carcinoma, and both should be considered malignant. These tumors are essentially the same as bladder neoplasms arising as they do from similar embryological structures. The papilloma, by its tendency to form implantations, frequently involves the ureter and bladder thus demonstrating its potential malignancy. Like the bladder papilloma it, also, tends to undergo carcinomatous changes. Again, as in the bladder, epidermoid carcinoma of the kidney pelvis occurs and is frequently secondary to chronic irritation such as infection and calculus.

Adult tumors of the renal parenchyma, for practical purposes, may be regarded as cancer. These neoplasms still lack a satisfactory histological classification because of their characteristic tendency to show various types of cellular structure in different portions of the same tumor. In general, however, many of these tumors show a cellular structure in which the cortex of the adrenal gland is strongly suggested (Grawitz), and this fact accounts for the term hypernephromata being generally applied to them, since their origin has been considered due to misplaced portions of the adrenal gland. Further histological study by competent pathologists, however, has thrown considerable doubt on such an explanation of the origin of these tumors and the present tendency is to regard them all as carcinoma. They are all definitely malignant.

These neoplasms of the kidney cortex are composed of large, clear cells of polygonal shape which contain fat and glycogen, arranged about a fine capillary stroma. Microscopically, their tissue is yellowish in color and interspersed with areas of necrosis and hemorrhage. They arise from any portion of the parenchyma which they invade and distort. Although often of large size when first seen, such tumors are usually surrounded by a thin capsule in those areas where invasive growth has not yet occurred. They are, therefore, only locally malignant during a considerable period and this is important since operation during such a period affords a favorable chance of cure. Extension of the tumor growth outside this capsule is especially prone to penetrate venous channels with prolongation of tumor cells to the renal vein and vena cava.

Extension of tumor growth is by direct invasion of neighboring structures, by the blood stream, or by the lymphatics. Invasion of the veins is especially common and results in the enormous enlargement of venous collaterals so commonly encountered at operation upon these tumors. By invasion of nearby structures the tumor mass becomes fixed in its position in the flank and at times the duodenum on the right side or the colon on the left is involved. When the tumor spreads by the blood stream metastases may be found anywhere in the body. Secondary involvement of bone is so common that in any obscure instance of bone tumor a primary renal neoplasm should be considered. Spread of the tumor by the lymphatics results in early involvement of regional lymph nodes along the vascular pedicle of the kidney and interferes at times with accurate clamping of the renal artery and vein during nephrectomy.

Incidence

Excepting the embryonal type of tumor found in infancy, malignant growths of the kidney occur most frequently from the fortieth to the sixtieth year.

Symptoms

The three outstanding symptoms of renal neoplasm have been traditionally, tumor, pain and bleeding. Whereas it may have been necessary at one time that all these signs be present to justify a diagnosis, this is no longer true. By employing all the resources at hand, such as the X-ray, cystoscopy, and intravenous pyelography, a much earlier diagnosis of this condition is made in the presence of any one of these symptoms, and indeed occasionally in the absence of all of them.

Unfortunately, renal tumors at an early stage produce such trivial symptoms that they often are disregarded by both patient and doctor. Since it is true that these tumors remain encapsulated for an appreciable length of time it is important that an adequate examination be made to reveal their presence as early as possible in the course of the disease. No symptom, however slight, should be disregarded.

Tumor, as a sign of renal neoplasm, necessarily appears late. The high position of the kidney and its covering of the ribs and thick muscles frequently renders a large mass impossible to palpate. Such signs as irregularities in the contours of the kidney by X-ray or a median displacement of the colon may suggest the diagnosis. In general these tumors are not evident to the examining hand until late in the course of the disease.

Pain is an inconstant and variable symptom. Its presence is more likely due to spasm of the pelvis or ureter to expel blood clot than from the presence of a tumor mass. A dull ache in the loin is often due to the size of the tumor but more frequently to adhesions to neighboring structures from the extension of the growth or inflammatory changes. Severe neuralgic pain is an evidence of extension to adjacent nerve trunks. In many instances a tumor of the kidney is known to have been present for years with no pain.

Blood in the urine is by far the most significant symptom of renal tumor. Hematuria is present in 80 per cent of these cases and is the first sign of disease in at least half. Spontaneous, painless bleeding from the urinary tract demands immediate and adequate examination in every instance. This bleeding is characteristically intermittent in character and the fact that the bleeding ceases must give no false hope of security to doctor or patient. Adequate examination of the patient while bleeding does at times afford extremely valuable information which may not be obtained at any other time. Cystoscopic evidence of unilateral renal bleeding is easily obtained at this time and in the absence of stone is extremely suggestive of tumor.

In addition to the great importance of gross blood in the urine the importance of microscopic blood must be further emphasized. As gross bleeding demands adequate examination so does persistent microscopic hematuria. The presence of but a few blood corpuscles in the urine on repeated examinations is of extreme importance and may be the first sign of renal tumor. Hematuria, gross or microscopic, means stone, tumor or tuberculosis in the majority of instances. Painless hematuria then is the one outstanding symptom of this disease.

The diagnosis of renal tumor is made by cystoscopy and X-ray. The bladder as a source of the bleeding is eliminated by cystoscopic examination. The kidney pelvis is visualized by pyelography, by means of the ureteral catheter or intravenous injection. The advent of more recent methods of visualizing the kidneys by intravenous dyes places pyelography within the ability of all, and while this method is not always sufficient to establish the diagnosis of tumor it is usually at least sufficiently suggestive to demand that further study be made. Interpretation of results by either of these methods is difficult at times but in most instances the deformities produced by encroachment of the tumor on the calices and pelvis are quite characteristic.

Once the diagnosis of renal tumor is made nephrectomy should be attempted. X-ray therapy offers nothing as a method of controlling tumor growth. Routine studies for metastases should be carried out before operation, such as roentgenograms of the chest, spine and pelvis. The presence of metastatic disease does not necessarily contraindicate operation since nephrectomy may stop uncontrollable hemorrhage or pain, and distant metastases have been successfully controlled or removed. Nephrectomy is the proper treatment for tumors of the renal pelvis and, where the tumor is papillary, total ureterectomy is necessary to control the spread of tumor implantations.

A recent statistical study of the operative results of renal tumor are those of Judd and Hand from the Mayo Clinic. In a series of 367 cases, 106 lived for from 3 to 22.5 years, about 29 per cent.

THE LEUKEMIAS
By Francis T. Hunter, M. D.
Boston, Massachusetts

The leukemias may be defined as universally fatal neoplastic-like hyperplasias of the reticulo-endothelial or the myeloid cells, accompanied usually by the presence of tumor-like cells in the peripheral blood stream. The etiology is entirely unknown. For clinical purposes they may be divided into acute and chronic types and, depending upon the cell from which the tumor arises, into two separate groups, lymphatic leukemia and myelogenous leukemia.

Acute Leukemia

Acute leukemia is more common in younger people, usually between the ages of fifteen and forty, whereas the chronic leukemias occur chiefly between the ages of thirty and sixty. Acute leukemia may have a sudden onset or may be preceded by prodromal symptoms of weakness and lassitude. It may first manifest itself by prolonged bleeding after tooth extraction. The patient soon develops purpuric spots on the skin and mucous membranes, slight enlargement of the lymphatic glands of the neck, axillae and groins, and the spleen becomes moderately enlarged. A fever ranging from 100° to 103° is almost always seen at some time during the course of the disease. Towards the termination there may occasionally be sloughing ulcers or gangrene of the mucous membranes. Examination of the blood shows a white count ranging from 10,000 to 100,000, consisting almost entirely of extremely young white cells, which are usually classified as lymphoblasts. It is doubtful whether it is worth while to attempt to assign these cells to the lymphatic or to the myeloid series, as in either case the disease runs the same course. A gradually progressing anemia is also noted in the great majority of cases. It is highly important to differentiate this disease from the superficially similar condition known as infectious mononucleosis. In the latter, however, purpura and prolonged bleeding are practically never seen and all cases recover. A new test consisting of titering the patient's serum for the presence of heterophile antibodies may serve to distinguish these two diseases and should be employed in case of doubt.

Treatment. There is no available treatment. Arsenic has been tried; high voltage X-ray therapy has been employed in some cases, but the rapidly fatal termination in six to eight weeks does not seem to be modified in the least. On the contrary, high voltage X-ray or arsenic, instead of improving the patient, may be distinctly detrimental.

Chronic Myelogenous Leukemia

Chronic myelogenous leukemia is a neoplastic-like disease arising from the primordial leucocytes of the bone marrow and spleen and, in contrast to acute leukemia, is usually fatal in from two to four years. Cases of a mild type have been known which have lived as long as seventeen years. The onset is usually gradual, the symptoms consisting of fatigue, weakness, and loss of weight. The patient frequently notices enlargement of the spleen, but ordinarily he does not consult a doctor until many months have gone by. When examined, anemia may or may not be present. The most important physical finding is the grossly enlarged spleen, which may vary from a few centimeters below the costal margin to a size which completely fills the abdomen. Examination of the blood presents an easily recognizable picture. The white cells may vary from 10,000 to 800,000 per c.mm. and show all stages of development of the polymorphonuclear leucocytes from the myeloblast to the adult form. The changes in the red cells may simulate those of pernicious anemia. A most important variation of this disease, because it is frequently overlooked, is the so-called *aleukemia* phase; this shows the same pathology in the bone marrow as the more classical type, but in the peripheral blood there may be few or no abnormal cells. This peculiarity may explain certain supposed cases of pernicious anemia which do not respond to liver therapy. In both phases of myelogenous leukemia the basal metabolic rate is usually elevated. If in doubt a biopsy of the sternum will establish the diagnosis.

Treatment. Many types of therapy have been tried, but those which have proved most efficacious are arsenic in the form of Fowler's solution or high voltage X-ray therapy. Arsenic improves some cases, but the borderline between an effective dosage to reduce the height of the white count and the point of toxicity of the drug is illy defined and frequently the patient will not tolerate a sufficient amount to produce the desired effect upon the hematopoietic organs. However, should the patient be unable to go to an institution which is equipped to give high voltage X-ray treatment, it may be tried. The treatment of choice, however, is high voltage X-ray therapy administered by an experienced operator. The object of treatment is not to prolong life, because this seems never to happen, but to keep the patient in good clinical condition so that he may be enabled to carry on his normal every-day activities without symptoms. To accomplish this the patient must be seen at routine intervals, not more than two months apart, and X-ray therapy instituted when the patient's condition and his blood picture demand it. Such therapy usually allows a patient to lead a normal life for the first two to three years of the disease; however, towards the last six months of life its effect is less pronounced. The so-called aleukemic phases referred to above are much more difficult to handle. Treatment of any sort is frequently unsatisfactory. It is important not to give this class of patients too much X-ray treatment as the already low white count may go down in a most alarming manner. Recently a few cases have been tried with "spray" therapy to the body as a whole with somewhat better results than the former method of treating the spleen in a concentrated field. It is too early, however, to determine whether this method will prove valuable.

Chronic Lymphatic Leukemia

There seems to be no consensus of opinion as to the relationship of the lymphatic group of tumors to each other and to Hodgkin's disease, reticulo-cell sarcoma and lymphosarcoma. Some cases of typical chronic lymphatic leukemia may, at post mortem, show sarcoma-like invasion of various organs. Cases that appear to be early Hodgkin's disease histologically may later show leukemic blood changes. The same holds true of lymphosarcoma. As Hodgkin's disease and lymphosarcoma have been discussed in another paper, I shall confine myself, as nearly as possible, to the leukemias.

Clinically *chronic lymphatic leukemia* has a varied appearance. The classical description is that of general glandular enlargement, splenomegaly, and a high white count in the peripheral blood consisting almost entirely of lymphocytes. Another form of the disease has been called *aleukemic lymphatic leukemia* because of the fact that the white count is only slightly elevated, normal or even subnormal, and the differential count shows a preponderance of lymphocytes. A third type is the so-called *pseudoleukemia* of Cohnheim. This shows the same clinical picture of enlargement of the glands and splenomegaly, but on examination of the blood there may be practically no abnormality depicted except a moderate anemia. A fourth type of the disease is the so-called *mycosis fungoides*, which is a lymphomatous tumor originating in the skin and subcutaneous tissues, later producing glandular and splenic enlargement and not infrequently a leukemic or subleukemic blood picture towards the end. As a general rule lymphatic leukemia and its allied conditions occur in a somewhat older age group than myelogenous leukemia. It is a curious fact that the older the patient, the more benign the course of the disease tends to be. The diagnosis is usually easily made, but in the "pseudoleukemia" or "mycosis fungoides" type a biopsy is necessary.

Treatment. Arsenic has been used in this group of diseases, but with nowhere near the success obtained with its use in myelogenous leukemia. The therapy of choice is high voltage X-ray for the deeper lesions and low voltage X-ray therapy for superficial skin lesions. Each case is variable in its manifestations and may at times change from one variety of the disease into another. Therefore, it seems futile to insist upon any routine therapeutic procedure. Lowering of the white count by high Voltage X-ray therapy does not parallel the improvement of the patient's symptoms as closely as it does in myelogenous leukemia and it seems better, in the main, to treat the local tumor-like tissue by appropriate therapy rather than to pay too close attention to the condition of the blood; but a decrease in the number of blood platelets and the appearance of purpura or bleeding gums is usually a bad prognostic sign and indicates that the end is not far away.

CANCER OF THE LIP
By Ernest M. Daland, M. D.
Boston, Massachusetts

Chronic fissures and ulcers, areas of leukoplakia and keratoses of the lip are precancerous lesions and require treatment. If they do not respond to simple treatment, malignancy must be considered.

A keratosis is a thickening or scaling of the outer layers of the dry portion of the mucous membrane of the lip. The scale is thick and tenacious and it may be sensitive. It may become ulcerated and heal with difficulty. It is more common in men, particularly smokers. Cigarettes often stick to it and tear it off when removed, leaving an ulceration. Some keratoses may be softened and destroyed by the use of ointments while others require radium in mild doses.

Chronic ulcers and fissures of several weeks' duration and not responding to treatment must be viewed with suspicion and treated by radiation or excision.

Leukoplakia, which may be present inside the mouth as well as on the lip, is frequently caused or increased by the use of tobacco and may be cured by stopping its use. It is probably best treated by desiccation or coagulation if it does not respond to simpler methods within a short time. Radium is not satisfactory.

Cancer of the lip is about fifty times as common in men as in women. It is much more common on the lower lip than on the upper and is more serious when on the lower lip. It is rare for a cancer of the upper lip to metastasize to the cervical nodes. Lip malignancies are more common in users of tobacco and in individuals with foul mouths and bad teeth.

The differential diagnosis lies between syphilis, tuberculosis and chronic infection. A chancre may be detected by a proper dark field examination and by the extensive early acute glandular involvement. Tertiary syphilis gives a positive Wasserman test. In the presence of suspected cancer and a positive Wasserman, a biopsy must be done, for both syphilis and cancer may be present. Tuberculosis of the lip is rare and is secondary to tuberculosis of the lungs or larynx.

Ewing[1] describes two clinical types of epidermoid carcinoma of the lip, the papillary and the ulcerative infiltrating type. The papillary type is a wart-like elevated lesion situated on the epidermis and for a long period is unaccompanied by a deep or subepithelial induration. It extends slowly in all diameters, finally ulcerates, penetrates the underlying tissue, involves the nodes and then resembles the second type.

The second type begins as a broad thickening of the epidermal layer, with early dense infiltration of the deeper structures and with crater-like ulceration surrounded by a definite, indurated border. It advances more rapidly than the papillary type, involves the lymphatic structures earlier and is surrounded by an area of edema. It may become infected and often undergoes necrosis.

Basal cell carcinoma begins on the cutaneous border of the lip and acts like a skin cancer. It metastasizes to glands rarely and is treated like other skin cancers.

The typical lip cancer has a definite pearly border with a central crust or ulcer. *Gentle* palpation of the lip between the thumb and forefinger reveals an inelastic pearly area of induration if cancer is present. If no such area is felt, we probably are not dealing with cancer.

Biopsy will, of course, prove the diagnosis, but usually it is just as easy to remove the whole lesion as to do a biopsy. If biopsy is done, one should be prepared to proceed with the appropriate treatment at once.

Cancer may appear on any part of the lip. It is most serious when it extends onto the mucous membrane toward the gum or when it invades the mucosa at the corner of the mouth. However, the seriousness of cancer of the lip lies chiefly in the fact that it spreads into the lymph nodes of the neck with great rapidity. Cancer in the center of the lip metastasizes into the submental glands, then to the submaxillary glands on either side and to the upper and lower cervical groups, both superficial and deep. If the lesion is located on one side only, it may skip the submental glands and spread to the chain of glands on one side only.

External palpation for glands of the neck is not very satisfactory unless the glands are large. A better method is to insert the forefinger of one hand into the floor of the mouth lateral and anterior to the tongue and to palpate the tissues between this finger and the fingers of the other hand. One quickly learns to recognize the normal submaxillary salivary gland and to note the presence of other glands. The typical cancerous gland is hard, but the gland may be fairly soft during the early stages of invasion. Glands in the neck must be considered cancerous until proven otherwise.

Broders[2] and others have shown that there is a marked difference in the degree of malignancy in various lip cancers. Microscopically this shows up in the variation in the size and shape of the cells, the number of mitoses, the staining of the nuclei, etc.—in short the cells vary in the degree in which they tend to approach the normal lip structures. In Grade I are the warty, papillary lesions which are slow growing and metastasize rarely. At the other end of the scale are the Grade III lesions which are very malignant and metastasize early and widely.

Treatment

We may dismiss, in a word, the use of cancer pastes, cancer salves and "herb remedies." Valuable time is lost in fooling with these remedies of the dark ages. Radiation and surgery are the only weapons that are available to cure this disease. If electrosurgery is to be used, one must be radical in the amount of tissue destroyed. We doubt if desiccation destroys cells deep enough to produce a cure. If electrocoagulation is used radically enough, a considerable defect is made. Is it not better to excise the lesion and repair the defect in one stage, rather than be forced to do a plastic operation for the defect?

Many clinics advocate radiation rather than surgery. Radium is applied to the lip and X-ray to the cervical region. Occasionally X-ray is used exclusively. In general we do not believe that as good results are obtained by radiation as by surgery. We agree that cancer of the lip itself can be cured in many instances by radium and X-ray. We have no quarrel with the radiologist who is sufficiently trained to use adequate doses to really destroy the lesion. We have a quarrel with the partially trained physician who believes in the magic of radium and who does not use sufficient doses to effect a cure. Some of the local results of radium are excellent and produce very little scar or deformity.

When it comes to radiation of the cervical nodes rather than removing the glands we disagree absolutely. Many radiologists admit that they cannot cure cancer in the cervical nodes by radiation. Certainly it is true that by the technique formerly used, cures were rare. The treatment today is much more radical and it is quite possible that by the present technique more will be accomplished. However, we believe that the cervical nodes should be treated by surgical measures.

We advise surgical removal of all cancers of the lip either by a V or a rectangular incision, the excision to extend through the full thickness of the lip and to include at least one half inch of normal tissue on all sides of the lesion. If a wide excision of a large lesion is done it may be necessary to resort to a plastic operation to close the defect.

With the exception of the small lesions which, on removal, prove to be Grade I cancers, we advise a neck dissection on all cases if the physical condition warrants it. We include the large Grade I lesions in this group. If we suspect a Grade I lesion, it is removed under novocaine, otherwise the lip lesion and the glands are removed at one sitting, either under general or local anaesthesia. If the lesion lies well to one side of the lip, dissection of the glands on that side is sufficient. The presence of the lesion near the center of the lip calls for dissection of both sides of the neck down to the level of the bifurcation of the carotid. For lesions of long standing, wherever their location on the lip, bilateral dissection is indicated.

The Neck Dissection

A curved incision is made under the jaw from beneath the chin, on the opposite side, parallel with the jaw, back to the sternomastoid muscle. The skin and fat flaps are dissected upward and downward. The sternomastoid muscle is exposed as is the tip of the parotid gland and the angle of the jaw. The triangular space between these landmarks contains some of the upper cervical glands and should be cleared out. The dissection is carried down the sternomastoid muscle for about two inches. Then all the fat and glandular tissue is swept forward to beyond the midline. The internal jugular vein is cleared and the facial vein ligated. The platysma should be removed and all tissues up to the edge of the jaw swept forward. The external and anterior jugular veins are ligated and cut, the facial artery at its entrance into the submaxillary gland is divided and the submaxillary gland removed. The lower dissection passes just below the digastric muscle and tendon, follows up the belly of one digastric for a short distance, but then includes the tissues in the submental space, which lie between the bellies of the two digastrics. When the submaxillary gland is removed care must be taken not to cut the lingual nerve which lies along the upper border of the inner half of the gland. This is well covered by fascia and may be easily retracted and missed if not looked for. Drainage is accomplished through a stab wound at the lowest portion of the dissected area. The skin is closed. Very little deformity follows this dissection.

Results of Operative Treatment at the Massachusetts General Hospital

Two series of cases have been studied and reported in recent years, the first by Simmons and Daland[3] and the second by Shedden[4]. In the first series there were 187 cases but only 131 are available for final results. Local excision of the growth was done in 33 cases with 20 three-year cures (66 per cent). Removal of the primary growth combined with neck dissection produced 87 per cent three-year cures when no cancer was found in the glands (63 of 72 cases). When cancer was present in the glands, 5 of 19 patients (26 per cent) survived three years.

It is not always possible to tell by clinical examination whether the glands are involved or not. In 24 cases in this group, no glands could be palpated before operation and yet in six (25 per cent) they were found at operation. Palpable glands did not necessarily mean that cancer was present, for many of these palpable glands were found to be inflammatory.

Shedden in an analysis of a later group of 107 cases found but 38 per cent three-year cures in the cases on whom the lip alone was operated on. Dissection of the glands was done in the remainder of the cases but in only 10 per cent was cancer found. There were 88 per cent alive and well where no cancer was found and 57 per cent where cancer was present in the glands.

Combining these two series, giving 200 known results, the results were 49 per cent on the simple lip operation, 42 per cent where the glands were cancerous and 87 per cent when no cancer was present in the glands. However, these are three-year, not five-year cures. Figuring on the longer time the results would not be quite as good, although recurrence after three years is uncommon.

Results of Operative Treatment at the Pondville Hospital

Taylor[5] has reported the three-year end results of all cancers of the lip operated on at the Pondville Hospital between July 1, 1927 and July 1, 1929. He has recently secured the five-year results and found that no patients died of recurrence between the three and five-year periods. There were twenty-three patients operated on. No pathological report was obtained in two. Four patients died of other causes without recurrence of their cancer. One case was recurrent following operation elsewhere. This patient died following resection of the jaw. There were, then, seventeen primary cases available for end result study. All of these (100%) were free from disease at the end of five years. However two of these were not examined by a physician between the fourth and fifth years, but were free from disease when examined at the end of four years and are said to be free from disease at the end of five years.

Conclusion

1. Persisting ulcers, leukoplakia, or tumors of the lip may be cancer and must be treated as such until proven otherwise.
2. If the lesion is treated before it has spread to the glands and if only the lip is treated, there is a 60 per cent chance of cure. If treated equally early but combined with a dissection of the glands, there is a 90 per cent chance of cure.
3. The percentage of cures obtained in all operable cases which are traced five years is approximately seventy.
4. Inasmuch as many patients have inoperable lesions when they are first admitted, it is probable that not more than 50 per cent of all the patients with cancer of the lip who appear for treatment survive the five-year period.

Cancer of the Lip

TABLE I. *Excision only. No treatment of glands*

	Number of cases	Duration of cures	Per cent cured
Bloodgood (6)	11	5 years	63
Brewer (8)	—	5 years	66
Simmons and Daland	33	3 years	60
Shedden	12	3 years	38
Taylor	6	5 years	100

TABLE II. *Excision lip lesion with dissection of glands*
No cancer in glands

	Number of cases	Duration of cures	Per cent cured
Bloodgood	12	5 years	95
Sistrunk (7)	—	5 years	90
Brewer	—	5 years	92
Simmons and Daland	72	3 years	87
Shedden	52	3 years	88
Taylor	7	5 years	100

Cancer in Glands

	Number of cases	Duration of cures	Per cent cured
Bloodgood	12	5 years	50
Brewer	—	5 years	34
Simmons and Daland	19	3 years	26
Shedden	7	3 years	57
Taylor	3	5 years	100

Bibliography

[1] EWING, *Neoplastic Diseases*.

[2] BRODERS, *Squamous Cell Epithelioma of the Lip*, J. A. M. A. 74:656, Mar. 6, '20.

[3] SIMMONS AND DALAND, *The Results of Operations for Cancer of the Lip at the Massachusetts General Hospital from 1909 to 1919*, Surg. Gynec. & Obst. 35:766-771, Dec. '22.

[4] SHEDDEN, *The Results of Surgical Treatment of Epithelioma of the Lip*, Boston M. & S. J. 196:262-270, Feb. 17, '27.

[5] TAYLOR, *A Further Report of the Cases Admitted to the Pondville Hospital during Its First Two Years;* Am. Journ. Cancer, XXI, 3, July, 1934. Also unpublished report.

[6] BLOODGOOD, *Cancer of the Lower Lip.* Boston M. & S. J., 1914, CLXX, 49-51, *Carcinoma of the Lower Lip; Its Diagnosis and Operative Treatment*, Surg. Gynec. and Obst. 1914, XVIII, pp. 404 - 422.

[7] SISTRUNK, *The Results of the Surgical Treatment of Epithelioma of the Lip*, Ann. Surg. 73:521, May, 1921.

[8] BREWER, *Carcinoma of the Lip and Cheek*, Surg. Gynec. & Obst. 36:169-184, Feb. '23.

CANCER OF THE LIVER AND GALL BLADDER

By IRVING J. WALKER, M. D.

Boston, Massachusetts

Carcinoma of the gall bladder should be of interest to the medical profession, chiefly from the point of view of its prevention. Statistics indicate that carcinoma of the gall bladder has a definite relationship to the incidence of gallstones. Marchand (F. Beitr. z. Path. Anat. 17:206, 1895) reports 88.8 per cent of cases of carcinoma of the gall bladder showing stones. Deaver and Bortz (Jn. Am. Med. Assn. 88:619, 1927) find that in 903 cases of gall bladder disease, 1.5 per cent showed carcinoma of the gall bladder. Graham (Diseases of the Gall Bladder and Bile Ducts, Lea & Febiger, 1928) states that one in twenty-five who have gallstones will develop carcinoma of the gall bladder.

The mortality rate of operation for gallstones is somewhat less than the risk of developing carcinoma of the gall bladder should the stones not be removed. In view of the accepted belief that carcinoma in general may follow chronic irritation, it seems logical to believe that the presence of gallstones is the chief etiological factor in the production of carcinoma of the gall bladder.

The diagnosis of carcinoma of the gall bladder also offers interest, from the academic scope, of the possibility of making a positive diagnosis of carcinoma of this organ.

From the viewpoint of cure where the lesion exists, little can be said in favor of curative measures, either by surgery or radiation. If discovered by accident and early in its progress, where the lesion is localized within the lumen of the gall bladder, cholecystectomy may result in cure. However, because of its intimate relationship to the liver and the plentiful lymphatic association of the gall bladder, liver, head of the pancreas, and the lymph glands about the ducts, and since the growth is usually a rapidly growing adenocarcinoma, the progress of the disease is so extensive when discovered that attempts at cure are practically futile.

Carcinoma of the liver demonstrates itself as of one of two types, primary or metastatic. From the histological aspect, primary carcinoma of the liver may arise from the liver cell, the lining cell of the bile ducts, and the more unusual type of cancer of the liver, namely, that of the adrenal cell tumor which is occasionally primary in the liver.

Primary liver cell carcinoma is grossly found in one of two forms, the large solitary type, or that with multiple areas of tumor formation.

The relationship between cirrhosis and primary liver cell carcinoma has been recognized by pathologists for years. In sixteen autopsies demonstrating primary liver cell carcinoma at the Boston City Hospital, an accompanying cirrhosis was present in each instance.

Metastatic carcinoma of the liver as a terminal pathological picture of carcinoma in general, is a most common finding. Particularly is this so in relation to carcinoma of the breast, and especially in carcinoma of the intestinal tract and structures associated with the portal circulation.

The interest of the physician in metastatic carcinoma of the liver should be that of prevention by early recognition and removal of surface tumors and investigation of symptoms referable to deep seated organs or systems, in the hope that by recognizing carcinoma early cures may result.

The diagnosis of carcinoma of the liver, whether primary or metastatic, offers problems of interest, especially to those interested in diseases of the biliary tract. Without entering into the differential diagnosis of carcinoma of the liver, we offer the following clinical facts in instances of carcinoma of the liver:

(1) With attention focussed upon the liver as a site of pathology, the findings of a previous or recent history of carcinoma or suspicion of the same points toward the possibility of metastatic carcinoma of the liver.

(2) The knowledge of an existing cirrhosis with positive clinical evidence of an enlarging and nodular liver, and with the absence of a primary lesion of carcinoma elsewhere in the body, might warrant one in hazarding a diagnosis of primary liver cell carcinoma.

(3) A large nodular liver which is gradually increasing in size points towards carcinoma. The nodules themselves are often tender with nontender areas of normal liver tissue between the same.

(4) An elevation of temperature and increase in leucocytosis are not uncommon when the nodules are numerous and large. These findings are undoubtedly due to necrosis of the central position of the carcinomatous areas.

Surgery for confirmation of diagnosis of carcinoma of the liver, whether primary or metastatic, is attendant with considerable mortality, the latter being associated with the many aspects of disturbed metabolic process as demonstrated by blood chemistry findings.

PRIMARY CARCINOMA OF THE LUNG
By Edward D. Churchill, M. D.
Boston, Massachusetts

Carefully evaluated statistics appear to indicate that the incidence of primary carcinoma of the lung is increasing. Various causes have been invoked, among them the inhalation of tar dust from the roads and the influenza epidemic of 1918. The origin of pulmonary carcinoma is as obscure, however, as that of other neoplastic disease. There is no evidence to show that pulmonary tuberculosis plays any important role as a predisposing factor.

Classifications of primary carcinoma of the lung have been based on the appearance of the lesion in gross, the Roentgen ray shadows and the symptomatology. As these descriptions are usually based on advanced stages of the disease they are without special significance. A classification on the basis of cell type will be more informative as surgical specimens reach the pathologists.

Primary carcinomas of the lung are usually referred to as "bronchogenic", indicating the belief that they arise from the epithelial elements of the bronchial mucous membrane. A controversy exists as to whether the epithelial lining of the alveoli may give rise to cancer, but the question at the moment is hard to prove and equally difficult to disprove. The common types of primary carcinoma of the lung are (1) squamous cell carcinoma, (2) adenocarcinoma, (3) small cell type ("oat cell") and (4) polymorphic tumors composed of more than one type of cell.

The conception that primary carcinoma of the lung is highly malignant and peculiarly prone to widespread extension and metastases seems due largely to the fact that the disease is rarely diagnosed in its early stages. The present knowledge of the disease is largely based on autopsy findings of terminal cases. As a matter of fact the progress of the disease in certain cases appears peculiarly and oftentimes cruelly slow. The tumor spreads to distant sites by both lymphatic and hematogenous routes. The bronchial and mediastinal lymph nodes are invaded early. Blood stream metastases appear to find particularly favorable soil in the brain, the liver, the adrenals, and the kidneys.

As is the case with other tumors, carcinoma of the lung also progresses and kills by direct extension. Invasion of the mediastinum, the pericardium, the diaphragm or the chest wall may occur. The "degree of malignancy" as indicated by rapidity of growth and metastasis has not been adequately correlated with the histologic type of individual tumors.

Symptomatology

The clinical picture of primary carcinoma of the lung is very varied, depending upon the location of the tumor and particularly upon the presence or absence of pleural involvement and bronchial obstruction. *Cough* is usually the earliest and most constant manifestation of the disease. Frequently its onset is coincident with an acute respiratory infection which simply means that a partially obstructed area of lung has become infected at that time. The physician is frequently caught off his guard by this happening and must learn to appreciate that a cough that "hangs on" in a patient previously well demands careful diagnostic study. A tumor in close proximity to the visceral pleura may produce a *pleural effusion* preceded or not by "dry" pleurisy. The effusion may be serous but is characteristically bloody. When actual invasion of the pleura exists, tumor cells may be found in the sediment of the fluid.

Bronchial obstruction presents a train of events as important and as characteristic as those that attend obstruction of the bowel. A tumor that partially obstructs a sizeable bronchus may cause a *wheeze* noted by the patient and audible to the examiner as a sibilant rale. A partial obstruction may cause *obstructive emphysema* or trapping of the air behind the obstruction on expiration. X-ray films taken in full inspiration and expiration respectively may reveal this phenomenon. Recurrent attacks of so-called bronchopneumonia punctuate the case history. When the obstruction becomes complete, *atelectasis* of the corresponding area of lung occurs. The lung becomes "drowned" by the imprisoned bronchial secretions. The bronchi become dilated, and depending upon the type and virulence of the bacterial flora, pneumonitis or abscess formation results. The physical signs that attend complete bronchial obstruction are important to recognize as they are often an indication for bronchoscopic examination. The breath sounds are usually totally absent in contrast to the bronchial breath sounds characteristically heard with fluid. They may be present, however, but faint and vesicular in type. Resonance is impaired and tactile fremitus diminished, but usually not to a degree simulating the flatness and absent tactile fremitus of fluid. *Clubbing of the fingers* may be an early sign particularly when bronchial obstruction is present.

Ulceration of the bronchial mucous membrane gives rise to the *blood-streaked* sputum or *recurrent hemorrhages* so characteristic of carcinoma of the lung. The "prune-juice" sputum described in textbooks is observed but rarely. The hemorrhages not infrequently lead to the erroneous diagnosis of pulmonary tuberculosis — a diagnosis that should always be carefully scrutinized in the absence of a positive sputum or indisputable X-ray evidence of the disease.

Foul sputum and other symptoms of *lung abscess* may appear when a tumor undergoes necrosis and a bronchial fistula is established. Malignant disease must always be considered as a possible etiologic factor in spontaneously developing lung abscess.

Pain is produced when the parietal pleura is invaded by the tumor. Extension of a growth to the central portion of the diaphragm gives pain referred to the shoulder. Pain down the arm with partial ulnar and median nerve palsy and constriction of the pupil on that side occur with growths in the extreme apical region (superior sulcus tumor of Pancoast). A primary tumor or metastatic deposit may cause paralysis of the recurrent laryngeal or phrenic nerves on the involved side by direct invasion of these structures in the mediastinum. Esophageal obstruction and ulceration are rare.

Diagnosis

The diagnosis usually depends upon obtaining a careful history with or without suggestive physical signs, and is confirmed by Roentgen ray examination. Although X-ray films may at times establish a definite diagnosis, they frequently portray only the pleural effusion, the atelectasis or the obstructive emphysema that are produced by the primary tumor. Bronchoscopy may establish a positive diagnosis if a bit of the tumor can be removed for microscopic examination. Many tumors in the periphery of the lung or in the upper lobes cannot be reached with the bronchoscope so a negative examination in no way rules out the diagnosis.

Treatment

Until very recently primary carcinoma of the lung has been regarded as invariably fatal. To establish the diagnosis was to pronounce the death sentence for the patient. The suffering in the terminal stages is often extreme. The course of the illness may be prolonged and the patient's life be made miserable for months by severe pain, harassing cough, foul sputum, alarming hemorrhages and shortness of breath. Uncontrollable hiccoughs, headache and loss of vision from cerebral metastases, prostrating weakness from adrenal involvement may be mentioned as typical of other distressing sequelae that combine to make the patient's existence intolerable.

Fortunately, thoracic surgery has now advanced so that a chance of cure may be offered to certain patients and palliation to others.

Unless definite evidence of metastases or inoperable extension of the growth is at hand, patients suspected of having primary carcinoma of the lung should be subjected to open thoracotomy to determine whether the growth may be resected. An artificial pneumothorax may be of aid in determining operability. The extent of the opacity in an X-ray film is frequently not a true index of the size of the growth as the shadow may be due in part to collapsed or consolidated lung tissue. Actual resection of primary carcinoma of the lung is too recent an operation and has been performed too infrequently to warrant comment upon the results that may be expected. It has been repeatedly demonstrated, however, that an entire lung may be removed with operative recovery of the patient, and that single lobes may be removed with immediate palliation of distressing symptoms. The problem confronting the surgeon is that of all forms of malignant disease—earlier diagnosis to secure proper treatment at a time when the disease is still localized.

Treatment by *radiation* may be indicated for certain inoperable growths or in patients who are poor operative risks. Cases subjected to radiation therapy must be selected with some discrimination or the results may be injurious rather than palliative. X-ray necrosis of a tumor in an infected lung may cause a flare-up of pneumonitis, hemorrhages and an increase of cough and sputum.

PRIMARY TUMORS OF LYMPH NODES
By HENRY JACKSON, JR., M. D.
Newton, Massachusetts

The various primary tumors of lymph nodes may be grouped under the general heading, Malignant Lymphoma. Into this classification comes Hodgkin's disease, lymphosarcoma, reticulum cell sarcoma, lymphoblastoma, plasmoma and other rarer forms of lymph node tumors. For most practical purposes they may be grouped together. Their etiology is unknown. The majority of authorities regard them as true neoplasma. It is likely, however, that Hodgkin's disease is, at least in its early stages, an infection; and this disease is often found in association with active tuberculosis. There is very little evidence, however, that Hodgkin's disease is actually a form of tuberculosis as has been claimed by some. The various forms of malignant lymphoma affect all ages and both sexes. Hodgkin's disease affects principally young male adults.

The classical textbook picture of malignant lymphoma shows involvement of the cervical lymph nodes, but it is important to remember that the disease may affect any portion of the body. The lymph nodes may arise in the neck, axilla, groin or mediastinum and be the presenting symptom. They are seldom painful unless they press upon adjacent nerves or other structures. Frequently they increase and decrease in size spontaneously or coincidentally with upper respiratory infections. They may even temporarily disappear. These spontaneous fluctuations do not by any means indicate a benign lesion. Unless associated with obvious foci of infection, notably enlarged lymph nodes in adults should be regarded as malignant until proved the contrary. In consistence the lymph nodes may be soft, firm or hard. Very rarely are they stony hard; nodes of this nature being almost always due to secondary carcinoma. There are no safe criteria upon which enlarged lymph nodes due to lymphoma may be surely told from tuberculosis, although necrosis and sinus formation are rare in the former condition. A biopsy is the only way of making a diagnosis and if properly done causes no difficulty. Celloidin, or better still, paraffin sections should be examined. Only in rare instances can a proper and safe diagnosis be made on frozen material.

Malignant lymphoma may also, as has been indicated, involve the lymph nodes elsewhere in the body without necessarily manifesting itself in superficial lymphadenopathy. Mediastinal lymphomas are not uncommon. Their symptoms are usually weakness, shortness of breath, cough and more rarely pain. In some instances they may be symptomless. Involvement of the gastro-intestinal tract is not uncommon, particularly of the stomach and rectum. The symptoms of malignant lymphoma in these regions are those of carcinoma or ulcer and only a pathological examination can differentiate them from these other lesions. The disease frequently involves the skin where it may manifest itself by generalized itching or by a variety of cutaneous lesions. These may be single or multiple, are usually raised and sharply circumscribed and may be serpiginous. In color they vary from that of the normal skin through pink to deep purple. They are usually found in cases where there is lymphoma elsewhere. Rarely they may be the sole manifestation of the disease. Involvement of bone is common and lack of recognition of this fact may lead to serious diagnostic errors. As a rule, the osseous lesions are accompanied by evidences of the disease elsewhere, are destructive in nature and cause considerable pain. Much more rarely the condition may be confined to bone. In certain cases fever may be the main symptom of lymphoma and in the absence of notable peripheral lymphadenopathy the diagnosis may be very difficult. The fever may be of any type. One occasionally sees the Pel-Epstein type in which bouts of fever lasting approximately ten days follow each other after periods of apparent health at decreasing intervals until finally the fever becomes continuous. This type of fever is almost invariably associated with Hodgkin's disease. The other forms of lymphoma are rarely, except in the terminal stages, associated with fever of any moment.

Malignant lymphoma of the tonsil and nasopharynx is not rare and its chief symptom is sore throat; the chief sign, tumor of the tonsil or enlargement of the cervical nodes. The benignity of its onset not infrequently deludes the physician into a false sense of security. The disease runs, as a rule, a rapid and fatal course.

Malignant lymphoma may also involve primarily or secondarily the central nervous system, the genito-urinary tract or, indeed, any other portion of the body. Barring those cases which are associated with leukemia, examination of the blood is usually essentially normal in the early stages. There may, however, be a considerable degree of anemia, particularly in the Hodgkin's type and in this latter condition both the total white blood cell count and the polymorphonuclear cells are often abnormally high. In all types of lymphoma the basal metabolism is frequently elevated to a considerable degree, usually in the region of +20 to +60. This fact may be of diagnostic importance.

In all suspected cases an isolated lymph node should be excised and examined by a competent pathologist.

The main stay of treatment is radiation, usually in the form of high voltage X-ray. The details of this treatment must necessarily be left to the radiologist. In general, however, it may be said that approximately 600 R units are given to each involved area once a diagnosis has been made, and further treatment is given when, and if recurrence occurs or symptoms arise which might properly be attributed to the disease—and these, as has already been pointed out, may be of a most varied nature. Some authors feel that if the disease is sharply limited to a small area, radical surgery is indicated. If the patient is in good condition and relatively young, such a procedure, in the hands of a capable surgeon, certainly can do no harm. It goes without saying that general supportive measures, good hygiene and the adequate symptomatic treatment of symptoms as they arise constitute an important part in the care of the patient. Iron in the form of Feosol (grs. 6 a day) and cod liver oil may be indicated. Fresh air and moderate exercise are beneficial.

As a broad generality, these patients live between three and six years, but the type of the tumor, its site, the age of the patient, and other less well understood features so markedly affect the prognosis that any generalization is misleading in so far as the individual case is concerned. Each patient is a problem by himself.

There is some dispute as to whether a definite cure can result in this disease. Not a few patients are living and well eight to ten and even fifteen years after their initial symptoms and still show no evidence of recurrence. It must be remembered, however, that even after many years the disease may recur and death may ensue very rapidly in such instances. It is probable, however, that there are a few well authenticated true cures.

CANCER OF THE MOUTH
By CHARLES C. LUND, M. D.
Boston, Massachusetts

Incidence

Cancer of the buccal mucosa comprises about 10 per cent of cases of cancer coming to a cancer clinic and about the same per cent of cancer deaths. It is very definitely connected with sex inasmuch as over 90 per cent of the cases come in males.

Etiology

Broken, infected, and dirty teeth are an important cause of this form of cancer. Poorly fitting dentures with or without rough edges and irrespective of whether they are attached, such as bridge work, or removable, such as plates, also play a role in many cases. Equally important with dental irritation is the irritation caused by tobacco. Of the forms of tobacco used commonly, pipe smoking and chewing are apparently more serious than the use of cigars and cigarettes. Syphilis is also important in relation to the cause of cancer of the tongue, but not in relation to cancer in other parts of the mouth. It is because of these etiological factors that the disease occurs most in males and also in the poorest part of the population.

Prophylaxis

From the statements in the above section it is obvious what methods should be used for prophylaxis. There is no form of cancer that may be as surely prevented as this. The greatest contribution that can be made by the medical and dental professions in regard to buccal cancer is to see that septic, broken teeth, irregular and poorly fitting plates are promptly removed from the mouth, that excessive use of tobacco be stopped, and that syphilis be adequately treated. These measures should be undertaken whether there are signs of irritation present or not.

Appearance and Diagnosis

About one-half the cases begin in an area of leukoplakia. Leukoplakia is a definite premalignant lesion. It has the appearance of a white patch usually with a rather discrete border and frequently with very little thickness. The shape is quite irregular and the extent may be from a small area of a few millimeters to a widespread process involving most of the mouth. In some cases it may have a papillary appearance and reach a thickness of two or three millimeters. The cancer itself, in its earliest stages, may have a papillary appearance indistinguishable except in the microscopic slide from papillary leukoplakia, or it may begin as a small ulcer with a varying degree of infiltration and irregularity of the base. A third form begins as a small infiltrating tumor without ulceration. Any case may combine the characteristics of any two of these three types. Early involvement of the lymph nodes is frequent, and these may be definitely involved for some time before they are enlarged to palpation. Later, a large fungating and infiltrating mass fixes the tongue and the jaw, and the mass of glands in the neck reaches a large size and breaks down. In the early stages it may be distinguishable from gumma tuberculosis, actinomycosis, granulation tissue or benign tumor only on microscopic examination. As a class these cases develop very rapidly. A delay of only three to four weeks before starting proper treatment will reduce the chance of cure by one half. The diagnosis is frequently obscure in the early stages and the textbook methods of differential diagnosis only apply to moderately advanced cases. The more experience one has with these cases the less he comes to rely on clinical methods of diagnosis. In all diseased conditions in the mouth think of cancer. If any aspect of the lesion remotely suggests cancer have a consultation with a specialist or at a cancer clinic or take an adequate biopsy.

Location

The frequency of distribution of cases in different parts of the mouth is as follows: tongue, 41 per cent; floor of mouth, 13 per cent; inside of cheek, 15 per cent; upper jaw, 7 per cent; lower jaw, 15 per cent; and palate 9 per cent.

Pathology

Ninety-nine per cent of malignancy in the mouth is epidermoid carcinoma arising in the buccal mucosa. The rare forms are adenocarcinoma, carcinoma adenoides cysticum, adamantinoma, fibrosarcoma, bone sarcoma and, very rarely, metastatic carcinoma arising from the thyroid, the kidney, or elsewhere. If the epidermoid carcinomas are graded microscopically they will run from highly differentiated low grade processes to highly undifferentiated. The cases arising in the tongue and floor of the mouth, and especially those arising in conjunction with syphilis average a higher, more malignant grade than those in the other locations.

Treatment

Biopsy within the ulcer in cancer of the mouth can never do harm. It is therefore indicated and should be done in all cases before treatment is decided upon. Even when the diagnosis of cancer is obvious the biopsy helps to determine the grade of the tumor and, as will be seen later the treatment varies with the grading as well as the stage of the disease. Before undertaking treatment all mouth sepsis should be eliminated. Many dentists will refuse or oppose extractions in the presence of cancer, being afraid of the spread of the disease. This idea must be combated energetically, as either surgery or radical radiation treatment in the presence of mouth sepsis leads to disastrous results. If syphilis is present this should be treated at first only by giving adequate doses of potassium iodide. Later, after the preliminary reaction to surgery or radiation is over, further treatment with bismuth, mercury, or arsenic should be given. Never treat a case with a nodular or ulcerated lesion of the tongue for syphilis, even if the presence of syphilis is proved, unless a biopsy has ruled out cancer. Cases of combined syphilis and cancer are common and will at first appear to improve on antisyphilitic treatment. However, the cancer continues to progress even when the process as a whole is becoming smaller and may well reach an incurable state during the period the physician takes to discover that he is dealing with something more than a gumma. The use of tobacco should be stopped.

Operative Treatment

Primary surgical excision should be limited to a very small number of cases. First, those with small superficial Grade I lesions without enlargement of the lymph nodes. These should be removed widely by diathermy. At the same time any leukoplakia should be cauterized. At a separate sitting the lymph nodes in the neck should be dissected radically. Small to moderate sized lesions involving the bone or either jaw or of the palate should also be excised surgically. This will usually, in the case of the lower jaw, mean a complete resection of part of the jaw.

Radiation Treatment

All other cases and recurrences following the above operations should be treated by radiation. This is best done by giving from 2000 to 4000 R units of external X-ray treatment from a 200,000 volt machine within a period of a week or ten days. This will cause a very sharp skin reaction. At the end of a month following this treatment the case should be re-examined and gold seeds or platinum needles inserted into any areas of the primary lesion which still show activity. At this time further radiation may be indicated. Rarely two or three months after this treatment if the primary lesion has entirely disappeared, remaining small involved glands may be removed surgically.

Results

Five year "cures" of forty per cent of the cases treated should result from the treatment of primary lesions which are not over one cm. in diameter and in which the lymph nodes are not palpably involved. Fifteen per cent of "cures" should follow the treatment in lesions up to 2 cm. in diameter without palpable enlargement of the glands. "Cures" are exceptional in cases with glands more than one cm. in diameter or in which the primary lesion is more than two cm. in diameter and in cases in which recurrence has taken place following previous surgery or radiation treatment. Improvement in results of treatment as a whole will occur only following earlier adequate treatment and following more energetic radiation treatment than has been customary in the past. The figures of "cures" given above are based on results of cases treated for the most part by surgery six to ten years ago. We believe that modern radiation treatment will give better results. Preliminary data leads us to believe that at least twenty-five per cent of "moderately advanced" cases should be "cured" by radiation.

CANCER OF THE NASOPHARYNX

By C. H. ERNLUND, M. D.

Boston, Massachusetts

The nasopharynx is frequently the seat of new growths of benign as well as of malignant nature. Among the benign tumors are considered the polypi, papillomata, lipomata, adenomata, myxomata, angiomata, chondromata, osteomata, neurofibromata, teratomata, cysts, lymphomata, etc. The so-called juvenile nasopharyngeal fibroma is also placed in this category, although clinically it must be considered as malignant in character. The mixed tumors are considered benign by certain authors, malignant by others. It is generally believed, however, that since they frequently show malignant degeneration they should be considered as potentially malignant.

The malignant tumors of the region which we are discussing are, as a rule, very dangerous, and frequently metastasize long before the original tumor has caused any local symptoms to make the patient or his physician aware of its presence. Various forms of sarcomata are found, although the small round cell type and the lymphosarcoma predominate. The carcinomata are most often of the squamous cell or of the so-called transitional cell types.

It is important to remember that new growths in the nasopharynx are not necessarily primary in this region. The original growth may be found in the nose or its accessory sinuses, inasmuch as the lymphatics which drain this region pass via the lateral nasal wall to the retropharyngeal glands and thence to the deep cervical nodes. Only a few lymph channels continue directly to the latter lymph nodes. This fact is probably the reason for the erroneous but frequently made statement that tumors of the maxillary sinus seldom if ever metastasize.

Statistics show that men are more frequently affected than women; and it has been said that mesoblastic tumors are, as a rule, found more often in youth, whereas those of epi- or hypoblastic origin occur later in life.

Signs and Symptoms

There are, naturally, wide variations as far as signs and symptoms are concerned, depending upon the situation and size of the tumor, etc. An analysis made by New, of seventy-nine cases of malignant nasopharyngeal tumors, showed symptoms referable to the eye in twenty-one cases, to the ear in twenty-nine, to the nose and pharynx in thirty-eight, to the glands in the neck in fifty-one, to the Gasserian ganglion in four, to the jugular foramen in two. Eleven showed evidence of intracranial involvement.

Many tumors remain "silent" for a considerable period, and the first symptom noted may be enlarged cervical glands. Laterally situated tumors often produce deafness, due to encroachment on the eustachian tube. Repeated and severe hemorrhages are characteristic especially of the nasopharyngeal fibromata. Frequently there is a nasal catarrh and polypoid degeneration to be seen upon nasal inspection. Approximately one-fourth of the patients show neuralgia due to the involvement of the ninth, tenth, eleventh or twelfth cranial nerves or the sympathetic nerves. It often resembles tic douloureux, and is frequently referred to the eyes, ears, occiput or the side of the head. There may be more or less difficulty in opening the mouth, with or without enlargement of the cervical glands. If the tumor is very large, there may be characteristic voice changes. Extension to the meninges may cause symptoms similar to those found in tubercular meningitis with pronounced headache, drowsiness, vomiting, etc.

Diagnosis

A thorough examination of the nasopharynx requires a great deal of experience and more refinement of technique than can reasonably be expected of medical practitioners who are not engaged in the specialty of rhinology. One is particularly impressed by this in view of the findings reported by New in a publication dealing with malignant growths of the nasopharynx. Out of a total of seventy-nine patients, seventy-four had been operated upon for relief of symptoms without recognition of the primary growth as the underlying cause. Twenty-four had had the tonsils and adenoids removed, eighteen had had dissection of the cervical glands and twelve had had wisdom teeth removed. Various intranasal operations had been performed in nineteen patients and in one case a mastoidectomy.

It is impossible to make a correct diagnosis from appearance alone. The tumor may be sessile or pedunculated; the surface may be perfectly smooth or cauliflower-like. Microscopic examination of what may have appeared to be a benign papilloma revealed it to be a highly malignant epithelioma. A lymphosarcoma may resemble a benign mixed tumor. It is, therefore, of the utmost importance to obtain a specimen for microscopic diagnosis. It is also necessary to remove a portion large enough for the purpose, since certain growths vary considerably in different areas of their own masses. If the choanae are obstructed it is not unusual to find the nares filled with simple polypi, the removal of which may fail completely to show the true growth. On the other hand, extensive operations have been performed upon patients when the offending neoplasm was found after removal to be a granuloma.

Types of Tumor

As it would be futile to attempt here a detailed description of the many forms of neoplasms occurring in the nasopharyngeal region, only a few of the more common tumors will receive individual attention.

Nasopharyngeal fibroma (angiofibroma). This is often referred to as juvenile fibroma, as it usually appears in persons between the ages of eight and twenty-five. It occurs most frequently in boys, rarely in girls. The tumor does not form metastases and hence has been placed among benign growths. It is slow growing, and originates from the fibrocartilage of the upper cervical vertebrae, from around the anterior lacerated foramen or from the sphenopalatine fossa, and develops by extension. It may thus invade the cranial fossa, or find its way between the styloid and pterygoid muscles into the temporal fossa, or through the inferior orbital fissure into the orbit. It is often exceedingly vascular and one of its chief symptoms is repeated hemorrhage from the nose or pharynx. It seldom produces pain, but it makes its presence known chiefly by mechanical obstruction to normal breathing or interference with swallowing. A tendency to spontaneous disappearance is characteristic of it, especially after a portion of the tumor has been removed. Various methods of treatment have been advocated. If the tumor is pedunculated, it can occasionally be removed by the use of a snare, and by diathermy. In surgical procedure the fact that the tumor is apt to be exceedingly vascular necessitates extreme caution. Fibromata have also been successfully eradicated by electrocoagulation and by the use of high voltage X-ray and radium.

Sarcoma.—Primary sarcoma of the nasopharynx usually runs a very rapid course, and the first symptom noticed is frequently a swift and painless increase in size of the deep cervical glands. The round cell type appears to be the most common of the various forms of sarcoma. Lymphosarcoma is also common and seems to be as prevalent among persons above the age of forty as it is among those below this age. It appears as a hard, nodular, diffuse swelling of the pharyngeal mucosa and the lymphoid tissue of the pharynx. It soon ulcerates, however, and extends to the cervical nodes, cranial cavity, orbit, etc. It soon finds its way to the intestinal lymph nodes and important organs. If removed it almost invariably recurs.

Carcinoma.—In the examination of a group of one hundred tumors of the nasopharynx, it was found that 50 per cent were squamous cell carcinoma, 37 per cent transitional cell carcinoma, 15 per cent lymphosarcoma and 11 per cent lymphoepithelioma. The remaining 7 per cent were malignant adenoma and adenoid cystic epithelioma.

The carcinomata of the nasopharynx, like the sarcomata, usually run a very rapid course. The original lesion frequently remains very small, and there may be extensive metastases before it is discovered. This is specially true of the transitional cell type. These growths are derived from a specialized epithelium found in the pharynx and nose, covering lymphoid tissue deposits. Hence they have been called lymphoepitheliomata. They invade the lymph nodes very early, and the primary growth may remain undetected for months. These tumors are usually very sensitive to radiation, and should not be removed surgically, owing to the possibility of widespread metastases. The less malignant forms can sometimes be healed by electrocoagulation, but if surgical removal of them is attempted, it should invariably be followed by adequate radiation, either in the form of radium packs or high voltage X-ray.

Summary

In the above observations, in addition to a classification of nasopharyngeal tumors, an attempt has been made to emphasize in particular the extreme importance of competence and experience both on the part of the diagnostician and of the roentgenologist. A thorough, careful, objective examination should be made, and a very competent pathologist should be called upon to make the microscopic examination for diagnosis. The treatment should be determined by the location and character of the tumor, and if X-ray or radium is used, it must be in the hands of thoroughly capable people who have had experience in the treatment of tumors.

MALIGNANT TUMORS OF THE OVARY
By Joe Vincent Meigs, M. D.
Boston, Massachusetts

There are many different tumors of the ovary, some benign, some semi-malignant, and some very malignant. To outline the proper treatment for them all is a difficult undertaking. The diagnosis of ovarian tumors is usually not difficult. Pelvic examination will disclose masses easily palpated and most often moveable. They must be differentiated from pregnancy and fibroids. Often ovarian lesions are accompanied by pain due to torsion or pressure. Abnormal bleeding before and after the menopause is a frequent symptom.

Most epithelial tumors have a tendency to be bilateral and for that reason careful inspection of both ovaries must be carried out by the operating surgeon. Failure to recognize this fact or failure to remove both ovaries and the uterus in malignant cases has resulted in too many unnecessary recurrences and fatal end results.

It is perhaps advisable to group the tumors under their different clinical types and suggest the treatment best suited to each type. The most common tumors of the ovary are the papillary cysts, benign, semi-malignant, and malignant. Differentiation between these forms of growth is extremely difficult and a few rules to follow in their treatment are essential. If a tumor or cyst of the ovary contains serous, bloody serous, or thick mucoid material a careful search should be made for papillary projections both on the inside and on the outside of the cyst. If papillary areas are found on the outside of the cyst a complete removal of the pelvic organs must be seriously contemplated no matter what the age of the patient. If the papillary areas are non-adherent and no implantation can be found and the patient is young, conservative surgery can be considered if conservation of the pelvic organs is a large factor in the case. If, in addition, papillary areas are found in conjunction with solid masses in a cyst the chances of serious malignancy are much greater and total ablation should be carried out no matter what the age of the patient. Extensive peritoneal involvement does not necessarily mean hopelessness for there have been patients cured by a radical removal of as much of the malignant disease as possible followed by X-ray treatment. Radical surgery should be the rule and not the exception in papillary tumors of the ovary. In youth, papillary cysts with the papillary areas confined to the inside of the cyst can be treated conservatively, but it is far better to err on the radical than the conservative side.

Semisolid tumors of the ovary of the epithelial type must be considered as having a serious outlook, for these tumors are usually of devastating malignancy. To be able to classify the slowly growing from the rapidly growing is difficult enough for the pathologist, and the surgeon confronted with such a tumor must err on the side of radical surgery. These tumors sometimes have papillary masses within the cystic areas and solid masses of tumor tissue alongside. Or they may be made up of solid masses with a few cysts in the solid masses of tissue. They are difficult to differentiate in the gross from the benign type of granulosal cell cancer and other types of embryonal cancers, but a good general rule, unless a pathologist is near by to make an accurate diagnosis, is to treat them as of great malignancy and remove both ovaries and the uterus, including the cervix. Solid epithelial growths of the ovary, also difficult to separate from the benign type of rare tumors, call for radical surgery in every instance.

Solid or semisolid, firm tumors of the connective tissue type can be differentiated from sarcoma by the coarse strands of connective tissue that can be seen on a freshly cut surface. For fibromas or the solid connective tissue tumors conservative surgery is proper. Removal of the tumor from the ovary, if possible, or the whole ovary if necessary, is sufficient. The solid sarcoma of the ovary, a tumor which is friable yet hard, but which a knife handle will penetrate, must be treated in a most radical manner for it is of the severest type of malignancy. Its recognition is difficult without the presence of a pathologist but a hard, friable, solid tumor of the ovary with evidence of connective tissue origin is better treated radically than conservatively.

Teratomas of the ovary, tumors made up of varying amounts of embryonal and adult tissue are usually hard to recognize. If hair is found in one of these solid tumors the diagnosis is clinched; cheesy substances, cartilage, and bone also make the diagnosis evident. Such tumors are often not very malignant but they may be of rapid growth. The solid type necessitates radical surgery, removal of both ovaries and the entire uterus. There is no method to determine the rate of growth or the danger of conservatism so that for the safety of the patient complete removal is the proper procedure. It may happen that some of the rare types of tumors of the ovary of very slight malignancy will be treated radically, but if in doubt it is far better for the patient to remove than to leave behind.

Many tumors of the ovary are metastatic. All gastric cancers, breast tumors, cancers of the body of the uterus, etc., may be the site of an original lesion that has metastasized to the ovary. If solid, bilateral, freely moveable tumors are found that are large, kidney-shaped, and with small or large amounts of fluid in the abdomen, the surgeon should immediately investigate the stomach, small intestine, breasts, etc. Search for the original focus is important and when found the lesion causing the greatest discomfort should be treated. Papillary cysts or solid tumors of the ovary may be found to have arisen in a cancer of the body of the uterus. If such a tumor of the ovary is treated radically, as has been already suggested, and the uterus removed, the original tumor will be found and removed also.

Great care should be taken not to rupture any ovarion cyst or tumor as it is being removed. Although in a series of ovarian tumors at the Massachusetts General Hospital good results were found in those that had been ruptured, it is definitely better not to allow rupture and spilling of malignant contents in the abdomen. The puncture by trocar of huge cysts before removal is usually safe but should only be done in those lesions considered as benign or when it is felt that an incision from ensiform to pubis is contraindicated.

The diseased ovary should be removed and then opened by the surgeon so as to view the contents. This is a very necessary procedure and should be always carried out. At this time the inside of the cyst, whether solid or papillary can be carefully inspected and solid areas with tumor found along with other evidence of malignancy. Even if no pathologist is present a good idea can be obtained by the operating surgeon and the proper treatment carried out. Total removal of the pelvic organs for benign tumors will be far less in number than the lives saved by removal of solid, semisolid, or papillary tumors plus the other ovary and the uterus. It is well for all operators to become familiar with ovarian tumors and close inspection and observation of the diseased tissue will give a great deal of information.

The prognosis of malignant ovarian tumors is about as follows: The papillary cystadenoma will not recur, the malignant papillary cystadenoma has about a 26 per cent curability, the solid tumors have a five-year curability of about 10 per cent, the sarcomas even less, and the metastatic tumors the worst outlook. It is evident that ovarian tumors must be carefully inspected at operation if favorable results are to be obtained, and any neglect such as leaving in one ovary in a malignant case will be rewarded by the appearance of the tumor in the other ovary or uterus eventually. Conservative surgery in but few cases is wise and radical surgery is often conservative.

CANCER OF THE PANCREAS
By LELAND S. MCKITTRICK, M. D.
Boston, Massachusetts

Incidence

Primary cancer of the pancreas probably represents about 2 per cent of all malignant tumors, although Hoffman[1] estimates that it now represents about 3 per cent of these cases in the United States. Moreover, he calls attention to the fact that in 1915 the death rate for cancer of the pancreas was 1.1 per 100,000, whereas, in 1932, it was 1.8. It is more common in men than in women and is most frequently seen between the ages of forty and seventy, but may be found at any age.

Pathology

According to Ewing,[2] the lesion may be either a cylinder cell adenocarcinoma arising from the ducts, or a carcinoma simplex arising from the parenchyma. The former frequently represents a larger more localized, bulky tumor, whereas the latter is apt to be more diffuse. Leven,[3] in 382 collected cases, found that in 56 per cent the involvement was in the head, in 31 per cent it was diffuse, and in the remaining 13 per cent it was divided equally between the body and tail. Metastases occur most frequently in the liver and regional nodes. Multiple metastases to the peritoneum, abdominal and pleural viscerae may occur but are less common. Metastases to the bone are extremely rare.

In the gross the lesion is at times difficult to diagnose. Clinically, it is frequently confused with chronic pancreatitis. Microscopic examination of a specimen removed at operation is often disappointing, partly because of the difficulty in being sure that the specimen was taken from the tumor itself, partly because microscopic interpretations of a small section of pancreatic tissue may be difficult. Recently we had a case clinically diagnosed as carcinoma of the pancreas, which diagnosis the pathologist was able to make only after a careful examination of a number of sections.

Symptoms

The symptomatology of cancer of the pancreas depends to a large extent upon the location of the tumor. Early occlusion of the ampulla of Vater and resulting jaundice is commonly associated with involvement of the head, and appears rarely or late with involvement of the body or tail.

Characteristically, the patient with cancer of the head of the pancreas gives an indefinite history; the onset is insidious with loss of appetite, strength, and weight. Frequently these symptoms are disregarded until the onset of pruritis or actual jaundice. The patient most frequently seeks advice because of the itching or the jaundice, rather than because of loss of strength and appetite. The jaundice is usually slowly progressive, is not of sudden onset, and almost always occurs independent of an attack of pain. Progressive jaundice with an insidious onset, preceded by a story of anorexia of several months and

---
[1] Hoffman, F. L. — N. E. J. M., 1934, 21, 165.
[2] Ewing — W. B. Saunders Co., Phila., 1928, 745.
[3] Leven, N. L. — Am. Jour. Can. 1933, xviii, 852.

loss of strength — particularly when its occurrence is not immediately following an attack of upper abdominal pain — strongly suggests carcinoma of the head of the pancreas. Pain is usually present although seldom severe in the early stages, may be steady or intermittent, more like a soreness or distress, and nearly always in the epigastrium although it may be in the right hypochondrium. In almost every instance it is easily distinguished from the characteristic attacks which one associates with a stone in the common duct. Late in the course of the disease there may be definite duodenal obstruction with its characteristic vomiting.

Carcinoma of the tail of the pancreas has an entirely different symptom complex. The patient with cancer of the body and tail of the pancreas presents himself most frequently because of pain. This pain, usually in the left epigastrium, going around the left costal margin to the back, is severe, generally constant but may be intermittent, is accompanied by loss of weight, strength and appetite. There is no doubt in the mind of the examiner of the patient's extreme discomfort. Jaundice is rare. Duodenal obstruction does not occur and vomiting, therefore, is not a prominent symptom. Constipation is more common than diarrhea, particularly in those cases where the lesion involves the ampulla and there is jaundice.

Physical Findings

If there is jaundice, the presence or absence of a palpable gall bladder is of greatest importance. A dilated gall bladder is found in most cases of carcinoma of the head of the pancreas, when associated with jaundice. It may not be possible to palpate the organ but (except in cases where there is a pre-existing mechanical lesion which will prevent its dilatation) a large distended, dilated gall bladder will be found at operation or autopsy. Therefore, repeated attempts to palpate this organ should be made in a jaundiced patient. A palpable mass in the upper abdomen, not descending with respiration, usually with overlying tympany is felt in only a small percentage of cases. Except for the possible palpation of a mass, the physical findings in the involvement of the tail of the pancreas are usually negative.

Laboratory

The color of the stools is important, particularly in the presence of jaundice. Characteristically, the patient with definite jaundice has clay-colored stools. Occasionally, however, varying amounts of bile may pass through the ampulla, resulting in the presence of some color in the stool.

X-ray may be of value in the diagnosis of cancer of the head of the pancreas. A wide duodenal loop, due to the enlargement of the head of the pancreas around which the duodenum extends, is found in some cases but absent in many. It is of value both in carcinoma of the head and body of the pancreas in excluding organic pathology elsewhere. Cholecystograms are of no help, nearly always resulting in failure of the gall bladder to fill.

Differential Diagnosis

The most important differential diagnosis occurs in the cases with jaundice. Courvoisier observed that jaundice due to a stone in the common duct was usually associated with a contracted gall bladder, whereas that due to obstruction from carcinoma of the ampulla or head of the pancreas was accompanied by a distended gall bladder. *Progressive, painless jaundice, associated with a palpable gall bladder in almost every instance will prove to be associated with carcinoma of the head of the pancreas.* It may be very difficult to distinguish between an intrahepatic jaundice due to a cirrhosis and a jaundice due to carcinoma at the head of the pancreas when the gall bladder cannot be felt. A differential diagnosis cannot be accurately made. A palpable spleen, commonly associated with an intrahepatic jaundice is practically never seen with carcinoma of the head of the pancreas. An intrahepatic jaundice is frequently associated with varying amounts of color in the stools. A palpable liver may be present in either. Ascites is more common in cirrhosis but may also be present with malignant disease.

Catarrhal jaundice is more frequently seen in younger people. Its onset is more acute and its course distinctly shorter. Rarely will it be confused with the more serious lesions.

Jaundice due to a stone in the common duct is the most important lesion to differentiate from that due to malignancy. The so-called painless common duct stone very rarely occurs. In almost every instance a carefully taken past history will reveal a characteristic attack of upper abdominal discomfort or gas, possibly severe pain, as many as ten, fifteen or thirty years before. The writer has seen one case with absolutely painless jaundice where it was impossible to obtain a history of previous attacks of abdominal discomfort which could in any way be associated with, or suggestive of gallstones. The gall bladder will not be palpable. Recurrent chills are more commonly associated with stones than with obstruction due to malignancy.

In carcinoma of the body or tail of the pancreas, a diagnosis can rarely be made. It may be suspected in a reasonable percentage of cases and is usually proven either at operation or autopsy. Severe, unrelenting pain in the left upper abdomen, around the left costal margin and in the left back, associated with loss of weight, sleep, and appetite and unexplained after careful hospital investigation more frequently proves to be due to carcinoma of the pancreas than to any other disease and justifies such a diagnosis.

Treatment

The treatment of cancer of the pancreas is in most instances palliative only. There have been a few reported cases of successful removal of carcinoma of the body or tail of the pancreas. The intense distress from pruritis associated with jaundice and the importance of not overlooking a stone in the common duct justify operation in cases with jaundice where the operative risk is not prohibitive. Likewise, the uncertainty and discomfort associated with a carcinoma of the body and tail justify the more accurate diagnosis offered by exploration.

If the sedimentation rate of the red cells is 25 mm. in 30 min. or faster (Linton),* the patient is in danger of hemorrhage following operation. Calcium, glucose solution and transfusions afford the best protection against this complication.

At operation, it is our custom to do an anastomosis between a distended gall bladder and either the duodenum or the pyloric end of the stomach, depending upon which is most available. There should be no tension whatsoever of the suture line and the anastomosis should be made in the location that is technically most satisfactory.

Occasionally following this operation the patient may do well for a sufficiently long period to permit an obstruction of the duodenum to occur. We have seen a few cases where a gastro-enterostomy became necessary because of obstruction. This, however, is not common.

High voltage X-ray treatment may at times be helpful for relief of pain from carcinoma of the pancreas. Patients suffering severe pain

---

* Linton, R. R. — Annals of Surgery, 1930, 91, 649.

with this disease should have the benefit of at least one carefully given series of treatments. If no relief is obtained from a single series of treatments, their continuation will be unnecessary and unavailing.

Results

The results following cholecystgastrostomy or cholecystduodenostomy for carcinoma of the head of the pancreas with jaundice are satisfactory if the patients are properly selected and operation carefully carried out. The tremendous relief they experience justifies the risks of operation. The expectancy of life is not great. Most patients with cancer of the pancreas die within a year of the time they seek medical attention. On the other hand, not a few patients live one, two or three years. We have seen several patients operated upon with a diagnosis of carcinoma of the pancreas, and a cholecystenterostomy done, who were demonstrated a year after operation as a mistaken diagnosis, only to have the patients go downhill and die of carcinoma within the second or third year.

Summary

Carcinoma of the pancreas represents from two to three per cent of all cases of malignant disease. Approximately 50 per cent of the cases involve the head only.

Progressive, painless jaundice with a palpable gall bladder usually means a carcinoma of the head of the pancreas.

Persistent severe pain in the left upper quadrant, left costal margin and back, accompanied by loss of strength and weight, if not explained after careful hospital investigation justifies a tentative diagnosis of carcinoma of the body or tail of the pancreas.

In carefully selected cases, cholecystogastrostomy or cholecystduodenostomy are excellent palliative operations. Most cases live less than one year.

PROGRESS IN THE MASSACHUSETTS CANCER PROGRAM

HENRY D. CHADWICK, M. D., *Commissioner,*
Massachusetts Department of Public Health
and
HERBERT L. LOMBARD, M. D., *Director*
Division of Adult Hygiene,
Massachusetts Department of Public Health

Sufficient time has elapsed since the inauguration of the Massachusetts Cancer Program to warrant a critical analysis. Legislative authority for the program was enacted eight years ago last May, and the first State-Aided Cancer Clinic was opened in December of the same year. The early part of the period was one of organization, but since 1928 it has been largely one of consolidation, with few changes of importance in clinic management, activities, or policies.

The establishment of the Massachusetts Cancer Program had a threefold purpose: the care and treatment of individuals with cancer who could not otherwise receive adequate care; the stimulation of diagnosis and treatment at an early stage of the disease; and studies of the disease. The Pondville Hospital, with over one hundred beds now available and additional ones under construction, has attempted to meet the first of these requisites. While at times the waiting list has been long and some patients have found difficulty in early admittance, this part of the program has functioned. The medical and nursing service has been excellent, and the equipment adequate. The experience of the Hospital has demonstrated that a great deal can be done for cancer patients who have passed beyond the early, curable stage and have not yet arrived at the moribund one. By the judicious use of radiation and alleviatory operations, a large number of patients have found their sufferings greatly lessened, and many of them have been able to return to their homes to carry on some of their daily duties. This contribution has been more significant than the many cures effected at the Hospital or the care of the dying, as this service is one not carried on in the average hospital, and it might well be called a contribution of Massachusetts to the knowledge of improved cancer therapy.

The studies have continued throughout the period. They have comprised statistical research into the epidemiology of cancer, and surveys of its care and treatment. The Department has been aided by a money grant from the Rockefeller Foundation in one of the epidemiological investigations, and at all times has received the hearty co-operation of physicians, hospitals, and citizens in this work. The studies have contributed an important part to the composite program, and through them a better knowledge of the disease has been obtained.

The third phase of the program — the stimulation of early diagnosis and treatment of the disease — motivated the cancer clinic program. All educational activities directed toward either the profession or the public centered around these clinics, and the clinics themselves offered diagnostic service to the public and consultative service to the physician. The clinics were administered by committees appointed by the local medical societies and met in twenty-three hospitals in fourteen cities and towns.

The policy of the Department has been to encourage group diagnosis at these clinics. It has been felt that the combined opinion of the surgeon, radiologist, and pathologist, together with such specialists as were needed in an individual case, would be of far greater weight than the opinion of one man alone, and both the patients and the physicians would be benefited by this method. Moreover, such consultations over individual cases would be stimulating and contribute to the more general knowledge of cancer. The Massachusetts program endeavored, by concentrating the cancer cases among groups of physicians, to form centers where adequate clinical diagnosis and therapy would be available. It has been found that the general practitioner is more ready to send a patient to a group for consultation than to a single individual. One of the principal features of the program has been the development of a consultative service where expert advice could be obtained for the busy practitioner who, on the average, would see but very few cancer cases in any one year. In some clinics this has worked out well, and in others it has failed. Last year at the Pondville clinic nearly 75 per cent of all patients were referred by their physicians; and at the clinic doing the least consultative work, about 15 per cent. The failure of several of the clinics to offer group diagnosis was doubtless responsible for less confidence among the profession in the findings of these clinics.

In the early part of the program, the records requested were meager and largely consisted of the administrative phases of clinic management. At the inception of the clinic program of the American College of Surgeons, clinics were advised to increase their record system to cover a more detailed history of the individual case. A few of them have done this, but the majority have continued to use only the original forms. This has been a weak feature of the clinic program.

The clinics were established for diagnosis only, and the policy of the Department has always been that cases be referred back to the family physician with the advice of the clinic.

The educational activities for the control of cancer have been directed in two channels — one for the lay individuals, and the other to furnish facilities for physicians to obtain a better knowledge of the disease.

Education for the physician has consisted of special clinics in the various centers to which all physicians in the community were invited, special clinics in Boston, distribution of literature to physicians, and in some clinics a regular consultant from Boston. The Massachusetts Medical Society has, in addition, given a course in cancer.

Lay publicity has revolved around work done by the educational committees in the clinic centers. These committees have been composed of public-spirited individuals in the clinic centers. They have contacted newspapers for publicity and, in some cases, have made arrangements for speeches before certain organizations. In the main, their efforts have been directed upon newspaper publicity.

In the early part of the program there was considerable criticism of lay individuals preparing material for newspaper publicity and, to obviate this, material was furnished by the central office and sent to the clinics. This tended to dull the enthusiasm of the lay individuals as in many centers they found their work becoming nothing more than passing on to newspapers material furnished by the central office, and many of them wondered why the central office could not send the material directly to the newspapers. This was a justifiable criticism as the State Department of Public Health's contact with newspapers has always been good. Except in the presence of a special campaign of education in a given city, the work of the educational committees has become almost negligible and the Department has failed to utilize to the full, the enthusiasm of these interested individuals.

Social service has been an essential part of every clinic. While an occasional physician has resented the follow-up work of social service, generally speaking there has been a co-operative spirit.

Certain improvements should be made in the management of the cancer clinics. The attendance at the clinics showed that nearly one third of them had less than ten patients a year, and another third between ten and one hundred. Only eight of the twenty-three clinics had over one hundred patients.

The Massachusetts Medical Society furnished three special clinics for instruction of members of the clinic staffs. While interest was shown in these clinics, it was not nearly as great as was anticipated. Seven of the twenty-three clinics had a representation of less than 25 per cent of their staff, and the only clinics which made a good showing were those in Worcester where one of the sessions was held. It would seem that at least 75 per cent attendance should have been realized by every clinic at these meetings.

While group diagnosis has been stressed since the inception of the cancer clinics, at the present time eleven of the clinics do not have this and only five of them have a radiologist in attendance at the clinics, although the Cancer Advisory Committee has urged that the radiologist should always be in attendance to consult with the surgeons.

Eight clinics have attempted to do educational work among physicians and medical students, but the remaining clinics have done nothing in this matter. At least once a year it would be desirable for some effort to be made by every clinic to improve the quality of the service in its locality.

An attempt to evaluate the work being done by these clinics can be accomplished only through a study of the records. Each year since the inauguration of the program, as well as previous to this, cancer has been causing more deaths in the Massachusetts population. In 1927, the first year of the program, 5454 individuals were reported to have died of this disease and last year, 1933, the number had increased to 6382. Possibly some part of this increase has been due to improved diagnosis.

The situation, however, is not as discouraging as might be implied from these figures. The Massachusetts population is steadily growing older; the birth rate is dropping; immigration is being restricted; and public health measures are lowering the incidence of deaths from the communicable diseases among the young. A larger percentage of the population is found in the older age groups. If this change in the population is taken into account and the death rates for cancer for both sexes are adjusted accordingly, the increase between 1927 and 1933 is 4.1 per cent. The rate for males increased 10.2 per cent, but among the females there was no change. The chance for cure among females is greater than among males, due to the accessibility of cancer of the cervix and cancer of the breast. It would appear, therefore, that measures now being instituted against cancer have succeeded in preventing an increase among females beyond that due to aging of the population.

In the first year of the cancer clinics 1350 individuals sought advice; in 1933 this number had nearly tripled to 3921. The percentage distribution of cancer by type has changed only slightly over the period studied. Cancer of the skin comprised about one third of clinic admissions, cancer of the mouth about one fifth, breast about one sixth, and uterus about one tenth.

The nationality picture has changed. There is a tendency for the native born to comprise a larger percentage of the clinic attendance as the years go on. In 1928, 55.7 per cent were native born; in 1933, 63.5. Of the foreign-born groups, the Italians alone have shown a steady increase in attendance. In 1928 they comprised 1.7 per cent of the attendance; in 1933, 2.6. In the hospital study on chronic disease it was found that the foreign born used the hospitals to about the same extent as the native born, and made greater use of the clinics. In the period under discussion, the foreign-born population has decreased approximately 1.5 per cent, but the attendance of the foreign born at the clinics has decreased over 8 per cent. This is particularly disheartening inasmuch as approximately 45 per cent of cancer deaths are among this group.

A comparison of the first two and the last two years of the clinic attendance has been made to determine changes in important items. The total attendance increased 89.2 per cent. The number of patients referred by physicians increased 233.0 per cent; and those not referred by physicians, 39.5 per cent. The percentage with cancer increased from 21.6 to 24.0, and the percentage with precancerous conditions decreased from 11.3 to 10.7. However, the percentage with precancerous conditions referred by physicians increased from 21.0 in the first period to 50.1 in the second.

An important measure of the effectiveness of lay education is the duration between first symptoms and consultation with first physician. This figure measures the apathy on the part of the individual patient. In the first period, this duration in cancer patients was 6.0 months; in the second period, 6.1 months. This indicates that in spite of the large amount of publicity that has emanated from the Department and the educational committees, the individual with cancer waits as long before seeing a physician today as he did at the beginning of the program. This would be most discouraging were it not for the fact that the interval between seeing the first physician and presentation of himself at a cancer clinic has decreased. In the first two years this interval was 6.7 months; in the last two years it decreased to 3.6 months. As this interval largely measures the ability of the physician to recognize the seriousness of the situation and to refer the patient to the consultative clinic, it shows that the activities of the Department in providing means for furthering medical diagnosis have been appreciated by the profession.

In the first two years, physicians sent 51.4 per cent of all cancer patients to the clinics; and in the last two years, 66.1. The percentage of cancer patients coming to the clinics on their own account that consulted a physician but were not advised by him to go to one of the clinics decreased from 33.9 to 18.1; while the percentage that consulted no physician remained practically stationary, 14.7 to 15.5. Again this indicates a great improvement on the part of the physician.

The cancer patients who came directly to the clinics without consulting any physician came earlier than formerly. In the first period they waited 12.3 months; in the last period, 8.1 months. This figure shows that publication education has accomplished something, but the 8.1 months' delay in the last two years is considerably greater than the 5.7 months' delay of the patients who consulted physicians before coming to the clinics.

By due consideration of these various factors, it would appear that the improvement found in the cancer clinics is about 80 per cent due to the physicians of Massachusetts and 20 per cent to an improved public consciousness of the disease. Although not satisfactory, this is far better than the reverse for even if the public does not present itself at the cancer clinics until after the disease has been progressing for several months, it can be assured of much better treatment by the profession than it would have received eight years ago.

These findings indicate that a more concerted action is necessary to improve the public consciousness of cancer. Either our methods of publicity are wrong or there exists an apathy on the part of the public which cannot be overcome. To assume this latter alternative is to admit defeat in the program for cancer control; to change our method of approach seems both feasible and desirable. If an eight years' experience with one type of publicity has failed to arouse the public to the realization of its own responsibilities, another approach should be attempted; and until all possible approaches have been exhausted, it would seem unwise to declare that this cannot be done.

The public needs more first-hand information. Individuals need to be told more than "Go to your physician if you have lump in your breast." They should know why. Many of them are skeptical of such statements as "Cancer is not contagious," "Cancer can be cured," and "For all practical purposes, cancer is not hereditary." Everyone has seen cancer among his relatives or friends. Many an individual has seen several cases in a household, and the mere statement against heredity or contagion leaves him in an extremely doubtful frame of mind. Talking down to the American public will not result in confidence. The public is far more health conscious and far more interested in the "Why is it? How is it? What is it?" than many of the so-called health educators have assumed. Any physician talking with his patient, in a few minutes' time can explain many doubtful points about the disease. The points would be far better understood than the statements on the printed page.

With this in view, the Department is inaugurating a new policy for the Massachusetts Cancer Program. This is to consist of three major phases: reorganization of clinics; education through the medical profession; and the inauguration of Cooperative Cancer Control Committees in every town and city in the State.

Reorganization of Clinics

On the premise that cancer is a specialty, not of an individual physician but of a group of physicians, the clinic is to be primarily a consultation clinic, although no patient will be refused admittance to the clinic. There will be no publicity propaganda of any type urging an individual patient to come to the clinic. On the other hand, physicians will be constantly urged to send every person with cancer or suspected cancer to the clinic for advice. Here the combined opinion of the general surgeon, the radiologist, and the pathologist, together with the opinion of a specialist on the part of the body involved, when needed, will give the practicing physician information at no cost to himself or to the patient. The clinic will furnish diagnosis and outline the best method of treatment, and return the patient to his personal physician.

Physicians are invited and urged to attend the clinic conferences, and both listen and participate in the discussion of cases. Complete medical records are to be kept of all cancer patients. Copies of hospital records showing what happened to the patient after he left the clinic are to be incorporated. Thus, when the follow-up is completed, a medical as well as a social history of the patient from clinic admission to death will be available. The initial record of a non-cancer case is to be made, but no further records will be necessary. Medical records of precancerous conditions and benign tumors should be continued while the patient is under observation, and the diagnosis cleared up.

Each clinic must have, as a minimum, fifty patients a year to qualify as a Massachusetts State-Aided Cancer Clinic.

Each clinic is urged to hold a special clinic at least once a year and invite all physicians in the community.

As publicity methods for the clinics have ceased, the educational committees, formerly sub-committees of the cancer clinic committees, will cease to function as such, but will function as local Cooperative Cancer Control Committees.

Education Through the Medical Profession

The eight years' experience of the Massachusetts State-Aided Cancer Clinics has demonstrated that the most effective method of educating the public is through the local physician. The family physician, in a few minutes' time, can furnish his patient with a better idea of cancer than otherwise can be obtained. With this in view, the Department will concentrate its endeavors in furnishing the physician with the latest information on the disease.

The Cooperative Cancer Control Program

In every city and town in the State an effort will be made to form a local Cooperative Cancer Control Committee whose chief function will be to arrange for local physicians to address groups on the subject of cancer. These groups preferably should be small and organized so that the round table discussions may be general and intimate. The Committee should vary in size according to the type of locality, and should be composed of the local health officer where he is available, and a representative of every type or group—racial, fraternal, religious, and social. The Committee itself will be organized by the Department, but any interested individual may become a member. Each committee will be advised by the district health officer in its own community.

This is the present status of the Massachusetts Cancer Program. The policies outlined above are more than a change of emphasis—they indicate the natural evolutionary processes of progress in the work of cancer control through cooperation of the physicians and the public and improved diagnostic methods in the clinics.

CANCER OF THE PROSTATE
By George Gilbert Smith, M. D.
Boston, Massachusetts

Incidence

In any large series of obstructing prostates, from 15 to 20 per cent will prove to be malignant. Hugh Young estimates that of every hundred men who live to be sixty years of age, four will have cancer of the prostate. Although this disease is occasionally found in men in the early forties, its greatest incidence is between the ages of sixty and seventy.

Pathology

Cancer of the prostate is most frequently an adenocarcinoma; in about 85 per cent of cases, it begins, according to Young and Geraghty, in the posterior lobe—that is, in that portion of the prostate which lies beneath the floor of the prostatic urethra and is most accessible to rectal palpation. The tumor is usually of slow growth and may be confined within the prostatic capsule for a long time. Eventually it extends into the vesicles and may appear as nodules on the trigone or base of the bladder. Metastases occur in the regional lymph nodes—iliac and aortic—and are especially frequent in the spine and pelvis. The ribs and femora are next frequently involved. Visceral metastases usually occur only in advanced cases.

Symptoms

Carcinoma of the prostate develops silently. The presence of malignant disease in the gland does not of itself cause symptoms. The symptoms which do occur are of three types: (1) Obstruction to urination. This may develop late in the course of the disease, or not at all. According to Young, "obstructive urinary symptoms inaugurate the great majority of cases." Frequently the obstruction is caused by masses of hypertrophied prostate gland which develop independently of the malignant process. If the obstruction is due to the malignant process alone, cystoscopy shows no projection of the gland into the bladder, as is seen in hypertrophy; the bladder neck is rigid and tight, and the entire prostatic uretha is contracted and rigid. (2) The pain due to metastases in bones or to infiltration of nerve roots. These pains most frequently occur as dull, boring pains in the lumbosacral spine, radiating down the posterior aspect of the thigh. Whenever such pains are present in conjunction with a stony hard prostate gland, the diagnosis of cancer can be made almost with certainty, and one may be sure that the process has already extended beyond the capsule of the prostate. (3) Other evidences of malignancy, such as extreme cachexia, and nausea and vomiting. In a small percentage of cases, these general disturbances are the only symptoms; there may be no symptoms which point to the prostate as the original seat of disease. Edema of one leg caused by the pressure of metastatic deposits upon the iliac vein of the corresponding side may be one of the first signs noted. Hematuria is a late development in cancer of the prostate, not occurring until a nodule of growth has ulcerated into the prostatic urethra or into the bladder itself.

Diagnosis

The diagnostic procedure of the greatest value in this disease is rectal palpation. Cancer of the prostate, in practically every instance, is characterized by induration of cartilaginous firmness. Some observers speak of soft, medullary cancers, but I have never seen one. At times the malignant prostate is marked by edema of the overlying tissues, but even under such conditions there is a fixity and a sense of deep induration which is easily recognized. The induration may be localized in either lobe or may involve the entire gland. In later stages, it extends beyond the prostatic capsule and seems to make the prostate continuous with the lateral walls of the pelvis. The induration may extend into one or both vesicles, and in advanced cases may extend over the bladder base higher than the finger can reach. A hypertrophied prostate, on the contrary, is rather soft, elastic, well defined laterally and inferiorly, and can be definitely moved within the pelvis. The condition most difficult to differentiate from prostatic cancer is fibrosis due to chronic inflammation. In the latter condition, there is likely to be either a history of urethral infection or the finding of pus in the secretion expressed by massage. (One should avoid massaging a suspected cancer, unless the indications suggest strongly that the process is inflammatory). In doubtful cases, repeated examinations are likely to show variations in the degree of induration if it is due to inflammation, and a constant, definite induration if the gland is malignant.

X-rays of the lumbar spine and pelvis are valuable, as the presence of osteoplastic or osteoclastic areas in the bone support the diagnosis of cancer.

The early recognition of cancer of the prostate, during the stage in which cure is possible, can only be achieved if every man of forty-five or over is subjected to routine rectal examination at least once a year. It seems probable that in most cases of prostatic malignancy, the disease has clearly been in existence for several years before it has given symptoms. If we do not examine these patients until they develop symptoms, we shall lose many opportunities to detect this disease while it is still amenable to radical surgery.

Treatment

In early cases in which the growth is still confined within the prostatic capsule, total perineal prostatectomy and vesiculectomy as described by Hugh Young offers an excellent chance for cure. Cases suitable for this form of treatment form but a small percentage of those in which the diagnosis is made, but with more frequent rectal examinations, more cases should be identified while still in this stage. If the diagnosis is doubtful, the prostate may be exposed by perineal incision and a section removed for immediate examination. In a series of thirty-eight total prostatectomies reported by Young and one of forty-two cases reported by Smith, twenty-four cases in the first series and seventeen in the second were living and apparently well at the time the reports were made. Young reports eleven five-year cures.

In cases which have progressed beyond the stage of complete removal, the chief object of treatment is to remove the obstruction to urination, and to alleviate the pain caused by metastases. For the former, electro-resection is a most helpful procedure; in cases too advanced even for this, permanent supra-pubic cystostomy is indicated. For the relief of pain, deep X-ray therapy has proved to be most valuable. The use of radium in cancer of the prostate is still of doubtful value. Some surgeons are enthusiastic advocates of its use; others find it of little if any value. In my own experience, I have seen excellent results follow the use of gold seeds or platinum needles in perhaps one-fifth of the cases in which radium was employed. In the group of cases in which the malignant process has progressed just beyond the point at which total prostatectomy can be done, but in which the disease is still localized to the prostate and vesicles, the employment of radium would seem to be a rational procedure.

CANCER OF THE RECTUM AND COLON
By Daniel Fiske Jones, M. D.
Boston, Massachusetts

Little can be accomplished in the treatment of cancer without the cooperation of the laity, the physician, and the surgeon. This is as true of cancer of the colon and rectum as of cancer of any other organ. It is true that the surgeon must initiate the idea that cancer of the colon and rectum is operable, but he can do little else until the patient is presented to him by the physician. The patient often does not appreciate the importance of slight intestinal symptoms and of course believes that blood from the rectum is due to hemorrhoids. These two facts delay consultation with the physician for weeks or even months. The physician frequently loses time because he is not much interested in the disease and is therefore not on the lookout for it. He agrees with the patient too often that intestinal symptoms are due to indigestion or simple constipation and that bleeding from the rectum is due to hemorrhoids. He is not particularly interested in the condition because he thinks the end results are all bad and he cannot bring himself to go into the symptoms too carefully for fear he will have to advise an operation which may mean a colostomy. Many physicians still feel that the patient "might better be dead" than have a colostomy. I am quite convinced in my own mind that neither the family, the physician, nor the surgeon, unless he is experienced in this type of work, has a right to decide as to whether or not the patient shall have a colostomy. That should be decided by the patient and the surgeon experienced in these operations. If he has done many he can at least tell the patient that out of several hundred cases who have had a colostomy and removal of the growth, all have lived happily and contentedly.

After a group of physicians and surgeons had been told that many cases of carcinoma of the colon and rectum were never recognized one of the physicians found three cases within three months. He sent them all to a surgeon, who did nothing more than a colostomy. How is it possible to keep up the interest of the physician under such circumstances? The physician knows that the colostomy need be done only as a last resort and therefore has no stimulus to make an early diagnosis.

It is, I believe, useless and even harmful to the patient to speculate as to the causes of cancer of the colon and rectum. It may be said that certain families seem to be rather more susceptible to cancer than other families. It should be definitely impressed upon the minds of physicians and surgeons, however, that adenomatous polyps frequently become malignant. Removal of adenomatous polyps is therefore of the greatest importance, we believe, in the prevention of cancer of the colon and rectum.

While the prevention of carcinoma is of much greater value than any treatment known today, we know so little about the prevention of carcinoma of the colon and rectum that early diagnosis and treatment are of much greater importance. We are frequently told that the diagnosis of these cases is difficult and that patients do not present themselves until late. It is true that the diagnosis of carcinoma of the colon may be difficult, but the diagnosis of carcinoma of the rectum should be made in 100 per cent of the cases who present themselves. It is my belief that the great cause for delay in sending patients to the surgeon is the lack of interest on the part of the laity and physicians. Perhaps this lack of interest may be indicated by stating that there are 5,000 deaths from cancer in Massachusetts each year, and that 12 per cent or 600 of these are due to cancer of the colon and rectum. A very liberal estimate of the number of radical operations in the state yearly would be 175. This leaves 425 cases which have no radical operation. Some of them have a colostomy, but a fairly large percentage are so far advanced when a diagnosis is made that they are never seen by an experienced surgeon.

Up to twenty years ago one could not blame the physician for his lack of interest, particularly in regard to cancer of the rectum, because the mortality was high and the results were not good. Conditions have slowly improved, however, and in recent years statistics have been presented by numerous surgeons which show that the results in the cases operated upon for carcinoma of the colon or rectum are even better than those in the cases operated upon for malignant disease in other organs. The truth about the present situation is that cases still present themselves so late that many surgeons do not do a radical operation in more than 25 or 30 per cent of the cases seen. If a surgeon will operate upon those he thinks he can make more comfortable for from one to five or more years, he can operate upon about 60 per cent of the cases seen. The mortality has been much reduced and in the hands of experienced men it should be between 10 and 12 per cent for both carcinoma of the colon and carcinoma of the rectum, as contrasted with 15 to 20 per cent for carcinoma of the colon and 25 to 30 per cent for carcinoma of the rectum, the percentage formerly obtained. Of the patients who survive the operation, about 55 per cent live five or more years if 60 per cent of the total number seen are operated upon.

The textbooks are, I believe, partly responsible for the confusion in regard to diagnosis, and the medical schools are responsible in that they permit their students to leave the school and often the hospital with the idea that the most important cause of bleeding from the rectum is hemorrhoids. Physicians and patients are also responsible because they believe that every rectal or colon symptom is due to hemorrhoids and because they believe that the X-ray is always correct.

It is my belief that physicians should not be held responsible for the accurate diagnosis of carcinoma of the colon or rectum, but should be held responsible for sending patients to the surgeon when there are suggestive symptoms. All that it is necessary for the layman or physician to know is that any change in bowel habit or sensation and bleeding from the rectum, or bleeding alone from the rectum suggest carcinoma of the colon or rectum. The diagnosis should be made by an experienced surgeon. It is useless to clutter one's mind with the many textbook symptoms because many of them are valueless.

Carcinoma of the colon and rectum begins on the surface and therefore ulcerates and bleeds early. It is true that there is occasionally no bleeding, as in the narrow scirrhus type. In carcinomata of the right colon the blood is mixed with the feces, while in the lower portion of the left colon it may be on the outside until there is sufficient obstruction to produce liquid feces. Anemia may be the only symptom of a carcinoma of the right colon. This should be remembered in any secondary anemia for which no cause can be found. At least four stools should be examined for blood in any suspected case.

Constipation still holds the lead in the minds of many as an important symptom. In these days of oil and oil compounds, this symptom is rarely noted by the patient. He slips quietly from his normal constipated habit into frequent movements without noticing that the constipation has increased. Oils have delayed diagnosis from two to six months. The old compound cathartic pill used to cause so much pain in these cases that the diagnosis was made much earlier.

Diarrhea or, much better, frequent movements, is a much more frequent symptom than constipation, as noted by the patient, but it is frequently a late symptom. As the patient does not recognize the frequent small movements or passage of gas and blood and mucus as diarrhea, the physician should never ask the patient if he has diarrhea, but should ask the number of times he goes to stool.

Alternating constipation and diarrhea is another favorite textbook symptom, but it is of little value as it is rarely recognized by the patient. This time-honored symptom should be given up along with ribbon stools, loss of weight, and the age of the patient. Ribbon stool is due to the consistency of the stool and the shape of the sphincteric opening. Loss of weight occurs only after there is sufficient obstruction to cause loss of appetite. Carcinoma of the colon and rectum can occur at any age; about 5 per cent occur in patients between the ages of ten and thirty.

Pain is always considered by the laity to be an important symptom of cancer anywhere, but patients rarely admit any pain until very late in the course of the disease. In cancer of the rectum there is locally a feeling that the rectum has not been emptied and discomfort in sitting in many cases even when the growth is quite high. There is an "ache" across the sacral region frequently. Abdominal pain is much more frequent with carcinoma of the colon than with carcinoma of the rectum. This pain is due to either partial or complete obstruction and comes in attacks. Frequently these patients become immunized to the pain in spite of the fact that borborygmi may be heard quite easily. So frequently do patients deny having intestinal pain that one must inquire as to whether the patient is bothered much with gas. The intestinal pain is across the lower abdomen or in the right lower quadrant in all cases of cancer of the colon and rectum, except in those of cancer of the cecum and ascending colon when there is a backing up into the small intestine causing small intestine pain, that is, epigastric pain. When growths are very far advanced and there is involvement of the peritoneum by the growth or infection, the pain may be localized in the region of the growth.

In carcinoma of the rectum, proper rectal and proctoscopic examinations should make a correct diagnosis in 100 per cent of the cases. A proper digital examination will also not infrequently make the diagnosis in carcinoma of the sigmoid when it has fallen into the pelvis. Proctoscopic examination should always be made in suspected carcinoma of the colon, for while the growth will be seen only rarely, much can be learned. Blood seen coming from above is of great value; ulcerations, chronic ulcerative colitis, and adenomatous polyps can all be diagnosticated with accuracy. The proctoscope should be used to feel with as well as to see with.

The X-ray is of value in the diagnosis of carcinoma of the colon, but it should never be used until carcinoma of the rectum has been definitely excluded by digital and proctoscopic examinations. No X-ray of the colon should be depended upon unless made by a roentgenologist experienced in this work, and unless all other information, the history and physical findings are considered in conjunction with it. It is my belief that the average roentgenologist does not diagnosticate more than 40 per cent of the carcinomata of the rectum and between 60 and 70 per cent of the carcinomata of the colon.

Careful palpation of the abdomen should be done, as a mass can frequently be felt, especially in the cecum.

A diagnosis of diverticulitis made by the X-ray when it is associated with bleeding should rarely be accepted. As bleeding occurs in only 5 or at most 10 per cent of the cases of diverticulitis, the burden of proof rests upon the shoulders of the man who makes such a diagnosis.

Radium is suitable for the treatment of cancer of the rectum only in those cases in which the growth is inoperable locally, or because of metastases, or because the condition of the patient is not sufficiently good to stand the operation. It is useless in the treatment of carcinoma of the colon.

As a palliative measure, X-ray treatment of the growth locally is often of some value.

CARCINOMA OF THE SKIN
By GRANTLEY W. TAYLOR, M. D.
Boston, Massachusetts

Carcinoma of the skin is the most common carcinoma encounterd in a cancer clinic, and the carcinoma most easy to detect in its early stages. Furthermore, it is one of the most slowly growing carcinomas and presents metastases relatively infrequently, and as a rule only late in the course of the disease. In addition, in many instances skin carcinoma is preceded by a definite recognizable precancerous stage, which is also of long duration, and which is readily curable by appropriate treatment. Under these circumstances a death from carcinoma of the skin is usually the result of egregious neglect, and a reflection on the medical community where it occurs.

Etiology and Precancerous States

Probably the majority of skin carcinomas originate in keratoses on the exposed parts of the body. It is likely that exposure to actinic rays plays a prominent role in the causation of these keratoses. Keratoses themselves respond very well to mild doses of radiation, and the development of carcinoma is practically nil in keratoses which have been successfully treated. Skin carcinomas also originate in old scars, areas of radiation dermatitis, chronic ulcers, osteomyelitis sinuses, and arsenical keratoses; and in workers exposed to aniline, tar, and soot. They also may arise in areas of neglected or improperly treated chronic infections of the skin, notably lupus vulgaris and chronic leutic lesions. Proper treatment of these precancerous states will usually prevent the development of carcinoma. The occurrence of ulceration in a previously healed scar should excite suspicion, and every effort should be made to bring about healing of chronic ulcers and sinuses and areas of skin infection.

Diagnosis

The typical established carcinoma of the skin, with an ulcerated central area and a surrounding slightly elevated hard margin is readily identified. Earlier stages may present no ulceration but a scaling of crusting center with an underlying plaque-like induration. The earliest recognizable stage of basal cell carcinoma consists in a yellowish waxy elevated area. However, many cancers of the skin present no such typical picture. A fairly safe rule to adopt is that any open or crusting skin lesion which persists more than a few weeks under careful conservative treatment should be suspected of being carcinoma unless it can be proved to be something else. This rule to be sure would include syphilitic and tuberculous lesions of the skin, and a few other chronic dermatological conditions. All of these diseases which may be confused with carcinoma, call for accurate diagnosis to permit successful treatment. The practice of prescribing a simple ointment for a chronic ulceration, the cause and nature of which is obscure, should be abandoned.

Biopsy should be resorted to freely if the suspicion of carcinoma arises. A specimen can be removed from the edge of an ulcer, or several specimens from various parts of a large lesion. If care is exercised to avoid cutting into adjacent normal tissue there should be no danger to the patient in this procedure.

Another recourse for the practitioner who has relatively little experience in malignant disease is early consultation. With our present widespread diagnostic clinics, the responsibility of the practitioner is limited to suspecting the possibility of cancer and to referring the patient to a clinic or to a more experienced physician for consultation. The clinic is in a position to verify the diagnosis and to recommend appropriate treatment.

Treatment

The essence of the treatment of established cancer is complete destruction of the lesion. It should be borne in mind that carcinoma of the skin has often infiltrated the surrounding apparently normal tissues for a considerable distance. The exact method of destruction to be employed is influenced by the site of the growth and its extent, the nature and amount of previous treatment, and the experience and facilities of the operator. The disease can be destroyed by excision, electrocoagulation, or radiation. It should be remembered that destructive doses of radiation should be employed to effect a cure, and that smaller doses may result in apparent healing without affecting the deeper parts of the growth. In practice, radiation is employed for lesions about the face where surgical excision would cause considerable disfigurement. It is also sometimes used in extensive superficial lesions of the trunk, when surgical excision would be too formidable a procedure. Lesions overlying or involving the cartilages of the nose and ears are less satisfactory for radiation, because of the painful chondritis which may follow destructive doses.

The need for radical destruction is not confined to radiation. If a lesion is to be treated by excision, the operation must remove all the disease with a margin of normal tissues, even when such an operation involves sacrifice of important structures and results in considerable disfigurement. The operator should remember that unless cure is effected, these structures will be soon destroyed by the progress of the disease; and the disfigurement of prompt radical excision is less than that caused by advancing cancer.

Careful attention should always be directed to the regional lymph nodes, and these nodes should be examined at all follow-up observations. Lymph node dissections are not carried out in cases of cancer of the skin routinely. If the patients are willing to report for observation at frequent intervals, there is a reasonable chance of cure if dissection is deferred until enlarged nodes are apparent. Epidermoid carcinomas in certain regions, especially in relation to the mucocutaneous junctions, as the lip, penis, and vulva, are more apt to develop lymph node metastases. In these cases decision as to the need of dissection of regional lymph node areas is made on the basis of the extent of the local lesion, the degree of malignancy of the process as shown by microscopic examination, and the general condition of the patient.

Patients with foul ulcerated carcinomas of the extremities are very likely to present enlarged regional lymph nodes at the time of the original examination. These enlargements may be due to secondary inflammation rather than to carcinoma. The best policy in these cases is to deal with the primary lesion first. The lymph node areas can be dissected more safely at a later time, if enlargements persist.

But even the smallest skin carcinomas may metastasize; and search for involved nodes should be a routine part of follow-up observation. Facial lesions may involve nodes in the preauricular region, or on the lower cheek near the angle of the jaw, and sometimes this involvement first becomes obvious months or years after apparent cure of the primary focus of disease.

Melanoma

Pigmented moles and melanotic sarcoma originating in them, call for special recognition and treatment. It would be practically impossible to remove all such moles and unwise to attempt it. Pigmented lesions on the extremities, especially in relation to the nail beds, should be held under suspicion. Likewise moles situated in areas subject to irritation by the clothing or otherwise should be watched with care. Moles in these areas, and any others showing evidence of growth, irritation or ulceration, should be widely excised. Radiation, coagulation, and milder methods have no place in the treatment of melanoma. A pathological report of melanotic sarcoma is an indication for a radical dissection of the regional lymph node area; and, when it is feasible, for the removal of a strip of skin, fat, and deep fascia containing the lymphatic trunks between the primary focus of disease and the lymph node area.

It cannot be too strongly emphasized that moles should be left strictly alone unless they are subject to irritation or unless they show evidence of growth. When these conditions exist the treatment consists in wide radical excision.

MEDICAL SOCIAL SERVICE IN THE CANCER CLINIC
ELEANOR E. KELLY
Supervisor of Social Service
Massachusetts Department of Public Health

The function of the medical social worker is to aid the doctor in securing for his patient the utmost that medical facilities have to offer. Various terms are used by the professional worker in this field to describe these activities, but the general term "service" seems best understood by those outside her profession.

In some cases the service is carried out at the clinic or the patient's home through an interview with the patient, or member of his family. In other cases, further study of the social situation is indicated; these may necessitate interviews with other social organizations, hospitals and others.

The experience of the Massachusetts Cancer Program has, I believe, shown the value and need of such service.

The patient comes to the clinic, is met by the social worker who attempts to obtain some idea of the motivating causes that brought the patient to the clinic. The physician is seen and the diagnosis and methods of treatment are told the patient either by the clinic physician or the family physician of the patient.

The social worker again sees the patient and when necessary reinforces the physician's explanation. Sometimes when the patient has returned home he decides against treatment. A woman has been told she has breast cancer and needs radical operation. At home, however, a neighbor reminds her that Mrs. A died under operation or that Mrs. B was cured by a salve. The patient decides that perhaps she is better off without operation or that she may not have cancer anyway, and that besides, a radical operation will mean disfigurement. The social worker's task is to make the patient realize her condition and the possibilities inherent in prompt following of the doctor's orders. The patient may have been distraught upon hearing the diagnosis at the clinic and many questions which she did not ask the physician then can be presented to the social worker; the answers received usually result in acceptance of the physician's advice.

In many cases, it is necessary for the social worker to interpret to the patient's family his medical social need and help them work out with the patient his problem. An attitude of fear or hopelessness on their part, whether expressed or not, may discourage the patient to the point of his refusing treatment. I think now of one patient who lost her chance for cure because, although she was ready to accept treatment, the daughter could not bear to have her mother subjected to an operation.

Many patients can, of course, make all their own plans; others are unable, without assistance, to overcome difficulties which stand in the way of treatment. The mother who must leave her children alone may refuse hospitalization; the children must then be cared for until her return. Often just talking the matter over will enable a patient to work out his own problem. Sometimes, however, the social worker will herself need to initiate some plan. A man refused treatment because he had just secured work after many months of unemployment, and feared to lose time from work. With his consent, the social worker explained the situation to his employer, who recognizing its urgency, agreed to hold the man's job during the few weeks he would be under treatment.

Sometimes transportation to the clinic or hospital must be arranged or financial aid secured for a family when it is the breadwinner who is incapacitated.

Patients in an inoperable condition may need help in securing hospitalization, or in making some temporary plan if the chronic hospital has a waiting list. Adequate home arrangements for a patient who can not benefit by hospital care may also mean that that hospital bed may be given to a patient who does need treatment.

For the patient to whom the physician offered no hope of cure, the social worker can often do much in helping him to accept the truth and make the most of the remaining months. Work commensurate with' his strength may be found, recreation suggested, or perhaps a changed attitude brought about on the part of his family or friends whose discouragement does not escape him.

In a rooming house, a patient whose condition is offensive may be unwelcome and other plans will need to be made for him.

At work, a cured patient whose face has been seriously disfigured, may no longer be acceptable, and not only must other work be sought, but the patient helped to accept this new attitude of people toward him.

In following up patients after their treatment the social worker urges prompt return to the doctor when there seem to be recurrent symptoms. Precancerous conditions are also kept under observation, and here again the follow-up visit may be the means of sending the patient more promptly to his doctor at the slightest sign of trouble.

Many other types of social problem may accompany, or be caused by, a patient's illness, and in each case the social worker studies the particular need. She then utilizes existing community resources—social and other agencies—as well as the resources within the patient's own group, or within himself, in an effort to meet his need.

Thus the medical social worker is aiding the physician in his fight against a disease in which prompt carrying out of his orders is of such vital importance. She acts under the supervision of the doctor and is an auxiliary rather than an independent unit in the combat of disease.

The family physician of earlier days often acted as doctor, spiritual adviser and friend. The advancement of medical science and the trend of the times has forced him to relinquish, in many cases, some of his former activities. While/he still stands as the original social worker he is greatly aided by the medical social workers of today.

CANCER OF THE STOMACH
By FRANK H. LAHEY, M. D.
Boston, Massachusetts

Since carcinoma of the stomach is the most frequently encountered carcinoma, since its symptomatology is frequently so vague or even silent up to the time it becomes inoperable, it behooves us to particularly concentrate our efforts to arrive at earlier diagnoses of the condition than we are at present succeeding in doing.

The history of carcinoma of the stomach tends to be vague. Obstructive symptoms can result only when the pylorus, media or cardia is occluded and this occurs only after the disease has been present for a considerable time and when it is usually inoperable.

The disease is usually associated with diminished gastric acidity and so lacks the attention-directing element associated with hyperacidity, that is, hunger pain and pylorospasm. It thus possesses no early typical chain of symptoms due either to mechanical interference with motor function or chemical interference with physiological function. It can occur, however, in the presence of a normal gastric acidity and is, when acidity is present, often too far advanced to insure non-recurrence after surgery. Perhaps as constant complaints with this condition as any are distaste for food, weight loss, and vague, variable complaints of digestive difficulties. While it is true that the diagnosis of carcinoma of the stomach by history is often difficult, if not impossible, on the other hand, it is equally true that rarely will inoperable carcinoma of the stomach be found without a long past history of digestive difficulties that should have warranted earlier bismuth X-ray examinations of the stomach.

The outstanding clinical features of such symptoms of carcinoma of the stomach as do occur are their persistency and progressiveness. Digestive difficulties due to other causes quite constantly tend to be characterized by periodicity. Unexplained digestive difficulties persisting over several days, particularly in patients past thirty years of age, demand investigation by bismuth X-rays and gastric analysis and even faintly suspicious X-ray evidence demands repetition of X-rays at an interval and comparison with the originals.

One of the pressing needs for earlier diagnoses of carcinoma of the stomach is to educate the public to permit their doctors to have X-rays of their stomachs on suspicion. It is particularly important to stress here that the late diagnosis of carcinoma of the stomach does not require any special X-ray acumen but that the early diagnosis of lesions that are still operable demands the highest grades of X-ray skill and experience since such lesions will of necessity be small ones and will often present many diagnostic X-ray difficulties.

Doctors subconsciously refrain from advising X-rays of the stomach while but mildly suspicious of possible carcinoma of the stomach because they realize that the odds are all in favor of a negative X-ray report, because patients with unimpressive symptoms and a negative X-ray report tend naturally to assume that there was nothing the matter with them, as proven by the findings, that their doctor was an alarmist and that in view of the negative X-ray report the expense of the X-ray was unjustified. Such patients' attitude should rather be one of thankfulness for a negative finding, one of appreciation of the protective value of the examination, and realization that only by many negative findings can a few patients with early lesions be discovered at a stage when curable by surgery; that it may be their good fortune not to have a malignant lesion, but that it could likewise have been their misfortune to have a malignant lesion, but due to their doctor's wise precaution and thoughtfulness, to have had it thus discovered early, operable and curable. Patients sometimes by their unintelligent criticism of their properly cautious doctors unwittingly play a part in sealing their own doom.

This all involves a delicate balance between producing cancerphobia and complacently accepting cancer diagnoses which are too late. If a mistake is to be made, let us make it on the positive side and have patients a little too-cancer conscious rather than be a party to hiding from them the real facts. After all, most people who have cancer of the stomach are grown-up individuals with many business, social and family responsibilities, and a sentimental attitude of protecting them against the worry of possible cancer is hardly in accord with their obligations in life. In addition, under the present state of the situation, gratifying figures as to early diagnosis in cancer of the stomach have not been obtained.

The greater the number of women who frequently examine their breasts for lumps and who thus consult doctors early for lumps or suspected lumps in their breast, the better will be the end results in carcinoma of the breast. The greater the number of patients who permit themselves to be examined by bismuth gastric X-rays on the appearance of any digestive abnormality which persists beyond a few days, the greater the number of cases of carcinoma of the stomach which will be discovered in a sufficiently early stage so that there is a reasonable chance of curing them by subtotal or total gastrectomy.

No longer is the attitude that a large percentage of gastric ulcers become malignant acceptable or proven by experience. In fact, it has come to be accepted that but a small percentage of gastric ulcers become malignant, perhaps not over 5 per cent. This attitude, however, demands the most careful segregation of gastric lesions into what is an ulcer and what is malignancy. It demands that gastric lesions, not because of the proneness of gastric ulcer to become malignant but because of the commonness of malignant lesions in the stomach, must always be viewed with suspicion as to being possible carcinomata rather than ulcers. If doubt exists these patients must be repeatedly checked by X-ray, gastric analysis examinations of the stools for persistent occult blood, pointing to progress or regression of the lesion while under treatment, and so making it possible to segregate them into the malignancy group demanding radical surgery or into the ulcer group, many of which may be safely treated by conservative measures.

The location of a lesion of the stomach plays some part in the possibility or probability of gastric malignancy. In our experience all lesions of the greater curvature have proven malignant. So consistent has this been that we waste no time but submit lesions at this location immediately to surgery. Prepyloric lesions are likewise particularly liable to be malignant and the closer these lesions are to the pylorus, the more apt they are to be malignant. On the other hand, prepyloric spasm at this point closely simulates malignancy and benign ulcers likewise occur here, so that the decision for or against malignancy in prepyloric lesions demands most critical observation and is not as easy and simple to make as in lesions of the greater gastric curvature.

The impressive features of gastric lesions while under treatment and observation for possible gastric malignancy, indicating the probable presence of malignancy, are that in spite of all medical relief measures, gastric symptoms persist, in spite of medical relief measures occult blood persists or reappears in the stools, in spite of such measures the outline defect of the gastric lesion never completely disappears. The persistence of such events in a gastric lesion under observation and suspicion of malignancy places it, we strongly believe, in the group of probable gastric malignancy demanding surgery.

The treatment of carcinoma of the stomach is still solely surgical. Radical removal of one half, three fourths or even all of the stomach remains the only means by which we can hope to cure these patients. The operation is formidable, the mortality high and likewise the percentage of recurrence high, due to the fact that the operation is one of major magnitude, that it must be done upon patients often advanced in years and frequently with relatively late lesions, but is the sole hope for the patient with gastric cancer.

One sees roughly two types of carcinoma of the stomach. One, the common type which involves a local area of stomach, invades the peritoneal coat early and also involves the adjacent lymph nodes early. One sees also another type which by X-ray seems utterly hopeless because of its extensiveness but which on operative exposure proves in spite of its apparent extensiveness to be entirely free from obvious metastases in the lymph glands and in the liver. This is the linitis plastica or leather bottle stomach type of carcinoma. In this type of carcinoma the peritoneal coat is not widely involved. The spread of carcinoma is within the muscular walls of the stomach and the energy of the growth is apparently expended in local mural extension rather than distant metastases. It is in such cases that we have, in three cases, succeeded in doing total gastrectomy with anastomosis of the jejunum to the oesophagus, one case (operated on by Dr. Clute), which seemed hopeless, living comfortably and working three and a half years after total gastrectomy.

In a recent study by Dr. Sara M. Jordan and the writer of 168 cases of cancer of the stomach, some interesting figures became available. As will be expected, 54 per cent of the cases were found to occur between the ages of forty and fifty-nine years, 35 per cent between the ages of sixty and seventy years. The most important figures, however, are that 6 per cent occurred between the ages of thirty and thirty-nine years with an occasional one occurring between twenty and twenty-nine years. Therefore, one should not presume that the patient with digestive symptoms between twenty and thirty or thirty and forty is exempt from the suspicion of carcinoma of the stomach.

A small group of cases, proven to be early cases, were of interest as to how long symptoms had been present before the diagnosis was made. Of this group thirty-two or 60 per cent had had a history for six months or less while twenty-one or 35 per cent had had a history of six months or over.

As the result of our quite extensive experience with carcinoma of the stomach, we feel safe in stating that one cannot determine in any satisfactory manner the operability of the lesion from the length of the history.

As already stated, carcinoma of the stomach may be slowly or rapidly growing. In general, the patients with long histories will prove inoperable but on the other hand, in spite of long histories there will be some cases in which exploration will be justifiable and the lesion removable.

It was of interest for Dr. Jordan to ascertain that in but 42 per cent of the cases was epigastric distress found to be the chief complaint.

In the cases in which the lesion was found to be early and removable, a mass was palpated in the abdomen in 31 per cent of the cases and in 54 per cent of the cases which proved inoperable. To insure a high percentage of cures, however, the diagnosis should be made and the operation done before a mass is palpable.

At the present time, we have nine patients who are alive and in excellent health, who have had radical removal of all or portions of their stomachs for cancer over one year ago. One of these patients has gone seven and a half years following a partial removal of his stomach for a cancer; another, six years; and two have gone over two years; four are in perfect health, each having had radical removal of a portion of his stomach over one year ago.

WHAT THE PHYSICIAN SHOULD KNOW ABOUT CANCER OF THE THYROID

By HOWARD M. CLUTE, M. D.

Boston, Massachusetts

Cancer of the thyroid occurs in approximately 2 per cent of all the goiter patients that are operated upon. While this means that the actual incidence of malignant goiters in the community is not large, the fact remains, however, that there is a very definite number of cases of thyroid cancer which will be seen by physicians. Furthermore, since cancer of the thyroid in nine out of ten cases arises long after a primary tumor in the thyroid has been noted, it is obvious that more interest in cancer of the thyroid by the profession at large will reduce very appreciably the mortality rate from cancer of the thyroid.

It has long been apparent to physicians that certain types of malignancy in the thyroid were relatively benign, slow growing, and more or less amenable to treatment. It has been equally obvious that other cases of thyroid malignancy are extremely rapid in their course and entirely uninfluenced by treatment. It is our belief that these two types can be differentiated from the clinical history and the physical examination since our observations of thyroid malignancy have demonstrated that not only the histology of these groups is distinctive but also their clinical course can be readily predicted.

We divide thyroid cancer into three groups. In group I we have patients with low or potential malignancy. Here the mortality rate over many years is only 5 per cent. In group II are the patients with definite but not hopeless malignancy where the mortality over a period of years, however, is 55 per cent. In group III we have the patients with the hopeless and usually incurable malignancy where the mortality rate over a period of years is over 80 per cent.

It is of distinct value to the physician to realize that there are such clinical and histological groups of thyroid cancer since it is at once apparent that if a patient falls into group I he has a very excellent chance for living for many years after proper treatment of the thyroid malignancy. If he falls into group II he has, in our experience, if he is an early case, one chance in two of living five to eight years before he dies of cancer of the thyroid, and one chance in two of living for many years with no further difficulty. If, however, the patient falls into group III then we realize that the outlook is extremely bad, and that the mortality is over 80 per cent. Fortunately group I is the largest group of thyroid malignancy. Group II is the next largest, and group III the most serious group, is the least common type with which we deal.

The classical symptoms of cancer of the thyroid are really the symptoms of the final stages of thyroid malignancy. One reads in textbooks that cancer of the thyroid is recognized when a rapidly growing goiter shows irregular lobulation distorting the usual symmetrical shape of the thyroid gland, when hoarseness, stridor, choking and inability to swallow are present as the result of invasion of the larynx, the laryngeal nerves, the trachea and the esophagus.

While these certainly are symptoms of thyroid cancer and can readily be recognized as such, they do not deserve as much emphasis as do those symptoms which suggest the earliest stages of thyroid malignancy.

In the early stages of thyroid cancer just as in the earliest stages of cancer of the breast, there are no symptoms which are positive and diagnostic. The significant suggestive findings, however, which point to the possibility of cancer in the thyroid gland are the slow growth of an adenoma over a period of weeks or months with increasing firmness of the tumor. The occurrence of a sense of pressure in the neck with lack of freedom in the movement of the tumor on palpation, are also evidences that should at once suggest malignant degeneration in a thyroid adenoma.

Over 90 per cent of all thyroid cancer starts in a discrete, circumsized, encapsulated adenoma of the thyroid gland. When such an adenoma is present in the thyroid gland it should be recognized by the physician as the premalignant lesion of the thyroid just as much as he would recognize any encapsulated lump in the female breast as a precancerous lesion in the breast.

Of course all thyroid adenomas are not malignant nor do they become malignant, but in our experience at least six in every hundred are malignant when we remove them. The physician must realize that when he says to a patient that she need not worry about the lump in her neck until something happens to it, that he is saying that she need not worry about the six chances in a hundred that she has that this is now or will later become cancer.

Inflammation of the thyroid gland resembles cancer on examination, and sometimes the differentiation of thyroiditis from cancer of the thyroid is most difficult. In general, however, in thyroiditis the normal contour and shape of the thyroid gland is maintained. There is no eccentric outgrowth of nodules, and there is rarely a general fixation of the tumor in the thyroid to the surrounding tissues in the neck. It is true that in certain cases a final diagnosis is not possible until removal of tissue at operation is undertaken. In this type of case operation and biopsy should not be long delayed.

Hemorrhage into a thyroid adenoma may also produce a most confusing picture. Here, however, the diagnosis can be suspected because of the fact that the patient has a swelling in her neck which came up in the matter of a few hours or at most, a day. As a rule following unusual exertion an adenoma in the thyroid becomes markedly enlarged and acutely tender. The swelling frequently causes difficulty in breathing, and choking. Furthermore, within another few days this type of tumor tends to diminish in size which, of course, thyroid cancer never does without treatment. Here also in these uncertain cases excision of the tumor should be advised.

In general, thyroid malignancy is suspected then because of a firm, hard, discrete type of tumor in the thyroid gland, because of its recent growth, either slow or rapid, and because of secondary evidences of pressure such as difficulty in swallowing, breathing or hoarseness. Thyroid malignancy early leaves the normal contour of the gland and grows in an irregular and unrestrained manner to become adherent to adjacent structures. In a few cases the presence of enlarged lymph nodes near the goiter is suggestive of the presence of malignancy.

Cancer of the thyroid has the same incidence in sex as does goiter in general, occurring in our experience seven times as frequently in women as in men. Cancer of the thyroid may occur at any age. The youngest patient in our experience was a boy of nine years of age who died as the tumor invaded his trachea, his mediastinum and lung. It is very important, it seems to me, to stress the fact that 16 per cent of our patients with cancer of the thyroid were less than thirty-one years of age, and that more than one-third of all our cases occurred at forty-one years of age or below. Certainly this fact shows that our previous idea that tumors of the thyroid need not be removed until after forty was wrong. We now believe that all localized, encapsulated tumors of the thyroid should be removed when they are discovered.

What is the outlook for the patient with cancer of the thyroid? In a recent survey of the results in these patients we found that in the group I patients with the benign type of malignancy 7 per cent were dead of thyroid cancer or were at present suffering with a recurrence. Most important, however, in our experience, is the fact that no death or recurrence has occurred in the group I cases when any patient had been free of trouble for a year after operation. The group I types of tumors can usually be readily removed, and they are always highly susceptible to X-ray treatment. Recurrences are likewise very susceptible to X-ray and radium therapy.

Group II cancers of the thyroid are definite, clear cut malignancies, yet there is some hope of cure in these patients and much chance of long relief. The mortality of this group in our experience is 55 per cent. It is impressive, however, in reviewing the figures to note that over half of the patients who died from thyroid cancer died only after a period of three to five years from the time of their operation, and enjoyed excellent health in that interval. Group II types of thyroid cancer are quite susceptible to X-ray and radium therapy, and it is our feeling that early radical operation supplement by X-ray and radiation therapy will give much better figures in the future than we now can show.

The group III cancers of the thyroid are fortunately the least frequently seen since they are by all odds the most serious type of thyroid malignancy. It is this group of cancer of the thyroid patients that has given cancer of the thyroid its bad name in general. All these tumors are of rapid growth. They occur most frequently in middle and late life, and they are usually rapidly fatal. In a very large per cent of cases the entire time from the first appearance of the tumor until the patient's death is a matter of a year or less. These tumors are not completely removable by surgery. They are not affected in any great degree by X-ray radiation, and only to a moderate degree by radiation therapy. The mortality of the group III cases is 80 per cent with most of the deaths in the group occurring within a few months of the operation.

Improvement in the results in cancer of the thyroid can be obtained in two ways: First, by the more general recognition by physicians that an adenoma of the thyroid gland or a nodular goiter is a premalignant lesion, which should be removed and not watched; and second, by the more radical treatment of thyroid malignancy when it is apparent, by the use of surgery, diathermy, radium and X-ray therapy.

REPORT OF THE DIVISION OF FOOD AND DRUGS

During the months of July, August and September 1934, samples were collected in 241 cities and towns.

There were 1,681 samples of milk examined, of which 305 were below standard, from 14 samples the cream had been in part removed, and 35 samples contained added water. There were 98 samples of Grade A milk examined, 7 samples of which were below the legal standard of 4.00% fat. There were 1,191 bacteriological examinations made of milk, 827 of which complied with the requirements. There were 24 bacteriological examinations made of ice cream, 17 of which complied with the requirements.

There were 411 samples of food examined, 85 of which were adulterated. These consisted of 7 samples of stale eggs sold as fresh eggs; 11 samples of buttered pop corn seasoned with fat other than butter; 1 sample of frozen custard which was low in fat; 31 samples of hamburg steak, 9 samples of which contained sodium sulphite in excess of one tenth of one per cent and 3 samples were also decomposed, 19 samples were decomposed and 1 sample was also watered, and 3 samples contained a compound of sulphur dioxide not properly labeled and 1 sample was also decomposed and watered; 5 samples of sausage, 1 sample of which contained a compound of sulphur dioxide not properly labeled, and 4 samples were decomposed; 10 samples of liver and 1 sample of chicken legs, all of which were decomposed; 2 samples of Youma Bread which were falsely advertised as to starch content; 1 sample of fruit syrup which was incorrectly labeled; 1 sample of sweet relish which contained saccharin; and 15 samples of mattress fillings which contained secondhand material.

There were 38 samples of drugs examined, of which 2 were adulterated. These consisted of 1 sample of argyrol solution not corresponding to the professed standard under which it was sold, and 1 sample of spirit of nitrous ether which did not conform to the U. S. P. requirements.

The police departments submitted 251 samples of liquor for examination. The police departments also submitted 23 samples to be analyzed for poisons or drugs, 7 samples of which contained heroin, 2 samples contained heroin hydrochloride, 7 samples contained opium, 1 sample contained Quinine Sulphate Solution, 1 sample contained cannabis, 1 sample contained caramel, amyl alcohol and a balsam similar to balsam of Peru or talu, and 4 samples were analyzed for poisons or narcotics with negative results.

There were 75 cities and towns visited for the inspection of pasteurizing plants, and 234 plants were inspected.

There were 86 hearings held pertaining to violations of the laws.

There were 94 convictions for violations of the law, $2,175 in fines being imposed.

Nelson Beaubieu of Montague; Charles Bray and Peter Hagopian of Marlboro; George Porter of Deerfield; Mazie Berry and George Chapin of Salisbury; James B. Crane of Leominster; Adam Denosky of Lincoln; Rosa Deon of Brookfield; Josephine Hill and James H. McManus, Incorporated, of Concord; Agnes Ritchie of Oxford; and Joseph W. Ryan of Charlton, were all convicted for violations of the milk laws. Mazie Berry of Salisbury, and Adam Denosky of Lincoln appealed their cases.

Frederick U. Wells of Whately was convicted for misbranding milk. He appealed his case.

Russell Atwell of Norton; Elwood Miller and Claudino Olivera of Seekonk; David Rheault, 2 cases, of Lowell; Hazen K. Richardson of

Middleton; and Abraham Brox of Dracut, were convicted for violations of the pasteurization laws and regulations.

Samuel Tallent, Economy Grocery Company, Thomas Tillman, and Joseph Tapor, all of Springfield; Ettore Angilini and People's Public Market of Fall River; Samuel Wolf, 2 cases, Peter Gordon, 2 cases, Julius Smokler, 2 cases, Norman Ruttenberg, Robert L. Barron, and Max Most, all of Boston; Consumers Provision Stores, Incorporated, 3 cases, Samuel Hodes, North Main Market, Incorporated, H. L. Dakin Company, Incorporated, and Benjamin Parker, all of Worcester; Morris Goodfader, Edward Simons, Louis Levine, Louis Rosenberg, Rabinowitz Delicatessen and Lunch Company, and Joseph Popkin, all of Roxbury; Milton Gordon and George Rossyn of Waltham; Abe I. Wernick of Brighton; Max Andrews, 2 cases, Keve Kessler, and Public Foods Markets, Incorporated, of Malden, Arthur Corey, 2 cases, Fairburn's Market, Incorporated, 2 cases, William Ganem, 3 cases, Brockelman Brothers, Incorporated, 3 cases, all of Lawrence; Albert Feingold of Brookline; Benny Sack, 2 cases, and Woburn Provision, Incorporated, of Everett; Samuel Curley, 2 cases, and Joseph Gordon of Lowell; Arthur C. Parent and Bert Mencis of Haverhill; and Joseph Pasquale, 2 cases, of Newburyport, were all convicted for violations of the food laws. H. L. Dakin Company, Incorporated, of Worcester; Louis Levine of Roxbury; Abe I. Wernick of Brighton; William Ganem, 3 cases, of Lawrence; and Joseph Pasquale, 1 case, of Newburyport, all appealed their cases.

Leo A. Bianchi of Springfield; Arthur Corey of Lawrence; Rabinowitz Delicatessen and Lunch Company of Brookline and Roxbury; Ernest R. Dayon of Beverly; Samuel Polen of Waltham; Howard Bellevue of Old Orchard, Maine (in Brockton Court); and George Secol of New Haven, Connecticut (in Brockton Court), were all convicted for false advertising. Ernest R. Dayon of Beverly appealed his case.

Wilfred Charron of Fall River; Diamond Mattress Company of Woonsocket, Rhode Island; Benjamin Florence, Rubin Warshaver, and Abraham Boodman of Boston; Albert Sachs and Saul Taylor of New Bedford; Samuel D. Kerr of Salem; and Philip Orenstein of Springfield, were all convicted for violations of the mattress law. Wilfred Charron of Fall River; and Rubin Warshaver of Boston, appealed their cases.

In accordance with Section 25, Chapter 111 of the General Laws, the following is the list of articles of adulterated food collected in original packages from manufacturers, wholesalers, or producers:

Buttered Pop Corn seasoned with fat other than butter was obtained as follows:

One sample each, from Paul Flynn of Brockton; Elmer T. Leonard of Onset; Charles Thomas of Worcester; Andrew Boghoshian of Indian Orchard,; Howard Bellevue of Old Orchard, Maine; and George Secol of New Haven, Connecticut.

Two samples of Youma Bread which was falsely advertised as to starch content were obtained from D. L. Hamilton of Waltham.

One sample of fruit syrup which was incorrectly labeled was obtained from Rhode Island Sales Company of Providence, R. I.

One sample of frozen custard which was low in fat was obtained from Kohr Brothers of Revere.

One sample of sweet relish which contained saccharin was obtained from Cambridge Packing Company of Cambridge.

One sample of chicken legs which was decomposed was obtained from Barney Garfinkle of Everett.

Liver which was decomposed was obtained as follows:

Two samples from Brockelman Brothers of Lawrence; and one sample each, from Sirloin Stores and Frank Foti of Everett; Gardner Market (Brockelman Brothers) and Isador Solomon (City Public Market) of Gardner; Rood & Woodbury of Springfield; Ganem's Market of Lawrence; New Public Market of Allston; and Waltham Public Market of Waltham.

Sausage which was decomposed was obtained as follows:

One sample each, from Brockelman Brothers of Lawrence; Thomas Tillman of Springfield; Garland & Barburn of Brookline; and Harper's Market of Everett.

Hamburg steak which was decomposed was obtained as follows:

Two samples each, from Publix Food Markets, Incorporated, of Malden, and Samuel Curley of Lowell; and one sample each, from Premium Market, George Fairburn's Market, of Lawrence; Chestnut Market, Sirloin Stores, and Woburn Provision, Incorporated, of Everett; Louis Israel and Nathan Cohen of New Bedford; Harry Parker of Worcester; J. B. Blood Company of Malden; Joe's Cash Market of Boston; Stark Supply Company, Incorporated, of Roxbury; Joseph Gordon of Lowell; and Harry S. Kreamer of Hudson.

One sample of hamburg steak which was decomposed and also watered was obtained from Ganem's Market of Lawrence.

Hamburg steak which contained sodium sulphite in excess of one tenth of one per cent was obtained as follows:

One sample each, from Samuel Weinek of Roxbury; Keve Kessler of Malden; Allston Meat Shoppe of Allston; Eddie's Market of Boston; and Abraham Holland and Edward S. Lanagan of New Bedford.

Hamburg steak which contained sodium sulphite in excess of one tenth of one per cent and was also decomposed was obtained as follows:

One sample each, from Andrew & Ollman of Malden; Robert Kravitz of New Bedford; and Joseph Pasquale of Newburyport.

Hamburg steak which contained a compound of sulphur dioxide not properly labeled was obtained as follows:

One sample each, from McKinnon's Market and Norwood Provision Company, Incorporated, of Everett.

One sample of hamburg steak which contained a compound of sulphur dioxide not properly labeled and was also decomposed and watered was obtained from Ganem's Market of Lawrence.

Mattress filling which contained secondhand material was obtained as follows:

Eleven samples from Gerson Bedding Company of Lowell; 2 samples from Ideal Bedding Company of Boston; and 1 sample from Diamond Mattress Company of Woonsocket, Rhode Island.

There were seventeen confiscations, consisting of 25 pounds of decomposed fowl; 3½ pounds of decomposed beef steak; 100 pounds of decomposed frankforts; 774 pounds of decomposed, cooked ham; 85 pounds of decomposed hamburg steak; 6 pounds of decomposed luncheon meat; 137 pounds of decomposed pork loins; and 225 pounds of decomposed squid.

The licensed cold storage warehouses reported the following amounts of food placed in storage during June, 1934:—1,439,640 dozens of case eggs; 1,728,645 pounds of broken out eggs; 2,711,477 pounds of butter; 1,328,345 pounds of poultry; 3,282,473 pounds of fresh meat and fresh meat products; and 11,772,952 pounds of fresh food fish.

There was on hand July 1, 1934:—8,048,010 dozens of case eggs; 3,303,774 pounds of broken out eggs; 3,361,728 pounds of butter; 3,705,147¼ pounds of poultry; 8,046,104¼ pounds of fresh meat and fresh meat products; and 21,751,249 pounds of fresh food fish.

The licensed cold storage warehouses reported the following amounts of food placed in' storage during July, 1934:—439,680 dozens of case eggs; 1,028,048 pounds of broken out eggs; 3,689,854 pounds of butter; 1,392,058 pounds of poultry; 3,901,679½ pounds of fresh meat and fresh meat products; and 8,883,495 pounds of fresh food fish.

There was on hand August 1, 1934:—7,648,350 dozens of case eggs; 3,595,389 pounds of broken out eggs; 6,399,369 pounds of butter; 3,529,455¼ pounds of poultry; 8,470,119 pounds of fresh meat and fresh meat products; and 26,158,551 pounds of fresh food fish.

The licensed cold storage warehouses reported the following amounts of food placed in storage during August, 1934:—461,910 dozens of case eggs; 625,589 pounds of broken out eggs; 1,890,426 pounds of butter; 1,240,440 pounds of poultry; 4,015,814½ pounds of fresh meat and fresh meat products; and 9,431,244 pounds of fresh food fish.

There was on hand September 1, 1934:—6,882,720 dozens of case eggs; 3,476,928 pounds of broken out eggs; 6,796,664 pounds of butter; 3,161,118¼ pounds of poultry; 7,980,717¾ pounds of fresh meat and fresh meat products; and 28,749,573 pounds of fresh food fish.

MASSACHUSETTS DEPARTMENT OF PUBLIC HEALTH

Commissioner of Public Health, HENRY D. CHADWICK, M.D.

Public Health Council

HENRY D. CHADWICK, M.D., *Chairman*

GORDON HUTCHINS.
FRANCIS H. LALLY, M.D.
SYLVESTER E. RYAN, M.D.
RICHARD M. SMITH, M.D.
RICHARD P. STRONG, M.D.
JAMES L. TIGHE.

Secretary, ALICE M. NELSON

Division of Administration	Under direction of Commissioner.
Division of Sanitary Engineering	Director and Chief Engineer, ARTHUR D. WESTON, C.E.
Division of Communicable Diseases	Director, GAYLORD W. ANDERSON, M.D.
Division of Biologic Laboratories	Director and Pathologist, ELLIOTT S. ROBINSON, M.D.
Division of Food and Drugs	Director and Analyst, HERMANN C. LYTHGOE, S.B.
Division of Child Hygiene	Director, M. LUISE DIEZ, M.D.
Division of Tuberculosis	Director, ALTON S. POPE, M.D.
Division of Adult Hygiene	Director, HERBERT L. LOMBARD, M.D.

State District Health Officers

The Southeastern District	RICHARD P. MACKNIGHT, M.D., New Bedford.
The South Metropolitan District	GEORGE M. SULLIVAN, M.D., Stoughton.
The North Metropolitan District	CHARLES B. MACK, M.D., Boston
The Northeastern District	ROBERT E. ARCHIBALD, M.D., Lynn.
The Worcester County District	OSCAR A. DUDLEY, M.D., Worcester.
The Connecticut Valley District	HAROLD E. MINER, M.D., Springfield.
The Berkshire District	WALTER W. LEE, M.D., No. Adams.

PUBLICATION OF THIS DOCUMENT APPROVED BY THE COMMISSION ON ADMINISTRATION AND FINANCE.
15M. 12-'34. Order 3221.

INDEX

Abbott, Mrs. T. Grafton, Parent education in its relation to nursery schools	192
Advertise, It pays to, by Dorothea Nicoll	165
American Public Health Association, annual meeting	46
Art and health education, by John H. McCarthy	161
Arteriosclerosis, by Paul D. White, M. D.	13
Arthritis, by Robert B. Osgood, M. D.	23
Basic considerations of the junior high school course of study, by John P. Sullivan, Ph.D.	185
Bauer, Helen M., Social problems facing diabetic patients	114
Bigelow, George H., M. D., Coma	93
Resignation of	3
Blood pressure, Can High, be avoided? by Laurence B. Ellis, M. D.	11
Bragg, Mabel C., Conservation of the school health program	171
Bright's disease, The truth about, by James P. O'Hare, M. D.	15
Cancer	
Biopsy, Relation to tumor diagnosis, by Shields Warren, M. D.	216
Bladder, by Roger C. Graves, M. D.	217
Bone, by Channing C. Simmons, M. D.	220
Brain, by Gilbert Horrax, M. D.	225
Breast, by Robert A. Greenough, M. D.	227
Cervix, by George A. Leland, Jr., M. D.	229
Clinic, Lowell, by Lowell Clinic Staff	231
Educational program in, of the General Federation of Women's Clubs, by Mary R. Lakeman, M. D.	232
Esophagus, by Harris P. Mosher, M. D. and A. S. MacMillan, M. D.	234
Excerpts and statistics on, by Frances A. Macdonald, A. B.	235
Eye, by J. Herbert Waite, M. D.	244
Fundus, by Stephen Rushmore, M. D.	245
Historical trends in, by Eleanor J. Macdonald, A. B.	247
Jaws, by Varaztael H. Kazanjian, M. D.	265
Kidney, by William C. Quinby, M. D. and Fletcher H. Colby, M. D.	269
Leukemias, by Francis T. Hunter, M. D.	271
Lip, by Ernest M. Daland, M. D.	274
Liver and gall bladder, by Irving J. Walker, M. D.	278
Lung, by Edward D. Churchill, M. D.	279
Lymph nodes, by Henry Jackson, Jr., M. D.	282
Massachusetts Cancer Program, Progress in, by Henry D. Chadwick, M. D. and Herbert L. Lombard, M. D.	294
Mouth, by Charles C. Lund, M. D.	284
Nasopharynx, by Carl H. Ernlund, M. D.	286
Ovaries, by Joe V. Meigs, M. D.	289
Pancreas, by Leland S. McKittrick, M. D.	291
Problem, by Ernest M. Daland, M. D.	18
Prostate, by George G. Smith, M. D.	299
Rectum and colon, by Daniel F. Jones, M. D.	301
Skin, by Grantley W. Taylor, M. D.	304
Social service in, by Eleanor E. Kelly	307
Stomach, by Frank H. Lahey, M. D.	308
Thyroid, by Howard M. Clute, M. D.	311
Chadwick, Dr., Appointment of	3
Foreword to Cancer number	215
and Herbert L. Lombard, M. D., The Health Forum	202
Progress in the Massachusetts Cancer Program	294
Children fed by wholesale with an eye to each's particular need, by Clara Sharpe Hough	156
Churchill, Edward D., M. D., Cancer of the lung	279
Clute, Howard M., M. D., What the physician should know about cancer of the thyroid	311
Coffey, Ada Boone, R. N., Appointment of	4

Coffey, Ada Boone, R. N., Progressive health education — 135
Coffin, Susan M., M. D., Franklin County Demonstration, 1927-1933 — 197
   Health education through demonstration — 160
   Health education through prenatal and postnatal letters and other printed material — 155
Colby, Fletcher H., M. D. and William C. Quinby, M. D., Cancer of the kidney — 269
Conservation of the school health program, by Mabel C. Bragg — 171

Daland, Ernest M., M. D., Cancer of the lip — 274
   The cancer problem — 17
Denny, Francis P., M. D., Health education through a community health department publication — 137
Diabetes, by Elliott P. Joslin, M. D. — 56
   Camps (diabetic), by Priscilla White, M. D. — 111
   Child (diabetic) of today, by Priscilla White, M. D. — 103
   Coma, by George H. Bigelow, M. D. — 93
   Coma, by Alexander Marble, M. D. — 88
   Cost of treatment, by Elliott P. Joslin, M. D. — 81
   Discharge directions — 82
   Diets (diabetic) — 76
   Fractures in elderly diabetics, by Howard F. Root, M. D., Priscilla White, M. D., and Alexander Marble, M. D. — 101
   Gangrene and surgery in, by Howard F. Root, M. D. — 93
   Heredity of, by Priscilla White, M. D. — 103
   Historical trend of, by Eleanor J. Macdonald, A. B. — 57
   In Massachusetts, by Herbert L. Lombard, M. D., Anne A. Boris, and Sadie Minsky — 65
   Insulin and, by Elliott P. Joslin, M. D. — 81
   Laboratory, The, by Hazel Hunt — 88
   Pregnancy in, by Priscilla White, M. D. — 98
   Social problems facing diabetic patients, by Helen M. Bauer — 114
   Talks for diabetics, Outline of course of — 86
   Treatment of, by Elliott P. Joslin, M. D. — 74, 77
   Tuberculosis in diabetics, by Alton S. Pope, M. D. — 96
   What do people need to know about diabetes, by Mary R. Lakeman, M. D. — 117
   What the public should know of, by Elliott P. Joslin, M. D. — 20

Eat? What shall we — 43
Editorial comment: Visual methods in health education — 207
Elkind, Henry B., M.D., Health education in the field of mental hygiene — 153
Ellis, Laurence B., M. D., Can high blood pressure be avoided? — 11
Ernlund, C. H., M. D., Cancer of the nasopharynx — 286

Fatigue, Effects of, by John H. Talbott, M. D. — 28
Food and Drugs, Report of Division of:
   October-November-December, 1933 — 47
   January-February-March, 1934 — 127
   April-May-June, 1934 — 208
   July-August-September, 1934 — 315
Franklin County Demonstration, 1927-1933, by Susan M. Coffin, M. D. — 197

Gangrene and surgery in diabetes, by Howard F. Root, M. D. — 93
Graves, Roger C., M. D., Cancer of the bladder — 217
Greenough, Robert B., M. D., Cancer of the breast — 227
Gums bleed, Why, prepared by Massachusetts Dental Hygiene Council — 32

Health? What price, by Mary R. Lakeman, M. D. — 36
Health education and art, by John H. McCarthy — 161
Health education and our high school girl, by Albertine P. McKellar — 189
Health education
   Basic considerations of the junior high school course of study, by John P. Sullivan, Ph.D. — 185
   By a hospital dispensary, by Mary Pfaffman — 148
   By the Community Health Association, by Evangeline Morris — 139

Health education—Cont.
  From the aspect of the physical education director, by Carl L. Schrader . . . 179
  In a city health department, by Susan Murdock . . 142
  In the field of mental hygiene, by Henry B. Elkind, M. D. . 153
  In Massachusetts as pictured by 1933 statistics, by Fredrika Moore, M. D. . . . 194
  In the schools, by John P. Sullivan, Ph.D. . . 169
  Material, Preparation of, for the schools, by Jean V. Latimer, A. M. . . . 182
  Progressive, by Ada Boone Coffey, R. N. . . 125
  Supervisor of — responsibilities and training, by C. E. Turner, M. A., Dr. P. H. . . . 175
  Through a community health department publication, by Francis P. Denny, M. D. . . . 137
  Through demonstration, by Susan M. Coffin, M. D. . 160
  Through prenatal and postnatal letters and other printed material, by Susan M. Coffin, M. D. . . . 155
  Through the classroom teacher, by Mabel E. Turner . 177
  Visual methods in . . . 207
Health Forum, by Henry D. Chadwick, M. D., and Herbert L. Lombard, M. D. . . . 202
Health services of tomorrow, by Thomas Parran, Jr., M. D. . 120
Health teaching in the Y. W. C. A., by Rae E. Kaufer . . 146
Heart disease, by Samuel H. Proger, M. D. . . . 9
Hemorrhoids, by L. S. McKittrick, M. D. . . . 33
Horrax, Gilbert, M. D., Cancer of the brain . . . 225
Hough, Clara Sharpe, Children fed by wholesale with an eye to each's particular need . . . 156
Hunt, Hazel, The laboratory . . . 88
Hunter, Francis T., M. D., The leukemias . . . 271

It pays to advertise, by Dorothea Nicoll . . . 165

Jackson, Henry, Jr., M. D., Primary tumors of the lymph nodes . 282
Jones, Daniel Fiske, M. D., Cancer of the rectum and colon . 301
Joslin, Elliott P., M. D.
  Diabetes . . . 56
    Diets . . . 76
    Discharge directions . . . 82
    Insulin and . . . 78
    Treatment . . . 74, 77
      Cost of . . . 81
    What the public should know of . . . 20

Kaufer, Rae E., Health teaching in the Y W C A . . 146
Kazanjian, V. H., M. D., Cancer of the jaws . . . 265
Kelly, Eleanor E., Medical social service in the cancer clinic . 307

Lahey, Frank H., M.D., Cancer of the stomach . . 308
Lakeman, Mary R., M.D., Educational program in cancer of the General Federation of Women's Clubs . . . 232
  What do people need to know about diabetes? . . 117
  What price health? . . . 36
Latimer, Jean V., A.M., Preparation of health education material for the schools . . . 182
Leland, George A., Jr., M.D., Carcinoma of the uterine cervix . 229
Lombard, Herbert L., M.D. The radio . . . 44
  and Anne A. Boris and Sadie Minsky, Diabetes in Massachusetts . 65
  and Henry D. Chadwick, The Health Forum . . 202
  Progress in the Massachusetts Cancer Program . . 294
Lowell Cancer Clinic . . . 231
Lund, Charles C., M.D., Cancer of the mouth . . 284

Macdonald, Eleanor J., A.B., Chronic rheumatism	25
Historical trends in cancer	247
Historical trend of diabetes	57
Macdonald, Francis A., A.B., Excerpts and statistics on cancer	235
MacDonald, William J., M.D., Care of the skin	4
MacMillan, A. S., M.D., and H. P. Mosher, M.D., Cancer of the esophagus	234
Marble, Alexander, M.D., Diabetic coma	88
and Howard F. Root, M.D., and Priscilla White, M.D., Fractures in elderly diabetics	101
Massachusetts Dental Hygiene Council, Why gums bleed	32
McCarthy, Eleanor G., D.H., Protect your smile	168
McCarthy, John H., Art and health education	161
McKellar, Albertine P., Health education and our high school girl	189
McKittrick, Leland S., M. D., Cancer of the pancreas	291
Hemorrhoids	33
Medical social service in the cancer clinic, by Eleanor E. Kelly	307
Meigs, Joe Vincent, M. D., Malignant tumors of the ovary	289
Moore, Fredrika, M.D., Health education in Massachusetts as pictured by 1933 statistics	194
Morris, Evangeline, Health education by the Community Health Association	139
Mosher, H. P., M.D. and A. S. MacMillan, M.D., Cancer of the esophagus	234
Murdock, Susan, Health education in a city health department	142
Myerson, Abraham, M.D., Nerves	6
Nerves, by Abraham Myerson, M.D.	6
Nicoll, Dorothea, It pays to advertise	165
Nursery schools, Parent education in its relation to, by Mrs. T. Grafton Abbott	192
O'Hare, James P., M.D., The truth about Bright's disease	15
Osgood, Robert B., M.D., Arthritis	23
Parent education in its relation to nursery schools, by Mrs. T. Grafton Abbott	192
Parran, Thomas, Jr., M. D., Health services of tomorrow	120
Pfaffman, Mary, Health education by a hospital dispensary	148
Physical education director, Health education from the aspect of the, by Carl L. Schrader	179
Pope, Alton S., M.D., Tuberculosis in diabetics	96
Preparation of health education material for the schools, by Jean V. Latimer, A.M.	182
Proger, Samuel H., M.D., Heart disease	9
Protect your smile, by Eleanor G. McCarthy, D.H.	168
Pyorrhoea, by E. Melville Quinby, M.R.C.S., L.R.C.P., D.M.D.	30
Quinby, E. Melville, M.R.C.S., L.R.C.P., D.M.D., Pyorrhoea	30
Quinby, William C., M.D. and Fletcher H. Colby, M.D., Cancer of the kidney	269
Radio, The, by Herbert L. Lombard, M.D.	44
Rheumatism, Chronic, by Eleanor J. Macdonald, A.B.	25
Root, Howard F., M.D., Gangrene and surgery in diabetes	93
and Priscilla White, M.D. and Alexander Marble, M.D., Fractures in elderly diabetics	101
Rushmore, Stephen, M.D., What the physician should know about cancer of the fundus of the uterus	245

School health program, Conservation of the, by Mabel C. Bragg . 171
School lunch survey, by Mary Spalding . 156
Schools, Health education in the, by John P. Sullivan, Ph.D. . 169
Schrader, Carl L., Health education from the aspect of the physical
    education director . 179
Simmons, Channing C., M.D., Bone sarcoma . 220
Skin, Care of the, by William J. MacDonald, M. D. . 4
Smith, George Gilbert, M.D., Cancer of the prostate . 299
Social problems facing diabetic patients, by Helen M. Bauer . 114
Spalding, Mary, School lunch survey . 156
Sullivan, John P., Ph.D., Basic considerations of the junior high
    school course of study . 185
    Health education in the schools . 169
Supervisor of health education, responsibilities and training, by C. E.
    Turner, M.A., Dr.P.H. . 175
Surgery in diabetes, Gangrene and, by Howard F. Root, M.D. . 93

Talbott, John H., M.D., The effects of fatigue . 28
Talks for diabetics, Outline of course of . 86
Taylor, Grantley W., M.D., Carcinoma of the skin . 304
Teacher, Health education through the classroom, by Mabel E. Turner 177
Tuberculosis in diabetics, by Alton S. Pope, M.D. . 96
Turner, C. E., M.A., Dr. P. H., Supervisor of health education—re-
    sponsibilities and training . 175
Turner, Mabel E., Health education through the classroom teacher . 177

Visual methods in health education . 207
Waite, J. Herbert, M.D., New growths of the eye . 244
Walker, Irving J., M.D., Cancer of the liver and gall bladder . 278
Warren, Shields, M. D., Relation of biopsy to tumor diagnosis . 216
White, Paul D., M.D., Arteriosclerosis . 13
White, Priscilla, M.D., Diabetic camps . 111
    Diabetic child of today . 103
    Heredity of diabetes . 109
    Pregnancy in diabetes . 98
    and H. F. Root, M.D., and A. Marble, M.D., Fractures in elderly
        diabetics . 101

THE COMMONHEALTH

Volume 22   Jan.-Feb.-Mar.
No. 1   1935

TUBERCULOSIS

MASSACHUSETTS
DEPARTMENT OF PUBLIC HEALTH

THE COMMONHEALTH

QUARTERLY BULLETIN OF THE MASSACHUSETTS DEPARTMENT OF
PUBLIC HEALTH

Sent Free to any Citizen of the State

Entered as second class matter at Boston Postoffice.

M. LUISE DIEZ, M.D., DIRECTOR OF DIVISION OF CHILD HYGIENE, EDITOR.

Room 545, State House, Boston, Mass.

CONTENTS

	PAGE
George H. Bigelow, M. D.	3
Tuberculosis in 1934, by Kendall Emerson, M. D.	6
Tuberculosis in the Practice of Medicine, by Joseph H. Pratt, M. D.	7
The Differential Diagnosis of Tuberculosis, by Frederick T. Lord, M. D.	12
The Diagnostic Dispensary, by Alton S. Pope, M. D.	14
The Cure of Tuberculosis, by Ernest B. Emerson, M. D.	15
The Role of Surgery in Pulmonary Tuberculosis, by Edward D. Churchill, M. D.	18
Hospitalization of Tuberculosis in Massachusetts, by Alton S. Pope, M. D.	21
Diet in the Home Treatment of Tuberculosis, by Frederica L. Beinert	25
Extra-Pulmonary Tuberculosis, by Leon A. Alley, M. D.	27
Tuberculosis in Children, by Roy Morgan, M. D.	29
The School Tuberculosis Clinic Program in Retrospect and in Prospect, by Henry D. Chadwick, M. D.	33
Chadwick Clinic Results	36
Tuberculosis Case-Finding in Children of School Age, by David Zacks, M. D.	39
Summer Health Camps, by Frank Kiernan	42
Medical Supervision of Health Camps, by Carl C. MacCorison, M. D.	46
Teaching the Etiology of Tuberculosis, by Howard J. Leahy, A. M.	48
Policies and Routines for a Tuberculosis Nursing Service, by Helen C. Reilly, R. N.	50
Social Work for the Tuberculosis Patient, by Eleanor E. Kelly	57
The Decline in Tuberculosis, by Alton S. Pope, M. D.	60
The American Neisserian Medical Society	64
How Safe is Home, by Howard Whipple Green—Book Note	64
Report of Division of Food and Drugs, October, November and December, 1934	65

GEORGE H. BIGELOW, M. D.

In the passing of Dr. George H. Bigelow, who for eight busy years directed the destinies of the public health program in Massachusetts, the public health movement has lost a distinguished leader whose vision and enthusiasm blazed trails in the fields of social betterment, the state has lost a distinguished public-spirited citizen who brought honor to his community, and we his former associates in the Department of Public Health have lost as true and dear a friend as was ever granted to any man.

Coming to the post of state health commissioner under circumstances that might have frightened a man of less vitality and courage, Dr. Bigelow rapidly assumed a position of unquestioned leadership in his chosen work. There is no branch of public health today upon which he has not left his indelible imprint. To those fields of health protection that had been developed through years of experience he carried a breadth of vision that added new life and purpose. Thus he brought to the problems of water supply and waste disposal a determination that nothing should stand in the way of achieving the highest standards of excellence. He was uncompromising in his insistence that the public water supply should be of unquestioned purity, and intolerant of those who, for one reason or another, were willing to jeopardize so essential a factor in our present-day civilization. Largely as a result of his activities, plans were consummated (in 1926) for the largest water supply improvement in the history of the State — the extension of the Metropolitan supply to the Ware and Swift Rivers.

Equally firm was his insistence upon the highest standards of purity for the public food supplies. That shellfish, if obtained from improper sources, might be dangerous for human consumption he well recognized. That in his successful fight for protection of this type of food, he should make many enemies he also recognized, and none regretted it more than did he. Yet he carried through with this work, in the face of seemingly insurmountable obstacles, seeing only as his goal the protection and safety of the consuming public.

His crusade for clean and safe milk for Massachusetts will always be remembered among his friends and foes alike. Ever impatient with interests that placed commercial gain above human welfare, he was outspoken in his criticism of those supplies that were unsafe for human consumption. That as health commissioner he should have the responsibility for the conduct of a hospital where were treated many children crippled by tuberculosis obtained through milk, rankled in Dr. Bigelow's heart when he saw on all sides of him so many opportunities for further infection of other children. Thus he championed the program for the elimination of tuberculosis of cattle, even though he realized full well at the time that such was a far from popular cause. That his stand on this issue provoked hostile criticism served but to strengthen his determination that human life and its protection far transcended petty political and commercial interests. In this field at least he lived to see his victory with the virtual elimination of bovine tuberculosis from Massachusetts and already a substantial decline in resulting human infections. He also lived to see the day when through more extensive pasteurization, which he militantly championed, milk-borne disease had all but disappeared from the state.

In the field of tuberculosis he was always striving to bring about a far greater utilization of existing knowledge and facilities to the end that cases of the disease might be recognized earlier and thus afforded the benefit of modern care. He helped to organize and for eight years directed the development of the Chadwick clinics so that there has evolved today a sound and well developed program for the detection of childhood tuberculosis, a program that reaches out into all corners of the state, and available to all persons regardless of their station in life. In other fields of disease prevention, in the control of typhoid fever, the elimination of diphtheria through the furtherance of immunization, Dr. Bigelow gave unsparingly of his time and energy.

It was not solely, however, in his brilliant excursions along the accepted paths of public health endeavor that Dr. Bigelow achieved his many triumphs, but also in the blazing of trails in still uncharted fields of disease prevention and health promotion. When he assumed the post as health commissioner he found himself faced with a new type of public endeavor, a program of cancer control. There were no precedents to be followed, no one had explored the pitfalls to be avoided, none knew how best to chart the course in this new field. Under his guidance, and molded by his brilliance and breadth of vision there evolved a program that has been studied by visitors from all parts of the world, the first state public health program for cancer control. That this program should be still in its early infancy is inevitable from the nature of the problem and yet in the few years of his guidance there was established a firm foundation on which may be built the structure that will evolve in future years.

It was this challenge of cancer that focused his interests on the tremendous economic and sociological problems presented by other chronic diseases. He was troubled at the thought that with the rapidly expanding scientific knowledge of care and prevention of disease, there should be such a lag in the application of this knowledge to human needs. A firm disbeliever in state medicine he envisioned, however, a far broader program through which the hospitals, the medical centers and the official governmental agencies might cooperate in rendering through the family physician many essential diagnostic and therapeutic aids that today because of cost or inaccessibility are denied to many who are most in need thereof. As to so many others who have pioneered in the field of social betterment, it was not granted to him to see the accomplishment of his dreams. That many of them will one day be achieved for the permanent betterment of human life will in the future serve as monuments to the genius of the mind that dreamed such visions.

It would serve no special purpose to enumerate further the vast number of fields of endeavor upon which Dr. Bigelow left his imprint. To attempt to do so would be akin to calling the roll of public health work, for there was no factor no matter how large or how small that could affect the health of the people that escaped his attention. Long after his ideals shall have been achieved, and the influences that he sought to combat shall have vanished into oblivion, his constructive work will live as a tribute to his public devotion.

Far transcending the material accomplishments of his too short life, there will be left upon his associates the influence of Dr. Bigelow's personality. Those of us whose privilege it was to be intimately associated with him, to work shoulder to shoulder with him, to share with him in his plans, his dreams and his visions, knew him in a way that was not granted to those whose contacts were more casual. We knew him as a friend whose pleasure it was to help others. No man could ever have had a truer friend than did those of us privileged to work with him. As a leader, he inspired those around him through the example that he himself set by the brilliance of his mind and his unselfish sacrifice to his work. He constantly denied himself the personal pleasures and relaxation that might have meant so much to him, simply because he found on all sides of him problems that demanded of his time. No problem was ever too small or too large to merit his attention, no request too insignificant. In his devotion to his work he gave of his seemingly boundless energy, never complaining of his tasks but ever impatient when confronted with opposition based on selfish interests and insincerity.

The Department of Public Health takes this occasion to salute the memory of George Bigelow, an inspiring leader in the field of public health, a friend whose memory will ever be cherished in the treasure-house of remembrance, a public servant who at the sacrifice of himself strove ever upward toward the goal of the betterment and enrichment of human life. The world is far better and richer that he has lived therein.

TUBERCULOSIS IN 1934
By KENDALL EMERSON, M. D.
Managing Director, National Tuberculosis Association

The significant fact in the tuberculosis field during 1934 is the continued decline in the death rate despite the persistence of hard times with their accompanying privation, unemployment and lowered living standards. The low rate of 1933, 59.5 per hundred thousand for all forms of tuberculosis, will be bettered. It is estimated that a further drop of about four per cent will be shown bringing the mortality to approximately fifty-seven for 1934. Meanwhile Dublin forecasts a rate below fifty among selected insurance risks.

As a possible offset to this extraordinary record one must bear in mind that figures are based on expected increase of population since the 1930 census, an increase of which it is impossible to be certain. The situation is one giving strong color to the argument for an interim census this year. Aside from its value in verifying statistical data it would, of course, be a most serviceable method of giving temporary employment to a considerable group of those now out of work.

Even with the possible need of making some corrections there will be a substantial cut in last year's mortality rate for tuberculosis, a source of some surprise and much gratification to the epidemiologists. One may well speculate on the reasons for its occurrence. Certain it is that no single discovery, as has happened in the case of some other infections, can be held responsible for the present favorable situation. It is difficult to assign any cause other than the effect of the long continued and carefully planned campaign against tuberculosis which has been going on for so many years. Under the studied guidance of experts in the tuberculosis field, each step has been formulated with care and prosecuted with vigor. Defensive positions have been constantly consolidated and an active offensive has been pushed as rapidly as new weapons can be found and put into action.

Pure milk is one of the factors in the campaign, the importance of which is too seldom mentioned today. Not many years ago ten per cent of the tuberculosis deaths resulted from milk-borne infections. Today the figure stands at less than four per cent, due to the elimination of tuberculous cattle from herds, the widespread pasteurization of milk and clean handling of dairy products.

A second material factor most easily recognized is the phenomenal increase in sanatorium and hospital beds in this country since the beginning of the century. In 1900 their number was less than 6,000 while at present there are over 80,000 such beds if we include those in the veterans' hospitals. The effect of removing from circulation that number of potential distributors of the bacilli is amply obvious.

Yet even such undoubted contributing causes as these cannot be held solely responsible for the continued decline in death rate at a moment when past experience would surely lead to the expectation of a recrudescence of this ever-present, pandemic disease. The corner stone upon which the foundation of the campaign against tuberculosis was laid and upon which much of its structure has been reared, is popular health education. A major part of the success witnessed today may be fairly attributed to the wise dissemination, by doctors, by nurses, by the public health service, by social workers, by the volunteer health agencies, and by industrial groups, of easily-grasped knowledge of the laws of healthy living and the methods of avoiding infection. This sort of education has spread not alone through the teaching of what one shall not do, what risks one shall not invite, but also through positive instruction regarding diet, rest, recreation, household and factory sanitation and behavior habits in schools, colleges and universities.

It is easy to prove the benefits of clean milk from statistics. Common sense recognizes the safety first objective in the segregation of infectious cases. It is more difficult even approximately to appraise the value of a less tangible factor such as health education. But it would seem that the argument is tolerably clear. We are forced to admit even with all our effort the actual number of tubercle bacilli in the world today is incredibly vast. Certainly any survey will disclose the fact that there are still abundant living bacteria to be found in any large aggregation of people, and crowded living has become extreme as a direct result of the depression. While deaths from starvation have been mercifully rare, there can be little doubt that lowered standards of nutrition have prevailed among many of the unemployed and their dependents. Furthermore, anxiety and apprehension have played their role in breaking down the mental and physical resistance of the people. In short, conditions could scarcely be more propitious for a marked increase in the incidence of tuberculosis. Yet precisely the reverse is proving true.

There are two obvious conclusions to be drawn from these facts. The first of these is the evident need of intensifying the procedures of health education during a period of peril such as the present. We have apparently more than held our own thus far against unusual odds. To maintain this advantage may require new techniques, but it will certainly demand more energetic employment of those which have already proved their value.

The second interesting conclusion is perhaps a bit more speculative but it holds high promise for human welfare. If we can continue to drive down the death rate in the face of present handicaps it is entirely logical to assume that we can do better still under more favorable conditions by the full use of the weapons already at our command. This argument leads in just one direction, to the ultimate complete control of tuberculosis, just as we can now control smallpox, cholera, typhoid and diphtheria. The inference is even more promising than that, for ultimate control may not really be so far away. There is a growing faith that by a still greater concentration of forces another ten years may see man's oldest enemy, tuberculosis, finally erased from the list of serious communicable diseases.

TUBERCULOSIS IN THE PRACTICE OF MEDICINE
By JOSEPH H. PRATT, M.D.
Boston, Massachusetts

In spite of the remarkable reduction of the death rate since the turn of the century, tuberculosis, like the poor, is always with us. Too much stress is often laid upon this falling off in the number of fatal cases and too little on the great number of deaths from this preventable disease that still occur year after year. In 1933, over 71,000 died in the United States from this disease. Statistics from four states are not included in this figure. Jessamine S. Whitney, statistician for the National Tuberculosis Association, gives the number as 75,000 yearly, nearly one-half more than the American soldiers who died in action or of wounds in the World War. She makes furthermore the following impressive statement: "Of all communicable diseases in this country today, tuberculosis takes the greatest toll. It has a mortality ten times greater than diphtheria, and nearly a hundred times greater than infantile paralysis." The death rate varies according to sex and age. It rises sharply from the age of ten to twenty in girls. Pope found in the Massachusetts school clinics that pulmonary tuberculosis of the adult type was three times as frequent in girls as boys between the ages of 15 and 18. After twenty-five the death rate in young women slowly falls until forty-five. From fifty years onward there is a second rise. Among males in the U. S. Registration Area in 1930, deaths increased with each decade from the age of ten to fifty.

The latest figures from Massachusetts, those of 1933, give the death rate for pulmonary tuberculosis as 47.7 per 100,000. This represents a slight increase over 1932. The other New England states have almost the same death rate as Massachusetts. Maine only one death less per 100,000 and Rhode Island two more.

It is estimated that there are more than a half a million consumptives living in the United States today, and that over a million persons, chiefly children, are daily in contact with them and exposed to infection. These figures indicate the magnitude of the tuberculosis problem that still confronts the medical profession in these United States in the year 1935.

The contacts should be protected from infection. This cannot be done by the health authorities unless cases of tuberculosis are reported. It is the doctor's duty to report every case but it is one that is neglected. Although there are probably six or more active cases to each death the average in the whole country was 1.6 reported cases to each death in 1933. Rhode Island leads not only New England but the United States with 3.46 cases per death. Massachusetts stands quite high in the list with 1.76 cases per death while Vermont is near the bottom with 0.62 case per death. Maine stands second to Rhode Island among the New England states in this important matter of reporting cases of tuberculosis.

It is known that the incidence of the disease among children is less in New England than in some other parts of the country and Europe. Comparative studies with the intracutaneous tuberculin test made of school children in Philadelphia and in the environs of Boston showed that 51 per cent of the children examined between the ages of five and nine years in Philadelphia reacted and only 28.5 per cent in Massachusetts. From the ages of ten to fourteen 73.4 per cent of the former and 41.5 of the latter reacted. From fifteen years to nineteen years the percentage rose to 82.5 in the Philadelphia schools and to 62.6 in the schools near Boston. In St. Louis in a hospital for children using the von Pirquet method 43 per cent at ten years were infected. In a rural district of Minnesota the percentage of infections was very low, being not over 12 per cent at any period between five and fifteen years. In Vienna the highest percentage of infection was reported amounting to 72 per cent in children ten years old and 94 per cent at the age of fifteen.

The Chadwick Clinic in the past ten years has examined 400,000 school children in Massachusetts. Twenty-five per cent of these reacted to the von Pirquet tuberculin test. As a result of making roentgenograms of the children that were found infected, 261 cases of the adult type of pulmonary tuberculosis were discovered and 5,620 of the childhood type. Only 5.9 per cent of the children who were found by the tuberculin test to be infected showed evidence of long involvement by x-ray. During the last five years of the ten years' program, high school pupils as well as students in the grade schools were examined. The percentage of reactors in the former fell from 43 per cent in 1930 to 34 per cent in 1933 and in the latter from 26 per cent to 17 per cent.

Zacks has published a valuable paper on knowledge gained from the ten year program for school children in Massachusetts. The great importance of the roentgenogram of the chest was clearly shown. In 55 per cent of the cases of the adult type of tuberculous pulmonary disease the diagnosis was made by means of the x-ray film alone, there being neither symptoms or râles. In 19 per cent there were râles in addition to x-ray evidence of tuberculosis. Symptoms were present together with râles and a positive roentgenogram in 22 per cent, and symptoms and x-ray evidence of disease in 5 per cent. Râles occurred more frequently than symptoms, such as cough and sputum. Râles on the average appeared 2.6 years after the roentgenogram demonstrated the presence of the tuberculous lesion, while cough and expectoration were not present until three years after the diagnosis had been made by the x-ray.

These findings of the workers in the Chadwick Clinic are of the greatest practical importance. *For the first two or three years after the onset of the adult type of pulmonary tuberculosis, the children had no symptoms and appeared to be perfectly well.* The physical examination of the chest revealed nothing abnormal. In view of the apparent good condition of the children, family physicians as well as parents were loath to believe that the children were seriously diseased. There was a tendency to disregard the interpretation of the roentgenograms made by the examiners. What was the result? In less than five years, in 4.6 years to be exact, twenty-four of the one hundred and ten children whose records were analyzed were dead and in fifty-three of those living the disease was progressing.

It is to be hoped that all physicians in Massachusetts have learned from the results obtained in the Chadwick Clinic that treatment in all cases of adult type of pulmonary tuberculosis should begin before symptoms appear. The treatment should be strict bed rest in a sanatorium, if possible, and there are now available in this state seven hundred beds for children.

To delay treatment until the disease has passed beyond the minimal stage is to invite death. It has been found from a study of the results at the Westfield Sanatorium that in spite of prolonged bed-rest treatment the great majority of the children and adolescents admitted with moderately advanced or advanced tuberculosis die. Even when collapse therapy in the form of therapeutic pneumothorax is employed in addition to bed rest the results are poor (Morgan). These results in spite of the most approved treatment should arouse physicians and parents to the urgency of beginning treatment in patients with the adult type of lesion as soon as the diagnosis is made by x-ray in spite of the fact that the child may appear in perfect health at the time.

Prior to the publication of Zack's paper, McPhedran of the Phipps Institute in Philadelphia had shown conclusively "that pulmonary infiltrations may be discovered months and even years before pulmonary tuberculosis becomes manifest either by symptoms or by physical signs".

In Massachusetts, nodular lesions were found in 1.4 out of every 100 school children. They usually denoted a source of infection nearby. Children with this childhood type of disease are about six times as apt to develop the adult form of disease as those who react to tuberculin but exhibit no x-ray evidence of lung disease (Pope). The interval between the discovery of the nodular lesions and the development of an infiltration in the parenchyma was usually between three and four years in Zack's series. The influence that home contact plays in the development of the adult type of disease was shown by the fact that 73.9 per cent of the cases of the infiltrative type occurred in homes in which the children were exposed to the disease.

It is the duty of the family doctor either to remove the patient ill with clinical tuberculosis to a sanitorium or to a hospital or move the children to a place free from the danger of infection. In the nodular type of childhood disease sanatorium treatment is rarely necessary. It is, of course, essential that the child should be provided adequate rest, fresh air, good food and sufficient sleep. The child should be carefully watched and a roentgenogram made at least every six months. Recovery from the primary infection without impairment of health is the rule.

It was formerly thought that the early diagnosis of pulmonary tuberculosis could be achieved if patients were thoroughly examined when they first consulted a private physician or sought treatment in a clinic or dispensary. Hammon, however, pointed out many years ago that patients often do not seek medical aid until in an advanced stage of the disease. This is true in many instances I know from personal experience. Physicians are still often remiss in not making the diagnosis when first consulted. In a survey made by the National Tuberculosis Association in 1928, it was found that among 1500 patients interviewed the average time elapsing between the first recognizable symptom and the first visit to any doctor was five months and another five months before a definite diagnosis was given.

The latest published statistics from the Rutland State Sanatorium indicate that most patients still enter the sanatorium in an advanced stage of the disease. Among the patients admitted in 1925 and 1926, only 15.1 per cent were in the minimal stage, 32.7 per cent moderately advanced and 52.2 per cent advanced. (Langmuir, Williams and Pope.)

Chadwick and Morgan have shown how little value can be placed on the stethoscope in the diagnosis of early pulmonary tuberculosis. Breath changes without râles were found to be very unreliable. In a series of 440 cases with tubercle bacilli in the sputum, 79 showed no auscultatory signs. "The seriousness of delaying diagnosis in children until positive sputum is found is shown by the subsequent history of two hundred cases. A follow-up shows that but seven are known to be living, one hundred fifty-two are reported dead and forty-one are untraced. Of forty-nine cases with cavity shown by the roentgenogram at the time of admission, forty-five are dead, four are living, three of them well and one in only fair condition."

The proper procedure to be followed by every physician has been tersely summarized by Chadwick. "The way to detect early tuberculosis is always to think of it as a possibility in every person. Use a tuberculin test in all children up to fifteen years of age, and in some adults it is of value in differential diagnosis. Take a roentgenogram of all positive reactors in children and all other persons who are examined for pulmonary tuberculosis. Become skeptical of the value of the stethoscope in the diagnosis of pulmonary tuberculosis and put more faith in the roentgen ray".

If a patient is found to have pulmonary tuberculosis all children in the household should be tested with tuberculin and roentgenograms made of all reactors as well as of all adults in the family.

The technique of testing with tuberculin can be easily learned and it should be employed by all physicians in general practice. It is safe to prophesy that unfamiliarity with this test will soon be regarded as serious a shortcoming as inability to use a stethoscope has been in the past.

Variations have been found in the strength of American tuberculins. Physicians in Massachusetts can obtain, from the Antitoxin and Vaccine Laboratory of the Department of Public Health, Jamaica Plain, without expense, ampules of old tuberculin—O.T.—for diagnostic use. Directions for its use come with each ampule.

The Pirquet test is the simplest. The tuberculin is used as it comes in the ampule without dilution. All authorities are agreed that it is a less sensitive indicator of tuberculous infection than the intracutaneous (Mantoux) test but it corresponds approximately to the first dilution of the latter, 1-10,000. By using a second intracutaneous test with a dilution of 1-100 (1.0 mag. of Old Tuberculin) in cases which do not react to the higher dilution about 20 per cent more reactors will be found.

The technique for performing both types of tests is given with the ampules of old tuberculin supplied by the state. Physicians intending to use tuberculin tests are also referred to the recent booklet of the

National Tuberculosis Association, "Childhood Type of Tuberculosis, Diagnostic Aids", a copy of which can be obtained upon application to the Association. This also contains an excellent colored plate illustrating the different degrees of reaction.

Through connection with the Bingham Associates Fund for the Advancement of Rural Medicine, I have had the opportunity to follow the work during the past three years in the Control of Tuberculosis in Oxford County, Maine. When Dr. Hanscom assumed charge of the state tuberculosis institutions in 1932 there was such a large waiting list for admission to sanatoria that a period of six months or more elapsed before treatment was begun. By securing state aid for general hospitals to admit tuberculosis cases he was able to reduce the time between application and admission to a few weeks. In Oxford County, as soon as the diagnosis of tuberculosis is made, patients can at once be admitted to the Rumford Community Hospital. They remain there until a bed is available at the Western Maine Sanatorium at Hebron. During their stay at the hospital, treatment is supervised by Dr. Lester Adams, superintendent of the Hebron Sanatorium. He also holds regular clinics and demonstrations at the Rumford Hospital which are well attended by the physicians of Rumford and surrounding towns. Furthermore if therapeutic pneumothorax is indicated it is given by Dr. William T. Rowe of the hospital staff until the transfer of the patient to the sanatorium.

Dr. Hanscom, State Commissioner of Tuberculosis, appointed Mrs. June H. Hunter as a tuberculosis social worker in Oxford County in 1932. Her salary and expenses have been met by grants from the Bingham Associates Fund. Mrs. Hunter had previously ten years' experience as a social worker in the Emmanuel Church Tuberculosis Class in Boston. Her success there has been duplicated in Maine. So remarkable has been the co-operation of the doctors in Oxford County in the tuberculosis work that her aid has been sought in every case of tuberculosis that has been recognized by them. All cases have been x-rayed at the Rumford Hospital and all children that have been in contact with known cases of pulmonary tuberculosis have been given the tuberculin test and roentgenograms made of all reactors.

The Maine Public Health Association tested with tuberculin the children in the public and parochial schools in Rumford a year ago, and all reactors were x-rayed. Last summer when an open case of tuberculosis was discovered in a school child in Sumner, the superintendent of schools in that town assembled all the pupils who attended that school although it was vacation, and Dr. Atwood of West Buckfield performed the Mantoux test on 100 per cent of the school enrollment.

Conclusion

In the diagnosis of pulmonary tuberculosis a roentgenogram is essential in every case. Even when tubercle bacilli have been found in the sputum it is needed to determine the extent and character of the lesions.

When a case of tuberculosis is found it is the doctor's duty at once to have all adult members of the patient's household x-rayed, all children in contact with the patient at home or at school tuberculin tested, and roentgenograms made of all reactors.

The diagnosis once made, treatment should be instituted without delay. In the adult type of tuberculosis the patient should be given strict bed rest until admitted to a sanatorium. At the sanatorium, in addition to bed rest, some form of collapse therapy in the great majority of cases increases the chance of recovery.

THE DIFFERENTIAL DIAGNOSIS OF TUBERCULOSIS
By Frederick T. Lord, M. D.
Boston, Massachusetts

In general, such negative features of the history as absence of opportunity for contagion in the family or elsewhere, especially early in life, lack of occupational exposure to certain dusts and past or present freedom from hemoptysis "out of a clear sky", primary pleurisy, phlyctenular conjunctivitis, cervical adenitis, ischiorectal abscess or anal fistula are helpful in excluding tuberculosis. Deviations from the usual sequence and grouping of symptoms of the disease in the present illness must be noted. The limitations of physical examination make constant resort to the roentgen-ray desirable. Lateral as well as anteroposterior films, and films taken at the end of full inspiration and full expiration, are helpful in selected cases. Repeated search of the sputum should be made for tubercle bacilli. Bronchoscopy and lipiodol insufflation help to solve certain problems.

Childhood Types of Tuberculosis

Glandular Type. Films should be taken in the lateral as well as the anteroposterior view. It is difficult at times to make the distinction between normal structures in the mediastinum and lung roots, especially axially-radiated vascular channels, and tuberculous glands, and there is in consequence a considerable proportion of children with positive skin tests who must be regarded as under suspicion.

Diffuse or Nodular Pulmonary Tuberculosis in Children

Non-tuberculous infection with secondary adenitis may be confused with diffuse or nodular tuberculous lesions with associated tracheobronchial glandular involvement. Stormy onset, leucocytosis, negative tuberculin test and rapid subsidence of the pulmonary and glandular lesions may serve to suggest a non-tuberculous origin. Lymphoblastomata may be confused with tuberculous tracheobronchial adenitis. General glandular enlargement, palpable spleen, lack of calcium in the glands on x-ray examination, negative tuberculin test and rapid diminution in size or disappearance under x-ray radiation help in the differentiation.

Adult Types of Tuberculosis

The differentiation of acute lobar or pseudolobar tuberculosis from *non-tuberculous lobar pneumonia* is especially important in view of the importance of early specific treatment of certain types of pneumococcus infections. In contrast to pneumonic phthisis, *pneumococcus lobar pneumonia* usually occurs in previously healthy individuals. The onset is more explosive with shaking chill, rapid elevation of temperature, cough with tenacious rusty sputum and pain in the side. The presence of Types I or II pneumococci in the sputum speaks for pneumococcus lobar pneumonia. In rare instances, pneumococcus pneumonia may complicate pulmonary tuberculosis. The complex of initial symptoms with pneumococcus lobar pneumonia is seldom complete with acute tuberculous lobar pneumonia, which is only rarely observed and is to be ascribed to massive infection. Chill and pain are less common. Tenacious rusty sputum may occur, but purulent, greenish expectoration is more common. Hemoptysis may be an initial symptom. Pallor rather than cyanosis, unusual irregularity in the temperature curve, remittent or intermittent fever, failure to become afebrile at the expected time, absence of leucocytosis, physical and x-ray evidence of apical or subapical disease in addition to consolidation elsewhere are suggestive features. The sputum is usually positive for tubercle bacilli.

Chronic Ulcerative Tuberculosis. With *tracheobronchitis* following a "cold" the cough and expectoration usually last only a few days or weeks. In the more protracted types only thorough investigation will exclude tuberculosis. Bronchopneumonia due to other organisms than the tubercle bacillus in a small proportion of cases terminates in permanent damage to the bronchopulmonary tissue. Absence of features in the history suggesting tuberculosis, involvement of the lower lobes, lack of evidence of disease in the apical or subapical regions on physical and roentgen-ray examination and repeatedly negative sputum are in favor of a non-tuberculous affection.

Malignant disease is primary in the bronchi in a large proportion of the cases. A persistent cough following a "cold" may be the first manifestation. The cough is usually for a time dry and after some time mucoid or mucopurulent in contrast to purulent sputum earlier in the course of tuberculosis. At times, hemoptysis is the first symptom. Recurring hemoptyses at long intervals with complete freedom from significant symptoms in the intervals is more common with malignant disease. If malignant disease involves a large bronchus, dyspnea may be an early symptom. Wheezing may be noted by the patient and may be present only when lying on the affected side. Night sweats and fever are less common than with tuberculosis. On physical and roentgen-ray examination, evidence of obstruction emphysema or atelectasis may be found. Bronchoscopy is indispensable in determining the nature of the bronchial obstruction. With malignant involvement of the lung, absence of apical or subapical involvement is important in excluding tuberculosis. When the disease is primary in the hilus region there may be a dense shadow at the root with radial projections along the larger bronchi. Primary new growths arising elsewhere may appear as dense round or irregular shadows with well or ill-defined margins. At times malignant disease of the lung simulates miliary tuberculosis, with small, dense, sharply defined areas scattered through both lung fields. Their larger size, greater density and more sharply defined margins may serve to distinguish them from miliary tubercles.

Confusion of *bronchiectasis* with tuberculosis is likely to occur only in incompletely investigated cases. Profuse hemoptysis is common, but only rarely occurs as an initial symptom. An offensive odor to the sputum, repeated failure to find tubercle bacilli in the purulent expectoration, x-ray evidence of dilated bronchi at the bases after insufflation of lipiodol and absence of subapical involvement are important.

Lung abscess may be distinguished from pulmonary tuberculosis by its occurrence following operation on the upper respiratory tract, or under circumstances suggesting aspiration, foul odor to the breath and sputum, repeated absence of tubercle bacilli and presence of elastic tissue in the sputum and leucocytosis. On x-ray examination in typical cases the abscess appears as an irregularly rounded shadow of variable size, its margins sharply defined or fading gradually into the normal tissue with central radiance and fluid level.

The diagnosis of *pneumonoconiosis* due to the inhalation of silica is not difficult, but tuberculosis develops sooner or later in a large proportion of cases and recognition of the two diseases combined may be difficult or impossible. With silicosis there is a history of occupational exposure, dyspnea out of proportion to other symptoms, relatively insignificant physical signs, usual maintenance of the general nutrition and absence of fever. Chest pain, cough and expectoration, at times blood-streaked, and occasional small hemoptyses may occur. The x-ray appearances vary with the stage of the disease. There is, at first, increased density of the lung roots with increased linear markings therefrom and later evidence of fibrotic changes and emphysema with mottling due to discrete, sharply defined nodules throughout the lung fields, excepting the apices. The combination of silicosis and tuberculosis modifies the picture. There may be increase in the cough and expectoration, more abundant hemoptyses and loss of weight. On x-ray examination the nodular areas appear hazy in outline with a tendency to the formation of conglomerate masses. The subapical regions are then likely to be involved. Even repeatedly negative examinations of the sputum for tubercle bacilli do not exclude tuberculosis.

THE DIAGNOSTIC DISPENSARY
By ALTON S. POPE, M. D.
Director, Division of Tuberculosis
Massachusetts Department of Public Health

Under the Massachusetts statutes every city of fifty thousand population or over is required to maintain a dispensary for the discovery, treatment and supervision of needy persons afflicted with tuberculosis. Passed soon after the statute establishing the first State Sanatorium this Act recognized the obligation of the community for the discovery as well as treatment of tuberculosis, and endeavored to provide an agency for the supervision of cases financially unable to go to a private physician. Such dispensaries became the responsibility of the local board of health, and are in most instances operated by them, though the physician in charge is usually some doctor specially interested in the field of tuberculosis. Minimum requirements as to facilities, equipment and service are from time to time promulgated by the State Department of Public Health, and at the present time 46 cities and towns in the State are maintaining such tuberculosis dispensaries.

Although probably modeled on the English dispensary, which has there become the center of tuberculosis control work, the Massachusetts dispensary has followed a quite different path, and is in most instances an agency for the very essential nursing supervision of cases in their homes, and for the more or less routine examination of indigent patients referred by private physicians, and boards of health, and social agencies. In some places the interest and ability of the clinic physician have inspired the confidence of practicing physicians, and made it possible for the dispensary to take its proper place in the local control of tuberculosis, but too often it has ceased to meet a real need in the community.

Along with the local dispensaries there have developed in Massachusetts diagnostic out-patient departments at the various state and county sanatoria. These departments have not only the advantage of the services of the sanatorium staff—a group working continuously with tuberculosis—but also such special diagnostic aids as x-ray, which is rarely provided in the local dispensary. The demand for medical service depends primarily upon the confidence it inspires, and with these special facilities available it is not strange that more and more physicians have turned to the sanatoria for aid in the diagnosis as well as treatment of their cases. During the past year 122 physicians referred patients to Rutland alone for this purpose, and a total of over 4500 diagnostic examinations were made in the clinics and out-patient departments of the four state sanatoria.

To facilitate the development of this type of diagnostic service the Legislature of 1931 passed an Act authorizing the maintenance of outpatient departments in state and county sanatoria, and providing that on request of the board of health of any town, or group of towns, in its district a county sanatorium may supplement local facilities in furnishing diagnostic tuberculosis service in such town. Under this provision, in addition to their out-patient departments the state and county sanatoria are now maintaining 16 "consultation clinics" in cities and towns in the Commonwealth. These clinics are as a rule held once or twice a month in local general hospitals where x-ray facilities are available. Case records and nursing service are provided by the local board of health, and the medical staff by the county or state sanatorium. Cases are referred for diagnosis almost entirely by written request of local doctors, but may be sent by local boards of health if the patients have no family physician and are unable to employ one. In all cases referred by a physician the report is made directly to him and not to the patient, so that treatment and supervision remain the doctor's responsibility.

By this method it is becoming possible to secure increasingly early diagnosis of tuberculosis by making available to physicians for their indigent patients the x-ray facilities which had previously been beyond their reach. This is of special value in securing the thorough examination of household contacts of diagnosed cases of pulmonary tuberculosis. It is well recognized that a great part of the spread of tuberculosis occurs in the home. Years usually elapse between infection and the appearance of manifest tuberculosis, and if the diagnosis has to wait upon the development of symptoms and physical signs the disease has often progressed beyond the favorable stage when recognized, and further spread in the family has already taken place. Studies in Tennessee and Massachusetts have shown that over 20 per cent of the family contacts of tuberculosis patients also have the disease, and it is only by the discovery of these incipient cases and chronic, unrecognized sources of infection that we can hope to control tuberculosis.

The importance of early diagnosis and prompt treatment upon the prospect of recovery in the individual case is well recognized among physicians. A quantitative measure of this factor is given in the following table from a study of some 400 patients admitted to the Rutland State Sanatorium during the years 1925 and 1926, whose subsequent condition was determined in the summer of 1931. The figures speak for themselves, but it should be noted that more than one-half of the patients were in an advanced stage of the disease upon admission.

Present Condition of Tuberculosis Patients, According to Stage of Disease on Admission to Sanatorium

Present Condition	Minimal No.	%	Moderately Advanced No.	%	Advanced No.	%
Well	43	72%	58	44%	28	13%
Ill	7	11%	19	15%	17	8%
Dead	10	17%	53	41%	163	79%
Total	60	100%	130	100%	208	100%

The excess of tuberculosis in the lower economic levels, together with the special facilities required for early diagnosis, will probably require some form of local dispensary service for some time to come. Experience in Massachusetts has shown that a combination of out-patient and consultation clinic service from the sanatoria is more economical, far more effective in case finding, and more acceptable to patients and physicians than the service usually available in the local dispensary.

THE CURE OF TUBERCULOSIS
By ERNEST B. EMERSON, M. D.
Superintendent, Rutland State Sanatorium

There is no specific for the cure of tuberculosis—no magic serum, drug, operation or climate alone or together will prevail against the disease. In a broad sense, the treatment of tuberculosis is a mode of life and whatever remedial measures we may prescribe are only adjuncts to a mode of life fitted to the individual. What this mode of life shall be, and what palliative measures shall be prescribed, depend on the type of case, its duration, whether acute or chronic, the age of the patient and his economic status. The treatment of an early case in a young person is an entirely different problem from that presented by the chronic case of many years' duration.

For the early acute case bed rest and very likely some form of collapse therapy are indicated.

For the chronic case, possibly nothing more than a few weeks of rest, or a vacation, is indicated.

The earlier treatment is started, the better are the chances for recovery. In many instances, treatment is delayed for months, or possibly years, before the patient is aware he has the disease. The fault may lie either with the patient himself, through his ignorance of the symptoms and neglect to seek medical aid, or with the physician who has failed to recognize the disease in its early stages, or has not told the patient the whole truth.

There are two outstanding symptoms which may or may not indicate the onset of tuberculosis: Unusual fatigue after the day's work and a cough with or without expectoration. A cough lasting more than four weeks demands a careful investigation as to its cause, including x-ray, sputum examinations, and observation until it has disappeared and tuberculosis has been ruled out, or the presence of the disease has been determined. If such a procedure were universally carried out, many months, to say the least, of taking treatment in the sanatorium or at home might be avoided, and more patients restored to health than can possibly be cured at a later date.

Once the diagnosis is established, the patient should be told; not to tell him that he has the disease is wrong, for the only hope of a cure depends upon his intelligent cooperation.

The first step in the treatment is the education of the patient. He should be given some idea of what he has, what he may expect with or without treatment, and the reason why a routine life is prescribed for him. It is not necessary to explain to one with a broken leg why it must rest in a splint but it is necessary, in order to get the fullest co-operation, to explain to a patient why he must lie in bed to rest a "broken lung". The consumptive who is to win must possess a certain degree of intelligence, must cooperate with his physician and must have a fair degree of will power and determination. Intelligent co-operation cannot be secured unless he has, at least, some knowledge of the disease and the reasons for details of treatment, which may otherwise seem unnecessary or even absurd. Is it fair to expect him to obtain this knowledge by himself, and to get the proper point of view from the many instructive and valuable contributions available for his use? In some measure, yes, but are we not expecting too much of the average man, sent away to the country with a package of pamphlets and general instructions to rest and to take plenty of nourishment? This may be good advice for the chronic case but it is not a good prescription for an early or acute case with no background based on the practical experience of the trained consumptive. It is for this reason that, in most instances, a patient should have a preliminary course of instruction and treatment in the sanatorium where he may learn something of the disease and the underlying principles or reasons for his treatment. In the early stages, it is certainly much easier for the patient to take treatment with others traveling the same way than it is to lie in bed, in a corner room, and listen to the family jars and the words of condolence and pity of the neighbors.

Home treatment, or life on the farm with its milk, butter, fresh eggs and sunshine all have their place; in fact, home treatment makes up the major part of the program but should come after sanatorium treatment and not before.

What is meant by a mode of life? Broadly speaking, less work and more rest; less play and more rest; less worry and more optimism.

It is a shock to be told that one has tuberculosis and somewhat disconcerting to find one's self in a sanatorium. However, shortly after arrival, the patient discovers individuals who convey to him that there is a chance, and a little later, the patient finds himself improving, notes improvement in others, and optimism takes the place of fear and worry.

The essentials for the treatment of tuberculosis are rest, fresh air, proper food and regulated exercise. Not one may be omitted unless, possibly, the exercise. It is the proper adjustment of these simple measures, and not a change of climate, serums, or drugs, which brings about the desired results. The importance of fresh air is recognized, is easily prescribed, and is readily taken. Food fills a large place in the minds of many. Twenty-five years ago, patients were taught to stuff themselves with milk and eggs, and the idea still lingers. Both are excellent foods but should be taken at the regular mealtimes and not in the form of lunches, or as a cure for tuberculosis. A normally functioning digestive system is the patient's greatest asset and should not be abused. It may happen that more good will be derived from the skim milk and a cracker than from steak and onions.

Rest is the only measure in the treatment of tuberculosis which has stood the test of time. Rest is an indefinite term. It signifies anything from sleep to the substitution of some other activity either mental or physical. Without rest, all other measures in the treatment of the disease will likely fail. It is the bed rock of tuberculosis therapy, and the one remedy a patient will evade, if he can devise any form of excuse to outwit the doctor, or to deceive himself. This is not surprising insomuch as the average tuberculous patient has a sense of well-being seen in no other disease. This again suggests the education of the patient and the explanation of why rest throws less work upon the heart and lungs. There must be physical rest and, so far as possible, mental rest with the removal of care and worry. With the subsidence of symptoms, intensive rest is modified by the substitution of graded exercise. The meaning of exercise is as indefinite as that of rest. It begins when the patient sits up in bed and may end with long walks in the woods, and finally a return to the business of earning a living. There is little danger of prescribing too much rest and fresh air but there is some hazard in too much food or too much exercise. Overeating does more harm than good and overactivity may retard convalescence or undo the results of many months of rest.

A proper mental attitude is most essential. Mental attitude is a product of heredity, more or less modified by teaching, suggestion, observation, and the patient's own efforts to see life in its proper perspective. The patient must have the determination to get well, based upon faith in himself, in his physician, and the willingness to yield to the discipline of a new life.

The onset of tuberculosis is not definitely known, neither is it possible to say definitely when a cure is established. Between the diagnosis and the cure is a long interval—one to tax the courage of the most optimistic. During this time, when the patient looks well, and feels well, he is in the danger zone—a difficult period through which to carry him.

The foregoing outlines the fundamentals in the treatment of tuberculosis. Drugs are of no value whatsoever except in so far as they may relieve symptoms arising from time to time—a tonic, possibly, for loss of appetite, a cathartic for constipation, or a sedative for cough. Alcohol in any form is not indicated; it only masks the symptoms. Narcotics are similarly contraindicated except as prescribed for definite and positive indications; for this reason, cough syrups and various exploited nostrums should be avoided; they neither prevent nor cure tuberculosis. A change of climate is unnecessary and may even do harm—just as many are cured at home as abroad.

The question may be asked: What can the sanatorium do that cannot be done in the home? In one sense, nothing; there is no patent on the treatment; however, from experience gained from contacts with many patients from various walks of life, there is no doubt that it is practically an impossibility to carry out in the average home the routine which becomes commonplace, and an everyday affair, in the life of the sanatorium patient.

The patient's education begins on the day of admission, when he receives instruction from the nurse with regard to the disposal of sputum, his hours in bed, and other details; also a word of encouragement. The physician at the time of examination continues this instruction, and explains to him the why of it all. Later he has the opportunity of attending lectures, or talks by the staff, in which the history of tuberculosis, its pathology, symptoms and treatment are frankly discussed. He is encouraged to ask questions at all times. The teaching of tuberculosis does not result in morbid brooding, or undue apprehension with regard to the future; on the contrary, it teaches respect for the disease and not fear.

In no other disease have so many advances been made in treatment during the past few years as in tuberculosis. Collapse therapy in some form, artificial pneumothorax, phrenic nerve operations, thoracoplasty, and other forms of surgery, have unfolded a future for many otherwise destined for unknown years of invalidism with its inevitable end. Yet with all that surgery offers, it is only an adjunct to the general principles already outlined. Successful treatment still depends on an early diagnosis and that mode of life which has, as yet, not been displaced by any panacea.

With this background of sanatorium teaching, and practical experience, the intelligent patient is more or less qualified to go on with home treatment, which is merely a modified sanatorium regime, adjusted to the individual handicap.

THE ROLE OF SURGERY IN PULMONARY TUBERCULOSIS
By EDWARD D. CHURCHILL, M. D.
John Homans Professor of Surgery, Harvard Medical School
Consulting Surgeon, Rutland State Sanatorium

The term "conservative" has a dual meaning, and its use as a descriptive term in medicine is often not clearly defined. Physicians find satisfaction and a certain freedom from responsibility in clinging to what they term conservative measures. Patients like to think that they have a conservative doctor. In this sense conservative means a tendency to harbor healthy skepticism regarding new methods of treatment the dangers or lasting benefits of which may not yet be apparent. All intelligent and conscientious physicians should be conservative according to this definition.

A second, and equally significant definition of conservative measures is that they *conserve* the patient or protect him from the loss, waste and injury of disease. In this sense, all efforts of the medical profession are by definition intended as conservative.

The treatment of pulmonary tuberculosis has passed the point where a policy of inaction or postponement of active forms of treatment in the face of certain clear indications can be condoned on the grounds that it is the conservative thing to do. Collapse therapy is no longer an untried or experimental newcomer in the field of therapeutics. It is of proven value and must be employed frequently and oftentimes promptly if the physician is to be really conservative and protect his patient from further loss, injury or death from the disease.

Fortunately there are no longer two camps among those familiar with the disease and its effective treatment. The dangerous postponement of active measures of treatment when they are clearly indicated is now only a refuge for the ignorant, careless or blindly prejudiced. Under no circumstances can such folly be termed the conservative course.

If a person develops active pulmonary tuberculosis today, and becomes a resident of an up-to-date sanatorium, the chances are somewhat better than one out of two that some form of "collapse therapy" will be advised during the course of his illness. This by no means indicates that the long established method of treatment by rest in bed has been *replaced* by newer methods. Sanatorium regime is still the foundation for any form of treatment in tuberculosis. Collapse therapy is *supplementary* and *complementary* to treatment by rest, and is in no sense an *alternative* procedure.

What is "collapse therapy", when is it recommended and what is accomplished by it? In its acute pulmonary tuberculosis is a progressing infection in the lung and as such the general principles that ap to the treatment of infections anywhere in the body are applicableply

First of all, the condition of the body as a whole must be built up and powers of resistance improved so that natural defense mechanisms that tend to control and limit the disease are at their best. This is accomplished by the regime in a sanatorium where the patient is taught to cultivate physical and mental rest. The weight loss that almost invariably attends the onset of the disease is restored by a nourishing diet. These measures, particularly the bed rest, afford a certain amount of local rest to the diseased lung, by decreasing its movement. In many patients this regime alone is adequate to promote arrest and healing of the disease.

When the involvement of the lung is extensive or when the resistance of the individual is inadequate even under the most favored circumstances, it becomes necessary to provide additional rest for the diseased lung by some form of collapse therapy. The first recommendation is usually to induce an artificial pneumothorax.

A lung may be compared to an inflated rubber balloon in an airtight box. To collapse this balloon, air is injected into the box. When air is injected into the chest the lung drops away from the chest wall, becomes markedly reduced in size and its movements on respiration are restricted. A successful artificial pneumothorax frequently brings almost immediate relief from cough, hemorrhage, fever and the many other distressing symptoms of the disease. The lung may be kept collapsed by repeating the injections of air over a long period of time. The extent of the disease in the lung at the time the treatment is instituted usually determines the length of time that the lung should be kept at rest.

Not infrequently when air is first injected it will be found that the lung has become glued to the ribs by scar tissue. These adhesions form over the diseased areas and prevent retraction of just the portion of the lung that is most important to collapse. It is possible in many cases to cut these adhesions by a small operation and thereby achieve a complete collapse. If the adhesions are extensive it is not possible for an effective pneumothorax to be established and hope must be pinned on other measures.

A relatively simple operation that serves to rest and relax the lung is termed "phrenicectomy". The strongest muscle of respiration is the diaphram—a muscular partition that divides the thorax from the abdomen. It is possible to stop the motion of half of this muscle by crushing the phrenic nerve on the diseased side. This nerve is reached through a small incision just above the collar bone in the neck. This operation is extremely effective in certain cases—one danger, however, lies in the fact that too much has been expected from what is a relatively minor procedure. Its use in far advanced cases is usually disappointing.

Many patients are successful in arresting the progress and further extension of their disease but find themselves unable to repair the damage resulting from the infection. These patients find themselves in the so-called chronic stage of tuberculosis. Lung tissue has been destroyed, leaving cavities or excavations that are imbedded in scar tissue and densely adherent to the ribs. These cavities continue to discharge the tubercle bacillus so that the focus of infection remains a menace, not only to the patient but to the community. An individual at this stage may remain indefinitely under sanatorium regime without making further progress. Such a person may feel well enough to return to his work, but almost invariably suffers a relapse within a relatively short time.

Under such circumstances the problem of healing is essentially a mechanical one, and mechanical principles are utilized in the form of surgery. The ribs that form the rigid wall overlying the cavity are removed, thereby allowing the walls of the cavity to come together so that healing may take place. This operation is termed a "thoracoplasty" and is divided into stages depending on the number and length of ribs to be removed. The results of this operation have been peculiarly satisfactory and health has been restored to hundreds of patients for whom the possibility of every other form of treatment were exhausted.

The operation of thoracoplasty is rarely used during the acute progressive stages of the disease—its chief application is in the case of patients who have demonstrated an adequate resistance and have brought the extension of the disease to a halt but are unable to complete the healing process.

Although long sections may be removed from all of the ribs on one side, thoracoplasty is not a deforming operation. A former patient of mine worked for several months as a stenographer in a doctor's office. One day she was called upon to take a long dictation having to do with thoracoplasty. Although the doctor was surprised at her knowledge of the procedure, he never suspected that she herself had had the operation two years before.

From this brief description it will be seen that the introduction of collapse therapy has effected a revolution in the treatment of pulmonary tuberculosis. The course of every patient must be carefully followed and the appropriate measure or measures instituted at the opportune moment. "Every individual is as different in his disease or in his response to treatment as he is in his features and character" (Davies). The moves of the disease must be met by counter moves in therapy as a game of chess. When both lungs are involved the situation becomes doubly complex and doubly hazardous. Frequent x-ray examinations are necessary. Studies of the blood in addition to the temperature, pulse and weight, serve as an important index to the patient's resistance and the progress of the disease.

The physician and the surgeon stand shoulder to shoulder in facing certain problems. The point at issue is not surgical treatment as opposed to medical treatment, but the selection of the *proper* treatment for the individual case. The first concern is the selection of the patient who requires collapse therapy; second, the selection of the operation that is indicated; third, the choice of the proper time for its institution; fourth, making the operation safe and effective for the patient; and finally, careful supervision of the convalescence.

The efforts of the surgeon and the physician center about the welfare of the individual patient—from the standpoint of public health and the community at large the change in the treatment of the disease is vitally significant. First, a larger proportion of the patients will return to their homes with their cavities closed, thereby reducing the number of so-called "open" cases that serve to spread the disease. Second, with the seal of more complete and effective healing, repeated breakdowns will become less frequent. At the onset of each "breakdown", infection may be disseminated in the home or in the community. Third, many patients that would be forced to remain in institutions indefinitely at public expense, may be returned as useful members to their communities.

HOSPITALIZATION OF TUBERCULOSIS IN MASSACHUSETTS
By ALTON S. POPE, M. D.

Director, Division of Tuberculosis
Massachusetts Department of Public Health

Hospitalization for advanced cases of tuberculosis who could not be adequately cared for in their homes has in most places been the first step toward tuberculosis control. This, of course, did not take into consideration the fact that such patients usually were beyond the hope of permanent benefit, but did serve to remove a certain number of foci of infection from the home and community. In the past fifty years the prevention and treatment of tuberculosis have made tremendous strides, but hospitalization still remains the backbone of an effective control program.

Following Dr. Trudeau's demonstration of the possibility of successful treatment of tuberculosis at Saranac Lake, the whole trend of tuberculosis treatment was toward the mountains, and especially toward the West. High altitudes and dry climate were considered the essential features of success, and patients came to feel their only hope lay in migration to these distant and relatively expensive seats of healing. It remained for a group of Boston physicians to show that phthisis could be as effectively treated in Massachusetts as in Colorado, and thus make treatment and the possibility of cure available to every sufferer from the disease instead of the few financially able to afford it.

In view of these successful experiments at Sharon, the first State Sanatorium in the country was opened at Rutland in 1898. Here also results more than justified the hope of its founders, and treatment of tuberculosis was put on a practical and lasting foundation. From this beginning the hospitalization of tuberculosis in Massachusetts has made a steady and rapid growth until at the present time 4795 beds are available in federal, state, county, municipal and private institutions in the Commonwealth. Of these beds approximately 300 are provided for the treatment of extra-pulmonary tuberculosis, and 600 for the treatment of children. A list of the public sanatoria, together with the addresses and names of the superintendents, with rates charged, follows:

STATE SANATORIA

Name of Institution	Location	Number Of Beds	Rates Per Week	Superintendent
Rutland State Sanatorium (for adults in early and favorable stage of pulmonary tuberculosis)	Rutland	365	$7.00 to patient $10.50 to city or town	Dr. Ernest B. Emerson
Westfield State Sanatorium (for children only)	Westfield	270	$7.00 to patient, or city or town	Dr. Roy Morgan
North Reading State Sanatorium (for children only)	North Wilmington	290	$7.00 to patient, or city or town	Dr. Carl C. MacCorison
Lakeville State Sanatorium (for non-pulmonary forms of tuberculosis)	Middleborough	304	$7.00 for children (if paid by patient) $7.00 for adults (if paid by patient) $17.50 for adults (if paid by city or town)	Dr. Leon A. Alley
State Infirmary (for unsettled cases of tuberculosis)	Tewksbury	280	Free for unsettled cases	Dr. John H. Nichols

GOVERNMENT HOSPITAL

United States Veterans Hospital	Rutland Heights	472	For Veterans Bureau patients only. Apply to United States Veterans Bureau, Boston	Dr. R. L. Cook

COUNTY SANATORIA

Barnstable County Sanatorium	Pocasset (Bourne)	50	$7.00 to patient $9.10 residents—to town $28.00 non-residents	Dr. J. G. Kelley
Bristol County Sanatorium	Attleboro	60	$9.10 residents $28.00 non-residents	Dr. G. P. Smith
Essex Sanatorium	Middleton	360	$9.10 residents	Dr. O. S. Pettingill
Hampshire County Sanatorium	Haydenville (P. O. Northampton)	100	$12.00 residents $15.00 non-residents	Dr. F. E. O'Brien
Middlesex County Sanatorium	Waltham	252	$10.50 residents $28.00 non-residents	Dr. S. H. Remick
Norfolk County Sanatorium	South Braintree	138	$9.10 residents $28.00 non-residents	Dr. N. R. Pillsbury
Plymouth County Sanatorium	South Hanson	140	$9.10 residents $28.00 non-residents	Dr. B. H. Peirce
Worcester County Sanatorium	Worcester (Greendale Station)	125	$12.25 residents $25.00 non-residents	Dr. E. W. Glidden

22

MUNICIPAL HOSPITALS

Boston Sanatorium	249 River St., Mattapan	616	According to ability to pay—residents $28.80 non-residents	Dr. F. L. Bogan
Brookline Tuberculosis Hospital	Brookline	30	According to ability to pay—residents $21.00 non-residents	Miss Elizabeth A. McMahon
Cambridge Tuberculosis Hospital	Cambridge (Fresh Pond Hill)	80	According to ability to pay—residents $21.00 non-residents	Dr. S. B. Kelleher
Chicopee Tuberculosis Hospital	Chicopee Falls	25	According to ability to pay—residents	Miss Rachelle Frechette
Fall River Tuberculosis Hospital	Fall River	125	According to ability to pay—residents $25.00 non-residents	Dr. Ernest M. Morris, Health Commissioner
Burbank Hospital (Tuberculosis Ward)	Fitchburg	36	$17.50 residents and non-residents	Dr. Edwin R. Lewis
Holyoke Tuberculosis Hospital	Holyoke	18	$10.00 a week for residents	Miss Margaret G. Healey, R.N.
Lowell Isolation Hospital	Lowell	54	$15.00 residents $25.00 non-residents	Dr. J. J. McNamara, Acting Supt.
Sassaquin Sanatorium	New Bedford	116	$15.50 residents and non-residents	Dr. J. F. Brewer, Jr.
Health Dept. Hospitals (Tuberculosis Wards)	Springfield	60	$15.00 residents $21.00 non-residents	Miss Margaret St. Ledger, Acting Supervisor
Belmont Hospital (Putnam Ward)	Worcester	150	$10.00 residents $17.50 non-residents	Dr. May S. Holmes

Admission to state institutions is upon signed application from a licensed physician to the Department of Public Health. Admission to the county sanatoria is through the superintendents, with the approval of the board of health of the town of settlement. Patients are admitted to municipal sanatoria through the local boards of health. Charges for treatment at the various institutions have been indicated above. Perhaps the most farsighted provision in the Act establishing the Rutland State Sanatorium was that if a tuberculosis patient is unable to pay for his own care in a state sanatorium the board of health of the town of settlement becomes legally responsible for the cost of his treatment. Unsettled cases may be admitted to the tuberculosis division of the state infirmary without charge to either patient or town of residence. This principle has been carried through the rules for admission to all public sanatoria in the State, and has made possible the treatment of all cases needing hospitalization, regardless of social and economic status. In a disease like tuberculosis but a small proportion of patients can ever pay for the long and expensive type of treatment required, and only by making this available can the community hope to reduce the mortality from tuberculosis and limit the spread of the disease.

To stimulate the hospitalization of tuberculosis, and encourage the building of county and municipal sanatoria, the Subsidy Act was passed in 1911. This provides, in brief, that any city or town hospitalizing a bona fide case of pulmonary tuberculosis in a hospital approved by the Department of Public Health is entitled to a subsidy of $5.00 per week for such patient. The cost of the subsidy is, of course, distributed by the state tax, but the Act undoubtedly did stimulate the building of sanatoria. It furthermore makes it possible for the Department of Public Health to set minimum standards of treatment. In this way it has been possible to maintain certain requirements as to number of beds, type of buildings, equipment, medical staff and records, and to secure a certain uniformity in methods of treatment.

During the past decade, and especially within the past five years, the sanatorium treatment of tuberculosis has been greatly amplified by the extensive use of pneumothorax and other forms of collapse therapy. In 1934 fifty-five per cent of adult patients in state and county sanatoria in Massachusetts received collapse treatment in some form. What this means to the patient and its effect on the prognosis of tuberculosis is discussed in other papers in this issue. Suffice it to say here that it has greatly extended the possibilities of sanatorium treatment and has unquestionably been an important factor in bringing more patients to the sanatorium at a time when treatment offers the best chance of recovery.

Some ten or fifteen years ago the National Tuberculosis Association set a tentative goal of one bed to each annual death from tuberculosis. In Massachusetts this standard was passed some time ago when it was still very obvious that it fell far short of actual needs. At the present time there are approximately two beds for each annual death from tuberculosis in Massachusetts, and still we have a waiting list at several of our sanatoria. Paradoxical as this may seem it has continued while the death rate from pulmonary tuberculosis in Massachusetts has fallen 75 per cent since 1900. The answer lies in the steadily increasing demand for sanatorium treatment. Ten years ago it was found that some 35 per cent of all reported cases received sanatorial care. At present over 60 per cent of known cases receive hospitalization. If the death rate from tuberculosis continues to fall at the present rate it is difficult to say how much longer improved methods of case finding will bring an increasing number of patients to our sanatoria. It is, however, evident that for a long time to come its functions of treatment, of isolation of the open case and of education of the patient will maintain the sanatorium as the keystone of tuberculosis control.

DIET IN THE HOME TREATMENT OF TUBERCULOSIS
By FREDERICA L. BEINERT
Nutritionist, Division of Child Hygiene
Massachusetts Department of Public Health

The tuberculosis patient who is taking treatment at home, or who is waiting for admission to a sanatorium, or who has been discharged as an arrested case, deserves careful consideration since his problem is much more difficult to manage than that of the institutionalized patient. The importance of rest, fresh air and food in the treatment of this disease is well known, but do we realize the importance of contentment? With rest, fresh air and contentment provided for, we can expect much more from diet.

With economic pressure so marked as it is at present, it is useless to make the usual "necessary" demands in many instances. If the patient is a member of a family which is managing to eke out a barely sufficient existence, it is purely beside the point to cause extra worry and discontent by urging that he move to the country so that he may have an abundance of fresh air and sunshine. What if the home he is living in has no yard or porch? He knows that he can't possibly afford to get to the country. But, won't a little sympathetic talk on the value of rest in a room away from the family, and with fresh air and sunshine through an open window, make the patient feel more content with the fact that he's really helping himself at home even under many adverse circumstances?

Nowhere, however, does economic pressure seem so severe as in the consideration of dietary treatment. The very mention of "Special Diet" causes many a patient to shudder and remark even before hearing an outline of the diet, "Well, I know I just can't afford it."

The question of diet in tuberculosis is becoming more simplified. Because this is a "debilitating, febrile disease" with emaciation a prominent feature, the supreme effort has been made to force the patient to gain weight.

According to McLester:

"The effort is commonly made to induce the patient to gain weight at all cost; the more weight the better. Forced feeding is often the rule and marked gain of weight, even to the point of obesity, is looked on as a most satisfactory sign. This is an error. Gain in weight follows improvement, but improvement does not necessarily follow forced gain in weight. It is an obvious error always to regard obesity as an evidence of robust health."

This is a protest against the forced feeding treatment employed in the past. Lusk says, "Forced feeding is unnecessary and probably harmful. Since protein and carbohydrate increase metabolism and therefore the respiratory activity in tuberculous people to the same extent as in normal people, it is suggested that their intake be limited during periods when the disease is active in order to put the lungs at rest. The patient should be well nourished, but should maintain his body weight near the average or a few pounds only above it, instead of allowing himself to become excessively fat. The patient's weight may usually be maintained with 2500—3000 calories.

Carter, Howe, and Mason point out that among the symptoms of tuberculosis, the various disturbances of digestion rank a good second in importance as many of the incipient cases complain of gastro-intestinal symptoms such as gas, heaviness after meals, and often sour stomach. From this publication of 1921 also—"by the *older* method of stuffing the patients with food, particularly in using large amounts of milk [and eggs] the patients often develop symptoms of gastric atony. Fortunately this mistake is now (1921) more rarely seen, particularly where any sort of intelligent care has been exercised in the selection of a diet." Stoll in 1927 says, "Patients continue to be 'stuffed', nothwithstanding the fact that we have long since learned that our automobile has a much better 'pick-up' if we cut down the 'gas' to the point where combustion is most complete." "Mental inertia" is often the reason for the diet prescription—"take large quantities of milk and eggs"—a simple diet, to be sure, and one which requires no planning. But it is not a fair deal for the patient, especially when appetite and income (in many cases the principal obstacle nowadays) are considered.

The diet for the tuberculosis patient should be characterized as follows, according to McLester's classifications:

1. Ample—calories slightly more than the average requirement.
2. Well balanced with plenty of minerals, vitamins, and roughage.
3. The food should be simple, easily digested, and well prepared.
4. Plan the menu to meet individual needs.
5. Give explicit directions (for diet and rest).

The diet should be worked out with the attending physician according to the individual needs. A nutritionist in the community could help to plan the diet in relation to the budget situation of the family. The foods allowed in the tuberculosis diet are simple, and choice may be aided by the following list:

1. Milk in all forms. Not more than 1 quart a day. Given with meals, not as between-meal feedings.
2. Eggs—include in the diet. Do not feed as a diet extra. Cooked eggs are more easily digested than raw.
3. Cereals—all kinds—particularly the whole grains to provide vitamin B and bulk.
4. Fruits—all kinds—use fruit juices freely in cases complicated by anorexia.
5. Vegetables—all kinds, especially raw, green and yellow vegetables. Use freely for vitamins A, B, and C.
6. Meat or Fish—a moderate serving daily. Use beef, lamb, and liver most often.
7. Cream, butter, oils (such as cod or halibut liver oils) to provide calories and vitamin A.
8. Sugars—use small amounts to bring out flavor. Avoid concentrated sweets for they tend to spoil the appetite.

For the patient of moderate means, the following adjustments may prove helpful:

1. Use Grade B pasteurized, or canned evaporated milk.
2. Egg—four times a week.
3. Tomato juice as a substitute for citrous fruits. One serving of fruit each day.
4. One vegetable besides potato daily. Potato may be served once or twice a day. A raw vegetable—four times weekly.
5. A small serving of meat or meat substitute once a day. Cheese and legumes are good substitutes.
6. Butter at each meal. Cod or halibut liver oil. Peanut butter.
7. Brown sugar and molasses for sweets.
8. Bread with every meal—dark daily.

Save all the appetite for three regular meals. Between-meal feedings often tend to spoil the appetite, and they often upset the digestive system. Dr. Emerson of Rutland Sanatorium has shown that by changing over to a three-meal schedule, food complaints and gastro-intestinal disturbances were greatly reduced. The patients also gained weight more consistently and showed a tendency to eat more food at mealtimes.

Rest is closely related to diet insomuch as it plays such a large part in complete utilization of food in the body, so that it must be considered as a part of dietary treatment in tuberculosis. As Hawes says in his summary of diet in tuberculosis:

"A rest before and specially after each meal is essential. The dictum, 'Approach and leave each meal in a rested condition' is an extremely good one to stick to."

BIBLIOGRAPHY

CARTER, HERBERT S., HOWE, PAUL E., and MASON, HOWARD H. *Nutrition and Clinical Dietetics.* Second edition. Philadelphia: Lea and Febiger, 1921.
MCLESTER, JAMES S. *Nutrition and Diet in Health and Disease.* Second edition. Philadelphia: Saunders, 1931.
LUSK, G. *Science of Nutrition.* Fourth edition. Philadelphia: Saunders, 1928.
STOLL, H. F. "Mistakes We Make in Diagnosis and Treatment of Tuberculosis." *Boston M. and S. J.* Vol. 197, pp. 1017-1024, Dec. 1 '27.
LUSK, G. "Specific Dynamic Action" *J. Nutrition* Vol. 3, pp. 519-530, Mar. '31.
HAWES, J. B., Jr., "Diet in Tuberculosis" *J. A. M. A.* Vol. 93, pp. 452-454, Aug. 10, '29.
—— and STONE, M. J. "Progress in Tuberculosis, 1928-1929" *N. E. J. M.* Vol. 201, pp. 820-827, Oct. 24, '29.
EDITORIAL. "Vitamin D in Tuberculosis" *J. A. M. A.* Vol. 94, p. 414, Feb. 8. '30.
MAYER, E. and KUGELMASS, I. N. "Basic (vitamin) Feeding in Tuberculosis: preliminary report" *J. A. M. A.* Vol. 93, pp. 1856-1862, Dec. 14, '29.
MCCANN, W. S. "Protein Requirement in Tuberculosis" *Arch. Int. Med.*, Vol. 29, pp. 33-58, Jan. '22.
PATTEE, ALIDA FRANCES. *Practical Dietetics with Reference to Diet in Health and Disease.* Mt. Vernon, N. Y.: Author. 1931.
BOYES, G. R. and WHITE, J. S. *"Cod Liver Oil in Treatment of Tuberculosis" Brit. J. Tuberc.* Vol. 23, pp. 75-82, Apr. '29.
GILLETT, LUCY H. *"Nutrition and Tuberculosis" J. Outdoor Life,* Vol. 30, p. 9, Jan. '33.

EXTRA-PULMONARY TUBERCULOSIS

By LEON A. ALLEY, M. D.

Superintendent, Lakeville State Sanatorium
Middleboro, Mass.

As an early diagnosis in pulmonary tuberculosis is of supreme importance so is it also of great importance in any of the many and varied forms of extra-pulmonary tuberculosis.

Without an early diagnosis the opportunity for immediate treatment is lost and delay practically always means more destruction in the diseased part. Early lesions tend to heal much more quickly and with less loss of function of the part, and in the bony structures with much less deformity, than do the later more advanced lesions.

To receive the benefit of an early diagnosis the patient must not shut his eyes to symptoms that call for investigation on the part of his physician. He must cooperate to the fullest extent to make possible a diagnosis which may be most difficult or even impossible without the aid of biopsy material for laboratory study, complete and satisfactory x-rays, as well as skin and blood tests. In other words the patient must not be dissatisfied if even a few weeks may be required before the physician arrives at a definite diagnosis. The genito-urinary cases must have cystoscopic study with animal inoculation. The animal studies require from five to six weeks before they can be completed, and even then it may be necessary for the examination and guinea pig studies to be repeated.

As there is no royal road to recovery from tuberculosis and as proper treatment requires months or even years in some cases, an accurate diagnosis must be made before we subject the patient to the medical and surgical program necessary to assist nature in healing the results of the ravages of the tubercle bacilli.

Indications at this time all point to the necessity of general sanatorium treatment for any form of extra-pulmonary tuberculosis. The patient is primarily suffering from a general constitutional disease regardless of its local manifestations and no form of local treatment has thus far been devised to satisfactorily replace rest, fresh air, and the regular habits of living and diet as provided in a properly conducted sanatorium. To the above, heliotherapy, both natural and artificial, has been added and found to be of great value. Developments in the last few years in high intensity carbon arc lamps now make heliotherapy possible for the patient throughout the year. Light therapy combined with the other methods of general sanatorium treatment and surgery has resulted in a very definite shortening of the duration of sanatorium treatment in practically every type of extra-pulmonary tuberculosis. Plaster casts for adequate and complete immobilization of tuberculous bones and joints must be applied and supervised by those trained in this field of orthopedics. No one thing contributes more to stopping the progress of disease and encouraging healing in the orthopedic cases than proper immobilization by means of plaster casts.

The patient's disease, when conditions are favorable for intensive treatment, tends to stop its progress, symptoms subside and recovery begins. Surgery, in many cases, if applied at the proper time is indispensable. This is especially true in the orthopedic and genitourinary groups. Distressing and tragic results however have been noted in many cases where surgery has been used injudiciously at a time when the patient's resistance was low. Surgery used in those patients with active, progressive tuberculous disease, as in joints for example, has resulted in the wide spread of the disease in that region, as well as a definite tendency to metastasis to other parts of the body. When the vitality of tissues, or resistance, is lowered infection can lodge in and attack various tissues of the body at the same time and a terminal condition of meningitis is not rare in some of the above cases.

Months of general sanatorium treatment in preparing patients for surgery results in an excellent resistance to the disease and goes far toward insuring prompt postoperative recoveries. Fewer sinuses follow operations under these conditions and those that do form heal in a shorter time. The aspiration of tuberculous abscesses per se should be practiced faithfully and patiently as fewer sinuses follow this method of treatment than in those cases in which incision is used. The latter method of drainage in tuberculous conditions very frequently results in mixed infections of the tract and prolonged drainage and such sinuses resist healing for months and even years. The avoidance of sinuses and the early elimination of those that do form is to be desired, as the incidence of amyloid disease can then be kept at a minimum.

In those patients suffering from renal tuberculosis where early diagnosis has made possible the removal of the diseased kidney, while the opposite kidney is still apparently free from destructive disease, fairly prompt and complete recoveries may be expected. If, however, the disease has been allowed to go on until the bladder and other neighboring structures have become involved, the economic time factor and possibility of more than partial recovery become very serious. The lowered resistance of the patient incident to an extensively involved tuberculous kidney may easily result in the spread of the disease to the other kidney as well as the bladder.

Neglect of tuberculous eyes may result in irreparable loss of vision with its manifold handicaps. General sanatorium treatment produces striking improvement in most of these cases and the results are among the most satisfactory obtained in the treatment of extra-pulmonary tuberculosis.

While tuberculous adenitis may appear to be one form of tuberculosis in which the patient may feel that hospitalization for general treatment is indicated the least, the early arrest of any tuberculous lesion is important, not only for the patient's well-being and for economic reasons but also to prevent the very serious possibility of the disease spreading to other parts of the body where more vital structures may become involved. The longer the disease is permitted to smoulder in the lymphatics the greater the danger of metastasis. In every case of adenitis sufficient time should be allowed for whatever study is necessary to positively rule out non-tuberculous adenitis due to oral sepsis as well as the possibility of Hodgkin's disease. The non-tuberculous cervical adenitis cases following oral sepsis should be eliminated from the group as prolonged, intensive sanatorium treatment is unnecessary to produce recovery in these cases. The wide difference in the treatment of Hodgkin's disease and tuberculous adenitis requires no comment here.

The cause of acute, subacute, or chronic abdominal pains resulting from inflamed tuberculous mesenteric or retro-peritoneal glands can only be determined by exploratory laparotomy. There should be no hesitation in carrying out this procedure in those cases in which the diagnosis is obscure.

In those cases where active pulmonary and active extra-pulmonary lesions co-exist, patients should receive the benefit of treatment in the sanatorium best equipped for the care of the predominating lesion. Treatment for the other lesion can be carried on, but should be considered secondary to the more serious one.

The proper management of extra-pulmonary tuberculosis is a problem for the medical man and the surgeon as well as for those in specialized fields of orthopedics, urology, and ophthalmology. Oral conditions must be cared for by the carefully trained dentist. Feeding problems must be met, supervised, and corrected in malnourished adults as well as in children.

At Lakeville, group teaching, adjusted to the age and strength of the patients, makes it possible for the great majority of children to keep up with their regular schooling while in the sanatorium and upon their discharge to re-enter the grades they would normally have reached. For older patients university extension, occupational therapy and other special types of instruction, besides improving morale and relieving the tedium of sanatorium life, are of definite value in helping certain individuals to prepare themselves for suitable types of work on their return home.

TUBERCULOSIS IN CHILDREN
By Roy Morgan, M. D.
Superintendent, Westfield State Sanatorium

As usually encountered in childhood, tuberculosis may be divided into two forms; viz: the Childhood Type and the Adult Type. These two types differ greatly in most of their characteristics. These differences are due to the fact that an uninfected person reacts differently to the tubercle bacilli from a person who has been previously infected. The lesion produced by a first infection tends to absorb and to involve the regional lymph glands. The reinfection lesion does not often tend to absorb and does not involve the regional glands. The first infection produces a disease which is usually mild while reinfection produces a disease which is clinically very serious. The first-infection disease is known as the childhood type, while the reinfection disease is known as the adult type.

When a child's lung is first infected with tuberculosis, he develops an area of bronchopneumonia. This may be in any part of the lung. It is usually a small lesion but may be quite extensive. In a short time this lesion begins to resolve and the adjacent lymph glands become involved. The resolution is usually complete and requires a few months to two or three years. The absorption, however, is not complete in all cases. Sometimes there is caseation followed by fibrosis and eventually calcification. When the process is completed, the parenchyma of the lung usually appears normal and the only trace of the disease is one or more hard nodules in the lung known as primary lesions, and a few dense glands at the root of the lung.

The symptoms of childhood tuberculosis are not at all characteristic. The child may have an acute fever which could readily pass for an attack of grippe, or he may have an occasional temperature of 99 plus for awhile. Cough may be entirely absent. If present, it is usually slight and unproductive. There is little or no loss of weight though the child may fail to gain for awhile. There may be more or less malaise. There is often a change in the child's disposition. He may become dull and listless or he may be unusually nervous and irritable but in the majority of cases infection takes place without any perceptible symptoms or signs, and only the residual calcification or fibrosis is revealed when the child is x-rayed in school.

These lesions are usually so small that they give no physical signs, or if physical signs are present, they are not characteristic.

The diagnosis of the childhood form of tuberculosis offers some difficulty. The tuberculin test, if negative, is of great value in ruling out the disease. X-ray in many cases will show the presence of calcified glands or primary lesions, and in the presence of a positive tuberculin test this is sufficient to establish a diagnosis. If seen in the early infiltrative stage, there is some difficulty because the x-ray findings are not characteristic. The diagnosis in these is best established by serial x-ray and by the history. This requires some time, however, as the lesions absorb rather slowly. The diagnosis (in most cases) in the infiltrative stage may be established more quickly by injecting stomach washing into a guinea pig.

Prognosis

The immediate prognosis in childhood-type tuberculosis is very favorable. Usually the lesions are small and absorb entirely. The symptoms are slight and soon disappear, and the child is apparently as well as ever and remains well. In fact, the disease is so benign that the majority of cases pass through it without the condition being suspected. Even when the lesions are quite extensive, recovery is to be expected without leaving any traces more than a dense nodule or two at the site of the lesion, and some enlargement of the hilum lymph glands. The danger of childhood tuberculosis therefore does not lie in the immediate future, rather it lies in the fact that the child's reaction to the tubercle bacillus has been changed, and that if he is reinfected he will develop the adult form of the disease.

Treatment

If the child has fever or is in poor general condition, a period of bed treatment is advisable, otherwise only hygienic treatment is called for. The child should have regular hours with plenty of sleep, a good diet and fresh air, and it is important that his activities be curtailed. This can best be done by instituting "rest hours". He should be required to rest a few minutes before each meal and for an hour or hour and a half after dinner. These measures can usually be carried out at home provided the child has a good home, is under good discipline, and is not exposed in the home to an open case of pulmonary tuberculosis. If home conditions are poor, or discipline is unsatisfactory, sanatorium treatment is to be preferred. If there is an open case of tuberculosis in the home, the contact should be broken by removing either the adult case or the child to a sanatorium.

Adult Type

If the child after passing through this childhood type of tuberculosis be infected again, we have the adult type. Here the course is quite different. This time the lesion *may* resolve but is more prone to spread. It usually remains apparently latent for a time when there is a sudden or gradual spread of the disease. This may be followed by apparent improvement only to have a second spread later. For some time we may have these alternating remissions and exacerbations until finally the lungs are extensively diseased with cavity formation.

The symptoms, if present, of the adult-type of tuberculosis in children are, in the main, the same as in adult persons, but it is a surprising fact which should be more generally appreciated, how much disease by x-ray a child may have in his lungs with very few, if any, perceptible symptoms. Early in the disease there may be noticed a tendency toward weight becoming stationary or an actual slight loss in weight. Close questioning may also reveal an unexplained case of tiring, or actual fatigue. A ten-day temperature chart may show a slight afternoon rise in temperature. As the disease progresses, or if the involvement is rapid, symptoms make their appearance. These may be cough, expectoration, fever, chills, night sweats, frank hemorrhages from the lungs, loss of weight and chest pain. All symptoms, of course, do not make their appearance in all cases at once. On the whole, it may be said that cough, night sweats and chest pain are less common and less troublesome in children than in adults. High fever is common in exacerbation and in cavity cases.

Complications such as tuberculosis of larynx or bowels are quite rare in these cases. When present, it is almost always in the terminal stages.

The physical signs of adult-type tuberculosis are the same in the child and the adult. It should be remembered, however, that early cases usually present no physical signs, so that our real reliance is on the x-ray. The x-ray findings are the same as in adults except that in children the lesions tend to be softer, and we seldom find fibrosis or displacement of heart or trachea. Distortion of the diaphragm is also rare.

Prognosis

The prognosis of the adult-type of tuberculosis in children is extremely poor. Under treatment, in fact often with no treatment, these cases do remarkably well for a considerable period. A short period of treatment in bed in early cases will usually result in the disappearance of all symptoms and the patient will have the appearance of perfect health. Too often, however, this is deceiving, and after a few months to three or four years the disease spreads. It we use discharge figures from the sanatorium as a basis, the prognosis of adult tuberculosis in children will seem to be good. However, if an adequate follow-up is employed, allowing five to ten years observation, it will be found that the disease is extremely fatal. Our own figures from the Westfield State Sanatorium show a mortality of about 80 per cent based on five to ten-years' follow-up of cases treated by bed rest and ordinary sanatorium regime. It is to be hoped that collapse treatment will considerably alter these figures but more time is necessary to determine this point.

Prognosis varies somewhat with the extent of disease. Early cases, of course, are more favorable but even in the very early cases the prognosis is poor. They will respond well to treatment for awhile but they have a strong tendency to break down later. Sex seems to have nothing to do with prognosis.

Treatment

Treatment of adult-type tuberculosis in childhood is the same as the treatment of adult patients. In view of the low resistance during the early years of life, it is important that treatment be begun as early as possible and carried out carefully for a long period. Outside of general routine treatment, rest and collapse therapy form our only reliance at present. If bed rest alone is used, it should be continued for a long time. It is our practice to keep these cases under bed rest for a minimum of twelve months. This has given somewhat better results than we obtained by general sanatorium routine alone but the improvement has not been remarkable. Bed rest apparently gives very good results for awhile, but a great many patients will break down later in spite of prolonged treatment in bed. Many authorities recommend collapse therapy in all of these cases as soon as a diagnosis is made and this probably will be the generally accepted treatment in a few years.

As to the relation of the childhood and adult-type of pulmonary tuberculosis, two things are well established. First: the childhood type always precedes the adult type. Second: the childhood type in some ways alters the child's resistance so that a later infection will result in serious, often fatal, disease. There are two theories as to the method of reinfection. One theory holds that the childhood lesions which are apparently healed may contain living bacilli, and that these may be released in some way, thus causing an autogenous reinfection. The second theory holds that the child has been given a certain amount of protection by his first infection and that this is in fact a sort of vaccination which renders the child less liable to develop the adult type. If the adult type of disease does develop, it is because the child has been reinfected from contact with another case. At the present time, it seems impossible to prove either of these theories. A recent study of 1,000 cases from the Chadwick Clinic with positive tuberculin test and definite x-ray findings, showed that 3.5 per cent had developed the adult type in from five to nine years. Of 1,000 cases with positive tuberculin test but negative x-ray, 0.8 per cent had developed the adult type. In this age group, the average incidence of adult-type tuberculosis is 0.1 per cent. Whatever theory we hold, the figures strongly suggest that children with the childhood type are most likely to develop the adult type. Until more light can be thrown on the subject, it is better to carry on our T. B. campaign on the assumption that reinfection may occur either from within or without. That is, we should keep childhood type cases under close observation, and provide treatment where indicated. This should reduce the chance of reinfection from poorly healed lesions. At the same time the child should be protected from contact with open cases of tuberculosis.

THE SCHOOL TUBERCULOSIS CLINIC PROGRAM IN RETROSPECT AND IN PROSPECT

By HENRY D. CHADWICK, M. D.

Massachusetts Commissioner of Public Health

Dr. Eugene R. Kelley, Commissioner of Public Health, in 1924, published an article entitled "The Proposed Tuberculosis Prevention Program of the Massachusetts Department of Public Health". From this I quote:

"A new project, to be worked out on a state-wide scale and over a period of ten years is being launched in Massachusetts for the prevention of tuberculosis. The plan attacks the problem during childhood, when the disease is in the incipient, or beginning stage, and the outlook is favorable....

"This new program proposes to put into effect on a broad state-wide scale, the knowledge gained during the last twenty years as the result of continuous study, and now universally accepted by the medical profession, as to the period of life in which tuberculosis usually first gains a firm foothold.... It has been conclusively shown by the research of hundreds of workers the world over that there exist three distinct general types of the disease tuberculosis.... The first or the so-called infantile type of the disease found under two years of age is practically always in the nature of a general infection throughout the body and practically always fatal. The next type, the so-called juvenile type, found usually between five and twelve years of age, is the type or stage of the disease which shows a very low fatality. During this age period the disease is essentially one of the lymphatic glands and in the vast majority of cases is confined exclusively to these glands. The third and last is the adult type of tuberculosis. Here the disease has spread beyond the lymph glands and may attack any organ of the body and is most conspicuously found in the lungs, producing the familiar type known as consumption."

It was proposed to examine three groups: First, the children who were 10 per cent or more underweight; second, contact cases; and third, suspicious cases — children whose physical condition is considered unsatisfactory by teachers and physicians. It was calculated that 15 per cent, or 110,000 of the children then in the schools between the ages of five and twelve would come under this classification, and that over the ten-year period probably 200,000 would be examined. It was estimated that when the children were examined and checked by x-ray, about 8 per cent would show sufficient signs to justify a positive diagnosis and that these children would need to be placed under good hygienic conditions and their nutrition improved before reaching the critical period of adolescence, and that not more than one per cent of the total group selected for examination would require sanatorium treatment.

Such was the forecast made by Dr. Kelley ten years ago. The clinics were organized and examinations have been carried on in practically every city and town, in many of them twice, during the period 1924-34. After the first three years' experience, all attempts at selection were given up because it was found that tuberculosis was as frequently present in children who were average or overweight as among the underweights. The state of nutrition was not a criterion as to the presence or absence of tuberculosis and a denial of contact could not be relied upon. Therefore, children were accepted for examination regardless of weight or history of contact. The children were all given a physical examination and a tuberculin test. Later the tests were read and a roentgenogram was made of the chest of each positive reactor.

After five years this procedure was radically changed when it was realized that the examination with the stethoscope was in most instances a waste of time as but rarely did it reveal signs of tuberculosis even when present. The examination for other physical defects was in fact a duplication of the work of the school physician and could be discontinued. It was decided that thereafter the purpose of the clinics should be wholly tuberculosis case finding. The new plan consisted of first, using the tuberculin test to screen out the infected children, second, x-ray the positive reactors, and third, a physical examination of only those children whose roentgenograms showed evidence of disease. This plan had many advantages. The large clinic staff was broken up into units of one doctor and one nurse who worked together. A shorter period was necessary for the examination, and consequently the children lost less time from the classroom. The confusion resulting from large numbers of clinic personnel working at one time in a school building was avoided. The number of children who could be examined for tuberculosis by the same number of doctors was greatly increased as compared with the earlier plan. In the first five years 100,000 school children were examined and in the second five years 300,000.

When the objective is restricted to finding tuberculosis in children, the tuberculin test first, x-ray of the reactors second, and physical examination third is the most rapid and effective procedure. Dr. Kelley's estimate that 200,000 children would be examined in ten years would have been quite accurate if the plan had not been changed whereby it was possible to double this number.

The number of cases of adult type pulmonary tuberculosis found was small (261) but this was to be expected as a large proportion of the children examined were in the elementary grades. Only during the last five years were high school pupils included in the examination. The number of cases of childhood type tuberculosis found was 5,620, and in addition 12,323 others were classified as suspects. These were cases where the x-ray evidence indicated tuberculosis but was not sufficiently clear to make a definite diagnosis. Many of these children had a history of contact and being positive reactors it was desirable that they be kept under observation. All together, in these three groups, there were found 18,204 school children who were definitely tuberculous or showed some indication of tuberculosis. In other words, nearly 5 per cent of all the children examined needed definite medical supervision and some of them sanatorium care. In no other way could these handicapped children have been selected from the multitude until the disease had progressed to such a degree that symptoms made it apparent, and then we know from our experience that it would have been too late to expect favorable results from treatment.

The number of cases of adult type tuberculosis in grade school children was one in 3300, and in high school students one in 690. Where there was a history of contact the incidence of this type of disease was very much higher than in the non-contact group, but it so frequently happens that contact has occurred without obtaining a definite history of it that all children should be x-rayed who react to the tuberculin test to find whether or not there is demonstrable disease. When tuberculosis is found in a child a systematic effort should be made to find the source by making an x-ray examination of the members of the household. The number of childhood-type cases was 1.4 per cent of the whole number tested. This was much higher where there was a history of family contact. Besides the possibility of reinfection from outside sources, these children have to contend with their own focus of tuberculosis — a potential cause of subsequent disease of the more serious adult type.

Following is a tabulation of three groups of children examined in 1924 to 1927.

Group I —Negative tuberculin test; no x-ray taken.

Group II —Positive tuberculin test; x-ray negative. Because of history of contact or suspicious x-ray evidence, classified as suspects and listed for annual x-ray.
Group III—Positive tuberculin test; x-ray showing nodules or calcified nodes. Classified as childhood type and listed for annual x-ray.

Subsequent Tuberculosis History as found in February, 1933, Six to Nine Years after First Examination

	Number	Tuberculin Test	X-ray	% Developed Adult Type	% Contact
Group I	927	Negative	Not Done	0.22	11.7
Group II	405	Positive	Negative	0.74	61.0
Group III	850	Positive	Positive	3.4	39.8

From the tabulation it will be seen that the adult type of pulmonary tuberculosis developed fifteen times as often in Group III as in Group I and five times as often in Group III as in Group II. This, notwithstanding the percentage of known contacts that was nearly twice as high in Group II as in Group III. It would seem, therefore, that children with a positive tuberculin test plus a roentgenogram showing tuberculous nodules or nodes are decidedly handicapped with a condition from which subsequent pulmonary tuberculosis often develops.

Instead of calcified nodes or nodules in the lungs being an indication of healed disease that would substantially increase immunity, they are in fact a potential menace to the individual concerned; at least, that is so during the period of adolescence and young adult life. Furthermore, we may speculate that the high death rates that occur in the forties, fifties and sixties may in fact be due in some instances to a reinfection from these hidden foci of childhood tuberculosis.

Critics have stated that the actual number of cases of tuberculosis found in school surveys is too small to make such an examination worth while on account of the time consumed and the expense entailed. The answer to this argument is that in no other way can the 5 per cent of children who either have tuberculosis or indications of it be found until tubercle bacilli have made such inroads that the disease becomes manifest. Then it is unfortunately too late to do much in the way of treatment that is effective in arresting the process. Furthermore, the lectures that were given to teachers and to high school students about tuberculosis, preceding the examination, the teaching of the method of doing the tuberculin test and the interpretation of the roentgenogram to the local physicians to whom the children are referred if there is evidence of disease, must be considered the most practical form of health education. The 400,000 children who have been tested and the stration of tuberculosis case finding that will always be remembered.

Such a program carried out over ten years in all the schools in a statewide survey must have far-reaching results. The more than 18,000 tuberculous children discovered during these years will be kept under observation by the follow-up clinic physicians who will x-ray and examine them annually while they remain in school. The future of this school clinic service is assured by the transfer of the program to the county and state sanatoria. These institutions have added to their staffs so that the work may be carried on in a modified way. Instead of occasional examinations of all school children it has been decided to examine annually the pupils in the seventh, ninth and eleventh grades. By so doing three examinations will be made during the period of adolescence when tuberculosis shows its highest incidence and the adult type of the disease is more often found. It is expected that this will become routine procedure and carried on in cooperation with the school physicians.

Except for the follow-up clinic, the Ten Year Program has come to an end as a project of the State Department of Public Health. Its essential and most valuable features, however, will be continued as part of the field work of the sanatoria. This is in line with the purpose of the Department to make these institutions the centers of all tuberculosis activities in their respective areas.

CHADWICK CLINIC RESULTS
Grand Totals

	1924-1934
Enrollment of tested schools	991,113
Number given tuberculin (Von Pirquet) test	400,591
Per cent tested of school enrollment	40.0
Number of positive reactors to test	100,025
Per cent positive reactors of number tested	25.0
Number x-rayed	103,462
Number given physical examination	117,777
Number of adult type (pulmonary) cases found	261
Per cent adult type cases of number tested	0.065
	(1-1500)
Per cent adult type cases of positive reactors	0.261
	(1-380)
Number of childhood type (hilum) cases found	5,620
Per cent childhood type cases of number tested	1.40
Per cent childhood type cases of positive reactors	5.62
Number of suspect cases found	12,323
Per cent suspect cases of number tested	3.08

Note: The ratios written in parentheses above and in the tables hereafter are convenient approximations only and are not intended to be as accurate as the percentage figures they follow.

Grade and High School Groups
1930-1934

	Grade	High	Total
Enrollment of tested schools	308,765	88,198	396,963
Number given Tuberculin (Von Pirquet test)	201,725	49,925	251,650
Per cent tested of school enrollment	65.3	56.7	63.4
Number of positive reactors to test	42,016	18,640	60,656
Per cent positive reactors of number tested	20.8	37.3	24.1
Number x-rayed	43,580	18,875	62,455
Number given physical examination	11,143	3,057	14,200
Number of adult type (pulmonary) cases found	60	72	132
Per cent adult type cases of number tested	0.030	0.144	0.052
	(1-3300)	(1-690)	(1-1900)
Per cent adult type cases of positive reactors	0.143	0.386	0.218
	(1-700)	(1-260)	(1-460)
Number of childhood type (hilum) cases found	2,104	580	2,684
Per cent childhood type cases of number tested	1.04	1.16	1.07
Per cent childhood type cases of positive reactors	5.01	3.11	4.43
Number of adult type suspect cases found	56	37	93
Per cent adult type suspect cases of number tested	0.028	0.074	0.037
	(1-3600)	(1-1400)	(1-2700)
Number of childhood type suspect cases found	4,765	1,020	5,785
Per cent childhood type suspect cases of number tested	2.36	2.04	2.30

Notes: The last four years' figures only were used in compiling this table since uniform methods of examining and recording for both grade and high schools were employed during that period alone.

In this table and those following in which Childhood Type (Hilum) Cases and Chidhood Type Suspect Cases are compared in the Grade and High Schools the figures given do not show the true incidence of such childhood type involvement in the high school. Early in the Clinics there was established the policy of placing varying importance upon similar x-rays in this childhood type group according to the age and the physical and social condition of the child. Thus, a grade school pupil with childhood type disease by x-ray was definitely reported as such, while a high school pupil with a similar x-ray but with a negative physical examination and good home conditions was not necessarily so classified. Therefore, the figures given here for this group indicate in the high school a part only of the childhood type of tuberculosis as shown by x-ray.

Contact and Non-Contact Groups
1932-1934

	Contact	Non-Contact	Total
Number given tuberculin (Von Pirquet) test	2,305	116,818	119,123
Grade	1,827	90,469	92,296
High	478	26,349	26,827
Number of positive reactors to test	1,418	28,610	30,028
Grade	1,045	18,502	19,547
High	373	10,108	10,481
Per cent positive reactors of number tested	61.5	24.5	25.2
Grade	57.2	20.5	21.2
High	78.0	38.3	39.1
Number x-rayed	2,382	29,109	31,491
Grade	1,887	18,972	20,859
High	495	10,137	10,632
Number given physical examination	2,318	4,128	6,446
Grade	1,844	3,085	4,929
High	474	1,043	1,517
Number of adult type (pulmonary) cases found	16	26	42
Grade	4	9	13
High	12	17	29
Per cent adult type cases of number tested	0.694	0.022	0.035
	(1-140)	(1-4500)	(1-2900)
Grade	0.219	0.010	0.014
	(1-460)	(1-10,000)	(1-7100)
High	2.51	0.065	0.108
		(1-1500)	(1-930)
Per cent adult type cases of positive reactors	1.13	0.091	0.140
		(1-1100)	(1-710)
Grade	0.383	0.049	0.066
	(1-260)	(1-2000)	(1-1500)
High	3.21	0.168	0.277
		(1-600)	(1-360)
Number of childhood type (hilum) cases found	290	948	1,238
Grade	242	699	941
High	48	249	297
Per cent childhood type cases of number tested	12.6	0.812	1.04
		(1-120)	
Grade	13.2	0.774	1.02
		(1-130)	
High	10.0	0.945	1.11
		(1-110)	
Per cent childhood type cases of positive reactors	20.4	3.31	4.12
Grade	23.2	3.78	4.81
High	12.9	2.46	2.83
Number of adult type suspect cases found	8	31	39
Grade	4	19	23
High	4	12	16
Per cent adult type suspect cases of number tested	0.347	0.027	0.033
	(1-290)	(1-3700)	(1-3000)
Grade	0.219	0.021	0.025
	(1-460)	(1-4800)	(1-4000)
High	0.836	0.046	0.060
	(1-120)	(1-2200)	(1-1700)
Number of childhood type suspect cases found	351	1,509	1,860
Grade	296	1,185	1,481
High	55	324	379
Per cent childhood type suspect cases of number tested	15.2	1.29	1.56
Grade	16.2	1.31	1.60
High	11.5	1.23	1.41

Note: These figures are those obtained in the Clinics for nine months of the 1932-1933 school year and for the full ten months of the 1933-1934 school year.

First Five Years

	1924-1925	1925-1926	1926-1927	1927-1928	1928-1929
Enrollment of tested schools	57,483	184,091	163,411	47,626	53,260
Number given tuberculin (Von Pirquet) test	10,016	18,601	19,194	26,052	25,699
Per cent tested of school enrollment	17.4	10.1	11.7	54.8	48.3
Number of positive reactors to test	2,927	5,314	5,188	7,219	7,423
Per cent positive reactors of number tested	29.2	28.5	27.0	27.7	28.9
Number x-rayed	3,008	5,780	5,803	7,670	7,519
Number given physical examination	10,648	19,073	19,527	26,177	25,693
Number of adult type (pulmonary) cases found	31	19	29	8	11
Per cent adult type cases of number tested	0.310	0.102	0.151	0.031	0.043
	(1-320)	(1-980)	(1-660)	(1-3200)	(1-2300)
Per cent adult type cases of positive reactors	1.06	0.358	0.558	0.111	0.148
		(1-280)	(1-180)	(1-900)	(1-680)

	1924-1925	1925-1926	1926-1927	1927-1928	1928-1929
Number of childhood type (hilum) cases found	561	621	524	376	415
Per cent childhood type cases of number tested	5.61	3.33	2.73	1.44	1.61
Per cent childhood type cases of positive reactors	19.1	11.7	10.1	5.21	5.59
Number of suspect cases found	1,114	1,399	1,112	896	848
Per cent suspect cases of number tested	11.1	7.53	5.79	3.44	3.30

Notes: The Clinics for the first five years tested grade school pupils only. In the first three years of the Clinics the cases examined were from three selected groups: known contacts, underweights, and suspects referred by local physicians and school nurses. During the remaining seven years all children without selection were tested. Likewise, early in the Clinics more stress was laid on physical examination as a diagnostic procedure than later. In these facts lies the explanation of the higher percentage of disease found and the relatively greater number of physical examinations done during the first three years.

Last Five Years

	1929-1930	1930-1931	1931-1932	1932-1933	1933-1934
Enrollment of tested schools	88,279	99,472	101,455	92,080	103,956
Grade		81,509	80,695	69,321	77,240
High		17,963	20,760	22,759	26,716
Number given tuberculin (Von Pirquet) test	49,379	57,412	68,899	58,461	66,878
Grade		48,681	55,962	44,769	52,313
High		8,731	12,937	13,692	14,565
Per cent tested of school enrollment	56.0	57.8	68.0	63.5	64.8
Grade		59.7	69.4	64.7	67.8
High		48.6	62.3	60.2	54.5
Number of positive reactors to test	11,298	16,426	13,254	17,177	13,799
Grade		12,663	9,245	11,187	8,921
High		3,763	4,009	5,990	4,878
Per cent positive reactors of number tested	22.9	28.6	19.2	29.4	20.6
Grade		26.0	16.5	25.0	17.0
High		43.2	31.0	43.8	33.6
Number x-rayed	11,277	16,612	13,396	17,586	14,861
Grade		12,814	9,339	11,549	9,878
High		3,798	4,057	6,037	4,983
Number given physical examination	2,459	3,476	3,865	4,062	2,797
Grade		2,961	2,945	3,038	2,199
High		515	920	1,024	598
Number of adult type (pulmonary) cases found	31	33	55	22	22
Grade		14	32	7	7
High		19	23	15	15
Per cent adult type cases of number tested	0.063 (1-1600)	0.057 (1-1800)	0.080 (1-1200)	0.038 (1-2600)	0.033 (1-3000)
Grade		0.029 (1-3400)	0.057 (1-1800)	0.016 (1-6200)	0.013 (1-7700)
High		0.218 (1-460)	0.178 (1-560)	0.110 (1-910)	0.103 (1-970)
Per cent adult type cases of positive reactors	0.274 (1-350)	0.201 (1-500)	0.415 (1-240)	0.128 (1-780)	0.159 (1-630)
Grade		0.110 (1-910)	0.346 (1-290)	0.063 (1-1600)	0.078 (1-1300)
High		0.505 (1-200)	0.575 (1-170)	0.250 (1-400)	0.307 (1-330)
Number of childhood type (hilum) cases found	439	625	750	672	637
Grade		512	602	494	496
High		113	148	178	141
Per cent childhood type cases of number tested	0.890 (1-110)	1.09	1.09	1.15	0.953 (1-100)
Grade		1.05	1.07	1.10	0.949 (1-100)
High		1.29	1.14	1.30	0.969 (1-100)
Per cent childhood type cases of positive reactors	3.89	3.80	5.66	3.91	4.61
Grade		4.04	6.51	4.42	5.56
High		3.01	3.69	2.97	2.89
Number of adult type suspect cases found	11	20	32	25	16
Grade		13	20	17	6
High		7	12	8	10
Per cent adult type suspect cases of number tested	0.022 (1-4500)	0.035 (1-2900)	0.046 (1-2200)	0.043 (1-2300)	0.024 (1-4200)

Grade		0.027 (1-3700)	0.036 (1-2800)	0.038 (1-2600)	0.011 (1-9100)
High		0.080 (1-1200)	0.093 (1-1100)	0.058 (1-1700)	0.069 (1-1400)
Number of childhood type suspect cases found	1,065	1,654	2,086	1,469	576
Grade		1,482	1,663	1,141	479
High		172	423	328	97
Per cent childhood type suspect cases of number tested	2.16	2.88	3.03	2.51	0.862 (1-120)
Grade		3.05	2.97	2.55	0.916 (1-110)
High		1.97	3.27	2.40	0.666 (1-150)

Notes: The 1929-1930 Clinic examined 7,318 high school pupils, but separate records were not kept of them.

TUBERCULOSIS CASE-FINDING IN CHILDREN OF SCHOOL AGE
By DAVID ZACKS, M. D.
Supervisor of Tuberculosis Clinics
Massachusetts Department of Public Health

That tuberculosis can be found right in the schoolrooms of the Commonwealth, has been a startling revelation to most school authorities. How is this possible with compulsory medical inspection these many years? It is true, mortality reports convincingly show that tuberculosis kills yearly the very young and adolescents in greater numbers than any one of the common diseases of childhood. But these children who die! Are they not ill? Do they not have some symptoms that would exclude them and therefore could not possibly be a school problem at all? The answer is, nevertheless, there is tuberculosis in the schools, more particularly in the high schools. The problem is not a simple one, for there is no agent now available which will successfully immunize a child against tuberculosis as toxoid, for example, immunizes against diphtheria. The problem is complex for the reason that tuberculosis prevention at the present time is influenced so largely by such factors as poor economic and social conditions, superstitious taboos and emotionalism, an environment altogether beyond the power of medicine alone to control. The best that medicine can do and the least it should do is to discover the disease in its earliest manifestations.

The Massachusetts Department of Public Health, for the past 'ten years, has carried on an extensive case-finding survey throughout the Commonwealth. Based on the findings of this study,[1] it is possible to state the extent of the problem as follows: In children of high school age, pulmonary tuberculosis was found once in each 700 students tested or once in each 260 students sensitive to tuberculin. In children of grade school age, pulmonary tuberculosis was found once in each 3300 tested children or once in each 700 children sensitive to tuberculin. The childhood type of tuberculosis in high schools was found once in 80 students tested or once in 30 students sensitive to tuberculin. In the grade schools, the childhood-type of tuberculosis was found once in each 96 children tested or once in each 20 children sensitive to tuberculin.

These children cannot be found by the ordinary routine school inspection. The tuberculin test has to be applied in order to screen out those children who are sensitive to tuberculin and who are therefore infected with the tubercle bacillus. Tuberculin is a sterile broth cooked from tubercle bacilli and does not contain any germs, living or dead. This test, although known for many years, had fallen into disuse because, as a result of early reports of its use which seemed convincing, there spread the general belief among physicians that by the time chil-

---
[1] Studies on 201,725 Grade School and 49,925 High School students tested in the years 1930 to 1934 inclusive.

dren reached high school age, all would give a positive reaction. It is no wonder, therefore, that the test was not generally used as a diagnostic aid. But all children do not react positively to tuberculin! In Massachusetts, for instance, only one out of every four was found to give a positive reaction by the von Pirquet method of applying tuberculin.[4] If, to the tuberculin test, is added the x-ray, we have a highly efficient method whereby almost all discoverable tuberculosis of the lungs can be brought to light.

Tuberculin testing and x-raying the positive reactors in Massachusetts was initiated by the State Department of Public Health in 1924. The first year about 17 per cent of parents gave their consent for the test. In 1934 over 60 per cent of parents requested the examination. In every city, every town, every village in the state, not once but several times was the testing carried out.

Preceding the actual testing there was an educational campaign. Talks were given to groups of physicians, school and public health nurses, teachers, parent-teacher groups and clubs. There were announcements in churches and notices in newspapers. The "consent blanks" which the parents were asked to sign explained the significance of the tuberculin reaction and the value of the x-ray. By this means the purpose of the clinics was made clear to parents and the high school students. The demand for the clinics increased from year to year. The occasional critic quickly became silent. To the family physician, without whose cooperation the work could not be carried out, was demonstrated again and again the mute evidence of the x-ray shadows of unsuspected tuberculosis in adolescents who were presumably well and who gave no symptoms and who had no signs in the chest. Dispensary physicians who had never used the tuberculin-x-ray method for the detection of early tuberculosis gradually adopted the method as routine. It is by far more reliable than the physical examination of the underweight and physically inferior child; a method which often will label a child as tuberculous who does not have pulmonary tuberculosis at all and will miss nearly all of the really early cases. The few that are found by the physical examination are as a rule too far advanced to respond favorably to treatment.

Some have said that the cost of the tuberculin-x-ray method is too great for the comparatively small catch in this far-spread net. The cost in Massachusetts has been approximately $1.50 per child tested. If it is desirable to find pulmonary tuberculosis early there is no other method as satisfactory as this one. The cost is negligible compared with the cost of waiting for the adolescent to develop far advanced tuberculosis, infecting others in the process, and requiring far more costly treatment, which, in most instances, unfortunately proves useless. Frequently, too, unknown "contact" children are discovered by this method.

By means of the tuberculin test the children are immediately separated into two groups. Those who are sensitive to tuberculin "react" to the test and those who are not infected with the tubercle bacillus are "negative" to tuberculin. We have not been concerned with the negative children, except that for the past two years (1932 to 1934) all of the definitely known "contact" children were x-rayed and placed under observation, regardless of the reaction. With this exception it has been the routine to x-ray only the tuberculin-tested children. When that is done, these children fall into one of three groups:

    Group 1—Tuberculin sensitive, x-ray positive group.
        (a) Childhood-type tuberculosis
        (b) Adult-type tuberculosis.

---

[3] Studies on 400,591 tested children throughout the Commonwealth for the years 1924 to 1934 inclusive.

Group 2—Tuberculin sensitive, x-ray negative group.
Group 3—Non-tuberculous lesions, acute or chronic.

The x-ray appearance of changes in the lung in the childhood-type of tuberculosis is usually small, round, opaque nodules containing calcium. The nearby lymph nodes along the root of the lung and along the bronchi are also involved, and, in white children of school age, usually also calcified. These nodes are really the resting places of tubercle bacilli. They cause at this stage no visible disturbances in the body and therefore no symptoms or signs can be recognized by ordinary physical examinations of the chest. Nevertheless, these should be recognized as early phases of tuberculosis or as preparers for the later development of the destructive type of tuberculosis.

In a much smaller number of children in this group the x-ray shadow may be soft, homogeneous, and usually triangular with the base of the triangle toward the periphery of the lung. Its location is occasionally apical, but more often basal. Usually, however, the shadow of the lesion is in an interspace or two below the clavicle. In such cases the x-ray should be repeated within a month. By this time it may be found that the shadow has disappeared entirely and was due in all probability to some "acute infection" in the chest. A story of an acute "cold" sometime before the taking of the x-ray is usually obtained in these cases. This type of transient shadow will occur often enough to be a real stumbling block, and a diagnosis of tuberculosis should not be made on a single x-ray. If, on the other hand, the shadow is found to persist, the lesion is usually tuberculosis, the exact nature of which, whether childhood-type or the more serious adult-type, only the future and serial x-ray study will determine. Whatever the decision ultimately will be, bed treatment should be instituted at once. The apical fan-like shadows are almost always re-infection tuberculosis of the adult type. These will in most instances progress either slowly or rapidly and are on the whole dangerous lesions. The basal shadows are usually non-tuberculous, are almost always accompanied by a loose cough and expectoration and many râles are easily found on physical examination. Paradoxical as it may seem, when a school child coughs and expectorates a good deal, the condition is almost always non-tuberculous. It is not necessary to add that these children should be examined and a search made for the cause of this infection which is also likely to be chronic.

All agree that the adult-type of tuberculosis and the infiltrative childhood-type of lesion should be removed from school as they may be open cases and dangerous to the other children. Furthermore, these children are in need of the most careful treatment, preferably at a sanatorium. They need treatment even when they do not present a single symptom, feel well, and do not have any signs in the chest other than the x-ray evidence. It is often difficult and at times impossible to convince parents and even the family physicians, that these children who seem to be so well are really in need of sanatorium care. However, time has proven again and again the wisdom of this recommendation.

What is the significance of the calcified type of childhood tuberculosis? Conflicting statements have been made, perhaps too hastily, regarding children with the calcified type of childhood tuberculosis. Some say that the calcified lesions are of no significance except when they are unusually large or numerous and no further attention need be given to them. Others would place all of the tuberculin-sensitive children under observation with a yearly x-ray examination at least. As a result of the study in Massachusetts for the past ten years, data has been accumulated for the tuberculin-positive x-ray-positive children and the tuberculin-positive x-ray-negative children. This data, when fully analyzed, will be reported. It is my impression that re-infection tuberculosis of the adult-type has developed in a much greater proportion in the tuberculin-positive x-ray-positive group. Only rarely is pulmonary tuberculosis found to develop in the tuberculin negative group. As it is impossible with any degree of certainty to determine in advance those children who will ultimately develop pulmonary tuberculosis, it is desirable that all of the positive reactors be x-rayed at least three times during their school life.

What shall be our recommendation for the children who are found to have tuberculosis? I have already stressed exclusion from school and sanatorium treatment for those with adult-type dangerous lesions and the infiltrative lesions of the childhood type. For the children with tracheobronchial calcified type of lesions, our procedure is as follows:

A physical examination is made, not so much for the physical signs that may be found as for the opportunity of meeting the parents who are invited to be present. The recommendation finally made will depend partly upon the history, social, economic as well as medical, and partly on the general physical condition of the child. If the child is in poor general condition and a good regimen to correct this cannot be expected in the home, especially if there is a source of further infection there, a report is made to the local board of health and preventorium treatment is recommended for the child. If, on the other hand, the child's general condition is good, the home satisfactory, and if, moreover, no evidence of pulmonary tuberculosis is found in other members of the family, sanatorium treatment is not, as a rule, necessary. Instruction is given, however, regarding rest and diet by a nutritionist. All of these children are given a yearly checkup examination which includes a routine x-ray.

Theoretically, it is sound advice that children with the tracheobronchial type of lesion, particularly if they are also contacts, should refrain from gymnasium exercises and especially competitive sports. It is also desirable that they be given special periods of rest and extra nutrition. Practically, such advice is very rarely heeded and often resented by the high school group. No child wants to be singled out and set apart in school as physically inferior. He does not like his fellows to think that he is "different." In this sensitiveness there is a challenge to any health program that may be undertaken with any special group in the schools. For this reason, it is not wise to single out any group such as contacts or underweights for examination. Either all children should be tested or all of the children of certain designated grades. Then, again, although an urgent need exists, the schools of the Commonwealth in most instances are not equipped for the special care that may be necessary for this group of children in "open air rooms" or "open window rooms" where rest periods and hot lunches are provided in restful surroundings. At present the majority of the children with the calcified type of childhood tuberculosis remain in school under no special regimen except for a yearly checkup examination by the State Follow-Up Clinic. In these re-examinations, if a child is not doing well and remains physically below standard, a period of prophylactic treatment either at Westfield or at North Reading State Sanatorium is usually recommended.

SUMMER HEALTH CAMPS
By Frank Kiernan
Executive Secretary
Massachusetts Tuberculosis League

The Summer Health Camp in Massachusetts, as in many other states, has apparently become a permanent feature of the programs of tuberculosis associations. It should be said at the beginning that the summer health camp for contact children is a step in the direction of preventorium care. There is no question but that the ideal treatment for these children is an extended stay at a preventorium until their condition is such that there is a reasonable presumption that their resistance against adult-type tuberculosis has been built up to the point of maximum defense.

In any serious undertaking of this sort there is a philosophy either expressed or inchoate. The philosophy of the summer camp and its big brother, the preventorium, is that if you take children who have been infected with tuberculosis and place them in an environment designed to augment their strength and resistance, and if you surround them in this environment with adequate supervision, a scientifically devised nutrition program, an abundance of rest and moderate recreation, and if, after the children return to their homes, there is a careful follow-up both with the families and through the schools, the children will be given the maximum protection against the subsequent development of phthisis. The whole summer health camp project was entered into in this belief. Ten years' experience has apparently justified this underlying premise.

In Massachusetts there are eighteen summer health camps in which the tuberculosis associations play an active part. In most instances they are owned and operated by the local tuberculosis associations. In some instances they are owned by the county governments and operated by the tuberculosis sanatoria. There are other combinations in individual instances but in connection with all of the camps the tuberculosis associations play an important part in the selection of the children and in the follow-up.

Let us look at the sequence of events in any year in connection with the summer health camp. In February or in March the tuberculosis associations begin their preparations for the camp. These preparations include notification of the school physicians, community and school nurses in the area served by the camp that it will be operated as usual in the coming July and August. With the notification there is sent a list of specifications by which the children are to be selected. These include a statement of the classification of the children according to a plan devised by Dr. Henry D. Chadwick, State Commissioner of Public Health, and promulgated by the Massachusetts Tuberculosis League. The school physicians and nurses are urged to make up their lists if possible from contact children. Children recommended for camp care by the Chadwick Clinics are also placed on the list.

Arrangements are then made with the local tuberculosis sanatorium or with the state sanatorium in the area so that the children recommended are given a von Pirquet test, an x-ray and physical examination. The final selection of the group of children for the camp is generally left in the hands of the superintendent of the tuberculosis sanatorium.

After the list of eligible children has been made up the families are notified and specific directions sent to the parents. Here is the way one association in 1934 notified the parents of the fact that their child was going to the summer health camp.

Notice to Parents

We are very glad that your daughter is coming to our Health Camp at Sterling. We will take extra good care of her and do everything we can to make her happy and healthy.

We want the children to receive all possible benefits from the sun and to have a good time, so they wear few clothes during the day and we provide them. You will need to send only:

1 comb	2 pair of socks
1 toothbrush	An old winter coat
1 large tube of tooth paste	A hat for church
1 pair of play shoes	2 pair of pajamas with full name
1 pair of rubbers	written on them

The best children's specialists in Worcester visit camp every day to see the children. Counsellors, who are college girls trained in the care of children, will be with the children day and night.

You may telephone to us at any time (Sterling 88-4) and if your child is not sleeping or away on a walk with her counsellor, we will gladly call her to the phone.

Do come out to see us on visiting days because we will have something very special plannned for you. We want to see you and tell you how well all the children are and what they are doing and learning. Because of the danger of contagious diseases, we cannot have visitors under the age of 18 years. Please plan, if possible, not to bring any children. Please bring stamps, writing paper, "funnies," crayons, pencils or books. Things to eat make the children sick because we always have plenty to eat three times a day and their stomachs get too full if we are not careful. We shall look forward to seeing you on the visiting days listed below.

Visiting Days	Camp Opens	Camp Closes
July 22nd—3 to 5 p. m.	July 5th	August 2nd
August 19th—3 to 5 p. m.	August 3rd	August 31st

Enclosed please find a letter for your daughter.

Sincerely yours,
(Signed) M. ELEANOR HANSON, R.N.
Camp Director.

Meanwhile preliminary preparations are going on at the camp itself in the way of repairs, repainting of beds, overhauling of kitchens, examination of water supply, installation of new equipment and other items necessary to have the camp completely ready for the opening day.

If the camp is not located on the grounds of a county sanatorium, arrangements are made with a local physician for médical service. All the camps are supplied with a registered nurse. In many instances there is an additional nurse on the staff.

The task of selecting counsellors is an important and difficult one. The camp directors must be cautious to select counsellors who will not cause the children to indulge in exercises beyond their strength. At the same time the counsellors must be trained and equipped to keep the children happily engaged in recreational activities. For the most part, the counsellors at the camps are school teachers or students of schools of physical education. There are few men employed as counsellors at the summer health camps in this state.

The physical equipment of the camps is in the main composed of permanent buildings. At some of the camps the development has been upon a plan extending over a period of years. Thus at Norfolk county the camp, which is on the grounds of the Norfolk County Hospital, has developed from the tent stage in 1922 to a group of permanent buildings with a swimming pool and other recreational equipment in 1934 and caring for one hundred boys and girls.

While there are some slight local variations the camp programs in the main follow the following schedule:

A.M.
Rising bell 7:00
Setting-up exercises 7:20
Flag-raising exercises 7:30
Breakfast 7:40
Chores ....8:00— 9:00
Supervised play and craft work ....9:00—10:30
Special classes 10:30
Swimming 10.45
Rest ....11:15—12:20

P.M.
Dinner	12:30— 1:00
Rest in bed	1:15— 3:00
Handicrafts and games	3:15— 5:00
Supper	5:30— 6:00
Story hour and camp fire	6:30— 8:00
All in bed	8:00

This schedule it will be noted calls for thirteen hours rest in bed. Of these hours, two are given over to a rest period after dinner. In some camps the custom has grown up of a rest period of one-half to three-quarters of an hour preceding dinner and supper. The camp directors and counsellors are careful to plan their activities so that the children are in bed for the night at 8:00 o'clock in order that they may have eleven hours of unbroken rest.

In the camp of the Southern Middlesex Health Association an experiment is now in progress by which the camp children, numbering one hundred and ten, are divided into two groups, viz., the group that is capable of carrying the whole activities' program and the second group which, according to the recommendations of the physician who selects the children, is given a modified program of activities.

Over the years there is a manifest tendency which seems to be altogether salutary to make the camp regimen more quiet. To this end such games as baseball, volley ball and running races are being gradually eliminated. Swimming also is carried on under the strictest regulations. Counsellors have charge of small groups of children and go into the water with them.

Gains in weight, which at the beginning of the camps ten years ago seemed to be one of the main objectives, have in recent years assumed a minor place. Careful records of the weights of the children are kept from the day of their arrival at camp, but no effort is made in the case of any individual child to strive for anything more than normal increase.

The camp records themselves are carefully kept and show the reason for selection of the child, number of other children in the family, sanatorium care of other members of the family, progress in camp and recommendations of the visiting physician.

In all of the camps provision is made for immediate isolation of children who develop signs of illness. Any child with a temperature above normal or other symptoms is immediately put to bed and kept there until released by the physician. Accidents at the camps have been few. With trained nurses always in attendance, with physicians on call, and with the counsellors sensitive to the physical condition of their charges, the hazards are kept at a minimum.

Eight weeks' camp care is given in most instances. Anything less does not meet with the approval of either this League or the State Department of Public Health. Because of local conditions it is in some instances impossible to conduct the camp for both sexes for two months. A compromise is therefore worked out in which a group of boys is taken for the month of July and a group of girls for the month of August or vice versa. Whatever the local difficulties which prevent the operation of the camp for eight weeks for the same group of children, those in charge are endeavoring so to arrange matters that they will be able to care for one group for the entire season.

One of the interesting developments in camp administration is the gradual reduction of the number of visiting days. The camps which have been working at this problem for some years now have but one visiting day for parents in July and one in August. Children under eighteen are not permitted to go into the camps at any time. When parents bring children whom they cannot leave at home the children are segregated at a distance from the camp under supervision.

Dr. Frederick T. Lord, president of the Massachusetts Tuberculosis League, once said, "A camp is as good as its follow-up." Certainly there would be very little justification for all the time and effort and money expended in connection with the summer health camp project if the gains made at the time of the camp were not conserved by adequate supervision through the winter. Those in charge of the camps are conscious of the importance of this fact and are striving to secure a camp follow-up which will be completely satisfactory. There is some division of opinion as to whether a more effective follow-up can be carried on through local nurses or by the associations themselves. There are good arguments on both sides. There is, however, no argument as to the desirability of the follow-up and in the judgment of this writer the best follow-up is really a combination of follow-up by the local association's nurse in conjunction with the local school or community nurses.

From time to time the question has been raised as to whether the camps are justified. No one has yet, so far as I know, given a complete answer.

The camp, like the school, like the church, and like many other community enterprises, is based on faith. The dogma of this faith would probably read as follows: If you place children under the proper environment, instruct them in hygiene and health habits, supervise their living for two months, inspire them with the desire to conserve the precious asset of health and supervise them as closely as possible after they have returned to their homes, you have done a valuable thing in the building up of the child's resistance. Also it must be remembered that not only the physical child who has been selected because of the fact that he is a contact but "the whole child" has been under the influence of the camp director and counsellors for a period of not less than one month. This close association, both by example and direct teaching, has given the child training in fair play, in manual work, in swimming and in self control. Then there are gains in ways that are somewhat intangible. Camp directors are unanimous in their opinion that the children make progress in mental agility, initiative, love of the outdoors, understanding of the value of health, refinement and love of the beautiful. All of our camps also have religious services each Sunday.

Ten years' experience with the summer health camps has convinced me that while we cannot scientifically prove that the camps prevent tuberculosis we do know that they send the children back to their homes better physically, mentally and spiritually. It is with a knowledge of these things that we face the future more determined than ever to build the camps for a larger usefulness in the years to come.

MEDICAL SUPERVISION OF HEALTH CAMPS
By CARL C. MACCORISON, M. D.
Superintendent, North Reading State Sanatorium

Within the last fifteen years, twenty-two health camps have been built in Massachusetts, and a large amount of money spent yearly in health camp projects. Recently doubt has been expressed by some physicians and others as to whether this expenditure of money, time and energy is justified, from the standpoint of tuberculosis prevention. Probably a categorical answer to this question is not possible, but the study made this past year by a subcommittee of the Massachusetts Tuberculosis League relative to the operation of the summer health camps conducted by the affiliated organizations of the League strongly recommends the continuance of the camps, inasmuch as they "fill a definite community health need."

This committee also reports that "Inasmuch as the camps are organized, and to a great extent supported, through Seal Sale money, there is need of a set of minimum standards, which will recognize that they are primarily set up in the interest of the prevention of tuberculosis."

In all probability, the criticism directed toward the health camps has been due in large part to the lax method of selecting applicants, and for the medical care and supervision of these children once they are admitted to the camp. This is not in itself criticism of the camp idea, and those of us who are so deeply interested in tuberculosis prevention and the work being done in our health camps and preventoria, should make every effort to improve our methods and insist on close, discriminating supervision of the children in our charge.

The requirements for admission to the health camps should be rigid, and the following recommendations for selection of children, as approved by the Massachusetts Tuberculosis League, strictly adhered to:

"1. Children positive to tuberculin and with x-ray evidence of the childhood type of tuberculosis.
Only those with inactive and inextensive lesions are suitable for admission to summer health camps.
Children with evidence of activity are in need of sanatorium care or its equivalent and should not be admitted to summer health camps.

"2. Children, with or without known exposure to tuberculosis, suspected of the childhood type of tuberculosis with a reaction to tuberculin and suspicious x-ray findings.

"3. Children exposed to the disease and reacting to tuberculin but with negative x-ray findings.

"4. Reactors who have definite malnutrition."

There may be instances, however, where a nonreactor, who is a contact and malnourished, should be given consideration provided beds a e not needed for these children, who would fall under groups 1, 2 and 3.

Once having selected the proper children for the camp, our responsibilities have just begun. Each applicant should be Schick tested, and if susceptible to diphtheria, immunized at once. Immunization against smallpox should be a prerequisite for admission, and the Dick test, followed by immunization of susceptibles to scarlet fever is desirable. Every effort should be made to have all physical defects corrected in order that the child may receive the maximum benefit from the eight weeks' treatment.

At the time of admission, a careful check up should be made to see if the child has been recently exposed to any contagious disease, and on arriving at the camp, the camp physician should carefully inspect each child to note if he has a contagious condition of the skin or some other condition that would make it inadvisable for him to be admitted at that time.

The medical supervision in these camps not located on the grounds of a sanatorium should be in the hands of a competent resident nurse and arrangements should be made for a daily call by a physician, and this physician should be subject to call at any hour of the day or night.

Every camp should be provided with an infirmary, where the sick child can be isolated and properly treated. There should be a daily inspection of all children by the nurse in charge. This inspection should include examination of the throat, and skin of the chest and extremities. All questionable cases should be referred to the physician immediately and, if possible, admitted to the infirmary awaiting his arrival.

All children should have their temperature taken at least once a day, preferably in the late afternoon.

At the camp of the Southern Middlesex Health Association we have found it a distinct advantage to the child to group the little patients into two or more classes with further modification, if necessary, depending on their physical condition. This grouping should be influenced by the general physical condition of the patient, the degree of malnutrition, the presence of a very severe reaction to tuberculin, somewhat extensive evidence of pathology, as revealed by the x-ray, complications such as cardiac lesions, and possibly a very recent intimate contact with an open case of tuberculosis. We must constantly bear in mind that we are engaged in tuberculosis prevention, and that we are dealing with children who show evidence of infection. We should all agree that rest, not exercise, is our most valuable aid in dealing with this type of case.

All health camp programs should be submitted to a competent physician, preferably one familiar with the childhood type of tuberculosis, for his approval before they are adopted by the camp directors. Rest should be insisted upon before meals and there should be a rest period of from one and one-half hours to two hours after dinner. All children, thirteen years or under, should be in bed by eight o'clock and the older children by nine.

The diet should be carefully balanced and the planning be left to a person with some training in dietetics. Following is an outline of the dietary, which I believe should be followed:

At least one quart of milk daily as a drink per patient.
Potatoes once or twice every day with two other vegetables, one to be eaten green or raw; such as cabbage, carrots, lettuce, tomatoes, or uncooked sauerkraut.
Fruit twice a day, one of these raw.
One serving of whole grain cereal.
Whole grain bread.
One egg daily, if possible, or at least three or four times a week.
Meat or fish not more than once a day.
Dried beans, peas or lentils once or twice a week.
Butter and other fats; such as salt pork, lard or lard substitutes.
Sugar or molasses — two or three teaspoonfuls daily on or in food.
The hearty meal of the day should be at noon.

During the two months' period of treatment, visits of parents, relatives and friends should be restricted to those days set aside by the camp directors. On these visits every effort should be made to interest the parents in tuberculosis prevention, child hygiene and dietetics. This can be done by group teaching and has been successfully carried out for some time at the Prendergast Preventorium.

I believe that all camp activities should be confined to the close vicinity of the camp and the little patients should not be allowed to come in contact with outside children under the age of sixteen years. Every effort should be made to teach the children good health habits so that they may know how best to live under the home environment to which they must return.

To make either a summer health camp or sanatorium successful, we must have an efficient follow-up system. This work is the responsibility of the local nurse, but where a local nurse cannot be provided, or the follow-up not properly carried out, it should be taken over by the field worker of the organization supporting the camp.

TEACHING THE ETIOLOGY OF TUBERCULOSIS
By Howard J. Leahy, A. M.
Instructor of Science, Natick High School

Following the death of a friend some four or five years ago, a notice appeared in the local papers announcing the fact that Mr. B— had passed away Thursday as the result of a long, lingering illness. To those who knew that death had been due to tuberculosis, such a vague, secretive announcement appeared peculiar. Immediately this question arose — Why are deaths caused by pneumonia, appendicitis, arthritis, and the like entitled to any more open publicity than those caused by tuberculosis. However, further inquiry among friends and associates revealed that society, for no logical reason at all, has been accustomed to attach a stigma to victims of the so-called "dreaded diseases", for generations.

Several years ago a tuberculosis clinic was held at the high school at which I happened to be teaching. At this time, all students suspected of being infected with tuberculosis were given the tuberculin test. To their fellow classmates they were known as "T. B.'s" who were to be feared and watched with caution. Very few understood the real significance of the test and merely looked upon its victims as harborers of a fatal disease-producing spirit.

Future informal chats with the youths brought to light the fact that it was difficult for the "T. B.'s" to live down the unfortunate stigma. Here, I thought, was an excellent opportunity for some real constructive teaching concerning the causes, means of preventing, and methods of treating tuberculosis.

While fingering the pages of various physiology and health books I came upon a small compact pamphlet that had been presented to me by Miss Anna J. Foley, Executive Secretary of the Plymouth County Health Association. It was entitled "A Suggested Teaching Unit on Tuberculosis and Its Prevention", and had been devised by Miss Jean V. Latimer, Educational Secretary of the Massachusetts Tuberculosis League.

At first I looked upon the unit as just another teaching device designed to make life easier for the teacher. But, it was decided finally to give the suggestions a try in our biology classes at Bridgewater High School. Approximately eight weeks were spent in a detailed consideration of all that we could find about the disease itself, and those men and women who had devoted their lives to its conquest.

The response of the students was most surprising, for they seemed to take hold with more gusto than is customary when studying some remote biological or physiological phenomena. At their request, members of the class held informal debates and gave organized talks on the lives of Koch, Pasteur, Trudeau and others. The stimulating new ideas that they acquired in the classroom were carried home to the family where traditional misconceptions about tuberculosis were aired at the dinner table, in the parlor, and attacked by the young, aspiring scientists. Several boys told me that they had succeeded in convincing their elders that the disease was not inherited and could be prevented by appropriate measures undertaken at the proper time.

Others reported that fathers, mothers, brothers, and sisters spent many interesting minutes perusing the contents of such pamphlets as "The Common Cold", "The Tuberculin Test", "Tuberculosis and Its Relation to Public Health", "What is Tuberculosis", etc., that were taken home for an evening's study.

We succeeded in making the study of tuberculosis such a vital part of their lives that the conversation at lunch period, at school dances, and on the street, oftentimes turned to the topic. In other words, the classes became health conscious, particularly in regard to something that was formerly regarded with a certain amount of fear and misunderstanding.

The initial success achieved with the teaching unit prompted its use a second year with a few minor changes in method of approach. The reactions of the pupils were more stimulating than in the previous year.

These youngsters were experimentalists at heart. They wanted to actually demonstrate how diet could influence body health. Consequently, at their own expense several sets of white mice were procured and they tried out different kinds of diets on the animal subjects. Incidentally, the results of these preliminary studies suggested the projection of a large biological exhibit in June, 1934, covering all fields of the subject for the benefit of parents, friends, and other science teachers and students. In this way, we were able to show what one small school was doing to aid in the dissemination of proper knowledge regarding tuberculosis and other pertinent subjects. They came, they saw, and they gave satisfactory evidence of their intention to carry out similar plans in their own schools.

Today, with our movie projectors, opaque projectors, and microprojectors at Natick High School we can give a more enlightened course in "Tuberculosis and Its Prevention." We can show slides of actual tubercle bacilli, movies of sanatoriums, and pictures from a wide variety of texts illustrating other means of combating the disease.

It is to the late superintendent, Clifton C. Putney of Bridgewater and the present principal Meredith G. Williams of the high school there that I owe thanks for the faith they expressed in this new teaching unit for allowing me so much freedom in the planning of my routine. My progress at Natick High should be just as successful, for Superintendent Clifford R. Hall, and Principal Roy W. Hill are all keyed up to the situation and ready to assist in any way possible.

In conclusion, let me say that the teaching of the elements of tuberculosis prevention can be made of vital interest to high school students and that Miss Latimer's unit for secondary schools on "Tuberculosis and Its Prevention" has proved a most satisfactory guide in the development of such a plan.

POLICIES AND ROUTINES FOR A TUBERCULOSIS NURSING SERVICE

By HELEN C. REILLY, R. N.

Consultant in Tuberculosis Public Health Nursing
Massachusetts Department of Public Health

In tuberculosis as in diabetes success in treatment and prevention depends to a large entent upon a sound understanding by the patient of his own disease. Such understanding is seldom attained without thorough, sympathetic instruction of the individual over a considerable period of time. Obviously few physicians can spare the time required for that kind of teaching, and as a contact agent between doctor and patient the public health nurse holds a unique position in the campaign against tuberculosis. This is true in any capacity in which she may be employed whether in child hygiene, industry, bedside nursing, or board of health work. Results are attained when the public health nurse integrates her efforts with those of private physicians, local boards of health, schools, nursing organizations, social workers, industries, local hospitals, sanatoria, and life insurance companies. Generalization in nursing programs may be as ineffective as mass methods in dealing with patients, and a fundamental study of the individual community should be the basis for the development of any tuberculosis public health nursing program. The following outline may, however, be of some assistance as a guide in principles and details:*

I. Objectives

The following objectives in a public health nursing tuberculosis service are those prepared by the Committee on Field Studies and Ad-

---

*Acknowledgment is made to the National Organization for Public Health Nursing and New York University for certain material used in this paper.

ministrative Practice of the National Organization for Public Health Nursing.
1. To assist in finding all cases of tuberculosis and all contacts.
2. To assist in arranging for medical supervision and early diagnosis.
3. To assist in the securing of complete reporting of all cases of tuberculosis.
4. To secure and supervise nursing care in the homes.
5. To assist in securing institutional care.
6. To teach personal hygiene to the patient.
7. To secure examination, provide continuous supervision and teach personal hygiene to all contacts.
8. To assist in providing postsanatorium care and supervision.
9. To assist in providing the means of rehabilitation.

II. Essential Information Regarding Community

1. Tuberculosis situation in town:
    (a) Number of reported cases of tuberculosis
    (b) Number of reported deaths from tuberculosis.
2. Facilities for diagnosis of adults and children:
    (a) Clinics—location, days, hours.
3. Facilities for treatment; location and method of admission:
    (a) State and county sanatoria available for care of patients, pulmonary and other forms
    (b) Institutional and others means for rehabilitation.
4. Facilities for preventive treatment:
    (a) Summer health camps
    (b) Rest classes.
5. Cooperating agencies:
    Official and nonofficial agencies through which cooperation may be secured; i. e., municipal departments of health, education, and welfare, local and county seal sale committees, Red Cross chapters, visiting nurse associations, United States Veterans' Bureau, social workers, etc.
6. General information:
    State and local regulations for control of tuberculosis:
    (a) Care of nonsettled patients
    (b) Provision for supplies
    (c) Relief measures in general.
    State and local programs.
    Agencies distributing authentic literature.

Much of the above information may be secured through the local and state departments of health or the county health association.

The Massachusetts Department of Public Health distributes a helpful "Directory of Massachusetts Sanatoria for Tuberculosis" which contains a list of sanatoria in Massachusetts and information relative to location and cost per patient. "Home Care of Tuberculosis Patients" is another helpful abstract and is suitable for patients. Both of these may be secured by writing to the Division of Tuberculosis of the Massachusetts Department of Public Health.

III. Procedure to Secure Initial List of Cases

1. Secure list of reported cases from local board of health.
2. Secure list of deaths from all forms of tuberculosis from town clerk.
3. Secure list of tuberculosis cases and deaths from State Department of Public Health. Where a new service is being initiated a list of cases, and deaths for a five-year period should be obtained.
4. Sort cases and deaths according to physician who reported case or signed death certificate.

5. Visit each physician to obtain information regarding patient and approval to visit. Ascertain his wishes regarding instruction to be given.

6. Ask physician for names of other patients and contacts of deceased tuberculosis patients in need of follow-up.

IV. Case Finding

Diagnosis is the responsibility of the physician but the nurse is in an advantageous position to locate suspicious cases and contacts; her alertness to symptoms will mean earlier medical care. The following symptoms are suggestive and indicate investigation:

(a) Lassitude
 Loss of energy
(b) Weakness
(c) Cough
(d) Expectoration
(e) Loss of weight
(f) Loss of appetite
(g) Indigestion
(h) Night sweats
(i) Hemoptysis, either frank or streaking
(j) Pain in chest especially when aggravated by respiration and pleurisy with effusion
(k) Fever
(l) Rapid pulse
(m) Dyspnoea
(n) Hoarseness
(o) Nervous instability
(p) Slow recovery from other diseases

The public health nurse who is familiar with the above symptoms, will find many leads which, if followed, will reveal new foci of infection. When tuberculosis is found in a child, all adult members in contact with the child should be examined for the possible source of infection.

Early diagnosis is of the greatest importance in an effective tuberculosis program. The x-ray is the only measure that can be depended on for recognition of tuberculosis in a truly minimal stage, but it should be supplemented by physical examination and repeated sputum examination. Recent studies of tuberculosis deaths indicate that either tuberculosis is not being found early or, if found early, is not being reported, for 58 per cent of the deaths in Massachusetts for 1928 occurred within the first year of report.

The following conditions favor the development of active disease or the reactivation of a previously arrested case:

(a) Pneumonia, pleurisy, influenza, communicable diseases
(b) Pregnancy
(c) Mental and physical strain
(d) Insanitary living and working conditions
(e) Injury
(f) Dissipation
(g) Malnutrition
(h) Lack of sleep and rest, especially in children.
 It is very essential that school children should have periodic skin tests, and x-rays, if necessary, as a part of the school health supervision. This is particularly urgent for those children who have been in contact with active tuberculosis patients.

Nursing Supervision of the Active Case in the Home

Inasmuch as the treatment of tuberculosis follows along well defined lines, it is well for the nurse to be familiar with the following routines although the details of treatment will be ordered by the physician. The nurse will teach and interpret instructions to the patient as outlined by his physician.

1. Rest

Whether the rest prescribed is absolute or part time the points to emphasize are:

(a) Outlined hours for rest, both day and night; methods and conditions for absolute relaxation; place absolutely quiet; patient in recumbent position in open air or in well ventilated room; prevention of unnecessary fatigue.

Remember that very careful instruction is indicated in supervision of rest. Sitting in the open air, talking to visitors or other out-door activity does not constitute rest. *Absolute* rest always means rest in bed.

2. Exercise

Exercise should be carefully guided and should be considered as any physical effort on the part of the patient. The amount and kind should be decided by the doctor because exercise is considered treatment. As a rule none is allowed if there is a rise of temperature or an increase in pulse rate or, of course, after hemorrhage. Ordinarily in the treatment of tuberculosis, the term exercise conveys nothing more strenuous than walking.

3. Diet

Three well-balanced meals a day following the accepted principles of nutrition should be encouraged and are much better than forced feeding except in special cases.

Variety of food and different methods of preparation and serving play an important part in maintaining the patient's appetite.

4. Temperature

When specified by the doctor, the patient should be instructed as to the details for proper and accurate recording of his temperature. Temperatures are important in tuberculosis:
    (a) To assist in the establishment of proper diagnosis in suspicious cases.
    (b) As one of the ways by which activity of disease may be determined.
    (c) As a guide in directing the type and degree of exercise or work.

An accurate determination of the temperature of the patient taken by mouth can only be determined when the mouth has been free of any foreign substance such as candy, chewing gum or cold water for at least ten minutes before temperature is taken. Clinical thermometer should be left in patient's mouth under tongue for five minutes.

5. Cough

Instruct patient that coughing MAY BE CONTROLLED to a large extent unless sputum is raised; coughing tends to irritate the respiratory tract. WARN HIM NOT TO SWALLOW sputum.

6. Hemorrhage

The following information regarding hemorrhage may be given to some responsible member of the family if the physician approves or cannot be reached at once:

Hemorrhage is not often fatal. In the event that one occurs, call the physician at once. Put patient to bed immediately. One or two pillows may be placed under his head so that he is in a semi-reclining position. Keep him absolutely quiet, with ice cap to chest, and allow a small amount of cracked ice by mouth. Keep room well ventilated and cool and the patient comfortably warm. This is emergency treatment pending the arrival of the physician.

7. Bedside Care

If the patient is in bed at absolute rest, good nursing care is indicated. The nurse should teach such care by actual demonstration to the person who is responsible for patient.

8. Patient's Room

Separate bed is essential; separate room when possible. Room with two or more windows and southern exposure, is desirable. Furnishings should be simple and easily cleaned. Room arranged with view to cleanliness.

Teach damp dusting. Wash furnishings and floors with hot suds frequently. Cover broom with washable cover. Burn all sweepings.

Remove bed linen and patient's linen and immediately place in covered boiler. Boil thoroughly.

9. Precautions

See that patient has metal sputum box with fillers and pocket sputum cups. Fillers and paper napkins will be supplied for indigent patients by local boards of health. For bed patients too weak to use sputum box leave plenty of paper napkins (toilet paper may be used). Pin paper bag on bed within reach of patient and instruct him to use napkin only once and dispose of it in bag. Small paper squares can be bought very cheaply through the local druggist. Burn all paper sputum receptacles and boil metal sputum box frequently. Instruct patient to cover mouth with a paper napkin when coughing or sneezing and to avoid kissing. Children should be kept out of the room. Be sure the patient and his family realize the danger of sputum infection and thoroughly understand the necessary precautions. THE HANDS ACT AS A MEDIUM OF INFECTION. Patient or attendant should not put hands to mouth. Frequent and thorough washing of hands with careful attention to finger nails should be encouraged.

All dishes and utensils used by patient should be boiled and then washed as usual. Scraps of food from patient's tray should be burned. Separate dishes should be provided. Other personal articles which cannot be boiled should be kept in patient's room. This procedure is more of a problem with ambulatory patients but nevertheless is just as important.

10. Terminal Disinfection

Everything in the room and all articles used by patient that cannot be washed should be placed out-of-doors to sun for several days. Recommend use of plenty of soap and water and fresh air. Wash walls. Ordinary fumigation is of little or no value. If proper precautions have been observed all through illness terminal disinfection will be no problem.

11. Frequency of Nursing Visits to Active Cases

Frequency of visits to patients should be based on the condition found in each case. Home conditions, intelligence of the family and social and economic status should be the determining factors. Patients should be visited regularly and at short intervals until the nurse feels confident that instructions will be carried out both for the care of the patient and the protection of the contacts. As a rule, after the patient and family understand instructions, it is desirable to visit an active case once a month during the period of "cure." Apparently arrested cases or contacts where the active case has died should be visited occasionally, the intervals between visits being determined by circumstances. A patient who practices good health habits and who appreciates the importance of a regular thorough physical examination at least once a year and a chest examination following a prolonged cold or occurrence of suspicious symptoms may be trusted to safeguard himself; a patient who does not appreciate these factors will need regular supervision. No patient should be carried in the nurse's active file who is not visited at least once a year.

12. Sanatorium Care

A sanatorium is the ideal place for the majority of tuberculous patients, at least for a reasonable period of time. Every effort should be made to arrange such care when ordered by the attending physician. In homes where there are children, the removal of the patient to the sanatorium is important; in other homes where there are only adult contacts the sanatorium may well be considered a school at which he receives instruction in the care of himself and the protection of others. This point is a good one to emphasize and will often change the patient's attitude toward leaving home. Instruction should be given as to preparation for sanatorium care and aid given in securing proper clothing if necessary. Remember that through Mother's Aid, financial assistance may be granted for children while the father is curing for tuberculosis. This security for his family should help to relieve his anxiety and so contribute to his cure.

13. Postsanatorium Care

Prepare the home for the return of the patient by giving instruction regarding the needs of the patient; adjustment in home routines, in arrangements for suitable room, etc., should be made in advance of his return.

The postsanatorium patient will need careful help and guidance until he has adjusted himself to the greater freedom of home life. The greatest care should be given until a regime of living is well established to insure a continuance of the gain in health accomplished through sanatorium care.

If the patient is to return to work remember that the average occupation is not harmful. His earning power and his peace of mind must be considered before suggesting or encouraging new occupation. Very often adjustments can be made with the aid of the former employer which will make it safe to encourage the patient's return to the work to which he is accustomed. If the former occupation represents a health hazard a careful plan for new work should be made with the advice of the physician and the aid of such agencies for rehabilitation as are available.

The patient only works about one third of the entire day so it is well to consider the whole twenty-four when planning a sensible regime.

14. Health Supervision of Contacts

Acquiring the disease depends upon a number of factors:
- (a) The amount of infection received, especially as related to time over which exposure is effective.
- (b) Resistance of the body.
- (c) Health habits.

Inasmuch as the greatest danger of infection is during the infant and preschool age, these children should be given regular physical examination with x-rays of the chest at periodic intervals. Where the facilities are available, physical examination every three months is desirable. Intensive health supervision is essential in order to insure the maximum of resistance for this group of contacts. Standards for the health supervision of infants and preschool children are outlined in the handbooks of the Division of Child Hygiene, State Department of Public Health.

Tuberculin testing is primarily used to prove that infection has occurred and is an essential aid in confirming the diagnosis of tuberculosis in children. It is a helpful procedure in selecting the children who should be watched more carefully and who should have more frequent physical examinations and x-rays. A positive tuberculin test in children has greater significance than a similar reaction in adults. A negative tuberculin test, as a rule, signifies absence of a tuberculous infection. It is a rare occurrence that any child diagnosed as tuberculous has a negative tuberculin test. A positive tuberculin test accompanied by a negative x-ray in a patient without symptoms or positive physical findings means tuberculous infection and not active disease.

The length of the period over which contacts should be carried in a tuberculosis service should be determined by the physician.

15. Clinics

If permanent clinic service is not available, arrangements may be made through the superintendent of the state or county sanatoria for examinations in the out-patient department of the sanatorium. The success of all clinics is due in a large measure to the effectiveness of the field work of the public health nurse and to her relations with the local board of health, physicians and families with whom she works. Selection of cases and prompt follow-up work is more important than large attendance.

16. Records

Records for nurses are recommended by the National Organization for Public Health Nursing. All items on the record forms are of value in the careful supervision of the patient. Data should be accurately recorded not only at the initial visit but after each subsequent visit. When the physician does not wish the nurse to visit the patient, the nurse should ask the physician to complete the 4" x 6" State Department of Public Health record form. Suggestions regarding the use of records may be obtained by communication with the consultant nurse in the district.

VI. American Public Health Association Standards for Tuberculosis Work

The following standards for the appraisal of tuberculosis work are those developed by the American Public Health Association:

1. Reporting of Tuberculosis Cases:
    (a) Two new cases reported per annual average number of deaths.
    (b) Five known living cases per annual average number of deaths.
2. Clinical Service:
    (a) 15,000 visits to clinic per 100 deaths.
    (b) Three visits per patient registered.
    (c) Twenty-five per cent minimal cases of total diagnosed.
3. Field Nursing Service:
    (a) 5,000 home visits per year per 100 deaths.
    (b) Eight visits per case registered.
    (c) 1,000 visits per 100 deaths to postsanatorium cases.
4. Institutional Care:
    (a) 25,000 hospital patient days per 100 deaths.
    (b) Twenty-five per cent of total admissions minimal cases.
    (c) Ten per cent of total admissions children under 12 years of age.
    (d) Ten children per 1,000 grade-school population attending open air classrooms, preventoria or day camps at least six weeks.

VII. Bibliography

HODGSON, MRS. VIOLET. *Tuberculosis Nursing for Public Health Nurses.* Boston: Massachusetts Tuberculosis League, Inc., 1148 Little Bldg. 10 cents.

NATIONAL ORGANIZATION FOR PUBLIC HEALTH NURSING. *Manual of Public Health Nursing.* New York: Macmillan. 1932. $1.50.

GARDNER, MARY, R. N. *Public Health Nursing.* Second edition. New York: Macmillan, revised. 1925. $3.00

MYERS, J. A. *Tuberculosis Among Children.* Springfield, Illinois: Charles C. Thomas. 1930. $3.50.
HAWES, JOHN B. *Tuberculosis and the Community.* Philadelphia: Lea and Febiger. 1922. $1.75.
BROWN, LAWRASON. *Rules for Recovery from Pulmonary Tuberculosis.* Philadelphia: Lea and Febiger. 1928. $1.50.
WEBB and RYDER. *Overcoming Tuberculosis.* New York: Hoeber. $2.00.
MYERS, J. A. *The Care of Tuberculosis.* Philadelphia: Saunders. 1924. $2.00.
CHADWICK, HENRY D. and MCPHEDRAN, F. MAURICE. *Childhood Type of Tuberculosis — Diagnostic Aids.* New York: National Tuberculosis Association: 1930. 25 cents.

SOCIAL WORK FOR THE TUBERCULOSIS PATIENT

By ELEANOR E. KELLY
Supervisor of Social Service
Massachusetts Department of Public Health

There is probably no medical problem in which social service can be more effective than in tuberculosis, because both prevention and adequate treatment depend so largely upon control of the social and environmental factors.

More effective measures for case finding, and improved methods of treatment and care have caused a tremendous decrease in tuberculosis. General social measures which have brought about improved living and working conditions have also aided materially in control of the disease. There is still, however, much to be done along these lines. The physical and mental strain of these years of economic stress is lowering the resistance of many families and making them potential victims of such diseases as tuberculosis. Any social measures therefore which assure individuals of proper housing, adequate food and clothing, and freedom from undue fatigue and worry will be welcomed by the medical profession as valuable aids in the campaign against tuberculosis.

But the social worker has a responsibility not only toward these broad social measures but also in individual case work.

Greater awareness on the part of all social workers, of the problem of tuberculosis should aid in case finding, as well as in control of the individual case. Undernourishment, overcrowding, poor working conditions, suggest to the social worker a health menace, but ought more frequently to suggest a possibility of this particular menace—tuberculosis, and lead to physical examination of such families. The social worker placing out children, for instance, will want to be sure that she is not exposing them to unrecognized disease hazards and that the foster mother understands the child's health needs. In cases of children—or adults—who have been discharged from tuberculosis sanatoria, or have been under care at home for the disease, the social worker should keep in touch with the nurse who is following up the case, and report to her any changes she may observe in the health situation of that family. She can often aid the nurse too in securing consent of the family to examination of contacts and acceptance of sanatorium care.

In clinics and hospitals for tuberculosis, a large proportion of the patients present problems which call for the services of the medical social worker, and these are by no means all economic as is often believed. The patient who is told by the physician that he has tuberculosis and must undergo treatment, confronts a situation which is always difficult to face, whether his disease be in an early or late stage. It means a more or less complete reorganization of his present mode of living, and, even when the physician has explained the diagnosis and its implications, it is seldom possible for the patient to make immediately the mental adjustment necessary.

He may fear death and see no hope of anything else for him; or he may dread even more the life of inactivity which spells hope for the future but disappointment and worry now. He has a kaleidoscopic view of his business ruined or job lost, his family suffering deprivation, his own loneliness and enforced idleness. In tuberculosis there is also the great uncertainty as to the length of time necessary for treatment, a fact which complicates his making of plans, and which may be particularly irritating, for instance, to a person of decisive nature.

The patient's participation in treatment is essential, however, and the physician often calls upon the medical social worker to help influence the patient's attitude toward his disease and toward treatment. She can reinforce the physician's instructions when necessary and she can also secure for the doctor further information regarding the patient's social history, and the forces which are already influencing his attitude. If he has, for instance, previously met difficult situations with courage and resourcefulness, he may be expected to cooperate with the physician more readily than a patient who has never honestly faced facts. On the other hand this may be for him the "last straw" in a series of misfortunes. Other patients may show indifference, unwillingness to accept the diagnosis, hopefulness or despair—attitudes which appear to fall readily into groups for classification, but which in reality represent as many different types of character and need as there are individual patients.

The patient's behavior is often modified by the attitude of his family and friends toward his disease; the social worker may need to interpret to them the patient's medical social problem and in some cases attempt to change destructive to constructive attitudes. They may know someone who "was told he had tuberculosis when he hadn't." Especially is this true in the case of children, a neighbor commenting, "Why, that child's the picture of health. She couldn't possibly have tuberculosis!" Overambitious parents are sometimes reluctant to send a child away to a sanatorium, "just when she's getting along so well in school."

Ignorance and neglect are frequently responsible for delay in treatment for the child—especially the adolescent who is allowed to make his own decision regarding sanatorium care. The boy or girl of this age is a problem too in the sanatorium where the routine differs so greatly from that of his inclination!

The majority of parents are anxious for their children to have the benefit of treatment when they have been convinced of its necessity, but the children of the minority must also have their chance, and the social worker endeavors to make this possible.

Most adult patients when they have faced the truth, are anxious to take steps toward arresting the disease. Frequently, however, it seems impossible for them to take that first hurdle. The effort involved in making a long time plan for himself and family may be more than a patient has strength for—a mother who must leave her children to be cared for by others; the man whose wages are the family's sole income. They will sometimes "take a chance" unless someone can help them to work out a plan for the family.

A person who has always been independent finds it hard to accept the fact that he is no longer able to direct his own affairs; the social worker's approach to his problem must be skillful and understanding in order that he may not develop a feeling of inadequacy and discouragement which would interfere with his treatment.

Within the sanatorium, some patients fall readily into the routine, cooperating completely with the physician; others have a poorer chance of recovery because they are under some mental or emotional strain. The social worker endeavors in each case to learn whether the underlying cause is real or fancied trouble and what can be done about it.

The patient may be worrying about home or business, brooding over the trouble he is causing, and the possibility of having infected members of his family. He may need only reassurance—a visit from a member of his family, a letter from his employer, the knowledge that the nurse has had all the family examined and is keeping them under observation.

In other cases, however, more complex social situations are presented. Feeblemindedness, unemployment, invalidism, behavior problems, alcoholism—within the family, may become more significant now that the home has been broken. A relative may have to be found to care for children left alone, or a children's agency called upon to plan for them. It may be necessary to secure financial aid or to assist the family in budgeting its resources or later, in case the patient does not live, to help the family to make that difficult adjustment; or hospitalization may be required for another member of the family. These and many other needs the social worker attempts to meet.

She must now, however, relieve the patient or family entirely of responsibility. One of the most important factors in a patient's recovery is his own will to gain health, and many a patient has been induced to make the fight, by the knowledge that someone was dependent upon him. This incentive must not be entirely removed, but the responsibility should not be allowed to weigh upon him so heavily that it interferes with his treatment. In individual cases the proper adjustment of such problems often prevents the patient's leaving the sanatorium prematurely and makes possible the successful completion of his treatment.

It is important that patients upon discharge from the sanatorium should return to good living and working conditions, otherwise they may break down and be obliged to return for further treatment. In the Massachusetts State Sanatoria, before a child is discharged a social service report is made on the home situation. This enables the physician to determine whether the child can be safely discharged; if satisfactory after-care is not assured he may wish to prolong somewhat the period of sanatorium care.

The child returning to home and school, although discharged in good condition, will need careful and intelligent supervision in the home, proper food and sufficient rest. If the mother works all day leaving the child to his own devices; if there is not money enough to provide proper nourishment; if his room is dark, airless and crowded, some attempt must be made by the social worker to remedy these conditions. It is not uncommon to find a child given tasks beyond his strength, or an adult returning to working conditions which were contributing factors to his original breakdown. It is particularly difficult in these days to secure suitable employment for discharged patients, but every effort should be made towards rehabilitation.

The process is complicated by the fact that patients who have been in a sanatorium for many months—or years—frequently find it hard to adjust to a situation in which they no longer hold the center of the stage. Just as it was difficult to accept a period of inactivity and dependence, so now the return to independence presents a problem of mental adjustment, and sometimes finds the patient unready to take the initiative. The sanatorium has prepared him as far as possible for a resumption of his normal activities but he sometimes needs the social worker's help in the search perhaps for suitable employment, the reestablishment of a broken home, or the rebuilding of self confidence—the step toward that rehabilitation which indicates control of his medical social problem.

Thus social service makes it contribution—through individualization, making it possible for patients to secure early treatment, to continue as long as necessary and finally to readjust into the community.

THE DECLINE IN TUBERCULOSIS
By ALTON S. POPE, M. D.
Director, Division of Tuberculosis
Massachusetts Department of Public Health

We can speak with conviction of the widespread use of vaccination as the determining factor in the control of smallpox, and of such environmental factors as the protection and purification of water supplies, safe sewage disposal, and the pasteurization of milk as the agents responsible for the almost complete disappearance of typhoid fever in this part of the world: no such obvious cause appears for the equally remarkable decline of tuberculosis during the past seventy-five years.

On account of the notoriously incomplete reporting of tuberculosis no accurate record of living cases is available so that mortality rates furnish our best index to the real incidence of the disease.

CHART I
PULMONARY TUBERCULOSIS
MASSACHUSETTS
Death Rates, Male and Female, By 5 Year Periods 1849-1933

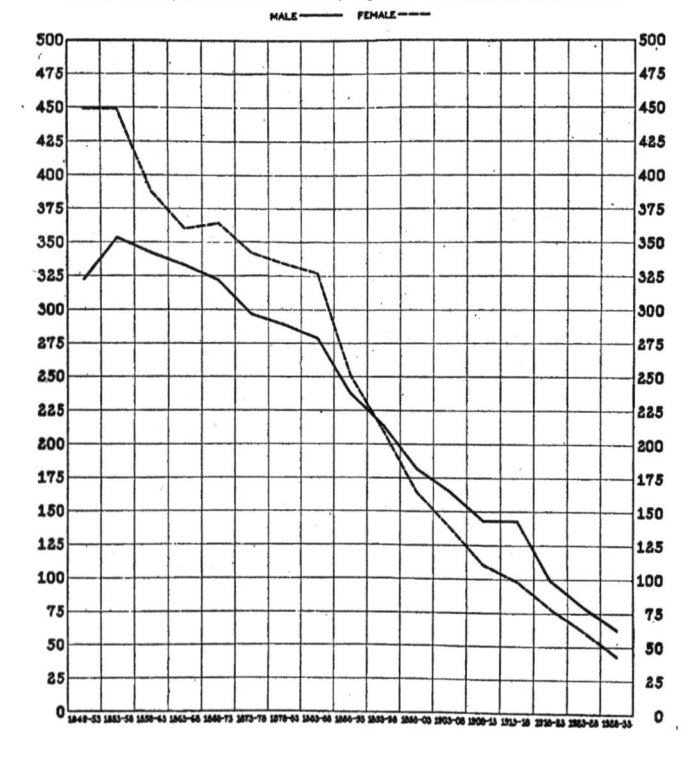

Perhaps the most remarkable thing in this record is the steady decline of the death rate for at least twenty years before the discovery of the tubercle bacillus, and its continued fall for some two more decades before organized control measures could be expected to play a determining part. How much of this decline is attributable to improvement in social and economic conditions may never be known, but there is every reason to believe that less severe physical labor, better housing, and a more adequate diet have been important factors. The much more rapid fall of the death rate among women during this period is notable and may well be due to the obviously greater relative improvement in living and working conditions for women during the past seventy-five years. In fact, data from certain parts of the world where women still routinely perform heavy manual labor strongly supports such an explanation.

By far the greatest saving of life has been among children under five years of age, where the apparent decline has been 97 per cent of the death rate in 1850. The lowest relative decline has been in the age group fifteen to thirty-nine, though even among young women of fifteen to thirty there has been a fall of over 50 per cent since 1900, compared with a stationary tuberculosis mortality in girls of the same age in England.

In the accompanying table are given the reported cases and deaths from pulmonary tuberculosis and other forms of tuberculosis since they have been reportable in Massachusetts, together with the corresponding rates. Although there has been a gradual rise in the ratio of reported cases to deaths it will be noticed that there are still scarcely two cases reported to each annual death, while there are in all probability nearly twice that number of new cases developing annually. In Cattaraugus County, New York, where case finding is intensive, there are regularly reported 3.5 new cases for each annual death from tuberculosis. In this connection it should be added that much confusion has arisen over this ratio of reported cases to deaths. On the basis of the Framingham Demonstration, Armstrong estimated that there are probably some ten *living cases in the community* for each reported death. By some this has apparently been construed to mean that there should be ten *new cases* reported annually for each death—a ratio totally at variance with all experience.

Table I
MORBIDITY AND MORTALITY FROM TUBERCULOSIS PULMONARY AND OTHER FORMS—1900-1933
MASSACHUSETTS

Year	Tuberculosis, Pulmonary Cases*	Case Rate	Deaths	Death Rate	Year	Tuberculosis, Other Forms Cases	Case Rate	Deaths	Death Rate
1900			5199	185.	1900				68.3
1901			5033	177.	1901				57.4
1902			4685	162.	1902				58.3
1903			4531	155.	1903				54.5
1904			4874	164.	1904				53.0
1905			4702	156.	1905				58.3
1906			4608	149.	1906				60.7
1907			4771	151.	1907				57.5
1908			4445	137.	1908				63.5
1909			4393	133.	1909				48.5
1910	7862	232.6	4503	133.2	1910				46.0
1911	7031	204.1	4418	128.2	1911				35.8
1912	7519	214.2	4212	120.0	1912	447	12.7	855	24.4
1913	7424	207.6	4180	116.9	1913	412	11.5	869	24.3
1914	7144	196.2	4171	114.5	1914	570	15.7	890	24.4
1915	8046	217.4	4194	113.3	1915	822	22.2	853	23.0
1916	7878	210.9	4467	119.6	1916	657	17.6	955	25.6
1917	8365	221.9	4559	121.0	1917	776	20.6	850	22.6
1918	7833	206.0	5078	133.6	1918	747	19.6	891	23.4
1919	6977	181.9	4145	108.1	1919	782	20.4	775	20.2
1920	6696	172.6	3645	93.9	1920	800	20.6	755	19.5
1921	6168	156.7	3272	83.1	1921	827	21.0	595	15.1
1922	5562	139.4	3167	79.3	1922	817	20.5	569	14.3
1923	5356	132.3	3062	75.7	1923	807	19.9	528	13.0
1924	5376	131.0	2953	72.0	1924	893	21.8	577	14.1
1925	5385	129.5	2883	69.3	1925	825	19.8	576	13.9
1926	5444	130.5	2961	71.0	1926	874	21.0	555	13.3
1927	5049	120.5	2774	66.2	1927	807	19.3	429	10.2
1928	4873	115.7	2690	63.9	1928	757	18.0	433	10.3
1929	4358	107.2	2561	60.5	1929	649	15.3	361	8.5
1930	4696	110.4	2423	56.9	1930	587	13.8	311	7.3
1931	4421	103.4	2306	53.9	1931	555	13.0	248	5.8
1932	3994	92.9	2041	47.5	1932	466	10.8	261	6.1
1933	3541	82.0	2058	47.7	1933	466	10.8	222	5.1

* Tuberculosis was not made reportable in Massachusetts till 1907 and notification was too incomplete to be significant before 1910.

It will be noticed that during this period the proportionate decline of extra-pulmonary tuberculosis has been even greater than that of the pulmonary form. In children this decrease has been especially marked and "abdominal tuberculosis" as a cause of death has practically disappeared. The comparative rarity of tuberculous meningitis and tuberculous cervical adenitis in children at the present time is too well known to pediatricians to require further comment, and probably can in large part be credited to the extensive pasteurization of public milk supplies.

Although the trend of tuberculosis mortality on a geometric scale shows little acceleration since hospitalization and the general public health program could be expected to be of significant influence there is much reason to believe they have had a real part in the continued decline in mortality. Experience indicates that after periods of rapid decline the mortality rates of communicable diseases tend to flatten out and that without the help of such limiting factors as immunization or reduction of sources of infection an equilibrium tends to be established between man and the invading organism.

As a result of this continued decrease tuberculosis has in the last twenty years fallen from first to seventh place among the leading causes of death. Since 1900 the mortality rate has fallen 75 per cent, representing a saving of over 5,000 lives per year in the Commonwealth. Yet even now tuberculosis is the cause of between four and five times as many deaths as all of the acute communicable diseases, excepting influenza and the pneumonias, and between the ages of fifteen and forty is still the most frequent cause of death. If to this is added the fact that the average case of tuberculosis has a duration of from two to three years some idea is afforded of the social and economic importance of the disease, even at the present time.

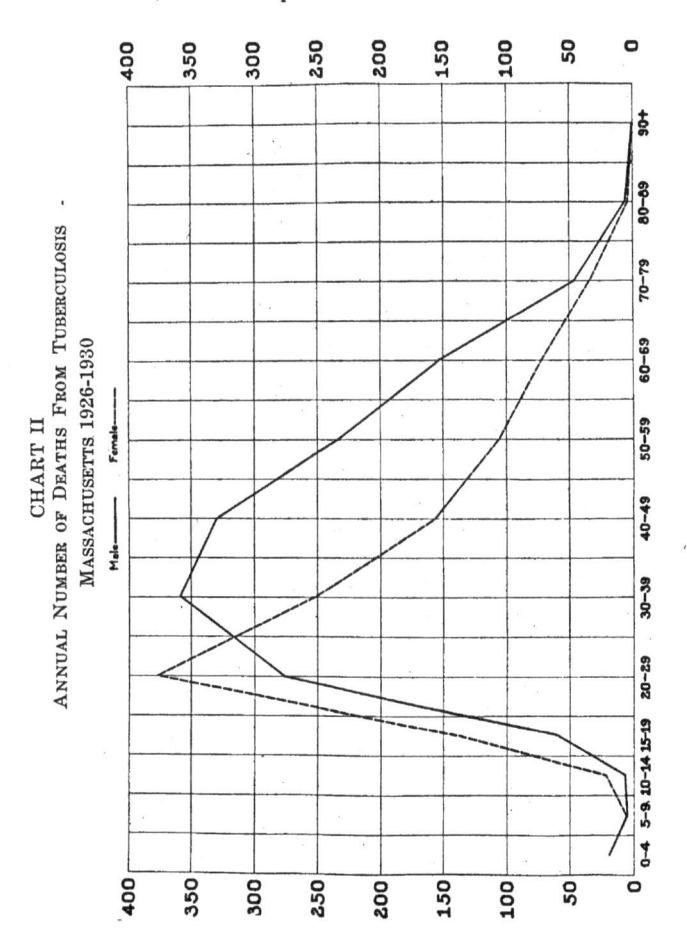

CHART II
ANNUAL NUMBER OF DEATHS FROM TUBERCULOSIS
MASSACHUSETTS 1926-1930

THE AMERICAN NEISSERIAN MEDICAL SOCIETY

The American Neisserian Medical Society was founded on June 12th, 1934. It is dedicated to the promotion of knowledge in all that relates to the gonococcus and gonococcal infections, that there may be attained improvement in the management of gonorrhea and a reduction in its prevalence. There are 115 charter members and the officers are:

Dr. Edward L. Keyes, New York, Honorary President
Dr. J. Dellinger Barney, Boston, President
Dr. P. S. Pelouze, Philadelphia, Vice-President
Dr. A. L. Clarke, Oklahoma City } Executive
Dr. Walter Clarke, New York   } Committee
Dr. R. D. Herrold, Chicago
Dr. N. A. Nelson, Boston
Dr. Oscar F. Cox, Jr., Boston, Secretary-Treasurer

The society plans to carry out the following program:
A. The scrutiny of the management of gonorrhea in both male and female.
B. Clinical and laboratory research in the diagnosis, medical and social pathology, and the treatment of gonorrhea.
C. Dissemination among the medical profession and the public of authoritative information concerning gonorrhea.

Membership is limited to:
A. Residents of the United States or its territories, Canada or Mexico.
B. Graduates of a medical school recognized by the American Medical Association.
C. Those who are engaged in some phase of the management of gonorrhea.

Invitation to membership is extended to all qualified physicians who desire to work for improvement in the management of gonorrhea. Application blanks can be obtained from the undersigned.

Oscar F. Cox, Jr., M.D., Secretary
475 Commonwealth Ave.,
Boston, Mass.

Book Note

How SAFE Is HoME by Howard Whipple Green. 50c. 48pp. Cleveland Health Council, 1900 Euclid Avenue, Cleveland, Ohio. 1934.

This is a summary of a study which tells the story of the part that accidents in general, and home accidents in particular played as the cause of death in the group analyzed. The variation in the importance of accidents as the cause of death is interesting. During the preschool years after the child can walk, accidental deaths were "nearly as important as pneumonia, 3 times as important as scarlet fever or diphtheria, and 5 times as important as whooping cough."

During early school life and up to 14 years accidents headed the list as the cause of death. Among adolescents the order of importance was tuberculosis, accidents, heart. From 20 to 24 years accidents dropped to third place, with tuberculosis and heart preceding. From 25 to 29 years accidents again took second place, preceded by tuberculosis and followed by heart conditions. From 30 to 34 years accidents were in the third place. From 35 to 39 years accidents were in fourth place because of cancer entering into the field and were again third in the age group 40 to 44. The age group 45 to 49 years was most affected by heart and cancer, with accidents and cerebral hemorrhage equal in the third place, and tuberculosis and pneumonia also equal as the fourth most important cause of death.

A special study was made of 1094 persons who died from home accidents during the five and one-half year period. Falls were the most common cause of death in this group with burns second. Sixty-three per cent of the falls were of persons 60 years or over, while burns were most important among children, 46 per cent being due to this cause in the group under 15 years of age.

Regarding injury from accidents which do not kill, during a single month, 2,253 persons went to the Cleveland hospitals for emergency treatment. Of these, 855 were home accidents.

As the author says, it does seem as though a large proportion of all fatal home accidents could be prevented.

REPORT OF DIVISION OF FOOD AND DRUGS

During the months of October, November and December 1934, samples were collected in 223 cities and towns.

There were 994 samples of milk examined, of which 92 were below standard, from 9 samples the cream had been in part removed, and 8 samples contained added water. There were 42 samples of Grade A milk examined, 1 sample of which was below the legal standard of 4.00% fat. There were 693 bacteriological examinations made of milk, 632 of which complied with the requirements. There were 378 bacteriological examinations made of ice cream, 288 of which complied with the requirements. There were 7 bacteriological examinations made of lobsters, all of which complied with the requirements; and 3 bacteriological examinations of candy were made, 2 of which did not comply with the requirements.

There were 1,124 samples of food examined, 102 of which were adulterated. These consisted of 1 sample of butter which was rancid; 1 sample of chocolate drink which was low in fat; 19 samples of cream cheese, 16 samples of which contained gelatine, 1 sample contained foreign fat, and 2 samples contained foreign fat and gelatine; 4 samples of sour cream which contained gelatine; 21 samples of eggs, 8 samples of which were stale eggs sold as fresh eggs, 7 samples were cold storage not marked, and 6 samples were decomposed; 2 samples of imitation vanilla not distinctly labeled as such; 3 samples of frozen desserts which were low in fat; 1 sample of maple butter which was very deficient in maple; 1 sample of stew chicken which was decomposed; 9 samples of pickles, 4 samples of which were sweet relish all of which contained benzoate of soda not marked and 3 samples also contained saccharine, 3 samples were decomposed, and 2 samples contained saccharine; 10 samples of cream, 2 samples of which were low in fat, 7 samples contained foreign fat, and 1 sample contained gelatine; 17 samples of hamburg steak, 5 samples of which contained a compound of sulphur dioxide not properly labeled and 1 sample was also watered, 3 samples contained sodium sulphite in excess of one tenth of one per cent, and 2 samples were also decomposed, and 9 samples were decomposed and 2 samples were also watered; 7 samples of sausage, 5 samples of which contained a compound of sulphur dioxide not properly labeled and 1 sample was also watered, 1 sample contained sodium sulphite in excess of one tenth of one per cent., and 1 sample was decomposed; 3 samples of buttered pop corn seasoned with fat other than butter; 1 sample of celery which was misbranded; and 2 samples of confectionery in which organisms of the B Coli group were present.

There were 52 samples of drugs examined, of which 9 were adulterated. These consisted of 3 samples of argyrol solution not corresponding to the professed standard under which they were sold, 1 sample of lime water, 3 samples of magnesium citrate, and 2 samples of spirit of nitrous ether, all of which did not conform to the U. S. P. requirements.

The police departments submitted 140 samples of liquor for examination. The police departments also submitted 33 samples to be analyzed for poisons or drugs, 6 samples of which contained opium, 13 contained heroin, 1 contained cannabis, 2 contained morphine, 1 contained gelatine, 1 contained heroin hydrochloride, 1 sample of pills were throat lozenges, 2 samples of candy were analyzed for bacteria, 1 sample of which was found to contain B coli, and 6 samples contained no drugs or poisons.

There were 61 cities and towns visited for the inspection of pasteurizing plants, and 222 plants were inspected.

There were 153 plants inspected for the manufacture of ice cream.

There were 78 hearings held pertaining to violations of the laws.

There were 53 convictions for violations of the law, $1600 in fines being imposed.

Jesse Oliver of South Westport; Arthur Vigneault of Haverhill; Stanley Antoski and Andrew Kareta of Ludlow; Charles L. Woodland of Watertown; and Morris Calcia of West Sterling, were all convicted for violations of the milk laws.

Lincoln Stetson of Abington; United Farmers Cooperative Creamery Association of Everett; and Chester A. Burkinshaw of Salem, were all convicted for violations of the pasteurization laws and regulations.

Hillside Dairy Company, Incorporated, of Marlborough was convicted for violation of the Grade A Milk regulations.

Central Meat Market and Provision, Incorporated, of Southbridge; Fred H. Willard, 2 cases, of Worcester; Clayton M. Hager of Somerville; John A. Levy of Lynn; Joseph Waldman, Samuel Weinck, Stark Supply Company, and Harry Brock, all of Roxbury; Publix Food Market, Incorporated, and Frank Foti of Malden; Norwood Provision Company, Incorporated, John N. Harper, Jr., and Woburn Provision Company, Incorporated, 2 cases, all of Everett; Belaine Roberts of Shrewsbury; Dave Levy and David Shuman of Boston; Hyman Press of Dorchester; and Harry Kramer of Hudson, were all convicted for violations of the food laws. Central Meat Market & Provision, Incorporated, of Southbridge; John N. Harper, Jr. of Everett; Publix Food Market, Incorporated, of Malden; and Samuel Weinck of Roxbury, all appealed their cases.

General Fruit Store, Incorporated, of Worcester; Andrew Boghoshian of Indian Orchard; Herbert W. Cook of Springfield; Harry Lessner of Malden; Samuel Pietrella of Everett; and H. Winer Company, Incorporated, of Boston, were all convicted for false advertising. General Fruit Store, Incorporated, of Worcester, appealed their case.

Rose Lochiatto and Thomas Screnci of Boston were convicted for misbranding.

Clayton H. Hager of Somerville; Ashley W. Partridge of Lexington; The Puritan Ice Cream Company of Boston, Incorporated, of Forest Hills; and J. G. Turnbull Company, Incorporated, of Greenfield, were all convicted for violations of the frozen dessert law.

Hyman Fogel of Boston was convicted for a violation of the drug law.

Nicolas Caraminas of Springfield was convicted for violation of the cold storage laws.

Stanley Sekscencksi of Holyoke was convicted for violation of the slaughtering laws.

Gerson Bedding Company, 2 cases, of Lowell; Harry Gladstone and Saul Schlager of Malden; Morris Goldstein of Haverhill; Providence Mattress Company of Providence, R. I.; Eagle Upholstery Company

Incorporated, of Boston; and Isaac Bartfield of Worcester, were all convicted for violations of the mattress laws. Morris Goldstein of Haverhill; Eagle Upholstery Company, Incorporated, of Boston; and Isaac Bartfield of Worcester, all appealed their cases.

In accordance with Section 25, Chapter 111 of the General Laws, the following is the list of articles of adulterated food collected in original packages from manufacturers, wholesalers, or producers:

One sample of butter which was rancid was obtained from The Borden Sales Company, Incorporated, of Boston.

Buttered pop corn seasoned with fat other than butter was obtained as follows:

Two samples, from Ernest R. Doyon of Beverly; and one sample from Herbert W. Cook of Springfield.

One sample of celery which was misbranded was obtained from Thomas Screnci & Rose Lochiatto of Boston.

Heavy cream which was low in fat was obtained as follows:

One sample each, from The Great Atlantic & Pacific Tea Company of Somerville, and A. Brox of Dracut.

Seven samples of cream which contained foreign fat were obtained from Fred H. Willard of Worcester.

Sour cream which contained gelatine was obtained as follows:

One sample each, from Springfield Butter Company of Springfield; National Creamery of Somerville; National D Store of Dorchester; and from the Store at 93 Millbury Street, Worcester.

Cream cheese which contained gelatine was obtained as follows:

Six samples from I. Fine of Mattapan; 3 samples from Springfield Butter Company of Springfield; 2 samples from F. W. Willard of Worcester; and one sample each from M. Winer Company and Rabonovitz of Mattapan.

One sample of cream cheese which contained foreign fat was obtained from Fred W. Willard of Worcester.

Two samples of cream cheese which contained foreign fat and also contained gelatine were obtained from Fred W. Willard of Worcester.

Two samples of frozen desserts which were low in fat were obtained from Hager's Ice Cream Company of Somerville.

Imitation vanilla not distinctly labeled as such was obtained as follows:

One sample each, from Granite Chemical Company of Quincy; and David Halperin of Cambridge.

One sample of maple butter which was very deficient in maple was obtained from Maple Butter Company of Boston.

Hamburg steak which contained a compound of sulphur dioxide not properly labeled was obtained as follows:

One sample each, from Hyman Press of Dorchester; Barney Stem, and American Beef Company, of Boston; and Boston Beef Market of New Bedford.

Hamburg steak which was decomposed was obtained as follows:

One sample each, from Edward Bloom of Newburyport; New York Butchers of Boston; Fred Guylialmo of East Boston; Taunton Public Market of Taunton; Jack Miller of New Bedford; Square Market of Roxbury; and Clinton Market of Lynn.

Hamburg steak which was decomposed and also contained water was obtained as follows:

One sample each, from Vincent Lombardo of East Boston; and Second National Store of Roxbury.

Hamburg steak which was decomposed and also contained sodium sulphite in excess of one tenth of one per cent was obtained as follows:

One sample each, from Woburn Provision Company of Everett; and Nathan Greenbam of Amesbury.

One sample of hamburg steak which contained sodium sulphite in excess of one tenth of one per cent. was obtained from Israel Snyder of Boston.

Sausage which contained a compound of sulphur dioxide not properly labeled was obtained as follows:

Two samples from A. L. Scheu & Company of Boston; and one sample each, from Arthur Giberti & Morris Rubin, and Moscardini Brothers, of Boston; and McLellan's Market of Springfield.

One sample of sausage which contained sodium sulphite in excess of one tenth of one per cent. was obtained from Hyman Alpert of Boston.

One sample of sausage which was decomposed was obtained from Central Meat Market & Provision, Incorporated, of Southbridge.

Three samples of sweet relish which contained benzoate not marked and also contained saccharine were obtained from Harvard Pickle Works, Incorporated, of Cambridge.

One sample of sweet relish and one sample of pickles, both of which contained saccharine, were obtained from Harvard Pickle Works, Incorporated, of Cambridge.

One sample of sweet relish which contained benzoate of soda and not so marked was obtained from Harvard Pickle Works, Incorporated, of Cambridge.

There were ten confiscations, consisting of 85 pounds of decomposed chickens; 644 pounds of decomposed cooked ham; 4,000 pounds of decomposed cooked spiced ham; 161 pounds of decomposed cooked luncheon meat; 120 pounds of decomposed cooked pigs' feet; 110 pounds of dried out lamb; 25 pounds of lamb that bore no inspection stamp; 120 pounds of dried out veal; 1,500 barrels of decomposed pickles; and 51 barrels of decomposed pickles.

The licensed cold storage warehouses reported the following amounts of food placed in storage during September, 1934,—488,160 dozens of case eggs; 210,350 pounds of broken out eggs; 1,175,716 pounds of butter; 1,284,798 pounds of poultry; 4,181,055½ pounds of fresh meat and fresh meat products; and 5,918,600 pounds of fresh food fish.

There was on hand October 1, 1934:—5,594,940 dozens of case eggs; 2,988,846 pounds of broken out eggs; 6,663,665 pounds of butter; 3,465,- 335½ pounds of poultry; 8,199,108¾ pounds of fresh meat and fresh meat products; and 27,183,051 pounds of fresh food fish.

The licensed cold storage warehouses reported the following amounts of food placed in storage during October, 1934:—388,740 dozens of case eggs; 351,155 pounds of broken out eggs; 822,398 pounds of butter; 1,423,096½ pounds of poultry; 3,624,794½ pounds of fresh meat and fresh meat products; and 3,419,777 pounds of fresh food fish.

There was on hand November 1, 1934:—3,791,400 dozens of case eggs; 2,548,557 pounds of broken out eggs, 5,584,413 pounds of butter; 3,792,305¾ pounds of poultry; 8,002,588¾ pounds of fresh meat and fresh meat products; and 23,656,300 pounds of fresh food fish.

The licensed cold storage warehouses reported the following amounts of food placed in storage during November, 1934:—262,170 dozens of case eggs; 671,456 pounds of broken out eggs; 486,327 pounds of butter; 2,130,626 pounds of poultry; 6,927,345 pounds of fresh meat and fresh meat products; and 7,947,311 pounds of fresh food fish.

There was on hand December 1, 1934:—2,033,730 dozens of case eggs; 2,305,818 pounds of broken out eggs; 2,809,181 pounds of butter; 5,015,543¾ pounds of poultry; 15,302,847 pounds of fresh meat and fresh meat products; and 24,538,857 pounds of fresh food fish.

MASSACHUSETTS DEPARTMENT OF PUBLIC HEALTH

Commissioner of Public Health, HENRY D. CHADWICK, M.D.

Public Health Council

HENRY D. CHADWICK, M.D., *Chairman*

GORDON HUTCHINS.
FRANCIS H. LALLY, M.D.
SYLVESTER E. RYAN, M.D.
RICHARD M. SMITH, M.D.
RICHARD P. STRONG, M.D.
JAMES L. TIGHE.

Secretary, ALICE M. NELSON

Division of Administration	Under direction of Commissioner.
Division of Sanitary Engineering	Director and Chief Engineer, ARTHUR D. WESTON, C.E.
Division of Communicable Diseases	Director, GAYLORD W. ANDERSON, M.D.
Division of Biologic Laboratories	Director and Pathologist, ELLIOTT S. ROBINSON, M.D.
Division of Food and Drugs	Director and Analyst, HERMANN C. LYTHGOE, S.B.
Division of Child Hygiene	Director, M. LUISE DIEZ, M.D.
Division of Tuberculosis	Director, ALTON S. POPE, M.D.
Division of Adult Hygiene	Director, HERBERT L. LOMBARD, M.D.

State District Health Officers

The Southeastern District	RICHARD P. MACKNIGHT, M.D., New Bedford.
The South Metropolitan District	GEORGE M. SULLIVAN, M.D., Stoughton.
The North Metropolitan District	CHARLES B. MACK, M.D., Boston
The Northeastern District	ROBERT E. ARCHIBALD, M.D., Lynn.
The Worcester County District	OSCAR A. DUDLEY, M.D., Worcester.
The Connecticut Valley District	HAROLD E. MINER, M.D., Springfield.
The Berkshire District	WALTER W. LEE, M.D., No. Adams.

THE COMMONHEALTH

Volume 22
No. 2

Apr.-May-June
1935

PERSONAL HYGIENE

MASSACHUSETTS
DEPARTMENT OF PUBLIC HEALTH

THE COMMONHEALTH

QUARTERLY BULLETIN OF THE MASSACHUSETTS DEPARTMENT OF
PUBLIC HEALTH

Sent Free to any Citizen of the State

Entered as second class matter at Boston Postoffice.

M. LUISE DIEZ, M.D., DIRECTOR OF DIVISION OF CHILD HYGIENE, EDITOR.
Room 545, State House, Boston, Mass.

CONTENTS

	PAGE
Clinical Psychology and Medicine, by Ives Hendrick, M.D.	73
Conserving the Sight, by William F. Snow, M.D.	75
Prevention of Deafness—Rear your Ear to Hear, by Dorothy Case-Blechschmidt, M.D., F.A.C.S.	78
Care of the Teeth, by Eleanor G. McCarthy, D.H.	80
Some Facts One Should Know about the Skin, by Loretta Joy Cummins, M.D.	82
The Care and Hygiene of the Feet, by Lloyd T. Brown, M.D.	85
Curious New Discoveries about Sleep, by Donald A. Laird, Ph.D., Sci.D.	87
Satisfaction Guaranteed, by Alma Porter	91
Suggestions for Students Who Are Preparing Their Own Meals, by Helen Knowlton	95
Meals for One or Two—To Those Who Eat Alone, By Dorothea Nicoll	97
Well Groomed, Well Kept, by Marion B. Gardner	102
Hobbies, by Lucy Wright	105
Ventilation—Air Conditioning—Heating, by Arthur D. Weston	107
Lighting for Seeing, by M. Luckiesh and Frank K. Moss	111
The Preservation of Foods in the Household, by Hermann C. Lythgoe	114
Gonorrhea and Syphilis in the Public Schools, by N. A. Nelson, M.D.	118
Editorial Comment:	
Vision of School Children	119
Back Issues of The Commonhealth	120
Book Notes:	
Comparability of Maternal Mortality Rates in the United States and Certain Foreign Countries	121
Report of the Division of Food and Drugs, January, February, March, 1935	122

CLINICAL PSYCHOLOGY AND MEDICINE
By IVES HENDRICK, M. D.
Boston, Massachusetts

Today a widespread interest in social and emotional problems of the individual, as well as the diseases to which they give rise, is generally apparent in medical discussion. In part, this is perhaps a "backwash," a negative result of the forward march of scientific medicine in solving the problems of physical illness. As the futilities of the "shotgun" prescription, the fallacies of medical traditions, the absurdities of many supposedly remedial diets and surgical treatments have become more obvious, dissatisfaction with the multitude of problems for which research had no experimental and statistically valid answers, increased. A generation of scientifically trained physicians turned away, at first, from such problems as marital incompatibility, vocational failure, psychoneurotic symptoms, and the suffering of those whose physical examinations were irrelevant. They tended to lose interest in what could not be objectively understood, nor experimentally verified.

Extensive interest revived, partly at the insistence of leaders in psychiatry; and partly because internists have independently become more and more certain that many organic symptoms, even in conditions involving structural pathology—gastric ulcers, Graves' disease, asthma, dermatitis, abnormalities of menstruation, to mention only a few—were the end results of a series of events in which emotional tensions, acute and chronic, were often contributory or decisive etiological factors. In the last analysis, it seemed that similar defects in the individual's capacity to deal with psychological problems resulted in some people in character problems, in some in hysterical, obsessional or anxiety symptoms, and in some in a chronic and harmfully excessive stimulation of one or another portion of the autonomic systems. Here the interests of internist and clinical psychologist converged; the answer of the internist becomes the problem of the psychiatrist.

The psychiatrist has not answered all these problems yet, nor can he assure the internist of an effective, permanent cure of a large percentage of cases, nor commend a simple therapeutic formula easily and quickly administered without thorough specialized training. But he can fairly state that the last decades of psychological investigation have laid a firm foundation for the building of a psychopathology unanticipated a generation ago; that a beginning has been made in understanding the causes of conditions unclarified by organic research. Moreover, there are today psychotherapeutic methods for dealing with the etiology of psychological problems; the effectiveness of these methods far surpasses any efforts to influence them permanently by persuasion, suggestion, pseudo-organic therapy, or even by an abundance of human sympathy.

It was inevitable that the scientific ear of clinical psychology should develop a century later than the unshackling of medicine and philosophy. The problems of the psyche are far more complex. Tradition had surrounded them with a wall of illusion and a moat of taboos. Man's love of these prejudices was the last of the citadels of superstition to surrender to the march of science. Few, if any, medically trained psychologists are inclined today to a dualistic assumption that mind and body are mutually independent. Their data indicate that mental and emotional experience are the effects of concomitants of physiologic function. But there is a complexity and refinement of the organic functions involved in mental experience or social behavior with which physiologic methods, involving the isolation of relatively simple processes, cannot yet cope. The results of such studies have yielded little of clinical value in the treatment of the more complex problems of personality, though inevitably that day will come. In consequence, many psychiatrists have in this century accepted psychological data as the raw material of their investigation, the results have justified the methods, but, as they deal with a class of phenomena in which physicians are very superficially trained, they are often perplexing to those in other departments of medicine. What cannot be heard or seen, or palpated is not infrequently looked upon as of doubtful value by those unfamiliar with the subject.

Complex psychological problems cannot be as extensively reproduced by animal experimentation as those of organic medicine, for they represent, in the last analysis, the struggle of primitive instinct and the restraints of civilization. The neurotic person is he who has failed to subdue sufficiently his individualistic needs to the restraints of human society. He remains in part a child, requiring the pleasures of the moment even though excessive suffering be the price. This suffering of the neurotic is the result. Such an individual manifests similar phenomena to those which impel our species to find in war an immediate gain and a release of passion, even though our intelligence disclaims an eventual advantage.

The investigations of psychological problems have led, therefore, in two general directions. The first has been the study of the effect of special environmental factors upon a given individual and the treatment of his problem by guiding him in the selection of environment and in the appraisal of its responsibilities. The second has devolved from the method of psychoanalysis, which has shown that often what seems to be a personal problem, accidentally resulting from an environmentally determined distress, is a repetition of emotional situations of childhood which the adult cannot recollect. The environmental situation of the adult is then shown to be more the result of his personality than a cause. The demonstration that human behavior is frequently determined by psychological functions of which the individual is unaware, that a reasoned motive is often a disguise for an unknown and rationally inacceptable motive, and the intensive study of the interactions of such unconscious motives and conscious behavior—these discoveries constitute an epoch in the history of science.

Psychologically conditioned pain can seldom be dealt with effectively by common sense or exhortation. Many such patients who seek relief are as intelligent as their physician, as qualified to formulate a plan of how life should be lived as he. The neurotic problem itself proves that there are mental factors at work more decisive than the patient's will to be well and his own logical appraisal of the consequences of his unwilled behavior. It is often as inaccessible to volition, and generally as uncontrolled by reason, as many functions of the internal organs. The first therapeutic task of the physician, after he has dealt with the patient's physical hygiene is, therefore, to help the neurotic patient to recognize without humiliation and denial these facts; his second, to provide a better understanding, or at least to comprehend that which the patient himself can offer—to concede first to himself and then to his patient, that the most naive, unmediated comments of a human being may reveal more about the nature of his suffering than all that anatomy, chemistry and terminology can yet provide.

A second vital contribution of modern psychiatry to general medicine is the clear differentiation of the "primary neuroses" and the "secondary gain." Though the cause of the neurosis is unconscious, its effects are not; after a neurosis has developed, most individuals tend to exploit it to obtain whatever additional pleasures they can, among the most obvious of these "secondary gains," pleasure in the symptoms.

childish demands for attention, a predilection for new diagnoses and treatments, a preference for being cared for and dependent. Only the specialist usually distinguishes the factors which contribute to the original neurosis from those which are secondary and generally much more obvious. The primary causes often require special psychological methods to demonstrate. Treatment which ameliorates symptoms and other neurotic manifestations of the moment is often the result chiefly of the patient's pleasure in the treatment. The ultimate result is therefore to encourage the habit of illness.

In practice, therefore, an adequate appraisal of the problem may often leave the physician between the Scylla of denying treatment and the Charybdis of unwittingly providing new inducements to be ill. These everyday dilemmas are further complicated by the imperative need of the neurotic individual to produce suffering for himself, however he may resist and deny it. Harsh reprimand, the execution of the notion "Spare the rod and spoil the adult of imperfect maturity," may satisfy his need to suffer and thereby unconsciously encourage him to exploit his illness as effectively as pleasingly individualistic diets, or the easily developed love of a well-run hospital. The intelligent management of such problems is, indeed, one of the rarest of medical arts, so long as the complex of psychological factors is inadequately appraised. It is, therefore, generally best to deal as directly as one's knowledge of clinical psychology, and especially unconscious psychology, allows with the primary neurosis itself. Only ignorance of modern psychology can today justify the notion that it is good medicine to treat an hysterical paralysis by suggestion and neglect the total personality, to advise as to sexual relations and not inquire why an individual has failed to develop normal marital relationships without instruction. For the symptom or complaint is not the disease itself; they are indications of a spontaneous repair. This is why other symptoms or environmental difficulties recur when only the symptom is treated and the fundamental emotional conflicts are neglected. What often seems by comparison with more fortunate people, or with an arbitrary standard of "normalcy", unfortunate and absurd, is actually the best solution of which an individual with a given unconscious problem is capable. A marriage which has seemed the source of otherwise unnecessary tribulation, or a group of obsessions which interfere with daily tasks, are often shown by analysis of the unconscious to be the least undesirable results of the neurosis, when its basic nature is revealed. As an ankylosis supplies but protects from a dangerous infection, so the neurotic suffers from his obvious handicaps, but adopts the least painful solution of which he is capable so long as the primary neurosis is uncured.

CONSERVING THE SIGHT

By WILLIAM F. SNOW, M.D.

National Society for the Prevention of Blindness
New York City, N. Y.

Among the greatest advances in medicine during the past twenty-five years has been the tremendously increased attention given to the prevention of disease. The whole health conservation movement has enlisted the efforts of teachers, social workers and many lay groups, in addition to physicians, nurses and health officials. The old saying that "an ounce of prevention is worth a pound of cure" applies particularly in any discussion of the conservation of children's eyesight; for the worst tragedy of blindness or seriously defective vision lies in the fact that, in most cases, such a disaster is avoidable.

The amount of needless blindness that may be found in China, India,

Egypt and in some of the European countries is appalling. Although the exact number of the blind in the world is unknown, it is estimated to be somewhere between three and five million. In the United States, the blind population is approximately 100,000.

During the past few years the Child Welfare Committee of the League of Nations has concerned itself with the possibilities of protecting children's eyesight. A practical means of assisting visually handicapped children—which has particularly interested the League—is the special educational technique employed in sight-saving classes. These classes, which originated in England, have become most widely adopted in school systems throughout the United States; they may be found also in France, Germany, Austria, Denmark, and several other European countries. Dr. F. Humbert, Secretary-General of the International Association for Prevention of Blindness, in a recent report says:

"In most countries, children who can still make use of their remaining eyesight are either sent to schools for the blind, or if their parents refuse to allow this, have no means of education or development. They suffer either through being assimilated among the totally blind or through being regarded at school and in everyday life as backward, simply because they have been unable to acquire knowledge commensurate with their intellectual abilities."

To the child with seriously defective vision, the sight-saving class offers not only an opportunity for education, but also the chance to keep his eye condition from growing worse. Moreover, in the vocational guidance that is offered in such classes, the child is taught to realize his own possibilities and his own limitations, and is guided to select occupations that will not only be practicable for him but will not increase his eye difficulties.

There are many other ways, in addition to sight-saving classes, through which the sight of children is being conserved. It is most significant and encouraging that the public is learning that proper protection of the eyes—like safeguarding growth and development of the teeth and other parts of the body—should begin long before the child is born. The prenatal examination of mothers and their treatment and care play a large part in providing children with normal healthy eyes. Such protection of the eyes in pregnancy and during infancy and early childhood lays a foundation for good vision in the years to come. The sooner defective vision can be discovered and eye diseases recognized, the greater the chance of overcoming the resulting handicap of poor vision.

One of the brilliant achievements of the movement for prevention of blindness and the conservation of vision is the control of ophthalmia neonatorum—a disease usually known as babies' sore eyes. Every year there has been a decrease in the amount of blindness from this cause, as a result of the widespread use of prophylactic solutions in the eyes of infants at birth. This is now compulsory nearly everywhere in the United States although a few states have not yet made it obligatory. Many of the blind adults today lost their sight needlessly because a prophylactic solution was not used in their eyes at birth. During the past twenty-five years, at least 3,000 men, women and children in the United States have been saved the tragedy of loss of sight, and of life in institutions for the blind, because of ophthalmia neonatorum. This was accomplished largely through the use of prophylactic solutions at birth. Under conditions of thirty or more years ago, they would not have escaped. This estimate is based on the fact that blindness due to ophthalmia neonatorum among new admissions to schools for the blind has decreased 75 per cent in twenty-five years.

Under ideal conditions, every child's eyes should be tested before he enters school. But it is not yet possible to do this in all communities. It is, however, practicable to accomplish this for the school age groups; and every effort should be made to learn the child's vision ability early in the first year of school and follow this initial examination by observation in subsequent years. Many children have failed to be promoted and have been considered stupid, when in truth they were unable to see well enough to learn. The child whose vision is too poor to allow concentration may easily become a behavior problem. Time may well be spent—and ultimately saved for both the child and teacher—in vision testing as a screening process, to select, at least, the more obvious cases needing the attention of eye physicians.

The National Society for the Prevention of Blindness estimates that approximately 20 per cent of school children have defective vision. The causes of these defects are, of course, many. Some are due to abnormalities in the physical development of the eye, or to permanent damage caused by disease. It is certain, however, that in many instances faulty vision is the result of bad hygiene, wrong use of the eyes or neglected medical care and attention which those responsible should have provided as soon as the need was discovered. It is also true that a considerable proportion of these conditions could still be remedied or improved. The National Society issues many interesting pamphlets and letters of advice to parents on all these phases of sight conservation.

The eye is a more delicate and more complicated mechanism than the finest watch in the world. The best watch can be bought for a few weeks' pay, but a human eye that will see cannot be bought for all the money in the world. Yet thousands of parents every day expose their children's eyes—and their own for that matter—to hazards to which they would not think of exposing the inner mechanism of a watch. Few people would think of giving a small child a hammer and a watch to play with at the same time; yet at this moment there are undoubtedly thousands of youngsters playing with sharp pointed scissors, with matches or with materials which rubbed into the eyes may cause inflammation or injury.

Children are easily susceptible victims of eye accidents of all sorts. Surveys disclose an amazing variety of injuries. The mishaps include such odd accidents as a wound from the fin of a fish and a peck from a pet rooster held in the lap. A little girl was so interested in observing her mother in the wonderful process of making pancakes that she was struck in the eye by flying grease from the pan. In a recent case a table fork being used to untangle badly knotted shoe laces slipped and cut an eye. The Fourth of July week always records a heavy toll of eye accidents.

Adolescent boys and girls seem to be especially afflicted by eye accidents; perhaps this is because they are most active at that age. Eye hazards stand high among the casualties of athletic sports, and in mechanical and chemical trades. Every eye injury, from accident or from other cause, should receive prompt and continuous medical attention until the wound is entirely healed. Probably more eyes are lost from neglect of prompt and proper medical treatment than from the injuries themselves.

Eye physicians recognize three cardinal principles of first aid after eye injuries. The first of these is cleanliness; next, prompt rest for the eye; and, third, medical care by a competent physician, in consultation when necessary with the ophthalmologist. These principles apply even if the injury is slight, and they are imperative with serious eye injuries. What can be accomplished by application of these principles has been demonstrated by their application in industries which have heavy eye hazards.

An objection frequently raised by parents, when glasses are advised for their children, is the possibility of breakage and the danger of broken fragments of glass entering the eye and doing it serious damage, or even destroying sight. The same danger is recognized when glasses are worn by older children and adults in their various sports as well as in work. Recently, however, the use of non-shatterable glass for spectacles has been inaugurated. The advantage of such glasses will readily be appreciated for near-sighted children, where it is so important to get them away from books and to get them interested in outdoor life and various types of sports.

If we neglect the eyes of the children of today, we shall be responsible for a large amount of defective vision and total blindness among the men and women of tomorrow. And loss of sight is, without question, one of the most unfortunate afflictions which may come to any individual; and one of the most costly afflictions from the standpoint of public burden.

It is important, of course, to avoid frightening parents about dangers to eyesight. It should always be remembered that tragic as it is to have constantly a hundred thousand blind persons in our population, and many times that number of needlessly handicapped by eye defects, this total is only a small portion of the whole population and is growing smaller year by year. What we all need to do as citizens is to help these individuals who are gallantly doing their work against limitations from which we have fortunately been spared, and join forces to prevent the oncoming generations from similar handicaps. It is also important to remember that there must be no lessening of activities in this field of conservation during these depressing years.

If you wish further information about conserving the sight of children, write to the National Society for the Prevention of Blindness, 50 West 50th Street, New York City.

PREVENTION OF DEAFNESS — REAR YOUR EAR TO HEAR

By DOROTHY CASE-BLECHSCHMIDT, M.D., F.A.C.S.
Surgeon, Woman's Hospital
Philadelphia, Pa.

Happy are those who reach middle age "sound eared" as well as "clear eyed."

Although the progressive development of catarrhal deafness is noted in adult life it is an undisputed fact that the incipient stages are found in childhood. It is conceded by authorities that in any attempt to prevent deafness the most hopeful point of attack is childhood through *The Prevention of. Colds*—*The Removal of Diseased Tonsils* and adenoids, which are so often responsible for recurring colds in the head with a coexistent eustachian tube congestion; through the *Removal of Bad Teeth* which may be the foci of infection and are frequently presenting a toxic handicap; through the *Treatment of Sinus Infection*, the *Correction of a Badly Deviated Septum* or the *Removal of any and all Mechanical Obstructions* found in the nasal passages which interfere with proper drainage of the upper air tract and their communicating accessory sinuses or which occasion, due to mechanical blockage, faulty breathing. All these conditions must be first corrected if we hope to make any headway in the prevention of deafness. There is continuously a normal outflow of secretion from the mucous glands with which the lining membrane of the nasal passages and sinuses is so richly supplied. When a blockage occurs, either *Congestive, Mechanical* or *Allergic* in type, we find a perfect medium prepared for the development and proliferation of bacteria.

The usual variety of germs ever present in the nasal passages of even healthy robust individuals are often harmless until congestion or obstruction occurs creating the moisture and food for strengthening their aggression.

A nasal allergy (hay fever) certainly needs attention and faulty diet, faulty elimination and bad hygiene are well known contributory causes to deafness.

In addition to the glandular structure of the mucuous membrane, we must consider the blood supply and the part the sympathetic nervous system plays in the gymnastics of the blood vessels and blood spaces not only found in the lining of the nasal cavities but in that of the sinuses as well and especially in the mucous lining of the eustachian tubes, a tract or passage from the throat to the middle ear. Paralysis of either the vaso-constrictors or the vaso-dilators even temporarily can be brought about by "over gymnastics" of these little filaments. A blow on the head or over the ears, exposure to cold on the nape of the neck, wet feet, exposure to cold after overheating of the body from physical exercise, overeating of sugar, constipation and poor hygiene all tend to produce this condition. An increased amount of blood in these parts particularly the blood of passive congestion tends to produce an overgrowth of tissue especially the lymphoid structures in the nose and throat.

So intricate and involved and interrelated are these delicate structures in themselves that in the presence of bacterial infection a prompt and efficient treatment should be instituted by those best able to advise and care for such patients because even the so-called cold, if neglected, may produce far-reaching consequences.

Improper blowing of the nose may force the infected secretion into the middle ear through the eustachian tubes or into one or more of the accessory sinuses. If the inflammation does not subside—abscess in these structures may occur. The nostrils should never be compressed when giving the nose a blow. The handkerchief, or better, the tissues should be held loosely about the nose and the secretion forced gently outward through both sides (both nostrils).

In nasal douching the danger of spreading these infections in the same way is so great that no douching should be done without proper instructions and on the advice of the physician. (The same is true of ear douching.) The sniffing of salt water or any of the ordinary washing solutions advertised so widely is a pernicious, dangerous procedure and imperils not only the ears but the sinuses as well.

So much has been said and written to the public about germs that one begins to feel that the laity are becoming indifferent to germ infections in the head. This is evidenced by the oft-repeated phrase "only a cold in the head." This does not, however, apply to the few who are so germ conscious and who repair at stated intervals to the doctor for vaccine treatment to prevent colds. While naturally the laity is most interested in getting relief or cure promptly it is impossible to prevent colds in the head or ear affections with attendant deafness unless the people are educated to an understanding of these relationships and give their intelligent cooperation. How often a man in the prime of life is denied life insurance because of a kidney disease which had its inception in childhood (perhaps an abscessed ear, diseased tonsils or sinusitis). Abscess of the pelvis of the kidney (pyelitis) is frequently traced to an infection in the nose, throat or ears. Infections in the appendix or gall bladder are often due to infections in the upper respiratory tract which spread either directly or through the blood stream or through the lymphatics. Acute rheumatic fever and arthritis are also well known far-reaching consequences so that the entire gamut of infection may be part of the same identical picture— each presenting a part or a stage of the same infectious pathologic process.

So important is the watchful care of the nose and throat (the gateway of the body) that children with the mildest head cold should be put to bed and have prompt care and attention. An ear that has abscessed should be treated until all purulent discharge has cleared up and the eustachian tube congestion has been relieved.

Overfed and undernourished children should be given a properly balanced diet. Swimming for children with ear infections should be prohibited. The delicate child with the poor-toned vasomotor system should have the regular tub bath followed by a short cold friction rub. There is nothing better to prevent colds so common to the delicate child than graduated cold friction rubs provided these be given in a warm room, and a good circulatory reaction obtained in each instance.

While the prevention of progressive catarrhal deafness in later life should be started in childhood, the writer believes that the so-called permanent deafness in adults due to otosclerosis (hardening) with fixation of the stapes and nerve deafness which may be due to a variety of causes and which are so hopeless when developed, may also be influenced by early promotion of healthy noses and throats in children.

CARE OF THE TEETH
By ELEANOR G. MCCARTHY, D.H.
Consultant in Dental Hygiene
Massachusetts Department of Public Health

What you eat and when you go to the dentist are, of course, personal matters, but for this article I have chosen the older meaning of personal hygiene and have confined the discussion to the home care of the teeth.

Good nutrition is fundamental and the need of dentistry, especially for children, is both universal and difficult to obtain. For this reason the home care of the teeth has had to be somewhat neglected by public health authorities, if not by the dentifrice manufacturers. The latter have helped to create the public demand for clean teeth and the movies give daily witness to the beauty of a "protected smile". All of which is excellent. The task for dentistry and public health is to follow this with more detailed information as to "the commonsense of mouth care" so that, once stirred, the public will not waste its millions on luxurious accessories or expect to cure disease by a careful toilet.

Toothbrushing

To begin with children. Last week a former schoolmate asked me, "Does brushing teeth prevent decay—isn't it largely a matter of proper food?". (This mother had studied nutrition). On the other hand, when I ask mothers at our Well Child Conferences, "The children brush their teeth, don't they?", many times the answer is, "Yes, but I finish for them, for I do a better job". (These mothers still feel that cleanliness prevents decay).

Our advice to all mothers is to help the children to do the brushing for themselves—it is part of the task of growing up. If you have time, play inspector to encourage thorough brushing rather than finishing for them. Clean teeth are desirable even though cleanliness does not prevent decay.

When should they begin? There is no set rule—when all twenty baby teeth are through the gums is one good rule— when the child is interested and you have time to teach him is another. At Nursery Schools children start brushing their teeth at two and a half years but this may not be possible at home.

Remember that the "tough crusted" bread, toast, fruit and raw vegetables, which are being recommended now for all children, help to keep their teeth naturally clean. Using fruit rather than pastry and cake for dessert makes the toothbrush less important for the three, four and five-year-old.

As remembering is the hardest part of toothbrushing when you are forming the habit, "how often" is a question deserving some thought. As "twice a day" is more or less expected in the first grade we suggest that brushing at night be the first step. When this is mastered add brushing after breakfast. Brushing the teeth after the noon-day lunch is equally logical even though the child may have to give it up later. Playing with the brush and "brushing every time they are near the bathroom" is often the result of beginning when there wasn't time to teach.

Buy the smallest toothbrush you can find and even then, if the brush is too big for a particular mouth, do not be afraid to cut off a row or two of tufts with a razor blade. Except for size, the best children's brushes are like the longer brushes—stiff, with plenty of space between the groups of bristles.

If you are helping the children to do a good job you will want to watch two places—the inside surface of the lower molars and the outside surface of the upper molars. In the first case the tongue, and in the second, the cheek gets in the way of the brush. With "just water" is the way to start; later a toothpowder or paste may be added. A little salt, or salt, soda and borax combined, as described presently, are good. Commercial toothpowder and mild (non-medicated) toothpastes are pleasant but expensive.

Looking in a mirror helps—no matter what your age. As soon as you have your own brush you need a separate hook or holder as well as a proper respect for other people's brushes which you may be prompted to try.

During the first few years of school, care of the teeth is still largely a matter of forming the habit of regular cleaning and of getting used to the pleasantness of a clean mouth. Using only your own brush and brushing without being reminded can be expected at this age if training began before school.

Up to now, the usual brushing back and forth has been accepted with all the emphasis placed on acquiring the habit. Dr. Gesell of Yale says that it is just as easy for a little child to brush his teeth up and down as crosswise. So, children can have their attention drawn to this *good* method as soon as you or the teacher have time to teach them. As the permanent teeth come in, the teeth are apt to be crowded and a method of cleaning which will reach the in-between surfaces of the teeth becomes important. Here, again, a small brush is essential. Place the brush, handle tipped toward the teeth, on the gums and brush up and down, with short vigorous strokes. This means learning to use just your wrist rather than your whole arm.

In Junior and Senior High School, students are shown the little "juggly motion", used with the upward or downward stroke, which forces the bristles in between the teeth and massages the gums. Gum massage becomes increasingly important as the children grow older.

School children can give their toothbrushes the care which any bristle brush needs—frequent washing with soap and warm water, and placing to dry in the sun. Shining teeth have no film and, no matter what toothpowder you use, you need a dry brush to cut the film. Older children are using two brushes so that each one has a good chance to dry. It is more economical in the long run.

A toothpowder that you can make at home is:
1/3 cup salt
1/3 cup baking soda
1/3 cup borax

Put through a sieve to mix thoroughly.
Add ½ teaspoon or more of oil of peppermint, wintergreen or other flavoring.
A good mouth wash can be made from this by using one teaspoon of the powder mixture in one glass of water.

If money is limited, we advise spending it for Cod Liver Oil (liquid or capsules) and dentistry, instead of expensive toothpastes and mouth washes.

Older school children will want to know the safe use of dental floss or heavy thread to remove bits of food that may stay wedged between the teeth after careful brushing. Winding the floss or thread around the two forefingers and sliding it up and down between the teeth is safer than using a sharp point of any kind.

In high school the first signs of future gum troubles are often found. The loss of teeth from decay causes poor bites or malocclusion. Malocclusion and crowded teeth are often responsible for gums that recede or become inflamed and even bleed—especially is this true when the gums are affected in certain areas of the mouth. Gums that are generally soft, tender and apt to bleed are often caused by a lack of Vitamin C foods* in the diet.

Toothbrushing which includes gum massage is important for the adult, for by increasing the circulation and by the actual rubbing you improve the tone and the toughness of the gum tissues. This helps to keep the edge of the gum close to the neck of the tooth and prevents infection from pathogenic bacteria.

In adult life then, daily care becomes more and more important in offsetting the effects of natural wear and tear. Clean teeth continue to be most desirable from the aesthetic point of view, and gum massage, either by the brush, foods, or the finger, essential for the health of the gums.

During the period from high school on, professional cleaning by a dentist or dental hygienist is often needed once, twice (or more often) a year to remove tartar. If tartar is present, gums cannot be kept healthy by home brushing and massage.

At times of physical illness and special strain, such as pregnancy, the teeth need extra care in cleaning as a heavy film may form from digestive disturbances.

When the gums are diseased, careful cleaning of all the tooth surfaces and massage of the gums with simple or medicated pastes become, according to the periodontist, a very important part of his treatment and the cure.

At no time is the careful daily cleansing of the teeth the only factor or the most important factor in maintaining their good health. It is most desirable aesthetically at all ages, as it contributes to the health of the teeth and gums and is an essential part of the treatment of gum disease. Most teeth require constant care by you and the dentist and all teeth need the care that comes from within—from good food and wise living.

*Citrous fruits, tomatoes, green leafy vegetables are richest in Vitamin C.

SOME FACTS ONE SHOULD KNOW ABOUT THE SKIN
By LORETTA JOY CUMMINS, M.D.
Boston, Mass.

Unless one has been afflicted with some skin disease, or been associated with someone who has been suffering from such a condition, her chief interest in skin is in learning what she can do to increase its beauty. It is very commendable that everyone today is interested in improving her appearance as much as possible; we want to encourage that, but there is a great deal for women to learn about the true facts of how to properly care for the skin and hair.

This is a simple statement of scientific facts. In the first place, one must remember that the skin is not merely the covering of the body. It is an organ of the body and as such must be given the consideration one would give to any other organ. It is a secreting organ. In the skin over the surface of the body, there are millions of tiny glands of two types: oil glands and sweat glands. These are pouring out their secretions onto the surface of the body during the whole twenty-four hours These secretions are taken care of through evaporation and absorption by the clothing. I will not go into the details of the structures and functions of the skin, but I do want to correct the idea so many have that the skin is merely a covering of simple cells. The skin is vitally connected with the whole system and is not a thing apart. One's general health is reflected in the skin in many ways: many cases of diabetes are first discovered by the dermatologist; focal infections of various kinds and gland disturbances are unearthed in our search for the causes of some skin eruptions. The care we take of our whole body is of great importance to the skin. If one would have a beautiful clear complexion one must observe all the laws of general hygiene; proper amount of bathing, exercise, diet, sleep, etc. The importance of bathing would be thoroughly understood if everyone knew the amount of secretion poured out onto the skin every twenty-four hours. The average normal person should take a daily bath in order to keep the pores free and clear. It is an amazing fact that so many persons would think they were very unclean if they didn't wash their body every day, but they are satisfied to go days or weeks without washing their face. Now the skin of the face is exactly the same as that of the body but is more exposed to dust and dirt so why not wash it with soap and water too? I am speaking now of the average normal skin; I allow there are many sensitive, delicate skins, but generally when a normal person cannot use soap and water on her face, it is because she is using too strong or too drying a soap, or many times because she has an idea that creams are better. Creams have their place, but they do not take the place of soap and water. Now just a word about nourishing the skin: The average woman is very gullible and will believe anything told her by a clever person selling cosmetics. The skin cannot be fed locally. There is no such thing as a skin food. The skin can be creamed and softened but it has no power of assimilating or digesting a local application; the only nourishment it gets is from the blood. The skin is filled with a fine network of blood vessels which brings it all its nourishment. Remember the only means of feeding the skin is through the stomach.

The causes of skin diseases are both external and internal. Many persons still hold the old idea that every skin eruption is due to something in the blood. There are many conditions which are purely localized. I want to speak briefly of a group of conditions which have quite recently been found to be of local origin, due to the fungus infection: First there is a condition which for years was considered an eczema: it is seen both in infants and adults. It occurs most commonly behind the ears, in the bend of the elbow, under the arms and in the groins. In many of these cases we find the organism by examining scrapings under the microscope. It is mildly contagious and a very small area on the hand of the mother or any person caring for a child may produce an eczema-like eruption on the child. The following case from our clinic at the Massachusetts General Hospital illustrates this point. A child eight months old had eczema off and on since it was one month old. The eruption was on the face, arms and legs. The skin tests were negative and changes in diet had no effect. It cleared up under local treatment but would reappear. There were short intervals of freedom from the eruption. One day when the nurse was making a house visit, the mother showed her a spot on her hand and stated she had had an itching eruption on her hand off and on for years. This was reported, and on the next visit to the hospital the mother's hands were treated and cleared up. Since then the baby's eczema has remained cured. The child was undoubtedly infected from the mother.

Another fungus condition is commonly seen on the hands and feet. It occurs as small water blisters which first appear deep in the skin on the side of the fingers, on the webs of the fingers and palms of the hands. On the feet they appear between the toes, producing a thickened whitish appearance of the skin, or peeling and fissures, or deep seated vesicles. Occasionally the skin on the palms and soles becomes thickened and calloused areas form. The name of this condition is epidermophytosis. It is a form of ring worm but has none of the appearance of the ordinary ring worm. The condition is very common to quite a large per cent of people who have it in a very mild form. At times the fungus goes into a spore or rest state causing the condition to temporarily clear up and later it develops and the eruption appears again. These outbreaks and remissions are quite characteristic. There is a great effort being made to prevent the spread of this very troublesome condition which is very commonly picked up in shower baths, swimming pools, bath houses and any place where people walk around barefooted. Many new cases appear every year at the close of the camp season. Another condition which is in this same group is plantar warts. A plantar wart is a small thickened callous-like area developing on the soles of feet. They are often very painful. There have been real epidemics of plantar warts in some of our colleges. Some of the smaller lesions clear up with the application of proper ointments but generally they require treatment with either x-ray or radium.

I am very glad to have this opportunity to give a word of warning about exposing the skin unnecesarily to the irritating rays of the sun. Nature has provided us with a body covering which is marvelously constructed. It will stand a great deal of abuse in most cases, but after a certain length of time it will show the effects of these abuses. Sunlight is very beneficial in certain cases and in certain amounts, but repeated exposures to the irritating rays of the sun produce degenerative changes which may lead up to the early development of serious skin diseases.

People leading outdoor lives like farmers, policemen, chauffeurs, etc., often show age changes quite early. After the age of thirty-five, every man and woman must be on the lookout for these signs. They start as roughened light brownish spots on any part of the face and hands. These may remain quite small for months or years with only a slight amount of roughness. They may come off at times and later reappear. These spots are called keratosis and in themselves are simple age changes but they are the potential sites of skin cancers and should be properly treated before they show any signs of degeneration.

Everyone naturally dislikes to hear anything about cancer but why shun hearing facts which, if understood, will bring health and happiness to us all. It is an appalling fact that between three and four thousand persons die every year in the United States of cancer of the skin and we, as skin specialists, know there should not be one death. There is no condition in dermatology more satisfactory to treat than the beginning skin cancer, because with the proper application of radium the results are marvelous. One must look out not only for these gradual new developments, but also for any degenerative change taking place in a mole or wart. Any skin lesion should be removed, no matter how simple it is if it is subjected to repeated irritation.

THE CARE AND HYGIENE OF THE FEET

By LLOYD T. BROWN, M.D.

Boston, Massachusetts

There are certain fundamental principles in the care and hygiene of the feet which should be understood and appreciated by everybody. The first of these, and the most important, is that the feet are a part of the whole human body, and are, therefore, affected by the condition of the body itself, as well as by the condition of the feet. It is not to be wondered at, therefore, that when the body has gone through a severe sickness or through any strain which has greatly weakened it, such as a considerable increase in weight or a sudden decrease in weight, that the feet not uncommonly become strained or painful when they are once more put to work. Such conditions as pregnancy or long illness, the change of occupation from a sedentary to a standing or a walking job or a change from the soft roads of the country to the hard sidewalks are very common causes of painful feet.

The next fundamental principle is the way or the position in which the feet are used. By this is meant whether the so-called weight-bearing lines show good or bad mechanical position of the feet in relation to the legs and the rest of the body. To understand this it must be realized that the feet are made up of a series of bones which are put together like a pile of blocks, and that there is motion between each one of these blocks; that the blocks are not placed directly one on top of the other, but are placed enough off center so that if there were no muscles or ligaments to hold them they would fall over to the inner side. The reason for this seeming mistake on the part of the builder is that with the blocks placed off center whenever the foot is put on the ground there is a spring-like action which takes the jar off the rest of the body. If they were placed on the exact center there would be no more spring to the foot than there is to a wooden leg or to a stilt such as the children walk around with. Because of this off-center position, it is easy to see that it must be the muscles and ligaments which keep the bones from falling apart, and therefore, it is these which get all the strain in walking. The strength of the muscles and ligaments are entirely dependent upon the general condition of the body as a whole. Thus it is possible to see the reason for the first of the fundamental principles which have been mentioned.

In order to appreciate what is meant by the weight-bearing lines of the feet, it must be recognized that there are four kinds of motion of the foot on the leg; the up-and-down motion used in walking, and the side-to-side motion which is most easily done when there is no weight on the foot. When the weight is put upon the foot there is always a tendency for the foot to roll over on the inner side instead of staying at the strongest point, which is about in the middle between rolling inward and rolling outward. When the foot is at the middle point, or the strongest position, a line drawn downward from the center of the knee cap will pass through the second toe. When the foot is too far rolled inward, the line will pass to inner side of the great toe and if rolled outward the line will pass through the outer toes. From the point of view of potential strain, the latter position is less of a strain than when the foot is rolled too far inward.

With these facts in mind, the answer to the question of whether the correct standing position is with the toes turned outward or with the feet parallel, and whether it is better to walk with the feet straight ahead or turned outward, does not offer any difficulty. If the toes and the knees point in the same direction, the feet are being used in their strongest position and the muscles are all getting their equal share of the work, and this position can be maintained whether the feet are turned outward or whether the feet are pointed straight ahead. If, however, the knees point to the inner side of the great toes and the feet are rolled over on the inner side, there must be an unequal muscle balance with a consequent more or less strain of the muscles and ligaments.

So far nothing has been said about the much abused term Flat Foot. There are just as many different kinds and shapes of feet in the world as there are different kinds and shapes of faces, or noses, or heads, or any other parts of the body. Some feet naturally have very high arches, and some have very low ones. This may be a racial, or a family trait. The important thing to recognize, whether the feet be high, medium, or low-arched is, are they being used with good or bad weight-bearing lines.

The two factors which lead to faulty weight-bearing lines are ignorance of what good weight-bearing lines are, and the kind of shoes which are worn. It is not possible to go into the question of what is a good shoe and what is a bad shoe, because no two people will ever agree on every detail. There are certain points, however, which are important. The shoe should be long enough so that the width of the thumb can be placed between the end of the longest toe and the end of the shoe. It should be no wider than the ball of the foot, as too great width has a tendency to allow spreading of the anterior arch. It should fit snugly around the heel. There should be plenty of depth on the inner side of the shoe directly over as well as back of the great toe joint. (This is a condition not commonly found in shoes.) There should be no narrowing in of the outer side of the shoe half way between the little toe and the heel, as is so commonly done, because the foot is normally and anatomically wide in this part. When it comes to the question of the height of the heel, there is opportunity for much discussion. It has been found that because of the hard floors and sidewalks a heel is better than no heel. From the mechanical and anatomical point of view about an inch heel for men and an inch and a half heel for women gives the best results.

Stockings play an important part in the function of the feet. Stockings which are too short can so crowd the toes together that the help which should be given to the rest of the foot by the toe muscles is greatly impaired. This, combined with faulty shoes and faulty weight-bearing lines, may lead to flat anterior arches and callouses and corns. Callouses and corns develop because of irritation of the foot on the shoe just as a callous will develop on the palm of the hand when a person is doing some unaccustomed work with a rake or a hoe. If the position of the foot in walking is changed either by the type of shoe used or, more effectively, by changing the weight-bearing lines of the foot in walking, the callouses will disappear. The same is also true with corns.

When it comes to the question of the greater value to the foot of silk or rayon or cotton or woolen stockings, this is largely an individual matter. What does well for one may be not so good for another. The important point is that the stockings should not be too short, nor too long, as the latter may make creases which will tend toward callouses. The feet themselves should be given the same hygiene, such as cleanliness, as is given to any part of the body. It is important that they should be thoroughly dried after each washing, as moisture between the toes may lead to maceration, and provides a fertile soil for infection with the condition called Athlete's Foot. When such a condition develops, and does not heal with the ordinary measures, it is wise to consult a physician as infection may become superimposed and may lead to serious consequences.

In closing it may be stated that it is not the height of the arch which may be the cause of the foot trouble. It is a question of the way the foot is habitually used. There are many people in the world who have such a flat foot that the print of the foot on the bathroom floor shows no arch at all and yet they have never had and probably never will have, any foot trouble. If, however, a foot, be it high or low arched, is used in bad weight-bearing lines over long periods of time, and if combined with this there is a marked increase or loss of weight, or a change of occupation from a sedentary to a standing or walking job, or if there is a general run-down physical condition, the picture is then all set for trouble with the feet provided something occurs which upsets the equilibrium between symptoms and no symptoms.

CURIOUS NEW DISCOVERIES ABOUT SLEEP*

By DONALD A. LAIRD, Ph.D., Sci.D.
Psychological Laboratory
Hamilton, N. Y.

Sleeping seems to be such a natural thing to do that most persons believe they are doing a pretty good job of it. True, we may be unconscious for eight, nine, or even ten hours, and feel that since we are getting so much sleep, it must be a pretty good sign.

But modern science has an unpleasant way of showing what a poor job we are really doing at many things we think could not be improved. Take the great amount of rickets a few years ago, for instance, as an example of thousands of people eating poorly although they thought their diets were good and wholesome And now we are finding that our sleep is in much the same status.

A dozen or so laboratories have been studying sleep during the past ten years, and science has learned a tremendous amount from these painstaking investigations. Everybody can learn a great deal of practical value from this work, also, and undoubtedly improve their sleep beyond what they had ever anticipated as a result.

That the average person needs this improvement was strikingly shown in a recent report in the "Medical Record." Forty per cent of well-educated and successful Americans, it was disclosed in this report, feel tired on getting up mornings. After a night of good sleep they should have awakened feeling well rested and even peppy, yet only eleven per cent woke up feeling this way. American sleep certainly does need improving.

Dr. Fred A. Moss, of George Washington University, has shown that the quality of sleep we get is just as important as the hours of sleep. Sleep has depth as well as mere length, and "how well" we sleep is perhaps even more important than "how long" we sleep.

Love, Chess, Excitement are Enemies to Sleep

Evening excitement, we have found in our laboratory, is one of the surest ways to give us a poor night's sleep. After witnessing an exciting football game one afternoon, for instance, a young man moved 140 times during the night; ordinarily he moved 86 times.

The worst disturbance of sleep we have yet discovered in the laboratory, however, was one night when a young man telephoned his fiancee in another city at 9.30. He was told that she was out, and would not be back home until between one and two in the morning. At 10:30 he went to bed in the laboratory, but moved almost two hundred times that night. As a rule he moved only 72 times. He did not awaken during this especially restless night, but the emotional disturbance—

---
*Reprinted through the courtesy of THE AMERICAN WEEKLY.

worrying about his "heart" being out—raised havoc with his sleep.

Slight emotional excitement taken to bed with one has also been found to disrupt the normal calm relaxation of sleep. A chess game in the evening, for a person who takes chess seriously, is as much a sleep disturber as an evening of bridge. And Dr. Samuel Renshaw and his associates at Ohio State University, have found that the sleep of orphan children is made more restless when they leave the institution to see a motion picture in the evening.

Even a child's birthday party, or some punishment during the day, will upset his sleep.

The antidote for this widespread enemy of sleep, for this emotional thief which steals some of the needed relaxation away from our sleeping hours, is to calm down mentally and emotionally before going to bed. We should prepare mentally for sleep, just as we have to prepare mentally to write a letter applying for a new job. We should slow down our thinking, forget serious or exciting things—in short, make our minds as blank as that of the wartime flapper. Feebleminded folk sleep better than brainy ones because their minds are more naturally empty and the moron does not need to make his mind a blank before going to bed since it is blank both day and night. One price that is paid for brains is troubled sleep, and although the feebleminded sleep most, it is the person with brains who needs the best sleep.

A hot bath—a real soaking—for at least five minutes helps to calm down emotions and makes sleep better. This helps so much to calm people down, in fact, that in hospitals for mental patients those who are abnormally excited are kept in a continuous bath of this sort all day and all night, smoking, eating, and reading in the tub until they are calmed down.

Empty Stomach or Color Scheme May be Disturbers

It also helps if the colors in one's bedroom are primarily blues or greens. These are calming colors, and in some mental hospitals they have special rooms furnished throughout in these colors to help calm excited patients. Yet the most used colors in American sleeping rooms are reds and yellows, which are the exciting colors.

The color of our sleeping room does its work before we get into bed. Once our eyes are closed and the lights out, of course, the color does not matter. But it does matter in gently guiding our emotional background during the half hour or so while we are preparing for the night's rest.

Another thief of our sleep's good quality is hunger pangs during the night. Four or five hours after the evening meal our stomachs are empty. Dr. Anton J. Carlson, of the University of Chicago, and Dr. Walter B. Cannon, of Harvard University, have conclusively shown that when the stomach is pretty well emptied of food these intense contractions of the entire stomach wall start in, and they keep up until food is put into the stomach. These intense contractions, which occur about four times an hour with an empty stomach, are what we "feel" as hunger pangs. They are probably one cause of children being cross and hard to manage late in the afternoon.

But during the night these thieving pangs make people move. Dr. Tomi Wada, working both at Johns Hopkins University and at Columbia University has found that many of the big moves made by people during their sleep follow by just a few seconds the appearance of these hunger contractions. The persons he experimented upon had a tiny balloon in their stomach all night long with which hunger pangs were registered.

With the sensitive somnokinetograph, or sleep-movement-recorder, we are now using in the laboratory, it is found that the average grown-up moves on an average of ten to twelve times an hour. Probably three or four of these moves which show disturbed sleep—one fourth—are caused by hunger pangs.

The only way to get rid of these sleep-robbing hunger pangs is to have food in the stomach. And experiments have shown that a light lunch of easily digested foods, eaten just before going to bed, makes adults sleep better than usual for them. A generous bowl of crackers and milk or corn flakes and milk eaten as a bedtime snack makes people move six per cent less than usual during the night. This is a pleasant way to get a six per cent dividend on our sleep, but it helps most only the first half of the night since the stomach is again empty some three to four hours after eating such a light lunch.

That is one reason why some scientists advocate sleeping only four hours at a time, but sleeping twice every twenty-four hours.

But having something on our mind and nothing in our stomach are not the only thieves of our rest units during the night. Noises, especially when they are irregular and unusual disturb sleep. The steady hum of traffic in the big city may, indeed, help sleep in a hypnotic-like fashion. But the brief screech of taxicab breakes, the whistles of a locomotive, a newsboy crying his extra edition, the policeman's whistle are real enemies of rest.

Light Sleepers Should Occupy a Room Alone

Many persons who are worried about waking up during the night for no apparent cause really have no reason for worrying about their sleep. It is not something intrinsically wrong with them that caused this wakefulness in many instances. They were awakened by some passing and unusual noise. But people awake gradually, and by the time they are wide enough awake to know what is going on, the noise which is the actual cause of their wakefulness can no longer be heard.

Some time ago, for instance, a gentleman wrote me that he was no longer able to sleep well. His only complaint was that he would awaken with great accuracy at 3.45 each morning. Almost a human alarm clock. He was worrying about this, and feared it might be just the beginning of serious trouble. I suggested that he set his alarm clock at 3.30, and get up at that time, go to his window, and listen closely for fifteen minutes.

At almost precisely 3.44 he was astonished to hear some noise in the next-door house. In just a few seconds the neighbor's front door opened, the man of the house stepped out, and the screen door slammed shut.

The very day he first noticed his "sleep disturbance" a new family had moved in next door. The husband's work required him to leave the house at approximately 3.45 each morning. The noisy exit had been awakening the man who got in touch with me, but by the time he was fully awake the last echo of the slamming screen door had died away. Little wonder that he was starting to worry about a serious sleep disease. For most disturbances of sleep some such cause can be found, although not always are they so simple and obvious.

Another person sleeping in the same room is also a sleep thief. Every time another person snores or moves in the same room, our sleep is disturbed. The way another person can disturb sleep is clearly shown in the section of an actual record of sleep movements of the men, Russell and Howard, sleeping in separate twin beds, but in the same room. Howard is the "lighter" sleeper, and his sleep is disturbed many times when Russell moves in the adjoining bed. Only the soundest sleepers should allow someone else to sleep in the same room.

Just how to discover a sound sleeper is a problem for the gods on

Olympus to fight over. While the average adult moves from ten to twelve times an hour, we have records in the laboratory from apparently normal persons who consistently averaged twenty moves each hour for week after week. There should be no argument about this person being at least a fitful sleeper if not a light sleeper. We have not yet found anyone who consistently averaged less than five moves an hour, and we have records from dozens of persons.

I suspect that many people think they are sound sleepers, however, when they are merely poor sleepers. On being called in the morning they are so slow waking up and in getting the cobwebs out of their head that they misjudge themselves to be sound sleepers. The truth, more likely, is that they simply haven't had enough good sleep and nature is attempting to have them take a few more needed winks. To be a good sleeper we should wake up mornings without needing to be called, feeling well-rested and energetic—something that not half of the population does.

Will our sleep be better if we sleep on the right or on the left side? For a while, a few years ago, it was a superstitious belief that we should sleep on our right side to prevent the heart from being crowded during the night. Then it was discovered that people who were right-handed were right-sided in many ways; not only were they also right-footed but actually used their right eye rather than their left. So the idea received some theoretical support that right-handed people would get better sleep if they slept on their right side. And left-handed people, of course, should sleep on their left side if there was anything in this theory.

But people don't sleep on one side. Before morning comes they sleep on all sides. Of the ten to twelve moves the average sleeper makes each hour, some three to four are major changes of position, where they turn from one side to the other, or onto their back or face.

Irregular Bedtime as a Prime Cause of Insomnia

It still matters a little, however, on which side you go to sleep. Richard Stradling has completed work in this laboratory which shows that habit helps in going to sleep, and that right-handed people usually have the habit of going to sleep on their right side. Once asleep, of course, the nightly whirligig of three to four turnabouts per hour begins, but there is the old demon of habit which helps going to sleep if we always go to bed on the same side. This is another aspect of the old saying that someone got up on the wrong side of the bed.

Habit is important through all of our sleep, not only in the side we go to bed on. Some people have the habit of irregularity in their bedtime which makes their sleep poorer when they go to bed early on some rare night. In the laboratory we make our subjects go to bed regularly at 10.30 for night after night. Every last person who has been under this routine says it is the wisest thing they learned. Going to bed early is not so important as going to bed at the same time each night, and on the same side each night.

We have also found that one night of the week is the worst for most persons' sleep. That is Sunday night. Sleep this night is at such low par largely because it is not just a day of rest, but it is also a day of neglecting the usual habit around which each individual life is strongly organized. Blue Monday can be better understood in view of Sunday night treating us to the most disturbed sleep of the week.

Some folks who have begun to worry about developing insomnia have been pleasantly surprised to find that instead they were neglecting a habit. These occasional nights, for instance, when it is difficult to go to sleep and we count sheep, stick a foot out from under the covers, get up and do setting-up exercises (a very unwise thing to do, by the way), hoping to coax a few winks quicker. These fitful going-to-sleep spells often happen when we have gone to bed much earlier than usual for us, or when we have taken a nap during the afternoon or early evening.

They also often occur when we get into bed on the wrong side.

SATISFACTION GUARANTEED
By ALMA PORTER
Assistant Supervisor of Physical Education
State Department of Education

Putting aside for the moment the learned and scholarly dissertations on recreation, the wise use of leisure time and the changing social order, this seemingly indisputable simple fact still remains: each one of us turns hungrily toward individually satisfying activities which have nothing whatever to do with earning a living. Just to suggest a few of the outstanding and much-advertised brands occupying some of our attention are the "movies," the theatres, the dance halls and night clubs, the ball games, the Coney Islands and Revere beaches, the automobile trips and wayside camps, the great pleasure-cruise ships, the clubs and lodges and resort hotels, and the gay parties. Then if one could add to that list all of the things which all of the people do in this country to "pass away time", there would be told the great story of a determined and aggressive effort not only to work for a living but to play in that life. Unquestionably this urge toward satisfying activity exists in the face of a more or less overwhelming conviction that leisure time activities are little more than sporadic amusement and entertainment just to take up slack and so leave us with few standards. The question then is: what individually satisfying activities are satisfactory in terms of well-balanced living?

That this natural and wholesome desire to play and to create is befogged is tragically true if one may believe the books and articles, controversies and discussions on the matter; befogged by worry, by economic and religious tradition, by bad or rather shall we say incomplete education, by a misunderstanding of essentials to well-balanced living; that it is only a fog and not a blotting-out is encouraging, as evidenced by the same books, and articles, controversies and discussions.

There is fogginess because worry of any kind tends to upset all life balances, and in the last few years worry about present lacks and future insecurity for millions has come to be their ever-present portion. There is uncertainness because of the work tradition and religious tradition of the country, which to all intents and purposes says, "this is a working country—we have no leisure time to waste and no leisure class to waste it." The Puritan tenets still spring up with their subtle suggestions that great joy in the life of this world, in and of itself, may jeopardize one's unrestricted admittance into the next. There is misunderstanding because in the midst of a commercially-amused country there has been no general acceptance of the great need to *educate* for a satisfying and skillful avocational life and for joyous healthful leisure-time activity. There is confusion because we have conceived, been forced perhaps to conceive, of life as successful in proportion to its hours of labor and its family, if not individual, accumulation of money.

No one wishes to minimize the personal and social need for hard and productive work; the need for a deep-rooted life plan whether it is called religion or ethics, the need for accepting responsibility, the need for substantial and fundamental education in the tool subjects, the need for money-earning and money-planning. Far from that! But in addition this constant urge for individually satisfying activity which has nothing to do with earning a living should provide a great incentive, a great power, to learn and to use all through one's life from birth to death "things to do," which enrich life and make it worth living even under the most adverse conditions of poverty and ill health and discouragement. We have not scratched the surface of that incentive and power because we have by and large accepted entertainment as a substitute for activity.

Until quite lately there has been no concerted effort to educate for leisure. Indeed we have been loathe to admit either the leisure or the need for its education. Commercialized amusement or even much of the uncommercialized amusement and entertainment have demanded no change in education front, and hardly more than compromise with traditional prejudices, since it took care of itself so to speak and made no public demand. *Education* for leisure has come slowly because it has forced the recognition of an undesired and perhaps permanent change in a social order in which most of us, at least in optimistic moments, have had a degree of faith.

So today there are at least two great problems of leisure time. First, the emergency problem growing out of an out-moded work tradition in an electrically industrialized country and its attendant unemployment, few with educated abilities to use long hours of leisure well, even if acute worry were not present, no money to buy entertainment, all resulting in a sad social chaos bolstered up here and there with public money invested in recreation programs and in other constructive programs. Second, the long-time problem, largely a children's problem with its solution based on the prophesy of a different work-leisure relationship going forward into an indefinite future and dependent upon a changing philosophy in our homes, schools, churches, and communities. This forward-looking plan involves recognition not only of this urge toward a more vital creative and social activity, but of the need for providing a more generous education which accepts the challenge of a newer time.

Perhaps it is in order here to again point out that the emergency leisure-time problem in this depression is acute for the hearts and souls of men if not for their bodies; the problem of how to bring up well-balanced and keen youth is critical in this time of stress and future uncertainty, but each one of us, young and old, has a modicum of leisure, a desire to do, and yet so pitifully little education or opportunity to make that doing productive and satisfying. Recent surveys show that the great difference between what people do and what they really wish they knew how to do, is not the vast difference between going to a "movie" and wanting to go on a 'round the world cruise involving much money. It is rather the difference between reading the funnies in a newspaper every day and wanting to learn to draw and sketch; between desultory talk with the neighbors and wanting to learn dramatic art; between watching someone else play tennis and golf, dance and hike out-of-doors, and wanting to learn to play tennis or golf and have opportunity to dance and hike; between listening to radio programs, good and bad, and wanting the satisfaction of playing in an orchestra; between watching father work at a carpenter's bench in the workroom and wanting to handle tools one's self; between appreciating someone else's lovely garden and wanting a pot of petunias on one's own window sill. This shows an open gap so wide that courage and great faith in a newer kind of educational opportunity which provides both for appreciation and participation is going to be needed to help close it.

To return then to the first problem—what is being done to fill that gap, recreationally speaking, in an effort to stem the tide of discouragement for adults, people used to working for money, or for the young adult who is ready and waiting to take his place in a working world which does not want him? This is not an easy task in the face of a fairly general feeling about play for and by adults, and their hesitance about seeking even the opportunities offered. Nevertheless in the last several years there has been a great increase in these opportunities and the acceptance thereof. So we see communities with their own money opening up their schools for professional and vocational study, for avocational activities, and for play of all kinds with the social centers and playgrounds cooperating. The Federal Government has expressed its faith in these ventures and has paid for service of its own to communities which requested it and conformed to certain regulations. The churches, the social agencies, and private organizations have combined in a great effort to provide programs for the advantage and enjoyment of the people of the country. Families in neighborhoods have contrived and struggled to keep its people active and relatively content at home.

We shall probably never know what such opportunities have meant by way of steadying people who must forget, if only for a moment, their frantic worry. What it may have meant to the man or woman even in the midst of great trouble, aching to make music, or sketch, or study current world problems, or learn to build gardens, or make over big clothes for little people, or take down an engine, or learn to budget an infinitesimal pay envelope, we can guess only if we ourselves have been touched with ambition.

In a broad sense, then, there has been a great concerted effort to do as much as possible for as many as possible by every agency organized to help in the country, seconded by the Government. It is too much to say that this is the reason why the people during the depression have been on the whole patient and friendly, but hopefully it may have played its small part in making a bad strain a little less bad. Remnants of it may even go on living when more stable times come.

On the other hand, one of the sad things of the past few years is the dilemma of the young adult. Brought up to believe in general education, specific preparation, a job, a marriage, a family, at the age of 23, 24, 25, he has his education, he is somewhat specifically prepared, but he is an adult living in his parents' home, with no job, no marriage, no family—his normal life cycle broken. Perhaps this is one reason why so many of our young adults are in mischief, why there are thousands of them "on the roads", why the average age in disciplinary institutions is about 19, why the newspapers record dreadful disorder coming at the hands of young boys and girls. Not all youth is delinquent, as some would have you believe, but the situation is critical enough to make one ask what the schools, the homes, the churches and the communities have been doing in the last twenty years that this thing could happen. All these youngsters have passed through our hands. We brag about our homes, and schools, and churches, and communities. What have we done, or what have we failed to do to cause such waste motion among young people? "Movies," the lack of good old hellfire and damnation religious fervor, broken homes and bad environment, no jobs, brought up in one kind of a world only to find another waiting; all of these and many, many more reasons are bandied about. Perhaps no one knows. The important thing is that a great cross-section of youth is in a serious plight, not because it is inherently vicious, but because we have somehow failed to give it stability and balance, wisdom in choice and power to think clear and straight.

All of which brings us to a second problem. Recreation and avocational educational programs are not going to save the world, but the many related activities incorporated into a deeper and broader education for children from birth in homes and schools, churches and communities will hopefully play their part well for the newer generations which very soon will take the reins from our hands and show us how the world is run.

The term recreation is essentially an adult word and not a child word; it implies a relationship with adult labor rather than with childhood activities. It is for this reason that there is a slight distinction made between suggested recreation activities in the first problem and activity programs in the second.

Our four great institutions if one may for the moment include the community as a unified institution, must and are thinking in terms of providing, each in its own way, opportunities for developing appreciations as well as for participation in individually satisfying activities. There are the orchestras and the glees, garden clubs and arts and crafts, active games and dancing, dramatic clubs and splendid libraries in the schools and churches and communities. These are taught not as things separate, but as part and parcel of the educational program. Playgrounds have proved themselves worth their weight in gold, not only as a safe place for children to play, but as a constructive agent for the teaching of socially-acceptable behaviors.

Homes, the most important institution of all, are thinking more than ever of providing security for children, security in the love of parents and their place in his world. Homes more than ever are providing for the work and play of its children with backyard playgrounds, work benches, quiet rooms for study and reading, and, quite consistently, better health routines are coming to be integral parts of the child's way of living. The homes of the "good old days" provided in many ways for its children with its chores, its handcrafts, its animals, its out-of-doors; and its demands on the skill and loyalty of all the family. Today homes must provide in a sense artificially, for these things, and encourage the schools and communities and churches so to do also.

What have we then to summarize? First, there is the unquenchable desire to do things—individually satisfying activities which have nothing to do with earning a living. The catch is that so many of the satisfying things that we do are hardly worth the doing except for a moment of time and for an amount of money. It becomes then a problem to reawaken in the adults of today a desire to take part in activities which bring groups of people together in a common interest; to rebuild the old love of making and doing things with the hands; to encourage the old urge to "talk things over together" and to use discrimination in the choice of commercial entertainment.

Since no one knows what lies ahead for us or for our children these children must learn not *what* to think so much as *how* to think, and in addition must be fortified, through our great institutions with sturdy bodies and capable minds, with skills and appreciations for the long leisure hours which are prophesied, with a healthy desire to be with people in socially acceptable ways, and with the power and courage to make their choices on high levels; all these that the cycle of normal living best suited to the time may go on in the newer generations, unbroken. "The world is not a 'prison house' but a kind of spiritual kindergarten where millions of bewildered infants are trying to spell God with the wrong blocks."—Edward Arlington Robinson. But how fortunate that they are trying to spell "God".

By HELEN KNOWLTON
Division of Home Economics, Massachusetts State College
Amherst, Massachusetts

Introduction

The following plan for students preparing their own meals, either singly or in small groups, was first formulated for students at Massachusetts State College in the winter of 1935. College students living in cities would have market facilities which would make possible much more variety in fresh fruits and vegetables as well as wide choice in baked products. The menus are planned for adequate nutritive value as indicated under "Do You Eat What You Need Before You Eat What You Want?" Their cost is low. They are intended to take little time and include few formal recipes.

No heat other than surface units is required. Two of these units are desirable, and a double boiler is almost essential. Students who wish more cooked desserts can easily prepare simple variations of tapioca or cornstarch puddings. The use of a refrigerator is necessary in warm weather and would make possible, at all seasons, more economical buying in larger quantities, and safe use of left-overs. If an oven is available, much more variety would be possible.

The menus represent types. The breakfasts are standardized including always fruit, cereal, bread, beverage. An egg is used if not found elsewhere in the day's meals. The luncheons have different kinds of hot dishes except number 5 which is a cold meal suited to a noon with limited time, as it can be ready in advance. The hot dishes include two egg dishes, a vegetable on toast, a warm sandwich, a chowder, and a cream soup. Each luncheon has a salad or crisp vegetable. The desserts are simple. Sometimes a salad is used. The dinners furnish always a vegetable other than potato with varied protein main dishes. The desserts are mostly fruit to simplify preparation.

Do You Plan To Eat What You Need Before You Eat What You Want?

YOU NEED:

1. Milk, at least 1 pint daily. One quart is safer.
2. Vegetables, three servings (½ cup each) daily. Vegetables other than potatoes at least two servings daily. One, a green or raw vegetable.
3. Fruits (count canned or fresh tomatoes here). Two or more servings daily. Fresh in preference to canned or dried.
4. Meat, fish, eggs, cheese, dried peas and beans. One or two servings daily. An egg a day, if possible. Meat or fish once a day when possible.
5. Whole grain products, one or more servings daily. At least half of cereals and breads whole grain. Hot whole grain cereals or shredded wheat give most nutriment for cost in breakfast cereals.
6. Butter and other fats, about 3 ounces daily, equal to 6 good sized "pats".
7. Sugar and sweets, only enough to add flavor.
8. Water, 6 to 8 glasses daily, two before breakfast.

Do You Plan To Save Money On Food?

1. Buy pink canned salmon. It is cheaper than red and has more flavor.
2. Use beef or lamb stews to lower your meat bill and to save cooking vegetables separately.
3. Haddock and cod are among the cheapest fresh fish.
4. Pig or beef liver costs less than that from calves.

5. If you can, without spoilage, buy large cans of tomatoes, other vegetables, and fruits instead of small ten-cent kind.

6. Medium-sized oranges (Florida) are cheaper for juice than large ones.

7. Buy regular American cheese in bulk. It is cheaper than the factory package cheeses.

8. Extend peanut butter with at least equal quantity of water or milk, adding a little salt. It spreads better and is creamy instead of sticky.

9. Use fresh fruit and vegetables when in season. Quickly cooked vegetables are spinach and other tender greens, cabbage, cauliflower, asparagus, peas, turnip, carrot, squash, parsnip, string beans.

10. Buy canned foods in tins rather than in glass.

Do You Plan Your Food By The Day?

Breakfast	Luncheon	Dinner
1. Orange Rolled Oats—Toast Coffee or milk	Scrambled Eggs—Cole Slaw Rye Bread—Jam Milk	Lamb (or beef) Stew (Potatoes, Carrots, Onions) Crackers Canned Pears—Cookies Milk
2. Prunes Shredded Wheat—Toast Boiled Egg Coffee or Milk	Stewed Tomatoes on Toast Pear and Cottage Cheese Salad Bread—Milk	Fried Haddock—Boiled Potatoes Beets (canned) Carrot Sticks—Bread Ice Cream—Milk
3. Canned Pineapple French Toast with Karo Coffee or Milk	Toasted Rye Bread Cheese Sandwich Celery Cocoa—Cookies	Pork (or beef) Liver Mashed Potatoes—Carrots Bread Sliced Bananas with Top Milk Milk
4. Raisins cooked in Wheatena. (Cook twice amount, put in cups and use for dessert at night) Toast—Coffee or Milk	Salmon Chowder—Crackers Cabbage and Pineapple Salad Milk	Bacon and Eggs Boiled Potatoes—Turnip Lettuce Salad Molded Wheatena and Raisins with Top Milk Milk
5. Stewed Apricots Cornmeal Mush with Brown Sugar (Cook twice amount, and use fried in No. 6) Toast—Coffee or Milk	Potato, Egg and Celery Salad Wheat Bread Chocolate Cornstarch Pudding Milk	Creamed Dried Beef on Toast Canned Tomatoes Boiled Rice and Raisins with Top Milk Milk
6. Apple Sauce Fried Cornmeal Mush with Karo Toast Coffee or Milk	Egg Poached in Cooked Tomato served on Toast Ginger Cookies—Milk	Baked Beans—Dark Bread Cabbage and Apple Salad Prunes Milk
7. Banana Shredded Wheat—Toast Fried Egg Coffee or Milk	Cream of Celery Soup Crackers Raw Carrot and Peanut Butter Sandwich Canned Fruit	Creamed Codfish Boiled Potatoes—Spinach Celery Apple Pie or Turnover Milk

Do You Plan By The Week?

Food Groups	Adequate Diet at Minimum Cost	Proportion of Dollar	Adequate Diet at Moderate Cost	Proportion of Dollar
1. Milk and cheese	30c. to 35c.	1/4 or more	25c. to 30c.	1/4 or more
2. Fruits and vegetables	25c. to 20c.	Not more than 1/4	30c. to 25c.	1/4 or more
3. Lean meat, fish and eggs	15c.	About 1/7	20c. to 15c.	Not more than 1/5
4. Bread, flour and cereals	15c.	About 1/7	10c.	About 1/10
5. Fats, sugars and accessories	15c.	About 1/7	15c. to 20c.	About 1/6

If you spend only $3.00 each week		If you can spend $4.00 each week	
1. Milk and cheese	$.90	1. Milk and cheese	$1.00
2. Fruits and vegetables	.75	2. Fruits and vegetables	1.20
3. Lean meat, fish, eggs	.45	3. Lean meat, fish, eggs	.80
4. Bread, flour, cereals	.45	4. Bread, flour, cereals	.40
5. Fats, sugars and accessories	.45	5. Fats, sugars and accessories	.60
	$3.00		$4.00

The booklet, "Your Guide", published by the Massachusetts Department of Public Health and endorsed by the Massachusetts Department of Public Welfare has been prepared for home-makers who have to budget closely. Grocery orders are given for families from one to ten, with plans for hot weather and cold weather meals, school lunches, and recipes.

This booklet is being given out by home economic teachers, nurses, nutritionists, and welfare workers.

MEALS FOR ONE OR TWO

To Those Who Eat Alone

By DOROTHEA NICOLL

Consultant in Nutrition
Massachusetts Department of Public Health

No matter how simple your meal, or how varied the collection of odds and ends that must be assembled, meal time should mean more than just a chance to satisfy the "inner man". It is a time for relaxation and comfort! Open the window while you are getting things together, and fill the room with lively fresh air—it will warm up more quickly for the change.

If you cannot seem to work up an interest in eating even then, take time out for rest. Drop on to the bed, close your eyes, and be as "limp as a rag" for at least five minutes—or longer. Think of nothing, look at nothing, move nothing, just loaf! You may be sure that this short rest can do much for your appetite, nerves, and disposition.

Arrange your food attractively, using a gay napkin or colorful dishes. Sit down comfortably in the most pleasant part of your room. Give yourself an air of dining! Even the simplest food will taste better than if you snatched it hastily from the corner of the bureau, or ate it absentmindedly while you hustled around.

Plan to take plenty of time for at least one, if not all, of your meals. Read the latest book, look over the fashions, scan the newspaper, or repeat poetry to yourself — but above all take your time — *Enjoy Yourself!*

A Plan for Meals

When you have only a little money for food, it is more necessary than ever that all three meals be well chosen. Not only do you need enough food to prevent that "hollow" feeling—but, more important still, it must have all the vital health factors as well. If you use milk, potatoes, some green or yellow vegetables and dark bread or cereal every day, you will be able to have tasty as well as nutritious meals. And, incidentally, you will be getting the most food value for your money.

Plan like this—Each Day:
  1 pint of milk—fresh or evaporated—plain or in cooking
  1 potato
  1 other vegetable—canned or fresh—raw ones often
  1 serving of orange, grapefruit or tomato—raw or canned
  1 serving of dark cereal
  2 or more slices of bread, preferably whole grain
  2 tablespoons of butter

Each Week:
  Eggs—on 4 to 7 days
  Cheese—on 1 or 2 days
  Meat or fish—on 3 or 4 days
  Lettuce, spinach, kale, or cabbage—on 3 or 4 days
  Prunes or apricots—on 3 or 4 days

For breakfast—depending on your time and appetite:
  Fresh or cooked fruit, if possible
  Cereal with milk—use a hot one in winter
  Bread or toast with butter
  Milk, cocoa, or coffee
    Eggs, bacon, or other meats add considerably to the cost as well as the size of the meal.

Lunch or supper:
  Soup or chowder, creamed or scalloped dish, egg dish, salad, or sandwich
  Bread or toast with butter
  Milk, cocoa, or tea
  Dessert of fruit, milk pudding, simple cookie, or a sweet gives a finishing touch but is not necessary.

Dinner:
  Main dish—choose one of these—
    Meat, fish, hearty chowder or stew, cheese or egg dish, or baked dried beans or peas.
  Potato—unless in main dish
  Cooked vegetable, or a salad or both
  Bread and butter
  Simple dessert
  Beverage

Shopping for One or Two

Product	Suggested Purchase
Milk, bottled—pasteurized	1 pint per person daily
Milk, canned—evaporated—for emergency shelf	Or 1 large can every other day if in place of bottled milk
Butter—tub or roll butter cheaper than print	½ pound
Salad Oil—corn and cottonseed oil cheaper than olive	½ pint to 1 pint—smaller bottle costly
Eggs—fresh, grade A or selected storage	1/3 to ½ dozen weekly
Cheese—cottage, in bulk—least food value	¼ to ½ pound
American	By pound or package
Cream	Package or bulk
Grated and Imported	Most expensive and really a luxury
Bread—white, whole wheat, rye, raisin, graham, cracked wheat	Small loaf

Product	Suggested Purchase
Rolls—Parker House, French, sweet rolls, coffee rolls, buns, muffins, etc. (More expensive than bread)	½ dozen or 1 to 2 days' supply
Crackers—whole wheat, graham, soda, saltine	Bulk — ½ pound — or small package
Breakfast foods—Ready to serve	Smallest package of desired variety
Breakfast foods—To be cooked	Smallest package of desired variety
Macaroni, spaghetti, noodles	½ to 1 pound carton — cheaper in bulk
Rice	1 pound carton — cheaper in bulk
Molasses—light, medium, or dark	1 pound 2 ounce can
Sugar—granulated, powdered or confectioners—store in tin brown—store in breadbox	1 pound carton
Syrup—cane, maple, or sorghum syrup	Small can—avoid mixed syrups
Coffee—in cans or bulk	1 pound
Tea—black, green, or oolong	¼ to 1 pound
Cocoa—domestic or Dutch	¼ to ½ pound
Chocolate— unsweetened cake	½ pound
Mayonnaise	2-4-8 ounce bottle
Spices—pepper, ginger, cinnamon, clove, celery salt	2 ounces
Extracts—vanilla, lemon	2 ounce bottle

Vegetables—fresh	Way Purchased	Amount of Serving
String beans—green or wax	1 pound	¼ pound per serving
Lima beans	1 pound	½ pound per serving
Beets	Bunch	1-2 per serving
Beet greens	On bunch, or pound	½ pound per serving
Cabbage—green or white	Pound	½ pound per serving
Carrots	Bunch or pound	¼ pound or 1/3 bunch per serving
Cauliflower	Head	¼ medium head per serving
Celery	Bunch	¼ bunch per serving
Lettuce—leaf, Boston, iceberg	Head	¼ head per serving
Onions—Bermuda, Spanish, Texas	Pound or bag	¼ pound per serving
Peas, green	Pound (or qt.)	½ pound (or 2/3 qt.) per serving
Potatoes—3-4 in a pound	5 pounds	¼-1/3 pound per serving
Spinach	½ pound	¼ pound per serving
Squash—summer	Single	¼-½ squash per serving
Squash—winter	Pound	½ pound per serving
Tomatoes	4 in pound or single	¼ pound or 1 medium per serving
Turnips	Pound or single	¼ pound per serving

Fruits—fresh	Way Purchased	Amount of Serving
Apples—cooking	Pound or single	¼-1/3 pound per serving
Bananas	About 4 to 1 pound	1 banana per serving
Berries	Box—½ pint—1 pint and 1 quart	¼ quart per serving
Cranberries	Pound or pint	¼ pound or ½ pint per serving
Grapefruit		½ medium per serving
Oranges — 2-3 days' supply—most economical		

Fruits—dried	Way Purchased
Dates—pitted or unpitted	½ pound bulk or 1 package
Apricots—bulk or package	½ pound or 1 package
Prunes—bulk or package	½ pound or 1 package
Raisins	1 pound package

Canned fruits or vegetables are often cheaper and more economical than fresh, particularly in the winter. The food value is comparable to the fresh, and they save time in preparation and storage space.

Common Sizes of Cans—for One

8 ounces	1 cup	2 servings
Picnic or No. 1 Eastern	1 1/3 cups	2-3 servings
No. 1 tall	2 cups	3-4 servings
No. 2	2½ cups	4-5 servings

Canned foods in the small sizes are a help in keeping down waste and food costs. Compare the price on your fresh product with the canned and be sure to take into consideration your time for preparation and cooking. Also look out for waste, such as pods on peas, tops on carrots, etc. Reckon the cost of the finished product—not the one you buy at the store. Buy the size can you can most easily use. Watch sales—sometimes you can pick up bargains in price or variety—particularly if your grocer knows your preferences.

Foods Quickly and Easily Prepared

Milk—milk toast, cocoa, egg nog, milk shakes, milk soups or chowder, junket.

Eggs—boiled, scrambled, omelet, salad, in white sauce with toast or potato.

Meat and Fish—chopped meat cakes, liver and onions, pork chop with apple rings, broiled and boiled fish, creamed salmon, sardines, sliced ham sandwiches. Bouillon cubes, in hot water or with water from cooked vegetables—or from various vegetables.

Store cheese—Sandwich, plain or toasted, Welsh Rarebit, in white sauce on potato or vegetables, in macaroni, with tomato.

Cottage or Cream cheese—plain, in sandwich, salad with green pepper or fruit, on crackers.

Peanut Butter—sandwich, milk soup, tomato soup, stuffing for dates.

Vegetables—raw, boiled, creamed, soup, chowder, salad, salad sandwiches. It is economy to use carrots, spinach, cabbage, and yellow turnip raw often in sandwiches, salads, or as a relish. They give twice as much health protection as when cooked. If vegetables are cubed or shredded, then cooked in a small amount of water in a tightly covered pan, they will be done in about ten minutes. Using this water from cooked or canned vegetables for soup or gravy gives extra food value.

Salads—cole slaw, cabbage and apple, salmon salad, pineapple salad, banana salad, raw carrot and apple, chopped lettuce or cabbage with leftover fruit or vegetable.

Fruit—sliced oranges, apples, stuffed dates or prunes, sliced bananas, grapes, pineapple in salads, various combinations or plain.

Desserts—custards, junket, French toast, fruits, fruit or molasses cookies, gingerbread.

(Adapted from "Nutrition Notes") Lucy Gillett

Unusual Sandwiches from Common Foods

Grated orange peel and brown sugar with a little orange juice or soft butter for a sweet sandwich.

Raw chopped celery leaves, raw spinach or raw carrots with mayonnaise or cream cheese.

For tasty crisp sandwiches—

Use the one lone strip of bacon left from breakfast—or those two sardines—that last bit of the canned salmon or tuna fish with a bit of green vegetable. Chop the final four dates—and mix with cottage or cream cheese.

Toast the bread of your favorite sandwich for a change—or toast the finished sandwich.

Try a sandwich plate—three or four small sandwiches—all different—with a glass of tomato juice or a cup of bouillon—and an apple to top it off. It takes but a small amount to make one of these sandwiches, and the number is decided only by the extent of your appetite or your pantry.

"Eating Out"

Although it is apt to be slightly more expensive to eat in a restaurant than at home, you can have meals that are not only thrifty but satisfying, too. Just make sure that your three meals measure up to the general meal plan, especially in the amount of milk and raw fruits or vegetables. As a rule it is somewhat cheaper to buy fruit and eat it in your room than to order it with breakfast. This would leave a choice of cereals, toast or muffins, and a beverage for a simple, inexpensive breakfast. The combinations chosen according to weather, appetite. or pocketbook are many and varied. The "hungry souls" will have to decide between seconds on cereal or bread and the more expensive egg and meat dishes.

Luncheon menus will depend on the time available and the sort of dinner you wish. The simplest luncheon usually consists of a hearty dish, dessert, and a beverage. These main dishes may be soup, stew, salad, creamed or escalloped dish, eggs, or one of the many sandwiches. This seems to be a good time in which to get that egg you could not afford for breakfast, or the raw vegetable in salad or salad sandwich, which will not be included in the plate dinner tonight. All milk soups and creamed dishes, cheese sandwiches, and custards help to increase the milk, particularly if you find it difficult to drink that glass of milk each day. Desserts will vary from raw fruit, custard, gelatine desserts, to pies and ice cream.

Dinner should be chosen with an eye to getting meat, fish or baked beans or peas—potato—and at least one vegetable. When possible, extra vegetables, particularly the raw ones, are an excellent "buy." "Plate dinners" or "Specials" are often more economical than "a la carte" meals.

When money is really scarce, it may be necessary to do without desserts for one meal, or even for all. In this case keeping fruit in your room is the sensible answer.

By choosing dark breads instead of white, and fruit or milk puddings instead of rich desserts, and gingerbread or fruit muffins instead of frosted cakes, you will get much more for your money. Dr. Mary Swartz Rose of Columbia University has worked out a series of menus for the single person at fifty cents a day. This can be arranged quite easily if two of the meals are eaten in your room. Here are two suggested menus.

Breakfast in Room

Man		Woman	
1 pint milk	5c.	1 pint milk	5c.
¼ loaf whole wheat bread (sliced)	2c.	1 shredded wheat biscuit	1c.
		1 orange	3c.
1 banana (possible two)	3c.	1 tbsp. sugar	¼c.
	10c.		9¼c.

Luncheon in Cafeteria

Baked Beans	10c.	Egg salad sandwich	15c.
Cold slaw	5c.	1 glass milk	5c.
2 cookies	5c.	Apple (bought outside)	3c.
1 glass milk	5c.	2 pcs. chocolate	2c.
	25c.		25c.

Supper in Room

1 pint milk	5c.	1 pint milk	5c.
½ loaf whole wheat bread	4c.	1 cup tomato juice	3c.
1 ounce dried beef	3c.	¼ loaf bread	2c.
1 ounce butter	1½c.	10 prunes (previously soaked)	5c.
¼ can tomato juice	1½c.		
	15c.		15c.

WELL GROOMED, WELL KEPT

By MARION B. GARDNER

School of Household Economics, Simmons College
Boston, Massachusetts

Did you ever go to a horse race and bet on that shining black, well-groomed horse, the one with the red ribbon in a short braid at the neck, or possibly that little bay with the green tie in his tail, or the iron gray, sturdy looking steed. I wonder just which one appealed to you the most and why? Was it the shiny, well-combed coat, the trimmed mane and tail, or the tilt and pride of the horse's head which made you say enthusiastically, "That's my horse! I'm sure he is good looking enough to win any race."

Good looks comes of being well kept and is comparable to well groomed; they go hand in hand, and one works only when it has the other for a pleasing and progressive result. Your horse cannot win a race unless he is properly and proportionately nourished. Correct food gives the skin the proper coloring and adds a softness and a luster to the hair, while the proper amount of rest makes the animal hold his head high and inspires him with a vivaciousness which assumes success just as you with pride and joy can hold your head and shoulders erect, when you have been correctly fed, had sufficient rest and are gowned with the correct lines in your clothes as well as the proper colors for your type and figure.

People, like delightful race hores, are of different fundamental structures. Their personalities and individualities differ so that they are each and everyone different from the other. However, there is some generalization which can be done so as to group the type of structures. Some are small and petite; others are tall, thin and lean. The medium size is that "just right" size, not too tall, not too stout or too big, while the contrast to this type is that big, broad-shouldered, boney female. The excess of flesh gives the structure such form that one must adopt lines for the short, stout. Many people are combinations of that type, but generally speaking, this is not true.

On the fundamental body framework is the note of interest; namely in the head, and the head coloring determines another classification of color which is graciously given to all but not so generally improved on by every one. There are those rare colorful blondes, ash blondes, more often made by bleaching, and the fair blondes who have lost many of the golden lights from their hair. The brunettes are the dark-haired people; they may have dark brown, brown-black, or blue-black hair. Between the blonde and brunette classes is the large intermediate classification, not a blonde or a brunette, but they were when younger, either one or the other, and now they are called intermediate (the half-way type). The auburn type has many groups; those with brilliant lights in the hair, the light auburn whose hair is just off the golden brown, toward orange; the dark auburn with hair that charms the world. Those dark reddish brown lights are like an old oriental copper water jar. The remaining type is the gray-haired, the disheartening head that has been discussed and always tried to be improved upon since the beginning of man until within recent years, when gray hair has become popular. There are the brunette gray, blonde gray and auburn gray, but, of course, the most charming bit of crowning glory is that delightful white, well-groomed head. Usually this person has been a brunette in youthful years for brunette hair turns a clearer, more even gray or white. To the head is added the enriched coloring of the eyes, the seat of brightness and expression, and is the basic measurement for the colors of the face and the costumes. In spite of the eye coloring which is usually brown, blue or gray, the skin is just as important, for its color, texture and quality depend much on the climatic conditions, food and rest. The skin may be colorful (pink and clear) or fair with little less pink, or sallow, with some yellow, and often the skin, as a person grows old, takes on a tone called dark sallow.

With this wide classification and just to make it more complicated is that definite, positive quality known as personality which cannot be overlooked in the application of color to figure. Personalities differ, and in so doing, give us definite colors for these kinds. The mannish, courageous, unemotional, business-like woman would naturally wear dark values of colors such as blue-green, green-blues, purple or black and white. Bright colors would be used very sparingly. The swift, vivacious, alert, active movements of a person would require peppy, bright colors which radiate cheer and keep in step with the person. She would avoid dull tones. The unassuming person who is most informal, amiable and easily approached would wear shades of green, old rose and dull tones of yellow (brown) to express radiating friendliness. The opposite to the unassuming type is the serious minded, reserved, formal, dignified and difficult to approach. She would wear reserved colors, dark tones with serious positive touches. The demonstrative who is dramatic, changeable, moody and emotional would wear striking colors. She usually disregards formality of color knowledge thus securing unpleasant effects in her costumes quite the opposite from the demure, reserved, delicate one who wears those charming pastel tones which express her femininity. There are, of course, combinations of these personalities mentioned, but we must keep in mind that all personalities are factors in the selection of colors for the individual.

Color is a vast subject and in order to do the subject justice, one should avoid prejudices and be open minded to what color may or may not suit her type and personality. A great dislike for a color usually comes from unpleasant association. Color may be becoming to eyes, hair and complexion but antagonize temperament. Therefore, it is unwise to permit personal preferences to limit one's selection. Colors in themselves have power to do many things. They suggest anger, confusion, depression, kindness, love, dignity, etc. The French were the first to realize the importance of the color symbolism in costume and named each dress creation according to the emotion expressed.

There are many general ideas upon which to build your foundation knowledge of color harmonies, but in order to combine colors one must first understand there are six colors on the color wheel; three primary colors and three secondary, the latter being made from the primary. Red, orange, yellow, green, blue and violet are the alphabet of the color world and are the colors upon which all hues (name of the color) are built. There are many methods of securing color combinations, but I do not have space or time to relate them here. Two or more bright colors should rarely be placed next to each other unless neutral colors separate them for they destroy the intrinsic value of each other. Small touches of black are great harmonizing agents and are effectively used in accents instead of bright colors. In large masses such as with the race horses, lower tones such as black, gray, bay (dull brown) are their background colors and intense colors in their ribbons have been used for accents. This is true in dress except in rare instances. Colors used as they appear on the color wheel in their fullest intensities (brightness) do not make a pleasing harmony no matter what combination is used. The hue, value and intensity relation must be changed and skillfully controlled before a delightful, enthralling effect will be secured for a costume of constant wearing.

The most interesting part of costume work is the selection of color combinations either in a general or a specific way. Before applying color to a specific type as before mentioned, I here list a couple of color combinations. Two or three colors around the color wheel such as yellow and yellow-orange used in combination are most interesting providing the yellow is pastel and the yellow-orange is a middle value or vice versa; with an accent of dark orange (brown) the costume has become much alive by value contrast. Colors are more easily harmonized if the color is used in singleness or slight doubleness with touches of value contrast. A color combination for a dark spring print might be a red purple background with a light lavender flower, a gray-rose flower of middle value with leaves of blue-green. All these colors have blue in them, and the blue is the definite harmonizing agent. Should this color, blue, be a becoming one for the selector, it should, of course, show its predominance in her wardrobe. Other interesting combinations can be found that will add the necessary change to prevent monotony in the wardrobe. Any coloring feature of the face is intensified in costume color by the repetition of that color or by its complementary colors (opposite on the color wheel) or by its analagous (adjacent color). Blue and blue-green add blueness to the blue or hazel eyes. It is a well known fact that the most pleasing harmony with the features is the repetition of the color in a costume, of at least one of the most attractive color features, hair, eyes, or complexion.

The most fortunate type as to color wearing is the intermediate, as before mentioned, with colorful skin and brown eyes. Her color range is greater than any other type. For her summer wardrobe she might wear spring green crepe with touches of dark brown. Should the brunette of blue-black hair, colorful skin and gray eyes wish to wear this spring green color, she would add a dash of Pompeian red. The golden blonde might don a grotto blue frock with an accent of midnight blue. A brown brunette could wear a raspberry color of monochromatic color harmony (light to dark of one color). The more varied the contrast, the more charming the frock. The gray hair, hazel eyes and fair skin might wear lupin blue with a touch of weigelia (light rose). There are endless effects one can secure by the selection of colors, but to select the charming colors, the one that does just the right thing to the wearer is an art acquired only by long-time study and working with colors. Don't let a salesgirl tell you, "That is beautiful on you", for she may be looking at the price tag or out the window as she influences you to buy. Analyze yourself; know your own coloring; study your figure and the reaction of color on your personality. With all of these factors in mind, you can select for yourself the color which adds both to your beauty and charm.

HOBBIES

By LUCY WRIGHT

Federal Emergency Relief Administration
Boston, Mass.

Hobbies appears at first rather a mild subject, and one that may quite innocently be discussed all by itself. It has a way, however, before you get very far with it, of disclosing paradoxes and unexpected developments. Your hobby may even stir a sense of grievance in others. Stephen Leacock, in a recent article on "First Call for Spring", fairly begs those of us who "love Nature" to keep it to ourselves! Probably ie has suffered from other people's hobbies. Let it be admitted, then, from the start, that it *is* best, if you have a hobby, to "keep it dark" or at least to manage it very carefully in relation to other people's time, space, and taste! This is really sound. For if there is any one earmark of the hobby, it is that hobbies as such are affairs between the hobby-rider and his own self, or between him and the universe at large, and not a part of his bread and butter traffic with his fellowman. A hobby is indeed an affair in which what one is doing, and what one wishes to do, coincide, and this may or may not include others. It may, of course, be an altogether gregarious affair, but that does not alter the situation. If gregarious affairs are an individual's hobby, it should still be kept a secret from the world at large—that is, if one really wishes to practice the art of hobby riding with distinction and reveal the secret only at vital moments.

The whole subject of the relation of hobbies to *time*, to one's own time as well as to other people's time, is of great importance. Your hobby may bring you under social disapproval, especially if it is of the public variety and appears to impinge upon time that should properly be devoted to your vocation. There was Mrs. Jellaby, the character in Dickens, who was so interested in "sending moral pocket handkerchiefs to the heathen" that she had to neglect her own family. An extreme individualist will no doubt defend this and pursue his hobby at any cost, even brandish it in the face of a disapproving world. I am only insisting that he must know what he is doing and have the will and strength to take the consequences when his hobby becomes a social boomerang.

Hobbies presupposes a vocation in contrast to an avocation. It is usually not the word to describe the effort of unemployed men and women to keep themselves occupied in times of business depression. Hobbies require a sense of freedom that sufferers from unemployment can hardly be expected to feel. It symbolizes free action of free people. Some of the unemployed achieve this, but that is part of miraculously fine living in the face of ordeal that appears in the life about us now and then like flowers in the desert. To many of us, economically unproductive occupation in time of responsibility and need is a species of torture. Even as I say this, however, I think of the place of gardening in many a life before and during depression, and almost take back what I have said. A hobby is, in any case, an affair in which process is more than result, and person more than either. For this reason it must require a background of comparative economic security. The great opportunity of the moment in this country arises with the promise of wider margins of leisure through shorter working hours for great numbers of people. This is the time which may be turned to constructive or creative account, if we will.

One of the interesting facts that has become clear in this period of depression is that hobbies may become *convertible* into vocations by chance, at least, though not perhaps when they are so designed "by malice aforethought"! Hobbies should remain in the class of things unpredictable as to outcome. Any transformation that takes place should come about casually or we defeat the purpose and place in life of the hobby element—with its sense of timelessness. I recall being told at the World's Fair that one of the great dahlia exhibits represented the former hobby, now the vocation, of an unemployed chemist, and I was told that the models of engines and other rolling stock of a great railroad represented the boyhood hobby, now the vocation, of an unemployed civil engineer. Many of us have heard that the lovely doll-houses that appeared on the market recently in architectural styles of different periods are the present work of a group of older men who, but for this development, would have been among the unemployed. Women who marry should surely be possessed of an adequate hobby to return to as hobby or vocation after the family is raised. A mother whose early hobby had been swimming, turned breadwinner by necessity when her children were nearly grown, became a successful teacher of swimming. I met a mother of two children who were invalids and of two who were well. She was looking for an Egyptian primer. "When I get this family raised," she explained, "I'm going to be an archaeologist."

Most paradoxical of all the facts about hobbies is the truth that some people appear to have little or no need of them. When Adolph Ochs, the great newspaper publisher, died recently, this was one of the sentences that stood out in the course of the sixteen columns of obituary notice of his life: "The publishing of *The Times* was his avocation and his hobby as well as his vocation." I have heard the superintendent of a woman's reformatory say, "My hobby is adult education in a woman's reformatory." Hobby in this sense is evidently a quality, or element, in one's work itself that carries with it exceptional individuality, something over and above the official requirements that characterizes the day's work of such men and women, and makes constant demands upon a great range of their powers. Very likely they have minor hobbies in addition. In fact, it is not unusual to discover that people have a cluster of hobbies—birds, hepaticas, and ferns, or mountain climbing, carpentry and modelling; or they may have changing hobbies, in the sense that one grows out of another—an interest in trees, in kinds of wood, in uses of wood, in furniture, in restoring antique furniture.

The most characteristic type of all is the single hobby. This may be participation in choral music or folk dancing; collecting models and pictures of bridges; the artist's creation of fairy gardens; the chemist's noon-hour experiments in inventing a fiery serpent; the tracing through the ages of the history of an idea—like "Know thyself"; the study of a single character, like Cecil Rhodes, widening to international proportions the field of children's reading; the continuous fostering of a cause, like the cooperative movement; experiment with group leadership—each of these and countless more may be an adventure or quest running like a thread of gold through a lifetime.

The important point is that the word hobbies represents an idea and is a word of great transitional value. At the present time this word carries a weight of meaning, probably disproportionate to its strength, but profoundly significant in the life and thought of our country. Presently it may shift its burden to more adequate words and phrases. but at the moment it carries with it a sense of age-long recognition of values in life outside the competitive economic world. It is a recognition infinitely older, probably, than the use of the word hobbies itself. Perhaps the word should be surrendered for use only in relation to mere hobbies—sports, games, whimsical and refreshing pursuits. For what we distinguish as creative or constructive hobbies, some other word implied in part by avocations and in part by our discussion of the possibilities of adult education, should and will be found.

However that may be, we are steadily coming to a recognition of the constructive and creative uses to which leisure time may be put, and the significance for individual and community living of the kind of use made by adults of these margins of time. Shall we pass our leisure time in the casual use of modern inventions, in emptying the contents of our minds to each other without discrimination and in keeping up to date with commercial recreations? Shall we even content ourselves with the cultivation of mere hobbies? Or shall we bring up our children and train ourselves to uses of leisure time that are creative or constructive in the individual personality, or that may contribute some new bit that was lacking to science or to art, or that has promise for widening areas of understanding in human relationships, personal and civic? Upon the answer much depends for the race of spiritually full-grown beings we may become, if we will.

VENTILATION — AIR CONDITIONING — HEATING

By ARTHUR D. WESTON

Chief Engineer, Division of Sanitary Engineering
Massachusetts Department of Public Health

A recent committee of the American Public Health Association defined air conditioning as—

"The maintenance by any suitable means of any desired atmospheric conditions (during occupancy)".

When asked the question—

"Should not the words 'air conditioning' be used instead of 'ventilation'?" two of the five members answered "No" and two answered "Yes" and one gave no answer.

The committee of the American Society of Heating and Ventilating Engineers in a report on ventilation standards, submitted in June 1932, defined ventilation and air conditioning as follows:

"Ventilation: the process of supplying or removing air by natural or mechanical means to or from any space. Such air may or may not have been conditioned." "Air Conditioning: the simultaneous control of all or at least the first three of those factors affecting both the physical and chemical conditions of the atmosphere without any structure. These factors include temperature, humidity, motion, distribution, dust, bacteria, odors, toxic gases and ionization, most of which affect in a greater or less degree human health or comfort."

As suitable ventilation and air conditioning are impracticable without some means of heating or cooling then heating must be considered in connection with either of these subjects.

As early as 1888 the Commonwealth of Massachusetts interested it-

self in the proper ventilation of public buildings, especially schoolhouses, and following the enactment of Chapter 149 of the Acts of 1888 it became the duty of the then State District Police to see that—
"Every public building and every schoolhouse shall be ventilated in such a manner that the air shall not become so exhausted as to be injurious to the health of the persons present therein."

Rufus R. Wade was the Chief of the District Police (now Department of Public Safety) at that time and under his supervision the first comprehensive systems of ventilation in schoolhouses in this State were installed. The ill effects from poorly ventilated rooms were then believed to be due to the toxic influence of carbon dioxide concentration resulting from exhalation from those occupying the rooms. Chief Wade had the benefit of the early studies of Parkes in England and De Chaumont, the works of Dr. John S. Billings, published in 1884, the work of Robert Briggs of the American Society of Civil Engineers, the work of Prof. S. Homer Woodbridge of the Massachusetts Institute of Technology, the work of the Boston Board of Health under Dr. S. H. Durgin, and that of A. C. Martin, Architect, and Dr. J. G. Pinkham for the then Massachusetts State Board of Health. Chief Wade, in agreement with others, felt that the carbon dioxide content of the air should not be permitted to exceed 800 to 1200 parts per million and after considerable discussion relative to the desirability of requiring larger amounts finally specified that the amount of fresh air supplied in the ventilating systems should not be less than 30 cubic feet per minute for each occupant.

The early regulations enforceable under the State Police have been amended from time to time and the regulations now enforceable by the Commonwealth of Massachusetts in matters of ventilation and air conditioning are those printed by the Inspection Division of the Department of Public Safety under the provisions of Chapter 143 of the General Laws. These regulations relate to theatres, public or special halls, auditoriums and school-houses, and copies of them may be secured upon application from the Department of Public Safety, State House, Boston. In general they permit the use of any source of heating supply which does not contaminate the air and which does not conflict with any building or fire ordinance. For the ventilation of theatres, public or special halls and auditoriums these regulations require suitable devices including ventiducts, dampers, etc., so as to provide for the removal of at least 2½ cubic feet of air per minute for each foot of area of the auditorium and gallery floors and to supply an equal amount of fresh air with, of course, suitable means for heating the air so as to maintain a temperature of 65 degrees F in zero weather. These regulations provide that the velocity of air entering the ventiducts shall not exceed 500 feet per minute and that the velocity entering the auditorium horizontally shall not exceed 350 feet per minute. Provision also is made for an improved plenum chamber system of ventilation, if required.

In the case of schoolhouses, the requirements are somewhat more rigid as the minimum capacity of the system must be capable of providing a fresh air supply for the schoolhouse classrooms of 30 cubic feet of air per minute per occupant and for the removal of an equal volume. In assembly halls, gymnasiums, including galleries, the capacity for supplying and removing the air must be equal to 2-½ cubic feet per minute for each square foot of floor space, and for locker rooms, lunch rooms, emergency rooms, natatoriums and shower rooms 1-½ cubic feet per minute for each square foot of floor space. Provision also is made for maintaining a temperature in the classroom, recitation and assembly rooms at the breathing plane above the floor of 68 degrees F, and in toilet rooms, corridors, passages and for certain manual training rooms, stairhalls, wardrobes, gymnasiums and play houses a temperature of 60 degrees F, and in showers, training rooms and laboratories 50 degrees F. These temperatures are based on a temperature of zero on the outside.

There has been considerable discussion as to the reasonableness of the requirement of 30 cubic feet of fresh air per minute per pupil. So far as can be determined by this Department this requirement is based on the early decisions of Chief Wade of the Massachusetts District Police. As early as 1913 the conflict of opinion as to the proper amount of fresh air to be supplied was great among hygienists, engineers, architects and educators. In school houses there was also some question as to the actual need of other than window ventilating systems and there was a very definite question in the minds of many as to the wisdom of installing expensive systems of ventilation if they were not to be used. Moreover, it had come to be generally known that the danger to health from toxic poisoning from cumulations of impure air in classrooms was not great and that the real value of ventilation and air conditioning was the comfort afforded the room occupants. Because of these many differences of opinion, the Department of Public Health was requested by the Commissioner of Public Safety to advise him in the matter of revising the regulations of his department. In order to clarify the situation, Dr. George H. Bigelow, then Commissioner of Public Health, called a meeting of educators, engineers and others interested and following this conference he appointed a committee of such experts as the following:

Philip Drinker and C. P. Yaglou of the Harvard School of Public Health,
Prof. Gordon M. Fair of the Harvard School of Engineering
Prof. Thomas R. Camp of the Massachusetts Institute of Technology.

As a result of the work of this Committee new standards were adopted by the Department of Public Health on September 20, 1932, and were submitted under date on September 27, 1932, to the Commissioner of Public Safety. These proposed standards read as follows:

"**Section I—Air Temperature and Humidity**

The condition of the air in such occupied space in which the only source of contamination is the occupant shall be maintained at all times during occupancy at a comfortable 'effective temperature'.

The effective temperature shall range between 64 degrees and 69 degrees when heating or humidification is required, and between 69 degrees and 73 degrees when cooling or dehumidification is required. It is desirable that the relative humidity shall not be less than 30 per cent nor more than 60 per cent in any case.

These effective temperatures shall be maintained at a level of 36 inches above the floor.

Section II—Air Quality

The air in such occupied spaces shall be at all times free from toxic or disagreeable gases and fumes and shall not contain odors and dust in objectionable amounts.

Section III—Air Motion

The air in such occupied spaces shall be in sufficient motion to maintain a reasonable uniformity of temperature and humidity, but not such as to cause objectionable drafts in any occupied portion of such spaces. (An air motion of more than 50 feet per minute within the range of effective temperature prescribed is ordinarily considered objectionable).

Section IV—Air Distribution

The air in all rooms and enclosed spaces shall, under the provisions of these requirements, be distributed with reasonable uniformity.

Section V—Air Quantity

The quantity of air used to ventilate the given space during occupancy shall always be sufficient to maintain the standards of air temperature, air quality, air motion and air distribution as herein required. Sufficient air to meet the above standards shall be taken from an unpolluted outdoor source through a window or other opening supplied with air of suitable quality unless effective means for the removal of objectionable odors and impurities are used. Nothing in this section shall be construed as preventing occasional flushing of rooms with outside air.

Section VI—Definitions

Effective Temperature and its Measurement—Effective temperature, sometimes known as the thermal index of atmospheric conditions, is an experimentally determined index of the degree of warmth or cold felt by the human body in response to temperature, humidity and the movement of the air. It is a composite index which combines the readings of temperature, humidity and air motion in a single value and may be determined from thermometric charts, copies of which may be obtained by making applications to the Department of Public Safety, Room 24, State House, Boston. (The Department of Public Safety should be equipped with copies of charts similar to those published in the American Society of Heating and Ventilating Engineers Guide, 1932, page 392.)

Relative Humidity—Relative humidity is the measure of the per cent saturation of the air with water vapor. It is the ratio of the actual amount of water vapor in a unit volume or unit weight of air at any given temperature to the maximum amount of water vapor which the air would hold at the same temperature when fully saturated with moisture. It may be determined from the dry and wet bulb temperatures, readings taken with a sling psychrometer, and using the Carrier psychrometric chart for computation.

Air Motion — Air motion is the velocity of air current in rooms and should include not only the linear movement of the air but also the turbulence or eddying currents produced by air changes. The air movement or turbulence in occupied rooms should be determined by means of the Kata thermometer. (The velocity of the air is not likely to fall below 10 feet per minute which is adequate even in tightly sealed rooms if there is a temperature or pressure difference between the air inside and outside the room.)

Since the adoption of these standards many advances have been made relative to air conditioning and ventilation as a result of the work of Prof. William F. Wells of the Harvard School of Public Health and C. P. Yaglou of that school. Wells demonstrated that thousands of droplets containing streptococcus viridans and micrococcus catarrhalis are expelled by sneezing into the atmosphere, and he found these organisms in the air of crowded rooms in large numbers several hours after the sneezing. The possibility of polluting the air to such an extent by sneezing certainly is a new thought and one which must be considered in any system of ventilation and air conditioning. Yaglou in his studies found that the average American adult of average habits and personal hygiene requires a minimum of about 15 cubic feet per minute of fresh air to dilute odoriferous organic matter to a concentration that will not be objectionable to persons entering the room from the outside air. Yaglou found that unwashed recirculated air has no effect on the odor intensity and that it was the quantity of fresh outdoor air that counted. He found that the air requirement for odor dilution of grade schools where children are present between the ages of 10 and 14 years is much greater than the requirement for adults, but the whole problem depends upon the particular habits of personal hygiene of those present. He also found that the higher the room temperature above the comfortable degree the higher the fresh air requirements per person. Depending upon the condition of the occupants, an air supply of from 15 to as high as 50 cubic feet per minute might be necessary. Yaglou is of the opinion that each building and type of occupant should be considered in any ventilation and air conditioning scheme rather than to apply a yard stick based on average conditions. Because of this new light on air conditioning and ventilation brought out in the studies of the School of Public Health and also because of the strong difference of opinion between engineers and architects relative to the need of revising the existing standards of the Department of Public Safety on heating and ventilation of schoolhouses, General Daniel Needham, former Commissioner of Public Safety, established a committee the latter part of 1934 with a view to revising the ventilation standards of his Department. This committee is a representative group of hygienists, engineers, architects and educators. Up to the time of writing this paper no final conclusions had been reached by that committee. Accordingly, the standards of the Department of Public Safety, printed as form B-1 and published in accordance with Chapter 143 of the General Laws are the only regulations enforceable relative to heating and ventilation of schoolhouses in this State.

LIGHTING FOR SEEING

By M. LUCKIESH AND FRANK K. MOSS

Lighting Research Laboratory: General Electric Company
Nela Park, Cleveland

This is a half-seeing world because the eyes are so often defective, partially disabled by inadequate light and improper lighting and dulled by misuse and the steadily increasing demands of exacting visual work. The enormous increase in the number of newspapers, magazines and books which has taken place in modern civilization is but a single example of the increasing use of the eyes for difficult visual work. On every hand are found other cases of increasing use and abuse of the eyes. Our modern mode of living, although it may be admirably suited to civilized man's desires and ambitions, is not necessarily best nor ideal for his inherited physical being. Certainly the prevalence of defective vision indicates that modern life is not generally ideal for the well-being of the eyes. In this "machine age" the human machine is sometimes neglected. It is in need of a few adjustments to fit it better for its tasks.

Much has been done to save the eyes of infants by means of medical care and of adults by mechanical protection from hazardous industrial operations. These are largely measures of prevention. Of the millions who begin life with normal eyesight, why is it that relatively few reach maturity with perfect eyes? If eye defects could temporarily be changed into comparable degrees of crippled legs, one would be greeted with a heart-rending spectacle! Standing on the street of a city one would see a continuous parade of persons limping along— some slightly, others on crutches, still others in wheel-chairs. Every other person passing by would be perceptibly crippled. Certainly it is worthwhile to prevent or to minimize or even to counteract by other means as much of this defectiveness of vision as possible.

Although the modern age imposes certain abuses upon the eyes, its sciences have developed effective corrective measures if they were widely appreciated and skillfully utilized. The optical and medical professions have made many advances in preventing and correcting defective vision and through lighting development ideal lighting is available to assist the eyes in their arduous tasks.

Seeing is the result of a partnership of lighting and vision. If eyes are defective, proper lenses are available for compensating the defects and for relieving the eyes of some of the strain and fatigue. Eyes without light are sightless. Eyes with inadequate light are inefficient, easily fatigued and defective vision is invited. Ideal lighting is essential if we are to see clearly, quickly and comfortably. Ideal lighting demands an adequate quantity of light and proper lighting free from glare. Since the eyes evolved for use under the abundance of daylight, they are entitled to more than the primitive artificial lighting exhibited in inadequate light and improper lighting so commonly encountered.

The unit of intensity of illumination is easily defined. If a surface is placed one foot from an ordinary candle so that the rays of light fall perpendicularly upon the surface, or nearly so, the intensity of illumination is about one *footcandle*. The intensity of illumination will be the same whether the surface is a white paper, a black cloth, a colored bookcover, or anything else. However, it will be noted that these various surfaces will appear of different brightnesses. The object of light is to produce brightness and the latter depends upon the reflection of the object. On a horizontal surface outdoors the intensity of illumination reaches a maximum of 10,000 footcandles at midday on a clear day in summer. On an overcast day it is often several thousand footcandles; and when in the open the intensity is as low as 1000 footcandles, the day is considered as a dull or dark one. Indoors and at a window the intensity of illumination is commonly as high as 300 footcandles, but at a distance of a few feet from the window it may be only a few footcandles. Almost everywhere in the indoor work-world artificial light is in use and the average intensity of illumination is only a few footcandles—and one footcandle is common. In view of these facts the following recommendations of intensities of illumination are considered as conservative.

100 Footcandles or more—For very severe and prolonged tasks, such as fine needlework, fine engraving, fine penwork, fine assembly, sewing on dark goods and discrimination of fine details of low contrast, as in inspection.

50 to 100 Footcandles—For severe and prolonged tasks, such as proofreading, drafting, difficult reading, watch repairing, fine machinework, average sewing and other needlework.

20 to 50 Footcandles—For moderately critical and prolonged tasks, such as clerical work, ordinary reading, common benchwork and average sewing and other needlework on light goods.

10 to 20 Footcandles—For moderate and prolonged tasks of office and factory and when not prolonged, ordinary reading and sewing on light goods.

5 to 10 Footcandles—For visually controlled work in which seeing is important, but more or less interrupted or casual and does not involve discrimination of fine details or low contrasts.

0 to 5 Footcandles—The danger zone for severe visual tasks, and for quick and certain seeing. Satisfactory for perceiving larger objects and for casual seeing.

It is a very simple matter to obtain desirable intensities of illumination. In a bridge lamp there is a 60-watt lamp. About one foot from it the photometer or footcandle-meter registers 80 footcandles, and at two feet, about 20 footcandles. On replacing this lamp with a 100-watt lamp more than 150 footcandles are obtained at a distance of one foot and 100 footcandles at a convenient distance for reading, sewing, etc. Before the mirror in the bathroom the intensity of illumination is 40 footcandles from two 60-watt lamps in diffusing shades, one on each side of the mirror at the height of the face. A 500-watt portable lamp in the bathroom provides mild ultraviolet and penetrating infrared radiation for health purposes. Three feet from it the photometer registers 1000 footcandles! How easily such an intensity of illumination is obtained and how hopelessly low the common intensities of illumination indoors really are. Such comparisons aid materially in demonstrating the value of quantities of light which are natural to us as seeing-machines, because we are still products of outdoor environment.

It is seen that levels of illumination of 100 footcandles and more, obtained easily and inexpensively with artificial light, are still meager compared with common daylight intensities, but they are far above those found almost everywhere in the indoor world. In homes low-wattage lamps are prevalent. It is difficult to find a boudoir lamp for the bedside in which a 100-watt lamp can be inserted. In railway stations, where one passes the time reading, less than a footcandle usually prevails at night. In many of the old stations this is not exceeded much in the daytime. Few schools have more than five footcandles of artificial light. Progressive stores, offices and factories may have five to ten footcandles and, in rare cases, 20 footcandles; but, for the most part, the artificial world is scarcely emerging from the age of candles in the intensities of illumination on visual tasks.

The eyes of children demand all the assistance that science is capable of providing. Young eyes in the formative period are easily injured. In an attempt to compensate for poor lighting, objects to be seen are held too close to the eyes and the defect of nearsightedness is a common result. Improper lighting causes children and even adults to assume awkward postures in order to see better. Thus habits are formed which place abnormally severe strains upon the ocular muscles, Lighting skillfully employed assists in acquiring correct postures, thereby eliminating useless and detrimental muscular strain. Then there are old eyes to consider. They need more light than average adult eyes. The same is true of imperfect eyes. Still, even normal adult eyes are seldom provided with ideal lighting.

As the eyes of adults grow older, many changes occur which should be considered. The pupils are smaller and more light is necessary. The lens of the eye becomes less flexible with age and a book must be held farther away in order to be in focus. In this case the reading matter is not so easily seen and eyeglasses and better lighting become increasingly helpful. Science has proved that good lighting helps those most who need help most.

The eyes are remarkable for their ability to adjust themselves for a variety of conditions. No other piece of apparatus can approach them in their marvelous range of adaptability and sensitivity. They are slow to complain of their need for glasses and for better lighting. Therefore, they are being penalized for their ability to overcome unfavorable and injurious conditions. Even though eyes can see some objects at low levels of illumination and defective eyes can see to some extent without glasses, they should not be sentenced to do so for long periods daily. An automobile may climb a steep hill in low-gear; but no sensible motorist will drive a car for hours in "low". It is built for continuous operation in "high". An automobile has the advantage of complaining in very positive ways against mistreatment. The eyes are penalized because they do not always complain and, when they do, they are likely to complain indirectly and indefinitely. We should be considerate of our eyes because they are so considerate of us—and they are invaluable.

THE PRESERVATION OF FOODS IN THE HOUSEHOLD

By HERMANN C. LYTHGOE

Director, Division of Food and Drugs
Massachusetts Department of Public Health

A few centuries ago, the Europeans were endeavoring to find a short route to India, and in so doing discovered America, which, however, did not solve the problem. The reason for desiring the short route to India was to obtain spices for the purpose of preserving food.

These voyages were made before the days of modern refrigeration. In those days, meat from animals killed in the summer time must of necessity have been eaten on the day the animal was killed, except possibly among the ultra-fastidious, when the meat was allowed to "hang" and become "ripe." The usual methods of preserving food at that time were by salting, smoking, and treatment with spices and vinegar. These methods of preservation are still applied, although to a large extent it has become commercialized.

We have our commercial warehouses for the storage of fruit and vegetables, which are located in many instances in the neighborhood of the point of production. We have our cold storage warehouses for the preservation of meats, fish, and eggs, which are located most extensively at the point of consumption. We have our creameries located at the point of production, and the meats which are salted and smoked are so prepared usually in the neighborhood of the slaughterhouses.

There is a certain amount of preservation of food in the household by the process of canning, in the case of fruits and home grown vegetables; in the preparation of pickles, both sweet and sour, by the use of vinegar and spices; but there is practically no salting and smoking of meats carried on in households, except occasionally on the farm.

The methods of commercial preservation of food are now so efficient that sound food may be purchased by any householder who has the price. After this food is purchased, it is essential for the householder to maintain it in a satisfactory condition until it is consumed. The health authorities have made regulations which will assure the purchaser that he is purchasing sound food.

The milk dealers have in the past justifiably criticised the bacteriological and sanitary regulations of boards of health because the dealers saw no practical reason for excessive cleanliness on their part and for delivering the milk at a low temperature when after delivery the milk was allowed to remain on the doorstep in the sunlight for several hours, and then, after being brought into the house, was poured into a dirty pitcher and not kept cool. Many complaints brought by householders against milk dealers have been caused by improper handling of the milk by the householder.

A few years ago, one of my neighbors requested me to recommend a milk dealer, which I declined to do. He ascertained the name of my milk dealer by direct question and passed that name on to one of his neighbors. Subsequently, I was in company with both of these persons and I asked one of them how his milk supply was. He replied that it was exceptionally good, but the other man said he wished the milk dealer would put a little more cream in the milk. I told him that a recent sample collected by the milk inspector showed that the milk contained more fat than was required for Grade A milk and that the bacterial content was considerably less than the maximum specified for such milk. He was therefore obtaining milk superior to Grade A milk at the price of market milk. About a week later, I received from my neighbor the answer to the above criticism. The maid was removing the cream for her morning cup of coffee.

A similar but more pathetic complaint was received from a woman, who stated that the baby was showing signs of malnutrition. She gave me the name of the milk dealer, and I knew from the analyses of samples collected by the inspector that the milk was produced and sold in accordance with the law. After a little questioning, she said, "Of course I take the cream off the milk for my husband's coffee." I advised her to feed the baby first, and give the baby the milk with all the cream on it, and then if the baby showed signs of malnutrition, to consult a doctor.

Milk should be brought into the house as soon after delivery as possible, and it should be immediately placed in the refrigerator, preferably in the bottle in which it was delivered. When some of this milk is desired for use, the cap should be removed from the bottle; the entire contents of the bottle transferred to a clean receptacle and again transferred to the bottle; and the portion to be used should be removed. The cap should then be placed upon the bottle and the bottle again placed in the refrigerator. This process should be repeated whenever more milk is subsequently desired, and in this way every person using the milk will get his share of the cream, and, by reason of the low temperature, will get milk with a bacteria count almost as low as when delivered by the dealer.

The deterioration of food in the household is largely due to high temperatures, and the foods which most rapidly so deteriorate are milk, fish, meat, and eggs. There are two varieties of household refrigerators now in use, one variety using ice and the other using mechanical refrigeration. The mechanical refrigeration is the most efficient of the two because the refrigeration unit is operated at a much lower temperature than that of the ice refrigerator. The temperature of an ice box cannot be reduced to 32° Fahrenheit, which is the melting point of ice. You cannot put water into an ice-operated refrigerator and freeze it. Such refrigerators during the extremely hot weather will rarely bring the temperature of food below 60°, even after standing overnight.

The average refrigerator is not constructed upon sound scientific principles. It is well known that cold air is heavier than hot air. The old fashioned ice box, which was in use about fifty years ago, was built in accordance with this principle. This ice box opened at the top and was an insulated compartment in which the ice and the food were placed. Persons using the ice box, therefore, were obliged to lift up the heavy cover and stoop over and occasionally move the ice and move the shelves, but it certainly was the most efficient of the ice refrigerators.

The new type of refrigerator, which came into use about fifty years ago, had vertical doors, and when the doors were opened the cold air went out of the box and was replaced by the warm air of the room. This type of refrigerator superseded the old type because it was preferred by the women, principally because it was easier to operate and easier to keep clean.

Most of the mechanical refrigerators for household purposes are built upon this same unsound principle. You can readily demonstrate this by standing in front of the door of your refrigerator. Open the door and feel the current of cold air around your feet. For this reason it is advisable to keep as much food as possible in your refrigerator so that there will be less cold air in the refrigerator to fall out when the door is open.

Food is spoiled by the growth of bacteria or similar plants. A low temperature will retard the growth of bacteria, and this is the principle used in the cold storage of food. Food which is frozen solid and kept at a temperature below zero will be edible after being kept under such conditions for years.

One class of food which is subject to very rapid deterioration is chopped meat. The process of putting the meat through a meat grinder introduces bacteria. It furthermore creates a large surface favorable to the growth of such bacteria and introduces air spaces which act as insulators and prevent the meat from becoming properly cooled if placed under refrigeration. Food of this character had best be prepared in the house and should be cooked as soon as possible after it has been chopped.

Dilute sugar solutions are frequently decomposed by the presence of yeast. Sweet cider is an example of this type food. The deterioration in this case is caused by the production of alcohol and carbon dioxide from the sugar by the growth of the yeast. Strange to say, this particular form of decomposition is not objectionable to many people.

Moulds are somewhat different from yeast and bacteria in their decomposition action, and, furthermore, low temperatures do not always prevent their growth in foods so infected. This form of infection is liable to occur in the summer time upon bread. The bread may be infected when purchased, but the infection may not be sufficiently intense to be noticed. If the infected bread is allowed to remain in the house for a sufficient length of time, the mould growth soon becomes apparent to the casual observer. This growth is most intense during hot humid weather, and it is extremely difficult to control. If the bread box becomes infected with mould, this infection will contaminate any bread which may be placed in the box. The box so infected must be thoroughly cleaned. It must be treated with scalding water and had best be dried in the sunlight, and care should be taken that no more mouldy bread is placed in the box.

The Department has received numerous complaints regarding alleged sickness from the consumption of mouldy bread, although it is a fact that the moulds themselves are harmless. In one instance, the complainant was honest about it and stated that the baker carried insurance and she wanted some of it.

There are, however, mouldy foods which are highly prized, as, for example, certain varieties of cheeses, specifically, Roquefort, Gorgenzola, and Stilton. In consuming cheeses of this character. it is customary to eat the mould. If cheeses of this character are kept in the refrigerator, they are liable to contaminate the refrigerator, with subsequent contamination of foods on which the presence of mould is not desired. Because of this, it is advisable to frequently wash and clean the refrigerator.

Meat is sometimes aged. This meat is kept in a cooler above the freezing point, and, as a rule, it becomes mouldy on the outside. This mould is removed from the meat before it is cooked, and the meat must be cooked as soon as possible after being removed from the cooler. The changes which have taken place in this meat are not due to bacteriological action, and the meat is not decomposed in its ordinarily accepted chemical sense. It is, however, inadvisable to age meat in your own ice box.

The preservation of fruits and vegetables is quite different from the preservation of other highly perishable foodstuffs. Much fruit is gathered before it is ripe, and it is allowed to ripen during transit. The exception to this is the citrous fruits, which do not ripen after being picked from the trees. Each of the fruits and vegetables requires its own particular mode of storage, and it is rather difficult for the average householder to store any large quantity of this material in a house which does not have a specially constructed vegetable closet. Peaches, for example, will deteriorate very rapidly, and pears will deteriorate more rapidly than apples. Potatoes, onions, and turnips can be stored for a considerable time without spoilage. Some vegetables, as for example, potatoes, are spoiled by freezing. Cabbages can, to a slight extent, stand freezing without spoiling. Numerous studies of this nature have been made and are applied extensively in the commercial world, the purpose being to stop the waste which would otherwise occur because of faulty storage, transportation, and handling of perishable foodstuffs.

So called "food poisoning" is largely due to an infection of the food with certain types of bacteria. Infections of this character may cause sickness in from twenty-four to forty-eight hours after the food is eaten, but the sickness seldom occurs prior to twenty-four hours after eating. It is usual for persons to quite naturally place the blame upon the last meal instead of upon a meal eaten one or two days before. A person complained about sickness due to eating hamburg steak. There were three persons in the family—a child who did not have hamburg steak for supper, a young man, and the mother. The sickness occurred about 1:30 A. M. The young man who made the complaint was informed of the above fact regarding food poisoning, but he was requested to furnish the name of the dealer from whom the hamburg steak was purchased for the purpose of inspecting the character of meat being sold by this dealer. The young man then telephoned his mother, and during the course of the conversation remarked, "That's what he told me." He then hung up the receiver and stated that there was no need of making the investigation. His mother had informed him that his married sister and her husband were taken sick at about the same time. They were not in the house when the hamburg steak had been eaten. They were at his house the night before, when all except the young child had eaten chicken croquettes, homemade.

If sickness is caused by the presence of bacteria, it takes some time for them to develop in the body to the extent sufficient to cause sickness. If, however, the sickness is caused by the development of a toxin, which is very unusual, its presence can be determined by the odor of the material before cooking. In this instance, however, cooking is liable to kill the toxin, and even then the food may be safe to eat.

Food sickness is usually caused through the consumption of salads containing considerable protein, such as lobster salad or chicken salad, when the lobster or the chicken has been handled in an unsanitary manner by the person who prepared and infected the material, and because of the large surface of the meat, the bacteria have had an excellent chance to grow. Food of this character is eaten without any subsequent cooking, and consequently, if it contains any bacteria of an infective type, it is liable to produce sickness. Persons handling food for others to eat should handle such food in a clean manner, using clean utensils, and should store the food in a clean refrigerator at a low temperature. By adhering to this practice, sickness caused by so called "food poisoning" would be greatly reduced.

118
GONORRHEA AND SYPHILIS IN THE PUBLIC SCHOOLS*
N. A. NELSON, M. D.
Assistant Director, Division of Communicable Diseases
Massachusetts Department of Public Health

There is too much misunderstanding and resultant confusion, almost to the point of hysteria, over gonorrhea and syphilis in the public schools. It is time that those who have to do with the schools and school children familiarized themselves with the facts.

Syphilis
Syphilis may be either congenital or acquired. About fifteen per cent of the acquired infections occur in boys and girls of from fifteen to nineteen years of age. It may be presumed, therefore, that an occasional case of acquired syphilis may be found in high school children. It is dangerous in non-sexual contacts only during the early (primary and secondary) stages, during which open lesions may be present in the mouth and on exposed parts of the body. Fortunately modern antisyphilitic treatment causes these lesions to heal within a few days, and to remain healed if continued to a satisfactory conclusion. The later stages of acquired syphilis are not communicable in ordinary contacts, but may be in sexual intercourse.

So far as acquired syphilis is concerned, it is entirely safe to apply the following procedures:

1. A child with primary or secondary syphilis should be excluded from school (and kept at home) until proper treatment has caused the lesions to heal. In most cases this will require from one to three weeks. Return to school should then be permitted, provided proper treatment is continued and there is no recurrence of lesions under treatment.
2. If a child has late syphilis, the possibility of transmitting the infection through non-sexual contacts is so remote as to deserve little or no consideration, except that provision should be made for treatment for the sake of the child's health and to prevent the possible spread of infection through sexual intercourse.

Congenital syphilis is communicable through non-sexual contacts only during the first few days or weeks or, at the very most, a few months after the birth of the infected child. At school age there is no danger whatsoever of transmission of a congenital infection through social or occupational contacts. So far as can be discovered, congenital syphilis is rarely, if ever, transmitted even in sexual intercourse. There is some evidence that a congenitally syphilitic child may be born to a mother who has a congenital infection.

The exclusion of a child from school because of congenital syphilis (except for esthetic reasons when there are obnoxious open lesions) is absurd. Treatment should be provided, however, since serious eye, ear and central nervous system damage may otherwise result.

Gonorrhea
Gonorrhea is acquired by adult females and by males, whether children or adults, only through sexual intercourse or some form of sexual practice. Exceptions are so rare as to constitute epidemiological curiosities. No child over the age of puberty, whether male or female, will acquire gonorrhea as a result of school contacts. Girls under the age

*Adapted from an article by the author in the Bulletin of the Massachusetts Society for Social Hygiene, March, 1935.

of puberty are susceptible to infection with gonorrhea through intimate contacts not necessarily of a sexual nature. These contacts are of such a nature that they take place only at home or in child-caring institutions. They do not occur in school. There is no evidence that school toilets have been vehicles of transmission of the infection.

There is no doubt that gonococcal infections will be found in school children. More than 10 per cent of these infections in the female are in girls under 14 years of age, and 20 per cent are in girls from 15 to 19 years of age. Ten per cent of all gonococcal infections in the male are in boys from 15 to 19 years of age. Except for some infections in girls under the age of puberty, these have been acquired through some form of sexual practice, and not through school or occupational or social contacts.

However, public opinion is opposed to the presence, in school, of a child known to have a frank gonorrheal discharge. For that reason it may be necessary to exclude children with gonorrhea until treatment has caused the discharge to stop. Thereafter they should be permitted to return to school, provided treatment is continued to a satisfactory conclusion. During the period of exclusion they should be strictly supervised, since idleness may afford ample opportunity for the sexual dissemination of their infections.

Editorial Comment

Vision of School Children.—A very interesting article has been published by Doctor William Thau of Boston in The Eye, Ear, Nose and Throat Monthly, Vol. XIV, No. 3 (April, 1935) based on the examination of the vision of 16,383 children in different schools in an area of 45 miles.

In this article Dr. Thau gives the findings of these examinations. He has submitted to us further figures which cover 25,261 children. The following are the findings:

152 eyes which saw mere shadows or fingers from 1 to 3 meters (from 1 to 3 yards)

142 eyes which saw 1/50 (saw in 1 meter what a normal eye sees in 50 meters)

104 eyes which saw 2/50 (saw in 2 meters what a normal eye sees in 50 meters)

81 eyes which saw 3/50	565 eyes which saw 5/30
81 eyes which saw 4/50	937 eyes which saw 5/20
294 eyes which saw 5/50	1427 eyes which saw 5/15
711 eyes which saw 5/40	1891 eyes which saw 5/10

Dr. Thau finishes his article with the following remarks:

(1) In this country every child is required by law to attend school which is therefore an excellent filter of our future citizens.

(2) By carefully examining every child in the schools an abnormal eye condition can be detected in time and a more serious complication avoided.

(3) Positive results along these lines can be obtained only when an experienced eye physician examines the children's eyes.

(4) Such examinations if performed in every school (public or other) periodically and at least once a year, cannot be overestimated as a means of improvement and preservation of the children's sight.

Back Issues of the Commonhealth. We are glad to be able to announce that single copies of the following issues are available upon request—while the supply lasts:—

1928
Rabies	April
Venereal Disease	July
Nutrition	October

1929
Milk	January
School Hygiene	April
Tuberculosis	July
Adult Hygiene	October

1930
Child Hygiene	January
The Deaf and Hard of Hearing	April
Diphtheria	July
Public Health Nursing	October

1931
The Business Woman	January
Sanitation	April
Lobar Pneumonia	July
White House Conference	October

1932
Dental Hygiene	January
Rural Health	July

1933
Cancer	January
Control of Gonorrhea and Syphilis	April
Epidemiology	July
The Handicapped	October

1934
Adult Hygiene	January
Diabetes	April
Health Education	July
Cancer	October

COMPARABILITY OF MATERNAL MORTALITY RATES IN THE UNITED STATES AND CERTAIN FOREIGN COUNTRIES

A study of the Effects of Variations in Assignment Procedures. Definitions of Live Births and Completeness of Birth Registration, by Elizabeth C. Tandy, D. Sc. Children's Bureau Publication No. 229.

This study is based on a representative sample of "1073 deaths associated with pregnancy and childbirth" that occurred in the United States during the year 1927. "Information in regard to 477 deaths that included one of every type and one of every combination of circumstances represented in the sample was sent abroad and the deaths were classified as puerperal or nonpuerperal by the statistical offices in charge of classification of cause of death in accordance with the rules in force in these offices." The countries making the assignments were Australia, Canada, Chile, Czechoslovakia, Denmark, England and Wales, Estonia, France, Irish Free State, Italy, Netherlands, New Zealand, Northern Ireland, Norway, Scotland, and Sweden.

In addition, the study was based on information obtained from the manuals for assigning cause of death and numerous official reports.

According to Dr. Tandy, the study shows "First: That the methods of assignment in use in Australia, Netherlands, New Zealand and Scotland are similar to that of the United States, and the official maternal mortality rates are directly comparable within a small margin of error: that under the method of Denmark a larger number of deaths would be assigned to the puerperal state and the rate for the United States would be significantly higher than it is now; that under the methods of the other countries included in the study — Canada, Chile, Czechoslovakia, England and Wales, Estonia, France, Irish Free State, Italy, Northern Ireland, Norway and Sweden—a smaller number of deaths would be assigned to the puerperal state and the rates for the United States would consequently be somewhat lower. Second: That differences in methods of assignment are insufficient to explain the high maternal mortality rate of the United States as compared with foreign countries. The official figure of the United States, which in the last few years has exceeded that of every country except Scotland, remains high no matter what method of assignment is used."

This study raises a number of interesting points. There is the familiar question of age—the death rate in the age group 20-24 was 4.5; in the age group 30-34 it was 6.9; 35-39, 10.1; 40-44, 13.5; and for those over 45 it was 20.1. Thirty-five per cent of the United States mothers were thirty or over. Is it not possible that the mothers in foreign countries were younger?

The size of family also may have some relation to the maternal mortality rate. The rate for primiparae in the United States is not available. In our study of maternal mortality in Massachusetts, we found that 38% of the deaths were primiparae. If the same percentage held for the country the rate would have been 8.3. Thirty-two per cent of the white native born mothers were primiparae and 22% of the foreign born. Larger families abroad would mean younger mothers and a smaller proportion of primiparae.

Then there is the question of color or nativity. Considering only white mothers the maternal death rate was reduced from 6.5 to 5.9 which was the same as the rate for all white foreign born in the United States. The maternal death rate for the foreign born in the United States has been consistently lower than the rate for the whole United States. This bears out the common report that American women generally have a harder time at childbirth than foreign women. Also a larger proportion of native born women are probably in the well-to-do group where one might expect a higher proportion of hospital and operative deliveries than among the foreign born women who are often poor and delivered at home. The difference between the rates for native and foreign born is increased when the rates are adjusted to the age distribution of 1917. In 1917, 41% of the white foreign born were 30 or over and in 1927, 50%.

According to Dr. Tandy, the rates for the Netherlands are comparable with those of the United States. Are the Netherlands really so much ahead of the United States in regard to obstetrics that they cut our maternal death rate in half? Norway, Sweden, France, and Italy also cut our rate in half although their methods of assignment are acknowledged to be different. The only encouraging statement is that unlike most foreign countries, the United States had rates that were considerably lower in 1932 than 1925.

Dr. Tandy estimated rates for the United States according to the method of assignment in the different countries. What rates would the United States assign to the foreign countries especially if we could obtain full information from the physicians?

If the gist of Dr. Tandy's study is that inferentially at least the medical care in maternal cases in the United States is not as competent as that of foreign countries, the argument used is a non sequitur because of the many other conditions that affect maternal death rates and that are hidden in gross rates. In other words, no deduction seems justifiable from Dr. Tandy's study.

—ANGELINE D. HAMBLEN.

REPORT OF DIVISION OF FOOD AND DRUGS

During the months of January, February and March 1935, samples were collected in 202 cities and towns.

There were 1,405 samples of milk examined, of which 247 were below standard, from 14 samples the cream had been in part removed, and 28 samples contained added water. There were 1,042 bacteriological examinations made of milk, 987 of which complied with the requirements. There were 227 bacteriological examinations made of ice cream, 193 of which complied with the requirements. There were 7 bacteriological examinations made of cream, 5 of which complied with the requirements. There were 6 bacteriological examinations made of lobsters, all of which complied; 1 bacteriological examination of candy which complied; 6 bacteriological examinations of powdered chocolate, all but one complied; 1 bacteriological examination of powdered milk which did not comply; 4 bacteriological examinations of empty tonic bottles, all of which did not comply; 1 bacteriological examination of butter which did not comply; 1 bacteriological examination of frozen eggs which did not comply; and 3 bacteriological examinations of canned meat, 1 of which did not comply with the requirements.

There were 696 samples of food examined, 130 of which were adulterated. These consisted of 4 samples of butter, 2 of which had a cheesy odor, and 2 were low in fat; 1 sample of dried fruit which contained sulphur dioxide and was not properly labeled; 1 sample of stale eggs sold as fresh eggs; 1 sample of frozen egg yolk which contained sugar; 5 samples of ice cream, 2 of which were low in fat, and 3 were misbranded; 5 samples of maple butter, 3 of which were incorrectly labeled, and 2 contained starch one of which also contained reducing sugar; 5 samples of hamburg steak, 1 of which was falsely advertised, 1 contained a compound of sulphur dioxide not properly labeled, and 3 samples were decomposed, one of which also contained a compound of sulphur dioxide not properly labeled; 7 samples of sausage, 6 of which were decomposed, and 1 contained lung tissue; 40 samples of olive oil, all of which contained cottonseed oil and 15 samples were also misbranded; 17 samples of pickles, 8 of which contained benzoate and were not properly labeled, 1 of which also contained saccharine, and 9 samples contained saccharine; 16 samples of cheese, 2 of which contained india gum, and 14 contained mineral oil; 14 samples of sour cream, 4 of which contained india gum, and 10 contained annatto; 5 samples of cream, all of which contained foreign fat; 1 sample of vanilla extract which contained coumarin; 4 samples of vinegar, 3 of which were misbranded, and 1 sample contained less than the required amount of acidity; 1 sample of maple syrup. which contained cane sugar; and 3 samples of mattress fillings which contained secondhand material.

There were 22 samples of drugs examined, of which 5 were adulterated. These consisted of 5 samples of lime water which did not conform to the requirements of the U. S. Pharmacopoeia.

The police departments submitted 177 samples of liquor for examination. The police departments also submitted 16 samples to be analyzed for poisons or drugs, 3 samples of which contained opium, 5 contained heroin, 5 contained heroin hydrochloride, 1 contained ergot and 2 contained cannabis.

There were 56 cities and towns visited for the inspection of pasteurizing plants, and 226 plants were inspected.

There were inspected 50 plants for the manufacture of ice cream.

There were 91 hearings held pertaining to violations of the laws.

There were 58 convictions for violations of the law, $1,550 in fines being imposed.

Henry S. Ashley of East Longmeadow; Arthur H. W. Stimson of Northampton; Frank Alger of South Easton; Charles Pervier, 3 cases, of Sturbridge; John Semas of Taunton; and Paul Louis Sykes, of Abington, were all convicted for violations of the milk laws. Arthur H. W. Stimson of Northampton appealed his case.

Konstanty Neizgoda, 2 cases, and Patrick Bresnahan of Holyoke; and Margaret Forbes of Melrose, were convicted for violations of the pasteurization laws and regulations.

National Creamery Company, Incorporated, 2 cases, of Somerville; William Winer, Arthur Giberti, Angelo Moscardini, American Beef Company, Incorporated, Dominic Maio, Peter Meo, Dominic A. Previte, 2 cases, and Henry Pasquale, all of Boston; Jack Miller of New Bedford; Harvard Pickle Works, Incorporated, 2 cases, of Cambridge; Nathan Greenbaum, 2 cases, of Amesbury; David Hill and Mrs. Rose Moro of Framingham; Herbert P. Gustafson of Gardner; Sarah Snyder of Mattapan; Louis Ballestraccio, 4 cases, Dominic Morano, Dominic Palermo, and Consumers Provision Company, all of Worcester, were all convicted for violations of the food laws. Consumers Provision Company of Worcester, and Nathan Greenbaum, 1 case, of Amesbury, appealed their cases.

Angelo Gatis of New Bedford, and Peter Meo of Boston, were convicted for false advertising.

Louis Ballestraccio, 4 cases, Dominic Morano, and Dominic Palermo, all of Worcester; and Dominic Previte, Dominic A. Previte 2 cases (4 counts), and Dominic Maio, all of Boston, were convicted for misbranding. Dominic A. Previte of Boston appealed his four counts.

Badger Farms Creameries of Newburyport, and Kalashian Brothers of Worcester, were convicted for violations of the frozen dessert law.

William Kocokinski of Webster was convicted for violation of the cold storage law.

Jackson Furniture Company of New Bedford; Samuel Pristau and Sunshine Bedding Company of Boston; and Benjamin London of Malden, were all convicted for violations of the mattress law.

In accordance with Section 25, Chapter 111 of the General Laws, the following is the list of articles of adulterated food collected in original packages from manufacturers, wholesalers, or producers.

Two samples of sweet butter which were low in fat were obtained from N. Y. Cut Rate Grocers, Incorporated, of Dorchester.

Butter which was decomposed was obtained as follows:
One sample each, from People's Market, and Red and White Store, of New Bedford.

Two samples of maple butter which contained starch were obtained from Maple Butter Company of Boston.

Cream which contained mineral oil was obtained as follows:
Three samples from Fellsway Cheese Company of Stoneham, and 2 samples from F. H. Willard of Worcester.

Thirteen samples of cheese which contained mineral oil were obtained from Fellsway Cheese Company, Incorporated, of Boston.

Two samples of ice cream which were low in fat were obtained from Hager Ice Cream Company of Somerville.

Three samples of ice cream which did not bear the manufacturer's name upon the carton were obtained from Joseph B. Fash of Charlestown.

One sample of extract of vanilla which contained coumarin was obtained from Roma Extract Company of Boston.

Three samples of vinegar which were misbranded were obtained from Food Specialty Company of Worcester.

Pickles which contained saccharine were obtained as follows:
Three samples from Harvard Pickle Works, Incorporated, of Cambridge, and 2 samples from National Pickling Works of Dorchester.

Pickles which contained benzoate not marked were obtained as follows:
Four samples from Food Specialty Company of Worcester, and 1 sample from M. Di Minnio & Sons of Fitchburg.

One sample of pickles which contained benzoate not marked and also contained saccharine was obtained from Harvard Pickle Works, Incorporated, of Cambridge.

One sample of sausage which contained lung tissue was obtained from John Pasquale of Boston.

Sausage which was decomposed was obtained as follows:
One sample each, from Mrs. Rose Moro, and New Hollis Market of Framingham; Consumers Provision Company of Worcester; and Malden Square Market of Malden.

One sample of hamburg steak which contained a compound of sulphur dioxide not properly labeled was obtained from Hager & Houghton of Gardner.

One sample of hamburg steak which contained a compound of sulphur dioxide not properly labeled and was also decomposed was obtained from Ganem's Market of Lawrence.

Hamburg steak which was decomposed was obtained as follows:
One sample each, from Warshaw's Market, and Ganem's Market, of Lawrence.

Olive oil which contained cottonseed oil and was also misbranded was obtained as follows:
Three samples from Dominic A. Previte of Boston; and 1 sample each, from Antonio Previte & Figlio, Catania Oil Company, Alberti Importing & Exporting Company, Incorporated, and Dominic Maio, all of Boston; Louis Ballestraccio of Worcester; and Georgia Calvi of Springfield.

Olive Oil which contained cottonseed oil was obtained as follows:
One sample each, from Romo Importing Company of Springfield; Genoa Packing Company, Joseph Verdi Company, Alberti Importing

& Exporting Company, Ameo Oil Company, Metropolitan Sales Company, and Frank Borgia, all of Boston; and Rex Olive Oil Company of Worcester.

Two samples each, from Louis Ballestraccio of Worcester; Gloria Chain Stores, Incorporated, of Newton; and Joseph Meo of Boston.

Three samples each, from Dominic Previte of Boston; and Joseph Pensavelle of Somerville.

One sample of olive oil which was misbranded was obtained from Cosmos Food, Incorporated, of Lynn.

There were nine confiscations, consisting of 3 pounds of decomposed chicken; 25 pounds of decomposed fowl; 8 pounds of decomposed calves' liver; 30 pounds of decomposed hamburg steak; 25 pounds of decomposed pork sausage; 2,000 pounds of decomposed salt cod; 100 pounds of decomposed salt cod; 9,750 pounds of decomposed salt herring; and 600 pounds of decomposed salt herring.

The licensed cold storage warehouses reported the following amounts of food placed in storage during December, 1934:—266,055 dozens of case eggs; 334,590 pounds of broken out eggs; 398,703 pounds of butter; 4,447,427¾ pounds of poultry; 5,760,958 pounds of fresh meat and fresh meat products; and 3,238,765 pounds of fresh food fish.

There was on hand January 1, 1935:—737,490 dozens of case eggs; 1,936,372 pounds of broken out eggs; 948,525 pounds of butter; 8,057,-788 pounds of poultry; 13,771,992 pounds of fresh meat and fresh meat products; and 21,296,969 pounds of fresh food fish.

The licensed cold storage warehouses reported the following amounts of food placed in storage during January, 1935:—243,210 dozens of case eggs; 309,831 pounds of broken out eggs; 440,960 pounds of butter; 1,977,194 pounds of poultry; 3,622,411 pounds of fresh meat and fresh meat products; and 3,847,933 pounds of fresh food fish.

There was on hand February 1, 1935:—43,770 dozens of case eggs; 1,384,738 pounds of broken out eggs; 759,405 pounds of butter; 8,-241,913¾ pounds of poultry; 12,548,599 pounds of fresh meat and fresh meat products; and 17,217,836 pounds of fresh food fish.

The licensed cold storage warehouses reported the following amounts of food placed in storage during February, 1935:—30,510 dozens of case eggs; 795,207 pounds of broken out eggs; 621,645 pounds of butter; 2,228,862 pounds of poultry; 4,050,355 pounds of fresh meat and fresh meat products; and 3,647,672 pounds of fresh food fish.

There was on hand March 1, 1935:—20,250 dozen of case eggs; 1,-283,322 pounds of broken out eggs; 899,505 pounds of butter; 7,821,-078¾ pounds of poultry; 12,690,719 pounds of fresh meat and fresh meat products; and 11,175,706 pounds of fresh food fish.

MASSACHUSETTS DEPARTMENT OF PUBLIC HEALTH

Commissioner of Public Health, HENRY D. CHADWICK, M.D.

Public Health Council

HENRY D. CHADWICK, M.D., *Chairman*
GORDON HUTCHINS.
FRANCIS H. LALLY, M.D.
SYLVESTER E. RYAN, M.D.
RICHARD M. SMITH, M.D.
RICHARD P. STRONG, M.D.
JAMES L. TIGHE.

Secretary, ALICE M. NELSON

Division of Administration	Under direction of Commissioner.
Division of Sanitary Engineering	Director and Chief Engineer, ARTHUR D. WESTON, C.E.
Division of Communicable Diseases	Director, GAYLORD W. ANDERSON, M.D.
Division of Biologic Laboratories	Director and Pathologist, ELLIOTT S. ROBINSON, M.D.
Division of Food and Drugs	Director and Analyst, HERMANN C. LYTHGOE, S.B.
Division of Child Hygiene	Director, M. LUISE DIEZ, M.D.
Division of Tuberculosis	Director, ALTON S. POPE, M.D.
Division of Adult Hygiene	Director, HERBERT L. LOMBARD, M.D.

State District Health Officers

The Southeastern District	RICHARD P. MACKNIGHT, M.D., New Bedford.
The South Metropolitan District	GEORGE M. SULLIVAN, M.D., Milton.
The North Metropolitan District	CHARLES B. MACK, M.D., Boston.
The Northeastern District	ROBERT E. ARCHIBALD, M.D., Lynn.
The Worcester County District	OSCAR A. DUDLEY, M.D., Worcester.
The Connecticut Valley District	HAROLD E. MINER, M.D., Springfield.
The Berkshire District	WALTER W. LEE, M.D., No. Adams.

PUBLICATION OF THIS DOCUMENT APPROVED BY THE COMMISSION ON ADMINISTRATION AND FINANCE
[M. 6-'35. Order 4851.

THE COMMONHEALTH

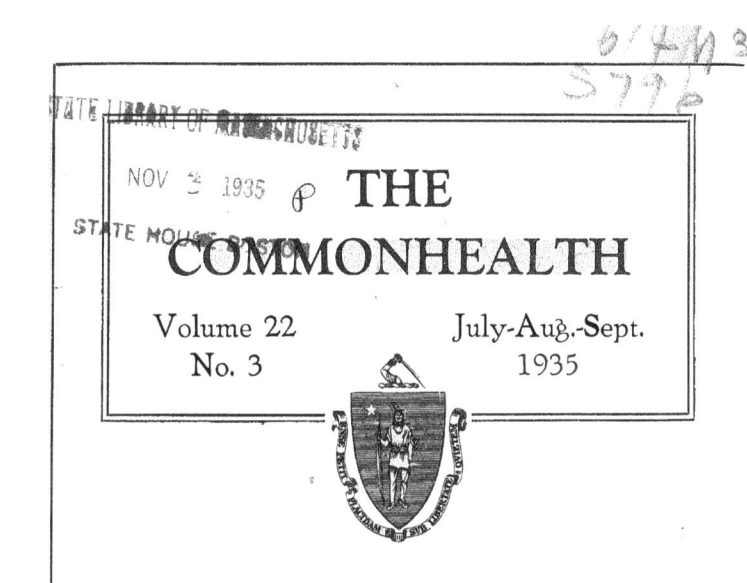

Volume 22   July-Aug.-Sept.
No. 3   1935

Handbook for Physicians

MASSACHUSETTS
DEPARTMENT OF PUBLIC HEALTH

THE COMMONHEALTH
QUARTERLY BULLETIN OF THE MASSACHUSETTS DEPARTMENT OF
PUBLIC HEALTH
Sent Free to any Citizen of the State
Entered as second class matter at Boston Postoffice.

M. LUISE DIEZ, M.D., DIRECTOR OF DIVISION OF CHILD HYGIENE, EDITOR.

Room 545, State House, Boston, Mass.

CONTENTS

	PAGE		PAGE
FOREWORD	129	Typhus Fever	166
COMMUNICABLE DISEASES	130	Undulant Fever	166
General	130	Whooping Cough	166
Reporting	130	Gonorrhea and Syphilis—General	167
Quarantine Requirements	131	Syphilis	167
Diagnostic Laboratories	133	Gonorrhea	169
Wassermann Laboratory	133	Legal provisions	173
Local diagnostic laboratories	134	INDUSTRIAL DISEASES	175
Hospitalization	134	CHILD HYGIENE	175
Biologic products	135	Prenatal letters	175
Regulations re distribution	135	Postnatal letters	176
Sensitivity	136	Educational material	176
Popular pamphlets	139	BLIND	177
Specific Diseases	139	CANCER	178
Anterior Poliomyelitis	139	Diagnosis	178
Chicken Pox	142	Treatment	178
Diphtheria	143	MENTAL DISEASES	180
Dog Bite	144	Diagnosis	180
Dysentery (Amebic)	146	General Out-Patient Clinics	180
Dysentery (Bacillary)	146	Child Guidance and Adjustment Clinics	180
Epidemic Cerebro-Spinal Meningitis	147	Habit Clinics	182
German Measles	148	Mental and Mental Hygiene Clinics	182
Gonorrhea	148	Feeblemindedness Clinics	183
Lobar Pneumonia	149	Treatment	183
Malaria	151	Insane persons	183
Measles	151	Epileptics	186
Mumps	152	Dipsomaniacs	187
Ophthalmia Neonatorum	152	Feeblemindedness	188
Paratyphoid Fever	153	PUBLIC WELFARE	190
Rabies	153	The State Infirmary, Tewksbury	190
Scarlet Fever	153	Massachusetts Hospital School, Canton	190
Septic Sore Throat	154		
Smallpox	154		
Syphilis	155		
Tetanus	155	REPORT OF DIVISION OF FOOD AND DRUGS, April, May, June 1935	191
Tuberculosis	155		
Typhoid Fever	164		

FOREWORD

HENRY D. CHADWICK, M.D.
Commissioner of Public Health

The purpose of this issue of The Commonhealth is to assist the physicians of Massachusetts toward the more effective utilization of certain of the community resources that are at their disposal. So many and so varied are the services that the physician may command to aid him in the proper care of his patient, that it has seemed suitable that the Department should attempt in this way to classify some of these aids and indicate how they may be utilized to the fullest advantage. There have been included in this booklet only those that have a particular bearing upon the public health, purposely omitting many that have but an individual importance. The Department realizes that in this its first attempt in this direction, mistakes and omissions will inevitably occur. It is the Department's hope, however, that if this booklet helps to fill the need for which it was intended, it may later be revised and expanded, keeping in touch with inevitable changes, and adding those features that experience shows should not have been omitted. The Department will, therefore, welcome all comments, criticism and suggestions on the data here presented.

COMMUNICABLE DISEASES

REPORTING: The following diseases are reportable in Massachusetts:

Diseases Declared by the Department of Public Health of Massachusetts to be Dangerous to the Public Health and Reportable Under Provisions of Sections 6, 7, 109, 111 and 112 of Chapter 111 of the General Laws:—

Actinomycosis
Anterior Poliomyelitis
Anthrax
Asiatic Cholera
Chicken Pox
Cholecystitis of Typhoid Origin
Diphtheria
Dog-bite

Dysentery:—
  a. Amebic
  b. Bacillary
Encephalitis Lethargica
Epidemic Cerebro-spinal Meningitis
German Measles
Glanders
Gonorrhea
Hookworm Disease

Infectious diseases of the eye:—
  a. Ophthalmia Neonatorum
  b. Suppurative Conjunctivitis
  c. Trachoma

Leprosy
Lobar Pneumonia
Malaria
Measles
Mumps
Paratyphoid Fever A
Paratyphoid Fever B
Pellagra
Plague
Rabies
Scarlet Fever
Septic Sore Throat
Smallpox
Syphilis
Tetanus
Trichinosis
Tuberculosis (all forms)
Typhoid Fever
Typhus Fever
Undulant Fever
Whooping Cough
Yellow Fever

All reports except of gonorrhea and syphilis should be made to the board of health of the community of residence. Telephone reports should be confirmed in writing. Cards for such reports can be obtained from most boards of health. Gonorrhea and syphilis should be reported directly to the State Department of Public Health, 546 State House, Boston, using special forms obtainable from the Department. (See under these diseases for details of reporting, p. 167.)

ISOLATION AND QUARANTINE: Each city and town determines its own quarantine requirements. In case of doubt inquire of the board of health of the town in which the patient lives. The physician is not entitled to modify these requirements. The following requirements, recommended by the State Department of Public Health, represent general practice throughout Massachusetts, though minor details may differ in certain communities:

QUARANTINE REQUIREMENTS
RECOMMEND BY THE MASSACHUSETTS DEPARTMENT OF PUBLI HEAL

DISEASE	MINIMUM PERIOD OF ISOLATION OF PATIENT	CONTROL OF CONTACTS			PLACARD
		ADULTS	IMMUNE CHILDREN	CHILDREN NOT IMMUNE	
Anterior Poliomyelitis (Infantile Paralysis)	Two weeks from onset of disease, and thereafter until acute symptoms have subsided.	Note 1.	Until two weeks have elapsed from date of last exposure.	Until two weeks have elapsed from date of last exposure.	Yes.
....	One week from appearance of eruption and thereafter until all crusts have disappeared.	No restrictions.	No restrictions.	No restrictions.	No.
iphtheria	One week from date of onset and thereafter until 2 successive negative cultures, taken at least 24 hours apart, from both nose and throat, have been obtained.	No restrictions save Notes 1 and 2.	If immune as shown by a Schick test or on the basis of a previous attack of the disease, may return to school provided they live away from home, or case is hospitalized, and if two consecutive negative nose and throat cultures taken at an interval of not less than 24 hours have been obtained.	Until one week has elapsed from date of last exposure and until 2 negative nose and throat cultures taken at an interval of not less than 24 hours have been obtained.	Yes.
Epidemic Cerebro-Spinal Meningitis (Cerebro-Spinal Fever)	Two weeks from onset of disease, and thereafter until all acute symptoms have subsided.	Note 1.	Until ten days from date of last exposure.	Until ten days from date of last exposure.	Yes.
erman Measles	One week from appearance of rash.	No restrictions.	No restrictions.	No restrictions.	No.
Measles	One week from appearance of rash.	No restrictions save immune school teachers. These handled as non-immune children.	No restrictions. (Note 3)	Exclusion from school for 16 days from date of last exposure.	No.
Mumps	One week from onset of disease, and thereafter until all swelling of salivary glands has disappeared.	No restrictions.	No restrictions.	No restrictions.	No.

131

RECOMMENDED QUARANTINE REQUIREMENTS—Continued

	Minimum Period of Isolation of Patient.	No restrictions save in certain occupations. (Notes 1 and 2)	No restrictions if away from home. (Note 3)	Unless child lives away from home one week and continues to live away from home, cannot re-enter school.
Scarlet Fever	See following page for Period of Isolation of Patient.			Yes.
Smallpox	Three weeks from onset of disease and thereafter until all crusts have disappeared and skin has healed.	Note 4.	Note 4.	Yes.
Typhoid Fever	One week after subsidence of clinical symptoms and thereafter until two successive negative stool and urine cultures, secured at an interval of at least one week, have been obtained, provided that a person who continues to be a carrier may be released under supervision of and after special permission by the Board of Health.	No restrictions save for food handlers. (Note 5)	No restrictions.	No.
Whooping Cough	Three weeks from beginning of spasmodic cough.	No restrictions.	No restrictions. (Note 3)	Exclusion from school two weeks from last exposure.	No.

NOTES

1. School teachers shall be subject to the same restrictions as school children. Food handlers and others whose occupation brings them in contact with children have no restriction if they live away from home.
2. Food handlers living in a family in which a case of diphtheria or scarlet fever exists shall be subject to the same restrictions as children.
3. A child shall be considered as having had the disease if so shown by the records of the Board of Health or by a sworn statement from the parent or guardian that the child has had the disease elsewhere.
4. Contacts shall be quarantined until three weeks have elapsed from the date of last exposure unless immunized by a previous attack, by a recent successful vaccination, or showing the immunity reaction.
5. Food handlers living in a family in which a case of typhoid fever exists shall be excluded from their occupation so long as they continue to live in the same house in which the case exists.

Scarlet Fever—*Uncomplicated cases*—three weeks from date of appearance of rash. Careful attention should be given to nose and throat to detect existence of discharge or inflammation before considering case as uncomplicated. If upper respiratory tract symptoms appear during month after release from isolation, precautions should be re-established.

Complicated cases—four weeks and thereafter until abnormal discharges shall have ceased, swollen glands subsided, or three successive cultures of abnormal discharge shall have been found free of hemolytic streptococci.

DIAGNOSTIC LABORATORIES: The State Department of Public Health maintains a Bacteriological Diagnostic Laboratory at 527 State House, Boston (Telephone, Capitol 4660; Sundays and holidays, Capitol 4665). Containers for shipment of specimens to the laboratory may be obtained through local board of health. Directions for collecting and shipping the specimens are inside the container and should be followed carefully for best results. Specimens are accepted only from physicians, dentists, hospitals and recognized health agencies. All *positive diagnostic* diphtheria cultures, *positive diagnostic* Widals or typhoid cultures, *positive* Type I or II pneumonia sputa, *positive* meningococcus reports and *positive* gonorrheal eye smears are reported by telephone or telegraph at State expense. All other reports are made by mail. No charges are ever made for laboratory examinations. No chemical examinations are made. The following bacteriological examinations are made:

Amebic dysentery
Anthrax cultures
Diphtheria cultures
Dysentery agglutination
Dysentery cultures
Gonorrhea smears
Malaria smears
Pneumonia typing
Spinal fluid for:
Meningococci
Pfeiffer's (influenza) bacillus
Pneumococci
Streptococci
Tubercle bacilli

Streptococcus cultures
Tuberculosis fluids for guinea pig inoculation
Tuberculosis sputum
Typhoid cultures
  Widal reaction
Undulant fever agglutination
Vincent's Angina smears
Weil-Felix reaction

Wassermann Laboratory: This laboratory, located in the Harvard Medical School, 25 Shattuck Street, Boston, (Telephone, Longwood 2380), is maintained by the State Department of Public Health. Special containers for blood samples should be obtained directly from the laboratory or local board of health. The following tests are made in this laboratory:

Blood for Hinton test
Spinal fluid for Wassermann
Blood for gonococcus complement fixation
Animal heads for rabies
Pathological tests for State Division of Livestock Disease Control.

Local diagnostic laboratories are maintained by boards of health in some communities. Not all the above examinations are done in each laboratory. When sending specimens to these laboratories, the special outfits furnished by them should be used. Local laboratories are maintained in the following cities and towns:

Arlington	Fitchburg	Needham
Ayer	Framingham	New Bedford
Boston	Gardner	Newton
Brockton	Gt. Barrington	Northampton
Brookline	Haverhill	Pittsfield
Cambridge	Holyoke	Somerville
Chicopee	Lawrence	Springfield
Clinton	Leominster	Waltham
Dedham	Lowell	Wellesley
Fall River	Lynn	Worcester

HOSPITALIZATION: The Board of Health may, if it sees fit, order hospitalization of any case of communicable disease. Before hospitalizing any case the physician should consult with the local board of health, in order to avoid subsequent misunderstandings as to hospital charges. Care of cases of communicable diseases may be obtained in the following hospitals:

Attleboro	Sturdy Memorial Hospital
Boston	Boston City Hospital (South Dept.)
Boston	Children's Hospital
Boston	Massachusetts Memorial Hospitals (Haynes Memorial)
Brookline	Board of Health Hospital
Fall River	Fall River General Hospital
Fitchburg	Fitchburg Isolation Hospital
Gardner	David Parker Municipal Hospital
Greenfield	Franklin County Public Hospital
Haverhill	Haverhill Contagious Hospital
Lawrence	Lawrence General Hospital
Lowell	Lowell Isolation Hospital
Lynn	Lynn Isolation Hospital
Malden	Malden Contagious Hospital
New Bedford	New Bedford Isolation Hospital
Northampton	Cooley Dickinson Hospital
Pittsfield	Sampson Memorial Hospital
Plymouth	Jordan Hospital
Pocasset	Barnstable County Infirmary
Salem	Health Department Hospital for Contagious Disease
Somerville	Somerville Contagious Disease Hospital
Springfield	Health Department Hospital
Vineyard Haven	United States Marine Hospital *
Waltham	Waltham Hospital
Worcester	Belmont Hospital

* Principally from the Marine Service, but occasionally local cases have gone there in emergency.

In addition to these hospitals, many general hospitals accept cases of typhoid, infantile paralysis, and epidemic meningitis.

BIOLOGIC PRODUCTS for aid in the diagnosis, prevention and treatment of communicable diseases are distributed free of charge by the State Department of Public Health. Most of the larger communities have made local arrangements for distributing stations where fresh products may be obtained at all times. As these are perishable products and their cost is borne by the tax levy, it is requested that due regard be given to avoid wastage through overstocking. Products furnished by the State, directly or through stations, are:

Diagnostic

Schick Test Solution   Old Tuberculin (undiluted)

Preventive

Diphtheria Toxin-Antitoxin   Silver Nitrate Solution
Diphtheria Toxoid   Smallpox Vaccine
Placental Extract   Sodium Citrate Solution
                                    Typhoid Vaccine

Therapeutic

Antimeningococcus Serum   Diphtheria Antitoxin
Antipneumococcus Serum (see under lobar   Scarlet Fever Streptococcus Antitoxin
pneumonia, p. 149)

REGULATIONS FOR DISTRIBUTION OF BIOLOGIC PRODUCTS

All biologic products are distributed under the following conditions:

1. Distributing stations must supply and use adequate refrigerating facilities for storage of products.

2. The delivery of diphtheria and scarlet fever antitoxin, smallpox vaccine, typhoid-paratyphoid vaccine, Schick test outfits, diphtheria toxin-antitoxin mixture and toxoid, and tuberculin is limited to boards of health, except as noted below.

3. A board of health not equipped to act as a distributing station may designate a hospital or drug store as its agent, but may not designate more than one agency.

4. A board of health may maintain more than one distributing station but products will be delivered by this Department to only one place in each town or city, unless needed for emergency use.

5. Hospitals of over 100 beds may obtain products by sending a messenger to the Antitoxin and Vaccine Laboratory for them.

6. Antimeningococcic serum will be distributed only through hospitals (or stations) selected by the Commissioner. In case of an epidemic, other distributing points may be established by the Commissioner.

7. Physicians may obtain prophylactic products and therapeutic products for immediate use by calling at or sending a messenger to the laboratory for them.

8. Delivery of products through channels other than those authorized above may be made if the Director of the Division of Biologic Laboratories considers the exigencies of the situation warrant.

9. District health officers will inspect biologic products on hand at distributing stations at least twice a year and will report their inventory and findings to the Antitoxin and Vaccine Laboratory.

10. These regulations are effective on and after June 1, 1935.
11. These regulations do not apply to State institutions.

SENSITIVITY

Whenever giving an injection of any biologic product, epinephrine should be available for treatment of any possible reaction. Although rare, reactions have been encountered even with intracutaneous injections.

Precautions Advisable in the Administration of Serums and Antitoxins

Reactions of various types may follow the parenteral administration of a foreign protein, such as horse serum, if the person has a natural or acquired hypersensitivity to the protein injected. Therefore, serum therapy should be employed only when definitely indicated and only by those equipped to combat such reactions as may occur.

I. Acute Anaphylactic Type of Reaction. These reactions, although infrequent, are of the utmost importance, because they may prove fatal. They may follow the administration of even minute amounts of serum in extremely hypersensitive persons, and may occur following the injection of serum by any route. The symptoms are dyspnea, cyanosis, urticaria, lumbar or abdominal pain, and collapse, any or all of which may begin within a few moments to an hour or more after the injection. Treatment consists in the injection of fresh epinephrine, 1:1000 dilution, the dose of which is 1 cc. (15 minims) for an adult, correspondingly less for a child, repeated within a few minutes if necessary; together with the application of measures designed to combat shock—artificial respiration, warmth, etc.

Such reactions may usually be avoided by observance of the following precautions which are designed to detect hypersensitive persons and lessen the dangers of serum administration.

A. History. Before the injection of serum, patients should be asked whether they have had asthma, hay-fever, eczema, urticaria, or angioneurotic edema. A positive history of these conditions is of importance only in suggesting the need for caution because such individuals probably have an allergic tendency.

A history of previous serum treatments (diphtheria, tetanus, or other antitoxin, antimeningococcic or antipneumococcic serum, diphtheria toxin-antitoxin mixture, etc.) and their sequelae should also be obtained. If rapid or severe reactions followed earlier administrations of serum, similar reactions may or may not occur again, but preparations should be made to combat them if serum is given.

B. Tests for Hypersensitivity. Tests are of more importance than history; and at least one such test should be done on each patient who is to receive serum. The ophthalmic test, in suitable cases, is probably a more reliable indicator of those individuals who may have severe reactions than is the intradermal test. Tests should not be done nor any serum administered unless fresh epinephrine solution is at hand, preferably in a syringe.

1. Ophthalmic Test. Observe both eyes carefully for any evidence of inflammation of the conjunctivae. Then put a drop of undiluted horse serum (if available; if not, use the serum it is planned to inject) in the conjunctival sac of one eye, leaving the other eye as the normal control. A positive reaction is indicated by itching, watering, and a diffuse reddening of the eye within 30 minutes. Severe reactions may be controlled by the instillation of a few drops of epinephrine, 1:1000 dilution. This test is of no value in young children, for they may wash out the serum by crying. In adults with marked injection of the conjunctivae it may prove difficult of interpretation.

2. Skin Test. If only one syringe is available, first make a control injection by injecting enough physiological saline solution *into* (not under) the skin of the anterior surface of one fore-arm to give a small elevation. In the corresponding location on the other arm, inject a similar amount of a 1:100 dilution of normal horse serum, having previously ejected some of the diluted serum from the needle to rid it of any water which may have remained from the sterilizing process. (The elevations caused by the injections tend to disappear within a few minutes if the test is negative, but the one produced by the serum may not disappear quite so quickly as the other.)

In hypersensitive patients the elevation at the site of serum injection rapidly enlarges within 5 to 20 minutes, becomes urticarial in appearance and is surrounded by a zone of erythema. Pseudopodial extensions of the central wheal are considered evidence of the higher and more dangerous degrees of sensitivity. Reactions usually subside within an hour or two.

C. *Use of Information derived from Tests.* The evidence provided by these tests is not infallible but is the best obtainable with our present knowledge. The eye test is not as sensitive as the intradermal, but the latter apparently is capable of detecting degrees of hypersensitivity below the level of clinical importance. Although occasionally hypersensitive persons may not react to either test, such individuals appear to be rare. Consequently, it is always advisable before beginning serum treatment to have epinephrine ready for injection.

1. Serum may be administered by any route to persons who do not react to these tests (or to either test, if only one is done). If serum is given intravenously, the first dose should not exceed 5 cc. and should be given very slowly, taking several minutes to administer the first cubic centimeter and at least one minute more for each additional cubic centimeter.

2. A positive eye test is so nearly an absolute contra-indication to intravenous serum therapy that no serum should be given by this route except after consultation. Intravenous serum administration probably

should not be undertaken at all in these patients except possibly in a hospital, for severe reactions may be expected.

3. Positive eye test is also a sufficient contra-indication to the administration of serum by any other route to warrant the precautions (consultation and hospitalization) advised in the preceding paragraph.

4. The import of positive skin tests is probably less than that of positive eye tests, but the same precautions are advised, particularly if the skin test is strongly positive.

5. If the tests give doubtful reactions or if the administration of serum is decided upon in spite of positive tests, the subcutaneous injection of a dose of epinephrine (5-15 minims of 1:1000 dilution) given a measured six minutes before the serum is a procedure which has been used with success and which appears to be rational.

6. The practice of desensitizing hypersensitive patients by the administration of repeated graduated doses of serum, starting with minute amounts (0.005 cc. more or less) subcutaneously and giving increasing doses at intervals of approximately one-half hour, is no longer recommended.

7. All patients receiving serum should be kept under close observation for not less than 30 minutes and preferably at least 45 minutes, during which time a physician should be immediately available.

8. Fresh epinephrine solution, ready for administration, should be at hand in a syringe whenever serum is administered. The dose is 1 cc. (15 minims) for an adult, correspondingly less for a child. It should be given if the patient complains of lumbar or abdominal pain or shows evidence of urticaria, dyspnea, cyanosis or collapse. The dose may be repeated within a few minutes if necessary, and may be given intravenously. Artificial respiration may be required and measures to combat shock (the application of heat, etc.) instituted if collapse occurs.

II. Thermal or "Chill" Reactions. These occur after the intravenous administration of serum and are seen most frequently with antipneumococcic serum, possibly because it is given intravenously more often and in larger doses than other serums. If the patient develops a chill, which when it appears at all usually begins within twenty minutes to one and one-half hours after any dose, the advent of hyperpyrexia should be watched for. Should hyperpyrexia develop, immediate treatment is essential. Epinephrine is of no use at such a time, but procedures advocated for the treatment of heat stroke are indicated, such as the use of ice packs, the application of sheets wrung from ice water, and ice water enemas. Venesection may be of use should pulmonary edema develop.

III. Serum Sickness. This is characterized most often by urticaria, but fever, enlarged glands, and joint pains are other common signs. It may come on any time up to four weeks after serum therapy, most commonly between the fourth and tenth days. Although this complication is disagreeable for the patient, it is not serious. Epinephrine may be given to allay discomfort, but its effect is of short duration. Cold applications lessen the annoyance of the urticaria. Large does of salicylate have also been recommended.

IV. Arthus Phenomenon. A local reaction, not incited by infection but going on to necrosis, at the site of subcutaneous or intramuscular injections occurs rarely. Serum injected within a period of several days to a few weeks or months after a previous injection is more likely to cause such reactions than is serum given either a few hours or days or some months or years after an injection. Such reactions are said to be most likely to occur if the patient shows signs of serum sickness at the time of injection. The possibility of such reactions should be kept in mind to avoid confusing them with local abscesses.

POPULAR PAMPHLETS: Available through Department of Public Health, 546 State House, Boston. Popular pamphlets are available on the following subjects:

Diphtheria
Infantile Paralysis
Measles
Rabies
Vaccination
Whooping Cough

ANTERIOR POLIOMYELITIS
(Infantile Paralysis)

DIAGNOSIS:

Preparalytic cases—Based on clinical findings, supplemented by lumbar puncture and spinal fluid examination. Under special circumstances, Department of Public Health will furnish consultant diagnostic service but only upon request of attending physician, where family is unable to afford a private consultant. Requests for such assistance should be made directly to Department, Telephone, Capitol 4660. During July, August and September, night and week-end requests may be made through Kenmore 8100.

Paralytic cases—Based on clinical findings. Special consultation service is not furnished by Department in such cases.

TREATMENT:

Preparalytic cases—Convalescent serum in limited quantities is available for treatment of preparalytic cases. Is of no value in cases where there is any paralysis or weakness of muscles; of very questionable value in preparalytic cases. Should be administered intravenously. Such serum may be obtained if physician has performed a lumbar puncture, certifies as to spinal fluid findings and certifies as to absence of paralysis or weakness of muscles. Small supplies of serum are available in the following hospitals and health agencies:

City or Town	Hospital or Health Agency
Attleboro	Sturdy Memorial Hospital
Ayer	Nashoba Associated Boards of Health
Beverly	Beverly Hospital
Boston	Boston City Hospital (South Department)

City or Town	Hospital or Health Agency
Boston	Boston Dispensary (Out-Patient only)
Boston	Floating Hospital
Boston	Children's Hospital
Boston	Massachusetts Memorial Hospital (Haynes Memorial)
Boston	Massachusetts General Hospital
Brockton	Brockton Hospital
Cambridge	Cambridge Hospital
Fall River	Fall River General Hospital
Fitchburg	Burbank Hospital
Framingham	Framingham Hospital
Gardner	Henry Heywood Memorial Hospital
Gloucester	Addison Gilbert Hospital
Great Barrington	Southern Berkshire Health District
Greenfield	Franklin County Isolation Hospital
Haverhill	Haverhill Contagious Hospital
Holyoke	Holyoke Hospital
Lawrence	Lawrence General Hospital
Lowell	Lowell General Hospital
Lynn	Lynn Isolation Hospital
Malden	Malden Contagious Hospital
Nantucket	Nantucket Cottage Hospital
New Bedford	St. Luke's Hospital
Newburyport	Anna Jaques Hospital
Newton	Newton Hospital
North Adams	North Adams Hospital
Northampton	Cooley Dickinson Hospital
Oak Bluffs	Martha's Vineyard Hospital
Pittsfield	House of Mercy Hospital
Plymouth	Jordan Hospital
Pocasset	Barnstable County Sanatorium
Salem	Health Department Hospital
Springfield	Springfield Isolation Hospital
Taunton	Morton Hospital
Ware	Mary Lane Hospital
Worcester	City Hospital

Paralytic cases—During acute stages—symptomatic and supportive with special reference to prevention of contractures. In cases of respiratory paralysis, placing patient in a respirator may be of life-saving value. Respirators are located in following hospitals:

Beverly	Beverly Hospital
Boston	Boston City Hospital
Boston	Children's Hospital
Boston	Massachusetts General Hospital
Boston	Massachusetts Memorial Hospital
Fall River	Fall River General
Fall River	Union Memorial Hospital
Holyoke	Carpenter Isolation Hospital
New Bedford	St. Luke's Hospital
Newton	Newton Hospital
Salem	Salem Hospital
Springfield	Isolation Hospital
Worcester	City Hospital

After acute stage—orthopedic care. In addition to the orthopedic clinics in certain hospitals, special clinics for care of paralyzed cases are maintained by or in conjunction with the Harvard Infantile Paralysis Commission as follows:

Arlington Clinic Visiting Nurse Assn. 707 Massachusetts Ave. Arlington Centre, Mass.	Wednesday P.M.
Beverly Clinic Public Health Dispensary 84 Cabot Street Beverly, Mass.	Wednesday A.M. and P.M. Alternate weeks
Cambridge Clinic Avon Home 1000 Massachusetts Ave. Cambridge, Mass.	Monday and Wednesday A.M.
Haverhill Clinic Board of Health Rooms City Hall Haverhill, Mass.	Wednesday A.M. and P.M.
East Boston Clinic Health Unit Paris Street East Boston, Mass.	Friday P.M.
Lawrence Clinic Child Welfare Rooms City Hall Lawrence, Mass.	Monday A.M. and P.M.
Lowell Clinic Lowell Guild 17 Dutton Street Lowell, Mass.	Wednesday A.M. and P.M.
Lynn Clinic Lynn Hospital Lynn, Mass.	Tuesday P.M.
Malden Clinic Malden Dispensary Malden, Mass.	Saturday A.M.
North Adams Clinic Board of Health Rooms North Adams, Mass.	Friday P.M.; Saturday A.M. once every 3 months
Quincy Clinic Quincy Dispensary High School Ave. Quincy, Mass.	Monday A.M. and P.M.
Somerville Clinic Old Police Station Bow Street Somerville, Mass.	Thursday P.M.

Waltham Clinic
   Waltham Baby Hospital
   755 Main Street   } Tuesday P.M.
   Waltham, Mass.

Hospitals and institutions admitting paralyzed cases for special care are:

City or Town	Name of Institution	Restrictions
Baldwinsville	Hospital Cottages for Children	Under 14
Boston	Industrial School for Crippled Children	Day School
Canton	Massachusetts Hospital School for Crippled Children	Between 5 and 15
Egypt (Scituate)	Children's Sunlight Hospital	Children 2-6 Adults 16-35
Newton Center	New England Peabody Home for Crippled Children	Under 12
North Dartmouth	Sol-E-Mar	Under 14
Springfield	Shriners' Hospital for Crippled Children	Under 14

Applications for admission to these hospitals should be made directly to the Superintendent (Sol-E-Mar admitted through St. Luke's Hospital, New Bedford).

ISOLATION AND QUARANTINE: (Consult regulations of local board of health. See p. 130.)

Cases—Usually two weeks from onset of disease, and thereafter until acute symptoms have subsided.

Contacts—Usually until two weeks have elapsed from date of last exposure.

PREVENTION:

Passive immunization—No method of proven value. Convalescent serum not available for this purpose. Parental whole blood has been tried without proven results.

Active immunization—No safe and proven method yet available.

CHICKEN POX (Varicella)

DIAGNOSIS: Based on clinical findings.

TREATMENT: Symptomatic and supportive.

ISOLATION AND QUARANTINE: (Consult regulations of local board of health. See p. 130).

Cases—Usually one week from appearance of eruption and thereafter until all primary crusts have disappeared.

Contacts—Usually no restrictions.

PREVENTION:

Passive immunization—Convalescent serum and placental extract have been used for passive immunization. (See p. 136).

Active immunization—No practical method of active immunization available.

DIPHTHERIA

DIAGNOSIS: Clinical condition, usually with laboratory confirmation. Nose and throat cultures for diagnosis may be sent to local or State Bacteriological Laboratory, 527 State House, Boston, outfits obtainable at local board of health. Positive diagnostic reports telephoned or telegraphed prepaid. (See p. 133.)

TREATMENT: Antitoxin furnished free by State through local boards of health. Available in 5,000 and 10,000 unit vials.

Amount of Antitoxin in the Treatment of a Case of Diphtheria

	Mild Cases Units	Mod. and Early Severe Units*	Severe and Malignant Units*
Infants, 10 to 30 lbs. in wgt. under 2 yrs.	3,000-5,000	5,000-10,000	7,500-10,000
Children, 30 to 90 lbs. in wgt. under 15 yrs.	4,000-10,000	10,000-15,000	10,000-20,000
Adults, 90 lbs. and over in wgt.	5,000-10,000	10,000-20,000	20,000-50,000
Method of administration advised	Intramuscular	Intravenous	Intravenous

* When given intramuscularly use the larger amounts indicated.

Cases of laryngeal and naso-pharyngeal diphtheria, moderate cases still active and seen late at the time of the first injection, and moderate cases of diphtheria occurring as a complication of the exanthems should be classified as "severe cases."

In mild and early moderate cases the antitoxin should be injected by means of a sterile hypodermic syringe into a suitable muscle instead of under the skin, because absorption takes place about three times as rapidly from muscles. For intravenous administration, the injection may be made into the vein on the flexor surface of the elbow. Antitoxin for intravenous use should be highly potent and should show no sediment or turbidity. It must be warmed to body temperature and given slowly. *All cases should be skin tested for sensitivity before giving serum.* (See p. 136.)

ISOLATION AND QUARANTINE: (Consult regulations of local board of health. See p. 130.)

Cases—Usually one week from onset and thereafter until two successive negative cultures from nose and throat taken at least 24 hours apart shall have been obtained.

Contacts—*Immune* contacts (those who have had diphtheria, have been immunized, or have a negative Schick test) usually quarantined until negative cultures obtained; *susceptible* contacts until one week from last exposure has elapsed, and negative cultures obtained.

PREVENTION:

Passive immunization—May be obtained through injection of 1,000 units of antitoxin. (See p. 136.) Does not last more than two to four weeks. Not usually recommended if contacts can be kept under observation.

Active immunization—All immunizing solutions should be given by subcutaneous injections preferably over the deltoid region. (See p. 136.)

Toxoid may be given in three doses (0.5, 1.0, 1.0 cc.) at three week intervals. Alternative, though less desirable, injection schedules are three doses at one week intervals or two doses at one month interval. Reactions no more severe though level of immunity somewhat reduced. Toxoid is the immunizing agent of preference under the age of ten years. Best age for immunizing a child is at age of six months. Toxoid contains no horse serum, and is more effective and acts more rapidly than does toxin-antitoxin; it produces more severe local and systemic reactions in adults and older children. Toxoid is furnished by State through local board of health.

Alum toxoid—May be given in single injection. Produces high level of immunity. Usually causes a lump in arm that lasts for several weeks with occasional sterile abscess. Not furnished by State at present.

Toxin-antitoxin—Is still used very extensively though being rapidly replaced by toxoid. Given in three injections of 1 cc. each at one week intervals. Toxin-antitoxin is the immunizing agent of choice for use in persons above the age of twelve. Furnished by State through local board of health.

SUSCEPTIBILITY: May be determined by Schick test. Usually omitted in small children, as this group is usually susceptible. All children above age of 12 should be tested before immunization as many are immune by this age. Schick test useful six months after immunization as a check on effectiveness of injections. Material furnished by State through local board of health. Inject 0.1 cc. toxin on right arm, and 0.1 cc. heated toxin for control on left arm, all injections *into but not through the skin*. Observe reactions on fourth day. (See p. 136.)

DOG BITE

REPORTING: All cases of dog bite, whether or not requiring antirabic treatment must be reported to the local board of health. (See p. 130.)

RECOMMENDED PROCEDURE:

The dog—(1) *Do not permit anyone to kill the dog*; if it is killed at once, it may be impossible to determine promptly whether or not it was rabid.

(2) *Keep the dog under observation for two weeks.* When the case is reported to the board of health, the animal inspector will care for this. If the dog is well at the end of two weeks, the possibility of transmission of rabies at the time of biting may be dismissed.

(3) *If the dog becomes sick* have it examined by a veterinarian.

(4) *If the dog dies* have head sent to Wassermann Laboratory, Harvard Medical School, 25 Shattuck Street, Boston, Telephone, Longwood 2380. This is a State laboratory, examination being made without charge.

The patient—(1) *Cauterize* wound, if possible, with fuming nitric acid. Iodine, mercurochrome, and similar antiseptics do not cauterize, nor are other cauterizing agents effective.

(2) *Antirabic treatment*: The law requires that "the board of health of any city or town shall, on recommendation of the state department of public health, furnish free of charge antirabic vaccine and the treatment of persons as to whom said department recommends such treatment." In accordance with this statute, the Department recommends antirabic treatment for the following patients:

1. TREATMENT IMPERATIVE:

    Persons bitten by or intimately exposed to the saliva of
    a. A clinically rabid animal.
    b. An animal the head of which was found positive for rabies on laboratory examination.
    c. An animal the head of which was found suspicious for rabies on laboratory examination.

2. TREATMENT ADVISED in the following instances unless the circumstances surrounding the bite are such that in the opinion of the attending physician there is no possibility of rabies in the individual case:

    a. Persons bitten on the head should be treated at once regardless of the condition of the dog. Treatment may be discontinued at the end of seven days provided dog is still well and is kept under observation for seven additional days, treatment to be resumed if dog shows signs of rabies during this period.
    b. Persons bitten by or intimately exposed to the saliva of
        (1) An animal the head of which was in such condition on reaching the laboratory that it could not be examined and was therefore classified as unsatisfactory.
        (2) A lost animal, that is an animal which could not be restrained for a clinical observation period of fourteen days or the head of which could not be submitted for laboratory examination.
        (3) An animal which was killed without being held for examination and without subsequent examination of the head.

ATTENTION: Before beginning antirabic vaccine treatment, obtain vaccine from board of health. Do not purchase vaccine directly as the board of health is not responsible for cost of vaccine which it has not purchased. To avoid possibility of subsequent dispute as to costs of treatment, obtain authorization for this from board of health. The State does not furnish antirabic vaccine.

ANTIRABIC VACCINE: The vaccine at present recommended by the Department of Public Health is that prepared according to the Semple method (phenolized virus). Fourteen injections are usually adequate for simple bites on the trunk and extremities. When the bite is on the head or neck, or there are severe multiple lacerations, twenty-one injections are desirable. All injections are given subcutaneously, preferably in a different site each day to avoid local soreness; the abdominal wall is a frequent site for the injections.

DYSENTERY (Amebic)

DIAGNOSIS: Clinical findings with laboratory confirmation through examination of fecal specimens.

Vegetative stage of amebae—For best results it is necessary to examine freshly passed specimens, such examination being possible only if patient is hospitalized or sent to laboratory. If local hospital is not equipped for such tests, patient, if ambulatory, may be sent to Department of Tropical Medicine, Harvard Medical School, a fee being charged for such examination. A fixed smear of a freshly passed fecal specimen may be sent to State Bacteriological Laboratory, 527 State House, Boston. Special containers for this purpose are available through local board of health. (See p. 133.) For satisfactory results, directions as to mailing and fixing of smears must be followed carefully. Do not send patient to State Laboratory.

Encysted stage of amebae—Stool specimens may be sent to State Bacteriological Laboratory, 527 State House, Boston. Special containers for this purpose are available through local board of health.

TREATMENT: Numerous specific amebicides available. See New England Journal of Medicine, *209*, 1071, 1933 (November 23).

ISOLATION AND QUARANTINE: (Consult regulations of local board of health. See p. 130.)

Cases—Usually no restrictions during acute stage as vegetative forms are non-infectious. Release from medical supervision should be conditioned by stool examinations for cysts. Carrier should not be employed as food handler.

Contacts—Usually no restrictions.

PREVENTION: No method of immunization available.

DYSENTERY (Bacillary)

DIAGNOSIS: Based on clinical findings with laboratory confirmation. Some strains of dysentery baccilli cause merely a transient diarrhea in healthy adults, or children above twelve years. Stool specimens may be sent to local or State Bacteriological Laboratory, 527 State House, Boston. For best results specimen should be taken early in the disease and from a diarrheal specimen. Agglutinins may often be found in blood after first week of disease. For dysentery agglutination test send at least 5 cc. of blood in sterile test tube to State Bacteriological Laboratory, 527 State House, Boston. (See p. 133.)

TREATMENT: Symptomatic and supportive. In Shiga type (rare in Massachusetts), antitoxin may be of use. Not furnished by State.

ISOLATION AND QUARANTINE: (Consult regulations of local board of health. See p. 130.) Usually same precautions as for typhoid fever.

PREVENTION: No practical method of active and passive immunization available.

EPIDEMIC CEREBRO-SPINAL MENINGITIS (Meningococcus Meningitis)

DIAGNOSIS: Clinical findings supplemented by lumbar puncture and spinal fluid examination. If the spinal fluid is cloudy, it is usual practice to treat with antimeningococcic serum until the laboratory rules out this diagnosis. Specimens of spinal fluids should be examined by direct smear and culture. If local facilities for such examination are not available, spinal fluid may be sent to State Bacteriological Laboratory, 527 State House, Boston. Positive reports telephoned or telegraphed prepaid. (See p. 133.)

TREATMENT: Antimeningococcic serum furnished free by State through certain hospitals or boards of health. All cases should be tested for sensitivity before giving serum. (See p. 136.) Dosage depends upon the amount of spinal fluid withdrawn. Twenty to forty cc. may be given intraspinally; in general 5 to 10 cc. less than the amount of spinal fluid withdrawn. Frequency varies with individual case (see circular accompanying serum). Intravenous serum is recommended in meningococcemia cases. Authorities differ on the value of intravenous serum in meningitis. If the patient fails to respond to serum, culture of spinal fluid should be sent to Antitoxin and Vaccine Laboratory, 375 South Street, Jamaica Plain, for check against serum. Antimeningococcic serum may be obtained through the following hospitals and boards of health:

City or Town	Hospital or Board of Health
Athol	Board of Health
Attleboro	Sturdy Memorial Hospital
Ayer	Community Memorial Hospital
Beverly	Beverly Hospital
Boston	Boston City Hospital
Boston	Carney Hospital
Boston	Children's Hospital
Boston	Massachusetts General Hospital
Boston	Massachusetts Memorial (Haynes Memorial)
Brockton	Brockton Hospital
Cambridge	Cambridge Hospital
Chelsea	Chelsea Memorial Hospital
Clinton	Clinton Hospital
Concord	Emerson Hospital
Fall River	Fall River General Hospital
Fitchburg	Board of Health
Framingham	Framingham-Union Hospital
Gardner	Henry Heywood Memorial Hospital
Gloucester	Addison Gilbert Hospital
Great Barrington	Fairview Hospital
Greenfield	Franklin County Public Hospital
Haverhill	Gale Hospital
Holyoke	Providence Hospital
Hyannis	Cape Cod Hospital
Ipswich	Cable Memorial Hospital

City or Town	Hospital or Board of Health
Lawrence	Lawrence General Hospital
Leominster	Leominster Hospital
Lowell	St. Joseph's Hospital
Lynn.	Lynn Isolation Hospital
Medford	Lawrence Memorial Hospital
Milford	Milford Hospital
Nantucket	Nantucket Cottage Hospital
New Bedford	St. Luke's Hospital
Newburyport	Anna Jaques Hospital
Newton	Newton Hospital
North Adams	North Adams Hospital
Northampton	Cooley Dickinson Hospital
Norwood	Norwood Hospital
Oak Bluffs	Martha's Vineyard Hospital
Pittsfield	Sampson Memorial Hospital
Plymouth	Jordan Hospital
Provincetown	Board of Health
Quincy.	Quincy Hospital
Salem	Salem Isolation Hospital
Southbridge	Harrington Memorial Hospital
Springfield	Springfield Health Department
Taunton	Morton Hospital
Ware	Mary Lane Hospital
Webster	Webster District Hospital
Westfield	Noble Hospital
Woburn	Choate Memorial Hospital
Worcester	Board of Health

ISOLATION AND QUARANTINE: (Consult regulations of local board of health. See p. 130.)

Cases—Usually two weeks from onset of disease and thereafter until all acute symptoms have subsided.

Contacts—Usually until ten days from date of last exposure.

PREVENTION: No practical method of active and passive immunization available.

GERMAN MEASLES (Rubella)

DIAGNOSIS—Based on clinical findings.

TREATMENT—Symptomatic.

ISOLATION AND QUARANTINE—(Consult regulations of local board of health. See p. 130.)

Cases—Usually one week from appearance of rash.

Contacts—Usually no restrictions.

PREVENTION—No practical method of immunization available. Convalescent serum and placental extract have been used for passive protection. (See p. 136.)

GONORRHEA

(See Gonorrhea and Syphilis, p. 167.)

LOBAR PNEUMONIA

DIAGNOSIS—Clinical and x-ray findings. Over half of all cases in adults are due to type I or II pneumococci.

Typing—Advisable in early cases, for those with type I or II infection may be helped by serum treatment. Select specimen of freshly raised sputum; do not be content with saliva as oral cavity may contain pneumococci of type different from that causing the pneumonia. Sputum should be sent to nearest laboratory equipped for typing. Typing service available at all times through State Bacteriological Laboratory, 527 State House, Boston. (See p. 133.) All sputa showing type I or II pneumococci reported by telephone or telegraph prepaid. Send sputum in special containers available through boards of health, or in any sterile container. Do not use tuberculosis sputum outfits as these contain carbolic acid that destroys pneumococci, making typing impossible. In addition to typing facilities available through State Department of Public Health, pneumococcus sputum typing may be secured through the following hospital laboratories, the charges for the same depending upon the hospital:

City or Town	Hospital
Ayer	Ayer Community Memorial
Beverly	Beverly
Boston	Peter Bent Brigham
Boston	Beth Israel
Boston	Boston City
Boston	Boston Dispensary
Boston	Carney
Boston	Faulkner
Boston	Massachusetts General
Boston	Massachusetts Memorial
Boston	New England Deaconess
Brockton	Brockton
Cambridge	Cambridge
Cambridge	Cambridge City
Chelsea	U. S. Naval
Clinton	Clinton
Fall River	Fall River Board of Health
Fall River	Fall River General
Fall River	St. Ann's
Fall River	Truesdale
Fall River	Union
Fitchburg	Burbank
Framingham	Framingham-Union
Gardner	Henry Heywood Memorial
Great Barrington	Fairview
Greenfield	Franklin County
Haverhill	Gale
Holyoke	Holyoke Hospital
Holyoke	Providence Hospital
Newburyport	Anna Ja'ques
Lawrence	Lawrence General

City or Town	Hospital
Lowell	Lowell General
Lowell	St. John's
Lowell	St. Joseph's
Lynn	Lynn
Malden	Malden
Marlboro	Marlboro Hospital
New Bedford	St. Luke's
Natick	Leonard Morse
Newton	Newton
North Adams	North Adams
Northampton	Cooley Dickinson Hospital
Norwood	Norwood
Peabody	J. B. Thomas
Pittsfield	House of Mercy
Pittsfield	St. Luke's
Quincy	Quincy City
Salem	Salem
Southbridge	Harrington Memorial Hospital
Springfield	Mercy
Springfield	Springfield
Springfield	Wesson
Westfield	Noble Hospital
Worcester	Hahnemann
Worcester	St. Vincent's
Worcester	Worcester City
Worcester	Worcester Memorial

TREATMENT—Specific serum is available for only type I and II pneumonias. Serum is available through State Laboratory or through any of above listed hospital laboratories under following conditions:

(1) Sputum or other material from the patient shall first be typed by the laboratory and shown to contain type I or II pneumococci, and

(2) The physician shall certify that the patient has not been ill with pneumonia longer than 96 hours (4 days), and

(3) A report will be made to the State Department of Public Health on form enclosed with serum.

Under the above conditions 60,000 units of concentrated antipneumococcic serum (Felton's antibody solution) will be issued for type I pneumonia, and 100,000 units for type II. Additional serum is available only under one of the following conditions:

(a) *Bacteremia*—blood culture positive for type I or II pneumococci.

(b) *Pregnancy* or delivery within seven days previous to onset of pneumonia.

(c) *Continued fever*—if, within eighteen hours after *beginning* of serum treatment, the patient's temperature remains above 102°F by rectum (101°F by mouth).

(d) *Recurrent fever*—if, following the initial temperature drop induced by serum, the patient's temperature, within 48 hours of *beginning* such treatment, rises to 102°F by rectum (101°F by mouth).

ADMINISTRATION OF SERUM—See circular accompanying serum. Directions should be followed in detail.

ISOLATION AND QUARANTINE—Usually no restrictions.

PREVENTION—No accepted method of active or passive immunization available.

MALARIA

DIAGNOSIS: Clinical condition with laboratory confirmation. Smears for diagnosis may be sent to State Bacteriological Laboratory, 527 State House, Boston. Special containers available through local boards of health. (See p. 133.)

TREATMENT: Symptomatic and supportive. Specific drugs.

ISOLATION AND QUARANTINE: (Consult regulations of local board of health. See p. 130.) Usually no restrictions except precautions as to screening of patient.

PREVENTION: No practical method of active and passive immunization available.

MEASLES (Rubeola)

DIAGNOSIS: Based on clinical findings.

TREATMENT: Symptomatic and supportive.

ISOLATION AND QUARANTINE: (Consult regulations of local board of health. See p. 130.)

Cases—Usually one week from date of appearance of rash. Isolation important for patient to reduce incidence of complicating pneumonia.

Contacts—*Immune* contacts, usually no restrictions; *susceptible* contacts, usually kept from school for 16 days from date of last exposure. Some schools permit child to attend school for one week after first exposure, then exclude until 16 days after last exposure.

PREVENTION:

Passive immunization and modification—Passive immunization (complete protection) is of no permanent value, lasting only two to four weeks, after which the patient is as susceptible as before the injection. It is desirable in hospitals, and for sick, debilitated children, or very young children. The purpose of *modification* is to obtain a mild measles which is usually devoid of complications and usually leaves a permanent protection. All injections are given intramuscularly. (See p. 136.)

May be obtained through:

(1) *Convalescent serum*—Usually not obtainable except in certain hospitals. For prevention 3 cc. during first four days after exposure*; for modification four to seven days. Inject intramuscularly in buttocks, lateral aspect of thigh, or between scapulae.

(2) *Adult whole blood*—Less certain in result. For prevention 30 cc. blood during first four days after exposure*; for modification four to seven days. Department of Public Health furnishes through local board of health ampoules of 4% sterile sodium citrate solution which may

be used in the syringe to prevent coagulation of the blood. (See p. 135.) Preliminary grouping of blood is not necessary as injection is intramuscularly; do not give intravenously without blood grouping. Injections are given in buttocks, lateral aspect of thigh, or between scapulae.

(3) *Placental extract* (Immune Globulins—Human)—For prevention give during first four days after exposure*; for modification four to ten days. Furnished for study purposes by State Department of Public Health. (See p. 136.) Given by intramuscular injection; do not give intravenously.

Active immunization—No practical method available.

MUMPS (Epidemic Parotitis)

DIAGNOSIS: Based on clinical findings.
TREATMENT: Symptomatic and supportive.
ISOLATION AND QUARANTINE: (Consult regulations of local board of health. See p. 130.)

Cases—Usually one week from onset of disease, and thereafter until all swelling of salivary glands has disappeared.

Contacts—Usually no restrictions. Males of age of puberty or older should be protected from exposure because of danger of complicating orchitis.

PREVENTION: No practical method of active or passive immunization available. Convalescent serum has been tried where available.

OPHTHALMIA NEONATORUM

REPORTING—All cases showing inflammation, swelling, redness or abnormal discharge of the eyes within two weeks of birth must be reported to the board of health. ("If either eye of an infant becomes inflamed, swollen and red, or shows an unnatural discharge within two weeks after birth, the nurse, relative or other attendant having charge of such infant shall report in writing, within six hours thereafter, to the board of health of the town where the infant is, the fact that such inflammation, swelling and redness of the eyes or unnatural discharge exists."—(General Laws, Chapter 111, Section 110). Also "if either eye of an infant whom or whose mother a physician, or a hospital medical officer registered under section nine of chapter one hundred and twelve, visits becomes inflamed, swollen and red, or shows an unnatural discharge within two weeks after birth, he shall immediately give written notice thereof, over his own signature, to the board of health of the town————." (General Laws, Chapter 111, Section 111).

DIAGNOSIS—Smears for possible gonococci should be obtained. May

---

*Determination of date of exposure. Measles is communicable three days before the appearance of the rash. Therefore, the date of appearance of the rash in the patient being known, the date of first possible exposure of the contact is three days earlier.

be examined in local laboratory or sent to State Bacteriological Laboratory, 527 State House, Boston. Usual gonorrhea outfits, obtainable through local boards of health, should be used for this purpose. Positive results are telephoned or telegraphed prepaid. (See p. 133.)

TREATMENT—The General Laws of the Commonwealth require that the local board of health upon receipt of a report of a discharging eye as above described "shall take such immediate action as it may deem necessary, including, so far as possible, consultation with an oculist and the employment of a trained nurse, in order that blindness may be prevented."

ISOLATION AND QUARANTINE—Aseptic nursing precautions to prevent spread of possible infection to other eye or to eyes of attendants.

PREVENTION—Silver nitrate solution for instillation in the eye at time of birth is furnished in wax ampoules by State Department of Public Health. Obtainable through hospitals and boards of health.

PARATYPHOID FEVER
(Same as for Typhoid Fever, p. 164.)

RABIES
(See Dog Bite, p. 144.)

SCARLET FEVER

DIAGNOSIS: Based on clinical findings. Throat cultures of no practical value.

TREATMENT: In most cases along general medical lines. Antitoxin furnished free by State through local board of health. *All cases should be tested for sensitivity before giving serum.* Serum reactions follow scarlet fever antitoxin more frequently than with diphtheria antitoxin. (See p. 136.)

ISOLATION AND QUARANTINE: (Consult regulations of local board of health. See p. 130.)

Uncomplicated Cases—Usually three or four weeks from onset. If upper respiratory tract infection develops during following month, reestablishment of isolation precautions desirable. Nose and throat cultures of little practical value in determining release from isolation.

Complicated Cases—Usually until abnormal discharges shall have ceased. Repeated negative cultures of discharge may warrant earlier release. Nasal discharge especially dangerous and frequently overlooked.

Contacts—*Immune* contacts usually not quarantined if living away from patient. *Susceptible* contacts usually quarantined until one week from date of last contact with patient. Nose and throat cultures of no practical value.

PREVENTION:

Passive immunization—Use of antitoxin for this purpose not generally recommended owing to frequency of serum reactions. Some local boards of health have limited supplies of convalescent serum which may be obtained for protection of family contacts of reported cases.

Active immunization—Dick toxin given in five subcutaneous injections at one week intervals produces high level of protection. (See p. 136.) Dick toxin is not furnished by State or local health departments.

SUSCEPTIBILITY: May be determined by Dick test. Inject exactly 0.1 cc. into the skin; observe 20-24 hours. (See p. 136.) Any redness 1 cm. or more in any diameter indicates susceptibility. Dick test material is not furnished by State or local health departments.

SEPTIC SORE THROAT

Is probably not a definite disease entity. Usually includes severe sore throats of streptococcal origin. Abnormal incidence of sore throats in practice of any physician should be reported to local board of health for investigation as to possible spread through milk. Persons with sore throats should not be permitted to work around milk supplies.

SMALLPOX (Variola)

DIAGNOSIS: Based on clinical findings.

TREATMENT: Symptomatic and supportive.

ISOLATION AND QUARANTINE: (Consult regulations of local board of health. See p. 130.)

Cases—Usually three weeks from onset of disease and thereafter until all crusts have disappeared and skin has healed.

Contacts—Usually quarantined until three weeks have elapsed from the date of last exposure unless immunized by a previous attack, by a recent successful vaccination, or showing the immunity reaction.

PREVENTION:

Passive immunization—No satisfactory method available.

Active immunization—Smallpox vaccine virus furnished by State through local boards of health. (See p. 135.) Virus must be kept cold until used (do not carry it in coat pocket). Multiple pressure method advised instead of scarification. (See directions accompanying vaccine). Acetone or alcohol is preferable for cleansing skin; avoid medicated alcohols. *Do not cover site of vaccination with a dressing or shield.*

When to vaccinate—The first year of life is ideal time to perform vaccination, as reactions are least severe and complications at a minimum. Massachusetts law requires that "an unvaccinated child shall not be admitted to a public school except upon presentation of a certificate . . signed by a registered physician designated by the parent or guardian, that the physician has at the time of giving the certificate personally examined the child and that he is of the opinion that the physical condition of the child is such that his health will be endangered by vaccination." The supreme court has ruled that a school committee may require renewal of such a certificate as often as every two months.

SYPHILIS
(See Gonorrhea and Syphilis, p. 167.)

TETANUS
DIAGNOSIS: Clinical findings with aid of spinal fluid examination. No bacteriological test available.
TREATMENT: Antitetanic serum. Not furnished by State.
ISOLATION AND QUARANTINE: No restrictions.
PREVENTION:
Passive immunization may be obtained through injection of antitetanic serum in certain wound cases. All cases should be tested for sensitivity. (See page 136.)
Active immunization with tetanus toxoid may be considered for those whose contacts entail an abnormal risk of infection. Not furnished by State.

TUBERCULOSIS
DIAGNOSIS. Diagnosis in early stages based usually on x-ray findings, with or without laboratory data and symptoms or physical signs.

1. *Sputum*—may be sent to local or to State Bacteriological Laboratory, 527 State House, Boston. Outfits obtainable through local boards of health. (See page 133.)

2. *Tuberculin Test*—Old Tuberculin for diagnostic purposes only is furnished for Von Pirquet or, after dilution, for Mantoux test by the State through local boards of health. (See page 135.) See accompanying tuberculin instructions. Saline solution for making dilutions not furnished by the State. Positive tuberculin test indicates tuberculous infection, but gives no indication as to activity of process.

3. *X-Ray Service*—Patients unable to afford private x-ray service may be referred to state and county tuberculosis hospitals (see page 159) by their family physicians. Reports made only to referring physician

4. *Diagnostic Out-Patient Departments*—are maintained at all state and county sanatoria. (See page 159.)

5. *Consultation Clinics*—Consultation clinics to which physicians may refer patients for examination are maintained by state and county hospitals in many communities. Patients accepted only on reference by physician, board of health, or other health agency. Reports made only to referring physician or agency. Consultation clinics are maintained as follows:

Consultation Clinics

City or Town	Location	Time	Auspices
Athol	Memorial Building	4th Wed. 2 P.M.	Rutland State Sanatorium
Ayer.	Community Memorial Hospital (for Nashoba Health District)	4th Wed. 2 P.M.	Middlesex County Sanatorium

City or Town	Location	Time	Auspices
Gardner	Municipal Tb. Dispensary	1st Wed. 2 P.M.	Rutland State Sanatorium
Great Barrington	Fairview Hospital	4th Tues. 9 A.M.	Westfield State Sanatorium
Greenfield	Greenfield Hospital	3rd Tues. 9 A.M.	Westfield State Sanatorium
Haverhill	Municipal Tb. Dispensary	3rd Wed. 2 P.M.	North Reading State Sanatorium
Hyannis	Cape Cod Hospital	3rd Tues. 1:30 P.M.	Barnstable County Sanatorium
Lawrence	Municipal Tb. Dispensary 37 Jackson Street	2nd Wed. 2 P.M.	North Reading State Sanatorium
Medford	Lawrence Memorial Hospital	Appointments thru Board of Health	Middlesex County Sanatorium
Milford	Milford Hospital	2nd Wed. 2 P.M.	Rutland State Sanatorium
Nantucket	Nantucket Cottage Hospital	4th Thurs. 3:30 P.M. every second month	Barnstable County Sanatorium
Newton	Newton Hospital	Appointments thru Board of Health	Middlesex County Sanatorium
North Adams	North Adams Hospital	4th Wed. 9:30 A.M.	Westfield State Sanatorium
Provincetown	Town Hall	2nd Friday	Barnstable County Sanatorium
Salem	5 St. Peter Street	3rd Mon. 2 P.M.	Essex Sanatorium
Southbridge	Harrington Memorial Hospital	3rd Wed. 2 P.M.	Rutland State Sanatorium
Vineyard Haven	Martha's Vineyard Hospital	4th Fri. or Sat. 1 P.M.	Barnstable County Sanatorium
Worcester	Worcester County Sanatorium	1st Tues. 2 P.M.	Worcester County Sanatorium

6. *Local Clinics*—Tuberculosis diagnostic clinics, independent of state or county sanatoria, are maintained by local boards of health as follows:

Local Clinics

City or Town	Location	Time	Auspices
Adams	20 Center Street	Monday 6-7 P.M.	Adams Board of Health
Arlington	Dr. Pratt's Office 385 Massachusetts Ave.	By Appointment	Arlington Board of Health
Attleboro	Sturdy Memorial Hospital	Wed. 4-6 P.M.	Attleboro Board of Health
Beverly	84 Cabot Street	Week days 8:30-5 P.M., Thurs. Eve. 7:30-8:30 P.M.	Beverly Board of Health
Boston	12 Health Units under supervision of the Boston Health Dept.		Boston Health Department
Brockton	Board of Health City Hall	Fri. 4-6:30 P.M.	Brockton Board of Health
Brookline	Town Hall Room 23	Tues. 2-3 P.M. Fri. 7-8 P.M.	Brookline Board of Health

City or Town	Location	Time	Auspices
Cambridge . .	1481 Cambridge Street	Tues. and Sat. 10-12 A.M., Thurs. 7-9 P.M.	Cambridge Board of Health
Canton	Health Centre 473 Washington St.	First Fri. each month 5 P.M.	Canton Board of Health
Chelsea	Board of Health	Thurs. 2:30 P.M. (by arrangement)	Chelsea Board of Health
Chicopee	City Hall	Wed. 2-4 P.M. Fri. 7-9 P.M.	Chicopee Board of Health
Clinton . .	Municipal Building Church Street	Tues. 4-5 P.M. Fri. 7:30-8:30 P.M.	Clinton Board of Health
Dedham . .	National Bank Building, Room 11	Second and last Fri. each month at 5 P.M.	Dedham Board of Health
Everett	40 Hancock Street	Tues. 8 P.M. Fri. 4 P.M.	Everett Board of Health
Fall River.....	City Hall Annex 66 Third Street	Tues. 7-8 P.M. (adults) Sat. 11-12 A.M. (children)	Fall River Board of Health
Fitchburg	444 Water Street	Wed. 7-8:30 P.M. Sat. 3-4:30 P.M.	Fitchburg Board of Health
Framingham	Memorial Municipal Building	Thurs. 7-8:30 P.M.	Framingham Board of Health
Gardner . .	City Hall, Room 9	Fri. 4 P.M. Tues. 4 P.M.	Gardner Board of Health
Gloucester	Board of Health	Mon. 7-8:30 P.M. Thurs. 3-4:30 P.M.	Gloucester Board of Health
Haverhill .	Board of Health 6 Court Street	Mon. 7-9 P.M. Fri. 4-6 P.M.	Haverhill Board of Health
Holyoke ...	City Hall Annex	Mon. 6-7 P.M. Fri. 4-5 P.M.	Holyoke Board of Health
Lawrence . .	City Hall	Daily 1-2 P.M. (none on Wed.)	Lawrence Board of Health
Leominster	City Hall, West Street, Room 7	Mon. 3-4 P.M. Mon. 8-9 P.M.	Leominster Board of Health
Lowell....................	Board of Health	Tues. 4-5 P.M. (children) Thurs. 7-8 P.M. (adults)	Lowell Board of Health
Lynn	Lynn Hospital	Mon. 3 P.M.	Lynn Board of Health
Malden	351 Main Street	Wed. 7-9 P.M. Fri. 3-5 P.M.	Malden Board of Health
Marlboro	City Hall	Mon. 4-5 P.M. Fri. 6-7 P.M.	Marlboro Board of Health
Medford .	Dr. Lanigan's Office	(by appointment)	Medford Board of Health
Methuen .	Board of Health	Tues. 3-4 P.M. Tues. 6-7 P.M.	Methuen Board of Health
Milton .	101 Blue Hill Parkway	First Wed. of each month at 4 P.M.	Milton Board of Health

City or Town	Location	Time	Auspices
New Bedford	Olympia Building Purchase Street	Mon. and Sat. 2-3 P.M. Wed. 5-6 P.M.	New Bedford Board of Health
Newburyport	2 Harris Street	Wed. 9-12 A.M.	Newburyport Board of Health
Newton	Newton Hospital	Second Mon. of month 2-4 P.M.	Newton Board of Health
North Adams	Municipal Building	Tues. 4-5 P.M. Fri. 4-5 P.M.	North Adams Board of Health
Northampton	Memorial Hall, Main Street	Fri. 4-5 P.M.	Northampton Board of Health
Norwood	Municipal Building, Room 11	Thurs. 5:30 P.M.	Norwood Board of Health
Peabody	Board of Health	Thurs. 3:30-4:30 P.M.	Peabody Board of Health
Pittsfield	House of Mercy Hospital	Thurs. 10:30-12 A.M.	Pittsfield Board of Health
Quincy	22 High School Avenue	Thurs. 6-7 P.M. (adults) Sat. 9-11 A.M. (children)	Quincy Board of Health
Revere	453 Broadway	Tues. 7-8 P.M. Fri. 4-5 P.M.	Revere Board of Health
Salem	5 St. Peter Street	Wed. and Sat. 2:30 P.M. (winter) Sat. 2:30 P.M. (summer)	Salem Board of Health
Southbridge	Town Hall	Mon. 4-6 P.M.	Southbridge Board of Health
Springfield	Tb. Hospital Building 1414 State Street	Mon. 4-5 P.M. Wed. 6-7 P.M.	Springfield Board of Health
Taunton	City Hall	Tues. 11-12 A.M. Fri. 7-8 P.M.	Taunton Board of Health
Wakefield	Board of Health	Second & Fourth Tues. 3:30-4:30 P.M. First & Third Fri. 8-9 P.M.	Wakefield Board of Health
Walpole	Lewis Manufacturing Company, West Street	Third Fri. of each month at 5 P.M.	Walpole Board of Health
Watertown	Board of Health	Thurs. 2:30-4:30 P.M.	Watertown Board of Health
Webster	Town Hall, Main Street	Thurs. 4:30-6:30 P.M.	Webster Board of Health
Westfield	City Hall	Mon. 4-5 P.M. Wed. 7-8 P.M.	Westfield Board of Health
Winchester	9 Mt. Vernon Street	Thurs. 2-4 P.M.	Winchester Board of Health
Woburn	City Hall	Thurs. 7-8 P.M. Fri. 4-5 P.M. (children)	Woburn Board of Health
Worcester	Worcester City Hospital	Mon. 9-12 A.M. Thurs. 9-12 A.M.	Worcester Board of Health
	Belmont Hospital	Wed. & Sat. at 9 A.M.	Worcester Board of Health

7. *School Clinics*—Designed to detect tuberculosis in school children. Examinations are usually made in 7th, 9th, and 11th grades and upon written request of parents. Procedure followed in such clinics as follows:
1. Tuberculin test (Von Pirquet) on all children whose parents sign request slip.
2. X-ray of all reactors. X-ray service furnished by state, county, or city sanatoria staff.
3. Physical examination of all cases found positive by x-ray. All reports are made to physician designated by parents, and to board of health and school committee.

TREATMENT. Cities and towns are financially responsible for treatment of tuberculosis provided patient is unable to pay for same.

Pulmonary Tuberculosis—Adult. Patients having a legal settlement and unable to pay for care are referable to state, county, or city sanatoria. For those able to pay, hospitalization may be found in private sanatoria, at county sanatoria, or at Rutland. The following hospitals and sanatoria are maintained in whole or in part for adult pulmonary tuberculosis:

Federal Hospital

Name of Institution	Location	Number of Beds	Rates per Week	Superintendent
United States Veterans Hospital	Rutland Heights	472	For Veterans Bureau patients only. Apply to U. S. Veterans Bureau, Boston	Dr. R. L. Cook

Application should be made to United States Veterans Bureau, Federal Building, Boston, Massachusetts.

State Sanatoria

Name of Institution	Location	Number of Beds	Rates per Week	Superintendent
Rutland State Sanatorium (for adults in early and favorable stage of pulmonary tuberculosis)	Rutland	365	$7.00 to patient $10.50 to city or town	Dr. Ernest B. Emerson

Procedure for Admission. Application on blank obtainable from local board of health or from Department of Public Health, 519 State House, Boston, Mass., should be made out and signed by attending physician and forwarded to Department at above address. The Department will arrange for approval of local board of health as to financial responsibility for those unable to pay.

State Hospital

Name of Institution	Location	Number of Beds	Rates per Week	Superintendent
State Infirmary	Tewksbury	280	Free for unsettled cases	Dr. John H. Nichols

Accepts unsettled cases from all parts of the State.

Procedure for Admission. Application on blank obtained from local board of public welfare or from Department of Public Welfare, 30 State House, Boston, Mass., should be filed with the State Department of Public Welfare.

County Sanatoria

Procedure for Admission—Special application blanks obtainable through local boards of health or directly from sanatoria, should be filled out by attending physician and returned to the superintendent of the sanatorium, who will arrange for approval of local board of health.

Name of Institution	Location	Number of Beds	Rates per Week	Superintendent
Barnstable County Sanatorium	Pocasset (Bourne)	50	$7.00 to patient $9.10 residents—to town. $28.00 non-residents	Dr. J. G. Kelly
Bristol County Sanatorium	Attleboro	60	$8.10 residents $28.00 non-residents	Dr. G. P. Smith
Essex Sanatorium	Middleton	360	$9.10 residents	Dr. O. S. Pettingill
Hampshire County Sanatorium	Haydenville (P.O. Northampton)	100	$12.00 residents $15.00 non-residents	Dr. F. E. O'Brien
Middlesex County Sanatorium	Waltham	252	$10.50 residents	Dr. S. H. Remick
Norfolk County Sanatorium	South Braintree	138	$9.10 residents $28.00 to non-residents	Dr. N. R. Pillsbury
Plymouth County Sanatorium	South Hanson	140	$9.10 residents $28.00 to non-residents	Dr. B. H. Peirce
Worcester County Sanatorium	Worcester (Greendale Station)	125	$12.25 residents $25.00 to non-residents	Dr. E. W. Glidden

Municipal Sanatoria

Procedure for Admission. Application blanks obtainable from and returnable to local city health department.

Name of Institution	Location	Number of Beds	Rates per Week	Superintendent
Boston Sanatorium	249 River St. Mattapan	616	According to ability to pay for residents. $28.00 to non-residents.	Dr. F. L. Bogan
Brookline Tuberculosis Hospital	Brookline	30	According to ability to pay for residents. $21.00 to non-residents.	Miss Elizabeth A. McMahon
Cambridge Tuberculosis Hospital	Cambridge (Fresh Pond Hill)	80	According to ability to pay for residents. $21.00 to non-residents	Dr. S. B. Kelleher
Chicopee Tuberculosis Hospital	Chicopee Falls	25	According to ability to pay—residents	Miss Rachelle Frechette

Name of Institution	Location	Number of Beds	Rates per Week	Superintendent
Fall River Tuberculosis Hospital	Fall River	125	According to ability to pay for residents $25.00 to non-residents	Dr. Ernest M. Morris, Health Commissioner
Burbank Hospital (Tuberculosis Ward)	Fitchburg	36	$17.50 residents and non-residents	Dr. Edwin R. Lewis
Holyoke Tuberculosis Hospital	Holyoke	18	$10.00 a week for residents	Miss Margaret G. Healey, R.N.
Lowell Isolation Hospital	Lowell	54	$15.00 residents $25.00 non-residents	Dr. J. J. McNamara Acting Supt.
Sassaquin Sanatorium	New Bedford	116	$15.50 residents and non-residents	Dr. J. F. Brewer, Jr.
Health Dept. Hospitals (Tuberculosis Wards)	Springfield	60	$15.00 residents $21.00 non-residents	Miss Margaret St. Ledger, Acting Supv.
Belmont Hospital (Putnam Ward)	Worcester	150	$10.00 residents $17.50 non-residents	Dr. May S. Holmes

Private Sanatoria

Procedure for Admission. Application to be made directly to sanatorium.

Name of Institution	Location	Number of Beds	Rates per Week	Superintendent
Channing Home	198 Pilgrim Rd., Boston	27	Sliding scale up to $14.00 to patients. $14.00 to city or town	Miss Elizabeth Pelton
Central New England Sanatorium	Rutland	100	Sliding scale at main division. $35. to $60. at private branch	Dr. Bayard T. Crane
Summit House	Rutland	25	$30. to $40. Special rates to cities and towns	Mrs. Ethel M. Brown (Visiting Physicians Dr. V. J. Alexandrov & Dr. J. B. Hawes, 2nd)
Wachusett Cottage	Rutland	14	$26.50 to $31.50	Mrs. Minnie G. Clark (Visiting Physicians, Dr. V. J. Alexandrov & Dr. J. B. Hawes, 2nd.)
Charles Carroll Sanatorium	Rutland	6	$29. single room $24. double room	Mrs. Charles E. Carroll (Visiting Physicians Dr. V. J. Alexandrov & Dr. J. B. Hawes, 2nd.)
Sullivan Cottage	Rutland	10	$23.00 and up	Mrs. Mabel Sullivan (Visiting Physicians, Dr. V. J. Alexandrov & Dr. J. B. Hawes, 2nd.)

Name of Institution	Location	Number of Beds	Rates per week	Superintendent
Sharon Sanatorium	Sharon	50	$20.00 for women $15.00 for children	Dr. Walter A. Griffin
Balfour Sanatorium	Sharon	25	Sliding scale $15.00 to $35.00 Average $25.00	Mrs. Bernice F. Balfour
Pittsfield Tuberculosis Hospital	West Pittsfield	14	$15. to patient $12. to city or town	Miss Edith M. Safford
Frederic S. Coolidge Memorial Home	West Pittsfield	8	$15. to patient $12. to city or town	Miss Edith M. Safford

Pulmonary Tuberculosis—Children. Provision for hospitalization is made at North Reading and Westfield State Sanatoria as follows:

Name of Institution	Location	Number of Beds	Rates per Week	Superintendent
North Reading State Sanatorium (for children only)	North Wilmington	290	$7.00 to patient or city or town	Dr. Carl C. MacCorison
Westfield State Sanatorium (for children only)	Westfield	270	$7.00 to patient or city or town	Dr. Roy Morgan

Conditions for Admission:

1. Patient must be under 17 years of age.
2. Family must have a bona fide residence of at least six months in Massachusetts.
3. Patient accepted regardless of prognosis or settlement.

Procedure for Admission. Application blanks obtainable from local board of health or from Department of Public Health, 519 State House, Boston, should be filled out by attending physician and returned to Department at above address.

Summer Camps and Preventoria (See page 163.)

Extra-Pulmonary Tuberculosis. All types of extra-pulmonary tuberculosis (bone, gland, kidney, intestinal, skin, eye, etc.) are acceptable at Lakeville Sanatorium.

Name of Institution	Location	Number of Beds	Rates per week	Superintendent
Lakeville State Sanatorium (for non-pulmonary forms of tuberculosis)	Middleboro	304	$7.00 for children $7.00 for adults (if paid by patient) $17.50 for adults (if paid by city or town)	Dr. Leon A. Alley

Conditions for Admission.

1. Patient must have a bona fide residence of at least one year in Massachusetts.
2. Settled cases take preference over non-settled.
3. All ages accepted.

Procedure for Admission. Application blanks obtainable from local board of health or from Department of Public Health, 519 State

House, Boston and returnable to the Department at above address. Fill in diagnosis and recommendations under "Remarks" (and only such other spaces as are applicable).

ISOLATION AND QUARANTINE—*Cases*. Special precautions should be observed as to disposal of sputum. Active cases with positive sputum should not be kept in homes where there are children.

Contacts. No special restrictions. Periodic check-up with aid of x-ray is advisable for all family contacts to detect early cases of tuberculosis. If family is unable to pay, this may be obtained through out-patient department or consultation clinic of the tuberculosis sanatorium (see page 159 and 155).

PREVENTION. No practical method of immunization available. Separation of contacts (especially children) from open cases of tuberculosis is most effective means of limiting spread.

SUMMER CAMPS AND PREVENTORIA are maintained by certain tuberculosis associations. Are intended for care of children shown to have tuberculous infection but without evidence of active disease. Preference is given to contacts of known cases of tuberculosis. Admission is on application of family physician to secretary of respective association. The following camps and preventoria are maintained in Massachusetts:

Location	Boys or Girls	Auspices	Apply to
Ashburnham (So. Ashburnham)	Girls	Northern Worcester County Public Health Association, Inc.	Mrs. Dorothy C. Hemingway, 12 Grove Street, Fitchburg
Attleboro	Both	Bristol County Public Health Association, Inc.	Mrs. Mary C. Putnam, R.N., Bristol County Court House, Taunton
Bolton	Both	The Public Health Association of Southwestern Middlesex County, Inc.	Mr. Franklin D. MacCormick, 214 Concord Street, Framingham
Boston (Mattapan)	Both	Boston Tuberculosis Association, Inc.	Miss Bernice W. Billings, R.N., 554 Columbus Ave., Boston
Bourne (Pocasset) Barnstable County Sanatorium	Both	Barnstable County Public Health Association	Dr. Julius G. Kelley, Pocasset
Boxford	Both	Lawrence Tuberculosis League	Miss Kate T. Fuller, 31 Jackson Street, Lawrence
Braintree	Both	Norfolk County Hospital	Dr. Nahum R. Pillsbury, So. Braintree
Cambridge Shady Hill School	Girls	Cambridge Tuberculosis and Health Association, Inc.	Mrs. Mabel Greeley Smith, 689 Massachusetts Ave., Cambridge
Dighton	Both	Fall River Anti-Tuberculosis Society	Dr. George C. King, 150 Purchase St, Fall River
Hanson (So. Hanson) Plymouth County Hospital	Both	Plymouth County Health Association, Inc.	Miss Anna J. Foley, R N., 106 Main Street, Brockton

Location	Boys or Girls	Auspices	Apply to
Middleton Essex Sanatorium	Both	Essex County Health Association, Inc.	Miss Vera Griffin, R.N., 222 Cabot Street, Beverly
Northampton (Leeds)	Both	Hampshire County Public Health Association, Inc.	Mrs. Geneva F. Rockford, R.N., Memorial Hall, Northampton
Pittsfield	Girls	Berkshire County Tuberculosis Association, Inc.	Mrs. Gertrude E. Brown, R.N., 16 South Street, Pittsfield
Salem (Salem Willows) Fort Lee	Both	Salem Association for the Prevention of Tuberculosis	Miss Edith J. Barker, R.N., 5 St. Peter Street, Salem
Sharon (Lake Massapoag)	Both	Southern Middlesex Health Association, Inc.	Miss Mary C. Hoisington, R.N., 661 Massachusetts Ave., Arlington
Sterling (Sterling Junction)	Boys	Southern Worcester County Health Association, Inc.	Mr. Arthur J. Strawson, Room 508, 5 Pleasant Street, Worcester
Westfield (Provin Mountain)	Both	Hampden County Tuberculosis and Public Health Association, Inc.	Mr. Henry P. Coor, 145 State Street, Springfield

TYPHOID FEVER

DIAGNOSIS: Clinical condition with laboratory confirmation.

Laboratory tests:

a. *Blood culture*—Usually positive in the first week; sometimes as late as fifth week in severe cases.

b. *Widal reaction*—May be positive by the end of first week; usually not until end of second week.

c. *Stool culture*—Usually not positive until in third week of disease.

d. *Urine culture*—May be positive in the second week in a small percentage of cases.

All specimens for above tests may be sent to local or State Bacteriological Laboratory, 527 State House, Boston, special outfits obtainable through local boards of health. (See p. 133.) Positive *diagnostic* reports telephoned or telegraphed prepaid.

TREATMENT: Symptomatic and supportive.

ISOLATION AND QUARANTINE: (Consult regulations of local board of health—See p. 130.)

Cases—Usually one week after subsidence of clinical symptoms and thereafter until two successive negative stool and urine cultures, secured at an interval of at least one week, have been obtained, provided that a person who continues to be a carrier may be released under supervision of and after special permission of the board of health. Specimens obtained prior to one month after onset of disease should be considered as of diagnostic value only, and not as criteria for release. As two negative cultures are not a guarantee that patient has not become a carrier, it is recommended that a stool culture be obtained once a month for one year after recovery.

Contacts—Food handlers living in a family in which a case of typhoid fever exists are usually excluded from their occupation so long as they continue to live in the same house in which the case exists, and thereafter until usual incubation period has elapsed. Stool and urine cultures should be obtained from these and all other members of the family to find possible carriers. It is recommended that all family contacts with a case of typhoid be immunized against typhoid as soon as the case is recognized.

PREVENTION:

Passive immunization—No practical method available.

Active immunization—Vaccine provided by the State Laboratory through local board of health. (See p. 135.) (Vaccine contains killed typhoid, paratyphoid A and paratyphoid B bacilli). Three subcutaneous injections (0.5 cc., 1.0 cc., 1.0 cc.) at intervals of seven to ten days. Children in proportion to their weight; those under fifty pounds, one-half the adult dosage. (See p. 136.) Injection of one cc. each year may be used for those constantly exposed.

Typhoid vaccination is especially indicated for:
1. Family contacts of a typhoid case.
2. Family contacts of a typhoid carrier.
3. Physicians.
4. Nurses.
5. Laboratory workers.
6. Institutional inmates.
7. Campers.
8. Those traveling in areas where they may not be certain as to safety of water, milk, and food supplies.

CARRIERS: Two classes of carriers are generally recognized.
1. *Convalescent carriers*—those shedding typhoid organisms in feces or urine during first year after infection.
2. *Permanent carriers*—those shedding typhoid organisms in feces or urine one or more years after infection. Certain proven carriers are unaware of previous typhoid, apparently becoming carriers as result of mild unrecognized infection.

RESTRICTION ON CARRIERS:
1. All typhoid carriers are reportable to the local board of health, usually as a cholecystitis of typhoid origin.
2. No typhoid carrier may be employed in a food handling capacity.
3. All typhoid carriers are subject to regulations of local board of health.
4. All known typhoid carriers are visited twice annually by representatives of State Department of Public Health.

TYPHUS FEVER

DIAGNOSIS: Clinical findings with aid from laboratory through Weil-Felix reaction. For this test send 5 cc. of blood in sterile test tube to State Bacteriological Laboratory, 527 State House, Boston. (See p. 133.)

TREATMENT: Symptomatic and supportive.

ISOLATION AND QUARANTINE: Precautions as to vermin.

PREVENTION: No practical method of active and passive immunization available.

UNDULANT FEVER (Brucella Infection)

DIAGNOSIS: Based on clinical findings with support of laboratory findings. For *blood culture* and *agglutination reaction* send 5 cc. of blood in *sterile* test tube to State Bacteriological Laboratory, 527 State House, Boston. (See p. 133.) Special containers for this purpose available through local boards of health (the tubes in the State Wassermann oufit are *not* sterile). *Significance of agglutination reactions—*

1/15 — of no significance
1/45 — of questionable significance
1/135 and higher — of diagnostic significance

TREATMENT: Symptomatic and supportive. Vaccines of questionable value.

ISOLATION AND QUARANTINE: Usually no restrictions.

PREVENTION: No practical method of active and passive immunization available. Most infections in Massachusetts contracted from raw milk.

WHOOPING COUGH (Pertussis)

DIAGNOSIS: Based on clinical findings. Use of cough plates is valuable in early diagnosis. Requires use of fresh plates and exposure to spasmodic cough. Cough plates are not available through State or board of health laboratories. White blood counts and differential counts are also used as aids to diagnosis. Such tests are not performed in State or board of health laboratories.

TREATMENT: Symptomatic and supportive.

ISOLATION AND QUARANTINE: (Consult regulations of local board of health).

Cases—Usually three weeks from beginning of spasmodic cough. Some boards of health have permitted earlier release from strict isolation provided the patient is attended by a responsible adult to prevent association with other children.

Contacts—*Immune* contacts, usually no restrictions; *non-immune* contacts, usually exclusion from school two weeks from last exposure.

PREVENTION:

Passive immunization—No practical method available.

Active immunization—Favorable results in preventing or reducing severity of subsequent infection have been reported through use of different vaccines. Vaccine prepared according to method of Sauer requires six injections (one in each arm for three successive weeks). Not of proven value. (See page 136.)

GONORRHEA AND SYPHILIS

REPORTING:—(All of the following reports may be made on the same form.)

1. *All forms and all stages of gonorrhea and syphilis* shall be reported directly (and only) to the State Department of Public Health, 546 State House, Boston, on forms provided by the Department for that purpose. Business reply envelopes are provided for mailing the reports to the Department. *These envelopes are to be used for no other purpose.* Every case is to be reported, whether or not it may have been reported by, or is to be referred for treatment to some other physician, clinic or hospital. The name of the patient is not to be reported except as hereinafter provided (see 3 and 4).
2. If the patient was in consultation previously with another physician over the same infection, the present physician shall notify the other of the patient's change of medical advisor. Otherwise the previous physician will be expected to *report the patient* to the Department as a delinquent in treatment.
3. Patients who discontinue treatment prematurely and who are not known to be under treatment elsewhere, shall be reported by name and address to the Department *within one week* of the missed appointment in case of primary or secondary syphilis, congenital syphilis with active lesions, syphilis in pregnant women, and acute gonorrhea; and within two weeks of the missed appointment in all other cases.
4. Patients with lesions of primary or secondary syphilis on exposed parts of the body or in the mouth, who are employed in any occupation requiring direct contact with other persons (barber, hairdresser, manicurist, waiter, waitress, nursemaid, domestic, etc.) shall be reported by name, address and occupation, to the Department, unless the attending physician will assume the responsibility for seeing that the patient discontinues such occupation until the lesions are healed.
5. The attending physician shall attempt to identify the source of the patient's infection, and shall report the name and address of the source of infection to the Department, within two weeks of identification unless, in the meantime, the said source is known to be under medical care.

SYPHILIS

DIAGNOSIS:—(Literature available from the Department on request.)

1. *Darkfield examination.* The diagnosis of primary syphilis frequently depends upon darkfield examination of serum from the lesion, for the spirochete, as blood tests may be negative in the early days of this stage. All syphilologists and most of the clinics in the State (see Clinics, p. 171) are prepared to make darkfield examinations. The patient must be sent to the examiner's laboratory. Prompt diagnosis of primary syphilis is of paramount importance to the patient and to others. *Seronegative primary syphilis is practically 100% curable.* Seropositive primary syphilis is from 90% to 95% curable. Secondary syphilis is from 70% to 90% curable. Cure is progressively more difficult and prognosis less favorable with lapse of time.

2. *Blood tests.* Serological examinations (Hinton tests) are made at the State Wassermann Laboratory, Harvard Medical School, 25 Shattuck Street, Boston (see p. 133). *There is no charge.* At least 5 c.c. of blood should be withdrawn from the patient's vein, into a clean, dry, sterile syringe and transferred to a clean, dry, glass tube. Tubes and mailing containers may be obtained from local boards of health or their authorized distributing stations or directly from the Wassermann Laboratory. Unless all apparatus which comes into contact with the blood is clean and dry, hemolysis or contamination may make the specimen useless.

The Boston Health Department and the Brockton City Laboratory perform Wassermann tests for physicians in those cities. Containers for specimens which are to be sent to those laboratories should be obtained from them.

3. *Spinal fluid examination.* The State Wassermann Laboratory performs only the Wassermann test on spinal fluids. Cell counts must be made as soon as possible after the fluid is withdrawn. Colloidal gold tests and chemical analysis are *not* made at the State laboratories. At least 5 c.c. of fluid should be sent to the Wassermann Laboratory for the Wassermann test. The regular blood specimen outfit may be used, but the tube should first be boiled and a sterile rubber stopper inserted in place of the usual cork stopper.

TREATMENT:—(Literature available from the Department on request.)

1. *Arsenicals.* The Department provides arsphenamine, neoarsphenamine and sulpharsphenamine free of charge for the treatment of syphilis. Mail requests to the Antitoxin and Vaccine Laboratory, 375 South Street, Jamaica Plain. The Department reserves the right to withhold arsenicals from physicians who neglect to report their cases of syphilis.

Arsphenamine (606) must be alkalinized with normal sodium hydroxide solution before use. Detailed directions accompany each package. The sodium hydroxide solution is *not* supplied by the Department.

Neoarsphenamine (914) becomes very toxic after exposure to air for more than 15 or 20 minutes. Should be used at once after opening ampoule.

Sulpharsphenamine is prone to cause arsenical dermatitis if used intravenously, and should be given intramuscularly (in the buttocks). The arsenicals are supplied by the Department in the following sizes:—
Arsphenamine (For intravenous use only) 0.4 gm., 0.6 gm., 3.0 gm.
Neoarsphenamine (For intravenous use only) 0.45 gm., 0.6 gm., 0.9 gm.
Sulpharsphenamine (For intramuscular use) 0.3 gm., 0.4 gm., 0.6 gm., 1.0 gm., 3.0 gm.
Double distilled water (*not* supplied by the Department) should be used in making solutions of the arsenicals. Apparatus must be both clean and sterile or avoidable reactions may occur.

2. *Bismuth* and *mercury* preparations (including Bismarsen) are not supplied by the Department.

3. *Tryparsamide* (for the treatment of neurosyphilis) is not supplied by the Department.

4. *Malaria* and other fever therapy is available for the treatment of neurosyphilis at the Boston Psychopathic Hospital and several of the State Mental Disease Hospitals (see section on Mental Diseases, p. oo). Commitment may be voluntary or by court order. Blanks for either may be obtained from the superintendents of the mental disease hospitals or from the Department of Mental Diseases.

LITERATURE:—(See p. 170.)
CLINICS:—(See p. 171.)
CONSULTATION:—(See p. 173.)
PATIENTS UNABLE TO PAY FOR MEDICAL CARE:—(See p. 173.)

GONORRHEA

PROPHYLAXIS OF GONORRHEAL OPHTHALMIA NEONATORUM

Silver nitrate (1% solution), in individuals ampoules, is provided by the Department of Public Health, free of charge. Supplies may be obtained from local boards of health or their authorized distributing stations. There is accumulating evidence that sole dependence upon prophylaxis at birth is dangerous and that gonorrhea should be diagnosed in the mother and so treated that exposure of the baby's eyes will not occur.

DIAGNOSIS:—(Literature available from the Department on request.)

1. *Smears.* Smears for organisms resembling the gonococcus may be sent to local board of health laboratories or to the State Bacteriological Laboratory, Room 527, State House, Boston. Outfits, consisting of glass slides, swabs and mailing containers, may be obtained from local boards of health. (See p. 133.) Smears should be taken from the male urethral meatus and, when indicated, of the prostatic secretion. In the adult female, smears should be taken from *Skene's glands* (*after thorough massage*) and from *within the cervical canal* (*after thorough cleansing of the cervix with cotton or gauze*). In the female child, smears should be taken in the small cul-de-sac just in front of the hy-

men. It is advisable to moisten the cotton swab and twist it firmly between the fingers before taking the smear, to prevent loss of the material by absorption into the swab. Smears should be made evenly and about the size of a dime. State Laboratory reports are made as to pus-content of the smears as well as of the presence or absence of organisms resembling the gonococcus. *If organisms resembling the gonococcus are found in smears from the eye, the report is made by the State Laboratory by telephone or telegraph.*

2. *Schwartz-McNeil* (complement fixation) tests are made at the State Wassermann Laboratory, Harvard Medical School, 25 Shattuck St., Boston. At least 5 c.c. of blood should be withdrawn from the patient's vein, into a clean, dry, sterile syringe and transferred to a clean, dry, glass tube. The regular Hinton test outfit may be used for mailing the specimen to the Laboratory, but *it must be plainly indicated that the test wanted is for gonorrhea.* If both the Schwartz-McNeil and Hinton tests are desired, send at least 10 c.c. of blood and indicate clearly that both tests are desired.

TREATMENT:—(Literature available from the Department on request.) The Department does not supply any therapeutic preparation or equipment for the treatment of gonorrhea.

LITERATURE:—(See below.)
CLINICS:—(See p. 171.)
CONSULTATION:—(See p. 173.)
PATIENTS UNABLE TO PAY FOR MEDICAL CARE:—(See p. 173.)

LITERATURE

The following literature is available on request for the more detailed information of the physician as to the diagnosis, treatment and control of gonorrhea and syphilis, reactions to treatment, significance of blood tests, etc., and for the information and instruction of the patient.

FOR THE PATIENT
1. Information for the Male with Gonorrhea
2. Information for the Female with Gonorrhea
3. Information for the Male or Female with Syphilis
4. The Difference Between Tweedledum and Tweedledee

FOR THE PHYSICIAN
1. Minimum Standards for the Diagnosis, Treatment and Control of Syphilis
2. The Management of Syphilis in General Practice
3. Syphilis and the Wassermann Reaction in Pregnancy
4. Congenital Syphilis
5. Diagramatic Interpretation of Blood Tests in Syphilis
6. The Economic Aspects of the Management of Syphilis
7. The Epidemiology of Syphilis and Gonorrhea

8. What is to be done about Gonorrhea and Syphilis?
9. Minimum Standards for the Diagnosis, Treatment and Control of Gonorrhea
10. Gonococcus Infection in the Male
11. The Laboratory in the Diagnosis of Gonorrhea
12. The Clinical Diagnosis of Gonorrhea in the Male
13. The Clinical Diagnosis of Gonorrhea in the Female

CLINICS IN MASSACHUSETTS FOR THE TREATMENT OF GONORRHEA AND SYPHILIS.

COMPILED BY THE MASSACHUSETTS DEPARTMENT OF PUBLIC HEALTH
Cooperating With
THE UNITED STATES PUBLIC HEALTH SERVICE

BOSTON

Beth Israel Hospital—330 Brookline Avenue
Syphilis: — Men and Women ... .. Mon., Wed., Fri., 8:30 A.M.-10:30 A.M.
Gonorrhea: — Men and Women ... .. Tues., Thurs., Sat., 8:30 A.M.-10:30 A.M.

Boston City Hospital—818 Harrison Avenue
Syphilis: — Men and Women ...... Tues., Thurs., Sat., 8:30 A.M.-10:30 A.M.
Gonorrhea: — Men .... Daily 8:30 A.M.-10:30 A.M.
Women ... . Tues., Thurs., Sat., 8:30 A.M.-10:30 A.M.

Boston Dispensary—25 Bennet Street
Syphilis: — Men and Women ... Mon., Wed., Thurs., Sat., 8:45-10:30 A.M.
Mon., Wed., Fri., 6:00 P.M.-8:00 P.M.
Gonorrhea: — Men . .. . Daily 8:45 A.M.-10:30 A.M.
Mon., Wed., Fri., 6:00 P.M.-8:00 P.M.
Women .... Tues., Fri., 8:45 A.M.-10:30 A.M.
Mon., Fri., 6:00 P.M.-8:00 P.M.

Boston Psychopathic Hospital—74 Fenwood Road
Neurosyphilis: — Men, Women and Children .. Tues., Sat., 8:30 A.M.-10:00 A.M.

Carney Hospital (Out Patient Skin Dept.)—140 Dorchester St. (S. Boston)
Syphilis: — Men and Women ... Tues., Thurs., Sat., 9:00 A.M.-12:00 M.

Children's Hospital—300 Longwood Avenue
Syphilis: — .... Children . ... Fri., 8:30 A.M.-11:00 A.M. by appt. only

Massachusetts General Hospital—Fruit Street
Syphilis and Gonorrhea: — Men and Women . Daily 8:00 A.M.-10:00 A.M.

Massachusetts Memorial Hospitals—88 East Concord Street
Syphilis: — Men and Women . .... Mon., Wed., Fri., 8:30 A.M.-11:00 A.M.
Tues., 5:00 P.M.-7:30 P.M.
Gonorrhea: — Men and Women Mon., Wed., Sat., 9:30 A.M.-10:30 A.M.
Tues., 5:00 P.M.-7:30 P.M.

N. E. Hospital for Women and Children—Dimock Street (Roxbury)
Syphilis: — Women and Children .Tuesday 9:00 A.M.
Gonorrhea: — Women and Children .Thursday 9:00 A.M.

Peter Bent Brigham Hospital—721 Huntington Avenue
Syphilis: — Men and Women .. Mon., Wed., Fri., 1:30 P.M.-4:00 P.M.
Gonorrhea: — Men and Women .... Daily 9:00 A.M.-11:00 A.M.

BROCKTON

Brockton Hospital—680 Center Street
Syphilis and Gonorrhea: — Men . . ... Friday, 6:00 P.M.   Mornings by
Women .... Tuesday, 6:00 P.M.   appointment

CAMBRIDGE

Cambridge Hospital (Out Patient Dept.) 330 Mt. Auburn Street
Syphilis: — Men and Women .... Thursday, 9:00 A.M.-10:00 A.M.
Cambridge City Hospital—1483 Cambridge Street
Syphilis and Gonorrhea: — Men and Women   Friday, 9:00 A.M.-10:00 A.M.

FALL RIVER

Board of Health Clinic—City Hall Annex, Third Street
Syphilis and Gonorrhea: — Men and Women   Mon., Wed., Fri., 6:30 P.M.-8:00 P.M.
Union Hospital—538 Prospect Street
Syphilis: — Men and Women ....   Mon., Thurs., 9:30 A.M.
Gonorrhea: — Women . . ..Mon., Thurs., 9:30 A.M.

FITCHBURG

Burbank Hospital—Hospital Road
Syphilis and Gonorrhea: — Men and Women   Tues., 6:30 P.M.-7:30 P.M.

HAVERHILL

Board of Health Clinic—6 Court Street
Syphilis: — Men and Women   Thurs., 12:00 M.-1:00 P.M. and 8:00 P.M.-9:00 P.M.
Gonorrhea: — Men and Women Tues., 12:00 M.-1:00 P.M. and 8:00 P.M.-9:00 P.M.

HOLYOKE

Holyoke Hospital—Beech Street
Syphilis and Gonorrhea: — Men .... Mon., 5:30 P.M.-7:00 P.M.
                          Women   Thurs., 4:30 P.M.-6:00 P.M.

LAWRENCE

Board of Health Clinic—130 Oak Street
Syphilis and Gonorrhea: — Men . ..Thurs., 11:00 A.M.-1:00 P.M. and 8:00 P.M.-10:00 P.M.
                          Women   Mon., 11:00 A.M.-1:00 P.M. and 8:00 P.M.-10:00 P.M. And by Appointment

LOWELL

Board of Health Clinic—Corner Kirk and Page Streets
Syphilis and Gonorrhea: — Men ...... Mon., 8:30 A.M. and Fri., 6:30 P.M.
                          Women   Tues., 6:30 P.M. and Thurs., 8:30 A.M.

LYNN

Board of Health Clinic—Lynn Hospital
Syphilis and Gonorrhea: — Men and Women   Tues., Fri., 9:00 A.M. and 6:00 P.M.

NEW BEDFORD

Board of Health Clinic—519 Olympia Building
Syphilis and Gonorrhea: — Men .. . Mon., Fri., 4:00 P.M.-6:00 P.M.
                          Women   Tues., 4:00 P.M.-6:00 P.M.
                                   Thursday by appointment
Gonorrhea: — Women and Children   Tues., Fri., 10:00 A.M.-11:00 A.M.

NEWTON

Newton Hospital—2014 Washington Street (Newton Lower Falls)
Syphilis: — Men and Women   Wednesday 9:00 A.M.
Gonorrhea: — Women . .   . Thursday 9:00 A.M.

PITTSFIELD

House of Mercy Hospital—741 North Street
Syphilis and Gonorrhea: — Men and Women   Tues., 11:00 A.M.–12:00 M.
                                          Fri., 5:30 P.M.–6:30 P.M.

QUINCY

Board of Health Clinic—Quincy Dispensary, High School Avenue
Syphilis and Gonorrhea: — Men .... Friday 5:45 P.M.–6:45 P.M.
                         Women .... Thursday 5:45 P.M.–6:45 P.M.

SPRINGFIELD

Springfield Hospital—759 Chestnut Street
Syphilis and Gonorrhea: — Men   .... Tues., 4:30 P.M.–6:00 P.M.
                         Women   .... Thursday, 4:30 P.M.–6:00 P.M.

WORCESTER

Worcester City Hospital (Out Patient Dept.)—162 Chandler Street
Syphilis and Gonorrhea: — Men and Women. Wed., 6:30 P.M.–7:30 P.M.
                         Men and Women   Mon., Wed., Fri., Sat., 8:30 A.M.–
                                                                10:30 A.M.

Memorial Hospital—119 Belmont Street
Syphilis: —   Men and Women   Mon., Thurs., 9:00 A.M.
Gonorrhea: —   Men   Tues., Thurs., Sat., 11:00 A.M.
                Women   Mon., Wed., Fri., 10:00 A.M.

CONSULTATION

The Department welcomes requests for information concerning any phase of the management of gonorrhea or syphilis. A considerable number of physicians who have had wide experience in this field are always ready to assist the Department in its consultation service. Physicians are urged, also, to make use of the consultation facilities that are available in the various clinics throughout the State.

The Department is prepared to send speakers on the management of gonorrhea and syphilis to any medical society meeting at any time.

PATIENTS UNABLE TO PAY FOR MEDICAL CARE

Under the communicable disease law (Chapter 111 of the General Laws) and, specifically, under Section 117 (as amended by the Acts of 1935), boards of health are required to provide treatment for indigent persons suffering from gonorrhea or syphilis. The board of health may decide where the patient shall be treated. No physician may contract with a patient for treatment, in behalf of the board of health, without the specific approval of the board of health.

RECORDS AND REPORTS OF GONORRHEA AND SYPHILIS TO BE CONFIDENTIAL

Section 119, Chapter 111, General Laws:—Hospital, dispensary, laboratory and morbidity reports and records pertaining to gonorrhea or syphilis shall not be public records, and the contents thereof shall not be divulged by any person having charge of or access to the same, except upon proper judicial order or to a person whose official duties, in the opinion of the commissioner, entitle him to receive information contained therein. Violations of this section shall for the first offence be punished by a fine of not more than fifty dollars, and for a subsequent offence by a fine of not more than one hundred dollars.

DISCLOSURE OF CERTAIN INFORMATION NOT SLANDER OR LIBEL

Section 12, Chapter 112, General Laws:—Any registered physician or surgeon who knows or has reason to believe that any person is infected with gonorrhea or syphilis may disclose such information to any person from whom the infected person has received a promise of marriage or to the parent or guardian of such person if a minor. Such information given in good faith by a registered physician or surgeon shall not constitute a slander or libel.

INDUSTRIAL DISEASES

The laws of the Commonwealth provide that ". . . every physician treating a patient whom he believes to be suffering from any ailment or disease contracted as a result of the nature, circumstances or conditions of the patient's employment . . ." shall report the same to the State Department of Labor and Industries. Blanks for reporting the same may be obtained from the Division of Industrial Safety, 473 State House, Boston.

CHILD HYGIENE

PRENATAL LETTERS—A series of letters to the expectant mother regarding the hygiene of pregnancy is available through Department of Public Health. Letters are nine in number, one for each month of pregnancy. First letter is accompanied by booklet "Baby and You", covering care of infants. A special letter to the "expectant father" goes directly with one of the letters, accompanied by pamphlet "The Great Imitator", a discussion of syphilis. All letters mailed directly by the Department at regular intervals to all names on prenatal registry. This registry is strictly confidential and is used for no other purpose. Requests to place name on registry for prenatal letters are accepted from physicians, clinics, hospitals, nurses, social workers, and expectant parents. All requests should be made to Department of Public Health, Division of Child Hygiene, 545 State House, Boston, Telephone, Capitol 4660. Sample set of letters and pamphlets will be mailed on request to professional workers.

POSTNATAL LETTERS—A comparable series of twenty-four letters covering care of first two years of life. Letters emphasize importance of regular medical and dental supervision. Accompanying these letters are following special letters and pamphlets:

    Special letters: Cancer in relation to birth injuries. Importance of examination of mother following confinement.
    Pamphlets: Diphtheria prevention.
        Vaccination.
        "Being a Parent", including list of booklets on habit training, prepared by Massachusetts Department of Mental Diseases.
        "One to Six", booklet summarizing child care up to time of school entrance.
        "Cooking for Health", booklet containing useful menus and recipes for home use.
        "How to Judge Nutrition".

Postnatal letters are sent routinely to all names already on registry for prenatal letters. Requests to have such letters sent directly to patients may be made to Department of Public Health, Division of Child Hygiene, 545 State House, Boston, Telephone, Capitol 4660. Sample letters and pamphlets sent on request.

EDUCATIONAL MATERIAL—Popular pamphlets on child hygiene are available as follows, requests to be made through local board of health or directly to Department of Public Health, 546 State House, Boston:

Aids to Bowel Movement
Attention! Stand Tall
Care of the Child in Cold Weather
Care of the Child in Hot Weather
The Care of the Teeth
Diet from Birth to Two Years
Feeding the Preschool Child
Feeding the School Child
Food for the Teens
Healthful Living for the Teens
How to Judge Nutrition of Children
Normal Gain in Height and Weight, 7-14 Years
Suggestions for Care during Pregnancy
Supplies Necessary for Confinement
Ten Rules for Healthful Living
Watch Your Step
Baby and You

One to Six
Are You as Attractive as Nature Intended?
A Child Entering School Should Be Able to:
Cooking for Health
Food Ways to Health
For Your Teeth and Gums
Good Eating Habits
A Health Creed
Keeping Baby Dry
Keeping Well
Minerals and Vitamins
Protecting Two
Sensible Sun Baths
Your Baby's First Teeth
Your Second Teeth

(See p. 139 for list of pamphlets on communicable diseases.)

ASSISTANCE TO THE BLIND AND CONSERVATION OF VISION

OPHTHALMIA NEONATORUM (See p. 152.)

ASSISTANCE TO THE BLIND: The Division of the Blind in the State Department of Education is established to assist those with defective vision. Although reporting of such cases is not compulsory, it is advisable that all persons with a vision of 20/200 or less, and children with 20/70 or less be reported to this Division, 110 Tremont Street, Boston, Telephone Liberty 6006. Assistance offered through this Division not obtainable unless patient is so registered. For those patients so registered, assistance is available through following sources:

1. *Visiting teachers* contact those becoming blind in adult life, giving home instruction in reading by touch, and in chair caning, sewing and other handwork.

2. *Workshops for the blind*—Six such workshops are maintained, in Cambridge (two,—one for men and one for women), Fall River (one), Lowell (one), Pittsfield (one), and Worcester (one). Work carried on here includes caning of chairs, manufacture of rugs, mops, and fine art fabrics.

3. *The Blind Handicraft Shop*, 73 Newbury Street, Boston,—Maintained for purpose of selling the work of the blind, all money, after deducting cost of sale, going to the producer.

4. *Relief funds*—Limited relief funds are available to certain individuals as supplements to inadequate incomes from other sources.

The Division of the Blind also cooperates with local school departments in establishment of Sight-Saving Classes for those having vision so impaired as to handicap normal school progress. Inquiries about such classes may be made to the Division or to local school department.

INSTITUTIONS:

1. *Perkins Institution and Massachusetts School for the Blind*, 175 North Beacon Street, Watertown—Limited to children of normal mentality, 5 to 19 years of age, with vision of 20/200 or less in both eyes. Applications may be made directly through the Division of the Blind, 110 Tremont Street, Boston.

2. *Boston Nursery for Blind Babies*, 147 South Huntington Avenue, Boston—Receives blind children up to 5 years of age. Applications may be made through the Division of the Blind, 110 Tremont Street, Boston.

CANCER

Under the provision of Chapter 391 of the Acts of 1926, the Department of Public Health maintains clinics for the diagnosis of cancer, and operates the Pondville Hospital for its treatment.

DIAGNOSIS:

State-aided clinics for the diagnosis of cancer are maintained in conjunction with certain hospitals and medical societies. Although no patient may be refused admission to such clinics, they are designed primarily as consultation clinics to which physicians may refer suspected cancer cases for examination. All cases are referred for treatment to the physician designated by the patient as the family physician. No treatment is offered in any clinic. No charge is made for clinic examination except for special laboratory and x-ray tests charged according to financial status of patient. Medical staff of clinic selected from local medical group, usually with provision for outside consultants when needed for special cases. State-aided cancer clinics are conducted in the following hospitals:

Boston	Beth Israel Hospital
Boston	Boston Dispensary
Brockton	Brockton Hospital
Fitchburg	Burbank Hospital
Gardner	Henry Heywood Memorial Hospital
Gloucester	Addison Gilbert Hospital
Greenfield	Franklin County Hospital
Lawrence	Lawrence General Hospital
Lowell	Lowell General Hospital
Lynn	Lynn Hospital
New Bedford	St. Luke's Hospital
Newburyport	Anna Jaques Hospital
Norfolk	Pondville Hospital
North Adams	North Adams Hospital
Northampton	Cooley Dickinson Hospital
Pittsfield	St. Luke's Hospital
Springfield	Springfield Hospital
Worcester	Memorial Hospital

TUMOR DIAGNOSTIC SERVICE: Tumor specimens for pathological examination may be sent to the Tumor Diagnostic Laboratory, Huntington Memorial Hospital, 695 Huntington Avenue, Boston. Laboratory maintained jointly by Department of Public Health and Harvard Cancer Commission. No charge made for tumor examination. *Pathological specimens other than suspected tumors should not be sent to this laboratory;* the State makes no provision for such examinations. Containers for shipment of tumor specimens may be obtained from local boards of health or from State Department of Public Health, 527 State House, Boston.

TREATMENT:

Local hospitals—Arrangements for treatment in local hospitals must be made directly with hospital. Consult with local social agencies or board of welfare if patient is unable to afford treatment. Social workers attached to State-aided clinics will assist in arranging for care of patients referred from such clinics.

Pondville Hospital—Maintained by State Department of Public Health for treatment of cancer in patients unable to obtain adequate care elsewhere. In addition to usual medical and surgical care, hospital is equipped for radium and x-ray therapy. Cancer in all stages accepted but preference for admission given to patients that may be cured or benefited by treatment. Admission to hospital is on application by family physician, on blanks obtainable from the Hospital, the Department of Public Health, local boards of health, or overseers of public welfare. Applications properly filled out should be sent to Pondville Hospital, Dr. George L. Parker, Superintendent, Wrentham, Telephone, Walpole 386. Patient must have been a resident of Massachusetts for at least two of the three years preceding date of application. Charges $10.50 per week, no extra charges for x-rays or special treatments. If patient or relatives unable to pay, cases are supportable by local boards of public welfare.

Incurable cases—Cases not requiring surgical or other special treatment are accepted at following hospitals, application in each case to be made directly to hospital:

    Boston—Long Island Hospital, Long Island, (Boston patients only)
    Cambridge—Holy Ghost Hospital for Incurables, 1575 Cambridge Street
    Fall River—Rose Hawthorne Lathrop Hospital, Bay Street
    Tewksbury—The State Infirmary (See p. 190)

EDUCATIONAL MATERIAL: Cancer bulletin containing selected abstracts of current cancer literature is mailed periodically to all physicians requesting the same of Department of Public Health. Popular pamphlets on cancer are obtainable also from Department. All requests for cancer bulletin or popular literature should be sent to Department of Public Health, 546 State House, Boston.

MENTAL DISEASES

DIAGNOSIS:

General Out-patient Clinics—Conducted by staffs of State Mental Disease Hospitals. Appointments to be made in advance through respective hospitals. Clinics are held as follows:

City or Town	Institution or Other Agency	Time	Auspices
Boston	Boston Psychopathic Hospital	Daily except Sunday, 9 A.M.–12 M.	Hospital staff
Boston	Massachusetts Memorial Hospital	Tuesday, 10 A.M.–4 P.M.	Westborough State Hospital
Danvers	Danvers State Hospital	(By appointment)	Hospital staff
Fitchburg	City Hall	Second Wednesday of month, 3 P.M.	Gardner State Colony
Foxborough	Foxborough State Hospital	(By appointment)	Hospital staff
Framingham	Municipal Building	Third Monday of month, 7 P.M.	Westborough State Hospital
Gardner	Gardner State Colony	(By appointment)	Hospital staff
Grafton	Grafton State Hospital	Saturday, 9 A.M.–12 M.; other days by appointment	Hospital staff
Lowell	St. John's Hospital	First Tuesday of month, 7 P.M.	Westborough State Hospital
Monson	Monson State Hospital	(By appointment)	Hospital staff
Northampton	Northampton State Hospital	Daily 9:30–11:00 A.M.; 1:30–4:30 P.M.	Hospital staff
Waltham	Department of Public Welfare, City Hall	Second Tuesday and third Wednesday, 7 P.M.	Westborough State Hospital
Westborough	Westborough State Hospital	Daily except Saturday and Sunday, 2–5 P.M.; first Sunday in month, 3 P.M.	Hospital staff
Worcester	Worcester State Hospital	(By appointment)	Hospital staff

Child Guidance and Adjustment Clinics—Conducted in various communities by staffs of State Mental Disease Hospitals. Appointments to be made in advance through respective hospital. Clinics are held as follows:

City or Town	Institution or Other Agency	Time	Auspices
Bedford	Union School	(By appointment)	Grafton State Hospital
Belmont	Junior High School Bldg.	First and third Mon. 9:30 A.M.–3:30 P.M.	Grafton State Hospital
Bolton	Emerson School	(By appointment)	Grafton State Hospital
Boston	Boston Psychopathic Hospital	Daily except Sun., 9–12 M.	Hospital staff

City or Town	Institution or Other Agency	Time	Auspices
Boston	Boston Psychopathic Hospital	Daily except Sat. and Sun. after 2 P.M. by appointment	Hospital staff
Carlisle	Highland School	(By appointment)	Grafton State Hospital
Concord	High School Bldg.	First and third Wed. of month, 9:30 A.M.–3:30 P.M.	Grafton State Hospital
Fitchburg	Academy Street School	Mon. and Fri. 1:30–4:00 P.M.	Gardner State Colony
Framingham	Municipal Bldg.	Mon., 1–5 P.M.; Sat. 9:30 A.M.–4:30 P.M.	Westborough State Hospital
Gardner	Prospect Street School	Tues. 1:30–4:00 P.M.	Gardner State Colony
Grafton	Grafton State Hospital	Sat. 9–12 M.	Hospital staff
Grafton	Superintendent of Schools	(By appointment)	Grafton State Hospital
Groton	High School Bldg.	(By appointment)	Grafton State Hospital
Harvard	Union School	(By appointment)	Grafton State Hospital
Haverhill	High School, Summer Street	Sat. 9–11 A.M.	Danvers State Hospital
Holyoke	Skinner Clinic, Holyoke Hospital	Wed. 1–3:30 P.M.	Northampton State Hospital
Hudson	Superintendent of Schools	(By appointment)	Grafton State Hospital
Lancaster	Superintendent of Schools	(By appointment)	Grafton State Hospital
Leominster	Junior High School Bldg.	Fri., 9:30 A.M.–3:30 P.M.	Grafton State Hospital
Lexington	High School Bldg.	Tues., 9:30 A.M.–3:30 P.M.	Grafton State Hospital
Littleton	Superintendent of Schools	(By appointment)	Grafton State Hospital
Lowell	Lowell General Hospital	Wed., 2 P.M.	Div. of Mental Hygiene, Dept. of Mental Diseases
Lynn	Child Welfare House, 15 Church Street	Tues., 9:30–11:00 A.M.	Danvers State Hospital
Maynard	Roosevelt School	(By appointment)	Grafton State Hospital
Melrose	Calvin Coolidge School Main Street	Thurs., 9:30–11:30 A.M.	Danvers State Hospital
Natick	High School Bldg.	First and third Thurs. 9:30 A.M.–3:30 P.M.	Grafton State Hospital
Newburyport	Health Centre, Harris Street	Second and fourth Fri. of month, 2–4 P.M.	Danvers State Hospital
Northampton	People's Institute	Wed., 4–6 P.M.	Northampton State Hospital
Northbridge	Superintendent of Schools	(By appointment)	Grafton State Hospital

City or Town	Institution or Other Agency	Time	Auspices
Norwood	Norwood Hospital, Washington Street	Third Tues. of month, 3-5 P.M.	Medfield State Hospital
Orange	Visiting Nurses' Rooms	First Wed. of month, 1:30-4:00 P.M.	Gardner State Colony
Quincy	Quincy High School, Coddington Street	Thurs., 2-4 P.M.	Medfield State Hospital
Salem	Pinkham Memorial, Hawthorne Blvd.	Mon. 2-4 P.M.	Danvers State Hospital
Springfield	Springfield Hospital	Mon., Wed., and Fri., 2-5 P.M.	Monson State Hospital
Stow	Superintendent of Schools	(By appointment)	Grafton State Hospital
Upton	Superintendent of Schools	(By appointment)	Grafton State Hospital
Worcester	21 Catherine Street	Daily 9 A.M.-5 P.M.; Sat. 9-12 M.	Worcester State Hospital

Habit Clinics—Conducted in several communities by staff of Department of Mental Diseases, Division of Mental Hygiene, 163 State House, Boston, Telephone, Capitol 7320. Appointments to be made in advance through Department or Hospital. Clinics are held as follows:

City or Town	Institution or Other Agency	Time	Auspices
Beverly	Health Center, Cabot St.	Wed., 9-11 A.M.	Danvers State Hospital
Boston	Boston Dispensary, 25 Bennet Street	Wed. and Thurs., 9:30 A.M.	Division of Mental Hygiene
Boston	New England Hospital for Women and Children, Dimock Street, Roxbury	Thurs., 9:30 A.M.	Division of Mental Hygiene
Boston	West End Health Unit, 17 Blossom Street	Wed., 2:30 P.M.	Division of Mental Hygiene
Lawrence	Lawrence General Hospital, Garden Street	Tues., 2 P.M.	Division of Mental Hygiene
North Reading	North Reading Sanatorium	First Tues. of month, 2 P.M.	Division of Mental Hygiene
Norwood	Norwood Hospital, Washington Street	Fri., 9:30 A.M.	Division of Mental Hygiene
Quincy	Woodward Institute, Hancock Street	Thurs., 2:30 P.M.	Division of Mental Hygiene
Reading	Reading High School	Tues., 10 A.M.	Division of Mental Hygiene

Mental and Mental Hygiene Clinics—Conducted in several communities by staff of State Mental Disease Hospitals. Appointments to be made in advance through respective hospital. Clinics are held as follows:

City or Town	Institution or Other Agency	Time	Auspices
Attleboro	Sturdy Memorial Hospital, Park Street	Last Mon. of month, 1:30-4 P.M.	Taunton State Hospital
Boston	*Boston Psychopathic Hospital	Tues. and Sat., 8:30-10:00 A.M.	Hospital staff
Boston	Boston Psychopathic Hospital	Last Mon. of month, 7 P.M.	Foxboro State Hospital
Boston	Massachusetts Memorial Hospital	Wed., 10 A.M.-4 P.M.	Westborough State Hospital
Brockton	Brockton Hospital	Wed., 2-4 P.M.	Foxborough State Hospital
Fall River	City Hall Annex, Third Street	Wed., 9:30-12 M.	Taunton State Hospital
Greenfield	Franklin County Hospital, High Street	Third Thurs. of month, 1-3 P.M.	Northampton State Hospital
Lawrence	International Institute, 125 Haverhill Street	First and third Fri., 9-11 A.M.	Danvers State Hospital
Lynn	Lynn Hospital	Wed., 2-4 P.M.	Danvers State Hospital
New Bedford	Olympia Bldg., Purchase and Elm Sts.	Wed., 1:30-4 P.M.	Taunton State Hospital
North Adams	Board of Health, Summer Street	Second Thurs. of month, 1-3 P.M.	Northampton State Hospital
Pittsfield	House of Mercy Hospital	Fourth Thurs. of month, 1-3 P.M.	Northampton State Hospital
Springfield	Board of Health Rooms	First Thurs. of month, 2-4 P.M.	Northampton State Hospital
Taunton	Taunton State Hospital	Thurs., 10-12 M.	Hospital staff

* Neurosyphilitic clinic.

Feeblemindedness Clinics—Conducted at State Schools for the Feebleminded. Appointments to be made in advance through School. Clinics are held as follows:

City or Town	Institution	Time	Auspices
Belchertown	Belchertown State School	Wed., 9-11 A.M.; 1-4 P.M.	Hospital staff
Waltham (Waverley)	Walter E. Fernald State School	Thurs., 9 A.M. by appointment	Hospital staff
Wrentham	Wrentham State School	Wed., 8:30 A.M.	Hospital staff

TREATMENT: All hospitalization of mental disease patients is under supervision of Massachusetts Department of Mental Diseases, 167 State House, Boston, Telephone, Capitol 7320.

INSANE PERSONS:

Emergency hospitalization—In emergencies, the superintendent of any institution for the insane (see p. 185) may receive without an order of commitment for a period of not more than five days persons certified by two legally qualified physicians to be dangerously insane. (See p. 184 for definition of "legally qualified physician"). Application blanks for emergency hospitalization obtainable from hospital in question.

Voluntary application—Any person whose mental condition is such as to render him competent to make voluntary application may be received by the superintendent of any institution for the insane (see p. 185), and detained as a boarder and patient until after three days' written notice of his intention or desire to leave. Application blanks for voluntary application may be obtained from hospitals for the insane or from Department of Mental Diseases, 167 State House, Boston.

Temporary care—The superintendent of any institution for the insane (see p. 185) may, upon written request of a
- (a) Licensed physician,
- (b) Member of a board of health,
- (c) Sheriff or deputy sheriff,
- (d) Selectman of a town,
- (e) Local or State police officer, or
- (f) Agent of Boston Institutions Department

receive and care for a period not exceeding *ten* days any person needing immediate care and treatment because of mental derangement other than delirium tremens or drunkenness. Any such patient found by the superintendent of the institution to be not suitable for such care must be removed from the institution immediately by the person requesting his reception. Application blanks for temporary care may be obtained from hospitals for the insane, or Department of Mental Diseases, 167 State House, Boston.

Temporary commitment for observation—A person may be committed to a State or Federal hospital (see p. 185), or to the McLean Hospital (see p. 185) for a period not exceeding *thirty-five* days in order to observe the person's mental condition. Commitment for observation is through same legal procedure as for regular commitment (see next paragraph). Application blanks may be obtained from hospitals for the insane, from clerks of courts, or from Department of Mental Diseases, 167 State House, Boston.

Commitment—Except in emergencies, for observation, or temporary care, or on voluntary application, no person may be received at any insane hospital, public or private, except upon an order of commitment from one of the following:
1. Justice of the superior court,
2. Judge of probate for Suffolk County,
3. Judge of probate for Nantucket County,
4. Justice or special justice of a district court (except municipal court of city of Boston).

Requirements for Commitment:

1. Filing with one of above-mentioned judges a certificate signed by two properly qualified physicians certifying as to insanity of said individual. Blank forms for such certificate may be obtained from the clerk of courts, the State Mental Disease Hospitals, or from Department of Mental Diseases, 167 State House, Boston. Only those physicians are "properly qualified" to sign certificates of insanity who
    - (a) Are graduates of a legally chartered medical school or college,
    - (b) Have been in actual practice of medicine for three years since graduation,

(c) Have been in actual practice of medicine for the three years immediately preceding the signing of said certificate,
(d) Are registered in Massachusetts to practice medicine, and
(e) Satisfy the judge as to standing, character and professional knowledge of insanity

2. Issuance of an order signed by one of above-mentioned judges stating that
   (a) Person committed is insane,
   (b) Person committed is a proper subject for treatment in a hospital for the insane.
   (c)-1. Person has been an inhabitant of the Commonwealth for the six months immediately preceding commitment, or
   2. Provision satisfactory to the Department of Mental Diseases has been made for person's maintenance, or
   3. Person would, by reason of insanity, be dangerous if at large.

Hospitals Accepting Mental Patients
Federal Hospitals

City or Town	Institution	Superintendent
Bedford	Veterans' Administration Facility	Winthrop Adams, M.D., Superintendent
Northampton	Veterans' Administration Facility (North Main Street)	F. E. Leslie, M.D., Superintendent

In addition to regular forms of application as above listed, special application must be made to Veterans' Administration, Federal Building, Boston.

State Hospitals

City or Town	Institution	Superintendent	Post Office Address
Boston	Boston Psychopathic Hospital	Clifford D. Moore, M.D. (Chief Executive Officer)	74 Fenwood Rd Boston
Boston	Boston State Hospital	James V. May, M.D.	Dorchester Center
Danvers	Danvers State Hospital	Clarence A. Bonner, M.D.	Hathorne, Mass
Foxborough	Foxborough State Hospital	Roderick B. Dexter, M.D.	Foxborough
Gardner	Gardner State Hospital	Charles E. Thompson, M.D.	East Gardner
Grafton	Grafton State Hospital	Harlan L. Paine, M.D.	North Grafton
Medfield	Medfield State Hospital	Earl K. Holt, M.D.	Harding, Mass.
Northampton	Northampton State Hospital	Arthur N. Ball, M D.	Northampton
Taunton	Taunton State Hospital	Ralph M. Chambers, M.D.	Taunton
Waltham	Metropolitan State Hospital	Roy D. Halloran, M.D.	Waltham
Westborough	Westborough State Hospital	Walter E. Lang, M.D.	Westborough
Worcester	Worcester State Hospital	William A. Bryan, M.D.	Worcester

Private Hospitals

Financial responsibility for patients admitted to private hospitals is, in all cases, a personal matter between the patient or his relatives and the hospital. There is no State or local subsidy for such cases.

City or Town	Institution	Superintendent	Post Office Address
Arlington	Ring Sanatorium and Hospital, Inc.	Barbara T. Ring, M.D., Med. Supt.	Arlington Heights
Belmont	McLean Hospital	Kenneth J. Tillotson, M.D.	Waverley

Town	Institution	Superintendent	Post Office Address
Boston	Glenside	Mabel D. Ordway, M.D.	6 Parley Vale, Jamaica Plain
Brookline	Bosworth Hospital	Arthur Berk, M.D.	166 Lancaster Ter., Brookline
Brookline	Bournewood Hospital	Geo. H. Torney, M.D.	300 South St., Brookline
Melrose	Dr. Reeves' Nervine	Fred B. Jewett, M.D.	283 Vinton St., Melrose Highlands
Wellesley	Channing Sanitarium	Donald Gregg, M.D.	Wellesley Ave., Wellesley
Wellesley	Wiswall Sanatorium	Edward H. Wiswall, M.D.	203 Grove St., Wellesley
Westwood	Westwood Lodge	William J. Hammond, M.D.	Westwood

EPILEPTICS:

Sane epileptics—Voluntary application—Any person who is certified to be subject to epilepsy by a properly qualified physician (see p. 184 for definition of "properly qualified physician") and who desires to submit himself to treatment, who makes written application therefor, and whose mental condition is such as to render him competent to make such application (or for whom application is made by parent or guardian) may be received at the Monson State Hospital or a private hospital licensed to receive such patients. (See below.) No such patient may be detained more than three *months* after having given written notice of his intention or desire to leave the hospital. Blanks for voluntary application may be obtained from the hospitals or from the Department of Mental Diseases, 167 State House, Boston.

Insane epileptics—Any insane person who is subject to epilepsy, and is not a criminal, inebriate or violently insane, may be committed to the Monson State Hospital, or to a private hospital licensed to receive such patients. Commitment through same procedure as for insane persons. (See p. 184.) Application blanks obtainable from clerks of courts, hospitals, or Department of Mental Diseases, 167 State House, Boston.

Dangerous epileptics—Epileptics who are dangerous to themselves or others by reason of epilepsy may be committed to the Monson State Hospital in the same manner as provided for commitment of dipsomaniacs and inebriates (see p. 187). Application blanks obtainable from clerks of courts, hospitals, or Department of Mental Diseases, 167 State House, Boston.

Hospitals Receiving Epileptics
State Hospital

Town	Institution	Superintendent	Post Office Address
Monson	Monson State Hospital	Morgan B. Hodskins, M.D.	Palmer

Private Hospitals

Financial responsibility for patients admitted to private hospitals is, in all cases, a personal matter between the hospital and the patient or his relatives. There is no State or local subsidy for such cases.

In addition to the private hospitals listed on p. 185, the following are licensed to receive epileptics:

City or Town	Institution	Superintendent	Post Office Address
Newton	Woodlawn Sanitarium	Ewan A. Robertson, M.D.	500 Crafts St., West Newton
North Andover	Kittredge Farm	Joseph Kittredge, M.D.	North Andover

DIPSOMANIACS, INEBRIATES AND DRUG ADDICTS:

*Admission—Voluntary application—*The trustees, superintendent or manager of any institution to which a dipsomaniac, an inebriate, or one addicted to the intemperate use of narcotics or stimulants may be committed, may receive and detain therein as a boarder and patient any person who is desirous of submitting himself to treatment and who makes written application therefor and is mentally competent to make the application. No such person may be detained more than three days after having given written notice of his intention or desire to leave the institution. Application blanks obtainable at institution, or Department of Mental Diseases, 167 State House, Boston.

*Temporary care—*The superintendent or manager of any institution to which a dipsomaniac, an inebriate, or one addicted to the intemperate use of narcotics or stimulants may be committed, may receive and care for in such institution, as a patient for a period not exceeding fifteen days, any person needing immediate care and treatment because he has become so addicted to the intemperate use of narcotics or stimulants that he has lost the power of self control. Application blanks obtainable at institution, or at Department of Mental Diseases, 167 State House, Boston.

*Commitment—*Is made in same manner as above under Mental Diseases (see p. 184). In addition to judges there listed as empowered to commit patients, commitments of dipsomaniacs, inebriates, and drug addicts may be made by a judge of the municipal court of Boston. Commitment may be to the State Farm at Bridgewater, to the Massachusetts Reformatory for Women, to the McLean Hospital, or to any private institution licensed by the Department of Mental Diseases for the care of insane, inebriates and drug addicts. Certificate signed by two properly qualified physicians (see p. 184 for definition of "properly qualified physician") must accompany application for commitment. Application blanks obtainable from police departments, clerks of courts, or institution.

Hospitals Receiving Dipsomaniacs, Inebriates and Drug Addicts
State Institutions

City or Town	Institution	Superintendent	Post Office Address
Bridgewater	State Farm	Dr. Wm. T. Hanson, Medical Director	Bridgewater

Financial responsibility for patients admitted to private hospitals is, in all cases, a personal matter between the hospital and the patient or his relatives. There is no State or local subsidy for such cases. In addition to the private hospitals listed on p. 185, the following hospitals are licensed to receive inebriates and drug addicts:

City or Town	Institution	Superintendent	Post Office
Boston	Private Hospital	Frederick L. Taylor, M.D.	45 Center Street, Roxbury
Boston	Washingtonian Home	Hugh B. Gray, M.D.	41 Waltham Street, Boston
Boston	Grove Hall Institute	Geo. C. Moore, M.D.	222 Townsend St., Roxbury

FEEBLEMINDEDNESS:

Admission to State Schools

Voluntary application—Application to be made by parent or guardian of feebleminded person; application to be accompanied by certificate of properly qualified physician (see p. 184 for definition of "properly qualified physician") stating under oath that he has examined said person within five days of signing certificate and that, in his opinion, the person is a fit subject for such school. Application blanks obtainable from superintendent of School for the Feebleminded, or from Department of Mental Diseases, 167 State House, Boston.

Observation—Application to be made by parent or guardian. Patient to be detained for observation for a period not exceeding thirty days to determine whether or not feebleminded. Application blanks obtainable from superintendent of School for the Feebleminded, or from Department of Mental Diseases, 167 State House, Boston.

Court commitment—May be made by any judge of probate within his county. Application to be made directly to court, forms obtainable from clerks of courts, superintendents of School for Feebleminded, or from Department of Mental Diseases, 167 State House, Boston. Application should be accompanied by physician's certificate (see Voluntary Application) certifying as to examination made within *ten* days of signing certificate.

Commitment to Department of Mental Diseases—If an alleged feebleminded person is found, upon examination by a properly qualified physician (see p. 184 for definition of "properly qualified physician") to be a proper subject for commitment, the judge of probate for the county in which such person resides or is found may upon application commit him to the custody or supervision of the Department; but no person shall be so committed unless the approval of the Department shall be filed with the application for his commitment. Such patients are not hospitalized but are supervised in the community by the Department of Mental Diseases.

Schools Accepting Feebleminded Patients
State Schools

City or Town	School	Superintendent	Post Office Address
Belchertown	Belchertown State School	Geo. E. McPherson, M.D. Med. Supt.	Belchertown
Waltham	Walter E. Fernald State School	Ransom A. Greene, M.D. Med. Supt.	Waverley
Wrentham	Wrentham State School	C. Stanley Raymond, M.D. Med. Supt.	Wrentham

Private Schools

Financial responsibility for patients admitted to private schools is, in all cases, a personal matter between the school and the patient or his relatives. There is no State or local subsidy for such cases. In addition to the private hospitals listed on p. 185, the following schools are licensed to received feebleminded patients:

City or Town	School	Superintendent	Post Office Address
Arlington	The Freer School	Miss Cora E. Morse	31 Park Circle, Arlington Heights
Barre	Elm Hill Private School and Home for the Feebleminded	Geo. A. Brown, M D.	Barre
Halifax	Standish Manor	Miss Alice M. Myers	Halifax
Lancaster	Perkins School of Adjustment	Franklin H. Perkins, M.D.	Lancaster
Newton	Clarke School	Miss Edith G. Clark	16 Summit St., Newton

INSTITUTIONS UNDER DEPARTMENT OF PUBLIC WELFARE

THE STATE INFIRMARY, Tewksbury, maintained by State Department of Public Welfare, 37 State House, Boston.

A general hospital, primarily for care and treatment of poor and indigent persons having no legal settlement, suffering from acute and chronic diseases. Special venereal, tubercular and maternity wards. Minors not admitted without approval of Division of Aid and Relief. Special provision made for any person who has been a resident of Commonwealth for not less than two years and who is affected with any incurable disease except mental defect or leprosy. Admission subject to regulations established by Department. Insane persons are not admitted.

The Department, through its Division of Aid and Relief, has authority of supervision and discharge of patients; certificates of admission are issued by Boards of Public Welfare, and in Boston by Institutions Department. Persons infected with diseases dangerous to public health are admitted to Infirmary only upon request of Boards of Health and with approval of Division of Aid and Relief. Said approval is generally confined to persons ill with tuberculosis and venereal diseases.

MASSACHUSETTS HOSPITAL SCHOOL, Canton, provides care and schooling for crippled and deformed children of Massachusetts between five and fifteen years of age who are mentally competent to attend public schools; girls taught cooking, sewing, general house work, laundering and a few assigned to office work, telephone desks, typewriting, etc.; older boys taught farming, gardening, care of poultry, work in dairy, baking, engineering, carpentry, painting, shoemaking, automobile driving. Expenses borne by pupils when able, or by those bound by law to maintain them, or by city or town of their settlement whose Boards of Public Welfare request their admission, or by the Commonwealth.

REPORT OF DIVISION OF FOOD AND DRUGS

(As required by law (General Laws, Chapter 111, Section 25) the following report is published in the Department bulletin.)

During the months of April, May and June 1935, samples were collected in 265 cities and towns.

There were 2,552 samples of milk examined, of which 465 were below standard, from 22 samples the cream had been in part removed, and 18 samples contained added water. There were 980 bacteriological examinations made of milk, 775 of which complied with the requirements. There were 295 bacteriological examinations made of frozen desserts, 257 of which complied with the requirements; 1 bacteriological examination of cream which did not comply with the requirements: 1 bacteriological examination of evaporated milk and candy, both of which complied with the requirements; and 4 bacteriological examinations of empty tonic bottles which did not comply with the requirements.

There were 690 samples of food examined, 81 of which were adulterated. These consisted of 1 sample of cheese which contained vegetable gum; 1 sample of extract of lemon which was misbranded; 17 samples of hamburg steak, 9 samples of which were decomposed and 1 sample also contained sodium sulphite in excess of one tenth of one per cent, 6 samples contained a compound of sulphur dioxide not properly labeled and 3 samples were also decomposed, and 2 samples contained sodium sulphite in excess of one tenth of one per cent; 3 samples of sausage, 1 sample of which contained starch in excess of 2 per cent, 1 sample contained sodium sulphite in excess of one tenth of one per cent, and 1 sample was decomposed; 8 samples of pickles, all of which contained sodium benzoate and were not properly labeled, 1 of which also contained saccharine; 5 samples of sweet relish which contained sodium benzoate and were not properly labeled; 31 samples of olive oil, 16 of which contained cottonseed oil, and 15 contained color; 9 samples of vinegar, 8 of which contained less than the required amount of acidity, and 1 sample was misbranded; 5 samples of scallops which were decomposed; and 1 sample of maple syrup which contained cane sugar.

There were 50 samples of drugs examined, of which 3 were adulterated. These consisted of 1 sample of argyrol below the specified concentration, and 2 samples of spirit of nitrous ether which did not conform to the U. S. P. requirements.

The police departments submitted 134 samples of liquor for examination. The police departments also submitted 28 samples to be analyzed for poisons or drugs, 9 samples of which contained opium, 6 contained heroin, 2 contained heroin hydrochloride, 3 contained Cannabis Sativa, and 8 contained no narcotic drugs or poisons.

There were 84 cities and towns visited for the inspection of pasteurizing plants, and 282 plants were inspected.

There were 93 plants inspected for the manufacture of ice cream.

There were 72 hearings held pertaining to violations of the laws.

There were 44 convictions for violations of the law, $655.00 in fines being imposed.

Alfred Fickert of North Middleborough; Ernest Freeman, 2 cases, of Lexington; Mary Iannacci and Nicholas Iannacci of Woburn; Antone Yanacek of Acushnet; Edward S. Briggs of Blackstone; J. J. Newberry Company of North Adams; Richard Murray of Lincoln; and Lorenzo Dean of Boylston, were all convicted for violations of the milk laws.

Barden Cream Company, 2 cases, and Gifford Chapman, 2 cases, of Quincy; Hilaire Lavoie of Ludlow; Ernest Harnisch and Fred Miller of Methuen; and Arthur Turner of North Hanover, were convicted for violations of the pasteurization laws and regulations. Barden Cream Company, 2 cases, and Gifford Chapman, 2 cases, of Quincy, appealed their cases.

Harvard Pickle Works, Incorporated, Carl's Market, Incorporated, 2 cases, Max Comman, and Simon Gordon, all of Cambridge; Cesare Ruggeri of Webster; N. Y. Cut Rate Grocery Company and National Pickling Works of Dorchester; The Great Atlantic & Pacific Tea Company of Marlborough; Joseph Ganem & Sons, 2 cases, of Lawrence; Jack Miller and Joseph Greenstein of New Bedford; John Pascarelli, Carl Carelli, and Food Specialty Company of Worcester; and Gregory Nicholas and William Kline of Lynn, were all convicted for violations of the food laws.

Frank Borgia of Boston was convicted for misbranding.

Festus L. McCann of West Berlin was convicted for false advertising.

Peter Vergos of Natick, Jackson's Incorporated, 2 cases, of Springfield, and Peter Shmeligian of Marlborough, were convicted for violations of the frozen dessert law.

Antiseptic Mattress Company of Lynn was convicted for violation of the mattress law.

Charles Sharek of New Bedford was convicted for violation of the drug law.

In accordance with Section 25, Chapter 111 of the General Laws, the following is the list of articles of adulterated food collected in original packages from manufacturers, wholesalers, or producers:

One sample of lemon extract which was misbranded was obtained from Roma Extract Company of Boston.

One sample of maple syrup which contained cane sugar was obtained from State Restaurant, Incorporated, of Fall River.

One sample of vinegar which was misbranded was obtained from Food Specialty Company of Worcester.

Vinegar which contained less than the required amount of acidity was obtained as follows:

Two samples from John Galante (Tileston Specialty Company) of Everett; and 1 sample each, from Edward Bloom of Newburyport, and Progress Pickling & Vinegar Company of Fall River.

Sweet Relish which contained sodium benzoate not marked was obtained as follows:

Three samples from Delmer M. Jewett of South Deerfield; and 1 sample from Caroline C. Anthony of North Quincy.

Pickles which contained sodium benzoate not marked were obtained as follows:

Two samples each, from Delmer M. Jewett of South Deerfield, and Growers Outlet, Incorporated, of Greenfield; and 1 sample from Nicholas Pappas of Bridgewater.

One sample of sweet pickles which contained sodium benzoate not marked and also contained saccharine was obtained from Harvard Pickle Works, Incorporated, of Cambridge.

One sample of sausage which was decomposed was obtained from C. Grimaldi of Chelsea.

One sample of sausage which contained starch in excess of 2 per cent. was obtained from Joseph Greenstein of New Bedford.

One sample of sausage which contained sodium sulphite in excess of one-tenth of one per cent. was obtained from Pasquale Guglielmo of East Boston.

Hamburg steak which was decomposed was obtained as follows:

One sample each, from Jack Miller of New Bedford; Handy Dandy Stores Incorporated of Haverhill; Liberty Market, Central Market, and Jacob Geller, all of Newburyport; City Meat Market and O. L. Bowman & Sons of Salem; and Cy's Market of Cambridge.

Hamburg steak which contained a compound of sulphur dioxide not properly labeled and was also decomposed was obtained as follows:

Carl's Market Incorporated of Cambridge; M. Baum (Boston Market) of Chelsea; J. Shavitsky (Spic & Span Market) of Revere.

Hamburg steak which contained sodium sulphite in excess of one tenth of one per cent was obtained as follows:

One sample each, from People's Market and Rich's Market of North Adams.

One sample of hamburg steak which contained sodium sulphite in excess of one tenth of one per cent and was also decomposed was obtained from Quality Market of Chelsea.

Hamburg steak which contained a compound of sulphur dioxide not properly labeled was obtained as follows:

One sample each, from Ideal Market of Cambridge; William Kline of Lynn; and Walter Rich of North Adams.

Olive oil which contained cottonseed oil was obtained as follows: Two samples each, from James Pepe of Lawrence; and A. L. Mihaloplos & Company (George Arminis Company, Boston, wholesaler) of Boston; and one sample each, from Anthony Morakis of Cambridge; Ameo Oil Company of Boston; Cesare Ruggeri of Webster; Gregory Nicholas of Lynn; Carl Carelli, L. A. Manyi, Incorporated, and John Pascarelli, all of Worcester; Shaheen Touma, George Abdulla, Lawrence High School Market, and Frank Commisuli, all of Lawrence.

Olive oil which contained color was obtained as follows: Five samples from George Armenis Company of Boston; 3 samples each, from J. S. Contas Brothers, Incorporated, and Edmond Caruso of Boston; 2 samples from Cara Donna Packing Company of Boston; and 1 sample from Jacob Pollen of Boston.

There were seventeen confiscations, consisting of 25 pounds of decomposed butter; 100 pounds of decomposed beef; 30 pounds of decomposed beef; 50 pounds of decomposed corned beef; 214 pounds of rancid pork; 40 pounds of decomposed shoulders; 25 pounds of decomposed veal; 30 pounds of decomposed veal; 135 pounds of unstamped veal; 50 pounds of decomposed frankforts; 15 pounds of decomposed sausages; 363 pounds of decomposed butterfish; 145 pounds of decomposed halibut; 1960 pounds of decomposed sea scallops; 200 pounds of decomposed squid; 625 pounds of decomposed squid; and 80 pounds of wormy flour.

The licensed cold storage warehouses reported the following amounts of food placed in storage during March, 1935:—887,100 dozens of case eggs; 692,397 pounds of broken out eggs; 425,939 pounds of butter; 914,524 pounds of poultry; 2,652,356 pounds of fresh meat and fresh meat products; and 4,877,102 pounds of fresh food fish.

There was on hand April 1, 1935:—759,990 dozens of case eggs; 1,204,949 pounds of broken out eggs; 337,604 pounds of butter; 6,077,747 pounds of poultry; 11,883,115 pounds of fresh meat and fresh meat products; and 6,596,801 pounds of fresh food fish.

The licensed cold storage warehouses reported the following amounts of food placed in storage during April, 1935:—2,616,180 dozens of case eggs; 678,045 pounds of broken out eggs; 488,004 pounds of butter; 1,059,930 pounds of poultry; 4,458,690 pounds of fresh meat and fresh meat products; and 5,720,678 pounds of fresh food fish.

There was on hand May 1, 1935:—3,244,770 dozens of case eggs; 1,132,543 pounds of broken out eggs; 202,815 pounds of butter; 4,445,640 pounds of poultry; 9,248,610 pounds of fresh meat and fresh meat products; and 6,609,278 pounds of fresh food fish.

The licensed cold storage warehouses reported the following amounts of food placed in storage during May, 1935:—2,109,480 dozens of case eggs; 1,125,715 pounds of broken out eggs; 983,952 pounds of butter; 1,253,655 pounds of poultry; 2,852,995 pounds of fresh meat and fresh meat products; and 15,933,887 pounds of fresh food fish.

There was on hand June 1, 1935:—5,188,260 dozens of case eggs; 1,342,292 pounds of broken out eggs; 917,638 pounds of butter; 3,428,794 pounds of poultry; 7,239,027 pounds of fresh meat and fresh meat products; and 16,976,647 pounds of fresh food fish.

MASSACHUSETTS DEPARTMENT OF PUBLIC HEALTH

Commissioner of Public Health, HENRY D. CHADWICK, M.D.

Public Health Council

HENRY D. CHADWICK, M.D., *Chairman*

GORDON HUTCHINS RICHARD M. SMITH, M.D.
FRANCIS H. LALLY, M.D. RICHARD P. STRONG, M.D.
SYLVESTER E. RYAN, M.D. JAMES L. TIGHE.

Secretary, ALICE M. NELSON

Division of Administration	Under direction of Commissioner.
Division of Sanitary Engineering	Director and Chief Engineer, ARTHUR D. WESTON, C.E.
Division of Communicable Diseases	Director, GAYLORD W. ANDERSON, M.D.
Division of Biologic Laboratories	Director and Pathologist, ELLIOTT S. ROBINSON, M.D.
Division of Food and Drugs	Director and Analyst, HERMANN C. LYTHGOE, S.B.
Division of Child Hygiene	Director, M. LUISE DIEZ, M.D.
Division of Tuberculosis	Director, ALTON S. POPE, M.D.
Division of Adult Hygiene	Director, HERBERT L. LOMBARD, M.D.

State District Health Officers

The Southeastern District	RICHARD P. MACKNIGHT, M.D., New Bedford
The South Metropolitan District	HENRY M. DEWOLFE, M.D., Quincy.
The North Metropolitan District	CHARLES B. MACK, M.D., Boston.
The Northeastern District	ROBERT E. ARCHIBALD, M.D., Lynn.
The Worcester County District	OSCAR A. DUDLEY, M.D., Worcester.
The Connecticut Valley District	HAROLD E. MINER, M.D., Springfield.
The Berkshire District	WALTER W. LEE, M.D., No. Adams.

PUBLICATION OF THIS DOCUMENT APPROVED BY COMMISSION ON ADMINISTRATION AND FINANCE
12M. 9-35. Order 5562.

THE COMMONHEALTH

Volume 22   Oct.-Nov.-Dec
No. 4   1935

RADIO NUMBER

MASSACHUSETTS
DEPARTMENT OF PUBLIC HEALTH

THE COMMONHEALTH

QUARTERLY BULLETIN OF THE MASSACHUSETTS DEPARTMENT OF PUBLIC HEALTH

Sent Free to any Citizen of the State

Entered as second class matter at Boston Postoffice.

M. LUISE DIEZ, M.D., DIRECTOR OF DIVISION OF CHILD HYGIENE, EDITOR.
Room 545, State House, Boston, Mass.

The Massachusetts Department of Public Health conducts three radio broadcasts each week, two given by members of the Department, the third by the Massachusetts Medical Society under the auspices of the Department. This number contains samples of broadcasts given in the past year.

CONTENTS

	PAGE
Public Health in Massachusetts in 1934, by Henry D. Chadwick, M.D.	199
Preventive Medicine From Your Family Physician, by Alexander S. Begg, M.D.	203
Infantile Paralysis, by Gaylord W. Anderson, M.D.	206
Ear, Nose and Throat Diseases, by Charles I. Johnson, M.D.	209
Collapse Treatment in Tuberculosis, by Alton S. Pope, M.D.	213
Illness and Character, by Leroy E. Parkins, M.D.	215
Child Hygiene, by M. Luise Diez, M.D.	218
Violence and Public Health, by Lincoln Davis, M.D.	222
The Darkness of Ignorance, and The Fog of Prudery, by N. A. Nelson M.D.	226
Boston of 1800, by Eleanor J. Macdonald, A.B.	229
Cancer, by Ernest M. Daland, M. D.	234
Topography of the State of Massachusetts, by Arthur D. Weston, C.E.	237
Tired Legs From Altered Circulation, by Hilbert F. Day, M.D.	240
The Biological Laboratory, by Elliott S. Robinson, M.D.	244
Jim Has a Stomach Ache, by John Birnie, M.D.	245
Food Fads, by Hermann C. Lythgoe, S.B.	248
Adult Hygiene, by Herbert L. Lombard, M.D.	251
The Progress of Medicine, by Elliott C. Cutler, M.D.	255
Book Note:	
The Work Of The Sanitary Engineer, by Arthur D. Martin	258
Report of Division of Food and Drugs, July, August and September, 1935	259
Index	264

PUBLIC HEALTH IN MASSACHUSETTS IN 1934

By HENRY D. CHADWICK, M. D.

Commissioner of Public Health
Massachusetts Department of Public Health

The year just passed has left a very favorable health record for the people of the Commonwealth. The general death rate has been low. There have been no serious epidemics. Infantile paralysis was at the third lowest level ever recorded in the State. Scarlet fever reached the lowest level since 1922. Diphtheria and typhoid fever reached new low points and there was a reduction of 165 deaths from tuberculosis.

Of the other and less serious communicable diseases, measles, whooping cough, German measles, and chicken pox show an increased incidence. Measles was widespread and over 44,000 cases were reported, more than ever before in a single year. Whooping cough caused 125 deaths and was at the head of the list of fatalities from children's diseases. Measles comes next with 91 deaths, scarlet fever third with 76 deaths, and fourth comes diphtheria with 50 deaths. If we check back fifteen years to 1920, we will see that great progress has been made in the control of these diseases that have always been a menace to children. Whooping cough in 1920 caused 546 deaths, in 1934 but 125. Measles, in 1920, was the cause of 352 deaths, and in 1934 but 91. Scarlet fever caused 214 deaths in 1920, and 76 in 1934. Diphtheria in 1920 caused 591 deaths, and in 1934 but 50. These four diseases caused the deaths of 1603 children in 1920 and of 343 in 1934, a reduction of 78 per cent in fifteen years. Gratifying as this showing is, it can be much improved if we put into general practice the present knowledge of how to prevent them.

Most children are susceptible to whooping cough and because it is so generally prevalent it is difficult to avoid exposure. This communicable disease is peculiar in that the incidence and mortality are higher among girls than boys. The most dangerous period to have whooping cough is in the first year of life. Most deaths occur between one month and twelve months and in the first year of life about 60 per cent of all the deaths from this disease occur. Parents should do everything possible to prevent infants from exposure to the disease. The longer it can be postponed the better, as it is but rarely fatal after five years of age. A whooping cough vaccine is being used to a limited extent to immunize children against this disease and reports as to its effectiveness are very encouraging. It would be a great boon to parents and children if a way is found to prevent this distressing and oftentimes fatal disease.

There is good news to report about measles. After several years of laboratory study and trial, a placental extract has been prepared that promises to control measles. It can be used to prevent or modify the disease, depending upon the time the extract is given in relation to exposure. If given within four days the disease will be prevented. If given after the fourth day and up to the appearance of the rash it will modify the attack and make it so mild in some cases that the children hardly know they have measles. The best procedure is to prevent measles in infants and delicate children, that is, postpone the disease to a more favorable time. With the others, permit them to have measles in a mild form and so make them permanently immune from attack. This extract is now available to physicians in the State at the Department of Public Health laboratory at Forest Hills.

Scarlet fever fortunately is now usually mild in form but often leaves serious complications and should be avoided when possible. Scarlet fever toxin is available and is being used more and more for immunization against that disease. The results in children's institutions where it has been used routinely for several years are so good that scarlet fever has been practically eliminated. Also, nurses who care for scarlet fever patients in hospitals are now given this protection.

Diphtheria

This is a disease that is rapidly disappearing. To have reduced the annual number of deaths from over 500 to 50 is indeed a triumph. Cases, and especially deaths from this disease are now a reproach to any city or town. Communities where boards of health and physicians are alive to their responsibilities protect their children by giving them diphtheria toxoid or toxin antitoxin early in life. The best time to give them this treatment is during the second six months of life, as 65 per cent of all deaths from diphtheria are among preschool children. Take warning from this and if you have a child six months old or older take it to a doctor for diphtheria protection. Many boards of health are sending out cards to parents when their baby reaches its six-months' birthday reminding them that it is immunizing time. Most boards of health will provide the ways and means for those unable to afford to pay for these treatments.

Now that we have reviewed the common communicable diseases which affect children, we will take up those that are common to all ages.

Typhoid Fever

If we go back in the records twenty-five years we find that this disease afflicted about 3500 persons a year and caused the deaths of 400. Contrast that picture with last year, when there were only 135 cases in the whole State, with but 13 deaths. This item of progress in public health comes about to a large extent by improved sanitation. The polluted water and infected milk that were the chief sources for spreading the germs of the disease have been largely eliminated. The public water supplies are free from sewage contamination and close supervision is maintained over them. Of the 355 cities and towns of the State, 241, with 97.3 per cent of the population, have public water supplies. One hundred and twenty-one municipalities have sewerage systems. No other factors have done so much to improve and conserve the health of the people as the development of pure water supplies and their protection by the installation of sewerage systems. Milk, which in the past has caused many outbreaks of typhoid fever, is now handled in a more sanitary way on the farm and distributed to the consumer in clean bottles. Furthermore, about 70 per cent of the milk consumed in Massachusetts is pasteurized and 85 per cent of the people live in localities where pasteurized milk is available. This safeguard has prevented many persons from contracting typhoid fever, scarlet fever, septic sore throat, dysentery, and gastro-enteritis. In the last seven years there have been nineteen outbreaks of these diseases just mentioned traced to milk marketed in a raw state. Altogether, there were 1790 cases and 75 deaths resulting from these milk infections that could have been avoided if the milk had been pasteurized. Why should people persist in drinking raw milk with its attendant dangers when they can have the disease germs killed, if any were present, by having the milk heated to 142°F and held there for thirty minutes, as is done in pasteurization. Most of the food we eat is heated to a much higher degree than that in pasteurization and we think nothing of it. When it comes to safeguarding milk by heating even to a moderate degree, some people violently protest and seem to think it is a sacrilege to doubt the cow's good faith in the production of her food product. Sometimes a well-intentioned cow has an infected udder which results in an abscess, and the streptococcus which causes this condition gets into the milk with disastrous results to the people who consume it in its raw state. This streptococcus causes mastitis in the cow and septic sore throat in humans who not infrequently die from the infection. Sometimes a milk handler is a typhoid carrier and infects the milk with typhoid fever germs. He is no more conscious of this than the cow is of the concealed abscess in the udder. Pasteurization is the only safeguard the consumer has against these serious infections. Fourteen cities and towns in the State now have ordinances in effect requiring that all milk sold be pasteurized or certified, and eight others have passed such resolutions that will soon become effective. Sanitary measures such as these that make for better health are steadily making progress.

Pneumonia

Pneumococcus serum made at the State Laboratory and distributed to doctors for treatment of certain types of lobar pneumonia has been used in a large number of cases in the last three years with very satisfactory results. There are over thirty varieties of this pneumonia germ, but the serum is effective in only two types, called Type I and Type II, and then only if used within the first four days of the disease. When the doctor is called to see a patient and finds pneumonia, a specimen of sputum is obtained and sent to the laboratory for typing. If the Type I or Type II germ is found, serum should be given at once. When this is done, the deaths from pneumonia are greatly reduced and this is the most effective treatment now available for this very serious disease. It must be emphasized, however, that only when given early is the serum effective. Therefore, when one has a bad cold on the chest or symptoms of congestion of the lungs, call a doctor as soon as possible.

Tuberculosis

The number of deaths from tuberculosis last year was approximately 2000. In 1900 it was 7000 and the old Bay State has a million more population now than it had at that time. This disease is rapidly being brought under control. The x-ray has been the most valuable aid in finding cases, and modern methods of treatment, by collapsing the diseased lung with air and by surgery, have restored many patients, who were formerly considered hopeless, back to health. The school clinics formerly conducted by the State Department of Public Health have been taken over by the state and county sanatoria. Members of the medical staffs of these institutions will examine the junior and high school students in their immediate neighborhoods. The seventh, ninth, and eleventh grades will be examined annually, which will give three examinations during the period when tuberculosis most often makes its appearance in children.

Rabies

One of the difficult problems that confronts the health officer today is rabies. An unusually large number of mad dogs are at large in Massachusetts, especially in the central and eastern parts of the State. About 1000 persons have been bitten by dogs and have been obliged to take the Pasteur treatment. One child, bitten on the face. was not treated and died from rabies. To protect the people we must protect the dogs. This can be done best by giving them one dose of antirabic vaccine each year. Several cities and towns have been holding clinics for dog vaccination and large numbers have been given this protection. It should be done all over the State and it is especially necessary in infected areas. If vaccination, or restraint of all dogs not so protected, was required throughout the State, rabies would soon be brought under control. I am sure the dogs would approve of this method if they could express an opinion because rabies is 100 per cent fatal for them and for humans too if the Pasteur treatment is not given promptly.

Two new health districts of ten towns each have recently been organized. One of these is the Nashoba district, centering about Ayer, and the other is in the Southern Berkshire section, with Great Barrington as the center. Each is a voluntary association entered into by vote of the towns for the purpose of maintaining an adequate public health department at minimum cost. A group of small towns by combining their resources can employ a physician trained in modern public health methods who will give these communities all the advantages that can be had from a city health department. It is to be hoped that other groups of towns will form similar health districts. An expenditure of about $1.00 per capita is necessary to finance a good health program provided the population in the area is not much below 20,000. This includes the services of a health officer, public health and school nurses, a sanitary inspector, and milk laboratory. Such a health department would do a great deal toward preventing illness and death from communicable disease, save much expense for hospitalization of contagious cases, and improve the general health and well-being of the community. Many states have county health departments instead of one for each municipality as is customary in Massachusetts. That plan has many advantages for the small towns as has been illustrated by the Cape Cod Health Bureau which comprises all the towns in Barnstable County. It is in effect a county health department, in which the towns have organized on a voluntary basis. There are other counties in the State where a similar type of organization would be a vast improvement over health work now being done in many of the small communities.

The practice of public health is a specialty, like other branches of medicine. A doctor needs special training and experience to become a good health officer. A city can afford to employ such a physician. Towns, however, by grouping together can pool their health expenditures and thereby have sufficient money to employ the services of a competent health officer. This is the trend of thought of public health administrators in these times in order to get the most effective service for the money expended.

PREVENTIVE MEDICINE FROM YOUR FAMILY PHYSICIAN

By ALEXANDER S. BEGG, M. D.

Boston University School of Medicine

This series of broadcasts which is being conducted by the Department of Public Health of the Commonwealth of Massachusetts and the Committee on Public Education of the Massachusetts Medical Society is made possible through the co-operation of the National Broadcasting Company. It is to be regarded as an evidence of the continuing interest of the public in matters which pertain to health. Responsibility for the health of the people is a matter of utmost concern to the State and Massachusetts may be justly proud of the work which has been done within its borders in this, as in other fields of science. Reference has already been made in these broadcasts to other work being undertaken by the Commonwealth through its excellent Health Department and it is now my privilege to discuss a phase of the health problem which must always be a personal one between the individual and the physician.

There was a period a few years ago when it appeared that the family physician was rapidly disappearing from the picture and many people regretted the passing of what was called "the old family doctor," that lovable and dramatic figure who has furnished the material for so many delightful stories. It has been found, however, that while the tall hat and the horse and buggy have disappeared, the family physician is still the most important link in the health chain. There is a very evident return to an older belief that the close personal relations between the family doctor and his patients is essential to the best results in any program for improving the health of the people.

Since it is impossible to go into all of the phases of the family doctor's work and, since it is the State's desire to improve health by preventing disease, I shall deal particularly with this topic.

One of the oldest of our common expressions is that which states that "an ounce of prevention is worth a pound of cure." Everyone is willing to accept this as particularly true in connection with health, but the trouble is that most of us are inclined to think of such things in terms of the other fellow, for whom we are always anxious to do something. Of course, this is not the case. The truth of the statement applies equally to you and to me. It is also true that the matter of prevention is apt to be regarded as an academic affair, one about which there are so many opportunities for glittering generalities. Again the truth is that it is a common everyday affair. Prevention when applied to health is nothing more or less than the common-sense application of well-known principles which have been learned from years of experience and from many sources. The definition might really be shortened and we might say that the prevention is the common sense of medicine. There is nothing mysterious about it!

The knowledge of prevention in medicine is *not* something which is confined to specialists. Every family physician is fully aware of its possibilities and of the details of most of its practical applications. Unfortunately it is not customary for doctors to volunteer much information along these lines to their patients lest they be misunderstood and thought to be attempting to increase their business. However, with a little intelligent insistence from the patient many of these things will come to the fore. Then too a great many of the preventive measures have now become routine and are carried out by the physician with little or no discussion--they are a part of the day's work.

I would not for a moment deny the need for the services of a specialist when such services will be useful, but there is always a danger in a patient going directly to a specialist without first having discussed the matter with his family doctor and having obtained his advice, since the family doctor can advise concerning the need and can often be most helpful to the specialist because of his better acquaintance with the whole story.

Perhaps this is the time to ask a question. Have you a family physician? If not, as a matter of ordinary self-protection would it not be a good plan to give this some thought? Do you know personally a medical man and do you have confidence in him? After all, this matter of confidence is of the greatest importance. If you know of no one, there are a few points which may help you. A well-trained doctor should be a graduate of a good medical school and should be familiar with the fundamental sciences of anatomy, chemistry, physiology, bacteriology and pathology. He should have received adequate instruction in clinical subjects and should have had an internship in a proper hospital. A doctor with such training has an opportunity through his professional magazines and journals to learn of the newer things as they develop and through his medical society meetings he has an opportunity to discuss current medical problems with the other physicians in his community. I cannot place too much emphasis upon the need for thoroughness in the training of the family doctor; his work demands it.

The family physician should know the family intimately. He should be acquainted with the living and working conditions of the individual members of the family, as well as with such physical and mental hazards as may exist. He is the one who can best appreciate the personalities involved and can give the proper setting to the important backgrounds of of heredity and social position. As a matter of fact, he is the one individual who should combine the necessary professional knowledge and the proper appreciation of the other important factors which are so necessary in meeting the problems you present to him. Usually, if he does not possess this thorough knowledge of your situation, it is because you have not fully co-operated with him by giving him the information he seeks. What we would like to obtain is complete co-operation between the physician and the patient.

I would now like to call your attention to a monthly publication which is carefully prepared by the American Medical Association to give to the public authoritative information about all kinds of health matters. This magazine is called "Hygeia" and information concerning it may be had by writing to the American Medical Association in Chicago, Illinois. I speak of this magazine because it discusses from time to time matters which are of vital importance to the health of the people. The information that it contains is carefully checked and is authoritative.

Now let us consider a few of the preventive measures with which your physician is familiar and which he is making use of in his daily work. Of course, there are other measures equally important, but time permits me to mention only a few.

Most mothers now know what is meant by the term "prenatal care" and realize that there are signs and symptoms in the expectant mother which may indicate dangers, and complications can be controlled or prevented from causing serious damage to mother or child. This the physician tries to do and his efforts will be more successful if he has the opportunity to see the patient early in pregnancy and to observe her carefully as her term approaches. Then, also, he has an opportunity to apply safeguards during confinement and finally, in the aftercare, he can in most cases prevent such calamities as hemorrhage and infection in the mother and blindness in the child.

Since children have been mentioned, it should be emphasized that the physician's part in the first few months of the child's life should be an important one. Constant vigilance is needed. Weight and growth must be observed, feeding supervised, and, at the proper time, preventive measures against diphtheria and smallpox must be instituted.

After the child is in school there will be a certain amount of supervision by school physician and nurse and obvious defects and tendencies may be called to the attention of the parents, but it is the family physician who should be consulted at intervals so that, with his knowledge of past history and environment, he can be on the lookout for conditions possibly not quite so obvious. You will find him willing and anxious to co-operate with the school authorities.

Teeth must be watched, nose and throat looked after, growth and posture observed, mental habits noted, as well as a host of other conditions. Your physician may need the help of a specialist in some of his preventive work, but he will tell you about it, if he does.

And so we go on past childhood into the adolescent age when so much can be accomplished by an intelligent physician, aided by the family efforts, but time is short and there is still something to be said to many of you, who have gotten along a bit farther in life. All diseases cannot be entirely eliminated and it may well be that your kind of prevention may consist of checking or altering something you have already so that you may add materially to your span of years.

Such diseases as diabetes and pernicious anemia may now be favorably altered by appropriate treatment. Tuberculosis no longer needs to be a fatal disease in many instances. Many cases of cancer may be cured when discovered and properly treated in the early stages.

What about your weight, your posture, your exercise, your digestion? You have your car inspected and your watch regulated. Isn't it a sensible thing to have yourself looked over once in a while? And don't make the intervals too long.

It is said that one of the first duties of citizenship is the conservation of one's health and it is the suggestion of the Department of Public Health that this can best be done by taking advantage of the advice and counsel which only your physician can give. Talk it over with your doctor.

INFANTILE PARALYSIS

By GAYLORD W. ANDERSON, M. D.

Director, Division of Communicable Diseases
Massachusetts Department of Public Health

During the past summer, the occurrence of infantile paralysis has, unfortunately, caused far more excitement and apprehension than the situation actually warranted. We are so helpless to prevent the spread of this infection, and the crippling that it so often leaves behind is so distressing and heart-rending, that it is little wonder the public should be somewhat panic-stricken when the disease occurs in the community. Unfortunately, in our panic and apprehension regarding the rare and occasional case of infantile paralysis, we have overlooked the far greater damage caused by the more common yet more serious measles or whooping cough. It is suitable therefore that in this broadcast under the joint auspices of the Massachusetts Medical Society and the State Department of Public Health, we should give some consideration to some of our popular fears and misconceptions about infantile paralysis.

I have already remarked that the popular fear this past summer was out of all proportion to the real seriousness of the situation. As a matter of fact, 1935 would not under ordinary circumstances be thought of as a particularly bad infantile paralysis year. The fact is that the public was all set for infantile paralysis. An outbreak developed in North Carolina in May and spreading out to Virginia, Maryland and other neighboring states made the eastern part of the country apprehensive as to what might occur elsewhere. Thus, the later and unrelated development of cases in New England and New York found a public already on edge so that any case caused greater apprehension than in most years.

It is true that the official records show a very high number of cases reported in Massachusetts, confined very largely to the eastern half of the State. It is also true that as compared with other years, and even as compared with some other states, these figures bulked large. But did this really mean that the disease was that much more prevalent in Massachusetts. The answer is decidedly "No!" because of the fact that many mild nonparalyzed cases were being reported this year that in other states and in other years were not being so recorded. A number of years ago the only way that infantile paralysis was diagnosed was on the basis of the actual paralysis which might or might not be lasting. But medical science progresses so that as years have passed we have more and more learned how to recognize the mild forms of the disease, that are so mild that no paralysis develops at any time. It is obvious that if these are counted in one year and not in another, the figures for the year in which they are counted will appear large as compared with those for the year when they are not counted, especially if they bulk large in the total number of cases. In 1916 almost all the cases were paralyzed. In some states this year over 90 per cent of the cases were paralyzed. But in Massachusetts the number that were paralyzed amounted to less than half of the total, and in some sections to barely one-fourth. It is obvious, therefore, that the official figures announced from day to day gave a distorted picture of the real prevalence of the disease as compared with other years and other states. So much for the present year.

What, briefly, do we know about this disease? There can be no doubt today that the disease is a true infection, caused by a living organism known as a filterable virus. This fact has been so well substantiated by so many different workers that it needs no further confirmation. The evidence is also overwhelming to show that this virus spreads from person to person, usually through the nose and throat secretions, and that in all probability healthy carriers are the principal spreaders of this as of certain other diseases. It is also apparent that most of us become immune to the disease before we reach adult life, an immunity which most observers believe is due to contact with the germs resulting in mild undiagnosed infections which may be infantile paralysis in its mildest form without the slightest suggestion of any paralysis at any time. It is increasingly apparent that only in rare instances do those exposed to the germs develop a severe paralyzing form of the disease and that this is because of some constitutional factor that makes the individual more susceptible to the paralytic effects, whereas other individuals may escape without paralysis. Some have even suggested that this constitutional factor may run in families. Regardless of the correctness of this latter theory, there can be little doubt today as to the soundness of the observation that infantile paralysis is a disease spread essentially from person to person and in which only a small faction of those exposed to the germs develop a recognizable form of the disease, the rest apparently developing a resistance to it.

In order to explain some of the apparent anomalies of the disease some have suggested that insects or other animals might be responsible for its spread. The hand of suspicion has also been pointed at fruits and vegetables. It has been popularly supposed that a frost or the advent of cold weather would stop an outbreak. Such hypotheses have overlooked the well-established fact that when infantile paralysis begins in a community it spreads by regular progression into neighboring communities, just as when a stone is dropped in a clear pool of water the ripples spread in all directions. In those sections where the disease begins early it will end early, and in those where it begins late it will not end until late. But the progression of the disease through any community is just as steady and regular as is the spread of an epidemic of measles.

Such thoughts do not, of course, tell us how to escape infantile paralysis. In fact, no one knows how to do it today. The most recent attempt has been through the use of various vaccines, but it cannot be said that these have been shown to be effective or safe. In the meantime, however, if we only keep in mind a few of the well-established facts about the disease we can at least avoid many of the foolish and useless measures that fear and panic so often prompt in us.

Finally a word of comfort and advice to those whose misfortune it has been to have a child paralyzed by the disease. One of the most fascinating and hopeful stories of medical achievement could be told about work that has been done in restoring to those crippled by the disease the normal or an effective use of the crippled parts. Paralysis is no longer a warrant that spells permanent disability, but rather it is the spur to bring forth the best in the surgeons and the parents to restore that child to normal life. I mention the parents advisedly for they play as great a role as does the patient or the surgeon, for on them falls the all-important task of carrying out the directions carefully given for the daily care of the patient. And upon them rests the necessity for a faith and an optimism that will keep steadfastly toward the goal of recovery through the application of sound and well established medical and surgical practices without departure into the tempting yet treacherous field of pseudomedicine that purports to offer quick cures for conditions that require time, skill and patience. There is no short cut to recovery for the paralyzed. The road to recovery is long, without obvious change from day to day, from week to week or even from month to month. It is little wonder then, that parents may be lured to attempt cures that are held out as promising so much in so short a time, unmindful of the fact that a muscle damaged by infantile paralysis needs slow and painstaking development lest it be permanently damaged by having too great burden placed upon it. The best advice that can be given to the parents in such cases is that they select a physician in whom they have the utmost confidence and let him guide their steps along the long path that is before them in restoring to their child the normal function of the paralyzed parts.

The message of infantile paralysis is thus not one of hopelessness. It is true that so far as regards escaping the disease, one cannot avoid a somewhat fatalistic point of view, as he does about other diseases such as influenza, meningitis and the like. Perhaps some day medical knowledge will progress to the point where control will be possible as for smallpox, typhoid and diphtheria. In the meantime, however, the principal attention must rest upon restoring normal function to those crippled by the disease, a line of endeavor in which remarkable and outstanding achievements have been made by medical and surgical science.

EAR, NOSE AND THROAT DISEASES

By CHARLES I. JOHNSON, M. D.

Boston, Mass.

The most frequent illness among all classes in the temperate zone, is the common cold, or upper respiratory infection, and it causes more loss of time from work and school than any other disease. Investigations in isolated districts of the Tropics have shown that colds are self-limited infections of about a week's duration, and in these isolated districts, there are practically no complications. The cause is a germ too small to be recovered and is passed from person to person by contact. However, in our crowded cities essentially every cold is complicated by secondary invaders or germs, usually the streptococcus or pneumococcus because these germs are omnipresent. It is these secondary invaders that cause all the troubles following colds, such as sinusitis, tonsillitis, bronchitis, pleurisy, pneumonia, abscessed ears, mastoiditis, and meningitis. The cold makes the soil fertile and these enemies of mankind go to work insidiously. Almost any acute disease we might mention starts with symptoms that resemble a cold or upper respiratory infection, viz., scarlet fever, measles, chicken pox, mumps, appendicitis, typhoid fever, etc.

Certain individuals and even families seem predisposed to colds. They "catch cold at every opportunity," often three or four times a year, and with repeated colds sooner or later get some of the complications.

It is highly advisable for such predisposed individuals to procure good medical care and study to know if there is some underlying weakness or disease that makes them more subject to colds than others. Some of these conditions may be chronic tonsillitis or adenoids, anemia or internal gland disturbance. Even if nothing wrong has been found, much can be done. The general resistance can be built up by proper diet, sufficient rest and sleep, avoiding fatigue, crowded places and keeping away from people with colds, taking moderate exercise, cod liver oil and other vitamins, and frequently vaccines may be of help in building up resistance against these complications of colds.

It is possible to get a severe throat or sinus or ear infection without the preceding cold, viz. Trench Mouth or Vincent's Angina can be dangerous and it is spread by public dishes and glasses or contact. All of you are familiar with swimming ears and sinuses or abscessed ears and infected sinuses contracted in salt or fresh water bathing. The swimming ears and sinusitis are caused by infected water getting into sinuses or the middle ears from the nasal side and never come from water getting into the ear canals, unless there is a perforated ear drum.

Many systematic diseases may manifest themselves in the throat as ulcerations or inflammatory changes. Pernicious anemia, leukemia, syphilis, the comparatively new disease of agranulocytosis, where the white corpuscles disappear from the blood stream, and advanced kidney disease are examples of this. In people past fifty cancer of the throat may show distinct throat symptoms.

Tonsils and adenoids are removed by general practitioners, surgeons and specialists everywhere, at all ages and for various reasons, but it seems fair to say that repeated attacks of tonsillitis with swollen glands are the best indication that the tonsils should be removed. Repeated earaches with ear-abscess formation are frequently remedied by a tonsillectomy and adenoidectomy, removal of tonsils and adenoids, particularly the latter. Recurrent colds may not be too favorably affected by removal of the tonsils and adenoids even though the tonsils appear large and chronically infected. The tonsils may need to be removed, but the operation may not prevent future colds.

At the House of the Good Samaritan, where acute rheumatic fever is being investigated in a most thorough fashion, we do tonsillectomies, removal of tonsils, when indicated on well selected cases. The tonsils are never removed during activity of the rheumatic fever as shown by elevation of the temperature and pulse rate and laboratory tests, but always during a period of quiescence. If tonsillectomy and adenoidectomy, removal of the tonsils and adenoids, is done during activity, it causes the rheumatic fever to flare up and is harmful. If the rheumatic fever child is susceptible to upper respiratory infections or colds and sore throats, the rheumatic fever is helped by tonsillectomy and adenoidectomy, removal of tonsils and adenoids, which is done in a quiescent stage, to the extent that upper respiratory infections are lessened or tonsillitis is avoided. There seems to be some definite relationship between the unknown cause of rheumatic fever and repeated upper respiratory infections or colds, the cause of which is also unknown.

At the Channing Home excellent results have been obtained in building up the well selected tubercular patients, by doing local tonsillectomies.

The tonsils removed have been found, in the laboratory, to be infected with tuberculosis and yet the tissues heal perfectly. In one case, a chronic tuberculous peritonsillar abscess or Quinsy sore throat with a constantly draining pathway was cured immediately by tonsillectomy, removal of tonsils, and because of the selection, for operation, of cases with definitely diseased tonsils, the general condition has been improved in every single case. Let me reiterate that the tonsillectomy, removal of tonsils, is done on these tubercular patients in an attempt to free them from colds and sore throats thereby raising their resistance and not for removal of tuberculous tissue.

At Peabody Home, the crippled children are given the benefit of a tonsillectomy and adenoidectomy, removal of tonsils and adenoids, where the indications are proper and frequently they are benefited as shown by a gain in weight, appetite and less susceptibility to upper respiratory infections. In these crippled children, it is often difficult with their braces and casts, to find a position in which the operation can be done.

It is better to wait until the age of four or five years for a tonsillectomy unless the indications are clean cut, but adenoids are often removed of necessity and with benefit in children under one year of age. Occasionally a poorly selected candidate for a tonsillectomy and adenoidectomy, removal of tonsils and adenoids, is made worse by the operation. That is, instead of a periodic cold or slight sore throat they periodically develop croup or bronchitis.

The indications for tonsillectomy, removal of tonsils, in adults are somewhat different than in children, for in adult life focal infection plays a greater role. By focal infection, we mean a local diseased area such as infected tonsils, teeth, or gall bladder causing or abetting arthritis, bursitis, neuritis, muscular rheumatism, heart and kidney disease, ulcer of the stomach, colitis, or appendicitis. I do not believe that sinusitis or chronic mastoiditis, particularly the latter, so often act as foci of infection, although recently an office patient was repeatedly cured of hives for twenty-four hours when her infected sinus was emptied, only to contract hives again when it filled up. With a cure of the sinusitis, the hives entirely disappeared.

There are a variety of types of arthritis, and in some types removal of foci is contraindicated, viz. gout, so it is very important to classify and study each case.

In the acute infectious arthritis, where sudden onset of joint pains occurs in an otherwise normal individual, removal of foci usually brings pleasing results.

I will mention electro-coagulation or diathermy removal of tonsils only to damn the procedure and say that I do not feel it should be used on any type of tonsils.

Any cold that hangs on longer than a fortnight should be investigated by your doctor, particularly if there is headache or yellow discharge from the nose, as these symptoms may be due to sinus infection and as early sinus disease is much more easily cured than chronic sinusitis. The sinuses are hollow spaces in the bones of the face and head that connect with the nose and their chief functions are to warm the inspired air and give resonance to the voice. Infection of these sinuses besides occasionally leading to serious brain disease or mastoids, may interfere with one's vocal resonance and lead to chronic nasal discharge, deafness, asthma or chronic hoarseness and cough. Prevent the colds or care for them and you will likely prevent much sinusitis. Once you have developed a sinus infection, treatment is necessary but very seldom is surgery needed in cases properly cared for from the onset. If spraying the nose with shrinking solutions, using mild antiseptic irrigations, etc. will not bring about an immediate cure, it may be necessary to remove a piece of the turbinate bone or correct a deviated septum in order to obtain proper ventilation and drainage. These are minor procedures and may obviate chronic sinusitis. "Once a sinus, always a sinus" is true only in a small percentage of these cases and we feel that some unknown factor is lowering the tissue resistance in this group, preventing a cure or else the operator is too timid to do a complete and thorough operation.

Chronic progressive hoarseness not following upper respiratory infections may be caused in adults by tuberculosis of the larynx which practically always is part of lung tuberculosis, or in older people by cancer, and at any adult age by syphilis.

Nasal obstruction is caused by adenoids, spurs or deviations of the middle partition or nasal septum, sinusitis and in children a common cause of unilateral nasal obstruction with discharge, is a bean or peanut or pencil eraser in one nostril.

As we have already mentioned, abscessed ears and mastoids are usually preceded by the upper respiratory infections, but in many cases come as a result of swimming. Prevent or take care of the upper respiratory infection and avoid too much diving and waterlogging of the tender membranes of the nose and you will prevent many mastoids. When an individual develops an earache, the ear should be examined by someone familiar with ears and in a great many cases of earache early opening of the drum will relieve pain and prevent mastoiditis. Repeated ear abscesses may lead to a certain amount of deafness as will chronic sinusitis and frequent colds, but simple mastoidectomies, that is, the type of operation done for ears draining not over one to two months, and when properly done, will prevent deafness. The old adage—"Running ears are all right so long as they run," is incorrect because any chronic discharging ear can suddenly explode into meningitis or brain abscess and only your specialist is capable of caring for these. Headache with a chronic running ear may be an ominous symptom.

Removing the tonsils and adenoids prevents deafness to the extent that the chronic congestion and swelling of the Eustachian tubes is lessened. The Eustachian tubes are small passageways between the back of the nose and the middle ears. It is only through these openings that the middle ear is ventilated or drained of its natural secretion, the ear drums being altogether intact.

Scarlet fever and measles often result in ear abscesses and mastoids, and ear infection during these contagious diseases should be especially watched to avoid chronically draining ears and deafness. In mumps there is a powerful toxin which may affect the inner ears and mumps is one of the most common causes of unilateral deafness in childhood. Mumps should be taken seriously because of its many curious complications.

You often hear nowadays of the glands of internal secretion chiefly through the thyroid; goitre is usually where there is too much secretion from the thyroid and myxedema is where there is too little. In this latter disturbance, myxedema, we often get deafness which may be cured by taking thyroid extract, so your medical man or your children's pediatrician should know that your internal glands are functioning properly.

There are over ten million deaf people in the United States and more than three million school children, many of whom can be helped.

COLLAPSE TREATMENT IN TUBERCULOSIS

By ALTON S. POPE, M. D.

Director, Division of Tuberculosis
Massachusetts Department of Public Health

New hope has come to the tuberculosis patient in the past few years in rumors that something could now be done for the "hopeless" case. This "something" has sometimes been referred to as "gas treatment" or "air", or as "surgery." Broadly, it may be included in the term "collapse therapy." Specifically, collapse treatment consists of three procedures, or modifications and combinations of the three: Pneumothorax, phrenic nerve cutting, and thoracoplasty. The aim of all three is the same: To allow the diseased lung or part of the lung to collapse so it may heal.

During the past century innumerable "cures" for tuberculosis have been brought forward only to be discredited by experience. Serums and chemicals have raised the hopes of the consumptive till he is rightly critical of every new treatment proposed. Out of this welter of trial and error three principles of treatment have emerged, proper diet, fresh air and rest; and the greatest of these is rest. When quiet, a normal person breathes some sixteen to eighteen times a minute; when he walks, this rate is increased; and when he runs, it is greatly increased. By complete rest in bed the activity of the lung can be reduced to a minimum. This is the essence of rest treatment in tuberculosis.

Collapse treatment is essentially an extension of rest to the diseased lung. In pneumothorax air is gradually introduced into the chest cavity, between the lung and the chest wall, till the lung shrinks down to a ball no larger than a man's fist. It does not expand in breathing, the circulation nearly stops and the diseased part can heal. At the beginning of pneumothorax it is necessary to introduce additional air into the chest every few days to keep the lung collapsed. Later the interval between refills can be increased to one or two weeks or longer. After a year or two, if all goes well, the lung is allowed to re-expand and takes up its work as before.

In a certain number of cases where a fairly good collapse has been obtained with pneumothorax the cough continues and the temperature does not come down to normal. Often in such instances the x-ray shows a cavity in the lung still held open by adhesions so that healing cannot take place. To meet this condition Dr. Jacobaeus, a Swedish physician, has developed an operation known as pneumolysis. This ingenious procedure consists of introducing into the chest cavity on one side a tiny electric light. On the other side of the chest an electric cautery is introduced between the ribs and by skillful manipulation narrow adhesions which prevent complete collapse of the lung are burned through. Only a small proportion of pneumothorax patients need this type of operation, but in properly chosen cases it greatly increases the effectiveness of collapse.

The phrenic nerve operation is another method of resting a diseased lung. When the nerve is cut, the diaphragm, the floor of the chest, rises some two to four inches and the lung on that side is compressed by about one-fourth to one-third. This again reduces the work of the lung and favors healing.

In more serious cases where the lung cannot be sufficiently collapsed by either of these measures, it is sometimes possible to get a permanent collapse by removing a part of the ribs on one side in what is known as the thoracoplasty operation. Breathing is, of course, carried on by the other lung. No deformity is noticeable through the clothing and the use of the arm on the affected side is not interfered with.

Thoracoplasty is usually attempted only on patients whose disease cannot be checked by simpler measures. Yet in properly chosen cases it often brings about an arrest of the disease when the outlook was otherwise hopeless. Over 100 patients at Rutland have had thoracoplasties, and nearly all have made excellent recoveries.

It was an English physician, Dr. James Carson of Liverpool, who over a hundred years ago first made the observation that a rather surprising number of recoveries from tuberculosis took place in patients who suffered whole or partial collapse of one lung. Another Englishman, Dr. James Houghton, was the first to collapse a lung artificially, as treatment. After him Italian and German doctors took up the treatment and perfected the technique of pneumothorax. Dr. J. B. Murphy of Chicago introduced the procedure in America. A Boston man, Dr. Cleaveland Floyd, Director of the Boston Tuberculosis Clinics, was called to Saranac Lake, in 1911, to give pneumothorax treatment to Dr. Trudeau. Since then its use has gradually increased, but only the last eight to ten years have seen its widespread application in this country.

Since we must all breathe to live, it is obvious that all forms of collapse therapy must be largely limited to the patient with one good lung. If the second lung is seriously involved, collapse of the other side throws a double load upon it and tends to hasten a fatal outcome. Also the diseased lung may be so tied to the chest wall by adhesions that collapse is impossible. Roughly only about two-thirds of all tuberculosis patients are suitable for collapse treatment. Furthermore, all forms of chest surgery call for some special training and the best of medical and surgical judgment is required. It is not a trifling matter to collapse a lung and without proper precautions serious results may ensue. Recent studies by the American Sanatorium Association show that in a large series of cases satisfactory pneumothorax could be obtained in only about forty per cent of the cases attempted, yet among this forty per cent the death rate was only one-seventh that of the patients with incomplete collapse.

At the Rutland State Sanatorium pneumothorax treatment was started about 1915. Limited at first to a few special cases its use has been gradually extended with our growing knowledge of the procedure. Three years ago it became necessary to add a special medical and surgical building to care for the collapse therapy work at the institution. In the development of chest surgery at Rutland we have been especially fortunate in having the guidance and assistance of Dr. E. D. Churchill of the Massachusetts General Hospital. At first all major operations were performed by Dr. Churchill as staff consultant. Since the opening of the Medical and Surgical Building all collapse procedures except thoracoplasties are being carried out at the Sanatorium.

At present approximately 70 per cent of the patients at Rutland are receiving some form of collapse treatment. Of these about two-thirds have pneumothorax alone. At Rutland, however, collapse therapy is never a routine procedure. Each case is brought up several times at staff conferences and only after all the possibilities have been carefully weighed is a decision made. Even after collapse has been secured the patient must be closely watched with fluoroscope and x-ray to be sure the lung does not re-expand nor complications occur. On account of lack of sufficient sanatorium beds, a few cities have recently begun starting collapse treatment in ambulant patients. Besides subjecting unsupervised patients to certain rather definite risks, such a procedure seems a direct contradiction of the principle involved; namely, to give the diseased lung a degree of rest which cannot be secured by bodily rest alone. For, it should be remembered, collapse therapy is not a panacea in itself, but rather a valuable adjunct to the fundamental procedures of proper diet, fresh air, and mental and physical rest.

With the increasing use of collapse therapy it becomes more important than ever that cases of tuberculosis be discovered early. Where the disease has been going on for months or years the lung is often so adherent to the chest wall that no collapse can be secured by pneumothorax. Also if both lungs have become seriously involved, collapse therapy is out of the question. Massachusetts sanatoria offer a grade of medical and surgical treatment for tuberculosis not excelled anywhere, but if we are to use these resources effectively the man on the street must be ready to avail himself of modern facilities for the diagnosis of tuberculosis including x-ray, and the tuberculosis patient must be willing to go to the sanatorium at the time when he can benefit most by any form of treatment.

ILLNESS AND CHARACTER
BY LEROY E. PARKINS, M. D.
Boston, Mass.

I will consider the subject of illness and character from the viewpoint of how character may affect one's health either for good or evil. By illness, I mean deviation from a normal, happy, and healthy state of being. By this definition one does not have to be sick in bed to be considered ill. Everything in existence is in a process of building up or tearing down; the human body combines these two processes in a most amazing way. Our health is measured by the delicate balance between these two forces. These forces include the mental and spiritual aspects of life, as well as the material conditions such as disease and accidents, which may impair our health. We might term any disease an accident, since we do not in sane moments intentionally inflict ill health upon ourselves.

Our knowledge of the causes of the disease and the breakdown of health has increased remarkably, especially since the middle of the nineteenth century when bacteria were discovered by the great French scientist, Louis Pasteur. Various other conditions may bring about illness; for instance, we do not know the cause of cancer; many eminent scientists are working earnestly to discover this secret. I firmly believe that the cause of cancer will ultimately be found. About one-half of all sick people are mentally ill; one-half of all hospital beds are for patients who have mental disease. It is to the credit of the human race that we have come to realize that these people are not possessed of demons, but are spiritually and mentally sick. As long as people consider the soul, mind, and body as separate units and deal with them as independent realities, much confusion must exist. After all, when we are sick, we are sick more or less all over. It has been said that even a philosopher cannot be philosophic when he has the toothache; I think this is right; what he needs and wants is a good dentist, not soothsaying with pleasant phrases.

I wish to encourage you to have a great faith in your own powers to overcome the major as well as the minor accidents of life. No life worth living is without some difficult problem. Vicissitudes are frequently the measuring rod of our will power. A succession of inspiring names comes before us to give us reason for renewing our faith that even the major accidents in life may be overcome. Who would trade his eyesight for fame or immortality? Blindness is considered a great cross. We look to the blind Milton as an inspired soul. He achieved wonderfully in spite of this infirmity. In this valley of everlasting shadows great souls are often born. So many people have read Robert Louis Stevenson's beautiful stories; he had eyes to see, but lived through many years with tuberculosis. His indomitable character rose high above his physical accident, and he achieved well.

Beethoven, the master musician and composer, was stone deaf, and he has left us a priceless gift in his music. Heine, the great poet, was half paralyzed; he wrote his inspiring poems while lying flat on his back. Gibbon, the great historian, wrote a history of the world although he was a chronic invalid.

Among our own friends and acquaintances you no doubt know many people who are making a success in spite of infirmities and disease. Do not pity people too much—rather give words of encouragement; help them to have courage to endure pain. At least be cheerful; help them to feel that they may inspire others by their own example of cheer and hope; fortitude is a virtue worth cultivating.

Frequently a doctor sees people with a long illness or chronic invalidism approaching and he wonders how they will accept the situation. Certainly I feel much more optimistic and hopeful when the patient exhibits sterling ideals of character. It gives the doctor inspiration to seek and find the causes of disease in order to give the needed advice for regaining health. It is like nailing your colors to the mast; your ship must not go down except with the colors flying. It matters not so much how long we live as how we live.

It has been my privilege to see various excellent surgeons operate, and it is a well-known fact that surgeons do not like to operate on people who think they are going to die. If an overwhelming fear creeps into the heart and mind of a person it may actually retard quick recovery. This is an example of character in a crisis. As doctors we talk of reserve force; we know there is such a thing and we label this force with such names as glucose, glycogen, adrenalin, and other equally pleasant names. Emerson says that character is a reserve force which acts directly without means; we like to count on this force too in waging a war on disease.

I suppose fears of one kind or another rob a great many poeple of much reserve force in a crisis. So often our fears are ungrounded; yet we must wonder until we know. Doctors are often embarrassed by well-intentioned friends or relatives by being asked not to tell the patient if he or she has a "serious disease." If you have confidence enough in a doctor to call him, please have confidence in him to say what is best for the patient. Our teaching is to always consider the patient's needs, comfort, happiness, and general well-being first of all. A good doctor would be the last one to cause grief or unhappiness to patient or relatives. I have told many people that they had various diseases and have never seen anyone yet who flinched. I first ask a patient if he wants to know what is wrong. If he doesn't want to know. of course he is not told, unless quarantine laws make it necessary. In dealing with intelligent responsible people, I have never seen anyone who was distressed by being told the truth about themselves if they wished to know. A kindly explanation in understandable language does much to dispel anxiety and fears; it also gives reassurance and strength to the spirit.

Dr. Joslin says concerning the treatment of diabetes, that knowledge counts, but knowledge alone will not save the patient. He says diabetes is a disease which tests the character of the patient, for successful treatment demands wisdom, honesty, self control, and courage. These virtues are among the essentials of a good character.

Character is also one of the main ingredients in the cure of many other diseases. Tuberculosis is known universally as a serious disease, but it can be helped and frequently arrested if the patient assumes responsibility and exercises obedience to the known laws for recovery. It is necessary to have will power to rest, sleep and eat properly. Oftentimes no medicine is necessary and the physician finds his chief function is to inspire hope and courage in the patient to do the simple things necessary to regain health and strength.

One of the popular things to do is to diet for one reason or another. Rarely should one start on any strict program of dieting without a doctor's advice. Following any diet program that restricts our liberties is a test of character. Temptation comes at least three times per day. You can banish most of the temptation by realizing that you are an individual person who has his own life to live. Don't make the mistake of comparing yourself to someone else. We each have a standard or ideal of living entirely distinct from all other people in the world. Fortunately most of the time our likes and needs are very similar; this allows us to get automobiles and breakfast foods at reasonable prices. But, suppose you are told to eat this or omit that food. Here you set your standard anew and this should no longer be a temptation. When driving on a well-marked highway we do not attempt an excursion into side roads and expect a quick arrival at our destination—we lose time both going off the road and returning. Living up to our best standard of life pays big dividends in health and personal satisfaction.

Also, it is well to consider that what is best for you is usually best for everybody. If you fail to care for yourself by proper thinking, sleep, rest, and eating, it may make you less efficient or retard complete recovery from illness, thus adding expense and anxiety for yourself and maybe your family and friends.

Our character is a great reality; it is ourselves, built of the past and crystallized in the present; it is the substance which casts our shadow into the future; it is the spark that glows when the body fades. The great thing about character is that it is a continuous building process; it can be improved, added to, and beautified—or it may rust, decay, and crumble from neglect. Life at its best is a continuous growth of ourselves in character. A good character is the true foundation for the best health of mind and body; it is the keystone of spiritual happiness.

I would urge and advise you all to think and act sanely even in the presence of danger and disease. I am firmly convinced that we are greater than anything that can happen to us, so with a rising courage meet life as it comes. Emerson said: "Nobody can cheat you out of ultimate success but yourself." A victorious life may be lived in spite of vicissitudes and infirmity. May your insight into your personal problems be better and your courage rise high to meet each new day, whatever it may bring.

CHILD HYGIENE

By M. Luise Diez, M. D.

Director, Division of Child Hygiene
Massachusetts Department of Public Health

The program for child care is largely one of education—education for the community and for the parent as well as for the child. It has been very interesting to watch during recent years the nation-wide progress in adult education, a very significant social movement, particularly so when we realize how much of it is based on consideration of the health of the child in its many aspects and through the various age groups, beginning with the period before birth through the period of adolescence.

The larger program for child welfare aims to instruct the parents in the best methods for the protection of child health, mental and physical, and to assist in bringing about these environmental conditions which will have the most favorable influence on the child.

When possible and practicable, the health department should assume the leadership in this, cooperating with those agencies within the community which are also interested in child welfare. To do this the community must make it possible—it is a community problem.

Informed public opinion helps to make a cooperative community and will afford facilities for leadership by providing trained personnel and an adequate budget for the official agencies, and support for the nonofficial agency.

Due consideration should be given to the non-official agencies working in the field of health, child health particularly, for they have contributed and are contributing large sums of money yearly to the public health field and are giving valuable assistance.

In considering programs of health activities for the child we find there is shown a steadily progressive but unequal development. For the infant and the school child in the elementary grades, a fairly equal development of program is found, but as yet it is far from adequate. When we consider two or rather three very important periods in the child's life—the prenatal, preschool and adolescent—we find a situation which is being met inadequately.

Every community has a definite responsibility for intelligent care of the potential and expectant mother to insure her a safe pregnancy, a well-conducted labor, careful nursing and postnatal supervision with the minimum of danger to herself and her child. To accomplish this, there must be an analysis of existing conditions with a carefully planned program and a community prepared and organized to accept and apply the program.

Education of the various groups in the community is a necessary feature of the program and in order to reach these groups it must be well thought out and adapted to the levels you desire to reach. This is done by lecture, radio, classes, through films, exhibits, posters, by the printed word, by demonstration and consultation—all to be done by those who are qualified to teach.

The inclusion of maternity hygiene in a public health program is necessary if we are going to solve our child problem intelligently.

Research work carried on in the field of public health as well as in the field of obstetrics, clearly points out to us the factors involved which must be met before we can conserve the health of the mother and prevent the fearful waste of child life and the maiming and crippling as well. How much of a problem in your own community are maternal deaths, to say nothing of the chronic illnesses, if they can be measured; how much of a problem are stillbirths—these numbers are showing very little general decrease, yet we know they can be reduced materially. What is your prematurity rate and what is the rate of those who die before they are a month old? And after you *do* know this, what are you going to do about it?

The time has passed when we can afford to sit complacently by and ignore the situation. Our efficiency will be measured by the success we show in bringing about reduction to the minimum in these rates.

Whatever method employed, it must include prenatal care, skilled attendance at delivery and afterwards by physician and nurse, with cooperation on the part of the individual concerned, her family and the community.

The facilities provided should be skilled medical care, prenatal nursing, which should be available for everyone in the community who desires it, prenatal clinics if the needs of the community warrant it, adequate hospital service and also bedside nursing should be provided through suitable organizations. With these and individual and group instruction, you have set up a maternity program through cooperative effort.

The period of the child's life before birth is perhaps the most complex of its life, at least it is the period of most rapid growth and development and is dependent upon the mother wholly.

The next most critical period is the first month of life, but it is difficult to reach the child at this time unless contact has been made previously.

Early registration of births may assist the health department to do this through its nursing staff, but the welfare of the child at this time lies in the hands of the physician, the hospital, the nursing attendant and the family, and until all assume the responsibility our early death rates will remain much the same.

The health program for the infant and preschool child is still not receiving its proper emphasis in the community program. Although our death rates have decreased for the age group from one month to one year, there are other problems of this group that have not been met and that come well within the scope of health departments. Among these are sanitation and housing, safe milk supply and control of communicable disease. There is a close relationship between the amount of public health effort expended and the saving of child life and prevention of sickness. Infant feeding, an educational problem, as is also prevention of respiratory diseases that are taking the lead now with the lessening of gastro-intestinal diseases, vaccination against smallpox and immunization against diphtheria, continuous medical supervision with prompt correction of defects, parental instruction for guidance and training of the child should be the concern of the health department whether carried on directly through its own personnel or through others. The medical, social and educational aspects of the task cannot be separated and should apply to all age periods. Care of the preschool child is a problem whose handling has been made easier by definite knowledge, except perhaps in the more rural areas, but it is being neglected by those whose public duty it is, and this neglect is an economic waste.

For the preschool group there should be provided an intensive project in dental hygiene. To be entirely effectual this should be incorporated in the maternity program and carried through all the age groups including the adult. Prevention of dental defects is the only solution of the stupendous problem that faces us all today.

Every public health worker must have a comprehensive understanding of the subject and its application to do effectual work in his or her field.

As mental hygiene touches upon all the activities of life, it has a significant place in health work and should have its place in a community program closely associated with the physical health program.

The child's path through life is beset with many difficulties which necessitate constant adaptation and adjustment in his emotional life and oftentimes added to this there is further need because of physical handicaps. Every assistance should be given by the health agency to have established in the community such facilities as may bring about a coordinated program for child adjustment.

Those children who are handicapped by irremediable defects such as the crippled child and others should be given special services.

The preschool program is directed more or less toward building a foundation of health that will fit the child to receive its formal education through the school.

Again it is interesting to have seen develop through the years the serious efforts that have been made to accomplish this, largely through local efforts stimulated by national movements.

At present the nursery school with the kindergarten offers an opportunity for work with the younger group and may assist in bridging the serious gap in child care that exists at the beginning of school life.

Adolescence is a period during which we can least afford to withdraw our help thereby losing the opportunity for giving further knowledge. The mental hygiene of this age group is particularly important and the community program should include this group.

Health hazards arise as soon as the child enters industry, consequently the child in industry is the responsibility of the health department. Recreation for the child from the preschool period through adolescence may not be the immediate concern of the health department, but it should be of interest as a community project and will be found to be an important adjunct to its own program.

The Division of Child Hygiene offers assistance through its staff and its educational material, to communities and individuals interested in promoting the health of the child and carries on a definite state-wide program of education.

VIOLENCE AND PUBLIC HEALTH

BY LINCOLN DAVIS, M. D.

Boston, Mass.

Today everyone is interested in health. This is manifest in the number of health talks, health meetings, and health columns in the newspapers which everywhere greet the eye and ear. The enormous progress made in the control and prevention of disease is one of the triumphs of modern civilization. This could never have been achieved by the medical profession or the public health services alone without the active cooperation and support of the general public. An educated and enlightened public is willing to accept the discomfort of vaccination in order to eliminate smallpox, and cheerfully endures many other uncomfortable measures to prevent the spread of infectious disease. The taxpayer willingly supports huge expenditures for public sanitation, for pure water supplies, safe sewage and waste disposal, food inspection, etc.

As a result of this spirit of cooperation on the part of the people with the health authorities and the medical profession, many epidemic diseases which in the past decimated the population, such as plague, smallpox, cholera, dysentery, yellow fever, typhus and typhoid fever, have been practically banished from the land. As the cause of one germ disease after another has been discovered, and methods of prevention or control secured, the mortality rates of the acute infectious diseases have shown a steady and striking decline. Influenza alone of the great infectious epidemics remains uncontrolled, and at intervals still rages unchecked throughout the civilized world.

There has been similar progress in sanitation and hygiene, and rules of rational living, unknown to our forefathers, are generally understood and accepted by the great mass of our people. Infant mortality in particular has been strikingly reduced by the dissemination of knowledge as to the proper feeding of infants.

As a result of all this progress, the span of life has been lengthened fifty per cent in the last hundred years. A century ago, a newborn child had a life expectancy of forty years, while a baby born today has an expectancy of sixty years of life. As long as man is mortal, the end must come eventually, the human machine must necessarily wear out in time. As a result of the prolongation of life by the elimination of many acute diseases which attack particularly children and young adults, there has been a relative increase in the mortality rates of the diseases of the elderly, the so-called degenerative diseases, the wearing out processes, such as hardening of the arteries, heart disease, kidney disease, and apoplexy. This increase is to be expected and must be accepted as a part of our human fate.

There is one factor in the mortality figures, however, which presents a striking contrast to the decline shown by diseases in general. This factor is a very important one, but for some strange reason it seems to be regarded by the public, which is so alert and responsive in matters of public health, with almost complete apathy.

I refer to the factor of external violence as a cause of death. This shows not only a relative, but an actual increase, and has now reached in this country truly frightful proportions.

The mortality statistics of the Census Bureau of the United States for the year 1930, the last year for which full official figures have been published, show over 95,000 deaths from accidents, over 18,000 suicides, and over 10,000 homicides, a total of over 124,000 violent deaths. These three forms of violent death together account for more victims than any single cause in the international classification of causes of death, with the single exception of heart disease. Cancer, pneumonia, kidney disease, tuberculosis, each of these grim reapers falls below the figures for external violence.

It is a striking fact that for those in the active period of life, from twenty to forty-five years of age, deaths by violence exceed any other cause of death.

The great epidemic scourges of the past fade into comparative insignificance. There were in the United States during the year 1930, no deaths from yellow fever, plague, or cholera. There were 35 deaths from typhus, and 165 from smallpox. None occurred in Massachusetts. There were somewhat over 1,000 fatal cases of infantile paralysis. The mortality figures for cancer, which presents perhaps our greatest health problem today, have shown in the last year or two an encouraging trend towards reaching a climax, and even indicate a slight decline, no doubt the result of the active educational campaign directed to the spread of knowledge as to the early symptoms of the disease and the importance of early treatment.

There are in the United States over 11,000 persons, the victims of homicide each year, two-thirds of these fatalities are caused by firearms. In the state of Massachusetts I am glad to say the homicide rate is only one-fifth of that for the country as a whole. In the year 1930 there were four cities of over 100,000 inhabitants in the United States with no homicides. Of these four, three were in Massachusetts. The homicide rate is six times higher in the negro population than in the white, and consequently the southern states show a much higher rate than the northern. The homicide rate for white people in the United States is about three times as high as in Canada, and ten times higher than England, and nearly thirty times higher than the Netherlands, which has the lowest rate in Europe. There has been a slight decline in the homicide rate noted in the last two years, but the figures are still appallingly high, and show that the United States of America is the most lawless civilized country on the globe as regards the willful taking of human life.

The prevalence of homicide is not exactly a public health problem. It is one of great complexity involving governmental, economic and social conditions, heredity, home life, environment, training and education. The scientific study of delinquency and criminology is in its infancy. A sound program of prevention can only be evolved after most careful study; but an aroused public opinion can demand that immediate steps be taken by the proper authorities to initiate a program to remove this reproach to our civilization.

The problem of suicide is more closely related to public health than is homicide. The record of the United States is better in this respect in relation to other countries. The rate in the United States is about one-half of that for the countries of Central Europe, and about the same as for England. Here again Holland has the lowest rate in Europe, about one-half the rate of the United States. In the colored population the rate is from one-half to one-tenth of that for whites. About 18,000 people die every year in this country by suicide. The estimated figures for the last year indicate that a slight decline has set in, but the number of people who destroy their own lives is a severe indictment of present-day conditions, and calls for the best efforts of every social and welfare agency to combat it.

It is the heavy toll of fatal and nonfatal accidents, however, that I wish to call to your particular attention. In 1930 there were over 95,000 fatal accidents of all kinds in the United States. The number is now estimated to be above 100,000. Of these, the fatalities caused by the automobile far exceed any other cause. There were 29,000 deaths caused by automobiles in 1930. It is estimated that for the year 1934 the number reached 35,000. Following the automobile in order of mortality are falls, drowning, burns, railroad accidents, and accidental shooting. Each year accidental drowning claims the lives of more than 7,500 persons in the United States. Four thousand are killed in railroad accidents, 3,000 die as the result of the careless handling of firearms mostly while hunting.

The nonfatal accidents which involve untold suffering, disability, and economic loss, are almost beyond calculation. The number injured by automobiles annually is estimated at almost a million, of whom one-sixth are children. The insurance companies estimate that the cost of industrial injuries alone is over five million dollars annually.

Of all forms of death it would seem that accidental deaths should be the most preventable, except those resulting from the uncontrollable convulsions of nature such as cyclones, earthquakes, floods, tidal waves, landslides, lightning, etc., which in this fortunate land have been factors of relatively minor importance. The blame is not to be laid on nature but on man. The high speed mechanized civilization of today is destroying its thousands and maiming its hundreds of thousands by direct external violence.

The human eye and hand and brain has not changed since the days of the ox cart. Meanwhile, the speed of living has been increased at least twenty-fold. No one advocates a return to the ox cart days, and we must rely on human training to control the modern mechanisms which human genius has invented, but which uncontrolled become veritable monsters of destruction.

In the investigation following so many of our great disasters it is the human element which is most often found to be at fault.

We hear a great deal about measures to promote social security, but what about security for life and limb? What is being done about that? A very notable improvement in the rate of industrial accidents and fatalities has resulted from the cooperative efforts of government, industry, labor, and the medical profession. This is certainly gratifying and encouraging and shows what can be done when conditions can be controlled.

The constantly mounting number of automobile accidents is our most acute and difficult problem right now. I have no solution to offer. It will require the intelligent co-operative efforts of our governing bodies, and of all forward looking agencies, professions and individuals to achieve a solution of this problem. The first step is certainly to awake the public conscience. Let the facts be broadcast far and wide and over and over again.

Automobile fatalities have been repeatedly compared to the casualties of war, and it is shown that the modern motor car has put the ancient god of war to shame. In the battle of Gettysburg the casualties on both sides were 5,664 killed and about 34,000 wounded. The carnage and maiming of a Gettysburg is reenacted every two months on our highways in these peaceful times. There is no valor, heroism or patriotism to mitigate this awful sacrifice to the automobile. Lives are snuffed out and limbs crushed and broken as the result of carelessness, recklessness, intoxication, and the mania for speed. Innocent children and feeble old men and women are too often the victims and still the slaughter goes on unchecked. Why is it allowed? Surely something can be done about it.

There are many agencies actively at work on this problem. Safety first campaigns promoted by humanitarian organizations all over the country are doing valiant work. Many public officials and the large insurance companies are also doing their utmost. The newspapers are certainly giving ample publicity to the prevalence of violence in our midst, and yet the general public remains strangely unmoved. Great bodies move slowly but once started their movement becomes irresistible. The vital spark to start the movement must be generated in the individual conscience. Let each one of us take this matter to heart, and resolve, whether driver or pedestrian, in taking to the road to exercise the utmost care and vigilance, to moderate undue haste, to observe sobriety, and to be considerate of the rights of others.

A stricter observance of the simple tenets of the Golden Rule would go far towards easing the problem.

THE DARKNESS OF IGNORANCE AND THE FOG OF PRUDERY

BY N. A. NELSON, M. D.

Assistant Director, Division of Communicable Diseases

The night before Christmas, in 1930, the Massachusetts Department of Public Health broadcast the story of an enormous public health problem, the control of gonorrhea and syphilis. Today, the Department is broadcasting on that subject for the eighth time.

Within the past year, one of the national broadcasting systems would not allow Dr. Thomas Parran, Jr., to mention syphilis, in a talk on health problems he had been asked to give, to the people of the United States. Dr. Parran is the Health Commissioner of New York State, and for several years he was Assistant Surgeon General of the United States Public Health Service, in charge of the control of syphilis and gonorrhea in the United States.

New Englanders are credited, by those who do not understand New Englanders, with a particularly annoying and stubborn form of prudishness. It is interesting, therefore, to compare Dr. Parran's experience with that of the Massachusetts Department of Public Health. Several New England newspapers, and at least three broadcasting stations, have given space or time to the discussion of this particular public health problem. This station, W. E. E. I., has worked with the Department for many years. At no time has it hesitated to allow the Department to discuss the control of gonorrhea and syphilis with you. Apparently, you have been as willing to hear what your Health Department has had to *say*, as this station has been willing to let the Department *say it to you*.

Some one has said that "prudery is like a wig; it is *used* to cover up a bald spot". The reluctance of some of those who control the major channels of public information, to permit discussion of this particular health problem, arises from a thorough misunderstanding of it, and an almost abysmal ignorance of the facts.

Syphilis is by no means invariably synonymous with sin. The National Health Council says that two per cent of all the children in the United States were born with that disease. It is well known to health authorities that among every hundred people who have syphilis ten will be found who were born with it. It is also well known to health authorities that if all the women who have syphilis could be adequately treated, at least during pregnancy, no more children would be born with this disease which makes them blind, deaf, feebleminded, insane and crippled, or kills them even before they are born.

How does it happen that so many children can have syphilis? The answer is pathetically simple. Well over half of the women who have the disease, are respectable, married women. Most of them were infected, after marriage, by husbands who thought they were cured before they married or who had no idea that they had syphilis. It is of course *true* that the *promiscuous* women keep the disease alive in the community, but the *innocent* victims of infection among women far outnumber the promiscuous.

Briefly, the outstanding facts concerning syphilis are these:—

1. One out of every ten or twelve persons in the United States now has or at some time has had the disease.
2. The United States Public Health Service has found that there are at least half a million new infections with syphilis in this country every year.
3. Most infections with syphilis occur in young men and women between fourteen and thirty years of age. Sixty out of every hundred infected are men and forty are women. Ten of the hundred were born with the disease.
4. About five per cent of all infections with syphilis occur through such ordinary personal contacts, as kissing.
5. Syphilis is no respector of person, wealth, social standing, intelligence or morals. The sons and daughters of the best families are marrying into syphilis.
6. Syphilis can be cured if treatment is begun at once and is kept up faithfully. Its progress can be arrested by proper treatment, in almost any case. The spread of the disease can be prevented to a very great extent by the proper treatment of those who have it.

A short time ago the Radio Health Forum, in discussing eye infections in the newborn, said, "The most serious cases of infection of the eyes at birth are those caused by the germs of gonorrhea, which are sometimes present in the birth passages of the mother."

Serious as the infection of a baby's eyes may be, its occurrence is only one part of the enormous public health problem which gonorrhea has become. For years public opinion has demanded the use of "drops" in the eyes of every newborn baby, so that although thousands of women have the disease, the infection of babies' eyes has been almost entirely prevented wherever this precaution is used. If public opinion can accomplish *that much* toward the control of this disease surely it can solve the problem of how to control *all* gonorrhea.

Since 1918 there have been 97,000 cases of gonorrhea reported to this Department. More than 20,000 of these infections were in women. Four times as many men and at least ten times as many women have it as are ever reported to the health department. Actually, more than half a million infections must have occurred in Massachusetts in that time, or more than 30,000 a year. There is no other communicable disease, except the common cold, which is as prevalent as gonorrhea.

Study of these reports shows that one hundred out of every thousand females who have the disease are girls under fourteen years of age. Many of them are babies. The great majority of these girls were infected by older members of their families or attendants who had the disease. Girls under the age of puberty can catch gonorrhea by sleeping with a mother or sister who has it or in other innocent contacts. At least one-tenth of the whole problem of gonorrhea in the female is accounted for by the innocent and accidental infection of these little girls and babies.

Further study shows that, as in syphilis, the great majority of women who have gonorrhea are the innocent victims of disease acquired after marriage. Their husbands thought themselves to be cured before they married.

Fortunately, except in little girls, gonorrhea is rarely ever spread other than through sexual relationships. Of course those relationships may be perfectly moral as between husband and wife. There is no need for alarm, therefore, that the disease may be spread through ordinary social contacts and occupations. If that were possible, not a single one of us would have escaped infection.

The control of gonorrhea depends upon a number of things, important among which are:—

1. The early recognition of infection. This is of great importance in women, who rarely suspect that the mild, early symptoms are due to this disease. The later stages of gonorrhea are very serious in women and cause "pus-tubes," "inflammation of the pelvis," "inflammation of the womb," sterility, and a multitude of other "female troubles," many of which lead to serious operation.
2. Immediate treatment by an experienced physician. Too many men depend upon drug store treatment, which may cause the eventual disappearance of the chief symptoms. The disappearance of symptoms is no evidence of cure of the disease.
3. The thorough examination, by a competent physician, of all those who are about to marry.

It must be said, however, that the eventual control of syphilis and gonorrhea, will depend upon something more fundamental than the mere discovery and treatment of those who are already infected. The story has been told of a city which was built upon a very high hill. One side of this hill was a sheer precipice, a dizzy drop of several hundred feet. Frequently strangers, losing their way at night, fell over the cliff. Many were badly injured and some were killed. The city fathers were sadly disturbed over this situation and met in solemn conclave. After some discussion it was voted to build a splendid hospital at the foot of the hill, to provide competent doctors and nurses and suitable ambulance service. *Thus they* would *solve* the problem by offering the best service in their power to give, to the unfortunate victims of the hill.

We smile at such *ridiculous* procedure. Why not build a good, strong fence at the *top* of the cliff and install an electric light or two, and so prevent the weary and confused traveller from falling over!

It is worth while, of course, to provide treatment for the unfortunate victims of gonorrhea and syphilis, but as a permanent solution of the problem, it is like building a hospital at the bottom of the hill. Better put up some lights and build a fence. Suppose, then, we begin turning the light of knowledge upon this problem. Suppose we expose the underlying social causes to the bright glare of publicity. Suppose we begin the building of a good, stout fence of sex education and sex hygiene and sex character, at the *top* of the hill. Then, perhaps, we may spare our boys and girls the awful fall over into the valley of gonorrhea and syphilis and unmarried motherhood and all the other evils that lie before them in the now dismal darkness of ignorance and fog of prudery.

BOSTON OF 1800

BY ELEANOR J. MACDONALD, A. B.

Statistician, Division of Adult Hygiene
Massachusetts Department of Public Health

Boston at the time of the establishment of the first health department differed so from the Boston of today that a general pen sketch of it will give us a background for subsequent development. Imagine an open air banquet on State Street, Boston, in the middle of January! This was the way the spirit of the French Revolution affected Boston citizens in 1793. A thousand-pound ox, roasted whole, with gilded horns, was drawn through the streets on a large wagon and served, along with several hogshead of rum, to a large gathering of the men of the town. The "Boston Centinel" reported discreetly that the banquet was an enjoyable affair, made especially so by the presence of bevies of beautiful women smiling encouragement from the balconies and windows of nearby houses; but history has had to record that the banquet broke into an uproar and that at the end large pieces of the ox were thrown about, some, it is said, even in the direction of the bevies of beautiful women.

The topography of the town was entirely different from the Boston of today. The town was a peninsula and Back Bay, as such, did not exist. A creek divided the central part of Boston from the tidewater. A mill pond existed at the north end where the North Station now stands. Boston had three hills, only one of which now remains—Fort Hill in the southern part of the town, Copp's Hill in the north end, and Beacon Hill. Beacon Hill was twice as high as it is today and was used as a common pasture ground. Nearly every family in the neighborhood pastured a cow or two there for its daily needs. An amusing story of the period has been recorded of Mrs. John Hancock. Her husband invited Admiral d'Estang to breakfast. The Admiral asked permission to bring three hundred officers with him. Without a moment's hesitation Mrs. Hancock sent her servants to Beacon Hill with instructions to milk all the cows there. If they were questioned, she advised them to send the questioner to her. The neighbors considered it a very good joke even if it did mean that they had no milk or cream for breakfast.

The change in men's clothing from that period to this is even more astonishing than that of the women's. Men wore caps in the privacy of their homes and blue damask dressing gowns. Wigs, cocked hats, scarlet coats and embroidered waistcoats were accepted fashions. Self expression in clothes among them even found an outlet in such styles as lace ruffles, silk stockings, polished shoes with buckles—which were made so as to be interchangeable for either foot, and broadcloth business suits of a light shade. Following the French Revolution there was a noticeable French influence in clothing. Breeches and stockings were discarded for pantaloons. Boots with yellow tops were worn by men of advanced years, while the younger people wore half boots made of elastic leather.

At this time there were about nineteen thousand citizens in Boston. Most of them were of English descent, and the general attitude towards education and culture was definitely English in tone. There was one general exception to this rule, and that was in the matter of music. Until 1800 the music of New England may be summed up as "one monotonous and barren type—the Puritan Psalmody!" As recently as 1810 very few musical instruments of any sort were to be found even in private homes. In the population of Boston, of six thousand families, not fifty pianofortes could be found.

"Many of the peculiarities of Puritanism had been softened, and so much of the old severity as remained supported the moral standards which the God-fearing founders of the State had raised." The political disturbances did not prevent the Bostonians from enjoying with relish their sober amusements. The Boston Theatre and the Haymarket Theatre were opened in 1794 and 1796 respectively. The shop of Balch, the hatter, was the general gathering place for men in the town. There were several lotteries. Stately minuets and lively contre dances were popular, as were hearty dinners in rooms lighted by great glowing logs in the fireplaces and flickering candles.

There was a marked deference then to age that is hard to imagine today. Even in the intimacy of family life children addressed their parents as "honored mama" and "honored papa." The difficulty to the eyes of reading in the wavering lights of the candle made the evening a time for conversational gatherings which were educational to all who listened for they were led by the men of age, experience, and wisdom.

Children were taught reading, writing, arithmetic, spelling, accent, English grammar and composition. Girls were admitted to school for only one half of the year. In 1817 it has been estimated that in Boston and Cambridge all the public libraries could present only sixty thousand volumes. This gives an idea of the limited resources for individual study.

Traveling and all secular employments, save those of necessity and mercy, were prohibited on the Sabbath. Another custom that has passed out of existence was the excessive mourning period that followed a death. Those who lost parents wore mourning for three years and widows never removed it. Every funeral procession must pass the town house and travel on a portion of the main street. The Boston Dispensary opened about this period. There were as yet no hospitals.

Boston was not only an industrial city at the time, but also a seaport and financial center. Upon its two banks one quarter of the population of the United States depended for financial and commercial capital. Shipbuilding had been extensively carried on but just now was beginning to decline. Any day of the early nineteenth century about eighty-four sailing vessels could be seen at two of the most active wharves, and the whole port of Boston would contain about 450 boats.

There were three mills—for meal, lumber, and chocolate. In 1794 twenty-five hundred pounds of chocolate were manufactured daily. There were industries for brass cannon, bells, earthen vessels, calico printing, a glass company, manufacturers of combs, clocks, mathematical instruments, soaps, candles, beaver hats, fish hooks, and rope. There were eighteen distilleries and seven sugar refineries. Rum and sugar were manufactured. A windmill was used for cutting the cardboard at the principal factory.

The sewers were drains for the cellars and land, were owned by private individuals, and ran to the nearest water. The human excreta was not allowed in the sewers until 1833. The water supply was derived from wells which were situated on the slopes of the three hills. The water was hard and sometimes polluted. The neighbors quarreled over their supplies, for the deeper wells took the water away from the shallower ones. In 1795 the Boston Aqueduct Company was incorporated to bring the water in from Jamaica Pond. The pipes consisted of wooden logs with holes bored in them. They frequently leaked, and this supply became inadequate in 1816.

The advance in the field of preventive medicine in Boston up until 1800 was not commensurate with the advance in other lines. Business was expanding. Education was becoming more inclusive. Banking and shipping were striding ahead. Yet in the midst of this progress people were dying, in most cases, before they had reached the period of greatest usefulness. Slightly less than one seventh of the inhabitants were over the age of forty-five.

Compare the change in the times—the early twentieth century in which 70 per cent of all deaths occurred after the age of forty, and the nineteenth century in which only 30 per cent occurred after this age. The diseases naturally were different as they were largely confined to the young and very few cases of such diseases as apoplexy, heart disease, and cancer were noted. Tuberculosis and infantile diseases comprised about one third of all deaths.

George Washington was a representative figure of the period that led to the first Board of Health. He did not live in Massachusetts, although he was a frequent visitor. He had to contend with many of the hardships of the Revolutionary Period in actual service, but then when he was at home he was in better circumstances than many of his Massachusetts contemporaries. Let us consider his health record and see what were the health hazards of the age.

George Washington had smallpox when he was nineteen years of age. Eleven years before his birth and thirty years before he contracted the disease, the inoculation method for the prevention of smallpox was introduced into this country. If Washington had been inoculated he would not have had the disease so severely, nor would he have had the pockmarks which disfigured him all the rest of his life. Later he developed a severe attack of dysentery. He was bothered most of his life with malaria, infected sinuses and teeth, rheumatism, and frequent colds. It is probable that he died of diphtheria, although some surmise that it may have been laryngitis.

The possibilities of health available today were conspicuously absent in this period. Health conditions in Boston became so bad that the public at last was aroused and demanded some governmental action to preserve the lives of the people against the recurring and increasingly violent epidemics. In 1792 there was a severe epidemic of smallpox. Great alarm was felt when the disease appeared, and inoculation became more common. The "Communications" of the Massachusetts Medical Society said of the epidemic, "The consequence which ensued constituted a scene of confusion and wretchedness which no one, who was a witness of it, could have viewed without horror and commiseration. It is to be hoped for the cause of humanity, that the inhabitants of Boston will never again experience this calamity.". In this epidemic 8,346 individuals had the disease and 198 died. Ten thousand six hundred and fifty-five inhabitants of Boston had previously had the disease. Only 483 of those who had never had the disease escaped and about 262 of these did so by moving out of town.

Four years later, Boston was visited by a typhus epidemic. So great was the anxiety that many of the dead were buried at night so that the town, as a whole, should not know how extensive death from the disease had become. Typhus was most prevalent in the crowded and poorer sections of the town.

In 1798 yellow fever appeared in Boston. It is believed that many more of the inhabitants would have fallen victim to this scourge if eight thousand of them had not moved into the country. One of the doctors estimated that three hundred deaths occurred. Another doctor stated that he had 103 patients and lost eleven. If the same ratio occurred throughout the town, there were probably nearly three thousand sick with the disease. The inhabitants themselves believed that the disease was caused by the filthy condition of the streets and docks which were littered with decayed animal and vegetable matter.

It is probable that this epidemic of yellow fever compelled the creation of the Board of Health in 1799. On February 13th of that year, the town of Boston was empowered to choose a Board of Health. The first meeting of the Board was held at Faneuil Hall, March 9, 1799. John Folsom was chosen Secretary and Paul Revere was chosen President. In Paul Revere's opening address to the Board he said, "Selected by you our Neighbors and Fellow Townsmen to the important office of a Board of Health, at a time when our feelings and sensibility have been keenly wounded in consequence of the fatal sickness that pervaded the Capitol, we have been anxiously employed to devise the best measures best calculated to retard, if not wholly to prevent a return of the like distressing scene. After consulting Medical Men and comparing their Opinions with our Own, we this Day present to you a Plan, which we trust if carried into effect, will, under the guidance of a kind Providence, lead to the attainment of this desired object; for notwithstanding the diversity of opinions respecting the real origin of the late fever, there can be no doubt but a rigid attention to cleanliness, and immediate removal of foetid substances in the town will, by correcting the Atmosphere, have a great tendency to impede its fatal progress, should the fever again make its appearance. . . .

"We know we can depend on your support to carry out our duties. . . .

"Money will be needed to carry on the work. . . . .

"A Committee has been appointed to compare Massachusetts and the United States laws with the power and duties of the Board, and to report what regulations they make in consequence of the same."

The original records of this Board of Health are preserved in the Boston Public Library and are very enlightening. Inasmuch as filth was supposed to have been the cause of yellow fever, a great deal of time and energy was devoted to sanitation. The records are filled with notations about scavengers, collection of excreta, care of hogs, and placing of slacked lime in graves under and in the walls of churches. One of their regulations that seems strange today follows: "That the Inhabitants would absolutely refuse to buy or eat any fresh meat brought in for sale that is blown up with the foul and impure breath that has passed the human lungs." This referred to a practice over two hundred years old of blowing the meat to make it swell and seem fat and fair.

Paul Revere continued as head of the Board of Health until 1801. Most of the work of the Board was devoted to quarantine and care of those with infectious diseases, either at home or on Rainsford Island. At the last meeting of the Board under his direction in 1801, thanks was officially voted to Paul Revere for all the arduous work done by him as President.

The following summer, 1802, there was another outbreak of yellow fever. There was no explanation of its cause as frequently several in one family would contract the disease, and in other cases the attendants of the sick would not contract it. In spite of this, some still maintained that it was spread by filth.

Bibliography

Bills of Mortality, 1810-1849, City of Boston. Printed for the Registry Department, 1893.
Original Reports of the Boston Board of Health, 1799, 1800, 1801, 1802.
Shattuck, Lemuel; Banks, Nathaniel P., Jr., and Abbott, Jehiel: Report of the Massachusetts Sanitary Commission, 1850.
Wells, Walter A. The Case of George Washington, Esq. Hygeia Magazine, Vol. 12, No. 2, February, 1934.
Whipple, George C.: State Sanitation. Vols. I and II. Harvard University Press, Cambridge, 1917.
Winsor, Justin (Edited by): The Memorial History of Boston. 1630-1880. Vol. IV. James R. Osgood and Company, Boston, 1881.

CANCER

BY ERNEST M. DALAND, M. D.
Boston, Mass.

The subject of cancer is of vital importance to everybody in this State. For many years Massachusetts had the highest cancer death rate in the Union, and even now it ranks among the highest. One of the reasons for this high rate is the ignorance of the public as to the nature and course of cancer. Another is the fear of cancer and the tendency to put off medical consultation for fear that the physician will make a diagnosis of cancer. Let us, then, consider just what cancer is.

Every organ of the body is made up of different kinds of cells—the basic units of all life. Viewed under the microscope all muscle cells show certain traits common only to muscles, the cells of the skin have characteristics of their own, the cells lining the stomach and producing gastric juices have still a different appearance. These cells vary in their size, shape and structure according to the function that they are going to have in a given organ.

A normal cell has a comparatively short life. It becomes worn out from hard work and dies. The cells which remain must fill the vacancy and each does this by a process of division into two cells, each of which is able to grow into a mature cell. Repair is a normal function which goes on day and night. It is possible to examine a section of an organ and determine whether normal cell division was going on at the time the tissue was removed.

As long as there is a balance between the number of cells dying and the number of new cells being formed, the organ is normal. However, sometimes the cells reproduce themselves faster than their mates die. There is, then, an accumulation of cells, similar to the parent cells, in the midst of an organ, growing so wildly and with such rapidity that they do not have any work to do. This is the mechanism of tumor formation. To sum it up: a tumor is a mass of cells similar to the parent cells, growing without control and having no function.

Certain types of tumors grow for a time and then stop. In some cases a capsule forms about the tumor to restrain it and support it. These tumors may be harmless except for pressure on some nerve or organ and except for their unsightliness. They are spoken of as benign or non-malignant tumors. However they may change into the other group of malignant or cancerous tumors which we shall consider next.

The next group of tumors are more serious problems. They are made up of cells which are not content to stay in one place—they grow right into an organ, push aside and replace important normal cells and interfere with the function of the organ. Thus the important secreting cells of the stomach become replaced by cells with no function and gastric digestion is impaired. But this is not the worst feature. These tumors send off cells into the blood or into the lymphatic circulation, thence to neighboring or distant parts of the body. On their arrival in their new locations they continue to grow as rapidly as in the first organ. They retain sufficient of the original characteristics of the mother tumor to allow them to be recognized microscopically. Such tumors are malignant tumors or cancers. They are dangerous to life if they are not checked. Thus it will be seen that all cancers are tumors, but not all tumors are cancers. Again we must remember that the well-behaved benign tumor may suddenly change into a cancer.

Rapidly growing tumors demand a large supply of food and because the food is brought in the blood a new system of thin-walled blood vessels is hurriedly built up. If the tumor grows faster than the blood vessels grow, the part of the tumor the farthest away from the normal blood vessels will suffer, will become gangrenous and will die. This accounts for the ulceration and sloughing of many cancers. Secondary infection may enter these ulcerations and then the same precautions must be taken by the patient and his family that would be taken with the discharge from a boil. There is no reason for the isolation of a cancer patient or for keeping his dishes or bedding separate if common sense precautions are taken with the discharges. There is no contagion of the cancer itself. Cancer is an individual disease in each person; no two cancers are alike or act alike. Heredity plays no part whatsoever in determining whether or not a person develops cancer. The occurrence of several cancers in the same family must be a chance occurrence. Inasmuch as about one person in ten who now dies after reaching the age of forty-five dies of cancer it is to be expected that occasionally two or more cases would occur in the same family.

We do not know the exact cause of cancer. There is no evidence that it is caused by bacteria or any other type of organisms. The men who have made the most extensive investigations of cancer believe that some chemical change goes on in the body and causes the cells to become abnormal. We do know that many cases of cancer follow long standing irritation. People with foul mouths and uncared for teeth are much more likely to develop cancer in their mouths than others who take proper care of their teeth.

The symptoms from cancer vary according to the organ in which it originates, that is cancer of the stomach may give indigestion and cancer of the bowel may cause severe constipation or stoppage. It is important for you to know that pain is not a usual symptom of cancer. If pain does occur it usually means that the cancer is far advanced. Each year hundreds of patients with advanced cancer, when asked why they have done nothing about it say, "It did not pain me." Do not wait for pain!

Any lump that appears in any part of the body, any unilateral change in shape of a structure like the breast is probably a tumor and it must be suspected of being a malignant tumor until proven otherwise. A microscopic examination must be made of every lump which a physician removes. Nearly every hospital has facilities for making this examination, or the state laboratory will make it for your physician. It is important to know whether the lump removed was a cancer or not. If it was a cancer, a more extensive operation may be necessary. If the cancer was in the breast, the whole breast should be removed together with the muscles under the breast and the glands in the armpit. In many hospitals the pathologist who makes the microscopic examination is present at the operation, watches the surgeon remove a piece of tumor and then makes an immediate examination. After learning the correct diagnosis the surgeon knows whether he must do a major operation or a minor one.

Any abnormal bleeding or ulceration, any sudden change in digestive or bowel habits call for medical advice to rule out cancer. Sudden increase in size or change in appearance of a long-standing mole is reason enough to see your doctor. The raised, thickened blemishes on your face, which do not respond to simple treatment may be skin cancers. These are very mild conditions compared with internal cancers. They are easily seen, readily examined and can be treated satisfactorily. Not all of the conditions I have mentioned will be cancer. It may be that your physician will tell you that you have no tumor and no cancer. He must make the decision and not you.

It is sometimes said that so much talk about cancer will scare many people and make nervous wrecks out of them. We do not want to scare the people who have not got cancer, but those who have it must be scared into doing something about it. Delay is what is keeping the Massachusetts cancer death rate so high. In recent studies in this State it has been found that patients wait an average of eight months after noticing something wrong before they consult a physician. If your child had pneumonia, would you expect your physician to cure him if you waited several days before calling him? If you suspected appendicitis, how long would you delay? Cancer may make such progress in eight months that nobody can cure it.

Cancer can be cured if it is diagnosed and treated early. The earlier you apply for treatment the greater your chances of being permanently cured. You are not the one who should be doing the watching. Let your physician take that responsibility. Even if you are one who has delayed for several months, there is still a chance that you may be cured. You may be certain that there is no chance of cure if you do nothing about it, however. You hear about your friends and neighbors who die from cancer. You do not hear so much about the thousands of patients who are treated early and cured of their cancers.

Ninety-five per cent of all skin cancers are now being cured when treated within a few months of onset. Early breast cancer has seventy-five per cent cures, lip cancer has eighty-five per cent cures and so on down the line. Of course there will be some inconvenience and some discomfort entailed in getting your cancer treated. However, this is a mere drop in the bucket compared to the pain and worry that you will have if you let it go untreated.

The only methods of treatment of cancer that accomplish results are operation, x-ray treatment, radium treatment or combinations of these three. Valuable time will be lost and your chance of cure decreased if other methods are tried. There is no known internal medicine that has the slightest effect on cancer. Do not be gullible and try the secret remedy that your neighbor tells you about. Each year thousands of these remedies are passed out to the public. Much damage is done and they are all found to be useless. Remember that the medical profession is as anxious to find the cause of cancer and new methods of treating it as you are. Let the trained scientists try out the new methods in the ways they see fit. Do not experiment on yourself.

If you wish to read more on this subject, a pamphlet called "The Whats and Whys of Cancer" may be obtained by applying to the Massachusetts Department of Public Health at the State House, Boston.

TOPOGRAPHY OF THE STATE OF MASSACHUSETTS

BY ARTHUR D. WESTON

Director, Division of Sanitary Engineering
Massachusetts Department of Public Health

The Department of Public Health has recently received many requests for information concerning the elevation of land in different parts of the State. Presumably these requests are made because the applicants believe that living on a high point of land is particularly beneficial to health. This assumption according to the health officers connected with this Department, is not well founded and in this connection I might quote the following statement prepared by the Deputy Commissioner of Public Health.

"In the earlier days, considerable importance was attached to the question of altitude in the treatment of tuberculosis. The reason back of this was the supposition that a high altitude coupled with the somewhat dry climate that usually accompanies it furnished an air which was beneficial to tuberculosis patients. Consequently, many tuberculosis sanatoria were built in such localities, as evidenced by the extensive development of sanatoria in Colorado and especially in the southwest.

"That an extremely dry climate or a high altitude was not necessary for the adequate treatment of tuberculosis was demonstrated by Dr. Trudeau, who was considered insane by his friends when he went to the Adirondacks during the winter in an attempt to regain his health, which was greatly impaired by an active tuberculosis. More recently it has been shown that tuberculosis can be adequately cared for at the ordinary altitude, and that even the slight elevation of the Adirondacks is not necessary. The outstanding work of this nature was that carried on in Sharon, Massachusetts, by Dr. Bowditch and his associates.

"When attention became fixed upon the value of sunlight as a factor in the treatment of bone and joint tuberculosis, new life was given to the idea of altitude, it being supposed that the ultra-violet rays would be greater under such circumstances. Actual scientific measurements of these rays show, however, that there is no mysterious benefit from seeking high altitudes in the treatment of tuberculosis which is not obtained at lower elevations."

However, it is of importance for prospective home owners and others to select a site of residence which will be sufficiently high to permit adequate drainage and where the land is free from dampness, especially swamp lands, and for this reason our radio address today will concern the physical characteristics of the State so far as they relate to the general topographical conditions. It should be borne in mind that high elevations are not necessarily free from swampy areas and may result in serious problems of water supply.

If one were to examine a relief map of Massachusetts, he would see three belts of highland and four of lowland sloping generally in a southerly and easterly direction.

The State is drained by two great rivers, the Connecticut and the Merrimack and by many smaller streams. In most cases the streams flow in a southerly direction through the State with the exception of the Merrimack River which enters Massachusetts from the north and flows in an easterly direction along the border into the Atlantic Ocean. Even this river according to our geological records had its outlet originally in Boston Harbor.

In the easterly part of the State there are the Charles and Ipswich River valleys where the streams flow northeastward into the sea, while in the southeast section there is the Taunton River which has its outlet in Narragansett Bay and the Quinebaug and Blackstone Rivers having outlets in Long Island Sound. Along the western border of the State is the Housatonic River rising in the vicinity of Hinsdale and flowing in a southerly direction to Long Island Sound, and the Hoosick River which has its source in the town of Lanesboro and which flows in a northerly and westerly direction into the state of New York.

There are three main divides between the different river systems of the State. One of these divides extends nearly through the middle of the State and divides it roughly in halves. The second, which is parallel to it, crosses the State about 10 to 15 miles from the westerly boundary. Between these two divides lies the Connecticut River basin. A third divide, which cuts the eastern half of the State into nearly equal parts, has an average westerly course from the sea to the Connecticut Valley. This divide separates those streams which flow directly into Long Island Sound from those that enter the Connecticut River and those that flow northeastward into the Atlantic Ocean.

Each highland or upland is due to the prevalence in it of rocks that are hard and resist the wear of streams and weather, and in contrast each lowland is due mainly to the presence of rocks that are weak and yield most readily to the elements. Plateau surfaces are characteristic of the State; several of them are plainly seen in each upland and there are four grand belts of depressed rocks or basins, corresponding roughly to several areas of sedimentary rocks.

There are seven topographic districts which have been formed in the State as the result of the geological conditions. These districts named in order from west to east are: the Taconic Range, the Housatonic Valley, the Green Mountain Highlands, the Connecticut Valley, the Central Upland and the Eastern Lowlands. The Taconic Range is located along the westerly border of the State and has its highest summit in Mount Greylock located at an elevation of some 3,500 feet above mean sea level. It contains other high peaks, such as East Mountain, elevation 2,660 feet, and Berlin Mountain, elevation 2,800 feet, and such altitudes as Mount Everett, near the southwest corner of the State, of 2,620 feet above sea level.

The Housatonic Valley has an elevation of some 1,100 feet above mean sea level at the head of the Housatonic and Hoosick River valleys and an elevation of 570 feet above mean sea level at the boundary between Massachusetts and Connecticut, while in the middle of this valley there are such mountains as the Lenox Mountain, 2,150 feet, and Tom Ball Mountain, some 1,900 feet, above sea level.

The Green Mountain Highlands include the Berkshire Hills. These highlands rise above the Housatonic Valley on the west and the Connecticut Valley on the east and consist of a plateau belt of lands about 25 miles wide extending southerly across the State. The northwesterly part contains the Hoosac Mountain, near the Vermont boundary, one of the most prominent high points of land in the State, which has an elevation of about 2,800 feet. In the western part of these highlands, in Berkshire County, is what is know as the Berkshire Hills. About one-half of these highlands is more than 1,500 feet above the sea, and much of the area is higher than 2,000 feet above sea level.

The Connecticut Valley, which lies to the east of the Green Mountain Highlands, is roughly triangular and is about four miles wide at the northerly boundary of the State, and 20 miles wide at the southerly boundary. This valley includes the Chicopee and Millers Rivers, tributaries of the Connecticut River, on the east, and Deerfield and Westfield Rivers on the west. The Connecticut River enters the State at an elevation 180 feet above sea level and leaves the State 67 miles downstream at an elevation of 42 feet above sea level. There are ranges in this valley, for example the Holyoke Range, which has a summit in Mount Tom of over 1,200 feet, and Mount Nonotuck about 1,100 feet above mean sea level; while there are many rolling hills around its margin with heights of 500 to 650 feet and of 300 to 340 feet above mean sea level. The greater part of this valley is less than 300 feet above mean sea level.

East of the Connecticut Valley is what is known as the central upland which includes the high part of the State between the Connecticut River Valley and the low lands in eastern Massachusetts. This belt is about 34 miles wide at the north and 20 miles wide along the Connecticut border. The westerly part of this upland rises to some 700 to 900 feet above the Connecticut Valley and there are peaks and hills in the valley; for example, Mount Wachusett, about 2,000 feet, Watatic Mountain, 1,850 feet, and Mount Grace, 1,625 feet, above mean sea level. In general, the plateau is slightly lower toward the south, the summits at the north being about 1,200 feet above sea level and those at the south about 1,100 feet.

East of the central uplands are the eastern lowlands. The general elevation of this section is from 200 to 300 feet above mean sea level although some of the lower sections are 110 to 160 feet above mean sea level. There are some peaks, however, in these eastern lowlands which rise, for example, at the Blue Hills of Quincy and Milton to 500 to 640 feet and Moose Hill in Sharon to 560 feet above sea level.

Along the coast is the coastal plain, which for the most part is but a few hundred feet above mean sea level, although there are peaks like Manomet Hill in Plymouth, 394 feet, while on Martha's Vineyard certain hills rise to 200 feet above mean sea level.

The Engineering Division of the Department of Public Health is well equipped with maps showing the topography of the State and will be pleased to supply information upon request.

TIRED LEGS FROM ALTERED CIRCULATION

BY HILBERT F. DAY, M. D.

Boston, Mass.

Tired legs are due to many causes, but the most frequent cause is varicose veins. When we have varicose veins we have a variation from normal circulation in the veins of the legs, hence the title of this talk.

Some of the other causes of tired legs are: flat feet, heart or kidney disease, diseases of the bones, arteries, or nerves.

Flat feet may be acquired from not giving the feet proper exercise, or from congenitally poor arches. Improper shoes are also a cause.

Heart disease may become so serious that the heart is not doing its whole work. Then there is a swelling of the limbs with an increased amount of fluid in the tissues which we call edema.

Certain kidney diseases cause edema when the kidneys are not functioning sufficiently well.

Chronic infection of the bones of the legs usually follows an injury.

The best medical men now are in thorough agreement that no treatment of varicose veins should be instituted unless preceded by a thorough physical examination. As tired legs can be due to many causes, it certainly would be bad practice to start treating a patient for one disease and later find out that he had another as well.

Physical examination should include a careful history of the patient and his family, particularly his parents. It is interesting to know whether either father or mother suffered from the same symptoms as the patient. The examination should include temperature, weight, height, urine examination, blood pressure, examination of the heart and lungs and of the abdomen. This will tell how well the heart and kidneys are functioning. The examination of the abdomen is important, particularly to rule out the possibility of some abdominal tumor causing pressure which in turn might aid in the development of varicose veins or cause swelling of the limbs.

In order to understand varicose veins, we must have an idea of what the circulation of the leg normally is, for varicose veins are abnormal. The arteries of the body and of the limbs carry blood away from the heart and into the tissues of the body to support and nourish them. The blood which flows through the arteries is rich in oxygen but becomes changed after it passes through the tissues at a distance from the heart. This blood returns to the heart through veins. The arteries are essentially pipes which have no partitions or valves in them and the flow of blood through these arteries is a matter of direct transmission from the heart. The veins, on the other hand, are thinner-walled pipes and in order to prevent back-flow have valves which normally allow the passage of blood only in one direction; that is, towards the heart. When these veins become stretched, the valves become incompetent, or destroyed, and the column of blood then falls back by the force of gravity into the smaller branches of the veins. This causes gradual destruction of the tissues which they are supposed to nourish because bad blood is not properly removed. These large valveless veins are useless because they then fail to function as veins in carrying blood towards the heart, and, in fact, such circulation as remains is often in the reverse from normal direction. Therefore, the individual would be very much better without these varicosed veins.

Immediately you will say, "How will blood from the legs get back to the heart if these veins are not working?" Fortunately for us, there is a double set of veins in the leg. Besides the superficial veins, which are covered only by fat and skin and are the ones that become varicosed, there are the deep veins, which are situated between the muscles of the leg. The contraction of these muscles squeezes the blood upward in the proper direction and prevents enlargement of these deep veins. We must think of the veins which have become varicosed as reservoirs of stagnant blood. This being so, it is correct to advocate their obliteration or removal.

A natural question which might arise in your minds is, "How do these veins happen to become diseased?" I am inclined to think that a certain proportion of people are born with weak-walled veins. In other words, they inherit veins which easily become over-distended and thus destroyed and unable to perform their natural function. Many individuals develop varicose veins from undue pressure; such pressure as might occur during pregnancy, or because of an abdominal tumor, or from straining and lifting. Restricting bands around the legs, such as tight garters, are often a cause. At this point I should say that I strongly disapprove of circular garters and think that both men and women should support their socks or stockings by side garters. Certain stores sell men lateral or side garters which are very satisfactory.

Without the foregoing more or less scientific description of varicose veins, you may all recognize them as large, irregular, blue channels, standing out from the lower leg or thigh, such as are popularly known as "very coarse" veins. You may notice one or two such veins in the calf and pay very little attention to them, but the destruction having started, it progresses. At first the symptoms noted are those of aching in the legs which develops a few hours after standing and increases until there is real fatigue and you have what we call *"tired legs."* This would not be so bad if the disease stopped there, for it would be possible for you to wear a bandage or stocking and thus give extra support to the circulation and overcome the symptoms of fatigue. Most people do not care to take that trouble and leave these large, visible, veins untreated and towards night they are apt to find a little swelling of the ankles which disappears during rest and reappears the next afternoon.

The next thing which happens is a discoloration of the skin due to the continued bad circulation and poor nourishment of the tissues. An itching condition with roughening of the skin develops, which is called varicose eczema. This, if allowed to go untreated, may be carried into the next phase where there is an actual breaking down of the tissues and an ulcer formation. Finally, the sufferer has a disagreeable, discharging, smelly sore on the leg. This generally brings even the most neglectful person to the doctor's care. When this has happened, you will naturally ask how could these unhappy results have been avoided. Sometimes they cannot be avoided, but if we are careful not to restrict the circulation of the leg by tight garters and take care to support leg circulation during pregnancy by proper bandaging, some of the destruction can be escaped.

Now as to *treatment,* when it comes to discussing the treatment of varicose veins, we realize that satisfactory treatment is aimed towards doing away with and preventing these useless channels. The symptom of tired legs can be somewhat relieved (if this fatigue is due to varicose veins) by proper bandaging, but that is a difficult thing to do well, as it means daily proper application of a supporting bandage. Elastic stockings, in my opinion, are only satisfactory for a short time because they stretch and then do not adequately support circulation. Bandages, elastic stockings, laced canvas stockings, etc., are only useful in relieving the symptoms by supporting the circulation, but they are not curative. To cure varicose veins, they must be removed or obliterated because they are merely reservoirs of bad blood with the normal circulation reversed; that is, blood dropping down from the body, rather than being carried towards the heart.

Twenty years ago, the only method we had for removing such veins was by surgery. At that time, a very extensive operation with incisions from the foot up the lower leg to the thigh was done. This was a tiresome and lengthy procedure and left the patient with tremendous scars up and down the leg which was operated on and entailed a two-weeks' stay in a hospital. Even then if the operation was not done by a good anatomist and the external system of veins was not completely removed, new veins would develop and after a period of time this process might have to be repeated.

Now let me tell you about newer methods. About ten years ago, we became interested in a method of treating varicose veins which was being largely used abroad. It was called the "injection treatment of varicose veins" and its object was to inject into an abnormal vein fluid which would destroy the walls of that vein and form in the vein a sterile clot. This clot stays in place because of the destruction of the lining of the vein, this frayed lining becoming intimately involved in the clot. When the sterile clot had thoroughly healed, the vein as a channel was destroyed and finally contracted down to a thread-like cord. This method has proved eminently successful and at present at least 125 people a week are being treated by injection in a single Boston clinic.

At first, we only injected one vein at a sitting. Now some of us inject many veins, thus diminishing the number of times the patient has to have treatment. The great advantage in this method of treatment is that it is essentially ambulatory; that is, the patient does not have to give up his ordinary routine of life, but can go to a clinic or the doctor's office for a treatment and return to his regular occupation. Naturally, you will ask how many treatments you may have to have, and my answer would be, "Enough to successfully obliterate all varicose veins." After three or four treatments, the relief of fatigue in the legs and absence of visible large veins make the patient think that he is cured and he may stay away until new veins appear. New veins will appear unless the complete channel of the diseased or dilated vein has been obliterated. Therefore, adequate treatment, controlled by the doctor, is absolutely essential. We think even if the patient has to go back to his doctor at two or three-year intervals for check-up, he is much better off than if he had to spend two weeks in a hospital following a tedious operation.

During the last few months, we have become convinced that certain cases do better if, with the injection of large veins of the lower leg there is combined a minor operation; that is, the tying off of the superficial system of veins of the legs at its upper limit. This tying off can be safely and painlessly accomplished using a local anesthesia such as novocaine, the patient staying in the hospital only twenty-four hours.

If this condition of the legs has become so bad that in addition to varicose veins there is an ulcer, the treatment of the ulcer should be carried along at the same time we are destroying the diseased veins. Newer methods of treatment of varicose ulcers have been developed within the last few months.

The newer methods of treating varicose veins and varicose ulcers have relieved the surgical clinics of Boston tremendously. People now receive treatment for their veins in many instances before ulcers have appeared and after ulcers have developed they are relieved more speedily and more permanently than they used to be.

In my opinion, varicose veins are the most common cause of tired legs. This disease should now be cured simply, practically painlessly, quickly and without loss of time. If you are suffering from tired legs, don't delay consulting a surgeon. Let *him* find out why you are suffering and tell you *how* to be relieved.

THE BIOLOGICAL LABORATORY

By ELLIOTT S. ROBINSON, M. D.

Director, Division of Biologic Laboratories
Massachusetts Department of Public Health

The discovery of germs just over fifty years ago began the period of the greatest advances in Medicine in the history of the world. Not long after germs were discovered, it was found that serum from adults contained substances which attacked disease germs. Shortly thereafter serum from an animal immunized against a disease germ was shown to protect other animals from that particular germ, and likewise to protect human beings. When it was found that animals could produce such serums for us, thereafter they were available in unlimited quantity.

The discovery of diphtheria antitoxin in 1894 led directly to the founding of the Antitoxin and Vaccine Laboratory because the State Board of Health wanted to make available to the people of Massachusetts this new remedy for the treatment of diphtheria. Dr. Theobald Smith, one of this country's most eminent bacteriologists, was placed in charge of this work and remained at the head of it for about twenty years. Then Dr. Milton J. Rosenau directed the work of the laboratory for a period of years and was later followed by Dr. Benjamin White, both of whom have been prominent figures in this state.

During these years, as medical science has advanced, product after product has been added to the list of useful ones made at the laboratory. On the other hand, it has always been the practice to distribute only those that are of proven efficacy, believing that it is better to be a little slow to accept a new product than to accept one too quickly only to have to give it up when its value proves to be very small. Not only have new products been added from time to time but better methods of making old ones have been found. Some of these new methods have come from discoveries of others engaged in similar work but many of the improvements have been made by discoveries made by workers at our own laboratory. It is the continual aim of the laboratory to increase the potency of its products and decrease the discomfort which sometimes follows their administration.

The Antitoxin and Vaccine Laboratory is located at Forest Hills on the grounds of the Bussey Institute and adjacent to the Arnold Arboretum. It consists of a laboratory and two stable buildings. The laboratory and stable were built about twenty years ago and additions were made in 1927.

The manufacture of diphtheria antitoxin is a complicated procedure requiring the employment of highly trained bacteriologists and chemists. A detailed description of the method is beyond the scope of a broadcast such as this.

Besides making diphtheria antitoxin the laboratory also manufactures scarlet fever antitoxin, used in the treatment of that disease; a serum for the treatment of some forms of meningitis, and a serum for treating certain cases of pneumonia. In addition it makes the toxoid and toxin-antitoxin mixtures used in the prevention of diphtheria, the vaccine used to prevent typhoid fever, and that to prevent smallpox, as well as the Schick test material to detect susceptibility to diphtheria and the tuberculin used in determining the presence of tuberculosis. When infantile paralysis is present in the state, the laboratory aids in preparing the convalescent serum used in treating patients with this disease.

Some idea of the work done may be gained from the fact that between seventy-five and one hundred thousand individual packages are made up each year. These are distributed to physicians, hospitals, and boards of health throughout the state to aid them in preventing or treating communicable diseases.

State laboratories such as this are not common in this country, for there are laboratories doing a similar scope of work only in two other states—New York and Michigan.

The high potency and the harmlessness of the products made not only by this laboratory but also by all other such laboratories in the country is assured by the close supervision of all procedures by the United States Government. For many years the laboratory has had a license from the National Institute of Health in the United States Treasury Department, whose officers make an annual inspection of the plant, examine its products, watch its procedures to make sure that everything is done according to regulation. Some of the products must be sent to Washington for final testing. This strict supervision gives further assurance that Massachusetts has available the best materials for treatment and prevention that can be made.

JIM HAS A STOMACH ACHE

By JOHN BIRNIE, M. D.
Springfield, Mass.

Jim has a stomach ache. This is a statement often heard and the maker of it is not particularly alarmed. A stomach ache is an unavoidable though disagreeable commonplace annoyance like flies or mosquitoes.

Stomach ache is a good old fashioned expression but hardly a medical one. To the person using it, it may mean something very definite. To the person listening it may mean little. It usually denotes a pain, of varying intensity, located anywhere below the breast bone on the front of the body proper. The boundaries between stomach ache and back ache are rather indefinite. The severity of the ache may vary from slight discomfort to a pain of such intensity as to be unbearable. People vary widely in their reaction to pain—that which seems excruciating to one may be borne with equanimity by another. It is a difficult thing to describe a pain but we are often asked to do so. We use the terms sharp, shooting, boring, darting, dull, constant, intermittent, grinding and so on. The descriptive adjectives used vary with one's vocabulary and with one's imagination. What the doctor wishes to know is whether the pain came on slowly or suddenly, whether it is mild or severe, whether it is constant or intermittent, and whether it remains in one place or moves about. We are all very indefinite in our attempts to locate abdominal pain. Ask someone where he has a pain and he will move his hand uncertainly over his entire upper abdomen or will start poking himself with his fingers until he finds a particular spot, saying —"There it is." He is really confusing tenderness with pain. Stomach ache or to be more exact—abdominal pain—is only one symptom and may mean much or little. The doctor in making his diagnosis considers all the other things which may or may not accompany the stomach ache. I say "may not accompany" for often the absence of one or more common symptoms or signs may rule out some possibilities under consideration. Pain in any part of the body means that something is wrong with the human mechanism. Pain in the abdomen, stomach ache, means something is wrong but it may not necessarily mean that the derangement is within the abdomen. Pain is often referred; that is— trouble in one location manifests itself by producing pain in another and often distant location. Pain in the abdomen is frequently caused by an abnormal condition in the chest. Certain forms of heart disease may herald themselves by causing severe abdominal pain without any accompanying discomfort in the region of the heart itself. Pain in the abdomen, especially in children, may proclaim the onset of pneumonia. The doctor may be uncertain for a time as to whether the patient is suffering from pneumonia or from appendicitis. X-rays will tell us nothing about appendicitis but they will tell us much about pneumonia. Do not misunderstand me. I do not mean that when the doctor says you have appendicitis that you should insist upon having an x-ray examination to be sure that you haven't pneumonia. This confusion in diagnosis is not common and the doctor has many other ways of confirming his opinion. Certain forms of poisons produce stomach ache. Chronic lead poisoning is one—the so-called "Painter's Colic." Stomach ache is often the first warning of impending diabetic coma, the unconsciousness which precedes death from diabetes. If the condition is recognized in time, and insulin is used properly, the onset of coma may be prevented. Knowledge and speed are necessary to avert this catastrophe. All of the organs situated within the abdominal cavity, and there are many of them, may cause a stomach ache. Each organ may do this in several ways and in combinations of these ways, so that the resulting causes of stomach ache are rather numerous. An organ may simply not be working normally, causing pain. It may be inflamed, causing pain. It may be the seat of a tumor, causing pain. If it is a hollow organ it may burst, causing pain. It may be injured, causing pain. It may be moved out of its normal position, causing pain. You can readily see that the underlying causes of abdominal pain—stomach ache—are many. It is really wonderful that a doctor can make an accurate diagnosis, and he usually does, when we realize what a large number of combinations may cause stomach ache. The problem is further complicated by the fact that he is dealing with organs hidden from sight and touch. The reason that he can do so well is because he has at his command the knowledge gained by millions of workers laboring throughout the centuries. He calls to his assistance facts gleaned from every branch of science. When one realizes that a doctor, so equipped with special knowledge gained by years of study, training and experience, has difficulty in determining the cause of a particular stomach ache, isn't it presumptuous for a layman or a person not so trained to guess at the cause of a stomach ache and, worse yet, attempt to treat it? For some unaccountable reason numerous non-medical persons feel themselves fully capable of diagnosing disease. Having made a diagnosis, of course it is a very easy matter to treat the ailment. Nearly everyone has a pet remedy for this or that condition. They cannot conceive that it takes much brains to treat a common stomach ache. Such a one would not think for a minute that he could tell a manufacturer how to manage his business or an executive how to run his railroad. When his automobile develops an unexpected knock or an unfamiliar rattle, he takes it to a trained mechanic who is expected to locate the trouble and remedy it. Our amateur doctor knows too much to tamper with an expensive, intricate, finely adjusted piece of mechanism—yet he does not hesitate to tinker with an infinitely more intricate and finely adjusted mechanism, a mechanism far more wonderful than anything man ever has or ever will devise.

The old adage that "things are not always what they seem" is particularly true of stomach ache. Nearly everyone has been strongly advised of the fact that pain in the lower right side of the abdomen may mean appendicitis. As a rule a person with such a pain seeks medical advice promptly. The lay public has been reasonably impressed with the danger which may arise from neglected pain in the lower right side. What they do not know is that the pain of appendicitis frequently manifests itself first as pain in the pit of the stomach, pain in the upper portion of the abdomen which later moves down to the lower right side. It is while this pain is in the upper position that infinite harm may be done with injudicious medication. The dangers of this amateur drugging are not confined to cases of appendicitis but apply equally well to numerous other cases of stomach ache. Inflammations need to be soothed and quieted, not stirred up and aggravated by physics. A real stoppage of the bowels, often difficult of diagnosis and dangerous to life, is rendered much more dangerous by a single dose of castor oil or salts. Even the mild milk of magnesia may become T. N. T. in untrained hands. Many lives which might have been saved have been sacrificed by the careless use of laxatives. If you feel that the bowels must be emptied in a case of a stomach ache, administer a rectal injection. It can do little harm and it is just as effective as a dose of physic by mouth. If one cannot empty the bowels from below, he cannot empty them by pushing from above. If you do employ an injection, use only warm soapy water in small quantities, never over eight ounces at one time—the amount of fluid which will fill the ordinary glass tumbler. Never use force in giving an injection. If you use a rubber bag to hold the fluid, it should not be elevated more than one foot above the patient as he is lying down. Nearly everyone suffering from a stomach ache immediately thinks it is caused by something that he has eaten. To be sure food poisoning does occur, but I am glad to say that in these modern times it is a rare occurrence. Your Board of Health is bending every effort and employing every known means to insure your health against injury from impure foods and from improper handling of foods which have been delivered in a pure and uncontaminated condition. Many of the laws upon our statute books, both state and national, were enacted to insure the purity of all foods delivered to you —foods free from harmful preservatives or deleterious substances. There is another incident which must always be taken into consideration when we are confronted with a stomach ache, and that is the element of time. Certain diseases and conditions which produce stomach ache progress very rapidly to a dangerous or fatal stage. It is absolutely true that numerous complications within the abdomen which are amenable to treatment at the time of their inception are hopeless after a few hours have elapsed. Many a doctor has been unjustly criticised for the unfortunate outcome of a stomach ache when his hands were tied at the outset because of the delay in summoning him. I do not wish you to think that I am trying to impress you unduly with the dangers lurking behind a stomach ache. I do wish you to realize that the symptom should not be regarded lightly and considered the announcement of a trifling ailment—something which, though disagreeable or even painful, will right itself in a few hours—something which can be cured with a hot water bag and a dose of physic. Stomach ache is nature's warning, not to be lightly disregarded. She never lies. The truth is there if we can but read it.

What I have said has been in an endeavor to point out to you and emphasize two dangers which lurk behind a stomach ache, an attempt on my part to warn you so that you may avoid two common errors—errors which in the past have cost many human lives. Do not temporize or procrastinate with a stomach ache. Do not give a dose of physic to a person with a stomach ache.

FOOD FADS

BY HERMANN C. LYTHGOE

Director, Division of Food and Drugs
Massachusetts Department of Public Health

Peculiarities in the individual consumption of food may be put into two classes: first, those resulting from personal idiosyncrasies; and second, those resulting purely from fads and fancies. Individual idiosyncrasies are well known. Some persons have idiosyncrasies against spices. Others again have idiosyncrasies against certain fats, particularly those showing more or less rancidity. Some have idiosyncrasies against meat which is slightly aged. Others have idiosyncrasies against alcohol, which are different from the ordinary intoxicating peculiarities of this chemical.

Among the former employees of the Food and Drug Division of the Department of Public Health was an Inspector who had an idiosyncrasy against aged meat, and for that reason he never ventured to pass judgment upon the wholesomeness or unwholesomeness of meat. Another employee of the Division has a slight idiosyncrasy against rancid fats, and for that reason never ventures to pass judgment upon the taste of butter. A personal friend of the writer has an idiosyncrasy against certain nuts, particularly pistachio nuts, and for that reason abstains from all food which is liable to contain any nuts. Persons having these idiosyncrasies naturally become acquainted with them and so fix their food habits that they do not eat the material which is liable to cause trouble. There are, however, lots of fads which are fads pure and simple.

Some years ago, I had a meal with a number of people and the question of drinking water with meals was under discussion. One person stated that the only time, in his opinion, to drink water was with meals, and he drank water at no other time. Two other persons at the same meal stated that in their opinion water should never be drunk at meals but should be taken between meals.

A more serious fad is the raw milk fad, and because of this fad it is extremely difficult for cities and towns to enact regulations requiring that market milk be pasteurized. Persons who have drunk raw milk all their lives and have not as yet been killed by it will protest to the Health Department against the enactment of regulations which will protect them from diseases disseminated by raw milk. Small dealers selling raw milk will protest against the enactment of such a regulation because there has never been any disease traced to the milk which they sold, and also possibly because the cost of pasteurizing milk would be liable to be sufficient to put them out of business.

During the past three or four years, there has been a popular misapprehension that the use of aluminum utensils will cause cancer. This statement has been published in newspapers and periodicals under the names of persons responsible for the statement. The Department has been unable to obtain any information to substantiate any of these statements.

Years ago, a controversy between the manufacturers of cream of tartar baking powder and the manufacturers of alum baking powder was carried on. The manufacturers of the cream of tartar baking powders spent considerable money trying, unsuccessfully, to show that alum baking powder was poison. In connection with this controversy there were numerous attempts to legislate some of these baking powders out of existence, and in one or two instances there were arrests for political corruption.

It is a fact that all the chemical ingredients of all baking powders when used to excess are toxic, but when used in small quantities are harmless. In New England the preference is for the cream of tartar type of baking powder. In the South the preference is for the straight alum powder. The law requires the package to bear a statement of the ingredients, and the purchaser can therefore use his best judgment as to what kind he shall use.

Aluminum is a fairly common constituent of many natural food stuffs, such as corn, wheat, rye, oats, parsnips, carrots, potatoes, and

it has been estimated that in the course of one day an adult person will ingest approximately three grams of alum as alum phosphate. In making this computation, aluminum utensils, alum baking powder, or agate ware utensils were not taken into consideration.

There is also a perennial controversy as to the relative merits of white bread and black bread. The fact that most of the bread consumed is white bread is indicative of the preference of the public for this type of bread. White bread contains more food value and is more easily digested than black bread. It is a fact that the coarse bran of the black bread acts as a laxative because of the presence of a comparatively large quantity of indigestible material. These statements should not be construed as advising against the consumption of black bread. If you like this type of bread eat it but do not feel that you must eat it if you do not like it.

There is another popular misconception which may be called a fad —that pure whiskey is a wholesome article of diet, whereas impure whiskey is not. All whiskey is 99.4 per cent alcohol and water, and the other 0.6 per cent consists of fusel oil, acids, aldehydes, esters, coloring matter, and material that may be extracted from the cask in which the whiskey was stored. Some years before prohibition, when there was a controversy between the manufacturers of so-called straight whiskey and blended whiskey, a statement was made that the average person preferred a blend but he wished to believe it to be a straight whiskey, and because of this peculiarity there was very little so-called straight whiskey sold in New England. So-called straight whiskey is produced by aging freshly distilled 50 per cent alcohol in an oak barrel for four years, during which period the fusel oil content is almost doubled, and at the same time aldehydes, esters, acid, and furfural are produced. These by-products of fermentation and of aging will cause a measurable increase in the toxicity of the alcohol, but if a person tried to consume sufficient whiskey to damage himself by means of these by-products, he would be killed by the alcohol before the by-products had any effect upon him. The blended liquor formerly was made from pure 50 per cent alcohol to which was added a certain amount of straight liquor together with flavoring substances and coloring matter and the mixture was diluted to a concentration of 45 per cent alcohol. The fusel oil content of the blended liquor was lower than the straight liquor. The straight liquor had a concentration of 50 per cent alcohol. The dangerous ingredient of liquor is alcohol, notwithstanding the faddist idea that it is the impurities which are dangerous.

About fifteen years ago, when popular articles regarding vitamins were extensively published, the general public became vitamin conscious, and this consciousness was responsible for the commercial exploitation of vitamins, more particularly in the form of proprietary medicine. During the past five or six years there has been a change, and at present there is a commercial exploitation of certain types of foods, which may or may not have been reinforced by additional vitamin concentrates.

It is a strange fact that by following the dictates of our appetites we can invariably obtain all the vitamins and other dietary essentials to keep us alive, and it is only by this peculiarity that plants and animals are in existence today. There are times when selected food is necessary, but the selection of this type of food had best be done under the advice of a skilled dietitian or a physician rather than under the advice of a person who wishes to sell something.

ADULT HYGIENE

By HERBERT L. LOMBARD, M. D.

Director, Division of Adult Hygiene
Massachusetts Department of Public Health

QUESTION.—Doctor, I read in the paper the other day that public health measures during the past fifty years had caused the average age at time of death of the population to increase twenty years. Is this true?

ANSWER.—There has been an increase in the average age at time of death of all individuals. This has been caused largely by saving the lives of babies and little children who formerly died of communicable disease, digestive disturbances, and tuberculosis. This has caused the average age of time of death to increase. There has been no increase, however, among the group over fifty. They are living no longer than they did fifty years ago.

QUESTION.—Will public health work change the situation?

ANSWER.—There is a possibility that the expectancy of life over fifty may be slightly increased but it is extremely improbable that many years will be added to the lives of members of the over-fifty group. Public health activities are directed to increasing the *health span* rather than the life span. At the present time a large number of individuals in the over-fifty age group are sick for years prior to death. If we can cut down the length of illness so that they live as well individuals until a short time before death we shall have accomplished much. That is the purpose of the Division of Adult Hygiene.

QUESTION.—How do you know that people are sick for long periods prior to death?

ANSWER.—During the past three years we have been conducting an extensive survey in Massachusetts and have records of nearly fifty-thousand individuals over the age of forty. We find that more than one fourth of all men and women over forty are sick with some chronic disease and many of them had this complaint for years.

QUESTION.—What are the principal sicknesses that you found in the survey?

ANSWER.—About one third of the sick individuals complained of rheumatism, about one sixth of heart disease, and about one twelfth of arteriosclerosis or hardening of the arteries. Cancer, which kills a large percentage of individuals over forty, does not form a large percentage of sickness as it is a disease of relatively short duration while many of these other diseases incapacitate for many years.

QUESTION.—Have you any idea of the money loss from chronic sickness in Massachusetts?
ANSWER.—We estimate that about forty-two million dollars each year is lost in wages. If we add to this the cost of medical care and nursing care, the figure is much greater. Eight million dollars per year is lost in wages by individuals with rheumatism.
QUESTION.—What are you doing to prevent these diseases?
ANSWER.—At the present time we are studying the reasons for the cause of many of these diseases. We know the cause of some. Others we do not and for the next few years a great part of our work will be in trying to find the reasons why some people have chronic disease and others do not. In this study we are using the material which we collected in our three-years' survey.
QUESTION.—Must we wait until your studies are completed before anything can be done for this group?
ANSWER.—By no means. Our present knowledge, if applied to the populace at large, will accomplish much. Probably we will not be able to prevent the occurrence of some of these diseases, but we can at least delay it and arrest the condition if it has already begun. Take cancer, for example—we are unable to prevent the occurrence of this disease in many individuals, but if an individual has an early symptom, goes to the physician and has the lesion treated, we can promise a cure in many cases. With diabetes, an individual who adheres to the advice of his physician can live as long as if he did not have the disease. Two thirds of the cases of rheumatism can be either arrested or cured. If we wait until the disease is no longer in the early stage the situation is entirely different. Chronic disease is, by and large, a race against time.
QUESTION.—What do you consider hygienic living, doctor?
ANSWER.—Hygienic living includes the proper food, proper exercise, and proper relaxation.
QUESTION.—I am particularly anxious for advice about diet. My breakfast consists of coffee and toast; for lunch I have a sandwich and coffee: and for dinner—soup, potato, meat, bread and butter, and coffee. I am not gaining any weight. Is this all right?
ANSWER.—Your diet is very poor. It is not well balanced between acid and alkaline producing foods. Furthermore, certain of the vitamins are taken in far too few quantities. You need more food at breakfast as the greater part of the work has to be done in the daytime and you need food for its accomplishment.
QUESTION.—I don't quite understand what you mean by acid and alkali, doctor.
ANSWER.—The meats, breads, starches and sugars when broken up in the body form acids, while the fruits and vegetables become alkalis. You need a mixture of the acids and the alkalis in your system.
QUESTION.—What about the vitamins, doctor?
ANSWER.—Everyone should eat protective foods. These contain vitamins in sufficient quantity for proper body functioning. Milk, fruits,

cabbage, tomatoes, lettuce and greens are the principal foods of this class. Every individual should consume at least a pint of milk daily. Some of this may be in soup, a part of it in coffee and on cereals. In addition, at least two helpings of the other protective foods should be taken. Tomatoes and cabbage are particularly good if eaten raw. A diet without these foods is apt to greatly impair the health of the individual.

QUESTION.—I do not wish to gain weight. I am afraid of overeating, doctor.

ANSWER.—None of the protective foods have many calories. However, if your weight is not what it should be, with a better diet your weight may decrease. I think we are too prone to measure proper weight by yardsticks that are none too good. What is overweight in one individual is not overweight in another. The leaves on the trees vary in size, animals vary in size, all nature shows variations, and it is to be expected that individuals will vary. There are limits beyond which it is desirable not to go. If an individual is greatly overweight or greatly underweight he is more apt to develop some disease. I think the greatly underweight group is fully as apt to become sick as the greatly overweight. A change in weight is of more importance than either over- or underweight. If you have noticed a sudden change it is well to consult your physician as to the meaning of this. I am not advocating obesity but some variation from the weight-height scale should not cause worry.

QUESTION.—What about tea and coffee, doctor?

ANSWER.—The excessive use of either of these drinks should not be indulged in. I have known individuals who drank nine or ten cups of tea and coffee daily. This is certainly too much.

QUESTION.—Does smoking harm us?

ANSWER.—Again I think it is the amount of smoking rather than the fact whether or not you are a smoker. There is some evidence to believe that cancer of the mouth is more apt to occur in those who are excessive smokers than in those who are not. Everyone who smokes should have his teeth cleaned at frequent intervals by a dentist, probably at least four times a year.

QUESTION.—I suppose exercise is good, doctor, yet I find I am often tired the next morning after vigorous exercise.

ANSWER.—Exercise, like everything else should be in moderation. If carried to the point where one is overtired the next day it has probably been overdone. The man of forty-five and over cannot perform the same amount of physical exercise that he did at the age of twenty. He should moderate his exercise based on his previous habits. The more sedentary the occupation, the more moderate should be the physical recreation as the years increase. For a man to sit at his desk during the year and then in his two weeks' vacation to go into violent athletics is very dangerous. Running for trains when one is not in the habit of running is another form of exercise that may cause serious consequences. As we grow older we must realize that we cannot do the things we were accustomed to do in early life. Moderate exercise, however, is good.

QUESTION.—What about fatigue, doctor?

ANSWER.—There are different kinds of fatigue. One is caused by over-exertion of the muscles and one by nervous energy. If an individual is chronically tired it indicates that something is the matter. A careful examination should be made by a physician to determine the type of fatigue. If an individual has a physique enabling him to do only an 80 per cent job and he is doing a 100 per cent job, fatigue is bound to occur. The physician's examination may show that his body is not functioning properly either through lack of certain glandular secretions or perhaps poisons from an infected tooth or tonsil. If the individual is below par and attempts to do more than his body will allow, fatigue is bound to occur. Then there is the other type where nervous energy is being used up. A man may be tired at the end of the day and yet be able to attend a dance, and dance every dance until midnight. That type of fatigue is nervous and that individual needs relaxation. Few of us have a sufficient amount of rest. This is one of the most important items in hygiene. An individual demanding more rest may often try to improve his body tone by more food and, as a result, an undue amount of fatness may occur. Frequently, these individuals, if given more rest, will find they require less food.

QUESTION.—What other suggestions have you, doctor, regarding proper hygiene?

ANSWER.—I would try to avoid tight clothing and would try to have as good posture as possible. Poor posture is often responsible for many of the discomforts of life.

QUESTION.—What about cold baths?

ANSWER.—Some individuals react very well to cold baths while others do not. If the bath is followed by a glow and sense of well-being, it is beneficial. If it is not, it shows that the individual should not take them throughout the year. Speaking of baths, an excessively hot bath is just as dangerous as a cold one. I knew one individual who came near fainting in the bath tub several times and when the temperature of the water was taken it was found to be far in excess of that which an individual should have. The ordinary warm bath should be not much warmer than the body itself.

QUESTION.—I am subject to colds. What can I do about it?

ANSWER.—Colds are contagious and apparently they give little immunity to subsequent ones. Different individuals, however, vary in the number of colds they have. You should keep your body in the best physical condition, and so far as possible, keep away from other persons who are coughing and sneezing. When you get a cold, go to bed if your temperature rises. Trying to work with an infection present is one of the easiest ways to bring on complications. With a cold you should be careful of drafts, wet feet, and chilling. Pneumonia often follows a cold plus exposure. Moreover, there is a greater strain on several of the vital organs during the process of a cold. Stay in bed until your temperature is normal. The same advice applies to any acute infection. We are willing to go to bed with severe infections, but with the seemingly mild ones like colds and tonsillitis, we may try to work. Such a practice is folly.

QUESTION.—Has the Health Department any reading matter for free distribution on the subject of Adult Hygiene?

ANSWER.—We have a large number of pamphlets on various phases of of this question, and are glad to send them to anyone making a request. These pamphlets cover some of the chronic diseases of adult life, as well as detailed information on hygienic living. One of the best of these pamphlets is "Successful Living." If you, or any of your friends, desire these pamphlets will you kindly indicate the phase of Adult Hygiene that interests you so that we may send you a satisfactory selection.

THE PROGRESS OF MEDICINE

BY ELLIOTT C. CUTLER, M. D.

Boston, Mass.

Matters which relate to the public health concern all and interest everyone. Life insurance statistics show us that, of babies born today in the United States, fifty-four out of every one hundred may expect to attain the age of sixty-five, whereas thirty years ago only forty-one attained this limit. The increase in the duration of life has come about in spite of a great increase in deaths due to accidents and suicide.

This extension of life with all the added happiness it has brought parallels the progress of modern medicine, and it would appear that the basis of this great scientific advance should be generally known. The conservatism of the profession of medicine has forced the public to learn about disease and life in many cases through inaccurate newspaper reports and backstairs gossip. Fortunately there is a growing tendency to teach something concerning life and our bodies in the primary schools of today. Our children now know that storks do not bring babies, that a rabbit's foot won't prevent scarlet fever if the individual contacts another with this disease, that trees have cancer, and that animals have diseases very similar to ours.

Modern medicine begins with the discovery of bacteria as the cause of infectious diseases. Our illnesses are largely those due to tumors, of which cancer is but a single variety; those due to infection, a group now coming under our control; those dependent on a disorder of the mind; and those due to an over or under functioning in some one or more of our internal organs, frequently a ductless gland.

The treatment of injury, whether there be broken bones or not, is obviously the mechanical replacement of the parts. The only difficulty in this field is the avoidance of infection. Wounds and broken bones which do not become infected usually heal promptly. The treatment of tumors is based upon the observation that all tumors start from a single cell which suddenly divides rapidly and multiplies without relation to any functions it is to perform. Treatment must be the early destruction of this cell and its offspring before they reach a tumor of great size or spread elsewhere in the body. Such destruction is usually accomplished by surgical excision or by x-ray or radium treatment, methods which kill the tumor cells. Disorders of metabolism and the over or under functioning of important viscera are controlled by understanding the function of the parts of the body.

Knowledge of physiology, that is the study of the functions of our various organs, has come about through correlating studies upon people after death in relation to their signs and symptoms before death, and then proving this relation by animal experimentation. The control of diabetes by insulin which has added years of comfort to the lives of countless thousands of diabetics is an example of this type, and is due entirely to animal experimentation. In fact, man could never have brought about this advance without these animal investigations. It was found that removing the pancreas in dogs gave them diabetes. Various fragments of the pancreas were then carefully studied until the part was found which controlled sugar metabolism. This is now manufactured in bulk and called insulin.

Similarly, feeding experiments using dogs showed us what elements in food benefited the red cells in our blood. These observations, when modified and used in man, taught us that the use of liver would benefit patients with pernicious anemia, and another group of sick people are restored to a happy and useful life.

Thus, a study of the use and work of the organs in animals under controlled circumstances has given us the greatest part of our knowledge of how our own bodies work; how we digest our food; how our nervous system functions, and how the circulation is maintained.

Another great step forward has been made in the use of drugs. Thus, in early medicine, concoctions of all kinds of flowers and herbs were made and given to the sick. Many of these did little more than nauseate the patient. Gradually more concoctions that were effective were critically studied in laboratories where the few but really useful preparations were singled out. This sort of study meant a great number of observations of the effect of single drugs in varying doses upon animals. But from this work results our present accurate appreciation of drug therapy. The advantage to men of the benefits from a full and scientific appreciation of the effect of digitalis alone cannot be overestimated, and hundreds of drugs are now safely and sanely used because of such investigations.

But perhaps man's chief debt to animal investigation lies in the realm of infectious diseases. The science of bacteriology began between 1860 and 1880 with the experiments of Pasteur and Koch. Preceding that time, disease was generally thought to originate spontaneously within our bodies. Gradually it was shown that bacteria were the cause of many diseases and that the transmission of these bacteria from one person to another spread the infection. The work which proved the relation of different bacteria to different infectious diseases such as diphtheria, typhoid, pneumonia, scarlet fever, cholera, etc. was largely carried out upon animals. Blood, sputum, or the excreta of sick people was placed in media suitable for the growth of bacteria; this infected material was then injected into animals and the bacteria when they had multiplied there were again recovered and grown upon suitable media. Thus by the use of animals, man established the definite causal relationship between all infectious diseases and bacteria. Thus he was able to separate the many kinds of bacteria and show the specific relationship of different bacteria to different diseases. For example, the typhoid organism causes typhoid fever, not pneumonia or diphtheria. This has led to a great extension of life and to a lower death rate, and has immeasurably increased man's opportunity to live long and in comfort.

This discovery of bacteriology gave us clean water supply, uninfected milk supply, better sewage and garbage control, taught us how to can food safely and why refrigeration is essential to the preservation of fresh food. The science of bacteriology enters into all walks of life. It has greatly benefited animals themselves, for it has led to the control of hog cholera, Texas fever of cattle, the infectious diseases of poultry, and many of the disorders of our pet dogs, including rabies and distemper.

Bacteriology has benefited man in so many ways that we cannot now even enumerate them. Perhaps its relation to modern surgery is as striking as any example we could give. Preceding our appreciation of bacteria as the cause of infection there was no real surgery. Legs were amputated, the bladder was operated on for stone, pus was let out of the chest, the superficial tumors were burned off, but you should know that most of these wounds became horribly infected. The surgeon unaware of bacteria, knew nothing of sterilization and carried infection on his clothes and on his instruments from patient to patient. The same conveyance of infection occurred at the birth of children, and puerperal septicemia or "childbed fever" was one of the great causes of death until bacteria were discovered and their relation to this disease established.

As a matter of fact, infection was so common in hospitals, where the transference of bacteria from one patient to another was much more likely to happen because of the close and immediate contacts between infected people, that the public developed a horror of hospitals, an antipathy which is now being gradually effaced. Hospitals instead of being havens of refuge where cleanliness and asepsis make them the safest place for the sick patient, were truly dangerous places for the sick. The doctors knew this also and Volpeau, the great French surgeon, wrote that "a pin prick is a door open to death, a door which widens with the slightest use of the knife!"

All this has now been done away with. Men, having learned of the relation of bacteria to disease, having reproduced the diseases in animals, soon learned, first by the use of drugs and later by the use of heat, how to sterilize materials and thus rid them of bacteria and infection. Today the surgeon performs his task in a field rid of all bacteria by several methods of sterilization. The skin is sterilized by antiseptic drugs, the linen and dry goods are sterilized by being heated in a container where steam is under pressure, and the instruments and gloves are boiled. Now, the surgeon, having learned asepsis, has only to learn the control of hemorrhage in order to be able to operate in any cavity of the body with safety.

There are about ten thousand surgeons in the United States operating almost daily. All the procedures which they perform from the cure of simple rupture in the little baby to the removal of a tumor in the brain, are made possible because only a generation ago Pasteur and a few other pioneers in the field of science established by animal experimentation the relation of bacteria to infection.

The lives saved by surgery, the reduction in the death rate at childbirth, from diphtheria, from typhoid fever, and the general extension of life in the last seventy years rests squarely upon the science of bacteriology. No single gift to man can ever bring him greater release from suffering, and to the individuals and methods which developed this science every living human being will always owe the deepest debt of gratitude.

BOOK NOTE

THE WORK OF THE SANITARY ENGINEER By ARTHUR J. MARTIN, 472 pages *MacDonald & Evans, London*, 1935

Although the author states on the title page that this new handbook is intended for the use of students in sanitary engineering and others concerned with public health, an examination of it shows much of value for the trained sanitary engineer. The references to old English public health laws alone make the book of great value and it is most gratifying to find in it such complete references to the work of the Royal Commission on Sewage Disposal.

Part I contains an historical review of the science of sanitary engineering and various English acts relating to the public health as well as discussions of local appropriations, the work of public works departments and the relation of certain trust institutions, engineering societies and foundations to sanitary engineering work.

Part II is a reasonably complete textbook on water supply and also contains some very interesting references to British water acts.

Part III deals with the subject of drainage and sewerage.

Part IV, devoted to sewage disposal, contains many valuable references to the work of the Royal Commission on Sewage Disposal including the standards of purity which have been set up as a result of their work. The chapter on trade wastes is particularly valuable to those who are interested in the work of preventing stream pollution.

Part V discusses the collection and disposal of refuse and garbage and Part VI, drainage, flood control and erosion.

"The Work of the Sanitary Engineer" is up-to-date in its references and a valuable addition to the library of any engineering school or public health engineering office.

REPORT OF DIVISION OF FOOD AND DRUGS

During the months of July, August and September 1935, samples were collected in 203 cities and towns.

There were 1,647 samples of milk examined, of which 290 were below standard, from 17 samples the cream had been in part removed, and 3 samples contained added water. There were 1,004 bacteriological examinations made of milk, 693 of which complied with the requirements. There were 237 bacteriological examinations made of frozen desserts, 180 of which complied with the requirements; 2 bacteriological examinations of meat which complied with the requirements; 5 bacteriological examinations of bread flour, 2 of which complied with the requirements; and 13 bacteriological examinations of empty tonic bottles, 6 of which did not comply with the requirements. There were 137 samples of ice cream analyzed for pounds of food solids per gallon, of which 4 samples were below the standard.

There were 654 samples of food examined, 69 of which were adulterated. These consisted of 1 sample of fruit cookies which contained worms; 17 samples of eggs, 12 samples of which were decomposed, 3 samples of stale eggs sold as fresh eggs, 1 sample adulterated by the addition of water, and 1 sample adulterated by the addition of water and salt; 4 samples of frozen desserts, consisting of 3 samples of ice milk which were low in fat, said samples having been advertised as "ice cream", and 1 sample of ice cream low in fat; 33 samples of hamburg steak, 10 samples of which contained a compound of sulphur dioxide not properly labeled and 4 samples were also decomposed, 2 samples contained sodium sulphite in excess of one tenth of one per cent and 1 sample was also watered, 2 samples contained water, one of of which was also decomposed, and 19 samples were decomposed, 1 of which also contained water and lung tissue, and 2 of which also contained sodium sulphite in excess of one tenth of one per cent; 1 sample of hamburger sandwich which contained a compound of sulphur dioxide not properly labeled; 3 samples of sausage, 1 sample of which contained a compound of sulphur dioxide not properly labeled, and 2 samples were decomposed and 1 sample also contained a compound of sulphur dioxide not properly labeled; 3 samples of fowl which were decomposed; 1 sample of vinegar which contained less than the required amount of acidity; 1 sample of buttered pop corn seasoned with fat other than butter; and 5 samples of mattress fillings which contained secondhand material.

There were 59 samples of drugs examined, of which 1 was adulterated. This was a sample of hydrogen peroxide which did not conform to the U. S. P. requirements.

The police departments submitted 128 samples of liquor for examination. The police departments also submitted 22 samples to be analyzed for poisons or drugs, 4 samples of which contained heroin, 2 contained heroin hydrochloride, 1 contained reducing sugar, 1 contained formaldehyde, 1 contained chloral hydrate, 1 contained sodium borate and boric acid, 1 contained cannabis, 1 sample was ergot, 1 sample was bicarbonate of soda, 8 samples were analyzed for arsenic with negative results, and 1 sample was analyzed and contained no alkaloids, no cyanide and no heavy metals.

There were 83 cities and towns visited for the inspection of pasteurizing plants, and 232 plants were inspected.

There were 35 plants inspected for the manufacture of ice cream.

There were 90 hearings held pertaining to violations of the laws.

There were 65 convictions for violations of the laws, $1,495 in fines being imposed.

John Behilo and Ignace Budrewicz of Greenfield; Donald Kirchner of Pittsfield; Dennis Boriea of Worcester; Anselmo Chiurri of Leominster; and Stanley Luinis of Brockton, were all convicted for violations of the milk laws. Dennis Boriea of Worcester appealed his case.

Badger Farms Creameries, 2 cases, of Newbury; Abraham Brox, 2 cases, and Guy H. Richardson of Dracut; Anthony Rogers, 3 cases, of North Andover; and William Hogg of Whitman, were convicted for violations of the pasteurization laws and regulations. Anthony Rogers of North Andover appealed 1 case.

Hazen K. Richardson, 2 cases, of Middleton; and Whiting Milk Companies, Incorporated, of Nantasket, were convicted for violations of the milk grading law.

Workers Cooperative Union, Incorporated, of Lawrence, was convicted for falsely labeling milk as to the fat content.

Fairburns, Incorporated, 2 cases, Benjamin Gross, 2 cases, Brockelman Brothers, Incorporated, and Isaac Lisman of Lowell; Jacob Geller of Newburyport; Growers Outlet, Incorporated, Sam's Market, Incorporated, and John Klys of Springfield; Sam Gordon and Robert Kravitz of New Bedford; Handy Dandy Stores, Incorporated, of Haverhill; Frank S. Hollis, 2 cases, of Chelsea; Kennedy & Company, Incorporated, Boston; Pasquale Guylielmo of East Boston; Growers Outlet, Incorporated, of Greenfield; Delmer M. Jewett of South Deerfield; William K. Kline, 2 cases, Harry Baker, 2 counts, Louis Goldman and David Steinburg of Lynn; Max Common, Simon Gordon, and United Meat Market of Cambridge; Patrick Foley, and Hudson Market, Incorporated, 2 cases, of Hudson; and Harold Lampert of Somerville, were all convicted for violations of the food laws. Jacob Geller of Newburyport; Pasquale Guylielmo of East Boston; and Harold Lampert of Somerville, appealed their cases.

State Restaurant, Incorporated, of Fall River; and M. Winer & Company, Incorporated, of Hull, were convicted for false advertising.

Demetrios Gonnaris of Arlington, James R. Sullivan of Brockton; Arthur F. Watkins, 2 cases, of Peabody, Filomena Acampora of Worcester; and General Ice Cream Company, Incorporated, of North Abington, were convicted for violations of the frozen dessert law. General Ice Cream Company, Incorporated, of North Abington, appealed their case.

Dominic Mastroianni, 2 cases, and John Shaker of North Adams, were convicted for violations of the soft drink law. John Shaker of North Adams appealed his case.

George Harvey of Clarksburg, and Walter Naleski of Auburn, were convicted for violations of the slaughtering laws. Walter Naleski of Auburn appealed his case.

George Gersmann of Worcester, and Providence Mattress Company of Providence, R. I., were convicted for violations of the mattress law.

In accordance with Section 25, Chapter 111 of the General Laws, the following is the list of articles of adulterated food collected in original packages from manufacturers, wholesalers, or producers:

Hamburg steak which was decomposed was obtained as follows:

One sample each, from Ganem's Market and Brockelman Brothers of Lawrence; N. Somers of Springfield; Everybody's Market of Indian Orchard; Grade A Market, Fairburns, Incorporated, and Brockelman Brothers, of Lowell; Abraham Holland of New Bedford; Taunton Public Market of Taunton; Harold Lampert of Somerville; Foley's Market of Hudson; Simon Gordon and United Meat Market of Cambridge; Olympia Square Market and Modern Market of Lynn.

Hamburg steak which was decomposed and also contained a compound of sulphur dioxide not properly labeled was obtained as follows:

One sample each, from John Raggieri of Somerville; Hudson Market of Hudson, Legion Market of Lynn; and City Public Market of Lowell.

One sample of hamburg steak which was decomposed and also watered was obtained from Ganem's Market of Lawrence.

Hamburg steak which was decomposed and also contained sodium sulphite in excess of one tenth of one per cent was obtained as follows:

One sample each, from City Public Market (Benjamin Gross) of Lowell, and Robert Kravitz of New Bedford.

One sample of hamburg steak which was decomposed, also watered, and contained lung tissue, was obtained from William K. Kline of Lynn.

Hamburg steak which contained a compound of sulphur dioxide not properly labeled was obtained as follows:

One sample each, from Louis Israel and Sam Gordon of New Bedford; Sam's Market of Springfield; and Fairburn's, Incorporated, of Lowell.

One sample of hamburg steak which contained water was obtained from Ideal Market (Max Common), of Cambridge.

One sample of hamburg steak which contained sodium sulphite in excess of one tenth of one per cent was obtained from William K. Kline of Lynn.

One sample of hamburg steak which contained sodium sulphite in excess of one tenth of one per cent and was also watered was obtained from Beverly Market (Joseph Pevritsky) of Beverly.

One sample of hamburger sandwich which contained a compound of sulphur dioxide not properly labeled was obtained from White Tower Hamburger of Cambridge.

One sample of sausage which contained a compound of sulphur dioxide not properly labeled was obtained from Anna Juskiewicz of Palmer.

One sample of sausage which was decomposed was obtained from Brockelman Brothers of Lowell.

One sample of sausage which contained a compound of sulphur dioxide not properly labeled and was also decomposed was obtained from Growers Outlet of Springfield.

One sample of fruit cookies which contained worms was obtained from Kennedy & Company, Incorporated, of Boston.

One sample of ice cream which was low in fat was obtained from New York Eskimo Pie Company of Springfield.

One sample of vinegar which was low in acidity was obtained from Samuel Herman of New Bedford.

Mattress filling which contained secondhand material was obtained as follows:

Three samples from Franklin Textile Company of Boston, and 2 samples from Providence Mattress Company of Providence, Rhode Island.

There were ten confiscations, consisting of 1715 pounds of decomposed fowl; 462 pounds of decomposed fowl; 309 pounds of decomposed butterfish; 734 pounds of decomposed butterfish; 439 pounds of decomposed butterfish; 7,300 pounds of decomposed butterfish; 190 pounds of decomposed eels; 1,700 pounds of decomposed grey sole; 1,200 pounds of decomposed grey sole; and 5,900 pounds of decomposed grey sole.

The licensed cold storage warehouses reported the following amounts of food placed in storage during June, 1935:—1,083,480 dozens of case eggs; 1,380,252 pounds of broken out eggs; 4,869,364 pounds of butter; 1,440,627 pounds of poultry; 2,347,430 pounds of fresh meat and fresh meat products; and 13,742,055 pounds of fresh food fish.

There was on hand July 1, 1935:— 6,006,420 dozens of case eggs; 1,918,135 pounds of broken out eggs; 5,257,373 pounds of butter; 3,450,206 pounds of poultry; 6,313,218½ pounds of fresh meat and fresh meat products; and 25,563,455 pounds of fresh food fish.

The licensed cold storage warehouses reported the following amounts of food placed in storage during July, 1935:— 438,360 dozens of case eggs; 1,493,178 pounds of broken out eggs; 4,945,964 pounds of butter; 1,182,238 pounds of poultry; 3,006,364 pounds of fresh meat and fresh meat products; and 10,992,321 pounds of fresh food fish.

There was on hand August 1, 1935:— 6,011,580 dozens of case eggs; 2,649,981 pounds of broken out eggs; 9,519,526 pounds of butter; 2,987,464 pounds of poultry; 5,327,620½ pounds of fresh meat and fresh meat products; and 30,955,123 pounds of fresh food fish.

The licensed cold storage warehouses reported the following amounts of food placed in storage during August, 1935:— 246,750 dozens of case eggs; 816,613 pounds of broken out eggs; 1,539,722 pounds of butter; 1,021,087 pounds of poultry; 2,757,254½ pounds of fresh meat and fresh meat products; and 9,534,133 pounds of fresh food fish.

There was on hand September 1, 1935:— 4,944,990 dozens of case eggs; 2,696,035 pounds of broken out eggs; 9,778,615 pounds of butter; 2,378,495 pounds of poultry; 4,801,164 pounds of fresh meat and fresh meat products; and 32,657,117 pounds of fresh food fish.

MASSACHUSETTS DEPARTMENT OF PUBLIC HEALTH

Commissioner of Public Health, HENRY D. CHADWICK, M. D.

Public Health Council

HENRY D. CHADWICK, M. D., *Chairman*

GORDON HUTCHINS
FRANCIS H. LALLY, M. D.
SYLVESTER E. RYAN, M. D.
RICHARD M. SMITH, M. D.
RICHARD P. STRONG, M. D.
JAMES L. TIGHE

Secretary, ALICE M. NELSON

Division of Administration . . Under direction of Commissioner.
Division of Sanitary Engineering . Director and Chief Engineer,
ARTHUR D. WESTON, C. E.
Division of Communicable Diseases Director,
GAYLORD W. ANDERSON, M. D.
Division of Biologic Laboratories . Director and Pathologist,
ELLIOTT S. ROBINSON, M. D.
Division of Food and Drugs . . Director and Analyst,
HERMANN C. LYTHGOE, S. B.
Division of Child Hygiene . . Director, M. LUISE DIEZ, M. D.
Division of Tuberculosis . . Director, ALTON S. POPE, M. D.
Division of Adult Hygiene . . Director,
HERBERT L. LOMBARD, M. D.

State District Health Officers

The Southeastern District . . RICHARD P. MACKNIGHT, M. D., New Bedford
The South Metropolitan District . HENRY M. DEWOLFE, M. D., Quincy
The North Metropolitan District . CHARLES B. MACK, M. D., Boston
The Northeastern District . . ROBERT E. ARCHIBALD, M. D., Lynn
The Worcester County District . OSCAR A. DUDLEY, M. D., Worcester
The Connecticut Valley District . HAROLD E. MINER, M. D., Springfield
The Berkshire District . . . WALTER W. LEE, M. D., No. Adams

INDEX

	PAGE
Adult Hygiene, by Herbert L. Lombard, M.D.	251
Air Conditioning—Ventilation—Heating, by Arthur D. Weston	107
Alley, Leon A., M.D., Extra-Pulmonary Tuberculosis	27
Amebic Dysentery	146
American Neisserian Medical Society	64
Anderson, Gaylord W., M.D., Infantile Paralysis	206
Anterior Poliomyelitis	139
Bacillary Dysentery	146
Begg, Alexander S., M.D., Preventive Medicine from Your Family Physician	203
Beinert, Frederica L., Diet in the Home Treatment of Tuberculosis	25
Bigelow, George H., M.D.	3
Biological Laboratory, by Elliott C. Robinson, M.D.	244
Biologic Products	135
Birnie, John, M.D., Jim has a Stomach Ache	245
Blind, Assistance to the	177
Book Notes:	
Comparability of Maternal Mortality Rates in the United States and Certain Foreign Countries	121
How Safe is Home, by Howard Whipple Green	64
Work of the Sanitary Engineer	258
Boston of 1800, by Eleanor J. Macdonald, A.B.	229
Brown, Lloyd T., M.D., The Care and Hygiene of the Feet	85
Camps, Medical Supervision of Health, by Carl C. MacCorison, M.D.	46
—Summer Health, by Frank Kiernan	42
Cancer	178
—by Ernest M. Daland, M.D.	234
Care and Hygiene of the Feet, by Lloyd T. Brown, M.D.	85
Case-Blechschmidt, Dorothy, M.D., F.A.C.S., Prevention of Deafness—Rear Your Ear to Hear	78
Chadwick, Henry D., M.D., Public Health in Massachusetts in 1934	199
—School Tuberculosis Clinic Program in Retrospect and in Prospect	33
Chadwick Clinic Results	36
Character, Illness and, by Leroy E. Parkins, M.D.	215
Chicken Pox	142
Child Hygiene	175
—by M. Luise Diez, M. D.	218
Churchill, Edward D., M.D., The Role of Surgery in Pulmonary Tuberculosis	18
Circulation, Tired Legs from Altered, by Hilbert F. Day, M.D.	240
Clinical Psychology and Medicine, by Ives Hendrick, M.D.	73
Clinics:	
Cancer	178
Gonorrhea and Syphilis	171
Infantile Paralysis	141
Mental	180
Tuberculosis	155

	PAGE
Collapse Treatment in Tuberculosis, by Alton S. Pope, M.D.	213
Commonhealth, Back Issues of	120
Communicable Diseases	130
Comparability of Maternal Mortality Rates in the United States and Certain Foreign Countries (book note)	121
Conserving the Sight, by William F. Snow, M.D.	75
Cummins, Loretta Joy, M.D., Some Facts One Should Know About the Skin	82
Cure of Tuberculosis, by Ernest B. Emerson, M.D.	15
Curious New Discoveries About Sleep, by Donald A. Laird, Ph.D., Sci.D.	87
Cutler, Elliott C., M.D., The Progress of Medicine	255
Daland, Ernest M., M.D., Cancer	234
Darkness of Ignorance and the Fog of Prudery, By N. A. Nelson, M.D.	226
Davis, Lincoln, M.D., Violence and Public Health	222
Day, Hilbert F., M.D., Tired Legs from Altered Circulation	240
Deafness, Prevention of—Rear Your Ear to Hear, by Dorothy Case-Blechschmidt, M.D., F.A.C.S.	78
Decline in Tuberculosis, by Alton S. Pope, M.D.	60
Diagnostic Dispensary, by Alton S. Pope, M.D.	14
Diagnostic Laboratory	133
Diet in the Home Treatment of Tuberculosis, by Frederica L. Beinert	25
Diez, M. Luise, M.D., Child Hygiene	218
Differential Diagnosis of Tuberculosis, by Frederick T. Lord, M.D.	12
Diphtheria	143
Dispensary, Diagnostic, by Alton S. Pope, M.D.	14
Dog Bite	144
Dysentery	146
Ear, Nose and Throat Diseases, by Charles I. Johnson, M.D.	209
Editorial Comment:	
Back Issues of The Commonhealth	120
Vision of School Children	119
Educational Material	139, 146
Emerson, Ernest B., M.D., The Cure of Tuberculosis	15
Emerson, Kendall, M.D., Tuberculosis in 1934	6
Epidemic Cerebro-Spinal Meningitis	147
Extra Pulmonary Tuberculosis, by Leon A. Alley, M.D.	27
Feet, Care and Hygiene of the, By Lloyd T. Brown, M.D.	85
Food and Drugs, Report of Division of:	
October-November-December, 1934	65
January-February-March, 1935	122
April-May-June, 1935	191
July-August-September, 1935	259
Food Fads, by Hermann C. Lythgoe, S.B.	248
Foods, Preservation of, in the Home, By Hermann C. Lythgoe	114
Gardner, Marion B., Well Groomed; Well Kept	102
German Measles	148
Gonorrhea	167, 169, 173
and Syphilis in the Public Schools, by N. A. Nelson, M.D.	118

	PAGE
Handbook for Physicians	127
Heating—Ventilation—Air Conditioning, by Arthur D. Weston	107
Hendrick, Ives, M.D., Clinical Psychology and Medicine	73
Hobbies, by Lucy Wright	105
Hospitalization of Communicable Diseases	134
of Tuberculosis in Massachusetts, by Alton S. Pope, M.D.	21
How Safe is Home, by Howard Whipple Green (book note)	64
Illness and Character, by Leroy E. Parkins, M.D.	215
Industrial Diseases	175
Infantile Paralysis	139
by Gaylord W. Anderson, M.D.	206
Jim Has a Stomach Ache, by John Birnie, M.D.	245
Johnson, Charles I., M.D., Ear, Nose and Throat Diseases	209
Kelly, Eleanor E., Social Work for the Tuberculosis Patient	57
Kiernan, Frank, Summer Health Camps	42
Knowlton, Helen, Suggestions for Students who are Preparing Their Own Meals	95
Laird, Donald A., Ph.D., Sci.D., Curious New Discoveries About Sleep	87
Leahy, Howard J., A.M., Teaching the Etiology of Tuberculosis	48
Lighting for Seeing, by M. Luckiesh and Frank K. Moss	111
Lobar Pneumonia	149
Lombard, Herbert L., M.D., Adult Hygiene	251
Lord, Frederick T., M.D., The Differential Diagnosis of Tuberculosis	12
Luckiesh, M. and Moss, Frank K., Lighting for Seeing	111
Lythgoe, Hermann C., S.B., Food Fads	248
—Preservation of Foods in the Household	114
MacCorison, Carl C., M.D., Medical Supervision of Health Camps	46
Macdonald, Eleanor J., A.B., Boston of 1800	229
Malaria	151
Maternal Mortality Rates, Comparability of, in the United States and Certain Foreign Countries (book note)	121
Meals, Suggestions for Students who are Preparing Their Own, by Helen Knowlton	95
Meals for One or Two—To Those Who Eat Alone, by Dorothea Nicoll	97
Measles	151
German	148
Medical Supervision of Health Camps, by Carl C. MacCorison, M.D.	46
Medicine, Progress of, by Elliott C. Cutler, M.D.	255
Meningitis, Epidemic Cerebro-Spinal	147
Mental diseases	180
Morgan, Roy, M.D., Tuberculosis in Children	29
Mortality (maternal) rates, Comparability of, in the United States and Certain Foreign Countries (book note)	121
Moss, Frank K., and Luckiesh, M., Lighting for Seeing	111
Mumps	152
Nelson, N. A., M.D., The Darkness of Ignorance and the Fog of Prudery	226
—Gonorrhea and Syphilis in the Public Schools	118
Nicoll, Dorothea, Meals for One or Two—To Those Who Eat Alone	97

	PAGE
Nose, Ear and Throat Diseases, by Charles I. Johnson, M.D.	209
Ophthalmia Neonatorum	152
Pamphlets on Cummunicable Disease	139
Paratyphoid Fever	153
Parkins, Leroy E., M.D., Illness and Character	215
Physician's handbook	127
Pneumonia, Lobar	149
Policies and Routines for a Tuberculosis Nursing Service, by Helen C. Reilly, R. N.	50
Poliomyelitis	139
Pope, Alton S., M. D., Collapse Treatment in Tuberculosis	213
—The Decline in Tuberculosis	60
—The Diagnostic Dispensary	14
—Hospitalization of Tuberculosis in Massachusetts	21
Porter, Alma, Satisfaction Guaranteed	91
Postnatal Letters	176
Pratt, Joseph H., M.D., Tuberculosis in the Practice of Medicine	7
Prenatal Letters	175
Preservation of Foods in the Household, by Herman C. Lythgoe	114
Prevention of Deafness—Rear Your Ear To Hear, by Dorothy Case-Blechschmidt, M.D., F.A.C.S.	78
Preventive Medicine from Your Family Physician, by Alexander S. Begg, M.D.	203
Progress of Medicine, by Elliott C. Cutler, M.D.	255
Psychology (clinical) and Medicine, by Ives Hendrick, M.D.	73
Public Health, Violence and, by Lincoln Davis, M.D.	222
Public Health in Massachusetts in 1934, by Henry D. Chadwick, M.D.	199
Public Welfare, Institutions under	190
Quarantine Requirements for Communicable Disease	131
Rabies	153
Reilly, Helen C., R.N., Policies and Routines for a Tuberculosis Nursing Service	50
Reporting of Communicable Disease	130
Robinson, Elliott C., M.D., The Biological Laboratory	244
Role of Surgery in Pulmonary Tuberculosis, by Edward D. Churchill, M.D.	18
Satisfaction Guaranteed, by Alma Porter	91
Scarlet Fever	153
School Tuberculosis Clinic Program in Retrospect and in Prospect, by Henry D. Chadwick, M.D.	33
Septic Sore Throat	154
Sight, Conserving the, by William F. Snow, M.D.	75
Skin, Some Facts One Should Know about the, by Loretta Joy Cummins, M.D.	82
Sleep, Curious New Discoveries about, by Donald A. Laird, Ph.D., Sci.D.	87
Smallpox	154
Snow, William F., M.D., Conserving the Sight	75
Social Work for the Tuberculosis Patient, by Eleanor E. Kelly	57

	PAGE
Some Facts one Should Know About the Skin, by Loretta Joy Cummins, M.D.	82
Stomach Ache, Jim Has a, by John Birnie, M.D.	245
Suggestions for Students Who Are Preparing Their Own Meals, by Helen Knowlton	95
Summer Health Camps, by Frank Kiernan	42
Surgery, Role of, in Pulmonary Tuberculosis, by Edward D. Churchill, M.D.	18
Syphilis	167, 173
Syphilis and Gonorrhea in the Public Schools, by N. A. Nelson, M.D.	118
Teaching the Etiology of Tuberculosis, by Howard J. Leahy, A.M.	48
Tetanus	155
Throat, Ear and Nose Diseases, by Charles I. Johnson, M.D.	209
Tired Legs from Altered Circulation, by Hilbert F. Day, M.D.	240
Topography of the State of Massachusetts, by Arthur D. Weston, C.E.	237
Tuberculosis:	155
Collapse Treatment in, by Alton S. Pope, M.D.	213
Cure of, by Ernest B. Emerson, M.D.	15
Decline In, by Alton S. Pope, M.D.	60
Diet in Home Treatment of, by Frederica L. Beinert	25
Differential Diagnosis of, by Frederick T. Lord, M.D.	12
Extra-Pulmonary, by Leon A. Alley, M.D.	27
Hospitalization of, in Massachusetts, by Alton S. Pope, M.D.	21
Policies and Routines of a Tuberculosis Nursing Service, by Helen C. Reilly, R. N.	50
The Role of Surgery in Pulmonary Tuberculosis, by Edward C. Churchill, M.D.	18
School Tuberculosis Clinic Program in Retrospect and Prospect, by Henry D. Chadwick, M.D.	33
Social Work for the Tuberculosis Patient, by Eleanor E. Kelly	57
Teaching the Etiology of, by Howard J. Leahy, A.M.	48
Case-finding in Children of School Age, by David Zacks, M.D.	39
In Children, by Roy Morgan, M.D.	29
In 1934, by Kendall Emerson, M.D.	6
In the Practice of Medicine, by Joseph H. Pratt, M.D.	7
Typhoid Fever	164
Typhus Fever	166
Undulant Fever	166
Ventilation—Air Conditioning—Heating, by Arthur D. Weston	107
Violence and Public Health, by Lincoln Davis, M.D.	222
Vision of School Children	119
Wassermann Laboratory	133
Well Groomed, Well Kept, by Marion B. Gardner	102
Weston, Arthur D., C. E., Topography of the State of Massachusetts	237
—Ventilation—Air Conditioning—Heating	107
Whooping Cough	166
Wright, Lucy, Hobbies	105
Zacks, David, M.D., Tuberculosis Case-Finding in Children of School Age	39

5M. 12-'35. Order 6281.

THE COMMONHEALTH

Volume 23　　　　Jan.-Feb.-Mar.
No. 1-4　　　　　　1936

NUTRITION
IN THE COMMUNITY

THE COMMONHEALTH
QUARTERLY BULLETIN OF THE MASSACHUSETTS DEPARTMENT OF
PUBLIC HEALTH

Sent Free to any Citizen of the State

Entered as second class matter at Boston Postoffice.

M. LUISE DIEZ, M.D., DIRECTOR OF DIVISION OF CHILD HYGIENE, EDITOR.
Room 545, State House, Boston, Mass.

CONTENTS

	PAGE
The Community Nutritionist, by Mary Spalding, M. A.	3
The Training of the Nutritionist, by Alice F. Blood, Ph.D.	5
Present Trends in Nutrition, by E. V. McCollum, Ph.D., Sc.D.	6
The Place of the Nutritionist in the Public Health Program, by W. G. Smillie, M. D.	11
The Nutritionist with the Board of Health in a Small Town, by Curtis M. Hilliard, A. B.	15
The Nutrition Worker and Nurse in a Family Health Program, by Blanche T. Dimond, B. S. and Ann Richardson, R. N., B. A., B. N.	18
An Itinerant Nutritionist in a Country Town, by Dorothy Hager, B.S.	22
The Contribution of the Food Clinic to the Community, by Frances Stern	32
The Nutritionist on the Itinerant Clinics, by David Zacks, M. D.	36
Nutrition on the Well Child Conference, by Susan M. Coffin, M. D. and Frederica L. Beinert, B. S.	40
A Smile from Araxie, by Ruth L. White, B. S.	47
A Dental Nutrition Program in a Community, by M. M. Brown, R. N. and Dorothea Nicoll, B. S.	50
Group Conferences with Expectant Mothers, by Charlotte Raymond, B. A.	54
A Nutrition Program in a Public Welfare Organization, by Sue E. Sadow, B. S.	56
A Budget Case, by Florence Genevieve Dorward, B. S.	61
One School's Nutrition Problem, by Catherine Leamy, M. S.	65
Publicity for a Community Nutrition Program, by Albertine P. McKellar, B. S.	68
The Nutritionist Says It with Exhibits, by Dorothea Nicoll, B. S.	71
Maternal Deaths in Massachusetts	73
Book Notes—	
Lobar Pneumonia and Serum Therapy by Frederick T. Lord, M. D. and Roderick Heffron, M. D.	73
The Facts About Certified Milk	74
Report of Division of Food and Drugs, October, November, December, 1935	75

THE COMMUNITY NUTRITIONIST
BY MARY SPALDING, M. A.
Consultant in Nutrition, Massachusetts Department of Public Health.

"There never was a time when the nutrition of the people was more critically important, not even excepting the war. A slow thing, the change in the eating habits of a people, and critically needed quickly. May this number of The Commonhealth help somewhat in the quickening process."—Dr. George H. Bigelow—April 1932, Nutrition Number of The Commonhealth.

This is still true in 1936. To meet this problem certain Massachusetts communities wished assistance in making plans for a nutritionist. In preparing for them the following outline I was fortunate to be able to discuss it with outstanding and experienced nutritionists such as Miss Lucy Gillett, who has built up the practical nutrition service of the A. I. C. P. for the welfare of New York City, Miss Mary G. McCormick, who is building up the health education in the schools of New York for their Department of Education, as well as able community nutritionists in Massachusetts. Our Nutrition Advisory Committee—Dr. Alice Blood, Mrs. Annette T. Herr, Professor Curtis M. Hilliard, Professor Murray P. Horwood, Dr. Florence McKay, Dr. Howard F. Root, Mrs. Octavia Smillie, and Miss Frances Stern—have also considered this outline from their various points of view and made generous suggestions. Because of the need to fit the nutritionist's work with that of her co-workers in the community, Dr. Stevens, Director, and Miss Woodbury, Supervisor of Nurses in the Berkshire Health Unit, and our own staff have assisted. We nutritionists ask help from physicians, nurses, dentists, psychiatrists, social workers, and teachers, as well as the lay people in the community. In turn we feel we can contribute a practical service from our experience and knowledge that will be of real use to the public health. Actual demonstrations by two of our nutritionists are being carried—one in a rural county health unit of about 10,000 people and one in a city of about 40,000. Now in order to make this outline alive, physicians and educators working with nutritionists, and nutritionists have contributed concrete examples of their work for this number of The Commonhealth.

The Community Nutritionist

The community nutritionist is a pioneer who is more and more proving her worth in public health through practical teaching of positive nutrition. In this way she fills a gap in the group of community workers. Her work differs from the dietitian in that she does not work from the institution, but in the community as does the public health nurse. The nutritionist stresses more the preventive measures than the curative. What she does will depend on the community's needs and desires. In various communities she may work with one or more of the following organizations and in the following ways.

Organizations Served

Public Health Departments, Public Welfare Departments, Departments of Education.

Private organizations—such as Visiting Nurse Association, Dental Infirmary, Out-Patient Clinics, Red Cross Chapter, Family Welfare Association, Tuberculosis Association, Health Centre.

In City

The nutritionist in the city might serve in a certain district or do the work of one organization in the city.

She should be responsible to the director of the employing organization, even though sometimes she might be loaned to other organizations.

In the small city or large town with a Community Council she might serve all organizations directly under an advisory committee from the Council.

In Rural Towns

The rural nutritionist might be an itinerant nutritionist and serve in a unit, such as a county health unit, or a group of townships.

She should be responsible to the director of the unit.

The nutritionist should have representation on the Community Council.

An understanding of individual, family, and community problems and backgrounds. Acquired through—

A four years' course in an accredited school of home economics—or its equivalent—with a major in food and nutrition.

Practical experience and training in family case work and in teaching to get a social viewpoint and first hand experience.

Additional training as a student dietitian in a food clinic or hospital is of value.

Her Personal Qualifications

Considerable experience and background so as to understand her resources and adapt her subject matter to the different types of individuals she serves.

Tact and adaptability, sincerity and understanding to gain confidence. Good health.

Ability to speak convincingly and to make graphic material, so as to interest and acquaint the community with what she does.

Her training, experience, and personal qualifications should be adapted to the organization and community served.

Her Salary

An amount depending on the community or county's funds, the type of nutritionist desired, and the salaries of commensurate positions.

Expenses should include an adequate amount for records, exhibits, and transportation.

THE TRAINING OF THE NUTRITIONIST
BY ALICE F. BLOOD, PH. D.

Professor of Home Economics
Simmons College, Boston, Mass.

There are two recent published reports which provide a background for the discussion of the training of the nutritionist. Nutrition Service in the Field by the Sub-committee on Nutrition of the White House Conference on Child Health and Protection, and Nutrition and Public Health in the Quarterly Bulletin of the Health Organization of the League of Nations*. Although the latter leans heavily on the White House Conference Report and on conversations which Mr. Aykroyd had with various nutritionists when he was in this country, it is nevertheless of special interest as representing the appraisal by an astute observer of a development which is chiefly American.

In reading either of these summaries one is struck by the equal emphasis which is laid on personal qualifications and on training. In this, as in other professional work where it is desired that the practices of large numbers of people be modified as the result of education, it is vital that the leader have the desire and the capacity to understand other people's problems, and the ability to arouse in them the "will-to-do." This is equally compatible with a quiet steadiness or with vivacity of temperament, but is always accompanied in the effective person by a strong sense of the human value of her undertaking. Because the work of the nutritionist is new in the community few jobs are ready-made and the worker needs to have a good self starter, a keen eye for opportunities, and a persuasive tongue.

As far as formal training is concerned, it seems to be generally conceded that the minimum foundation is a familiarity with the principles of nutrition and ability to handle food preparation problems equivalent to that provided by a major in food and nutrition in a well organized home economics course.

This implies a good background of chemistry, physiology, and bacteriology for the training in nutrition and food. The student should also have a strong minor in the social sciences including economics, psychology, sociology, and education, and covering the relevant practical aspects of these subjects, such as budgets, the social resources of the community, and practice teaching, preferably in the health field.

The colleges and universities that are particularly interested in this field are finding it possible to provide specialized training either at the graduate level or in the senior year of college. If the course is given by someone with wide experience in the field of applied nutrition and if opportunity is found for field work in one or more suitable organizations, much can be done to prepare the prospective worker for a job. At the least, such courses should reveal the students who have real aptitude in this field.

Hospital training after college is generally recognized as contribut-

---
*June, 1935.

ing to the preparation of the nutritionist, but a hospital course which is devoted in large part to administrative problems is certainly not ideal. The plan, recently accepted by the American Dietetic Association, which recognizes a program which is chiefly devoted to food clinic problems is a big step in the right direction and it is hoped that developments here will be rapid. By no means, however, are all nutritionists engaged with the problems of the sick and there seems urgent need that more opportunities for apprenticeship (preferably on a minimum wage) be created in those organizations employing nutritionists whose concern is chiefly with economic problems and health education.

PRESENT TRENDS IN NUTRITION*
BY E. V. MCCOLLUM, PH. D., SC. D.
Professor of Chemical Hygiene, School of Hygiene and Public Health Johns Hopkins University, Baltimore, Md.

Recent progress in nutrition has called attention to the variation in the biological value of proteins, that is, that some are much more valuable to the body than others. Those of meat, milk, and eggs are more efficiently used for body building than are those of peas and beans. Hence, for good growth and development in the child and for prolonged well-being in the adult some meat, milk, eggs, fish, poultry, cheese or game should be included in the daily diet.

The importance of the minerals is equal to that of the proteins. In fact, abnormalities and ill health are certain to occur if any one of the essential dietary constituents is omitted. The minerals we hear most of are calcium, phosphorus, iron, and iodine, not because they are more important than the others, but simply because their distribution in foods is such that their presence in adequate amounts assures a sufficiency of the remaining necessary minerals. The necessity of calcium and phosphorus for normal bone and tooth development, of iron and copper for the building of red blood cells, of iodine for the prevention of goitre, has been dramatically demonstrated in human beings and experimental animals. Only recently have we learned that too little manganese causes a perversion of maternal instinct in the rat; that too little magnesium produces violent spasms and death in rats and cows, and that too much fluorine in drinking water causes marked abnormality and defacing of the tooth surfaces.

The novelty of the discovery of the vitamins created much enthusiasm in the public and in the minds of some eclipsed entirely the importance of proteins, fats, carbohydrates and minerals. The name "vitamin" itself is a mystifying one. The fact that such extremely small amounts of the vitamins are necessary renders them all the more interesting. There appear to be several new vitamins yet to be studied, but we now know a great deal about six of them and about the part they play in maintaining normal health. We distinguish two distinct classes of vita-

*The author spoke at the Section Meetings of the Massachusetts Home Economics Association in Springfield and Worcester and was so good as to send us his paper for publication.

mins, one of which is associated with fats and oils, and the other, never so associated, but which is dissolved out of natural foodstuffs by soaking them in water. The former are called fat-soluble vitamins, the latter water-soluble vitamins. The best known fat-soluble vitamins are A-D-E and F. The best known water-soluble vitamins are B-C-G and lactoflavin, an indispensable food element which is not yet called by a letter of the alphabet as are the other vitamins.

During the earlier years of vitamin researches we did not know the chemical nature of any of them, so it was convenient to designate them by the letters of the alphabet. As knowledge has increased it becomes more desirable to give them definite names which tell something about them. We now know several of them in pure crystalline form, and one has been made in large quantities by chemists in the laboratory. It is only a matter of time when all of them will be manufactured like soap or the perfumes.

Vitamin A is now known to be formed by cleaving in the middle of the molecule the yellow pigment which gives carrots their color. This pigment, called carotene, occurs in all yellow and green vegetable products. After the molecule is split, a molecule of water is combined at the point of cleavage, and thus two molecules of the vitamin are formed. The vitamin itself does not occur in plant products, but only its precursor or mother substance, carotene. When we eat the pigment our livers divide the molecule and add the water and make the vitamin, which is a colorless, oily substance. The vitamin itself has been prepared in considerable amount by distilling concentrates of halibut or herring liver oil in high vacuum. Chemists are, therefore, familiar with its appearance and properties.

Unfortunately vitamin A has been called the "anti-infective" vitamin. It is no more entitled to this distinction than are some of the others. It is true that experimental animals such as the rat develop a condition strikingly similar to our severe head colds when greatly depleted of their vitamin A store. It has not been proven, however, that low vitamin A intake causes one to be susceptible to the common cold. What we actually know is that even moderate shortage of the vitamin in the diet impairs the health of the mucous membranes of the nose, throat, mouth and elsewhere, so that they probably form less effective barriers against the invasion of micro-organisms which are ordinarily not disease-producing, but which we should keep out of the underlying tissue.

The most important fact pointing to the wisdom of taking daily a diet rich in carotene or vitamin A is the well-established observation that impairment of the eyes due to A deficiency does occur. It has been known for years that in the rat, vitamin A deficiency causes impairment of vision in subdued light. It has been shown that when the eyes are used in bright light the visual purple, a pigment in the retina, is destroyed by bleaching. This purple pigment is necessary for acuity of vision in twilight or skyshine at night. People who run short of vitamin A show poor vision at night. This condition is of fairly frequent occurrence, as has been shown by Drs. Jeans and Zentmire of the University of Iowa. About one-fourth of the children they examined showed impairment of vision which cleared up in most cases in a few days on the administration of cod liver oil, which is fairly rich in vitamin A. There is much evidence that many people do not take sufficient vitamin A.

The significance to health of vitamin D is now too well known to need description. The existence of this vitamin was not known until 1922, and now it is almost universally administered to infants and children for the safeguarding of their bone development. It is of greater significance for health, however, than merely the prevention of rickets. The rachitic infant gets several diseases easily to which he would be relatively immune were he free from the rachitic taint.

Vitamin D was first demonstrated in cod liver oil. It is now known that there are at least five distinct anti-rachitic substances. There are at least two vitamin D's in fish liver oils. That from the blue-fin tuna is different from that in cod liver oil Another anti-rachitic substance is produced by the action of ultraviolet light on a substance, ergosterol, prepared from yeast. This is different from either of the anti-rachitic substances in fish oils. In addition to these forms, two others have been prepared from a substance called cholesterol, which is prepared from brain. Probably a number of other distinct anti-rachitic agents will be discovered in the next few years.

It does not appear that there is much choice between these different forms of vitamin D for the protection of human infants. The irradiation of foods apparently forms the same vitamin D as is in viosterol, sold in the drugstores, and made by irradiating ergosterol of yeast.

Every infant and child should receive some extra vitamin D during the colder months when sunshine is not readily available because of lack of outdoor life, excessive smoke in the city atmosphere, heavy clothing, etc. There is much evidence that the structure of the teeth is much improved in infants which receive vitamin D. There is also much reason to believe that the provision of the proper amount of D raises the résistance of the teeth against decay or dental caries. There is no difference of opinion among authorities on the question of the advisability of every expectant or lactating mother taking some vitamin D regularly. Irradiated milk is now available in most cities, and is a good source of the vitamin, but cod liver oil is still preferred by most physicians for infants. Vitamin D consumption for the promotion of the general health, especially during the months when sunshine is at a premium, is well established as advisable.

The importance of vitamin E to human welfare is still in a state of uncertainty. We actually know little about it except that it is necessary in rats and guinea pigs for the health of the young during prenatal life. Practically nothing can yet be said about its role in human fertility, though there is accumulating some evidence of a suggestive nature.

Vitamin F has been found to be a fatty acid which looks like salad oil. Its chemical name is linoleic acid. Its physiological role is as yet little understood, but it is known to be essential to life and health. A few years hence we can say much more about it than now.

Vitamin B has recently been prepared in crystalline form in considerable amount and chemists are now studying its molecular architecture, so we shall soon know much more about its chemical nature than we now know. Although very widely distributed in natural foods, it occurs generally in quantities so sparingly that it is necessary to plan the diet with intelligence in order to secure as much of it as we should have. The disease beri-beri has for many centuries been one of the principal causes of disability, and is now perhaps about seventh in the order of importance among human diseases the world over. Deficiency of B causes damage to the nervous system, and secondarily to the muscles and organs.

It is well known that milk is rather poor in this vitamin, so there is a growing tendency among medical men to supplement the diets of infants with some rich source of this vitamin. This is probably a wise policy. It is equally clear that many persons convalescing from illness need more than the normal amount of vitamin B since it is used up faster during fever, and the sick person often eats little and becomes seriously depleted as respects this substance. Loss of appetite is one of the first symptoms of B deficiency, and its administration has remarkable effect on the desire for food.

Vitamin C is now generally called ascorbic acid. It is especially important for the health of the capillary blood vessels and arteries. It is most abundant in the adrenal glands, brain, and organs. Not only has this vitamin been isolated from natural foods, but several methods for synthesizing it from certain common sugars have been perfected. It is now manufactured chemically to the extent of pounds at a batch, and bids fair to become a moderately cheap chemical. Professor King of the University of Pittsburgh has made many important studies on the human subject in relation to vitamin C needs. The vitamin can now be estimated quantitatively in tiny sections of any tissue suitable for microscopic examination. Professor King finds that a great many people have much less ascorbic acid stored in their tissues than they should have.

An important observation made by Dr. Rinehart is that when guinea pigs are depleted of ascorbic acid and are then injected with a culture of an organism frequently found in human cases of rheumatism, the animals develop most of the symptoms characteristic of that disease. Guinea pigs which have been given an abundance of ascorbic acid previously are immune to doses of the organism which produce severe lesions of rheumatism in C-deficient pigs. This is, of course, a demonstration of susceptibility to rheumatism rather than a demonstration of cure. At the Rockefeller Institute for Medical Research the administration of ascorbic acid to patients suffering from rheumatism has not been found to be of any considerable benefit. These highly suggestive studies cannot now be fully evaluated, but they point to an important principle in nutrition, viz., that the state of nutrition, when allowed to fall below the optimum for health, makes one susceptible to disease to which he would be immune if on a better plane of nutrition. It is not finally established that the experimental rheumatism in the guinea pig is analogous to that disease in man, but at any rate, prevention is far better than cure, and these studies illustrate well how progress is made in safe-guarding human health by diet.

Vitamin G has a most interesting history. The late Dr. Joseph Goldberger established that pellagra, a disease afflicting about two hundred thousand people in America, mostly in the Southern states, was due to some vitamin deficiency. About three years ago it was demonstrated that the greenish-yellow pigment which gives the characteristic color to the whey formed when cottage cheese is made is an indispensable food principle. This pigment is called lactoflavin. It has been prepared by many chemists in pure crystalline form and has been synthesized in the laboratory. There are similar or identical flavins in egg white, liver, kidney, yeast, etc. This substance, while indispensable to health, and effective in very small amounts, is not a preventive against all the symptoms of rat pellagra. The pellagra-preventive principle is now demonstrated to be of a multiple nature and one part of it is colorless, and one is probably lactoflavin. There is a difference of opinion among certain investigators as to whether lactoflavin should be called vitamin G (the British call it B_2). The exact relation of this pigment to our physiological processes is not yet known, but in animals, health fails rapidly when the pigment flavin is omitted from the diet, and recovery follows its restoration to the food.

There are probably at least, two or three more vitamins to be discovered.

The experimental study of these substances is a thrilling experience, and many years must elapse before the chapters on nutritional science in which they are concerned are finally completed.

The spectacular nature of the discovery of a list of nutrient principles which were so elusive, and whose effects were so remarkable, has tended to overshadow the other phases of practical dietetics. We still need the structural materials supplied by proteins, the energy supplied by fats and carbohydrates, and the regulatory effects of the twelve or more inorganic elements which are indispensable components of the normal diet. These are just as important as the vitamins although not so well advertised.

It is not necessary for the enjoyment of optimal health for one to become vitamin minded or mineral minded, or to be a close student of foods and nutrition. Expert dietitians have simplified practical nutrition by telling us about the combinations of foods which are so constituted as to make good each other's deficiencies and form a good health-promoting diet. The most important foods for supplementing the cereals, tubers, roots, fruits and sugar, so as to provide what they lack, or contain in inadequate amounts, are milk, leafy vegetables, eggs, and the glandular organs such as liver, kidney, sweetbread, etc. Many years ago I distinguished these as the "protective" foods. The ordinary meats are of exceptional importance for certain purposes as supplemental foods. If the daily diet is built up around a sufficiency of the "protective" foods the rest may be selected with a view to satisfying the appetite. "Eat what you would after you have eaten what you should."

THE PLACE OF THE NUTRITIONIST IN THE PUBLIC HEALTH PROGRAM

BY W. G. SMILLIE, M. D.

*Professor of Public Health Administration
Harvard School of Public Health*

Thoughtful leaders in the field of public health have just begun to realize the important place that proper nutrition must occupy in the promotion of health of the individual and the community. This tardy recognition of an obvious need is due in part to the fact that clinical disease entities produced by faulty diet do not play a significant role in morbidity and mortality statistics. Beri-beri, scurvy, pellagra and night blindness are not encountered frequently in the medical clinics. They have relatively little public health importance in most parts of the United States. The really important issue which the health department executives in the United States must face is the necessity for proper nutrition of each individual during the period of growth and development.

We are a most fortunate nation in one respect. Faulty nutrition in the United States is not due to a basic lack of essential nutritional elements, nor to faulty distribution, storage and refrigeration of food.*

The essential food elements are abundant and easily procured. Poor nutrition is due, in great part, to a failure to utilize properly these readily available foods. It is true that this failure to utilize the readily available essential food elements is due in some degree to low purchasing power of a certain proportion of families.** By and large, however, it is due to a lack of knowledge and understanding of the simple elementary principles of good nutrition.

This limitation of knowledge is not confined to the parents and their children. School teachers, public health nurses and health officers, and including also staff members of the voluntary health and welfare agencies frequently do not realize their responsibilities or opportunities in this field. The hiatus in knowledge on the part of both those who desire to teach and aid, and those who are the recipients of this assistance is three-fold in nature.

(a) A failure to grasp the importance of the influence of proper nutrition upon normal development and optimum growth.

(b) Failure to recognize nutritional deficiency when it exists.

---
*One exception to this rule is the natural iodine deficiency of a large zone in the North Central States.
**The U. S. Department of Agriculture has estimated that one third of the population cannot afford even a minimum adequate diet.

(c) Lack of an elementary knowledge of the basic principles of normal bodily food requirements.

A simple example of our lack of perspective and understanding serves to illustrate these points. We have encouraged the development of extensive programs of preventive dentistry under public health auspices. Dental clinics have been organized, dentist and full-time dental hygienists have been employed, and elaborate programs for correction of dental defects have been developed, with no thought of the utilization of a nutritionist in a dental hygiene program. Yet the only effective method that is available at the present time for actual prevention of dental defects is through proper nutritional methodology.

Most authorities have accepted the tenet, as an established principle of government in relation to the public health, that it is the function of the official health service to act not only as a police agency in protection of the community against an invasion of infectious disease, but also to do everything in its power to **promote individual and community health**.

If this principle is accepted, we must, of necessity, agree that the promotion of a proper nutritional status in the individual and the community is an important governmental function.

How can this desirable condition be achieved? Is it solely a public health function? If the poor nutrition of any individual is due to the low purchasing power of the family, the matter becomes a public welfare function. If wholly due to lack of knowledge, and if best results are to be secured by instruction of the children, then the whole subject should be assigned to the Department of Education. This academic question may be discussed indefinitely, but one conclusion has already been clearly determined for us. Practical experience in this field has shown that no single agency should be asked to carry the complete responsibility. Rather, a co-ordinated plan should be developed in which the various official and non-official agencies participate. The initiative should come from the health department. The local health department will give direct service and the state should furnish advisory service and leadership.

What then is the place of the nutritionist in the health department?

The State Health Department

The **State Health Department** should assume the leadership in this field. A well qualified nutritionist should be attached to the state health department staff. She may be assigned to:

(a) The division having responsibility for local health service development.

(b) The Division of Child Hygiene.

In one state at least the nutritionist is attached to the Division of Health Education—a very logical arrangement.

The state nutritionist should be an outstanding leader in her field. Her functions are educational and advisory. She works through the local health departments and also through her colleagues on the state staff. Her major activities will include:

(1) Aid to local health departments and local welfare departments also, in formulation of their plans for adequate nutritional programs.

(2) Preparation of popular educational material for general use throughout the state. This will include press releases, pamphlets, radio talks, material to be used for instruction in public schools, exhibits of all sorts, as well as other publicity which is dignified and effective.

(3) Education of local health department personnel concerning the technique of their nutritional activities. Both group classes and individual conferences are effective methods of instruction of local health department personnel. The personnel of local voluntary agencies may well be included in these instructive exercises.

The Nutritionist in the Local Health Program

Every local health department should have the benefit of the advice of a trained and competent nutritionist. Here direct service is given and direct results are secured. Where possible, the nutritionist should be a full-time employee of the health department. She should possess the necessary technical qualifications. In addition, she should be a good teacher and should also have had social service experience. Her various duties and activities may well include the following projects:

1. Preparation of the educational material for the community at large. This work will include talks to parent education groups, women's clubs and other organizations that are interested in public health affairs.

2. Organization of the nutrition work in the public schools.
   a. Conferences with the teachers concerning the content of their teaching material that may relate to nutrition.
   b. Education of the children through the school lunch program.
   c. Mid-morning supplementary food for undernourished children.
   d. Parent conferences.
   Certain school children will be found, on school medical examination, to be definitely undernourished. The nutritionist may set aside certain hours at the school for consultation with parents of those children that require special attention.

3. Consultation with the public health nurses concerning the special dietary problems encountered in the course of their daily work. The nutritionist may hold group conferences with the nurses and use illustrative cases to instruct them so that they will recognize the nutritional needs of their patients and be able to give suitable instruction to those intrusted to their care. The nutritionist will occasionally make home visits at times with a nurse, or other health or welfare workers, to solve a specially difficult problem or to instruct the visitor.

4. Participation in maternal hygiene and prenatal programs.

5. The dental hygiene program will, perforce, include nutrition work as one of its most important constituents.

Nutrition Clinics

Three types of nutrition clinic are frequently developed:

1. Clinics in conjunction with the general child hygiene clinics.

This plan is well suited to the "Health Center" development in some of the larger cities.

2. Clinics for special instruction of parents of malnourished children.

3. Therapeutic nutritional clinics, usually attached to and sponsored by a larger hospital or outpatient dispensary.

Nutrition Camps

A few official health departments sponsor summer nutrition camps. Usually, however, these camps are run under the auspices of voluntary health agencies. The effectiveness of these nutrition camps can be greatly augmented, if the regimen is carried out under the supervision of a competent nutritionist.

Organization of a Nutrition Service

Larger municipal health departments cannot afford to be without the services of a full-time nutritionist. In general, a proper distribution of personnel requires one nutritionist for each twenty-five to thirty public health nurses; or, if considered in relation to population, one nutritionist per 100,000 inhabitants. She is of general aid to all divisions, but is most frequently attached to the Division of Child Hygiene.

In communities smaller than 100,000 two plans have been followed:

1. Nutritional advice and assistance have been supplied to the local health department through the State Health Department. The state nutritionist spends a certain proportion of her time with each of the various local health departments guiding and assisting the local personnel in formulation of their programs.

2. Some smaller communities have secured the service of a full-time nutritionist through the cooperative utilization of her services by both official and non-official agencies. The Department of Public Welfare secures her guidance in its work relating to care and proper nutritional supervision of the indigent.

Voluntary agencies utilize her services for supervision of summer camps and other nutritional activities. The Department of Education may share in the program, and in some instances the local hospital employs her on a part-time basis to organize the therapeutic food clinics for out-patients. All the various organizations share in the cost of the nutrition work. The administrative difficulties encountered in this loosely knit type of organization are obvious, but not insurmountable.

In one small city the local Red Cross has taken as its responsibility the cost of supplying the city with a competent nutritionist. The Red Cross does not utilize the nutritionist directly, but assigns her to the various organizations that require her services. This is an excellent temporary arrangement, but does not place the responsibility for the service where it belongs, namely, upon the official health and welfare agencies.

An ideal administrative arrangement from the nutritional standpoint for smaller communities would be the allocation to a single governmental agency of all governmental functions relating to public health and public welfare under a single administrative head. The nutritionist would be employed as a full-time member of the department and would be fully occupied in the multitude of official duties that would come within her scope in the two related fields of promotion of the public health and the public welfare.

THE NUTRITIONIST WITH THE BOARD OF HEALTH IN A SMALL TOWN

BY CURTIS M. HILLIARD, A. B.

Professor of Biology and Public Health
Simmons College, Boston, Mass.

The field of public health work is an expanding one. As science gives us new evidence regarding the extremely complex individual and environmental factors that determine health and disease, or that affect the degree of health enjoyed by the individual or by a community, we should be prepared to make practical use of these facts in our health programs. There is always a lag between scientific knowledge and its effective use. Official public health work, depending as it does on the enlightenment of a community in health matters to make it acceptable, commonly has to wait for private agencies to do the exploring and pioneer work in new and interesting projects. It is further necessary to educate first the lay officials of each town or community to the need of such projects, and the diversity of situations in which they may be helpful, before freedom can be obtained to establish them in the community. It has been thus with nutrition work applied on a general and community basis.

The Massachusetts Department of Public Health recently issued a two-page bulletin entitled "The Community Nutritionist." This announces in a challenging way that a new type of community servant, whose work is comparable in its method of operation to that of the public health nurse, is prepared to enter the field; that the well-trained nutritionist with the preventive and community, or social point of view can make a definite contribution to the promotion of public health and possibly to the prevention of the development of specific diseases. The nutritionist today is being trained not only to plan appetizing, economic, and well-balanced diets, or to serve in hospitals or diabetic clinics to plan meals, or instruct sick persons in their specific food problems, but she is trained to be a health educator and social worker in a restricted field. As such, her advice may prove helpful to the welfare agencies of the community in judging the need and worthiness of given families. She is better acquainted with the actual food problems of those families which she has contacted.

The Wellesley Board of Health conceived that the newer type of nutritionist had a definite field of usefulness during the so-called depression, to work with the Board of Public Welfare, the local stores, and those receiving public aid, so that a maximum use of the limited food budget might be obtained. The uninstructed family might commonly think of the food budget in terms of bulk, and as satisfying their appetites, rather than in terms of real food value and health requirements. The local chapter of the Red Cross gave financial aid to this project.

With the nutritionist working in the community, there quickly arose other individual and family health situations where it seemed to us that the nutritionist had special helpful knowledge and could be of specific aid. For example, we look upon the family in which there is a case of tuberculosis as one which needs continual advice so that the health of contacts may be maintained at a high level. Regardless of whether malnutrition, as such, predisposes to tuberculosis or not, the general opinion still prevails that those in good physical health are less liable to break down than those who are below par in health. Therefore, all of our families with a history of tuberculosis were given to the nutritionist to provide what information and help might seem most desirable. In the majority of these cases the work became preventive, for often the child having tuberculosis had been subjected to so much care and training that his food habits were the best in the family. It was, therefore, the brother or sister, also exposed to the risk of infection, who most needed guidance and encouragement in proper nutrition.

School dental clinics should be centers of health information as well as places to provide specific dental prophylaxis or treatment. The relation between diet and dental caries is well established. Nutrition education should receive major emphasis from the standpoint of prevention, and while the dental physician and nurse attendant may give instruction to the little children who visit the clinics, nevertheless, to make the advice effective, mothers must be taught the importance of food to the teeth, and cooperation between the child and parent must be established. The dental physician for the past two years has been selecting cases of dental caries which, in his opinion, are essentially due to defective metabolism, and has turned these cases over to the nutritionist who has followed them up. A control group is being carried, and while it is far too early to have any conclusive evidence as to the value of this work, it is safe to say that the results so far appear promising.

Although the nutritionist has not definitely engaged in the school health program of physical examination and general follow-up of children, she has been given certain selected cases, who, in the opinion of the school nurses, would profit by her services and advice. In many of her home visits she has discovered children who are much more in need of nutritional aid than those she had been asked to follow up by the board of health or the school department. At the present time, she has under her supervision over two hundred individuals.

As the program of nutrition has grown, we have come to realize that the nutritionist's most useful work is in stimulating, and giving advice to various groups of people who in turn are able to use this information in their own work. For example, school teachers in the primary grades are constantly aware of children in their classes who are sent to school without appropriate breakfasts, or who are not getting enough sleep, or who are emotional or nervous types that require special attention in the home to keep their metabolism up to standard. By meeting with the teachers in the various buildings two or three times during the school year for discussion and conference, the nutritionist can make many suggestions which can be used by the teachers in their health education program in the classroom. The teacher may also give special attention to individuals and offer advice and encouragement to parents regarding a particular child. Similar work can be done with those in charge of school lunches to advise with them regarding menus that give proper balance, ways of encouraging the consumption of milk and vegetables by playing them up and making them more attractive, and supplying lists of inexpensive foods to be either bought in the lunchroom or brought from home in the lunch box. Also, work with the school nurses and the private nursing association in the community by conference and definite cooperation or participation in their work, makes the nutritionist a valuable agent.

We are convinced that the nutritionist, specially prepared by education or experience, has a useful and important function in public health work in the small community as well as in large cities. She should serve chiefly as a consultant and educator, confining case work to a minimum of special or unusual situations or for demonstration purposes.

One major difficulty is that full-time work is not justified in smaller communities. This same situation is met in other fields of public health work and its solution would seem to lie in cooperative or union health areas. Whether a formal general arrangement for health work was entered into or not, the same nutritionist might be employed on a part-time basis by two or more communities. One nutritionist could competently serve a population of 50,000 in a reasonably concentrated area. The costs of her work would be repaid many fold in the return that needy people would get for their food expenditure in terms of food value, and in terms of more abundant health and disease prevention, her services likewise would amply repay the community. We believe it will be only a matter of time and experience before this type of trained person will be considered as necessary in the personnel of a health department staff as the public health nurse or milk inspector.

THE NUTRITION WORKER AND NURSE IN A FAMILY HEALTH PROGRAM

BY BLANCHE T. DIMOND, B. S.
Nutrition Supervisor

ANN RICHARDSON, R.N., B.A., B.N.,
District Supervisor
Community Health Association

In the past few years the need for nutrition teaching has been increasingly recognized by public health authorities as one of the gaps in a public health program. Such authorities in the field of public health as Dr. Wilson G. Smillie and Dr. C.-E. A. Winslow constantly stress this need. Public health nursing organizations represent widespread community machinery for family health teaching. A number of these agencies have convincingly demonstrated the increased effectiveness of their work by the addition of nutrition workers to their staff. It is, of course, quite generally accepted that the nurse's knowledge in this special field is too limited to develop a sound teaching program and she needs the constant advice and assistance of a trained nutrition worker.

The qualifications of a nutrition worker in the public health field should be carefully considered. The first essential in her preparation is a thorough scientific knowledge of her subject which entitles her to be considered as an expert. In addition she should have a planned field experience in order to have a clear conception of public health objectives. She needs too, not only a knowledge of teaching methods but the special ability to simplify scientific principles and adapt her teaching to various economic and mental levels.

The nutrition worker has three functions in a public health nursing organization. First, she needs to give the nurses scientific data regarding the adequate normal diet required for building health and keep them constantly stimulated by information regarding the newer developments in the field. This is knowledge which the nurse uses on every single visit. Second, she helps the nurse solve one of the most difficult problems; i. e., finding the best plan of spending the food money. Third, she assists the nurse in the planning of special diets, such as diabetes, anemia and gastric ulcer, which have been ordered by physicians. She knows how to adapt these diets to racial customs, personal idiosyncrasies, and family income.

Since nutrition as a part of a public health program is comparatively new and methods are constantly changing, it is probably more convincing, in considering a nutrition program, to discuss the problem in terms of a plan which has been found practical in one agency[*] rather than in terms of general principles. It is appreciated, of course, that this is not presented as an ideal plan.

In the experience of the work of this organization one of the com-

[*]Community Health Association, Boston, Mass.

mon mistakes in developing a nutrition program is in expecting miracles of one worker. Her effort, like that of every other person, when spread too thin becomes ineffective. Over a period of years it has been found that the nutrition worker gives the most valuable assistance to a nursing group when the number is limited to not more than ten or fifteen nurses to one nutrition worker. In a smaller group of nurses it would be possible to do more intensive work and become an even more valuable community worker.

The plan of nutrition work in this agency* is this:

1. With individuals—individual problems in family diet or budget planning.

With groups—classes for expectant mothers and Low Cost Food Demonstrations.

2. With the staff—individual consultation regarding problems of particular patients.

With the group—regular conferences on subjects helpful to them in their family teaching, or on newer developments in research.

3. Preparation of teaching material for the use of nurses and patients.

4. Consultations with outside agencies usually on budget problems.

The program of the nutrition worker with the patients offers a great variety of opportunity for teaching. At the classes for expectant mothers the nutrition worker and the nurse share equally in the responsibility. The nurse gives talks on prenatal care, preparation for delivery, baby's clothes, etc., and at alternate classes the nutrition worker talks on the prenatal diet, the mother's daily plan of work, budget, and marketing. At each class refreshments are served, always to illustrate some dietary point, such as the use of milk, fruit or vegetables. That this teaching is effective is evidenced by the fact that nurses visiting in the homes after Mother's Club find the mothers preparing for their families the very same foods demonstrated at the club.

Families whose incomes have been drastically reduced have found it imperative to consider more carefully how they spend their food money and are as grateful for this kind of assistance as they are for nursing care in a sickness emergency. To meet this need it has been found more effective to do this teaching by a course of demonstrations to groups of interested women.

In this course there are seven lessons demonstrating the actual preparation of the family dinner and teaching the daily food requirements for children and adults. In the process of preparation, continuous teaching is carried on in food values, economical buying and attractive preparation. One of the most difficult problems in working with low cost food is to make it sufficiently attractive to the family. Therefore, we place special emphasis on this point, stressing contrast of color and texture of the foods. Even a mother with the most limited knowledge of meal planning can easily see that a dinner of hamburg

*Community Health Association, Boston, Mass.

loaf, buttered carrots, scalloped potatoes and apple brown betty is more attractive than one of creamed codfish, parsnips, mashed potatoes and tapioca cream. The cost of the meal, varying from 48-60¢. for a family of five, is a very important part of the discussion.

These groups have been held in homes, churches and community centers. The place is not important so long as it is possible to demonstrate methods which are practical in the home. A very satisfactory group was that assembled by a young Italian woman in her home. She belonged to a group of Italian women who, all with young families, were very much interested in the health of their children. Once a week these women meet in the sunny kitchen of their hostess, and sitting around the table, they watch the nutrition worker preparing a low-cost dinner, using the home equipment. Explaining each step as she works, she leads them into a discussion of their food customs, showing wherein their way is good, or where a newer way is better. While the dinner cooks, they plan the breakfast and luncheon which would provide the daily food requirements. They are all very proud of their use of the menus given in previous lessons, whether or not their children liked them, and the cooperation of their husbands. One of them reports: "My husband said to me while I was making those graham muffins, 'This is the first time since we've been married, Concetta, that you have taken any interest in the housekeeping.' He is so pleased that I'm not opening cans and that we are having more nourishing food than before and that we're not spending so much money." Gaily they exchange menus and new suggestions to make the meals attractive and economical.

The work of the nutrition worker with the family is of great importance, but even more far-reaching in numbers is her work with the nurses whose opportunities for service of this kind are endless. The nurse's scope is so wide that given proper stimulus and education regarding the newer developments of nutrition work, every family which she contacts must learn from her something which can be carried over into the health of the whole group. The nutrition worker gives her talk to the group of nurses in her office. Nutrition conscious, the nurse, equipped with facts, perhaps, as to the importance of milk in every diet, can give to the prenatal patient the facts about the development of the baby's bones through calcium; to the maternity, the importance of milk for the proper breast feeding of her baby; to the acutely ill, nourishing fluids; the chronic, building up resistance; to the child, growth. When we visualize more than a hundred nurses going to perhaps a thousand homes daily, the influence of this teaching seems infinite.

Never is there a better opportunity to teach, never is the family more receptive than when there is illness in the home and the nurse, working side by side with the mother, helps to bring the child back to health.

More and more the practical demonstration method is replacing verbal instruction, and nutrition becomes more vital when the nurse shows the mother just how to prepare fluids for the man with pneumonia, carrot straws for the child who needs but hates vegetables, and how much better cocoa tastes when made with milk. Every home needs just this kind of teaching, and every nurse given the proper stimulation by the nutrition worker will find these opportunities daily.

When the nurse finds a special problem, too rapid gain in weight during pregnancy, a diabetic diet, not fully comprehended by the patient, the nurse and the nutrition worker get together on the problem, and the nurse brings to the family the help it needs. Perhaps if the solution is very detailed, the nutrition worker can give the needed help more efficiently. Working together in this way, a larger number of patients can be helped.

Nurses and social workers of other agencies are constantly discovering families which need help in planning the expenditure of money. This type of teaching is increasingly in demand. Both because such visits require more time and because it is a specialized kind of teaching, these cases are handled by the nutrition worker. As a basis for this work, figures are prepared twice a year by the nutrition staff of the Boston Community Health Association. These figures show the adequate minimum allowance for each member of the family, for food, clothing and other items of the budget. The food prices are based on averages in twenty-two Boston grocery stores and clothing prices in four of the stores selling low cost, good quality merchandise. These patients may have adequate or inadequate incomes. Since the depression, the proportion of inadequate cases has been increasing. Examples of both follow:

Mrs. S., the mother of four undernourished children, was trying to feed her family on an income of $12.00 a week. The family diet included only one can of evaporated milk each day, few vegetables and fruits, no dark bread or cereals, and very little or no butter. The children were rather fussy eaters, disliking dark bread and detesting cereal. Better health habits were introduced into this family through the children's enthusiasm for sport heroes. At each visit something was given the children to stimulate their interest, literature on the health rules in sport, charts, and stars for improvement. The mother, as well as the children was very interested and followed the suggestions carefully. She became interested in planning the meals, made menus a week in advance, learned about food values, and became very alert in finding food bargains. In this way she increased the family milk supply to twelve quarts of fresh and ten cans of evaporated milk each week, has taught the children to eat dark bread and cereal and has increased the fruit, vegetable and butter intake. It is easy to see that the children are healthier now and the mother is convinced that food plays a great **role in health.**

In general such teaching requires five or six intensive visits, but the number and content of the visits are entirely dependent on the caliber of the family. Quite a different plan was made for the family of a professional person where the budget was adequate but poorly managed so that they owed $1200. This patient was brought to our attention by the nurse, who found the wife so overwhelmed by bills that she could see no way to plan for her approaching confinement. By arousing the interest of the husband in budget plans, and going over the expenditures with the husband and wife together, the family reduced their bills $600 in a year. This was accomplished by apportioning amounts to be paid weekly in bills, cutting down on unnecessary spending and careful buying of wholesome food. This case was carried intensively at first, then with lengthening intervals between visits and finally with three month check-up. All of the children improved greatly in health and appearance, though much less money was being spent for food.

The correlation of these two workers, nurse and nutrition worker, makes it possible to carry nutrition teaching into many homes every day.

AN ITINERANT NUTRITIONIST IN A COUNTRY TOWN
BY DOROTHY HAGER, B. S.

Prologue

A picture, however sketchy, of the town in which Miss Hager worked may serve to show how she fitted into the total school health situation and what were the difficulties which she had to meet.

The little town of X, with a population of about 2,000 and a school population of approximately 400, has been particularly hard hit by the depression, the only industry there having moved away at the beginning of the depression. Some of the people have found work in surrounding towns, many are on relief or working on WPA projects.

The town is rural in type— the people are Polish, Irish, French-Canadian and Armenian. There is no town water supply, no resident physicians, no clinics or hospitals, but there is a bus line to neighboring cities with these facilities. A local nurse gives one day a week to the schools and there is a community council of about sixty members which has interested itself enthusiastically in raising funds for and in administering a dental clinic for the children.

In 1935 one of the State Department of Public Health physicians was asked to act as school health supervisor.

A brief survey of the situation showed need for work along four major lines—examination of the children, working out feasible methods for obtaining correction of defects, improvement of the sanitary conditions of the schools, and the development of a program of health education.

The health examinations revealed poor nutrition of "the hidden hunger" type to be the difficulty most in need of attack, underlying as it does problems of teeth and posture, as well as growth.

Meetings were held with teachers and parents to discuss the results of the examinations, and the parents, with a little leading, expressed a wish to have help with their nutrition problem. Interested organizations were found to sponsor financially not only some tonsil clinic work but a more far-reaching event—the employment of a nutritionist for three months, and the Community Council financed the dental work. So with the concentrated effort of everyone, a program of health rehabilitation started. Here are the results:

	Jan. 1935	Jan. 1936
Children with major defects	91%	56%
Poor nutrition	28%	16%
Poor posture	18%	6%
Carious teeth	84%	27%
Defective tonsils	24%	14%
Defect of nose	9%	4%

—FREDRIKA MOORE, M. D.
Massachusetts Department of Public Health.

* * * * * *

When I came to the town for the summer, I felt a tactful, friendly approach to the people was necessary.

From the health records left by Dr. Moore last spring I made a list of all the children who had been checked for nutrition defects. There were one hundred and eighty-nine. This list I arranged by school grades and again by families. The first list was for my use in making up clubs and in grouping the children; the second list was for my use in making home visits. Many of the families in town are related, and I found cousins with the same name rather confusing. The one hundred and eighty-nine children were finally sorted out into about one hundred and five families.

Then there was the problem of streets. At this time the school nurse was a great help. She offered to go with me to the homes of the preschool children who had been found by the dentist to have poor teeth.

Everywhere I went—during those first few days and later on throughout the summer—I was met with a pleasant welcome. The people seemed glad to talk about themselves and their families. Perhaps it was because of the unemployment situation that they had so much time to visit. I often felt that the only people in town who felt at all rushed were the girl who had a paper route and I. There were a few exceptions to this in the Hill district where mothers of large families went to the mills for a half day's work and then came home to wash and iron and bake and clean. Even these women had time to visit if they could go on with their ironing while they talked.

The children had enthusiasm and interest for things familiar to them; but they hesitated to try the unknown. Even girls studying at the State Teachers College said they did not like to try new things to eat. (These young women helped Miss Hager with clubs.)

In order to form clubs and classes I had to get to know the people. This meant a certain amount of give and take in the way of conversation. The people were just as curious about me and what I did, where I lived and ate, and what I hoped to do in the future as I was about the size of their families and pocketbooks, what they raised in their gardens, fed their children, burned for fuel and did with their leisure. Only they were more polite about inquiring.

To compare notes on patchwork quilts with a French grandmother, and to urge Victoria to take a postgraduate course at high school since she was unable to find work; to admire Blanche's crocheting and Helen's apron and the polish that Mrs. S. was putting on her car; to loan Dorothy my own favorite cook book; to praise the collection of coins Kenneth brought to school and to accept gracefully the duplicate Chinese copper he gave me; to examine the hooked rugs that Mrs. H. had made; to listen to, and intelligently question the local history as given by the man who was (supposedly) repairing the fire alarm at school; to ask about life in Poland or France; to inquire about the recipe for Danish cabbage, and spiced carrots, and macaroni as a Frenchman made it—all this seemed to be necessary for the establishment of that goodwill feeling which I hoped might lead to opportunities for teaching nutrition. Doing these odd jobs—giving people rides up and down the Hill in the rain, or taking a group of 4-H Club girls to a grange meeting, going out of the way to take a man with a lame ankle up to camp to see his son, saving cellophane for the war veteran who made belts, and giving the leftover salad of carrots and cabbage to a worker for lunch—all these good will "wedges"—reminded me of the old rhyme:

"Do the task that's nearest
Though it's dull at whiles."

Some days I would wonder when nutrition was to be taught. Then the next evening the woman whom I had taken down town in the rain would come to one of the meetings and the girl to whom I had loaned a magazine would offer to help with one of the children's clubs. Or a busy housewife would come to the door as I brought her children up the hill to tell me about the new dish she was making for lunch out of green peppers and tomatoes. When I stopped to tell some one where her sister, a rural school teacher in Vermont, could get information on hot lunches, I would be told that her daughter had made at home the creamed carrots and green peppers which we had tried at school and that on the second day they warmed-up what was left with a can of beans and "it was simply delicious." It is then that you begin to think things are happening.

All this has been rather detailed in explanation, but so was it time consuming in fact. The work of a nutritionist, like that of any teacher, seems to be slow and needs frequent repetitions. At the end of twelve weeks in the town I felt as though a start had been made—the way paved for further enlightenment—and that is all. (Miss Hager will go in again next summer.)

When I made the first home visits, I spoke of the possibility of forming clubs for the boys and girls. Most mothers thought the idea a good one, but wondered—mildly and politely, of course—how the children would take to it. But after the girls started to come on Wednesday morning—the older ones—and Wednesday afternoon—the younger ones —they kept on coming and bringing their sisters and friends. The cooking room would comfortably accommodate twelve. We usually had sixteen or eighteen and sometimes ran as high as twenty-six. Picnics went up to thirty and thirty-eight, but that generally meant sisters and cousins and neighbors. It really seemed too bad to turn any away for lack of space although efficiency suffered with so many cooks. Some who came were well nourished and this mixture helped to put the club meetings on a basis of good times rather than one of health.

The girls decided to watch their weights during the summer. Some gained and some did not. All of the girls saw that excessive exercise—such as going swimming at the reservoir every afternoon—either resulted in no gain at all or in a loss of weight. Going swimming at the reservoir meant a two-mile walk each way by the road in the shade or a mile and a half in the sun along the railroad track. The swim generally lasted an hour or more. Whenever possible I spoke of how fine it would be if there were a suitable swimming place nearer the center of town. The water at the reservoir is good; but there is no real supervision of the younger children and in some places the ground goes off quite suddenly. The long walk in the sun and the long time the children spend in the water use up more energy than many of the children have. There is also no place to dress except in the woods and a deserted ice house. A supervised playground in the middle of the town with a wading pool for the little children would be an excellent thing.

To return to the girls and what they did at their club meetings—they all seemed interested in cooking. There has been no school instruction in this for the last few years because there has been no home economics teacher. The 4-H Club teaches only canning and sewing and encourages gardens.

Among the foods we prepared in the cooking classes were:

Milk drinks
    Vanilla milk shake and eggnog with fresh whole milk and a chocolate drink and raspberry shake with evaporated milk.
Salads
    Cabbage chopped with onion and green pepper.
    Cabbage chopped with pineapple.
    Carrots ground up with raisins and orange juice.
A sandwich loaf of dark and white breads with fillings of
    Chopped hard boiled eggs and cucumbers
    Chopped cabbage and green pepper and
    Chopped carrots and peanuts and mayonnaise.
An uncooked lemon pie with condensed milk in the filling and graham crackers crumbled for the crust.
Creamed carrots and green peppers.
Baked bean soup.

We also made several inexpensive salad dressings and a chocolate syrup to be used in milk drinks. At one meeting we had moving pictures. At another we had a picnic. Each girl brought her bread and butter (the quality and size of the slices were strange to see) and necessary cup and spoon. We had hoped to cook outdoors but continued dry weather made it inadvisable to have a fire. So we prepared a sandwich filling of chopped carrots and cabbage and took along jam for the sweet part of the meal. Evaporated milk and chocolate syrup made the drink. The last meeting actually did take the form of an outdoor meal. We climbed to the highest place in town, made a fire and cooked a milk and vegetable chowder. The girls found suitable sticks and baked biscuit twists over the fire. We had a sandwich filling of raisins, carrots, oranges, and peanuts which they spread between their slices of bread and butter. About forty-five girls were reached through these cooking classes and picnics at different times.

The girls were quite reasonable about trying new dishes—even when they had their doubts as to the flavor. There were a certain number of dislikes; but the results on the whole were very favorable. Quite a number of girls reported making the dishes at home afterward and told how much their families enjoyed them. Some surprised themselves by liking new and strange things— green peppers—carrots—evaporated milk. One girl said, "When you serve the Baked Bean Soup, don't give me any beans. They make me sick." She had not seen the whole mixture go through the sieve, so when I poured the soup for her I said, "Just juice for you. Let me know how you like that." "Oh", she said, "It's good without the beans." When we explained to her that she had eaten the whole mixture—beans, tomatoes, and all, she laughed as much as the rest.

Forming clubs for the boys was an entirely different matter. In some communities I know boys have been interested in camp cooking, but it is not so here. I do not mean that they could not be so interested; but at first they seemed wary of anything which might be termed "sissyish." These towns have a reputation in the valley of being "tough" towns. I saw no other evidence of it than this—that the boys objected to any approach that would class them with the girls.

Several small groups of boys of the seventh and eighth grade variety would come around to see me now and then. They would weigh themselves and measure each other, examine the collection of rocks and shells in one of the classrooms, look through the library books for something about scouts or animals or birds, talk about their collections of foreign stamps or coins, or the Civil War guns the man down the street had shown them — anything but health. They used the library books for an excuse, but they came for other reasons. One day they came to see moving pictures. Later they came and tried a little soap carving suggested by one of the movies. After this we all drank lemonade through peppermint sticks—a very noisy but pleasant pastime. When we borrowed a collection of rocks to be found in Worcester County and some stuffed birds from the Natural History Museum in Worcester, the boys came around to see them. At another time they came to see the charts and bird houses loaned to us by the Audubon Society of Boston.

These same boys who might have been annoying when I showed moving pictures in the town hall one evening were kept busy counting the crowd and giving out leaflets about bananas, oranges, and soap carving. They had decorated the hall before the performance and had a feeling of responsibility which kept them on their best behavior. A few of them followed the girls on our two picnics and hung around to exhibit their skill as imitators of Tarzan. The girls were somewhat afraid that the boys would fall into the chowder and put out the fire, but it seemed to me more likely that they would get a little camp cooking in a secondhand fashion and be interested enough to try it later themselves. The basis of most of the town's picnics is a plentiful supply of hot dogs. When we gave them a chance, the boys were only too glad to sample our biscuit twists and sandwich fillings.

A certain group of, younger boys—about nine years of age—came quite regularly to the school on Thursday afternoons. We made magazine puzzles one week and went swimming and had a picnic at another meeting. I managed to pack nine of them and all the lunch into Timothy—my green roadster—and so saved us all a four-mile walk. After a half hour's swim we stopped by the spring and made a drink of chocolate syrup and evaporated milk which we drank with our peanut butter, raisin, and dark bread sandwiches.

I had thought the children might be interested in a white rat experiment to show the value of milk as a source of nourishment. These younger boys made cages of screening laced up with copper wire set into large enamelware baking dishes. Pie tins were covers, and muffin cups were food containers. The rats were named Pat and Mike. Pat was to have water with his whole wheat bread crumbs and Mike was to have milk. The boys drew lots to see who should care for the rats from week to week. Of course we had to consider which families liked pets of this sort and which did not. It was interesting to see each week how Mike had grown and how smooth his fur was. Pat was thinner and his coat was rough. The rats served their purpose, and the children saw the results.

I called at the home of one of the boys later in the summer and the mother told me how well Junior was doing with his Swiss chard and milk. I thought how nice it was that I had made at least one impression. Then they—mother and father both—went on to tell me how the comic section of the Sunday paper had emphasized the strength of Pop Eye and its relation to spinach and milk. So it is questionable at present whether dietary changes are due to Pop Eye or to the nutritionist.

Early in the summer when I got together a group of the older boys and tried to discover some common interest which I might use as a basis for health teaching, I realized that what they really needed was a man leader who would take them hiking and camping and perhaps bring health into the program in an indirect manner. The boys were interested in a Boy Scout Troop and called themselves Scouts although no effort was made to form a regular troop. After much effort on the part of everyone we found a leader—a young man who had just finished college. He was hoping to find work teaching in the fall and agreed that a little experience in club work would not be out of place. He played baseball with the boys and finally their interest centered on camping.

A camping spot was found quite near to the reservoir and not too far from the drinking water. About twenty-two boys and three leaders stayed at the camp from Sunday evening to Friday afternoon. Potatoes were contributed by the boys; canned mutton, hamburg and veal, evaporated milk and butter came from the E. R. A. supply; and the seventy-five cents which each boy brought with him covered the cost of the rest of the food. I bought most of the food, planned the meals, and prepared a few of them. The boys laid out a fine camp and kept it clean. They made an excellent fireplace, picked berries, swam, played ball and quoits and fixed up a place for jumping.

It was the first experience some of them had ever had camping out and being away from home with others their own age and with no women around. The boys were enthusiastic about the camp, talking about it long after they were back in town. They learned a little something about the cooperation necessary in group life and the independence one needs away from home as well as having a glimpse of the pleasure that outdoor living can be. Since they were hungry they ate what was served with very little fussing. The meals were usually one dish affairs; one that I remember was macaroni and tomatoes, bread and butter, raw carrots, gingerbread and chocolate milk drink.

Camping presents an opportunity to teach health in an indirect manner which seems to carry over better than more formal teaching. Between thirty and forty boys were probably reached in one way or another during the summer. This number—as also with the number given for the girls—does not include the children who came to meetings at the Hill.

The library books for the children are all kept in the school and are usually inaccessible during the summer. (Perhaps they have not always been kept in the school, however.) The principal gave us permission to use them this summer, and nearly one hundred were loaned to the children who came to club meetings. In August a collection of twenty-five books was borrowed from the library of the State Department of Education. These were loaned to the children of the Hill district.

The Hill children between the ages of eight and ten were invited early in the summer to come to the school on Tuesday mornings, and soon the group grew to include brothers and sisters from four to fourteen. Two very attractive Polish girls—sisters—both through high school—came nearly every week to help. We weighed the children several times and read stories to them about children in other countries. The children colored pictures of vegetables and other foods, drew pictures on the blackboard, made up health games and acted out a play for which they made their own costumes. Usually there were about twenty present. The time between ten and twelve o'clock would go very quickly and occasionally we met twice a week.

Their last meeting was a party. In spite of a pouring rain twenty-eight were present. We sang songs, wore crepe paper hats, and read original and appropriate verses about Paul Potato, Stasia Squash, Cecile Carrot, and Rene Radish. Then there was cream of tomato soup with a few kernels of popcorn on top, and clown cookies made of crackers decorated with marshmallow faces, raisin features and peppermint stick hats. A few minutes in the oven had melted face and hat enough to spread.

The Mothers' Meetings in the Hill School were well attended. Usually seven to ten families were represented. Samples were passed around and leaflets given out. The use of milk was stressed because so many mothers claimed they could not afford to buy any more. They did not seem to realize how necessary it was for proper growth and development. Some of the women in this district have as many as twelve children; all are very hard workers in their gardens and with their housework. A few could not spare the time to come to meetings more than once or twice. One woman had a daughter fourteen years old with a crippled arm who could do very little housework. Then there were three boys and two younger girls. This woman worked as an inspector in a mill in the next town. She left home between five and six in the morning and came back sometime during the afternoon. Then she had the housework to do after that. Doris came to the meetings, and we would send samples of the food over to her mother. Some women did not understand English well enough to come to the meetings; in a few of these cases the grown-up daughters came instead. Those who did come seemed to look upon the meetings as social occasions and came quite as much for the opportunity of seeing each other as for the chance of learning nutrition. I generally planned so that the girls in the cooking classes made more than enough of whatever it was. Then I had the extra amount for samples at the Hill in the evening. In this way we had a variety of salads, sandwich fillings, drinks, salad dressings, and simple desserts made with evaporated milk, samples of nut margarine and soup.

The women of this district had asked for information on canning and through the Extension Service the methods of canning peaches and tomatoes were demonstrated. To gain publicity for the demonstration we had held a poster contest among the 4-H Club canners. Six posters were made and Helen received the prize. Her poster had been placed in the post office window and the other five in five stores about town.

To "put up" eighty quarts of corn plus beets and pickles, carrots and beans and tomatoes is an ordinary affair among many of these people. Last year one woman—with the help of her daughter—"put up" five hundred quarts of garden products for her family of eight. And they used it all. The gardens began to supply tomatoes quite early in August and I remember one day saying to a woman that I was planning to talk about good breakfasts. "Well", she said, "Our tomatoes and cucumbers are ripe now and this morning we had tomatoes and cucumbers and bread and butter and the children had milk to drink". Surely tomatoes and cucumbers count as fruit, but I would never have thought of that meal myself. This showed quite clearly the value of letting other people talk first.

The meetings for mothers in town were not so well attended. We were not so regular about holding the meetings as we were at the Hill, because other public affairs interfered. The meetings that we did have were similar to those at the Hill.

For two weeks I was able to show moving pictures by combining the service offered by a film company of New York City and the State Department of Public Health. One showing of pictures was given at the Town Hall and one hundred and ten children and forty-five adults were present. Another showing at the Hill brought out thirty-five children and twenty adults. Also there were various showings at school for smaller groups. The interest shown was remarkable considering the educational value of the pictures and the fact that they were silent except for my frequent interpretations.

Late in August I spent several days figuring supplies and equipment and costs for a proposed project to provide a hot dish lunch for school children during the winter. It was hoped to give work to three people in this way and a hot dish (some milk and vegetable combination such as corn chowder) to about one hundred children. Considering that a large number of the Hill children have to bring their lunch to school throughout the year and that in the bad weather others bring theirs, it would be an excellent idea to have such a project go into effect. It would also give an opportunity to teach certain health habits such as handwashing before eating and the introduction of new foods into the diet.

One talk was given for the women of one of the churches at a meeting they held late in July. There were about twenty people present. Leaflets on economical foods were distributed and posters on health work were shown. The women were very much interested in what I was trying to do with the children in club work. Mention was made of outdoor cooking and some bulletins were passed out.

The people need education in economy. A woman who has twelve children and a husband to feed and care for on twenty-three dollars or less a week should not be buying three pounds of haddock for seventy-four cents for one meal just because "the children don't like canned salmon very well." (The next Friday they had sardines.)

The men in all the stores in town have told me that those who should buy cheap food buy just as expensively as the others. They also buy in small amounts, losing a few cents each time. When children do the shopping, as is necessary in a family of twelve or fourteen, the most economical purchases are not made. When there is no cash, one must run an account and lose a little more.

I think some educational work could be done with the storekeepers. It seems as though they carried many of the most expensive brands of canned goods, cheese, and meat. One man told me that no one will buy soup bones and stew meat and that when he has two grades of frankfurters, he sells more of the higher priced variety.

I talked to the teachers the day school opened and spoke about what I had been doing during the summer. I gave them many posters and projects to use in connection with geography and history. I tried to explain a little about the most recent theories of health education—"health is a result of a way of living," and not a subject to be taught by itself. But I think the teachers want more information on this matter.

As I said earlier in the report, I feel as though a start had been made —a few results shown. Of the one hundred families that I hoped to work with—seventy or seventy-five were called on during the summer, and met with in the clubs. In addition to these, perhaps fifteen or twenty other families were met in some way or other. There is room for a great deal more work to be done. This nutrition work means changing attitudes and ideas so that the people themselves will want to change their habits, and this is slow work. It means offering them anything that will show the way to a more abundant life.

It has been very interesting work. The people have been so appreciative and—at least, verbally—cooperative that I have enjoyed working with them. Those who were in a position to help me always seemed glad to do so.

Olga, a little Polish girl, told me the other day about the lilac bush by their wall. It had been a large one at the entrance to their front yard. To widen the road, her father had cut it down—"all but a little piece he left for remembrance." Somehow I can't help hoping that a way will be found to keep a little nutrition work going in the town— "just for remembrance." It is so very easy to forget about lilacs and good living.

Epilogue

As a follow-up of the school lunch project started by Miss Hager, a nutritionist from the State Department of Public Health assisted the WPA supervisor in estimating under federal specifications the requisitions for the year's supply of food and equipment. In the central schoolhouse, an unused basement room was converted into a clean, cozy looking, eating place by the efforts of the three WPA relief workers, and a carpenter from the relief rolls. In spite of handicaps, such as carrying every bit of water from outside into the lunchroom, and working without a sink, a hot dish is provided to about one hundred children daily, and more in bad weather.

HELEN INMAN DUFF
Massachusetts Department of Public Health

THE CONTRIBUTION OF THE FOOD CLINIC TO THE COMMUNITY
BY FRANCES STERN
Boston Dispensary

As I begin to write of the dietitian in the Food Clinic, and her relation to community work, I have before me an issue of the Journal of Home Economics of a quarter of a century ago. Not only in that publication, but in books, lectures and courses, Mrs. Ellen H. Richards stressed the relation of nutrition to public health. She declared the homemaker to be the health officer of the home. She coined the word "euthenics," by which she meant the science of controllable environment, and in a book with that title* she outlined the environmental factors that bear upon nutrition.

Influenced by association with Mrs. Richards and Miss Isabel F. Hyams, and from close observation of the patient both in the clinic and in the home, the writer became convinced that food guidance and the interpretation of the relation of food to the body's health, growth and activity were an essential part of the medical treatment of the outpatient.

The opportunity came during war time to test the worth of this belief, and with the cooperation of the Administration of The Boston Dispensary, the first food clinic was opened in 1918.

In 1935 we received the Quarterly Bulletin of the Health Organization** of the League of Nations with the title "Nutrition and Public Health." The authors write, "The remarkable advance of the science of nutrition during recent years demands a new orientation of public health activity," and again, "The problem of malnutrition is largely a social and economic problem and, as such, concerns politicians, economists, agriculturists and social workers as closely as it concerns the medical profession," and I add, the dietitian and nutritionist. The authors note also that the Food Clinic has reached its highest development in the United States.

Early in the depression period Mr. Frank E. Wing, Director of the Boston Dispensary, made the statement that competent authorities estimated the number of visits to all clinics in the United States, for the year 1930, to be as great as 40,000,000.

The thousands of such patients suffering from diseases or faulty food habits that dietary measures would help—are they receiving dietary care as a recognized part of the medical treatment of the ambulatory patient?

Certainly the increasing belief and interest of physicians, and of workers in allied fields, is stimulating the growth and development of food clinics in this country and abroad. The American Dietetic Association has recently approved a course of training in the very special technique that food treatment of the outpatient demands.

---
*Richards, Ellen H., Euthenics, Barrows, Boston, 1912.
**Et. Burnet and Aykroyd, W. R., Nutrition and Public Health, Vol. IV, No. 2, June 1935.

Let us enter a Food Clinic and observe its procedure. It is furnished in accordance with the belief that a cheerful environment, with things of interest and beauty in it, and reflecting friendliness and sympathy, will encourage the patient to feel at ease and assure him of receiving understanding treatment. It helps him, in private conference with the dietitian, to talk quite unreservedly of himself and his family, his home, his work, his habits, his difficulties and hopes—the environmental factors that affect nutrition and that the dietitian will make use of in adapting the diet plan to the patient's needs.*

The patient's record, containing the findings of the medical examination, laboratory tests, and treatment in other clinics, with the physician's diagnosis and his recommendation for food treatment, gives the dietitian the necessary data on which to base the diet. Then with the aid of an outline for taking a nutritional history** the dietitian gathers data for a study of the influence of environmental factors: the income and how far it allows for an adequate diet, and whether in applying it to the purchases of the various necessaries of life the patient is protecting sufficiently his food requirements; the nationality and religion, and the difficulties that arise in trying to adhere, in the new community, to dietary laws and cherished age-old practices in the choice and preparation of food, often resulting in unhappy attempts at adaptation; the ability of the homemaker or provider to choose foods that are economical and yet meet body needs, and to prepare them in an appetizing manner, even with poor facilities; the adequacy of the meal that is eaten away from home, and the conditions under which it is eaten; the household arrangements for sleep and the practice of proper sleep habits; the demands upon energy that the type of home entails; the type and accessibility of toilet facilities; the arrangement of mealtimes in relation to the requirements of occupation; the opportunity which the community affords for recreation and the enjoyment of sunlight; mental attitudes and ability; family relationships and food likes and dislikes.

Then the dietitian assembles the data that will give her a comprehensive picture of the patient's life at home, in the community, at school, at work, and at play. How and what is she to teach the patient about food and his body needs, while adjusting her teaching and the diet plan to his daily requirements and to his understanding? For to him must be transferred, in a large measure, the responsibility for carrying out the diet in the interim of his visits to the clinic.

It can be done with the aid of materials for visualization, and these the Food Clinic has sought to assemble and develop. With the leaflet* that shows the skeleton and the foods that provide calcium, the circulatory system and the foods that provide iron, the muscular system and

---

*Stern, Frances, The Nutritionist Looks at Mental Hygiene, Mental Hygiene, Vol. XIV, No. 1, 1930.

**Nutritional History form No. 173 may be obtained from Miss Stern, Boston Dispensary. The form includes an outline for a detailed Nutritional History — Child, from a Personal, Family, School, House, and Neighborhood point of view, including income, meals, foods, attitudes, intake, purchasing, hygiene, and education.

*Feed Your Body To Protect Your Health — N. E. Dairy & Food Council, 51 Cornhill, Boston.

the protein foods, the body displaying energy and the foods that supply carbohydrate and fat, and the body in health and vigor and the foods containing vitamins, even the patient who cannot read understands the relation of food to the body's growth and development, activity and vigor. The leaflet shows him that certain foods, such as milk, serve the body in several ways and, consequently, are of great value in the diet. He learns to evaluate different foods according to the contributions they make to body needs, and uses familiarly the terms calcium, iron, protein, carbohydrate, fat and vitamins. Attractive methods have been evolved for teaching these elements of nutrition to the child.

A picture or drawing of a scale illustrates the balance to be maintained between the food intake and the output of energy. The patient understands that "What I Eat" must balance "What I Do". With various illustrations he is led to see why, with reference to his particular need for food treatment, it may be necessary to modify his food intake in amount, kind or consistency, in order to compensate for the deviation in normal functioning of the body part affected.

The food order for the day is written out for the patient, listing foods in kinds and amounts, with choices for variation, and sometimes with menus and recipes. Wax models of foods are used to visualize to him the amount of servings allowed. In his Food Diary the patient will keep a record of his meals, which he and the dietitian will study together at his next visit to the clinic.

But does the patient spend the income to the best advantage for purposes of health, and would a little guidance help him? The dietitian asks him to keep on a special form a record of his expenditures for a week, and again this is studied and discussed with him on his return visit.

On the basis of the dietary recommendations in the valuable bulletin by Stiebeling and Ward* the Food Clinic has developed another helpful form which the patient can use as a guide in selecting the foods that will provide for each member of his family, whatever its size and the ages of its members, an adequate diet at minimum cost per week.

Thus the dietitian educates the patient over a number of visits, to go back into the community with an elementary knowledge of the principles of nutrition and economical buying, and capable of self-guidance in the selection of an adequate diet.

But more than the patient is involved in food treatment. What is the attitude of the home people? They must cooperate; and so the family, too, must be carefully educated.

When it is revealed during the food treatment that the patient needs care in other clinics, or that he or his family is unable to provide the food that effective treatment requires—so often the case—or that adjustments are desirable in the home or school or occupational environment, the Food Clinic turns to the social worker and again there is contact with the community.

---
*Stiebeling and Ward, Diets at Four Levels of Nutritive Content and Cost — U. S. Dept. of Agriculture, Circular No. 296, November 1933.

There is affiliated with the Food Clinic in The Boston Dispensary another service which helps to transmit health knowledge—the Health Education Department* which teaches food and health habits to patients, especially to children, as they wait for treatment in various waiting rooms. Gathered about a table, in an attractive environment, the children discuss with a teacher the way in which a food constituent —calcium, protein, food iron, the vitamins—or a health habit helps the body. It is done happily and informally with repeated emphasis on principles through things which the child enjoys—the story, game, experiment, motion picture and handwork. Adult patients and guardians are always interested listeners.

Mothers' meetings, held once a month, bring the principles of child health directly to the parent and the home, to the betterment of family food and health habits. And with the help of the Food Clinic, exhibits are developed and loaned to various health agencies in the community.

The following is quoted from a report prepared by Mr. Michael M. Davis concerning the clinics in New York City: "In the course of a single year, about 2,500,000 people suffer incapacitating illnesses. Of the three to four million persons who annually seek medical attention while not sufficiently ill to be in bed, about one million secure it from doctors practicing in clinics, but the bulk of such service is rendered privately in doctors' offices." It is certain that to many physicians, nurses and social workers the help of the community nutritionist is not available.

To meet this need, the Food Clinic again renders service. To medical and dental students and graduates, to nurses, dietitians and other students of public health problems in the fields of home economics, social service, education and other forms of community service it gives instruction, and opportunity for observation and practice in applied dietetics.

Thus the Food Clinic reaches out far and deeply into the community, through the education of its patients and their families, and through the training of health workers in the community. And always it is in the spirit of Dr. Francis W. Peabody that the dietitian attempts to conceive of her service as community dietitian: "What is spoken of as a 'clinical picture' is not just a photograph of a man in bed; it is an impressionistic painting of the patient surrounded by his home, his work, his relations, his friends, his joys, sorrows, hopes and fears."**

---
*Health Education by a Hospital Dispensary by Mary Pfaffman, The Commonhealths July—Aug. —Sept. 1934.
**Peabody, M. D., Francis Weld, Doctor and Patient, Macmillan Co., New York, 1930.

THE NUTRITIONIST ON THE ITINERANT CLINICS
BY DAVID ZACKS, M.D.
Chief of Clinics
Massachusetts Department of Public Health

I have been asked for an opinion as to the value of the nutritionist and nutrition in itinerant clinics such as the Chadwick School Clinics. Is the nutritionist a stark necessity or a useless luxury? Has she proven her worth in such clinics? Should she be retained or added to the staff of school clinics which are gradually replacing the popular Chadwick Clinics? I shall first relate briefly my own experience on this subject.

My first introduction to the problem of nutrition occurred in 1924 when I became examiner in the School Clinics. For some reason, then unknown to me, a nutritionist formed an integral part of the clinic unit. In medical school I learned the physiology and chemistry of digestion. It was taken for granted, I presume, that the food intake would always be adequate in quantity and quality. I do not recall for certain any instruction regarding adequacy of food intake, balanced diet, growth diet and food deficiencies, except in the interesting and spectacular clinical entities such as beri-beri, scurvy and rickets. The sun was still unbottled. Vitamins were, of course, unknown. Later, in Pediatrics, I learned to my surprise that a child seven per cent underweight for its age and height was a sick child. To "cure" this "sick child" there was a formula—"The parallelogram of Forces." These "Forces" made such a vague impression upon me that I was warned one day by the instructor that unless I could dispel my mental fog, I should "flunk" the course. This was a new experience as I had never failed in any subject before. I cite this incident to show that not only was I innocent of any knowledge in nutrition, but had, perhaps, an unconscious prejudice against the subject.

Then I was introduced to nutritionists and to nutrition. A part of the child's physical examination was to estimate whether the nutrition was good, fair or poor. I was glad of the word "fair" as I could hide my inexact knowledge in that inexact word. Instinct told me also that "fair" would least antagonize the mothers who might have some objection to calling their children poorly nourished. Poor nutrition has an unfortunate connotation. To many mothers it means poor, lazy mothers, poor cooks, poor managers, poor providers, poor homemakers. I also found myself repeating to each mother (sometimes also father) who accompanied the child—"Now, please, before you go, I want you to talk to our Nutritionist about your child's food habits and personal hygiene." Unwittingly, I became a propagandist for the Nutritionist.

Soon I wanted to know what it was that the nutritionist was talking about so intimately, confidentially, and at such length, with these mothers; so I accompanied the children with their mothers and "listened in." I found the Nutritionist taking an inventory of the child's food intake, its quality, its quantity. Did the child have a quart of milk every day or its equivalent? And two vegetables (one raw) besides potato? And two fruit helpings at least? In other words, the Nutritionist stressed in the food intake—milk, vegetables, fruit, water—made suggestions about the right amount of fish, meat, eggs, cereals, dark bread and butter. She spoke about the value of rest and proper bedtime. She used a sensible standard as a yard-stick, made verbal suggestions which she wrote down on a special report for the mother to take home for reference. A copy of this report was also given to the School Nurse for her information. This was Health Education—personal, intimate, carried to the home by two routes—the child and the parent.

The standard by which the growing child's food intake is checked is reproduced below. With this as a flexible guide, the individual's gross diet inadequacies may be determined and suggestions for corrections made.

A Measuring Stick for a Family's Meals

MILK—1 qt. a day for each child—or at least 3 cups. 1 pt. a day for each adult. 1 qt. a day for the nursing or pregnant woman.

VEGETABLES—1 raw vegetable each day. Potato. An additional vegetable, especially of a green or yellow color.

FRUITS—Orange, tomato, grapefruit or pineapple each day. An additional serving of fruit—fresh, canned or dried, each day.

BREADS AND OTHER CEREALS AND CEREAL PUDDING—"Dark" bread or a "whole grain" cereal for at least one meal each day. (Size and number of servings vary with energy needs.)

EGGS—1 a day for children and adults if possible.

MEATS, FISH, CHEESE, PEAS, BEANS—A serving of one of these a day.

FATS—Butter at every meal for children, and for adults, if possible. Fish liver oil, especially for children.

SWEETS—For flavor in small quantities. As an extra at the end of a meal. Molasses, honey, brown sugar and maple syrup, sometimes in place of white sugar. Fruits are good sweets.

PLENTY OF ADDITIONAL FOODS—To meet the calorie needs.

WATER—About four glasses a day for children. About six to eight glasses a day for adults. (Plenty of water is important for the best use of food. The amount of water needed depends upon activity, the weather, and the size of the person.)

REGULARITY—Eating meals at regular times makes for a good appetite and a healthy digestive system.

LEISURE AT MEALS—Makes for family companionship and good digestion.

GOOD APPETITE—Is aided by rest and outdoor activity.

At times, I went to dinner or to lunch with the Nutritionists. I noted with pleasure that they were not food faddists. From example, I personally began to increase the use of milk, vegetables, fruit, and decreased the amount of fish and meat. In secret, I wanted to gain two or three inches in height. I expected a miracle, you see. What happened was a painless personal reduction of fifteen pounds in weight as a matter of course and without any magical formulæ or radio health crooners.

I became the nutritionists' friend. I turned to them for help with the varied health problems which, to my surprise, I found existing in school children. If dental caries are due to deficient diet, then many children are on a deficient diet. If fatigue posture is due to an inadequate diet, then many children are on a poor diet. If the periodic rate of gain and the regularities of growth in height, and weight give evidence of an adequate diet, then children are found in the schools on an inadequate diet. If constipation is the result of faulty diet, then many of the children in school receive faulty diets. If deficient food intake in growing children is a fault, then many children have incorrect diets for growth, stamina, and that desirable surplus for the occasional emergency demand in illness.

Granting that there is at present no practical method of judging nutrition of children which has the stamp of scientific authority, shall we do nothing until the exact measuring stick will have been found? Of course not! Let us make an examination into the dietary of the child as an obvious first step in determining the adequacy of intake. We know the desirable quantities of the various food sources for insuring ample intake and therefore we can determine gross inadequacies at least, using such knowledge as we find:

Three children in every thousand come to school without breakfast.

Thirty-three in every hundred need better breakfasts.

Ten in every hundred need better lunches. (Of those who either bought their lunch or brought their lunches to school with them, thirty-six in every hundred needed more sleep.)

Forty-two* in every hundred had poor food habits. These poor food habits were due first (67%) to inadequate quantity and quality because of economic stress, and second (33%) to poor home discipline.

A very large number of children need immediate dental work. (Of this number, 50 per cent could not afford to have this done and 50 per cent was due to parental neglect.)

I believe that the success of an educational program of this type may be measured by the reaction of the parents, nurses, and the older children themselves. With this in mind, 167 school nurses were asked these questions:

1. Do you consider the Nutritionist an essential part of the Chadwick Clinics?

2. Have the parents been helped by the Nutritionist?

3. Has the Nutritionist helped in solving individual economic problems?

4. Has the Nutritionist aided you in teaching the value of rest?

---

*It may be of some interest to record that in 1927-1928, 13% of the families could not follow the minimum recommendations for economic reasons. In the school year 1928-1929, this was 8%; in the school year 1929-1930, it was 19%; in 1930-1931, 20%; in 1931-1932, 30%; in 1932-1933, 34%; in 1933-1934, 31%; and in 1934-1935, 30%.

5. Has the Nutritionist supplemented your health education program?

The answers were almost a unanimous "yes" to questions 1, 2, 4 and 5. Question 3 was, perhaps, a bit ambiguous. What was meant was help in solving individual economic problems as far as can be done by intelligent budgeting of the low income, to get the most food value for the money available. The nurses also made some voluntary comments:

1. "In my home visits to parents, they quoted the nutritionist and seemed to have received much help and had confidence in her suggestions."

2. "The parents value and appreciate the services of the nutritionist and so do the School and Health Departments. I have also gained much by her service."

3. "I consider a nutritionist so valuable that I wish we could have her with us all of the time."

4. "In passing out the report cards, I have found that parents speak very highly of the help given by the nutritionist."

5. "The material she gave pupils I had already given them as the State supplies me with it. However, the discourse with parents and pupils deepens local interest in nutrition."

6. "The nutritionist was always valuable but is needed more than ever at this time when people are reducing food for lack of money."

Mothers who have faithfully attended the Clinics from year to year, were asked to state in what way the nutritionist's advice has been helpful to them. The replies were generally flatteringly favorable. These are typical replies:

"The nutritionist must have helped as the child's (health) habits are so much better."

"The nutritionist's advice has helped very much. The use of raw vegetables when fruit was high, as a source of vitamin C, was new."

"Nutritionist has helped in low cost, balanced meals. Information applied to all of the family."

"I look forward to the Clinic for encouragement to go on. It helps with my problems at home."

"We have tried to buy more milk instead of meat since the nutritionists told us we get more for our money in that way."

"They (children) won't listen to me, yet when you tell them to rest, they believe it is more important."

"When you state a definite bedtime, it is a big help to me."

"Marion has tried to learn to like everything since she talked with the nutritionist."

High school pupils tell us that as a result of their talks with the nutritionists, they have taken better care of their teeth, have gone to bed earlier, have improved their food habits regarding milk and vegetables, fruit, cereal, and dark bread. They have improved personal hygiene with regard to water inside and out, for better care of their skin in particular.

My own experience these past twelve years with school children has taught me the need for health education, not only for the children in the schools, but for their parents as well. The children's diets are far too often either insufficient in amount, inadequate in kind, or faulty because of poor food habits. The stigmata of faulty food intake are—dental caries, fatigue, and lag in the gain of weight rate. Nutrition is certainly a basic science in the field of "preventive medicine." Until such time as health education becomes more generally accepted in the school curriculum, any special clinics having to do with the health of school children come face to face with the problem of nutrition. Unless an attempt is made to meet this problem, the clinics cannot be completely successful. Those responsible for itinerant school clinics should consider seriously the addition of a nutritionist to the clinic staff. There is ample evidence, it seems to me, that the nutritionist is a very useful addition to any clinic having for its objective the prevention of disease.

NUTRITION ON THE WELL CHILD CONFERENCE
BY SUSAN M. COFFIN, M.D., *Pediatrician*
and
FREDERICA L. BEINERT, B.S., *Nutritionist*
Massachusetts Department of Public Health

The nutrition teaching problems met at the Well Child Conference are as many as the children who attend. Most of the Conferences are held in rural areas, though there are occasional demonstrations in urban communities. The parents accompanying the children represent all walks of life and all economic levels. In one town, Mrs. Jones, driving into the center of town from her farm several miles away with a horse and buggy, has the first appointment for Jane. Following comes Mrs. Falkowski with Wanda, walking down the dusty road from her house on the edge of the tobacco field. The third appointment is for Mrs. Arnold with James and baby John. Mrs. Arnold is the wife of a lawyer whose offices are in the nearby city. Each of the mothers has an opportunity—sometimes the first one ever—to talk over her child's diet, to discuss difficulties in feeding habits, and to ask for assistance in managing her food budget.

The most common defects found among children seen at our Well Child Conferences are those related to nutrition. These include dental defects, for we consider active tooth decay and multiple caries as evidences of faulty nutrition.

It is realized, of course, that other factors than food enter into the nutrition picture. Malnutrition is not necessarily a question of lack of food due to poverty. It may mean a lack due to indifference or lack of information, leading to poorly balanced meals and faulty family food habits. Marked cases of malnutrition sometimes appear in families of abundant means as well as in those less fortunate.

Dietary deficiencies with subsequent nutritional defect may be due to one or several of many causes. Important roles are played by poor prenatal diet, poor postnatal diet, lack of breast feeding, or lack of sufficient protective foods during infancy and the preschool years. Poor prenatal nourishment may, of course, have been due to the mother's inability to retain or properly assimilate food during pregnancy, or it may have been due to her lack of sufficient knowledge as to the necessary building foods for her good and that of her baby. The protective diet for mothers during pregnancy needs a large amount of attention, and receives constant mention by the physician and nutritionist at the Conferences. So many mothers still do not realize that proper food at this time helps to save their own teeth, guards their health, and helps start sound teeth and bones for the coming child. Many curious notions are met as to what a pregnant mother should or should not eat—and they die hard!

During the first year of life the infant may have had a physiological disturbance affecting the assimilation of foods. He may have refused new foods when they were offered to him, and may not have been encouraged to learn to like them. These same dislikes may have carried over to the preschool years. The food habits of the older members of the family maybe poor examples for the young child to copy. We are so often called upon to teach the fact that food likes and dislikes are not inherited but copied. Nutrition information given at the Conference thus discusses not only the diet and food habits of the child who attends, but the food habits of the whole family.

So many of the dietary inadequacies (or insufficiencies) met in the Conferences are found to be due to poor food habits. Each mother spends from twenty to forty-five minutes with the nutritionist. She has heard the physician's comments and recommendations made during the stripped examination, and on these the nutritionist bases many of her suggestions. Both the physician and the nutritionist emphasize the important relationship between adequate food, rest and sleep. This is rarely sufficiently realized in the home. The tired child is not a "good eater" and there are many tired children seen—children who never get "slept out," who are never quite ready to get up in the morning, even at this early age.

So many poor food habits are met that it is hard to isolate them. Many of the children hesitate to taste a new food because they are given a too large serving. The nutritionist suggests that a "taste" will do, and the size of serving gradually enlarged with the increase in the child's liking for the food. Just as many times, the parents try to "make" the child eat a food because it is "good" for him when they themselves make no effort to eat it. Such an example is not a good one for preschool children to follow. "Don't talk about food at the table" is a good rule for many families. It is so often possible for the parent to learn to like the food with the child. Not unimportant by any means, though rarely considered, is help given in varying diet, and in getting the most out of what food is obtainable. Poor food habits may result from "sameness" in diet. Meals are a three-times-a-day job and need all the variation possible. This need not mean expensive additions or extra fussing. Often a vegetable cut in a new shape, a gay bit of color added to the familiar prepared dish, a new high colored plate for serving, care to avoid repetition of a food within too short a time—all of these simple helps increase the "eye appeal" of food and thus the appetite. Cereal twice a day has ceased to be the rule, and many children eat better suppers when they are served a cream soup or a vegetable instead.

A copy of recommendations made at the conference is given to the mother and a report of all recommendations given to the local nurse to aid in home follow-up. When the Demonstration is at an end, and the town plans taking over the Well Child Conference, we help find in the community the person best prepared and suited to carry on the nutrition end of the work. This person may be the community nutritionist, an extension worker with definite training in nutrition, or a dietitian or home economics teacher with a background of clinic experience.

Chart No. I. (see page 44) shows in part the nutrition findings and recommendations of all Well Child Conferences for the past four years. The nutrition condition of the child was judged by the physician; the suggestions for increased intake of specific foods made, for the most part, by the nutritionist. The latter applied to those families in which there was not sufficient food and to those children who were not eating the food provided for them. In many cases in which active tooth decay was found, special suggestions were made for increased intake of the protective foods and lessened intake of sweets. Advice on food budget adjustment was given to families on low income when it was desired.

An analysis shows the following points:

A decrease in the number of children considered to be in "good" nutrition condition from 1932 to 1933; a slight improvement from 1933 to 1934; a tendency toward "holding its own" for 1934 and 1935.

There has been a small steady increase in the number of recommendations for increased intake of milk. There was a slight decrease from 1932 to 1934 in recommendations for more fruits, and an abrupt increase from 1934 to 1935.

The number of recommendations for the use of more vegetables was fairly constant for 1932, 1933, 1934 and abruptly increased for 1935.

The number of families requesting advice on budgeting food expenditures increased to nearly double from 1932 to 1935.

Figures showing the number of recommendations for the increased use of foods containing whole grains, and the number of families on welfare relief have been studied only for the last two years, but in both cases there was an increase from 1934 to 1935.

For all Well Child Conferences the following constants have been retained:

The same physician and nutritionist worked together during most of the four-year period.

The time of year was the same annually for the various towns, including principally the months of March through July. This allowed a good average between families seen during each spring when the fruit and vegetable market prices were high with home canned food supplies low, and those seen during the time when garden produce was plentiful.

The geographic distribution of towns was essentially the same for the four years. However, in 1933 a three-year demonstration began in a town of 24,525 population changing considerably the total number of urban families seen on the Conferences.

Charts II and III (see pages 45 and 46) show the analysis of nutrition Conferences held in two adjacent towns for a three-year period. Chart II represents a decidedly urban population (24,525) in contrast to the semi-rural population (1,859) represented in Chart III.

A summary shows improvement in the nutrition picture for the urban area from 1932 to 1935 as evidenced by an increased number of children judged "good." There was, however, a slight shift in emphasis among the children showing nutrition defect, from "slight" defect to an increased number showing a "moderate" defect. This indicates a tendency toward more marked nutritional defect when such defect is noted.

The figures for the semi-rural area show a marked increase in the number of children showing "good" nutrition, and a corresponding decrease in the marked nutritional defects.

In both towns the number of recommendations for the increased use of milk varied in interesting contrast. For the urban group there was an increase in recommendations from 1933 to 1935. In the rural town there was a *decrease* in recommendations for the same period. A similar comparison is shown by the recommendations for the use of more fruits and vegetables.

In both towns there was a decrease in budget cases from 1933 to 1934, and then a sharp increase for 1935.

In all cases it is to be hoped that improved nutritional condition of the children, as well as improvement in the number of recommendations for more protective foods were results of nutrition teaching: the personnel of the group seen in the rural town did not vary so greatly as that seen in the large town so this seems a possible conclusion.

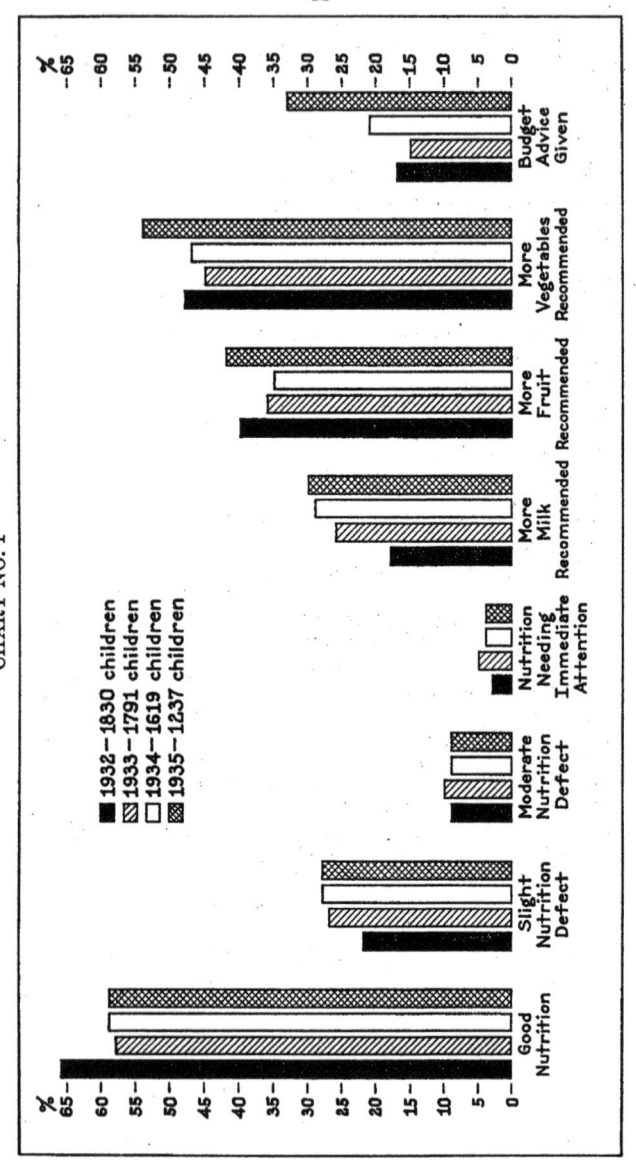

CHART NO. 1

CHART NO. 2

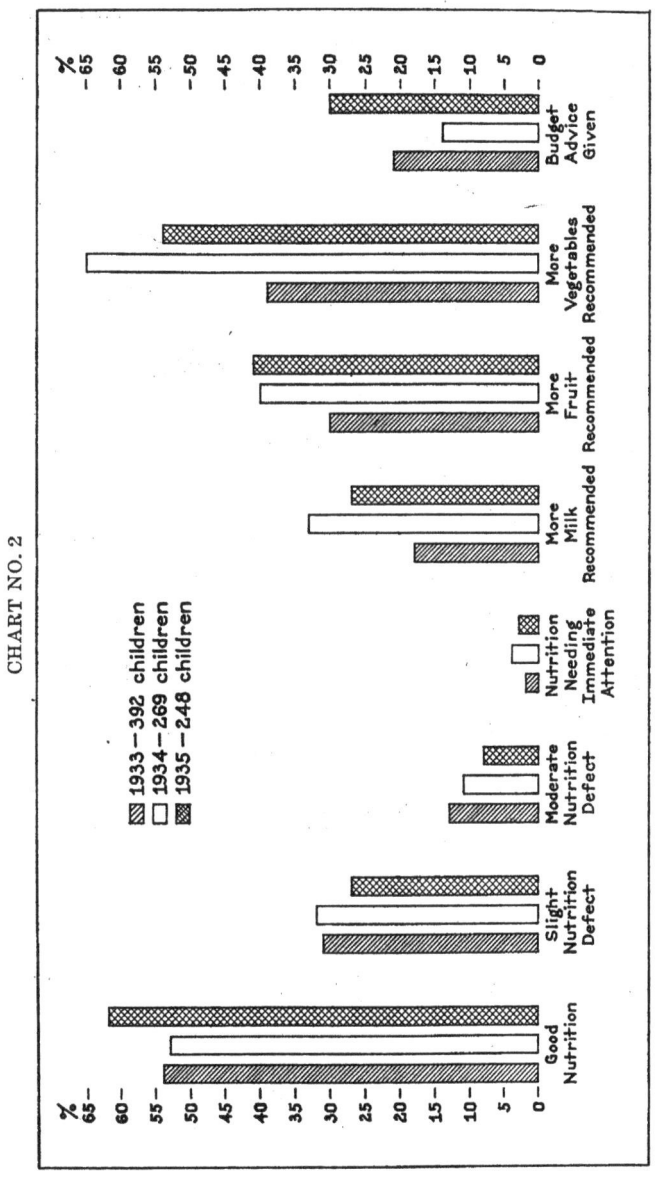

CHART NO. 3

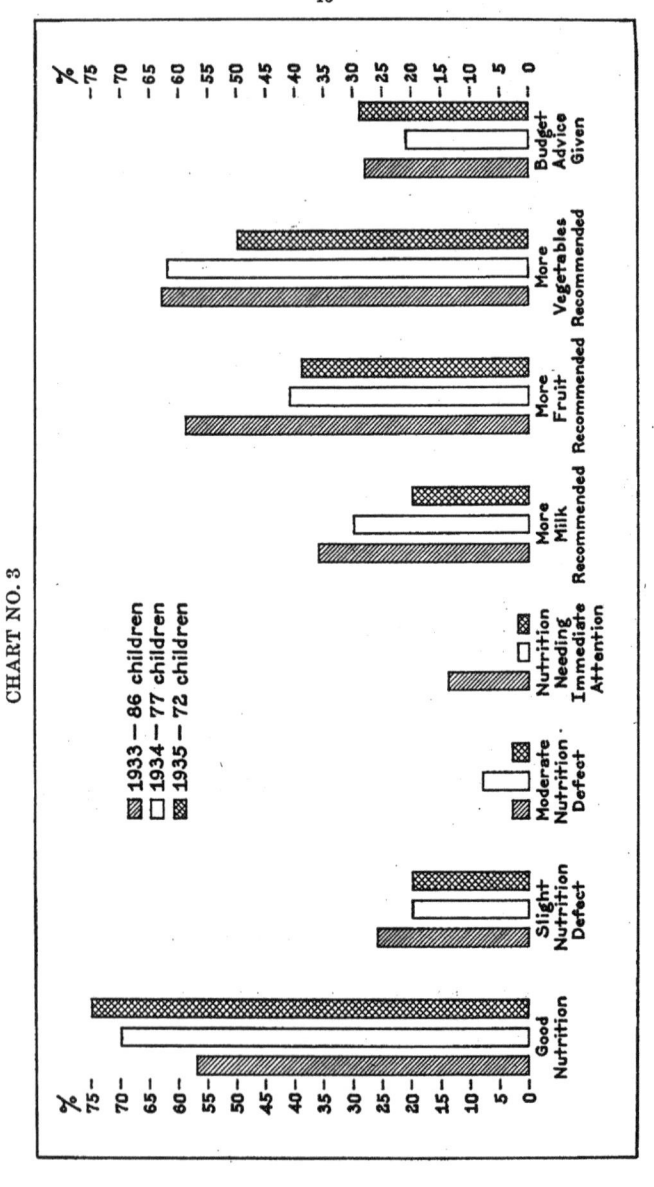

A SMILE FROM ARAXIE
A Dental Nutrition Case
BY RUTH L. WHITE, B.S.
Chief, Nutrition Department
Forsyth Dental Infirmary for Children

"Extensive decay. Refer to Nutrition Department." So wrote the dental interne who, one day in January 1932, had just completed a filling for black haired, seven year old Araxie at the Forsyth Dental Infirmary for Children.

A letter signed by the dentist went promptly to Araxie's home. On the following week they came to the Clinic—Araxie with quaint, irrestible charm in her dark eyes and her mother, an intelligent, serious woman showing in her expression the old-world sadness of her race.

Her husband had come to this country from Armenia in 1907 and she five years later, she told the Clinic history-taker. Other facts were related with anxious precision. When Araxie was born after eight long years of waiting for a baby, the doctor said that she must be the only child. During pregnancy her mother had "lived on air," eating practically nothing because of persistent nausea. Before her pregnancy everyone had admired her teeth but soon after Araxie's birth they began to decay. The baby was breast fed for one month, then put on a formula by the doctor at the clinic who supervised her care and feeding for the first twelve months. Araxie's only illnesses were measles when she was four years old and chicken pox when six. Her mother's own conception of the present situation was told briefly in the troubled phrase, "she just won't eat."

Dental conditions were recorded, the chart indicating extensive caries in ten deciduous teeth and definite areas of decalcification about the gingival surfaces of seven teeth. The gum tissue was red and spongy.

Next came the physician's examination with these notations:— Harrison's groove, hypertrophied tonsils, flabby muscles, constipation— and the recommendations, "Refer to Nutrition Department. Tonsillectomy needed. More outdoor play."

In the nutrition conference which followed, Araxie, her mother, the dentist who referred her to the Department, and the nutrition worker participated. Several interrelated problems which may be summarized as follows gradually became apparent:

Teeth so carious that mastication was painful.

A diet inadequate in milk, vegetables (cooked and raw), fresh fruits, eggs and butter.

Constipation.

Parents' overprotective attitude regarding food habits. Araxie was fed measured spoonfuls by her mother. Both parents constantly pleaded with her to eat and offered food at frequent intervals between meals.

Lack of outdoor exercise. Because of fear of accident or contagion, her mother would not allow her to leave the yard, and looked out of the window "every five minutes," calling her into the house at the end of half an hour.

Several concrete suggestions regarding more freedom in play activities and mealtime attitudes and habits were agreed upon in conference fashion. There is true science in the old adage, "hunger is the best sauce for appetite."

Alone at the Clinic a week later, the mother gave a proud report. The new play schedule had lead Araxie far afield and her father had cooperated by inviting her to meet him "past a crossing, too" as he returned home from work each night. Not much improvement in appetite was evident, but said Araxie's mother with courage and resignation, "We will wait." One day the following week, her husband was called to his office telephone. "Araxie just said that she was hungry!" came his wife's voice. It was the first time in her life!

On the third Clinic visit, Araxie came too. The conference this day concerned the diet itself, how foods could build the new teeth growing in her jaws and could help, even, to save and strengthen the decayed ones in her mouth. In pleasant cooperation, Araxie and her mother, the dentist and the nutritionist worked out her daily food needs, making use of familiar dishes but adding more of the protective foods to her usual diet.

Week by week the dental treatment was carried out. Caries in one tooth was so deep that extraction was necessary. Amalgam and cement fillings were placed in the cavities which could retain filling materials. Seven teeth so badly broken down that fillings were impractical were kept under careful observation. A prophylaxis was given.

It has been four years since that first Clinic day. Slowly, habit and dietary adjustments have been made. Comparison of the day's meals reported on Araxie's earliest and latest visits gives some indication of her changed program:

January 1932
Breakfast
　Whole wheat bread　½ slice
　Milk　1 small glass
　(Taken under protest)
　Egg
10:30 a.m.
　Milk　½ pint
　Graham crackers　2

January 1936
Breakfast
　Orange juice　¾ cupful
　Egg　1
　Whole wheat bread
　　with butter　1 slice
　Whole wheat bread
　　with cheese　1 slice
　Milk　1 glass
10:30 a.m.
　Apple　1

Noon Meal
  Chicken soup with
    rice   ½ cupful
  Chicken sandwich on
    whole wheat bread ½ sandwich
3:00 P.M.
  Saltines   4
4:00 P.M.
  Apple   1

Night Meal
  Matzoun (clabbered
    milk)   ½ cupful
  Pilaf with chicken
    broth   2 tablespoon-
                              fuls
7:45 P.M.
  Milk   1 glass

Noon Meal
  Lamb   1 small
                              serving
  Lima beans cooked in
    olive oil   ½ cupful
  Lettuce with olive oil
    dressing   5 leaves
  Milk   1 glass
  Whole wheat bread
    with butter   1 slice
4 P.M.
  Apple   1

Night Meal
  Spaghetti with tomato
    sauce   ¾ cupful
  Matzoun (clabbered
    milk)   1 cupful
  Whole wheat bread
    with butter   1½ slices
  Milk   1 glass
7:30 P.M.
  Milk   1 glass

Tonsils were long ago removed and constipation corrected. Growth has progressed at a satisfactory rate. There have been lapses, to be sure, from the schedule outlined. At one time, for example, Araxie's mother was ill for four months and meals cooked by her father and herself were "not so very good." But interest and effort have been steady and whole-hearted.

And the teeth, true to modern scientific belief, have seemed a barometer of body changes, a measure of the success of the new regime. In the four-year period, only one new cavity has appeared in the deciduous teeth. Only one deciduous tooth has been prematurely lost due to deep caries. The exposed dentine in the other six carious teeth under observation has become extremely hard, the carious process being definitely arrested. These teeth have been retained in healthy condition and have performed their normal function for a normal length of time. Recurrence of dental caries has taken place in two six-year molars around margins of fillings placed previously in January, 1932 but the permanent teeth which have erupted since that time are well formed and sound. Gum tissue has become pink and firm.

"A fine record," the dentist said last month, as he studied the dental chart. But the most convincing record is the change in Araxie's smile.

A DENTAL NUTRITION PROGRAM IN A COMMUNITY

BY M. M. BROWN, R.N., *Director of Health*
Department of Health and Physical Education, Reading, Mass.
and
DOROTHEA NICOLL, B.S., *Nutritionist*
Massachusetts Department of Public Health

Introduction

In any nutrition program the whole child must be considered. This is especially true where work such as the following is attempted, in which children are selected on the basis of just one nutrition defect. Many nutrition studies have been based on underweight children, but since over ninety per cent of our school children have dental defects this seemed a fertile field for work of widespread interest to the community.

This work is based on three accepted facts:

(1) The close relation a child's diet and daily regime bear to his dental condition as well as to his physical health.
(2) The need of more closely correlating nutrition and dental services in planning dental programs in the future.
(3)* The success of the nutritionist in helping to correct and prevent tooth defects at the Forsyth Dental Infirmary.

Problem

Attempts along this line have been made even on a community-wide basis. A plan which would furnish a combined service of nutrition supervision and dental care, through the cooperation of the State Department of Public Health in providing the nutrition service, was worked out a year ago with a school nurse in a nearby community. The plan was eagerly seized upon as a means of helping to reduce the incidence of dental caries as well as to relieve a situation which had developed as a result of inadequate facilities for dental correction. For in spite of the fact that the community has a dental clinic, which operates two full days a week, the service has been inadequate for all those in need of this form of dental service. Moreover, it was felt that nutrition work which was done in the interest of dental health among school children would have a carry-over value in the form of improved general health and would affect not only the school group but other members of the community, including the preschool and adult groups.

Community

With this specific end in mind, the following program has been developed and is being carried on in a semi-urban community of about eleven thousand population, consisting mostly of native-born Americans, with a small foreign element of French-Canadians. The community is largely residential, the only industries being two small rubber

---
*Retardation of Dental Caries in Out-Patients of a Dental Infirmary—Percy R. Howe, D.D.S. Ruth L. White, B.S. Milton Rabine, D.D.S. American Journal of Diseases of Children—November 1933, Vol. 46, Part 1, pp. 1045-1049.

shops, a necktie factory, and a stove foundry. The people, for the most part, belong to the average income group, with approximately seven per cent of the population receiving aid from either local or federal funds.

Preliminary Procedure

In working out the details of the program, it was found that the only item that involved additional expense was the dental examination. There was no school dentist, and the school committee had pledged its support to the program provided no expense was involved. The problem, then, became one of financing the dental survey. This problem was taken by the school nurse to a health committee, composed of representative lay women, which acts as an auxiliary agent to the school health program. Through the generosity of the visiting nurse association, members of which are also on the health committee, the fifty dollar appropriation, which the health committee makes annually to the visiting nurse association to help support the preschool clinic, was diverted to the dental nutrition program to pay for the dental examination. The dental nutrition program thus became a community project involving the school, the health committee, and the visiting nurse association.

The next step was to interest the local dentists and to secure their cooperation. This was done through a meeting of the dentists with the dental clinic committee and the visiting nurse at the office of the school nurse. Mrs. Eleanor McCarthy, former state dental hygienist, outlined the dental plan, and Dr. Mark Elliott of the Forsyth Dental Infirmary and Miss Dorothea Nicoll, Nutritionist with the Massachusetts Department of Public Health, described the results of previous experiments along this line. The aim to be accomplished and the methods and records to be used were explained. The dentists expressed their desire to cooperate and their willingness to keep uniform records so that the results could be easily evaluated.

Organization

The dentists from the local dental clinic were employed to examine the teeth of the pupils from grade one through twelve. The teeth were checked, not from the point of view of selecting those children in need of dental care, but from the standpoint of selecting those with mouth conditions, cavities, and past decay indicative of a nutritional deficiency. The examination was made rather hurriedly as the pupils filed past the dentist. In most cases a tongue depressor was all that was necessary but in some cases, especially in identifying decalcification areas, an explorer and mirror were used. A portable sterilizer, therefore, was a necessary part of the equipment for the examination. The dentists were assisted by the school nurse, who arranged the time and place of the examination and recorded the findings of the dentists.

A total of 987 cases were discovered in the dental survey. Because of the inability to handle such a large group, it was finally decided to select 335, including 83 cases with gingival fillings, 208 with decalcification areas, and 44 with many fillings, for intensive follow-up. Because of lack of time the number was reduced to 104 children, representing as many kinds of problems as possible. Following the selection of cases, notices were sent to the parents of these cases, asking them to come to the school to talk over the dentists' findings. As the parents were interviewed by the school nurse, the children were referred to their respective dentists for verification of the examining dentists' findings and for dental care if necessary. In order that each dentist might know which cases were coming in as a result of the survey a list of his patients was sent to him following the interviews with the parents. The private dentist, in turn, made out a chart for each child coming to him.

Nutrition Service

The nutritionist started by contacting each dentist to talk over the mouth condition of the children who had come in for examination. A total of 35 children took the initiative of going to their own dentists. With a lengthy list due to be cared for at the clinic, she took as many of these as time would allow, selecting those whose records showed the greatest need nutritionally. This group numbered 69. The total number of children reached was 104—51 boys and 53 girls from all grades in school. They represented 83 families.

All these children had extensive caries—39 also had inflamed or puffy gum tissue, and 55 had fair or poor occlusion. Each child's dental condition was recorded on the nutrition blank for reference during the home visit.

Before starting home visits the nutritionist discussed the family with the school nurse in order to have an idea of the size of the family, the financial condition, and expected cooperation. This paved the way for a much more individualized home visit than is otherwise possible where only one visit can be made. A blank for recording all the food eaten at meals and between meals for three days was given to each child. Then the nutritionist, using a special record on which to fill in the amount of different kinds of food, the sleep, appetite, food habits, and special problems of the child, made the home visits. Sometimes these were filled out with the mother, and sometimes outside of the home. The nutritionist took considerable time with each mother, talking about the child's teeth and explaining how teeth grow and how food affects them, using diagrams and photographs.

Of course many other problems came up for discussion—how to get a fussy child to eat, more rest for the overexcitable one, less candy for many of them, and how to feed ten children as adequately as possible on twelve dollars a week. Besides the two leaflets on teeth, "Eating for Teeth" and "The Care of Your Teeth," the nutritionist gave pamphlets on child feeding and recipes to the mother, always underlining the particular points needing to be emphasized.

A survey of the records at the end of the visits showed the following facts:

> Two-thirds of the families were in fair or poor economic situation which, of course, influenced the diet greatly.

Most of the children had their meals regularly, but only two-thirds had really good appetites.

Only one-half had good eating habits, and over one-third had too little sleep and rest—two factors that have a close relationship.

As to the food:

One-third had less than one pint of milk a day, and one-half had too few eggs.

Only one-half had vegetables other than potato every day and raw vegetables, particularly, were lacking.

Over one-third had fruit daily—many of them using the raw fruits, but the majority had them only occasionally.

There was no lack in meat, and the amount of dark breads and cereals was surprisingly high.

Where sweets were concerned—at least half of the children had too many.

Only a few were taking cod liver oil, that great help in tooth-building.

Thus, with a diet lacking in milk and fruits and vegetables—yet too high in sweets—it is easy to see why so many children were having difficulty with their teeth.

The nutritionist also met with a group of expectant mothers at the visiting nurse's office, and had individual conferences at the school with the mothers who brought their entering-school children for registration.

Conclusion

At the present time the cases which have been under nutrition supervision are being re-checked by their respective dentists.

As soon as this work is completed, another meeting of the dentists, the nutritionist, and lay people will be called by the nurse to review the work that has already been done and to formulate plans for the future. Mouth charts again will be collected and analyzed by the nutritionist, and home visits will be made on all cases with the hope that considerable improvement has been made since the recommendations of last year.

After the results of this year's work the group will know better how to plan for the continuation and growth of this corrective and preventive service by the dentists and the nutritionist in the community, so that these children may be benefited as are those who have the opportunity of working with the nutritionist at the Forsyth Dental Infirmary.

GROUP CONFERENCES WITH EXPECTANT MOTHERS

BY CHARLOTTE RAYMOND, B.A.

Community Nutritionist, Newton, Mass.

The Community Nutritionist has a great opportunity to help in the educational crusade for protection of mothers. Individually and in groups she can teach not only parents but the community at large the importance of competent medical supervision for expectant mothers and the relation of proper diet and other factors to the health of mother and child.

Group work with expectant mothers has certain definite advantages for both worker and mothers. To the busy nutritionist attempting to meet community needs, time and distances are important factors. More individuals can be reached in groups in a given time than any other way. More equipment for demonstration can be gathered in a central location—equipment which couldn't be taken easily from house to house. As visualization is an important part of teaching, demonstration materials add greatly to the value of group work. A fact often overlooked or minimized is the social value of such gatherings. Many women, owing to financial stress have almost no recreation, no chance for social contacts outside of neighborly visiting. Mothers' Clubs offer not only opportunities to learn, but also recreation which is so needed. Psychologically many people respond better in groups and points can be discussed impartially without personal implication—points which an individual alone might resent. Interest is often so stimulated in groups that individuals seek further help, and then more work can be done on the basis of the individual needs. Nor can one overlook the value and importance of the practical experiences and contributions which mothers themselves make—thus increasing their own sense of adequacy and helping each other.

The importance of proper food in the prenatal and nursing period cannot be overestimated from the standpoint of both mother and child. All too often, in order to supply the demands of a rapidly developing new life, the mother's body must yield its own materials—materials which could have been supplied in a dietary carefully planned to include everything necessary to build the child and protect the mother. As evidence of this needless sacrifice one has only to consider the teeth of a large majority of mothers. The old saying "a tooth for every child" is not without basis, but in the light of modern scientific knowledge it is a disgrace that this waste of a mother's own body and health should go on. A well planned diet supplying adequate essentials for the development of the child and the protection of the mother will go a long way towards eliminating this waste. As nutrition is a composite of food eaten, with its digestion, assimilation and utilization there are sometimes instances where despite an adequate dietary intake faulty body mechanics may cause malnutrition. One then sees the same process of sacrifice of the mother's bones, teeth, tissues and blood to meet the increasing demands of the child which is growing so fast. If a mother's health is so undermined, even when one is sure she is taking an adequate diet, then further investigation should be made to determine why the food is not being utilized. Fortunately the average woman, who eats a simple, easily digested, adequate diet, gets plenty of sleep, rest, fresh air, exercise and recreation, as suggested by her doctor, can come through the prenatal and nursing periods without undue drain upon her physical resources.

How, then, is one to teach the vital importance of proper diet, the needs of the bodies of mother and child, the selection and preparation of food to meet these needs, the related factors as rest, sleep and routine, which aid in the establishment of good nutrition as a whole? The community with its organizations and resources will largely determine how this education is to be carried out, but no possibility should be overlooked. Groups of expectant mothers may be reached through such organizations as hospital prenatal clinics, Visiting Nurse Associations and health departments and units, but only those women under medical supervision should be allowed to attend. A nutritionist cannot take the responsibility for patients who are not under a doctor's care. Such patients, coming to group conferences should be told why prenatal care is so important and then urged to go to a doctor, or clinic, at once, with the understanding that unless this is done they cannot come to future meetings.

This education, as well as education in the responsibility of the community to see that each mother has an opportunity for proper prenatal, delivery and postnatal care, can be carried out by a nutritionist through such groups as women's clubs, churches, parent-teacher associations, through newspapers, radio, exhibits and any other available resources.

The creation and development of a new life is a story which can be classed with the wonder of miracles. In this age of rampant mechanization one is so often overawed and thrilled by the creation of buildings, or machines, or ships, that the human body is taken as a matter of course. And yet no device of man's ingenuity can begin to compare in complexity, efficiency and beauty to the human body. It is likewise true that people pay far more attention to the development and care of property than to planning for the building and preservation of far greater treasures—life and health.

The teaching of health habits and proper food can be prosaic and uninteresting, or it can be made dynamic and inspiring, especially to expectant mothers whose bodies are creating the miracle of life. As the fascinating story of the development and functioning of the individual is unfolded in simple, but skillful ways, and the relation of food, rest, exercise, posture (among other things) to these processes becomes clear, mothers are increasingly interested, not only in thinking of these things, but also in planning how they may best be accomplished. An x-ray of a baby about to be born, or of just the baby's jaw, showing the first teeth completely finished before birth, is a far more telling argument for proper food than hours of lecture. From a simple understanding of one's body, and the role which food plays in its building and maintenance throughout life, comes readiness for the next step—the knowledge of selection of food best suited to the body's needs. Gradually the mother can realize the limitless possibilities of her position in life, her responsibility to herself, her children and society, the opportunity for the use of all her powers of intelligence and imagination. She realizes that to be a good wife and mother is a job requiring the best in her—a job second to none in importance and in its stimulating interest. Once she can feel important—a vital part of life and society—the drudgery and routine do not always seem out of all proportion to the results. Willingly she learns how to care for herself, her children, her family; how to plan to make her money go the farthest in health protection; how to be an intelligent, understanding parent in the training of children; how to accept and be glad of her responsibility. It is within the power of the nutritionist to kindle and foster this conception of motherhood, as she teaches the overwhelming importance of food in the prenatal and nursing periods, desirable dietary habits, and food selection in terms of financial, racial and environmental factors.

A NUTRITION PROGRAM IN A PUBLIC WELFARE ORGANIZATION

BY SUE E. SADOW, B.S.

Supervisor of Nutrition Service, Family Service Division
City of New York Emergency Relief Bureau

Since such a large proportion of our population is on relief of varying degrees of inadequacy, the first problem that must be faced is the possible jeopardizing of the good health of these families. This places upon the community the responsibility for finding some method of preventing the breakdown of the physical well-being of such a large group. What can the nutritionist, especially equipped with the knowledge and practice of nutrition, contribute towards safeguarding the health of so many individuals?

The forward looking Federal Emergency Relief Administration recognized as early as 1933 the necessity for the participation of the trained nutritionist in the relief program and requested State Administrations concerned with relief to seek the services of fully qualified nutrition specialists to assist with family budget, food, and nutrition problems. This can be interpreted as a recognition by the Federal Government of the need for applying to a national situation, knowledge in nutrition, gained from recent researches. They realized the danger of the breakdown of health due not only to insufficient funds with which to purchase adequate nourishment, but also to the lack of knowledge on the part of the general public regarding the best expenditure of funds available. This called for a program which would utilize and adapt all the nutrition information available to preserve good health, and to restore what had been lost.

In New York City the Nutrition Program was initiated less than two years ago. To be sure, one nutritionist was included on the staff when the Emergency Relief Bureau was first organized in December 1931. At this time her duties were limited to the formulation of the allowance schedule used in figuring family budgets and to the supervision of food stores authorized to redeem food vouchers presented by relief clients.

The program as it has been developed to the present time calls for a nutritionist in each District Office with the supervisory staff at Central Office. Each nutritionist is a trained Home Economist.

Duties of Nutritionist

As a member of the staff in the District Office, the nutritionist assumes full responsibility for the teaching of budgeting and is consulted on all cases where adaptation of the allowance schedule seems necessary for case work reasons. In the nutritionist is invested all information regarding policies of budgeting and changing of allowance schedules due to variation in living costs. She must be constantly aware of current living costs and checks these against the budgetary allowances to determine their adequacy. She participates in the periodic collection of prices in her district of food and other commodities allowed in the budget. When general re-budgeting of all cases is necessary, from time to time, it is the nutritionist who gives the instructions and interpretations. This supervision is most essential, because it is one method of insuring uniformity in interpretation of the allowance schedule and is one of the best means of controlling relief funds.

With relief allowances just sufficient to cover the barest essentials of food, rent, fuel and light, and cleaning supplies—with the knowledge that by the time families apply for relief they have exhausted all resources and many are in a depleted condition physically, the administration agreed that cod liver oil was a necessary supplement to the low cost dietary and should be provided for all children under three years of age and for other individuals for whom it was considered necessary. The nutritionist has the full responsibility for authorizing cod liver oil allowances. There are approximately 47,500 individuals for whom this valuable food is provided.

Teaching of Staff

Although control of family budgeting, computation of special diets and authorization of cod liver oil play an important role in the program, the nutritionist functions most effectively as a teacher to staff members in consultation on individual cases and in participation in the regular training program established in each district office. In consultation she is able to impart to the investigator such nutrition information as applies directly to the case in question. Teaching by this method of individual treatment has the most far reaching influences and makes possible widespread dissemination of knowledge among families who otherwise might not have the opportunity to obtain this kind of assistance. At these conferences the investigator frequently acquires for the first time factual information which stimulates his interest, he becomes "nutrition conscious" and learns how to apply this newly acquired knowledge to other similar situations. He becomes enthusiastic about the constructive help he is able to give families by bringing them specific instruction either in the market list showing the variety and quantities of food the family can buy for the relief allowance, recipes of dishes based upon racial food tastes, suggestions for correcting wrong diet practices, dietaries for different age groups, nutrition of children, food value or special diet needs in relation to the total food budget. This awakened interest and belief in what the nutritionist has to offer and the positive results achieved in many instances in a short period of time, motivates the investigator to such an extent that he refers more of his cases and in innumerable instances seeks help with his personal food and budget problems. In addition to the individual conferences, nutrition talks form a part of the general education program of the District Office.

Meeting with small groups of staff members at regular intervals, the nutritionist discusses with them recent developments in the field of nutrition and their application to the low cost dietary. Much has already been accomplished in overcoming personal prejudices as the groups acquire more and more scientific information, by means of these talks and exhibits which are frequently set up to supplement the information and guide the staff further. It is not only interesting, but gratifying to observe the change of attitude on the part of staff, as they themselves observe changes which have taken place in family dietaries, as a result of their efforts. The need for educating our staff impresses itself upon us by the many questions asked, revealing their own lack of knowledge and prejudices.

Much has been accomplished in individual cases and investigators report back enthusiastically such incidents as seeing the market list, which was prepared for the family, tacked up on the kitchen wall and used as a guide for purchasing from week to week; of family's statement of more variety because the housewife sees things listed which she never thought about before.

Records contain reports by investigators of the nutrition information they have given clients. Frequently without the nutritionist suggesting it, they ask families who are not managing well to keep records weekly of expenditures and bring these to the nutritionist for analysis and suggestions.

Community Resources

Acquaintances and contact with all community resources for the purpose of obtaining their cooperation and making it possible to function most effectively for the welfare of clients, is the responsibility of each district nutritionist. As contacts have been built up and community relationships established, there has been increasing recognition of the value of the services which these specialists offer, and they are constantly being called upon to participate in community activities centering around the health of the constituency.

Most important is the relationship that has been established with hospitals.

Special Diets and Hospitals

The number of patients attending clinics has steadily increased until it has reached proportions almost beyond the capacity of hospitals to meet the demands made upon them. Since many of these patients are also recipients of relief, it is necessary for hospitals and the Home Relief Bureau to work together on a cooperative basis. Thousands of patients have been found to be suffering from nutritional diseases and in need of special diets. These cases are referred to the nutritionist in the District Offices. She studies the diagnosis and recommendations made by the clinic. She reads the family case record for the purpose of acquainting herself with the whole family situation, the length of time on relief, the family's ability to manage on the allowance, the health history of all members of the family and the racial food habits. From this analysis, the nutritionist is better equipped to plan the special diet, figure the cost, make recommendations for the best expenditure of the food money and best management of the income. Frequently it is necessary for her to interpret to the patient, the diet recommendations made by the doctor in the clinic.

Twenty-three thousand special diets are being provided for clients under care of the Emergency Relief Bureau with an extra cost above the normal food allowance of $78,000 per month or nearly one million dollars per year. The need for supervision of such huge expenditures is recognized and the nutritionist takes her place as an important member on the staff. She is responsible not only for making provisions for the diet, for exercising control over the continuance or discontinuance of a special diet allowance and to this end keeps the case work staff informed as to when a report on the condition of the patient is due. Medical follow-up reports are due every three months. Dependent upon the new recommendations, the diet is continued or discontinued. This also grants an opportunity to determine improvement in health conditions as a result of increased allowance and education. Thus through the cooperative efforts of doctor, dietitian, medical social worker and nutritionist, a plan has been developed in the best interest of the patient and is one which can be recommended to other communities.

Further Community Cooperation

Cooperation between nutritionist and the community has extended beyond the hospital and includes schools, parent-teacher associations, health centers, baby welfare stations, churches, visiting nurses associations, settlements, etc. Individual programs have been developed by each nutritionist to suit the needs of the locality in which she works and these vary in accordance with the community resources available in the district. In those localities where there is a dearth of resources of any kind the nutritionist develops food and nutrition classes and teaches the preparation of various dishes possible on the relief allowance. Food values, costs and budgeting are discussed and general nutrition information given. The depots from which Surplus Foods provided by the Federal Government are issued, have also been utilized in some districts as teaching centres.

Distribution of Nutrition Information

The Educational Assistant on the staff of the Nutrition Service, plans, formulates and writes much of the educational material prepared especially for use of clients on Home Relief. District nutritionists, organized into special committees and utilizing their experiences in district offices with staff and clients, have written some of the leaflets and prepared exhibits used as aids to nutritionists for teaching purposes. Thousands of these leaflets have been distributed among clients by our visitors. In reception rooms of each of our District Offices this educational material is displayed and quantities have been taken by applicants. Encouraging stories of its usefulness to clients are frequently brought to our attention and often the visitors are requested to bring additional copies on subsequent visits to the home. The visitors have appreciated being given something which—as they have expressed it—they can take and hand to a client, knowing that it contains concrete and helpful information relating to specific problems.

Conclusion

The duties of a nutritionist in a public agency and the variety of her functions have been set before you. The need for putting into practice to a much greater extent existing knowledge in nutrition and for more widespread nutrition education has been stressed.

One cannot leave a discussion of this nature without emphasizing the importance of adequacy of relief allowances. If we are to accept the general belief, that for years to come a large number of these families will remain on relief, or at best will be compelled to live on greatly reduced incomes, then we must be foresighted enough to measure the effects upon health of long years of inadequate funds with which to purchase essentials. Is it not the duty of communities to face squarely the fact that millions of unemployed individuals throughout the country will not be re-employed in private industry? If this is so, then what results can we anticipate in terms of physical and mental health if the amount of relief given continues to be just enough for bare existence? Families are entitled at least to a minimum standard of living which will maintain standards of health and decency. Nutritionists in relief agencies must create a consciousness of this need, and work toward the establishment of a minimum adequate relief standard which will make it possible for families to maintain themselves healthfully and respectably. Inadequate allowances make it even more necessary for us to exert all efforts in the direction of intensive guidance in food selection and more extensive education in nutrition.

Administrations, relief workers, and all socially minded groups are constantly raising the question of the results of such a nutrition program. The most that can be said of any preventive program is that in years to come the results will be measured in the general state of health of our people. At this time it is only possible to point out that hundreds of thousands of individuals have been enlightened in a subject with which they have not been conversant before. This number have now been exposed to nutrition information either through lectures, classes, direct contact with nutritionists in the discussion and planning of family budget and diet problems, or by a study of nutrition leaflets carried into the homes by our visitors, or through special diets. Changes in dietary habits are constantly reported. Two weeks after the establishment of a food and nutrition class in a Puerto Rican neighborhood it was noticed that the local grocer, catering only to Puerto Rican trade had taken in a supply of whole-grain breads. The customers began to demand it. Already we have corrected food prejudices among our staffs and many of our clients. We have contributed toward eradicating fads, made our people more substantially health conscious and aware of the science of nutrition. Through our educational literature and teaching, we have made it possible for the low income and relief group to get more and better nourishment for their money.

Scientific literature as well as other publications contain a sufficient number of reports on human dietary studies convincing enough of the importance of correct feeding. With the results of these studies as evidence, it is indicated that all our energies need to be directed toward the establishment of adequate relief standards, so that sufficient nourishment can be purchased, and toward the development of a broad educational program which will result in improved health of our communities, more varied and therefore more interesting diets, and eventually decreased cost of medical care and above all happier family relationships.

A BUDGET CASE
BY FLORENCE GENEVIEVE DORWARD, B.S.
Nutritionist, Visiting Nurse Association
Springfield, Massachusetts

"I don't see how I can manage. I have just about enough to get the food and pay the rent now, and John came home last night and said he was in for another 10 per cent cut. We owe for all our coal, and I promised to pay two dollars a week but I haven't a cent and they will not let me have any more. I owe the milk man and my sister-in-law let me borrow twenty-five dollars from her to pay on the back rent."

This sad tale was sobbed out to the Visiting Nurse when she went to see Raymond, who had a severe cold. Miss Jack was very understanding and suggested that they talk over the whole situation to see if some order could not be brought out of the chaos. They discussed the whole economic situation in detail and with paper and pen in hand obtained the following information.

Mr. Black regularly earned $24.50 but it was hard to make it stretch for the needs of a family of five.

Edwin was nine, Louise six, and Raymond two and a half years old.

They were paying $20 a month for a four-room tenement, and insurance cost $1.50 weekly made up from several small industrial policies on each member of the family.

The electric light bill averaged $1.40 a month, and although they burned coal, they had to drop 25¢ in the quarter meter each week for gas.

Fuel had been put in by the ton at the beginning of the summer but they owed for that.

Carfare was $1.00 a week.

These expenses were met as they came due, but no plan was made ahead to meet them. Mrs. Black had no knowledge of what she spent for food. The week the rent was due, food was scarce; during other weeks the food was more plentiful. Clothes and household supplies were bought when possible. Her sister-in-law gave help in furnishing the children with clothing from time to time. The sad part was that the husband's wages had never been enough. Mrs. Black gave Miss Jack the following list of bills.

The Morris Plan. They promised $3 weekly on a bill amounting to $116.

Dr. Brown had been promised $1 weekly on his bill of $23.

There was still $25 to pay on the furniture.

Coal had cost to date $45 on which nothing had been paid.

Besides the $25 borrowed from the sister-in-law for back rent, they also owed the landlord $60.

A milk bill of $11.85 was also charged against them.

"Now, don't you worry," soothed Miss Jack, "the very first thing to do Mrs. Black, is to determine right now to turn a new leaf. Play a game, challenge yourself that you will meet certain expenses that will not exceed $24.50. How many things do you have? Let us count: rent, electricity, gas, coal, food, household supplies, carfare, insurance, clothing, and personal expenses, and let us not forget health. Besides, I suppose we had better add "Bills." That makes twelve places for $24.50. Of course there are others that it could go for, but if you can be a good sport, and enter into the spirit of this game, you will find that for a few weeks we can account for only the bare necessities.

"Now, what I will do is to discuss it with our nutritionist, who knows much more about budgeting than I do, and see what she would suggest. And, what you should do, is to keep a list of all your accounts this week, beginning today, and I will come to see you next week. Do not be discouraged. Just make up your mind to see this through."

A week later Miss Jack returned, and found that Mrs. Black had caught the spirit, and was getting some enjoyment out of what was to be a long and tedious task. She had kept the accounts, and oh, how revealing!

"Why, do you know, Miss Jack, I would not have believed it, if any one had told me how many little ways money can slip away foolishly."

"Yes," said Miss Jack, "that is why it is necessary to keep accounts, for it makes us plan a bit more carefully. I had a long conference with our nutritionist and we went over all the points of your income and your expenses. She finally suggested this plan.

"You will probably find that a plan will have to be made new each week until the emergency expenses are met. She also suggested, after talking with one of the Family Welfare workers, that if you are willing to talk this whole situation over with them there is a bare possibility of lumping all your bills and taking them to the Credit Bureau with the exception of the Morris Plan. The Credit Bureau is maintained by the Chamber of Commerce but by special arrangements they have cooperated with the Family Welfare Organization, and, if given a list of the bills, they will write to your creditors, and make the payments directly to them for you. They do not pay your bills, but it makes it easier for you, in that you pay them a definite sum each week. Before making that decision, you should talk it over with your husband. You will find that this budget idea will work much better if you get everybody in on it. Even the children would like to help. Tell them what you are doing. You might even make some sort of a bargain with them, so that they would have three or four cents each week, instead of pleading for a penny every now and then.

"A plan is the key to the whole problem. I have brought along envelopes so that we can divide up the money as we plan it. I find this about as helpful as any way, for, unless you put your money aside, it has a way of getting spent without your realizing it. It may be that you have a better plan, if so, try it.

"First, plan to whom the money will go when it does come.

"Second, plan for where it will be put when it comes, that is, in envelopes or boxes.

"Third, plan for paying or spending each item.

"When I went to our nutritionist she helped me work out the following plan. I want you to look it over and see what you think about it, and what changes you would make."

Food	$8.50	Husband	.75
House	.50	Insurance	1.50
Rent	5.00	Health	.50
Fuel	2.25	Incidentals	1.00
Electricity	.35	Bills	3.00
Carfare	1.00		
		Total	$24.35

"Perhaps some of these items need a bit of explaining. The item marked "House" has reference to the soap and cleaning powders, etc., which one has to buy almost every week. You might add that item to food, and call it $9.00 for groceries. Every three months we have an extra week, and at that time you would pay the extra $5 for rent to the landlord.

"We have put down $2.25 for fuel; the 25c is for gas. If by chance you do not use the full $2 each week for coal, you might drop it into the envelope marked "Bills." I am sure that once you have learned to set aside each week's expenses, you will find it very helpful. Your husband receives $1.75 and pays for his own carfare, newspaper and cigarettes. You will notice that the item marked "Health" is only 50c. This will take care of a few simple household remedies. Such things as doctor and dentist charges we will arrange for when necessary, perhaps through clinics, if Dr. Brown is willing. There will also be such incidentals as church, recreation, and pennies for the children, etc.

"Now we know, Mrs. Black, that this budget plan is not complete, for we have not arranged for clothing. But you told me before that your sister-in-law was very good about helping out with that item, and I thought, perhaps you might feel like letting her in on this plan of ours. She might become so interested that she would be glad to help you make good on it."

"Oh, I am sure she would," said Mrs. Black. "You don't know how much I appreciate this help, Miss Jack, and I think your outline or plan is very good, but I do have one or two suggestions. I think I can get along on less than $9 for groceries. And then, too, if I don't spend the 50c for health couldn't we put that into the envelope marked "Bills?" You see I am really anxious to get these accounts paid as soon as possible. You have suggested only $3 for bills and I have promised the Morris Plan that much."

"Mrs. Black, what item in that budget provides the most for the strength and health of your family? Don't you think it is food? I can't stay now to tell you just how important I think it is, but on my next visit we will talk more about it. But just let me warn you now that if you cut too low on the food account you will not be providing the necessary foods for health. I do not think you should take that health money either, to swell the amount for bills. I have just one more suggestion before leaving, and that is, have your husband go to the Morris Plan with our plan and talk it over with the manager, and see if he would be willing to make some adjustment so that you could pay $2 instead of the $3 arrangement. Suppose you keep accounts again this week and next time we will talk more about foods."

A week later Miss Jack called and brought with her a grocery order which she and the nutritionist had worked out together in conference. "Our nutritionist explained that the grocery order is the real backbone of the health situation in your home," said Miss Jack. "You see health is very important and food is one of the chief things that keep us healthy. We need certain foods that build bone and teeth, certain other foods that give us life and energy and keep us warm, and, of course, you want the family to have the foods that help us to resist disease and make us grow. So, you see, planning meals is quite a job. Our nutritionist says she can tell a great deal about the health of a family by their grocery order and I guess she is right."

"Oh, yes you can," said Miss Jack. "I will help you and if we find some things that we don't know, we will ask the nutritionist who is always glad to help. I would suggest that you try to follow this order, which she has planned and see how you come out. She has some recipes for inexpensive meat dishes which I will bring on my next visit. I would also suggest that you plan to do most of your shopping only twice this week and that you do it yourself, making out your list and getting the prices from different stores first. Children do not understand how to buy groceries and grocers may send things that you would not have selected had you done the shopping yourself."

It took some time, of course, to accomplish the budget so that it was running smoothly, but Mrs. Black was in earnest and proved to be a very cooperative homemaker and mother. After discussing the situation with her husband, they decided to go to the Family Welfare and inquire about the Credit Bureau. The worker in that organization helped them to move to a small cottage where the rent though no more gave the family more rooms in the house and a yard in which the children could play. That Agency also made contact with the credit bureau and backed up the nurse in her efforts to straighten the finances. Having established very pleasant contacts, and being very much interested in the financial progress, the Family Welfare worker made several friendly visits and bolstered up the sometimes waning spirits of the Blacks.

The nutritionist also made one or two visits with Miss Jack and suggested economic cuts in food, without diminishing the food value. Evaporated milk was found to be a great saving. It was used for soups, puddings, etc. Cereals were bought in bulk at a grain store. Mrs. Black learned to use the tops of green vegetables in soups, or for greens, etc.

It took quite an effort to get the menus planned ahead of time and then make the grocery order meet the needs. The one thing which pleased Miss Jack as much as anything was the success Mrs. Black had made of having the whole family take part. Even Mr. Black had become quite interested in the family finances. He now paid the house bills himself such as rent, electricity, gas, etc. and once a week both Mr. and Mrs. Black went over the accounts together and found it was rather fun to play this game of "finance." Even the children caught the spirit and saved the pennies given them "to help mama."

ONE SCHOOL'S NUTRITION PROBLEM
BY CATHERINE LEAMY, M.S.
Nutritionist, Massachusetts Department of Public Health

The town of X has a high school enrollment of about four hundred students. Two hundred and twenty of these students come from rural areas at such distances that it is necessary for them to come by bus for eight-thirty classes, remain at school for the lunch hour from eleven-fifty to one o'clock and leave again by bus at three-fifteen. This situation makes the necessity of a substantial noon lunch for each student obvious.

The high school has recognized the need of a school lunch for many years. At first a cafeteria was provided which was given on a concession basis to an elderly woman, untrained, but considered a good cook. This woman believed in feeding the children what they wanted in the form of jelly doughnuts and hot dogs, giving the cafeteria a rather unsatisfactory reputation. When she died, another experienced cook took over the management, still on a concession basis. Under her guidance the cafeteria continued its previous policy unsuccessfully. It was then decided that the home economics teacher should cooperate with the manager, help plan the meals, and assist in buying. This system proved unsatisfactory, for the manager resented a young teacher's suggestions and guidance. Finally the cafeteria was again given to the manager unconditionally, but in the meantime it had become more and more difficult to make both ends meet. Finally the school committee had to guarantee the manager a small amount of money for each day, and eventually had to pay that amount regularly. When the school committee's appropriation was cut, the school lunch, which was at that time patronized very little, seemed a good point at which to economize, and it was definitely discontinued in June 1935.

In November, with the cooperation of the superintendent of schools, a survey was made of school lunch conditions. The superintendent, nutritionist, and school nurse made out a lunch questionnaire—a copy of which was given to each pupil. Through these questionnaires it was possible to discover what each student had for lunch since every student filled out a blank and passed it back unsigned. It was found that more coffee and tonic were consumed than milk, hot lunches were practically non-existent, and desserts were consumed in abundance, as the chart below clearly portrays.

Survey Figures

Milk	5%	Fruit	77%
Coffee	5%	Vegetable	10%
Tonic	10%	Pie	24%
Hot dish	4%	Cake	83%
White bread	88%	Ice cream	29%
Dark bread	12%	Candy	30%

The conditions under which these lunches are eaten are most unfortunate. Some of the girls eat their lunches in five classrooms, with teachers in charge, while the boys, under the supervision of a male instructor, eat either in the old lunchroom now used as a classroom, or on the street corner. Each noon several young people can be found in the drug stores, in Freddie's, a bar and restaurant combined, in Woolworth's buying candy, or just hanging around. If the students who eat their lunch at school do not want to study all during the noon hour, they must leave the building by twelve-thirty, another reason why so many students are found on the streets every noon.

It was thought that the conversion of the auditorium into a recreation hall might alleviate the difficult situation somewhat. However, cramped conditions made it necessary to use the auditorium for a classroom, and the fact that the seats were nailed down further hindered the usefulness of the room.

Since making the survey, every effort has been made to re-establish the school lunch. The results of the survey were discussed by the nutritionist with all the prominent women's organizations. She talked with the high school lunch students; the problem has been discussed with the school committee. The results of the survey have been published in the local paper. The survey showed clearly the need for a

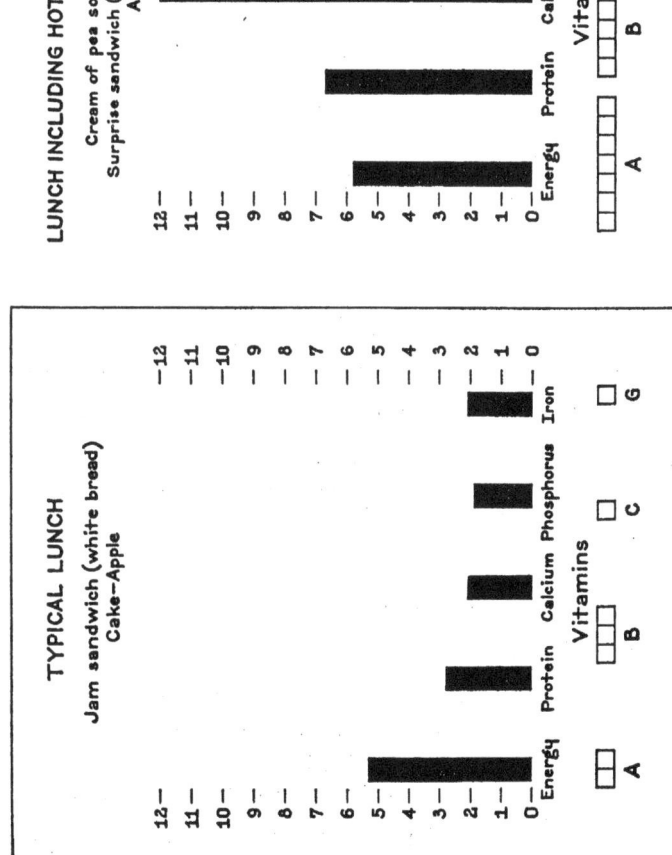

TYPICAL LUNCH

Jam sandwich (white bread)
Cake—Apple

LUNCH INCLUDING HOT DISH AND VEGETABLE

Cream of pea soup (made with milk)
Surprise sandwich (carrot and dark bread)
Apple

school lunch. Since a new appropriation has been made through the town meeting to the schools, it is hoped that the lunch can again be resumed.

If the typical lunch as shown by the survey figures was changed by simply introducing a hot dish and changing a jam sandwich into a vegetable sandwich, the startling difference in food value portrayed below would be overcome. Such a change in the average lunch could be brought about through the installation of a very simple cafeteria service.

Without question it will be necessary not only to stimulate the interest of parents but also that of teachers and students if a new cafeteria is to succeed in 1936. Changes may have to be made to arrange lunch periods which will accommodate all the lunch students in the small cafeteria. Care will have to be taken to serve well prepared, suitable, and attractive lunches so that the number of patrons will steadily increase instead of decrease as in the past. The lunchroom to succeed will have to become a school cafeteria rather than one in which only the manager is interested.

PUBLICITY FOR A COMMUNITY NUTRITION PROGRAM
By ALBERTINE P. MCKELLAR, B.S.
Public Health Education Worker
Massachusetts Department of Public Health

The necessary publicity at present, for the organization of a community nutrition program is that having to do with the nutritionist.

Publicity—to introduce her to many who have never head of "this pioneer who is more and more proving her worth in public health, through practical teaching of positive nutrition."

Publicity—to explain in minute detail her enumerable valuable services.

Publicity—to convincingly prove that a nutritionist is essential to the community intending to provide modern methods and employ members of up-to-date professions to meet its responsibility for the general health and welfare of its citizens.

Introduce the Nutritionist

The objectives, then, of this timely publicity are:
1. To attract attention to arouse community interest in the need for the nutritionist.
2. To explain meticulously her possible services
   and
3. To give convincingly justifiable proof of her value.

The Nutrition Advisory Committee has Publicity Responsibility

The nucleus of persons in a community, usually made up of representatives of the organization the nutritionist would serve forms the Advisory Committee to the Nutritionist. The very first duty of this committee, then, is this publicity project—the job of selling the nutritionist and her services to the community. A person with newspaper reporting experience is a valuable member of the Committee in addition to the representative of the schools, the medical, dental profession, the Department of Welfare and an influential lay member of the community who generally serves as chairman.

Publicity Agencies and Methods

1. *The Newspaper* is the most available and most important publicity agency. It would carry the main portion of the publicity project. There is value in having the newspaper articles appear in the same place in the paper each time. Oftentimes the editor will not only make that possible but will arrange for a special heading—such as are suggested below:

"Meet the Nutritionist"
>A series of articles describing her training and experiences, accomplishments in other communities.

"Why We Need a Nutritionist"
>A series of articles explaining various community conditions based upon information secured through surveys—school lunch —eating habits, growth of school children—welfare food budget, border line cases needing assistance, etc.

"How a Nutritionist Would Help"
>This series signed by well known community leaders from—
>>The Board of Health
>>>Nutrition conferences with mothers at prenatal— baby—Well Child Conferences—Summer Round Up.
>>>Special diet case—tuberculosis, malnutrition, rickets, scurvy, dental defects, etc.
>>The Board of Welfare
>>>Food budgets—marketing prices and suggestions— meal planning.
>>>Budget consultation with special cases.
>>The School Department
>>>Assistance with planning of adequate lunches.
>>>Teaching, especially when there is not home economics teacher.
>>>Personal conference with children or their parents.
>>The Visiting Nurse Association
>>>Individual conference.
>>>Special cases.
>>>Staff education.

Any other organization in the community such as the Family Welfare Association, the Y. W. C. A., the youth organizations, list ways that the nutritionist would be of assistance.

A similar series might follow—
"A Nutritionist Would Help Me"
Written by a physician
>dentist
>nurse
>dental hygienist

teacher
welfare worker
lunchroom manager
lay community leader
mother
grocery man
restaurant manager

Editorial comment, has very special value and if possible to secure is most worthwhile.

2. *The Flyer*—a printed or mimeographed sheet explaining the nutritionist and her services is another valuable publicity agency—distribute:

Copy in newspaper.
House to house (Boy or Girl Scouts or 4-H Club assistance)
Send to President of each community organization requesting that it be read before a meeting.

3. *The Exhibit* is the simplest and most accurate method of education and reaches persons who would *not* read the paper or go to a lecture. It has an important place in any publicity plan.

A vacant store window in the center of the community offers a splendid opportunity to use this visual type of education.

Pictures or simple miniature figures showing the services of the nutritionist:

At the Well Child Conference
In the home
In the school
In the group.

Ribbons coming from the central exhibit or picture to various signs explaining the service in detail.

Example:
  Central exhibit:
    Either picture of nutritionist in home or room in miniature with nutritionist having conference with mother.
    Ribbons coming from the central interest—the picture or miniature setup and the following signs:
    Signs:
      "Help with good meal planning and preparation"
      "Help with family budgets"
      "Helps mother plan special diets recommended by physician"
      "Suggests ways to induce baby to eat"
      "Helps with preschoolers' food and nutrition habits"
      "Helps to adjust racial customs to good meal planning"

"The Nutritionist Helps to Stretch your Food Dollar"—including marketing and cooking suggestions—is another possible series of exhibits to arouse interest and appreciation of the community.

Conclusion

A well planned publicity program will play a large part in the acquisition of a community nutritionist. Helpful references for such a plan are:

Articles in this issue of The Commonhealth
"The Community Nutritionist" { Massachusetts Department of
"Suggestions for Publicity" { Public Health
"13 Stations Bring Good Luck to Boston"—J. P. Marquand
(Boston Transcript—February 8, 1936—5c)

THE NUTRITIONIST SAYS IT WITH EXHIBITS

BY DOROTHEA NICOLL, B.S., *Nutritionist*
Massachusetts Department of Public Health

There is no question of the value of visual education today. The nutritionist, primarily a teacher, can well profit by the experience of other educators and incorporate visual educational methods in all phases of her program.

Exhibits—whether simple or elaborate—offer one of the best means of making the message "stick." It is much easier to read a book that has pictures—to remember facts that have been demonstrated. Recipes are certainly more tempting when the actual food is there "in person." It is fine to know that molasses is an excellent source of iron, but there is nothing like a whiff of freshly-baked gingerbread to make folks want to eat molasses. So with exhibits—the nutritionist adds glamour to common sense and makes teaching material much more interesting and inviting.

Where would a nutritionist use exhibits? First—right in her office. Gay covers on her nutrition books, flowers, a poster—non-technical material just invites the mother who is waiting to peek inside. Stolid, scientific-appearing tomes may be necessary for reference, but for the public—make nutrition facts inviting even to the passerby. With an extra table, or window ledge, or top of a bookcase—why not use a poster and articles to point out the pennies saved by buying canned tomatoes instead of fresh oranges, or making homemade oatmeal cookies instead of buy the "frosting sandwiches."

Next, there's the school. Why not collaborate with the lunchroom manager or the classroom teacher in making good school lunches popular? When speaking before a Parent-Teacher Association meeting, why not display a collection of different kinds of dark breads that might be used for lunches packed at home? Is there a special spot in the lunchroom dedicated to teaching the whys and wherefores of an "A" lunch? And what classroom teacher or school nurse does not welcome assistance in making food and health lessons a bit more fascinating? There is a first class opportunity to educate not only the youngsters but the teachers.

Classes of all kinds are the natural "stamping-ground" for the exhibitor. The weekly mothers' class—or the monthly study club—the Italian girls' supper club—the Campfire girls, striving for the homecraft badge—the Boy Scouts camp cookery crowd: how they welcome the person who uses graphic exhibits instead of just talking. Can they handle it? Smell it? Taste it? Look at the pictures? Perhaps even borrow it until next week? This is the easiest kind of exhibit to use because it is an integral part of a talk or discussion. It does not necessarily need to be self-explanatory. It will, like all other such material, be simple and pertinent to the topic of the day: No exhibits— just for the exhibit's sake—they are teaching tools!

Any exhibit that is placed for the casual passerby to glance at should be unusually well planned. It must attract attention, then hold it long enough to get the message over. But most important of all it must have such a clear, concise setup that, "he who runs may read" and still digest the truth of the matter.

Probably the most vital exhibit the nutritionist plans is the one which introduces her to the community and keeps people informed about what she is doing. Is there a spare window in an empty store or at the office where a weekly exhibit may be placed? It needs an advantageous spot and prompt, regular exchange of subjects to keep the attention of the community. If there is a local paper, why not try for space and have the exhibit and weekly article tie up together? Those window-shoppers who get down town will still have the information even though they do not read the paper.

What would go in such an exhibit? Perhaps a photograph or a silhouette—who the nutritionist is—and what she does. Show her discussing prices with the grocer, judging lunches with the fifth graders, in personal conference with a group of high school seniors, comparing recipes with Mrs. Jones, advising mothers at the well child conference, adjusting a diet with the doctor and public health nurse, planning a budget with a young couple, or speaking to the Lions' Club. A whole series of such case-study stories will do much to inform a community where to turn for help in nutrition. Not only the poster but actual articles can be used in such a display. Mrs. Jones' prize recipe for salmon chowder stands beside a red arrow pointing to the cans and prices noting the bargains in canned salmon and evaporated milk this week.

Then, too, there are the multitude of nutrition facts that Tom, Dick and Harry should know and use. Try interpreting some of the latest scientific findings into everyday language. Show the comparative value and cost of the vitamin A and D products. Who should take them and why? What about raw sugar—and other food fads? Give a sound basis for judging what Mr. Smith reads in the paper or Mrs. Jones hears on the radio. How can vegetables be prepared to save the most minerals and vitamins? What is the difference between a No. 2½ can and a No. 3. Is it really true that "cat" salmon is any good? What is the best buy in apples this week? Should a three-year old have cheese or baked beans?

Experiment with a "Did You Know That" series. Show charts of the improvement in food and health habits of some of the Junior High hygiene class. Or astonish the "natives" with the variety of dried beans, peas, and lentils that their foreign born neighbors enjoy, and don't forget to include some of their luscious recipes and the prices.

Are there a few hints on getting a fussy, finicky child to eat?

"But," I hear you say, "all this takes money and time." Certainly, but so does travel, and you don't get there if you don't use it. Probably the best substitute is ingenuity and imagination. That alone will carry you some distance. Interested groups can often be inveigled into giving donations, or local merchants to lend food or articles. At any rate it is well worth a struggle, for it accomplishes miracles in goodwill and confidence.

There is an old saying, "You can lead a horse to water, but you cannot make him drink." Only too true, in trying to teach health facts —but why not try feeding him salt beforehand? A few grains of salt —in the form of a lively exhibit—will make the job much easier.

Suggestions, leaflets, (and even fresh plaster cabbages) for exhibits are available at Massachusetts Department of Public Health, Room 522, State House, Boston. Mass.

MATERNAL DEATHS IN MASSACHUSETTS

Int. List No.		1931		1932		1933		1934	
	Total maternal deaths	408		369		389		317	
140									
141	Abortions (with and without septic conditions and including hemorrhages)	42	10%	30	8%	35	9%	28	9%
144	Puerperal hemorrhage	49	12%	57	15%	56	14%	45	14%
145	Puerperal septicemia								
148	(includes puerperal phlegmasia alba dolens, embolus, sudden death)	157	38%	140	38%	139	36%	131	41%
146	Toxemia								
147	(includes puerperal albuminuria and eclampsia)	93	23%	70	19%	67	17%	59	19%
142	Others	67	17%	72	20%	92	24%	54	17%
143									
149									
150									
	Maternal mortality rate per 1,000 live births		5.9		5.4		6.1		5.0
	Infant mortality rate per 1,000 live births		54.8		53.1		51.9		49.2

BOOK NOTES

LOBAR PNEUMONIA AND SERUM THERAPY by Frederick T. Lord, M.D. and and Roderick Heffron, M.D. $1.00. 91 pp. The Commonwealth Fund.

This book purports to be nothing more than a brief handbook regarding the serum treatment of lobar pneumonia. It is designed to present in a small space, and in simple and direct manner, the essentials of what the general practitioner must know to guide him in the intelligent use of concentrated pneumonia serum. In the achievement of their purpose the authors have been extremely successful. After an introductory statement of the fundamental problems involved, and a brief discussion of a few of the immunologic factors in pneumococcus infection, the authors devote the remainder of the small volume to the details of the use of serum. Due attention is given to typing, testing for sensitivity, administration of serum and treatment of serum reaction. The style is simple and direct, and the use of the book is facilitated by numerous tables, graphs, margin annotations and a complete index.

That much of the volume is based upon the results of the Department's pneumonia study over which the junior author had immediate supervision, precludes the Department from a critical review of this volume. The Department cannot, however, hide its justifiable pride at the thought that this volume was one of the outgrowths of this study. There has long been a need for a handbook of this sort. In adding this volume to its already distinguished series of publications the Commonwealth Fund, which so generously supported the Massachusetts pneumonia study, has made another signal contribution to the better health of the community.

THE FACTS ABOUT CERTIFIED MILK (As explained by the American Association of Medical Milk Commissions, 1265 Broadway, New York City). 14 pp., 1936.

This is a small and interesting booklet of fourteen pages, outlining in some detail the story of the origin and present status of certified milk. It also gives a summary of a few of the regulations, specifically those relating to the health of the animals and the health of the employees and to the laboratory control of the milk. There is also a description of the production of Vitamin D Certified Milk, which incidentally, was the first "Vitamin D" milk sold in Massachusetts.

The booklet states that in June, 1935, the Association voted to include permissive pasteurization of certified milk in the Méthods and Standards. This is a distinct advance, and persons who can afford to pay the price will be able to obtain milk which is produced under the best sanitary conditions from cattle which, as far as practicable, are known to be free from disease, handled by employees who, as far as possible, are known to be healthy, and then protected by pasteurization.

A little additional information relative to certified milk in Massachusetts may be of interest. It was ascertained some years ago that the Medical Milk Commissions were not actively supervising the production of this milk, and consequently legislation was adopted, giving the Department of Public Health the right to make regulations, and also requiring that the Department approve contracts between the producer and the Commission.

Since the Department of Public Health has had some control over these certified dairies, eight have gone out of business as far as the production of certified milk for Massachusetts is concerned. Two of these farms voluntarily ceased producing certified milk. The other six ceased producing such milk either because the Department refused to approve the certificates or because the Commissions in cooperation with the Department declined to renew the certificates because of repeated violation of the regulations.

There are at present six dairy farms furnishing certified milk for sale as such in Massachusetts. One farm located in Bennington, Vermont, furnishes a small amount of certified milk which is sold in Pittsfield, the bulk of the milk from this farm being sold as certified milk in Albany and Troy. Another farm located in Wilton, New Hampshire, furnishes part of its supply to the City of Boston. A third farm, located in Whately, furnishes this type of milk in the Connecticut Valley. A fourth farm, located in Spencer, furnishes this type of milk to Worcester and Springfield. Two other farms, located in Beverly and Needham, furnish the bulk of the certified milk sold in Greater Boston.

The Medical Milk Commissions of Massachusetts are now taking pains to see that the dairies operating under their supervision are operating as required. All but one of the dairies supplying Massachusetts with certified milk are equipped with pasteurizers, and approximately 60 per cent of the certified milk sold in Massachusetts is sold as Certified Milk Pasteurized.

REPORT OF DIVISION OF FOOD AND DRUGS

During the months of October, November and December 1935, samples were collected in 249 cities and towns.

There were 1,443 samples of milk examined, of which 117 were below standard, from 8 samples the cream had been in part removed, and 8 samples contained added water. There were 1,033 bacteriological examinations made of milk, 899 of which complied with the requirements. There were 9 bacteriological examinations made of cream, 7 of which complied with the requirements; 216 bacteriological examinations of ice cream, 183 of which complied with the requirements; 14 bacteriological examinations of sherbet, 9 of which complied with the requirements; 4 bacteriological examinations of well water, all of which did not comply with the requirements; 3 bacteriological examinations of empty bottles, all of which complied with the requirements; 2 bacteriological examinations of feathers, 1 sterile and 1 unsterile, both of which complied with the requirements; and 1 bacteriological examination was made of frozen treat. There were 151 samples of ice cream analyzed for pounds of food solids per gallon, of which 6 samples were below the standard.

There were 799 samples of food examined, 100 of which were adulterated. These consisted of 3 samples of butter which were moldy and 1 sample was also rancid; 11 samples of eggs, 5 samples of which were decomposed, 1 sample of stale eggs sold as fresh eggs, 4 samples of cold storage eggs not marked, and 1 sample of frozen egg whites which contained added water; 19 samples of hamburg steak, 5 samples of which contained sodium sulphite in excess of one tenth of one per cent, 1 sample of which was also decomposed, 7 samples contained a compound of sulphur dioxide not properly labeled, and 7 samples were decomposed; 24 samples of sausage, 7 samples of which contained starch in excess of 2 per cent, 11 samples contained a compound of sulphur dioxide not properly labeled, one of which was also decomposed, 3 samples contained sodium sulphite in excess of one-tenth of one per cent, one of which was also decomposed, and 3 samples were decomposed, one of which was also rancid; 4 samples of relish and 1 sample of pickles which contained sodium benzoate and were not properly labeled; 1 sample of heavy cream which was below the legal standard in fat; 8 samples of olive oil, 6 samples of which were colored to conceal inferiority, and 2 samples were misbranded; 2 samples of maple butter which were misbranded; and 27 samples of mattress fillings which contained secondhand material.

There were 153 samples of drugs examined, of which 17 were adulterated. These consisted of 1 sample of alcohol which was adulterated by the addition of water, 8 samples of argyrol which did not conform to the professed standard under which they were sold, 1 sample of camphorated oil, 5 samples of spirit of nitrous ether, 1 sample of lime water, and 1 sample of tincture of iodine, all of which did not conform to the requirements of the U. S. Pharmacopoeia.

The police departments submitted 123 samples of liquor for examination. The police departments also submitted 62 samples to be analyzed for poisons or drugs, of which 1 sample contained iron, 1 sample contained oil of savin and oil of tansey, 1 sample contained ergot, 3 samples contained quinine, 2 samples contained quinine and caffeine, 1 sample contained morphine, 2 samples contained morphine and heroin, 11 samples contained heroin, 39 samples contained no alkaloids, no narcotics and no heavy metals, and 1 sample of alleged alkaloidal drug was in insufficient amount for identification.

There were 112 cities and towns visited for the inspection of pasteurizing plants, and 513 plants were inspected.

There were 5 plants inspected for the manufacture of ice cream; and 83 investigations made relative to narcotic licenses.

There were 110 hearings held pertaining to violations of the laws.

There were 57 convictions for violations of the law, $1,430 in fines being imposed.

Clover Hill Farms, Incorporated, and S. S. Kresge Company of Fitchburg; and Dominic Shukis of Bedford, were convicted for violation of the milk laws.

Leroy F. Gould of Framingham, Jacob Shick, 2 cases, of Watertown, and Mary Iannacci and Thomas F. Lydon of Woburn, were all convicted for violations of the pasteurization laws and regulations.

Charles Battaglia and David Cohen of Cambridge; City Public Market, 2 counts, of Lowell; Economy Grocery Stores, Incorporated, of Dorchester; Ganem & Sons of Lawrence; The Great Atlantic & Pacific Tea Company of Gloucester; Sam Lipsky, Incorporated, 2 cases, of Brookline; Samuel Berger of Salem; Nathan Somers and A. H. Phillips, Incorporated, of Springfield; Peter Stathis of Holyoke; Taunton Public Market of Taunton; Charles Shapiro of Somerville; A. H. Phillips, Incorporated, 2 cases, of Chicopee; Stephen A. Sotre of Webster; Anthony Brodecki of Southbridge; and Zenon Forcier of Providence, R. I., were all convicted for violations of the food laws. Sam Lipsky, Incorporated, of Brookline appealed one case.

Fall River Dairy Company, and Manuel R. Soares, of Fall River, were convicted for violations of the milk grading law. Fall River Dairy Company of Fall River appealed their case.

Post's Taste-T-Foods, Incorporated, of Newton was convicted for a violation of the bakery law.

M. Brown & Sons, Incorporated, of Boston, was convicted for delivering, and Edward B. Steen of Somerville, was convicted for using decomposed eggs in the manufacture of food products. Edward B. Steen of Somerville appealed his case.

Economy Grocery Stores, Incorporated, of Dorchester, was convicted for a violation of the cold storage laws.

Manuel Batista of New Bedford was convicted for violation of the false advertising law.

Robert A. Somers of Boston was convicted for violation of the drug laws.

Jacob Pomeratz of Indian Orchard, and A. H. Phillips, Jr., of Springfield, were convicted for obstruction of an inspector. A. H. Phillips Jr., of Springfield, appealed his case.

David Earnest of Boston; Morris Freedman of Waltham; Samuel Kreplick of Worcester; Sherman & Feinberg, Incorporated of Chelsea; Louis Young of Brockton; George Greene of Roxbury; Leo Meltzer, 2 cases, of Fall River; Saul Taylor of New Bedford; Hyman Lanes, Jack Lanes, and George Cohen of Lynn; and David Hecht of Dorchester, were all convicted for violations of the mattress laws.

John A. Carlson, Melvin H. Cross, John Farrell, Gulf Refining Company, Rudolph O. Werme, and Albert B. Westlund, all of Worcester; and Sears Roebuck & Company of Lynn, were all convicted for violations of the wood alcohol law.

In accordance with Section 25, Chapter 111 of the General Laws, the following is the list of articles of adulterated food collected in original packages from manufacturers, wholesalers, or producers:

Butter which was moldy was obtained as follows:

One sample each, from A. H. Phillips, Incorporated, at Springfield; and A. H. Phillips, Incorporated, at Chicopee.

Two samples of maple butter which were misbranded were obtained from L. & D. Maple Products Company of Hartford, Connecticut.

Olive oil which was misbranded was obtained as follows:

One sample each, from Ferrari Brothers, Incorporated, of East Boston; and Joseph Pollen of Boston.

Three samples of relish which contained sodium benzoate and were not properly labeled were obtained from Providence Pickling Company of Providence, R. I.

Two samples of pickles which contained sodium benzoate and were not properly labeled were obtained from Peerless Products Company of Pawtucket, R. I.

Frozen desserts which were low in pounds of food solids per gallon were obtained as follows:

Two samples each, from White House Ice Cream Company of Cambridge; and Hager's Ice Cream Company of Somerville.

Hamburg steak which contained a compound of sulphur dioxide not properly labeled was obtained as follows.

One sample each, from Babcock Market of Brookline; Brookfield Market of Chelsea; Grand Central Market of Haverhill; Ganems Market of Lawrence; National Meat Market (Sarah Snyder) of Boston; and Barron's Market of Cambridge.

Hamburg steak which was decomposed was obtained as follows:

Two samples from Central Square Market of Cambridge; and one sample each, from Hyman Bean (Little Wonder Market), and New England Market, Incorporated, of Cambridge; The Great Atlantic & Pacific Tea Company of Gloucester; Benjamin Roman of Boston; and World Beef Company of Fall River.

One sample of hamburg steak which was decomposed and also contained sodium sulphite in excess of one-tenth of one per cent was obtained from Boston Cash Market of Boston.

Hamburg steak which contained sodium sulphite in excess of one-tenth of one per cent was obtained as follows:

One sample each, from Sam Lipsky, Incorporated, of Brookline; Stanley Sigda of Holyoke; Boston Market of Chelsea; and Blackstone Supply Company of Boston.

Sausage which contained starch in excess of 2 per cent was obtained as follows:

Two samples from Ferry Provision Company of Boston; and one sample each, from Anthony Brodecki of Southbridge; Omaha Packing Company, Incorporated of Boston; Peter L. Berlo of South Boston; Essem Packing Company of Lawrence; and Globe Provision Company of Fall River.

Sausage which was decomposed was obtained as follows:

One sample each, from Boston Cash Market of Boston; Ruth Ginsberg (Plymouth Market) of Salem; and Silverman's Market of Holyoke.

Sausage which contained a compound of sulphur dioxide not properly labeled was obtained as follows:

Two samples each, from Stella Chain Stores of Revere; and Charles Cierquci of Boston; and one sample each, from Stella Chain Store of Haverhill; D. Petrini & Son, Benjamin Chaffin and New Tunnel Market, all of Boston; and Julius Hershman of Lynn.

One sample of sausage which was decomposed and also contained sodium sulphite in excess of one-tenth of one per cent was obtained from Dominick Ciotti of Malden.

One sample of sausage which was decomposed and also contained a compound of sulphur dioxide not properly labeled was obtained from Peter Stathis of Holyoke.

There were thirteen confiscations, consisting of 20 pounds of decomposed hamburg steak; 18 pounds of decomposed hamburg steak; 24 pounds of immature veal; 40 pounds of decomposed veal; 327 pounds of decomposed boneless veal; 600 pounds of decomposed soft cheese; 620 pounds of decomposed soft cheese; 400 pounds of decomposed soft cheese; 270 pounds of decomposed soft cheese; 880 pounds of decomposed soft cheese; 78 pounds of decomposed soft cheese; 277 pounds of decomposed soft cheese; and 100 pounds of decomposed shrimp.

The licensed cold storage warehouses reported the following amounts of food placed in storage during September, 1935:—322,890 dozens of case eggs; 766,188 pounds of broken out eggs; 859,073 pounds of butter; 1,611,770 pounds of poultry; 2,271,801½ pounds of fresh meat and fresh meat products; and 8,439,309 pounds of fresh food fish.

There was on hand October 1, 1935:—3,706,350 dozens of case eggs; 2,719,114 pounds of broken out eggs; 8,940,677 pounds of butter; 2,976,536 pounds of poultry; 4,364,140 pounds of fresh meat and fresh meat products; and 30,649,586 pounds of fresh food fish.

The licensed cold storage warehouses reported the following amounts of food placed in storage during October, 1935:—349,260 dozens of case eggs; 436,575 pounds of broken out eggs; 679,281 pounds of butter; 1,284,101 pounds of poultry; 3,481,539½ pounds of fresh meat and fresh meat products; and 10,266,756 pounds of fresh food fish.

There was on hand November 1, 1935:—2,622,090 dozens of case eggs; 2,346,740 pounds of broken out eggs; 6,934,426½ pounds of butter; 3,008,932 pounds of poultry; 4,538,177½ pounds of fresh meat and fresh meat products; and 29,418,682 pounds of fresh food fish.

The licensed cold storage warehouses reported the following amounts of food placed in storage during November, 1935:—268,950 dozens of case eggs; 516,464 pounds of broken out eggs; 792,657 pounds of butter; 3,220,437½ pounds of poultry; 3,919,178½ pounds of fresh meat and fresh meat products; and 7,181,298 pounds of fresh food fish.

There was on hand December 1, 1935:—1,599,510 dozens of case eggs; 2,121,930 pounds of broken out eggs; 3,860,824½ pounds of butter; 4,905,358½ pounds of poultry; 5,191,272¾ pounds of fresh meat and fresh meat products; and 26,783,888 pounds of fresh food fish.

MASSACHUSETTS DEPARTMENT OF PUBLIC HEALTH

Commissioner of Public Health, HENRY D. CHADWICK, M.D.

Public Health Council

HENRY D. CHADWICK, M.D., *Chairman*
GORDON HUTCHINS.   RICHARD M. SMITH, M.D.
FRANCIS H. LALLY, M.D.   RICHARD P. STRONG, M.D.
SYLVESTER E. RYAN, M.D.   JAMES L. TIGHE.
Secretary, FLORENCE L. WALL

Division of Administration	Under direction of Commissioner.
Division of Sanitary Engineering	Director and Chief Engineer, ARTHUR D. WESTON, C.E.
Division of Communicable Diseases	Director, GAYLORD W. ANDERSON, M.D.
Division of Biologic Laboratories	Director and Pathologist, ELLIOTT S. ROBINSON, M.D.
Division of Food and Drugs	Director and Analyst, HERMANN C. LYTHGOE, S.B.
Division of Child Hygiene	Director, M. LUISE DIEZ, M.D.
Division of Tuberculosis	Director, ALTON S. POPE, M.D.
Division of Adult Hygiene	Director, HERBERT L. LOMBARD, M.D.

State District Health Officers

The Southeastern District	RICHARD P. MACKNIGHT, M.D., New Bedford.
The South Metropolitan District	HENRY M. DE WOLFE, M.D., Quincy.
The North Metropolitan District	CHARLES B. MACK, M.D., Boston.
The Northeastern District	ROBERT E. ARCHIBALD, M.D., Lynn.
The Worcester County District	OSCAR A. DUDLEY, M.D., Worcester.
The Connecticut Valley District	HAROLD E. MINER, M.D., Springfield.
The Franklin County District	WALTER W. LEE, M.D., No. Adams.
The Berkshire District	HAROLD W. STEVENS, M.D., Great Barrington.

PUBLICATION OF THIS DOCUMENT APPROVED BY THE COMMISSION ON ADMINISTRATION AND FINANCE
5500. 4'-'36. Order 7591

THE COMMONHEALTH

Volume 23   Apr.-May-June
No. 2   1936

REPRINT NUMBER

MASSACHUSETTS
DEPARTMENT OF PUBLIC HEALTH

THE COMMONHEALTH

QUARTERLY BULLETIN OF THE MASSACHUSETTS DEPARTMENT OF
PUBLIC HEALTH

Sent Free to any Citizen of the State

Entered as second class matter at Boston Postoffice.

M. LUISE DIEZ, M.D., DIRECTOR OF DIVISION OF CHILD HYGIENE, EDITOR.
Room 545, State House, Boston, Mass.

CONTENTS

	PAGE
History of the Department, by Eleanor J. Macdonald, A.B.,	83
The Supervisor of Health Education — Responsibilities and Training, by C. E. Turner, M.A., Dr. P.H.	124
Suggestions for Integrated Health Teaching in the Primary Grades, by Jean V. Latimer, A.M.	127
Basic Considerations of the Junior High School Course of Study, by John P. Sullivan, Ph.D.	132
The Charm Course, by Albertine P. McKellar	138
Lunch in a Country School, by Mary Spalding, M.A.	141
The Vegetable Cupboard for the Country School, by Mary Spalding, M.A.	148
Recreation, by Alma Porter	150
The Use of Leisure, by Helen I. D. McGillicuddy, M.D.	154
The Cure of Tuberculosis, by Ernest B. Emerson, M.D.	156
The Role of Surgery in Pulmonary Tuberculosis, by Edward D. Churchill, M.D.	160
Approved Prophylactic Remedy for Use in the Eyes of Infants at Birth	163
Resolution Adopted by the Joint Committee on Health Problems in Education of the National Education Association and the American Medical Association	164
Book Note: Syphilis and Its Treatment, by William A. Hinton, M.D.	165
Report of Division of Food and Drugs, January, February, March, 1936	166

A HISTORY OF THE MASSACHUSETTS DEPARTMENT OF PUBLIC HEALTH

ELEANOR J. MACDONALD, A.B.,
*Statistician, Division of Adult Hygiene,
Massachusetts Department of Public Health.*

General Background

On June 21, 1869, an act establishing a State Board of Health in Massachusetts was passed by the Legislature. In this simple statement is expressed the culmination of the concentrated efforts of years, and sociological trends extending back for centuries.

That such a trend was in the air both here and abroad is undeniable. What had happened in America after the Revolutionary War and what happened in England at the same time were inevitable antecedents of the recognition that public health was a governmental responsibility. The method of meeting the administrative demands of this new field was worked out differently, but interrelatedly, here and in England. To clearly visualize one, the other must be understood. The distinctly different personalities of the pioneers in this work had an important bearing upon the evolution of their respective plans. It will be noticed that although the final gesture in the passage of public health legislation might have been fear of an epidemic, the work leading to its passage was sound and deliberate.

The gradual permeation of ideas, not based on sudden calamities but on the acts and thoughts of sincere and foresighted men working for years for an ideal, and adapting to that ideal the results and zeal of other workers in the field, is responsible for organized public health as it is today. The immediate causes, however, were varied, and would never have resulted in permanency without the rational underlying trend.

The Board of Health, established in Boston in 1799, known as the "Paul Revere Board of Health," was an aftermath of a severe outbreak of yellow fever in Boston. The "Report of the Massachusetts Sanitary Commission, 1850" prepared by Lemuel Shattuck, was authorized because of the fear of a cholera epidemic. Since the disease was reported at quarantine in New York harbor in 1848 and the memory of the 1832 epidemic was still fresh, the statement of Abbott that, "It was this condition of affairs which undoubtedly led the Massachusetts legislature of 1849 to enact a resolve calling for the appointment of a commission to make a sanitary survey of the state and to report upon the same," is readily understood. The first State Board of Health that actually functioned was in Massachusetts, and Dr. Wolcott said that it had its inception because of an outbreak of typhoid fever in a girls' school, in which the wife of a prominent state official was interested.

Events of apparently no individual importance were happening in the first half of the nineteenth century that should be understood if the whole gradual development is to be understood. The Humanitarian Movement was launched in England at a time in her history when even the most conservative of the population were forced to realize that antiquated social, physical, and economic conditions as they were had reached a saturation point, and must be improved. This great emotional surge was accompanied by a movement less humane in initial impulse, but not less important in end result. This was the Utilitarian Movement sponsored in England by Jeremy Bentham. Edwin Chadwick, under the direct influence of Jeremy Bentham, made his famous "Report on the Sanitary Condition of the Labouring Population of Great Britain" in 1842.

It is remarkable that England, with her rich literature and growing world influence, should have been one of the last European nations to take active steps in the establishment of measures to safeguard the health of the people. Since 1350, France had been taking cognizance of the sanitation of the environment. These measures were more or less objective at first. Public health, as it exists today, did not begin to be known in France until the first decade of the nineteenth century. At this period the several German states were evolving a form of preventive medicine that was centralized and efficient. The development of a health program in the United States followed the lines of planning of the concept of England rather than that of Germany or France. It was not in imitation of any system, however, but was developing contemporaneously, in constant touch with its own and other nations' progress.

Edwin Chadwick

In 1828, in the "Westminster Review" for April, appeared an article dealing with the expectation of life and the influence of environment, written by Edwin Chadwick, Esquire, of the Inner Temple, a barrister-at-law. The purpose of the article was "to exhibit the present state of the information possessed relative to the casualties of sickness and mortality, and the conduct of the government respecting the departments of the public expenditure appropriated as means to diminish the evil effects of these casualties." Whipple calls this one of the events that marked the "dawning twilight of sanitary improvement."

This first article, which was followed by many others on such questions as pauperism and mendicity, attracted the attention of Jeremy Bentham, who was then quite an old man. During the last year of Bentham's life Chadwick lived at his home and came into daily contact with his ideas on questions of government and reform. Owing to his intense interest in these questions, Chadwick, in 1832, the year of Bentham's death, was appointed an Assistant-Commissioner to inquire into the workings of the Poor-Law. In 1833, he was appointed a Royal Commissioner to examine the conditions of factory children.

It must be remembered that this interest in health, to which most individuals today are thoroughly accustomed, just one hundred years ago was thought to be a new idea, the peculiar product of an enlightened age.

The famous Chadwick Report of 1842 on the sanitary condition of the labouring population of Great Britain, was the result of a careful survey and was one of the most important precursors of the establishment of the General Board of Health of 1848. Chadwick himself worked so zealously for the cause of the General Board of Health that the credit for its eventual establishment belongs to him. He was convinced that drainage, removal of all refuse of habitations, streets, and roads, improved water supplies, corrected ventilation in homes and places of employment as a preventive of disease, abatement of nuisances, and the promotion of civic, household, and personal cleanliness were the primary and most important measures, and at the same time the most practical, and within the recognized province of public administration. This General Board of Health had little real authority except in an advisory capacity.

The development of the public health movement in America had run parallel to the English plan for several years, and then had developed its own definite characteristics.

The Early Public Health Movement in America

The early public health movement in America may be said to have begun with the enactment, in 1648, by the General Court of the Massachusetts Bay of a statute providing for maritime quarantine, because of the prevalence of disease in the West Indies. The act was repealed the next year when the epidemic stopped. There were many other acts during the seventeenth and eighteenth centuries having to do mainly with the prevention of contagion. Toward the end of the century, the appearance of severe epidemics of influenza, smallpox, scarlet fever, and yellow fever attracted the attention of the medical profession and stimulated the attempt to find the cause of these diseases. Noah Webster popularized the idea that infectious diseases were caused by the emanations from such nuisances as decaying animal and vegetable matter. Once this idea was established, the logical legislative approach to a solution of the problem was nuisance abatement.

This accounts for the passage on June 22, 1797, in Massachusetts, of the health act of greatest importance to the development of public health in America. It was a law providing for the formation of health organizations in towns and gave these local boards of health the authority to abate nuisances which they considered dangerous to the public health. This law was copied throughout the State and the country. Boston, Salem, Marblehead, Plymouth, Charlestown, and Lynn were among the first towns to establish boards of health under this authority. This idea of the cause of disease persisted for years, and relegated the idea of contagion to the background.

One outstanding exception to the general rule was the development of the prevention of smallpox. Inoculation, as a preventive, progressed with great rapidity from its introduction in 1721. In 1792, in Boston alone, eight thousand individuals were inoculated. Gradually, vaccination supplanted inoculation. A new precedent was set by Milton, Massachusetts, in 1809, when free vaccination was given to all its inhabitants. Other communities followed this example. This accounts for the less general prevalence of smallpox in proportion to that of other diseases of this period.

Lemuel Shattuck

This post-Revolutionary period witnessed the development of the great founder of public health institutions in America—Lemuel Shattuck. He had always been a student of conditions. As a young man he taught school and established a system of keeping school records that is, with slight variation, still in existence. Even' at this stage in his career he was interested in the collection and tabulation of data, most of which he interpreted inductively and published.

Genealogy interested him from childhood, as did history. He later remarked that to him a history of events alone was not a real history. History, he felt, to justify its existence, should contain the homely facts about environment, health, and customs of each successive generation. In Concord, Massachusetts, where he was in business with his brother for a period of ten years, Shattuck wrote a history as he felt it should be written, and his "History of Concord" is considered an excellent piece of work.

The study of his own genealogy revealed to him how carelessly town records were kept and even how devoid of interest in family background many families were. As he rounded out his own family tree, he thought of a method whereby all families might more readily keep the important members and events listed. He published this shortly before his active public life began.

In Boston, where he moved in 1834, he became immediately prominent in public affairs. In 1837, his plan for arranging, printing, and preserving the Boston city documents went into effect. He felt very strongly that the terrific amount of sickness which the State's citizenry had come to consider part of normal life would throw the people into consternation, and even action, if this data were presented to them. The records were so poorly kept that nowhere was this evidence obtainable, and each community kept its records in its own way so that the data in one place could not be compared with the data in another. In 1842, through his intense effort, an act was passed which established the present system of registration of births, marriages, and deaths. These laws were revised in 1849 under his direction.

His interest in statistics, which had governed his various activities, had led, with the cooperation of others similarly interested, to the formation of the American Statistical Association in 1839. This same instinct for discovering the complete picture behind his figures led to his sanitary survey of Boston in 1845. He used a new plan and one which is still the foundation for census collection. Originally, a census was an enumeration showing simply the age and sex of the population. According to Shattuck's plan, information was sought concerning the health, age, sex, and marital and economic status of every individual. This plan gives the statistician a complete picture of the state of health of a community, and points out the direction reform should take, if it is needed. His work in this survey, which was called the "Census of Boston in 1845," was considered so effective that he first advised concerning, and later actually drew up, the act of Congress which gave

Federal authority for the census. The most important item of interest in this survey was not the Federal recognition of its merit, but the sudden realization by Shattuck of the state of health of the people. His early motive was to obtain a picture, but when he saw the picture it became apparent to him that something must be done.

In Boston, Massachusetts, in 1800, seven years after Shattuck's birth, 70 per cent of the population died before the age of forty. Instead of improving as knowledge advanced and as the metropolis of Boston, in particular, became more and more famous for her enlightened medical training, conditions became worse, until in 1845, 84 per cent of the population was dead before it reached the age of forty. It becomes clearer when it is realized that of every one hundred people born ninety years ago, only sixteen passed the age of forty. In his report on the subject, Shattuck stated that in 1830 there was one death for every forty-eight people in the State each year. Ten years later, there was one death annually for every thirty-nine. Shattuck compared his Boston figures with those obtained from some of the towns in which he had lived previously, and found that environment made a difference in the total death rate. The rural population had a lower death rate than the urban, although even in cities those living under better conditions were more comparable with the more prosperous farming class, than those who lived in squalid factory districts or tenement houses.

The Shattuck Report, 1850

In 1848, the American Statistical Association, through the influence of Shattuck's sincere interest in public health, appointed a committee which was directed to urge the Legislature to make a sanitary survey of the entire State of Massachusetts. From 1848 to 1849, during which years he was a member of the State Legislature, Shattuck worked for the passage of this act. As with Chadwick in England, he did not work alone. The medical profession joined in this movement through the Massachusetts Medical Society, and sent in petitions asking that the survey be made. On May 2, 1849, an act appointing a Sanitary Commission was passed.

Mr. Shattuck had carried the request of the petitioners through all its stages. There were then three political parties in the State,—the Whigs, the Democrats, and the Freesoilers. The Governor appointed one from each of these parties to be the Commission,—Mr. Shattuck, Dr. Jehiel Abbott of Westfield, and Nathaniel P. Banks, Jr. of Waltham. Mr. Shattuck was chairman, and the master spirit of the Commission. He was the most familiar with and interested in the plan, and was expected to do the whole work.

It is generally recognized that he did the work and wrote the report practically unassisted. On April 25, 1850, this monumental document of five hundred pages was given to the General Court with a bill advising its adoption. Both were tabled and Shattuck died before the report was resurrected to be used as the guide by the founders of the State Board of Health in Massachusetts.

The introduction of the report gave a comprehensive picture of the history of sanitation abroad and at home. Then came the proposed plan. This was followed by a list of reasons why the plan should be accepted, and ten hypothetical objections were raised and answered. The report closed with an appeal to every individual, group, and governing body of the State, to throw aside partisanship and effect a solution to the problem of preventable disease and to the misery of the large and growing masses.

There were conditions, not at first apparent, which had to be corrected before the public could be ready for the acceptance of this report. It was a period of intense pride in liberty of thought and action, of intense insularity and town consciousness. Many physicians felt that this layman had no right in the field of preventive, or any other kind of medicine and objected to his suggestions. It should not be assumed, however, that the medical profession, as a group, took this attitude. Most of the generous and persistent effort that took place between the time of Shattuck's report and the establishment of the State Board of Health in Massachusetts was carried on by members of the medical profession who had the vision to see, with Shattuck, the advantages to the masses of organized preventive medicine.

Shattuck's complete confidence in the future of preventive medicine, in a period that had yet to learn of bacteriology, is one of the most visionary of his attitudes. Speaking editorially for the Commission, he said, "We believe that the conditions of perfect health, either public or personal, are seldom or never attained, though attainable;—that the average length of human life may be very much extended, and its physical power greatly augmented;—that in every year, within this Commonwealth, thousands of lives are lost which might have been saved;—that tens of thousands of cases of sickness occur, which might have been prevented;—that a vast amount of unnecessarily impaired health, and physical debility exists among those not actually confined by sickness;—that these preventable evils require an enormous expenditure and loss of money, and impose upon the people unnumbered and immeasurable calamities, pecuniary, social, physical, mental, and moral, which might be avoided;—that means exist, within our reach, for their mitigation or removal;—and that measures for prevention will effect infinitely more, than remedies for the cure of disease."

Mr. Shattuck's recommendations are so comprehensive that some of them have yet to be effected. He recommended that the public health laws be revised and a State Board of Health be established. His report advocated changes in the law and new laws to establish both State and local boards of health, together with various directions pertaining to these. The inquest laws were to be changed. Authority for quarantine of ships was advocated. Supervision of the insane was to be transferred to the State Board of Health. The Constitution was to be altered regarding the census, and subjects for enumeration at this census were included. Public registration of births, marriages, and deaths, and a uniform nomenclature of deaths were suggested. The local boards of health were advised to buy books for information, to study sanitary conditions in their relation to water systems, drainage, dwellings, and public buildings. That nuisances should be prevented and sanitary surveys undertaken, that vaccination should be furnished, and that the boards of health should make house-to-house visits to learn of disease were recommended. An effort to effect a conciliatory, rather than a compulsory, course was advised. Tuberculosis control through scientific study of the problem was suggested. The collection and dissemination of material concerning public and private health was repeatedly advocated. Institutions for the training of nurses and individuals interested in sanitary science were recommended. Physicians were advised to keep records of their cases. Adulterated and patent medicines were to be controlled by the State Board of Health. Families were advised to keep records of their sickness and to care for their children from the standpoint of health, while clergymen were to make public addresses on health at least once a year. His recommendations cover practically every field in public health.

The briefest outline of the table of contents brings graphically to the mind the unexampled foresight of this famous document. Under Section III, entitled "Plan for a Sanitary Survey of the State," the following fifty measures are discussed in detail:

I. Revision of the Health Laws of the State
II. General Board of Health recommended
III. Composition of the Board of Health
IV. Secretary of the Board of Health
V. Local Boards of Health recommended
VI. Officers of Local Boards of Health
VII. Sanitary Rules and Regulations
VIII. Compulsory Measures
IX. Books for the use of Boards of Health
X. Annual Reports of Boards of Health
XI. Printing and exchanging Documents
XII. Census or Enumeration of the Inhabitants
XIII. Alteration of the State Constitution
XIV. Registration of Births, Marriages and Deaths
XV. Atmospheric Observations
XVI. Causes of Disease and Causes of Death
XVII. Laying out new Towns
XVIII. Public Buildings regulated
XIX. Manufactories and Private Dwellings
XX. Over-crowded Lodging-houses and Cellar-dwellings
XXI. Public Squares and Ornamental Trees
XXII. Special Sanitary Survey of different places
XXIII. Mill-ponds and Stagnant Water
XXIV. House-to-house Visitation
XXV. Observations concerning Sickness in general
XXVI. Observations concerning Sickness in Schools
XXVII. Periodical and Special Vaccination
XXVIII. Observations concerning Consumption
XXIX. Abatement of Nuisances

XXX.	Sanitary Evils of Intemperance
XXXI.	Inquest on Dead Bodies
XXXII.	Insane and Idiotic Persons
XXXIII.	Interment of the Dead
XXXIV.	Emigrant Ships and Seamen
XXXV.	Quarantine Regulations
XXXVI.	Sanitary Evils of Foreign Emigration
XXXVII.	Sanitary Associations recommended
XXXVIII.	Tenements for the Laboring Classes
XXXIX	Public Baths and Wash-houses
XL.	Refuse of Towns, for manure
XLI.	Abatement of the Smoke Nuisance
XLII.	Physicians' and Apothecaries' Prescriptions
XLIII.	Adulterated Food and Drugs
XLIV.	Establishments for the Education of Nurses
XLV.	Education in Sanitary Science
XLVI.	Professional Records of Physicians
XLVII.	Clergymen interested in Public Health
XLVIII.	Sanitary Observations in Families
XLIX.	Sanitary Science useful to fathers and mothers
L.	Personal Sanitary Examinations

Under Section IV, the reasons for approving the plan are discussed at length under the following headings:

I. Because it is a practical measure
II. Because it is a useful measure
III. Because it is an economical measure
IV. Because it is a philanthropic and charitable measure
V. Because it is a moral measure
VI. Because the progress of the age demands it
VII. Because it involves an important duty

This preliminary work in the development of the institution of public health in Massachusetts and, subsequently, through the example of Massachusetts, in the rest of the country, has been considered in detail because it explains the permanence and soundness of this science. It was a foundation laid in reason and security based upon demonstrable facts. The actual passage of the bill may have been accidental; the reasoning which brought it to that stage in its development certainly was not. This was all the more remarkable in view of the comparative youth of the country and its seemingly limitless possibilities for expansion.

The Period Between 1850 and 1869; Dr. Edward Jarvis

The man who filled the gap between Shattuck's work in 1850 and Bowditch's work in 1869 was Dr. Edward Jarvis. He was born in Concord in 1803 and was descended from an Englishman who came to Boston in 1661. He was graduated from Harvard College in 1826, and from Harvard Medical School in 1830. He practiced medicine in Concord. While there he became acquainted with Lemuel Shattuck and through him developed a fondness for vital statistics. Although he was an active practitioner in medicine, his dominating interest seemed to have been more sociological. He wrote many articles on the necessity for establishing health departments, boards of charity, and hospitals for the insane. In 1859, Lemuel Shattuck, his friend, died. Following the Civil War, Jarvis was delegated by the United States Government to work out the statistics of the census of 1860. From this time on, Dr. Jarvis's whole life was devoted to social and public health problems.

The work of Dr. Jarvis is best summarized in the tribute given to him by Dr. Walcott who said, "He was one of the great sanitary leaders of his day, especially in that department of the science which alone gives a secure foundation for preventive medicine, that is, a correct body of vital statistics. Massachusetts, as you well know, second only to Great Britain among the English speaking people, established a state system of vital statistics and Dr. Jarvis was one of the active promoters of the legislation which accomplished this result.

"At a later date he was chairman of a committee of the Massachusetts Medical Society which enlisted the aid of the medical profession in the preparation of that great report of the year 1850, made by Lemuel Shattuck to the Legislature of Massachusetts, a report which laid out a scheme for the sanitary administration of the Commonwealth which the State has only now been able to accomplish.

"It seems to me a sufficient praise for any man of my profession to say that he served in a company of men of the quality of Lemuel Shattuck, Dr. Henry I. Bowditch, and Dr. George Derby, and of these men Dr. Jarvis was an honored and trusted associate."

State Board of Health (June 30, 1869 to June 30, 1879)

On June 21, 1869, an act establishing a State Board of Health in Massachusetts was passed. This act authorized the appointment of seven persons who should constitute the Board of Health and Vital Statistics. The Board was instructed to take cognizance of the interests of health and life among the citizens of the Commonwealth, to make investigations regarding the people and regarding causes of disease, epidemics, and sources of death, together with the effects of locality, employment, and economic status on the public health. It was also instructed to examine and report the effect of the use of intoxicating liquor as a beverage.

It is interesting to note that in this act four important activities of health departments are mentioned: 1, vital statistics; 2, communicable disease control; 3, epidemiology; 4, sanitation.

The first Board of Health was composed of three physicians, a lawyer, a civil engineer, an historian, and a business man. Dr. Henry I. Bowditch was chosen chairman and Dr. George Derby, secretary. In the early days the Board met four times a year, in a committee room of the State House, while the routine work of the Board was carried on in Dr. Derby's private office. The advisory powers of the Board, which have been carried down through the various administrative units to the present Department, were evident at the very beginning. A general circular which set forth these principles was mailed to the mayor of every city, to the board of health where one existed, to the selectmen of every town, to every member of the Legislature, and to every clergyman and physician in Massachusetts. "To the Boards of Health of the several Cities and Towns of Massachusetts:

"The undersigned have recently been appointed by the governor and council, to constitute the 'State Board of Health,' under an Act passed by the last legislature.

"In entering upon our duties, which are rather advisory than executive, we desire to establish such communication with the local boards having this important subject in charge, that all may work together for the common advantage of the people, for the prevention of disease, and for the prolongation of life.

"We believe that all citizens have an inherent right to the enjoyment of pure and uncontaminated air, and water, and soil; that this right should be regarded as belonging to the whole community; and that no one should be allowed to trespass upon it by his carelessness, or his avarice, or even by his ignorance. This right is in a great measure recognized by the State, as appears by the General Statutes.

"If these were strictly and impartially enforced, we should have a condition of public cleanliness, and of public health, which would make Massachusetts a model for all other communities. That this has not been done depends upon many causes, some of general, and others of purely local operation.

"It has been doubted, whether the public mind is sufficiently aware of the dangerous elements around us; whether the connection between filth and disease is as yet proved to the public satisfaction; whether the people are convinced that undrained land is unwholesome to live upon.

"All these doubts of the public intelligence have impeded the operation of our laws.

"It is thought also that local and private interests have often been so strong as to paralyze the action of the health authorities.

"But we hope and believe that a better time is coming; and we confidently look to you to put in force the powers which the laws have placed in your hands.

"Among these laws we would particularly call your attention to—

"General Statutes, chapter 26, in which are comprised stringent provisions relative to the abatement of nuisances, to vaccination, to contagion, and to offensive trades.

"Also, to chapter 49, section 151, relative to the sale of milk produced from cows fed upon the refuse of breweries or distilleries, and to the sale of milk rendered unwholesome by any cause.

"Also, to chapter 166, in which the law is given relative to the sale of unwholesome provisions of all kinds, whether for meat or drink; the corruption of springs, wells, reservoirs, or aqueducts; the sale of dangerous drugs, and the adulteration of drugs of every sort.

"It will also be seen, on reference to chapter 211 of the Acts of the year 1866, that it is in the power of any person aggrieved by the neglect of the board of health of any city or town to abate a nuisance, to appeal to the county commissioners, who can in that case exercise all the powers of the board of health.

"Chapter 253 of the Acts of 1866 authorizes boards of health to seize and destroy the meat of any calf killed when less than four weeks old.

"Chapter 271 of the Acts of 1866 authorizes boards of health to appoint agents, to act for them, under certain restrictions.

"The legislature of 1868 passed two Acts of great importance to the public health, to which we would respectfully and earnestly ask your attention. The first, chapter 281, 1868, applies only to the city of Boston, and relates to tenement and lodging houses, placing them under very strict regulations, for the public good.

"The second, chapter 160, is of general application. It provides that in any city or town, lands which are wet, rotten or spongy, or covered with stagnant water, so as to be offensive, or injurious to health, shall be deemed a nuisance, to be abated by the board of health of such city or town. In case they refuse to act, appeal may be made, by persons aggrieved, to the superior court or any justice thereof, who may appoint three commissioners with powers equal to those possessed by boards of health.

"We confidently look to you for the enforcement of these laws.

"We believe that public opinion will fully support you in so doing.

"We will give you all the help in our power.

"There is a great work before us, which, if carried out in the letter and spirit of the laws referred to, we cannot doubt will justify the wisdom which framed them.

"In making this our first communication to the boards of health of the various cities and towns of the Commonwealth, we sincerely hope that it may serve as the opening of friendly and helpful relations between us, and that it will lead to reforms, the effects of which will be evident in the improved condition of public health.

"Communications addressed to our Secretary, Dr. George Derby, State House, Boston, will be at once acknowledged, and will be laid before the State Board of Health at their next meeting.

"Very respectfully, your obedient servants,
      HENRY I. BOWDITCH,
      GEORGE DERBY,
      ROBERT T. DAVIS,
      RICHARD FROTHINGHAM,
      P. EMORY ALDRICH,
      WARREN SAWYER,
      WILLIAM C. CHAPIN.
        State Board of Health."

In the early years of the Board many subjects were investigated. Among these were studies on consumption, prevention of disease, slaughter houses, improper housing, use of alcohol, various epidemics, the sale of poisons, adulteration of food, and even the effect on women of the constant use of treadles on sewing machines.

In 1870, a circular letter was sent to every city and town requesting that a medical correspondent be designated to keep the Board informed of what was happening in the city or town.

The Offensive Trade Act of 1871. The offensive trade act of 1871 was the first act of the Legislature that gave executive powers to the Board. It authorized the Board, after due notice and hearing, "and if, in the judgment of the Board, the public health or the public comfort and convenience so required," to order parties to cease and desist from further carrying on such trades or occupations.

In the 1871 report of the State Board of Health appears a sixty-nine page report on "An Inquiry Into the Causes of Typhoid Fever, as it Occurs in Massachusetts." In preparing this report, the Board obtained the opinions of physicians all over the State "concerning the relation of cause and effect in typhoid fever as they have watched it." After summing up the information received in this way, as well as from death records and study of the literature, the Board stated:

"The single continuous thread of probability which we have been able to follow in this inquiry leads uniformly to the decomposition of organized (and chiefly vegetable) substances as the cause of typhoid fever as it occurs in Massachusetts.

"Whether the vehicle be drinking-water made foul by human excrement, sink drains, or soiled clothing; or air made foul in enclosed places by drains, decaying vegetables or fish (Swampscott), or old timber (Tisbury), or in open places by pigsties, drained ponds or reservoirs, stagnant water, accumulations of filth of every sort, the one thing present in all these circumstances is decomposition.

"And may not the influence of soil charged with vegetable remains, in the season of heat and of drought, be also referred to the same cause? Although not yet proved, it is exceedingly probable that a rich and fertile soil in which decomposable substances are retained near the surface by any cause, whether a clay subsoil, or a ledge of rock, or a protracted drought, is a soil favorable to the production of this special disease."

Even at this late date, and in spite of the work done by Budd, the State Board of Health in Massachusetts and the majority of the physicians of the State did not yet appreciate the relationship between excreta from typhoid patients and the subsequent disease.

Professor William Ripley Nichols of the Massachusetts Institute of Technology made several investigations for the Board, relative to water and sewage. In 1871, he examined the water of Mystic Lake which supplied Charlestown and several cities north of Boston. Following this, he went to England to learn the latest developments there in stream pollution and water supplies, and for many years following, continued work along these lines. Professor Nichols was not the only expert employed by the Board. Phineas Ball, in 1873, studied possibilities of utilization of sewage. James P. Kirkwood made extensive investigations of stream pollution in 1876, and other experts assisted the Board. In 1877, Pasteur's paper on anthrax laid the real foundation for the germ theory of diseases. The bacillus typhosus was seen by

Eberth in 1880. Spirillum cholerae was discovered by Koch in 1883. The problem of how water contaminated by sewage had caused epidemics was solved and the logical course was indicated which culminated in the act providing for the purity of inland waters in Massachusetts.

General Supervision of Water Supplies, 1878. In 1878, the authority previously referred to of having "general supervision of water supplies" and of investigating the pollution of them and its causes was granted and was executive in nature. The Board was empowered to issue orders for the prevention of such pollution.

Dr. George Derby. Dr. George Derby died in 1874, and Dr. F. W. Draper became the temporary secretary, to be followed by Dr. Charles F. Folsom. Dr. Derby had held such an important place in the establishment of preventive medicine in Massachusetts that a word must be said about him at this point. In 1866 he had begun to edit the registration reports of Massachusetts. These publications established such a reputation for excellence both at home and abroad, that he was the only man who was suggested for the position of secretary of the State Board of Health when it was established in 1869. At his death, Dr. Bowditch, chairman of the Board, wrote of him as follows:

"We remember his genial and commanding presence; his indefatigable zeal in everything that was ordered by the Board. We were sure of him, as the most reliable person we could have. How much the present position of the Board, as a motive-force in the community, depends on his really wonderful faculty of meeting and of moulding men, we shall never exactly know. For my own part, words would fail me to give my idea of the debt we owe to him. He guarded our honor and safety with so jealous a care that sometimes I was inclined to think him unduly cautious. I never had any forebodings in regard to the safety and ultimate success of the Board, for I believe that State, or Preventive Medicine, has taken so deep a root in the conscience of the English-speaking race, that hereafter, boards of health, or in other words, boards for the prevention of disease, must forever exist; and they will have more and more weight upon the policy of states and of nations, as well as upon the private habits of individuals."

One of the most famous letters of the Board was Dr. Bowditch's in which stress was laid on personal hygiene, housing, nutrition, clothing, exercise, bathing, education, and work.

A large number of reports were published by the Board in the ten years of its existence. The data for many of these were collected by the questionnaire method, and this frequent communication with physicians kept the profession in close touch with the Board.

The first ten years were in the nature of a study period. Everything that had to do with the State was subjected to scrutiny: the population and its health, the prevalent diseases, the sanitation of homes and environment, the common nuisances, the water and sewage problems, the schools and their ventilation, and the disposal of the dead.

At the end of ten years, under the chairmanship of Bowditch and the Secretaryship of Derby and Folsom, the State Board of Health came to an end. It had carried out its mandate to "take cognizance of the interests of health and life" of the people. It had disseminated knowledge about the public health, had stimulated legislation, had aroused to activity the local authorities and had, in short, justified its existence and acquired State-wide confidence.

State Board of Health, Lunacy and Charity
(July 1, 1879 to May 26, 1886)

On July 1, 1879, the State Board of Health, Lunacy and Charity was formed. This combined administrative boards whose duties, though somewhat allied, should have been distinct entities. This Board was originally composed of nine members, of which three constituted a committee of health of the new Board. These men had been members of the original State Board of Health.

In 1880, Dr. Henry P. Walcott was appointed health officer and given executive charge of the public health work. This health committee had as secretary and executive officer, Dr. Folsom of the old State Board of Health. The public health committee was soon changed to five members, plus a health officer. Later, in December, 1882, Dr. Walcott resigned as health officer to become chairman of the committee on health, and Dr. Samuel Abbott was appointed health officer in his place. The act of 1882 to prevent the adulteration of food and drugs extended the executive power granted in the offensive trade act of 1871 and the act of 1878 concerning the general supervision of water supplies. During this period, important work was carried on. Stream pollution was studied, as was sewage. The Massachusetts Drainage Commission was appointed in 1884. As a result of the labors of the Board of Health, Lunacy and Charity, an act was passed to build an abattoir at Brighton. This was after years of agitation on the subject.

The error of the combination of the Health, Lunacy and Charity Board soon became evident. In 1883 there was so much dissension in the Board that the report was signed by only six of the nine members. Dr. Bowditch served on the new Board for a short time and then resigned in protest. A brief account of Bowditch is indicated here because of his vital part in the development of the whole program.

Dr. Henry Ingersoll Bowditch. Dr. Henry Ingersoll Bowditch, the chairman of the first Board of Health, was one of the first authorities in this country on diseases of the lungs. He had studied medicine under the famous Dr. James Jackson of Boston and later in Paris under the great Louis. His knowledge, acquired in Paris, in the use of the stethoscope, aroused his interest in lung disorders and he was famous for his work on consumption, its predisposing causes, and methods employed in the treatment of complications. His first paper on the subject appeared in 1852. Ten years later, his most important contribution to the history of medicine, an article upon soil and moisture as the cause of consumption, was published in the transactions of the Massachusetts Medical Society under the title "Consumption in New England." Largely as a result of his studies, he began to feel that the State should take an active part in the investigation of all disease and on April 2, 1866, a committee of the House of Representatives reported that it was expedient to establish a State Board of Health. Three years later, largely through the efforts of his friends, the Honorable Thomas H. Plunkett of Pittsfield, Massachusetts, and Mrs. Plunkett, the Legislature voted to establish a State Board of Health. He was an active member of this Board until it was merged in the Board of Health, Lunacy and Charity.

In 1874, he published an article in the Fifth Annual Report entitled "Preventive Medicine and the Physicians of the Future." Two years later, he was asked to read, at the International Medical Congress in Philadelphia, an address upon "State Medicine and Public Hygiene in America." He had found through study that the conditions of preventive medicine were in a deplorable state throughout the country, and thus he presented them. In describing his sensations before delivering his address, an interesting picture of the man himself is presented. He said, "After working many months, I felt that I had gained one point; viz., of showing our utter neglect of everything like state preventive medicine. I felt that I had a truth, which, unpalatable as I supposed it would be to most of my hearers, must be told. 'You have got to hear this, my friends,' thought I, 'so help me God!' Judge of my surprise when the above resolutions were offered—the first by Dr. Atlee on the day the address was delivered, and the last two on the succeeding day. I indeed felt gratified, but my innermost thought was of thankfulness that I had been called thus to strike a blow in behalf of the sacred cause of preventive medicine."

In 1879, Bowditch was appointed one of the first members of the National Board of Health by the President. This organization included some of the foremost scientists in the country. Although his active participation in the Massachusetts State Board of Health ended in 1878, his interest in public health work continued until the time of his death. His is one of the outstanding names in the corner-stone of preventive medicine in the United States.

Dr. Charles Follen Folsom. Dr. Charles Follen Folsom was assistant to Dr. Bowditch as a young man and it was through Dr. Bowditch that he later became secretary of the Board and followed Dr. Bowditch as a member of the National Board of Health. He discontinued his connection with the Board of Health, Lunacy and Charity the year after Bowditch's resignation. Dr. Folsom's work as secretary is not his only claim to importance in this field as his investigations connected with public water supplies, sewage disposal, vital statistics, and mental diseases, are among the outstanding achievements for which the early Board of Health was noted. Whipple described him in the following words, "Dr. Folsom had had a wide experience with men, with books, and with affairs. He had a good memory, a good sense of humor, and a fondness for a good story, as well as the capacity to tell one, characteristics which, combined with his real love for his fellowmen, made him a highly acceptable companion. The grip that he had upon his friends was shown by a testimonial of nearly seventy of his friends and patients who, wishing to express their grateful appreciation of Dr. Folsom's unfailing care and skill as a physician and their admiration for him as a man, presented Harvard University with a fund of ten thousand dollars for the establishment in the Medical School of the Charles Follen Folsom teaching fellowship in hygiene or in mental and nervous diseases."

State Board of Health (May 26, 1886 to July 7, 1914)

In 1886, the Board of Health, Lunacy and Charity came to an end and the State Board of Health was reorganized with Dr. Henry P. Wolcott as chairman. On the Board was Mr. Hiram F. Mills, civil engineer of Lawrence. In the succeeding years, the work carried out by this new Board was phenomenal. Among the most important responsibilities of this Board were those imposed by act 274 of 1886 which replaced the act of 1884, and enlarged the powers of the Board relative to the purity of inland waters to such an extent that it became obligatory for all cities, towns, or firms to obtain the advice and consent of the State Board before they could build systems for water supplies or sewage disposal.

Soon after the establishment of the new Board, a circular was sent to local boards, physicians, and other persons interested, defining the proposed scope of work.

"COMMONWEALTH OF MASSACHUSETTS
State Board of Health,
13 Beacon Street, Boston, July, 1886

To all persons interested in the Preservation of the Public Health in the Commonwealth of Massachusetts:—

"In compliance with the provisions of the Acts of 1886, chapter 101, the undersigned have been appointed by the Governor and Council as a State Board of Health.

"The present Board enters upon its work with a much broader field before it than that of its predecessors, powers of a more decidedly executive character have been conferred upon it, and its duties have been made more exacting and comprehensive. We desire at the outset to establish such relations and communications with the local Boards of Health that all may work together for the common advantage of the people, for the prevention of disease, and for the prolongation of life.

"The rights of the people to pure air, soil, water and food are recognized by the laws of the Commonwealth; and various statutes have been passed to secure the enjoyment of these rights, and to prevent their infringement by any individuals, corporations or municipalities, either from ignorance, carelessness or selfishness.

"This Board is charged to some extent with the duty of enforcing these rights and preventing and punishing any violation of them; having for this purpose powers co-ordinate with those of the local Boards of Health.

"The business of investigating and gathering information as to any matter pertaining to the public health and of diffusing such information among the people is also included in its functions.

"Among the matters of which it thus takes cognizance are:—

"1. The causes and prevention of infectious diseases. For this purpose the State Board is given co-ordinate powers with local Boards of Health. (See chap. 80, sects. 1 and 2, Public Statutes.)

"The rapid advance in the knowledge of the nature and causes of infectious diseases in recent years has an important bearing upon the legitimate work of Boards of Health. Greater familiarity with this subject is therefore essential to the successful operation of such boards.

"2. The suppression of nuisances, including the regulation of noxious and offensive trades. (Chap. 80, sect. 93, Public Statutes; chap. 107, sect. 2, Public Statutes.)

"3. The collection and diffusion of information relative to industrial hygiene, or the effects of different occupations, industries and domestic pursuits upon people at various ages, and under various conditions of life.

"4. The hygiene of schools, school-buildings and public institutions.

"5· The examination and investigation of public water-supplies and public ice-supplies, and the prevention of their pollution. (Chap. 80, sects. 103, 104, 105, Public Statutes; chap. 274, Acts of 1886; chap. 287, Acts of 1886.)

"6. The investigation of drainage and sewerage systems or plans, so far as they relate to the public health. (Chap. 274, Acts of 1886.)

"7. The disposal and transportation of the dead.

"8. The inspection of food, drugs, and other articles affecting the public health. (Chap. 263, Acts of 1882; chap. 289, Acts of 1884.)

"9. Inquiries into the causes and means of prevention of insanity.

"10. Inquiries relative to the amount of intemperance from the use of stimulants and narcotics, and the remedies therefor.

"11· The protection of human life.

"12. Investigations as to the infectious diseases of animals, so far as they affect the public health, e.g., hydrophobia, trichinosis, glanders, anthrax, etc.

"Your attention is hereby respectfully called to the enclosed copy of the very important statute entitled 'An Act to protect the purity of inland waters.' (Chap. 274, Acts of 1886.)

"Communications should be addressed to the Secretary, Dr. Samuel W. Abbott, 13 Beacon Street, Boston.

"Respectfully,
HENRY P. WALCOTT,
ELIJAH U. JONES,
JULIUS H. APPLETON,
THORNTON K. LOTHROP,
FRANK W. DRAPER,
HIRAM F. MILLS,
JAMES WHITE,
State Board of Health.

SAMUEL W. ABBOTT, *Secretary.*"

For the purpose of carrying out the provisions of the act concerning the purity of inland waters more fully, a regular system of chemical analyses of all the domestic water supplies in the State was organized under the charge of Professor T. M. Drown of the Massachusetts Institute of Technology. At the same time the services of Mr. George H. Parker were secured for the purpose of making examination of the same waters with reference to the presence of algae and other forms of vegetable life, which were present in the different water supplies.

The early office of this Board was at 13 Beacon Street. The Board divided the work among committees governing finance, publications, contagious diseases, water supplies and drainage, public institutions, food and drugs, legislation and legal proceedings, health of towns, and correspondence with local boards of health. The construction of the sewage system for draining the Mystic and Charles River valleys became a reality, and according to Whipple, "may be regarded as a child of the State Board of Health." In the first year of the new Board an engineering department was organized with Joseph P. Davis, consulting engineer, Frederick P. Stearns, chief engineer, X. H. Goodnough and others, assistant engineers. The second year of the Board, a committee on the registration of vital statistics was added.

In 1886, the General Court adopted the recommendations of the Massachusetts Drainage Commission, which for two years had been studying the pollution of Massachusetts rivers, and turned these additional functions over to the State Board of Health. Associated in this work were Hiram F. Mills, engineer, Professor Thomas M. Drown, consulting chemist, Professor William T. Sedgwick, biologist, Allen Hazen, a chemist and engineer, Harry W. Clark, chemist, George W. Fuller, bacteriologist, Edwin O. Jordan, bacteriologist, and others. The conclusion of the first report of the Board read as follows:

"In order to make the series of examinations above outlined, including monthly analyses of all waters used for domestic supply in the State, and biological examinations of certain waters injuriously affected by animal life, together with chemical analyses of other inland waters, to conduct contemplated experiments upon the purification of sewage and refuse from industrial establishments, to make the necessary investigations in order to advise cities, towns, corporations and individuals in regard to the best method of assuring the purity of intended or existing water supplies, and the best method of disposing of their sewage, and to carry out the other provisions of Chapter 274, the Board estimates that the sum of $30,000 will be required."

The Lawrence Experiment Station, 1887. The Lawrence Experiment Station, planned by Hiram F. Mills, was established in 1887 and was one of the greatest accomplishments of this Board. During the early years of its operation, this station was a guide for engineers in matters pertaining to sewage disposal.

Clark and Gage, in their report on the work done at Lawrence, said, "It may be said fairly that the investigations at the Lawrence Experiment Station laid the foundation for the scientific treatment of sewage

nd have given the initiative for similar investigations in this and
ther countries."

Sedgwick writes of the early work of this station, "For this purpose,
number of large wooden tubs or tanks built of cypress were cau-
iously filled with different soils, ranging from muck and garden loam
n the one hand, through fine sand and coarse sand to mixed gravel
stones, coarser materials, and pebbles on the other. The soil or sand to
be tested was in each case supported by a stratum of stones and gravel,
and underdrained through an effluent pipe which emptied into a large
measuring basin. The sewage was also measured as it flowed on at
the top, and the whole experiment was under control in every respect.
Each tank, or 'filter,' was sixteen feet in diameter, or one two-hundredth
of an acre in area, and the filtering material in each case was five feet
in depth. The sewage to be experimented with was drawn from one of
the main sewers of the city of Lawrence, and was ordinary domestic
city sewage, free from manufacturing wastes. No experiments of this
kind had ever before been undertaken on such a scale or with so much
care. For the first time in the history of science, engineers, chemists,
and biologists worked together under the direction of a master in hy-
draulics, toward one common end,--the promotion of the public health.

"The results crowned the endeavor. Intelligent bystanders, who saw
the sewage flowing upon the filters, at the outset unhesitatingly predicted failure. They felt certain, and did not hesitate to express their
belief, that in a fortnight, at the latest, the filters would become clogged
and foul, and the whole neighborhood pestilential. They did not know
that Berlin, the German capital, disposed of all its sewage upon land.
They forgot that the farmer once a year, or oftener, manures his fields
with filth, and that the hungry earth receives the gift with open mouth,
devours it, and soon cries out for more. As soon as a few days had
passed, and the filters had become established, the effluent began to
grow bright and clear. Chemical analyses showed that the out-put
was now purified sewage, comparatively free from odor, and poor in
organic matters. Bacterial analyses showed that while earlier, as
sewage, it was swarming with the germs of putrefaction and decay, it
now contained only a few bacteria. Further studies revealed the fact
that the foulness of the sewage was not held back as by a strainer; but
rather that as wood by a slow fire is turned to ashes, the organic matters here were slowly reduced to mineral substances. No disagreeable
odor developed, and the filters showed no signs of clogging. Thus the
very name 'filter' became a misnomer. The bystanders were amazed,
and could not repress their feelings of surprise and admiration."

English scientists have attributed the idea of the contact bed and
trickling filters, which are in general use in England, to experiments
conducted at Lawrence. Clark's experiment on purification of sewage
by aeration with compressed air was seen by Dr. Gilbert Fowler of
Manchester, England. He carried the idea home to his associates,
Lockett and Arden, and their work produced the activated sludge process.

Public Water Supplies, 1890. In 1890, water purification was begun at Lawrence and in the course of years various studies on different phases of sanitary engineering were carried on. The Merrimack River water was used. This water was similar to that filtered in Europe which supplied such cities as London and Berlin. Hiram F. Mills, Allen Hazen, George W. Fuller, Harry W. Clark, Professor Thomas M. Drown, and Professor William T. Sedgwick, the men associated with this work at Lawrence, became famous throughout the engineering world. By means of small experiments, they determined the practical nature of various purification processes.

Based on plans made by Mills, Lawrence built a sand filter to purify its drinking water. This filter, put in service in 1893, was the first filter built in America for the express purpose of reducing the death rate of the people and is biologic in principle. "The slow sand filter," according to Norton, "depends on the formation, on the surface of a sand bed, of a slimy gelatinous mass composed of a variety of organisms and their metabolic products. This material acts as a bacterial filter. The slow sand filter is a highly efficient mechanism for removal of bacteria from water." The typhoid fever rate was reduced 79 per cent following the installation of the filter, and the death rate from all causes, 10 per cent.

The increase in public water supplies in this country, and the improvement in their quality, has been phenomenal. Prior to 1800 there were only sixteen public water supplies in the United States: one in New Hampshire, five in Massachusetts, one in Rhode Island, two in Connecticut, three in New York, one in New Jersey, one in Pennsylvania, and two in Virginia. In 1850, only eighty-three public water supplies were in existence, one of which was Lake Cochituate, which had been diverted to Boston's use in 1848. The Boston water supply was increased in 1878 by the addition of the Sudbury River, and twenty years later by the Nashua River at Wachusett. When the Wachusett Reservoir was built, it was the largest artificial water supply reservoir in existence. Eventually, Goodnough and other engineers saw that Wachusett would not supply the needs of the Metropolitan area of Boston. A tunnel, thirteen miles long, was constructed to the Ware River at Coldbrook. This supplies additional water to the Wachusett Reservoir. Within a few years, a tunnel from the Ware River to the Swift River was completed, and one of the largest reservoirs in the world is now being constructed.

The outline of the growth of the public water supply in this State has been briefly considered at this point because it was this Board of Health that visualized its expansion.

In 1894, this program was studied and planned by Frederick P. Stearns, chief engineer of the State Board of Health. On recommending the plan in the annual report, Dr. Walcott, head of the State Board of Health, said in part, "The very great merit of the plan now submitted is to be found in the fact that this extension of the chain of the metropolitan water supplies to the valley of the Nashua will settle forever the future water policy of the district, for a comparatively inexpensive conduit can be constructed through to the valley of the Ware River, and beyond the Ware River lies the valley of the Swift; and, in a future so far distant that we do not venture to give a date to it, are portions of the Westfield and Deerfield rivers, capable, when united, of furnishing a supply of the best water for a municipality larger than any now found in the world."

From 1886 to the present time public water supplies have been introduced into the cities and towns of the State at a fairly uniform rate until now cities and towns, with about 97 per cent of the population of the State, are supplied in this way. The engineers engaged by the Board of Health, and later by the Department, have had in their charge the safeguarding of the water supplies. In 1886, with the establishment of the water supply and sewerage department, eight applications in regard to water supply and sewerage were received. Some idea of the expansion of this phase of the work alone may be realized when it is observed that by 1900, the number has increased to 104 applications and by 1935 to 686 which necessitated 1058 replies.

Food and Drug Laboratory, 1891. Until 1891, the analytical work entailed by the food and drug act had been carried on in private laboratories. This year, under the direction of Charles P. Worcester, a laboratory was established by the Board at 994 Washington Street. Four years later, the food and drug laboratory was established at the State House.

Diseases Dangerous to the Public Health Made Reportable, 1893. In 1893, a statute was passed which made reporting of "diseases dangerous to the public health" to the State Board of Health within twenty-four hours compulsory for local boards of health. The diseases which came under this heading included smallpox, scarlet fever, measles, typhoid fever, diphtheria, membranous croup, cholera, yellow fever, typhus fever, cerebrospinal meningitis, hydrophobia, malignant pustule, leprosy, and trichinosis.

Columbian Exposition at Chicago, 1893. In 1893, the subject of public hygiene was represented at the Columbian Exposition at Chicago by exhibitions of the work of state and local boards of health. None of these exhibits created more favorable comment than that of the State Board of Health of Massachusetts. Of the total of ten thousand square feet of space to be allotted to this subject, Massachusetts obtained six hundred and twenty square feet. The Board then directed the preparation of an exhibit representing the progress of public hygiene in the State. This consisted of a complete set of reports of the State Board of Health from 1869 to 1891, special reports, circulars upon infectious diseases, sets of blank forms in use by the Board, the manual of health laws, reports of city boards of health for 1892, charts and diagrams illustrating such phenomena as the death rate for a series of years, the effect of density of population on the general death rate, the rates of special diseases, and seasonal mortality rates. There were maps giving geographical distribution of diseases. The engineering section having water supply and sewage control in its care presented a complete and perfect replica of the Lawrence Experiment Station, to the scale of one half inch to the foot, a sand sieve, steam sterilizer, thermostat galvanized iron filter, complete battery of stills, sections of sand filters in glass tubes, apparatus for determining the color of waters, bacteria stand, with tubes, and charts, photographs, and maps showing details of the many phases of its work. The section of food and drugs sent charts showing ratios of adulteration of milk, other kinds of food and spices in the State, of the ratio of expenditures for food, clothing, rent, and fuel in different countries, and of allied subjects. It also presented samples of pure food, adulterants, and models of trichinae. Professor W. T. Sedgwick went to Chicago and installed the exhibit. Thousands of individuals visited the exhibit during the Fair and especially during the week of the Congress of Public Hygiene. The exhibit received very favorable comment in the various medical and sanitary periodicals in the United States and in foreign countries.

Commission Appointed to Plan Improvement in Charles River, 1893. This was the year in which a commission, composed of the State Board of Health and the Metropolitan Park Commission, studied and reported favorably upon the plan for beautifying the Charles River by building locks to control the water level, which would prevent its being a mud-flat when the water was low. The plan went further and considered the beautifying of the river's banks.

Act Passed Requiring Reporting of all Deaths in Towns of Over Five Thousand, 1894. In 1894, an act was passed which required all cities and towns of over five thousand population to send an annual report of all deaths to the State Board of Health. The office of the Board was established in the State House in 1894. This was also the year in which the secretary of the Board, Dr. Samuel Abbott, began his famous annual analysis of the vital statistics of Massachusetts. Dr. Abbott began his first paper on the subject as follows: "Among the duties which were proposed and carefully defined by the Massachusetts Sanitary Commission of 1850 as properly belonging to a general or State board of health, special prominence was given to that of supervising the vital statistics of the State.

"The intimate connection between the vital statistics of a State or nation and its public health must be everywhere acknowledged, since the former constitutes the only accurate measure of the efficiency with which public health measures have been administered. An annually increasing demand made upon the Board for information relative to the vital statistics of the State makes it necessary to supply this information through the annual reports of the Board."

The Establishment of the Antitoxin and Bacteriological Laboratories, 1895. In 1894, Dr. Walcott, following the example of New York City, wished to establish a laboratory where antitoxin could be manufactured

was such a drastic change from previous custom. The work was begun in 1894 on a tentative basis, but in 1895, Theobald Smith, one of the foremost of American scientists, became director of the newly established antitoxin laboratory. He had been the chief of the Division of Pathology in the Bureau of Animal Industry at Washington, D. C. His official title was Pathologist of the Board of Health in Massachusetts. The Board was able to obtain his services through the gift of Dr. George F. Fabyan, who endowed the Fabyan Chair in Comparative Pathology at Harvard Medical School. Dr. Smith was the first incumbent. For the next nine years, Dr. Smith used the laboratory in the Bussey Institute which was part of a bequest of the late Benjamin Bussey to Harvard College. Dr. Smith made a European trip to study the latest developments in vaccine. In addition to the manufacture of biologicals, Dr. Smith made many scientific investigations, among which his remarkable work on human and bovine tuberculosis should be mentioned.

The act creating the Board in 1869 had required it to "take cognizance of the interests of health and life among the citizens of the Commonwealth," and it was under this provision that the Board had provided, in 1895, for the supply of antitoxin to be used in the State to lessen the mortality from diphtheria. In connection with the same work, a bacteriological laboratory was established for the purpose of experimental work in the investigation of some of the infectious diseases; namely, for the diagnosis of diphtheria and tuberculosis, and for the examination of the blood of patients suspected of having malaria.

The Beginning of Tuberculosis Control as a State Problem, 1895. On June 5, 1895, in accordance with the provisions of Chapter 503 of the Statutes of 1895 of the Massachusetts Legislature, a bill was approved for the establishment of a so-called "Massachusetts Hospital for Consumptives and Tubercular Patients," and a board of five trustees was appointed by the Governor and Council. This was the first instance in America of the foundation of·a state institution for the treatment of tuberculosis. At first this sanatorium was for advanced and hopeless cases. Gradually, it altered its policy and admitted early cases with a chance of cure.

Although in the early years the program of tuberculosis control was not administratively in the hands of the Board of Health, it cannot be unrelated from the work of the Board, and many years later it was incorporated with the Massachusetts Department of Public Health. In the famous 1850 report, Lemuel Shattuck specifically stated that it was imperative that the Massachusetts Legislature recognize the need for "particular observation and investigation of the causes of consumption and the circumstances under which it occurs," on the ground that "if consumption is ever to be eradicated or ameliorated it can only be done by preventive means and not by cure." The first chairman of the State Board of Health, Dr. Henry I. Bowditch, had acquired an international reputation as an authority on pulmonary consumption because of his investigation of the influence of soil moisture on the prevalence of consumption in New England. He indicated the future policy of the Board of Health in his first address before it in September, 1869, in the statement that one of the fundamental principles of a board of health was "to take care of the public health, to investigate the causes of epidemic and other diseases, in order that each citizen may not only have as long a life as nature would give him, but likewise as healthy a life as possible."

Dr. George Derby, the Board's first secretary, had, previous to his appointment, attracted much attention for his statistical work on pulmonary tuberculosis. In his first report, he stated, "If there is any one disease which more than another would seem to favor the views of the advocates of the predestined and the inevitable, it is that terrible scourge, far more to be dreaded than cholera, consumption. It has been regarded as a special mode intended by Providence to reduce a redundant population, as feeble trees in a forest are crowded out of existence by their more vigorous neighbors. And there is much in the history of the disease which makes such arguments plausible. It is found everywhere in civilized communities, in the South as well as the North, seeming to be generally distributed. Yet the kind of investigation of its natural history and of its causes which we are able to make in these latter days, through the aid of vital statistics, and by the comparison of great numbers of cases, shows that this is far from being true, and places us directly upon the path leading to a discovery of the conditions under which it originates--conditions which, when fully recognized, may be avoided. That its causes are many is certain; that some of them are obscure, and even quite unknown as yet, is very probable. But others are fully revealed, and are influencing practice and saving life."

He went on to emphasize the importance of fresh air. "Fresh air, by day and by night, strong and nourishing food, dry soil on which to live, sunlight and warm clothing are the means of saving many lives which would have been hopelessly lost in the preceding generation . . . Let in the sunlight, and never mind the carpets; better they should fade than the health of the family."

In the report of the Board for 1871 was a reply to the Legislature of 1870 concerning the comparative health of minors employed in various industries. About 40 per cent of all deaths between the ages of fifteen and nineteen in Massachusetts was due to pulmonary tuberculosis. At first it appeared that the mortality was the same among factory children as among the general population, but when it was learned that upon becoming ill the children withdrew and were lost sight of, it became apparent that the mortality was probably higher among the children in factories. In every annual report of the Board of Health, thereafter, there was either a paper on some phase of the tuberculosis problem or, at least statistical reference to the disease.

In 1895, a widely read circular was issued by the Board furnishing information to the public on the nature of pulmonary consumption, the conditions which favor its spread, and the best methods of preventing it, and the Board of Health began the free examination of the sputum or other material for the bacilli of tuberculosis. These specimens came from all over the State.

Abbott's Report on "Vital Statistics of Massachusetts from 1856 to 1895," 1896. In the 1896 report of the Board, the famous paper of Abbott on the "Vital Statistics of Massachusetts from 1856 to 1895" was published.

In January, 1897, the laboratory for water analysis was transferred from the Institute of Technology to the State House, where ample provision was made for this work upon the fifth floor of the new extension. Mr. H. W. Clark, chemist of the Board, who for several years had had charge of the laboratory at the Lawrence Experiment Station, was placed in charge of the laboratory at the State House. The work on water and sewage, and on drainage of certain marshes, progressed with creditable rapidity throughout this period.

Whitney's Report on Cancer, 1899. In the report of 1899 it was stated that an investigation was in progress having "reference to the causes and conditions prevailing throughout the State in connection with the existence of cancer among the population." The statistical section of the study was entrusted to Dr. W. F. Whitney. The report of the Board of Health for 1900 printed the conclusions of Whitney's famous and often referred to paper on cancer.

In 1900, the Board of Health of Massachusetts sent some material to the Paris Exposition for display. The following year, the Board used the same exhibit at the Pan-American Exposition at Buffalo.

Blood Tests of Typhoid Suspects Added to Work of Bacteriological Laboratory, 1900. In 1900, bloodtests of typhoid suspects were added to the work of the bacteriological laboratory which had formerly been limited to the diagnosis of diphtheria, tuberculosis, and the examination of the blood of individuals suspected of having malaria.

Distribution of Smallpox Vaccine Authorized, 1903. In 1903, the Legislature authorized the distribution of smallpox vaccine in addition to antitoxin.

Dr. Samuel Abbott's Death, 1904. In 1904, Dr. Samuel Abbott, after eighteen years with the Board, died. It was through his office that all the clerical work of the Board had been carried on. He was an authority in vital statistics as well as in medicine. The Registration Reports of Massachusetts from 1886 to 1890 were edited by him, and to him also belongs the credit for the excellence of the statistical matter in the reports of the State Board of Health. His paper on the "Past and Present Condition of Public Hygiene and State Medicine in the United States" is invaluable. In the words of his friend, General Morris Schaff, "Dr. Abbott came near being the most ideal public servant that this Commonwealth ever had or ever will have in her service."

In 1905, the Legislature passed a resolve authorizing the State

Board of Health "to cause a public exhibition to be made of the various means and methods used or recommended for treating and preventing tuberculosis, now recognized as a communicable and preventable disease." This was held in Horticultural Hall, Boston, from December 28, 1905, to January 7, 1906, inclusive. Every interested person and society was asked to make this educational exhibit effective for the citizenry of the State. The total attendance was 25,953 persons, or a daily average of 2,355 persons. Special meetings were held at the same time and every class and type of individual in the State was reached. The next year the Board of Health drew attention to the influence of the dusty trades on tuberculosis. This was one of the main reasons for the act of the Legislature apportioning the State into fifteen health districts, in each of which a State Inspector of Health was appointed.

State Inspectors of Health Appointed, 1907.

This occurred in 1907 and greatly expanded the work of the Board. It brought the Board into much closer contact with the local communities. This was the first time in the United States that health work had been carried on in this way. Since then, other states have copied this example.

The value of the State Health Inspectors may be appreciated by an excerpt from one of the annual reports, "Of the many duties imposed by the Legislature upon the State Inspectors of Health, none are of greater importance or more far-reaching in their effects upon the conservation of the health of the inhabitants than is the requirement that the State Inspectors of Health inform themselves concerning all influences that are or may be dangerous to the public health within their districts, and to gather all possible information relative to the prevalence of communicable diseases and to co-operate with the local health authorities in their eradication. Acting in an advisory capacity, the State Inspectors of Health have co-operated with the local boards of health throughout the State and have assisted them in various ways. Frequent conferences were held by the State Inspectors of Health with the local boards of health in the various districts. These conferences were often asked for by the local health officials who have come to rely on advice and guidance from the State Inspectors of Health in dealing with local health problems. In their dealing with local health problems the State Inspectors of Health had often to meet town officials, finance commissions, influential citizens, and physicians practicing in various communities. The range of subjects along which assistance was rendered to local boards of health covered almost every problem on health matters which is apt to come up in any community."

Creation of the State Board of Labor and Industries, 1912. In 1912, the Legislature enacted a law creating a State Board of Labor and Industries. All the duties of the State Inspectors of Health relative to the enforcement of laws in factories, workshops, and mercantile establishments were transferred to the new Board on June 1, 1913. The transferred duties included the inspection and licensing of tenement-house workrooms where work is done on wearing apparel; the enforcement of the provisions relative to proper water closets for women in mercantile establishments; the enforcement of all the provisions relative to cleanliness, ventilation, and washing facilities in all industries; the investigation of lighting conditions in factories and workshops and eye injuries to operatives; the enforcement of laws relative to the purity and use of water for humidifying purposes, and the regulation of humidity and temperature of the atmosphere in textile factories; the prohibition of the use of suction shuttles in factories; the regulation of conditions relative to the employment of women in core rooms; the constant appraisal of the health of all minors employed in factories; and the exclusion of minors from occupations injurious to health.

Of the duties imposed on the State Inspectors of Health by the original act of 1907, and by subsequent legislation, the following duties remained in force: information was to be gathered concerning all influences that might be dangerous to the public health, and concerning the prevalence of tuberculosis and other diseases dangerous to the public health; knowledge was to be disseminated as to the best methods of preventing the spread of such diseases, and steps were to be taken to effect their eradication; the State Board of Health was to be aided in the enforcement of laws relative to the maintenance of isolation hospitals, tuberculosis hospitals and tuberculosis dispensaries, and in the enforcement of laws relative to furnishing drinking water on passenger trains; examinations were to be made of school buildings, police station houses, houses of detention, jails, houses of correction, prisons and reformatories; and, finally, the Inspectors were to perform such duties as the State Board of Health might impose upon them from time to time.

Study of Rabies, 1910; Silver Nitrate Furnished for Use in Eyes of New Born, 1910. An intensive study of rabies was begun in 1909. It was found that it would be more expensive for the State to manufacture the material for the Pasteur treatment than to buy it. Beginning in 1910, the laboratory furnished silver nitrate for use in the eyes of the new born as a preventive of blindness. Dr. Smith resigned from the laboratory in 1914, and the work was carried on under the supervision of Dr. Milton J. Rosenau, Professor of Preventive Medicine and Hygiene in the Harvard Medical School.

End of State Board of Health, July 7, 1914. July 7, 1914, was a very important date in the history of the health movement in Massachusetts. On that day the State Board of Health came to an end, and with it the service of two of the men who had made health history in this State. One was Hiram F. Mills, a civil engineer, and the other was Henry P. Walcott, a physician. These two men had worked together continuously for the State Board of Health for twenty-eight years since 1886. Previous to that time, Dr. Walcott had served for six years as health officer and Board member.

Hiram Francis Mills. Hiram Francis Mills was an hydraulic engineer and sanitary expert. He was in general practice for eleven years in Boston and his name is connected with such engineering feats as the Bergen tunnel of the Brooklyn Water Works, the famous Hoosac tunnel in western Massachusetts, and the construction of the dam across the Deerfield River. As an expert in his chosen field, his services have been in demand throughout the country and the results of his work are found in many states. In 1886, Mr. Mills was appointed a member of the State Board of Health and remained with it until the Board went out of existence in 1914. Throughout this long period, he devoted his time and study to the State without remuneration. He was chairman of the Committee on Water Supply and Sewerage, and it was under him that the famous Experiment Station at Lawrence was built in 1892, on land owned by the Essex Water Power Company for which Mr. Mills had been an agent and engineer for several years. This was the first large scientifically designed municipal filter in America. An immediate decrease in the death rate from water borne typhoid fever followed its installation. In addition to its local benefit, it has been the pattern from which similar filters have been built all over this country and in Europe. To Mr. Mills is due much of the credit for the purification of our water supplies, with the consequent betterment of the public health.

Henry Pickering Walcott. Henry Pickering Walcott attained outstanding recognition in every field in which he was interested. To name but a few, he was chairman of the Board of Trustees of the Massachusetts General Hospital, a member of the Corporation and twice acting president of Harvard University, chairman of the Metropolitan Water and Sewerage Board, as well as chairman of the State Board of Health for the duration of its existence.

Dr. Walcott's services to the State were memorialized by 2,200 members of the medical profession in the State upon the termination of his connection with the State Board of Health. Among other important comments, the memorial stated, "Since the re-establishment of the State Board of Health in 1886, under your chairmanship, it has been the custom of the legislature to refer all important sanitary questions to that Board for investigation and advice, instead of creating special commissions, as obtains in many states. This custom, under your wise administration, has doubtless saved much money to the State and, at the same time, secured sanitary improvements recognized in all civilized countries as the best of their class.

"The investigations and recommendations of the Board have commended themselves to the legislature and in general have been carried out ultimately as presented.

"From 1886 to the present time, you have been constantly and steadfastly facing these great and grave problems. Since 1895, when the State Board of Health made its report to the legislature, presenting a plan for the water supply of the City of Boston and the surrounding cities and towns, have been added to your responsibilities those of a commissionership on the Metropolitan Water Board. You have borne the responsibilities both of recommendation and of execution. . . .

"You have met the responsibilities then assumed with such wisdom, discretion, and rare modesty, as to make the task of your successor who would uphold the standards bequeathed to him a difficult one indeed."

It is impossible to enter into detail in the life of this pioneer in health work. The accomplishments of the Board from 1886 to 1914 speak for themselves.

The State Board of Health had been enlarged in its scope by several statutes in the years since its establishment. The duties of the original Board were of an advisory nature. Gradually, these had expanded to include executive powers. The addition of such acts as the one which gave the Board co-ordinate powers with local boards of health were enacted periodically, thus increasing the executive functions of the Board. By 1907, when Health Inspectors were added, these executive powers had differentiated and were well enough established to cope with the great expansion in policy of that year. The advisory nature of the Board was still its strongest feature, and has remained unimpaired through the several reorganizations. These were the forces that led to the establishment of the State Department of Health.

State Department of Health (July 7, 1914 to December 1, 1919)

On July 7, 1914, the State Department of Health was created. This replaced the old Board of Health and inaugurated a new era in health administration. The act authorized the appointment of a Commissioner of Health and a Public Health Council of six members. The duties of the Council were to make and promulgate rules and regulations, to take evidence in appeals, to consider plans and appointments required by law, to hold hearings, to submit annually to the General Court and to the Governor a report including recommendations as to health legislation. It was to have no administrative or executive function. The Commissioner of Health was to administer laws relative to health; prepare rules and regulations for the consideration of the Public Health Council; with the approval of the Council appoint and remove division directors, district health officers, and other employees; and perform all executive duties.

In the State Department of Health there were to be such divisions as the Commissioner of Health, with the approval of the Public Health Council, determined. In place of the Health Inspectors of the former Board, District Health Officers were authorized who had all the powers of the inspectors and, in addition, were to act as representatives of the Commissioner of Health and, under his direction, were to secure the enforcement within their districts of the public health laws and regulations.

Dr. Allan McLaughlin, of the United States Public Health Service, was appointed by Governor Walsh as the first Commissioner of Health of Massachusetts. At the request of the Governor, Dr. McLaughlin had been granted a leave of absence from the service of the United States Government.

The divisions first organized included Administration, Sanitary Engineering, Water and Sewage Laboratories, Food and Drugs, Communicable Diseases, Biologic Laboratories, and Hygiene.

Diagnostic Facilities for Diagnosis of Venereal Disease Established, 1914. In 1914, laboratory facilities for the diagnosis of venereal disease were provided. The Wassermann Laboratory was established June 1, 1915. A circular letter was sent to all the District Health Officers, to all the institutions under the control of the State Board of Charity, the State Board of Insanity, the Board of Prison Commissions, and a special issue of the "Public Health Bulletin," to every physician in the State announcing the inauguration of this service. In the first six months of its existence, the laboratory examined a total of 6491 specimens. The annual report of the Department for 1915 gave an intuitive account of the meaning of this extension of service: "The prompt recognition and treatment of syphilis is a public health problem of the first importance. It means a decrease in the incidence of those obstinate late manifestations of the disease which affect the heart, the blood vessels, the brain and spinal cord, the results of which are usually serious and often incurable, or may only be relieved after great suffering and expense to the patient, his family or the Commonwealth, if he becomes a public charge. It means a decrease in the number of miscarriages and stillbirths, and in the congenital syphilitics who either die early or are often greatly handicapped constitutionally. It prevents in many cases needless major surgical operations by correctly diagnosing a syphilitic condition. In all of these instances a correct Wassermann test gives larger value than the sum total of all other methods used in the diagnosis of the disease."

Division of Hygiene Established, May 1, 1915. The Division of Hygiene was created May 1, 1915. As this was a new departure from precedent, the division had to work out its own aims and policies. It devoted itself first to a statistical study of infant mortality. A lecture service was organized, with the cooperation of the Division of Communicable Diseases, which included talks and stereopticon lectures on such subjects as child welfare, how to keep well, milk, public health nursing, cancer, tuberculosis, pure food, school hygiene, and the care of the teeth. The division constructed an infant welfare exhibit which was shown in many places. Two public health nurses were placed on the staff of this division and were the nucleus of the subdivision of public health nursing established four years later. The Division of Hygiene stimulated the introduction of the various health weeks which have become increasingly popular. The first year of its existence, it made a study, through the District Health Officers, of the question of school hygiene. It took over the editing of the regular monthly bulletin and prepared the booklet, "The Baby and You," for distribution. The following year a nutritionist was added to the staff. This division was established to educate the public so that the lag between existing and applied knowledge might be shortened.

In 1916, the Division of Animal Industry transferred its diagnostic service to the Division of Biologic Laboratories. The General Court of

1916 authorized the expenditure of ten thousand dollars for a product similar to salvarsan for free distribution in the Commonwealth.

Pneumonia Made Reportable, 1917. In 1917, the Department made pneumonia reportable. The same year, the manufacture and distribution of anti-pneumococcus serum for Type I and Type II pneumonia was begun.

Venereal Disease Program Planned, 1917. The problem of venereal diseases received much attention because of the wartime effort to effect its control. The details of a program for handling the reporting of gonorrhea and syphilis was formulated in 1917. By this year, the furnishing of free diagnostic facilities was an accomplished fact. Although efforts were being made to establish a State-wide chain of fifteen venereal disease clinics, this was not accomplished until later. An attempt was also made to prohibit the dispensing of remedies for these diseases by druggists, except upon the written prescription of a physician. Many of the druggists in the State voluntarily consented to abstain from this practice.

Subdivision of Venereal Disease Established, 1918. By 1918, the interalliance of the venereal disease program of the War Department, the United States Public Health Service, the Commission on Training Camp Activities, and the State Department of Health in Massachusetts and other states, was accomplished. It was during 1918 that the Federal Government passed the Kahn-Chamberlain law which divided one million dollars annually among the states for anti-venereal disease work under regulations laid down by the United States Public Health Service and conditional upon each state appropriating an equal amount. This State accepted its share until three years later, when Congress failed to appropriate the money. The manufacture of arsphenamine reached the factory stage this year, and approached a regular quantity production sufficient for all the needs of the State. A subdivision of venereal disease was formed by the Division of Communicable Diseases and twelve State-aided venereal disease clinics were established.

Teaching of Hygiene Introduced into the Schools, 1918. A study of the draft had shown that from one third to one fourth of those examined suffered from physical defects that might have been prevented or corrected if detected in childhood. The Division of Hygiene, in cooperation with the State Board of Education, introduced the teaching of hygiene into the schools in an effort to solve the problem.

Dr. McLaughlin was recalled to the United States Public Health Service in 1918 on account of the World War, and Dr. Eugene R. Kelley, the director of the Division of Communicable Diseases, formerly Commissioner of Public Health in the state of Washington, was appointed his successor.

Influenza Epidemic, 1918. The most disastrous epidemic the State ever had was the influenza epidemic of 1918. The early records indicated that the initial point of invasion into the country was among the naval units within this State. Massachusetts suffered greater proportional infection and fatality than any other state. Over fifteen thousand deaths occurred, exclusive of deaths among the military forces, and four hundred thousand persons were ill from the beginning, in the second week of September, to December 1. Early in the epidemic, influenza was added to the list of notifiable diseases. The war had made a great drain upon the medical and nursing personnel of the State. An appeal was sent to the Federal Government for aid. On September 30 the United States Public Health Service sent assistant surgeon M. S. Draper, with seven commissioned officers as assistants, to Massachusetts. In addition, physicians and nurses from all over the country came and gave unsparingly of their energy and knowledge. The influenza epidemic demonstrated that some coordinating agency should assist persons temporarily unable to care for themselves, to find help until they could be readjusted in normal conditions. Dr. Kelley recommended the study of medical social service as a possible means of approach to this problem.

Department of Public Health (December 1, 1919 to———)

In 1919, a reorganization of the Department was authorized. The name was changed to the Department of Public Health and the four State tuberculosis sanatoria and the Penikese leper hospital were placed under its supervision. The same year, the Legislature appropriated money for cancer investigations. This permitted the Department to co-operate with the Harvard Cancer Commission in furnishing pathological diagnosis.

Mouth Hygiene Added to Educational Work of the Division of Hygiene, 1919. The subject of mouth hygiene was added to the educational program of the Division of Hygiene in 1919. The same year, in carrying out Dr. Kelley's plan for determining ways of safeguarding the health and life of mothers and infants, the Division of Hygiene, with the aid of the District Health Officers, made an intensive study of midwifery in Massachusetts.

Division of Tuberculosis Established, January 1, 1920. On January 1, 1920, the Division of Tuberculosis was established. This replaced the former board of trustees for hospitals for consumptives and took over the departmental work on tuberculosis done previously by the Division of Communicable Diseases.

Survey of Seaport Cities and Towns for Potential Bubonic Plague, 1920. The Legislature, in 1920, directed the Department to conduct a survey of the seaport cities and towns to see what measures were necessary for the prevention of bubonic plague. Four rat trappers were employed and the waterfront of the city of Boston trapped. Six thousand two hundred rats were caught. None of the rats was found to be infected.

The leper hospital at Penikese Island was closed in 1921, and the patients removed to the federal institution at Carville, Louisiana. This same year, the name of the Department bulletin became "The Commonhealth."

Maternal and Infant Hygiene Activities Extended and Radio Broadcasting Begun, 1922. In lieu of accepting money for the Sheppard Towner act, the Legislature appropriated money for the Department of Public Health to extend the maternal and infant hygiene activities in 1922. In June, 1922, the Springfield Westinghouse Company offered the use of its station to the Department of Public Health for broadcasting health talks. This was the beginning of the radio educational program.

An intensive drive to prevent diphtheria was inaugurated this same year. Over ninety-five thousand doses of toxin-antitoxin were distributed.

Ten-Year Tuberculosis Program for Detection of Tuberculosis in Children Begun, 1924. The ten-year tuberculosis program for the early detection of tuberculosis in children, named the Chadwick Clinics, after its founder, Dr. Henry D. Chadwick, received legislative approval and was begun in 1924.

Twenty years of research by thousands of workers had shifted the emphasis in tuberculosis from the obvious pulmonary cases of adults to the earlier or more incipient stage in which it is to be found in the lymphatic nodes of children. This usually occurs in children under twelve years of age. From experience, it was found that their resistance to tuberculosis could be built up by sanatorium treatment which comprised fresh air and sunshine, regulated physical activity, sufficient sleep, and an adequate and well planned dietary.

This led to the practical consideration of the problem. Tuberculosis in adults is a very serious and often fatal disease. It is decreasing but, nevertheless, constitutes a major item of expense for the State, community, family, and individual. It represents, in many instances, an extension of a previously existing tuberculosis in childhood of an entirely different nature. The childhood type of tuberculosis is relatively easy to control and treatment, if instituted early, will prevent the development of the more serious adult pulmonary type of the disease.

Dr. Chadwick, through his observation of the children at Westfield, felt that cases of childhood type tuberculosis might be detected by physical examination before symptoms obvious enough had developed to necessitate a visit to the physician. He was impressed by the subnormal condition in development and nutrition of many of the children admitted to Westfield. The superintendent of the Westfield public schools agreed to allow him to make an examination for the presence of tuberculosis of a group of children falling below the standards of weight and height, together with children known to have been exposed to tuberculosis in their homes. The work was very thoroughly carried out and cases similar to those in the sanatorium were found attending school. Recognizing the statistical fallacy of basing far-reaching conclusions on an inadequate sample, the Department cooperated in carrying out the same plan in other communities.

It was estimated that 15 per cent of the children in the schools of Massachusetts between the ages of five and twelve were in the three groups: either 10 per cent or more underweight or underheight for their age, either contact cases exposed to tuberculosis at home, or children whose physical condition was considered unsatisfactory by teacher or family physician. On this basis, there were, in 1923, 110,000 children in these groups in the State and it was estimated that about 8 per cent of them would show some evidence of tuberculosis if examined by tuberculin test and X-ray of the reactors. In other words, from eight to nine thousand children would be discovered in this way who should be placed under better hygienic conitions, thereby hoping to prevent the development of the serious adult form of tuberculosis.

The Chadwick Clinics were organized and a staff of physicians, nutritionists, and nurses were appointed to carry out the plan. The closest cooperation existed between this staff and the family physicians, to whom all positive and suspicious cases were referred. Local boards of health with their dispensary and nursing staffs, the school departments with their physicians, nurses, and nutritionists, and the summer camps and preventoria, played important parts through their enthusiastic participation.

Cancer Study, 1925. In 1925, under legislative authority, the Department studied the cancer situation in Massachusetts. In the same year occurred the death of Dr. Eugene R. Kelley, who was succeeded by the Deputy Commissioner, Dr. George H. Bigelow.

Dr. Eugene R. Kelley. Dr. Kelley had guided the Department through several years of progressive development. He had the vision to sponsor the school clinics on a State-wide scale, to see the value and extend the field of technical health education, to carry out the additional responsibility of State supervision of food handling and food handlers, to coordinate the activities of the several divisions by centralized administration, to join in the nation-wide move for the development of infant, child, and maternal hygiene, to work out the administrative details for the development of the venereal disease campaign which received such initial impetus by the wartime focus on the subject, to urge the continuance of the progress in sanitary engineering, and to recognize and accept the responsibility of cancer and other chronic diseases as a potential public health problem. It would be hard to match such a record of achievement.

Establishment of Cancer Program, 1926. In 1926, the Legislature authorized the inauguration of the cancer program. This program had five main features: a tumor diagnostic service, statistical research for the evaluation of the problem, clinics for group diagnosis of suspected or actual cancer, the Pondville Hospital for providing the best known methods in diagnosis and treatment of cancer, and education for the dissemination of exact information concerning cancer to every individual in the State with the hope of eventually sublimating the current groundless fears and phobias. It was a new departure from established lines and extended the scope of public health to include chronic disease.

Hinton Test Introduced, 1927. In 1927, Dr. William A. Hinton, chief of the Wassermann Laboratory, devised a serological test for syphilis that has proved to be simpler and more sensitive than the Wassermann test.

The Status of Milk. By 1927, cities representing 47 per cent of the population of the State required that milk sold within their borders be either pasteurized or from tuberculosis-free cows. The septic sore throat epidemic of July, 1928, in one of the communities not requiring milk of this nature, was caused by drinking raw milk from a cow found to be grossly infected with a hemolytic streptococcus, and brought the advantages of pasteurized milk graphically to the attention of the citizenry of the State. It did not effect immediate State-wide results, however, although Dr. Bigelow made a continuous and valiant fight for universal pasteurization or for the use of milk from only non-tuberculous cows. At the present time thirty cities and towns, with a population of more than two million, have an ordinance in force which requires that all milk sold in these communities be either pasteurized or certified.

Chronic Disease Survey, 1929. In 1929, a morbidity study, information for which was obtained in house-to-house surveys in Winchester and Shelburne Falls, was published. This was the experimental step in the study of chronic diseases which culminated in the volume entitled, "Cancer and Other Chronic Diseases in Massachusetts," by Bigelow and Lombard.

Establishment of Health Units and of Divisions of Child and Adult Hygiene, 1929. In 1929, legislation was passed permitting several small towns to unite and form a health district so that the smaller communities could obtain the benefit of health supervision by trained personnel at a minimum cost. This same year, the Division of Adult Hygiene was formed and some of the activities previously carried on by the Division of Hygiene were transferred to it. The former Division of Hygiene became the Division of Child Hygiene. The Division of Adult Hygiene began, in 1929, an intensive three-year study of chronic disease throughout the State. The knowledge of the prevalence of cases rather than deaths from chronic disease, their economic distribution, their interference with work, and the resources for their diagnosis and treatment was necessary as a basis for the whole program of adult hygiene.

Mr. X. H. Goodnough. The Department lost, through retirement, Mr. X. H. Goodnough, who, as chief engineer for the Department since 1886, had guided the development of the public water supplies and supervision of inland waters from the beginning. Largely through his foresight and direction, about 97 per cent of the people of the Commonwealth now have safe water supplies and water-borne outbreaks of disease are no longer to be feared.

In 1930, the Commonwealth Fund made a grant to the Department to be used to organize rural towns into health districts. Two such districts are now operating, one in Southern Berkshire centering about Great Barrington, and the other the Nashoba district centering about Ayer. The Rockefeller Foundation assisted financially in the statistical and epidemiological study of tuberculosis.

Program for Pneumonia Control, 1931. In 1931, the Commonwealth Fund again assisted the Department financially in a program for pneumonia control. In view of the high mortality from lobar pneumonia, attempts at some control had been in progress for several years. The Department had been working in a few hospitals with a concentrated antibody solution which seemed to offer hope for success. The grant from the Commonwealth Fund made it possible to continue and extend this work.

Infantile Paralysis Service, 1931. During the summer and fall, 1428 cases of infantile paralysis caused an emergency service to be developed in the Department that was noteworthy. Over six hundred previous sufferers volunteered their blood to help those afflicted. The Department, in cooperation with the Harvard Infantile Paralysis Commission, saw in consultation 75 per cent of those affected in the Connecticut Valley where the epidemic was centered.

In 1931, the Rockefeller Foundation gave financial assistance for a comprehensive three-year study on cancer and arthritis.

Dr. George H. Bigelow. Dr. George H. Bigelow left the Department in 1933 to assume directorship of the Massachusetts General Hospital and was succeeded by Dr. Henry D. Chadwick. Dr. Bigelow had been Commissioner since 1925, and had served the Department for several years before his appointment as Commissioner. When he assumed leadership, the Department of Public Health was adapting itself to the rapidly increasing growth of administrative and advisory duties which had been granted to it since 1914. The State and country were just emerging from the first post-war economic depression only to be plunged into the second and more lasting depression of the last several years. These external conditions had a very definite bearing on the whole policy of the State, and Dr. Bigelow was acutely conscious of their actual and implied potentialities.

He was an able, fearless administrator. If personal effort could have achieved the immediate passage of laws to allow only pasteurized milk or milk from non-tuberculous cows to be sold, or the immediate and possible eradication of rabies, to mention only two of the projects for which he fought against overwhelming odds, these things would have been accomplished years ago. He saw the advantages of medical social service and incorporated this addition to the Department. He worked for proper scientific shellfish control. He established health units and a Division of Adult Hygiene, the first of its kind in the United States. He obeyed the legislative mandate concerning cancer control with characteristic enthusiasm, even though he questioned its place in the field of preventive medicine. The Department, under his leadership, made notable contributions epidemiologically and otherwise to many fields of research, particularly in chronic disease. The work of every division was broadened, and every division and individual felt the influence of his enthusiasm. The tradition of his predecessors to lead to new heights by personal example was nowhere better demonstrated than in Dr. Bigelow.

Harry W. Clark. Mr. Harry W. Clark retired in 1933. For forty-five years he had worked as chemist in health work for the State. He was a pioneer in the scientific discovery of methods of water, sewage, and industrial waste treatment and purification. His contributions in this connection and in matters pertaining to environmental control have made him and, through him, the Massachusetts Department of Public Health, famous throughout the world.

Silicosis Study, 1933. Under Chapter 43 of the Resolves of 1933, the Commissioner of Public Health was made a member of the Industrial Disease Commission to study the incidence of the disease silicosis in the granite and foundry industries. A comprehensive study of working conditions was undertaken. "This involved the study of the kinds and size of dust particles, their concentration in the air being inhaled by different classes of employees, and the evidence of disease that could be attributed to the conditions to which the workmen were exposed in the course of their employment." When needed for diagnosis, X-rays were taken. The study was the most comprehensive of any in the country on this subject. It was recognized that the installation of dust removing devices and periodic X-ray examination of the men would decrease the health hazard and effect the early detection of tuberculosis common among workers in these industries.

Completion of Fourth Year of Pneumonia Study, 1934. The pneumonia study completed its fourth year in 1934, and the evidence showed definitely that the lives of many patients ill with Type I and Type II pneumonia had been saved by the use of the serum.

The Rockefeller Foundation continued in its support of the cancer study, and also assisted in financing the work of tabulation and study of the records obtained in the ten-year program for the examination of school children which completed its last year in 1934.

Results of the Chadwick Clinics, 1934. The decentralization of the work of the Chadwick Clinics was begun this year. The county sanatoria, the State sanatoria, and some of the larger cities are taking over the work and will continue it in effect. The results may be stated as follows: "Briefly, we may say that 400,000 school children have been examined. These clinics have been held in practically every city and town in the Commonwealth and in some of them twice. This extensive program has brought the subject of tuberculosis, its diagnosis and treatment to the attention of parents, teachers, nurses and doctors and has created, we believe, a consciousness of the problem of tuberculosis which is bound to be of the greatest value in the application of further control measures. It is practical health education."

Study on Value of Placental Extract in Control of Measles, 1933. The Commonwealth Fund made a grant to Harvard Medical School for a study to be carried out jointly by the Pediatrics Department of the Children's Hospital and the Department of Public Health on the value of placental extract in the control of measles. In a series of one thousand children exposed to measles and treated with this extract, in about 95 per cent of the cases the attack was prevented or at least modified. This was considered very encouraging.

Ten-Year Plan for Increasing the Natural Recreational Facilities of the State, 1933. The Department of Public Health, in association with the Department of Conservation and the Metropolitan District Commission, prepared a ten-year plan for increasing the recreational facilities of the State.

The Revised Cancer Program, 1934. In October, 1934, a critical analysis of the cancer program was undertaken to determine its advantages and shortcomings. Certain large areas of the State were so far removed from a cancer clinic that attendance was almost impossible. Several new clinics were added so that now practically every individual in the State lives within twenty-five miles, at least, of a cancer clinic. The clinics themselves were improved. Frequent local teaching clinics, conducted by recognized authorities on cancer, were added. The educational program was fundamentally changed. It was recognized that the general education in cancer that had gone on for years was excellent because it had laid the foundation in the public mind for the acceptance of the more specific and personal instruction which would have to follow before the results of education would become tangible in shortened delay between observed symptoms and adequate therapy. The family physician was made the central force in the new plan. The organization of a cooperative cancer control committee in every city and town in the State was begun. Each of these committees includes representatives of all organizations in the community. Each individual member is asked to arrange with the organization that he represents for at least one meeting a year at which cancer will be discussed by one of the local physicians.

Massachusetts State Health Commission, 1934. A very important step in public health planning was taken with the appointment by the Governor of the Massachusetts State Health Commission. A study of the reports of the Department, under its several names, shows that careful planning has been the underlying basis of its advance from the beginning. Dr. Eugene R. Kelley and Dr. George H. Bigelow had both felt that the time had arrived to survey the health policies of the State, but this was not attempted until 1934. In October, 1934, the Massachusetts Central Health Council, an organization composed of fifteen public and private State-wide health agencies, appointed a committee to stimulate interest in and take the necessary legislative action for a survey of health practices of Massachusetts. A grant of ten thousand dollars was secured from the Commonwealth Fund to defray the cost of the study. The members of the Commission were as follows:

Dr. Henry D. Chadwick, State Commissioner of Public Health.
Dr. Winfred Overholser, State Commissioner of Mental Diseases.

Dr. Charles E. Mongan, President, Massachusetts Medical Society.
Professor Curtis M. Hilliard, President, Massachusetts Health Council and Professor of Biology and Public Health, Simmons College.
Dr. Wilson G. Smillie, Professor of Public Health Administration, Harvard School of Public Health.
Dr. Alexander S. Begg, Dean, Boston University School of Medicine and Secretary, Massachusetts Medical Society.
Professor Samuel C. Prescott, Dean of Science and Professor of Industrial Biology, Massachusetts Institute of Technology.
Dr. Dwight O'Hara, Chairman, Public Health Committee, Massachusetts Medical Society and Professor of Preventive Medicine, Tufts College Medical School.
Dr. David D. Scannell, Chief of Surgical Staff and President of Senior Staff, Boston City Hospital.
Dr. Francis X. Mahoney, Health Commissioner, City of Boston.
Dr. Charles F. Wilinsky, Deputy Health Commissioner, City of Boston and Executive Director, Beth Israel Hospital.
Dr. Gerardo Balboni, Physician, Home for Italian Children and Member of the Staff of the Massachusetts General Hospital.

The Commission has appointed committees with a total personnel of nearly one hundred and fifty to consider individually the problems of the several branches of public health. The purpose of the present Commission is to study existing health laws and practices, with a view to improving them, and to anticipating the expansion of the next fifty years. In 1850, Lemuel Shattuck, through the same method of approach, gave us our present plan. Today, a notable group is planning for the future.

Conclusion. The Public Health Council has continued the tradition of the former organizations since 1869 of making policies and giving advice. The work of all the individual divisions, and of the Department as a unit, has continued along constantly changing and improving lines, following the example of an adaptable flexibility to changing conditions set forth by its pioneers. The details of the epidemiological work done in communicable disease and cancer, of the intensive disease control and preventive work done in communicable disease, of the engineering work being carried on to higher peaks of excellence, of water purification and sewage control, of the tuberculosis program, of the far-reaching educational activities of child hygiene and of adult hygiene, of the assistance being rendered the physician in innumerable ways,—all these are the work of the Department of Public Health. It has expanded by statute and by popular demand, until it now has a constant influence on the life of every individual in the State. The advantages accruing from the efforts of this group of workers trained to anticipate and care for any exigencies of health in the State have been accepted as a natural heritage and taken for granted, and yet it is only eighty-eight years since a State holiday was declared to celebrate the introduction of Cochituate water to Boston!

STATE BOARD OF HEALTH
June 30, 1869, to June 30, 1879

Service began	Name	City or Town	Occupation	Length of Service in Years	Service ended
1869	Henry I. Bowditch	Boston	Physician	10	1879
1869	George Derby	Boston	Physician	5	1874*
1869	P. Emory Aldrich	Worcester	Lawyer	4	1872
1869	William C. Chapin	Lawrence	Manufacturer	3	1871
1869	Warren Sawyer	Boston	Business	5	1873
1869	Richard Frothingham	Charlestown	Historian	11	1879
1869	R. T. Davis	Fall River	Physician	10	1879
1872	G. V. Fox	Lowell	Lawyer	2	1873
1874	J. C. Hoadley	Lawrence	Civil engineer	5	1879
1874	Thomas B. Newhall	Lynn	Business	6	1879
1874	David L. Webster	Boston	Manufacturer	6	1879
1874	C. F. Folsom	Boston	Physician	5	1879

*Died in office

STATE BOARD OF HEALTH, LUNACY AND CHARITY, COMMITTEE ON HEALTH
July 1, 1879, to May 26, 1886

Service began	Name	City or Town	Occupation	Length of Service in Years	Service ended
1879	Henry I. Bowditch	Boston	Physician	1	1879
1879	R. T. Davis	Fall River	Physician	4	1883
1879	J. C. Hoadley	Lawrence	Civil engineer	3	1882
1880	Alfred Hosmer	Watertown	Physician	2	1882
1880	Thomas Talbot	Billerica	Lawyer	4	1884
1880	George P. Carter	Cambridge	Business	3	1883
1882	Henry P. Walcott	Cambridge	Physician	1	1883
1882	John Fallon	Lawrence	Business	4	1886
1882	Edgar E. Dean	Brockton	Physician	2	1884
1883	Charles E. Donnelly	Boston	Lawyer	3	1886
1883	Reuben Noble	Westfield	Business	2	1885
1884	Samuel A. Green	Boston	Physician	2	1886
1884	Edward Hitchcock	Amherst	Physician	2	1886

STATE BOARD OF HEALTH
May 26, 1886, to July 7, 1914

Service began	Name	City or Town	Occupation	Length of Service in Years	Service ended
1886	Henry P. Walcott	Cambridge	Physician	28	1914
1886	Hiram F. Mills	Lawrence	Civil engineer	28	1914
1886	Julius H. Appleton	Springfield	Manufacturer	4	1890
1886	Frank W. Draper	Boston	Physician	15	1901
1886	Thornton K. Lothrop	Beverly	Lawyer	—	—
1886	Elisha M. Jones	Taunton	Physician	7	1893
1886	James White	Williamstown	Business	1	1887
1887	Theodore C. Bates	No. Brookfield	Manufacturer	1	1888
1889	Joseph W. Hastings	Warren	Physician	5	1894
1890	John M. Raymond	Salem	Lawyer	1	1892
1891	Gen. Morris Schaff	Pittsfield	Soldier	2	1892
1893	James W. Hull	Pittsfield	Insurance	9	1911
1893	Gerard C. Tobey	Wareham	Lawyer	9	1911
1893	Charles H. Porter	Quincy	Insurance	8	1911
1895	Julian A. Mead	Watertown	Physician	10	1914
1902	John W. Bartol	Boston	Physician	5	1907
1907	Robert W. Lovett	Boston	Physician	8	1914
1911	Clement F. Coogan	Pittsfield	Business	3	1914
1911	Joseph A. Plouff	Ware	Lawyer	3	1914
1911	C. E. McGillicuddy	Worcester	Lawyer	3	1914
1913	Milton J. Rosenau	Brookline	Hygienist	2	1914

STATE DEPARTMENT OF HEALTH
July 7, 1914, to December 1, 1919
DEPARTMENT OF PUBLIC HEALTH
December 1, 1919, to———

Commissioners

Service began	Name	City or Town	Occupation	Length of Service in Years	Service ended
1914	Allan J. McLaughlin	United States Public Health Service	Physician	4	1918
1918	Eugene R. Kelley	Boston	Physician	8	1925
1925	George H. Bigelow	Milton	Physician	8	1933
1933	Henry D. Chadwick	Newton	Physician	—	

PUBLIC HEALTH COUNCIL

1914	William T. Sedgwick	Boston	Biologist	7	1921
1914	George C. Whipple	Cambridge	Sanitary Engineer	9	1923
1914	Milton J. Rosenau	Brookline	Hygienist	1	1915
1914	William J. Gallivan	Boston	Physician	5	1919
1914	David L. Edsall	Boston	Physician	7	1921
1914	Joseph E. Lamoureux	Lowell	Physician	10	1924
1914	John T. Wheelwright	Boston	Lawyer	5	1919
1919	Warren C. Jewett	Worcester	Retired	6	1925
1920	Sylvester E. Ryan*	Springfield	Physician	—	
1921	Roger I. Lee	Boston	Physician	13	1934
1921	Richard P. Strong*	Boston	Physician	—	
1923	James L. Tighe*	Holyoke	Engineer	—	
1924	Francis H. Lally*	Milford	Physician	—	
1926	Gordon Hutchins*	Concord	Engineer	—	
1934	Richard M. Smith*	Boston	Physician	—	

*Present incumbent.

BIBLIOGRAPHY

Abbott, Samuel W.: The Past and Present Condition of Public Hygiene and State Medicine in the United States. Wright & Potter Printing Company, Boston, 1900.

Annual Reports of the State Board of Health of Massachusetts. 1870-1879.

Annual Reports of the State Board of Health, Lunacy and Charity of Massachusetts. 1880-1886.

Annual Reports of the State Board of Health of Massachusetts. 1887-1914.

Annual Reports of the State Department of Health of Massachusetts. 1915-1919.

Annual Reports of the State Department of Public Health. 1920-1933.

Bowditch, Henry I.: Public Hygiene in America. Little, Brown, and Company, Boston; Trübner and Company, London, 1877.

Chadwick, Sir Edwin: Report on the Sanitary Condition of the Labouring Population of Great Britain. W. Clowes & Sons, London, 1842.

Jones, Dorsey D.: Edwin Chadwick and the Early Public Health Movement in England. Vol. IX, No. 3. New Series No. 197, February 15, 1931. University of Iowa, Iowa City, Iowa.

Kiernan, Frank: Massachusetts State Health Commission. The New England Journal of Medicine. Vol. 213, No. 19, November 7, 1935.
Locke, Edwin A., (Edited by): Tuberculosis in Massachusetts. Wright & Potter Company, Boston, 1908.
Manual of Health Laws, Massachusetts, 1929.
Prescott, Samuel C. and Horwood, Murray P.: Sedgwick's Principles of Sanitary Science and Public Health. The Macmillan Company, New York, 1935.
Ravenel, Mazyck P.: (Edited by): A Half Century of Public Health. The Nichols Press, Lynn, 1921.
Sedgwick, William T.: Principles of Sanitary Science and the Public Health. The Macmillan Company, London, 1902.
Shattuck, Lemuel: Report of the Sanitary Commission of Massachusetts, 1850. Dutton & Wentworth, Boston, 1850.
Simon, Sir John: English Sanitary Institutions. Cassell & Company, Limited, London, Paris, New York and Melbourne, 1890.
Whipple, George C.: State Sanitation. Vols. I and II. Harvard University Press, Cambridge; Humphrey Milford, Oxford University Press, London, 1917.

THE SUPERVISOR OF HEALTH EDUCATION—RESPONSIBILITIES AND TRAINING*

BY C. E. TURNER, M.A., DR. P. H.

*Professor of Biology and Public Health
Massachusetts Institute of Technology*

"Health education should be in charge of the teacher under the sympathetic guidance of an efficient advisor or supervisor of health education, equipped with special and adequate professional training for this complex task."

This statement from the conclusions of the White House Conference on Child Health and Protection presents the combined opinion of national leaders in child health and in education. Why is such supervisory service needed, or, in other words, what are the responsibilities of such a supervisor?

The school department as well as the home must play its part in the health education of the child. When the child enters school we help to improve his health practices by direct training. As he goes through the grades we must continue the training and supply health information from grade to grade in accordance with his interests, responsibilities and mental capacity. The health education program must be a properly coordinated unit at all school levels and it must be so organized that each year presents a new approach with fresh interests to the child. The first responsibility, therefore, which can be adequately met only by a trained supervisor of health education is to establish a unified program of health training and instruction throughout the school system and to make this an integral part of general education.

*Reprinted from *The Commonhealth*, Vol. 21, No. 3, July-Aug -Sept. 1934.

There is need of health education supervision after the program has been set up if it is to function efficiently. A teacher can teach subtraction without knowing higher mathematics but he cannot answer correctly the questions of children in the field of health without a sound basic knowledge of physiology, hygiene and sanitation. The child asks "Does milk give me red blood?" The answer is "No." But behind that answer is a knowledge of nutrition on the part of the teacher that includes the information that iron is an essential element in which milk is deficient. Health education requires such a range of technical knowledge that special supervision is needed to see that health facts and not health fallacies are taught.

The importance of method in health education should not be undervalued. We are training as well as instructing. Inducing a child to get enough sleep is not at all like hearing a spelling lesson. Definite periods for hygiene are set aside beginning with grade four and must be wisely used, but health facts alone do not motivate health behavior. Much of the health training program must be scattered through the school day or developed in connection with opening exercises, school lunches, activity and rest. Without supervision and inspiring leadership these activities become haphazard, ineffective or nonexistent. The second responsibility of the health education supervisor, then, is to aid the classroom teacher in developing devices, subject matter, and methods for measuring the results of the health education program.

We have said that health education needs to be made a part of general education. It should also be made an integral part of the school health program. Some of the child's most valuable educational experiences come from a contact with the physician and the nurse. The teachers should know the nature of these experiences, help to prepare children for them, assist children to interpret them clearly and encourage children to act upon them wisely. The third responsibility of the health education supervisor, therefore, is to integrate the work of the classroom teacher with the other elements of the school health program. Such a person is a "Health Educator and Coordinator." Because he facilitates the work of the other health experts and because his constructive and creative leadership is reflected in the work of the whole body of classroom teachers, it is probable that the activities of no other health worker are productive of greater health benefits per dollar expended.

Training

There seems to be general agreement with the statement of the White House Conference that "supervisors of health education should have the usual training and experience of classroom teachers with a master's degree, or the full equivalent, in health education." Such a person "should be well trained in the sciences fundamental to health and in modern trends in supervision and curriculum building; and should have at least three years' experience in classroom teaching." In several schools it is now possible to secure a master's degree or its equivalent, the certificate in public health (C.P.H.) in the field of health education.

Training requirements for health education supervisor are naturally divided into three phases: (1) training in health, (2) training in education, and (3) training in school health administration. If we are to develop a school health program for which the public health profession, the educators and the community have respect, supervisors must be trained soundly in educational method, subject matter and administrative principles.

Training in health should include a knowledge of the structure and function of the human body. This means a basic knowledge of modern physiology, built upon a background of biochemistry, gross and microscopic anatomy. The individual should also possess adequate training in nutrition, which rests primarily upon chemistry as a basic subject. A sound knowledge of mental hygiene, social hygiene and safety education is especially important.

In the public health field, knowledge ought to include general and sanitary bacteriology, the principles of municipal sanitation and public health administration, the biology of communicable diseases, and a sufficient knowledge of vital statistics to allow the supervisor to interpret the health status of the community and the state. We should add here some knowledge of public health social work, bordering on the field of social case work.

A thorough knowledge of child psychology, educational psychology and educational method is required if the supervisor is to command the respect of the teacher and contribute effectively to class activities when he visits the classroom. Furthermore, the supervisor needs a sound knowledge of the curriculum, its nature, its development, and its operation. The understanding of the individual differences in children, physical and mental, should be a part of his equipment, as well as a sound knowledge of the principles of modern supervision in the public school.

It is wise to insist upon teaching experience preparatory to work in health education supervision. The teaching profession like any other prefers to accept leadership and directions from a person with distinctive training and successful experience in its own professional field.

Instruction in school health administration will naturally be a part of the special graduate training of the supervisor. Specific training in the development and supervision of health education is a most important aspect. It is not possible for the supervisor of health education to be a physician, a nurse, a nutritionist, a dental hygienist, and a physical educator. It is not necessary that he should know the technique of the specialists who are working in the school. It is necessary that he understand what these various groups are doing and, more especially, how the classroom program in health education can be related to the medical, nursing, dental, physical education and nutrition services.

Obviously, some professional maturity is necessary for this field of work. A year of special work will supplement quite successfully the previous training for (1) the graduate of a teachers' college who has majored in science (chemistry, biology, and nutrition), or (2) the graduate of the liberal arts college who has a major in education with a minor in these sciences, or (3) the graduate in physical education from a school giving the bachelor's degree, or (4) a nurse with a bachelor's degree. It will be seen that nutritionists are included under the second classification. Some nurses who are also graduates of teachers' colleges have made outstanding contributions in this field of work. A one year program of study is adequate for persons with these different kinds of previous training only if it is arranged individually for each student to supplement previous training with courses in the special subjects needed.

A thorough training in school health administration will provide opportunities for study in a school or department of public health which has relatively broad offerings in that field and in a school or department of education. From two such departments it is possible to build up a program of study which, when supplemented by special work in health education with practical teaching and when further supplemented by specific instruction in school health administration, provides a background upon which the individual can build a satisfactory professional experience.

We shall do well to remember in any consideration of this sort, that there is no substitute for native intelligence and that no program of study can make a person of limited ability into a professional worker of superior capacity. We should expect to find occasional individuals possessing high native intelligence, the ability to work well with other people, and the ability to profit by experience, who will have developed superior pieces of work in public school systems without ever having completed all of the desirable training requirements suggested above.

SUGGESTIONS FOR INTEGRATED HEALTH TEACHING IN THE PRIMARY GRADES

BY JEAN V. LATIMER, A. M.
Coordinator in Health Education
Massachusetts Department of Public Health

The vital question of arousing the child's interest in Health Education has for over a decade received much consideration both from educators and public health authorities. Significant progress has been made in the growing realization that health teaching may be integrated with the general school curriculum. Hence, schools today are talking about "health in the elementary curriculum" as well as "a health education curriculum."

Particularly in the primary grades is it advantageous to have the health program built around the child's everyday activities. Young children are not interested in health as a subject, but through the work of the school in promoting child growth through the right kind of experiencing, health as one of the necessary qualities of life may unconsciously permeate all that children do. The natural tendency, especially of the primary grade child, to regard all experiences as a part of a total experience makes it pertinent to integrate health teaching with the large learning situations which, in turn, are integrated and unified around wholesome living.

Just how does health teaching articulate in such a plan and what are the possibilities for teaching health as part of the large comprehensive teaching-learning units?

Below are some suggestions as to the broad possibilities for an integrated health program in the first three grades, where the central theme of the general curriculum is built around an exploration of the child's immediate environment. Since health is an essential factor to be considered in all phases of daily life, an alert teacher, in the development of other classroom learning situations, will, herself, find innumerable similar opportunities.

In the first grade where the general activities are centered around the central ideas of home and school life, health may be tied up with things children are already interested in. "Building and furnishing a house," and "carrying on household activities through the play of children with one another or with dolls" are examples of such units. In developing the activity, "Cooking and Serving Meals," as a part of the unit concerned with household activities, the best foods for a child's breakfast may be discussed. Pictures illustrating desirable foods may be drawn or cut out from magazines. Play setting the table and serving breakfast, dinner and supper. It is desirable to emphasize the combination of essential foods rather than over emphasizing one undesirable food. While in the primary grades there should be no formal teaching in regard to nutritional values, the teacher can nevertheless do much toward making desirable foods attractive and popular.

In considering other aspects of home life, a daily review of items of health routine with informal discussion of individual accomplishments may be made. Talk with the pupils in an informal way concerning "What you usually do when you get up in the morning before coming to school." Discuss healthful experiences carried on in the home, such as sleeping with windows open, eating leafy vegetables, bathing regularly, cleaning teeth, visiting dentist and doctor. Some of such home life experiences may be dramatized in the classroom.

In order that each health experience may become an integrated part of the child's total experience, enlist his interest in playing the entire health game at home from morning to night. As the children give the rules such as—be clean, drink milk, eat fruits and vegetables, sleep in the house with windows open, these may be written on the board. Posters illustrating such practices may be made with rules plainly lettered and tacked on the walls for reference. Flash cards of the rules can also be made and individual members of the class may dramatize each one in order to see if they understand the meaning. As a part of the language work, a health vocabulary may be developed. The vocabulary should include the external parts of the body, the common names of the foods, such as cereals, milk, bread, fruit, vegetables, etc., and the words relating to sleep, rest, cleanliness, play, sunshine and fresh air.

It is desirable that all daily health habits should be taught *in toto* so that the entire pattern may more likely become a part of the young child's neuro-muscular mechanism. Each item such as food, sleep, fresh air, cleanliness, and so forth is to be discussed at the opening of the school year rather than taking them up as separate health topics during special months. A plan of teaching which emphasizes the topic of fresh air in September, food in October, cleanliness in November, and so forth, is to be discouraged in the primary grades.

"Caring for Pets," is another unit within the area of the first grade which in its development may have many inherent health values. For example, the conditions which make for the growth and welfare of the pet, will involve similar elements as for the child, such as food, fresh air, sunshine and cleanliness.

"Making and Caring for Doll Clothes" may lead to a consideration of the child's own clothing, and the health factors involved. A playlet, "How I Dress for the Rain," may be developed as one means of emphasizing the use of raincoat, umbrella and rubbers.

As a part of the unit on "Making the school a safer, cleaner, and more attractive place to live" plan housekeeping projects. As an activity, children may be assigned individual tasks for assisting in keeping the classroom clean. Discuss the problems involved with the children themselves. Help the child to learn the best ways of keeping all books and materials neat and clean - emphasizing that the child's first responsibility is to take care of his own things and to be neat and orderly in whatever he does. Arrange with class the facilities for hanging up wraps, placing rubbers and umbrellas in the proper place. Take a trip through the school hall, the school buildings and the school grounds and observe the location of ash cans, playground equipment, toilets, and so forth. In practically every school it is necessary for primary pupils to be given some information as to use and care of school toilets. The teacher should secure the co-operation of the school nurse for carrying out such instructions.

Discuss the pupil's share in the care of the assembly hall and other parts of the school building and grounds. Compose and read stories about the trip after it is over. Discuss the proper disposal of paper, trash, etc. In the care of the halls, observe the building and woodwork, plan to keep the corridor walls clean. Discuss the use of door mats at the entrance. Compose and read stories about the use of the hall.

Discuss the reasons for drinking fountains. Practice with the class the proper use of the drinking fountain. In schools where there is no drinking fountain individual cups are necessary. First-grade children often must be taught how to use the drinking fountain properly. In this connection the value of water drinking as a health rule may again be emphasized. Arrange during the day for regular time for water drinking.

In the second grade, as the child has enlarged his experience and has developed an increasing control over the tool subjects in the curriculum, there are even greater opportunities for health teaching. The larger teaching-learning unit, "Planning and equipping a library corner," may include the addition and the use of health materials and health readers.

Also, in the second grade, as the child's environmental consciousness is extended to include certain aspects of the local community, units concerning the functioning of community health may include the work of the school doctor and the public health nurse. The public health nurse may be invited to visit the primary classroom and talk to the children informally about her work. There are teaching opportunities in having a classroom visit from the school doctor to explain why we have school health examinations - why should physical defects be corrected -- why should a child go to the dentist to have his teeth filled even if they have not started to hurt. After such visits and discussions, stories may be written about the work of the public health nurse and the school doctor. The children may dramatize "the school doctor is coming to examine us." The primary teacher can do more than anyone else in the school health education program to help the children to develop the attitude that the doctor and the school nurse are their friends and to make them interested and cooperative in the work of the school medical service.

In the second grade, a unit on farm life which includes emphasis on the health habits of animals, is within the interest and experience of this age level. "Making a school garden" is another unit which offers many health potentialities. If such a large project cannot be developed the teacher and pupils may at least grow one vegetable out-of-doors.

Also observing the growth of plants in the classroom may be a means of teaching the factors which are necessary for the growth of both plants and children. Emphasis may thus be placed on the value of sunshine, fresh air and water.

Teaching in regard to foods may be included in the larger teaching-learning activity of giving a school party. The pupils may plan the guests to invite, the invitations to be written, things to do at the party and refreshments to serve which are both inexpensive and nutritious. In one school the children cooked and prepared applesauce as an example of a wholesome dessert. The children may also serve the food. Similarly, planning a picnic in which the foods for the luncheon are prepared and served, is another illustration of integrating health teaching with a large teaching-learning situation.

In the third grade a continued emphasis is still placed on getting into practice a complete program of personal daily health habits. But in the health teaching a growing sense of the child's own responsibility regarding the health phases of his experiences is to be stressed.

An extension of the child's interpretation of health relationships in the community is also to be undertaken. In the study of "being a community helper" in the second grade a first introduction has been made to the topic of protection against disease by having visits and talks from the public health nurse and the school doctor. Children should not be made anxious about sickness nor should they be constantly warned of the dangers of disease germs. Theoretically, there should be no teaching about germs in the primary grades but even second and third-grade children will often introduce the topic themselves, having heard the word at home. The teacher should treat such topics, when they come up, in a casual way. She should not get involved in trying to give too detailed an explanation. A communicable disease had best simply remain a "catching disease" but even the young child can learn to appreciate that he must do his share in the control of the common communicable diseases by obeying quarantine signs and regulations; staying at home when he is sick, especially when he has a common cold; being immunized against smallpox and diphtheria and by the development of other habits which may assist in preventing him from contracting and spreading communicable diseases.

For example, the child should learn to wash his hands before eating and after going to the toilet -- he should be taught to use his own handkerchief, toothbrush, wash rag, towel, etc. He should learn that it is an unclean practice to use such articles belonging to other people. He should drink from the fountain without touching his lips to the bubbler or he should have an individual drinking cup. He should refrain from biting fruit, candy or gum which belongs to other children. He should know better than to eat fruit which has been handled by dirty hands or picked up from the street.

To those who hold a mature concept of health subject matter such topics may seem too difficult for the primary pupil. However, it should be kept in mind that the child does not need to master all aspects of a health topic at the time he has his first teaching experience regarding it. Each health experience needs only to be rounded out in the fullness that is valuable to the child at a given age and enlarged as he grows older.

In the third grade, a large teaching unit concerned with the sources of the local food supply, which includes planning and taking a trip to the local food markets, is well within the scope of the interest and experience of the child. Investigation as to methods of transportation of foods will prove exceedingly interesting. Classroom discussion may be pertinent of such questions as "Why are we not able to have fresh vegetables and fruits all winter?" Constructing and operating a play grocery store is another example of the opportunity for teaching health through a larger learning situation. A study of the farm which has been referred to for the second grade, may be enlarged to include the local food products. A discussion of the value of cereal as an essential part of the child's breakfast may lead to an enlarged study of wheat.

Thus, the problem of health teaching in the primary grades would seem to be that of guiding the everday doings of the child into worthy and fruitful channels. In such a plan children learn about health in relation to the everyday things they are doing, they develop health skills through daily practice and health knowledge through solving interesting health problems.

Such a theory of health teaching is sometimes called a theory of integration -that is, all the health learnings are integrated and unified around wholesome living.

BASIC CONSIDERATIONS OF THE JUNIOR HIGH SCHOOL COURSE OF STUDY*

BY JOHN P. SULLIVAN, Ph.D.
Supervisor of Health Education
Boston School Department

The need of organized courses of study in junior high schools is evident in the light of recent findings. The Research Department of the National Education Association finds in a curriculum study that health instruction is offered at least once a week as a required subject in nearly all junior high school grades. Even in the ninth grade it is offered as a constant in more programs than is any other subject except English.[1]

In the light of this authoritative information it is hard to understand the wholesale lack of courses of study in the junior high schools. In a survey completed in Massachusetts[2] it was found that only thirty-two per cent of the junior high schools had health courses of study.

The course of study is an important educational vehicle for unifying, coordinating and grading health content. It is equally necessary in the secondary grades as in the elementary. "A course of study consists of specifications and directions relating to educating children. Without a course of study a teacher works more or less in the dark. Although individually the teachers of a school system may be capable, industrious, and conscientious in their work, they will not, except by accident, coordinate their efforts in the best way unless they are provided with a good course of study."[3]

It can be truly said, that the course of study, supplemented by appropriate textbooks and teaching aids, is the best guarantee of what any particular school system aims to do in health teaching and training.

In the actual construction of a course of study for junior high schools, the supervisor finds himself in a veritable thicket of advocated theories.[4]

Charters[5] and Bobbitt[6] would stress present needs of society as the starting point in making a course of study. Miriam[7] would emphasize the construction from the viewpoint of paidocentric (child centered) development. Bonser[8] would suggest a course based on fundamental life needs. They are not completely adequate. They fail in so far as they do not go beyond the orbit of present-day conditions and experience.

The job-analysis is urged by some educators as the most desirable method of determining the elements for the course of study. This method of determining such elements is open to criticism. While it

---
*Reprinted from *The Commonhealth*, Vol. 21, No. 3, July-Aug.-Sept. 1934.
[1] Creating a Curriculum for Adolescent Youth. Research Bull. of N. E. A., Vol. VI, No. 1, p. 52.
[2] Report, "Health Education Survey"—Mass. Tuberculosis League.
[3] Monroe, W. S., Making a Course of Study, p. 4.
[4] Cocking, W. D.—Administrative Procedure in Curriculum Making.
[5] Curriculum Construction, Chapt. I.
[6] How to Make a Curriculum, Chapters II-III.
[7] Child Life and Curriculum, Chapt. I.
[8] Elementary School Curriculum, Chapt. I.

is doubtless true that careful analysis of what children do is a valuable contribution, nevertheless as a basis for procedure in course of study construction it fails in that it investigates the activity as it is now rather than as it should be. This is a fundamental error in procedure and would tend to strengthen and continue present practices, whether desirable or undesirable.

The following suggested procedure in constructing the junior high school course is based on the practices presented by the committee of the National Society for the Study of Education,[9] and supplemented by the biological and psychological principles and the laws of learning.[10]

Based on these the following procedure was undertaken in constructing the Boston course of study in health education for the junior high school grades:

1. Statement of objectives.
2. Examination of present courses of study.
3. Judgment of teachers and masters on selected topics.
4. Experimental teaching.
5. Health information test and teacher questionnaire for minimum of essentials and grade placement.
6. Course of study committee to bring course to completion.

The objectives as outlined by the Joint Committee[11] were the results of the best scientific investigation, and served as the objectives of this course of study:

1. To instruct children and youth so that they will conserve and improve their own health.
2. To establish in them the habits and principles of living which throughout their school life, and in later years, will assure that abundant vigor and vitality required for the greatest possible happiness and service in personal, family, and community life.
3. To influence parents and other adults, through the health education program for children, to adopt better habits and attitudes, so that the school may become an effective agency for the promotion of the social aspects of health education in the family and community as well as in the school itself.
4. To improve the individual and community life of the future; to insure better second generation and a still better third generation--a healthier and fitter nation and race.

Dividing the field of health instruction into some of the major topics generally taught points to the range of placement. Table I shows the specific placement of the topics in some ten courses of study issued during the period 1927 to 1932. Four of the courses were for grades seven, eight and nine; six courses pertained to grades seven and eight.

While the grade placement of some topics varies, the placement of certain topics is found to be constant in median practice: home and school hygiene, for example, are taught almost entirely in the seventh

---

[9] 26th Yearbook, National Society for the Study of Education, Foundation of Curriculum Making. Part II—p. 11-28.
[10] Basic Considerations of the Course of Study in Health Education. Education, Dec. 1933.
[11] Health Education.

grade, the nervous system in the eighth, and disease prevention and bacteria in the eighth and ninth. Is it not a reasonable assumption that the grade placements shown to be fairly constant in median practice, might suggest the most feasible placement?

These topics were sent to a representative group of junior high school masters and teachers. They were asked to group them under appropriate teaching units and assign the grade they thought best in the light of their experience. From the results of this source and with a realization that the foundation upon which to lay a health education course of study is a knowledge of the objectives for which you are going to train, the individual you are going to train, and the condition under which training is to be given, a mimeographed copy of a "Working Outline in Health Education for Grades VII, VIII, and IX"[12] was prepared for experimental teaching. The following topic headings are suggestive of the experimental work considered suitable for the junior high schools.

Grade VII — Topic Headings
School Hygiene
Home Hygiene
Community Hygiene
Budgeting Time
Safety
Alcohol, Tobacco, and Patent Medicines
Vacation Time

Grade VIII — Topic Headings
Foods
Digestive System
Circulatory System
Respiratory System
Nervous System
Bony and Muscular System
Special Senses

Grade IX — Topic Headings
Public Health Agencies
Disease
Food Control
Health Heroes
Vocational Hygiene
Mental Health
Safety

This "Working Outline in Health Education" was distributed to some forty-nine schools having junior high classes for experimental teaching. At the end of the year two check-ups on the outline were offered. One was a health information test and the other a questionnaire to the teachers. This gave an approximate reaction from the teachers and pupils. These two sources afforded definite information and in the

[12]"A Working Outline in Health Education for Grades VII, VIII, IX" Boston School Dept. Boston.

light of these two reactions, certain modifications were considered on the outline. These modifications necessitated the following changes. Physiology was divided among grades VII, VIII, and IX, and not concentrated in grade VIII. Furthermore, physiology topics were made to fit more appropriately the respective units. Thus bones and muscles were the physiological basis of the unit on posture. The following phases were made constant in all three grades, food, alcohol and tobacco, safety and first aid, mental health, and vacations. Personal hygiene was recommended for grade nine. Omission of vocational hygiene was considered as it was thought that personal hygiene would cover this phase sufficiently. The special senses were found too difficult for grade eight and more appropriate for the unit on personal hygiene in grade nine.

Out of the experience of this experimental teaching grew the necessity for realigning certain topics and for a more exhaustive study of the content. A course of study committee was then appointed by the superintendent to work under the direction of the supervisor of health education to further the "Working Outline" into a tentative course of study. The organization of this committee consisted of two groups. The construction committee, composed of representatives from intermediate and senior high schools, was responsible for the actual construction. This committee worked in subcommittees according to grades developing objectives, content, activities, problems, references and the philosophy underlying the program. The supplementary committee composed of representatives from fields allied to health education acted in an advisory capacity to the construction committee. This cooperative undertaking made for a better understanding of the objectives of each field and prevented unnecessary overlapping of content.

In setting up the most desirable type of organization the committee agreed on the unit plan, with each unit allotted to an appropriate time for completion. This time element was one of the results of the experimental teaching. Furthermore it was suggested by a majority of the teachers in answering the questionnaire. Each unit began with the title and unit aim, followed by the specific objectives and basic activities. The course had table of contents, a list of the committees, and the Massachusetts Education Laws referring to health instruction and training. The teaching units followed, organized by grades. At the rear of the course a bibliography of pupil and teacher texts was added.

The following units represent the contents of the completed Tentative Course of Study as it is in use now:

Course of Study by Grades

GRADE VII
Unit I—Health Education in School and other Public Buildings
Unit II—Planning Time
Unit III—A Model Home
Unit IV—Health Education in the Neighborhood

    Unit   V—Elementary First Aid
    Unit   VI—Effects of Alcohol, Tobacco, and Patent Medicines
    Unit   VII—Vacation Time

GRADE VIII
    Unit   I—Introduction to Year's Work
    Unit   II—Posture and Its Needs
    Unit   III—Nutrition
    Unit   IV—The Digestive System
    Unit   V—The Circulatory System
    Unit   VI—The Nervous System and Mental Health
    Unit   VII—Vacation Time

GRADE IX
    Unit   I—Importance of Health
    Unit   II—Mental Health
    Unit   III—Personal Health
    Unit   IV—Diet
    Unit   V—Drugs, Tobacco, Alcohol and Narcotics
    Unit   VI—Bacteria and Preventable Diseases
    Unit   VII—Health Heroes
    Unit   VIII—Safety
    Unit   IX—First Aid
    Unit   X—Public and Private Health Agencies

The supervisor supplemented this course with teaching aids. The list consisted of films, prepared simple experiments, models, graphs, and a library of approved source material. The films, with projectors and screens, prepared experiments, and charts are furnished the teachers on request. The library of approved source material is in the hands of each health education teacher. In addition the master of each school purchases the textbooks and other aids from his per capita allowance.

Thus the course of study, suitable texts and desirable teaching aids serve as a criterion of how one large school system is solving the health education program in the junior high school grades.

TABLE I

Grade Placement in Health Topics in Junior High Schools

Topics of Health Teaching	A	B	C	D	E	F	G	H	I	J
Bones	7	8	—	—	8	7	8	8	7	7
Budgeting Time	—	7	7	—	—	—	—	—	—	—
Cells	7	8	—	—	—	—	7	9	—	—
Circulatory System	7	8	8	8	8	8	8	7	7	7
Cleanliness	—	7	7	—	7	—	—	7	—	—
Clothes	—	—	9	—	9	—	7-8	9	—	7
Community Hygiene	9	7	9	7	7	7	7	7	7	8
Digestive System	7	8	8	8	8	8	8	7	8	8
Disease—Bacteria	9	—	9	8	9	—	—	9	8	8
Fresh Air—Sun	—	7	—	—	7	7	7	7	—	—
Food	8	8	8	7	9	7	8	8	8	8
Health Heroes	9	7	8	8	9	—	—	9	8	8
Home Hygiene	7	—	7	7	7	8	—	7	—	7
Home Nursing	8	—	9	—	—	—	—	9	—	—
Industrial Hygiene	9	—	9	—	9	—	—	9	—	8
Joints	7	8	—	—	8	—	8	—	—	—
Mental Health	9	—	—	—	7	—	—	9	—	7
Muscles	7	8	8	8	7	7	8	8	7	7
Narcotics—Tobacco—Alcohol	9	—	7-8-9	7	7-8-9	—	7-8	7-8-9	7-8	8
Nervous System	8	8	9	—	8	8	8	8	8	8
Personal Hygiene	9	7	7	—	9	—	7	7	—	—
Rest—Sleep—Exercise	8	7	8	7	7	7	7	8	8	8
Posture	8	8	8	8	7	8	8	8	7	7
Respiratory System	7	8	7	8	9	7	8	7	7	7
Safety	8	7	7-8-9	7	8	7	7-8	8	7-8	7
First Aid	9	7	7-8-9	7	8	8	7-8	8	7-8	—
School Hygiene	7	7	7	—	8	—	—	—	7	7
Skin	8	8	9	7-8	7	7	7	9	—	—
Special Senses	8	8	9	8	9	8	—	9	8	8
Vacation Time	—	7	7-8	—	—	—	—	—	—	—

THE CHARM COURSE
BY ALBERTINE P. MCKELLAR
Public Health Education Worker
Massachusetts Department of Public Health

The interest in Charm holds - and grows. The 'teen-age girl really listens—not in sophisticated boredom but intently, even enthusiastically. She eagerly asks questions, discusses material, challenges statements and then, often convinced that there is a relationship between many of her most desired possessions and the old commonplace, perhaps forgotten, health habits, she changes or begins anew various health practices. So very much she wants vivaciousness, a clear complexion, shining eyes, a pleasant smile, and an alert, physically fit, poised body that wears clothes well - all essential to her conception of charm - and all, she finally realizes, once she has seen the light through the fog, are undeniably dependent upon her manner of daily living.

Material

The course in Charm is an outgrowth of the material used previously in the 4H Club Charm School. Fundamentally it is, of course, a unit in personal hygiene adorned, enlivened, and made more palatable with the magic of charm. In from three to six sessions Charm is discussed in relation to health - health in relation to complexion, posture, smiles, pep, personality, popularity, grooming - all of these in relation to sleep and rest, food, exercise, posture, cleanliness and finally summed up in a last question-box period for practical everyday application to everyday problems.

Exhibits so vital to present-day teaching are an important part of the material. There is a portrait of a lovely high school girl, truly a possessor of charm that never fails to awe and inspire, and a color type book prepared by the Jordan Marsh Fashion Center showing correct color selection for various types. The Charm Tools and the Protect Your Smile exhibits, the Food Composition charts and a new food selection exhibit showing the changes in the regular menu necessary for gaining or losing weight are used in the course to maintain interest and to more graphically present facts and procedures.

The material as well as the method of presentation has undergone constant change during the past three years in an unceasing endeavor to keep apace with the newest interest and fads of the 'teen.

A study of the unsigned questions placed by the girls in various question boxes throughout the State last year showed them to be as follows:

    30% on skin, complexion, make-up, care of hair such as—Is eye make-up dangerous? Does constipation have any relation to poor complexion, etc?

    30% on boy and girl relationships - problems of growing up such as—Is it wrong to want to know the so-called facts of life? Is it wise to have a steady boy friend in high school? What about petting, etc?

10% on so-called health questions such as—Must menstruation be painful? Questions regarding the many products advertised profusely over the radio - How is it possible to do all the things we have to and want to and have enough time left for sleep, etc?
10% on weight control - and for the first time a few more than half were inquiring how to gain - rather than how to lose!
10% on grooming - choice of colors, appropriateness of dress for various occasions - hair arrangement, etc.
10% related to smoking and drinking.

Carrying out suggestions of the girls, at the end of the course, mothers in several places were invited to a special meeting when the course was explained to them. Attendance at this meeting has varied greatly, in one high school practically 85% of the mothers were present, while in others only a very few came. At one of the Neighborhood Houses where some fifty girls had attended the course, seventy mothers came. On the whole, the mothers have been most cordial and expressed encouraging appreciation. A resume of the material given the girls is presented to the mothers, together with an idea of the subjects covered by the questions submitted. The most is made of this opportunity to urge the mothers to allow the girls to choose their own clothes and to make the home a happy, friendly place, to which a girl may bring her friends —both girl and boy. They hear about the girl who said that she simply couldn't understand her mother's attitude - that all her life she had taught her to be fair and honest and truthful, but now as a junior she was not allowed to have boy friends, she must even refuse an invitation to the high school dances. She had tried to talk it all over with the ridiculous answer - that she was still a little girl - and so she said "I say I'm going to the library, but I don't! Telling the first lie was hard but now they come easily - but gosh! I hate it, - why does she make me?"

Requests for Course

A few small high schools in 1933 first requested some special work for the girls. Last year in twenty-two high schools at least four sessions were held. The Dean of Girls in two city schools requested single discussions. The girls in four other towns held after-school meetings that were surprisingly well attended. Teachers in several vocational schools asked for more detailed presentation of the same material. A junior college and two county agricultural schools have had the course.

Requests came from outside the schools. Six Neighborhood Houses in Boston and one in West Springfield offered the course to their older girl members. A group of unemployed girls coming to the Boston Y.W.C.A were given three sessions as a part of a refresher course and a club of girls in one of the large Boston churches graciously requested a series of discussions. Several Girl Scout Mother and Daughter Banquet Committees, the Junior Achievement League in Springfield, a 4H Personality Club and the Girl's League in New Bedford and Agawam asked for a meeting on Charm.

Results

In the schools, occasionally the girls are asked to answer an unsigned questionnaire. Here is the data taken from those submitted in one high school:

Did you like the course?   Yes - 299   No - 1
Why?   Learned new things - 125
    Generally interesting - 108
    Acquired different viewpoint - 30
    And "Learned a great deal which may be of help to others in my family as well as myself" - "Because it gave me a better outlook on what we have to face and I think that at last some of the older people are trying to understand us" - "It helped me to become more interested in the big things of life and to become a better liked girl."

Which meeting did you enjoy most?
    The question period is invariably the most popular meeting, with the first session on "What is Charm" second, and "Complexions" and "Smiles" in order.

Have you made any changes in your daily habits?   Yes - 279   No - 20
What changes?
    Improved dental care - 168
    Improved care of complexion - 82
    Improved food habits - 77
    Giving more thought to appearance - 37
    Getting more sleep - 19
    Changed my actions toward boys - 16
    Think I've improved my personality - 9
    And "Decreased my smoking," "Given up smoking," "I've changed my opinions about things in general and I've come off my high horse about various stands I took," "I've been helped to overcome shyness especially when I'm around older people."

Do you think such a course should be given high school girls?
    Yes - 299   No - 0

Has this course made you interested in studying further in health education?   Yes - 283   No - 1

In one of the vocational groups - this answer appeared - "I enjoyed the course because it made me really want to do some of the things I'm supposed to do."

The outside-of-school groups are less formal and are attended voluntarily. Maintaining interest in these primarily social groups is naturally more difficult than with the girls in school who are given a free period for the meetings. With these extra curricular groups, the material or its presentation must not in the slightest way resemble classroom procedures. Questionnaires were not given to them and consequently no definite results were recorded. In compensation though, there is greater freedom in these groups allowing ample opportunity for consideration of personal problems - not cut short by end of period bells or the departure of school buses. Then too, in these groups confidences are invited by a certain permeating ease and friendliness seldom discernible in the more formal school groups.

Conclusion

In the Charm Course a very special effort is made to present health in practical, understandable terms - as a vital worthwhile asset within the reach of the majority of us - health in terms of attractiveness, enthusiasm, popularity and efficiency - health that is essential to the poised, capable, charming woman.

LUNCH IN A COUNTRY SCHOOL*

BY MARY SPALDING, M. A.
Chief Consultant in Nutrition
Massachusetts Department of Public Health

Is the school lunch having the benefit of a consultation service from a skilled lunchroom manager, as the plans for the new school are being drawn, or is it still entrusted solely to the architect and the equipment salesperson together with the superintendent and perhaps a school committee?

Before a modern hospital is built, the superintendent, the head of the medical staff, the supervisor of nurses, the dietitian and other department heads are called to discuss various parts of the plant with the architect, so he may have the benefit of their trained viewpoints. Such forethought for all new schools would do away with the makeshift lunchroom found tucked away in an unattractive and inconvenient corner of the smaller school, even of the new consolidated school of today.

Able Manager is Needed

Schools are cutting building costs to essentials. To one interested in an adequate noonday meal for children, the lunchroom in the country school to which children come from a distance, is indispensable. It is essential for the service of the right kind and amount of foods for growing children, and it offers an opportunity to teach the children to choose foods wisely with regard to their needs and pocketbooks.

An able school lunch manager is needed to foster the development of the lunchroom and to adapt it to the children and teachers served. Few small schools can employ a full-time person for this job. The home economics teacher may give part of her time.

A school of 100 can afford a part-time person. Some schools are fortunate in finding a local person who can handle purchasing, preparation and cooking of foods in large quantities without losing sight of the nutrition value of foods and their presentation in popular form.

The lunchroom has the advantage of arousing child and teacher interest. Health and social activities may be built up with the lunchroom. Children may assist with menus, with the preparation of certain dishes

*Reprinted from the Nation's Schools, June, 1936.

and even with the decorating by making tables, chairs and curtains. In this way the lunchroom becomes their own room.

Help From Community

When the community has been kept informed of the needs of the lunchroom, it has joined in the support of the lunch by contributions of canned goods and winter vegetables and fruits for the lunch cupboard and by donations towards lunches for needy children.

In one lunchroom I know, for example, a small group consisting of a school committee member, the lunchroom manager and a few friends put up vegetables and fruits for the year. They gathered these in the fields to get half rates, with the object of giving wholesome foods to children and keeping out of debt.

Teachers give support through health education with the children, using the lunchroom as a practice field. The principal plans with the manager, teachers and children for a pleasant lunch hour.

In Massachusetts the department of public health employs a nutritionist to assist with school lunches as part of its school hygiene work. She helps the lunchroom manager with details of equipment, buying, arrangement and bookkeeping. This nutritionist has many requests for help. Of course, she cannot take the place of the good manager who gives daily service, but she can render practical assistance to the manager, the school committee and the superintendent. The employment of such a person by state departments of education or of health is of real economic as well as of health value.

Staggering Lunch Periods

Real ingenuity is needed in many of the old country schools. In some it has been shown by staggering lunch periods when a small room does not offer sufficient space for all pupils to sit and eat. This means more supervision by teachers, but many volunteer their help. In a few schools the women of the neighborhood assist in service and supervision as a community project.

Not only is space for eating likely to be lacking in these old schools but also space for storage and refrigeration. A vegetable cellar, a new cupboard and a refrigerator have actually provided savings by making it possible for the manager to buy in quantity. Changes can sometimes be brought about in old schools at a minimum of expense or by volunteer labor.

It is suggested that boy and girl leaders hold lunch and recreation clubs at the noon hour. Such clubs might save part of the lunches that go into the wastebasket so boys can play ball. They would also divert the nickels to milk instead of to chocolate bars, or make popular a better sandwich than a mustard sandwich.

As the school lunch is one of the pupils' three meals per day, it concerns closely the home. Some managers (See "Parents Check School Menus," The Nation's Schools, February, 1936) win parent cooperation by sending home menus for a week. In this way the day's meals may be better rounded, and the manager may buy more exactly.

In Massachusetts the departments of health and education held a week's conference for lunchroom managers at Fitchburg State Teachers College during the summer of 1935. This year the department is organizing a conference for less experienced managers from country towns asking townspeople to provide transportation to reduce the cost to the manager. At the conference the manager will have a chance to buy, prepare, and serve lunches, to keep accounts and to learn tricks of salesmanship - not only to "keep out of the red" but to help in building up better nutrition for the children served.

The following material has been prepared by the nutrition service of the state department of health in order to meet some needs of the schools and to keep the public informed:

For teachers in one and two-room country schools: "The Hot Dish for the Country School."

For lunchroom managers in small schools: "Three Weeks' Spring Menus," with recipes based on a fifteen-cent lunch, which is the amount a survey showed the children had to spend.

For children in elementary grades: "A Measuring Stick for a Good School Lunch," "Food for the School Child" and "Keeping Well."

For high school children: "Food Value Posters," "Food for the Teens," "Healthful Living" and "Cooking for Health."

For superintendents and community leaders: survey card to find the needs.

Articles on the growth and development of lunchrooms have appeared in various state publications. Posters representing lunches in different countries are available as a loan exhibit.

Some typical spring menus selected from the three weeks' menus prepared by the state department of health are given on following pages.

Typical Spring Menus*

Day	Quantities for 25	Quantities for 100	Recipes
MONDAY Escalloped Cabbage and Cheese	Cabbage, shredded coarsely—10 lbs. White sauce, medium—1¾ qts. Fat—4 tbsps. Cheese—¼ lb. Salt—2 tbsps. Bread crumbs—2½ cups	Cabbage, shredded coarsely—40 lbs. White sauce, medium—7 qts. Fat—1 cup Cheese—1 lb. Salt—½ cup Bread crumbs—2½ cups	*Escalloped Cabbage and Cheese* Boil cabbage until tender. Add fat, salt and grated cheese to white sauce. Arrange cabbage in baking dish, cover with cheese sauce and top with bread crumbs. Brown lightly in hot oven.
Bran Muffins	Shortening—½ cup Sugar—½ lb. Eggs—3 Bran—¼ lb. Sweet or sour milk—1 pt. Flour—4 cups Soda—1 tsp. Salt—1½ tsps. Baking powder—3 tsps.	Shortening—2 cups Sugar—2 lbs. Eggs—12 Bran—1 lb. Sweet or sour milk—2 qts. Flour—16 cups Soda—1 tbsp. Salt—2 tbsps. Baking powder—3 tbsps.	*Bran Muffins* Cream shortening and sugar. Add eggs. Mix and sift flour, soda, baking powder and salt. Add bran to creamed mixture, then milk alternately with dry ingredients. Pour into greased muffin tins and bake in moderate oven (375° F.) for twenty minutes.
Stewed Apricots	Apricots—2½ lbs.	Apricots—10 lbs.	*Stewed Apricots* Soak over night. Stew with little water and sugar. Use two slices of lemon to bring out flavor.
TUESDAY Lettuce, Egg and Macaroni Salad	Eggs—2 doz. Macaroni (cooked)—4 cups Lettuce—3 heads Mayonnaise—1 cup	Eggs—8 doz. Macaroni (cooked)—12 cups Lettuce—12 heads Mayonnaise—1 qt.	*Lettuce, Egg and Macaroni Salad* Hard cook the eggs. Chop eggs, macaroni and outside lettuce leaves. Add mayonnaise. Serve on lettuce leaves.
Dark Bread and Butter Sandwich	Bread—2 1¼-lb. loaves Butter—½ lb.	Bread—8 1¼-lb. loaves Butter—2 lbs.	

Ginger Bread

Fat—⅔ cup
Sugar—¾ cup
Egg yolks—5
Molasses—1½ cups
Sour milk—1½ cups
Flour—5¼ cups
Cloves—1 tbsp.
Soda—1½ tsps.
Cinnamon—2 tbsps.
Ginger—1 tbsp.
Salt—¾ tsp.
Baking powder—1½ tsp.

Fat—3 cups
Sugar—3 cups
Egg yolks—20
Molasses—4½ cups
Sour milk—4½ cups
Flour—21 cups
Cloves—4 tbsps.
Soda—4½ tsps.
Cinnamon—8 tbsps.
Ginger—4 tbsps.
Salt—1 tbsp.
Baking powder—2 tbsps.

Hot Ginger Bread

Cream butter, add sugar. Add beaten eggs, molasses, and beat well. Sift together dry ingredients and add alternately with sour milk. Pour into greased and floured tin. Bake at 350° F. about forty minutes.

[App]le Fluff

Apples—6
Egg whites—6
Sugar—¾ cup

Apples—24
Egg whites—24
Sugar—3 cups

Apple Fluff

Pare apples and grate. Beat egg whites stiff but not dry. Add sugar gradually, a few drops lemon juice, then grated apples.

WEDNESDAY
Vegetable Chowder

Bacon—½ cup, diced
Onions—2
Vegetables, cubed—8 cups
Water—4 cups
Milk—2 qts.
Salt—1½ tbsps.
Pepper—1 tsp.

Bacon—2 cups, diced
Onions—6
Vegetables, cubed—30 cups
Water—16 cups
Milk—8 qts.
Salt—6 tbsps.
Pepper—1 tbsp.

Vegetable Chowder

Fry out bacon. Add sliced onion and cook until slightly brown. Add vegetables in any combination desired. Potatoes, carrots, turnips, celery and peas are good. Tomatoes may also be added. Add water and cook vegetables until tender. Watch carefully to prevent burning. Add scalded milk and season to taste with salt and pepper.

[Rad]ishes

Radishes—6 bunches

Radishes—24 bunches

Radishes

To add interest cut into roses: cut off greens and cut down from top in petal form. Soak in ice water.

Prune Whole Wheat Muffins	Prunes, stoned—2 cups Prune juice—2 cups Butter—2 tbsp. Eggs—2 Sugar—2 cups Whole wheat flour—4 cups Soda—2 tsps. Baking powder—1 tbsp. Salt—½ tsp.	Prunes, stoned—8 cups Prune juice—8 cups Butter—½ cup Eggs—8 Sugar—8 cups Whole wheat flour—16 cups Soda—2½ tbsps. Baking powder—3 tbsps. Salt—2 tsps.	*Prune Whole Wheat Muffins* Stone prunes into mixing bowl. Add warm prune juice to butter and add to stoned prunes. Add beaten eggs, sugar, then dry ingredients. Bake in greased muffin tins at 400° F. for twenty-five minutes.
Sliced Bananas and Milk	Bananas—2 doz. Milk—2 qts.	Bananas—8 doz. Milk—8 qts.	*Sliced Bananas* Slice bananas just before serving.

THURSDAY

Corned Beef Hash	Cooked corned beef, chopped—8 cups Potatoes, cold, boiled—12 cups Salt—2 tbsps. Pepper—2 tsps. Milk—to moisten Onion—1 medium	Cooked corned beef, chopped—8 qts. Potatoes, cold, boiled—12 qts. Salt—½ cup Pepper—3½ tbsps. Milk—to moisten Onions—2 medium	*Corned Beef Hash* Buy lean corned beef. Combine beef and potatoes. Season. Add chopped onion. Moisten with milk. Put in hot pan with a little fat spread evenly. Cook over low heat.
Escalloped Tomatoes	Tomatoes—1 No. 10 can Salt—1 tbsp. Fat—¼ cup Pepper—¼ tsp. Sugar—2 tbsps. Stale bread crumbs—1 pt. Onion, grated—2 tbsps.	Tomatoes—4 No. 10 cans Salt—¼ cup Fat—1 cup Pepper—1 tsp. Sugar—½ cup Stale bread crumbs—2 qts. Onion, grated—½ cup	*Escalloped Tomatoes* Put the tomatoes, salt and onions into a buttered baking dish. Add the bread crumbs and butter. Bake until crumbs are brown.
Baked Indian Pudding with Raisins	Milk—4 qts. Cornmeal—1 cup Molasses or brown sugar—1 1/3 cups Eggs—4 Salt—1 tbsp. Cinnamon—1 tsp. Ginger—2 tsps. Seeded raisins—1 cup	Milk—16 qts. Cornmeal—4 cups Molasses or brown sugar—5 1/3 cups Eggs—16 Salt—¼ cup Cinnamon—1 tbsp. Ginger—3½ tbsps. Seeded raisins—1 qt.	*Baked Indian Pudding with Raisins* Cook the milk and cornmeal over hot water twenty minutes, stirring occasionally. Add beaten eggs, molasses, salt, ginger and raisins. Pour into a greased baking dish and bake slowly for two hours.

FRIDAY

Creamed Codfish
Codfish, salt—4 cups
Milk—1 qt.
Eggs—½
Butter—¼ cup
Flour—½ cup

Codfish, salt—4 qts.
Milk—4 qts.
Eggs—16
Butter—2 cups
Flour—2 cups

Creamed Codfish
Separate the fish into very small pieces and leave in cold water to cover for three hours, changing water three times. Heat the milk in a double boiler; add the codfish, well drained, and cook for ten minutes. Mix the butter with the flour until a smooth paste is formed, then stir it into the milk stirring until thickened. Cook ten minutes. Take the dish from the heat; add the beaten egg and stir well.

Raw Spinach Slaw
Cabbage, shredded—2½ qts.
Raw spinach, chopped—4 qts.
Carrots, grated—2 cups
Vinegar—2/3 cup
Salt—1½ tbsps.
Salad oil—¼ cup

Cabbage, shredded—7 qts.
Raw spinach, chopped—6 qts.
Carrots, grated—2 qts.
Vinegar—1¾ cup
Salt—½ cup
Salad oil—1 cup

Raw Spinach Slaw
Soak prepared vegetables in cold water. Just before serving drain and add seasonings.

Gelatine with Fruit
Raspberry gelatine—13 oz.
Water, hot—5 qts.
Bananas—2 doz.

Raspberry gelatine—52 oz.
Water, hot—20 qts.
Bananas—8 doz.

Gelatine with Fruit
Dissolve gelatine in hot water. When it begins to set add the sliced bananas.

The combination cost of these lunches is approximately 15c, or 5c per child. These menus are to be supplemented by one-half pint milk for each child.

*These menus are selected from three weeks' menus prepared by the Nutrition Division, State Department of Health, Boston.

THE VEGETABLE CUPBOARD FOR THE COUNTRY SCHOOL*
MARY SPALDING, M.A., B.S.**

Need

Dr. Davies, formerly of the Amherst State Experiment Station, in studying food habits of Massachusetts children, found that even country children do not eat enough vegetables—those foods that the White House Conference says exert such a profound influence on growth and well-being.

Cause

Why this poverty in the supply of vegetables? Vegetables have rather decided flavors. It is a little harder to interest children in them, but who has not seen a boy or a girl pull a carrot from the garden or eat a tomato with relish? A little boy in the Well Child Conference, the other day, said that he ate all his cabbage but the bones. Boys and girls do learn to like vegetables.

Is it because vegetables have no special "backers"? Milk has the Dairy Council, fruits have the big fruit companies. Cereal companies have sent out stories written by real writers for children. These organizations supply posters and graded material for teachers so that the children always have interesting matter to remind them to eat these foods. Vegetables do not have such strong supporters.

These may be the reasons. Have you studied the Boston food supply for 1931? This shows a promising increase in vegetables sold in this city market, but only 17 per cent of the total vegetables and fruits were trucked into Boston from Massachusetts farms. Even July peas came in large quantities from Idaho and Washington, carrots in large amounts from California and Texas and a large supply of cabbage the first of the year from Texas. Farmers do not feel like buying products that they can raise themselves. Yet, in many cases they have not produced enough for their families. The Extension Service is doing an astonishing amount to encourage the canning and storage of vegetables. More parent and school education is needed.

Value

Food economists recommend even in the very low cost food budgets that children should have every day, tomatoes, a green or yellow vegetable, a fruit or an additional vegetable (raw). The White House Conference reports that green vegetables generally should make up 15 to 20 per cent of the day's calories. They should be a regular part of each day's diet, beginning with one tablespoon of sifted pulp for the child under a year, and increasing gradually to one-half cup, then to two cups.

In all diets, especially in the low cost diets, vegetables must be count-

---
*Reprinted from *The Commonhealth*, Vol 19, No. 3, July-Aug.-Sept. 1932
**Mary Spalding, M.A., B S., is the Consultant in Nutrition of the Massachusetts Department of Public Health. Miss Spalding supervises the work of five nutritionists, and is responsible for the preparation of all the Department nutrition material. She has during the past months given particular attention to the emergency nutrition problem. A vegetable cupboard for each rural school is a splendid idea, and Miss Spalding gives some very practical suggestions.

ed on to supply the iron and copper which are too often lacking in children's foods. Immature seeds of plants such as lima beans and peas and thin, green leaves, such as beet tops and spinach, are excellent sources. Tomatoes are invaluable for Vitamin C, deficiency of which is shown too quickly in the condition of gums and teeth. Dr. Sherman warns us that this vitamin is one that must not be forgotten this year. In our Well Child Conferences the effect of Vitamin C deficiency is already too evident. Raw vegetables such as cabbage and raw spinach, so good in salads and sandwiches, give some of this important vitamin and also are rich in Vitamin A and Vitamin B.

Cooking has much to do with the value of the vegetable. Much Vitamin C may be destroyed by cooking or by the addition of soda. Tomato bisque, for instance, does not need soda; it can be made without curdling by combining the milk and tomato at the same temperature. Vegetables put in boiling water retain more of their mineral and vitamin content than those put in cold water. Some of our scientists are working, at the present time, on the seemingly simple problem of better cooking of vegetables.

The Vegetable Cupboard

This year of much scarcity, cannot home-makers who have been looking ahead, share some of their shelf of canned vegetables for that "noon hot dish"? Country children who are growing and active need three square meals, one of which should be the school lunch. How well a good, hot, tomato bisque goes with a cold, concentrated sandwich brought from home! Each week some parent might send to the school raw carrots, tomatoes or cabbage so that these, too, could help out the daily raw vegetable supply. This would not mean much in money, but would mean a tremendous amount in protecting the children within your neighborhood from anemia, constipation, and tooth and gum troubles. Is not the vegetable hunger of the children a need that country men and women may undertake to fill by taking pride in stocking a school cupboard with vegetables?

Moreover, the children will not only have a wholesome lunch, but will learn a life-long lesson in the importance of eating vegetables each day. It may well be that Massachusetts boys and girls may be stronger for this forethought of their parents.

Dr. Ray Lyman Wilbur thinks that one of the reasons Pacific Coast athletes seem to excel over those in the East may be because they have fresh foods each day of the year.

RECREATION*
ALMA PORTER
Assistant State Supervisor of Physical Education

After all, leisure time is a part of life—a part which should be expected to enrich and color what otherwise is often a mere existence. That for years the leisure of children and adults has been recognized as a problem, as a time of potential mischief, is, of course, true; that there should be a concerted effort toward education for its better use, or as a matter of fact, recognition of the need of such education, is so new an idea as to be quite staggering.

There seems to be no question in the minds of those who have studied children, or who work with children, that their play life is an essential part of their very being. From the time when the baby kicks and squirms with his every inch, or reaches a wavering, uncertain hand toward the bright thing held by his mother, all through childhood and into adult life there is this urge toward play. There is this urge toward interesting, soul satisfying activity, which in the growing child is unquenchable, but which has been considered all through the ages as superfluous, certainly, and even a little suspicious in adults.

However, there is some recognition that play is not a particularly unpleasant, mischievous thing which a child concocts to annoy his parents and his teachers, but a vital something which serves as a background, a natural opportunity for that physical growth which must come through activity, and for social growth which must come through "give and take" with his kind. Joseph Lee once said, in effect, that children do not play because they are children, but they have childhood that they may play.

The play of the very young child is a fascinating study, about which all too little is known. It is fairly safe to say, however, that opportunity and facility for those play activities which seem to be natural for small children are so seldom made available for them, either by parent or community, that anyone interested in the play of children may well focus some of his attention there.

These little people are surprisingly strong as well as surprisingly active, and most of them, if they are well, take the utmost pleasure in a few activities which seem to have a definite relationship to their growth, physical and social. They like to creep and roll; they like to walk; they like to climb; they display the deepest interest in all sorts of little things which they can handle and investigate; they like and need companionship; they have an insatiable curiosity which they need opportunity to use, and they have a power of persistence which is not short of marvelous. This delightful curiosity as to what they can do with themselves, as to what they can do with all the queer things this world offers to an adventurous spirit, this persistence until they get satisfaction—complete baby satisfaction—in activity, help to make up a very nice world, a very pleasant place in which to be.

*Reprinted from *The Commonhealth*, Vol. 18, No. 1, Jan.-Feb.-Mar. 1931.

And yet these strange adults, who might very well provide opportunities for this pleasant, satisfying world, are so busy entertaining this same baby that it is no wonder that it becomes a puzzling place to him. A fat brown baby, who was sitting on the beach, illustrates this point. With infinite pains he was filling his little pail with sand, using a big spoon clumsily, but persistently, completely absorbed and happy. His oversolicitous mother, who had thoughtfully provided the sun suit, the pail, the spoon, the beach, and even the baby, leaned over him, emptied his pail, filled it brimming full and set it down before him. The effect was immediate, disastrous, and noisy. Unfortunately, the fat, brown baby did not want a full pail. He had nothing to do with it after it was full, but he had wanted to fill it. That was his own idea, and it would have afforded him glowing satisfaction to accomplish it.

It would seem that children through life are rather well entertained, and largely in artificial ways; to fail to recognize the difference between play and entertainment is to fail to provide opportunity for natural activity, which means growth and happiness. Unfortunately, the results last through life.

The White House Conference sums it up: "Since play forms the chief, and indeed the only activity of the preschool years, it follows that the neglect of the recreation and physical education of the preschool child constitutes a serious flaw in any system of child care and protection. A child's occupations are his whole existence; he is always at work during his waking hours. 'His play is the formative element of the early period, producing independence, self-direction, joy of accomplishment—three basic principles of early life. For this education he needs: a suitable and safe place for his activities; adequate play material; good companionship; sufficient supervision to prevent harm, or accident, yet not enough to take away the opportunity he needs for self-direction and spontaneity.' (Baldwin). Absence of motive, stimulus, or opportunity for normal play activity, results in retarded and unsatisfactory physical and mental development."

Now the relation of the play life of children to the leisure time of adults is evident. To be trite and platitudinous, "As the twig is bent, so is the tree," or to suggest the old Methodist warning for the upbringing of its religious students: "He who playeth when he is young will play when he is old," is to encourage us to believe that since we cannot eliminate either the play urge or its expression, that we had better build on its wisely and take joy in it. The play life of the adult is just as important as the play life of children—a little different in emphasis, a little different in conception, but a part of life which is real living—often in this rather badly adjusted economic life of ours the only real life.

Unquestionably the attitude toward recreation and leisure time is changing. The old idea that joy in life, play and happiness were incurably wicked—inventions of Satan—is going. This feeling, which had its inception in the old religious teachings, is strong even in the present day,— we call it conscience, but it is really a distrust of joy in life which has been handed to us. But faith in those things which mean richer and deeper appreciations of life is coming—is already here.

To go back a little, there are reasons why this problem of leisure time has crept so persistently into modern life. In the "good old days" of this country, the actual labor involved in supporting a family, feeding it, clothing it, and keeping it warm, was a twenty-four hour business. Not only the father and the mother were so burdened, but the children likewise had chores—long, hard jobs of work—which contributed to the need and comfort of the family. Today, not only are the families kept warm, and fed and clothed by infinitely easier methods, but the industrial situation of the machine age has limited the number of hours a man may work; even, unfortunately, has made it impossible for many of them to work at all. All this means that both adults and children have leisure hours thrust upon them with proportionately greater possibilities for trouble. Without adequate understanding and education for its use, there are not only greater possibilities for trouble but it becomes almost impossible to stay out of it.

So, to speak broadly, all people have leisure time—large quantities of it. They all do something with it, good, bad or indifferent. Where did they learn to do those things? The fact, and it is a fact, that they do learn the things they engage in is encouraging, for four places are largely responsible, and to a certain extent, open to educational suggestion—the home, the school, the church, and the street.

There was a time when the home was the center, the social center of life; the church, the moral force; the school, a place of dull preparation which didn't prepare, except in terms of the so-called tools of learning; the street, as a place of undesirable social contact, of less importance in considering the child's life than at the present time. As we conceive it now, it was an attempt to cut his life into four neat parcels, from which he might be expected to draw adequate and protective information to meet the needs of his experience, sometimes difficult experience.

Today the effort to draw the first three together and to reform the fourth is evident,—experimental, to be sure, but nevertheless evident. The school has attempted to do its part by building up in the last ten years seven big objectives which they have called the cardinal principles— interesting in the light of the time-honored Three R's—health, worthy home membership, efficient use of the tools of learning, ethical character, vocational education, worthy use of leisure time, and good citizenship. An amazing list, when one gives thought to it, that the school presumably a place to inspire children to work, and only work, should, among the seven, set down, as one great objective of its existence a plan to help them, as children and adults, to use leisure time as a part of life, as recreation, is beyond the comprehension of many of those who feel that the new school is built on fads and fancies.

As a matter of fact there are not so many great categories of things that people engage in during their leisure time—entertainments and parties, theatre and movies, outdoor and indoor sports and games, the arts and crafts, reading and mischief. And they have learned to do these things in terms of their dispositions and tendencies, their financial opportunities, and their education.

There is the person known to everyone, who, except when he is forced into action, does nothing. Sometimes he "sets and thinks," but generally he just "sets." Who can tell why? There is the other extreme—that person who never under any circumstance can enjoy himself by himself, who has no resource within himself, whose whole life is a round of excitement created by other people, largely in artificial ways. Edna St. Vincent Millay speaks of this person, perhaps even with justification:

"My candle burns at both ends,
It will not last the night;
But, ah, my foes, and oh, my friends—
It gives a lovely light!"

Somewhere between those two lie you and me.

The financial issue is largely one of degree and standard. The rich and the poor do very much the same kind of things, and if the first lays its emphasis on luxury, the latter certainly does on getting the most out of an opportunity. They both go to the movies, they laugh and cry at the same pictures, indeed, in the same places. They drive cars on the same roads; they bathe in the same ocean; they laugh at the same jokes, and love and quarrel in much the same old human way.

And education—what is it doing to help? One thing, largely—attempting to give opportunity for participation in, and appreciation of wholesome activities which meet the peculiar needs and tendencies of individuals, that are within reasonable financial bounds, and which may be provided for all kinds of people everywhere. It is impossible to give a survey of all that is being done to make happiness in leisure time possible, but study the programs of the schools with their efforts toward fine appreciation of the arts, the crafts, the development of physical education programs in school and after school, and the literature. Watch what the museums and art galleries, the libraries, the big recreation associations, the playgrounds, the home magazines, the industries, the church, the newspapers, and, occasionally, even the movies are doing to support the argument that leisure time may be an asset but that too often we have permitted it to be a liability. And then watch the juvenile courts, the delinquency records, and the pathetic missteps of youngsters. Emphasis on education and facility for leisure time is unquestionably the keynote of the future.

People will do something—those "somethings" are learned. So let the home, the school, the church, and yes, even the street, teach.

In an article published in "Recreation," a publication of the National Recreation Association, called "Recreation and Living in the Modern World," and written by Abba Hillel Silver, D.D., the situation is interpreted this way: "Do you know what we need for real living? We need beauty and knowledge and ideals. We need books and pictures and music. We need song and dance and games. We need travel and adventure and romance. We need friends and companionship and the exchange of minds—mind touching mind, and soul enkindling soul. We need contact with all that has been said and achieved through the cycles of time by the aristocrats of the human mind and hand and soul."

THE USE OF LEISURE*

HELEN I. D. MCGILLICUDDY, M. D.
Educational Secretary
Massachusetts Society for Social Hygiene

One of the most interesting questions under discussion at the present time is the "Use of Leisure." On one hand we have those people who declare they have no leisure; on the other hand, those who have too much. Every normal person hopes for leisure, hopes for some spare time in which he may express himself, recreate himself.

While there has always been a leisure class, not all persons have had leisure. In ancient Greece every free boy had an opportunity to develop in his school work a taste for athletics, music, drama, oratory. Leisure was for free male citizens only. So, too, in ancient Rome.

During the Middle Ages, recreation was more widespread. Knights gave tourneys, there was fencing and hunting. Festivals were celebrated by outdoor sports, fairs and pageants. The village people gathered in the Common, and danced on the green. This, in a word, was community recreation.

With the coming of the Puritans to this country, life became very serious. Their struggles with the forces of nature, the rocks, trees, climate and Indians gave them little time for play. As a result, work became the business of life. No longer was there any community recreation, no longer any spare time. So has come commercialized recreation.

What do we do when we have spare time? We do the thing we like to do, we are more revealed in play than in any other way.

Dr. M. J. Exner of the American Social Hygiene Association has said—"Probably nothing influences the individual more profoundly than the way he spends his leisure. Direct the play hours of the young wholesomely and you will need to have little concern about their character."

Studies have shown that we form our habits for leisure during our school years, so that leisure is largely an adolescent problem. Yet no society has solved the problem of outlets for the impulses of youth. Dr. Luther Gulick, the father of the Playground and Recreation Association of America, just before his death said:—"There is not yet a single community in America adequately prepared to handle the recreational life of its people."

We all have seven play instincts: creation, rhythm, fighting, hunting, nurture, curiosity, and team play. The Ancients had Gods dedicated to these instincts: Mars, of War; Diana, of Hunting. As children we grow through play; as adults we sometimes make our work play. Living as we do in a machine age, our ideas of play have changed. We

---
*Reprinted from *The Commonhealth*, Vol. 18, No. 1, Jan.-Feb.-Mar. 1931.

work at high tension all day, we want jazz, speed and excitement at night. Therein lies the danger.

Jane Addams in "Spirit of Youth and the City Streets" has said:—"Only in the modern city have men concluded that it is no longer necessary for the municipality to provide for the insatiable desire for play. Never before in civilization have such numbers of young girls been suddenly released from the protection of the home. Apparently the modern city sees in these girls only two possibilities, both of them commercial—first, a chance to utilize by day their labor power in its factories and shops, and then, another chance in the evening to extract from them their petty wages by pandering to their love of pleasure."

Because Social Hygiene is concerned with the building up of family life and sound leisure activities, a study was made by the American Social Hygiene Association of what the modern girl does with her leisure. One of the most illuminating questions was the following:—"What would you do with your spare time if you had your choice?"

There were 1,516 girls who answered this question and they reported 3,402 items of activity in which they would like to participate.

These choices fall into three general classifications:
1. Educational and creative or constructive activities chosen by ·42%.
2. Organized athletics and outdoor activities by 30.5%.
3. General sociability, passive forms of amusement by 27.5%.

Do girls do what they like to do? In this study 74% were gratified to some extent. The study continues:—"It is important for those planning leisure time activities for girls to know if those from the various foreign groups are especially interested in one type of activity."

Most of the girls in this study preferred reading. As they grow older if they do not have access to good books they may lose interest in reading and turn to magazines of no literary value.

In the study one fourth were not able to do what they desired to do. The question is asked will they later lose their desire for constructive forms of recreation or turn their interest to unsocial activities?

Woods and Kennedy in "Young Working Girls" stated that normal recreational provision should consist of one half holiday, in the open, one evening devoted to a club, one evening for attendance on a party, theatre, or motion picture show, and an occasional red letter event in addition.

What then shall we do with our leisure? The best of refreshment or the worst of mischief is likely to happen in leisure hours. How to make leisure recreative is the problem. Perhaps we read, or dance, go to the theatre, or the pictures. Why not do other things? Read "Recreation in Boston." There you will find cruising afoot, bird and flower walks, historical walks, outdoor sports and outdoor games. Within an hour's ride from Boston there are more than fifty golf courses and many tennis courts. Facilities for horseback riding, boating, and for folk dancing are present.

If our work is creative we find in it opportunities for self-expression. If it is not, then through music, art, drama may we find self-expression.

This means cultivating a taste for the best. A love for the best is twin born in the soul. It means developing a taste for beauty, the blue sky, the sun, the twinkling stars, the lovely moon, the tumbling brooks, the lakes, the rivers, the mountains, the beautiful flowers, the trees, all speak of beauty to us. This beauty finds response in our creative spirit —it helps to recreate us—to enjoy some of our leisure time.

Tell me what you do in your leisure time, and I will tell you what sort of a person you are!

Bibliography

ADDAMS, JANE, *The Spirit of Youth in the City Streets.*
WOODS AND KENNEDY, *Young Working Girls.*
EXNER, M. J., M.D. *What is Social Hygiene?*
JOURNAL OF SOCIAL HYGIENE, Vol. XVI, No. 6—*June* 1930.
SIZER, JAMES PEYTON, *The Commercialization of Leisure.*
VAN WATERS, DR. MIRIAM, *Concerning Parents.*
PROSPECT UNION ASSOCIATION, *Recreation in Boston.*

THE CURE OF TUBERCULOSIS*

BY ERNEST B. EMERSON, M. D.

Superintendent, Rutland State Sanatorium

There is no specific for the cure of tuberculosis—no magic serum, drug, operation or climate alone or together will prevail against the disease. In a broad sense, the treatment of tuberculosis is a mode of life and whatever remedial measures we may prescribe are only adjuncts to a mode of life fitted to the individual. What this mode of life shall be, and what palliative measures shall be prescribed, depend on the type of case, its duration, whether acute or chronic, the age of the patient and his economic status. The treatment of an early case in a young person is an entirely different problem from that presented by the chronic case of many years' duration.

For the early acute case bed rest and very likely some form of collapse therapy are indicated.

For the chronic case, possibly nothing more than a few weeks of rest, or a vacation, is indicated.

The earlier treatment is started, the better are the chances for recovery. In many instances, treatment is delayed for months, or possibly years, before the patient is aware he has the disease. The fault may lie either with the patient himself, through his ignorance of the symptoms and neglect to seek medical aid, or with the physician who has failed to recognize the disease in its early stages, or has not told the patient the whole truth.

There are two outstanding symptoms which may or may not indicate the onset of tuberculosis: Unusual fatigue after the day's work and a cough with or without expectoration. A cough lasting more than four weeks demands a careful investigation as to its cause, including x-ray, sputum examinations, and observation until it has disappeared

*Reprinted from *The Commonhealth*, Vol. 22, No. 1, Jan.-Feb.-Mar. 1935.

and tuberculosis has been ruled out, or the presence of the disease has been determined. If such a procedure were universally carried out, many months, to say the least, of taking treatment in the sanatorium or at home might be avoided, and more patients restored to health than can possibly be cured at a later date.

Once the diagnosis is established, the patient should be told; not to tell him that he has the disease is wrong, for the only hope of a cure depends upon his intelligent cooperation.

The first step in the treatment is the education of the patient. He should be given some idea of what he has, what he may expect with or without treatment, and the reason why a routine life is prescribed for him. It is not necessary to explain to one with a broken leg why it must rest in a splint but it is necessary, in order to get the fullest cooperation, to explain to a patient why he must lie in bed to rest a "broken lung". The consumptive who is to win must possess a certain degree of intelligence, must cooperate with his physician and must have a fair degree of will power and determination. Intelligent cooperation cannot be secured unless he has, at least, some knowledge of the disease and the reasons for details of treatment, which may otherwise seem unnecessary or even absurd. Is it fair to expect him to obtain this knowledge by himself, and to get the proper point of view from the many instructive and valuable contributions available for his use? In some measure, yes, but are we not expecting too much of the average man, sent away to the country with a package of pamphlets and general instructions to rest and to take plenty of nourishment? This may be good advice for the chronic case but it is not a good prescription for an early or acute case with no background based on the practical experience of the trained consumptive. It is for this reason that, in most instances, a patient should have a preliminary course of instruction and treatment in the sanatorium where he may learn something of the disease and the underlying principles or reasons for his treatment. In the early stages, it is certainly much easier for the patient to take treatment with others traveling the same way than it is to lie in bed, in a corner room, and listen to the family jars and the words of condolence and pity of the neighbors.

Home treatment, or life on the farm with its milk, butter, fresh eggs and sunshine all have their place; in fact, home treatment makes up the major part of the program but should come after sanatorium treatment and not before.

What is meant by a mode of life? Broadly speaking, less work and more rest; less play and more rest; less worry and more optimism.

It is a shock to be told that one has tuberculosis and somewhat disconcerting to find one's self in a sanatorium. However, shortly after arrival, the patient discovers individuals who convey to him that there is a chance, and a little later, the patient finds himself improving, notes improvement in others, and optimism takes the place of fear and worry.

The essentials for the treatment of tuberculosis are rest, fresh air, proper food and regulated exercise. Not one may be omitted unless, possibly, the exercise. It is the proper adjustment of these simple measures, and not a change of climate, serums, or drugs, which brings about the desired results. The importance of fresh air is recognized, is easily prescribed, and is readily taken. Food fills a large place in the minds of many. Twenty-five years ago, patients were taught to stuff themselves with milk and eggs, and the idea still lingers. Both are excellent foods but should be taken at the regular mealtimes and not in the form of lunches, or as a cure for tuberculosis. A normally functioning digestive system is the patient's greatest asset and should not be abused. It may happen that more good will be derived from the skim milk and a cracker than from steak and onions.

Rest is the only measure in the treatment of tuberculosis which has stood the test of time. Rest is an indefinite term. It signifies anything from sleep to the substitution of some other activity either mental or physical. Without rest, all other measures in the treatment of the disease will likely fail. It is the bed rock of tuberculosis therapy, and the one remedy a patient will evade, if he can devise any form of excuse to outwit the doctor, or to deceive himself. This is not surprising insomuch as the average tuberculous patient has a sense of well-being seen in no other disease. This again suggests the education of the patient and the explanation of why rest throws less work upon the heart and lungs. There must be physical rest and, so far as possible, mental rest with the removal of care and worry. With the subsidence of symptoms, intensive rest is modified by the substitution of graded exercise. The meaning of exercise is as indefinite as that of rest. It begins when the patient sits up in bed and may end with long walks in the woods, and finally a return to the business of earning a living. There is little danger of prescribing too much rest and fresh air but there is some hazard in too much food or too much exercise. Overeating does more harm than good and overactivity may retard convalescence or undo the results of many months of rest.

A proper mental attitude is most essential. Mental attitude is a product of heredity, more or less modified by teaching, suggestion, observation, and the patient's own efforts to see life in its proper perspective. The patient must have the determination to get well, based upon faith in himself, in his physician, and the willingness to yield to the discipline of a new life.

The onset of tuberculosis is not definitely known, neither is it possible to say definitely when a cure is established. Between the diagnosis and the cure is a long interval—one to tax the courage of the most optimistic. During this time, when the patient looks well, and feels well, he is in the danger zone—a difficult period through which to carry him.

The foregoing outlines the fundamentals in the treatment of tuberculosis. Drugs are of no value whatsoever except in so far as they may relieve symptoms arising from time to time—a tonic, possibly, for loss of appetite, a cathartic for constipation, or a sedative for cough. Alcohol in any form is not indicated; it only masks the symptoms. Narcotics are similarly contraindicated except as prescribed for definite and positive indications; for this reason, cough syrups and various exploited nostrums should be avoided; they neither prevent nor cure tuberculosis. A change of climate is unnecessary and may even do harm —just as many are cured at home as abroad.

The question may be asked: What can the sanatorium do that cannot be done in the home? In one sense, nothing; there is no patent on the treatment; however, from experience gained from contacts with many patients from various walks of life, there is no doubt that it is practically an impossibility to carry out in the average home the routine which becomes commonplace, and an everyday affair, in the life of the sanatorium patient.

The patient's education begins on the day of admission, when he receives instruction from the nurse with regard to the disposal of sputum, his hours in bed, and other details; also a word of encouragement. The physician at the time of examination continues this instruction, and explains to him the why of it all. Later he has the opportunity of attending lectures, or talks by the staff, in which the history of tuberculosis, its pathology, symptoms and treatment are frankly discussed. He is encouraged to ask questions at all times. The teaching of tuberculosis does not result in morbid brooding, or undue apprehension with regard to the future; on the contrary, it teaches respect for the disease and not fear.

In no other disease have so many advances been made in treatment during the past few years as in tuberculosis. Collapse therapy in some form, artificial pneumothorax, phrenic nerve operations, thoracoplasty, and other forms of surgery, have unfolded a future for many otherwise destined for unknown years of invalidism with its inevitable end. Yet with all that surgery offers, it is only an adjunct to the general principles already outlined. Successful treatment still depends on an early diagnosis and that mode of life which has, as yet, not been displaced by any panacea.

With this background of sanatorium teaching, and practical experience, the intelligent patient is more or less qualified to go on with home treatment, which is merely a modified sanatorium regime, adjusted to the individual handicap.

THE ROLE OF SURGERY IN PULMONARY TUBERCULOSIS*

BY EDWARD D. CHURCHILL, M. D.

John Homans Professor of Surgery, Harvard Medical School
Consulting Surgeon, Rutland State Sanatorium

The term "conservative" has a dual meaning, and its use as a descriptive term in medicine is often not clearly defined. Physicians find satisfaction and a certain freedom from responsibility in clinging to what they term conservative measures. Patients like to think that they have a conservative doctor. In this sense conservative means a tendency to harbor healthy skepticism regarding new methods of treatment the dangers or lasting benefits of which may not yet be apparent. All intelligent and conscientious physicians should be conservative according to this definition.

A second, and equally significant definition of conservative measures is that they *conserve* the patient or protect him from the loss, waste and injury of disease. In this sense, all efforts of the medical profession are by definition intended as conservative.

The treatment of pulmonary tuberculosis has passed the point where a policy of inaction or postponement of active forms of treatment in the face of certain clear indications can be condoned on the grounds that it is the conservative thing to do. Collapse therapy is no longer an untried or experimental newcomer in the field of therapeutics. It is of proven value and must be employed frequently and oftentimes promptly if the physician is to be really conservative and protect his patient from further loss, injury or death from the disease.

Fortunately there are no longer two camps among those familiar with the disease and its effective treatment. The dangerous postponement of active measures of treatment when they are clearly indicated is now only a refuge for the ignorant, careless or blindly prejudiced. Under no circumstances can such folly be termed the conservative course.

If a person develops active pulmonary tuberculosis today, and becomes a resident of an up-to-date sanatorium, the chances are somewhat better than one out of two that some form of "collapse therapy" will be advised during the course of his illness. This by no means indicates that the long established method of treatment by rest in bed has been *replaced* by newer methods. Sanatorium regime is still the foundation for any form of treatment in tuberculosis. Collapse therapy is *supplementary* and *complementary* to treatment by rest, and is in no sense an *alternative* procedure.

What is "collapse therapy," when is it recommended and what is accomplished by it? In its acute stage pulmonary tuberculosis is a progressing infection in the lung and as such the general principles that apply to the treatment of infections anywhere in the body are applicable.

First of all, the condition of the body as a whole must be built up and powers of resistance improved so that natural defense mechanisms that

*Reprinted from *The Commonhealth*, Vol. 22, No. 1, Jan.-Feb.-Mar. 1935.

tend to control and limit the disease are at their best. This is accomplished by the regime in a sanatorium where the patient is taught to cultivate physical and mental rest. The weight loss that almost invariably attends the onset of the disease is restored by a nourishing diet. These measures, particularly the bed rest, afford a certain amount of local rest to the diseased lung, by decreasing its movement. In many patients this regime alone is adequate to promote arrest and healing of the disease.

When the involvement of the lung is extensive or when the resistance of the individual is inadequate even under the most favored circumstances, it becomes necessary to provide additional rest for the diseased lung by some form of collapse therapy. The first recommendation is usually to induce an artificial pneumothorax.

A lung may be compared to an inflated rubber balloon in an airtight box. To collapse this balloon, air is injected into the box. When air is injected into the chest the lung drops away from the chest wall, becomes markedly reduced in size and its movements on respiration are restricted. A successful artificial pneumothorax frequently brings almost immediate relief from cough, hemorrhage, fever and the many other distressing symptoms of the disease. The lung may be kept collapsed by repeating the injections of air over a long period of time. The extent of the disease in the lung at the time the treatment is instituted usually determines the length of time that the lung should be kept at rest.

Not infrequently when air is first injected it will be found that the lung has become glued to the ribs by scar tissue. These adhesions form over the diseased areas and prevent retraction of just the portion of the lung that is most important to collapse. It is possible in many cases to cut these adhesions by a small operation and thereby achieve a complete collapse. If the adhesions are extensive it is not possible for an effective pneumothorax to be established and hope must be pinned on other measures.

A relatively simple operation that serves to rest and relax the lung is termed "phrenicectomy." The strongest muscle of respiration is the diaphragm—a muscular partition that divides the thorax from the abdomen. It is possible to stop the motion of half of this muscle by crushing the phrenic nerve on the diseased side. This nerve is reached through a small incision just above the collar bone in the neck. This operation is extremely effective in certain cases—one danger, however, lies in the fact that too much has been expected from what is a relatively minor procedure. Its use in far advanced cases is usually disappointing.

Many patients are successful in arresting the progress and further extension of their disease but find themselves unable to repair the damage resulting from the infection. These patients find themselves in the so-called chronic stage of tuberculosis. Lung tissue has been destroyed, leaving cavities or excavations that are imbedded in scar tissue and densely adherent to the ribs. These cavities continue to discharge the tubercle bacillus so that the focus of infection remains a menace, not only to the patient but to the community. An individual at this stage may remain indefinitely under sanatorium regime without making further progress. Such a person may feel well enough to return to his work, but almost invariably suffers a relapse within a relatively short time.

Under such circumstances the problem of healing is essentially a mechanical one, and mechanical principles are utilized in the form of surgery. The ribs that form the rigid wall overlying the cavity are removed, thereby allowing the walls of the cavity to come together so that healing may take place. This operation is termed a "thoracoplasty" and is divided into stages depending on the number and length of ribs to be removed. The results of this operation have been peculiarly satisfactory and health has been restored to hundreds of patients for whom the possibility of every other form of treatment was exhausted.

The operation of thoracoplasty is rarely used during the acute progressive stages of the disease—its chief application is in the case of patients who have demonstrated an adequate resistance and have brought the extension of the disease to a halt but are unable to complete the healing process.

Although long sections may be removed from all of the ribs on one side, thoracoplasty is not a deforming operation. A former patient of mine worked for several months as a stenographer in a doctor's office. One day she was called upon to take a long dictation having to do with thoracoplasty. Although the doctor was surprised at her knowledge of the procedure, he never suspected that she herself had had the operation two years before.

From this brief description it will be seen that the introduction of collapse therapy has effected a revolution in the treatment of pulmonary tuberculosis. The course of every patient must be carefully followed and the appropriate measure or measures instituted at the opportune moment. "Every individual is as different in his disease or in his response to treatment as he is in his features and character" (Davies). The moves of the disease must be met by counter moves in therapy as a game of chess. When both lungs are involved the situation becomes doubly complex and doubly hazardous. Frequent x-ray examinations are necessary. Studies of the blood in addition to the temperature, pulse and weight, serve as an important index to the patient's resistance and the progress of the disease.

The physician and the surgeon stand shoulder to shoulder in facing certain problems. The point at issue is not surgical treatment as opposed to medical treatment, but the selection of the proper treatment for the individual case. The first concern is the selection of the patient who requires collapse therapy; second, the selection of the operation that is indicated; third, the choice of the proper time for its institution; fourth, making the operation safe and effective for the patient; and finally, careful supervision of the convalescence.

The efforts of the surgeon and the physician center about the welfare of the individual patient—from the standpoint of public health and the community at large the change in the treatment of the disease is vitally significant. First, a larger proportion of the patients will return to their homes with their cavities closed, thereby reducing the number of so-called "open" cases that serve to spread the disease. Second, with the seal of more complete and effective healing, repeated breakdowns will become less frequent. At the onset of each "breakdown," infection may be disseminated in the home or in the community. Third, many patients that would be forced to remain in institutions indefinitely at public expense, may be returned as useful members to their communities.

APPROVED PROPHYLACTIC REMEDY FOR USE IN THE EYES OF INFANTS AT BIRTH*

The Massachusetts Department of Public Health, in accordance with the provision of Chapter 115 of the Acts of 1936, approved the following "prophylactic remedy" for the treatment of the eyes of infants at birth: A one per cent filtered solution of silver nitrate, U. S. P., in distilled water, stored in ampoules for single use, the ampoules to be protected against penetration of light and provided that if the ampoule must be broken, it shall not be made of glass or other shatterable material which might cause injury to the eye, and further provided that the ampoule or its container shall bear an expiration date which shall not be later than six months after the date of preparation of the solution and that no solution shall be used after said date of expiration.

Under the provisions of Chapter 115 of the Acts of 1936, no prophylactic remedy may be used, after June 4, 1936, for the treatment of the eyes of infants at birth which is not furnished or approved by the Department of Public Health.

The Department recommends the following procedure for the protection of an infant's eyes against infection at birth:

1. Every pregnant woman, concerning whom there is the least suspicion of gonococcal infection, should be so treated for the infection, both during pregnancy and at delivery, that the birth canal may be as free as possible from the gonococcus during the birth of the baby.
2. The following order of procedure is recommended for the use of the prophylactic in the baby's eyes:
   (a) Clean the skin of the four eyelids with cotton pledgets moistened in boric acid solution, using separate pledgets for each eye.
   (b) Thoroughly irrigate the conjunctival sac of each eye with boric acid solution, using a sterile soft rubber ear syringe.
   (c) Retract the eyelids, digitally, and instill one drop of a one per cent solution of silver nitrate into each eye, preferably near the outer canthus, and allow the solution to remain in contact with the conjunctiva for at least two minutes.
   (d) Irrigate the conjunctival sac of each eye with sterile normal salt solution to prevent chemical conjunctivitis.

*Reprinted from the *New England Journal of Medicine*, Vol. 214, No. 21, pp. 1067—1068, May 21, 1936.

(e) Secure the services of an ophthalmologist upon the first appearance of suppurative conjunctivitis and insist upon a bacteriological report on the conjunctival secretions.
3. Precautions:
Since corneal abrasions promote ulceration in the presence of the gonococcus, great care must be taken to avoid contact between the cornea and the finger manipulating the eyelids, the irrigating syringe or the eyedropper, if the above recommended procedure is carried out.

HENRY D. CHADWICK, M. D.,
Commissioner of Public Health

May 12, 1936.

RESOLUTION ADOPTED BY THE JOINT COMMITTEE ON HEALTH PROBLEMS IN EDUCATION OF THE NATIONAL EDUCATION ASSOCIATION AND THE AMERICAN MEDICAL ASSOCIATION
June 1936

Moved by Bauer, seconded by Leland:

Whereas: At the annual meeting of the Joint Committee on Health Problems in Education of the National Education Association and the American Medical Association held at St. Louis, Mo., February 25, 1936, a presentation was made by Major Joel I. Connolly, of the Chicago Board of Health, relating to possible health hazards in apparently modern plumbing installations in public buildings, and

Whereas: It was manifest in the said presentation that plumbing fixtures which have been generally regarded as safe and sanitary in design may in fact constitute a real and serious health hazard by reason of the danger of back siphonage and contamination of water supply mains, and

Whereas: The probability exists that such apparently modern, safe and sanitary plumbing installations may exist in numerous school buildings in the United States, and

Whereas: The existence of such apparently safe, modern and sanitary plumbing installations and reliance upon them brings about a sense of false security, therefore, be it

Resolved: By the Joint Committee on Health Problems in Education of the National Education Association and the American Medical Association that this Committee apprehends the possibility of danger to the health of school children from apparently safe, modern and sanitary plumbing installations in school buildings, and be it further

Resolved: That the said Joint Committee earnestly recommends to all school boards and school executives that surveys be instituted by competent engineers to ascertain whether or not the danger of back siphonage and consequent pollution of water supply mains exist in plumbing installations within their jurisdictions, and that such surveys be followed by prompt corrective measures, and be it further

Resolved: That these resolutions be offered for publication to all journals dealing with public health, health education and general education.

Book Note

SYPHILIS AND ITS TREATMENT by William A. Hinton, M. D., Formerly Chief of the Syphilis Clinic and Director of Clinical Research at the Boston Dispensary, he is now Chief of its Laboratory Department, Chief of the Wassermann Laboratory of the Massachusetts Department of Public Health. He is also Instructor in Preventive Medicine and Hygiene and in Bacteriology and Immunology, Harvard Medical School. 304 pp. New York: The Macmillan Company. $3.50.

This book is intended for the general practitioner, the public health worker, and the medical student. It is, therefore, written in simple, relatively non-technical language and every technical term is defined. For this same reason the rarities are left out. This steering of a middle course, as it were, is of definite advantage to this group of readers, who are not, therefore, confused with useless details; yet the reader is always directed to larger books and toward consultation with specialists for help in meeting the rare and serious complications.

The author has had unusual training in pathology and throughout has tried to describe the lesions by their underlying pathology, especially is this true in regard to treatment. Expressing very vividly the need of considering the patient regarding his syphilitic pathology and general physical background, he emphasizes that the aim of treatment is not to work blindly for negative blood tests regardless of the damage to the patient, but it is so far as possible to restore the injured parts to normal function, to render the patient safe as regards transmitting the disease, and to prevent the patient from fresh outbursts. As he explains it, "the physician will succeed most often in controlling syphilis if he administers a few carefully chosen drugs promptly, intensively, continuously for a long time, and with a minimum of inconvenience and expense to the patient."

In spite of his particular interest in the laboratory phases of the problem he has been careful to keep them in their place. The book is very well and very consistently done and should be owned and studied by all who plan to treat syphilis from the point of view of the general practitioner.

—AUSTIN W. CHEEVER, M.D.,
Boston, Mass.

REPORT OF DIVISION OF FOOD AND DRUGS

During the months of January, February and March 1936, samples were collected in 295 cities and towns.

There were 1,229 samples of milk examined, of which 82 were below standard, from 12 samples the cream had been in part removed, and 9 samples contained added water. There were 1,485 bacteriological examinations made of milk, 1,292 of which complied with the requirements. There were 11 bacteriological examinations made of cream, 9 of which complied with the requirements; 113 bacteriological examinations of ice cream, 112 of which complied with the requirements; 4 bacteriological examinations of canned goods, all of which complied with the requirements; 3 bacteriological examinations of spring water, 5 bacteriological examinations of tonic, all of which complied with the requirements; 3 bacteriological examinations of tonic bottles, all of which did not comply with the requirements; 9 bacteriological examinations of food samples from flood areas which did not comply with the requirements; and 10 bacteriological examinations of mattress fillings, all of which complied with the requirements. There were 97 samples of ice cream analyzed for pounds of food solids per gallon, of which 3 samples were below the standard.

There were 1,048 samples of food examined, 315 of which were adulterated. These consisted of 63 samples of cheese in which gum was present; 4 samples of canned goods which were decomposed; 29 samples of pickles which contained sodium benzoate and were not properly labeled; 1 sample of celery which was misbranded; 1 sample of cordial drops, the cordial in which contained sodium benzoate and was not marked; 7 samples of sour cream in which gum was present; 1 sample of fish which was rancid; 60 samples of olive oil, 54 samples of which contained tea-seed oil, and 6 samples contained cottonseed oil; 44 samples of hamburg steak, 10 samples of which contained a compound of sulphur dioxide not properly labeled, 4 of which were also decomposed, 32 samples which were decomposed, 4 of which also contained sodium sulphite in excess of one-tenth of one per cent, and one also containing added water; 1 sample contained added water, and 1 sample contained sodium sulphite in excess of one-tenth of one per cent; 24 samples of sausage, 12 samples of which contained a compound of sulphur dioxide not properly labeled, 1 of which was also decomposed, 9 samples which were decomposed, 4 of which also contained sodium sulphite in excess of one-tenth of one per cent, 1 sample contained lungs, 1 sample contained starch in excess of 2 per cent, and 1 sample contained sodium sulphite in excess of one-tenth of one per cent; 51 samples of soft drinks, 41 samples of which were artificially colored and were not properly labeled, 9 of which also contained sodium benzoate and were not properly labeled, and 1 of these samples also had an insect floating in the contents, 3 samples were in dirty bottles, and 7 samples contained sodium benzoate and were not properly labeled; and 30 samples of mattress fillings which contained secondhand material.

There were 76 samples of drugs examined, of which 9 were adulterated. These consisted of 4 samples of argyrol which did not conform to the professed standard under which they were sold, 1 sample of lime water, and 4 samples of spirit of nitrous ether, all of which did not conform to the requirements of the U. S. Pharmacopoeia.

The police departments submitted 164 samples of liquor for examination. The police departments also submitted 13 samples to be analyzed for poisons or drugs, of which 1 sample contained codeine, 1 sample contained opium, 1 sample contained heroin hydrochloride, 2 samples contained morphine, 2 samples of weed were not cannabis, 3 samples of cigarettes, 2 of which contained cannabis and 1 sample did not, 1 sample of white powder contained heroin, 1 sample was opium with char and partial decomposition products of opium, and 1 sample of liquor contained no narcotics or injurious substances.

There were 106 cities and towns visited for the inspection of pasteurizing plants, and 430 plants were inspected.

There were 109 hearings held pertaining to violations of the laws.

There were 99 convictions for violations of the law, $3,045 in fines being imposed.

William Benedict of Fitchburg; Angelo Boura of Waltham; Ernest T. Cabral and Antone Silva of North Westport; Matias S. Medina of Brockton; Arthur Pezold of Lynn; Guy Amrheim, and James Bekus & Charles Contas of South Boston; Philip Blanchard of Worcester; George Chronopoulas and Aristedes Poleprone of Boston; and Louis Battaro of Mattapan, were all convicted for violations of the milk laws. Ernest T. Cabral and Antone Silva of North Westport appealed their cases.

James Boturas of Haverhill was convicted for violation of the milk grading law.

Whiting Milk Companies of Charlestown, and New England Dairies, Incorporated, of Boston, were convicted for selling milk with a fat content less than specified.

B. L. Cummings of Arlington was convicted for violation of the pasteurization regulations.

Nathan Baker of Haverhill; George Jamgochian, National Creamery Company, Incorporated, and Louis Kumin, 2 cases, of Somerville; New England Market, Incorporated, of Cambridge; Dominick Ciotti of Malden; Benjamin Bornstein of Dorchester; Morris Marienberg, 3 cases, Pasquale Buonaguiro, 2 cases, Bernard L. Kolovson, 2 cases, Alphonse Iavazzo, 2 cases, Edward Rood, Hyman Alpert, Nathan M. Alpert, Charles Cerqua, Benjamin Chaffin, Samuel Dechter, Max Most, and Salvatore Savini, all of Boston; Pasquale Guylielmo of East Boston; Henry Abrams, Broadway Market, Incorporated, Peter L. Berlo, W. T. Grant Company, Edward Skiddell, and Benjamin Goldberg of South Boston; World Beef Company, Incorporated, Michael Borowik, and Michael J. Dwyer of Fall River; Barney Cohen, Samuel Gordon, and Joseph Lipman of New Bedford; Essem Packing Company of Lawrence; Nathan Somers, Michael Tokarsky, and Samuel Kutzenko's Market of Springfield; Anthony Marcello and Nino B. Moro of Milford; Erasmo Capobiano of Quincy; and Ernest Carino of Medford, were all convicted for violations of the food laws. National Creamery Company, Incorporated, of Somerville; Edward Rood, Nathan M. Alpert, and Pasquale Buonaguiro, 2 cases, of Boston; and W. T. Grant Company, and Edward Skiddell, of South Boston, all appealed their cases.

Leo Letalien of Fall River; and William Di Pietro of Milford, were convicted for violations of the drug laws. William Di Pietro of Milford appealed his case.

Omaha Packing Company, Incorporated, of Lowell, was convicted for violation of the sanitary food law.

Freedman's Bakery, Incorporated, and Carl Freedman, of Roxbury, were convicted for violations of the bakery regulations.

Marijan Dworakowski and Frank Kucgarski of Easthampton; Anthony Dyjak and Stanley Rapalus of Ludlow; Bondsville Water Company of Bondsville; Wincenty Matera and Walter S. Nogg of Palmer; and Edward Niles of Thorndike, were all convicted for violations of the law and regulations relative to the manufacture and bottling of carbonated non-alcoholic beverages.

Arminio Francesconi of Milford; S. S. Kresge Company of Greenfield; Charles E. Goldman of Norwell; Louis Liebman of South Sudbury; and Sears Roebuck & Company of Salem, were all convicted for violations of the law relative to methyl or wood alcohol.

John Chiatreres, 2 cases, of Springfield; and Louis Cramer of North Adams, were convicted for violations of the slaughtering law.

Max Abramson and Alexander Stroum of Dorchester; George Gershman of Worcester; Empire Parlor Furniture Company, Incorporated, of Roxbury; Max Goldstein and Hub Mattress Company, Incorporated, 2 cases, of Boston; Jennie Agonoski of Charlestown; Israel Weiner of Lynn; Osiason, Incorporated, of Fall River; Springfield Mattress Company, Incorporated, of Springfield; Julius Rubin of New Bedford; Abraham Moretsky of Chelsea; Harry Berman and Philip Lederman of Beverly; and Young Brothers Mattress Company, Incorporated, of Providence, Rhode Island, were all convicted for violations of the mattress laws. Max Abramson and Empire Parlor Furniture Company, Incorporated, of Roxbury; Harry Berman and Philip Lederman of Beverly; and Jennie Agonoski of Charlestown, appealed their cases.

In accordance with Section 25, Chapter 111 of the General Laws, the following is the list of articles of adulterated food collected in original packages from manufacturers, wholesalers, or producers:

Sour cream in which gum was present was obtained as follows:

Three samples from M. Winer & Company of Boston, and 1 sample each, from M. Winer & Company of Revere, Mattapan, and Fall River; and Mayflower Creamery Company, Incorporated, at Boston.

Cheese in which gum was present was obtained as follows:

Ten samples from Mayflower Creamery Company, Incorporated, at Boston; 7 samples from National Creamery Company of Somerville; 5 samples from M. Winer Company of Boston; 5 samples from Berkshire Creamery Company of Pittsfield; 2 samples each, from New York Cut Rate Grocery Company of Mattapan, National Dairy Products of Springfield, Borden Sales Company of Boston, and Shefford Cheese

Company of New York; 4 samples from Fairmont Creamery Company of Boston; and 1 sample each, from M. Winer Company of Springfield, Worcester, Revere, and Mattapan; S. Salvate of New Bedford; Mayflower Butter & Cheese Company, Incorporated, at Springfield; and Columbia Cheese Company of Newark, New Jersey.

Pickles which contained sodium benzoate and were not properly labeled were obtained as follows:

Four samples each, from Louis P. Labbee and Quality L. & B. Store, of Fall River; 2 samples, from N. E. Wholesale Grocery Company of Fall River; and 1 sample each, from Limas De Cambra and Fall River Trading & Finance Company, of Fall River; P. Berlo and W. T. Grant Company, of South Boston; National Pickling Works of Roxbury; and Taunton Public Market of Taunton.

Olive oil which contained tea-seed oil was obtained as follows:

Seventeen samples from A. Accardi Company of Boston; 10 samples from Cara Donna Packing Company of Boston; 8 samples from Cosmos Food Stores, Incorporated, at Lynn; 6 samples from Ameo Oil Company of Boston; 4 samples from Lo Conte Brothers, Incorporated, at Boston; 2 samples each, from A. De Luca & Company of New York, and Cantania Oil Company, Incorporated, at Boston; and 1 sample each, from M. De Robbio & Sons of Providence, Rhode Island, and E. G. Sophis of Lowell.

Olive oil which contained cottonseed oil was obtained as follows:

Two samples from Louis Bellestraccio of Worcester; and 1 sample each, from Cosmos Food Stores, Incorporated, at Lynn; and Marianna Messina of East Boston.

Hamburg steak which was decomposed was obtained as follows:

Two samples each, from Murry's Market and Second National Market, of Roxbury; and 1 sample each, from Original Indian Orchard Market, Jacob Pomeratz, and Community Market, of Indian Orchard; A. H. Phillips, Incorporated, Kutzenko's Market, and Michael Tokarsky, of Springfield; New York Butchers, Stark Supply Company, Incorporated, and Transfer Market, of Boston; Morris Abrams (Taylor's Market), Mohican Market, William's Market, and Peter L. Berlo, of South Boston; Jack Miller, Samuel Gordon, Joseph Lipman, Phillip Kaler, and Barney Cohen, all of New Bedford; Waltham Provision Company and Maurice Spector of Waltham; Consumer's Provision, Incorporated, at Worcester; Sam Lipsky of Brookline; Manhattan Market of Allston; and Puritan Public Markets, Incorporated, at Brockton.

Hamburg steak which contained a compound of sulphur dioxide not properly labeled was obtained as follows:

One sample each, from First United Market and Food Mart, Incorporated, at Somerville; Broadway Market, Incorporated, at South Boston; Barney Lass of Boston; Hyman Weisman of Lynn; and Economy Market of Fall River.

One sample of hamburg steak which contained sodium sulphite in excess of one tenth of one per cent was obtained from Mohawk Market of Boston.

Hamburg steak which contained a compound of sulphur dioxide not properly labeled and was also decomposed was obtained as follows:

One sample each, from Hub Meat Stores Company of Somerville; and Henry Abrams of South Boston.

Hamburg steak which contained sodium sulphite in excess of one tenth of one per cent and was also decomposed was obtained as follows:

One sample each, from Singer's Market and National Cash Market of Boston; and Edward Skiddell & Benjamin Chook of South Boston.

One sample of hamburg steak which contained water was obtained from Samuel Kline of Lynn.

One sample of hamburg steak which contained sodium sulphite in excess of one tenth of one per cent, was decomposed, and also contained water was obtained from Ideal Market of Boston.

Sausage which was decomposed was obtained as follows:

One sample each, from Washington Public Market of Boston; Morris Abrams and W. T. Grant Company of South Boston; Pasquale Guglielmo of East Boston; Hub Meat Stores Company of Somerville; The Little Market of Medford; and Standard Market of Lynn.

Sausage which contained a compound of sulphur dioxide not properly labeled was obtained as follows:

One sample each, from A. H. Phillips Company and Somers Market of Springfield; Stella Chain Store of South Boston and Quincy; Mike Pisella of Quincy; Max Goldberg of South Boston; Peerless Market of Boston; Gloria Chain Stores, Incorporated, and Moro's Market of Milford; and Puritan Public Markets, Incorporated, at Brockton.

One sample of sausage which contained sodium sulphite in excess of one tenth of one per cent was obtained from Genoa Packing Company of Boston.

One sample of sausage which contained starch in excess of two per cent was obtained from P. W. Rounsevell, Incorporated, at Boston.

One sample of sausage which contained lungs was obtained from Salvatore Savini of Boston.

One sample of sausage which contained a compound of sulphur dioxide not properly labeled and was also decomposed was obtained from Michael Ricci of Beverly.

One sample of sausage which contained sodium sulphite in excess of one tenth of one per cent and was also decomposed was obtained from Al's Meat Market of Boston.

Three samples of ice cream which were low in pounds of food solids per gallon were obtained from National Ice Cream Company of Boston.

Soft drinks which were artificially colored and were not properly marked were obtained as follows:

Three samples each, from White Eagle Bottling Company of Everett; and Crescent Star Beverage Company, Incorporated, at Charlestown; 2 samples each, from Metropolitan Bottling Company and Blue Ribbon Bottling Company, of Roxbury; Pocasset Bottling Company of Fall River; Phillips Bottling Company of West Everett; Wilben Bottling Company of Worcester; and Parkdale Beverage Company of Boston; and 1 sample each, from Boston Club Bottling Company and Dorchester

Bottling Company, of Dorchester; Red Star Bottling Company of East Boston; Will Bell Bottling Company of Boston; Liberty Bottling Company of Fall River; Glaser Beverage Company, Incorporated, American Products Company, Washington Beverage Company, Incorporated, Queen Wachusett Company, Worcester Soda Company, Incorporated, National Bottling Company, Worcester Orange Crush Company, and Mountain Dry Beverage Company, all of Worcester; Colonial Beverage Company, Incorporated, at Cambridge; and American Bottling Company of Somerville.

There were 20 confiscations, consisting of 420 pounds of butter; 100 pounds of frozen eggs; 3,945 pounds of beef; 9,779 pounds of beef; 851 pounds of veal; 2,337 pounds of poultry; 77,885 pounds of pork; 175 pounds of beef and pork; 150 pounds of mixed meat; 100 pounds of chocolate liquor; 40 pounds of cake; 81 pounds of cocoa; and 144 pounds of cocoa, all contaminated by flood water; 25½ pounds of immature veal; 45 pounds of underweight veal; 250 pounds of decomposed frankforts and bologna; 614 pounds of unstamped pork; 6 pounds of decomposed liverwurst; 2,890 pounds of decomposed sea perch; and 580 pounds of decomposed sea perch.

The licensed cold storage warehouses reported the following amounts of food placed in storage during December, 1935:—247,290 dozens of case eggs; 537,557 pounds of broken out eggs; 453,055 pounds of butter; 3,846,800 pounds of poultry; 2,443,805½ pounds of fresh meat and fresh meat products; and 4,815,109 pounds of fresh food fish.

There was on hand January 1, 1936:— 744,120 dozens of case eggs; 1,945,045 pounds of broken out eggs; 2,008,059 pounds of butter; 7,363,787 pounds of poultry; 5,906,973½ pounds of fresh meat and fresh meat products; and 21,778,220 pounds of fresh food fish.

The licensed cold storage warehouses reported the following amounts of food placed in storage during January, 1936:— 121,500 dozens of case eggs; 444,245 pounds of broken out eggs; 298,710 pounds of butter; 2,187,019 pounds of poultry; 2,723,331 pounds of fresh meat and fresh meat products; and 2,624,762 pounds of fresh food fish.

There was on hand February 1, 1936:— 185,850 dozens of case eggs; 1,697,996 pounds of broken out eggs; 1,162,268 pounds of butter; 8,076,104 pounds of poultry; 6,421,752 pounds of fresh meat and fresh meat products; and 13,275,187 pounds of fresh food fish.

The licensed cold storage warehouses reported the following amounts of food placed in storage during February, 1936:— 28,170 dozens of case eggs; 508,410 pounds of broken out eggs; 169,968 pounds of butter; 893,270 pounds of poultry; 2,522,803 pounds of fresh meat and fresh meat products; and 5,178,435 pounds of fresh food fish.

There was on hand March 1, 1936:— 1,920 dozens of case eggs; 1,261,479 pounds of broken out eggs; 763,729 pounds of butter; 7,031,429 pounds of poultry; 5,980,605½ pounds of fresh meat and fresh meat products; and 8,112,109 pounds of fresh food fish.

MASSACHUSETTS DEPARTMENT OF PUBLIC HEALTH

Commissioner of Public Health, HENRY D. CHADWICK, M.D.

Public Health Council

HENRY D. CHADWICK, M.D., *Chairman*

GORDON HUTCHINS.
FRANCIS H. LALLY, M.D.
SYLVESTER E. RYAN, M.D.
RICHARD M. SMITH, M.D.
RICHARD P. STRONG, M.D.
JAMES L. TIGHE.

Secretary, FLORENCE L. WALL

Division of Administration . . Under direction of Commissioner.
Division of Sanitary Engineering . Director and Chief Engineer,
  ARTHUR D. WESTON, C.E.
Division of Communicable Diseases Director,
  GAYLORD W. ANDERSON, M.D.
Division of Biologic Laboratories . Director and Pathologist,
  ELLIOTT S. ROBINSON, M.D.
Division of Food and Drugs . . Director and Analyst,
  HERMANN C. LYTHGOE, S.B.
Division of Child Hygiene . . Director, M. LUISE DIEZ, M. D.
Division of Tuberculosis . . . Director, ALTON S. POPE, M.D.
Division of Adult Hygiene . . Director,
  HERBERT L. LOMBARD, M.D.

State District Health Officers

The Southeastern District . . RICHARD P. MACKNIGHT, M.D., New Bedford.
The South Metropolitan District . HENRY M. DE WOLFE, M.D., Quincy.
The North Metropolitan District . CHARLES B. MACK, M.D., Boston.
The Northeastern District . . ROBERT E. ARCHIBALD, M.D., Lynn.
The Worcester County District . OSCAR A. DUDLEY, M.D., Worcester.
The Connecticut Valley District . HAROLD E. MINER, M.D., Springfield.
The Franklin County District . . WALTER W. LEE, M.D., No. Adams.
The Berkshire District . . . HAROLD W. STEVENS, M.D., Great Barrington.

PUBLICATION OF THIS DOCUMENT APPROVED BY THE COMMISSION ON ADMINISTRATION AND FINANCE
5500. 8-'36. Order 8381.

THE COMMONHEALTH

Volume 23   July-Aug.-Sept.
No. 3   1936

DENTAL HEALTH

MASSACHUSETTS
DEPARTMENT OF PUBLIC HEALTH

THE COMMONHEALTH

QUARTERLY BULLETIN OF THE MASSACHUSETTS DEPARTMENT OF
PUBLIC HEALTH

Sent Free to any Citizen of the State

Entered as second class matter at Boston Postoffice.

M. LUISE DIEZ, M.D., DIRECTOR OF DIVISION OF CHILD HYGIENE, EDITOR.
1 Beacon Street, Boston, Mass.

CONTENTS

	PAGE
A Review	175
Dental Health Education for Children, by George E. Davis, D.D.S.	179
Trained Teachers of Health, by John J. Desmond, Jr., A.M.	186
A Visual Presentation of the Value of Dental Service, by Henry B. Taylor	188
What Dentists Should Do about Nutrition, by Florence B. Hopkins, M.D., D.M.D.	191
Retardation of Dental Caries in Out-Patients of a Dental Infirmary, by Percy R. Howe, D.D.S., Ruth L. White, B.S., and Milton Rabine, D.D.S	194
Food Fallacies and Nutritional Quackery. Report of the Committee on Nutritional Problems, American Public Health Association	198
How Greenfield Is Solving the Dental Health Problem, by Harold R. Lamb, D.M.D.	204
Our Dental Hygiene Program, by Jennie W. Ball	206
Do You Know about the Volta Bureau?	209
Report of Division of Food and Drugs, April, May and June, 1936	210

A REVIEW

It is most difficult to keep one destination in mind and always steer a course, despite storms and unfavorable currents and head winds, to avoid the rocks of prejudice and the shoals of indifference, and to eventually approach port. Important side issues sometimes completely fog the way but the public health worker, like a navigator, must consult the charts and compass to keep off shoals and reefs. He must read the log of his predecessors carefully and intelligently.

When a new skipper comes aboard his first job is to take his bearings and find out whether his ship is sound and well found. If he has never sailed this run before it would be necessary to read previous logs and comments by previous captains. In studying reports of other workers in dental hygiene in past issues of *The Commonhealth* it seemed that a brief review of some of this material would be most interesting, and it should be enlightening and inspiring to all of us that from the beginning the leaders in the dental hygiene movement have been so well agreed on the best course to sail that we may safely use their charts today.

—FLORENCE B. HOPKINS, M.D., D.M.D.,
Massachusetts Department of Public Health.

September 1920

"Probably there is no stronger argument for the oral hygienist than the draft figures, which showed that over one-fifth of the men called in the first draft in Massachusetts were rejected because of defective teeth, in spite of the fact that dentistry has been practiced in some form for hundreds of years. When one realizes that such conditions have a direct bearing on the physical and mental efficiency of the individual, there can be no question as to the need for some one to educate the people in preventive dentistry."

—EVELYN C. SCHMIDT, D.H.,
Health Instructor in Mouth Hygiene,
Massachusetts Department of Public Health.

"It is of the uttermost importance that the growing child should be taken to the dentist for frequent examination. Beginning at the age of three years a careful inspection should be made at least every three months."

—WILLIAM RICE, D.M.D.,
Dean, Tufts College Dental School.

"The results of examinations of school children's teeth show very bad mouth conditions. We do not need to spend time and energy in making examinations for record purposes as the results are uniformly bad. What can be done to help this condition? Without the cooperation of parents and children little can be accomplished."

—WILLIAM PARKER COOKE, D.M.D.,
Professor Preventive Dentistry and Oral Hygiene,
Harvard Dental School.

July 1926

In a backward check-up, it was found that 82 per cent of the children in the eighth and ninth grades who received treatment in the first, second or third grade have four six-year molars in good condition, while 11 per cent have three good six-year molars. Those six-year molars which are missing are from those who either were a little early in erupting these teeth or were the last to receive treatment at the end of the third grade and consequently were obliged to lose their first molars at that time.

"If it is possible to conserve 93 per cent of six-year molars in cases in which only a portion received sufficiently early and systematic care, we certainly can expect to raise the proportion very easily, could we treat every child not later than six years of age.

". . . In 1915, one six-year molar to every three teeth was extracted; this was gradually reduced by early attention to one in five, in 1918. In 1924 only one six-year molar in each two hundred teeth was extracted in a group which had consistently received sufficiently early attention."

—Harold DeWitt Cross, D.M.D.,
Director, Forsyth Dental Infirmary.

"The dentist who finds himself unable to cope with the peculiar requirements of children's dentistry cannot excusably seek the solution of the problem by the route of neglect. He should be thankful if there is a pedodontist within reach. If such special service is not obtainable he has but two courses open: fit himself to efficiently face the demand or turn the patient over to another general practitioner who is so fitted."

—Edwin N. Kent, D.M.D.

"Two or three hours per year in three to five appointments is generally sufficient to obtain the maximum of prevention and the minimum of operative repair work for normal children in good physical tone, seen between the age of two and three years."

—Edward F. Sullivan, D.M.D.,
Secretary, Massachusetts Dental Hygiene Council.

"Specialists in the diseases of children probably realize, even more than the profession at large, how much harm diseases of the teeth and gums and malformations of the jaws and teeth do in early life. They know that diseased teeth, by interfering with proper mastication, and hence with proper digestion, disturb the nutrition and growth of the child and that the absorption of toxic substances from diseased teeth and gums is a not infrequent cause of disturbances of nutrition, as well as of diseases of the joints, heart and kidneys. They also know how much the nutrition and development of the child are hampered by the interference with mastication and nasal respiration caused by deformities of the jaws and teeth. They can, therefore, be counted upon to give even more enthusiastic support to these preventive measures which you advocate than the profession at large."

—John Lovett Morse, M.D.,
President, New England Pediatric Society.

"Dentistry attacked its problem from the wrong end, and stands before you today confessing that it is a relative failure from the standpoint of Prevention."

"I speak for myself alone in confessing that, after twenty-three years of general practice, no patient was better off than when he came to me; all had either fewer teeth, more fillings, or more substitutes and a lowered efficiency. It was the best service I could give, but the task was too overwhelming; the problem was not understood."

"The plan of procedure to meet this situation presented today is practical; it will work and give the results we look for; it will prevent a huge percentage of dental troubles. It has been proved in public clinic and private practice."

"You are not going to work yourself out of a job in the next hundred years; here will always be enough repair work to be done because of the public inertia nd indifference if for no other reason."

"Tomorrow the mother will come into your office and say, 'Will you give my hildren this service? The poor children in our town are getting it.'

"Your answer must be 'Yes' or 'No.'

"You may answer 'No' if you so decide for any sufficient personal reason, but our moral and professional obligation demands that you then refer her where he can get it done."

—FRANK A. DELABARRE, A.B., D.D.S., M.D.

"Every Board of Health or School Committee that employs a dental hygienist hould realize her value as an Educator and should arrange for her to talk to others' Clubs and other organizations as an important part of her regular program. Too often she is left merely to clean teeth or to talk to the children."

—ELEANOR GALLINGER, D.H.,
Assistant in Dental Hygiene,
Massachusetts Department of Public Health.

April 1929

"There should be a well planned program throughout all grades and age groups including the junior and senior high and normal schools.

"The school dentist and school dental hygienist should cooperate in the health work with proper emphasis on the preventive side of dentistry. The superintendent, principals and teachers should be interested and should correlate health with their classroom activities. Frequent conferences and discussions by the various groups are necessary. The interest and cooperation of the parents should be obtained by the school nurse and the teacher—thereby carrying the message of good health into the home and arousing community interest."

—EDITORIAL COMMENT—*"Why School Hygiene?"*

"The most rapid progress in the field program has come as a result of the adoption of the Forsyth policy for prevention of dental caries in the school clinics.

"The increase in interest in good teeth among children and parents and increased interest among dentists in working for little children is hard to estimate but herein lies our true progress.

"May 1939 find every community in Massachusetts with some definite plan for solving the problem of dental care for poor children, may every clinic be running on a preventive basis, may more families be properly fed and larger percentage of our 688,214 school children leave school with sound teeth in clean mouths at the end of the next ten years."

—EDITORIAL COMMENT—*"Ten Years' Progress in Dental Hygiene, 1919–1929."*

January 1930

"It is a little difficult to know where to start when speaking of Child Hygiene. One naturally thinks it begins with the infant when it is born but that is only an important episode and we must begin before this period. We start with the child—but with the child that is old enough to be taught his or her responsibility as a member of the family and a member of the community—the parent of the future in fact.

"I do not believe it is too early to begin this teaching in the upper class of the grade schools, for so many children do not go beyond these schools and there is no further opportunity to give the necessary training. Begin by teaching the child personal hygiene in all its phases with its relation to the community at large—the prevention of diseases, the establishment of good morals and good behavior with their bearing upon the future of the race and nation. Teach them what is meant by the family and the part the child is supposed to play in this institution. This can be done with simple understandable language and comparisons. The machinery you have is the Parent Teacher Association, health workers, public health nurses and members of the various professions that bear on these subjects.

"Carry the work through the higher schools, through the adolescent and young adult stages. Then you will have laid the foundation for healthy prospective fathers and mothers and for future citizens."

—M. LUISE DIEZ, M.D.,
*Director, Division of Child Hygiene,
Massachusetts Department of Public Health.*

January 1932

"The well child conference reaches children between the ages of two and four before decay has begun or before it has destroyed the teeth to the extent that they are beyond repair. It is, therefore, the logical starting point for a community dental service that is really preventive."

—ELEANOR G. MCCARTHY, B.S., D.H.,
*Consultant in Dental Hygiene,
Massachusetts Department of Public Health.*

"The problem of providing dental care to maternity cases is one which has been most neglected in dental practice."

"We are also advised that most dental operations may be performed with safety, that it is better to perform extractions with local or conduction anesthesia than with prolonged anesthesia, and that it is better not to submit the expectant mother to long and fatiguing sittings."

"Too often is dentistry left out of the picture in the organization of community and state health programs, not intentionally, but frequently because of failure to think of it and to provide the necessary finances. In this field there is a wonderful opportunity for training a larger and larger number of dentists in the knowledge of the dental problems of pregnancy."

—GEORGE H. WANDEL, D.D.S.,
*Supervisor, Bureau of Dental Health Education,
American Dental Association.*

"An analysis of past dental programs in different sections of the country shows that a rather alarming number of such programs have fallen short of their original goal. Some have died a natural death brought on by inherent weaknesses of organization. Still others, although continuing to flourish year after year, accomplish no lasting results because of paying insufficient attention to the educational opportunities at hand. Probably the biggest single factor leading to the failure of a dental program is the failure to lay a proper foundation preceding the inauguration of the actual demonstration."

—FREDERICK S. LEEDER, M.D., D.P.H.,
Medical Director, Southern Berkshire Health Unit.

July 1934

"The objectives as outlined by the Joint Committee were the results of the best scientific investigation, and served as the objectives of this course of study:—

1. To instruct children and youth so that they will conserve and improve their own health.
2. To establish in them the habits and principles of living which throughout their school life, and in later years, will assure that abundant vigor and vitality required for the greatest possible happiness and service in personal, family, and community life.
3. To influence parents and other adults, through the health education program for children, to adopt better habits and attitudes, so that the school may become an effective agency for the promotion of the social aspects of health education in the family and community as well as in the school itself.
4. To improve the individal and community life of the future; to insure a better second generation and a still better third generation—A healthier and fitter nation and race."

—JOHN P. SULLIVAN, Ph.D.,
Supervisor of Health Education,
Boston School Department.

DENTAL HEALTH EDUCATION FOR CHILDREN *

BY GEORGE E. DAVIS, D.D.S.

President, Board of Education, Floral Park-Bellerose Schools, Long Island
Member of the Board of Education, Sewanhaka Central High School,
Floral Park, Long Island

The purpose of this paper is to present a program of dental health education which can be established in the schools of the community.

There are very definite reasons for establishing such programs in the schools.

First, every child in the community attends school, and in the schools there are representatives of nearly every family in the community. A dental health education program in the schools will serve to raise the sanitary consciousness of the whole community.

Second, the conclusions reached by the Committee on Community Dental Service of the New York Tuberculosis and Health Association, after a survey of this situation, are a valuable guide. In the report of this committee on "Health Dentistry for the Community," the authors, Dr. I. Ogden Woodruff, President of the Association, and Dr. Alfred Walker, Chairman of the Committee on Community Dental Service, say, "In a program to provide adequate health dentistry for the community, prevention of oral disease and the correction of its consequences in children must be given first place; the curative treatment of oral diseases in adults must be given second place; the restoration of the organs of mastication by means of artificial treatment should have third place. The need of this last type of service, owing to the institution of preventive care, should decrease with each successive generation."

Third, there is at least some evidence to show that the best method of getting children to the state of continuous dental care is through the influence of the school.

---
* Reprinted from the *Dental Cosmos*, Vol. 78, June, 1936.
(Read before the Greater New York December Meeting, December 5, 1935, New York City.)

An investigation of the influence which brought children to attaining continuous attention to the teeth shows the following result in New York City:

School, alone	61 per cent
Home, without outside influence	27 per cent
School, plus some other influence	4 per cent
Social agency	3 per cent
Private practice	5 per cent

These figures are quoted from "A Study of Physical Defects among School Children," conducted by the American Child Health Association in cooperation with the Department of Health and the Department of Education.

I wish to speak briefly of the need for dental health education, then of a plan which is now operating, a method of teaching and the economic status of the program, but first I shall say something of the attitude of the schools toward dental health education.

(I) Evolution of the School Program

No program of dental health education can be established in a school without the consent and approval of the school authorities, so the attitude of those who control the schools is very important.

Great changes have taken place in our educational programs during the past few years. Educational programs have been established from primitive beginnings. When life was simple, its requirements were few and education was unhampered by complexities. As civilization advanced, life became more and more complex and, as a result, changes were made in these educational systems to meet these complexities. So in the various stages of civilization, educational plans which represent conflicting ideas and diverse ideals are found. But, as experience was gained through the years, progress was made, and we of the modern world are fond of the belief that we saved the best of all civilizations of the past and, upon the experiences of our forebears, have built an educational system which is superior, at least for our needs, to any that has gone before it. In the beginning we have the doctrine that the classics stood supreme as a training in culture values, but later there came the thought that this doctrine might be false and gradually there followed the popularization of education.

From the pioneers who first came to this country, we have inherited the principle of free education for all children, supported by a general property tax which brought about the establishment of schools, colleges and universities, founded upon the theory that education, largely at the public expense, should be accessible to all. From these beginnings there has sprung up all over the land a system of education of which we may all be proud.

There are two periods in American education in which we are especially interested. During the early days the curriculum was grouped mainly about the classics. Then there grew up the feeling that such studies were not practical and that education should be along lines of "learning by doing," vocational activities and specialization. As a result, the demand for the study of the classics has all but disappeared and the demand for the newer education has penetrated far down into the lives of those of tender years. Until recently the function of the elementary school was to train children to read and write and cipher, as these were the tools by which an education might be won. The curriculum was confined to the three R's, but now this curriculum is supplemented by adding certain subjects which are demanded by the newer training, such as art, music, domestic science, manual training, physical education and health of which dental health is a very important part.

The present favorable attitude of the New York Education Department toward health education and dental health education can be expressed by quoting from a recent bulletin of that department:

"Assuming that growth is the ultimate aim of education, we should set up educational objectives which will satisfy the conditions of growth. The first requisite of growth is health. Therefore health should be the first in our list of educational objectives.

"The health educational curriculum should be based on the underlying philosophy that health is a way of living—mentally, emotionally, socially and physically—and as such should not be handled as a special subject but should grow out of, and be a part of all child experiences in the home, school and community."

(II) Need for Dental Health Education

(1) Adults. Almost 100 per cent of the adult population is suffering from unsound teeth. The authors of "Health Dentistry for the Community" say: "It can be safely assumed that 100 per cent of the adult population is affected by oral disease."

The children of today are the adults of tomorrow, so the start to correct the dental situation must be made in the childhood years.

(2) School children. Examinations of the mouths of school children show appalling percentages of defects. In spite of the fact that research has disclosed various measures for the betterment of these conditions, the dental phase of the school health program still presents the physical defect which is most frequently encountered among children.

Surveys in schools in all parts of the country show an almost constant ratio of 97 per cent with defective teeth and an average of about six cavities per child. Only a small percentage of these children are receiving continuous dental care. The balance receive attention only occasionally and then only for the relief of pain, and in their mouths we may see the usual train of disaster, with open cavities, exposed pulps, alveolar abscesses, loose teeth, with consequent illness and absence from school, which cause failure and retardation and thus economic loss to the family and to the community.

(3) Pre-school children. The pre-school child of today will be the school child of tomorrow. His dental health problem will then be the problem of the school. The situation in this group is no better than in the school group.

In the DENTAL COSMOS, August, 1935, Dr. J. O. McCall says, "The wide spread of dental decay in the population is well known. Less generally realized is the fact that this insidious disease is attacking our population at an earlier and earlier age. Figures, compiled at the Guggenheim Dental Clinic in New York and obtained from other sources, indicate that about half the two-year-old children in our large cities have at least one cavity. The percentage affected and the number of cavities per child increases rapidly throughout the pre-school period, as shown in the following figures compiled from the files of the Guggenheim Dental Clinic:

Age	Per cent with cavities	Per cent with 7 or more cavities
2	53	17
3	81	39
4	92	56
5	97	61

"Children with more than seven cavities usually have at least one tooth requiring extraction because of an actual or incipient abscess. To find the means of preventing or even markedly reducing this most common disease of childhood will be an achievement worthy to be ranked alongside that of finding the philosopher's stone."

No one can doubt the need of a program of some kind for the betterment of conditions like these, and the program should begin by the second year at least.

(III) The Plan

The program proposed in this paper has been in operation in the Floral Park-Bellerose schools for five years. It was planned by Dr. Charles M. McNeely and the author, both of whom are residents of the school district. In developing this plan it was determined to make it distinctly educational in character as far as the school was concerned. All clinical work was to be done in the office of the dentist. It was also determined that the policy was to be *to educate the child into a sustained desire to have sound teeth and the habits and precautions necessary thereto.* Clinical service should be an incident and not the end of the program.

For several years previous to the introduction of this new plan, service had been rendered by dentists employed in the schools. This service was clinical. Examinations were made by the dentist, the results sent to parents, and any child whose parents consented and were willing to assume the expense was treated. Certain children who were unable to bear the expense were treated and the cost paid from other sources. As far as possible the worst cases were treated first and there was little or no follow-up of the remainder. So much time was spent on these worst cases that only a few could be treated. Five years of this program showed no reduction in the percentage of children affected or the number of cavities per child. A valuable service was rendered to certain individuals, but the situation as a whole remained static.

To establish a new plan, the cooperation of the Board of Education was sought as well as that of the school principals and the dentists of the community, and this cooperation was generously given. The idea of a dental program without clinical features seemed unique to every one who was approached. The dentists of the community offered their time to establish free clinics in the schools. This might have been a temporary advantage, but it was felt that it would militate against the educational phase as a school project. To make the program effective it would be necessary to develop in each child a sense of personal responsibility to maintain a healthy mouth. If a boy is taken out of his class and sent to a clinic and has his teeth put in order, whether he will or not, and free, he will get a valuable service, but nothing will be added to his habits or attitudes in overcoming pain resistance or expense resistance after he leaves school, and, after all, no child should be singled out for special service just because he is poor. But if a child is educated into a sustained desire to have sound teeth and the habits and precautions necessary thereto and selects his own dentist and earns his own fee, if necessary, he will take pride in doing this, and can be expected to develop a sense of personal care and self-reliance that will fortify him against neglect of his teeth or his health in any particular in later life.

Charity which gives something for nothing is not conducive to character building or good citizenship, especially in a public whose ideals of democracy place all on an equal basis. Operative dentistry is a valuable service and should be paid for, and it adds greatly to the self-respect of the child if this service is paid for, no matter how small the fee. Dentists in any community can usually adjust their fees so that every child can receive service.

(IV) Method of Teaching

Believing that dental health education should not be handled as a special subject, but should grow out of and be a part of all child experiences in the home, school and community, it was determined that classroom teachers should do the teaching under the leadership of the dental hygiene teachers and the supervision of the dental supervisor.

A dental hygiene teacher is a duly licensed dental hygienist who has also successfully completed certain courses in education which are prescribed by the New York State Education Department, who has been licensed by that department as a teacher and stands in the same relation to the school as any other teacher.

To establish this program in the schools, Dr. McNeely was appointed dental supervisor and also the writer. At the request of the dental supervisors, the Board of Education employed two dental hygiene teachers, Mrs. Pauline Newman for the high school and Miss Martha Breder for the elementary schools.

Examinations are made by the dental hygiene teacher, the children coming to the health room in small groups. The teacher is requested to be present so that she may use this opportunity to integrate this experience with the plan of dental health education. A permanent record card is made and retained in the school and notices sent to the parent. This notice directs the child to the dentist. When corrections are completed the dentist signs a card which is furnished by the school. These notices are very carefully followed up, and the whole force of the administration is brought to bear to get every child into the office of the dentist: telephone calls, home calls, visits of parents to the school, talks with the principal and any means available.

Many states have laws compelling pupil examinations. The New York State Education Law, Section 570, says "Medical inspection shall be provided for all pupils attending the public schools of this state."

So intent has been the effort to get these examinations made and procedures established, that the utilization of the results has been quite overshadowed. The chief purpose of the examination, which is relief of the condition found, was often not attained.

The report of the New York State Health Commission for 1932 reads:

"The physical examinations which are made each year of every school child represent useless expenditures unless steps are taken to correct defects found. Hundreds of thousands of dollars are spent annually in this state for the examination and reexamination of children, which discover and rediscover the presence of defects about which nothing is done, either by the parents or the school. Future efforts should be directed toward securing necessary care and treatment rather than routine examinations."

While the examination is being made, the pupil is instructed in dental health by the dental hygiene teacher. By means of models, extracted teeth, plaques and roentgenograms, the pupil is shown the purpose and care of the deciduous teeth, the value of sound teeth and the healthy mouth and correct hygiene of the mouth. The kindergarten, first, second and third grades receive prophylaxis as does the eighth grade, just before graduation.

The instructions of the dental hygiene teacher in personal hygiene can be held to a rigid accomplishment by the possibility of daily inspection by the classroom teacher. This daily action, if persisted in over a period of months or years, will lay very deeply certain habits which are fundamental in the final goal of all health teaching, which is to establish each pupil's own personal responsibility to maintain his health at such a standard that he will be *vocationally fit, socially acceptable and pathologically immune.*

The integration of the program with the rest of the school program is done by means of dental health teaching units. Some subjects such as general science, biology and domestic science lend themselves especially well to integration with dental health. Any subject may be integrated.

Our units are composed of specific objectives and topical discussion material. To quote from "A Unit in Mouth Health Teaching for General Science" by Mrs. Pauline Newman, Dental Hygiene Teacher, Sewanhaka High School:

Specific Objectives
(A) To learn what bacteria are.
(B) Where bacteria are found.
(C) Conditions necessary to growth.
(D) Common means for spread.
(E) Mode of attack on teeth and gums.
(F) Value of a clean mouth in prevention of disease.

Topical Discussion Material
Relation of diet to strong teeth.
Why are you afraid of a dentist?
Personality and health in getting a position.
The care of the teeth.
Relation of vitamins to the teeth.

In English, the value of sound teeth, properly aligned, can be shown in pronunciation, in the ability to speak understandingly; reading interest can be directed to stories about animals and their teeth and the pupil can be made "sound tooth" conscious. "Suggestions for a Teaching Unit in Mouth Health," prepared and directed by Anne Raymond and sponsored by the Oral Hygiene Committee of Greater New York, is an especially fine example of a teaching unit.

Dr. H. Shirley Dwyer carried on an experiment in a number of public schools in New York City. Dental health was integrated with the school curriculum without any professional aid. Dr. Dwyer was able to completely change the dental situation in these schools. These pupils were made "sound tooth" conscious and, instead of only a small percentage achieving corrections by a dentist and correct hygiene, the percentage rose to as high as 90 per cent in some schools. I think Dr. Dwyer proved the value of dental health education in this experiment.

(V) **Economics**

First, cost. This program costs but little more than the salary of the dental hygiene teacher. The materials used, such as models, plaques and booklets, are inexpensive, and most of them will be used year after year.

Second, economies.

(A) *To the School district:*

(1) Defective teeth are a very prolific cause of absence from school. Education service is rendered to every pupil enrolled whether or not the pupil is present. If the pupil is absent, this service is wasted. Absence brings about failure and retardation and re-education, which costs just the same as the original education.

(2) *Increased state aid:*
Financial aid is granted to all school districts under the provisions of the Freidsam Act. This act provides that there shall be paid $1,500 for every twenty-seven pupils in the elementary schools, $1,900 for every twenty-two pupils in the high school and $3,000 for every twenty-two pupils in the central high school, less sixty cents for every $1,000 of assessed values. These sums are computed, not on the enrolment, but on the daily attendance, so that each day's absence entails a loss of thirty cents in the elementary school, fifty-three cents in the high school, and seventy-two cents in the central high school. Defective teeth materially reduce State aid payments. Dental Health Education should pay dividends in money as well as health.

(B) *Economy to the child:*
Economy to the child and the family is evident. In the Thaddeus P. Hyatt Prize Essay of 1934 (Dental Cosmos, June, 1935), this fact was pointed out: "The final cost of preventive operative service for a child in a private office will total no more by the age of sixteen than the amount required to rectify that child's condition if coming to the dentist for the first time at the age of sixteen. However, if preventive service has been given from two to sixteen, that child may expect to have all his teeth, in good condition, and will have suffered no loss of function nor ill health of dental origin. Obviously this will not hold true of the patient who has come for treatment for the first time at sixteen years of age."

Dental health is true economy for all concerned.

Summary

(1) All children should be under the influence of dental health teaching and the logical place to do this is the school.

(2) The present dental situation furnishes a problem that is crying for solution, and there is very great need of correction.

(3) The dental health program should be educational in character. The function of the school is to teach and not to treat disease. The aim of education is growth and the first requisite of growth is health, so health should be the foremost of our educational objectives.

(4) Dental health should not be handled as a separate subject, but should grow out of and be a part of all child experiences.

(5) Dental health is true economy to the community, to the family and to the child, both as to finances and as to physical consequences.

(6) The problem of the pre-school child should be studied by educators and dentists, with the view to finding some means of getting this child under whole-

some health influence and into the hands of the dentist by the end of the second year at least.

(7) I have no thought that all dental caries or cavities will be eliminated by means of this suggested program, but I do believe that every child can be educated into the sustained desire to have sound teeth and the habits and precautions necessary thereto, and this program will get the child into the office of the dentist at the earliest possible age.

The author is indebted to the various persons who have been quoted and to Dr. Alfred C. Fones of Bridgeport, Conn., some of whose statements have been paraphrased and used in the preparation of this paper.

TRAINED TEACHERS OF HEALTH
BY JOHN J. DESMOND, JR., A.M.
Superintendent of Schools
Chicopee, Massachusetts

Should health as a subject in the curriculum of the public schools be taught as a separate course by a special teacher who has had specific training? What should be the qualifications and training of the special teacher?

The answer to these questions will be dependent upon what is accepted as the scope of health education in the schools. As defined in the "Course of Study in Health for the Elementary Schools in Massachusetts," health education means for the individual and his community the development of such attitudes, practices, and knowledge as will produce increased happiness; efficient, vigorous living; and social progress. Obviously a thorough program of health education will affect not only the individual but his home and his community as well. A knowledge of the importance and functions of the health services and health agencies is an essential part of a course in health.

A coordination of all the elements in the school curriculum which have any relation to the physical or emotional development of the individual would be properly within the sphere of health education. The requirement of the General Laws is that "physiology and hygiene, good behavior, indoor and outdoor games and athletic exercises . . . instruction as to the effects of alcoholic drinks and of stimulants and narcotics on the human system and as to tuberculosis and its prevention" shall be taught in all schools. Hygiene connotes more than personal health habits and routine. It embraces all the activities of health organizations and officials which seek to promote public health by the supervision of sanitation, purification of water supply, sewage disposal, inspection of food and milk supply, as well as prevention of disease, accidents, and industrial hazards. Obviously a thorough program of health teaching will affect not only the individual pupil but his home and community as well. The aim of health teaching is twofold: first, to inculcate habits of healthful living in the individual; second, to develop the knowledge and attitudes which will prompt the individual to promote healthful living in the family and in the community group of which he is now or will later be a member.

Few subjects in the curriculum have as broad an aim as health teaching. The language arts or the social sciences may have somewhat analogous aims, but in health teaching the whole aim must have the possibility of realization. By taking thought, Scripture admonishes us, we may not add a cubit to the stature. Who will deny, however, that we may add a decade to our natural existence, unmeasured happiness and productive efficiency to our whole life, by taking thought on the laws of healthful living. The achievement of such a result would be worth the effort and expense involved in the proper teaching of health. Among the most active leaders in health education are the large life insurance companies which expend large sums annually in the education of their policyholders and the general public on how to live. The publications of these companies contain in simple form useful material on such important subjects as sleep, exercise, nutrition, sanitation, disease, and accident prevention.

No one will question that the schools should be recognized as an agency for health education and have a responsibility for the teaching of these essential facts concerning personal health, as well as to furnish their pupils with full knowledge of how the various health agencies function for the benefit of the individual and the community.

The content of a complete course in health education, particularly in the secondary schools, could be accomplished effectively only through a separate unit course. To attempt to teach the subjects interdepartmentally through units in science and social studies destroys the coordination and tends to treat the subject as of minor importance. Health as a subject in the curriculum of the public schools has far more significance to the pupils than the academic subjects whose objectives may be confined chiefly to the individual's social and economic advancement. If it is essential to develop certain attitudes and habits as well as to furnish pupils with a body of useful knowledge, the treatment of health teaching incidentally with instruction in other subjects will not accomplish this object. Unfortunately, in many secondary schools, health education is given only in this form.

Health education in view of its importance to every school pupil has lagged behind the languages, fine arts, science, the social studies, and mathematics in the emphasis accorded it by educators. The chief reason appears to be that there is a lack of specially-trained teachers of this important subject. Where do we find in the liberal arts or teachers' colleges a curriculum designed to train teachers of health? Music, art, domestic science, manual training, physical education in its restricted sense are organized into either separate departments, or frequently into separate colleges. Student health courses with systematic lectures on personal hygiene including the psychological basis for sound health habits, the importance of frequent medical, dental, or optical advice are found in the first year curriculum of practically all colleges, but no provision is made for the pedagogical training of prospective teachers of health.

The general education of the teacher of health should be the equivalent of that of any academic teacher in the secondary school. In addition, specialized training prescribed by public health authorities and the medical profession should supplement the general education of the teacher. The most essential qualification should be a thorough conviction on the part of the teacher of the importance of health education and the willingness himself to follow what he teaches.

When such specially-trained teachers are available for each school system the development of health education is assured. The cooperation of the colleges and the department of public health could accomplish in a brief period of time the desired result.

A VISUAL PRESENTATION OF THE VALUE OF DENTAL SERVICE

BY HENRY B. TAYLOR

The London Life Insurance Company
Toronto, Canada

(With grateful acknowledgment to those members of the dental and medical professions without whose cooperation this and other similar charts could not have been developed.)

Speaking generally, people do not become sufficiently interested in health until their own health has been impaired or lost. What is, to the sick, extremely interesting reading matter, is usually quite boring to those in the enjoyment of health. But, since it is to the latter that the dental practitioner renders his greatest service, it becomes imperative that we find some method of overcoming this indifference or lack of interest and of imparting much needed and priceless knowledge of prevention through dental service.

The total yearly expenditure upon the cure and attempted cure of disease is so large as to be almost, if not altogether, beyond comprehension. Whatever the amount may be, it is generally conceded that a proper regard for the primary rules of health would cut it in half.

The vast amount, so needlessly spent, is one of the greatest and most deplorable of present-day economic wastes, the elimination of which would do much to banish the discontent that threatens our social structure. Imagine the nation-wide prosperity and contentment that would surely follow, could this money be spent on material comforts of life, rather than in an effort to recover the priceless thing we need never have lost and so often can never regain—our health.

Is it not obvious that if more adequate measures were taken to inform the public regarding vitally important health subjects there would not be the same widespread need for medical service? This need, all too frequently on the part of those who cannot pay for such service, presents an extremely urgent social problem. Greater consideration could well be given to preventive medicine, not only for the benefit of those who cannot pay for medical service, but for the benefit of the State and still more of those quite able and willing to pay.

Prevention of disease not only costs much less than does its cure, but also is possible to a much greater extent than is its cure—hence its greater economic value.

The members of the dental profession have it in their power to render and are now rendering a great service in the prevention of disease and in the elimination of the consequent economic waste of such disease. In the words of Sir William Osler, "There is not one single thing, in preventive medicine, that equals mouth hygiene and the preservation of the teeth."

With a full acceptance of and a constant belief in this as a fact, the accompanying chart * has been devised as a tangible instrument that will enable the members of the dental profession to render an even greater service than heretofore in this work of prevention.

In considering why it is important that the information contained in this chart should be brought to the attention of the public, reference is herewith made to the opinion expressed by an eminent American authority who said "It seems to me that a public health propaganda should be inaugurated to inform people of the dangers to their health that may arise from infected teeth and how these dangers may be avoided. Prophylaxis (prevention) should be the watchword."

* Endorsed by Massachusetts Dental Society.

Periodic Dental Examination

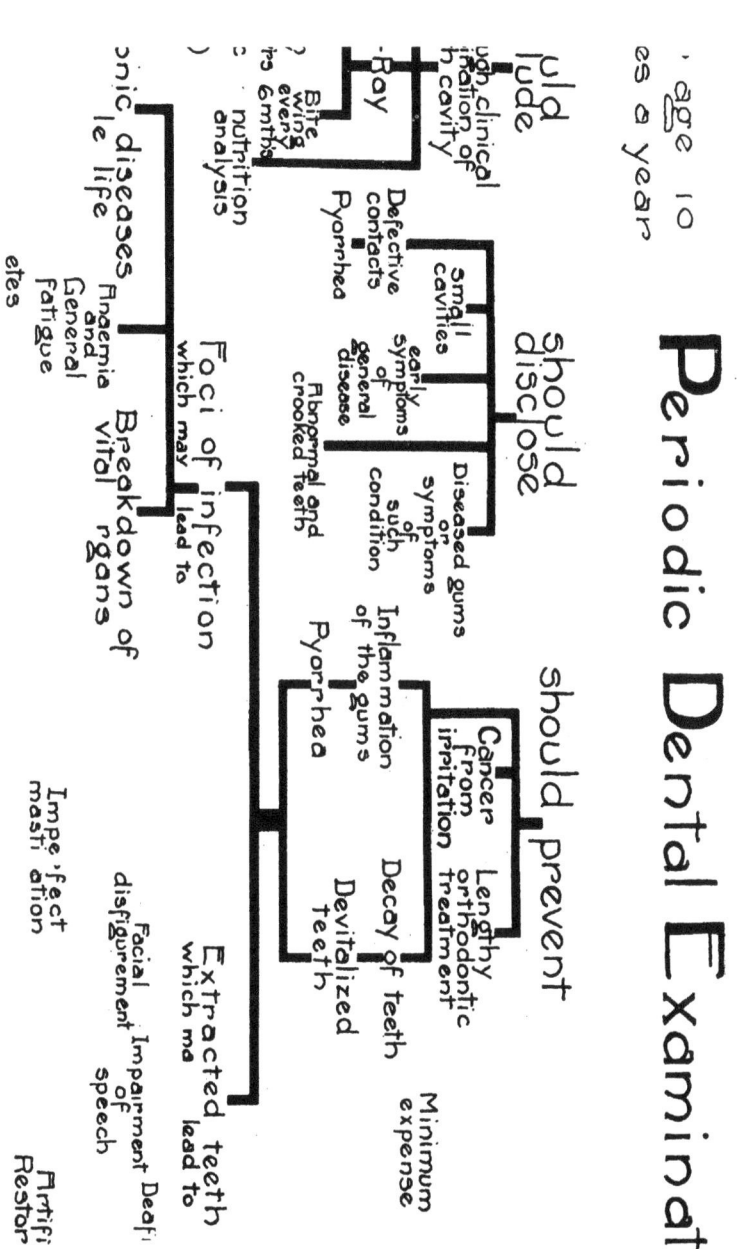

age 10 ... es a year

should include
- ...ugh clinical ...ination of ...h cavity
- X-Ray
  - Bite wing every 6 mths
- nutrition analysis

should disclose
- Small cavities
- Defective contacts
- Pyorrhea
- early symptoms of general disease
- Diseased gums or symptoms of such condition
- Abnormal and crooked teeth

should prevent
- Cancer from irritation
- Lengthy orthodontic treatment
- Inflammation of the gums — Pyorrhea
- Decay of teeth — Devitalized teeth
- Minimum expense
- Extracted teeth which may lead to
  - Facial disfigurement
  - Impairment of speech
  - Deaf...
  - Imperfect mastication
  - Artifi... Restor...
- ...onic diseases ...le life
  - Anaemia and General fatigue
  - ...etes
  - Foci of infection which may lead to Breakdown of vital organs

This chart is presented as an effective means of imparting such information to the public.

There are two main interests in life common to all normal human beings and these have been kept constantly in mind during the compiling of this chart.

1st. Our own economic and social status throughout life.

2nd. The preservation of our life and health.

It happens all too frequently that, in the struggle to maintain our own economic and social status, we may, through lack of knowledge or neglect, fail to correct the very condition which may be the cause of our economic downfall—loss of health and consequent loss of earning power. This chart shows how the care of one's teeth prevents needless suffering and disease, the destruction of earning power through loss of health and at the same time shows how such care will promote the things most cherished in life. Its wide distribution to the profession and the public should prove to be of inestimable value in the promotion of the two fundamentally important interests in life to which reference has already been made.

Periodic Dental Examination

It should begin at two years of age and, generally speaking, such an examination should be made four times a year until the child is ten years of age and after that at least twice a year.

The information contained in the chart herewith illustrated is presented under four subheadings:

1st. What this examination SHOULD INCLUDE.

There should, of course, be a very thorough clinical examination of the mouth cavity.

Prophylactic or preventive treatment.

It should be ascertained whether or not the patient is receiving food necessary for the growth of normal, strong, healthy teeth.

Next comes, perhaps, the most important thing in the entire chart indicating the need for a sufficiently frequent use of the x-ray. A full mouth x-ray should be taken every one to two years to discover, if present, any infection or abscessed condition at the roots of the teeth before such condition has produced the results set forth elsewhere in the chart and which may be prevented by the removal of the teeth. This will also disclose the presence of impacted teeth.

A Bite-Wing x-ray should be taken approximately every six months to discover the presence of small cavities which cannot be found otherwise. If efficient dental service is to be given there can be no doubt as to the necessity of x-ray practice, though the frequency of such examinations can be determined by the dental practitioner having a full knowledge of his patient.

2nd. What this examination SHOULD DISCLOSE.

Defective contacts or the meeting of the teeth in such a way as may lead to pyorrhea or imperfect mastication.

Small cavities, while they are still small and easily repaired.

Early symptoms of general disease.

The presence of abnormal and crooked teeth should be disclosed and corrected by orthodontic or other treatment.

Diseased gums or symptoms which may lead to such disease, indicating the need for curative or preventive treatment.

3rd. Next we come to that section of the chart showing what thorough and regular dental service SHOULD PREVENT.

Lengthy orthodontic treatment—If malposed or irregular teeth are corrected early in life, it should take less time to complete the operation in a satisfactory manner.

Cancer from irritation—This may result from either malposed or irregular teeth or teeth having jagged edges, generally from decay.

It should prevent pyorrhea and inflammation of the gums.

It should prevent decay of the teeth which if not arrested and repaired will result in devitalized teeth.

At this point indicated by the heavy black line, we have a condition which will lead either to extraction or the development of foci of infection, commonly known as abscessed teeth. If the devitalized teeth are allowed to remain and infection develops at the roots of the teeth serious systemic disorders are almost certain to follow. It may be in the form of some chronic disease as indicated on the chart, or the breakdown of some vital organ. This depends to a great extent upon the presence of some previously weak spot in the system, though not necessarily so.

Supposing, however, none of the disorders indicated do develop, then the infection draining into the blood stream, year after year, may result in anemia and fatigue or a generally weakened condition, developing into a susceptibility to infectious disease and in all probability a complete breakdown.

As shown on this section of the chart, the almost inevitable outcome of one or more of these disorders is the serious economic result—Greatly impaired or ruined Earning Capacity.

Coming back to the centre of the chart again, let us suppose that the devitalized teeth have been extracted without restoration having been made. Then we have an unnatural condition and without these teeth there will almost certainly follow imperfect mastication, and the stomach disorders indicated, bringing about malnutrition and an undermining of the health which will again lead to GREATLY IMPAIRED OR RUINED EARNING CAPACITY.

Extraction may lead to facial disfigurement, impairment of speech, possibly to deafness and certainly to expense that could have been avoided.

At the younger ages it may lead to the necessity for orthodontic treatment.

Where artificial restoration has been made it sometimes happens that, in spite of efficient service on the part of the dental practitioner, unforeseen circumstances may result in the conditions indicated in this section of the chart, the most serious being the possible development of cancer from a diseased or irritated condition of the soft tissues. This again would lead to GREATLY IMPAIRED OR RUINED EARNING CAPACITY.

In reviewing or summing up this section of the chart, it is obvious that most of the trouble referred to could be prevented by PERIODIC DENTAL EXAMINATION and efficient and regular dental service.

4th. In the remaining section of the chart we find some indication of what efficient dental service SHOULD PROMOTE.

First of all, greater care of the teeth resulting in MINIMUM EXPENSE.

How much better to detect and, at small expense, correct all cavities while they are small rather than wait until the decay has progressed to the point of devitalization and the development of infection with its resultant disorders and heavy medical expense and perhaps ruined earning capacity.

How much better, through the use of the x-ray, to find infection at the roots of the teeth, rather than be a victim of serious physical suffering and again of the resultant economic loss.

Periodic Dental Examination should promote minimum expense, attractive appearance and self confidence, freedom from suffering and dental disease, thorough mastication, good digestion and better assimilation leading naturally to good health, resulting in physical fitness for one's vocation and earning capacity unimpaired.

The opinion has been expressed by a medical man of the highest standing that "Dentistry has now been exalted to the highest rank in preventive medicine." The writer believes this to be a literal truth but, a truth either largely unknown, or its full significance appreciated by comparatively few well-informed, health-minded people.

Therefore, with the help of those professional men who have so generously cooperated, an effort has been made to develop an effective method of bringing about the general acceptance of this truth. By this visual method the practitioner or public health worker can present to the patient or the prospective patient, in readily acceptable form, a true concept of the intrinsic value of dental service, to the end that a vast amount of physical and mental suffering may be prevented, that society may be spared much of the tremendous economic burden of disease, that countless thousands may not, through loss of health, suffer the results of reduced or ruined earning capacity, but may live longer and enjoy life more fully.

(Arrangements will be made to supply these charts, printed in two colors, to the members of the profession or to any institution engaged in educational or health work.)

(Requests for these charts should be addressed to Henry B. Taylor, The London Life Insurance Company, Toronto, Canada.)

WHAT DENTISTS SHOULD DO ABOUT NUTRITION*

BY FLORENCE B. HOPKINS, M.D., D.M.D.

Massachusetts Department of Public Health

During the past three years, increasingly large numbers of dentists have appealed to the Forsyth Dental Infirmary for help in nutritional difficulties in their private practices. They know the need for such treatment, and are anxious to obtain for their patients the care which infirmary patients receive. Here all cases have a physical examination to rule out pathology. If special extra treatment is necessary, patients are directed where they may obtain it.

Many dentists and their patients who have availed themselves of this type of consultation are loath to accept the resources of a charitable institution. And properly so! Patients anxious to pay for private consultation are now barred by the unbreakable rule of Forsyth which does not accept persons able to pay for professional services. The above group are at present, through the courtesy of Dr. Howe, given a single consultation and referred to their family dentist with certain recommendations. Their future care, however, cannot be assumed by this wonderful institution, and there seems to be no other place to obtain it.

Many dentists have tried to get this done through the family doctor and have failed to get the cooperation they sought. They find, perhaps to their surprise, that the medical profession, as a whole, is not as keen to the question of nutrition as is the dentist; neither does the average physician quite grasp the idea that the dentist has such a broad conception of his work. The medical man is likely to

* Read before the Fall Meeting of the New England Dental Society—1935.

think of the dentist as one to seek when an extraction is expected to cure the otherwise incurable case of arthritis; not as the man who could have prevented the arthritis.

Speaking on nutrition, Dr. Miner said some medical men feel that this service is entirely without the dentist's province, but, "so far as actual training goes, dentists will get as much and perhaps more than the physician. Dentists have spurred some medical men to interest themselves in it."

Being keenly interested in this phase of the dental question, I have studied much dental and medical literature, seeking all that could be found on nutritional subjects. Aside from work on special diets in disease, the dental literature in the past five years has given much more space to nutrition than has the current medical, and all the good and comprehensive work published in medical journals has at least been abstracted in the dental ones. You can easily see, therefore, that the dentists who peruse their professional magazines carefully have a right to feel that they know as much on the subject as the general practitioner whose only recent postgraduate study has been his medical journal.

The council on Dental Therapeutics of the American Dental Association has recently made the following statement, in part: "In order to acquaint the dental profession with its own position, the following general statement of the council's position is given:

"Diet is recognized as a contributory factor in the formation and maintenance of sound teeth. Various experiments on large groups of children in this country have demonstrated that no single factor of those mentioned above is responsible for prophylaxis against or correction of caries, but that an adequate food intake containing all of these elements is essential.

"The essentials are usually furnished by well-balanced diets. If the diet is deficient in any one of these essentials, it may be corrected by the addition of foodstuffs known to be a source of the missing essential."

If this is the position to be taken by the dental profession, what are the dentists going to do about it? McLester in the August 11, 1934, issue of the Journal of the American Medical Association says that the day *was* when the physician advised what the patient must *not* eat; *now* he advises what the patient must eat.

"Then," you say, "the answer is simple; the dentist must tell his patient what to eat." Do you really know what your patient should eat? "Yes," you answer, "a well-balanced diet." And do you honestly know of what a truly well-balanced diet consists? Very likely many of your patients feel sure they know more about it than you do, for they have spent time and money to listen to such "teachers" as Drs. Hay, Jackson, Hauser, etc.

These men, while enemies of good medical practice, are reaping harvests, because people want to know what to eat for health and they know of no legitimate, ethical source of this knowledge. Can you tell your patients whether or not the diet facts these men propose are adequate and well balanced? Can you tell them some better dietary regime? If your patient drinks a pint of orange juice a day, he will surely get all the Vitamin C he needs; if he eats an egg a day and a dish of spinach, he will get enough iron; and if he drinks a pint to a quart of milk each twenty-four hours, he will get the calcium and phosphorus required; *but*, perhaps your patient cannot afford a pint of orange juice a day, what is to be done then? He may have asthma and can't eat eggs at all; he may absolutely refuse his spinach. Your patient may be a person who is keeping to a reducing diet and tells you that he must not drink much milk because it will make him too fat. What will be the answers to all these arguments? We could go on indefinitely with a long list of questions which patients may, and do frequently, ask concerning diet.

If the dentist knows the answers to these questions, where did he get the knowledge? Probably not one dentist in a thousand plans or prepares his own meals; so he has no practical experience in dietetics. Surely he did not get such training in dental school, and this is no criticism of these schools. You know and I know that even though we talk glibly about preventive dentistry, and even though we go so far as to admit that nutrition is an essential factor in the control of caries, it is still the dentist's chief function to do repair work, and the majority of dentists need all the training they get in crown, bridge, fillings, and extractions.

Since there is a limit to what can be crowded into an already full curriculum, there probably never can be a place made for an adequate course in dietetics in either medical or dental schools. There has been a tentative nutrition study program outlined by the American Association of Dental Schools which is, in their own words, to give the student an understanding of these principles with special emphasis on their dental relationship in order that he may be able:

"1. To care for his own health through the use of a proper diet.
2. To explain to patients the relation between diet and (a) the growth,(b) the development, and (c) the maintenance of the health of the mouth.
3. To cooperate with physician in suggesting diets that will correct faulty nutrition.

"This is not to say that the dentist should be qualified as, or presume to be, an expert nutritionist, nor should he prescribe definite dietary programs for his patients; but he should have a working knowledge of the general principles involved; so that he may recognize outstanding dietary defects and, in conjunction with the physician or pediatrician, suggest a type of diet that will correct the faults."

There is not an adequate undergraduate course in orthodontia, we admit that, and we send our orthodontia cases to one who has had a special postgraduate training; there is not an adequate undergraduate course in oral surgery; so we send our impacted molars and broken jaws to a specialist in this field; there is a course in bacteriology and pathology in school, but we use laboratories for diagnostic help.

Nutritional prescribing cannot be done on a fifteen-minute snap judgment. A superficial analysis on the part of the dentist often gives the wrong impression, and may do more harm than good. Only after infinite questioning and listening by one with a good understanding of methods of investigation is accurate information secured. An expert nutritionist is trained in these methods.

The interview requires a special technique and is time-consuming. In a general practice a dentist could hardly afford to give the time from his dental work. Too often the dentist is tempted to prescribe concentrates which might do harm, which, though they are needed at times, are at best poor substitutes for an adequate well-balanced diet. (Ketogenic diet and allergies, Paget's.)

It would not be worth the while of the general dentist to spend four years in medical school and one or two years in nutritional training before he took his dental course. However, in order to grasp the entire picture of nutrition in its broadest meaning, this would really be necessary, for nutrition is so much more than food. Substances are food when eaten but become nourishment only when they have been utilized by the body. (Rowe.) The many dentists who took the Metropolitan Dental Society study course two years ago saw what a large number of biological, physical and psychological factors entered into the actual absorption and utilization of each food element. Temperaments, family relations, habits of exercise and hygiene, blood conditions, kidney, liver, thyroid and pancreatic functions, infectious disease—all play their part in nutrition. These factors dentists justly feel are out of their province.

How then can a dentist fulfill his obligation to his patient? A report of the study of Medical Education in the United States for 1932 said, "The object of practice is to see that every patient receives a thorough study by his physician and advice when special experiments or treatment are indicated. In order to accomplish this, every well-trained doctor ought to be familiar with the ordinary methods of diagnosis, treatment, and prevention; and also with the indications, value and limitations of special examinations and treatments, and *where* they can be secured."

If, then, "Diet is recognized as a contributory factor in the formation and maintenance of sound teeth," and if the medical and dental professions must, of necessity, curtail their study of this special field, it must then be their duty to understand the value of this special treatment and know where and how they can secure it for their patients, even though this means that they create a demand for a new specialist, the nutritionist, in the profession. Only in this way can your private patients be given as good health service as the clinic patient is receiving today.

RETARDATION OF DENTAL CARIES IN OUT-PATIENTS OF A DENTAL INFIRMARY *

PRELIMINARY STUDY
PERCY R. HOWE, D.D.S.
RUTH L. WHITE, B.S.
AND
MILTON RABINE, D.D.S.
BOSTON

Introduction

The following study is already familiar to many readers of The Commonhealth. It is reprinted here in full because of the encouragement which it gives in the belief that an improvement in the habitual diet of children in their own homes can materially lessen dental decay.

The stimulus for the dental nutrition service which the State Department of Public Health has developed comes largely from this Forsyth report.
—FLORENCE B. HOPKINS, M.D., D.M.D.
Massachusetts Department of Public Health.

In the past few years, several reports have been made of the arrest of caries through dietary changes in various children's institutions in this country and in England. The strictly controlled conditions under which these studies have been conducted have caused the profession as a whole to be skeptical as to the feasibility of a similar project in the dentist's private practice, in which rigid regulation cannot be maintained. The preliminary findings of a recent survey carried on at Forsyth Dental Infirmary indicate that results similar to those reported from institutional studies may be secured by the practitioner who has a working knowledge of nutrition.

The case histories selected for this study were those of patients who had reported

*From the Forsyth Dental Infirmary.
Reprinted, with additions, from the *American Journal of Diseases of Children*, November, 1933, Vol. 46, Part I, pp. 1045–1049.

to the clinic conducted by the department of nutrition of the infirmary during an eight week period chosen at random. This period extended from February 1 to March 26, 1932. Cases were discarded whenever (1) the data were insufficient or (2) the initial visit to the clinic occurred during this period. These children had been under the supervision of the department for an average time of one and six-tenths years. Their ages ranged from 2 to 11 years inclusive. For purposes of study the patients were divided into two groups according to their cooperation in relation to the advice given during this time on problems of nutrition and habit-training. The number of cooperative patients was 104. The number of non-cooperative patients was 28.

Following the routine of the infirmary, a child, on completion of his dental work, is presented with a card which entitles him to attend the department of nutrition. Also, a member of the staff of the dental clinic may refer to the department any child whose oral condition suggests the possibility of a nutritional disturbance.

The routine of the department of nutrition is as follows for each patient: 1. The history of family health and of prenatal and postnatal conditions is taken. 2. A dental examination is made, cavities are charted, and the condition of the mouth is noted. 3. Physical examination is made by a pediatrician. 4. A conference on nutrition is held. Information as to present habits in relation to food and health is secured, and instruction given to the mother and the patient. 5. Follow-up appointments are made.

A survey in a clinic of this type presents certain obstacles not found in studies carried on in institutions, where accurate data may be kept as to the exact amounts of food consumed, and where a regimen of practices for health is maintained. For illustration of the latter point, the routine of an early bedtime established in an institution makes one contribution to good nutrition which is lacking in many homes. Recognition of such factors as the variability in incomes and in the truthfulness, intelligence and stability of the parents has not been important in the institutional studies previously conducted, but is essential in the interpretation of this report.

As to income, it must be assumed that the patients attending this clinic cannot afford to pay for the services of a private dentist. Incomes fluctuated to a greater extent during the period of this study than they would during a time of economic normalcy. Because of these facts, a diet which was considered optimal could not be prescribed in every case.

In clinical interviews, experience has proved that the truthfulness of the patients' statements may be substantiated in various ways. Frequently reliance must be placed on such subjective factors as the mother's enthusiasm regarding the changed condition of the child and the improvement in his disposition. The clinician's judgment of the sincerity of the parent is, however, supplemented by more tangible observations, such as the rate of growth and other findings of the pediatrician. We have learned that a child's own statement, made when he is unguided by the parent, is usually dependable—a fact for which provision is made in the clinical routine. We have found that repeated, varied and indirect questioning is effective in obtaining accurate information.

The success of an educational clinic of this type may be measured by the reaction of the parent to the advice given. It has been found that a period of from one to six months must be allowed for the mother and the child to become adjusted to the routine recommended. During this period, pathologic conditions are still in progress but are becoming retarded. Tissue changes seem to be seeking their normal threshold. In the computation of the following tables, nevertheless, allowance has not been made for this interval of adjustment.

Dental Findings

The progression of caries in the cooperative group was reduced 79.21 per cent, as indicated in the chart.

Method of Computation.—In item 1, table 1, the figures were compiled in the following manner: For all children above 4 years of age, an arbitrary age of 3 years (six months after the completion of dentition) was adopted in the computation of the average number of cavities a year before dietary regulation was begun. For children under 4, the age of 2 years was chosen. On this basis, the total number of cavities which were found when the child was admitted to the department of nutrition was divided by the number of years over the ages of 3 or 2.

The figures in item 2 were computed as follows: The number of new cavities which developed following the initial clinical visit was divided by the length of time intervening.

TABLE 1.—*Cooperative Patients*

Item 1.	Average number of years of possible decay before supervision was begun	3.2
	Average number of years of supervision	1.6
Item 2.	Average number of cavities per child per year before supervision was begun	3.51
	Average number of cavities per child per year during period of supervision	0.73
Item 3.	Average percentage decrease in caries per child	79.21

TABLE 2.—*Noncooperative Patients*

Item 1.	Average number of years of possible decay before supervision was begun	2.5
	Average number of years of supervision	1.6
Item 2.	Average number of cavities per child per year before supervision was begun	3.39
	Average number of cavities per child per year during period of supervision	3.83
Item 3.	Average percentage of increase in caries per child	12.97

The cavities listed as new came under the following classifications: (1) incipient caries, (2) recurrent decay around fillings, (3) exposure or abscess requiring extraction of tooth.

It will be observed that the number of cavities for each child in a year, during the period of supervision, is comparable with the average expectancy for the age of 6 years, as evidenced by the graph made from the records of children treated in the clinics for dentistry and extraction, but not in the department of nutrition. It must be considered that the number of cavities computed in table 2 represents an average for children ranging from the ages of 2 to 11 years. In the chart the figures represent the number of fillings and extractions yearly for children of an age in our departments for operations and extractions.

Dietary Findings

An analysis of the dietary changes which took place under supervision was made. This analysis was based on the record of the previous day's intake secured at each visit to the clinic, and also on the statements of the mother and child as to the average number of servings a week of the various foods. No attempt was made to define the size of the servings, but it must be granted that with the improvement in appetite, the size of the servings was automatically increased. In a large proportion of the cases, the parents' lack of understanding of child psychology had resulted in the loss of appetite. By far the most common cause of this anorexia is oversolicitation on the part of the parent, manifesting itself in various ways such as a constant display of emotion at the table, with an accompaniment of coaxing, feeding and bribing. In 68 per cent of the cases in the cooperative group, an improvement in appetite was noted, compared with 14 per cent in the noncooperative group.

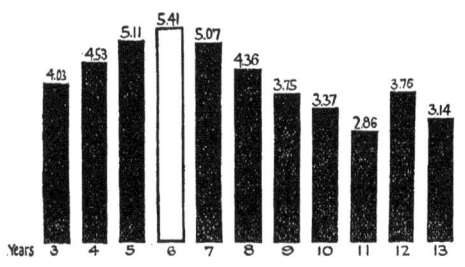

Average number of fillings and extractions per child at the Forsyth Dental Infirmary. Note that the high point of caries represented by the white column coincides with the average initial age of the children in the group studied.

TABLE 3.—*Comparison of the Optimal Diet and the Average Diet Consumed During Supervision*

	Milk, Glasses	Eggs, Number per Week	Meat or Fish, per Week	Fruit, per Day	Vegetables (Besides Potatoes) Number Servings per Day	
					Raw	Cooked
Optimal diet	4.00	7.00	5.00	2.00	1.00	1.00
Average amount consumed before supervision . . .	3.03	3.55	6.07	1.14	0.30	0.88
Average amount consumed during supervision . . .	3.66	4.29	5.91	1.82	0.58	1.42
Average percentage increase or decrease . . .	20.7 increase	20.8 increase	2.6 decrease	59.6 increase	93.3 increase	61.3 increase

The following daily diet was considered optimal for dental health: 1 quart (946 cc.) of milk; one raw vegetable (or canned tomato), with special emphasis on cabbage and tomato; at least two cooked vegetables, one of which may be potato; two servings of fruit, with special emphasis on oranges; one egg; meat or fish five times a week, and butter on vegetables and bread. An attempt was made to keep cereals and breads, because of their acid ash, as low as was consistent with the requirements for energy. Candy was allowed only at the end of the meal. Cod liver oil was not given as a routine, but was prescribed by the pediatrician in occasional cases.

Table 3 gives a comparison between the optimal diet and the average diet which was actually consumed during supervision, with the percentage of change from the former diet.

Summary

1. In the preliminary findings of a study of 132 patients followed for dietary supervision over a period of 1.6 years, an average reduction of dental caries of 79.21 per cent was observed in 104 cooperative patients. In 28 noncooperative patients, an average increase in dental caries of 12.97 per cent occurred. This increase compares with the expectancy for the average age of the group studied, which was 6 years.

2. The conditions under which the study was made strongly suggest that a similar project can be successfully carried out in the office of the dental practitioner

with a knowledge of nutrition and an understanding of methods of interesting his patients in dietary improvement.

Dr. G. T. Milliette rendered assistance in the compilation of this material.

Bibliography

1. Boyd, J. D., and Drain, C. L.: Arrest of Dental Caries in Childhood, *J. A. M. A.* 90:1867 (June 9) 1928.
2. Boyd, J. D.; Drain, C. L., and Nelson, M. V. Dietary Control of Dental Caries, *Am. J. Dis. Child.* 38:721 (Oct.) 1929.
3. Bunting, R. W.: Report of Successful Control of Dental Caries in Three Public Institutions, *J. Am. Dent. A.* 18:672 (April) 1931.
4. McBeath, E. D.: Experiments on the Dietary Control of Dental Caries in Children, *J. Dent. Research* 12:723 (Oct.) 1932.
5. Mellanby, M.: Diet and the Teeth, *Medical Research Council, Special Report Series*, no. 153, London, His Majesty's Stationery Office, 1931.
6. Mellanby, M.; Pattison, C. L., and Proud, J. W.: The Effect of Diet on the Development and Extension of Caries in the Teeth of Children, *Brit. M. J.* 2:354 (Aug. 30) 1924.
7. Mellanby, M., and Pattison, C. L.: Some Factors Influencing the Spread of Caries in Children, *Brit. Dent. J.*, 47:1045 (Oct.) 1926.
8. Mellanby, M., and Pattison, C. L.· The Action of Vitamin D in Preventing the Spread and Promoting the Arrest of Caries in Children, *Brit. M. J.* 2:1079 (Dec. 15) 1928.
9. Sprawson, E.: Preliminary Investigation of the Influence of Raw Milk on Teeth and Lymphoid Tissue, *Proc. Roy. Soc. Med.* 25:649 (March) 1932.

FOOD FALLACIES AND NUTRITIONAL QUACKERY*
REPORT OF THE COMMITTEE ON NUTRITIONAL PROBLEMS
American Public Health Association

The popular appeal, through the press and commercial advertisements, of matters relating to food and health has elicited wide popularization, and dissemination of information developed by scientific investigations in the field of nutrition. As a result, we have become as a nation "food conscious." The great popular demand for information about foods and dieting, together with the erroneous idea in many cases that nearly every disease and ailment can be cured by some system or other of dieting, has offered an unusually attractive opportunity for exploitation. During the last few years there has been an increasing amount of publicity, and exploitation of false and harmful statements foisted upon the public by dietary quacks, faddists, and so-called nutrition "experts." Some of them may be honest, but ignorant and misguided enthusiasts and fanatics. Many of them, however, are fakers, so-called "doctors," with little or no recognized professional standing, motivated by personal gain, who have selected this fruitful field for preying on the public.

Notwithstanding the large amount of popular scientific knowledge available in nutrition, the successful preying on the public by faddists and quacks has assumed alarming proportions. Influenced by promises, fanciful appeals to fear, and suggestion, many choose the courses offered by the faddist in preference to the advice of reputable authorities. Unfortunately, a large proportion of the population is unable to discriminate between the claims of the charlatan or ignorant faddist and

* Reprinted from American Public Health Association Year Book, 1935–1936.

those of investigators whose scientific contributions and knowledge have gained for them the position of outstanding authorities. Even physicians, nurses, teachers, medical students, and dietitians are numbered among the victims. Aside from mulcting thousands who can ill afford it, the exploitation of these dietary notions is a menace to public health, causing serious injury as a consequence of relying upon these false dietary systems for alleviating their ailments instead of seeking the timely aid of reliable medical assistance.

The most common subjects of the appeal which these quacks make are food combinations and incompatibilities. Based on entirely false representations, vicious systems of dieting which do much injury are given in books and pamphlets sold under high pressure salesmanship.

One of the most common and extensively proclaimed nutritional fallacies is that proteins and starches are incompatible and should be separated into distinct and separate meals. Based largely on this idea a system of dieting has been developed and featured in books and syndicated newspaper columns. A monthly magazine is devoted to this system. It is maintained that because starches require an alkaline medium for their digestion and proteins an acid medium, an antagonistic effect is developed when both are taken together which seriously interferes with the digestion of each of these classes of foods. One can look in vain through the writings of authorities in textbooks and journals for any scientific experimental data in support of this idea. The proponents ignore the fact that a large proportion of our staple articles of food contain both starch and protein. Adherence to this system would necessarily eliminate from the diet practically all products made from cereals and grains, such as bread, crackers, macaroni, cakes, pastries, etc. It would also exclude potatoes, beans, peas, and many other important foods. The cereal grains, wheat, rye, barley, oats, and corn, range in their protein content from 9 to 12 per cent or higher, and contain also about 60 per cent starch. Rice contains about 7 per cent protein and upward to 80 per cent of starch. Beans and peas are rich sources of both protein and starch, containing from 20 to 25 per cent protein and 40 to 50 per cent starch. Chestnuts range from 9 to 10 per cent protein and 20 to 30 per cent starch.

This absurd system would ban the time honored combinations which for generations have been recognized as wholesome and healthful, such as meat and potatoes, bread and milk, bread and cheese.

Investigators and authorities in the field of nutrition are practically unanimous in the opinion that there is no incompatibility between starches and proteins in the diet.

> Faddists have hit upon the idea that we should not eat starches and proteins at the same meal because starch digestion is interrupted in the acid stomach, acid being essential to peptic or stomach digestion of proteins. This is a fallacy. There is no significance in this interruption. The cat, dog, and cow have no starch-digesting ferment in their saliva, but they thrive on foods rich in starches. All their starch digestion takes place after the food has left the stomach and reaches the small intestine. Nature did not put these animals at a disadvantage in this respect. *McCollum and Becker*.[1]
>
> Much of what is said by food faddists relative to combinations of protein and carbohydrate is fallacy without any basis in scientific study. *Fishbein*.[2]

It has been shown that a mixture of carbohydrate and protein foods is discharged from the stomach in shorter time than protein alone, indicating that

> . . . the addition of carbohydrate to the diet accelerates digestion and the discharge of the gastric contents. *Cannon*.[3]

Studies by Rehfuss, Hawk, and others[4] on human gastric digestion in the stomach involving more than 1,000 studies on 200 normal men, in which a great variety of protein and starch combinations was used, failed to produce any evidence whatever of the incompatibility of these two classes of foods. In order to meet criticisms of the food faddists, that different results would have been obtained had the studies been made with chronic invalids instead of normal individuals, Rehfuss[5] has more recently extended the investigations to include a cross-section of medical invalids representing almost every variety of chronic illness encountered in a medical work service. Meat was used to represent protein, and potatoes to represent starch. The results of these studies involving hundreds of observations and representing a year's work in medical service, again demonstrated

> . . . the absolute inaccuracy of the statement that proteins and carbohydrates are incompatible in the stomach. . . .
> There is no evidence either in the literature or in my investigation to lead me to believe that proteins and carbohydrates are incompatible in the stomach. The danger of such teaching based on a lack of scientific evidence is manifest, and while it may be true that many individuals overeat and are presumably better by a reduction of carbohydrates, the unqualified acceptance of such a teaching can lead to the occurrence of serious malnutrition as well as to a lighting of tuberculosis and old infections.

We are also told to eat but one kind of starch at a time and one kind of protein. This is obviously so devoid of any scientific reason that it merits but a mere passing reference. All starches yield on digestion the same simple sugar, glucose. The end product is the same irrespective of the source of the starch. As to proteins, to eat one kind at a time is just what one should not do. Proteins differ in their nutritive value depending on their amino acid composition. Some proteins are lacking or deficient in certain amino acids which are nutritionally indispensable.

Nutritionally deficient or incomplete proteins should be supplemented with other proteins so that the amino acids lacking in the one will be supplied by the others in order to have an assortment of amino acids adequate to meet the requirements of the body. For example, the endosperm proteins of the cereal grains in general are deficient in lysine and trytophane, two amino acids indispensable for growth and normal nutrition. The proteins of meat, milk, eggs, and nuts, on the other hand, are excellent sources of these amino acids. The value of the cereal proteins in the diet is enhanced by inclusion of the latter protein foods in the diet. Instead of an incompatibility we have a supplementation.

Acidosis is a term that is frequently and effectively used by the purveyors of food fallacies in the exploitation of their books, literature, and dietetic systems. Nearly all diseases that afflict mankind can be found enumerated as the result of acidosis caused by eating "acid foods." Elaborate menus are offered for "alkali-forming" meals, and systems of dieting which can be had by purchasing their books or enlisting their services and special courses. The claim that acidosis, with all its dire effects, will result from eating bread and meat or certain combination of foods, such as proteins and starches, or fruits and starches, is entirely unsupported by scientific evidence.

Acidosis is usually a condition attending certain diseases, such as diabetes or kidney diseases, involving a faulty metabolism of the body.

There is no evidence that a preponderantly acid diet is injurious.

That the body reaction remains practically unaltered even when a wide range of amount of acid or base is ingested has been pointed out by Henderson.[6]

McCollum and Hoagland[7] found that long continued excess of acid-forming elements in the diet did not lead to any apparent injury.

The Committee on Foods of the American Medical Association in one of its recent decisions states that

> . . . acidosis is a name for a morbid condition of diminution in the reserve supply of fixed alkali in the blood and body fluids. Most people have no conception of the true meaning of the word and are quite likely to confuse it with gastric hyperacidity or "acid stomach," or to conceive of it as "acid blood," a condition which would be incompatible with life. The term "acidosis" is so little understood that its use in any advertising except that restricted to the medical profession is misleading and consequently disapproved.

As stated by Stone,[8] the term acidosis has become a popular fancy.

> . . . The belief that acid-ash foods are responsible for a variety of common symptoms such as gastric hyperacidity, lassitude, biliousness, acid mouths, headaches, nephritis, and high blood pressure carries one far afield. . . . The importance of the acid-ash diet as a factor in the etiology of disease has been overestimated.

Mariott[9] believes that ". . . acidosis is a rare condition and there is no good evidence that the regular taking of large amounts of alkaline-ash foods is of any special benefit." In his experience there is no evidence ". . . that an alkaline-ash dietary can effect the reduction of established arterial hypertension."

Arthritis is a disease which is commonly emphasized as resulting from improper food combinations and which readily yields to the particular dietetic system which is exploited. We are told to omit "acid fruits and vegetables"; to partake of only one type of food substance at a meal; to alter the acid-base balance of the diet; to use a low protein and carbohydrate diet. Carbohydrate restriction is based on a dietary rationale, the correctness of which has not been satisfactorily demonstrated by scientifically controlled experiments. The commonly so-called acid fruits, such as oranges, tomatoes, and grapefruit, contain weak organic acids which are easily oxidized in the body. These acids are chiefly present as salts of inorganic bases which are left in the blood as alkaline carbonates and really serve as available alkali to the body. The fallacy and inadequacy of these claims have been recently pointed out by Bauer.[10]

> One need make no conscious effort to maintain a basic diet in an arthritic person any more than in a normal one. . . . The prescribing of a low protein diet is a relic from the days when rheumatoid arthritis was confused with gout. There is no justification for the limitation of proteins in the dietary of a patient with rheumatoid arthritis. There are many reasons why it should be liberal.

Another fallacy which finds a prominent place in the armamentarian of the nutritional quack is that acid fruits should not be eaten at the same time with carbohydrate foods, including breads and cereal products, potatoes, squash, and sugars of every kind. These foods, we are reminded, require an alkaline medium for their digestion, and without the alkaline reaction of the saliva they would never be digested at all. This view ignores the well-known fact that only a part of the carbohydrate digestion occurs in the mouth and stomach as a result of the action of ptyalin in the saliva, and that there are active amylolytic enzymes in the intestines where carbohydrate digestion proceeds to completion. In fact, starch digestion can proceed favorably in a medium that is practically neutral. The relatively small amounts of the weak organic acids in fruits can have little or no significance in any interruption of starch digestion in the stomach where the hydrochloric acid of the gastric juice is many times stronger than the fruit acids.

Emphasis is laid by "experts" and exploiters of preparations offered for sale on the claim that the use of common table salt is responsible for Bright's disease, cancer, tuberculosis, high blood pressure, and other diseases and ailments.

The surmise that salt has some relation to high blood pressure has influenced to some extent the treatment of this disease. However, the work of O'Hare and Walker[11] lends no support to such a view. No relation was found to hold between blood pressure and the chlorides of the blood and plasma, and no effect on the systolic and diastolic levels was observed during wide variations in the amounts (0.5 gm. to 4 gm. daily) of salt taken in high pressure cases without nephritis. McLester,[12] in a series of controlled observations with patients having hypertension, was unable to note any improvement when a so-called "salt-free" diet was used. He believes, however, that in cases of hypertension complicated with nephritis the salt intake should be restricted "to that contained in the food as it reaches the table." While the avoidance of large quantities of salt in the diet of patients suffering from certain diseases may be advisable, there is no evidence that salt in the quantities generally used in the diet results in the development of such diseases as mentioned or is attended by any harmful effects.

We are told to avoid the use of dark meats or to limit our meat consumption to fish and fowl. The statement that white meat is less harmful than dark meat has no basis in fact.[12] This belief goes back to the days when gout was confused with other forms of arthritis, and that foods rich in purines yield uric acid with resulting gout, rheumatism, and acidosis. With the exception of the glandular organs, liver, sweetbreads, and kidneys, dark meat contains no more purine bases than does white meat. Fish and fowl contain as much, or more, uric acid-forming bases as beef, veal, lamb, and pork.[12]

It has been proved by numerous investigators [13, 14, 15, 16, 17, 18, 19] that the white of eggs is much less digestible when raw than when cooked. There is even evidence [20, 21, 22, 23] that raw egg white when fed to experimental animals will invariably produce toxic symptoms. Nevertheless, it is still not uncommon to find physicians and nurses prescribing raw eggs for invalids in the belief that they are more digestible and more easily assimilated than when cooked.

Among the dicta of faddists and food charlatans are many so fanciful and absurd that to the person of ordinary intelligence they need no refutation.

As illustrations of such fallacies may be mentioned the following: Tomatoes cause cancer; meat makes one sensuous and belligerent; mixtures of incompatible foods explode in the stomach; fish is a good brain food; garlic "purifies" the blood; cream should not be eaten with lobster, strawberries or pickles; fish and celery should not be eaten together; "dead foods" should be avoided in the diet.

Many different systems of dieting and treatments are advocated for weight reduction, some of which are merely scientifically unsound; others are positively harmful and dangerous. Many, eager to conform to the current prevailing fashion of being slender, adopt short-cuts to reduction advertised by food promoters and those interested only in their own personal gains, have done themselves harm, bringing ou weakness, nervous irritability, and anemia. Particularly to be deprecated is the use of salts and dangerous drugs. In reduction treatment the first consideration is curtailment of calorie intake, with the object of accomplishing a gradual loss of weight without sacrificing the amount of protein, vitamins, and mineral salts required for normal body needs, nor even of the calories needed as a source of energy for body temperature and for production of work. Many reducing menus are erroneously based on elimination from the diet of individual foods, such as potatoes, rice, cereal products, and butter. In order to assure an adequate balance of food factors essential for health and normal nutrition, it should be remembered that it is not the kind of food that should be restricted, but rather the quantity. As Mendel[24] has aptly stated, "Sanity in diet calls for moderation in eating rather than exclusion of any wholesome food. Even the slenderest persons need some energy for their daily undertakings."

It is only by a process of education that the public can be enabled to discriminate between the fallacies proclaimed by the food faddists and quacks, and the sound principles of nutrition established by reliable investigators. Public health officials are in an excellent position to render a great service in educating the general public along these lines, and in waging a concerted attack on the operations of these enemies of public health.

There is plenty of reliable literature available which can be effectively used in conducting such a campaign of education.

In addition to the references already cited in this report, there are given others[25], [26], [27], [28], [29], [30] which excellently cover the subject.

References

1. McCollum, E. V., and Becker, J. E. *Food, Nutrition and Health.* Lord Baltimore Press, 1933.
2. Fishbein, M. *Shattering Health Superstitions.* Horace Liveright, Inc., 1930, p. 57.
3. Cannon, W. B. The Passage of Different Foodstuffs from the Stomach and Through the Small Intestine. *Am. J. Physiol.*, 12:387, 1904.
4. Rehfuss, M. E., Hawk, P., et. al. *Am. J. Physiol.*, 1914-1920.
5. Rehfuss, M. E. Proteins Versus the Carbohydrates. *J. A. M. A.*, 103:1600. 1934.
6. Henderson, Y. Physiological Regulation of the Acid-Base Balance of the Blood and Some Related Function. *Physiol. Rev.*, 5:131, 1925.
7. McCollum, E. V., and Hoagland, D. R. The Effects of Acid and Basic Salts, and of Free Mineral Acids on the Indogenous Nitrogen Metabolism. *J. Biol. Chem.*, 16:299, 1913.
8. Stone, W. J. Dietary Facts, Fads and Fancies. *J. A. M. A.*, 95:709, 1930.
9. Mariott, W. M. The Uses of Proprietary and Medicinal Foods in the Hospital. *J. A. M. A.*, 94:1281, 1930.
10. Bauer, W. What Should a Patient with Arthritis Eat? *J. A. M. A.*, 104:1, 1935.
11. O'Hare, J. P., and Walker, W. G. Observations on Salt in Vascular Hypertension. *Arch. Int. Med.*, 32:283, 1923.
12. McLester, J. S. *Nutrition and Diet in Health and Disease*, W. B. Saunders Co., 1931.
13. Hosoi, K., Alvarez, W. C., and Mann, F. C. Intestinal Absorption, A Search for a Low Residue Diet. *Arch. Int. Med.*, 41:112, 1928.
14. Bateman, W. G. The Digestibility and Utilization of Egg Proteins. *J. Biol. Chem.*, 26:263, 1916.
15. Mendel, L. B., and Lewis, R. C. The Rate of Elimination of N as Influenced by Diet Factors. III. The Influence of the Character of the Ingested Protein. *J. Biol. Chem.*, 16:55, 1913.
16. Wolf, C. G. L. Some Human Digestion Experiments with Raw White of Egg. *J. Biol. Chem.*, 52:207, 1922.

17. Bayliss, W. M. The Nature of Enzyme Action. Longmans, Green and Co., 1908, p. 67.
18. Boaz, M. A. An Observation on the Value of Egg White as the Sole Source of Nitrogen for Young Growing Rats. *Biochem. J.*, 18:422, 1924.
19. Childrey, J. H., Alvarez, W. C., and Mann, F. C. Digestion Efficiency with Various Foods and under Various Conditions. *Arch. Int. Med.*, 46:361, 1930.
20. Salmon, W. D., and Goodman, J. G. Studies on the Raw Egg White Syndrone in Rats. *J. Nutrition*, 8:1, 1934.
21. Parsons, H. T., and Lease, J. G. Variations in the Potency of Certain Foodstuffs in the Cure of Dermatitis Induced in Rats by Dietary Egg White. *J. Nutrition*, 8:57, 1934.
22. Parsons, H. T. The Effect of Toxicity of Egg White of Various Heat Treatments. *J. Biol. Chem.*, 97:30 (July), 1932.
23. Stenquist, F. Raw and Cooked Egg White as Sole Nutrient for Growing Rats. *Deutsch. med. Wchnschr.*, 54:1920, 1928.
24. Mendel, L. B. *Food Facts*, 4:2 (May), 1934.
25. Sherman, H. C. *Chemistry of Food and Nutrition*. The Macmillan Company, 1927.
26. McCollum, E. V., and Simmonds, N. *The Newer Knowledge of Nutrition*. The Macmillan Co., 1925.
27. Mitchell, H. Food Fads and Fallacies. *J. Home Econ.*, 27:89, 1935.
28. Farren, M. R. Food Fads and Faddists, *Hygeia*, Oct., 1934, p. 885.
29. Eddy, W. H. Avoid Dietary Fads. *Good Housekeeping*, Aug., 1934, pp. 106, 130.
30. Rose, M. S. Belief in Magic. *J. Am. Dietetic Assn.*, 8:489, 1933.

D. B. Jones, *Chairman*	P. L. Day
E. V. McCollum	C. G. King
E. M. Nelson	H. T. Scott
F. L. Gunderson	

Members of the Committee.

HOW GREENFIELD IS SOLVING THE DENTAL HEALTH PROBLEM
BY HAROLD R. LAMB, D.M.D.
School Dental Clinician
Greenfield, Mass.

This article is being presented in an endeavor to show how we in Greenfield are getting the better of the problem of dental care in the schools. We have divided the article into two major headings; namely, system of handling patients, and methods of operative procedure.

System of Handling Patients

Our preschool examinations are held in mid-June in conjunction with the medical examination. Parents are notified through the press that all children about to enter kindergarten in September will be examined medically and dentally on a certain date. At this time we make definite appointments for all desiring dental clinic service, and the work is done during the following two or three weeks. This disposes of preschool work before the fall term and results in a high percentage of perfect teeth in the incoming kindergarten pupils.

In September and part of October all nine grades are examined. We have always done this, even when we were unable to offer treatment to the upper three grades, in the belief that an examination is an incentive to getting necessary attention outside the clinic. It also uncovers many urgent cases that have filtered through the grades without treatment, usually because of fear. We are now in a position to offer treatment to all underprivileged cases in the upper grades.

All cases are classified at the examination into A, B, and C cases (A minor cavities, B moderate attention, and C urgent attention). Teachers' lists are made out in duplicate, one of which is left with each teacher, and the other retained by us for reference and follow-up work. All blue cards showing need of dental work are made out and left with the teachers to be sent home by the pupils, but certificates are made out later by the dental nurse and delivered to the teachers in due course. This saves about half a day of examining time on the part of the dentist compared with our earlier method of delivering certificates at the time of the examination.

When operations are begun, all C cases are sent for first, throughout all buildings, and disposed of as far as possible. Next in line are the kindergarten and first two grades. The kindergarten is handled with comparative ease, because of preschool work in July. A thorough check is made on these grades in an effort to "dam up caries at its source." After this, A and B cases from all grades are handled in groups of six throughout the remainder of the school year, the lower grades having the priority.

The fine cooperation of the teachers and school nurse with the dental nurse makes for a smooth-running schedule with a minimum loss of time. The dental nurse takes a keen interest in follow-up work and cooperates with the school nurse who contacts cases and furnishes transportation when necessary. Emergency cases, which have diminished considerably, but are still numerous, are worked in as they present.

Methods of Operative Procedure

Since the purpose of this article is to show how we are making progress, I am including below only the methods of operating which have to do with rapid accomplishment. They are as follows:

1. We extract all teeth with pulp involvement. We have never undertaken to treat teeth except in rare instances where anterior teeth are involved. Years ago, the six year molars were the problem, and extraction of these teeth comprised a large proportion of the clinic work at that time. But now these teeth are being preserved by fillings, with only occasional extractions. The policy of extracting all pulp-involved teeth, together with a thorough combing of the first three grades has, in our opinion, brought about the solution of this problem.

2. We fill all fissure cavities, however small, and extend them wherever the fissures are deep or have failed to unite.

3. Arrested decay is common in deciduous molars. We let such conditions alone. In permanent molars if the arresting is complete, we also let them alone. The condition will remain unchanged indefinitely, or until such time as the patient will be able to have the necessary restoration made.

4. In certain cases where deciduous molars are slightly decayed, with only a short time to remain, we use a ten per cent solution of silver nitrate rather than spend the time in filling. These conditions will take care of themselves automatically, so we feel that with such limited time, it should be devoted to the most necessary work.

5. We spend only a minimum of time on deciduous anteriors.

By following the above outlined system of clinical procedure, we have succeeded in gaining ground each year over the annual influx of dental defects. Fourteen years ago the task appeared overwhelming and progress was so slow that it seemed impossible to ever get ahead. But steady hard work over the years, gradually bringing in more system, more education and more cooperation from all concerned, has resulted in more rapid gains, until the percentage of pupils entitled to certificates is now around 60 per cent, compared with an initial percentage fourteen years ago of 15 per cent.

We have been requested to submit this article in the hope that other dental clinicians may find something outlined therein, which may prove to be helpful.

OUR DENTAL HYGIENE PROGRAM
By JENNIE W. BALL
Hygienist, Park Avenue School Dental Clinic
West Springfield, Massachusetts

West Springfield is a progressive town of about 17,500 inhabitants. We have ten public schools—senior and junior high schools, eight elementary schools and two parochial schools.

Our town has one centrally located dental clinic in a new school building. The clinic is modern in every way and very well equipped. We are all certainly proud of it! Children in the various school buildings who need dental attention all come to this clinic.

Our dental program is scheduled the same as the school year; that is, we start in September and complete our work in June. We begin by examining the children's teeth in the classrooms. Until last year all children were examined including junior and senior high schools. Since the fall, examination is made by the dentist with the hygienist's assistance. This took considerable of the dentist's time away from the clinic. At that time the dentist did all emergency work in the upper grades as well as in junior and senior high schools. However, during the depression, the children who entered the grade schools had very little done by their family dentists —an average of four out of five children needing dental attention at the clinic. Thus, at present, all clinic work is limited to the first three grades only. A separate book is kept by the hygienist for each school. In the fall all students' names are entered in the books by the grades from one to six. In each grade the names are entered as the pupils are seated, row by row, by their respective teachers. The hygienist arranges an appointment with the principal of the respective school. The dentist arrives with the hygienist at the specified time and examines the pupil's teeth row by row. The hygienist enters the examination mark against the pupil's name, whether it is a cleaning, filling or extraction case, also whether it is temporary or permanent teeth which need attention. These records are kept in the clinic. This year we are also planning to enter the marks on the physical record charts so that the school department may have them for reference. The hygienist sends out Permit Cards to the parents of the children who need dental attention. The parents who wish their children's teeth attended to at the clinic express their willingness by signing and returning the card. The hygienist files these cards alphabetically in the clinic. Only children who have these cards on file receive appointments for clinic attention. When making an appointment for the dentist I usually select seven pupils for a morning appointment or six for an afternoon session. All emergency work is taken care of as it arises in grades I, II, and III. However, all regular work is done in grades I and II first, names taken in rotation. When grades I and II are completed then grade III is given attention. All appointments for the clinic are made with the principal. An older pupil accompanies the younger group to the clinic. The dentist saves as many of the children's teeth as possible by filling them. He extracts the badly decayed teeth. The children above grade III who need dental attention and can not afford a family dentist have their work done through the Teachers' Welfare Fund. Of course, the children whose parents are on welfare or soldiers' relief have their teeth attended to through that department.

The hygienist takes care of all the cleaning cases, doing grades I, II and III, respectively, operating on days when the dentist is not using the chair.

In the fall the hygienist presents a Dental Honor Roll to each class. All the names of the boys and girls who had perfect teeth, that is, free from decay or filled and cleaned at the time of the examination have their names entered on the Honor Roll. Certificates are given to the patients at the clinic as their cases are completed. The children bring the certificates to their teachers and teachers enter their names on the Honor Roll which is hung on the board or wall. The children are so proud to see it grow!

The hygienist divides her time equally between the clinic and classrooms. At each visit she inspects the children's teeth for cleanliness. This individual clean-teeth inspection is very important because if a child has an abscessed tooth or cavities in the six year molar, he is immediately sent to the clinic or referred to the family dentist. The hygienist has a small blackboard space in each classroom where she keeps a record of the clean teeth marks throughout the year. Of course, we all are trying for "100% clean teeth." The school which shows the best record throughout the year wins the Dental Banner. We have a lot of close competition. The hygienist awards the Banner in June to the school principal and it is kept in that school for the following school year. After the "clean teeth smiles" and inspection of teeth the hygienist gives a short talk to the class on dental hygiene or nutrition. A full period is taken with the visit but careful planning is done not to run over the period as that throws the teacher's regular work off schedule. Talks are given on temporary and permanent teeth and their structure, decay and how it spreads, abscessed teeth, why we have teeth, home care of teeth, use of paste or powder and regular visits to the dentist. Considerable time is spent on nutrition —vegetables and fruits are stressed. Children are taught the importance of milk in the daily diet. Some time is spent on vitamins in the upper grades. Also the children are shown specimens of x-rays and how to read them. We have toothbrush drills often in classes. We teach the up and down strokes as the lower grades seem to master that the easiest. I allow five minutes at the end of the period for discussion. Children usually have a lot of questions to ask or personal stories to tell. I find it difficult to get away, but am glad to know that the children are interested in my program and their teeth. I keep a book of some of the interesting questions asked me by the children and use them as the bases of my talks in the future. I vary my talks from year to year and also at each visit. I plan to illustrate my talks with colored posters or diagrams, especially so in the lower grades. Occasionally I give talks at junior and senior high schools in the health classes. I do this upon request of the health instructors when the class is studying about teeth and oral hygiene. In June each year I give the classes an oral examination. I am very much pleased how well the children remember the various subjects studied throughout the year.

I noticed in the past that some children are slow about replacing their worn-out toothbrushes with new ones and that a few of the first graders were without toothbrushes. I remedied this situation last year by selling toothbrushes at cost in classrooms. I distributed eleven hundred and fifty-eight junior-size toothbrushes.

Sad but true! Each year we have a few backward children in our programs. They either have badly decayed teeth or filthy mouths. Most of these children are newcomers in town and come from cities or towns where they do not have dental hygiene programs. These situations are ironed out very nicely by making a call and talking it over with the parents. Home visits are important in order to put over a perfect program.

We have excellent cooperation between our department and the school department. The principals are very interested in our work and allow the teachers time for daily questioning and inspection of teeth. This is important as it holds the children's interest in their teeth between the hygienist's visits. On the whole we make very good progress with our program and are pleased with the results.

DO YOU KNOW ABOUT THE VOLTA BUREAU?

"We consulted several specialists, and all of them confirmed our fears, but none offered any solution of our problem." Thus the mother of a small deaf child wrote to the Volta Bureau. The sentence might be quoted verbatim from many letters written by parents of deaf or hard of hearing children, or by hard of hearing adults.

The knowledge that deafness is present and that it is incurable comes with the force of a major calamity. It is so crushing in its effect that something positive in the way of help must be offered immediately, if the individual is not to spend desperate years in a bewildered effort to adjust himself. The parents of a deaf child must be told that the child can be taught to speak and can be successfully educated, and that this education may be begun at home immediately, even if the child is not more than two years old. The parents of a child whose hearing is only slightly impaired must be given advice as to his adjustment. The hard of hearing adult must be told about lip reading, about hearing aids, about social efforts in his behalf.

The Volta Bureau was established for the purpose of furnishing all this information to all who ask for it. Its services are free. Alexander Graham Bell, the son of a hard-of-hearing mother, the husband of a deaf wife, the lifelong friend of everyone handicapped by deafness, used the money received as a prize for inventing the telephone to found the Volta Bureau so that any one confronting the problems of deafness might be assured of help. Advice is given as to schools and preschool training, lip reading instruction, hearing aids, social contacts, psychological difficulties. While the Volta Bureau is not equipped to do employment service, it gives information in regard to the fields of activity that are open to the deaf and the hard of hearing.

The Volta Review, a magazine for parents and teachers of the deaf and for the hard of hearing, is on the reading table of many physicians. Pamphlets dealing with all phases of deafness except medical problems are available to all who ask for them. Lists of such pamphlets and sample copies of the magazine will gladly be sent free of charge. The Volta Bureau is located at 1537 35th St., N. W., Washington, D. C.

REPORT OF DIVISION OF FOOD AND DRUGS

During the months of April, May and June, 1936, samples were collected in 236 cities and towns.

There were 1,899 samples of milk examined, of which 230 were below standard, from 13 samples the cream had been in part removed, and 5 samples contained added water. There were 1,214 bacteriological examinations made of milk, 1,041 of which complied with the requirements. There were 377 bacteriological examinations made of ice cream, and 19 bacteriological examinations of sherbet, 369 of which complied with the requirements; 5 bacteriological examinations of raw cream, and 5 bacteriological examinations of pasteurized cream, 8 of which complied with the requirements; 10 bacteriological examinations of meat, 4 of which complied with the requirements; 4 bacteriological examinations of grenadine from flood area, and 4 bacteriological examinations of tonic, all of which complied with the requirements; 37 bacteriological examinations of empty bottles, 35 of which did not comply with the requirements; and 16 bacteriological examinations of mattress fillings, all of which complied with the requirements.

There were 901 samples of food examined, 168 of which were adulterated. These consisted of 25 samples of butter, 24 of which were low in fat, and 1 sample was moldy; 14 samples of cheese in which vegetable gum was present; 6 samples of eggs which were decomposed; 3 samples of olive oil which contained tea seed oil; 2 samples of sweet relish and 1 sample of pickles which contained sodium benzoate and were not properly labeled; 5 samples of grenadine syrup which contained sodium benzoate and were not properly labeled; 2 samples of vinegar which contained less than the required amount of acidity; 40 samples of soft drinks, 15 samples of which contained artificial flavor and were colored to conceal inferiority, and 6 of these samples also contained sodium benzoate and were not properly labeled; 7 samples contained sodium benzoate and were not properly labeled; 1 sample contained saccharine; 2 samples were in dirty bottles; 7 samples were orange beverage which were misbranded, 7 samples were orange soda which were deficient in orange, and 1 sample was orange juice which was colored to conceal inferiority; 28 samples of hamburg steak, 3 samples of which contained sodium sulphite in excess of one tenth of one per cent, 1 sample of which was also watered and decomposed, 2 samples contained a compound of sulphur dioxide not properly labeled, 1 sample of which was also decomposed, and 23 samples were decomposed, 1 sample of which also contained excess water; 11 samples of sausage, of which 6 samples were decomposed, 4 samples contained a compound of sulphur dioxide not properly labeled, and 1 sample contained starch in excess of 2 per cent; 1 sample of maple syrup which contained cane sugar; and 29 samples of mattress filling, of which 26 samples contained secondhand material, 1 sample contained oil, and 2 samples were improperly labeled.

There were 97 samples of drugs examined, of which 12 were adulterated. These consisted of 3 samples of rubbing alcohol, 1 sample of which was low standard, and 2 samples were misbranded; 2 samples of argyrol which did not conform to the professed standard under which it was sold; 1 sample of ammonia which bore no poison label; 1 sample of camphorated oil, 1 sample of lime water, and 4 samples of spirit of nitrous ether, all of which did not conform to the requirements of the U. S. Pharmacopœia.

The police departments submitted 180 samples of liquor for examination. The police departments also submitted 14 samples to be analyzed for poisons or drugs, of which 5 samples contained heroin, 3 samples contained morphine, 2 were cannabis,

1 charred cannabis, 1 sample of white powder contained no alkaloids, and 1 sample of meat and 1 sample of liquor were analyzed for cyanide, alkaloids and heavy metals, with negative results. One sample was candy containing arsenic.

There were 105 cities and towns visited for the inspection of pasteurizing plants, and 535 plants, operated for the pasteurization of milk, were inspected as well as 17 ice cream plants.

There were 128 hearings held pertaining to violations of the laws.

There were 83 convictions for violations of the law, $2,460 in fines being imposed.

James J. Gilgun of Malden; J. J. Newberry Company, George Stathacopoulos, and Walton Lunch Company of Boston; John Joacquin of Fall River; and Frank Pedercini of North Adams, were all convicted for violations of the milk laws. John Joacquin of Fall River appealed his case.

H. P. Hood & Sons, Incorporated, of Lynn; and Hazen K. Richardson of Middleton, were convicted for violations of the pasteurization regulations.

Hazen K. Richardson of Middleton was convicted for violation of the milk grading law.

Mohican Market, Harry Abrams, Morris Abrams, 2 cases, and Peter L. Berlo, 2 cases, of South Boston; P. W. Rounsevell, Incorporated, Abraham Kantor, Antonio Accardi, Jerry Caradonna, Dominick Meo, Louis Ruggerio, John Freni, John Gaeta, Abraham Black, David Shuman, Lo Conte Brothers, Incorporated, and Anthony Giacobbi, all of Boston; Hyman Racoff, Morris Bernstein, Stark Supply Company, Incorporated, Sigmund Waldman, and William Waldman, all of Roxbury; Max Bass and George Snyder of Lynn; Joseph Frank and John Fontes, and People's Public Market, Incorporated, of Fall River; Jacob Pomerantz and Ely Slotnick of Indian Orchard; A. H. Phillips and M. Winer Company of Springfield; Luigi Ballestracci, 2 cases, of Worcester; Kamel J. Ganem, Shaheen Kawash, and James Yameen of Lawrence; Simon Kronick, 2 cases, and William Dickenson of North Adams; and Benjamin Gross of Lowell, were all convicted for violations of the food laws. Mohican Market and Harry Abrams of South Boston; John Gaeta of Boston; and M. Winer Company of Springfield, all appealed their cases.

Luigi Ballestracci, 2 cases, of Worcester, was convicted for misbranding.

Lakin's Ice Cream and Sherbet Company, Incorporated, of Roxbury, was convicted for violation of the frozen dessert law.

Harry Kessler, 3 counts, and Abraham Zemen, 4 counts, of New Bedford; and Joseph Koza of Westfield, were convicted for violations of the bakery laws and regulations.

Will Bell Bottling Company and Simon S. Millman of Roxbury; Arthur Padgur of Boston; Jacob Phillips of East Boston; John E. Daly of Attleboro; Elk Spring Beverage Company, Incorporated, of Wakefield; John Machaj of Ipswich; and Mrs. Cscslawa Proudecki of Turners Falls, were all convicted for violations of the law and regulations relative to the manufacture and bottling of carbonated nonalcoholic beverages. Will Bell Bottling Company and Simon S. Millman of Roxbury; and John E. Daly of Attleboro, appealed their cases.

Simon Belson and Solomon J. Feldman of Dorchester; Amodeo Brothers, Incorporated, and Morse & Sturnick, Incorporated, of Boston; Irving W. Chaney of Manchester; Arthur H. Sinclair of Salem; and Stephen Karp of Cambridge; were all convicted for violations of the drug laws. Amodeo Brothers, Incorporated, of Boston appealed their case.

Joseph Schott of Easthampton was convicted for violation of the slaughtering law.

Abraham Boodman, Samuel Mover, Eagle Mattress Company, and Kane Furniture Company of Boston; Charlestown Furniture Company, Incorporated, of Charlestown; Samuel Rosen of Whitman; James Zanello of Plymouth; Isaac Bartfield of Worcester; David Hecht of Roxbury; Carl Schlager of Malden; Samuel Cohen of Manchester, N. H.; and Diamond Mattress Company, Incorporated, of Woonsocket, R. L; were all convicted for violations of the mattress laws. Isaac Bartfield of Worcester; and David Hecht of Roxbury, appealed their cases.

In accordance with Section 25, Chapter 111 of the General Laws, the following is the list of articles of adulterated food collected in original packages from manufacturers, wholesalers, or producers:

Butter which was low in fat was obtained as follows:

Four samples from M. Winer Company of Boston, 1 sample each from M. Winer Company of Newton Center, Springfield, and Worcester; 5 samples from Fairmont Creamery Company of Boston; 4 samples from Harding Creamery Company of Omaha, Nebraska; 2 samples from Charney Milk Company of Chelsea; 1 sample each, from Abraham Marshall of Chelsea; New York Cut Rate Store of Dorchester; and Mayflower Butter & Cheese Company, Incorporated, of Springfield.

Cheese in which vegetable gum was present was obtained as follows:

Four samples from Berkshire Creamery Company, Incorporated, of Pittsfield; 3 samples from Mayflower Creamery Company of Boston; 2 samples from Shefford Cheese Company of Syracuse, New York; and 1 sample each, from National Creamery Company of Somerville, and M. Winer Company of Boston.

Olive Oil which contained cottonseed oil was obtained as follows:

One sample each, from Growers Outlet, Incorporated, of Holyoke; and Diamond Drug and Magnesia Company of Cambridge.

One sample of olive oil which contained tea seed oil was obtained from Capone and Company of New York.

Sweet relish which contained sodium benzoate and was not properly labeled was obtained as follows:

One sample each, from Delmar Jewett of South Deerfield; and Albert C. Rower of South Boston.

One sample of pickles which contained sodium benzoate and was not properly labeled was obtained from R. J. Reynolds of Indian Orchard.

Hamburg steak which was decomposed was obtained as follows:

Three samples from Waltham Provision Company of Waltham; 2 samples from People's Cash Market of North Adams; and 1 sample each, from Hutchinson's Market, Abraham Kantor, and Sarah Snyder of Boston; William Steiman (United Food Store) of Webster; The Great Atlantic and Pacific Tea Company of Haverhill and Quincy; Morris Provision Company and Fanueil Hall Market of Waltham; First National Stores, Incorporated, of Peabody; City Public Market of Lowell Economy Grocery Stores Corporation of Franklin; Hudson Market, Incorporated of Hudson; People's Public Market of Fall River; Ganem's Market, U-Sav Market, and Franklin Market of Lawrence; and Arthur Bernard of Holyoke.

Hamburg steak which contained sodium sulphite in excess of one tenth of on per cent was obtained as follows:

One sample each, from Liberty Market of Newburyport; and Broadway Publi Market of Waltham.

One sample of hamburg steak which contained a compound of sulphur dioxide not properly labeled was obtained from Irving Kimmel of Boston.

One sample of hamburg steak which contained a compound of sulphur dioxide not properly labeled and was also decomposed was obtained from Samuel Smokler of Boston.

One sample of hamburg steak which was decomposed and also contained excess water was obtained from Carl Blasberg of Boston.

One sample of hamburg steak which contained sodium sulphite in excess of one tenth of one per cent, was decomposed, and also contained excess water, was obtained from Abraham Bell of South Boston.

Sausage which was decomposed was obtained as follows:

One sample each, from Waltham Provision Company and Progresso Cash Stores of Waltham; The Cudahy Packing Company of Lawrence; William Dickenson and George Parrino of North Adams; and John Froni of Boston.

One sample of sausage which contained a compound of sulphur dioxide not properly labeled was obtained from F. Astuti Market of Boston.

One sample of sausage which contained starch in excess of two per cent was obtained from Square Deal Market of Boston.

Soft drinks which were artificially colored and were not properly marked were obtained as follows:

Three samples from Commonwealth Whiskey Corporation of Boston; 2 samples from Wamsutta Bottling Company of North Attleboro; and one sample each, from Shawsheen Bottling Company and Columbia Bottling Company of Lawrence, and Louis J. Robbins of Worcester.

Soft drinks which contained sodium benzoate and were not properly marked were obtained as follows:

One sample each, from Goulding Brothers, Incorporated, of Whitman; Copes Ginger Ale of Taunton; Curran and Joyce of Lawrence; and J. F. and C. Leary Company of Newburyport.

Soft drinks which contained sodium benzoate and also were artificially colored and not properly labeled were obtained as follows:

Two samples each, from Peter Gwozdz and Ignatius J. Wojtaszek of Adams; and 1 sample each, from Herman S. Braum of Pittsfield, and Coleman and Keating Company, Incorporated, of Roxbury.

One sample of soft drink which contained saccharin was obtained from Hillside Bottling Company of Hudson.

Orange Beverage which was colored to conceal inferiority was obtained as follows:

Two samples each, from Coates Bottling Company and Wheeler Bottling Company, Incorporated of Lynn; and 1 sample each, from Henry Beverage Company of Lynn; Snow Crest Beverage Company of Salem; and Essex Bottling Company of Peabody.

Four samples of grenadine syrup which contained sodium benzoate and were not properly marked were obtained from Ruby California Products Company of Lynn.

One sample of syrup which contained sodium benzoate and was also artificially colored and not properly labeled was obtained from Red Star Beverage Company, Incorporated, of East Boston.

The licensed cold storage warehouses reported the following amounts of food placed in storage during March, 1936:—720,300 dozens of case eggs; 651,576 pounds of broken out eggs; 391,315 pounds of butter; 998,961 pounds of poultry; 1,445,090 pounds of fresh meat and fresh meat products; and 6,928,731 pounds of fresh food fish.

There was on hand April 1, 1936:—672,270 dozens of case eggs; 1,010,701 pounds of broken out eggs; 332,467 pounds of butter; 5,939,347 pounds of poultry; 5,385,361½ pounds of fresh meat and fresh meat products; and 7,405,451 pounds of fresh food fish.

The licensed cold storage warehouses reported the following amounts of food placed in storage during April, 1936:—2,512,080 dozens of case eggs; 1,082,615 pounds of broken out eggs; 507,608 pounds of butter; 1,005,948 pounds of poultry; 1,624,671 pounds of fresh meat and fresh meat products; and 9,648,780 pounds of fresh food fish.

There was on hand May 1, 1936:—3,012,330 dozens of case eggs; 1,172,680 pounds of broken out eggs; 259,083 pounds of butter; 4,696,944 pounds of poultry; 4,839,482 pounds of fresh meat and fresh meat products; and 11,334,557 pounds of fresh food fish.

The licensed cold storage warehouses reported the following amounts of food placed in storage during May, 1936:—3,373,680 dozens of case eggs; 1,685,687 pounds of broken out eggs; 1,204,686 pounds of butter; 1,138,107 pounds of poultry; 2,354,081 pounds of fresh meat and fresh meat products; and 14,860,209 pounds of fresh food fish.

There was on hand June 1, 1936:—6,193,710 dozens of case eggs; 1,895,467 pounds of broken out eggs; 946,635 pounds of butter; 4,101,301 pounds of poultry; 4,500,862 pounds of fresh meat and fresh meat products; and 19,167,156 pounds of fresh food fish.

There were twenty-seven confiscations, consisting of 165 pounds of Farmer cheese, which had soaked in dirty water in an ice box; 1,500 pounds of cheese, 20 pounds of cheese, 10 jars of cheese, 30 pounds of lard, 10 pounds of bacon, 30 cans of peas, several boxes of raisins, several cakes, 4 dozen cakes, 12 jars of horse radish, 2½ barrels of flour, 37 bags of flour, 1 barrel of corn meal, bread dough for about 400 loaves, 400 loaves of bread, 5 truckloads of mixed groceries, 72 crates of eggs, 250 boxes of butter, 864 pounds of butter, 480 pounds of butter, 15 pounds of butter, 720 pounds of oleomargarine, and 7,515 pounds of beef, all of which had been contaminated by flood water; 625 pounds of decomposed butterfish; 600 pounds of decomposed butterfish; and 125 pounds of decomposed pigs' feet.

MASSACHUSETTS DEPARTMENT OF PUBLIC HEALTH

Commissioner of Public Health, HENRY D. CHADWICK, M.D.

Public Health Council

HENRY D. CHADWICK, M.D., *Chairman*

GORDON HUTCHINS. RICHARD M. SMITH, M.D.
FRANCIS H. LALLY, M.D. RICHARD P. STRONG, M.D.
SYLVESTER E. RYAN, M.D. JAMES L. TIGHE.

Secretary, FLORENCE L. WALL

Division of Administration	Under direction of Commissioner.
Division of Sanitary Engineering	Director and Chief Engineer, ARTHUR D. WESTON, C.E.
Division of Communicable Diseases	Director, GAYLORD W. ANDERSON, M.D.
Division of Biologic Laboratories	Director and Pathologist, ELLIOTT S. ROBINSON, M.D.
Division of Food and Drugs	Director and Analyst, HERMANN C. LYTHGOE, S.B.
Division of Child Hygiene	Director, M. LUISE DIEZ, M.D.
Division of Tuberculosis	Director, ALTON S. POPE, M.D.
Division of Adult Hygiene	Director, HERBERT L. LOMBARD, M.D.

State District Health Officers

The Southeastern District	RICHARD P. MACKNIGHT, M.D., New Bedford.
The South Metropolitan District	HENRY M. DE WOLFE, M.D., Quincy.
The North Metropolitan District	CHARLES B. MACK, M.D., Boston.
The Northeastern District	ROBERT E. ARCHIBALD, M.D., Lynn.
The Worcester County District	OSCAR A. DUDLEY, M.D., Worcester.
The Connecticut Valley District	HAROLD E. MINER, M.D., Springfield.
The Franklin County District	WALTER W. LEE, M.D., No. Adams.

PUBLICATION OF THIS DOCUMENT APPROVED BY THE COMMISSION ON ADMINISTRATION AND FINANCE
10,900. 9-36. Order 8795.

THE COMMONHEALTH

Volume 23   Oct.-Nov.-Dec.
No. 4   1936

PARENT EDUCATION

MASSACHUSETTS
DEPARTMENT OF PUBLIC HEALTH

THE COMMONHEALTH

QUARTERLY BULLETIN OF THE MASSACHUSETTS DEPARTMENT OF PUBLIC HEALTH

Sent Free to any Citizen of the State

Entered as second class matter at Boston Postoffice.

M. LUISE DIEZ, M.D., DIRECTOR OF DIVISION OF CHILD HYGIENE, EDITOR.
1 Beacon Street, Boston, Mass.

CONTENTS

	PAGE
The need for parent education, by Mrs. T. Grafton Abbott	219
The job of being a parent, by Katharine Herring	220
Parent education and the well child conference, by Florence L. McKay, M.D.	223
The parent as the private physician sees him, by Warren R. Sisson, M.D.	226
Parents and dental hygiene, by Robert L. Robinson	229
What mothers want to know about child nutrition, by Dorothea Nicoll	230
Health supervision as parent education, by Marie L. Donohue	233
The community aspects of parent education in regard to settlement work, by Ethel Ward Dougherty	238
Community aspects of parent education through public libraries, by Edith H. Bailey	240
The church and parents, by Rev. Phillips Endecott Osgood, D.D., L.H.D.	244
The church and parent education—need and opportunity for development, by Rev. Richard J. Quinlan, S.T.L.	247
The home as a builder of character, by Rabbi Herman H. Rubenovitz	250
The private school and parent education, by Gladys Beckett Jones	253
The Froebel Centennial, by Lucy Wheelock	254
Parent education, by Arthur B. Lord	257
The need for co-operation between headmaster and parents in country day high schools, by J. Halsey Gulick	260
Educating the backward child, by Ada M. Fitts	265
Psychiatric aspects of parental education, by Bernice M. Henderson	269
Causes of first grade failure, by Lura Oak, Ph.D.	273
Parent education, by James A. Moyer	277
Health education becomes one of the social sciences, by Jean V. Latimer	279
The cardiac child, by Edith M. Terry	280
The program for services for crippled children in Massachusetts, by Edward G. Huber, M.D.	284
Report of Division of Foods and Drugs, July-August-September, 1936	290
Index	296

THE NEED FOR PARENT EDUCATION
By Mrs. T. Grafton Abbott
Consultant in Parent Education
Massachusetts Department of Public Health

Due to the rapidity of change in our present-day world we find that parents are more in need of help in understanding and evaluating the problems which confront them in child rearing than they have ever been before. Parenthood, as a profession, has not been dignified by training until within the last few years. It has always been taken for granted that parents should know all the answers, and should be, more or less, omniscient due to the fact that they had produced offspring. Of all the professions (and we regard parenthood as the greatest of all) parenthood has had the least and most inadequate training in preparation for the job. It is our purpose to furnish parents with sound principles which they may apply to their home and to their family situations. We are endeavoring to change the attitudes, the methods and the practices of parents in dealing with the problems of child training so that we may insure to them a better understanding, more effective practices and greater satisfaction in their tasks. In other words, we are trying to encourage, through parent education, an open-minded searching attitude on the part of those people engaged in bringing up children.

We are offering to parents, through our Division of Child Hygiene, a positive and progressive plan of study which will bring insight and skill in the anticipation and prevention of problems. We are endeavoring to impart knowledge in such a way that it may lead to a modification of the behavior of parents in relation to their children.

Parent education involves skills, techniques and methods in order that they may develop and become an art. The techniques are acquired through tested experience and the methods are based on a philosophy of life. Parents as educators have heretofore lagged behind and have leaned too heavily on teachers, nurses, doctors and educators. The information parents have received has been on a verbal scale and on an intellectual basis. It is important that we teach parents to assimilate the material offered them and to transfer this knowledge from the intellectual level to an emotional plane. In other words, we must help them to make adjustments in their own lives, in their marital relationships and in the field of parent-children relationships. We want to teach them how to apply material, of which there is a wealth, to the case of their own particular child and to give them an understanding of their children's impulses, desires and needs.

We find parents eager for training, but we find also a great lack in trained leaders to meet with such groups. Through our Division of Child Hygiene, we are endeavoring to meet this need by training a group of lay leaders in the field of parent education. We are encouraging parents to come together in groups in order that their family problems may be brought forth for discussion and for conscious consideration. We are asking them to evaluate past traditions in the light of present-day living.

We find parents in general rather fearful and insecure because of changing conditions. There are others who feel guilty or ignorant and those whom we find held by conflicts and unconscious motives. Still another group are inflexible or indifferent to change. The encouraging part of a parent education program is the great eagerness for knowledge in this field.

We find that parents need very definitely three things—first, a sense of confidence in themselves as teachers and educators; second, a need for practical help and information in the rapidly changing field of child psychology and rearing; and third, a need of social methods and understanding. Every parent's experience is valuable because it is individual and different from those of other members of the group, and by pooling experiences of parents we find each parent contributing some valuable factor which sheds light on the problems of other mothers. Too many parents are too emotionally tied to their situations and for them we need to develop objectivity in order to help them. Through this they will be able to become analytical about their problems and develop judgment in regard to the handling of their children without losing their sense of balance.

Through parent education we are attempting to awaken curiosity on the part of mothers and fathers and to stimulate their thinking through experimental procedures. Parents are not easy to modify. They are resentful of criticism; they are fearful of their neighbors; and often distrustful of their own judgment.

Through our program based on the needs of all parents, we hope to meet some of these problems through the collection of material, the evaluation and the distribution of it. We hope to act as a clearing center for information of interest to parents and those engaged in child rearing, and to help groups co-ordinate the interests in this field in their communities. We hope to furnish groups with leaders after we have trained the leaders, and for this purpose our State program in parent education is being planned.

THE JOB OF BEING A PARENT
By Katharine Herring
Brattle Street Nursery School
Cambridge, Mass.

Here is the baby. Out from him like rays from the sun go shafts pointing to his nurse, his doctor, the psychologists who write about him in books, the teachers at the school to which he will go. We call all these the experts. How greatly they influence this baby! Why bother with his parents at all?

In the modern nursery school, a part of the framework of experts built around the baby, teachers sometimes want to say, "Look at our little Jock. Have his parents done him any good? Would he be better off if we kept him at school for twenty-four hours a day and let his family visit him between two o'clock and five o'clock on Sundays?" And adjusting their spectacles they dive into the big steel file and pull up the records of Jock.

He is a neat little boy. His mother is pretty and beautifully dressed. When she takes Jock out with her she likes him to look smart. His shoes are without a speck of dust. His hair is tidy and his collar straight. He is three years old. "Excuse me, please," he says when he has finished his lunch at school and wants to leave the table and "Excuse me, please," he says, whenever he sneezes, which is often, because he has hay fever. Miss Wiggs brings out the clay. "I might get all dirty," says Jock, and his face is unhappy. Miss Wiggs uncovers the sand-box. "I guess I won't," says Jock, "I might get all dirty." He stands very still and orders the big people around when he wants things. "Miss Wiggs, bring me my hat; put on my mittens please, Miss Wiggs. No, you put the blocks away—I don't have to put my blocks away at home." Often he cries. His hanky is clean and carefully placed with a corner sticking out of his pocket. "Wipe my tears," whines little Jock, his hands hanging helplessly at his sides.

It is nice for a child to have pretty manners, but Jock's have been shouted into him by a fussy father, and his face has a strained look. He is too clean to be happy and too helpless to get along with the other three-year-olds. Shall we take him away from his parents? There are plenty of other cases like him in the big steel files.

Melanie, for example, is another child whose parents stand between her and any possible contact with the outside world. "She is so sensitive," they tell visitors, and Melanie, listening, looks slyly down her nose, planning to be sensitive whenever she gets a chance.

Challoner, four and a half years old, still wets his bed at night. His mother is trying contrary suggestion. "Go ahead, sir, make a nice wet bed tonight and mother can give you a lovely big spanking in the morning." Challoner is all mixed up, but he knows one thing—he hates grown-ups.

Shall we give up the parents then and turn these unhappy little people over to the psychologists and the nursery schools? Remember that these three cases tell the story of very confused parents dealing with very confused children. We can avoid being abrupt in scrapping the family system. Most parents are not like that. Besides, if you do away with the family, a child loses too much. It is a loss the experts cannot restore. The parents of a little child must stay on the job.

These parents can be helped by the experts, to be sure. They can read books or visit schools, where they learn to know the average child. Jimmy's streaks of temper then, his elaborate false stories, his sharp, "I won't," will not seem so terrible. All children do these things at two and three and four years old. Parents can turn to the experts, too, to learn what might be called parental techniques. Being a parent does not only involve leaving the baby alone when he cries, and removing his food when he is not hungry. It includes also, the use of a definite technique in weaning him in such a way that naughtiness at meal times does not arise, in teaching him how to feed himself, in dressing and bathing him. A good parent learns how to handle children expertly in all the ordinary situations which must be met at home. Common sense, experience, and turning to authorities on child care for criticism and advice is the way in which a wise mother learns her techniques. But there are other things fundamentally necessary to the baby which no expert can supply.

A baby needs security. He gets it at home. He needs individual affection. He gets it at home. He must grow on his own roots, feed from his own soil, get the unique family flavor to round off his heredity. This he can only do at home. No schools, no professionals can supply these things. It is a parent's job and falls most intensively in the first five years of a baby's life.

We all know that parenthood is a career. We all know that we should start getting ready for it long before the birth of the first baby. We seldom do our duty in that line, but we see it. Parenthood, however, is an odd sort of career in one way. The young doctor goes to medical school, studies, practices, digs in deeper and deeper into his chosen job. He reads medicine, thinks medicine, lives medicine until he is too old to work. The young lawyer goes to law school, studies, practices, digs in, reads law, thinks law, lives law. The vigor with which he does this is the measure of his success. If he was up to his knees in law at thirty, he is up to his ears at fifty, but what about the young mother? If she has a conscience she digs in to her career of motherhood long before her baby comes. After he is born she gives herself, her security, her affection, her wisdom to him intensely for the first two years. She shapes his manners, his outlook, his health, his thoughts. At two years old a small personality begins to peer out. There is a definite "I won't," someday, a strut, an independence, an interest in outside things and people. "My daddy," "my nanny," "my school," "my friend Billy," "my gang," become important one by one and "my mummy," fades a little to give place to these expanding interests. Mummy has been digging in to give her baby his start; now, unlike the doctor and the lawyer, she must begin to dig out. She must let her baby grow up, become independent of her step by step. If her family is large she can begin again on Baby Number Two and so on, until she becomes very skilled, but, if her family is small, her career at its fullest is over in a few years, and as her children's interests begin to expand, her own interests must also. This makes being a parent the most difficult career there is, calling for unselfishness and great wisdom. We see the parents who have failed often enough. Jean's mother is an example, because Jean is twenty-two, and if she is offered coffee at lunch, her mother calls quickly from across the room, "No, Jean does not take coffee, thank you; it keeps her awake." Jean looks annoyed but is too kind-hearted to object.

Parenthood does remain a career during all the child's growing years to this extent. A parent from start to finish must be a person his child can respect and imitate. Melanie is only just three and already she sees through her mother. On the first day of nursery school she wept a little and her mother, not brave enough to tell the truth, said in a fluttering voice, "I'll just step out a minute to speak to the head teacher, Melanie—I'll be right back."

After her mother had gone, Melanie stopped crying and said to Miss Wiggs rather grimly, "Mummy thinks she's fooling us. She won't be back—Nope." And she was right.

Ronny's mother is another example of this in a different way. Ronny is four years old and he is a very tense little boy, whose mother is eager for his proper growth and contentment. "Why won't Ronny concentrate in doing things with his hands?" she asks. "I've given him plenty of constructive toys because I thought they would steady him so much."

Ronny's mother is right and she has done all the right things to interest him in constructive work, except one thing—she herself is not interested; Ronny has never seen her bake cookies, make a dress, paint a picture, or work in the garden. Ronny has never seen his father mend the car or change a fuse. The car goes to the garage, the electrician fixes the fuse, and Ronny's mother smokes cigarettes fitfully, while his father listens to the radio.

The profession of being a parent is hard, even with help from the experts. The good parent studies techniques, digs into his job, digs out again tactfully just as he is getting most skillful; and finally is a superb person himself whom his child can be proud to copy.

PARENT EDUCATION AND THE WELL CHILD CONFERENCE

BY FLORENCE L. MCKAY, M. D.

*Assistant Director, Division of Child Hygiene
Massachusetts Department of Public Health*

The Well Child Conference is parent education for the preschool age group in its broadest sense. Here we have the education of mothers in child health and child behavior with definite and concrete suggestions in health and personal habit training.

One of the first steps in beginning preparation for the Well Child Conference is the formation of local committees of women to make the arrangements for space, equipment and appointments for the examination. Usually the consultant nurse for the district meets with the women's organization which is sponsoring the Well Child Conference and here begins Parent Education by the consultant nurse, for she describes the Well Child Conference in detail and the plan of assistance by the local committee. They in turn are taught how to approach the mothers when making appointments for the Well Child Conference.

To give a clearer view of what is done in the Well Child Conference, let us follow a mother and child through the conference routine.

The mother is first approached by the local committee or the local nurse to make an appointment for the examination of her child. Here is stressed the value of examination of well children at periodic intervals. For parents who are unaccustomed to periodic medical supervision this is an entirely new departure and a foundation for parent education in health. When the mother reaches the conference she goes first to the nurse who takes the history of the child, during which there is further teaching by the nurse, particularly on immunization and vaccination, communicable diseases and general health habits. The mother and child then go to the physician who makes a complete stripped examination, pointing out to the mother the defects found as well as the good points in the child's physical condition. Then follows a talk with the mother on the child's habits of play, of fresh air and sunshine, rest and sleep, elimination; bathing, and foods, as well as questions and instruction where needed on dependency, nail biting, sucking, enuresis, temper tantrums and masturbation. Of course, limited time prohibits detailed instruction on all types of habit training. The physician selects those where the need seems to be greatest. She may also refer the mother to such other member of the unit who has more time to give, as each member has had some training in this field.

Next, the dental hygienist is visited and the mother is shown the condition of the child's teeth and instructed particularly concerning dentition in later years (the six and twelve year molars and the wisdom teeth), in oral hygiene and the relation of foods to dentition. In the following conference with the nutritionist, food habits are gone into in detail, as well as eating habits. Here the mother is taught the values of protective and other types of food for the family and is given specific help in planning her food budget. Then the nurse goes over with the mother the complete visit and summarizes the defects and the recommendations that have been made and prepares the mother for the nursing visit.

Sometime after the conference the mother is visited by the nurse who is to do the follow-up. Here, further help is offered with any difficulties in health or habit training and the mother has an opportunity to ask questions that may have come up in her mind between her visit to the conference and the nurse's visit at the home. At the same time, arrangements for correction of defects are made.

Probably the problems most frequently met in the Well Child Conference are those of eating and sleeping habits, enuresis, temper tantrums, the problems of the nagging mother who discusses the child in his presence, the mother who asserts before her child her inability to cope with his discipline.

How are these problems met? When the mother enters the conference routine the nurse who takes the child's history gives the mother our Department pamphlet, "One to Six", writing the mother's name upon it. While instructing the mother the nurse marks with red pencil certain passages in the book which will pertain to the needs in the case in health and habit training, as evidenced by conversation during the child's history taking. This booklet goes with the mother to each of the unit members with whom she confers and each, in turn, marks additional passages. Then the mother takes the book home where she may read it entirely at her leisure or at least refer to the marked passages that especially concern her problems.

In addition to the actual instruction given by the physician, nurse, dental hygienist and nutritionist, there is the Well Child Conference exhibit which has in it material dealing with several of these problems. There are, for instance, posters on bed wetting, discipline, eating and sleeping habits. Literature published by our own Department is given to the mother with pertinent passages marked in red pencil. Whichever member of the Well Child Conference staff is available at the moment talks to the mother in detail about any subject in which she is particularly interested or which has been marked as a topic by one of the staff whom she has seen. As a part of the exhibit there is a group of books from which helpful information concerning the mother's problems may be obtained. These books are recommended to the mothers individually and also to the local library.

There is a great need for parent education in all parts of the State, particularly in rural areas. At every Well Child Conference there is a group of mothers, varying in size, who have very little idea of how to meet this need in their own families. In some conferences every mother has more than one problem in habit training. There are few mothers attending these conferences who have had any opportunity for study or training in rearing their children. Ideally, there should be opportunity for actual case work with many mothers. This is not practical in our Well Child Conference set-up because of the time-consuming quality of individual work. Wherever possible, cases needing individual work are referred to the mental hygiene clinics held by the Department of Mental Diseases but these are not sufficient in number to meet the needs.

Meeting with the mothers in groups would be the next best method and it is hoped the time may come when the mothers who attend the Well Child Conferences may be followed up by having group meetings in health and habit training. This is impossible at present because of lack of trained leaders in the field. The State Department of Public Health, through the parent education section of the Division of Child Hygiene, is planning to try to meet some of these needs in the future through training of lay leaders in parent education throughout the State.

THE PARENT AS THE PRIVATE PHYSICIAN SEES HIM
BY WARREN R. SISSON, M. D.
Boston, Massachusetts

The parent, as looked upon by the private physician, is the greatest asset at his command for the successful care of the child. The physician assumes, when a parent comes to him for medical counsel for his child, that a corporation has been formed consisting of those interested in the patient, namely, the parent, the child, and the physician. He assumes from the outset that it is a co-operative unit with a single purpose, namely, the welfare of the child. In this association, the physician acts as the director or leader and the parents are looked upon as the important co-operative members. The analogy is similar to the relationship which exists between a teacher and a pupil, and the physician in this case should be the most patient, understanding instructor.

It is assumed by the physician that he has been selected because of certain qualifications as a suitable person under whom the child can receive competent medical care. By the nature of our social order, this selection of leadership must be made by the parent and the physician must assume that the choice has been made advisedly. Unfortunately, this decision in many instances is not given sufficient thought and the relationship may soon be broken, sometimes with embarrassment and oftentimes with unfortunate results to all concerned, including the child. The qualifications of the private physician and his fitness for the particular medical situation are, of course, of the greatest importance. It is taken for granted from the outset that the physician is thoroughly trained professionally in his particular field. In passing, it is of interest to note that children's specialists are now "certified" in order to give parents greater protection against incompetency. Besides having recognized professional knowledge, the physician of a child must be in a particular degree endowed with the qualifications of a teacher and among these characteristics probably patience is the most important.

The private physician looks upon the parent as one who, under his guidance, will develop certain essential qualifications for co-operation. He recognizes that these qualifications will be developed many times only after years of education and contact, but he also realizes that the corporation of physician and parent for the medical care of the child can only be successful after these qualifications are established. Perhaps the first fundamental requirement looked for by the private physician is that the parent's physical and mental health be normal. It is obvious that a parent with any disease cannot be a successful administrator of health. In many instances, the parent may not be responsible for his health, but the private physician should first look upon him as one willing to put his own house in order as well as that of his child. The influence of a physical defect in the parent and its relationship to the child can be easily illustrated by such diseases as tuberculosis or syphilis. A child may be seen because of minor symptoms, such as failure to eat, loss of weight, or possibly fever. The physician learns that a few years previously the mother had a similar complaint, together with a productive cough. Examination of the parent reveals in the lungs a definite lesion of old tuberculosis which may well have been the cause of the child's condition, as evidenced by a positive tuberculin test. It is obvious that the correction of the parent's condition is of great concern to the physician and the child. In many instances parents have no demonstrable disease but their habits of living, their diet, and their exercise are totally inadequate for the production of good health. No physician and no parent can successfully supervise the health of a child unless he first follows recognized laws for maintaining good health himself.

Even more common and possibly more important are the existing mental and psychological attitudes of the parent which may interfere with the successful co-operation by the physician in the care of the child. Pregnancy sometimes causes not only profound changes of a physical nature in the mother but frequently is responsible for mental aberrations. Symptoms of children are frequently exaggerated at this period and the understanding physician must give the mother undue consideration in the evaluation and guidance of the child's health. The causes of the so-called abnormal psychological reactions of parents are legion and the physician must look upon these as important factors in influencing the mental and physical health of the child. Domestic situations, financial conditions, and marital relations are among those which not only may be causative factors for the child's symptoms but also may influence unfavorably their correction or amelioration. The period of child-bearing is almost a crisis in a parent's life. Physical expenditure of energy is accelerated, emotions are under tension, finances are under a strain, and at this period children are more susceptible to diseases. The physician should look upon the parent with sympathy. He should not be critical of these conditions, so often unavoidable. He should, by his experience, be the stabilizing agent and foster a co-operation upon which the child's welfare depends.

It is obvious that the physician must have the complete faith and confidence of the parent. This is a qualification of the corporation which the physician and parent have formed and is of vital importance for its success. This confidence cannot be demanded by the physician at the onset of his professional relationship with the parent. The fact that the parent has selected the physician signifies his desire to develop this confidence. The growth and consummation of this faith rest in a large measure upon the physician's personality, his professional ability, his patience, and his gift as a teacher. There are many factors which may weaken or sever this faith in the physician which are quite beyond his control. Gullible, easily influenced parents rely too often upon the advice of poorly informed friends and neighbors for their medical information. Relatives are a most offending group in this particular. The press with its unauthenticated medical information and the uncensored professional radio discussions, not to mention the advertising methods of patent medicines, all act in a conflicting manner in establishing this faith in the physician. The physician looks upon the parent as one who will learn to evaluate these extraneous influences and one who will learn to recognize authority in medical matters.

The development and preservation of the faith which the physician demands rest in a large degree upon an attitude of frankness on the part of the parent. There should be no inhibitions in discussing any subject which has a direct or indirect bearing upon the child's health. It is upon this information gained from open discussions that the physician is able to see the picture of the child's life in its entirety and formulate methods for his mental and physical health.

There is another point of view which is not generally discussed. In reality, however, the private physician looks upon the parent as one who will reward him adequately for his professional services. There seems to be a certain restraint upon the part of the physician in regard to his attitude towards finances. There is particularly a temerity in regard to the discussion of these matters. This subject, fortunately, is more frankly discussed than formerly and in many instances there is an improved financial basis. The child is different from the average patient in that he is unable to pay for his professional care. The private physician of a child, therefore, looks upon a parent as one who is responsible for the financial remuneration due him. The physician is cognizant of the fact that at this period of the parent's life his earning power is often at a low ebb and the financial demands are great. On the other hand, the physician may be in a similar position, a fact which is often overlooked. Few physicians are privately endowed and their efficiency is greatly impaired by financial problems which may arise from the failure of the parent to give him the necessary compensation. Here again, the private physician expects from the parent of the child for whom he is caring the same co-operation, confidence and frankness as displayed in their purely medical corporation which has been formed for the successful welfare of the child.

PARENTS AND DENTAL HYGIENE
BY ROBERT L. ROBINSON
Dental Surgeon
U. S. Public Health Service

The essential relationship of parents to dental hygiene can only be accomplished through education from scientific and reliable sources. Although most of the instruction of parents goes on in study groups, a significant phase can be carried on with individual parents by the medical and dental professions.

The various agencies, such as community centers, health clinics, well child conferences, visiting nurses, teachers and family social workers, should include the teaching of dental health. Without the parents having this knowledge very much is lost by any teaching of dental hygiene to the child because if the parents lack this knowledge most of the child's interest and co-operation is lost.

The dental profession should realize that time spent in instruction to parent and child is of equal value with time spent on any operative procedure. The essential points of most value that should be presented to parents relative to dental hygiene should include:

1. Instruction in the value of prenatal care, which must be adequate and continuous throughout pregnancy, particularly in reference to proper nutrition and its value in the foundation of sound teeth;
2. Following birth, two essentials are necessary to maintain health —first, the prevention of defects and disease, and second, the correction of defects as quickly as they are discovered which necessitates adequate and periodical physical examinations;
3. In reference to teeth it is just as important that deciduous teeth should receive the same care as permanent ones;
4. Adequate nutrition for the nursing mother is as important as prenatal diet, and the importance of correct subsequent diet of the growing child should be understood.

Through education and demonstration the present knowledge of the following main essentials should be stressed:

1. Formation of teeth and their contiguous parts.
2. Relationship of opposing teeth and proper formation of dental arches.
3. Necessary care of deciduous teeth and their retention until the normal time for replacement by permanent teeth.
4. Normal eruption of permanent teeth.
5. Necessity of reparative treatment regardless of how minor the defects for both deciduous and permanent teeth.
6. The necessity of proper care of surrounding tissues for healthy oral hygiene.
7. The relationship of oral health and general health.

WHAT MOTHERS WANT TO KNOW ABOUT CHILD NUTRITION
BY DOROTHEA NICOLL
Nutritionist, Massachusetts Department of Public Health

"Tell me, how many vitamins should Dolores be getting?" A young mother was settling herself in the chair beside me, eager for knowledge concerning the acme in child feeding. Such did the term "vitamins", heard over the air and seen in glowing, colorful magazine advertisements, mean to her. That, then, is what mothers want to know when discussing their children's best growth and development. With hardly an exception, each of the twelve hundred mothers I have talked with during the past seven months at the Well Child Conferences for children of preschool age held throughout the State by the Department of Public Health, wants to learn how to find the way to perfection in the nourishment of her child.

This desire does not generally make itself openly manifest, but there will be questions—"What can I do if he won't drink milk?"—or "Should he get the sun on his bare skin?" Yes, there are plenty of questions—"Will raw potatoes hurt Mary Jane?"—"Isn't soup for dinner and supper good for him?"—"How can I get Adelbert to play in the fresh air?"—"Am I doing wrong in buying margarine?" However, questions are not always ready, and confidence must be gained and friendliness established by the nutritionist. Then the mother will tell her problems. Even Mrs. Najewski will bubble over in broken English and point to pictures for help in conveying what she would like to know. When one hears, "Pie and coffee—mm—how he like for breakfast!"—"Not good?"—"He like", the need of this mother is felt. She is measuring the best by what her child particularly likes. We teach her scientific standards in everyday terms, showing her that boys and girls can learn to like foods that keep them healthy, and convincing her that when they are small is the best time for them to become acquainted with the appearance, flavor, and texture of different foods. Those dishes characteristic of her nationality need not be omitted but rather direction given to the wisest additions in this new country. For example, the Italian mother may make spaghetti for the family, but can learn to serve it to the youngest children with just a little butter instead of a peppery sauce.

Then there is, unfortunately, too often, the weary, somewhat discourage, somewhat overwhelmed mother who knows the children should be getting at least three cups of milk a day as well as other foods to help make good teeth, but exclaims, "How can I get these on my weekly grocery allowance!" It is seldom that suggestions of ways to get the most for the money in food value, help in marketing, meal planning, and food preparation will fail to remedy in some measure an extremely or apparently hopeless effort to feed a family on a low income. We do not relinquish our standards. We uphold the optimum not the minimum in nutrition. How to do it, that is what mothers want to know.

Other questions arising from the comfortable chat of the mother and the nutritionist, "How can I cut down in his candy eating?"—"Am I canning my vegetables so as to keep the most health value in them?" —"What do you suppose will give her an appetite?"—"What kinds of cereals are good?"—all show realization of the right foods and good eating habits. This interest in correct child nourishment is not surprising when we think of the generally aroused consciousness of the past few years in matters nutritional. Mothers fresh from mothers' club meeting or yesterday's radio broadcast greet me with, "Oh! This is what I'm going to enjoy". They want to know which vegetables to plant in their gardens, whether water drinking is necessary, what they can use some days instead of meat, how they can get Billy or Joan to try new foods. By putting in their own thoughts and ideas here and there they help to work out the answers with the nutritionist. Yes, some mothers are hindered by prejudice and old teachings, but if we kindle a spark of curiosity they emerge, find joy in learning, and "Tell me more—I want to give him the best I can", is the result of our attempt to understand each other's ideas.

Often what mothers want to know sounds really simple enough. Sometimes, however, the best answer to a question like, "How can I get Jackie to play in the fresh air?" is not quite so simple. Who can he play with—What can he play with—Where can he play—When can he play—Why doesn't he like to play—all these and more must be answered and considered before Jackie's fresh air play plan can be worked out. Then in every town some mother will ask, "What does cod liver oil do?" She knows its value by its name but wants to learn further the why and wherefore.

It is evident when mothers talk about whether or not to have the big meal at noon, new ideas for school lunch boxes, the amount of sleep needed, or the introduction of new foods to the baby that the household problem very nearly uppermost, if not uppermost, in their minds is this matter of child feeding. A surprising number of them worry because their child falls short of the weight listed as standard on the bright front of "the big scales down the corner" or listed as average or standard again on some one or other of the printed charts in circulation. The relief they express when they hear that there is no real standard weight, that a steady gain is the thing to be desired, that the normal child is the best child we can produce, is gratifying to say the least. Still more mothers worry because they would like to give Doris or Charlie something to eat around ten-thirty in the morning or three o'clock in the afternoon but are afraid it will spoil their next meal. When one tells them that some fruit, an apple, an orange, or a banana, for instance, will not interfere with their appetites because it stays but a short time in the stomach and therefore does not prevent hunger pangs, whereas the reverse is true of milk and starchy foods, they are quite taken with the thought. It sounds logical, and they will give it a try.

This shows us that our teachings must be far removed from improbable sounding flights of oratory. The keynote of that power to inspire another human being to pursue a changed course is co-operative understanding. In speaking on the subject of milk versus no milk or taking cocomalt, ovaltine, malted milk, or any of the several commercially prepared additions, the nutritionist does not expound, using abundant scientific terminology, the virtue of those constituents found in a nearly perfect food but rather in simple words, telling of rabbits and guinea pigs and many children watched for a long time, helps the mother come to the realization that milk is necessary in the making and keeping of good teeth and bones and for general health. That lack of enough milk definitely brings about a poorly nourished condition and that use of cocomalt or ovaltine, etc., is perfectly all right when Edward or Kenneth would not otherwise drink milk, and if buying this extra would not use up money that should be going for other protective foods like fruit and vegetables is easily understood.

Then there is the mother who is very diet-minded. She makes a fetish of giving her child just the right foods and "seeing that he takes them, too." What she wants to know ties up the physiological aspects of child feeding with the psychological. Our task is to impress upon her the necessity of building now for the future. "Provide the good foods", we say "let him choose, never force him to eat what he would discard, make mealtime a happy time." In this way no definite dislike of any food is built up, the child does not make use of mealtime to control his parents, and the parents do not have the chance to use it as an outlet for emotional strain or instability. A healthy child will choose an adequate diet if it is provided, and a child when hungry will eat. The immediate result, getting the food in, is far less to be desired than the remote result, the learning and practicing of good eating habits.

Once in a while the nutritionist encounters mothers who want to know what food their child who has asthma, eczema, nephritis, or some such disability should eat. She must teach these mothers that each child's problem is an individual one, and how very necessary it is to have a physician's specific diet prescription before any regulation of feeding can take place.

In every individual conference the need for follow-up is seen. This means another conference or two with the nutritionist before too long an interval, or repeated teaching by the public health nurse as she makes her follow-up home visit. She is able to refer the mother again to the nutritionist in instances where real improvement is not shown. Much is to be gained at the follow-up conference, both by the mother and the visitor since it so often takes place in the home. By now the mother has tried in her own home the practical suggestions which she and the nutritionist worked out together at the first conference. As Miss Lucy Gillett so aptly states, "Good growth in children needs intelligent thought and eternal vigilance."

HEALTH SUPERVISION AS PARENT EDUCATION

BY MARIE L. DONOHUE

Mental Health Supervisor
Community Health Association, Boston, Mass.

"See that high hill ahead, Mother? Well, when we get to it, it will flatten right down." This observation was made by my small nephew before he had reached his third birthday. The wisdom in that observation is obvious and yet, how many of us practice the philosophy that it suggests?

It is, I think, pretty universally conceded today that no education is more important than education for family life. This is only another way of saying parent education. If we could assist parents to use the wisdom and the philosophy contained in that brief sentence, "when you get up to that hill, it will flatten right down," much of the need of parent education today could be and would be eliminated. Much of our concern could be diverted into parent education in the various fields of life about which parents must have knowledge and understanding to function adequately and efficiently as parents.

All of us, I think, will agree that parent education is far too involved and concerned with the problems, the failures of parents, in the correcting and treating of problems that might have been prevented if we had had the opportunity, had taken the time, to educate early our young people as they embark on the road to build new families.

I am going to attempt to show how great is the opportunity of the Community Health Association of Boston to share in this much needed education of parents and also how it is using that opportunity, the opportunity for prevention as well as for cure.

The Community Health Association is an organization providing Boston with trained nursing service and health supervision. The nurses are ready to serve anyone in Boston no matter what his financial condition. The skilled nursing care includes communicable disease nursing, antenatal supervision, attendance at confinement, postnatal care, infantile paralysis after-care, nutrition service, mental health—an opportunity for opening channels for better social adjustment and advice and guidance in child training and social hygiene to meet the needs of better sex character training and also better family adjustment. All these divisions of the Association's service carry along with them the possibilities of health education, family health teaching.

Our opportunity and responsibility for parent education lies in all these various fields of health. Our health teaching is parent education in the very fundamentals of family life. As the Community Health Association has extended its services in all the various fields, it has become unusually well equipped to take in all sides of life. Its educational program has become more and more a skilled health supervision. The service begins with the antenatal period; it ends with the end of life.

What are some of the advantages that our nursing association has over other community organizations?

1. We are often the first professional person to whom the family turns. The nurse has the opportunity to get there first with the information. She begins her parental education before the family is really a family unit—before the arrival of the new baby.
2. We have already established a fine relationship. In almost all of these families we have rendered services in time of illness. Services rendered in illness are easily recognized, understood, appreciated. This establishes a relationship that creates trust and confidence. Patients very naturally bring to the nurse for solution all the problems that arise as the new family starts on its way—problems of health, problems of adjustment, various problems that arise naturally when children are born.
3. We have advisors and consultants in all the different health fields. The Community Health Association, recognizing that skilled nursing care of this type and health supervision in all the fields can only be effective by continuous education, employs on its staff special advisors and consultants in the different fields. It is the responsibility of these consultants to keep the staff up to date in orthopedics, nutrition, social hygiene, mental hygiene.
4. We have specially prepared reference material for our families. The special consultants are constantly preparing material for the staff in their role of parent educators. It is the responsibility of these consultants to modify and simplify the newer scientific facts, to work through these facts at levels easily understood and especially fitted to the needs and capacities of the parents served. We try to see ourselves as a part of the great laboratory for child study. We are sharing in the experimentation of the newer theories as they are evolved and are studying their effectiveness. We try to keep our minds open to scrap what is not successful, to keep ourselves really ready and willing to believe that nothing is final—nothing static.

Perhaps in no clearer way can you obtain an understanding of our service, the kind of parent education that our staff is doing day in and day out throughout the year, than by hearing Mrs. J's story. Mrs. J is only one of hundreds, yes thousands, of families served by the Community Health Association through the 365 days of each year.

Mrs. J was twenty-nine years old when she was referred to us a few months ago. She was referred by the hospital clinic for prenatal care. This is the situation that greeted our nurse on her first visit: Mrs. J, her husband, and three children were living in one of our drab tenement districts. They had recently moved, knowing little of the neighborhood and its facilities. The woman was so ill, so discouraged, so utterly miserable, that she was not able to function intellectually. She spoke of her fatigue, her inability to get anything done. She was vomiting almost constantly. She admitted that she could not get beyond herself, that she had no interest in her husband, in her children. And yet withal, she was able to see herself—the nagger, the irritable, unkind, unreasonable mother. With real misery she looked up at the nurse, bursting into tears, and said, "I just can't help it, that's all."

This is something of Mrs. J's history as it came forth spontaneously during our service to her family over a period of a few months. Mr. and Mrs. J were married in 1929. Since late 1930, Mrs. J had never known what it really was like to feel well, to be really rested: a long, miserable, first pregnancy, with a baby in July, 1931, another baby in December 1933, then a baby in October 1934. Previously Mrs. J had had private physicans for her pregnancies with hospital delivery. At each pregnancy however, she had been utterly miserable. During the last pregnancy she had marked toxemia, suffering through her entire pregnancy. At delivery she had had a long difficult labor.

Also contributing to the physical condition were Mrs. J's social and financial worries. Since marriage, things had gone rather badly for Mr. J. He was working regularly but earning, when we came into the picture, but $15 weekly with commissions. The commissions had fallen to almost nothing. This upset Mrs. J. She continued to worry and fret over this. The more she worried, the more she became upset. Her worries added to Mr. J's worries, and so we had a vicious circle, Mr. J becoming so worried and harassed that his efficiency was lowered, his money earnings less—and so on it went.

Their debts, at the time we became interested, seemed to them absolutely hopeless. It seemed to them futile to contemplate ever being square with the world again, ever looking forward to the time when they would be free from bills and bill collectors. Although fond of each other, they had become critical, nagging, fault-finding. Mrs. J. admitted she had given the children no consistent training. They had come so close together that she had never really had a chance to get on her feet. She was tired, exhausted, physically and mentally; and not even the fundamental habits of eating, sleeping and eliminating were established. The children were entirely dependent upon the mother—not one of them able to dress or feed himself. Mrs. J admitted screaming at the children, demanding at one time one thing of them, at other times making no demands. She was still so resentful, so antagonistic to this pregnancy that she did not wish prenatal care. It meant nothing to her, she said.

After our first or second contact with Mrs. J. she actually attempted suicide. No one was told of this until our nurse's next visit. She noted the scarred wrists of Mrs. J and casually commented upon them. Mrs. J broke down again and told the story of her worries and fears in even more detail. She agreed with the nurse that the doctor at the clinic should know of her deep discouragement and depression. The doctor agreed with us that Mrs. J needed psychiatric advice. We did get her in touch with a psychiatric clinic.

Over a period of a few months, of what did our services to the J family consist? What were the services we were equipped to give this physically frail little woman? There was nothing right in Mrs. J's life. She was really ill physically—not alone pregnant. Mentally she was harassed and driven, depressed enough to have at least made an attempt to end it all. The family were unable to meet any of their bills. Mrs. J's physical and mental condition were definitely showing their effect upon Mr. J and the children. Mr. J's health was suffering. Lack of the proper food, lack of sleep were taking their toll in his efficiency. The children were uncontrolled, undisciplined, entirely untrained. There was no order in the home, nothing was ever really finished. What education for family life did we bring to the J family? What was the value of our service?

Let me tell you of what our services consisted and let you judge of their value as Mrs. J judged them. Will you agree with her?

1. Our first service was in physical care. A frail, really ill, pregnant woman with marked toxemia, vomiting almost constantly. Above everything, she needed education for her own care during the remainder of her pregnancy.

    A proper diet was gone over with her carefully. This was interpreted and explained. Its relation to her vomiting and her toxic condition was made clear.

    A planned day was outlined. Every hour of the day was scheduled and planned. Rest, a little exercise out-of-doors, sleep were all arranged for, and the reason for these given Mrs. J.

    Some promise of an ease in the financial situation was given. The patient had been receiving irregularly some aid from a welfare agency. We asked the agency for co-operation in giving this aid consistently over a period of time—at least during the time we were trying to work out with the J family our health supervision, our budget planning and our child training program.

    The antenatal care included attendance at our Mothers' Club, a club for expectant mothers where prenatal teaching is given by our staff and also is included a demonstration of the various inexpensive foods that all pregnant mothers should be eating. Later, attendance at Low Cost Food class was arranged for Mrs. J. At these classes patients are taught by the trained Nutrition Worker. The kinds of food that are essential for health, how these foods can be obtained, even with a reduced income, are explained.

2. Service to the children: A pregnant woman's diet and the diet for three small children under five years can be almost one and the same. So an improvement in Mrs J's diet that was absolutely essential for her health was also an improvement in the children's diet.

    Preparation for the coming baby's health necessarily was made as Mrs. J cared for her own health. She was made to see that her physical condition, her proper diet, meant the baby's physical condition. This challenge given her was, almost from the start, accepted.

3. From the mental health angle, what were we able to do? Her almost immediate response to the physical routine planned for her, her acceptance of the diet, brought, of course, almost an immediate response in her physical condition. This, in turn,

brought an improvement in her mental state. She felt well enough to think of some one beyond herself. The whole subject of child training could now be discussed. Her ready response to her own care, her routine, her diet, naturally included care and routine and diet for the three little youngsters. This routine, the physical condition resulting, had its immediate response in the children's behavior. They were no longer screamed at, punished one minute, ignored the next. Their security and happiness were shown in laughter, gaiety and good feeling. With consistent effort on the part of mother and father, the fundamental habits showed progress toward real establishment. Rested, well-fed, properly disciplined children soon showed a real interest in becoming independent—wanting to do things for themselves, and the matter of dressing and feeding themselves became a real game.

4. The nutrition service given the J family has already been shown. The patient's physical condition was immediately improved by a good diet. The health of the whole family was improved. Preparation of the proper kinds of food also included the knowledge that the food could be purchased at less cost than the family had ever spent for food before. She learned that the food could be made to last throughout the week. The special service of budgeting brought this family a service that has meant much. They were pursued by bills and bill collectors. They gave excellent co-operation, excellent interest in every possible angle of working out the budget with the nutrition worker. The summary on the nutrition worker's record gives a picture of her feeling about the results.

"Mrs. J. made excellent progress with her budgeting. Mr. J was completely won over. The meals were well-planned from every standpoint, the substitutes often used by Mrs. J showing real thought, ingenuity and imagination. Her attitude toward the children seems completely changed. One sees no nagging of her husband. There is a real spirit of co-operation between Mr. and Mrs. J in the care of the home and the discipline of the children. Patience has worked wonders—the children now really dressing themselves, eating by themselves."

Surely the various services of the Community Health Association are brought together in this family. These services were given in a period of from four to five months. Tolerance, time, understanding were necessary. Willingness to let Mrs. J work through her irritation and resentments, to let her be herself in all her criticism and anger, willingness to stand by, to give her as much as she could accept, willingness to ignore some of the missteps, the discouragements, made it possible to carry through with Mrs. J. We were in the parent-child relationship with her, and we tried to be the wise parent who guided and interpreted and explained—not the parent who forced and dictated because we thought we knew what was best.

May I, in conclusion, quote the letter received this month, November

1936, by our district supervisor from Mrs. J? You can then answer my question—Is this type of parent education worth-while?

"This acknowledgment of your kindness is rather tardy, but I do want you to know how much I appreciate what you and members of your department have done for me. It was the easiest delivery I have ever had, and I am sure that the care I received, both before and after my little daughter was born, could not have been better were I in a position to pay for it.

P. S.—Please excuse delay in posting but the Nutrition Worker made no allowance for postage in the budget but *do I manage?* It has been an extremely interesting course and has certainly helped me to get untangled. As a child there seemed nothing quite as hopeless as getting untangled from a barbed wire fence, but when a collection of bills pile up—does a budget work wonders? Ask me!"

THE COMMUNITY ASPECTS OF PARENT EDUCATION IN REGARD TO SETTLEMENT WORK
By Ethel Ward Dougherty
Roxbury Neighborhood House

Somewhere in our planning for community betterment there apparently has emerged a weak point which grows increasingly important. For many years it seems to have been felt that emphasis must be placed on work with the oncoming generation, from the preschool baby through adolescence and youth. But the present increase in youthful lawlessness and serious juvenile delinquency indicates that this method has not accomplished the improvement in responsible behavior which it seemed to promise.

Two elements seem paramount in this apparent failure—first, poor community conditions, bad housing, unclean streets, vice, inadequate policing, and lack of supervised city recreational facilities; second, and the really vital point, is a family life which, careless or groping for understanding, has been unable to create a home situation which shall make for stability and wholesomeness.

Since 1930, a movement has been growing to give parental education a most important place in raising the standard of community life. Every worker with a problem preschool child knows that the problem lies not in the child but in a family situation. Every worker with a delinquent knows that the real cause of his social behavior lies in a home situation which cannot or will not meet the child's needs with reasonable control and understanding; which is too weak to strengthen the child's resistance to poor community factors.

If money expenditure and hard, devoted work were to be justified, it would seem that, with no lessening of effort for civic improvement or opportunities for children, the drive should be to make the parents "responsibility conscious"—in other words, parent education, organized and vital.

In some districts, where such a program is vitally needed, the settlements are the natural leaders. They know a larger number of people more intimately than any other agency. The close personal relationship existing between the settlement workers and the people of their district would seem to make the settlement the best starting points for an organized program.

Much of this the settlements are already doing efficiently and well. But there is not, as yet, a sufficiently coordinated program to make the thinking and the cooperative effort of the whole group strong. Is there not, however, already at work a skeleton of organization involving nursery and kindergarten mothers' groups which could be more consciously built into the program for the older age groups in the settlements. Could every range of group activity for children and young people have a corresponding parental interest group? The settlements have in the past through mothers' groups—fathers' groups and intimate family visiting of their membership done a great deal to extend education in the home. But I believe no settlement has ever done or could ever do without a tremendous increase of program and staff what it would feel to be a really adequate job. And yet, I believe we all feel that the primary responsibility rests on the shoulders of the parents—and that our responsibility is to see that it gets placed there fairly and squarely. Do not a community responsibility and a parental responsibility go hand in hand—one unable to progress faster than the other? And does not this involve a much extended and far more consciously organized parent education program than any of us have envisioned so far. The problem, it seems to me, is one for every settlement to work out. If the weak link in the chain of community life is parental recognition of the problems and possibilities involved therein, how can we bring that home to our own organization? In what community does *every* parent know just why the settlement exists—what the settlement is trying to accomplish for his child—what the parent's part is in making that child's program a success.

Could the day come when every children's group in the wider field of education—school, church and community—could be matched by a coordinating parents' group? Could every parent have such an understanding of the particular activity in which his child engaged that he would perforce recognize his own responsibility in the bargain? Could small groups of parents be called in to see what is going on—to know the reason why a given activity is included in the program—to be shown just what social attitudes and skills the settlement is trying to develop in that child and how, and why? Then on the basis of his better understanding could not the parent be encouraged to discuss and contribute to the program? Could not parents receive informal reports on the child's social progress with sufficient regularity so that a report did not always carry the connotation of failure, but might as often be the signal of success?

If a coordinating program involving all the scattered efforts in a community could be worked out in which the parents had responsible parts in the working of all the agencies, our community life might go forward, perhaps not faster, but on a much *sounder* foundation.

COMMUNITY ASPECTS OF PARENT EDUCATION THROUGH PUBLIC LIBRARIES

BY EDITH H. BAILEY

Teacher — Parent — Librarian

"What is a baby?" asked the teacher of a Child Study class.

"A little bundle of possibilities," was the accepted answer.

And a parent? One responsible for supplying right conditions, as a gardener does for his plants, for the development of these inherent possibilities of the child.

Of the importance of childhood there can be no doubt; for in the hands of youth is the Future. We have always known that. Society has recognized it by establishing many agencies for the help of children,—clinics and clubs, scouts and Y's, children's rooms in libraries, and our great system of schools—church schools and public schools—on which we have put our main reliance. And many a teacher, many a librarian or club leader or pastor deserves more thanks than he is ever likely to receive, for understanding and skillful help in the child's unfolding.

Yet society is not satisfied with its results. The teacher says, "What can I do against the steady pull of home environment?" The judge thunders, "The home is at fault." The pastor pleads, "We can do little without the co-operation of parents." Columbia University has made a most thorough and careful investigation, covering a five-year period, of the sources of the child's ethical and moral standards, with the overwhelming conclusion that the home has far and away more weight than all other influences combined. It is dawning on society in general that no other institution can replace, or even overbalance to any great extent, the home influence, which is constant and determinative.

Bruce Barton tells of riding in the engine of the Twentieth Century Limited, and of his surprise that the famous train seemed to go no faster than others he knew. He learned that the secret of its record lay not in speed but in steadiness, no stops, no slowing down and gradual working up of speed again, but a steady, everlasting keeping at it. So it is with the home. Its standards, its points of view, have done much decisive conditioning before the school age begins; every day its attitudes are more deeply impressed; it forms the enveloping atmosphere within which the child grows.

We are beginning, therefore, to hear something of the importance of *parent* education; and, so far, the most obvious, the most available agency seems to be the Public Library.

Long before a child reaches school age libraries can help the mother, first with books on infant care and nutrition, and on the forming of habits that give a firm foundation for mental health and social adjustment. More and more importance is being placed by psychologists on this preschool conditioning so often decisive in the whole later life.

Soon, if the mother has formed the library habit, she is asking for picture books, and simple songs and rhymes; later for bed-time stories; and sometimes for specific means for building up in her child some desired attitude, such as faith or courage, or for overcoming an undesirable trait, like fear or resentment.

Such a mother sends her boy or girl into the school environment with an already acquired bent toward beauty, in color and rhythm and mental images; and with a pleasant association with books, which are to have so large a share in the next stage of his life's expansion; and with wholesome social attitudes, unconsciously held, but almost instinctively held *to*.

Then comes the first great transition in the child's life, when he goes to school. Too many parents, some with relief, some with a tragic sense of loss, regard the new arrangement as a division of labor that leaves little but physical care to the home, and the whole responsibility for the child's mental life to the school. Not so. The school is the agency provided by society "to help parenthood out." The same is true of the library, of the various clubs to which the child may soon belong, even of the church, in its educational work for children and youth. The mother still has the supreme responsibility of her child's growth. Hers is the constant, unifying influence. She must keep all the threads in her own hands, accepting her privilege of weaving them together into a harmonious pattern. The character of the child, his reactions to experience, his impact upon his own social group—these are still pre-eminently in her keeping.

Interest is the word now, leading to co-operation and comradeship.

Here is a foreign-born mother, with little or no schooling herself, who is so thrilled with her boy's opportunity, and so proud of his attainment, that he himself catches her sense of the importance of his school work, and forges ahead in his class.

Another mother, disturbed that her son is not doing very well in the "regular" subjects, finds that he is fascinated with natural history, and particularly with reptiles. In spite of her instinctive aversion to snakes, she encourages his reading such books as Buck's "Bring 'em Back Alive" and Ditmar's "Thrills of a Naturalist's Quest" (adult books above his supposed mental age) and even allows him to collect specimens with his spending money. These books and experiments led to others more technical, and the boy who was considered a dullard is on the way to being a specialist. Of course, his work in the standard subjects is much improved, by the habit of concentration acquired where his interest is keen, and by his enhanced self-respect, his hope of being "somebody" after all, fostered by the fact that he knows more than his classmates in one line at least. Book reports and oral compositions, once his bugbear, now give him a chance to shine.

The freedom of choice allowed by most teachers for book reports is a grand opportunity for the ambitious parent of the quick-minded young person who is not kept sufficiently "on his toes" by the routine work of large classes. For example, a high school student became interested through a historical novel, in French history. Encouraged at home, she read a history textbook and all the collateral novels she could find. It proved quite possible to use her hobby as the basis for all book reports for the year whether the assignment was biography, travel or fiction. Thus the time so often frittered away in hurried reading of second-rate material was utilized for a definite advance in education.

In multitudes of cases, of which these incidents are only samples, the library is the indispensable ally of both home and school.

To realize how much library helps school work, one would have to know a community before and after the opening of a library. That experience the writer has had. Before, the teachers of the district agreed, in confidential moments, that on the whole the children were a backward lot, generally about two years behind in reading. Near the end of the first year of library privilege, the master of one of the schools called up to say, in a tone of excitement, "Come over to my office. I have something to show you." The "something" proved to be a record of reading tests taken at the beginning of the school year, and again in May. He had just completed his comparisons. Child after child he pointed out, as having gained two years in reading ability. Others had made eighteen or sixteen months. "And I find," he said, "that every one of those who has made more than a year's gain, is taking books from the library. Next year I shall require every child in my room to have a library card."

This record was told to one of the Sisters in the parochial school. "I am not surprised," was her comment. "I have noticed even more strikingly the improvement in written work. The children who read outside are expressing themselves better and, what's more, are finding much more interesting things to write about."

And yet there are still parents who forbid children to "take library" during the school term, for fear they will neglect school work. The right way, of course, is to utilize the library for home and school values, as did the three wise mothers mentioned above.

Summer vacation even more than the school year is the great opportunity for fruitful reading. So many children, glad as they are when vacation comes, are bored before it is over, unless it is given some worthwhile content. Some libraries have special summer projects, and some schools give school credit for summer reading vouched for by the librarian. One girl became interested first in the credit and then in the books, and reported on fifty titles during the summer. One of her chums was heard to tell another, "Angelina read fifty books this summer, and she says she had so much fun no one could stop her reading now if they tried." I don't know that anyone has tried, but she certainly has not stopped reading. I doubt if she ever will.

An attractive sixth-grade girl came to a certain library almost every evening at the supper hour when everything was quiet. She said, "I like to imagine myself the person I am reading about." (Do parents realize what *that* may be doing for character?) Soon we noticed that she was choosing over and over stories of girls in other lands—China, Italy, Ireland, France—quite indiscriminately. "Why do you especially like these books?", we asked, "because they are so different?" "No", was the quick answer, "because they are all so much alike after all." (How the hope of world peace might be advanced if that insight were general).

Sometimes the library folk catch these special tastes and encourage them, but how much safer for the parent to keep in touch with the child, the book resources, and the librarian—again, to keep the threads in her own hands and guide the weaving of the pattern.

Even if the library does not supply the incentive, the books are there for the wise parent to use. Mother and daughter can travel together by the book route, mother supplying maps and pictures and factual background for the stories that appeal to daughter, both getting their material from the library collection. Dad can start son off on handicraft books and give some help in construction; or encourage some other useful hobby that will make home interesting and Dad a pal, and keep the boy from the corner gang.

Is this parent education or child education you are talking about, the critic may be asking by now. I say they are inseparable. Clearly the uneducated parent, so-called, is learning much by thus keeping step with son and daughter. Tony, in the primary grades tells us he is teaching his mother to read English and she is teaching him Italian. He is proud of both sides of the reciprocation. The college-bred woman, even the ex-school teacher, can keep up with the times in teaching method and psychological theories, and, reading all around her child's assignments, expand her own outlook.

"Living with our children!" Yes, I believe in it. And I know that it is rewarding to both parent and child. In fact, I am confident that most people working with children and young people agree that wherever you find a child outstanding in scholarship, in musical or other special talent, or in personal charm or strength of character, behind him there is someone, usually a mother, who is pouring her life into his.

Yet Mother and Dad must be more than pals to their children. After all, their great value, apart from the security of their love, is in being friends of more experience and larger outlook and wider appreciations. Every bit of knowledge or skill or appreciation that makes them more worth-while persons makes them also better parents. For education and culture and character are conveyed much more by contagion than by conscious effort. "More religion is caught than ever can be taught," said Margaret Slattery; and her dictum applies to much besides religion.

A charming girl, when we complimented her on her fine selection of books, told us, "We children all like to read. I suppose we take after my father. You know, he only went to school about three years, but I think you would take him for an educated man, because he has read so much."

At this point of general culture, parent education merges with the whole field of adult education—a field far too large to be included here. Suffice it to say that on almost any subject you may wish to study your library will have something to contribute. If it has only a small collection of its own, it very likely has affiliations with a larger one from which it can procure material for your special needs. And always it can supply lists of desirable books: lists by age groups, lists by subject, lists of cheerful books for convalescents or of the best texts for the earnest student, lists that are practically study outlines for "Reading with a Purpose."

In addition to the help thus offered to individuals, some libraries are trying in various ways to serve parent *groups*. Lectures are sponsored on child study, usually in a series, according to age groups, or according to problems studied. The lecturers are willing to answer questions on individual problems, and the library staff follows up by recommending books.

Somewhere else the children's librarian addresses the kindergarten mother's meeting telling them of the best books on child training or of story collections suitable for telling to children of just that age. Or she is visiting the Community Mothers' Club, showing the newest picture books, and gift editions of children's classics, and inexpensive editions of good titles provided for flatter purses, all by way of aid in the Christmas gift problem.

It even happens that a church will give over an evening service to a library staff for council on worth-while reading, or ask for a selected deposit of books for the Lenten seasons. Community study classes have certain books "on reserve" for their groups.

This sort of service is in its infancy, but could be indefinitely expanded on demand.

Occasionally the library even takes the initiative in a community problem. One small branch, confronted with a discipline problem with a certain group of boys, realized that the difficulty arose, not from total depravity, but from sheer energy with no constructive outlet. A club was suggested to the boys, who were eagerly responsive. Co-operation of the "Y" in a neighboring locality gave leadership, and *then* community parents and older young men woke up with some valuable backing.

Libraries think of themselves as centres of opportunity in any community, and are eager for more extended usefulness. We believe that in the complex and disturbed period in which we live there is need of fullest co-operation among all educational forces, schools and churches, library and home, if the youth of our day are to develop all their inherent possibilities and become leaders tomorrow, capable of lifting civilization to a higher level.

THE CHURCH AND PARENTS
By Rev. Phillips Endecott Osgood, D.D., L.H.D.
Rector of Emmanuel Church, Boston

Not only do parents *become* parents but also they must *keep on being* parents. The latter duty is the continuous, always changing, always developing one. For it, then, more continuous education or helpfulness is needed than for any merely preparatory phase of parenthood. The church, to be true to its pastoral function, must deal continuously, constructively and patiently to keep the relationship of the senior and junior partners in the home a steadily enriching one for all concerned.

It is our glib, trite axiom that the home is the cornerstone of society; and it is a resigned and melancholy wail on all sides that this cornerstone is threatened with granulation. The first is surely a truth, if also a truism, but the second is not so passively to be accepted. We can do something about *that* danger. The church can and must occupy itself more with the home unit as a unit. The fact is, however, that the church itself has often unconsciously contributed a little to this granulation process by treating the members of the family individualistically, out of their relatedness.

Unconsciously, of course. Traditional church methods have only imperceptibly departed from the family norm, but now we realize that the church has come to gear its activities either to very individually personal religion or to age-graded and age-stratified programs, and that it has scanted family emphasis.

Scan the average parish menu of activities and approaches. Are they not mostly individuated? The elder congregation worships well nigh childlessly; the Sunday School is age-graded and likely to be a competitive, mutually exclusive alternative to church worship; the guilds are all of selective groups; the family pew is gone; the home has largely delegated religious education to the church; sponsors are mostly nonfunctioning in any vital way, etc., etc. In fact the Sunday timetable alone sets up the expectation that the family will be split up for the day's observances; and the week-day expectation is too prone to follow that pattern.

Quite obviously there are both program and pastoral projects which need new emphasis on the unities.

The program projects are in the interests of the unity before God, of which the family pew is both the symbol and a means, to help parents continuously to be parents in their churchly aspect. There can be no debate over the statement that companionship is more potent by contagion than teaching can ever be by didactic authority. In things religious companionship will be a more vital influence on both parents and children than preaching or instruction by itself. Any family unity is founded upon its unanimity in mutualizing things. The unbreakable home is what it is because of its membership one of another in shared ideals and practice.

Parents need to be urged to do their part in the restoration of the family pew. But the church must somewhat modify its program also. In our modern urban or rural conditions alike, the timetable must create the presupposition that parents and children may arrive at church together, sit through the worship portion of the service together (unless the littlest wrigglers are cared for in the nursery or kindergarten), get their instruction simultaneously (parents from the pulpit, boys and girls from church, school teachers in the parish house) and then all go home together with something in common to talk over and build on together through the week. It may take pressure on parents to bring the realization how much this comradeship will mean to their children, but that is a part of parental education. Given the opportunity of such comradeship the children are as likely to bring the parents to church as parents their children. There is no magic in the family pew alone, but there is potent miracle in the educive comradeship it enables.

Probably it is more effective pastorally to deal with individual parents than it is to have (e. g.) classes for mothers or discussion groups for "young marrieds". Although those groups are not to be discounted. Eager young mothers will gladly meet in groups to discuss child psychology, hygiene and home economics, but there must also be individuated follow-up on the part of the minister or other church representative to guarantee the application of even the most rudimentary principles in the given home itself. The minister who has clear ideas of the parent-child relationship will keep steadily hammering away on them in all his sundry contacts in his parishioners' homes. His parish calling will prove to be a traveling consulting diagnostician's amidst his people. What numberless projects can he suggest or aid into family ventures!

For example, what if parents allow the boys and girls to erect a "God's corner" or family altar. Not necessarily an elaborate shrine, but some table set apart for the family's religious books, with a sacred picture above it and perhaps a cross and candles, with fresh flowers on "occasions" and perhaps a seasonal symbol from time to time. Here the family prayers can be said (and they will be *family* prayers now more likely than only "hearing the children's prayers.") Here will center the emotions of the home's beauty of holiness. Here will be the continual reminder to both older and younger that there is a wholesome duty of spiritual valuations in the home's routine.

Parents can be urged to sacramentalize the major events of the home cycle. Christmas trees will have a *creche* near by or beneath their branches; when they are trimmed at last there will be a carol and a word of informal, interpretive seriousness and a word of prayer from the lips of all together? Thanksgiving Day will be dignified, if only by a more adequate moment of "grace at table", perhaps with hands joined meaningfully around the table in the circle of ingathered family completeness; with mention, too, of the absent and the lonely whom the family has also included in its generosities beforehand? Birthdays can have some informal hallowing as well as riotous parties? Hallowe'en can be interpreted without spoiling its games? Easter will be something more than an affair of bunnies and colored eggs? Just as each family builds up its own roster of little customs, traditions and family humor so it can be led to build up its home ceremonials, to the lasting sanctification of wholesomeness. In all this the church may act only as suggester, or it may provide guides and urgencies. How many a home has indeed been blessed and blest because the church's representative came into it to say "well done" when the "God's corner" had been established and to give *esprit de corps* by the information how many neighbor's homes were likewise provided.

On and on through the mounting crescendo of growing older in team play the church must always emphasize the family unit as basic. On and on through the days until boys and girls with the customs of their own home their norm grow to the moment when they go out from under the parental roof to found homes of their own. Homes of their own with the selfsame standards and endeavors for each and all and each for all and all for each therein. May the church be somewhat more the conscience of the home and its guide to solidarity, integrity and joy, together.

THE CHURCH AND PARENT EDUCATION—NEED AND OPPORTUNITY FOR DEVELOPMENT

BY REVEREND RICHARD J. QUINLAN, S.T.L,
Supervisor of Schools for the Archdiocese of Boston

The need and importance of parent education are very forcibly proclaimed by Pope Pius XI in his Encyclical on the Christian Education of youth. In this powerful document, which might be called the Catholic Charter of Parent Education, the Holy Father calls attention to the fact that the home is the fundamental educational agency and that parents are the prime educators of their children. He urges all Catholics to take a very active part in the growing movement for parent education and deplores the lack of preparation on the part of present-day parents for fulfilling their duties as educators of their children.

It has always been the teaching of the Catholic Church that the responsibility for the training of children rests primarily with parents. This principle is set forth in canon 1113 of the Church's Code of Law which declares "Parents are bound by a most serious obligation to provide to the best of their ability for the religious and moral education of their children, as well as for their physical and civic training as far as they are able and they are also obliged to provide for their temporal well-being." This law simply repeats what has always been an accepted principle of the Catholic Church that parents are primarily responsible for the education of their children and that all other educational agencies are merely extensions of the home.

It has now become a commonplace to say that we are living in a changing world. Whether we will it or not many time-honored customs and institutions no longer have a place in our modern way of living. The old fashioned home is rapidly disappearing. Life is more complex. Parents and children have been relieved of many of the responsibilities that formerly made for the development of individual character and responsibility. The growing tendency of both parents and children is to seek their recreation outside the family circle. All of this has made the task of rearing children more complicated and difficult. Parents have not responded to their new responsibilities. Many of them keenly realize their inability to cope with modern conditions and are sincerely looking for expert guidance and assistance. It was the realization of present-day conditions that moved Pope Pius XI to reaffirm the Christian principle that the home is the first and most essential school. When referring to the environment necessary for education His Holiness insists that "the first natural and necessary element in this environment is the family and this precisely because so ordained by the Creator Himself." "Accordingly," he adds, "that education as a rule, will be more effective and lasting which is received in a well-ordered and well-disciplined Christian family."

All education to be effective requires capable teachers. Today great attention is being given to the training of those who teach in our schools. This is as it should be. Yet every teacher knows that the school can accomplish very little for the child without the cooperation of the home.

When we consider the tremendous influence of parents in the lives of their children, we recognize at once the necessity of educating them for their sacred duties. They must also be qualified teachers. They must be prepared for the sacred responsibilities of parenthood. Pope Pius XI recognizes this necessity and very definitely calls attention to it. In strong and forcible language he condemns the lack of preparation on the part of many modern parents for the proper fulfillment of their parental duties. "We wish", he says in his Encyclical, "to call your attention in a special manner to the present-day lamentable decline in family education. The offices and professions of a transitory and earthly life, which are certainly of far less importance, are prepared for by long and careful study; whereas for the fundamental duty and obligation of educating their children, many parents have little or no preparation, immersed as they are in temporal cares."

Pope Pius XI is not satisfied with merely pointing out the failure of many of our present-day fathers and mothers to measure up to their parental responsibilities. He goes further and says that the only remedy for this condition is parent education. In strong and vigorous words, he says "For the love of Our Savior Jesus Christ, we implore pastors of souls, by every means in their power, by instructions and catechisms, by word of mouth and written articles widely distributed, to warn Christian parents of their grave obligations. And this should be done not in a merely theoretical and general way, but with practical and specific application to the various responsibilities of parents touching the religious, moral and civic training of their children, and with indications of the methods best adopted to make their training effective, supposing always the influence of their own exemplary lives."

The Holy Father's restatement of Christian educational principles points out clearly the need of parent education. Today among Catholics especially in the United States particular attention is being given to this subject. Evidence of this interest may be found in the fact that special courses in parent education are being introduced into the curriculum of an increasing number of Catholic colleges and universities, especially in colleges for women. A number of textbooks have been written to meet the demands of Catholic colleges for material to be used in parent education classes. Worthy of special mention is a recent publication entitled "Parent and Child, An Introductory Study of Parent Education" by Reverend Edgar Schmiedeler, O. S. B., and M. Rosa McDonough, Ph. D.

Catholic organizations have also accepted the challenge of Pope Pius XI and are devoting more and more attention to parent education. Such long established organizations as the National Catholic Educational Association and the National Conference of Catholic Charities are devoting much time and thought to the entire problem of parent education. The Catholic Rural Life Conference and the National Council of Catholic Women have appointed special committees to study this important problem and to organize definite programs for their respective groups.

For a number of years, the National Catholic Welfare Conference at Washington has carried on as one of the activities of its Social Action

Department, an organization known as the Family Life Section. This organization serves two purposes—first it acts as a clearing house or bureau of information in all matters pertaining to family life, and secondly, it acts as an agency for coordinating all activities which are beneficial to the family of which parent education is one of the most important. The Family Life Section of the National Catholic Welfare Conference has proved a most effective agency for increasing the interest of Catholics throughout the United States in parent education.

In September 1933, the Catholic Conference on Family Life was established. Membership in the Conference is open to all Catholics but the nucleus of the organization is made up of students of the family and of parent education. While parent education is given particular emphasis, it is not severed entirely from the general subject of the family. This is made clear in the "Aims" of the Conference and in certain of the resolutions which were approved at the first meeting of the Conference. The general aim of the organization is "The promotion by every means in its power of a wholesome and successful family life." Among the more specific aims are the following: "The promotion of a Catholic parent education movement that will emphasize all the various phases of child training within the home—religious, social, physical, mental and moral," and "the development and dissemination of a popular and an advanced literature on parent education." The particular resolution that deals with parent educations reads as follows: "Deeply appreciating the wisdom and the truth of the words of Pius XI in his Encyclical on Christian Education that 'that education, as a rule, will be more effective and lasting which is received in a well-ordered and well-disciplined family', and heartily deploring with him 'the lamentable decline in family education', we, the members of the Catholic Conference on Family Life, condemn as a perversion of the natural order of things modern efforts to make the merely supplementary educational agencies take the place of the home itself and we pledge to make it one of the chief and most active interests of the Conference to foster a well-founded and thoroughly Catholic parent education program. We feel that one of the most salutary things that can be done for the family life of our day is for the individual parent to assume again, in truly Christian fashion, his full duties and obligations as the educator of the little ones whom God has entrusted to his care." The Conference already has a large membership and publishes a most successful magazine known as "The Catholic Family Monthly."

Pope Pius XI directed his plea for parent education directly to the "pastors of souls." He did this because in the last analysis, the individual pastors have the greatest opportunity for bringing the parent education movement into the lives of the great mass of Catholic people. They are in daily touch with their people and have many excellent opportunities for furthering parent education. It is gratifying to note that in all parts of the country, pastors are following the directions of Pope Pius XI and are giving great impetus to the parent education movement. To accomplish this purpose, effective use is being made of parish organizations such as sodalities, mothers' clubs, parent teacher organizations and study clubs.

From the very dawn of civilization, religion has been recognized as the most powerful force in the lives of men and of nations. It was the realization of this fact that prompted the immortal Washington to say in his farewell address "Of all the dispositions and habits which lead to political prosperity, religion and morality are indispensable supports. In vain would that man claim the tribute of patriotism, who should labor to subvert these great pillars of human happiness, these firmest props of the duties of men and citizens—whatever may be conceded to the influence of refined education on minds of peculiar structure, reason and experience both forbid us to expect that national morality can prevail to the exclusion of religious principles." Much might be said of the great need for more religion in the American home of our day. The all-too-evident breakdown in the moral character of our American people can be traced directly to the decline of religious influence in the lives of too many of our American people. The typical American home of a century ago was one in which religion dominated. Like prodigal sons and daughters, we have wandered far away from the religious teachings and practices which meant so much in the home life of our fathers and mothers. The need of our day is more religion in our American homes. The child who is brought up in the holy atmosphere of a good Christian home will never wander afar from his duties to God and neighbor because of the example given him by God-fearing and virtuous parents. Parents, therefore, who manifest a deep and abiding love for each other and who are motivated in their daily lives by religious ideals and principles are maintaining in their homes the strongest and noblest of all educational agencies.

THE HOME AS A BUILDER OF CHARACTER
BY RABBI HERMAN H. RUBENOVITZ
Congregation, Mishkan Tefila
Boston, Mass.

A prominent British statesman once gave striking expression to a thought which, to my mind, has a direct bearing on the theme of this symposium. Said he, "The first problem of statesmanship is not international, neither is it national; it is personal. It is the problem of helping men and women attain to a life of discipline, of steady purpose and obedience to higher things." Paraphrasing this thought, we may well say that the first duty of government lies in the field of education and character building. But in this all-important task of the building of character, the religious factor is fundamental. Of all motives that make for moral courage and self control, the religious motive is the strongest. All the wisdom of man, his arts and his science, are sheer and utter vanity unless they are based on reverence, purity and kindliness, unless they are accompanied by cheerful submission to divine "Thou shalts" and "Thou shalt nots", unless they are prepared to make constant sacrifices of selfish inclination for the sake of principle.

More than ever before, our youth of today require a discipline more severe, more drastic, more hardening in spiritual things, so as to withstand the new barbarism which modern city life brings upon the masses of a nation. Too many of our newspapers and magazines, too many of the offerings of our theatres and moving picture houses, too many of the superficial and flashing allurements of our city streets, tend to poison the mainsprings of life and fritter away the soul. Only by inculcating in the souls of the young a living faith in God and a loyal obedience to divine laws, can we hope to stem the onrushing floods of animalism and heathenism which threaten to engulf our civilization.

Granting the truth of these premises, what then follows? The state cannot teach religion. In this country, we are happily committed to the principle of asbolute separation of Church and State. The government can provide schools and make school attendance compulsory but it must look to the home to supplement the educational work carried on in our schools, high schools and colleges, and to supply the religious element so necessary to its existence and security.

The family is in very truth the foundation of the social edifice. The home is the nursery of all the virtues. But for its stability and wellbeing, neither society nor the state could exist. According to Rabbinic teaching, parents stand toward their children almost in place of God. With them it largely rests to determine the moral destinies of their children. Conscientious parents must not be content with equipping their children only in body and mind for the battle of life. They will see to it that they have a moral and spiritual outfit likewise. It is the inalienable right of every child to be given not only the special training which will enable him to make a living, but also to be taught of God, since character can only be securely rooted in the fear of God. More than two thousand years ago, the psalmist summed up the entire matter in one brief sentence, "The Fear of God is the beginning of wisdom."

In this connection, one further truth must be stressed. Religion is not only individual, but it is also social. As mankind falls into groups, according to language, race and nationality, so also it falls into groups according to religion. The man who has no nation is not the richer but the poorer; so too, is he who has no religious community or brotherhood. Such a one has no point of departure and no home. He is without leverage or anchor. A historical creed exercises a certain momentum or impulse upon those who feel in conscious communion with it. Hence the importance, aye the necessity of belonging to a church and to a definite religious organization. For the same reason, it is not enough to tell children about God and religion in general. You would not tell children to be philanthropic and expect them to develop into socially minded and benevolent men and women as a result. They must first love their parents, brothers and sisters, friends and teachers. You must first give them definite objects for their love and devotion. So also they must learn to love God through the medium and with the help of the religious practices, rites and ceremonies of a particular religion. In all sorts of ways, religion and God will be made more living and real to them by their being taught the tenets and living in the atmosphere of a particular faith.

It is, unfortunately, a fact that even those parents who are affiliated with some established church or creed, are only too prone to shirk their obligations with reference to the religious phase of their children's education and to throw the entire responsibility upon their church and the church school. But these are not enough. In and from the home, the child starts; to the home the child returns. What is taught and what is not taught in the home, what is felt and what is not felt there, is of primary and permanent importance in the life of the human being. Parents must give some thought to religious matters themselves. Let them not be afraid to communicate to each other their religious problems and anxieties. It is often said that the most sacred objects bear talking about least. But it is also true that what is never talked about may be driven away from consciousness and memory. The pressure of the world and of things material, of business and of golf, of cooking and of washing, may cause the things of the spirit to be forgotten and ignored. Just as in questions of morality, it is all important to make children realize that their fathers and mothers, like themselves, are under the dominion of conscience and the moral law; that over both them and their parents alike rules the divine will and eternal righteousness; so in the sphere of religion, must they realize that religion is not something for children only, but for everybody, and that we are all children in the sight and in the presence of God.

As regards religious forms and ceremonies, the statement of Butler still holds true, "The forms of religion may indeed be there where there is little of the thing itself, but the thing itself cannot be preserved without the forms". It may be possible for some few chosen spirits to dispense with forms and still hold on to the essence of the religious life, but for the child this is utterly impossible, and of religious forms the most important is prayer. Judaism has always stressed and made much of religious services in the home. Family prayer is something between public and private prayer, and may be made to partake of the sanctity of both. Private prayer falls into desuetude if family prayers are neglected. The need for public worship will be maintained if family worship is faithfully observed.

The times are critical and the need is great. Upon each family and upon every household, a solemn responsibility falls. It is for the fathers and mothers of today to say what type of citizenship is to mold the future destinies of our country. Every child is a potential citizen. Are the men and women of tomorrow to have their lives fashioned by the love of God and of right or by indifference, materialism and worldliness?. It is only the American home of today which can give an answer to this question.

THE PRIVATE SCHOOL AND PARENT EDUCATION
By GLADYS BECKETT JONES
*Director, The Garland School
Boston, Mass.*

Consciously or unconsciously, all schools on the junior-college level are preparing young women to meet the problems of parenthood. The Junior College is often a terminal school and the alert administrator recognizes the importance of preparation for living while the student is still in an organized group. The background courses of Hygiene, Biology, Psychology, Sociology and Economics as presented by a Junior College curriculum may make a direct contribution to parent education, but whether or not these courses function in this way lies in the hands of the instructor, for his or her vision determines the interpretation of the subject matter.

In the planning of curriculum, the private school is often free to adventure in a new approach to an educational problem. It has the opportunity to experiment with the content of courses and the freedom to adjust the administrative problem of hours of work for class and field study. Since it has considerable leeway in planning the subject matter content of individual courses, it may introduce into several courses the subject matter of a comprehensive field such as that of parent education. This is valuable when the subject is new to the student and several approaches are needed to create the correct attitude.

From the point of view of a homemaking school, it would not be possible to teach parent education in a single course; it is a subject that must permeate most of the courses in the curriculum. Let me illustrate. I had luncheon recently with two instructors. One teaches "Child Guidance", the other "Child Development". As curriculum problems were discussed, it was evident that both instructors had training for parenthood as one of the chief aims in their course. On the following day a nutrition instructor bewailed the fact that her time was limited for the presentation of the nutritional problems related to feeding habits of children—problems that must be met by parents throughout their entire period of parenthood, whether it be with the first baby when he rebels at his nightly feeding of cereal or the adolescent when she consumes too much chocolate. The field of social development offers a fascinating opportunity for the social adviser to say to the faculty: "Let us give the kind of parties that we want our girls to give their daughters some day and let us have them so lovely that they will always set a standard. Decorations and refreshments may change, standards and social behavior will remain the same."

While many points of view in parent education are desirable, a terminal course or class is essential, for the material must be brought together and clarified. The title is of little importance. It may be "Parent Education" or it can be done equally well under the title of "Family Relationships" or "Family Council" or "Parent-Child Relationships" or "Child Guidance", but the leadership of the course matters tremendously. In the selection of personnel to present the varying aspects of parent education, careful choices will give gratifying results. The instructor who can carry through consistently his or her sincere understanding and appreciation of the problems involved in modern parenthood builds up within the student an attitude toward parent obligations that perhaps she is never able to express in words, but that she will carry through life.

It is important that the student realize the value of her own individual development; that what she is as well as what she does will have bearing on her relations with her children and that, while techniques are valuable, they do not in any way replace character, sound judgment and love for the child. A young parent may know the last word in the techniques of handling the problem of stealing but when confronted with the fact that the child is pilfering, love for the child and deep interest in his future development are just as important factors in the solution of the case as the technique.

In the secondary school, the student has been absorbed in the preparation of her lessons to meet the requirements of college entrance and when she reaches Junior College, the interpretation of educational material in relation to her own life seems to her at first not to have academic value. This attitude may prevail for a considerable length of time unless definite action is taken to break it down. Field work under trained supervision is one of the quickest ways to give the young person respect for the point of view she is acquiring. When a discipline problem has been successfully coped with there is no doubt as to the effectiveness of the training and it affords material for further class discussion and reading.

From past experience, it would seem advisable to give the student one-half school day an academic year for such field work and supplement it with two hours a week of class lecture and discussion. If, in addition, a course in family relationships and child psychology could be included, an excellent background is laid for successful parent-child relationships.

If the student can be given the picture of "the changing family in the changing world", she might not be dogmatic in her approach to adult groups and should be an excellent lay worker to promote the cause of Parent Education.

THE FROEBEL CENTENNIAL
By LUCY WHEELOCK
*Principal, Wheelock School
Boston, Mass.*

The Harvard Tercentenary celebration in 1936 has been called the most notable event in all educational history. Distinguished educators from all over the world gathered to honor the traditions of Harvard and to glorify its contribution to the leadership of this country.

Another educational anniversary is to be celebrated in 1937 which will attract less attention from the general public but which is most significant in marking educational progress. This is the centennial of the establishment of the first kindergarten by Friedrich Froebel in the little Thuringian town of Blankenburg. Blankenburg is a town almost as small as Nazareth, out of which the critics of nineteen hundred years ago doubted if any good thing could come. Out of the little town of Nazareth came an influence which shaped the history of the world and founded a Christian civilization. Out of the little town of Blankenburg has come an influence which is remaking our scheme of education and so remaking society. Is Froebel also among the prophets? He was and is the greatest of prophets because he was the first to recognize in practical form as well as in theory that children are first. In 1837 his was a lone voice crying in the wilderness; now it is heard around the world. His slogan, "Come, let us live with our children," has been often repeated; but our generation for the first time really gives heed to it.

Creative self-activity and social living are the ideals which the kindergarten has brought into the school system. These ideals will make the themes for the celebration of the Froebel Centennial in the training schools and colleges of education in the United States during 1937. Pageants and dramatizations will feature the early days of the kindergarten in Germany and in America, showing the costumes of the period in Froebel's homeland and reproducing some of the play activities of the groups of children gathered about their beloved friend and leader. Kindergarten progress will be traced to the present-day practice in many centers where children are learning how to play together, how to work together, and how to live together.

In 1840, Froebel made a plea to the women of Germany to "assist in the founding of an educational system for the nurture of little children which shall be named kindergarten on account of its inner life and aim." Mothers' clubs and meetings have been featured in kindergarten circles in this country from the early efforts of Elizabeth Peabody and others to enlist the cooperation of parents and citizens for the cause of early childhood education to the present day. Through the daily program of the kindergarten under a wise teacher children are forming good health habits which carry over into the home. To secure health of body and mind the home and school must work together. We hope the Parent-Teacher Association and other parents' organizations will participate this coming year in the centennial of Froebel's great contribution to childhood education. They can help us to secure the best conditions to promote kindergarten progress. Our "new" psychology confirms the teaching of Froebel that the first years of childhood are the most important for educational purposes. It emphasizes his belief that formation of right attitudes and a sound emotional life are the foundations of a good life. The mental hygiene authorities agree with his diagnosis of emotional states of childhood: whether a child is to be happy or unhappy, sullen or genial, gloomy or cheerful, helpful or hindering, is determined in the early years of life. Thus says Froebel, and our leaders in child study say the same today.

When school people really put children first in their educational plans, several things will happen: first, the best teachers will be given the children in kindergartens and in the lower grades. Our best normal schools and training schools now give a kindergarten-primary course which prepares teachers not only to teach subjects and to use modern and best methods; but, more important, to secure an understanding of a child's nature and needs. A glance at a list of modern textbooks assures us of this fact. One of my graduates wrote me that the best thing my school did for her was to make her see the need of an understanding heart. She said, "All I learned of methods and materials has been of value to me but when I remember the understanding heart, I get inspiration for my day's work."

The first demand today is for the best trained and finest teachers for the little ones; second, we must have a good environment. Some of us can recall the time when most of the school funds went to building and equipping high schools and later junior high schools, while primary grades were housed in any old building not needed for upper grades. Now some of the new buildings in Boston and vicinity give the best rooms to the kindergarten, with plenty of air and sunshine, window seats for plants, a fireplace, low blackboards and cupboards for each child. I picture as I speak two or three such rooms with a library corner with a low table covered with picture books, a doll corner behind a screen with a doll in residence, her bed, her chair, her table, her cooking stove and a set of dishes, by which one may begin to learn the arts of housekeeping. The modern schoolroom should have movable furniture which permits space and opportunity for free activity and for socialized work. Floor space for group projects is a necessity in every schoolroom.

The accounts which we have of the first kindergarten in Thuringia show Froebel with a group of children going to a fountain in the square, walking together to a hillside to play games, making a community garden on a terrace near the school. His plan was social and we are now realizing it.

Creative self-activity is the watchword of the kindergarten today and of the progressive school. We know play is a child's business, as earnest and real to him as is a man's business to the adult. The play spirit is not suppressed, but guided into desirable and worth-while activities. Geography is no longer a study of dots and lines on a map but an introduction to the life of the world. Picture maps of China with figures in Chinese costume and boats to carry tea and rice or other products down the rivers make China a real country. A Japanese student in a Brookline school made with a group of children a Japanese rice village in the sand box. There were Japanese fields and trees and walls and houses and little Japanese dolls for the workers. The children were greatly interested in the scene and one boy asked, "If I should go to Japan, would they know me?" Had not this little boy caught the spirit of the good brother and the good neighbor? If peace is to come, it must come through an education which removes misunderstanding and prejudice and gives knowledge and sympathetic understanding of all races in all climes.

We need not only efficiency and invention and better business in the world we are making. America has these in the first degree. We still lead the world in material prosperity, in wealth, and in industrial efficiency. We need to put into our world hope and faith and trust and an appreciation of those things which make life not only successful but happy and desirable and good. We have more leisure today for our workers than any other land and undoubtedly will have more in the future. Hoodlumism, speeding, and loafing are the resources of idleness. Leisure is undesirable unless well spent. The right use of spare time is a problem of education. The school has three contributions to make here:

1. Organization of the plays and games of children so that they gain through them the enjoyment of right recreation and the love of lawful activity;

2. Guidance of the creative and productive powers so that boys and girls not only *do*, but do *something;*

3. Appreciation of the arts which make life fine, so that love of beauty, love of the good and true, may become the possession of each child.

In achieving these aims we take the best means to secure a sound mind in a sound body. If our educational procedure secures for our children this health of mind and body, we need not fear for our future—for these children are to make the new order and the new world.

PARENT EDUCATION
By ARTHUR B. LORD
Superintendent of Schools, Vineyard Haven, Mass.

"It is not the education of children that
can save the world from destruction; it
is the education of adults."—H. G. Wells.

We may not fully agree with Mr. Wells's statement but everyone who has given thought to the subject will agree that if the education of children is to be successful, parents must be educated to appreciate the aims and methods of the present-day school.

A quarter of a century ago our conception of education was quite different from our conception today. Then, practically the entire high school program had for its ultimate aim the preparation for entrance to college. Attendance at college was out of the question for many boys and girls because of financial reasons. Many had no particular interest in going to college and so looked upon the training which the high school offered as a waste of time. There were other boys and girls who found it difficult, if not impossible, to do the work required by the restrictive programs offered. The result was that the high school was made up of a very selective group. Our people, however, gradually came to think of the public schools as a place where the young people of the community should be trained for worthy home membership, and to meet their obligations to society and to the state. With this conception of education the high school curriculum was expanded to meet public demand, and more and more boys and girls, with no particular desire for college, but with a desire for the broader training which the schools were offering, entered the high schools.

The same gradual change in secondary school aims and methods was also taking place in the elementary schools during the past two decades.

The result has been the development of the school system with aims and methods quite different from those of our youth.

The modern educative process centers about six fundamental life-needs, health, family life, economic adjustment, civic life, recreation, and religion. The individual child, however, holds the teacher's attention.

The school of today offers a wide range of opportunities for slow, so-called "normal" and gifted children. We shall not evaluate educational progress wholly by the "measuring stick" of academic learning. We shall not think of the child who fails to pass the academic standards of the teacher as a failure. We shall forget these standards and think of progress as a development of the child's individual abilities. We shall not endeavor to have all children of a given group do the same thing at the same time and at the same rate of speed, and we shall have fewer discouraged, disappointed children who have little love for school. As long as we feel sorry for the child who is not "college material", we cannot go far in training for character, good citizenship, happiness and contentment. To make real progress in educating the many children we must forget the traditional set-up of our school system with "college requirements" as the ultimate goal.

One of the very definite problems confronting the teacher and the school administrator is to bring a realization of the present-day educational aims and methods to parents.

The attention and interest of parents has been enlisted in various ways. The following are illustrations: A mimeographed letter addressed to parents from the superintendent enclosed with the first report card of the year: A meeting for parents and teachers with a general theme as: "The Health of the School Child" with a series of talks by experts such as "The School's Responsibility for the Child's Health", "Mental Hygiene of the School Child", "The Value of Immunization" and the year's program outlined by the school nurse. Other general themes may be treated in the same way. Another effective method of enlisting parental support is an evening session of school with a few classes demonstrating their work, an exhibit of written and other handwork and talks by teachers and principals explaining the aims which it is hoped will be attained.

Mothers' Clubs, School and Home Associations, and Parent-Teacher Associations may be most effective in parent education. Purposeful programs rather than those for entertainment should predominate. Such programs will include entertaining features given by pupils representing school activities, as one-act plays, debates, orchestras, bands, choruses, etc., but there will also be included short talks by teachers on such subjects as: "How Much Arithmetic?", "How We Teach Reading", "Why Study Latin?", "Aims of the English Department", etc. Outside speakers will be selected, who will bring messages of value to the members. Such subjects as I have in mind are illustrated by the following: "The Common Cold, Its Prevention", "The Nursery School", "Fatigue", "The Child and His Nerves."

The newspaper should not be overlooked as a means of parent education. Editors gladly print school news. Unfortunately the type of news sent in is not always of general interest. Parents most frequently ask teachers, "How do you do it?" or "Of what value is it?" A study of school news as it has appeared in papers* showed seventy-five and four tenths per cent dealt with such phases as: Attendance, Buildings and Building Programs, Business Management and Finance, Boards of Education, Parent-Teacher Associations and Extra-Curricular Activities. Twenty-four and six tenths per cent dealt with those phases shown to be of particular interest to parents: Pupil Progress and Achievement, Methods of Instruction, Health of Pupils, Courses of Study, Value of Education, Behavior. The wide popularity of Angelo Patri's syndicated articles would bear out this conclusion.

In communities where evening classes, Americanization classes or classes in English for the foreign born are maintained, community interest is often developed in the entire school system and the school becomes a community center. It thus reaches groups of people that otherwise would have very little idea of the methods and aims of modern education. The possibilities in this field have often been overlooked. These adult classes could be made a vital factor in parent education if they were linked up more closely with the school system.

For the parent who has some leisure time and a real interest, the courses offered by the state and county extension service and the several colleges provide a means of acquiring knowledge of child life and education. The wide range of courses offered and the large registration in such courses prove quite conclusively that many parents are taking their job seriously.

One of the new forms of adult education which has aroused widespread interest is the "Community Forum". The Federal Office of Education has fostered the idea and the response in such centers as Springfield and Newton in Massachusetts and in Manchester in New Hampshire, has brought out very clearly the possibilities which it offers. While its appeal is not entirely to parents, as subjects of general interest or often discussed, yet its contribution to parent education can be of immeasurable value. Carroll H. Wooddy, Director of the Des Moines, Iowa Forum in the Journal of Adult Education says in part:

"The procedures employed have followed well-established forms. City-wide forums have been built around a prepared address by an 'imported' speaker, whose remarks have been subjected to discussion by a panel composed of forum leaders in residence plus several representative citizens. Audience participation has been limited to questions offered after the conclusion of the panel discussion. Neighborhood forums now offer, first, a brief discussion of current events, then a prepared but often informal address by the leader, followed by free discussion. Mimeographed outlines of the address plus questions for study and a suggestive bibliography are provided. While forum attendants come to hear a well-rounded speech, they recognize the discussion period to be an inseparable part of the proceedings. As an added feature, a number of discussion study classes have been provided."

* B. M. Farley, *"What to Tell People about the Public Schools"*, Bulletin No. 355, Teachers College, Columbia University, 1929.

Every parent is interested in the welfare of his children. The school may well capitalize this interest. By doing so parents may be helped to understand the child and his needs more fully and thus act more intelligently. Parent education means closer cooperation between home and school, better child adjustment in family and school life and a clearer understanding of child life and its problems by both the parent and the teacher.

THE NEED FOR CO-OPERATION BETWEEN HEADMASTER AND PARENTS IN COUNTRY DAY HIGH SCHOOLS

By J. HALSEY GULICK

Headmaster, Proctor Academy, Andover, New Hampshire

There is probably no one who has such an excellent chance to help with parent education as the Headmaster of a Country Day School. He is in closer contact with the parents than the head of a boarding school could possibly be. The average parent of the average boy in boarding school sees the headmaster only on the first and last days of vacation, at which times he is so occupied that it is impossible for him to have any very satisfactory interviews. In the public schools, the principal has such an enormous number of parents descending upon him at all times that it is impossible for him to give many of them much help, especially as in many cases, he only knows the boys by sight. In a private school, if a parent is sufficiently dissatisfied with the school, he sees that the cause for complaint is remedied or he puts the child in a more satisfactory school. In a public school, the parent simply keeps on complaining.

It is regrettable that the parents who have the most fault to find with our school systems are usually the parents of children who are having a difficult time. Again and again I have seen children changed from one school to another because the parents felt that the school was not doing a satisfactory job, when the change should have taken place at home. Naturally parents are apt to be enthusiastic if their children are doing well. The same condition is found in almost every turn of our lives. As long as we are doing well, the conditions which make it possible seem to be satisfactory, but when trouble brews for us we assume there is something wrong with the organization.

I think this may be one of the reasons why school heads speak of the "parent problem". It really is a problem, and one which is frequently discussed among school heads. Because the fault-finding parents are speaking for the unusual child, the school heads are apt to think lightly of their criticism, and there is a tendency to pacify the parent rather than to search deeply for the cause. Parents, as a whole, should take a greater interest in the school, and especially the parents of children who have the ability and the adjustment to carry on school work with success.

I mention this situation, as an article such as mine is apt to be overlooked by the parents of successful children and only taken seriously by those who are having trouble.

The headmaster of a country day school can avoid much trouble by finding out immediately what the parent of a new boy considers the objective of a high school education. What does he want his child to gain during this four-year period? If his objective agrees with the headmaster's, they can work together from the start. Personally, I have found no better statement of the ideal of education than that given by Dr. Jacob Bigelow in an address before the students of Massachusetts Institute of Technology in 1865. Quoting from his speech, "The first steps in education should be for the parties most interested to study, and, as far as possible, to ascertain the peculiar bent and capacity of a boy's mind. This being done, he should be put upon a course of intellectual and physical training corresponding as far as possible to that for which nature seems to have designed him."

This ideal is a problem for the parents as well as the headmaster. Many heartbreaks could be avoided if the parents could be tactfully educated to this point of view. The family with the Harvard tradition should be prevented from forcing a non-academic boy through the traditional mould; the family with a name famous among doctors should consider carefully before urging their son to study medicine, and likewise the family with an industrial background should study the boy before encouraging an education suitable for industry. The Harvard boy may prove to be a poor scholar, when he might have been a mechanical genius: the doctor's son might prove to be a mediocre physician, while a life devoted to art would have brought success; and the son urged into industry might have been the scholarly type with a vocation of teaching indicated.

At the present time few schools and few parents study their boys to find their "peculiar bents". Rather we set up what we think is the average environment and attempt to educate every boy as an average boy. This failing, we hunt for the remedy. The remedy is almost always left until failure has been made evident. Obviously, there are many semi-failures, which never come to light, among boys who are able to assume the average characteristics in spite of their own "peculiar bent".

We have heard a great deal about an education for life, one which will fit our boys and girls to go out into the world, meet conditions as they are, and carry through with a degree of health, happiness, and success. Actually, however, what is the goal? The present goal is higher education, and in most cases college. In spite of the fact that only a small percentage of our high school graduates go to college, our high school work is still primarily based on the assumption of a college career. Some may disagree here, and, of course, there are exceptional schools, but by and large the work is based on the college requirements. Otherwise, what is the reason for the technical nature of mathematics, the sciences and many parts of the work in English and in foreign languages? These courses have been planned with the assumption that they will be followed by more advanced work.

Schools are judged by the percentage of children who do go to college. The ultimate goal is the college goal. Regardless of their "peculiar bent" the one goal is still there. Talk to any successful headmaster and he will boast about the unusually high percentage of his pupils who fulfill the college requirements. This places the school in good standing by the various boards of education. No matter if some of these pupils might have had a far saner and happier life with music, art, manual occupations, and many other types of work which do not require college and so might indicate a different type of high school course. In the last analysis, no matter what our personal feelings may be, our schools are judged on the basis of the college requirements, and the nationally recognized courses, as found in most high schools, lead to college.

Parents are probably equally to blame for this condition. They also think in terms of academic attainment. In their minds this is also the only goal. All other goals are secondary and should be considered only after failure with the first. Last year a parent sat in my office and almost wept because her boy was doing very poor work in his academic subjects. The fact is that this boy has shown very little scholastic aptitude. In the Aptitude Tests he was given a mark which would indicate that he was unable to complete the usual high school course. If he received passing grades he would be doing work far beyond that which could be expected. It had never occurred to this parent that the boy might have other aptitudes which would be valuable, aptitudes in which the boy might take real pride and follow through with success. To her the boy seemed bright enough at home and she was convinced of the fact that the boy could do the regular high school work. In her mind the fault was with the teachers. She was quick to see imagined mistakes in supervision, but very slow to study the boy and try to understand just what type of work would mean most to him in future years. She thought the boy bright enough, and rightly so; he has real possibilities, but not along the line of the typical scholastic work. The boy could excell in other directions.

If a boy takes piano lessons for a year or so and accomplishes very little, his parents may be disappointed but certainly not discouraged. They may finally admit that the boy has little musical ability and let it go at that. If he takes lessons in painting or work in the shop and also does poorly, they may again be disappointed but will finally admit that the boy has only a small amount of talent in these activities. But if the boy comes home with a poor report card in his academic subjects, his parents begin to show real concern. They will trot down and have a talk with the principal, or force the boy into more diligent home study. The boy is quick to see the signs of hopelessness in his parents' eyes, and if he is doing his best and is still below par in his marks, he may break from the reins of school and home and become a rebel. If he has the right stuff in him I should think he would. No live boy is going to continue in an environment of failure when he feels that he is doing his best. It would be my guess that a large percentage of the cases of maladjustment were caused by boys being forced into work which was not suited to their aptitude and their "peculiar bent".

Cases of maladjustment are not all on the side of those with low ratings in scholastic aptitude. In fact, probably the most serious cases are found in the top ranges of the school. Every headmaster can put his finger on case after case where boys of unusual scholastic ability have found it almost impossible to study in the regulation, day-by-day, plodding methods of the typical curriculum. It is just as severe for them to adapt themselves to the work arranged for the average as it is for those in the lower brackets. They need a type of course which will challenge their greatest efforts and keep their active minds working at top speed. Many of them can take the high school course in two or three years. There is even a record of one boy who went through Chicago University in eight months. For a boy of this ability it would be foolhardy to spread his work out over the usual four-year periods.

In the private school field there is another cause of maladjustment. During the depression the competition between schools for pupils has been even keener than in normal times. With the exception of a few outstanding schools most headmasters have been forced to carry on an active enrollment campaign, with magazine advertising in many cases, and almost always with elaborate sales catalogues, minor literature, and an efficient follow-up system. One of their most important jobs has been to *sell* the school collectively and also to the individual prospects. In many cases parents change schools because their boys have been doing poor work and they feel that a change will be the remedy. They either write or call on the new headmaster. In order to land the new boy, the headmaster, or his representative, is apt to make every attempt to please the parents by encouraging them to think that with the new school all the problems will be solved. Few attempt to convince the parents at this time that possibly some other type of schooling might be better; the need for new boys has been too great. As a result the parents enter the boy with unjustifiable confidence. Unless the new school has a program which is able to meet his individual needs the same difficulties are going to crop up and the parents will have the problem right back on their hands.

This difficulty is handled in many schools by marking the boy up. If they feel that he has less than the average ability the teachers will agree to increase his marks a certain percentage so that he may have the opportunity of passing. This inevitably does one of two things: it will give the boy a false confidence in his academic ability, or, if he sees what is being done and most boys do, he will lose respect for the marking system and feel that it is meaningless. Some new type of marking system is needed which will take into account individual differences, but certainly we do not want to make it appear that a boy has accomplished work which he has not really done. This does not encourage a boy toward his "peculiar bent", instead it puts a false label on his deficiencies.

For generations our schools have devoted their efforts towards scholastic attainment so it is natural that theoretical tests to discover scholastic ability should be developed far beyond those for other types of aptitude. Some day we may have adequate methods of discovering many aptitudes and finding them at an early age. When that time comes, we will be able to outline a far more intelligent school program.

Until then, however, we will have to use the inadequate tests at our disposal and supplement them by the trial and error method.

We are able to discover scholastic aptitude with some degree of accuracy, and in the majority of cases it is possible to pick out the boys who should definitely follow the typical academic type of career with the ultimate aim of college and further study. We are able to do this, and there is no excuse for keeping these boys in classrooms carried on for the average. They should be working hand in hand with other boys of the same ability, thus stimulating their efforts with lively discussions and a much more rapid rate of speed.

This group will, of course, prepare for college. Necessarily they will study the subjects set down by the various college entrance requirements. This could be varied as the entrance requirements become more liberal. Here again, the boys of varying ability should not be expected to follow the average group. Those with more ability should have a stimulating program which would tax their every effort. "Passing" should not be the aim, but rather high scholastic attainment. Boys should not be placed in a position of being able to loaf through their classes merely because the learning process is easy. If it is easy, they should be given subject matter which will keep them in the habits of work. The lack of this need for work has probably been the cause of many brilliant students failing after finishing school. They have difficulty in adjusting themselves to everyday life because they are not used to working. Things have been too easy for them, and they expect life to sail smoothly along. Hard work is a necessity for every type of school program, if at the end the boys are to find success.

Boys who lack this so-called "scholastic aptitude" should also be separated. Possibly they should be separated into a number of groups, each with different types of work and an entirely different goal. For the present, however, it would be a satisfactory improvement if we merely separate them from the boys headed for college.

This second group should follow a curtailed program which will only include the most important academic work. Why study French, when poor work is being done in English composition? Why go into Geometry when the fundamentals of Mathematics are still hazy? Why go into the advanced forms of Chemistry and Physics before the boy understands the simple forms of science as found every day in his immediate vicinity? Many of the advanced courses should be eliminated from the curriculum and greater stress should be placed on a more practical type of work. I would not advise specialized vocational training until a boy is well on in his school career, but he should go through a series of experiences which will give him the fundamental information for many types of work and the fundamental manual skills which will assist him in adapting himself to various physical occupations. Give him a thorough course in English, particularly composition, with outside reading devoted primarily to modern authors. Teach him to read the newspaper, and teach him to form his own opinions in regard to the biased information he will find. Compare similar subjects in one paper and another. If he has difficulty with handwriting, which has handicapped all his written work, teach him to use the typewriter, and for the first time he will have the glorious experience of expressing himself neatly on paper. At the same time, it may help his spelling.

In mathematics, go into the simple forms of bookkeeping and budgeting. Have him analyze the cost of the school plant, and make a report as to the use of the school dollar. Keep a daily chart of the costs of electricity and coal. Have a school bank and, so far as possible, have it run on professional lines. Many are the men who are unable to balance their own check books and yet have been given a passing mark in high school algebra. We can better prepare these boys for life by giving the type of mathematics that will have a definite bearing on their future lives. They must have solid, useful material for the highest attainment and, wherever possible, the application for the material they are studying should be close at hand.

But before a headmaster puts a boy into the non-college course, he educates the parents to his ideal of education. It is necessary to come to an agreement as to the boy's peculiar bent and how it should be encouraged. The parents must see that, though it may mean a future utterly different from that which has been planned for the boy from the cradle, it will mean the difference between an enthusiastic worker and a misfit who feels himself a failure. It is our inability to educate parents which has kept our school curriculum deep in the college preparatory rut. It is because we have, in the past, placed a stigma on non-college material, that enraged parents now refuse to let us change our curriculum drastically and place their boys in the non-college course. Until we can satisfy parents that the ultimate aim of education is to encourage a boy's "natural bent" and capacity; and until we are capable (and we will have to become more capable than we are now to prove it) of *determining* his natural bent and capacity, every fall term and every spring term will find the same group of parents up in arms.

EDUCATING THE BACKWARD CHILD
BY ADA M. FITTS
Director of Special Classes
Boston Public Schools

The problem of the backward child in the public schools is everywhere recognized as one that should not be neglected. Formerly the idea was to try to compel him by punishment or other means to take his place with grade pupils. We now know that he is to be accepted and dealt with as he is and that he forms a special problem to be solved by special methods. For that very reason he requires exceptional understanding and treatment. It is recognized that if these pupils are selected early, placed in small groups under a trained teacher, much can be done for them and the regular grades greatly relieved by the removal of the backward child.

Someone has said—"A teacher is a discoverer of boys and girls, discovering their powers and latent possibilities, discovering also their lack of power and latent possibilities, and devising ways and means of making up this lack." In the training of retarded pupils it is our privilege to attempt to overcome these handicaps and help others to realize that the backward child is not to be neglected but is to be dealt with as he is. The teacher attempts to form habits which will develop him to his capacity and which will give him ability and training for adult life. For the child who is slow, whose attention and power of concentration are poor, who has failed in school for several years and who is discouraged, the transfer to the Special Class is a privilege and an opportunity. It takes him out of an environment of failure and places him where his efforts will give him self-respect.

In every classroom there is a group of children who are not to be promoted—those who are behind because of prolonged absence from school, serious illness, behavior problems, as well as the mentally retarded, who have failed of promotion and to whom the grade teachers have given faithful work with little material benefit to the pupils and to the great disadvantage of the other children.

The Opportunity Classes are designed for these retarded pupils. The selection of those who are to enter such classes should be made by a trained expert after careful study of each individual. We cannot judge by appearance but in addition to intelligence tests the examiner should consider the school history of the child, his practical knowledge, personal history, physical condition and any other information available. Not until that has been done can the diagnosis be made. One can readily see how necessary it is to have the cooperation of parents, teachers and all interested in the child and to take every precaution against errors.

In order to overcome the natural reluctance of parents to placing their children in such a class, a personal interview should be arranged by the examiner in order to explain that because of slow mental development the child who has been two or more years in grade is still not up to the standard, and that an opportunity to advance more rapidly is to be available in a smaller group where the pupil is fortunate in having individual help and consideration. By these consultations, understanding and cooperation may be secured and a bond between home and school established.

Every parent wants to believe that his child is successful in all ways but we know that there are pupils who can get on only within the limits of their abilities, not beyond them. It is cruel to try to force a child who is handicapped to attempt to do what perfectly equipped children do easily. Cruel because the child is expected to do the impossible. Most parents are anxious and they desire to do what is advised but if there is prejudice and misunderstanding let us consider how this may be overcome and the ways by which the right attitude may be developed.

First of all the class should be for mentally retarded children of the improvable type. It is designed for those who require individual attention and the form of training that is, for them, educational. Low-grade cases do not belong either in the regular grades or in the opportunity classes.

Again, much depends on the teacher herself. She must have the personality necessary for this specialized and difficult work. She must be one who will win her pupils by inviting the parents to visit the classroom, by sending home samples of successful work, by visiting the home, especially when she has something good to report. In a word she must use every means to gain confidence and to become a trusted friend of the family.

Another handicap is the lack of understanding and sympathy on the part of other teachers and their normal pupils. They should be tactfully educated to have a respect for the class and its advantages.

Finally through acquired skill in academic studies, manual work and physical training, the special children themselves must gain reliance and self-respect through their school activities.

The candidates for special training are given examinations which show their degree of backwardness. These examinations determine mental age, special abilities and disabilities and show how far a child is likely to progress in school. It is important that the teacher know the mental ages of her pupils as the possibilities of school training at the different age levels are now quite definitely fixed. This determines the grade of work the child ought to be able to accomplish. In other words, the mental age tells what the pupil is able to do at a given time.

An example given by Dr. Walter E. Fernald explains what this means for an individual—"John is a boy who is fifteen years old. If he were normal he would have a fifteen-year-old mind and his intelligence quotient would be 100. A fifteen-year-old mind usually means the capacity for doing first year work in high school. The mental age of John is on the nine year level and at this mental age he should be capable of doing fourth grade school work. School tests showed that to be true. In other words, he was doing all he was capable of doing and a definite plan for his advancement must be made."

With the little children one should do what is possible and of value along academic lines, but experience has shown that backward children who succeed in life do so because they are able to do worthwhile work with their hands. This type of training begins with the younger pupils by the use of scissors, pencils, crayons, plastecine, paper folding and cutting and leads to more advanced work. Physical training is carried on by exercises, games, sports, etc.

Some parents object to manual work for these pupils but no less an authority than Angelo Patri says—"We are missing an opportunity if we insist on giving the same instruction to every child regardless of his tastes, abilities or needs. This is the time to teach handwork. I believe all children who are gifted with skillful hands should be trained to use them thoroughly and well." This is especially true of opportunity class pupils.

In addition to the academic, manual and physical training we need to put still more emphasis on social training and adjustments. Much can be done to strengthen desirable traits, to make the child self-reliant, honest and truthful. Success in adult life depends on courteous manners, intelligible speech, erect carriage and the like. Hence, the formation of good habits is stressed.

When there is but a single Opportunity Class in a district it is usually housed in a school building with normal pupils and cares for the younger children selected from the first three or four grades. As the children reach twelve or thirteen years of age they require more advanced work than is possible in the single classes. In many of the cities and large towns, this need is met by setting apart a suitable building and transferring to this Center the older pupils selected from the individual Opportunity Classes. Such groups are interested in the same projects, occupations and sports. Promotion to such a Center is something that corresponds to promotion to a high school from the grades and is a distinction much coveted by the pupils. Workrooms for carpentry, metal work and other forms of manual work are available for the boys. The girls are taught needlework, weaving, domestic science, etc. Every attempt is made to provide training of practical value in the life of these pupils.

While pupils are in school the teacher has a contact with the home but when they leave to go to work they are in need of a friend to advise, suggest, encourage and assist their efforts towards partial or entire self-support. The follow-up work is the next step of helpfulness to the pupil and his family. When a child reaches the age when he may legally go to work, he is given special attention and help in finding employment and is guided to the lines of work for which he is adapted. Many school systems provide an After-Care Worker who is the recognized link between the home, the school and the employer. There are thousands of retarded children who never come to the attention of society except in a favorable manner, but for the comparatively few who do not an important work is done by the After-Care Worker who follows up the court cases. Her recommendations are relied upon by the teachers concerned, by the relatives of the child and by the Judge. Probably no other phase of Opportunity Class work is more important than this social and after-care work. No city or state can afford to do without it for the children who yearly pass beyond the control of the schools.

Thus, by early recognition and placing in small groups, by providing the type of education suitable for the child's possibilities and his limitations, and by furnishing an After-Care Worker, the Opportunity Classes train the backward child for a place in the working world where many meet the problems of life with a fair degree of success.

PSYCHIATRIC ASPECTS OF PARENTAL EDUCATION
BY BERNICE M. HENDERSON
Educational Secretary, Massachusetts Society for Mental Hygiene
Boston, Mass.

• The current emphasis on parental education is justified from the psychiatric point of view when one realizes the growing significance which is attached to the home and more especially to parental attitudes in shaping the personality of the developing individual. For some time the school has placed increasing emphasis on the child as an individual, attempting to use many concepts drawn from the field of psychiatry and mental hygiene in changing its aim to teaching the child rather than teaching the subject. But when one considers that the average child between the ages of six and eighteen spends only about one-fifth of his life in school, one realizes that no matter how much wisdom and understanding goes into the school curriculum, no matter how satisfactory from a mental hygiene angle teachers themselves may be, it is still the home which is undoubtedly the most important environmental influence in the child's life. There has been a tendency on the part of many parents to shift their responsibilities to the teacher on the ground that by special training and experience she is more ably equipped to handle the child. This attitude, however, must be discouraged. Parents should be urged not only to accept their responsibilities but to attempt to gain a more thorough understanding of the needs of the child and methods of handling him that the child may make a satisfactory life adjustment, meeting life situations with a minimum of conflict and a maximum of satisfactions which are sociably acceptable.

From the psychiatric standpoint, what are some of the concepts which may be helpful to the parent, first, in general, as regards all children, second, in their efforts to understand and guide the individual child?

First of all, parents should accept their responsibility and recognize that mental health is as important as physical health, that the two are inseparable, that whatever affects the child's physical life also affects his intellectual and emotional life, and vice versa, that every child has problems to meet, particularly as he goes through stages that are more difficult than others; e. g., starting school, beginning high school, illness, and the like. Certain types of children require special handling at even other times. The important point for parents to bear in mind is that it is how the individual handles these situations as they arise during childhood and adolescence that determines his adult method of handling problem situations.

The emphasis in the mental hygiene field is always placed upon the child as an individual, made up of various components, physical, intellectual, and emotional. Each side of the child must be given due consideration in relation to the whole, and not one stressed at the expense of any other. The mother who decides that her exceptionally bright child is a budding genius and overevaluates his scholastic accomplishments should stop and consider the price her child may pay for these if achieved at the expense of a poor physique or inability to get on with his schoolmates. This parent must bear in mind that her child's natural egotism and self-centeredness must be gradually tempered with altruism and generosity. He must learn to forget himself in cooperative group work and games, to experience being a partner, a contributing member of the group, and to derive his satisfactions therefrom.

It is important for the parent to know her child, to understand his physical, intellectual, and emotional sides, and to work toward developing each to capacity. But it must be *his* capacity. Too much cannot be said of the crippling effect on the child's emotional development of holding him up to the achievements of a physically more robust or an intellectually superior brother.

In a large measure, the average parent has long been interested in the child's physical welfare and school achievement. It is in the field of the emotional life that parents have received less help, and it is to this phase of parent education that attention is now being especially directed. It may be pointed out to the parent that the home has the child for practically its entire time for the first few years of life, before he enters school. Not only this, but the influence of the home continues to exist parallel to that of the school. It is only natural that the child, dependent as he is physically and economically upon his parents, develops toward them deep emotional attitudes. Here it may be said that dependence activated by dislike or hate is as potent in the child's own emotional development as dependence activated by love. He cannot escape from the emotional aspects of parental ties. Both rejection and overprotection by the parent affect the child.

One of the chief functions of the home is to provide the child with a sense of security, physical, economic, and emotional. This may be done not only by giving the child a feeling of being loved and wanted but by providing in the home a controlled environment where stresses and strains are reduced to a minimum. There are naturally many such incidental to rapid physical growth, habit formation, and the numerous emotional adjustments which the child is obliged to make, but the parental attitude may reduce these to a minimum.

One way of providing such a controlled environment is by letting the child know in general what is and what is not expected of him. A few simple prohibitions, the reasons for which the child can understand, help diminish anxiety. Whatever regulations are made should be enforced with understanding. Every effort should be made to provide the child with reasons and standards which at this particular stage of development he is capable of comprehending. This gives him a basis on which, as he grows older, he is able to form standards and principles for himself.

A second important contribution of the home is to foster a gradually increasing independence, preserving at the same time normal affectional ties. The child must learn to stand on his own. Parents must stress self-reliance. The parent who does things for the child only because of the personal satisfaction derived may not realize the crippling effect it has upon the child. Certainly the child who has all his desires anticipated and everything done for him is at a disadvantage when he starts school with other children who have already learned a degree of self-reliance usual at their age. It must also be remembered that unforeseen events may temporarily or permanently withdraw the parent from the child who, if he has not learned a degree of self-reliance usual at his age, will have great difficulty in adjusting to the changed situation. Every child is bound to meet with both success and failure. Some experiences in both are essential for mental health, but the problem for parents is to prevent or minimize bad reactions from either. A failure may be turned into a situation having constructive as well as destructive meaning. Persistent criticism has usually disastrous results, especially if it is merely destructive, given with no helpful alternative suggestions. Children, as well as adults, respond favorably to encouragement, yet too constant praise may also be disastrous. The parent, especially with the young child, must be judicious in his use of praise lest the child work to attain praise rather than to derive satisfaction from actual accomplishment, for as he goes to school, where he is one of many, he cannot be praised for each thing he does. The sense of satisfaction through group achievement develops an ease of social relationships and makes them stimulating rather than irritating to the individual.

Parents may well consider other basic social attitudes which by imitation or suggestion the child acquires in the home. One of the most important of these is his attitude toward authority. The child, being highly imitative, soon takes on his parents' attitudes toward authority and carries these attitudes into the school and into his wider social life. It seems needless to mention that children's attitudes toward authority as vested in their teachers is often a direct reflection of the attitudes of their parents. If authority is exercised fairly, honestly, as a protective and guiding influence, children will conceive it as something to be respected rather than evaded or rebelled against. It is therefore well for parents to live up to the restrictions placed by society upon them if they expect their children to respect the rules of the home. Punishment, when necessary, should be commensurate to the offense and should be carried out so that the child realizes that it is the thing which he has done, not he himself, which the parent does not countenance. Punishment dispensed to relieve parental emotion does not help the child. It may rather make him sensitive, openly defiant, or he may be found merely substituting one undesirable form of behavior for another. Threats get parents nowhere, but add to the child's insecurity. The important point for parents to remember is that all behavior is purposive, that what a child does in a given situation is symptomatic of his total adjustment to that situation. If he offends, the first step is to understand why he does and then to honestly and fairly attempt to help him understand the situation. Not infrequently the problem of the child is merely a reflection of the problem or problems of the parent who should look to his own adjustment before taking it out on the child.

It must also be remembered that no two individuals react in the same way to a given situation and that the child who responds in an overt fashion, even though his behavior of the moment is undesirable, is potentially less of a danger to himself in terms of life adjustment than the sensitive, shy child who retires to a corner and takes it out on himself. The former is noticed and something is done; the latter may escape unnoticed and may either become resentful, antagonistic, and suspicious or he may learn to derive his satisfactions in a world of his own, removed from that of reality.

In all their contacts with the child, it is important that the parent respect his developing individuality. This is especially true of the adolescent who is called upon to make many adjustments before he has accumulated the experience, habits, and judgments necessary to give him a feeling of adequacy and sureness. What may seem fickleness or indecision may actually be an increased sensitiveness in the face of making new choices in the strains and stresses of his fast-changing life.

Again, it must be remembered that the child must be considered as an individual and also as a whole, physically, intellectually, and emotionally. His behavior must be evaluated in terms of his level of adjustment, his equipment and potentialities, not according to adult standards. While it is unfortunate for any one child in a family to be overprotected, specially privileged at the expense of others, it must be remembered that parents need to help the handicapped child to find adequate and legitimate compensations, so that the entire household need not revolve about him.

Not only the handicapped child, but the only child, the oldest, the middle, and youngest often present special problems, the significance of which parents cannot easily overlook.

Generally speaking, however, those parents who are themselves well adapted, who derive their own emotional satisfactions on a mature adult level rather than experiencing them vicariously through their children, will have those attitudes which aid rather than handicap the child. By co-operating with the school and by making use of such forms of parent education as are provided by adequately experienced individuals, they may assist the child to become a mentally healthy adult.

A discussion of psychiatric aspects of parent education should not be closed without mentioning that wherever group discussions are held, wherever programs for such discussion are planned, there is need of leadership by those whose experience and training adequately qualify them to understand these broader concepts in relation to the adjustment not only of the child but of the parent. Discussion without such direction may actually create problems or intensify those already in existence. A constructive, preventive program of parent education obviously calls for expert leadership.

CAUSES OF FIRST GRADE FAILURE
BY LURA OAK, PH. D.
Head of Research-Learning Project
Massachusetts Department of Public Health

It is not generally known that the highest percentage of all school failure occurs in the beginning year. That this fact has been overlooked and its importance disregarded can probably be laid to the age-old attitude of slight interest in the young child's educational status. There has been a traditional assumption that educational matters become serious as the child grows older, but the early stages of education appear so elementary and simple from the adult's point of view that they have not generally commanded much serious consideration. This attitude of neglect is gradually giving way to a heightened attention to all that affects the young child's welfare.

Upon entering the first grade of school one idea is uppermost in each child's mind: now he will learn to read. His parents likewise assume he will read and other social pressures are so imperative that every child would master reading if he had the ability to do so. The challenge of this beginning year becomes at once the first major undertaking of the young child's life. In a special way he has now set out for himself. True, he has already learned to talk and to walk but these skills he mastered without competition, without daily comparisons with others or assignments to be learned. Here at school he first meets his contemporaries in the great challenge to make his own way in the world. The climactic effect of this new adventure is to key him to succeed, and the heightened emotional coloring associated from the beginning with reading endeavor gives to the experience an extraordinary potency. What happens in this connection is important to each growing personality in molding attitudes toward self, toward others, toward school and toward life itself. To fail in this effort in the presence of others who succeed has the effect of undermining self-confidence, especially since a young child has no way of considering reasons why he cannot learn what others are mastering with ease and satisfaction. He accepts the inference that he is inferior.

To compensate for this inadequacy the child may turn to defensive and often anti-social conduct, seeking as best he can to maintain his self-respect and gain prestige within the group. Sometimes he tries the effect of boasting and bullying his schoolmates. Often he retires into a shyness and inner brooding which make him difficult to understand. In the personality profiles of many maladjusted individuals there is clear evidence that failure and frustration in the beginning year of school began the picture of unsocial conduct. The mental hygiene aspect of early school failure points to the highly significant bearing of this problem upon social as well as educational programs.

In the light of recent study and investigation much of the early failure and frustration are caused by factors which the parents and the school can certainly prevent. Except in cases which are very rare, involving severe organic deficiencies, every child can learn to read.

The new literature on reading readiness and on remedial instruction provide the guidance needed. It devolves then upon the parents and the schools to turn the new knowledge to the service of the boys and girls to the end that all may make a good school start. The following paragraphs present a brief description of the major causes interfering with first grade success and point to some of the ways in which the problem may be met.

First among the causes to be listed is the general immaturity of many of the first-grade entrants. There may be a lack either in the necessary physiological maturity or in the psychological readiness which together constitute the essential preparation for successful mastery in reading. For the physiological immaturity the remedy is usually quite simply that of time. For interferences in maximum growth and development during early childhood due to prolonged illnesses or to lack of adequate nourishment or exercise, a time extension should be provided so that nature may make up for these delays. Among the features of development shaping toward maturity in which growth may be temporarily retarded from one cause or another are postural steadiness, easy use of voice, and habitual visual concentration. Often a month will mark the difference between a state of immaturity and inadequacy for reading and a spurt in physical powers to the point where success may be confidently expected. Just as a child reaches a moment in his effort to walk when he dares to step off alone, so also he reaches a point in all-round development when he can safely accomplish what is required for reading. Someone has spoken of this as the "educative moment." To force him to try what he is yet unable to do is as unreasonable as to stand him on his feet and bid him walk before he has had the experience of creeping, of pulling up to chairs and of moving himself around by holding fast to objects. Unfortunately, the evidences of physiological development necessary to reading readiness are not so obvious as those that precede walking, but they are doubtless equally specific. For the present it is necessary to rely upon general criteria of development as they can be observed by parents and by the school authorities responsible for admitting first-grade entrants. The following checks may serve to guide such observation: Is the child physically well coordinated? Can he hold book-size objects steadily to observe them closely? Carry a plate of cookies? Keep time to music? Run and skip easily? Unless he has such development he will profit by days full of physical exercise and practice which use large muscles of the body. If there is gross physical incoordination and an obvious strain in body movement he is still unready for the finer muscle skills which reading will demand.

The other aspect of immaturity which characterizes many children who fail in first grade work is a meagerness of personal background. Children need a range of personal and social experiences which call for thinking and extended use of language. Some children have grown up in an environment unfavorable for learning many meanings, for gaining emotional independence and for developing their powers of thought and language. They are infantile in these respects even though they have passed a fifth or sixth birthday. Five or six years, after all, is a very short period of time in which, under maximal conditions, an infant beginning at zero ability is expected to master upright locomotion, a command of language and those personal and social adjustments which qualify him for part-time living outside his home. Unless he is sufficiently mature to endure separation from home without serious strains upon his affectional relationships he is distracted in whatever he tries at school. Until he can appreciate humor and enjoy, for example, a story like Little Black Sambo or the fanciful yarn of the Three Billy Goats Gruff, he is too immature to grapple with the words that make up reading content. The serious business of reading presupposes certain basal experiences in thinking and in living which each child needs as stock in trade. If there are gaps in his background in this respect they should be filled in before he is obliged to make the effort to read under conditions where failure is almost certain.

The guidance needed with respect to these two aspects of immaturity is equally the responsibility of the parents and the administrative offices of the school. As parents understand the deferred advantages which occur when reading waits for an all-round maturity they will cease the imperative demand for early reading and welcome in the school an effort to establish for each child whatever preparation he may need for "reading readiness." "Play" in school will not be frowned upon when the school intelligently interprets and directs it to the purposes of widening the child's horizon of meanings and experiences. One function of the nursery school, the kindergarten and all pre-primary groups should be to pave the way from one year to another for a broad base of experience and understanding leading to an all-round readiness to read. Nursery schools and kindergartens may be adjudged a menace or a boon to early childhood, depending upon the extent to which they encourage a wise and patient deference to the inexorable laws of wholesome growth and normal maturation. They should provide rich meaningful experiences without stimulating prematurely the concentration upon the finer motor skills of which reading heads the list.

Physical defects, especially those of the ear and the eye, constitute another major cause of failure. The symptoms of these defects are often too obscure to be readily detected. Tragic stories can be told of boys and girls too readily classified as dull who failed in school and found life miserable and discouraging when the underlying cause was some reparable defect in sight or hearing which could have been corrected in the beginning year of school. The only certain way to screen out cases such as these is to test all first-grade entrants and provide corrections that are needed. The hard-of-hearing child should always have a front row seat, not only that he may better hear the teacher's voice but also that he may clearly see her lips for whatever help this gives in understanding what is said.

Malnutrition also plays a part in lowering the child's responsiveness in school. Attention should be given to cases where undernourishment or lack of proper sleep and rest seem factors in the child's ability to hit his stride in school.

Finally, in listing the major causes of reading disability, it is necessary to add a group of causes which for want of accurate classification might be tentatively called "miscellaneous anomalies in learning." The group of children whose difficulty falls within this classification are baffling to parents and to teachers because they often present no evidence of inferior mental or physical powers. On the contrary, a number of children with exceptional endowments find reading a stumbling block out of all proportion to their evident accomplishment in mathematics and other non-reading activities. The limits of this article do not allow a detailed analysis of the several causes included in this group, but an outline of some general characteristics will be briefly given.

Among these anomalies which appear to interfere with reading and require special treatment is faulty functioning of the eyes. Though vision may be good in each eye, the behavior of the eyes in reading effort is inadequate. Eyedness, like handedness, is a factor which may interfere with maximal achievement. Sometimes there is a difference in the size and shape of the ocular images presented by the right and by the left eyes which is of sufficient disparity to interfere with reading. Ordinary corrections for refraction do not eliminate this difficulty and special correction must be given.

The eye, like the hand, needs experience and training for its part in school achievement. Sometimes the task is beset with interferences much like those which the left hand encounters in trying to propel a pen in right-hand fashion. For some children the need to look first toward the left and then to move the eyes in rhythmical sweeps across the page and back again is opposed to the natural tendency of the eyes to begin the other way, that is, at the right and move backward over the page. Children with this difficulty need to be detected very early and given special eye training exercises in order to master the left-to-right order of rhythmical movement. In most cases the teacher will be able to detect eye tendencies by facing the child and watching his eyes as he tries to read. Difficulties of this nature are by no means confined to left-handed children. They frequently appear in cases of crossed-dominance, that is, in left-handed, right-eyed individuals and in those who are right-handed but left-eyed. Occasionally they occur in the cases of right-handed, right-eyed individuals.

There are some children whose whole problem of orientation is especially difficult. They are confused by such concepts as in "front of" and "back of", "push" and "pull", "left" and "right". Such words as "team" and "meat", in which the letters are the same but reversed in order, appear identical and letters such as "p" and "q" cannot be differentiated. In addition to eye-training exercises, these children need help in mastering direction and space concepts through games and explanation.

One of the high spots in our present educational program is a focusing of attention upon remedial reading work throughout the schools.

One is forced to observe that the extent of reading disability from the grades to college is a sorry commentary upon the inadequate school program of the past which failed to establish successful reading habits in the early grades. The evidence of material and human waste points to the necessity of a thorough-going program of prevention. With excellent new literature in the field of reading readiness and in methods of teaching reading, and with new commercial aids to testing and to training, the young children now entering school should receive far better care than has been given in the past. A concentration of effort to prevent the unnecessary failure in first grade and to establish successful reading techniques from the start will go far toward assuring a generation of eager wholesome boys and girls who have confidence in themselves and in the future.

PARENT EDUCATION
BY JAMES A. MOYER
State Director of University Extension
Massachusetts Department of Education

The program of the Massachusetts Division of University Extension is so elastic that it may well be said that every man and woman in the State is a prospective University Extension student. The clerk, the mechanic, the housewife, the business man, the policeman, the fireman and the engineer, from the unlettered immigrant on the one extreme to the college graduate on the other—all are represented in the lists of students. This Division, which has always boasted of the fact that it is responsive to the needs of all the people, naturally emphasizes "parent education" as there is a real need for such training in present-day Massachusetts with its great foreign-born population. Indeed, the census of 1930 revealed that there are 596,423 Bay State children of fourteen years and under, born of foreign or mixed parentage.

Education is necessary in order to facilitate the transition from the customs, traditions and languages of the old country, to the ideals and language of this new dynamic civilization that is America. This does not mean, of course, that the culture of the past must be wholly abandoned in order to make room for the new, for there is, doubtless, much of value in the past. It does not mean, for instance, that the newly arrived Albanian mother must forget her native language and her ideal of the role of woman as a stay-at-home, and make a bee line to the Jonesborough Women's Bridge Club. It does mean, however, that since she has come to America to reside permanently, she must prepare herself to "do as the Americans do" to whatever extent is absolutely necessary. Adjustments must be made not only for their own sakes but for the benefit of the children and the community as a whole. The parents must learn to speak English if they are going to "keep up" with their American-born offspring. Naturally if the parent clings like a drowning man to the habits and language of the old country while his child is being made more American and different by the environment of the public schools, the playgrounds and his companions, there is bound to be an ever-widening breach between them. The child comes to think of his parent as old-fashioned, and he is ashamed of his European habits and customs. In the same degree that the parent loses contact with his child, he loses control of him. The situation results in a defensive attitude toward both parents and playmates, the home background becomes more difficult, rebellion against it leads to rebellion against all authority, and through anti-social activities and acts, the drift toward law-breaking is direct and inevitable. The loss of contact explains why it has been found that native-born children of foreign parents contribute more than their share to the criminal ranks* of the nation. The absence of parents' authority in the control of their children's behavior at the most impressionable years of their lives is a very serious handicap for the child.

The Massachusetts Division of University Extension has sought to remedy this particular situation by many courses on the subjects of "Adult Alien Education" and "English for Newcomers."

The parent education program, however, is not designed exclusively for the foreign parent. Native-born parents are beginning to realize that they, too, need training in bringing up their children. Child guidance clinics are being established in the larger cities and parents are coming more and more to realize that many of the causes of a child's misbehavior can be discovered and removed if they go about the task intelligently. Parents all over Massachusetts are demanding more University Extension courses on "Child Psychology", "Psychology of Adolescence" and "Mental Health". They want to understand their children, and to build up in the children confidence and trust in their parents.

Other courses are designed to provide the parents with the information necessary for a sturdy generation of children. Such courses include: "Hygiene of Maternity and Infancy," "Dietetics" and "Nutrition and Foods."

The parent education program includes many courses to help mothers make their homes more attractive in line with the new theory of the effects of the environment upon mental health. A number of courses in "Interior Home Decoration", "Home Garden Designing" and "Exterior Home Decoration" are offered.

Parents of children handicapped by deafness or mental retardedness have often sought and found help in University Extension courses in these fields.

One of the most valuable and unique parts of the entire Parent Education program is the courses which aim to enrich, indirectly, the lives of the children. The busiest individual is always the happiest and the child who has developed many interests will be too busy usually to get into trouble when he steps into adulthood. Many mothers realizing the importance of leisure-time activities in modern life are enrolling in courses on "Pre-School Music", "Music for Little Chil-

* *Parent Education for Crime Prevention* by Mrs. A. H. Reeve, No. 19 of Publications of National Commission on Enrichment of Adult Life, 1401 Sixteenth Street, N.W., Washington, D. C. (Price 5c).

BY JEAN V. LATIMER
Co-ordinator in Health Education
Massachusetts Department of Public Health

One of the immediate tasks ahead is that of co-ordinating the health education efforts of the school with those of the home and the community so that all function more effectively for the welfare of the child.

Since it is now generally conceded that the planning and functioning of the school health education program must be based on the total health needs of the individual child during the twenty-four-hour day, closer cooperation between the school and the home, of necessity, must be brought about. Health behavior must be consistent throughout the entire twenty-four-hour day of the child. In no other way will the habits, attitudes and information acquired in school become effective.

The methods used to bring about such co-ordination will vary with the resources of the community and the skill of those used in bringing about such relationships.

In the process of basing health education for each grade on the actual health needs of the child, teachers, parents and public health nurses will, of necessity come together. Individual conferences will be held with the school doctor, the principal, the teacher and the parent. The public health nurse, who, by her visits to the home, becomes the most influential liaison officer between the school and the home, will thus be brought into closer association with the school health education program. She, through individual parent education, will not only interpret the school health education program to the home but she will strengthen and enlarge it.

The presence of parents at the physical and dental examinations of their children is developing another channel for parent education.

It is desirable that a group of parents termed "Grade Mothers", be organized for each classroom and that during the year regular meetings of such groups be held, under the directions of the principal, the teacher and the public health nurse. In the large parent-teacher meetings, important as they are—it is impossible to develop the intimate type of parent education—so necessary for interpreting and evaluating the health education program and for meeting the needs of all age groups.

Groups of mothers organized for general study of child care and development, should, of course, emphasize the health needs of the child.

Use should be made of all adult educational groups as channels for establishing mutual understanding between the home and the school as to the objectives and methods of the entire school health education programs. The aims and methods for giving the child health protection through school medical service, through healthful school surroundings and by motivating desirable health behavior through health teaching must all be studied and evaluated together.

At the same time that the school is seeking to educate the child to better health standards, community health agencies will be adding to the parents' knowledge as to the factors which best promote child growth and development. Here the work of the community nutritionist is of great value.

How to direct teachers in service and those now in our teachers' colleges to individualize health education by basing health teaching on the actual needs of the children found in the classroom, is immediately before us. Suggestions for the discovery and handling of the health problems of school children are now being made.

Attainable goals are impossible without knowing and taking into consideration the child's social and economic background. But, while health teaching must be consistent with the facilities offered the child at home, it must nevertheless seek to bring about improvement.

Community health facilities must also be available so that the health motivations developed in school will not be lost.

The school health program thus reaches out into the community and becomes a part of its social organization. The health work of the school and the health department become aspects of one unitary educative process.

When the school, the home and community co-ordinate their several endeavors, then and only then, may we expect to realize our goal—"A Healthy Child in a Healthy Community."

THE CARDIAC CHILD
BY EDITH M. TERRY
Committee for the Home Care of Children with Heart Disease, Children's Cardiac Clinic, Massachusetts General Hospital

The head worker in a settlement house in one of our large cities recently made the statement that since life eventually forces obedience upon us, it is more important to teach a child to reason than to obey. With the diagnosis of heart disease, obedience to the doctor's orders is essential and should be immediate, but if the child is to accept long months of convalescence, a reasoning process must be established at the very start. How to establish this reasoning process successfully presents many difficulties to parents already fearful and perplexed.

If the doctor himself explains directly to the child the reasons for treatment, which in many instances must be complete bed care, the situation is greatly simplified. This allows the child to consider himself a factor in the situation, and presents cooperation to him as a privilege. Parents must always remember that emphasis should be placed at the start and continued during the illness on the fact that the child himself is the person most interested in his own recovery. He should be allowed to feel that the problem is his own, and that, although doctor, parents, and friends will help, he must really handle the situation himself. Children, like adults, rise to meet responsibility, and the importance of being a co-partner with one's father and mother, even in a project that involves sacrifice on one's own part, is worthwhile. He should be consulted as to ways and means, and no step should be taken without his understanding of it all.

The importance of explanations cannot be overestimated. Unnecessary worry over things easily explained make many childhood tragedies. Children seldom ask what this means, or that, and are keenly attuned to strange words and ideas. The medical lingo of the clinics, feared but not understood, has a strange fascination for small children, for whom even a mere physical examination at first presents strange associations.

Parents, too, are often bewildered by medical terms. Queer, indeed, are the directions passed on to the child after the return home from a clinic visit—directions so foreign to the junior partner's understanding that the result is bewilderment on his part, and often open rebellion. It is essential that the problem and subsequent treatment be understood before leaving the doctor's office, or the clinic. This understanding secured, the partnership between doctor and parents and child should start at once. The child who understands seldom begs to wait until tomorrow to begin.

Although his comprehension is necessary, parents have an equally important part to play in the venture. The necessary changes in the home routine must be made by them, and on their adult understanding and wise sympathy the child will depend on difficult days for courage.

In this type of partnership it is possible to make of days spent in bed an adventure that the child will remember as a time when he learned many new things, when he had a really good time, whether these days were spent in some hospital ward or in bed at home. It can be for him a time of character building; during his inactivity he will reveal new traits and develop others. The child who successfully goes through this experience keeps his normal place in his home circle and makes a satisfactory readjustment to his school group.

Let him keep his place at home by giving him simple things to do for other members of the family. He needs the satisfaction of sharing, the joy of giving; and too often brothers and sisters are forced to give up their own desires to meet those of the sick child. While he may be able to "lord" it over them, he often recognizes the unfairness of it all. Give him an opportunity to pass on to his friends the new things he is learning. Being in bed tends to increase the feeling of inferiority in a child. Let him keep his place in his group. The sympathy of the whole neighborhood turns towards the child who is ill, and in many instances he grows to feel that he should receive and need not, or cannot, give. One small boy kept his leadership in his group largely because what he was doing was so much more interesting than the street games of his friends that they gladly toiled up three flights of stairs to watch what he was about. Visiting must, of course, be regulated by the doctor. Sometimes the child must be protected from the ill-advised sympathy of members of the family and friends. Visitors should feel, however, that they are welcome, and although they stay but a few minutes, that there has been a worth-while exchange of interests.

Convalescence is just the time to start collecting. Let the child collect anything from tops of ginger ale bottles to stamps. Get his father and older brothers interested to help him with his hobbies. Fill a box with dirt and let him raise lettuce and parsley for the home table. Put carrots in water and let him watch them grow. Get him a bowl of gold fish, if there is money to spare. Turtles, too, can prove good companions even though they occasionally get lost in the bedclothes. Tell your neighborhood librarian about him and what his interests are. She will find books for him, and, if he loves to read, will cooperate to keep him happy. Ask the doctor if he may have a visiting teacher and apply for one from the principal of the school which he attends when he is well. There is no harder situation for the average child than loss of school work and associations. To be out of school for weeks may mean a year repeated; the "gang" goes on and he has to stay behind.

With partnership well established, the child usually improves under the simplest of home conditions and with little equipment. It is essential, however, that he have a room and bed to himself. Sunshine, too, is an important factor. Give him a bedside table and, if the doctor allows him to use his hands in simple craft work and games, a bed table. This table may be cut from a carton obtained from the corner grocery; all that is necessary is a flat surface with supports at either end. It should be high enough to prevent his stooping while at work. It serves as well for his tray at meal times. With a kitchen chair as a brace for pillows at his back, his bed table, and within easy reach of his hands, a stand containing his toys, games, books, and work materials, he will stay happily occupied for hours at a time, especially if the door is left open and he can hear the murmur of voices and feel himself still a part of the home life.

Rest is the best cure for the types of heart disease most common in childhood, and there must always be periods of inactivity when, with the door shut, the child tries, if not to sleep, at least to lie quietly. To make this rest time most effective, the hours he is allowed to sit up should be as interesting as possible. It is here that a program worked out with him is most helpful; get him to plan his day, and then see that he carries out his plans. Where there is systematic routine, days go by with surprising rapidity. Give him a clock; let him take his own rest periods, and run on schedule. This also prevents his constant calling for attention, and will foster his independence. Let him keep a

close at home.

As in every growing business, partners must constantly confer in regard to ways and means. For the child outside the usual give and take of family life, it is most important that times of conference be arranged for, with both father and mother. These times should be his very own, when with one or both parents he has a chance to talk over his day, to discuss the things that are troubling him, to reorganize his routine. It is well for his mother to recognize the fact that rest periods may be changed and even the hours of meals adjusted to the desires of the child if there is a real reason for so doing. In these quiet times surprising things come to the surface. To be a good listener is important and few have the art. If one sits quietly by a child's bed, one learns much of fears, disappointments, and joys. A rough, heedless boy will amaze one with a flash of spiritual insight, gone almost before expressed, but so truly there. He needs to talk with someone who understands; during days in bed one may learn to know one's child anew.

To fit all this into a mother's already overburdened life may seem to be an impossible task. It can be done, however, if, like her child, she, too, organizes her day and runs on schedule. As one mother has done, she can go to her room and shut the door for one hour while she sleeps, reads, or thinks. It is her time for refreshment; and, when the hour is up, she goes back to her family, ready to take up the burdens of the day and share her serenity of spirit. Part of a junior partner's responsibility may be to see that his mother gets the rest she needs and make it possible for her to have it.

One of the compensations of childhood is the ready adjustment that it makes to change. Children do adjust happily to bed life when they understand the reason for it all, have the security that comes from parents and friends who stand by, and have new interests that change dull days to bright ones. As one child said recently to her brother, in speaking of the many things she had learned during her convalescence, "It's fun to stay in bed when you have things to do."

THE PROGRAM FOR SERVICES FOR CRIPPLED CHILDREN IN MASSACHUSETTS

BY EDWARD G. HUBER, M.D.
*Assistant Director of Division of Administration
Massachusetts Department of Public Health*

The 74th Congress, in Part 2 of Title V of the Social Security Act of 1935, made an appropriation of $2,800,000 "for the purpose of enabling each State to extend and improve (especially in rural areas and in areas suffering from severe economic distress) . . . services for . . . providing medical, surgical, corrective, and other services and care, and facilities for diagnosis, hospitalization, and after care, for children who are crippled or who are suffering from conditions which lead to crippling."

In order to obtain this grant for Massachusetts a plan was evolved by the Department of Public Health which, after its approval by the General and the Technical Advisory Committees (both of which had been appointed by Dr. Chadwick) and by the officers of the Massachusetts Medical Society, was accepted by the Chief of the Children's Bureau, U. S. Department of Labor.

Accordingly, activity commenced. The Program for Crippled Children was placed in the Division of Public Health Administration. Since the keynote is close co-operation with the Massachusetts Medical Society the first step after organization of the central office was to visit the officers of the eighteen District Societies which make up the Massachusetts Medical Society. Preliminary letters had been written the presidents of these constituent societies by the Secretary of the Massachusetts Medical Society and by Dr. Chadwick, apprising them of the fact that they would soon be visited by representatives of the Department of Public Health for the purpose of explaining the program. These interviews were nearly all very satisfactory. In a few districts the president was the sole representative of his society at the conference. This occurred chiefly in districts which, being in the metropolitan area, are not intended to receive service as fully as are the rural areas. In the remaining districts a great deal of interest was aroused. After the first explanation of the program, we were asked to return and explain the plan to a larger group, and in about a dozen districts we were invited to address the entire society at a regular meeting.

The usual procedure was first to give the details of the plan in a fifteen or twenty-minute talk and then to answer questions and reply to arguments against the program. The opponents' main objection was that this is state medicine,—socialized medicine, and therefore iniquitous. It reminded one of a paragraph in Dr. Mustard's Introduction to Public Health. "Let any scheme for a medical arrangement be presented to a medical organization, and all opponents need to do is to brand it as 'state medicine'. . . . This term is one of respectability in most countries but to many of the official medical leaders in the United States it is anathema: the whipping boy to be castigated for any real or imaginary sins against the status quo, regardless of who committed the sins, or when or where or in what circumstances." Our answer was that we considered the program rather an evolution from the principle of the survival of the fittest to that policy of an enlightened civilization where the needy members of the community who otherwise would be neglected could be helped. And even if a liberal definition of the term would permit classifying "Services for Crippled Children" as socialized medicine, at least it is the type of state medicine which physicians should accept. For, since the tendency of the times is toward socialization, and socialization of medicine may be on the way, it is far better to have the evolution directed by the medical profession itself. As I have already stated and now wish to emphasize, this program is so much an activity of the Massachusetts Medical Society that the Department of Public Health regards itself as merely administering the program.

The fact that the Program for Crippled Children is embodied in the Social Security Act is another reason for the opposition. The more prominent features of that Act, those relating to old age and unemployment, are much in the limelight and because of some question of the constitutionality of those Titles, "Services for Crippled Children" participates in the anathema. However much may be said for or against Social Security (and at one large medical meeting the discussion following the talk disgressed at once to a one-sided political meeting) the fact remains that aside from the old age and unemployment provisions, the Act initiated a national program to protect and promote public health. As Surgeon General Parran says, "the distress which arises from sickness and death of the wage earners is one of the prime factors in contributing to social insecurity. Therefore a national effort to promote social security must include a serious attempt to prevent unnecessary disease and death." Social insecurity, as we all know, was the basis for the moves toward the extreme left in Russia and Spain.

Another argument we advanced to the medical profession was that "Services for Crippled Children" had, through legislation, already become an established procedure in the State. Many communities were very glad to get the aid for their needy and so co-operation might as well be state-wide, especially since the program is so largely in the hands of the medical profession.

Well over forty states have accepted federal aid for crippled children but the respective Departments of Public Health are administering the program in less than half of them. The probability is that in none of them is the co-operation with the medical profession more complete than in Massachusetts.

The program was accepted at once by practically all the District Medical Societies. In the two dissenting areas, objections were subsequently silenced when the Council of the Massachusetts Medical Society unanimously endorsed the program and the methods of the Department of Public Health in endeavoring to secure the co-operation of the Society.

"Crippled children" are defined in the State Plan as follows:

"For administrative purposes, the term 'crippled children' is understood to include those children under 21 years of age who are suffering from poliomyelitis, bone and joint tuberculosis, congenital defects, cardiac conditions, arthritis, and such other similar conditions as may lead to or have produced crippling, and which may be treated advantageously. It is planned to include children under the age of 21 years who require plastic operations following burns, accidents, congenital defects such as harelip, cleft palate, etc. It is not planned to include the care of children who are the victims of 'acute' accidents, or who require operations for hernia, or for the removal of tonsils and adenoids, nor is it planned to provide custodial care for children of low mentality or for other children."

In 1931 there was completed by the Department of Public Welfare a survey of crippled children which disclosed 6,141 such children under 21 years of age. This survey has been continued as an annual census, conducted by the Department of Public Welfare and the Department of Education, of handicapped children between the ages of 6 and 16 years. There are now on record as of September 1, 1936, 5,858 crippled children under the age of 21 years. These records, through the courtesy of the Commissioner of Public Welfare, are now kept for our convenience in one of the rooms of the Department of Public Health in the State House. They are the basis of the search for crippled children. Each record is being copied and classified geographically. In co-operation with the Division of Child Hygiene, lists of these crippled children are being distributed to community nurses and they ascertain the status of these children and will also inform the Division of Public Health Administration of hitherto unreported cases. In time, practically all crippled children should be known.

The procedure in setting up the initial clinic in each district was as follows:

After the selection of a consultant and the conclusion of satisfactory arrangements for clinic facilities with a suitable hospital, the field staff consisting of the Supervisor of Clinics for Crippled Children, a medical social worker, two orthopedic nurses and two physiotherapists have visited each area, taking with them the existing records of local crippled children. These workers then proceeded to look up the individual cases, ascertaining the status of the crippled individuals. If the patients have apparently been neglected, the names of the respective family physicians were obtained and report made to the supervisor. The latter then visited the designated family physician or physician of the patient's choice and discussed the child with him. If the physician decided the patient needed treatment and that the parents were unable to pay for it, he signed an application for the admission of the child to a clinic. This application was then referred to the committee of the District Medical Society whose duty it is to investigate the economic status of the patient and then to approve or disapprove the application. On approval, the patient was admitted to the clinic.

It is planned to have eleven state-wide clinics, located as follows:

Pittsfield, Greenfield, Springfield, Gardner, Lowell, Haverhill, Salem, Brockton, Fall River, Hyannis, and Worcester. The method of admission to these clinics will be as just described; that is, by an application signed by a physician and approved by the Committee of the District Medical Society. Each of these clinics will be conducted by an orthopedic surgeon who confines his practice to that specialty. Wherever possible an orthopedist residing in the clinic district has been selected for each district; it is also planned to utilize local hospital facilities to the fullest extent.

The consultants for the clinics are as follows:

Brockton	— Dr. George W. Van Gorder
Fall River	— Dr. Eugene A. McCarthy
Gardner	— Dr. Mark H. Rogers
Greenfield	— Dr. Harry R. Wheat
Haverhill	— Dr. Arthur T. Legg
Hyannis	— Dr. Paul Norton
Lowell	— Dr. W. Russell MacAusland
Pittsfield	— Dr. Francis A. Slowick
Salem	— Dr. Harold C. Bean
Springfield	— Dr. Garry deN. Hough
Worcester	— Dr. John W. O'Meara

These men, leaders in their specialty, have all been more than willing to contribute their time and skill to aid these needy cases.

The staff of "Services for Crippled Children," in addition to the field staff, includes the Assistant Director of the Division of Public Health Administration, a physiotherapist at the Lakeville State Sanatorium, a brace maker, and clerical assistants. The physiotherapist permanently stationed at the Lakeville State Sanatorium assists in the treatment of the victims of poliomyelitis who were recently authorized to be admitted there. The brace maker will also be at the Lakeville State Sanatorium in order to take care of the increased call for braces and other apparatus. The equipment of the brace shop has recently been augmented through aid from "Services for Crippled Children". In addition to this equipment, funds from the same service have provided a diaphragm respirator and a Hubbard tub for use in treatments.

Each clinic is operated entirely by the field staff of "Services for Crippled Children." The Supervisor and a Medical Social Worker are in attendance at each clinic, after having made all preliminary arrangements. The nurses and physiotherapists are each assigned an area including several clinic districts. They attend and assist at all the clinics in their respective areas and are responsible for treatments, follow-up care, and the numerous other incidental details in their respective areas. No local hospital is called on for personnel except

and either performs the operation himself or delegates that function to some one else. In any event, the consultant is responsible for all professional care. In other cases, the child may need a brace or other apparatus. Measurements are then taken and the brace shop at the Lakeville State Sanatorium proceeds to make the apparatus. A child may require physiotherapy only. If so, the physiotherapist either visits the home for that purpose at stated intervals or the patients from one community are taken to a central place for the convenience of the physiotherapist or to conserve her time. After discharge from hospital, patients may be returned to their respective homes if the social worker advises that the homes are suitable. If not, convalescent hospitals or homes are selected. Wherever the patient goes, follow-up work by the nurses is necessary. It is anticipated that the local nurses will render valuable assistance in such work by co-operating with the orthopedic nurses of the staff.

The Technical Advisory Committee has decided upon the following fee schedule:

$3.50 per day for hospital care
$2.00 per x-ray, with $10. maximum per patient
$10.00 operating room fee

Clinics have been held at the following places,—Pittsfield, Greenfield, Springfield, Haverhill, Salem, Hyannis, Lowell, Gardner, and Brockton. Fall River and Worcester Clinics are planned in the very near future, following which a schedule for state-wide clinics will be made, each clinic to be conducted at monthly or six-week intervals. This schedule, it is hoped, will be published in the New England Journal of Medicine, as well as in local newspapers. These newspapers have almost without exception gladly published information concerning the clinics. That this publicity has not been without results has been shown by the inquiries received by the Department of Public Health. At first most of these letters were requests for employment and for information regarding ways and means for securing a "fair" portion of the federal grant for various hospitals and institutions, but of late more and more requests for treatment of crippled children have arrived.

In the administration of the program so far three major difficulties have been encountered. The first and most important one is the resistance of the patient or of his family, or both, to accepting hospitalization. Some of the children seen at the clinics could be helped a great deal by operative procedures. But so far only two children, other than the poliomyelitis cases at the Lakeville State Sanatorium, have actually been admitted to hospital. The consent of the parents of one of them could only be obtained by assurances from the orthopedic consultant, the hospital authorities and the Department of Public Health, that she would receive every possible care and would in no sense be treated as a pauper. Most patients were not frank in voicing reasons why they would not consent to enter hospital for operation, but in at least two instances the patient seemed to fear he would be given a stiff joint in spite of the fact that assurances were given by all the personnel that only tendon operations were advised. One mother objected because she had been told that an operation on a tendon of the foot would weaken the child's brain. These objecting cases will of course be followed up to some extent, but the advisability of too strongly urging these patients to accept an operation is questionable. Experience has shown that even though an orthopedist has refrained from promising more than he could reasonably expect as a result of an operation, dissatisfaction on the part of the patient has followed because the result has fallen below what the patient wanted. This difficulty of persuading the patient to take a step from social insecurity toward social security would seem to contradict the quotation from Dr. Parran cited above but we feel that this program being comparatively new, needs to be more firmly established before results can be weighed.

A second difficulty is the fact that some of the committees of the district medical societies do not act with the celerity of others. And since the approval of the committee is a pre-requisite to the institution of treatment it may easily be seen that in some districts clinics may not be held so frequently as in others. In order to expedite the routine during the process of organizing clinics in the various districts, cases have been admitted to clinic on the signed request of a physician, or even on his oral request, before the committee has had a chance to investigate. Treatment was of course withheld until his approval was obtained. This has not proven satisfactory, for two reasons. As so frequently occurs, the cases where the planned routine was not carried out were the very ones which caused administrative embarrassment. The other reason why it seems advisable to obtain full approval for each case before the clinic, is that where physiotherapy or an apparatus is advised and accepted at the clinic, and the treatment is withheld while the committee investigates, the patient becomes discouraged or dissatisfied and may even refuse consent when approval is finally obtained, especially if that has been unduly delayed. These cases are not emergency cases and delay in admission to clinic is of no importance. In at least one other state the procedure for admission to clinic, as described in a recent Journal of the American Medical Association, is very much more cumbersome than the Massachusetts method.

The third difficulty encountered is the growing desire of local communities, and of some private as well as some public agencies, to cease the work for crippled children which they have been doing and to have it all done from federal funds. The small amount of money awarded Massachusetts (about $80,000 per year) is not sufficient to do this, and the Children's Bureau specifies that the Program for Crippled Children is to extend and improve existing services and is not to supplant any. Children suffering from bone and joint tuberculosis are to continue to be sent to the Lakeville State Sanatorium and to be paid for by the town of settlement. Where local charities are providing braces and other apparatus, or hospitalization, or physiotherapy, it is earnestly hoped that their aid will not cease.

In the nine clinics conducted to date, 113 patients have been seen. Operation has been advised for 34; physiotherapy for 33, and braces or other apparatus for 34. The other patients either needed no further treatment or were hopeless cases.

A satisfactory start has been made. Difficulties have arisen, as was to be expected, but these are being eliminated. The success of the program as outlined in the State Plan depends on the co-operation of the medical profession. The Department of Public Health is doing its utmost to further "Services for Crippled Children."

REPORT OF DIVISION OF FOOD AND DRUGS

During the months of July, August and September 1936, samples were collected in 205 cities and towns.

There were 1,734 samples of milk examined, of which 313 were below standard, from 8 samples the cream had been in part removed, and 19 samples contained added water. There were 1,319 bacteriological examinations made of milk, 1,035 of which complied with the requirements. There were 281 bacteriological examinations made of ice cream, 34 of which did not comply with the requirements; 1 bacteriological examination of pasteurized cream which complied with the requirements; 9 bacteriological examinations of empty bottles, 6 of which did not comply with the requirements; 10 bacteriological examinations of mattress fillings, 4 of which did not comply with the requirements; 5 sediment tests, 5 endo plates, 1 examination for bacillus coli, 2 bacteriological examinations of canned crab meat, and 1 bacteriological examination of orangeade, all of which complied with the requirements.

There were 658 samples of food examined, 114 of which were adulterated. These consisted of 9 samples of butter, 6 of which were low in fat, and 3 samples were rancid; 1 sample of candy which was misbranded; 2 samples of eggs which were decomposed; 2 samples of olive oil, 1 sample of which contained tea-seed oil, and 1 sample contained cottonseed oil; 1 sample of ham, and 1 sample of meat loaf, which were decomposed; 36 samples of hamburg steak, 20 of which were decomposed, 8 samples contained a compound of sulphur dioxide not properly labeled, 3 samples contained sodium sulphite in excess of one tenth of one per cent, 2 samples were watered, decomposed, and contained a compound of sulphur dioxide not properly labeled, 2 samples were decomposed and contained sodium sulphite in excess of one tenth of one per cent, and 1 sample contained a compound of sulphur dioxide not properly labeled and was decomposed; 14 samples of sausage, 6 of which were decomposed, 7 samples contained a compound of sulphur dioxide not properly labeled, 2 of which were also decomposed, and 1 sample contained sodium sulphite in excess of one tenth of one per cent; 27 samples of soft drinks, 6 of which contained a compound of benzoate not marked, 1 of which was also misbranded, 13 samples of orangeade which were colored to conceal inferiority, and 8 samples of orangeade which were misbranded; 16 samples of soft drink wash water which were deficient in caustic alkali; and 5 samples of mattress fillings, 1 sample of which contained oil, 1 sample contained oily mill sweepings, 1 sample contained secondhand material, and 2 samples were a mixture of secondhand and new material.

There were 92 samples of drugs examined, of which 23 were adulterated. These consisted of 3 samples of camphorated oil, 1 sample of lime water, 8 samples of spirit of nitrous ether, and 11 samples of sulphuric acid dilute, all of which did not conform to the requirements of the U. S.Pharmacopoeia.

The police department submitted 206 samples of liquor for examination. The police departments also submitted 71 samples to be analyzed for poisons or drugs, of which 2 samples contained morphine, 1 sample contained cocain, 4 samples contained cannabis, 20 samples contained heroin, 1 sample contained opium, 1 sample contained ergotamine tatrate, 2 samples contained white flour sold as a bug poison, 1 sample was identified as Hayden's Viburnum Compound, 4 samples contained no alkaloids, and 35 miscellaneous drugs which were free from narcotics.

There were 78 cities and towns visited for the inspection of pasteurizing plants, and 492 plants, operated for the pasteurization of milk were inspected, as well as 9 ice cream plants.

There were 50 hearings held pertaining to violations of the laws.

There were 114 convictions for violations of the law, $3,300 in fines being imposed.

Caracostas Brothers, Incorporated, of Boston; Frank Kaszowski of Dudley; Donald Kirchner of Pittsfield; Eleanor G. Noel of North Adams; William Rose of Taunton; Andrew Bashista of Westfield; Moses E. Ricker, 2 counts, of Rowley; John Stuhler of Edgartown; and Frank Smegeil of Belchertown, were all convicted for violations of the milk laws. Donald Kirchner of Pittsfield appealed his case.

Adam Schuster, 2 cases, and Whitcomb Farms, Incorporated, of Roslindale; and George S. Zervas of Ipswich, were convicted for violations of the pasteurization law and regulations. Whitcomb Farms, Incorporated, of Roslindale, appealed their case.

Westwood Farm Milk Company of Jamaica Plain was convicted for a violation of the milk grading regulations.

Antonio Accardi, 5 cases; Louis Ruggiero, 3 cases; 2 cases each, Paul Cionciola, Morris Rubin, Lo Conte Brothers, Incorporated, United Markets, Incorporated, Jerry DeRosa, and Harry Diamond; and 1 case each, Dominic Meo, Aaron Cohen, Dominic A. Previte, Harry Newman, Carl Blasberg, Abraham Chernois, Raffelle Sarno, Hyman Alpert, Sarah Snyder, Economy Grocery Stores, Incorporated, North End Meat Market, Incorporated, Joseph Reinholtz, Incorporated, P. W. Rounsevell, Incorporated, and Edward Rood, all of Boston; Peter Lombardi of East Boston; Abraham Bell, 2 cases, of South Boston; New York Cut Rate Grocers, Incorporated, and Albert Lagorio of Dorchester; Harry Lifshitz of Roxbury; Frank S. Hollis of Chelsea; Lester Swartz, 3 cases, of Brighton; Cosmos Food Stores, Incorporated, 5 cases, and Paul Booras, of Lynn; Arthur Cardin of Webster; Joseph Carbone, 2 cases, of Fitchburg; Samuel Gomez, 2 cases, and Valmore Vigeant, of Lowell; Edward Alpert, 3 cases, Morris Kenion, and Maurice Spector, of Waltham; Cudahy Packing Company of Lawrence; and National Cash Market of Holyoke, were all convicted for violations of the food laws. Cosmos Food Stores, Incorporated, of Lynn appealed 4 cases, Paul Booras of Lynn, 1 case; P. W. Rounsevell, Incorporated, of Boston appealed 1 case; Edward Alpert of Waltham appealed 3 cases; and Harry Lifshitz of Roxbury appealed 1 case.

Nick Costa, 2 cases of East Boston; and New York Cut Rate Grocers, Incorporated, of Dorchester, were convicted for violations of the sanitary food law. Nick Costa of East Boston appealed 2 cases.

Leo E. Costa of Dorchester was convicted for violation of the bakery regulations.

Grower's Outlet, Incorporated, of Greenfield was convicted for false advertising. The case was appealed.

Antonio Accardi, 5 cases, Louis Ruggiero, 3 cases, Lo Conte Brothers, Incorporated, 2 cases, and Dominic Meo, of Boston; and Cosmos Food Stores, Incorporated, 3 cases, of Lynn, were all convicted for misbranding. Cosmos Food Stores, Incorporated, of Lynn, appealed 3 cases.

Pallister Bottling Company, Incorporated, of Roxbury; Causeway Bottling Company of Boston; New Bedford Bottling Company of New Bedford; Ignatius J. Wojtaszek of Adams; Robert C. Albert and Samuel Kanter of Beverly; George A. Davis Company, Incorporated, of Gloucester; William Greenwood of East Pepperell; and Stanley Machaj of Ipswich, were all convicted for violations of the law and regulations relative to the manufacture and bottling of carbonated non-alcoholic beverages. Causeway Bottling Company of Boston appealed their case.

Paul Timberlin of Pownal, Vermont, was convicted for violation of the slaughtering law.

Chair City Upholstering Company, Royal Furniture Manufacturing Company, and Selig Manufacturing Company, Incorporated, of Gardner; Benjamin Malick of Lynn; Massachusetts Wool Waste Company and Eagle Upholstery Company, Incorporated, of Boston; and Standard Mattress Company, Incorporated, 2 cases, of Springfield, were all convicted for violations of the mattress laws. Massachusetts Wool Waste Company and Eagle Upholstery Company, Incorporated, of Boston; Standard Mattress Company, Incorporated, 2 cases, of Springfield; and Benjamin Malick of Lynn, all appealed their cases.

In accordance with Section 25, Chapter 111 of the General Laws, the following is the list of articles of adulterated food collected in original packages from manufacturers, wholesalers, or producers:

Butter which was low in fat was obtained as follows:

One sample each, from Smiley Brothers and Fairmont Creamery Company of Boston.

Two samples of butter which were rancid were obtained from Wellworth Market of Roxbury.

One sample of olive oil which contained cottonseed oil was obtained from D. A. Previte of Boston.

One sample of olive oil which contained tea-seed oil was obtained from DeLuca Company of New York.

One sample of ham which was decomposed was obtained from Abraham Chervis & Samuel Goldsmith of Boston.

One sample of meat loaf which was decomposed was obtained from Harry Lifshitz of Roxbury.

Hamburg steak which was decomposed was obtained as follows:

Two samples from Main Public Market, Incorporated, of Fall River; and 1 sample each from Arabelle Cummings of Swansea; Cohen's Market and Samuel Gordon of New Bedford; First National Store of Medford; Lester Swartz of Allston; The Great Atlantic & Pacific Tea Company of Greenfield and South Boston; Valmore Vigeant of Lowell; Economy Grocery Stores, Incorporated, Gray United Market, J. Reinholtz, Incorporated, North End Market, P. W. Rounsevelle, Incorporated, Carl Blasberg, Hyman Alpert, and Edward Rood, all of Boston; and Quality Market of Chelsea.

Hamburg steak which contained a compound of sulphur dioxide not properly labeled was obtained as follows:

One sample each, from Harrison Avenue Cut Price Market, Supreme Public Market, and Haymarket Provision Company, Incorporated, of Boston; Manhattan Market of South Boston; Sam Tillman of Springfield; Manuel Gomez of Lowell; Quality Cash Market, Incorporated, of Worcester; and People's Market of North Adams.

Hamburg steak which contained sodium sulphite in excess of one tenth of one per cent was obtained as follows:

One sample each, from Isaac Leisman of Lowell; Harry Berkovitz of Boston; and Rosenburg Brothers of Dorchester.

Hamburg steak which contained sodium sulphite in excess of one tenth of one per cent and was also decomposed was obtained as follows:

One sample each, from Sarah and Israel Snyder, and Morris Rubin of Boston.

Hamburg steak which contained a compound of sulphur dioxide not properly labeled, was decomposed, and also contained excess water, was obtained as follows:

One sample each, from Hub Poultry Company, and Harry Diamond of Boston.

One sample of hamburg steak which contained a compound of sulphur dioxide not properly labeled and was also decomposed was obtained from Phillip Kaller of New Bedford.

Sausage which was decomposed was obtained as follows:

One sample each, from Lester Swartz of Allston; Manuel Gomez of Lowell; United Market of Dorchester; People's Market, Incorporated, of Fall River; and The Great Atlantic & Pacific Tea Company of Springfield.

Sausage which contained a compound of sulphur dioxide not properly labeled and was also decomposed was obtained as follows:

One sample each, from De Rosa Meat Market of Boston; and Joseph Carbone of Fitchburg.

One sample of sausage which contained a compound of sulphur dioxide not properly labeled was obtained from Lester Swartz of Allston.

Orangeade which was colored to conceal inferiority was obtained as follows:

Two samples each from Hillcrest Dairy, Incorporated, and Anderson Brothers of Worcester; James Cooper of Rochdale; Meola Brothers of West Boylston; and Wheeler Bottling Company of Lynn; and 1 sample each, from John B. McManus of Worcester; and Stanley Raplus of Ludlow.

Soft drinks which contained sodium benzoate and were not properly marked were obtained as follows:

Two samples each, from Lovers Leap Company of Lynn; and F. W. Woolworth Company of Boston; and 1 sample from Snow Crest Beverage Company of Salem.

One sample of orangeade which was misbranded was obtained from San-Hi Ginger Ale Company, Incorporated, of West Natick.

One sample of orangeade which contained sodium benzoate and was not properly marked and was also misbranded was obtained from F. W. Woolworth Company of Boston.

There were five confiscations, consisting of 238 pounds of decomposed beef; 195 pounds of dried out beef livers; 40 pounds of decomposed lamb quarters; 90 pounds of decomposed frankforts; and 150 pounds of decomposed flounder fillets.

The licensed cold storage warehouses reported the following amounts of food placed in storage during June, 1936:—1,092,570 dozens of case eggs; 1,078,280 pounds of broken out eggs; 3,987,552 pounds of butter; 1,568,122 pounds of poultry; 2,705,482 pounds of fresh meat and fresh meat products; and 19,703,826 pounds of fresh food fish.

There were on hand July 1, 1936:—7,043,940 dozens of case eggs; 1,924,059 pounds of broken out eggs; 4,437,979 pounds of butter; 4,155,016 pounds of poultry; 4,695,112 pounds of fresh meat and fresh meat products; and 31,011,694 pounds of fresh food fish.

The licensed cold storage warehouses reported the following amounts of food placed in storage during July, 1936:—1,107,630 dozens of case eggs; 1,518,827 pounds of broken out eggs; 2,217,840 pounds of butter; 1,538,654 pounds of poultry; 2,394,187 pounds of fresh meat and fresh meat products; and 15,539,270 pounds of fresh food fish.

There was on hand August 1, 1936:—7,570,230 dozens of case eggs; 2,512,814 pounds of broken out eggs; 5,356,857 pounds of butter; 4,069,351 pounds of poultry; 4,497,809 pounds of fresh meat and fresh meat products; and 35,779,812 pounds of fresh food fish.

The licensed cold storage warehouses reported the following amounts of food placed in storage during August, 1936:—343,620 dozens of case eggs; 961,519 pounds of broken out eggs; 963,837 pounds of butter; 1,602,685 pounds of poultry; 2,963,082 pounds of fresh meat and fresh meat products; and 12,101,026 pounds of fresh food fish.

There was on hand September 1, 1936:—6,728,760 dozens of case eggs; 2,421,860 pounds of broken out eggs; 4,966,487 pounds of butter; 3,920,086 pounds of poultry; 3,961,635 pounds of fresh meat and fresh meat products; and 38,133,418 pounds of fresh food fish.

MASSACHUSETTS DEPARTMENT OF PUBLIC HEALTH

Commissioner of Public Health, HENRY D. CHADWICK, M.D.

Public Health Council

HENRY D. CHADWICK, M.D., *Chairman*

GORDON HUTCHINS. RICHARD M. SMITH, M.D.
FRANCIS H. LALLY, M.D. RICHARD P. STRONG, M.D.
SYLVESTER E. RYAN, M.D. JAMES L. TIGHE.

Secretary, FLORENCE L. WALL

Division of Administration	Under direction of Commissioner.
Division of Sanitary Engineering	Director and Chief Engineer, ARTHUR D. WESTON, C.E.
Division of Communicable Diseases	Director, GAYLORD W. ANDERSON, M.D.
Division of Biologic Laboratories	Director and Pathologist, ELLIOTT S. ROBINSON, M.D.
Division of Food and Drugs	Director and Analyst, HERMANN C. LYTHGOE, S.B.
Division of Child Hygiene	Director, M. LUISE DIEZ, M.D.
Division of Tuberculosis	Director, ALTON S. POPE, M.D.
Division of Adult Hygiene	Director, HERBERT L. LOMBARD, M.D.

State District Health Officers

The Southeastern District	RICHARD P. MACKNIGHT, M.D., New Bedford.
The South Metropolitan District	HENRY M. DE WOLFE, M.D., Quincy.
The North Metropolitan District	CHARLES B. MACK, M.D., Boston.
The Northeastern District	ROBERT E. ARCHIBALD, M.D., Lynn.
The Worcester County District	OSCAR A. DUDLEY, M.D., Worcester.
The Connecticut Valley District	JOHN J. POUTAS, M.D., Springfield.
The Franklin County District	WALTER W. LEE, M.D., No. Adams.

INDEX

Abbott, Mrs. T. Grafton, The need for parent education 219
American Medical Association, Resolution adopted by the Joint Committee on Health Problems in Education of the National Education Association and the 164
American Public Health Association, Report of the Committee on Nutritional Problems. Food fallacies and nutritional quackery . . . 198
Approved prophylactic remedy for use in the eyes of infants at birth . 163
Backward child, Educating the, by Ada M. Fitts 265
Bailey, Edith H., Community aspects of parent education through public libraries 240
Ball, Jennie W., Our dental hygiene program 206
Basic considerations of the junior high school course of study, by John P. Sullivan, Ph. D. 132
Beinert, Frederica L., and Coffin, Susan M., Nutrition on the Well Child Conference 40
Blood, Alice F., Ph.D., The training of the nutritionist 5
Book Notes:
    Lobar pneumonia and serum therapy, by Frederick T. Lord, M.D. and Roderick Heffron, M.D. 73
    Syphilis and its treatment, by William A. Hinton, M.D. . . . 165
Brown, M. M., R.N., and Nicoll, Dorothea, B.S., Dental nutrition program in a community 50
Budget case, by Florence Genevieve Dorward, B.S. 61
Cardiac child, by Edith M. Terry 280
Causes of first grade failure, by Lura Oak, Ph. D. 273
Character, The home as a builder of, by Rabbi Herman H. Rubenovitz . 250
Charm course, by Albertine P. McKellar 138
Church and parents, by Rev. Phillips Endecott Osgood, D.D., L.H.D. . 244
Church and parent education—need and opportunity, by Richard J. Quinlan, S.T.L. 247
Churchill, Edward D., M.D., Role of surgery in pulmonary tuberculosis . 160
Coffin, Susan M., M.D., and Beinert, Frederica, L., B.S., Nutrition on the Well Child Conference 40
Community aspects of parent education in regard to settlement work, by Ethel Ward Dougherty 238
Community aspects of parent education through public libraries, by Edith H. Bailey 240
Community nutritionist, by Mary Spalding, M.A. 3
Conferences, Group, with expectant mothers, by Charlotte Raymond, B.A. 54
Contribution of the food clinic to the community, by Frances Stern . . 32
Course of study, Basic considerations of the junior high school . . 132
Crippled children in Massachusetts, The program for services for, by Edward G. Huber, M.D. 284
Cure of tuberculosis, by Ernest B. Emerson, M.D. 156
Deaths, maternal, in Massachusetts 73
Dental caries, Retardation of, in out-patients of a dental infirmary, by Percy R. Howe, D.D.S., Ruth L. White, B.S., and Milton Rabine, D.D.S. 194
Dental health—a review 175
Dental health education for children, by George E. Davis, D.D.S. . . 179
Dental health problem, How Greenfield is solving the, by Harold R. Lamb, D.M.D. 204

Dental hygiene, Parents and, by Robert L. Robinson, D.D.S. . . . 229
Dental hygiene program, Our, by Jennie W. Ball 206
Dental nutrition program in a community, by M. M. Brown, R.N., and
    Dorothea Nicoll, B.S. 50
Dental services, A visual presentation of the value of, by Henry B. Taylor 188
Dentists, What, should do about nutrition, by Florence B. Hopkins, M.D.,
    D.M.D. 191
Desmond, John J. Jr., A.M., Trained teachers of health 186
Dimond, Blanche T., B.S., and Richardson, Ann, R.N., B.A., B.N., Nutri-
    tion worker and nurse in a family health program . . . 18
Do you know about the Volta Bureau? 209
Donohue, Marie L., Health supervision as parent education . . . 233
Dorward, Florence Genevieve, A budget case 61
Dougherty, Ethel Ward, The community aspects of parent education in
    regard to settlement work 238
Educating the backward child, by Ada M. Fitts 265
Emerson, Ernest B., M.D., The cure of tuberculosis 156
Exhibits, The nutritionist says it with, by Dorothea Nicoll, B.S. . . 71
Eyes of infants at birth, Approved prophylactic remedy for use in . . 163
Fitts, Ada M., Educating the backward child 265
Food and Drugs, Report of Division of:
    October-November-December, 1935 75
    January-February-March, 1936 166
    April-May-June, 1936 210
    July-August-September, 1936 290
Food clinic, Contribution of the, to the community, by Frances Stern . 32
Food fallacies and nutritional quackery, Report of the Committee on Nu-
    tritional Problems, American Health Association . . . 198
Froebel Centennial, by Lucy Wheelock 254
Greenfield is solving the dental health problem, How, by Harold R. Lamb,
    D.M.D. 204
Group conferences with expectant mothers, by Charlotte Raymond, B.A. . 54
Gulick, J. Halsey, The need for co-operation between headmaster and
    parents in country day high schools 260
Hager, Dorothy, B.S., An itinerant nutritionist in a country town . . 22
Health education becomes one of the social sciences, by Jean V. Latimer . 279
Health education, Supervisor of—Responsibilities and training, by C. E.
    Turner, M.A., Dr. P.H. 124
Health problems in education, Resolution adopted by the Joint Committee
    on, of the National Education Association and the American
    Medical Association 164
Health, public, History of the department of, by Eleanor J. Macdonald,
    A.B. 83
Health supervision as parent education, by Marie L. Donohue . . . 233
Health teaching in the primary grades, Suggestions for integrated, by

tion 191
How Greenfield is solving the dental health problem, by Harold R. Lamb, D.M.D. 204
Howe, Percy R., D.D.S., White, Ruth L., B.S., and Rabine, Milton, D.D.S., Retardation of dental caries in out-patients of a dental infirmary 194
Huber, Edward G., M.D., The program for services for crippled children in Massachusetts 284
Itinerant nutritionist in a country town, by Dorothy Hager, B.S. . . 22
Job of being a parent, by Katharine Herring 220
Jones, Gladys Beckett, The private school and parent education . . 253
Lamb, Harold R., D.M.D., How Greenfield is solving the dental health problem 204
Latimer, Jean V., Health education becomes one of the social sciences . 279
Suggestions for integrated health teaching in the primary grades . 127
Leamy, Catherine, M.S., One school's nutrition program 65
Libraries, Community aspects of parent education through public, by Edith H. Bailey 240
Lord, Arthur B., Parent education 257
Lunch in a country school, by Mary Spalding, M.A. 141
Macdonald, Eleanor J., A.B., History of the Department 83
Maternal deaths in Massachusetts 73
McCollum, E.V., Ph.D., Present trends in nutrition 6
McKay, Florence L., M.D., Parent education and the Well Child Conference 223
McKellar, Albertine P., B.S., Publicity for a community nutrition program 68
The charm course 138
Milk, The facts about certified (book note) 74
Moyer, James A., Parent education 277
National Education Association and the American Medical Association, Resolution adopted by the Joint Committee on Health Problems in Education of the 164
Need for co-operation between headmaster and parents in country day high schools, by J. Halsey Gulick 260
Need for parent education, by Mrs. T. Grafton Abbott 219
Nicoll, Dorothea, B.S., The nutritionist says it with exhibits . . . 71
What mothers want to know about child nutrition 230
and Brown, M. M., R.N., Dental nutrition program in a community . 50
Nurse, nutrition worker and, in a family health program, by Blanche T. Dimond, B.S., and Ann Richardson, R.N., B.A., B.N. . . . 18
Nutrition, Present trends in, by E. V. McCollum, Ph.D., Sc.D. . . . 6
Nutrition, What dentists should do about, by Florence B. Hopkins, M.D., D.M.D. 191
Nutrition, What mothers want to know about child, by Dorothea Nicoll . 230
Nutrition dental program in a community, by M. M. Brown, R.N., and Dorothea Nicoll, B.S. 50
Nutrition on the Well Child Conference, by Susan M. Coffin, M.D., and Frederica L. Beinert, B.S. 40
Nutrition program in a public welfare organization, by Sue E. Sadow, B.S. 56
Nutrition program, One school's, by Catherine Leamy, M.S. . . . 65
Nutrition program, Publicity for a community, by Albertine P. McKellar, B.S. 68
Nutrition worker and nurse in a family health program, by Blanche T. Dimond, B.S. and Ann Richardson, R.N., B.A., B.N. . . . 18
Nutritional quackery, Food fallacies and. Report of the Committee on Nutritional Problems, American Public Health Association . 198

Nutritionist, Community, by Mary Spalding, M.A. 3
Nutritionist, Itinerant, in a country town, by Dorothy Hager, B.S. . . 22
Nutritionist on the itinerant clinics, by David Zacks, M.D. . . . 36
Nutritionist, Place of, in the public health program, by W. G. Smillie, M.D. 11
Nutritionist says it with exhibits, by Dorothea Nicoll, B.S. . . . 71
Nutritionist, Training of, by Alice F. Blood, Ph.D. 5
Nutritionist with the board of health in a small town by Curtis M. Hilliard, A.B. 15
Oak, Lura, Ph.D., Causes of first grade failure 273
One school's nutrition program, by Catherine Leamy, M.S. . . . 65
Osgood, Rev. Phillips Endecott, D.D., L.H.D., The church and parents . 244
Our dental hygiene program, by Jennie W. Ball 206
Parent as the private physician sees him, by Warren R. Sisson, M.D. . 226
Parent, The job of being a, by Katharine Herring 220
Parent education, by Arthur B. Lord 257
Parent education, by James A. Moyer 277
Parent education and the Well Child Conference, by Florence L. McKay, M.D. 223
Parent education, The church and, need and opportunity for development, by Richard J. Quinlan, S.T.L. 247
Parent education, Health supervision as, by Marie L. Donohue . . 233
Parent education in regard to settlement work, by Ethel Ward Dougherty 238
Parent education, The need for, by Mrs. T. Grafton Abbott . . . 219
Parent education, The private school and, by Gladys Beckett Jones . . 253
Parent education through public libraries, Community aspects of, by Edith H. Bailey 240
Parental education, Psychiatric aspects of, by Bernice M. Henderson . 269
Parents, The church and, by Rev. Phillips Endecott Osgood, D.D., L.H.D. 244
Parents, The need for co-operation between headmaster and, in country day schools, by J. Halsey Gulick 260
Parents and dental hygiene, by Robert L. Robinson, D.D.S. . . . 229
Physician, private, Parent as the, sees him, by Warren R. Sisson, M.D. 226
Place of the nutritionist in the public health program, by W. G. Smillie, M.D. 11
Pneumonia, lobar, and serum therapy, by Frederick T. Lord, M.D. and Roderick Heffron, M.D. (book note) 73
Porter, Alma, Recreation 150
Program for services for crippled children in Massachusetts, by Edward G. Huber, M.D. 284
Prophylactic remedy, Approved, for use in the eyes of infants at birth . 163
Psychiatric aspects of parental education, by Bernice M. Henderson . 269

Retardation of dental caries in out-patients of a dental infirmary, by
Percy R. Howe, D.D.S., Ruth L. White, B.S., and Milton Rabine,
D.D.S. 194
Richardson, Ann, R.N., B.A., B.N., and Dimond, Blanche T., B.S., Nutrition worker and nurse in a family health program . . . 18
Robinson, Robert L., D.D.S., Parents and dental hygiene . . . 229
Role of surgery in pulmonary tuberculosis, by Edward D. Churchill, M.D. 160
Rubenovitz, Rabbi Herman H., The home as a builder of character . 250
Sadow, Sue E., B.S., Nutrition program in a public welfare organization . 56
School, private, and parent education, by Gladys Beckett Jones . . 253
Settlement work, Community aspects of parent education in regard to, by
Ethel Ward Dougherty 238
Sisson, Warren R., M.D., The parent as the private physician sees him . 226
Smile from Araxie, by Ruth L. White, B.S. 47
Smillie, W. G., M.D., Place of the nutritionist in the public health program 11
Spalding Mary, M.A., The community nutritionist 3
    Lunch in a country school 141
    Vegetable cupboard for the country school 148
Stern, Frances, Contribution of the food clinic to the community . . 32
Suggestions for integrated health teaching in the primary grades, by
Jean V. Latimer, A.M. 127
Sullivan, John P., Ph.D., Basic considerations of the junior high school
course of study 132
Supervisor of health education, Responsibilities and training, by C. E.
Turner, M.A., Dr. P.H. 124
Syphilis and its treatment, by William A. Hinton, M.D. (book note) . . 165
Taylor, Henry B., A visual presentation of the value of dental service . 188
Teachers of health, Trained, by John J. Desmond, Jr., A.M. . . 186
Terry, Edith M., The cardiac child 280
Trained teachers of health, by John J. Desmond, Jr., A.M. . . . 186
Training of the nutritionist, by Alice F. Blood, Ph.D. 5
Trends, Present, in nutrition, by E. V. McCollum, Ph.D., Sc.D. . . 6
Tuberculosis, Cure of, by Ernest B. Emerson, M.D. 156
Tuberculosis, pulmonary, Role of surgery in, by Edward D. Churchill, M.D. 160
Turner, C. E., M.A., Dr. P.H., Supervisor of health education—Responsibilities and training 124
Use of leisure, by Helen I. D. McGillicuddy, M.D. 154
Vegetable cupboard for the country school, by Mary Spalding, M.A., B.S. 148
Visual presentation of the value of dental service, by Henry B. Taylor . 188
Volta Bureau, Do you know about the 209
Well Child Conference, Nutrition on the, by Susan M. Coffin, M.D., and
Frederica L. Beinert, B.S. 40
Well Child Conference, Parent education and the, by Florence L. McKay,
M.D. 223
What dentists should do about nutrition, by Florence B. Hopkins, M.D.,
D.M.D. 191
What mothers want to know about child nutrition, by Dorothea Nicoll . 230
Wheelock, Lucy, The Froebel Centennial 254
White, Ruth L., B.S., A smile from Araxie 47
    and Howe, Percy R., D.D.S., and Rabine, Milton, D.D.S., Retardation
of dental caries in out-patients of a dental infirmary . . . 194
Zacks, David, M.D., Nutritionist on the itinerant clinics . . . 36

Lightning Source UK Ltd.
Milton Keynes UK
UKHW020557261118
332889UK00009B/1009/P